ENCYCLOPEDIA OF WORLD BIOGRAPHY

SUPPLEMENT

32

ENCYCLOPEDIA OF WORLD BIOGRAPHY

SUPPLEMENT

$\dfrac{\text{A}}{\text{Z}}$ **32**

GALE
CENGAGE Learning®

Detroit • New York • San Francisco • New Haven. Conn • Waterville. Maine • London

REF
920
ENC

GALE
CENGAGE Learning®

Encyclopedia of World Biography Supplement, Volume 32

Project Editor: James Craddock

Editorial: Tracie Moy, Jeffrey Muhr

Image Research and Acquisition: Leitha Ehteridge-Sims

Rights Acquisition and Management: Mollika Basu, Jermaine Bobbitt, Jackie Jones

Imaging and Multimedia: Sheila Spencer

Manufacturing: Drew Kalasky

For product information and technology assistance, contact us at
Gale Customer Support, 1-800-877-4253.
For permission to use material from this text or product,
submit all requests online at **www.cengage.com/permissions.**
Further permissions questions can be emailed to
permissionrequest@cengage.com

Gale
27500 Drake Rd.
Farmington Hills, MI, 48331-3535

ISBN-13: 978-1-4144-8084-8
ISBN-10: 1-4144-8084-9
ISSN 1099-7326

This title is also available as an e-book.
ISBN-13: 978-1-4144-8208-8 ISBN-10: 1-4144-8208-6
Contact your Gale sales representative for ordering information.

Printed in Mexico
1 2 3 4 5 6 7 16 15 14 13 12

CONTENTS

INTRODUCTION

The study of biography has always held an important, if not explicitly stated, place in school curricula. The absence in schools of a class specifically devoted to studying the lives of the giants of human history belies the focus most courses have always had on people. From ancient times to the present, the world has been shaped by the decisions, philosophies, inventions, discoveries, artistic creations, medical breakthroughs, and written works of its myriad personalities. Librarians, teachers, and students alike recognize that our lives are immensely enriched when we learn about those individuals who have made their mark on the world we live in today.

Encyclopedia of World Biography Supplement, Volume 32, provides biographical information on 175 individuals not covered in the 17-volume second edition of *Encyclopedia of World Biography (EWB)* and its supplements, Volumes 18, 19, 20, 21, 22, 23, 24, 25, 26, 27, 28, 29, 30, and 31. Like other volumes in the *EWB* series, this supplement represents a unique, comprehensive source for biographical information on those people who, for their contributions to human culture and society, have reputations that stand the test of time. Each original article ends with a bibliographic section. There is also an index to names and subjects, which cumulates all persons appearing as main entries in the *EWB* second edition, the Volume 18, 19, 20, 21, 22, 23, 24, 25, 26, 27, 28, 29, 30, and 31 supplements, and this supplement—more than 8,000 people!

Articles. Arranged alphabetically following the letter-by-letter convention (spaces and hyphens have been ignored), articles begin with the full name of the person profiled in large, bold type. Next is a boldfaced, descriptive paragraph that includes birth and death years in parentheses. It provides a capsule identification and a statement of the person's significance. The essay that follows is approximately 2,000 words in length and offers a substantial treatment of the person's life. Some of the essays proceed chronologically while others confine biographical data to a paragraph or two and move on to a consideration and evaluation of the subject's work. Where very few biographical facts are known, the article is necessarily devoted to an analysis of the subject's contribution.

Following the essay is a bibliographic section arranged by source type. Citations include books, periodicals, and online Internet addresses for World Wide Web pages, where current information can be found.

Portraits accompany many of the articles and provide either an authentic likeness, contemporaneous with the subject, or a later representation of artistic merit. For artists, occasionally self-portraits have been included. Of the ancient figures, there are depictions from coins, engravings, and sculptures; of the moderns, there are many portrait photographs.

Index. The *EWB Supplement* index is a useful key to the encyclopedia. Persons, places, battles, treaties, institutions, buildings, inventions, books, works of art, ideas, philosophies, styles, movements—all are indexed for quick reference just as in a general encyclopedia. The index entry for a person includes a brief identification with birth and death dates *and* is cumulative so that any person for whom an article was written who appears in the second edition of *EWB* (volumes 1-16) and its supplements (volumes 18-30) can be located. The subject terms within the index, however, apply only to volume 32. Every index reference includes the title of the article to which the reader is being directed as well as the volume and page numbers.

Because *EWB Supplement,* Volume 32, is an encyclopedia of biography, its index differs in important ways from the indexes to other encyclopedias. Basically, this is an index of people, and that fact has several interesting consequences. First, the information to which the index refers the reader on a particular topic is always about people associated with that topic. Thus the entry "Quantum theory (physics)" lists articles on people associated with quantum theory. Each article may discuss a person's contribution to quantum theory, but no single article or group of articles is intended to provide a comprehensive treatment of quantum theory as such. Second, the index is rich in classified entries. All persons who are subjects of articles in the encyclopedia, for example, are listed in one or more classifications in the index—abolitionists, astronomers, engineers, philosophers, zoologists, etc.

The index, together with the biographical articles, make *EWB Supplement* an enduring and valuable source for biographical information. As school course work changes to reflect advances in technology and further revelations about the universe, the life stories of the people who have risen above the ordinary and earned a place in the annals of human history will continue to fascinate students of all ages.

We Welcome Your Suggestions. Mail your comments and suggestions for enhancing and improving the *Encyclopedia of World Biography Supplement* to:

The Editors
Encyclopedia of World Biography Supplement
Gale, a Cengage Learning company
27500 Drake Road
Farmington Hills, MI 48331-3535
Phone: (800) 347-4253

ADVISORY BOARD

ACKNOWLEDGMENTS

Grateful acknowledgment is made to those publishers, photographers, and artists whose works appear in this volume. Following is a list of the copyright holders who have granted us permission to reproduce material in this volume of *EWB*. Every effort has been made to trace copyright, but if omissions have been made, please let us know.

PHOTOGRAPHS AND ILLUSTRATIONS APPEARING IN EWB, VOLUME 32, WERE RECEIVED FROM THE FOLLOWING SOURCES:

ALAMY IMAGES: Jean-Pierre Aumont, Kathryn Bigelow, Louis Bleriot, Charlie Christian, Manuel Chrysoloras, Concino Concini, Errol Flynn, Roland Garros, Allvar Gullstrand, Lasse Hallstrom, Eduard Hitzig, Tamara Karsavina, Andrei Kolmogorov, Ellen Kuras, La Malinche, Samuel Mudd, Fritz von Opel, Frederick Arthur Stanley, Primoz Trubar, John Vassall, Freddie Young, Viktor Zhdanov

AP WIDEWORLD PHOTOS: Baruch Blumberg, Glenna Collett Vare, Dorothy Harrison Eustis, John Heydler, Fritz Zwicky

ART RESOURCE: Romaine Brooks

BRIDGEMAN ART LIBRARY: Francesco Hayez

CORBIS: Mildred Cohn, Rowland H. Macy, Seymour Papert

EVERETT COLLECTION, INC. Dorothy Arzner, Jimmy Durante, Maria Montez

GETTY IMAGES Mel Allen, Roone Arledge, Alexander Bain, Francis Bebey, Gian Francesco Poggio Bracciolini, Donna Brazile, Paul Pierre Broca, Jimmy Cannon, Catherine of Braganza, Patrick Camoiseau, Steven Chu, Leonard Cohen, William Dieterle, Thomas S. Gates, David Gelertner, Josh Gibson, Cammi Granato, Carole King, King Curtis, Anne Lamott, Tom Lea, Lilly Ledbetter, Peggy Lee, Leiber & Stoller, Elmore Leonard, Bette Bao Lord, Effa Manley, Roger Maris, Frank McCourt, Jim McKay, Malcolm McLaren, Ved Mehta, Wallace Neff, Milorad Pavic, William D. Phillips, Sam Phillips, Rod Serling, George Steinbrenner, Howard Thurman, Sophie Tucker, Mikhail Tukhachevsky, Bob Uecker, Martha Washington, Phillip K. Wrigley

THE GRANGER COLLECTION, NY: Max Bodenstein

LEBRECHT MUSIC & ARTS LIBRARY: Antal Dorati, Paul Muni, Atahualpa Yupanqui

LIBRARY OF CONGRESS: Louisa Catherine Adams, Barack Obama, Frances Folsom Cleveland, Lucretia Garfield

NEWSCOM: Abbott and Costello, Forrest J Ackerman, Stephen Ambrose, Ralph Bakshi, Viola Desmond, Anatoly Dobrynin, Ella Grasso, Elie Greenwich, John Hearfield, Beth Heiden, Marilyn Horne, Oscar Kambona, Stanley Kramer, Violeta Parra, Ariel Ramirez, Rene Thom, Cesare Zavattini

REDUX PICTURES: Amos Elon, Cyrus Harvey, Alberto Vargas, Wilhelm Von Gloeden

REUTERS: Eric Cornell, Sergio Marchionne, Carl Wieman

SCHOMBURG CENTER FOR RESEARCH IN BLACK CULTURE: Victoria Earle Matthews

SHUTTERSTOCK: Saskia van Uijienburgh

UNITED NEGRO COLLEGE FUND: Almena Lomax

UNITED STATES GOVERNMENT: Sonia Sotomayor

OBITUARIES

The following people, appearing in volumes 1-31 of the *Encyclopedia of World Biography,* have died since the publication of the second edition and its supplements. Each entry lists the volume where the full biography can be found.

BENACERRAF, BARUJ (born 1920), American medical researcher, died of pneumonia in Boston, Massachusetts on August 2, 2011 (Vol. 27).

CHRISTOPHER, WARREN (born 1925), American Secretary of State, died in Los Angeles, California on March 18, 2011 (Vol. 4).

FERRARO, GERALDINE (born 1935), American politician, died of complications from multiple myeloma in Boston, Massachusetts on March 26, 2011 (Vol. 5).

FITZGERALD, GARRET (born 1926), Irish Prime Minister, died of a heart attack in Dublin, Ireland on May 19, 2011 (Vol. 5).

FORD, BETTY (born 1918), American First Lady, died on July 8, 2011 (Vol. 20).

HANDLIN, OSCAR (born 1915), American historian, died of a heart attack in Cambridge, Massachusetts on September 20, 2011 (Vol. 7).

HARWELL, ERNIE (born 1918), American baseball broadcaster, died of complications from bile duct cancer in Novi, Michigan on May 4, 2010 (Vol. 31).

HAVEL, VACLAV (born 1936), Czech playwright who became President of Czechoslovakia, died in the Czech Republic on December 18, 2011 (Vol. 7).

HEALY, BERNADINE (born 1944), American physician and administrator, died of brain cancer in Gates Mills, Ohio on August 6, 2011 (Vol. 7).

KEVORKIAN, JACK (born 1928), American pathologist and assisted-suicide advocate, died in Royal Oak, Michigan on June 3, 2011 (Vol. 19).

LUMET, SIDNEY (born 1924), American filmmaker, died of lymphoma in New York City, New York on April 9, 2011 (Vol. 22).

MAATHAI, WANGARI (born 1940), Kenyan environmental activist, died on September 25, 2011 (Vol. 18).

MARGULIS, LYNN (born 1938), American biologist and professor, died of a stroke in Amherst, Massachusetts on November 22, 2011 (Vol. 10).

GADDAFI, MUAMAR AL (born 1942), Libyan ruler, died in Sirte, Libya on October 20, 2011, (Vol. 6).

RITCHIE, DENNIS (born 1941), American computer programmer, died in Murray Hill, New Jersey on October 8, 2011 (Vol. 27).

SABATO, ERNEST (born 1911), Argentine novelist and essayist, died on April 30, 2011 (Vol. 13).

SZYMBORSKA, WISLAWA (born 1923), Polish author, died of lung cancer in Krakow, Poland on February 1, 2012 (Vol. 25).

TAYLOR, ELIZABETH (born 1932), American film actress, died of congestive heart failure in Los Angeles, California on March 23, 2011 (Vol. 15).

YALOW, ROSALYN SUSSMAN (born 1921), American physicist, died in New York City, New York on May 30, 2011 (Vol. 16).

YAMAMOTO, HISAYE (born 1921), Japanese-American author, died in Los Angeles, California on January 30, 2011 (Vol. 25).

Abbott and Costello

America's premier comedy team of the 1940s, Bud Abbott (1895-1974) and Lou Costello (1908-1959) were major stars in Burlesque, Vaudeville, radio, movies and television. Best remembered for the baseball-themed routine "Who's On First," the duo utilized razor sharp timing that pitted Lou's hapless stooge character against Bud's nervy con-man persona. Well-stocked with burlesque routines retrofitted for their own personalities, they achieved greater mainstream success than any of their predecessors.

Both Abbott and Costello seemingly had show-business in their blood. Costello, born Louis Francis Cristillo on March 6, 1908, was raised in Paterson, New Jersey. His father Sebastian Cristillo was an immigrant from Caserta, Italy who became a weaver after he moved to America in 1898. Married to Helen Rege, an Irish Catholic, they raised three children; Anthony (later called Pat), youngest sister Marie Katherine and young Lou, the middle child. According to Costello's daughter Chris in her memoir *Lou's On First*, young Lou voiced having show-business aspirations since the age of four. Inspired by Charlie Chaplin movies, he would play act for his friends at school and take every opportunity to draw attention to himself by making jokes in class. The latter often provoked his teachers to make the aspiring comic write on the blackboard repeatedly, "I'm a bad boy." Which later became one of his trademark catchphrases, "I'm a b-a-a-a-d boy!"

Unlike the character he would one day play in the movies, the roly-poly Costello was quite athletic in his youth—playing baseball, basketball, and winning 32 straight bouts as an amateur boxer. After graduating from high school, he worked in a local hat store while his brother Pat served in World War I. Upon his return, the sax playing elder sibling became a working jazz musician who eventually led his own band, Pat Cristillo and His Gondoliers. Realizing that a career in show-business was possible, Costello left for Hollywood in 1926. Sleeping in parked cars and working as a day laborer on the MGM and Warner Bros. lot, the struggling actor appeared in silent films as an uncredited stunt man and extra before he decided to head back east and get some real experience in live theatre. Broke in St. Joseph, Missouri, he saw a want ad for a "Dutch comic" at a local burlesque theatre and quickly applied. Hired by a desperate stage manager for a mere $16 a week, he wore a putty nose, baggy pants and delivered his jokes with a mock Dutch accent. As he grew more confident, the young comic dropped the exaggerated make-up and clothing and, following his brother's lead, changed his last name to Costello. When the burlesque manager would not increase his salary after a year, Costello quit and decided to try his luck in New York City.

In contrast to his future partner, Bud Abbott had been in the entertainment business nearly all his life. Born William Alexander Abbott on October 2, 1895 in Asbury Park, New Jersey, his parents were both circus people. Harry Abbott Sr. was an advance man for the Barnum & Bailey Circus while his wife Rae was a bareback horsewoman for the troupe. Eventually, the Abbotts left the circus and settled in Coney Island, where Abbott Sr. helped establish the Columbia Wheel, the first burlesque circuit. At age 16, young Bud worked as an assistant treasurer for the Casino Burlesque Theater in Brooklyn, where he was also used as a shill, hailing and steering customers into the establishment. One of Costello's later claims was that he chose Abbott out of the audience or, in another version, pulled him from the box office to work as his partner. In truth, Abbott became

a straight man when he began working with his wife, former exotic dancer Betty Smith, after their marriage in 1918. Blessed with a strong stage speaking voice—which grew gravelly in later years—a con man's demeanor and unshakably brilliant timing, Abbott found himself in demand as a partner for some of the better burlesque comedy acts of the time, such as Harry Steppe and Harry Evanson.

Became a Team

There exists some disparity about when Abbott and Costello formally became a team. Abbott's widow Betty claimed the team did not get together officially until 1936. Other sources say the two knew each other and occasionally worked together starting in 1931. Regardless, both men learned their craft inside and out on the burlesque circuit. In burlesque, the straight man was considered more important than the comic; he paced the act, reeled the comic in when he started ad-libbing too much and got the act on and off stage in an orderly fashion. On-stage, Abbott and other straight men would sometimes even slap a comic to get the funnyman's attention and bring their act to its punchline conclusion. As was the tradition with straight men of the era, Abbott received 60 percent of the money from his work with other comics. Yet once they officially teamed up, he and Costello were equal financial partners despite the fact that Costello made most of the creative decisions for the act.

The take-off points for most of the Abbott and Costello routines were the traditional sketches that many other comics had been spinning off of since the beginning of burlesque. "Mustard" "The Drill Sargent," "The Dice Game," "The Lemon Bit," "13 x 7 = 28" and their "Mudder/Fodder" sketch were modernized by comedy writer/gagman John Grant and personalized by the duo themselves. Even their most famous routine, "Who's on First" began decades earlier as "The Baker" (a man named Who) and had been done in different incarnations by such comic giants as Weber and Fields and Phil Silvers. At the time, most comics had a baseball oriented routine in their repertoire, and Abbott and Costello's redrafting of the old sketch into one about the national pastime, along with their rapid-fire delivery and rich comic interaction, made them a hit act overnight.

Radio Made Them Stars, Movies made Them Icons

Outgrowing burlesque, the duo began playing more vaudeville houses, stage shows and nightclubs in 1937. Possessing a lively act that featured snappy wordplay and slapstick pratfalls—Moe Howard of the Three Stooges claims to have seen Abbott studying his group's live shows—Abbott and Costello were an immediate hit with mainstream audiences. Their career received a valuable boost when they were signed to make regular appearances on the *Kate Smith Show* broadcast on CBS radio. It was there that Costello, in order to differentiate his voice from Abbott's, began to speak in a high voice and incorporate many of the vocal mannerisms and catch-phrases, such as "Hey Ab-b-a-a-a-a-tt!" and "I've been a b-a-a-d boy," that would make him a national star Initially, the show's producer Ted Collins did not want the comedians to do "Who's On First," deeming it too physical, but once the routine was aired, it proved a comic sensation.

By the summer of 1940, Abbott and Costello were starring in their own summer replacement radio series for NBC. Working in Fred Allen's time-slot, their mastery of wordplay—including some deliberately bad puns—and sound effect-aided slapstick with a touch of pathos made the show an immediate audience favorite. Beginning in 1942, the team enjoyed a regular prime-time slot sponsored by Camel cigarettes, and their part variety show/part sitcom boasted a cast that included singers Marilyn Maxwell and Connie Haines and longtime second banana Sid Fields. Mixing their vast array of vaudeville routines with popular songs of the day and a simple plot, the team's radio show remains their funniest, most consistent work. Their hot run was nearly cut short, however, when Costello contracted rheumatic fever, which damaged his heart and forced him off the air for half a season. In their place, Jimmy Durante—teamed with future *I've Got a Secret* host Garry Moore—used the opportunity to mount a late career comeback. Sadly, the night Costello returned to the radio show, his son Lou Jr. drowned, and although the pudgy comic went on with the show, his daughter Chris wrote that her father was never quite the same again.

The team began their film careers as supporting players in the 1940 release *A Night in the Tropics*. Buoyed by strong audience reaction, they were signed to a seven-year contract with Universal Pictures. Their first starring roles came with *Buck Privates*, which featured the Andrews Sisters singing the hits "Boogie Woogie Bugle Boy" and "Apple Blossom Time." With the dawning of World War II, audiences in need of a laugh saw Abbott and Costello in three more pictures that same year—including two more military spoofs, *In the Navy, Hold That Ghost,* and *Keep 'em Flying*. The following year, their antics in such comedies as *Ride 'em Cowboy, Rio Rita, Pardon My Sarong* and *Who Done It?* made them the top box office draws of 1942.

As structured by their manager Eddie Sherman, Abbott and Costello not only received a percentage of the profits for their work at Universal but were allowed to make a picture a year with other movie studios. Filming for Universal, MGM, Warner Bros. and United Artists, the team made thirty-seven feature films from 1940-1956. Though never a favorite of the critics, their pictures appealed to an ever growing audience of children, especially the later fright comedy releases *Abbott and Costello Meet Frankenstein, Abbott and Costello Meet the Killer Boris Karloff* and *Abbott and Costello Meet the Invisible Man.* Reportedly, the comedy team was not that well-behaved on the set, insisting on impromptu pie fights, time-consuming practical jokes and a fair amount of gambling in between takes. Further, Abbott's drinking became more serious during production of the later films and Costello—who never quite trusted Universal—often took home studio furniture and props to decorate his home.

Television Provided Their Last Hurrah

Following an incredibly successful decade that generated money from films, radio, live appearances and merchandising, Abbott and Costello's fortunes waned badly during the early 1950s. Costly lawsuits against their management, fellow investors and Universal Pictures went against them. Worse, in 1953, the IRS waded through their tangled finances and disallowed hundreds of thousands of dollars in business deductions. Suddenly, the team that had been awarded a special medal from the Treasury Department for selling War Bonds were forced to sell off everything they owned to pay back taxes. Both men were financially wiped out and the only solution was to add television to their already crowded professional schedule.

Hired by NBC as one of the revolving hosts of NBC's *Colgate Comedy Hour,* Abbott and Costello reprised a great many of their most famous routines with great success. Although they were rapidly being eclipsed by Dean Martin and Jerry Lewis as America's favorite comedy team, their version of the variety show was often better than the product supplied by the newcomers. In a bit of serendipity, Costello had helped Martin pay for a nose job before the singer became a star. Tightly scripted and brilliantly executed in front of a live audience, the show briefly reinvigorated their careers. Looking to capitalize on the newfound television profits, the team's own company produced fifty-two episodes of the syndicated sitcom *The Abbott and Costello Show.* Based on many of their old radio scripts, the first season's supporting cast included Sid Fields, Joe Besser, and Hilary Brooke. The second season mainly featured the team, Fields and the team's vast array of burlesque routines. Cheaply produced, the show was a solid hit and ran in syndication for nearly three decades. The team made a few more motion pictures together, including their swan song, the lackluster *Dance with Me Henry,* but their time had passed.

There had been squabbles between Abbott and Costello as far back as 1945, when, offended by Abbott hiring a maid that he had just fired, Costello did not speak to him off camera for nearly two years. Regardless, most accounts portray Bud and Lou as solid partners who genuinely respected one another. But as the 1950s wore on, Abbott's drinking, increasing attacks of epilepsy and need to take

time off—he was 10 years older than Costello—resulted in the amicable termination of their partnership in 1957. Costello continued to work steadily, appearing in Las Vegas with Sid Fields as Abbott's unofficial stand-in, as well as making numerous guest appearances on *The Steve Allen Plymouth Show* and giving respectable dramatic performances on episodes of *Wagon Train* and *General Electric Theatre.* His final motion picture *The 30 Foot Bride of Candy Rock,* co-starring Dorothy Provine, was released several months after the great comedian had died of heart failure on March 3, 1959. He was fifty-three years old and left behind his wife of twenty-five years, the former Anne Battler, and their three children.

Like his former partner, Abbott was continually hounded by the IRS and in a desperate attempt to pay his debts, he sued his former partner for a bigger share of the profits from their sitcom. Forced out of retirement in 1960, he teamed with musical comic/bit player Candy Candido, but the new pairing exhibited little spark and Abbott's failing health kept him from touring with the act. After a solid dramatic performance on *General Electric Theatre,* several strokes forced Abbott into a wheelchair. Living off a modest pension, he re-emerged in 1967, supplying his own voice on 156 episodes of Hanna-Barbera's syndicated cartoon series *The Abbott and Costello Show,* featuring the voice of Stu Irwin as Costello. Suffering from prostate cancer, Bud Abbott died of a stroke on April 24, 1974; he left behind his wife of 56 years, Betty Smith, and their two adopted children.

The works of Abbott and Costello continue to entertain audiences and inspire new comedians. Their radio shows are easily available on cassette tape and compact disc collections, their old films are shown often on cable stations such as Turner Classic Movies, and along with *The Abbott and Costello Show* TV shows, are available on DVD. In 1978, Harvey Korman and Buddy Hackett played the duo in the made-for-TV bio-pic *Bud and Lou.* In 1994, NBC honored the team with an entertaining retrospective, *Jerry Seinfeld Meets Abbott and Costello.* More importantly, their signature routine "Who's On First?" is still the most famous comedy routine of all-time, and has been given a place of honor at the Baseball Hall of Fame in Cooperstown, New York.

Books

Burr, Lonnie, *Two For the Show—Great Comedy Teams,* Messner, 1979.

Costello, Chris w/ Strait, Raymond, *Lou's On First,* St. Martin's Press, 1981.

Cox, Stephen and Lofton, John, *The Abbott & Costello Story—Sixty Years of "Who's On First?"* Cumberland House Publishing, 1990.

Franklin, Joe, *Joe Franklin's Encyclopedia of Comedians,* Bell Publishing, 1979.

Lackman, Ron, *The Encyclopedia of American Radio,* Facts on File, 2000.

McNeil, Alex, *Total Television,* Penguin Books, 1996.

Schochet, Stephen, *Hollywood Stories,* Hollywood Stories Publishing, 2010.

Smith, Ronald L., *Comedy on Record: The Complete Critical Discography,* Garland Publishing, 1988.

Online

"Abbott & Costello" *All Music,* http://www.allmusic.com/artist/abbott-costello/biography, (November 20, 2011).

"Bud Abbott," *Internet Movie Database,* http://www.idb.com/name/nm0007941/bio, (November 20, 2011).

"Lou Costello," *Internet Movie Database,* http://www.idb.com/name/nm0182579/bio, (November 20, 2011).□

Forrest J Ackerman

Forrest J Ackerman (1916–2008) influenced a generation of science fiction and horror movie filmmakers and writers. Often described as the ultimate archivist of both genres, Ackerman ran his own literary agency while amassing an astonishing collection of first edition books, B-movie props, and other paraphernalia. His most enduring contribution to popular culture, however, was his 25-year tenure as editor of the cult classic *Famous Monsters of Filmland,* a magazine devoted to horror and science fiction movies. *FM,* as it was known in shortened form, had an enormous impact on a generation of teen-aged readers in the 1960s and '70s, among them Steven Spielberg and Stephen King. "He was the world's biggest fan," King told the *New York Times.* "If you had been to his house, you wouldn't doubt it."

Ackerman's full name is sometimes given as Forrest James Ackerman, but he preferred to use the middle initial "J" without punctuation. He was born in Los Angeles on November 24, 1916, the son of an oil company statistician. He was six years old when he saw his first science fiction movie, *One Glorious Day,* a 1922 silent that starred Will Rogers. At age nine, he bought his first copy of a new magazine called *Amazing Stories,* launched by science fiction writer Hugo Gernsback. It was the first periodical to be entirely devoted to the literary genre that Gernsback had dubbed "scientifiction." "By the time he reached the final page, he had become America's first fanboy," wrote Daniel Zalewski about Ackerman in the *New Yorker.* "He started a group called the Boys' Scientifiction Club; in 1939, he wore an outer-space outfit to a convention for fantasy aficionados, establishing a costuming ritual still followed by the hordes at Comic-Con."

Ackerman soon started writing his own short stories. In 1932, the year he turned 16, he co-founded *The Time Traveler* magazine for fellow enthusiasts, and two years later launched the Los Angeles chapter of the Science Fantasy Society, a national organization created by Gernsback. In 1937 he met a 17-year-old Ray Bradbury, a newcomer to California and budding science fiction writer. As editor of the Science Fantasy Society's magazine *Imagination!,* Ackerman published Bradbury's first short story in 1938.

Ackerman spent some time at the University of California's Berkeley campus, but by the late 1930s was working as

a vari-typist, a bygone occupation that was a form of typesetting. He spent the World War II years near home, serving with the U.S. Army at its Fort MacArthur base in San Pedro, where he edited a military newspaper. In 1947 he formed the Ackerman Science Fiction Agency to broker the stories of Bradbury and other writers. Among his other clients was L. Ron Hubbard, the charismatic founder of the Church of Scientology.

Moved into the 'Acker-Mansion'

Ackerman and his wife, Wendayne Wahrmann, married in 1949 and lived in several Los Angeles-area properties, but at one point were forced to move into an apartment because Ackerman's personal library of science fiction publications and collection of movie memorabilia began to overtake their living quarters. In the 1950s and '60s they lived at 915 South Sherbourne Road, which was the original "Ackermansion," as Ackerman called it. Fans of science fiction stories and horror films began turning up at his home unannounced as far back as the early 1950s, as rumors of the breadth and scope of his collection circulated among the close-knit community of aficionados. He eventually started hosting a regular Saturday open house, giving tours through all the rooms and their various ephemera. His possessions included a trove of books on the mythical prehistoric land of Atlantis, an island city-state mentioned by the ancient Greeks that was said to have vanished under the sea. Ackerman's movie memorabilia included the cape allegedly worn by Bela Lugosi in the 1927 stage version of *Dracula* and the toy prop that director Ed Wood used as a stand-in for an alien spaceship in the 1959 B-movie *Plan 9 from Outer Space,* often cited as the worst movie ever made.

Though Ackerman had a fascination with similarly cheesy B-movies that came out of Hollywood during that era, his favorite film of all time was the 1927 future-dystopian masterpiece *Metropolis,* commonly hailed as one of the top achievements in silent-era cinema. Its director, Fritz Lang, was known for wearing a monocle eyepiece, and one of these found a permanent home in the Ackerman-sion's *Metropolis*-themed room. Ackerman also owned a pair of the pointy-ear prosthetics that Leonard Nimoy wore as the Vulcan Spock in the *Star Trek* television series. *Star Trek* creator Gene Roddenberry was friends with "Forry," as Ackerman was known, for many years.

In the 1970s Ackerman and his wife acquired a large four-story home in the Los Feliz section of Los Angeles. It was on Glendower Road, a few addresses down from one of the city's most infamous crime scenes: in 1959 a physician murdered his wife and attempted to kill his teenaged daughter, who escaped. The doctor killed himself, and the house was sold. No one ever moved into it, and its contents remained sealed up as they were in 1959 even 50 years later. The infamous Perelson house was a curiosity for true-crime enthusiasts for years, some of whom found their way over to the Ackermansion, which was decorated with a worthy Halloween display every year. But Ackerman and his wife bought their Los Feliz house because it had once been owned by Jon Hall, a B-movie star of the 1930s and '40s who had appeared in camp classics like *Cobra Woman* with Maria Montez.

Launched *Famous Monsters* Magazine

Ackerman's major contribution to film history was the low-budget magazine *Famous Monsters of Filmland,* which made its debut in February of 1958, had production values similar to those of the comic book industry, with its thin black-and-white pages and artful, eye-catching color cover. *FM,* as it became known, was "the first serious (but never solemn) magazine devoted to horror and science fiction movies," wrote Richard Corliss in *Time.* Its pages, written largely by Ackerman, featured "appreciations of old and new films, interviews with the genre's actors, directors, writers and special-effects men, all informed by the ripe musings and unabashed enthusiasm of its editor. The photos often came from Ackerman's archive; his collection was likely the world's largest in its category."

FM had a noteworthy 25-year run. "As crammed and chaotic as his house," wrote Michael Carlson in the London *Guardian,* the magazine "was an extension of his obsession, and found a huge young audience that shared it. He called himself 4E (Forry), a moniker that anticipated teenage text-messages decades before mobile phones." George Lucas of *Star Wars* fame was an avid reader of *FM,* as was Steven Spielberg. Future horror story writer Stephen King read it as a kid, and at the age of 14 sent Ackerman one of the first stories he ever wrote. Years later King, quoted in Ackerman's obituary in the *New York Times,* assessed Ackerman's impact in a few succinct words: "When you think of the size of the business, the dollar amount, that has sprung up out of fantasy, the people who made everything from 'Star Wars' to 'Jaws,' well, Forry was a part of their growing up. The first time I met Steven Spielberg, we didn't talk about movies. We talked about monsters and Forry Ackerman." The horror and science fiction genre had a particularly rich resonance for a new

generation of American youth raised on reruns of once critically dismissed television series and B-movies. "Kids these days identify with the monsters because the monsters were all victims of circumstance," Ackerman told journalist Jacquin Sanders for a story headlined "Creepy-Boppers" that ran in the *Boca Raton News.* "Frankenstein, the Hunchback of Notre Dame, the Phantom of the Opera . . . were all in worlds they did not control."

Made Cameos in Dozens of Films

Ackerman claimed to have coined the term "sci-fi" in the 1950s after the new craze in stereo systems, dubbed "hi-fi" for high fidelity. Actually the writer Robert A. Heinlein used it first, but Ackerman popularized it on the pages of *FM* and elsewhere. Over the years he co-authored or edited dozens of reference books on horror and science fiction films and authors, including *Ackermanthology: 65 Astonishing, Rediscovered Sci-Fi Shorts* and *Worlds of Tomorrow: The Amazing Universe of Science-Fiction Art.* He was so beloved a figure in Hollywood that it was standard practice for directors to give him a cameo in low-budget spectacles. His most visible part was as the popcorn-eating man sitting behind Michael Jackson in the movie theater scene in the 1983 hit video "Thriller," directed by John Landis, another longtime *FM* reader and Ackerman fan.

In the mid-1980s Ackerman loaned out some artifacts from his 300,000-piece collection to the Smithsonian Institution's "Yesterday's Tomorrows" exhibition on the impact of science fiction on American pop culture. Among his treasures was the monster costume used in the 1954 cult classic *The Creature from the Black Lagoon.* Ackerman told a newspaper reporter for the Nashua, New Hampshire *Telegraph* that the slime suit "was casually thrown away" after shooting ended. A member of the set's cleaning crew brought it home for his son. The youngster eventually sold the costume to a friend, who later donated it to Ackerman's trove. Ackerman told the same *Telegraph* reporter that he still had the original October 1926 issue of *Amazing Stories* that he had bought as a nine-year-old. He spent years pitching the idea for a museum dedicated to horror and science fiction films, to be located somewhere in the Los Angeles area, and though he had some support from local officials and prominent figures in the film industry, his museum idea was never realized.

For years he had engaged in legal battles with competing publications that tried to capitalize on the success of the *Famous Monsters of Filmland* with similar titles, and finally shuttered the publication in 1983. Several years later, he agreed to revive it with a business partner, but the deal soured and Ackerman's finances were drained further in an attempt to regain the rights to the original title. He was forced to sell the Los Feliz "Ackermansion" to defray legal costs, and later in life sold off large parts of his personal museum of horror movie and science fiction memorabilia to pay for mounting medical bills. Ackerman's wife died in 1990. Ackerman himself died of heart failure in Los Angeles on December 4, 2008, at the age of 92. In the Nashua *Telegraph* interview, he reflected back on his lifelong interest in science fiction and futuristic worlds. His personal archive "has permitted me to live a great deal in the future," he said. "I may not be around in 2001, but I've already been there."

Books

Painter, Deborah, *Forry: The Life of Forrest J Ackerman*, McFarland & Co., 2011.

Periodicals

Boca Raton News, January 26, 1971.
Guardian (London, England), December 7, 2008.
Hollywood Reporter, October 31, 2001.
Los Angeles Times, December 6, 2008.
New York Times, June 6, 1993; December 6, 2008.
New Yorker, February 7, 2011.
Telegraph (Nashua, NH), February 15, 1986.
Time, December 22, 2008.□

Louisa Adams

American First Lady Louisa Adams (1775–1852) spent four years in the White House during the presidency of her husband, John Quincy Adams. Among holders of the title, she is the sole First Lady who was not born on American soil, and along with Laura Bush is the only presidential spouse who was also the daughter-in-law of a sitting U.S. president. Adams's husband was the son of John Adams, America's second president and considered one of the nation's founding fathers.

Louisa Catherine Johnson was born on February 12, 1775, in London, England. Her father was Joshua Johnson, a tobacco merchant from Maryland whose brother Thomas would become that state's first governor and was also a signer of the Declaration of Independence. Adams's mother, Catherine Nuth Johnson, was English and produced six other daughters besides Louisa, plus one son. When war erupted between the American colonies and their British overlords in 1776, Joshua Johnson relocated his family to safety in Nantes, France. They lived there until 1783, and Adams and some of her sisters attended a Roman Catholic convent school. Her parents encouraged her creative talents, and she emerged as multilingual and musically gifted as a teenager. Adams's father became the first American consul in London in 1790 and the family resumed a comfortable, social engagement-focused lifestyle in the city.

Battled Abigail Adams

Adams actually met her future husband when she was four years old and he was a preteen, when John Quincy Adams was traveling with his father, who was then the American envoy to France. They met again in London in 1794, the same year that John Quincy Adams began his role as the U.S. ambassador to the Netherlands. His father was the vice president to George Washington at the time. The formidable matriarch of the Adams clan was Abigail Adams, one of the early heroines of American history. The wife of one president and mother of another, Abigail maintained a voluminous correspondence and diary during her event-filled lifetime, as did her husband and son. The Adams family papers make up a rich trove of detail about the Founding Fathers, the American Revolutionary War, and the first years of nationhood. They also provide a glimpse into scores of internecine family battles.

When John Quincy Adams developed an interest in Louisa as a potential spouse, Abigail tried valiantly to dissuade him by letter, writing that the Johnson daughter "inherits the taste for elegance which her mamma is conspicuous for," for Abigail had known the family from an earlier sojourn in London. She believed the half-English, French-speaking Louisa was far too European for her son, who was nevertheless nearing the age of 30 and had been expected to take a wife long before that age. Finally, all sides capitulated and the couple were married on July 26, 1797, at an Anglican church in London called All Hallows Barking.

Letters from their courtship reveal that Adams and her fiancé quarreled habitually; he could be dismissive and misogynistic in his treatment of her, and she was as headstrong as his mother, who had become First Lady earlier in 1797 when John Adams became America's second president. The couple spent the first years of their marriage in Berlin, as her husband was serving as the U.S. ambassador to Prussia. She endured several miscarriages and at least one stillbirth, and was pregnant a total of eleven times. Their first child, George Washington Adams, was born in Berlin on April 12, 1801. Later that spring the couple returned to the United States with their infant, where the former ambassador entered political life in earnest with a seat in the Massachusetts state senate. In 1803 he was elected to a U.S. Senate seat, and the family moved to Washington, D.C.

The Adamses' second son, named John after his father and grandfather, was born, propitiously, on July 4, 1803, the 27th anniversary of the proclamation of the Declaration of Independence. A third son, Charles Francis, arrived on August 18, 1807. John Quincy Adams's term in Congress ended the following spring, and he took a teaching job at Harvard College, his alma mater.

Sailed for Russia

In the summer of 1809 the Adamses sailed for Europe when a new U.S. president, James Madison, appointed John Quincy Adams as the first official ambassador to Russia. One of the most difficult trials that Adams endured as a political spouse was the decision to leave her two older sons in Massachusetts with their Adams grandparents; they were just eight and six years old. She took the youngest, Charles, with her on an 80-day sea voyage to St. Petersburg.

Adams struggled to contain costs on the meager ambassador's salary, where the expenses of servants and entertaining in the tsarist capital could prove ruinous. Even little Charles was expected to participate in the glittering round of gala dinners and formal balls that made up the St. Petersburg social whirl within the court of Tsar Alexander I: there were special costume events for children, where mothers were required to stand behind the chairs of their offspring for hours. On August 12, 1811, Adams delivered her fourth child, a daughter they named Louisa, and took a break from the hectic pace of social engagements. But the infant fell ill at six months and never recovered from a bout of dysentery. Little Louisa died a little over a month after her first birthday.

Adams was devastated. In addition to her own physical sufferings from so many pregnancies, plus recurring migraines, her marriage had never been a harmonious one. John Quincy Adams—despite a marked talent for international diplomacy at the highest levels—had an imperious streak toward his wife, and the couple quarreled when together and often via letter when apart, though their correspondence does show both expressions of love and a desire for a better marriage. Adams's depressed state was then further compounded by the troubles of a new war between Britain and the United States, the War of 1812. Then an even more calamitous event imperiled the Adamses' safety when France went to war with Russia, mounting an aggressive campaign that rolled eastward through the latter half of 1812. Some of the 500,000 troops of Napoleon's Grande Armée actually reached Moscow, but the rest were soundly defeated by the brutal Russian winter and forced to retreat.

Embarked on Epic Journey

Adams's husband departed St. Petersburg in April of 1814 for what appeared to be a brief journey over to Göteborg, Sweden, to negotiate the treaty that would conclude the U.S.-British War of 1812. Britain, however, objected to the site, and was able to win a change of venue to Belgium. Peace talks dragged on for several months, but finally the Treaty of Ghent was signed on December 24, 1814. A few weeks later, Adams's husband cabled for her to join him in Paris, either immediately or when better weather permitted easier sailing through the Baltic Sea. If she left soon, she could take the land route, he suggested, and Adams immediately opted for that, remembering a treacherous eleven-week journey five years earlier.

Adams spent the next three weeks planning her journey and arranging for their household goods to follow them to London, where her husband was to become the new U.S. ambassador to England. She was excited at the prospect of seeing her older sons, but in her journal she admitted, "My heart is torn at the idea of quitting for ever the spot where my darling lays," referring to her infant daughter's grave in St. Petersburg's cemetery for foreigners, according to *Russian Life*. She departed St. Petersburg with her seven-year-old son Charles, a French nursemaid she had just hired, and a recently released French prisoner of war, at 5 p.m. on Sunday, February 12, 1815, which was also her fortieth birthday.

Adams's journey was so impressive that it served as the subject of a 2010 book, *Mrs. Adams in Winter: A Journey in the Last Days of Napoleon*, written by Michael O'Brien. She and her young son traveled 2,000 miles by horse-drawn carriage for nearly six weeks during a season of ice, snow, and mud. The expense of the journey included a new six-horse enclosed coach called a berline. The horses had to be changed daily, a service that was arranged at the post-depots dotted along the way. They traveled the mail roads, and because there were few respectable inns along this route, they often slept inside the carriage. When they did stop to eat, innkeepers regaled her with tales of recent murders of travelers in the area. There were also perilous river crossings over thawing ice, and wrong turns that found them lost at night in dark, primeval forests where wolves and elk still roamed.

Crossed Several Points of Danger

Along the way, through Russia and the Baltic lands, then on through Germany and France, Adams and her party passed relatively recent battlefield sites, replete with acres of freshly dug graves, and even piles of bones and discarded uniforms. One respite came in Berlin, where the royal princess, now Queen Luise of Prussia, whom Adams had known from her time as an ambassador's wife, welcomed her with luxurious accommodations. Meanwhile, Napoleon had escaped from his Mediterranean exile on the island of Elba, and war across Europe loomed once again. In Germany, Adams's guards deserted her, fearful of being illegally conscripted into an army, and the rest of the journey through France was planned to avoid towns where troops were already mustering for battle.

Near Epernay, Adams's party was assaulted by a roving band of Grande Armée camp followers, who recognized the Russian-built berline and suspected it contained enemy Slavs. A mob surrounded the carriage and began hurling insults and calls for violence, but officers of Napoleon's elite Imperial Guard were fortunately present. Adams produced her documents and the crowd was informed that it was an American woman and her son. At that, the soldiers began shouting "Vive les Américains!" according to O'Brien's account, for the French and Americans felt a unique amity as new democracies. They were surprised when she opened the window as the carriage pulled out, waved her handkerchief and responded "Vive

Napoleon!'' in her perfect, nearly accent-less French. She finally arrived in Paris on the night of March 23, 1815, and over the next few weeks, her husband and others who listened to her tale of adventure were astonished at the courage and calm she had displayed under pressure.

Became First Lady

In May of 1815 the Adamses moved to London, where their two older boys finally joined them after a six-year absence. Two years later the family returned to the United States when John Quincy Adams was appointed Secretary of State in the cabinet of James Monroe. Seven years later, he made a surprise run for the presidency, and won it in a closely contested race. The couple moved into the White House in March of 1825, shortly after Inauguration Day. As First Lady, Adams kept a relatively low profile after the bruising campaign that had brought her husband to office. He ran for a second term in 1828 but lost to General Andrew Jackson, hero of the War of 1812 and his 1824 foe. The former president was elected a U.S. Representative from Massachusetts after leaving office, the only president to do this, serving for the last 17 years of his life.

There followed a dismal time for the Adamses, with reports that their eldest son, George, had fathered a child by a woman who worked as a domestic servant; shortly after the family left the White House, George disappeared from a passenger ferry off the coast of Long Island. Weeks later his body washed ashore, a presumed suicide. Their second son, John, died prematurely, too, in 1834. For much of her life Adams believed she had irreparably harmed her two sons by leaving them behind in 1809, though they had been in the solid care of her Adams in-laws.

Adams wrote a memoir of her 1815 horse-drawn trek from St. Petersburg to Paris in 1836. Her husband continued his political career almost until death's door: he collapsed on the floor of the U.S. House of Representatives as he stood to argue against a motion on February 21, 1848, and died two days later. Adams died four years later in Washington on May 15, 1852. When members of Congress learned the news, they voted to adjourn, which was the first time a session did so in honor of a woman. Adams's youngest son, Charles, was apparently unharmed by the adventure of his epic trip of 1815, and went on to a long career as a Republican politician and historian. It was through his efforts that the first U.S. presidential library, honoring both his grandfather and father, was created.

Books

Nagel, Paul C., *The Adams Women*, Oxford University Press, 1987.

Nagel, Paul C., *John Quincy Adams: A Public Life, a Private Life*, Alfred A. Knopf, 1997, p. 99.

O'Brien, Michael, *Mrs. Adams in Winter: A Journey in the Last Days of Napoleon*, Farrar, Straus & Giroux, 2010, p. 282.

Periodicals

Russian Life, September-October 2008.

Online

"Louisa Catherine Johnson Adams," White House.org, http://www.whitehouse.gov/about/first-ladies/louisaadams (December 13, 2014).

"Adams, Louisa Catherine Johnson," Massachusetts Historical Society, http://www.masshist.org/publications/apde/index/entry.php?g=71-00499#dca_note (December 14, 2011). □

Harold Melvin Agnew

American physicist Harold Agnew (born 1921) helped develop the United States' first atomic weapons, working on the Manhattan Project at Los Alamos.

From an airplane, Harold Agnew witnessed up close—or as close as you can possibly get—the destructive power of atomic weaponry. This devastating armament Agnew helped create. As a young graduate student, he was recruited to become a member of the Manhattan Project, a research and development enterprise that produced the first atomic bomb during World War II.

The project's result forever changed the world. The bomb it created represented the one and only time that atomic weaponry was deployed against a nation (Japan) during warfare, and it hurtled the world into a fearful new environment, where people wondered if global leaders would have a quick and nervous finger on the nuclear trigger.

On August 6, a B-29 aircraft launched from an airbase on Tinian, an island in the West Pacific region. This plane, called the "Enola Gay," carried the atomic payload, which it dropped on Hiroshima. It was accompanied by two other planes, "The Great Artiste" and an unnamed aircraft. "The Great Artiste" was equipped with instrumentation that would help measure the impact. Agnew was aboard this plane.

The Manhattan Project was located in Los Alamos, in a desert area in New Mexico. There, Agnew, an ever unapologetic proponent of nuclear weaponry, played a major role. As he told the BBC in a 2005 interview, "About three-quarters of the [United States nuclear arsenal] was designed under my tutelage at Los Alamos. That is my legacy."

Agnew takes pride in that legacy, but physicist Albert Einstein, whose research and theories helped lead to the development of the bomb (even though he did not take part in its creation) is famously quoted as saying, "If only I had known, I should have become a watchmaker."

Worked with Enrico Fermi

The physicist who helped forever change the world was born as Harold Melvin Agnew on March 28, 1921 in Denver, Colorado. His parents were Sam E. and Augusta Agnew. He received his undergraduate degree in chemistry from the University of Denver in 1942. That same year, in Chicago, Agnew joined a research group headed by Italian-born physicist Enrico Fermi, who would often later be referred to as the "father of the atomic bomb."

The association enabled Agnew to witness the first-ever controlled nuclear chain reaction (on December 2, 1942).

In the meantime, he had married Beverly Jackson (on May 2, 1942). The couple would have two children, a son and a daughter.

After witnessing the seminal chain-reaction event, Agnew moved to Los Alamos, to engage in the research and development activities with the Manhattan Project, which included a group of scientists commissioned to develop atomic weaponry. Working in the Experimental Physics division, Agnew was a project member from 1943 to 1946. In an interview for a PBS show called "The American Experience" (which aired in January 1999), Agnew recalled the environment in positive terms: "It was a fantastic place. You had the *crème de la crème.*

He also recalled the sense of urgency. Project members had a definite mission, he said. They believed that time was of the essence. "In the early [1940s], things were going very bad for the Allies," he recalled on the PBS program.

The project's "definite mission" he said, was to try and help end the war. In recent years, the idea has been advanced that the bombing of the Japanese cities was over-kill. Agnew never felt that way, however. The bomb, he believed, forestalled further wartime casualties. "Clearly, by the time we used the bomb in Hiroshima and Nagasaki the war was won, but it wasn't over, and there were a tremendous number of people still dying," he related in "The American Experience" interview. "If we had had an invasion, it would have been a real mess."

Flight Over Hiroshima

Agnew had a chance to view atomic bomb destruction from far above the ground-level. In his role as a member of the Experimental Physics Division at Los Alamos, Agnew was selected to be a member of Project Alberta (Destination Team) on Tinian Island. Specifically, this meant that he would be a scientific observer during this critical mission (as part of the 509th Composite Group). Flying on the B-29 aircraft, "The Great Artiste," he was accompanied by colleague Luis Alvarez (1911-1988), who developed the detonators for setting off the plutonium-based bomb. Alvarez would later receive the Nobel Prize (in 1968) for his contributions to elementary particle physics. Also on board was physicist Lawrence Johnston, who would also later witness the atomic explosion at Nagasaki.

From this safe position high above the earth's surface, Agnew's mission was to measure the yield of the atomic bomb explosion. For the "American Experience" television program, he related how this was accomplished: "I flew on the Hiroshima mission ... [and we felt] we ought to try to devise a way of measuring the yield—that's pretty tricky because you couldn't be on the ground. So we devised a method of dropping some blast gauges on parachutes and then telemetering the blast pressure of the impulse back to our plane, recording it, and then analyzing the results, and that's how we determined the yield."

Flying over Hiroshima, Agnew, Alvarez and Johnston looked down upon the mushroom cloud that once was a city. But Agnew believed the bombing was necessary, even if it costs the lives of many civilians. He told the BBC, "My honest feeling at the time was that they deserved it, and as far as I am concerned, that is still how I feel today. People

never look back to what led up to it [Pearl Harbor, Nanking] and there are no innocent civilians in war, everyone is doing something, contributing to the war effort, building bombs. What we did saved a lot of lives in the long run and I am proud to have been part of it."

Encountered Espionage

Development of the atom bomb led espionage activity, with secrets passed on to the Soviet Union. This would lead to the trials of Klaus Fuchs, who was later imprisoned, and Julius and Ethel Rosenberg, who were tried, found guilty and executed. In a 1998 interview printed on the *National Security Archive* website, Agnew described what he perceived as the impact of the espionage. "I think [it] helped the Soviets in the context of confidence," he said. "They clearly had the intellectual capability among their physicists, chemists, metallurgists, mathematicians to know how to make such a device once fission was discovered and they'd been working quite early on the theoretical aspects of it, but the real problem was, as impressed me was recovering from the devastation and the starvation and dislocation that they were able to put together this effort."

Fuchs worked at Los Alamos. After the war, he gave to the Soviets information about the development of the hydrogen bomb, which was an advance over the plutonium bomb. Agnew worked with Fuchs at Los Alamos and knew him well. "We weren't socially very much involved, although we lived in a quadruplex in Los Alamos during the war," he recalled in the 1998 interview. "Interesting enough when ... we flew the Hiroshima Mission and measured the yield, the person who helped me in analyzing the theory of what the yield was based on our blast measurements, was Klaus Fuchs, so essentially the last paper in which I was involved in Los Alamos before I went back to the University of Chicago was with Klaus Fuchs. People used him as a babysitter, he was a very polite, very quiet type of individual. No idea at all that he had this dual personality or this dual endeavor."

In the same interview, Agnew speculated about the kind of information that Fuchs provided the Soviets: "I gather the information he gave the Soviets was what we were doing, what our progress was and in the end a complete detailed drawing, schematic, of our first Nagasaki bomb, the plutonium bomb," he said, "everything including the lenses, lens design, mass of plutonium, actual dimensions, the whole thing."

Continued his Education after the War

After the war, Agnew returned to the University of Chicago, where he earned his master's degree in 1948. The following year, he received his PhD from the university, under the direction of Fermi (Agnew would later earn honorary degrees, in 1980 from the College of Sante Fe and in 1992 from the University of Denver).

Following his studies in Chicago, Agnew returned to Los Alamos and worked in the Physics Division. He eventually became the Weapons Division leader, a position he held from 1964 to 1970.

In 1970 he became director of the Los Alamos Scientific Laboratory. During Agnew's years as director, Los Alamos developed an underground test containment program, built the Clinton P. Anderson Meson Physics Facility, acquired the first Cray supercomputer, and trained the first-ever class of International Atomic Energy Agency inspectors.

In 1979, he left Los Alamos and became president of General Atomics (until 1983). During his career, Agnew also served as scientific advisor to SACEUR at NATO (1961-64), became a member of the President's Science Advisory Committee (1965-73), was chairman of the General Advisory Committee of the Arms Control and Disarmament Agency (1974-78), and was a White House science councilor (1982-89). In addition, he served as a New Mexico state senator, from 1955 to 1961. Later, he served as adjunct professor at the University of California, San Diego.

Received Many Honors

Along with his honorary degrees, Agnew received much recognition during his career. His awards include the Ernest Orlando Lawrence Award in 1966, an award that was established in 1959 to honor scientists who helped elevate American physics to world leadership. Also, along with Hans Bethe (a German-American nuclear physicist and Nobel laureate), Agnew was the first recipient of the Los Alamos National Laboratory Medal, which is the highest honor that Laboratory bestows (typically for pioneering work in the area of physics). In 1987, Agnew received the Enrico Fermi Award, which is given by the Department of Energy's Office of Science. According to the Department, the award is given to "encourage excellence in energy science and technology; to show appreciation to scientists, engineers, and science policymakers who have given unstintingly over their lifetimes to benefit mankind through energy science and technology; and to inspire people of all ages through the example of Enrico Fermi, whose achievements opened new scientific and technological realms, and the Fermi Award laureates, who continued in his tradition."

A Fermi Award winner receives a citation signed by the President of the United States and the Secretary of Energy, a gold medal bearing the likeness of Enrico Fermi, and a $375,000 honorarium.

Books

"Agnew, Harold Melvin," *American Men & Women of Science*, Gale, 2008.

Online

"Harold Agnew," *Nuclearfiles.org*, http://nuclearfiles.org/menu/library/biographies/bio_agnew-harold.htm (December 1, 2011).

"Harold Agnew," *Right Web*, http://rightweb.irc-online.org/profile/Agnew_Harold (December 1, 2011).

"Harold Agnew-Biography," *mphpa.org*, http://www.mphpa.org/classic/COLLECTIONS/LA-HAGN/Pages/biography.htm (December 1, 2011).

"Harold Agnew on: The Hiroshima Mission," *pbs.org*, http://www.pbs.org/wgbh/amex/bomb/filmmore/reference/interview/agnewhiroshima.html (December 1, 2011).

"Interview with Harold Agnew," *gwu.edu*, http://www.gwu.edu/~nsarchiv/coldwar/interviews/episode-8/agnew1.html (December 1, 2011).

"The Agnew Years 1970-1979," *lanl.gov*,http://www.lanl.gov/history/people/agnew.shtml (December 1, 2011).

"The Men Who Bombed Hiroshima," *BBC.co.uk*, http://news.bbc.co.uk/2/hi/americas/4718579.stm (December 1, 2011).□

Mel Allen

American broadcaster Mel Allen (1913–1996), the longtime voice of the New York Yankees baseball team, was one of the most recognizable figures in the world of sports during the middle of the twentieth century.

Allen introduced several phrases to the lexicon of baseball, including the now-ubiquitous "going ... going ... gone!" with which he described a home run for radio audiences. He began his career with the Yankees in 1939 and remained in their employ until 1964, except for a period of military service during World War II. Allen combined a classic radio voice, rich and clear, with a gift of gab that brought baseball to life for radio listeners but did not always translate well to the new medium of television. He influenced many of the next generation of baseball broadcasters, in some cases training them directly as they entered the Yankees' organization.

Raised in Observant Jewish Household

One of three children born to Russian Jewish immigrants Julius and Anna Israel, Allen was born Melvin Allen Israel on February 14, 1913, in Birmingham, Alabama. His father operated a clothing store for a time and also worked as a traveling salesman of shirts and other consumer goods; the family lived in several places around the South, eventually settling in the college town of Tuscaloosa, Alabama. The Allens' neighbor across the street was future Alabama head football coach Paul William "Bear" Bryant. Allen's way with words came partly from Julius Israel. "My daddy was a storyteller," he recalled, according to Richard Sandomir of the *New York Times*. Anna Israel was descended from a line of Jewish rabbis, and Allen remained an observant Jew; at parties for baseball players during his career, Anna Israel would use separate dishes when serving shellfish.

A precocious student, Allen entered the University of Alabama at 15. He had already served as batboy for a North Carolina minor league baseball team, and he saw his first major league game, enlivened by a home run from the great Babe Ruth, on a family visit to Detroit. Allen tried out for the football team but was instead offered the post of equipment manager and public address announcer for the team's home games. It was enough to learn the game, and when Birmingham radio station WBRC was gearing up for live broadcasts of Alabama games, the team's coach recommended Allen as a play-by-play announcer. "My only experience was in listening to [pioneering sportscasters]

Graham McNamee and Ted Husing,'' Allen recalled in an interview with historian Curt Smith quoted in the *New York Times.* "But even so, I passed the audition. . . . 'Course, from what I understand, I was the only one to audition.'' Allen made his on-air debut at WBRC in 1933.

The previous year, Allen had received his undergraduate degree from Alabama and enrolled at the University of Alabama Law School. He graduated and passed the Alabama bar exam. Allen "was a scholar at heart, at least originally,'' Yankees shortstop Phil Rizzuto reflected to Bill Pennington of New Jersey's Bergen County *Record.* "You know, he had a law degree. And so he had a sense of words and literature and how all that fits into a scene.'' But Allen had already begun to love broadcasting. On vacation with friends in New York in 1937, he decided to audition at CBS radio, where executives were already familiar with his Alabama football broadcasts.

Joined CBS Radio

He was hired at a salary of $45 a week—much to the displeasure of his father, who felt he was throwing away a professional education. To add insult to injury, CBS asked Allen to drop his surname of Israel; like many other Jewish figures in the sports and entertainment industries of the time, he agreed, taking the familial middle name of Allen as his last name. As a junior anchor at CBS, Allen stepped into a variety of roles, and especially enjoyed introducing live big-band broadcasts from New York hotel ballrooms. He began working sports broadcasts as an underling of Husing and sportscaster Arch McDonald, and he nearly landed a spot as the voice of the Washington Senators when that team's broadcast sponsor, Wheaties cereal, expressed a desire that he be hired. The sponsor was overruled, however, by Senators' owner Clark Griffith, who wanted pitching legend Walter Johnson for the job.

Allen's breakthrough came in 1939 when McDonald's chief assistant, Garnett Marks, twice read the name of sponsor Ivory Soap on the air as Ovary Soap, and was fired. Allen replaced him in June of 1939, and took over later in the 1939 season when McDonald moved to Washington. With the beginning of the 1940 season he became the Yankees' official lead announcer. The young broadcaster got a firsthand taste of baseball's emotional power when he met Lou Gehrig, then in the final stages of amyotrophic lateral sclerosis (later known as Lou Gehrig's disease), in the Yankee dugout. "Lou patted me on the thigh and said, 'Kid, I never listened to the broadcasts when I was playing, but now they're what keep me going,''' Allen recalled, as quoted by Sandomir. "I went down the steps and bawled like a baby.''

Allen also broadcast New York Giants' home games in 1940. After a 1941 hiatus caused by a sponsorship dispute, Allen returned to the Yankees' booth in 1942. In 1943 he joined the U.S. Army, serving for three years. On leaves from his post at Fort Benning, Georgia, he did play-by-play broadcasts for a few Alabama football games and was active on Armed Forces Radio. Fresh out of the army in 1946, and with sports broadcasting growing rapidly, Allen was courted by both the Yankees and the Giants. He signed an exclusive contract with the Yankees, agreeing to broadcast the entire season of 154 home and away games on radio station WINS.

Allen would remain the much-loved Voice of the Yankees until 1964, gaining a national following (and national detractors as well, among supporters of opposing teams) through his numerous appearances on World Series broadcasts during the Yankees' dynasty of those years; between 1951 and 1963 he was in the booth for 11 of 13 series. He was also frequently tabbed for the mid-season All-Star game. Sometimes he still announced other sports as well—football, boxing, and a range of sports news for Movietone newsreels (news shorts shown in movie theaters). "Mr. Allen's voice, distinctly Southern but a perfect fit for the Bronx, became synonymous with baseball's rhythms, its lazy summer afternoons, chilly Octobers and shadows creeping over Yankee Stadium's greensward,'' Sandomir wrote.

Coined Stock Baseball Phrases

Like other broadcasters of his era, Allen had his trademark phrases—repeated descriptions and exclamations that made him an instantly identifiable, comforting presence in listeners' lives. He was apparently the first to use the now-common "going . . . going . . . gone!'' to evoke the flight of a home run ball. He dubbed Yankees ace hitter Joe DiMaggio "Joltin' Joe,'' came up with nicknames for several other Yankees players, and delivered an enthusiastic "How about that!'' for almost any remarkable play. A count of three balls and two strikes elicited from Allen the question "Three-and-two, what'll he do?'' Home runs were "Ballantine blasts'' and later "White Owl wallops,'' after sponsors Ballantine beer and White Owl cigars, respectively; Allen's Southern huckster instincts never deserted him. But he was a literate, precise speaker who once quoted Henry Wadsworth Longfellow's poem "Song of Hiawatha'' in full during a slow stretch of a game.

From 1954 until 1964, Allen frequently shared the booth with fellow Southerner Walter Lanier "Red" Barber, who had moved to the Yankees organization from the crosstown Brooklyn Dodgers. The two men were cordial on the air but reportedly were not personally close. Their styles differed. Broadcasting historian Curt Smith, quoted by Warren Corbett of the *Baseball Biography Project,* said that "the Ol' Redhead [Barber] was white wine, crepes Suzette, and bluegrass music; Mel, beer, hot dogs, and the United States Marine Band." Allen's style was garrulous and enthusiastic, Barber's deliberate and folksy. Their personal lives formed a contrast as well; Barber was happily married, while Allen remained a single man-about-town. The pair were jointly recognized in 1978 with the inaugural Ford C. Frick Award of the Baseball Hall of Fame, which recognizes broadcasters' contributions to the game.

Allen generally made a successful transition to television in the 1950s, although he was sometimes criticized for filling his broadcasts with talk instead of letting the camera tell part of the story, as was possible in the new medium. Nevertheless, his unvarying "Hello, everybody, this is Mel Allen" introduction remained a fixture of the game well into the 1960s, and fans were shocked to find that he simply disappeared from the airwaves in the fall of 1964. No clear explanation for his firing has ever surfaced, and the Yankees organization maintained press silence about the situation. "They left people to believe whatever they wanted—and people believed the worst," Allen complained, as quoted by *The Sporting News.* "The lies that started were horrible: that I was a lush or had a breakdown or a stroke or was numb from taking medications for my voice." Some of the rumors stemmed from an episode in which Allen lost his voice during the broadcast of a 1963 World Series game.

Only 51, Allen found other work intermittently. He broadcast games for the Atlanta Braves and the Cleveland Indians, as well as for the University of Miami football team. But he was largely absent from top-level sports for a period lasting into the 1970s, and a *Sports Illustrated* writer stated that it was as if he had leprosy. In 1977 Allen returned to the Yankees as suddenly as he had departed, announcing several dozen games on the SportsChannel cable network. Beginning in 1977 he hosted the Major League Baseball–sponsored program *This Week in Baseball,* where the opening credits included an animated Mel Allen figure, complete with fedora hat, that delivered the "Hello, this is Mel Allen" greeting. He was inducted into the Radio Hall of Fame in 1988. In 1990 Allen appeared on a regular Yankees broadcast, becoming one of just four broadcasters (the others are Vin Scully, Ernie Harwell, and the Spanish speaker Jaime Jarrin) to call games in seven different decades. In poor health in the 1990s, Allen lived with his sister Esther in Greenwich, Connecticut. He died there on June 16, 1996, and was buried at Temple Beth El Cemetery in nearby Stamford, below a gravestone bearing English and Hebrew lettering.

Books

Borelli, Stephen, *How About That! The Life of Mel Allen,* Sports Publishing, 2005.

Encyclopedia Judaica, 2nd ed., Macmillan, 2007.

Smith, Curt, *Voices of Summer,* Carroll & Graf, 2005.

Periodicals

New York Times, April 27, 1990; June 17, 1996; June 26, 1996.

Record (Bergen County, NJ), June 18, 1996.

Sporting News, April 7, 1997.

Online

"Mel Allen," *Baseball Biography Project,* http://www.bioproj.sabr.org(September 10, 2011).

"Mel Allen," *Museum of Broadcast Communications,* http://www.museum.tv/rhofsection.php?page=160 (September 10, 2011).

Schwartz, Larry, "Mel Allen, legendary Yankees voice, dies at 83," *ESPN Classic,* http://www.espn.go.com/classic/s/moment010616_mel_allen.html (September 10, 2011).s☐

Stephen Ambrose

The American historian Stephen E. Ambrose (1936–2002) became one of his country's best-known nonfiction writers in the last quarter of the twentieth century.

Focusing mostly on military history, Ambrose produced highly readable accounts written from the perspective of the individuals who did the fighting. His books were best sellers. In the words of former U.S. Senator George McGovern, a World War II bomber pilot, Ambrose "probably reached more readers than any other historian in our national history." Ambrose also penned widely read biographies of political figures, including presidents Dwight D. Eisenhower and Richard Nixon. At the end of his life, Ambrose was plagued by charges that he had used the work of other writers without attribution, and that he had fabricated accounts of extensive meetings with Eisenhower during the preparation of the several books he wrote about the general.

Stephen Edward Ambrose was born on January 10, 1936, in Decatur, Illinois; his family's home was in the nearby village of Lovington, where his father was a physician. After his father joined the U.S. Navy during World War II, the family moved to Whitewater, Wisconsin. A good but not stellar student who enjoyed his four years of high school Latin, Ambrose was the captain of the football team and prom king. Graduating in 1953, he enrolled at the University of Wisconsin with the intention of studying medicine. A specific teacher, history professor William B. Hesseltine, reoriented his ambitions.

Inspired by History Teacher

"He was a hero worshiper, and he got us to worship with him," Ambrose said in a *Baton Rouge Sunday Advocate* interview quoted in the *New York Times.* "Oh, if you could hear him talk about George Washington." In order to involve his students in history, Hesseltine had them do original research, and Ambrose headed off to the Wisconsin State Historical Society to investigate the career of one

Charles A. Billinghurst, an obscure nineteenth-century Wisconsin politician.

Enthusiastically, he realized that he knew more about Billinghurst than anyone else. "Now what I soon learned was, the reason for that was that nobody else cared about Charles A. Billinghurst," Ambrose said in an Academy of Achievement interview. "And then what I learned after that was, 'But I can make 'em care if I tell the story right.' And that's how I got into history." With Hesseltine's encouragement, he switched his major to history, later saying that he had decided to do so within ten minutes of entering Hesseltine's classroom. He received a B.A. in 1957 from Wisconsin and moved to the University of Louisiana for an M.A. the following year, writing a thesis on Civil War general Henry Halleck, Abraham Lincoln's chief of staff. The thesis was published in 1962, becoming the first of Ambrose's eventual 25 books.

Began Teaching Career

Ambrose returned to Wisconsin and began a Ph.D. dissertation there on another Civil War military leader, Emory Upton. He joined the faculty at Louisiana State University in New Orleans (now the University of New Orleans) in 1960 and received his Ph.D. from Wisconsin in 1963. Ambrose taught at various institutions, including Johns Hopkins University and Kansas State University, but he spent much of his career at Louisiana State University in Baton Rouge. For Ambrose, teaching reinforced the skills necessary to write history compellingly. "There's nothing like having an eight o'clock class in a non-air-conditioned building at summer school in New Orleans, Louisiana, to sharpen your skills as a storyteller," Ambrose observed in the Academy of Achievement interview. "Because those kids come in there, and there's a big fan, a big floor fan rattling away over there, and they're in that heat...boy, you damn

well better learn how to tell a story." Indeed, it was Ambrose's gifts as a pure storyteller that would mark his writing over his entire career.

That storytelling could sometimes obscure aspects of Ambrose's own career. In 1964, while working on Eisenhower's presidential papers at Johns Hopkins, he wrote to the former president, suggesting the idea of a biographical account of Eisenhower's military career. He enclosed a copy of his Halleck biography. Later Ambrose would say that Eisenhower himself initiated contact between the two, but the date of Ambrose's initial letter makes it clear that this was not so. Despite Ambrose's self-proclaimed leftist views at the time, Eisenhower's team identified Ambrose as a potentially sympathetic biographer, and he was given access to Eisenhower materials—although only rarely to the former president himself.

The books that followed—*Eisenhower and Berlin, 1945: The Decision to Halt at the Elbe* (1967), *The Supreme Commander: The War Years of General Dwight D. Eisenhower* (1970), and later *Eisenhower: Soldier and President* (1990)—made Ambrose's reputation. They were straightforward, forceful narratives, full of action verbs, that elevated Eisenhower's reputation in the face of criticism the former general had received from both the political left and right. Ambrose's own views became more conservative over the years. In 1970 he was part of a faculty group that heckled President Richard Nixon during a speech at Kansas State, resulting in his being pressured to leave the university. But he ultimately began to adopt more traditionalist views, finding heroism in the actions of the military personnel and explorers that filled the pages of American history, and it was to those that he devoted most of his writing career.

Ambrose's commercial breakthrough came with a massive three-volume biography of President Richard M. Nixon, a project that marked the beginning of his long association with the New York publishing house of Simon & Schuster. *Nixon: The Education of a Politician, 1913–1962* appeared in 1987, *Nixon: The Triumph of a Politician: 1962–1972* in 1990, and *Nixon: Ruin and Recovery, 1973–1990* in 1991. Ambrose disliked Nixon initially, and had to be persuaded to undertake the project ("I don't even like the guy," he complained, according to the *Wisconsin State Journal*), but he ultimately became convinced that the positive aspects of Nixon's legacy outweighed the negative ones.

The other two principal areas of Ambrose's research were the colonization of the American West and the experiences of the American soldiers who fought in World War II. The latter thread in Ambrose's output began with 1985's *Pegasus Bridge: June 6, 1944,* and continued with one of his most successful books, *Band of Brothers: E Company, 506th Regiment, 101st Airborne: From Normandy to Hitler's Eagle's Nest.* Published in 1995, the book was adapted into a widely seen ten-part mini-series broadcast on the HBO cable television network. Ambrose's *Undaunted Courage: Meriwether Lewis, Thomas Jefferson, and the Opening of the American West* (1996) became his best-known book dealing with the West; it was stimulated by his close readings of the diaries of Western explorers Lewis & Clark. Throughout his career, part of the strength of Ambrose's writing came from its direct engagement with source materials.

That book, by Ambrose's own testimony, earned him more than $4 million, and by the mid-1990s he was a best-selling author, reliably issuing a new book nearly every year. He scored a new commercial triumph with 2001's *The Wild Blue,* which recounted the experiences of crews on B-24 bomber aircraft during World War II. The following year, controversy surfaced as *Weekly Standard* writer Fred Barnes detected word-for-word similarities (without quotation marks or direct attribution) between passages in *The Wild Blue* and in a 1995 book, *Wings of Morning,* by Thomas Childers. Ambrose issued an apology, stating that the mistake would be corrected in future editions of the book. Similar passages were found in several other Ambrose books; Ambrose responded that the controversy involved only ten pages out of around 15,000 in print. Columbia University history professor Eric Foner observed to the *New York Times* that "nobody can write as many books as he has—many of them were well-written books—without the sloppiness that comes with speed and the constant pressure to produce." Ambrose himself suggested that the scrutiny given his works resulted partly from resentment among professional historians who disdained his popular success.

In 2002 Ambrose was diagnosed with lung cancer, and on October 13 of that year he died in Bay St. Louis, Mississippi, where he had maintained a home for many years (he also lived in Helena, Montana). He had been married three times and had five children. Before his death he substantially completed a personal and professional memoir, *To America: Personal Reflections of An Historian.* That book and a historical novel for children, *This Vast Land,* were issued posthumously. Before his death, faced with mounting questions about the integrity of his work, Ambrose said, as quoted in the *Weekly Standard,)* "Screw it. If they decide I'm a fraud, I'm a fraud."

Those questions persisted after Ambrose's death. In 2010, Timothy Rives, deputy director of the Dwight D. Eisenhower Presidential Library and Museum in Abilene, Kansas, reviewed Eisenhower's schedule logs and found that they did not corroborate Ambrose's claims to have spent large amounts of time with the ex-president in the 1960s (for example, Ambrose told the Academy of Achievement that he had been with Eisenhower "on a daily basis for a couple years"). Rives found that Ambrose and Eisenhower apparently met only three times, for a total of five hours, each time with others present, and that several meetings referred to in Ambrose's footnotes apparently did not occur. Despite these questions about Ambrose's work, he remained one of American history's most popular writers. His chronicles of American military enterprises loomed large among the output of contemporary historians, who many times have focused on social and economic matters.

Periodicals

Military History, September 2010.
New York Times, October 14, 2002.
New Yorker, April 26, 2010.
Times (London, England), October 14, 2002.
Weekly Standard, May 3, 2010.
Wisconsin State Journal (Madison, WI), October 23, 2002.

Online

"Interview: Stephen Ambrose, Biography and Historian," *Academy of Achievement,* http://www.achievement.org/autodoc/printmember/amb0int-1 (September 2, 2011).
Rives, Timothy D., "Ambrose and Eisenhower: A View from the Stacks in Abilene," *History News Network,* http://www.hnn.us/articles/126705.html (September 2, 2011). ☐

José Argüelles

The American philospher and art historian José Argüelles (1939–2011) was associated with several milestones of New Age thinking, most notably the Harmonic Convergence event of 1987 and the apocalyptic prophecies applying to the year 2012, derived from the calendrical system of the Maya people of ancient Mexico.

Those two events, in Argüelles's mind, were linked: the Harmonic Convergence, which Margalit Fox of the *New York Times* described as "by all accounts the first large-scale multinational meditation in history," was intended by Argüelles as an attempt to stave off or at least lessen the effects of the coming apocalypse through a worldwide application of spiritual energy, devoted to imagining a new social paradigm. Argüelles argued that other measures as well, such as the replacement of the traditional Roman or Gregorian calendar with a new lunar-based system, might reorient humanity away from disaster. The founder of California's Whole Earth Festival in 1969, Argüelles is regarded as one of the key promoters of the idea that the world would end in 2012 according to Mayan prophecy—an idea disputed by many archaeologists specializing in the Maya culture.

Spent Early Childhood in Mexico

Argüelles was born Joseph Anthony Arguelles in Rochester, Minnesota, on January 24, 1939. His father, Enrique Sabino Argüelles, was a Mexico City policeman who claimed to have been the first officer on the scene after exiled Russian Communist leader Leon Trotsky was murdered with an ax. He met Argüelles's mother, Ethel, a Minnesota-born junior college Spanish major when she was on a school trip to Mexico City. Determined to be closer to Enrique Argüelles, she landed a job at the U.S. embassy in Mexico City. The couple married in 1929 and lived in Mexico City, returning to Minnesota in 1931 to give birth to Argüelles's older sister, Laurita, and again in 1939 for the birth of Argüelles and his twin brother, Ivan. As a child, Argüelles was a friend of the modern Mexican political leader Cuauhtemoc Cárdenas.

After the family moved to Minnesota, Argüelles found that as a Mexican American he encountered discrimination; he stopped speaking Spanish and tried to fit in, using the name Joe. But a family trip to Mexico in 1953 gave him a strong desire to reconnect with his Mexican heritage: he later traced his fascination with the Maya to a visionary experience he had while standing atop the ancient Pyramid of the Sun at Teotihuacán. He readopted the name José and added Spanish diacritical marks to his name. Argüelles earned a B.A. degree from the University of Chicago in 1961, surmounting a brief expulsion the previous year for, he recalled to Michael Moynihan of *New Dawn*, "being a full-blown beatnik, accused of being the ringleader of a pot-smoking set of thugs meant to undermine the freshman women."

With his art history degree, the only work Argüelles could find was an insurance sales job. He considered undertaking a road trip in the manner of hippie role model Jack Kerouac, but he was already envisioning writing major philosophical tracts inspired by his study of the Maya, and he felt that advanced degrees would give him added credibility. So he went on for M.A. and Ph.D. degrees at Chicago. Traveling to Paris in the mid-1960s to do research on neo-impressionist art, he experimented with the drug LSD and became convinced that he was a visionary.

Painted Mandalas

Nevertheless, Argüelles continued to combine his academic work and his interest in what would become known as New Age ideas. He switched his dissertation topic from neo-impressionism to the little-known French mathematician, psychologist, and librarian Charles Henry, whose ideas had influenced some of the Impressionist painters. Argüelles was able to publish his Ph.D. thesis, *Charles Henry and the Formation of a Psychophysical Aesthetic,* as a book in 1972. He continued to explore world spiritual traditions, and became interested in Buddhist art and in the work of Nicolas Roerich, a Russian explorer of Eastern religions. Argüelles met the Tibetan Buddhist leader Chogyam Trungpa Rinpoche in 1971, and began painting circular Buddhist-inspired patterns known as mandalas. His first book, published in 1972, dealt with mandalas.

Argüelles's first major contribution to New Age culture came in 1969, while he was on the faculty at the University of California at Davis. Students remembered him as an unorthodox but effective professor who introduced lectures by playing a Native American flute and talked about commonalities in non-Western artistic traditions. On Mother's Day weekend of that year, he asked students to create a live art event—a "happening" in the terminology of the day—that would express beauty and love for the earth. That first Whole Earth Festival consisted merely of a group that hung chimes in trees, burned incense, played guitars, sang, and danced, but by 2011 Argüelles's creation had grown into a California institution attracting some 30,000 people annually.

Leaving Davis for Boulder, Colorado, Argüelles continued to write, and traveled widely, often in the company of his wife, Lloydine. Argüelles, who struggled with alcohol addiction, was married three times; he had a daughter, Tara, and a son, Josh, who was killed in an auto accident in 1987 shortly after the Harmonic Convergence. In 1983 Argüelles and Lloydine created the Planet Art Network, an international network of art collectives described in the London *Daily Telegraph* as "a force for non-political change." The full development of Argüelles's ideas coincided with the rapid growth of New Age philosophies and other new, unorthodox forms of spirituality in the 1980s.

Organized Harmonic Convergence

The single effort for which Argüelles remains best known is the Harmonic Convergence, which occurred on August 16 and 17, 1987, and was satirized in the popular "Doonesbury" comic strip as the Moronic Convergence. As a way of forestalling the cataclysm that Argüelles believed was foretold by Mayan chronicles, he organized worldwide gatherings at spiritually significant geographical locations such as Sedona, Arizona, Glastonbury, England, and Ayers Rock, Australia. Participants gathered at sunrise, held hands, meditated, chanted, and hummed. According to Elaine Woo of the *Los Angeles Times,* Argüelles stated that a "minimum human voltage" of 144,000 participants was needed to derail the Mayan prophecies; exact estimates of crowd sizes were hard to come by, but thousands of people, including 1,500 in New York's Central Park, attended.

The ideas behind the Harmonic Convergence were expressed fully in Argüelles's 1987 book *The Mayan Factor: Path Beyond Technology.* That book set forth Argüelles's analysis of the Mayan calendrical system, in which he contended that the year 2012 would mark the end of a 5,125-year cycle. Around the winter solstice of 2012, Argüelles believed, the Earth would enter a new age, and the existing order might be cataclysmically destroyed (his prophecies varied on this point). Argüelles expanded on this point in some of his roughly two dozen books. One of the most successful was *The Word Thirteen Moon Calendar Change Peace Plan* (1995), in which he advocated the replacement of the 12-month, solar-based Gregorian calendar with a 13-month lunar system. "Art and beauty really will save the world," Argüelles told Moynihan, "but only if humanity returns to living in the perfect harmony of the Thirteen Moon Calendar and thus becomes synchronized again with the whole of the universal order of the cosmos."

Mainstream scholars studying Mayan culture dismissed Argüelles's ideas. "Although I have spent years studying Mesoamerican calendars, I must confess that I cannot understand even one of Argüelles's complicated-looking diagrams," Colgate University Maya expert Anthony Aveni said, according to Woo. Undaunted, Argüelles returned with books on a variety of subjects, such as *The 260 Postulates of the Dynamics of Time* (1996), *Living Through the Closing of the Cycle: A Survival Guide to 2012* (2003), and *The Mayan Calendar and the Transformation of Consciousness* (2004). A four-volume set of *Cosmic History Chronicles* was written with a companion, Stephanie South.

Although he wrote voluminously, little documentation exists on Argüelles's later years. He maintained homes in Palenque, Mexico, and in Ashland, Oregon, where he set up the nonprofit Foundation for the Law of Time and operated a bookstore. He began using the name Valum Votan, meaning closer of the cycle. As 2012 approached, he began to lay plans for another massive event resembling the Harmonic Convergence. Argüelles apparently also had a home or connections in rural central Australia; he was in that region, accompanied by South at what was described as a retreat, when he began to suffer from peritonitis. He died there on March 23, 2011. Argüelles's death was announced by the Foundation for the Law of Time, but no specific location was given.

Books

South, Stephanie, and Daniel Pinchbeck, *2012: Biography of a Time Traveler,* New Page, 2009.

Periodicals

Daily Telegraph (London, England), April 6, 2011.

Davis Enterprise (Davis, CA), May 7, 2011.

Independent (London, England), April 20, 2011.

Los Angeles Times, April 10, 2011.

New York Times, August 11, 1987; April 3, 2011.

Online

"José Argüelles," *Miracles & Inspiration,* http://www.miraclesand inspiration.com/arguelles2.html (November 2, 2011).

"José Argüelles (1939–2011)" 13moon.com, http://www.13moon. com/Votan-bio.htm (November 2, 2011).

"Michael Moynihan Speaks with José Argüelles," *New Dawn,* November-December 2002, http://www.newdawnmagazine. com/articles/michael-moynihan-speaks-with-jose-arguelles (November 2, 2011). □

Roone Arledge

The name Roone Arledge (1931–2002) is virtually synonymous with the rise of the ABC network to dominance in sports and news programming during the 1960s and '70s. The creator of both *ABC's Wide World of Sports* and *Monday Night Football,* Arledge was named president of the network's staid news division in 1977 in a move that generated tremendous controversy, both at ABC and in broadcast journalism itself. Predictably, Arledge made sweeping changes that reshaped American television viewing habits, first by introducing *Nightline,* the late-night news program, and then by finessing and perfecting the formula for fluffier, feature story newsmagazine shows like *20/20* and *Primetime.*

Roone Pinckney Arledge Jr. spent almost his entire life in New York City, where he was born on July 8, 1931. His parents, Gertrude and Roone Sr., lived in the Forest Hills section of Queens before moving out to Merrick, Long Island, where Arledge covered sports for his high school newspaper. The first television images he ever saw were at the 1939 World's Fair in Flushing Meadows, New York, when the new medium first went on public display. He graduated from high school in 1948 and entered Columbia University with the plan to major in journalism, but discovered the Ivy League school offered only a graduate-level program in the subject.

Graduated from Columbia

After graduating from Columbia in 1952, Arledge joined the DuMont Television Network, one of the first broadcasters in the United States. The company made superb state-of-the-art television sets, owned a string of stations along the East Coast, and produced its own programming. DuMont was an early rival to the National Broadcasting Corporation (NBC); the Columbia Broadcasting System was the third entrant to the medium. Arledge picked up some television production skills before he was drafted into the U.S. Army at the height of the Korean War. Fortunately, he served his time at a Maryland base as an announcer for the base's radio station. When he returned, he found the DuMont Network on the verge of financial collapse, and finagled his way into a job with NBC through his wife, Joan, who was among the team of administrative assistants who worked for David A. Sarnoff, president of RCA.

Arledge spent much of the 1950s as a producer and unit supervisor at NBC, running a myriad of programs, including a daytime hour aimed at mothers and their young children called *Hi, Mom!* that featured ventriloquist Shari Lewis and a sock puppet named Lamb Chop. Arledge's first live-remote directing job was the lighting of the Rockefeller Center Christmas tree in 1959, and he yearned to take cameras out into the world and create other, similarly exciting special event broadcasts. An ardent sports fan from an early age, Arledge was also disappointed by current standards of television sports, which he contended fell far short of conveying the genuine excitement of an athletic contest.

Jazzed Up College Football

In 1960 Arledge was hired by Edgar Scherick, a pioneer in teaming advertising sponsors with sporting event broadcasts. Scherick had sold his company to the final entrant in the national television network stakes, the American Broadcasting Company (ABC), and had become head of ABC's sports programming. Scherick hired Arledge just as the network was working on a deal with the National Collegiate Athletic Association (NCAA) to broadcast a select number of college football games on Saturdays. Scherick asked Arledge to draft a memo he could bring to the contract negotiations to generate some excitement about ABC's proposal. Arledge's typewritten notes contained all of his radical ideas, including multiple cameras, crowd shots, and cutaways to cheerleaders. "WE ARE GOING TO ADD SHOW BUSINESS TO SPORTS!," he asserted in the memo, according to his autobiography, *Roone: A Memoir.* "In addition to the natural suspense and excitement of the actual game, we have a supply of human drama that would make the producer of a dramatic show drool. All we have to do is find and insert it in our game coverage at the proper moment."

Scherick soon put Arledge in charge of *ABC's Wide World of Sports,* which debuted in 1961 and ran for an astonishing 27 years. The 90-minute weekly program had an unexpected impact, generating interest in little-known sports once thought to have mere lackluster regional followings. Arledge sent reporters and cameras out to cover collegiate track and field events, NASCAR auto racing, the U.S. Figure Skating Championships, tennis's Wimbledon Cup, and even gymnastics. He also devised the dazzling opening titles for *ABC's Wide World of Sports,* including longtime anchor Jim McKay's weekly voiceover pledging to bring viewers "the thrill of victory and the agony of defeat," which became a national catchphrase. "Almost every element of everyday sports production was inspired or enhanced by Arledge," declared veteran *Sports Illustrated* writer Frank Deford years later about the Emmy-winning Saturday afternoon staple. "Simple things like ambient sound, the tight, intimate shot—up close and personal!—and identifying graphics...were his ideas. So were advances like the handheld camera, cranes on golf courses, the underwater camera, the split screen, the camera on the basketball backboard and the three-announcer booth."

Created *Monday Night Football*

In 1964 Arledge was made vice president of ABC Sports, and played a key role in the network's decision to pay what was then a staggering $200,000 to secure the broadcast rights for the 1964 Winter Olympics held that year in Innsbruck, Austria. As the producer in charge, Arledge amped up the television coverage considerably, using behind-the-scenes interviews and picking out compelling athletes to profile, replete with visits to their far-flung hometowns. Ratings proved sufficient for ABC to bid successfully on the 1968 Summer Olympics in Mexico City.

Arledge was promoted to president of ABC Sports in 1968 after some other successes at the network. He had been heavily involved, for example, in broadcasting games of the fledgling American Football League (AFL), a rival to the National Football League (NFL), whose games were broadcast on CBS at the time. Arledge's innovative techniques helped the AFL build a solid fan base in several major markets, and the two leagues were eventually forced into a merger. Out of that deal came one of Arledge's most enduring career achievements, *ABC's Monday Night Football.* Because the now-enlarged NFL had struck deals with NBC and CBS for broadcast rights, Arledge went to NFL commissioner Pete Rozelle and asked for a Monday night game to be held, which ABC would carry.

Arledge's idea of a weeknight prime time football game had few supporters at first, but the program began pulling in a surprising number of viewers. Arledge hired a trio of commentators for the broadcast booth, whose banter helped make *Monday Night Football* one of the top-rated network shows for decades to come. The inaugural team consisted of Frank Gifford, an ex-New York Giants player who provided sober play-by-play commentary; retired Dallas Cowboys quarterback Don Meredith, known for his Southern drawl and folksy patter; and former labor attorney Howard Cosell, who had gained fame as a boxing announcer. The brash and opinionated Cosell seemed to attract an equal number of critics and admirers across America, but Arledge's hiring decision had been a smart one and ABC's Monday night ratings share escalated and held firm for decades.

Covered the 1972 "Munich Massacre"

During his years as head of ABC Sports, Arledge had revolutionized Olympics broadcasting, correctly judging that television audiences were more likely to tune in to see women's gymnastic events than men's weightlifting competitions. But the merging of sports and current events that shaped his career came unexpectedly and dramatically at the 1972 Summer Games in Munich, West Germany, when members of a Palestinian militant group gained access to the Olympic athletes' housing complex and held several Israeli athletes and coaches hostage before killing them in a botched escape attempt. Arledge was the producer in charge over 18 hours of the unfolding drama on ABC, which became one of the most dramatic events in the history of live television; he and his ABC team won an Emmy Award for their coverage.

In the spring of 1977 ABC's president, Leonard Goldenson, announced that Arledge was taking over the network's news division, too. This roiled staffers at ABC News, for Arledge was the first-ever head of a major network news division without any solid journalism credentials on his resume. Moreover, the network's nightly news broadcast, *ABC Evening News,* was flaming out after receiving a short burst of interest when Barbara Walters, who came over from NBC's morning staple *The Today Show,* became the first woman to co-anchor an evening news broadcast in America. On camera her co-anchor, veteran journalist Harry Reasoner, was barely able to contain his disdain for the experiment.

One of Arledge's first moves was to get rid of the Reasoner-Walters lineup in favor of a three-anchor broadcast he named *World News Tonight.* He put African-American journalist Max Robinson on the Chicago desk, sent a young Canadian named Peter Jennings to report from a London set, and installed gruff news veteran Frank Reynolds on the Washington desk. Arledge deployed his usual production tricks to generate appealing shots, in one instance lighting the Vienna Cathedral at night as a backdrop for a report on U.S.-Soviet arms treaty talks being held there. Other journalists in town to cover the summit were appalled, but such easy solutions to enlivening the news became commonplace in the industry within a few years. "What Arledge has done," assessed *New York Times Magazine* writer Desmond Smith in a profile on Arledge that was essentially a lengthy hatchet job, "is to isolate and package whatever may be the cathartic high point in any story. The result is that today there is a genuinely different 'look' to ABC television news, and a consistent editorial viewpoint—one that seeks out the passionate element in public life."

Put *Nightline* on the Air

Smith's article was notable for the scores of anonymous quotes from Arledge's competitors in the news business and even from colleagues inside ABC News, most of whom relished the chance to discuss Arledge's unfitness for the job of delivering serious journalism. It ran in February of 1980 just as Arledge's final, enduring contribution to ABC News was emerging. Three months earlier, Iranian university students had stormed the U.S. Embassy in Tehran and seized 53 Americans, demanding the return of the exiled Ayatollah Ruhollah Khomeini and the removal of the ruling Shah of Iran. The incident provoked international outrage, and tremendous debate in the United States about how to resolve the quagmire; U.S. president Jimmy Carter was widely judged to have lost his reelection bid a year later over his handling of the crisis. Arledge came up with the idea of a special nightly broadcast to follow the 11 p.m. news on ABC affiliates called *The Iran Crisis—America Held Hostage: Day [X]*, with the "X" increasing every day for the full 444-day duration of the hostage standoff. The program morphed into *Nightline* in March of 1980, and remained on the air—and a ratings success—more than three decades later.

Ted Koppel became the host of *Nightline* and one of ABC News's most respected journalists. Even Koppel, years later, told another *New York Times Magazine* writer that he was among the staffers who opposed Arledge's promotion to head of the news division. "The things we resented most about Roone when he came on were what ultimately hooked people," Koppel admitted to Julian Rubinstein.

Arledge's instincts for what viewers wanted to see helped turn ABC's sports and news programming slots into lucrative profit centers for the network. ABC was bought by Capital Cities Communications in 1985 for an astonishing $3.5 billion. A year later, Arledge was forced out as head of ABC Sports, and retired from ABC News in 1998. He wrote a memoir that was published a year after his death from prostate cancer on December 5, 2002, at the age of 71. The thrice-married Arledge, who favored safari jackets and cigars, was one of the most colorful personalities ever to work in television, but also one of the most prescient. "Every bit of research tells us that American people don't care a lot about foreign news," Arledge told Smith. "I just don't believe it. When you have a revolution in Iran and two months later you have gasoline lines in this country, people damn well better care. You've got to show them the connection, and you've got to show them the relevance."

Books

Arledge, Roone, *Roone: A Memoir,* HarperCollins. 2003, pp. 30–32.

Periodicals

American Journalism Review, January–February 2003.
Broadcasting, December 2, 1985.
Broadcasting & Cable, October 10, 1994.
New York Times Magazine, February 24, 1980; December 29, 2002.
Sports Illustrated, December 16, 2002. □

Dorothy Arzner

American filmmaker Dorothy Arzner (1897–1979) was one of the first woman directors during Hollywood's Golden Age. For a time, she was the only woman to make big-budget feature films at a major studio, and her singular career in the 1930s would remain somewhat of an anomaly for decades. She directed Paramount's first sound film in 1929, then went on to helm a string of melodramatic "women's pictures" that earned both critical acclaim and commercial success, and turned lesser known players like Katharine Hepburn and Rosalind Russell into stars.

Dorothy Arzner was born on January 3, 1897, in San Francisco, though she later shaved a few years from her age and asserted she was born in 1900, claiming that her vital statistics data had been lost in the infamous San Francisco earthquake and fire of 1906. But Arzner was likely already living in the Los Angeles area by then with her family: her father, Louis, ran the popular Hoffman Café at 215 South Spring Street, a favorite gathering spot for Hollywood studio executives, directors, and stars like Charlie Chaplin. Only recently had the U.S. film production industry shifted from New York and New Jersey to Southern California, where land was plentiful, landscape scenery varied, and the weather was almost always agreeable.

Began in Typing Pool

After graduating from the Westlake School for Girls in 1915, Arzner enrolled at the University of Southern California with a plan to enter medical school. She spent two years there before signing on as a volunteer with the Los Angeles Emergency Ambulance Corps when the United States entered World War I in 1917. She completed the course, but was never posted overseas. Her stint did serve to introduce her to the screenwriter and director who ran the civilian service operation, William C. DeMille, the brother of acclaimed director Cecil B. DeMille. William worked for one of the top studios of the era, Famous Players-Lasky, and in 1919 he hired Arzner as a typist. She was admittedly terrible at the job, and credited a sympathetic colleague for helping her on the sly.

Entranced by the movie business, Arzner was determined to move out of the stenography pool and up the chain at Famous Players, which eventually morphed into Paramount Pictures. She became a script clerk, then film

cutter, or editor, and found a mentor in Alla Nazimova, a Russian-born star who wielded enormous influence in crafting her own projects in the 1920s. Nazimova was said to have been romantically linked to two of Rudolph Valentino's wives, and this led to an offer for Arzner to edit *Blood and Sand,* Valentino's latest project in which he played a famous matador. Arzner did a particularly adept job on the bullfighting sequences, and was given increasing responsibilities for editing by James Cruze, who had moved from acting to directing Westerns. She worked on several pictures of his, including 1923's *The Covered Wagon,* and edited a comic serial titled *Ruggles of Red Gap,* about a proper English butler who is traded away in a poker game and winds up in a frontier town.

Within a few short years, Arzner was writing scenarios for other directors, and then entire screenplays. After one of her stories, *When Husbands Flirt,* did well at the box office in 1925, she felt ready to direct a movie of her own. Paramount executives were reluctant, however, and so she threatened to leave the studio for Columbia Pictures, which had offered her a contract. Paramount relented and asked her to stay on, promising to let her direct at some future date, but Arzner held firm and demanded that she be given an "A"-picture (top tier) directing job within a two-week time-frame, and they complied.

Trusted by Paramount

Arzner's directorial debut was *Fashions for Women,* a 1927 silent film featuring former vaudeville child performer Esther Ralston in her first starring role. The picture was a hit, and Arzner began a relationship with dancer Marion Morgan, who worked on the costumes for the Paris set. Morgan was the choreographer for *Ten Modern Commandments* and *Manhattan Cocktail,* two more silents Arzner directed over the course of 1927 and 1928. The pair were

among a number of successful Hollywood professionals who lived semi-openly as same sex couples, a remarkable breach in defiance of the conventions of the era. When Arzner made plans to build a home in a newly developed section of the Los Feliz neighborhood of Los Angeles—the area situated below the landmark "HOLLYWOOD" sign— her bank refused to give her a mortgage, so Arzner cashed in some of her investments. Her decision to sell her stock shares was prescient, for her holdings would have been evaporated in the Wall Street stock market crash that occurred a few months later in October of 1929.

Paramount's publicity department promoted Arzner as its first woman director. Her status was cemented when she was given the task of directing screen star Clara Bow in her first "talking" picture since the advent of sound; this would also be the studio's first foray into that realm. It was a period of perilous transition for some stars, who proved to have unappealing voices or problems with memorizing pages of dialogue. Bow, who had little formal schooling and a heavy Brooklyn accent, was understandably nervous and hoped to keep her ranking as Hollywood's No. 1 female box office star and her massively hyped status as "The 'It' Girl."

Arzner turned *The Wild Party* into box office gold, and Bow's reign continued. The 1929 release was set at a women's college and revolved around the carefree lifestyle of its student body, who exulted in the freedom of living away from their families. The most daring among them was Bow's Stella, who falls in love with a new professor, played by Fredric March, and becomes embroiled in a divisive campus scandal. *The Wild Party* was a major critical and commercial success, but compiled one more "first" in the annals of cinema history: the skittish Bow was afraid of the large microphones used to record dialogue, so Arzner devised a way to hang one overhead, attached to a fishing rod, which could follow the actors around and not distract them. This was the first boom microphone, which became standard equipment on film sets.

Drew Appealing Performances from Actors

Arzner's sixth movie as director, *Sarah and Son,* earned its star Ruth Chatterton a nomination for the Best Actress Academy Award. Arzner was quickly becoming known as a director who could help a performer reach major star status. She had done so with March, who appeared in his first leading role in *The Wild Party* and won the Best Actor Academy Award two years later for *Dr. Jekyll and Mr. Hyde*—made by another director. March also appeared in a 1931 movie of Arzner's, *Honor Among Lovers,* as a perennially absent corporate executive whose capable secretary, played by Claudette Colbert, essentially runs the company.

Merrily We Go to Hell, made during the depths of the Great Depression in 1932, was Arzner's tenth feature film. Film historians cite it as a classic example of the "Pre-Code" movie, works filmed or released before the stringent Hays Code went into effect. It starred March and Sylvia Sidney in a marital comedy with adultery as its running theme. When the Code went into full effect in 1934, Hollywood studios capitulated to conservative watchdog groups and turned out films in which sexual transgressions and criminal behavior were depicted on screen, but always punished appropriately in the end.

The fate met by Katharine Hepburn's character in *Christopher Strong* was a perfect example of Hollywood's new screen morality. Hepburn sought out Arzner to help resurrect a career that had showed some early promise after Broadway success, but then languished in Hollywood. In *Christopher Strong*, Hepburn played Lady Cynthia Darrington, a daring British aviatrix who is in love with the married politician of the title, played by Colin Clive. "Hepburn's lithe, strikingly androgynous and unique presence owns the film in all but title," wrote film critic Molly Haskell in the London *Guardian* about this 1933 classic. "Hepburn is convincing as a flyer, but even more unforgettable wearing that peculiar grasshopper costume, a satin jumpsuit with antennae popping from her head—the very image of an actress indifferent to convention, determined to be herself, matched by a director as determined and accepting of herself as she is."

Worked with Joan Crawford

Billie Burke played the cuckolded wife in *Christopher Strong*, and Arzner cast Burke in a supporting role in *Craig's Wife*, a significant success that propelled Rosalind Russell to stardom. The story of a domineering, acquisitive wife, the film was adapted from a Pulitzer Prize-winning drama of 1925 penned by George Kelly, the uncle of screen legend and future Monaco royal Grace Kelly. By this point Arzner had left Paramount and moved to Columbia, and she was profiled in advance of the movie's release by the *New York Times*. The article described her as "completely poised . . . with a reputation of being one of the quietest directors in Hollywood; her sets are conspicuously lacking in the quality of raucousness."

After the success of *Craig's Wife*, studio mogul Louis B. Mayer hired Arzner in 1937 to resurrect Joan Crawford's career. In Metro-Goldwyn-Mayer's *The Bride Wore Red*, Crawford was cast as a cabaret singer with a sketchy past "who pretends to be a lady when she is given an unexpected taste of Tyrolean high life," wrote Graham Fuller in the *New York Times*. Crawford's Anni/Anna "basks in the attention paid to her by a feckless playboy while his pretty, passive longtime fiancée suffers beside them. Arzner targeted not just man's insensitivity to woman but women's unkindness to women."

In 1938 Arzner became the first woman admitted to a new labor union, the Screen Directors Guild, which had been founded two years earlier by King Vidor. The organization later evolved into the Directors Guild of America (DGA). Her career as a director was winding to a close, however, and she made only two more movies in her career: *Dance, Girl, Dance,* a 1940 drama that featured Lucille Ball and Maureen O'Hara as two rival performers, and *First Comes Courage* in 1943, a wartime drama with screen beauty Merle Oberon as a Norwegian resistance fighter. While making the latter, Arzner came down with pneumonia and then decided to retire. She was in her mid-forties at the time, and had earned, saved, and invested enough to live comfortably at her expansive Los Feliz home, whose living room was so large that an entire Russian *corps de ballet* once performed there.

Arzner returned to the camera briefly in the late 1950s, when Joan Crawford—married to the president of Pepsi Cola—persuaded her to make a few television commercials for the beverage brand. For most of the 1950s Arzner taught courses in filmmaking at the Pasadena Playhouse, then at the Graduate Film School of the University of California—Los Angeles from 1959 to 1963, where a young Francis Ford Coppola was one of her students. A decade later, a new generation of women filmmakers rediscovered Arzner and her pioneering films, and honored her at the First International Festival of Women's Film in New York City in 1972. Three years later, the DGA gave her a special career achievement award. She died on October 1, 1979, in La Quinta, California. Film historian Judith Mayne wrote extensively on Arzner's place in Hollywood history, including a 1994 biography, *Directed by Dorothy Arzner.*

Books

Mahar, Karen Ward, *Women Filmmakers in Early Hollywood,* JHU Press, 2008, p. 206.

Mayne, Judith, *Directed by Dorothy Arzner,* Indiana University Press, 1994.

Mayne, Judith, *The Woman at the Keyhole: Feminism and Women's Cinema,* Indiana University Press, 1990, p. 98.

Periodicals

Guardian (London, England), January 9, 2004.

Los Angeles Magazine, February 1999.

New York Times, September 27, 1936; June 15, 1972; August 20, 1976; October 12, 1979; February 6, 2000.

Online

"Giving Credit," Directors Guild of America, http://www.dga.org/ (July 7, 2011). □

Jean-Pierre Aumont

The career of French actor Jean-Pierre Aumont (1911–2001) spanned seven decades through stage, screen, and television. He first rose to stardom in French cinema of the 1930s, then took his talents to Hollywood, where Metro-Goldwyn-Mayer put him in a few big budget productions. The 60-plus movies in which Aumont appeared range from the 1938 French *noir* classic *Hôtel du Nord* to a campy musical from 1947, *Song of Scheherazade;* in his later years he turned up in both François Truffaut's *Day for Night* in 1973 and the Diana Ross-Anthony Perkins drama *Mahogany.*

orn Jean-Pierre Salomons on January 5, 1911(some sources claim the year was 1909), Aumont came from a wealthy Paris family. His father, Alexandre, was descended from Dutch Jews and owned a profitable chain of linen stores called La Maison du Blanc. Aumont's

of France's leading writers, André Gide, several years earlier. Allégret had hoped to cast Olympic medalist and *Tarzan* star Johnny Weissmuller in the coveted lead role of a swim coach at an Alpine resort, but Weissmuller's Hollywood studio bosses refused to loan him out. Aumont was one of several young actors to audition for the part, and he won the role of Erik, a young man whose appealing looks and natural charm place him in the middle of a vexacious love triangle.

Lac aux Dames went on to become a classic of French cinema from this era. The film was a visual delight. Its lavish budget was bankrolled by a young scion of the Rothschild banking family, and it did well at the box office, bolstered by its picturesque mountain setting and lively dialogue written by another giant of French literature, Colette. It also made Aumont a star overnight, both in France and elsewhere. "Aumont makes of him a man at once to admire and with whom to sympathize," noted a *Times* of London review, while across the Atlantic *New York Times* critic Herbert L. Matthews asserted of Aumont, "There is a sincerity and simplicity about him which more than makes up for his lack of experience.... He never appears to be acting, or even conscious of the adoration that is a deserved tribute to a genuine and very masculine beauty."

mother, born Suzanne Berr, had done some acting before her marriage, and she was also the niece of veteran comic actor Georges Berr, who "did everything in his power to deter me from the theater," Aumont wrote in his 1976 autobiography, *Sun and Shadow*.

Studied at Paris Conservatory

Sent to a strict boarding school at the age of nine, Aumont announced his intention to become an actor after his grandmother—Berr's sister—had taken him to a performance at Paris's legendary Comédie Fraçaise. At 16 he began formal studies at the esteemed Conservatoire de Paris, and his first major break came when a well known French actor-director named Louis Jouvet signed him to the corps of players at the Comédie des Champs-Elysées in Paris.

Aumont's film debut came in *Jean de la Lune* (Jean of the Moon) in 1931. "Expecting that it would fizzle 'director' Jean Choux had entrusted the direction to his assistant. In my scene I'm asleep on a train on the knees of Madeleine Renaud, who regrets having left her husband for me," Aumont wrote in his autobiography. Aumont would reunite several more times on screen with Renaud, a classically trained actor and veteran of the stage. He also appeared in a 1932 romantic comedy with Anny Ondra, who was the wife of German boxing great Max Schmeling. The movie was *Faut-il Les Marier?* (Should We Marry Them?), but its production was halted when Aumont was unable to postpone his compulsory military service any longer.

Nabbed Part Meant for *Tarzan*

The film that turned Aumont into a star was actually his ninth appearance on the screen. *Lac aux Dames* (Ladies' Lake), released in 1934, was the work of filmmaker Marc Allégret, who had become the teenage companion of one

Appeared in Jean Cocteau Drama

That same year, Aumont also cemented his reputation as stage talent when France's most famous living playwright, Jean Cocteau, cast him in a new play at the Comédie des Champs-Elysées, titled *La Machine Infernale* (The Infernal Machine). Aumont starred as Oedipus in Cocteau's reworking of the great ancient Greek tragedy, and from this point onward he would alternate film and stage roles for the remainder of his career, branching out into television in the early 1950s.

Aumont appeared again with Simone Simon in *Les yeux noirs,* just before she left for Hollywood, where her best-known role would be in the classic thrillers *Cat People* and *Curse of the Cat People.* Aumont stayed in France and worked with a series of Russian émigré directors who had in some cases been trained under the great theater director Konstantin Stanislavsky. These films included *L'Equipage* and *Tarass Bulba,* the latter a 1936 release that co-starred him with another rising star of French cinema, Danielle Darrieux.

Aumont's best-known role from this period of his career came in *Hôtel du Nord,* a 1938 drama set at the titular Paris establishment with a large cast and intertwining plots. One of France's leading box office draws was the ingénue Annabella, and in *Hôtel du Nord* she and Aumont appeared as doomed lovers who plan to carry out a suicide pact in one of the rooms.

Fled France, Then Returned

World War II interrupted Aumont's screen career. Like many of his compatriots, he was devastated when France capitulated to Nazi Germany in May of 1940 after a brief and embarrassing attempt to repel an invasion, and he had been called up to serve that spring. Aumont's mother, however, had become gravely ill, and he was granted leave to see her. His absence coincided with the worst of the brief fighting, and he caught up with his unit as it retreated, finding his comrades in traumatized disarray. The unit was demobilized and Aumont fled to the South, which was France's unoccupied territory. His Jewish heritage placed him at risk, however, and he was fortunate to secure both a travel visa and a berth on a Portuguese liner bound for New York City.

In America, Aumont made his way to Hollywood, where studio executives had already expressed interest in working with him. He made two war movies for Metro-Goldwyn-Mayer, *Assignment in Brittany* and *The Cross of Lorraine,* both of which were released in 1943, and found himself the toast of wartime Hollywood. Hotly pursued by a number of prominent stars, Aumont became romantically involved with another European Jewish émigré, Hedy Lamarr, and the two were briefly engaged. Their tempestuous romance did not last, and Aumont entered into another whirlwind dalliance with Dominican-born María Montez. They were married on July 13, 1943, just before Aumont left to serve with the Free French Forces in North Africa. He took part in combat operations in Tunisia, then moved through France with his division as part of an Allied coalition of Free French, British, and American troops to retake France from the Germans. After being hit by shrapnel, Aumont was taken out of active combat duty and made an aide-de-camp to a Free French Forces general, Diego Brosset. On November 20, 1944, Aumont was riding in a jeep with Brosset when the general swerved to avoid a mined bridge in Vosges. The vehicle plunged into the gorge, and the already critically injured Brosset was carried away by the fast water, an event Aumont witnessed just as he freed himself from underneath the jeep.

Widowed in 1951

After the war, Aumont returned to Montez and Hollywood. He made a movie with Ginger Rogers, *Heartbeat,* in 1946 before starring as Russian composer Nikolai Rimsky-Korsakov in *Song of Scheherazade* opposite Yvonne DeCarlo a year later. DeCarlo had a long career in Hollywood, and is also famous for her role as Lily Munster on the hit television series *The Munsters* in the 1960s.

Aumont and Montez had a child, a daughter they named Maria Christina, before relocating to France. They starred together in *L'Atlantide,* also known as *Siren of Atlantis,* while Aumont began writing plays. In September 1951, while Aumont was winding up his scenes in a French comedy called *Les Loups chassent la nuit* (Wolves Hunt at Night), Montez died of an apparent heart attack in the bathtub of their home in Suresnes, France. Grief-stricken, Aumont submerged himself in work, taking as many jobs as possible, including television plays. One of the best-known movies from this period is a 1953 charmer, *Lili,* which starred Leslie Caron. The carnival tale featured Aumont as a handsome magician and Zsa Zsa Gabor as his assistant; the two are secretly married, a fact that devastates Caron's waifish orphan.

In 1953 Aumont appeared in a Philco-Goodyear Television Playhouse production of *The Way of the Eagle* as famed eighteenth-century ornithologist John James Audubon.

His co-star was American film star Grace Kelly, and the pair were linked romantically for a time before her engagement to Monaco's Prince Rainier. In 1956 Aumont married Italian film star Marisa Pavan, the twin of film star Pier Angeli. The couple would have two sons and work together in a number of films and plays. One of them was *John Paul Jones,* a 1959 costume drama from Warner Brothers in which Aumont was cast as King Louis XVI of France.

Appeared in Broadway Musical

Aumont put in a memorable turn on Broadway in the 1963 musical *Tovarich,* which paired him with British star Vivien Leigh in one of her last stage roles. Leigh suffered from manic depression and in a November matinee performance had what appeared to be a nervous breakdown on stage. "She began to claw me, slap me in the face," wrote Aumont in *Sun and Shadow.* He was forced to improvise when Leigh refused to deliver her next lines, "then Vivien came to the edge of the stage. She looked out at the whole auditorium and spoke carefully, enunciating each syllable: 'An actress has to think before answering,' and she walked off." In the finale, she came on stage but refused to waltz with him. Eva Gabor—the sister of Zsa Zsa—eventually replaced her, but the *Tovarich* production was soon shuttered. The experience did provide Aumont with other offers for singing roles, and he toured as a cabaret act for a time.

Solid roles for Aumont became scarcer as he entered his fifties. He appeared in a 1963 Disney movie and in a 1967 episode of *Flipper,* a television series about a dolphin. In 1969 director Sydney Pollack hired him for a World War II drama, *Castle Keep,* that co-starred Burt Lancaster and Peter Falk. One of his last choice parts came in François Truffaut's *Day for Night,* which also was released in France as *La nuit américaine.* The 1973 comedy also starred Truffaut himself as the director of a movie-within-a-movie, with Aumont as a famous French movie star. Two years later, Aumont was cast in a supporting role in the Diana Ross vehicle and Cinderella tale *Mahogany,* as an Italian noble who helps finance Ross's dreams of becoming a fashion designer.

Honored with Lifetime Achievement Award

Aumont had continued to write plays and short stories throughout his career. His French language autobiography *Le Soleil et Les Ombres* was published in 1976 and a year later in English translation. In 1981 he returned to Broadway to appear in a whodunit alongside Claudette Colbert, in *A Talent for Murder.* A decade later, France's Académie des arts et techniques du cinéma awarded him a César for lifetime achievement. His last roles came in productions of Ismail Merchant and James Ivory: he turned up in 1995's *Jefferson in Paris* and a year later in *The Proprietor.* He died on January 31, 2001, in Saint-Tropez, France, a few weeks after his ninetieth birthday. "The war taught me to judge things at their true value," he wrote in the final pages of *Sun and Shadow.* "I learned to appreciate a single cup of coffee, a single letter, a single proof of friendship."

Aumont was survived by Pavan and three children. One of their two sons, Patrick, became an antiques dealer in Santa Barbara, California. Aumont's daughter with Montez, Maria Christina "Tina" Aumont, had a long film career in Europe, appearing in Federico Fellini films, before her death in 2006.

Books

Aumont, Jean-Pierre, *Sun and Shadow,* with foreword by François Truffaut, translated from the original French edition *Le Soleil et Les Ombres,* by Bruce Benderson, W.W. Norton, 1977.

Turk, Edward Baron, *Child of Paradise: Marcel Carn and the Golden Age of French Cinema,* Harvard University Press, 1989, p. 141.

Periodicals

Guardian (London, England), January 31, 2001.

Independent (London, England), February 1, 2001.

New York Times, July 22, 1934; March 11, 1953; January 31, 2001.

Times (London, England), April 5, 1935.□

Richard Avenarius

The German philospher Richard Avenarius (1843–1896) was the founder of a school of philosophy known as empirio-criticism or critical positivism.

I n the words of the *Routledge Encyclopedia of Philosophy,* "[a] contemporary systematic treatment of Avenarius' work is sorely lacking." Avenarius was a major figure in his own time. His work anticipated some of the major themes of twentieth-century philosophy, and it seems to have influenced, positively or negatively, figures as prominent as Friedrich Nietzsche and Vladimir Lenin. Avenarius's ideas have links to those of other major philosophers, such as the American William James, whose works are grouped under the positivist label. Yet, especially outside of Germany, Avenarius remains little known. The sole major exposition of his work in English is a dissertation by the American scholar Wendell T. Bush, published in 1905.

Composer Wagner Was Godfather

Richard Heinrich Ludwig Avenarius was born into a German family in Paris, France, on November 19, 1843. The name Avenarius, which others in his family also used, was a Latin version of the German name Habermann. His father, Eduard Ludwig Friedrich Avenarius, was a co-founder of the Paris publishing firm Brockhaus, which specialized in German-language books. Artistically oriented young Germans who spent time in Paris became part of a circle surrounding the publisher; these included the poet Heinrich Heine and the opera composer Richard Wagner, who became Avenarius's godfather.

Avenarius's own interests, however, inclined less toward the arts than toward philosophy, in which he majored at the University of Zurich in Switzerland. Even as an undergraduate he was interested in the ideas of the seventeenth-century Dutch Jewish philosopher Baruch Spinoza and was impressed by the way Spinoza rigorously derived a broad set of philosophical and ethical ideas from a group of core logical principles. Avenarius traveled widely in his youth, but finally settled down at the University of Leipzig in Germany, writing a dissertation on Spinoza, *Philosophie als Denken der Welt gemäss dem Prinzip des kleinsten Kraftmasses* (Philosophy as Thinking of the World in Accordance with the Principle of the Least Amount of Energy Expended).

This dissertatation was well received, and Avenarius was appointed Professor for Inductive Philosophy at his alma mater, the University of Zurich. He remained there for the rest of his relatively short life, producing two major works, *Kritik der reinen Erfahrung* (Critique of Pure Experience, 1888–1890) and *Der menschliche Weltbegriff* (The Human Concept of the World, 1891). He also founded a philosophical journal, *Vierteljahrschrift für wissenschaftliche Philosophie* (Quarterly for Scientific Philosophy), editing it until he died. He had several students who carried forward his ideas after his death.

Emphasized Primacy of Sensory Experience

Avenarius called his own system of philosophy empiriocriticism (in German *Empiriokritizismus*). It was a branch of more general philosophical current known as empiricism, which emphasized the root of all human knowledge in human sensory experience, as opposed to innate or inborn ways of thinking. Avenarius's contributions were to link this idea in a detailed way to human communication and language, and to broaden it to encompass the functions of biological organisms. In brief, he tried to give empiricism a biological and a linguistic basis.

The basis of Avenarius's ideas was a systematic attempt to purge the idea of experience from any extraneous insertions (or "interjections") that divided the human and natural worlds into such categories as inner and outer or mind and matter. For him, mental and physical being were not two separate things, but related parts of the same thing, which he sought to reduce to a kind of algebraic system of expressions. The central idea of his exposition was the individual, who encounters not only a surrounding environment but also others who make statements about it. Avenarius called this basic form of human experience System C, which could denote the cerebrum (brain) or central nervous system.

The individual undergoes change, or experience, in two ways. First, System C may encounter variations in the environment (designated with the letter R), which will cause a stimulus or excite a nerve. Second, the individual may undergo variations in metabolism of nutrients; the process of metabolism in Avenarius's system was designated with the letter S. System C, in Avenarius's view, always attempted to keep R and S in balance—a process he called the vital maximum conservation of strength, or vital conservation maximum. The processes involved in the vital conservation maximum have their own term in Avenarius's philosophy: he called them independent vital sequences, which proceeded in three stages, summarized as pressure, work, and release.

The independent vital sequences proceed below the level of cognition or thought, but the same is not true of what Avenarius termed the dependent vital sequences, in which the human cognitive apparatus identifies a phenomenon or a problem. Like the independent vital sequences, the dependent vital sequences involve phases of pressure, work, and release, but in this case they involve cognitive conceptions, which may range all the way from simple perceptions to verbal concepts to ethical or aesthetic ideals. Conceptions in Avenarius's scheme could arise from simple stimuli or from the individual's perception that an excess of energy is present in a given situation and could be expressed in assertions.

Expressed Thought in Equation Forms

Such fluctuations of energy gave rise to what Avenarius called E-values, which he divided into two groups. One group consisted of elements; these were simple contents of sensation, such as perceiving that something was hot or green. The other involved what Avenarius called characters, which involved feelings and forms of awareness. These were further subdivided into affective (corresponding to what is generally meant by the word "feelings"), adaptive (involving perceptions of sameness or difference, believability or non-believability, certainty or uncertainty, known and unknown, and so on), and prevailing. Each of these was further subdivided into various forms and expressed in various equations.

How might human communication occur under this system? Avenarius believed that we presuppose what he called the principle of human equality, that when other humans make statements, we are able to generalize their experiences to our own by analogy. It is through this process that the E-values are recognized and named, giving rise to a new set of algebraic expressions involving the basic operations of language.

Avenarius's ideas, which even some professional philosphers have found idiosyncratically expressed, seemed to contain several of the key ideas of twentieth-century philosophy in embryonic form. His division of the E-values into elements and characters anticipated the distinction between cognitive and noncognitive elements found in the writings of several positivist philosphers. More generally, his rigorous attempt to exclude preexisting mental structures from perception preceded and likely influenced the idea of pure description advanced in the phenomenological philosophy of Edmund Husserl. Avenarius and his journal were widely read in the late nineteenth and early twentieth centuries. Among his critics was Vladimir Lenin, the founder of Soviet Russian Communism, whose ideas proceeded from philosophical bases; Lenin wrote an extended critique of Avenarius that attempted to go beyond the German's ideas, arguing that the external world or environment is completely independent of, and the ultimate source of, human knowledge.

Scholar Thomas H. Brobjer has also pointed to correspondences between the ideas of Nietzsche, who is not generally classed among the empiricists, and those of Avenarius. Nietzsche is known to have read and made extensive notes on Avenarius's dissertation, and he is likely to have been a reader of Avenarius's quarterly magazine as well. Nietzsche was a friend of Avenarius's brother Ferdinand, a bookseller, and for the first part of his career he was close to Wagner. Parts of Nietzsche's books *Beyond Good and Evil* and *On the Genealogy of Morals* appear to address points made in Avenarius's writings, and the principle of the will to power that appears in several of Nietzsche's books may have had at least a distant connection to Avenarius's vital conservation maximum. Avenarius died in Zurich on August 18, 1896.

Books

Brobjer, Thomas H., *Nietzsche's Philosophical Context: An Intellectual Biography*, Illinois, 2008.

Bush, Wendell T. *Avenarius and the Standpoint of Pure Experience*, Science Press, 1905.

Craig, Edward, *Routledge Encyclopedia of Philosophy*, Routledge, 1998.

Deathridge, John, introduction to *Family Letters of Richard Wagner*, University of Michigan Press, 1991.

Edwards, Paul, ed., *The Encyclopedia of Philosophy*, Macmillan, 1967.

Zusne, Leonard, *Biographical Dictionary of Psychology*, Greenwood, 1984. □

Tex Avery

One of Hollywood's zaniest and most influential animation directors, Fred "Tex" Avery (1908-1980) stretched the boundaries of his craft by simply applying his surreal imagination and sassy, slightly risqué sense of humor. Considered the anti-Disney, his joke-driven theatrical cartoons for Warner Bros., MGM, and Walter Lantz defied realism with their breakneck pacing and use of wild sight gags and visual puns that included elasticized eyeballs, steam spewing ears, and battered heads taking on the shape of frying pans and irons and popping back to normal. Further, his creative efforts helped define the comedic personalities of such cartoon icons as Bugs Bunny, Porky Pig, Daffy Duck, Elmer Fudd, Droopy Dog, and Chilly Willy.

Born Frederick Bean Avery on February 26, 1908 in Taylor, Texas, he was the son of Alabama-born George Walton Avery and Mississippi native Augusta "Jessie" Bean. The Avery side of the family claimed legendary frontiersman Daniel Boone as a descendent, whereas the Bean clan traced its roots to the infamous hanging judge of the old west, Judge Roy Bean. The latter could not be easily confirmed and, according to a quote on *IMDB.com* Avery's own grandmother warned him, "Don't ever mention you are kin to Roy Bean. He's a no good skunk!"

While attending North Dallas High School in 1926, Avery drew cartoons for the school newspaper and yearbooks. It was there that the young humorist first heard the expression, "What's Up, Doc?," which he would later use as Bugs Bunny's most famous catch-phrase. After graduation in 1926, he enrolled in a three-month course at the Art Institute of Chicago, did not like it and simply came home to the Dallas area, where he worked a series of odd jobs while experimenting with ideas for a newspaper comic strip. In 1928, he accompanied some friends on a trip to southern California and stayed. Initially, he pitched the ideas for his prospective comic strip to several local newspapers while supporting himself with day labor jobs such as unloading produce trucks and sleeping on a nearby beach.

Got His Start with Walter Lantz

In early 1929, a friend of a friend helped Avery find a job as a cel washer/assistant animator at Walter Lantz's studio at Universal. Although he felt that most of Lantz's artists could out draw him, the aspiring director compensated for his technical shortcomings by learning his trade from the ground up. After five years, he had mastered every phase of cartoon production, dabbled in gag writing, and was listed as an artist in the title cards of the *Oswald the Lucky Rabbit* cartoons—originally created by Walt Disney but Lantz's big moneymaker at the time. Nicknamed "Tex" in honor of his home state (and penchant for telling tall tales), Fred Avery lost the use of his left eye in an office paper clip fight, losing much of his playful nature in the process. Some speculate that the lack of depth perception after the accident gave his animation style its pleasingly surreal edge. Near the end of his tenure with Lantz, Avery was allowed to fully supervise two cartoons. Noting their success, he demanded more money. When Lantz refused, the young animator departed, fast-talking his way into a far better position both creatively and financially.

Made Bugs Bunny, Porky Pig, and Daffy Duck Cartoons

At age 27, Avery was hired by production chief Leon Schlesinger, whose *Looney Tunes* and *Merrie Melodies* cartoons were Warner Bros. response to Walt Disney's enormously successful *Silly Symphonies*. Although they were contemporaries, Schlesinger and Disney were poles apart in attitude about their respective companies: "We're businessmen," Schlesinger told *Time* in 1937. "Walt Disney's an artist. With us, the idea with shorts is to hit 'em and run. With us, Disney is more of a Rembrandt." By contrast, Avery was less enthralled with Disney's artistic gifts, thinking his output too sentimental.

Promising improved production output, Avery convinced the Warner Bros. honcho to give him complete responsibility for his own unit. After taking charge of the *Looney Tunes* series, which were initially made in black and white, he began forging a style of cartoon comedy that became Warner Bros. signature. Avery's early rubbery style owed much to the work of the Fleischer Brothers' *Popeye* and *Betty Boop* series. However, working in the Quonset hut dubbed "Termite Terrace" with such high-powered talents as Chuck Jones, Bob Clampett, Robert McKimson and Frank Tashlin, he employed faster pacing, sillier non sequiturs, adult style sarcasm, and more visual jokes than his competitors. The result was a style of cartoon humor that fans stil associate with Warner Bros.

Porky Pig was Avery's first successful retooling. Changing the character from the enormous hog in the 1936 black

and white *Golddiggers of '49* to the cute, never-say-die young pig appearing in *Picador Porky* who stammered "That's All, Folks!" at the end of every cartoon, Porky quickly became Warner Bros. biggest cartoon star. Titled a supervisor—the director credit would come a few years later—he introduced another popular character in *Porky's Duck Hunt,* the hyper-kinetic, anarchic Daffy Duck. Calling himself "that darnfool duck" and manically exclaiming "Woo-hoo, woo hoo, woo hoo!" as he inflicted mayhem on polite society, Daffy's character completely embodied Avery's philosophy that anything can happen in a cartoon. According to legend, Daffy's voice was inspired by producer Schlesinger's lisp.

Perhaps Avery's greatest achievement at Warner's came when he crafted the perfect personality for Bugs Bunny, a version of whom first appeared in the 1938 Ben Hardaway-directed *Porky's Hare Hunt.* Changing his own Egghead character into a slow-witted hunter named Elmer Fudd—voiced by Arthur Q. Bryan—Avery set up the perfect comic protagonist for Robert McKimson's rendering of Bugs in *A Wild Hare.* Chewing on a carrot in the style of Clark Gable in *It Happened One Night,* the Mel Blanc-voiced rabbit acted like anything but prey when faced with Fudd's shotgun. "We decided he [Bugs] was going to be a smart-aleck rabbit, but casual about it," Avery is quoted saying at *The Phrase Finder.* "That opening line of 'Eh, what's up, Doc?' floored them. They expected the rabbit to scream, or anything but make a casual remark. For here's a guy pointing a gun in his face! It got such a laugh that we said, 'Boy, we'll do that every chance we get.'" Avery only directed four Bugs Bunny cartoons, but his version of the cartoon rabbit is the one that resonated with movie audiences, making Bugs and the rest of the Warner cartoon characters movie, TV, and merchandising favorites for decades to come.

Among the 73 cartoons Avery directed for Warner Bros. were take-offs on fairy tales, travelogue parodies, and Hollywood caricature films. Creatively supportive of each other, the denizens of Termite Terrace all shared story ideas and gag ideas in meetings they called the "Period of the Big Yes." "There were no negatives allowed for the duration of the two-hour meeting," director Chuck Jones told *Time* in 1973. "If you couldn't say anything positive, you couldn't talk at all." Yet for all the creative bonhomie and comic spirit captured on screen, Avery was a perfectionist who put his heart and soul into every short film he did, even supplying an occasional character voice when necessary. So invested was the director in his creative vision, that when producer Leon Schlesinger insisted that he change the ending of *The Heckling Hare* from a lengthy triple fall off a cliff to a single fall, the director became enraged and promptly quit.

Moved to MGM

Sporting an enviable track record, Avery had no problem finding work. Joining Paramount for a few months in 1942, he collaborated with Jerry Fairbanks and Bob Carlysle on the studio's *Speaking of Animals* series of short films. Signing with MGM later that year, the director enjoyed far fewer budget limitations and more creative freedom. Creating under the aegis of producer Fred Quimby, Avery drew from MGM's entire animation talent pool—including William Hanna and Joseph Barbera—to craft the best sustained work of his career. Most of the director's cartoons list future novelist Heck Allen as the writer—Rich Hogan also wrote stories—but Allen himself has said that most of the eye-popping sight gags and clever twists were Avery's.

Avery's MGM debut was the Oscar-nominated *Blitz Wolf*, a Three Little Pigs parody in which the opening title card proclaims: "The wolf in this photoplay is NOT fictitious. Any similarity between this wolf and that [curse word symbols] jerk Hitler is intentional." Aside from some futuristic travelogue parodies, however, the director gravitated more towards quirky caricatures and funny animals such as Droopy Dog. Created in 1943 and originally called "Happy Hound," Droopy was a puny basset hound with a voice reminiscent of radio actor Bill Thompson's Wallace Wimple character on the *Fibber McGee and Molly* series. Indulging in some fourth-wall busting shtick, Avery had Droopy introduce himself in *Dumb Hounded* by looking directly at the audience and drolly deadpanning, "Hello all you happy people . . . you know what? I'm the hero." On the surface, Droopy seemed outmatched by every foe and circumstance, but no amount of evil could ruffle his low-key demeanor, and he used his wits and freakish out-of-proportion to his size strength to comedic triumph.

Droopy, the peripatetic Screwy Squirrel, or the *Of Mice and Men*-inspired bears George and Junior never proved as popular as the cast he had created at Warner's, but their inventive, wacky humor appealed to movie audiences of all ages. However, sometimes the adult allusions in Avery's cartoons got him into trouble. The swing era remake of Little Red Riding Hood, redubbed *Red Hot Riding Hood* featured a zoot suit clad wolf whose body suggestively stiffened when he caught sight of the sexy nightclub singer, Red Riding Hood. At the time, the adult-oriented visual gags were simply edited out by regional censors, but today that cartoon is regarded as a classic. Often, Avery's best work featured a deceptively simple gimmick, as in 1950's *Ventriloquist Cat,* wherein a cat discovers a device that allows him to throw his voice to misdirect an aggressive bulldog. Equally brilliant was 1947's *King Size Canary*, in which a cat, canary, and mouse grow increasingly larger thanks to a bottle of Jumbo Gro.

During his 12 year stint with MGM, Avery crafted sixty-eight cartoons that stretched the boundaries of humor and animation. Facing tough financial times, the studio completely phased out its animation department in 1955. Towards the end of his association with the studio, Richard Lah helped Avery direct some shorts and he remade a few of his classics for CinemaScope.

Created Chilly Willy and Kwicky Koala

Returning to Walter Lantz—riding high with the Woody Woodpecker series—Avery proved that he had lost none of his madcap genius. *Crazy Mixed-Up Pup,* the story of a dog and owner who receive each other's plasma and take on each other's personality traits, was particularly amusing. Of more lasting influence, was his final great big screen contribution, Chilly Willy. Although the director felt some

of the small, intrepid penguin's soul was lost in the transfer from the pencil test to the big screen, *Chilly Willy in the Legend of Rockabye Point* ranks with Avery's very finest work. That said, his reunion with Lantz would not last long. Another dispute over pay sent him packing, effectively ending his career in film animation.

While Hanna and Barbera, Jay Ward, and the Terrytoon crew were figuring out limited animation techniques for television, Avery decided to pay the bills directing animated commercials. Like Stan Freberg before him, Avery made memorable TV ads, including his spot for Raid insecticide or his now controversial ad for Fritos, featuring a stereotypical Mexican bandit known as the "Frito Bandito." He also fashioned a series of ads for Kool-Aid that featured the Warner Bros. characters i.e. Bugs, Daffy, etc. that he had helped create. However, during the 1960s and 1970s, his theatrical cartoons were shown regularly on television stations all around the country and, although some parents complained of the comedic violence, his work was held in high esteem by genre fans.

Hanna and Barbera lured Avery back to cartoons in 1980 to work as a story editor on the *Flintstone Comedy Show* and *The New Adventures of Tom and Jerry*. That same year he also created *The Kwicky Koala Show*, a CBS Saturday morning series that featured such colorful characters as Dirty Dog and Crazy Claws. It was his final project. Avery died of lung cancer at the Hanna-Barbera studios on August 26, 1980.

During the 1990s and 2000s, Avery has made new fans thanks to reissues of his work on VHS and DVD. In 1993, the director was paid tribute when a cowboy character was given his name for the animated series that featured none of the director's work, *The Wacky World of Tex Avery.* Far more satisfying artistically, *The Compleat Tex Avery*, a compilation of all of his MGM cartoons, was released on Laserdisc. In 2007, Warner Home Video released the critically acclaimed *Droopy: The Complete Theatrical Collection.* Further, such animated shows as *Tiny Toon Adventures, Animaniacs, Family Guy* and many programs on the Cartoon Network's late-night Adult Swim programming block seemingly live by Avery's creative credo: in a cartoon, you can do anything.

Books

McNeil, Alex, *Total Television*, Penguin, 1996.

Periodicals

Time, Dec. 27, 1937; Dec. 17, 1973.

Online

"Avery, Tex," *Film Reference.Com,* http://www.filmreference.com/Writer-and-Production-Artists-A-Ba/Avery-Tex,html , (January 20, 2012).

"The Compleat Tex Avery" *Modemac.Com,* http://www.modemac.com/cgi-bin/wiki.pl/The_Compleat_Tex_Avery, (January 21, 2012).

"Heck Allen," *Internet Movie Database,* http://www.imdb.com/name/nm/ 0020571/bio, (January 21, 2012).

''Leon Schlesinger,'' *Internet Movie Database,* http://www.imdb.com/name/nm/ 0772266/bio, (January 21, 2012).

''A Quickie Look At The Life & Career of Tex Avery,'' *Bright Lights Film Journal,* http://www.brightlightsfilm.com/22/texavery.html, (January 20, 2011).

''Tex Avery,'' *AllRovi.Com,* http://www.allrovi.com/name/tex-avery-mn0000992571, (October 25, 2011).

''Tex Avery,'' *Biography.com,* http://www.biography.com/print/profile/tex-avery-5540, (January 20, 2012).

''Tex Avery,'' *Internet Movie Database,* http://www.imdb.com/name/nm/ 0000813/bio, (October 25, 2011).

''Tex Avery 1908–1980,'' *Comedy Zone,* http://www.comedy-zone.net/cartoonists/avery-tex.htm, (January 21, 2011).

''What's up Doc?,'' *The Phrase Finder,* http://www.phrases.org.uk/meanings/406400, (January 22, 2012). □

B

Alexander Bain

Scottish psychologist, philosopher, and educator Alexander Bain (1818-1903), one of the most well known of British Utilitarians (who advanced a school of thought based the ethics of utility, or the usefulness of human concerns), was an early proponent of scientific psychology. Along with James Mill (and son John Stuart Mill), Bain was a major figure of British empiricism, a group that proposed that knowledge should be based on sensory experience and not introspection.

Scottish psychologist, philosopher, and educator Alexander Bain distinguished himself as British Utilitarian, a group of researchers and mind scientists who advanced a philosophical tenet that, as its name implies, outlines what is most useful—and, in turn—the most good for the individual. The underpinnings of the philosophy relate to what should be fundamentally good, whether this involves what can be considered happiness or what can be considered well being.

Rightness of action resides at the core of the philosophy; essentially, this leads to morality, and morality represents a measure that increases the welfare of living forms, most especially sentient life forms—that is, thought-filled life forms, such as humans.

Bain built upon the ideas of philosophers in seventeenth-century Britain, who advanced the main tenets of what was considered classical utilitarianism. Indeed, theirs was not a radical philosophy. Their tenets trace back to ancient Greece, specifically Plato.

In its more modern manifestation—advanced by proponents such as Jeremy Bentham (1748-1832) and Henry Sidgwick (1838-1900) and, most importantly, John Stuart Mill (1806-1873)—utilitarianism eventually aligned with social reform. Still, the philosophy was at once political and apolitical, and it merged the psychological with the physical–that is, human psychology with human physiology. Further, old-fashioned and Old Testament concepts of God had no place in this thought process. Utilitarianism philosophy resonates with modern thought, where the democratic and universal view of morality results in the greater good for the greatest number of people. A judgmental and punishing God is not an acceptable concept.

Utilitarianism has been often characterized as hedonistic; that is, best serving the individual and, of course, resulting in one's own pleasure. However, it may be more accurate to equate utilitarianism with consequentialism—a theory that advances ethical behavior.

Thus, the ideas advanced in Bain's era cannot be quickly pigeon-holed. Instead, they represent a blending. Classical utilitarianism—which Bentham and Mill promoted—can be readily translated into hybrid thought, referred to as act-consequentionalism, where the best actions enhance the happiness, and thus promote a full life, for sentient—or thinking—entities. The sanctity of thought and life is paramount.

A theory that embraces morality and virtuosity, consequentionalism closely relates to normative ethics, as normative thought focuses on righteous actions. Those embracing consequentialist thought believed that righteous action brings about the best consequences in the affairs of humankind.

Obviously, Alexander Bain did not advance such thought or pioneer the theories. Rather, he enhanced the thought already present in the world he was born into and, in the process, helped promote the understanding of the processes of the human body's most mysterious organ, the brain.

A Young Tradesman and Scholar

Bain was born on June 11, 1818 in Aberdeen, Scotland. He was the son of a struggling weaver who was faced with the care and feeding of four other children. To help support his family, the young Bain took up the weaving trade. But he was an inquisitive, curious individual, which led to his autodidactic pursuits. An autodidact is an individual who enthusiastically engages in self-learning, however informal it may be. With an unquenchable thirst for knowledge, the young Bain epitomized the autodidact, as he voraciously read books and absorbed the knowledge they provided. Indeed, Alexander Bain, not only epitomized what an autodidact should and could be, but also represented the potential of what an autodidact could achieve through self learning.

Today, someone like Bain would be called an "accelerated student," and his innate curiosity and intellectual gifts led to his acceptance into Marischal College, in 1836, where he pursued his intense focus on making at least some sense of the world in which he found himself. At this vibrant learning center, he studied mathematics, physics, and mental philosophy. Intuitive and highly intellectual, Bain sensed the way that each topic merged. Because of his versatile and eclectic acumen, he attracted the attention of a diverse group of influential educators including John Cruickshank (a mathematics professor), Thomas Clark (a chemistry professor), and William Knight (a philosophy professor).

Became a Renowned Academician

In 1840, at the end of his college education years, where he excelled in areas of philosophy, mathematics and physics, Bain contributed to the *Westminster Review,* a publication that served as a forum for so-called "philosophical radicals" such as Bentham, Charles Buller, Edward John Trelawny,

James Mill and John Stuart Mill. Through this activity, Bain made the acquaintance of John Stuart Mill, which would lead to a friendship that would last a lifetime. Like Bain, Mill was a proponent of pragmatism (a philosophic tradition that merged practice with theory) and empiricism (a theory based on the idea that knowledge is acquired through sensory experience). Bain would later write *John Stuart Mill: A Criticism, with Persona Recollections* in 1882.

Proceeding on his active and enthusiastic scholarly path, Bain—in 1841 at Marischal—substituted for the professor of moral philosophy who had taken ill. He would teach for three terms while still writing for the *Westminster Review.* Also, he helped Mill revise his book manuscript, *System of Logic* (1842).

In 1843, Bain published the first review of Mill's book. Then two years later, in 1845, Bain received a significant academic appointment: professor of mathematics and natural philosophy at the Andersonian University of Glasgow. But he found the education environment somewhat stifling, so he resigned from his position to focus on his writing. He still needed to support himself, however, so he moved to London, England and assumed a government board of health post. While in London, he became part of a distinguished group of intellectuals that included, among others, Mill and George Grote (who was a renowned historian).

Bain's writing efforts eventually resulted in his 1855 publication, *The Senses and the Intellect,* a large volume that proved to be his first major work. Bain followed this provocative and influential discourse four years later with *The Emotions and the Will.* As the titles of both works suggest, Bain was advancing ideas that psychology is best described, and understood, by laws of association. To underscore his ideas, he delineated a linkage that merged psychological and physiological processes. In his first work, and its chapter on the human nervous system, he helped advance the idea of that connection.

With these works, Bain became a prominent figure in the growing field of psychology. Still, he remained attached to philosophy, as he became an examiner in logical and moral philosophy for the University of London, and in moral science in the Indian Civil Service examinations.

Returned to the Academic Environment

But in 1860, Bain received another prestigious appointment: He became the chair of logic and English at the newly created University of Aberdeen in Scotland (which the Scottish Universities Commission formed by combining two colleges, King's and Marischal). Bain advanced education in both areas, as he helped prepare new and influential textbooks, particularly on grammar and composition. These include *Higher English Grammar* (1863), which he followed with the *Manual of Rhetoric* (1866), *A First English Grammar* (1872), and the *Companion to the Higher Grammar* (1874). In these texts, Bain expressed original ideas that would gain wide acceptance. At the same time, he addressed the existing deficiencies in the teaching of logic.

Bain's previously published works did not lend themselves well to the classroom setting, as they were large and very complex. In response, in 1868, he produced his *Manual of Mental and Moral Science,* which condensed his ideas into language and format much more accessible to the classroom.

Two years later, he published *Logic.* This 1870 work was also geared to students, and it advanced ideas originally proposed by John Stuart Mill; however, these were filtered through Bain's own ideas, particularly as to how logic principles related to different scientific studies.

Achieved Recognition

As his approach was innovative, Bain received recognition. In 1871, he was awarded an honorary degree of doctor of laws by the University of Edinburgh. Meanwhile, he continued writing. Two important works included *Mind and Body* (1872) and *Education as a Science* (1879), which was published as part of "The International Scientific Series."

As such, his twenty years at Aberdeen were quite productive, and his activities included the establishment of *Mind,* a journal focused on philosophic thought. It became one of the most prestigious publications of its kind. The first issue appeared in 1876, and Bain would contribute many important articles. He also provided the periodical with financial support.

In 1880, Bain resigned from his professorial role. His considerable influence, however, was underscored by the man who succeeded him: William Minto, who was one of Bain's most outstanding students.

Though retired from the academic setting, Bain continued writing. In 1882, he published *Biography of James Mill* and *John Stuart Mill: a Criticism with Personal Recollections.* In 1884, his collected articles and papers were published as *Practical Essays.* Later in that same decade, he revised his "Rhetoric" manual, and also produced a book, *On Teaching English,* a work geared toward educators who sought to comprehensively apply principles of rhetoric to literary criticism.

In 1894, Bain published a revised edition of *The Senses and the Intellect,* which updated his thoughts about psychology. But for Bain, the end of his career, and his life, was rapidly approaching. That same year, he would make his last contribution to *Mind.*

Died in Aberdeen

Then followed a final nine years spent in relative seclusion in Scotland. There, he died on September 18, 1903 at Ferryhill Lodge in Aberdeen, the city where he was born. Though he married twice, he had no children. His autobiography was published posthumously in 1904.

Bain was eighty-six years old when he died. He enjoyed a long and productive life, which came as a surprise to some who knew him, indicated William L. Davidson, a professor of logic and metaphysics at the University of Aberdeen, in an article that appeared in *Mind* following Bain's death. For Bain, in his younger days, was in "fragile and delicate in health," wrote Davidson. But Bain lived his life in a "methodical manner," continued Davidson. "There was a time for work and a time for exercise, a time for diet and a time for rest, to which he adhered."

This appears keeping in line with what Bain taught and wrote about. Even though he was influential in areas of philosophy,

logic and grammar, he is best known today as one of the founding fathers of modern psychology. Indeed, he was the first in Great Britain to link the mind to the body, the mental to the physical. He developed the psycho-physical parallelism theory, which formed the foundation of the works of modern psychologists.

Davidson summarized the full measure of Bain's contributions. With Bain's death, he wrote, "psychology has sustained a great loss; but so too has education and practical reform. It is rare to find a philosopher who combines philosophical with educational and practical interests, and who is also an active force in the community in which he dwells. Such a combination was here. Let us not fail to appreciate it."

Books

Borchert, Donald M., ed., *Encyclopedia of Philosophy,* Macmillan Reference USA, 2006.

Online

"Alexander Bain," *NNDB.com,* http://www.nndb.com/people/221/000100918/ (December 15, 2011).

"Alexander Bain (1818-1903)," *Scottish Philosophy.org,* http://www.scottishphilosophy.org/alexanderbain.html (December 15, 2011).

"Alexander Bain (1818-1903)," *The Victorian Web,* http://www.victorianweb.org/science/psych/bain.htm (December 15, 2011).

"Bain, Alexander," *New World Encyclopedia,* http://www.newworldencyclopedia.org/entry/Alexander_Bain (December 15, 2011).

"HT Talks: History & Theory of Psychology Evening Colloquium Series (Alexander Bain and Sigmund Freud—A Look at Two 19th Century Neural Network Models," *York University.com,* http://www.yorku.ca/httalks/?page_id=257 (December 15, 2011).

"Professor Bain," *Fair-use.org,* http://fair-use.org/mind/1904/01/notes/professor-bain (December 15, 2011). □

Ralph Bakshi

The Palestine-born American director and animator Ralph Bakshi (born 1938) was a pioneer in the creation of animated films aimed primarily at adults.

Bakshi remains notorious as the creator of *Fritz the Cat* (1972), the first animated film to receive an X rating from the Motion Picture Association of America (MPAA) agency. But his activity has extended far beyond that single film. In the 1970s and 1980s Bakshi created a series of animated features that were original, often controversial, and highly influential. The scatological and satirical aspects of contemporary television animation owe a great deal to Bakshi, both directly (Bakshi helped launch the career of *Ren & Stimpy* creator John Kricfalusi) and generally; when Bakshi began his career, animation was almost always considered a medium for wholesome family entertainment, but after the release of his major films,

animators had a much wider choice of ideas and story material.

Won Cartooning Award as Student

Of Turkish Jewish background, Ralph Bakshi was born in Haifa, now in Israel but then part of British-controlled Palestine, in October of 1938. His birthday has been reported as October 26 and October 29, but his own website does not list the day. Bakshi's family fled the worsening situation in the Middle East as World War II approached and moved to New York, settling in the impoverished Bedford-Stuyvesant neighborhood in Brooklyn. Bakshi showed artistic talent from the time he was a small child and enrolled at Brooklyn's High School of Industrial Arts (now the High School of Art and Design in Manhattan). He did well in his classes and even won an award for his cartoons upon graduating in 1957.

Landing a job with the suburban New York animation studio Terrytoons, Bakshi worked as a cel polisher and cel painter, doing animation drawings on his own time to improve his skills. He won a promotion to animator, he recalled on his website, by sitting down at an empty chair on the shop floor and claiming that he had been given the job. Soon he was not only living up to the position but exceeding expectations, producing drawings for such popular television cartoons as *Deputy Dawg* and *Mighty Mouse*. By his mid-20s he was regularly directing episodes of animated programs for Terrytoons, and in the mid-1960s he became the studio's creative director.

It was at about this time that Bakshi's rebellious streak began to show itself. Irritated by a request from CBS television to develop yet another superhero animated series, Bakshi responded by creating an unlikely set of antihero superheroes, including Tornado Man, Cuckooman, Ropeman, Strongman, and Diaper Baby. The move coincided, however, with an opening-up in the creative atmosphere of

network television in the mid-1960s, and Bakshi was given the chance to turn his set of characters into a series, *The Mighty Heroes,* which went on the air in 1966. The series lasted barely more than one season, but it put Bakshi on the Hollywood creative map.

Worked on *Spider-Man* Cartoon

After the demise of Terrytoons, Bakshi enjoyed a stint as head of a short-lived cartoon division operated by Paramount Studios. When that, too, was shuttered, Bakshi went back to New York and opened a small studio of his own, called Ralph's Spot. There he worked for producer Steve Krantz on animation for the original *Spider-Man* television series and produced advertisements for Fanta soft drinks and other clients. During the late 1960s he developed and pitched to Krantz the idea of an animated adaptation of the adult-themed *Fritz the Cat* comics penned by underground comics artist R. (Robert) Crumb. Although Crumb's then wife, Dana, was enthusiastic about the project, R. Crumb himself would later disparage Bakshi's adaptation, and the two men developed a long enmity.

When *Fritz the Cat* appeared in 1972, it was unlike any other animated feature up to that point. The film's title character, a human in cat form, was a college student who indulged frequently in sex and drugs, earning the film the first X rating in animation history. The film was technically fresh as well, with on-the-street recording of much of its audio track. Whether because of its sexual material, its cross-country road trip, or its anti-police attitudes, the film fit the spirit of the times and became a hit at the midnight showings presented in the 1970s by numerous campus film societies and urban film houses. Bakshi even earned an invitation to the prestigious Cannes Film Festival in France. Plans were in the works for a second *Fritz the Cat* feature, but due to disagreements with Krantz, Bakshi decided to pursue an original idea for his second feature, *Heavy Traffic.* Krantz did serve once again as producer.

Heavy Traffic, the story of a cartoonist navigating life on the streets and among some very unusual characters in New York, had its premiere at New York's Museum of Modern Art in 1973. Once again, Bakshi included adult themes, but this film avoided the X rating. Although Craig Butler of *AllRovi* felt that "the story itself is no great shakes and the dialogue is at times painful," he found "a genuine sense of urgency to the film, which gives it great energy and life." *Heavy Traffic* earned generally strong reviews and for many filmgoers remains the high point of Bakshi's achievement. Its mixture of live action and animation was unique at the time.

Released Controversial Satire

Perhaps unwisely, Bakshi followed this promising pair of films with a 1975 release, *Coonskin,* that generated almost enough controversy to derail his growing career. Although Bakshi intended the film in part as a satire of the violent so-called "blaxploitation" films of the day, it was difficult to tell where satire left off and stereotypes took over in its story of African-American drug dealers. After *Coonskin* drew protests from the Congress of Racial Equality and other civil rights organizations, it was withdrawn from circulation by the Paramount studio. Bakshi remained unapologetic about the film in later life, telling Gary Younge of the London *Guardian* that "I knew [the film] was going to be explosive. But those were particular times. If you were black then you were perfect, and if you were white you were supposed to be guilty."

Given the success of the *Lord of the Rings* film trilogy of director Peter Jackson in the early 2000s, it is surprising that little attention has been paid to Bakshi, who was the first to film J.R.R. Tolkien's fantasy epics. Bakshi's *Lord of the Rings* appeared in 1978, and he expressed annoyance when Jackson's films appeared. "My contract reads that I have all the sequel rights," he pointed out to the London *Express.* "But I think I'll let it go. I think Jackson is a good director but leaves a lot to be desired as a gentleman. No one has spoken to me, no one has shown me a foot of film, and I'm stunned about that from one film-maker to another." Bakshi's animation technique in the film, known as roto-scoping, dated back to the days of silent film.

Bakshi's films of the 1980s and 1990s have been less widely seen than his earlier releases. They included the rock music story *American Pop* (1981), *Hey Good Lookin'*, a 1950s street-gang tale that was made in the 1970s but not released until 1982, and the fantasy animation *Fire and Ice* (1983). Bakshi returned to the spotlight with his work on the 1987 animated television series *Mighty Mouse: The New Adventures,* which gained publicity when it came under attack by Christian fundamentalist minister the Rev. Donald Wildmon, who accused the series of promoting cocaine use (the titular mouse was seen in one episode sniffing a white flower and then behaving in an energized fashion). Bakshi strenuously denied the charge.

Bakshi made a few more films in the 1990s, but by that time his main contribution took the form of influence he exerted over younger filmmakers and television writers. Without the model of Bakshi's irreverent brand of comedy, such animated television series as *South Park* become more difficult to imagine. *Ren & Stimpy* director John Kricfalusi gained experience as a director working on the *Mighty Mouse: The New Adventures* series (Bakshi's title was creator). By the 2000s decade Bakshi was respected as an elder statesman of contemporary American animation. At a convention Bakshi attended in 2011, animator Jeaux Janovsky told Henry Hanks of *CNN* that Bakshi "showed us cartoons could be for grownups too, not just for the kiddies. Ralph has tackled a lot in his films: racism, violence, drugs, society, poverty, fantasy, life . . ." Bakshi, who admired both the do-it-yourself spirit of YouTube videos and Japanese animation, was planning a new film as of that year, a murder mystery entitled *The Last Days of Coney Island.*

Books

Gibson, John M., and Chris McDonnell, *Unfiltered: The Complete Ralph Bakshi,* Universe, 2008.

Periodicals

CNN Wire, September 22, 2011.
Daily Variety, February 21, 2003.
Express (London, England), December 20, 2011.
Guardian (London, England), May 14, 1999.
New York Post, March 5, 2008.
New York Times, April 27, 2008.
Seattle Post-Intelligencer, January 15, 2010.

Online

"Ralph Bakshi," *AllRovi,* http://www.allrovi.com/name/ralph-bakshi-p80464 (January 3, 2012).
"Ralph Bakshi Biography," *Ralph Bakshi Official Website,* http://www.ralphbakshi.com/ (January 3, 2012). □

Lester Bangs

Lester Bangs (1948–1982) spent most of the 1970s honing a reputation as one of rock music's most belligerent but eloquent critics. After leaving both *Rolling Stone* and *Creem* on bad terms, Bangs moved to New York City and immersed himself in the burgeoning punk-rock scene while writing for the *Village Voice.* "Bangs's writings are instantly recognizable, steeped in the subjective style of New Journalists," wrote Theo Cateforis in *The Rock History Reader,* "yet mixed with equal doses of his own unique cynical attitude, corrosive wit and expressive insights. For many, this intense, self-reflexive approach signified an unparalleled level of integrity in rock journalism."

Leslie Conway Bangs was born on December 13, 1948, in Escondido, California. His father, Conway Bangs, was a truck driver who drank heavily; his mother Norma coped with the unhappy marriage by immersing herself in the Jehovah's Witness church. By the time Bangs was nine, his father had vanished for good, and his mother told him one day that Conway had died in a fire. In 1960 mother and son moved to El Cajon, near San Diego, where he began to rebel as he entered his teens. The Beat Generation poets like Jack Kerouac and Allen Ginsberg inspired him to begin writing, and he picked up an intense interest in jazz music.

Following his graduation from El Cajon Valley High School in 1966, Bangs enrolled at Grossmont Junior College to study journalism, but soon fell in with a crowd of other aspiring writers, random drunks, and bikers. He abused a panoply of substances, including vodka, cough syrup, hallucinogenics, tranquilizers, and speed. When he wrote about witnessing a group sexual assault at the clubhouse of the local Hell's Angels motorcycle gang chapter aloud in his creative writing class—an episode that terrified him, though he was numbed by a mix of substances—both the teacher and the class were aghast, and he dropped out of college for good. He spent months watching television and listening to his Velvet Underground and Van Morrison records.

Wrote for Young *Rolling Stone*

Bangs was by then the prototypical music fan of his era. He bought whatever records he could afford and read anything he came across, and by 1969 several new publications had been founded to cover the genre. *Rolling Stone* magazine, founded in San Francisco in 1967, emerged as a major influence on the burgeoning counterculture scene. In early 1969, it ran an effusive story about a Detroit band called the MC5, whose manager, a local poet named John Sinclair, was touting them as a revolutionary new front in the history of sedition in America. Bangs bought the record, read the liner notes by Sinclair, and recognized them as lifted from the dialogue from *Wild in the Streets,* a shlocky 1968 movie about a rock band that manages to unleash actual political chaos in America. He sent his own scathing review of the MC5's *Kick Out the Jams* to *Rolling Stone* with a letter daring them to publish it, and they did. Greil Marcus, the magazine's first record-review editor, signed Bangs on as a freelance critic.

On the pages of *Rolling Stone* he championed musicians like Lou Reed of the Velvet Underground and Captain Beefheart, a.k.a Don Van Vliet, while dismissing the majority of major-label releases. At the time, he was still living in El Cajon and selling shoes at a local mall, but as the new decade started he fully immersed himself in the rock scene. The end of the 1960s was formally marked by the date December 6, 1969, when the Rolling Stones headlined a free music festival at the Altamont speedway in California. Bangs was in the audience when members of the Hell's Angels, hired as security, brutally beat to death an African-American man in the audience. He wrote about the incident in a 1973 article while covering the Stones on their 1972 tour. "It was great!" he remembered Altamont, with typical deadpan irony. "I remember the freaked-out kid shrieking 'Kill! Kill! Kill!' I remember the Angels vamping on him, too, and then seeing him passed in a twitching gel over the heads in the first few rows and then dumped on the ground to snivel at the feet of total strangers who would ignore him, because the Stones were coming on in a minute which would be two hours."

Reached Peak at *Creem*

That article appeared in *Creem* magazine, a daring new monthly out of Detroit that positioned itself as the antithesis to *Rolling Stone. Creem*'s publisher, Barry Kramer, offered Bangs a full-time job in late 1971 and he moved to Detroit. The magazine quickly developed a cult following, as did Bangs's lengthy articles, reviews, and even a fictional interview with the late Jimi Hendrix. Bangs was one of the earliest critics to hail Michigan native James Osterberg, a.k.a. Iggy Pop, as about as authentic as rock 'n' roll would ever become.

Bangs's most prolific years as a rock critic coincided with the genre's nadir, as rock bands became bloated, profit-making entities discovered, refined, and hyped by major labels. At both *Rolling Stone* and *Creem,* Bangs wrote scathingly of almost everyone, dismissing acts like Aerosmith, the J. Geils Band, and Alice Cooper as little more than hopeless poseurs. Record-company executives lured him into the scene with extravagant junkets, attempting to win him over by co-opting him into the rock 'n' roll lifestyle, but Bangs freely indulged in all the perks he was offered and still wrote sentences like this about Emerson, Lake and Palmer in a March 1974 issue of *Creem:* "The most insufferable snob, the most hateful patronization, is the one that's unaware, the guileless shiv," Bangs wrote as way of introduction to Carl Palmer's statement, " 'We hope if anything we're encouraging the kids to listen to music that has more quality.' "

After a trip to investigate Jamaica's reggae scene, courtesy of Island Records, Bangs left *Creem* after a falling-out with Kramer over health insurance, expenses, and other financial issues. Bangs moved to New York City in 1976, where he already had a strong following among members of the burgeoning punk scene. Poet-musician Patti Smith loved his work, and he wrote effusively of her 1975 debut album *Horses.* He was also an ardent fan of the Voidoids, an energetic New York band fronted by a singer named Richard Hell. Hell turned down a job offer in London to front the Sex Pistols, a cleverly packaged British import Bangs quickly disdained as a farce.

Immersed Himself in Punk Scene

In New York City, Bangs wrote about the punk scene for the *Village Voice* and, true to the genre's do-it-yourself ethos, decided he would start his own band. Teaming with a few other musicians as Birdland, Bangs easily landed a slot at CBGB's and fans turned up to see what he would do. As a writer, he had amassed a strong cult following; fans included not just Patti Smith but Chrissie Hynde, who was a music writer before forming the Pretenders, and Voidoids member Robert Quine, who played guitar for Birdland. Yet Bangs's exercise in actually being a musician himself left most perplexed. "It struck me that this guy had amazing taste as a critic, but when he was in a band, it was like the worst band I've ever seen in my life," musician Ian Hunter told Jim DeRogatis, the author of *Let It Blurt: The Life and Times of Lester Bangs.* "I didn't know what to say to him because it was so bloody awful."

The title of *Let It Blurt* was taken from the one single that Bangs's band issued, which in turn was a riff on the Rolling Stones' 1969 album *Let It Bleed.* As punk turned to New Wave, Bangs earned some income with a book on the band Blondie, then declared New York to be over and moved to Austin, Texas, in 1980. Only places far removed from the excess of the celebrity-entertainment complexes in New York and California, he argued, were going to produce any authentic new music in the coming decade. Prophetically, he also cited the Pacific Northwest as a potential new frontier.

In Austin, Bangs performed with a local punk outfit called the Delinquents, but his stint in Texas did not last, and he finally resolved to curtail what was then a legendary tolerance for alcohol and all manner of illicit and pharmaceutically manufactured drugs. Back in New York City in early 1981 he began attending Alcoholics Anonymous meetings. He tried to interest publishers in a tell-all of the rock world he titled *Rock Gomorrah,* but the potential legal quagmire scared off any of the major publishing houses.

On April 14, 1982, a New Jersey teenager turned up at Bangs's apartment to interview him for a high school journalism class assignment. At the time, Bangs was living in a building at 542 Sixth Avenue, near 14th Street, and his telephone had been turned off due to nonpayment. Jim DeRogatis conducted what would be one of Bangs's last interviews that day, and went on to a solid career as a rock critic himself in Chicago. "Good rock'n'roll is something that makes you feel alive," he told DeRogatis that day when the teen asked him to define the form. "To me, good rock'n'roll also encompasses other things, like Hank Williams and Charlie Mingus and a lot of things that aren't strictly defined as rock'n'roll. Rock'n'roll is an attitude; it's not a musical form of a strict sort. It's a way of doing things, of approaching things. Writing can be rock'n'roll, or a movie can be rock'n'roll. It's a way of living your life."

Bangs was found dead in the apartment on April 30, 1982, at the age of 33. His death was ruled an accidental overdose from a combination of Valium, Darvon, and cough syrup. True to form, the last piece of music Bangs listened to while still conscious became part of his legend: his opinion on *Dare* from the Human League would never be known.

Enjoyed Long Pop-Culture Afterlife

Bangs was resurrected by actor Philip Seymour Hoffman in the 2000 movie *Almost Famous* by filmmaker Cameron Crowe, who had also been one of Bangs's devotees and began writing reviews for *Rolling Stone* while still in his teens. Hoffman's appearances in the film are mere cameos, as the teenage Crowe, played by Patrick Fugit, phones Bangs from the road for advice. "Bangs, if he were he still alive, would certainly have had reservations about being depicted in a film where the spirit of 1970s rock'n'roll is evoked through a scene in which a fictional rock band bond on their tour bus by singing along to an Elton John track," asserted Nick Kent in the London *Guardian* newspaper. "Nevertheless, Philip Seymour Hoffman pulls off a complicated feat by letting us see Bangs's big romantic chump heart beating under his belligerent-looking black leather jacket and ragingly cynical rhetoric."

Even Kent was one of Bangs's young acolytes, writing about his visit to Detroit to spend time with the writer during the *Creem* years. "Certainly, rock criticism has never recovered from his passing," Kent mused as the 20th anniversary of Bangs's death loomed in 2002. "The genre quickly fragmented—much like the music it was reporting on—and most of the old school became content to pen windy, academic appreciations of their old favourites: the Beatles, Hendrix, the Sex Pistols, etc. No one wanted to rock the boat anymore or kick up the dust like Bangs used to. No one has tried to take his place, because they all recognise that what he achieved was unique and impossible to duplicate."

Books

Bangs, Lester, and John Morthland (editor), *Mainlines, Blood Feasts, and Bad Taste: A Lester Bangs Anthology*, Anchor Books, 2003.

Cateforis, Theo, *The Rock History Reader*, CRC Press, 2007.

DeRogatis, Jim, *Let It Blurt: The Life and Times of Lester Bangs*, Broadway Books, 2000.

Periodicals

Guardian (London, England), April 12, 2002.

Independent on Sunday (London, England), April 9, 2000. □

Jean Bartik

American computer programmer, Jean Jennings Bartik (1924-2011) helped change the world, as she was one of the early pioneers in the creation and deployment of software. At the time of her death, she was the last surviving member of the group of women who programmed the ENIAC, or Electronic Numerical Integrator and Computer, which became recognized as the first all-electronic digital computer.

The ENIAC (or Electronic Numerical Integrator and Computer) proved to be a major milestone in the evolution of modern computers. It was designed during World War II to calculate the firing trajectories for artillery shells. Its development and usage, however, proved too late for that. The war was over by the time it was introduced to the world. Still, it represented a major milestone in computer technology.

Indeed, when its capabilities were demonstrated at the University of Pennsylvania in February 1946, it created an enormous stir. Newspapers throughout the nation reported its capacity and capability. Although the excitement was justified, what was not justified was the lack of recognition of the women who contributed. Indeed, the men involved in the project were present at the event; not so the women who played roles in the development of this outstanding technological achievement. One of those women was Jean Jennings Bartik. But her contribution, or the impact it had on the world, cannot be denied.

A computer involves much more than just the people who build the hardware of the tool; it also involves its programmers—and Bartik helped lead a small team of women that provided programming for the ENIAC.

The 1946 oversight was fortunately addressed in Bartik's lifetime. She died in 2011, but in 2008, she was named a fellow by the Computer History Museum in Mountain View, California; and in 2009, Bartik received a Pioneer Award from the IEEE Computer Society.

Bartik was among the group of women (possessing strong math skills) recruited to plug in the wires and help set up the ENIAC machine. But they did more than that. They converted the math analysis into the process that made sense to this early generation computer—enabling calculation to flow through circuitry and eventually reaching completion. This was a complex undertaking, but the women proved up to the task. Essentially, they were the first to address the necessary issue of programming, indicated Paul E. Ceruzzi, a computer historian at the Smithsonian Institution. "They met the challenge," he said.

Raised on a Farm

Jean Bartik was born Betty Jean Jennings on December 27, 1924 in Gentry County, a rural area in Missouri, near Stanberry. She was the sixth of seven children of a farming family that placed great importance on education. "I come from a long line of school teachers and farmers," recalled Bartik, in an interview she gave late in her life for the Computer History Museum. "I had three brothers and three sisters. So I grew up in a big noisy family."

As this family was "noisy," Bartik's voice often got drowned out. "I never acquired any fame of any kind in my family," she revealed in the interview. But she did acquire local notoriety for her athletic skills, as well as her first taste of fame. "I was a good softball pitcher," she said in the same interview. "I went to a little one-room school, and you know that they have enough kids to play on a team. We played softball from the time we were in first grade. So it turned out that when I got to be in sixth and seventh grade, I could pitch better than anybody else."

A manager of the team in Stanberry, Missouri, heard about her pitching skills, and he asked her father if she could play for his team. Her father agreed, and Bartik became a local star. "There used to be stories about me in the newspaper," she remembered.

Attended College During Wartime

Bartik graduated from Stanberry High School in 1941 when she was sixteen years old. From there she attended Northwest Missouri State Teachers College (which would become Northwest Missouri State University) in Maryville. During her first year of college, the Japanese launched its attack on Pearl Harbor and the United States was plunged into World War II.

In college Bartik majored in mathematics. She was the only female math major at the time. She graduated in December 1944 with a bachelor's degree (later she would receive a masters in English from the University of Pennsylvania and an honorary doctorate of science from Northwest Missouri State University).

Applied Math Skills to Computers

In 1945, Bartik's faculty adviser came across an advertisement in a math journal that he felt would be perfect for her. The United States Army, according to the announcement, was recruiting math graduates for a war-related project taking place in Philadelphia, Pennsylvania. Bartik quickly and enthusiastically replied to the ad. For an interview that appeared on the About.com website, she recalled this period in her life: "There was a war on and women were doing everything, including being Rosie the riveter. I wanted to get out of Missouri and see some of the world. I wanted adventure, something new."

She was twenty-one years old, was accepted, and took a train to Philadelphia. She became a member of the computer programming staff at the University of Pennsylvania's Moore School of Engineering. There, she dropped the use of her first name Betty, which she had never liked. Also, at the University of Pennsylvania, she met William Bartik, an

engineer who was working on another wartime project. They married in 1946 (but divorced in 1968).

Bartik was one of six women who became human "computers," a term that later became programmers. The others included Betty Snyder Holberton, Kathleen McNulty Mauchly, Marlyn Wescoff Meltzer, Frances Bilas Spence and Ruth Lichterman Teitelbaum. Their job was to program the ENIAC, which was the world's first large-scale, fully electronic and general-purpose computer. It was a massive piece of equipment: It included 18,000 vacuum tubes, measured more than seven-hundred square feet and weighed 30 tons. It also had a challenging interface; Bartik and her female colleagues were confronted with hundreds of wires and three-thousand switches.

In her interview with About.com, Bartik described the complexities involved with the programming of the computer: "It was a parallel machine where we had to essentially build a central processor using program trays, digit trays, accumulators, multiplier, divider/square rooter, function tables, master programmer and I/O devices. We were the only group who programmed the ENIAC this way."

Enjoyed Vibrant Work Environment

Despite the challenges, Bartik was thrilled to be involved in such a project. "I thought I had died and gone to heaven," she told About.com. "I had never been around so many brilliant people in my life. My brain was running in high gear. I was in a world I had never dreamed of, yet I knew it was something I'd always wanted. We had no manuals for ENIAC."

For sure, the women were basically starting from scratch, learning as they went along—specifically learning how to program by studying logical block diagrams. "We gained the respect of the engineers from the beginning because we really knew what we were doing and we could debug better than they could because we had our test programs as well as our knowledge of the computer. It also laid down the background so I could do logical design on UNIVAC later on."

As she indicated, that would come later. In the meantime, the ENIAC, as Bartik would describe as quoted on about.com, was built to compute firing tables for Army Ordinance during World War II. She accurately described the specific problem the computer was designed to address: "For each new gun, tables are calculated to show the soldiers how to aim the gun to reach its target. It took a person at a desk calculator about 40 hours to compute one trajectory for one gun. A table consisted of hundreds of trajectories for different gun elevations, different altitudes, and different weather conditions."

Continued Working with Computers

Even though the end of the war essentially invalidated the computer's envisioned purpose, Bartik continued working with computers. In 1947, she became part of a group that converted ENIAC into a stored program computer, which represented a major development in computer technology. Also, with ENIAC designers John Presper Eckert and John W. Mauchly, she helped develop the UNIVAC, which was an early version of a commercial computer. It would be introduced in 1951. Bartik worked on micro-coded logic design and data backup.

As important as the ENIAC innovation was, Bartik found her work on the UNIVAC technology to be even more satisfying. "My favorite job was working on the design team for UNIVAC I," she told About.com. "I did some programming, but mainly I did logical design, putting in the check circuits and designing a backup for UNIVAC using cathode ray tube memory. It was microcoded."

Bartik would also work on the BINAC (hardware and software), which was a small computer developed for the Northrup Aircraft company.

Left the Computer Industry

Bartik stopped working on computers in 1951 so that she could focus on raising her three children (one son, two daughters). But she resumed her professional career in 1967. She engaged in programming and training. She also worked in technical publishing. She became an editor for Auerback Publishers, which produced materials related to high technology. In 1981, Bartik became a senior editor for communications services for Data Decisions, which was a Ziff-Davis company.

In 1985, she was laid off. By this time, she was sixty-one years old and she couldn't find another job in the computer industry. Both age and gender seemed to pose barriers to her re-entrance into the field, as her former husband would reveal. Faced with such professional obstructions, Bartik turned to another field: She became a real estate agent, and she worked in that field for twenty-five years.

She died of congestive heart failure on March 23, 2011 in Poughkeepsie, New York. She was eighty-six years old and living in a nursing home.

Received Recognition

Late in her life, Bartik received the recognition that she so well deserved. In 1997, along with her fellow female programmers who worked on the ENIAC, she was inducted into the Women in Technology Hall of Fame. That same year, she received the Augusta Ada Lovelace Award from the Association of Women in Computing. In 2001, her Alma Mater renamed its computer museum after her. The next year, she was bestowed an honorary doctorate from Northwest Missouri State University. In 2008, she received the Computer History Museum Fellows Award. In 2009, Bartik was honored with the IEEE Computer Society Computer Pioneer Award.

Such honors and awards helped redress the lack of recognition that Bartik and her fellow female computer programmers had suffered in 1946. Looking back on that post-war University of Pennsylvania ENIAC event, Bartik said that it did not trouble her too much at the time. In fact, for one conference, when she wrote a letter pointing out that no women had been invited to speak, she herself won an invitation and accepted the chance to share her knowledge and expertise.

At the same time, she didn't want to turn anything into a women's issue, even though she could have been well justified.

Kathy Kleiman, the founder of the ENIAC Programmers Project, which includes oral histories and film of the female mathematicians who worked on the computer, recalled Bartik in an online tribute found on the *Computer World* website. "I have two favorite memories of Jean," she said, after Bartik passed away, "one is my time with her listening to stories and learning about computer pioneers. The other is from 2008 watching Jean in the Google cafeteria, surrounded by young women from Google, with their heads together swapping stories and laughing. Systems change; challenges in computing, and triumphs, seem to be universal."

Periodicals

The New York Times, April 7, 2011.

Online

"Jean Bartik, last of the original ENIAC programmers, 86," *Computerworld.com*, http://blogs.computerworld.com/18018/jean_bartik_last_of_the_original_eniac_programmers_86 (December 1, 2011).

"Jean Bartik-2008 Fellow Award Recipient," *Computerhistory.org*, http://www.computerhistory.org/fellowawards/hall/bios/Jean,Bartik/ (December 1, 2011).

"Jean Bartik-Pioneer ENIAC Computer Programmer," *About.com Inventors*, http://inventors.about.com/library/inventors/blbartik1.htm (December 1, 2011).

"Jean Jennings Bartik," *Northwest Missouri State University*, http://www.nwmissouri.edu/compserv/Museum/JeanBartik.htm (December 1, 2011).

"Oral History of Jean Bartik," *Computerhistory.org*, http://archive.computerhistory.org/resources/text/Oral_History/Bartik_Jean/102658322.05.01.acc.pdf (December 1, 2011).□

Francis Bebey

The Cameroonian musician and writer Francis Bebey (1929–2001) was a trailbrazer in communicating West African music and culture to the wider world.

Bebey was one of the first individuals to record traditional African music within the structure of the music industry, and he had a rare ability both to participate in musical traditions and to stand outside them with sufficient perspective to write about them. His textbook, *African Music: A People's Art*, remained in print as of late 2011, more than 40 years after it was first published. As a novelist, playwright, radio producer, journalist, guitarist, and songwriter, Bebey worked tirelessly over his long career to bring the culture of his native Cameroon to the world. Most contemporary music-makers in the francophone countries of Africa owe him a debt, and he has even been called (by Radio France Internationale) "Africa's Renaissance Man."

Embraced African Musical Traditions

Francis Bebey (pronounced bay-BAY) was born on July 15, 1929, near Douala, which after the colony's independence

from France and Britain became the capital of Cameroon. His father was a Protestant minister, and the language spoken at home was French. Bebey grew up listening to Western classical music and playing several Western instruments, but it became clear in his teens that he had a special affinity for the guitar, and he switched to that instrument. He was taught to reject traditional African beliefs, but he was fascinated by a local shaman who spoke the regional language of Douala and used African music in ceremonies, and soon he was sneaking out to play African mouth bows and harps with friends. Very early in life, Bebey concluded that African traditions were worth preserving and celebrating.

Began Playing Professionally

By his teens, Bebey was already a working musician in Douala, playing the dance music known as *ashiko*. It was a close relative of Ghanaian and Nigerian highlife music, mixing jazz, Caribbean, and African rhythms into an infectious brew. Several new influences shaped his outlook after he won a scholarship to study languages at the Sorbonne university in Paris, France, in 1950. He discovered the first stirrings of Cameroonian literature. He heard the great Spanish classical guitarist Andres Segovia, and for the rest of his life critics would be impressed by the unusual guitar skills this encounter stimulated. He plunged into Paris's vital jazz scene, which already included some African musicians. At one point Bebey launched the career of fellow Cameroonian Manu Dibango, later the composer of "Soul Makossa" (sampled by Michael Jackson in "Wanna Be Startin' Somethin'"), by bringing him aboard Bebey's jazz trio; it was Dibango's first professional engagement.

Bebey moved to the United States in 1958 to study media and communications at New York University. His travels in the United States inspired his first composition for guitar, "L'été du Lac Michigan" (Summer on Lake Michigan),

and by the time he left, he could speak fluent English as well as French. Bebey returned briefly to Africa and helped launch a new French-language radio station in Ghana. He hosted a program called "Jazz Train" for a French overseas radio network. These experiences resulted in Bebey's first book, *La radiodiffusion en Afrique Noir* (Radio Broadcasting in Black Africa), published in 1963.

Worked with United Nations

During this period, Bebey first landed funding from the United Nations Educational, Scientific, and Cultural Organization (UNESCO) to study African music, and he began traveling around the countries of sub-Saharan Africa to learn more about their traditional musical genres. Returning to Paris, he worked for UNESCO as a program specialist, eventually rising to become head of the organization's music section. With stable employment, Bebey wrote prolifically during the 1960s. His musical studies reached fruition with the publication in 1969 of *Musique d'Afrique,* translated as *African Music: A People's Art* in 1975. For many years it was one of the few general surveys of African music available to Western readers, and although Bebey took some criticism for focusing most closely on the music of his native western Africa, the book remains a standard reference in its field.

Wrote Novels

Bebey's career as a fiction writer began in 1967 with *Le fils d'Agatha Moudio,* which was translated in 1971 as *Agatha Moudio's Son.* The novel traced the unfortunate multiple marriages of a Cameroonian man. Apparently it was not autobiographical; Bebey was married only once, to Jacqueline Edinguese in 1956, and the couple raised five children, Evidi, Christiane, Fanta, Francis Jr., and Patrick. *Le fils d'Agatha Moudio* won the Grand Prix Littéraire de l'Afrique Noir (Literary Grand Prize of Black Africa) in 1968.

After retiring from his UNESCO post in 1972, Bebey had more time to devote to writing. He produced five more novels, *Les petits cireurs* (The Little Shoeshine Boys), *Le roi Albert d'Effidi* (issued in English as *King Albert*), *La poupée Ashanti* (issued in English as *The Ashanti Doll*), *Le ministre et le griot* (The Minister and the Griot), and finally *L'enfant pluie* (Rain Child). Bebey also published several collections of short stories and a play, *Congrès de griots à KanKan* (Congress of Griots at KanKan, 1995).

During African literature's first burst of popularity, Bebey's fiction was widely read and critically hailed, but it is his musical legacy for which he remains best known. In the 1970s he formed his own label, Ozileka, and began to record his music in a home studio—neither of these being a common decision at the time. His first album was *Pièces pour guitare seule* (Pieces for Solo Guitar), released in 1968. Attesting to his popularity, Bebey's 1975 album, *Savannah Georgia,* appeared on the major Decca label; the all-instrumental release featured a mix of African percussion and synthesizer melodies. In 1976 Bebey released the comic album *La condition masculine* (The Masculine Condition), and the following year he won the Prix SACEM de la chanson française, roughly analogous to a U.S. Grammy award.

Learned to Play African Instruments

Bebey's career entered a new phase when he learned to play African instruments, something he had never done before the late 1970s. Among them were instruments of the Pygmies of Central Africa: the sanza, or thumb piano, and a small flute. Reviewing a 1995 Bebey concert, *New York Times* critic Jon Pareles wrote that Bebey's compositions drew on "glimmering, plinking patterns from the sanza and on the hooting syncopations of Pygmy music," with voice and the *ndewhoo* one-note flute alternating. Beginning with the 1982 album *African Sanza,* Bebey used that instrument in various contexts on most of his recordings.

Along with his orientation toward traditional music, however, Bebey remained open to collaborations with musicians of many kinds. His composition *Kasilane,* written for the experimentally minded Kronos Quartet, featured the mix of Pygmy flute and string quartet, and he wrote a classical work for sanza and cello. He composed the soundtrack for the highly regarded 1989 film *Yaaba* from Burkina Faso, and recorded or performed with musicians from U.S. film music composer John Williams to South African vocal harmony group Ladysmith Black Mambazo. In 1998 he appeared with Germany's Cologne Philharmonic Orchestra in a program called *Africa at the Opera.* Through all of these experiments, Bebey continued to develop his own guitar sound, sometimes striking its body to emulate the sound of pitched African drums or twisting the strings together to produce percussive effects.

Toured and Recorded Extensively

All this variety turned Bebey into a major concert attraction for the last part of his life, when he would often spend six months a year on the road. His sons Francis and Patrick, known as Toups, accompanied him on stage, and he would begin a segment of his shows in the manner of an African griot, using a traditional story to preface a musical piece. He mixed French, English, and several African languages as necessary in his presentation. Bebey maintained his Ozileka label and issued new music consistently through the 1990s; his albums included *Django Preface* (1991, dedicated to the memory of jazz guitarist Django Reinhardt), *Mwana* (1994), and the pair *Dibiye* and *Mbira Dance,* which jointly marked his 70th birthday in 1999.

In his final years, Bebey offered a broad, humanistic message of love and reconciliation in his concerts. In the words of *Afropop Worldwide,* "He often made the argument that art is not simply a diversion, but an essential feature of life—a civilizing force." Maintaining his concert schedule, he suffered a heart attack in Paris after returning from a tour of Italy. He died there on May 28, 2001. In the words of *Sing Out!,* "His contributions to AfroPop and traditional African culture are countless." A box set compilation of his music, *The Magic Box,* appeared that year on the Sony Classical label.

Books

Contemporary Black Biography, volume 45, Gale, 2001.

Periodicals

Independent (London, England), May 31, 2001.
New York Times, February 13, 1995; June 7, 2001.

Online

"Francis Bebey," *Afropop Worldwide,* http://www.afropop.org/explore/show_artist/ID/421/Francis%20Bebey (September 2, 2011).
"Francis Bebey," *Radio France Internationale,* http://www.rfimusic.com/artist/world-music/francis-bebey (September 2, 2011). □

Esteban Bellán

Cuba-born Esteban Bellán (1849-1932) became the first Latin to play in organized baseball in the United States. His career in America was brief, however: he turned professional in America in 1868 and then returned to Cuba in 1874, where he remained involved in the sport.

Esteban "Steve" Bellán is one of professional baseball's unsung pioneers. Many Major League baseball fans most likely do not know his name, but he assumed a major role in organized baseball's history: He broke the sport's first racial barrier, as he was the first Latin (he was Cuban) to participate in organized baseball in the United States. This took place in 1868, almost a century before African-American Jackie Robinson broke baseball's so-called "color barrier" when he joined the Brooklyn Dodgers in 1947.

Bellán's career was brief in the United States, lasting just six years in the late nineteenth century (from 1868 to 1873) and he was not what could be considered an "all star," but his historic impact is substantial nonetheless.

Bellán usually played third base (although many baseball historians now consider him a "utility" player—an individual that can field many positions). His career kept him involved with the National Association of Base Ball Players (1868-1870) and the National Association of Professional Base Ball Players (1871-1873), and he was a member of three teams: the Union Base Ball Club of Morrisania, the Troy Haymakers and the New York Mutuals. In 1874, he returned to his homeland of Cuba, where he became one of his country's first important player-managers.

Sent to School in America

Bellán was born in Havana, Cuba on October 1, 1849. His father was a Cuban native and his mother was born in Ireland sometime around 1820. Details about his early life are scant, but this much has been discerned: His family was wealthy, and this enabled his parents to send Bellán and his older brother, Domingo, to the United States for education.

This occurred in 1863, when Bellán was thirteen years old. He and his brother left Cuba at a time of political strife (Cuba was seeking independence from Spain). This led the brothers to New York City and St. John's College. The Jesuit preparatory school, which was established in 1841, would later become known as Fordham University, and it would come to include three New York State campuses: Rose Hill in the Bronx, Lincoln Center in Manhattan and Westchester in West Harrison. Bellán attended the Bronx (Rose Hill) campus. There, he studied English grammar. He remained at the school until 1868.

Bellán also played baseball for the Rose Hill Baseball Club, which was established in the late 1850s. At the time, baseball was an emerging sport, and St. John's had started its own scholastic team in 1859. Besides offering a Latin player (Bellán) a position on the team, Rose Hill's history included another significant milestone: On November 3, 1859, it played the first-ever nine-man team college baseball game in the United States (against St. Francis Xavier College). Nine men on the field would later become the professional baseball standard.

At the time, baseball was a wild and wooly sport: Consider a box score that appeared in *The New York Times*: In a June 18, 1868 game, Rose Hill defeated another New York team (the Actives) by a score of 36-34. Compare that to the typical modern day scores. Reportedly, Bellán garnered four hits and scored twice in this slugfest.

Left School to Play Baseball

Bellán left St. John's in 1868 when he was eighteen years old. He then played for the Union Base Ball Club of Morrisania. The team became commonly known as the Morrisania Unions. It was formed in the mid-nineteenth century and became part of the National Association of Base Ball Players (at the time Morrisania was a New York town, and it later became a neighborhood in New York City's Bronx borough). The club was one of the first organized teams in the New York City area and by the mid-1860s it became one of the best. Indeed, at the time that Bellán came on board, the Morrisania Unions were the NABBP champions. The team included shortstop George Wright, who was inducted into the National Baseball Hall of Fame in 1937. It has been speculated that Wright was partially responsible for recruiting Bellán—a move that helped launch Bellán's professional baseball career.

Bellán played but one season for the Morrisania Unions. By this time, he became known to teammates as "Steve," an Americanized version of his Latin name.

By today's baseball standards, he was somewhat small in terms of physical size: he stood only about five-feet six-inches tall and he weighed 154 pounds. But he capably fielded his position (third base, in baseball parlance, is called the "hot corner"). He played in the barehanded era, and he demonstrated a knack for grabbing hard-hit baseballs and then throwing to bases with unerring accuracy. During his American career, his batting average hovered around the .250 range, but he was noted for being a quick-footed base runner. His schooling in New York was most likely his first introduction to the sport, as baseball had not been introduced in Cuba until 1866, several years after Bellán left the country.

In 1869, Bellán became a member of the Troy Haymakers. He played third base for the New York-based team until 1872. A year earlier, the Troy Haymakers became part of the National Association of Professional Base Ball Players. The Association, which was formed in 1871, would evolve into the National League. The Haymakers would eventually become the New York Giants (and later the San Francisco Giants).

The team was originally called the Unions of Lansingburgh. It was established in the post-Civil War era (1866) and took its place among pre-war clubs including the Priams of Troy, Nationals of Lansingburgh, and Unions of Rensselaer County. The newer Unions of Lansingburgh team, when it became part of the NABBP, was a dominant force, winning about ninety percent of its games in its first five seasons. Legend has it that the team became known as the Haymakers after soundly defeating the New York Mutuals in a game. The outcome compelled one of the losing players to complain about being defeated by "haymakers." At the time, "haymakers," was a derogatory term for people raised on farms.

In 1871, the Haymakers lineup was filled with some of early baseball's best hitters—people like Bill Craver, Dickie Flowers, Clipper Flynn, Steve King and Lip Pike. While Bellán was not considered one of the team's more powerful plate performers (during the team's twenty-nine games, he only batted .250), he did come through with some outstanding individual game batting numbers. For instance, on August 3 of 1871, he batted 5-for-5 and drove in five runs. More importantly, he fielded his position expertly.

After Bellán left the Haymakers (the team had disbanded), he went on to play with the New York Mutuals for a year, playing third base for the most part. At the time, the NABBP excluded black baseball clubs and black players. This exclusion included Latin players, because of their complexion. Because his father was Cuban and his mother Irish, however, Bellán had a light complexion, which made it easier for him to traverse the racial barrier.

Returned to Cuba

In 1873, after he became a naturalized citizen of the United States, Bellán left the New York Mutuals and returned to Cuba. He played his final game in the United States (as a member of the New York Mutuals) on June 9, 1873. By this time, baseball was becoming organized in his homeland. Bellán helped further its development into one of the most popular sports among the citizens.

Back home, Bellán joined Club Habana, which would become the leading—and most famous—team in Cuba for a while. On December 27, 1874, Bellán's team participated in the first organized game played in Cuba, an event that he helped make happen. The team defeated Club Matanzas by an astonishing score of 51-9. The event took place at the Palmar del Junco Field, located in Pueblo Nuevo, Matanzas, Cuba. Bellán participated in the game as a catcher. He was considered a "utility" player, meaning that he could assume several on-field roles (throughout his career, Bellán worked as a catcher, infielder and outfielder). He contributed to his team's wildly high score: Bellán belted three home runs and crossed home plate seven times. He also batted in several runs for his team.

An additional historic note: The Palmar del Junco Field hosted the first baseball game where an American team went up against a Cuban team. No doubt, the region was excited by this event. American sailors brought the sport to the country in 1866.

By 1878, the Cuban League was established, but only a relatively few games were played during a regular season, Habana finished the 1879-1880 season with a 5-2 record, which was good for a pennant, but seven games is far lower than the modern Major League Baseball's 162-game regular-season schedule. Games were usually scheduled for Sundays and holidays, and the season schedule involved as few as three teams.

Bellán became the team's player-manager in 1878, a position he held until 1886. In his role, he helped lead the club to three Cuban League championships (in the 1878-1879, 1879-1880 and 1882-1883 seasons).

Subsequently, Cuban baseball professional development became hampered by disputes and feuds and, as such, no league games were played from 1880 to 1882. When activity resumed, Club Habana won another pennant (in the 1882-1883 season with a 5-1 record). Further disputes forestalled the 1883-1884 season. Bellán returned to the sport in the 1885-1886 season when, as a player-manager, he led Club Habana to a fifth-straight Cuban title (this time, the team recorded a 6-0 record). During Bellán's five-season leadership, Club Habana boasted a 21-6-1 record (indicating wins, losses, and a tie).

Died in His Homeland

As with Bellán's early life, Bellán's post-baseball life offers few details. Somewhere along the line, he left the game and severed contacts with the people that he knew—either fellow players or the Cuban sports press. In a 1911 newspaper article that detailed baseball in Cuba, there was no mention of his name.

Despite this, Bellán has come to be known as the ''father'' of Cuban baseball, based on his role in making the first organized Cuban baseball game happen, as well as for his success as a player-manager.

Bellán died on August 8, 1932 in Havana. He was eighty-two years old. He was not a completely forgotten man, however. A statue was erected in Havana to honor his contributions to the sport that he had come to love.

Periodicals

The Wall Street Journal, September 23, 2010.

Online

''19th Century Pioneers,'' *CubanBall.com,* http://www.cubanball.com/pioneers.html (December 2, 2011).

''Cuban Baseball-Estaban Bellan,'' *Fordham University Libraries,* http://www.library.fordham.edu/cubanbaseball/e_bellan.html (December 2, 2011).

''Morrisania Unions,'' *Baseball Chronology,* http://www.baseballchronology.com/baseball/leagues/NABBP/Clubs/Morrisania_Unions.asp (December 2, 2011).

''Steve Bellan,'' *The Baseball Biography Project,* http://bioproj.sabr.org (December 2, 2011). □

Kathryn Bigelow

Filmmaker Kathryn Bigelow (born 1951) became the first woman to win an Academy Award for Best Director for her 2009 drama *The Hurt Locker,* which also earned Best Picture honors at the 2010 ceremony. Known for her talent in crafting glossy, big budget action movies, Bigelow is the rare female filmmaker to direct such typical Hollywood fare. Her Oscar win also marked the first time in Academy Award history that a pair of ex-spouses competed against one another in the top two categories: Bigelow's ex-husband, James Cameron, was nominated for both Best Picture and Best Director for his sci-fi thriller *Avatar.*

Kathryn Ann Bigelow was born on November 27, 1951, and grew up in the San Francisco Bay area community of San Carlos. Her mother, of Norwegian heritage, was a graduate of Stanford University and worked as a librarian. Bigelow's father was a manager at a paint production facility. ''My dad used to draw these great cartoon figures,'' Bigelow recalled in an interview with *Newsweek* writer Jennie Yabroff. ''His dream was being a cartoonist, but he never achieved it, and it kind of broke my heart. I think part of my interest in art had to do with his yearning for something he could never have.''

Earned Art Degree

An only child, Bigelow was encouraged by her parents to be creative and independent-minded, which sometimes veered off into the realm of outrageous: once, she brought home a horse and convinced her parents to let her keep it in a nearby yard. She took art classes from an early age, and entered college at the San Francisco Art Institute at the height of the city's counterculture era. After graduating in 1972 she won a coveted slot at the Whitney Museum of American Art's Independent Study Program, and in New York City worked with a provocative conceptual art collective that went by the name ''Art & Language.'' She studied film theory and criticism at Columbia University's School of the Arts and made her first movie in 1978. The 15-minute work, shot on Manhattan's Lower East Side, essentially centered around a display of male aggression that would become the hallmark of her later films: two of her Columbia film theory professors, Sylvère Lotringer and Marshall Blonsky, debate the issue of violence in cinema as a pair of toughs come to blows in an alley fight.

Bigelow has said that the films of Sam Peckinpah and Martin Scorsese were a profound influence on her; those directors' works usually feature elaborate, even artfully executed scenes of violence. One of her first jobs in the industry was as a script supervisor on a little-seen low budget film that starred Deborah Harry, *Union City,* released in 1980. After that, Bigelow then moved to California at the urging of her artist friend, John Baldessari, to teach a course in B-movie directors at the California Institute of the Arts. That led to a

job with writer-director Walter Hill, who made the 1979 teen-gang classic, *The Warriors.*

Made Biker Movie

The first feature film Bigelow made was *The Loveless,* which she co-wrote and co-directed with Monty Montgomery, a producer who had been part of the *Union City* project and worked on the periphery of experimental film. Released in 1982, *The Loveless* centered on a gang of bikers on their way to the annual Daytona Beach races who are delayed in a small town in Georgia. The movie marked actor Willem Dafoe's screen debut, but failed to spark interest in any of Bigelow's other scripts.

Bigelow met James Cameron in the mid-1980s, not long after the largely self-taught Canadian-born filmmaker had scored a massive hit with *The Terminator,* one of the biggest box office releases of 1984. Cameron went on to make *Aliens* in 1986, another special effects dazzler, followed by *The Abyss,* an epic underwater sci-fi thriller. The couple were married on Martha's Vineyard in August of 1989, the same month that *The Abyss* was released. They were close friends of actor Bill Paxton, who had appeared in *Aliens.* Paxton was in a short-lived band called Martini Ranch, and Cameron directed a long-form video, a mock Western, for their song "Reach." Bigelow appears in it as one of an all-female bounty-hunting gang. Her only other screen credit came in *Born in Flames,* a futuristic thriller about a dystopian female-run socialist society that achieved cult status almost immediately after its 1983 release.

Gained Mainstream Success

In 1987 Bigelow made her own minor cult classic, a vampire-Western called *Near Dark.* It starred Paxton and Adrian Pasdar and premiered at the Toronto International Film Festival. *Variety* gave it a good review, noting that its chief merit was the fact its director "has undoubtedly created the most hard-edged, violent actioner ever directed by an American woman." That small success paved the way for Bigelow's first real Hollywood movie, the serial killer drama *Blue Steel.* Released in March of 1990, the movie starred Jamie Lee Curtis as a rookie cop who kills a robber in a supermarket holdup. The perpetrator's gun disappears during the chaos, however, and Curtis's character is accused of shooting an unarmed assailant. Actor Tom Sizemore, who has appeared in several of Bigelow's films, made his screen debut as the doomed robber in "the taut, frightening action scene that...shows off Ms. Bigelow's methods at their very best," wrote Janet Maslin in the *New York Times.* "It isn't necessary to believe 'Blue Steel' fully to find it gripping all the way through, and to be both fascinated and frightened by its icy, gleaming vision of urban life. For the audience, it's both a sobering and invigorating experience. For Ms. Bigelow, it's a breakthrough."

Blue Steel's performance at the box office won Bigelow some clout with studio executives, and she was determined to cast young actor Keanu Reeves in her next project, *Point Break.* At the time, Reeves was typecast as an affable stoner-type, and Bigelow pushed hard to convince producers that he would make an ideal action hero for the movie, which featured Reeves as a federal agent who goes undercover as a surfer in Hawaii to catch a masterful gang of bank robbers led by Patrick Swayze. Reeves would go on to appear in several big-budget action epics, including *Speed* and *The Matrix* franchise, thanks in part to *Point Break.* The movie was largely trashed by critics, but well-received by audiences. One notable sequence was a skydiving duel scene that earned Bigelow high marks for staging and direction.

Bigelow was divorced from Cameron in 1991, but it was an amicable split, and her ex-husband served as one of the producers on her next movie, *Strange Days.* This 1995 violent thriller starred Ralph Fiennes in a debauched future Los Angeles, and relied on some imaginative high tech gadgetry to drive the plot. It cost $42 million to make, but earned just under $8 million in domestic box office receipts. Because of that, Bigelow's career stalled for a time, and her next film, an adaptation of Anita Shreve's murder mystery *The Weight of Water,* was also panned by critics. Despite an all-star cast that included Sean Penn, its release was delayed for nearly two years.

Succeeded with Cold War Crisis Drama

Bigelow fared slightly better with her seventh movie, *K-19: The Widowmaker.* Released in the summer of 2002, the Cold War-set Russian submarine drama starred Harrison Ford and Liam Neeson in charge of a newly built nuclear sub and its crew. K-19 sets out on a top secret missile test in Arctic waters, but technical issues with its on-board reactor put the sub, the crew, and potentially the entire world in peril. The crew agrees to repair the reactor in alternating teams, to lessen the threat of radiation sickness, but the first pair of sailors emerges "scalded, vomiting, and doomed, like victims of an instant plague," wrote Anthony Lane in his *New Yorker* review, "and you can hear the otherwise restless audience freeze and gasp. Movies have become so adept at simulations of universal horror—the flash of white-out, the mushroom cloud—that it is salutary, and far more effective, to be reminded of the damage that can be done to a single body, delivering the whimpers without a bang.''

Other critics, however, were less than impressed with *K-19* and the Russian-accented dialogue. Its $90 million production budget did give Bigelow a new distinction, making it the most expensive movie ever directed by a woman. Seven years would pass between that movie and her next project, the Oscar-winning *Hurt Locker.* Based on a script by journalist Mark Boal, who was embedded with a bomb disposal unit in Baghdad in the first year of the Iraq War in 2004, *The Hurt Locker* was a grim, tense war movie centered on one of the U.S. Army's Explosive Ordnance Disposal units, who head out several times a day to investigate suspicious parcels. Bigelow filmed much of the action in Jordan in 2007, and the picture starred a passel of relatively unknown actors, led by Jeremy Renner as staff sergeant William James. ''Like most of Ms. Bigelow's most memorable characters, James has pushed against his own limits and then pushed some more,'' asserted *New York Times* film critic Manohla Dargis. ''He's a danger addict who walks directly into the abyss so he can hear the thump thump thump of his own ticking heart, itself an incendiary device. But war isn't a solitary act and James can only feed his habit by imperiling others: this is his tragedy and, by extension, ours.''

The Hurt Locker, released in the summer of 2009, was one of the year's unexpected cinema success stories. Critics raved about it, then the title started showing up on year-end ''best-of'' lists and began to win actual awards. David Edelstein, writing for *New York* magazine, wrote of its appeal as a war movie that broke new ground. ''The question of what the hell these good men are doing in a culture they don't understand with a language they don't speak surrounded by people they can't read hangs in the air but is never actually called,'' he remarked. ''Or is that why this movie rises above its preachy counterparts? Bigelow's triumph is to show why they don't call that into question themselves.''

Made Oscar History

On January 30, 2010, Bigelow made history as the first woman ever to win the Directors Guild Award for Outstanding Achievement in Feature Film. The elite award is generally considered a solid predictor of which movie will win the Academy Award for Best Picture—in 60 years, 54 movies have shared both honors—and publicists attempted to drum up interest in Bigelow's possible big win on Oscar night by playing up the fact that her ex-husband's *Avatar* was also up for several awards. At the 82nd Annual Academy Awards on March 7, 2010, both *The Hurt Locker* and *Avatar* won in several lesser categories. Barbra Streisand, who struggled for years to direct her first feature film, *Yentl,* was the presenter for the Best Director award. When Streisand opened the envelope, she said, ''Well, the time has come,'' according to the *New York Times,* and announced Bigelow's name.

Bigelow was already working with Boal on another project involving the hunt for fugitive al-Qaeda leader Osama bin Laden. That project was greenlighted a few days after bin Laden was found and killed in Abbottabad, Pakistan in May of 2011 in a Navy SEALs black-ops mission. Dargis, the *New York Times* film critic who has been one of Bigelow's most steadfast supporters, wrote about the significance of the director's 2010 Oscar win, asserting that the dual honors for Best Picture and Best Director ''didn't just punch through the American movie industry's seemingly shatterproof glass ceiling; it has also helped dismantle stereotypes about what types of films women can and should direct. It was historic, exhilarating, especially for women who make movies and women who watch movies, two groups that have been routinely ignored and underserved by an industry in which most films star men and are made for and by men.''

Periodicals

New York, June 21, 2009.

New York Times, March 16, 1990; January 10, 2010; March 8, 2010.

New Yorker, July 29, 2002.

Newsweek, June 29, 2009.

Premiere, August 2002.

Online

''Goddess of War,'' EW.com, January 1, 2010, http://www.ew.com/ew/article/0,,20333854,00.html (August 8, 2011).

''*Near Dark* (Review),'' Variety.com, December 31, 1986, http://www.variety.com/review/VE1117793441?refcatid=31 (August 9, 2011). □

Louis Blériot

Louis Blériot (1872-1936) was a prominent engineer and aviator. Best known as the first person to cross the English Channel in a heavier-than-air machine, Blériot was also instrumental in moving forward innovative designs in aircraft. Blériot designed thirteen aircraft, and two of those, the Blériot XI and the S.P.A.D. planes, were used extensively by the Allies during World War I.

L ouis Blériot was born on July 1, 1872 in Cambrai, France to a textile manufacturer. He received his engineering degree from L'Ecole Central in Paris in 1893. He eventually married Alicia Védère with whom he would have five children. Blériot made his fortune by inventing automobile headlights. Later on, he also invented foot warmers for car passengers and luminous license plates. These inventions made Blériot a very wealthy man, and at a very young age.

Dabbled in Aviation

Blériot began dabbling in aviation by towing gliders across the Seine. When he was in his thirties, Blériot began to design his own aircraft and taught himself to fly. The prominent airplane design of the time was a two-wing biplane. Among other interests, Blériot wanted to experiment with a single-wing airplane. This kind of design, thoeretically, would lead to less weight and therefore less drag, hopefully allowing for higher speeds and additional maneuverability. In addition, the pilot would have a freer field of vision. Unfortunately, Blériot's designs were generally considered to be fairly bad. While he improved his designs with trial and error, they were generally clumsy and sometimes never even made it off the ground.

Blériot's first airplane design was modeled off of a bird. Blériot believed that if birds flapped their wings to fly, then humans could do the same. This design failed. He later attempted to create a float-plane glider. In 1906, he established the first airplane factory in France.

Blériot eventually brought in another talented aviator, Gabriel Voisin, to help him design planes. These two worked together for several years. Voisin and Blériot had different visions for appropriate design ideas. Voisin was very interested in box-kite biplanes and Blériot was interested in working on a flattened flying cylinder. While they eventually built both planes to little success, these types of vast creative differences between the two led to their separation and eventually to them competing against one another.

Blériot's designs eventually began to improve with trial and error. He had a colossal failure with his tail-first monoplane, which flipped on the first trial. The pilot refused to ever fly it again and warned the other aviators in the area to the dangers. Because of this, Blériot started flying his own planes and was able to make a few small flights in this plane in April 1907.

Found Successful Design

Blériot's sixth airplane was nicknamed *La Libellule* or *The Dragonfly*. It included a 24-horse power engine with a propeller in the front. It included moveable control surfaces on the vertical stabilizer. Blériot had introduced something akin to ailerons on the wing tips. He also included a sliding seat so that the pilot could gain additional control of the aircraft by shifting his weight. When the plane debuted in July 1907 Blériot was able to get it off the ground for 25, 150, and 140 meters, which was considered a success at the time. Blériot was convinced that all he needed to improve the plane was a more powerful engine, so he installed one, and then promptly crashed the plane.

Later that year, Blériot designed the Blériot VII. This was the first monoplane with a front-mounted engine, an enclosed fuselage, a rear tailplane and rudder, a two-wheel undercarriage, and a tail wheel. Blériot gradually moved the rear wings further aft and made them smaller until they began to look like a modern stabilizer; unfortunately Blériot crashed the plane on December 18, 1907 before he had a chance to fully understand the proper size and positioning of the rear wings.

Blériot designed more than 13 aircraft in his lifetime. More than half of them would not fly or crashed when he flew them. Blériot survived more than 50 crashes in his lifetime. Eventually he sold his headlight business and decided to focus solely on aircraft.

In 1908, Blériot created the world's first true monoplane: the Blériot VIII. There were many features that had never been seen before on a plane. There was one long single wing. There was a tail with both vertical and horizontal surfaces. It had moveable control surfaces that were precursors to later ailerons. It was not particularly aerodynamic and it was slow and awkward, but it did have the smooth lines of future planes. There was also a 50 horsepower engine that moved a four-blade propeller. On October 31, 1908 Blériot flew 30 kilometers from Toury, France to Artenay, France and back. The news of this impressive flight was overshadowed by the fact that Henri Farman had flown 27 kilometers in his Voisin biplane only the day before.

Blériot's most notable design was a remodeled Blériot VIII and was named the Blériot XI. It had a maximum weight of about 500 pounds and a maximum range of about 50 miles. The fuselage was partially covered and the pilot sat on a wooden seat with only a leather strap for a backrest. It had no instruments, not even a compass. The wings were detachable for easier transport, it had a three-cylinder engine and could run for about a half-hour. It would be the plane that Blériot would fly across the English Channel, and it would eventually come to be used as the main French training aircraft during World War I.

Crossed the English Channel

In 1909, the London *Daily Mail* offered a £1000 prize for the first flight across the English Channel by a "heavier-than-air machine." Blériot did not need the money, but he was interested in the publicity. He entered with his Blériot XI monoplane, and he was underestimated by the competition because of his often-unsuccessful plane designs.

In Blériot's 1936 obituary, *The Washington Post* would say of attitudes about flight at the time that, "when Louis Blériot flew the English Channel from Calais to Dover, the airplane was regarded as an oversized kite with a motor, and fliers were looked upon as queer individuals with a distaste for life." Blériot was about to change all of that.

Three European pilots entered: Hubert Latham, Count de Lambert, and Blériot. De Lambert was delayed by airplane trouble. Lamtham made his first attempt on July 19, 1909. His plan crashed but was salvageable, so Lantham remained in Calais and was still there on the morning of July 25, 1909.

That morning Albert Le Blanc, a businessman and friend of Louis Blériot, woke him very early in the morning with the news that the weather was good. At 4am, Blériot took a short test run, about fifteen minutes, around Calais, landing where he would need to take off for England. Blériot had to wait, though, as the guidelines set down by the *Daily Mail* stated that the flight needed to take place between sunrise and sunset. Waiting for sunrise, Blériot had a routine take-off from Calais at 4:35am on July 25, 1909. Lantham, who was still in Calais waiting to attempt another flight, watched Blériot take off from his hotel room window.

Blériot would later say that the most unnerving part of his journey was when he was over the Channel. The French had provided a carrier to watch out for the pilots, but Blériot quickly flew over it and, as he had a previous injury from a test flight, he was not optimistic that he would survive a crash into the water. In addition, Blériot had no instruments, not even a compass, to guide him from shore to shore and could have easily gotten lost when both shores were out of sight.

Luckily, Blériot made it safely to Dover, England. The wind over the Channel had taken him slightly off course and he needed to correct it when he was able to determine his location. The wind also caused him problems upon landing, twirling Blériot around until he cut the engine and fell 65 feet to the ground.

This flight won Blériot the London *Daily Mail* prize and made him a media sensation. Blériot took a boat back to France, only to discover that he needed to return to London immediately for a dinner at the Savoy hotel in London, thrown for him by the London *Daily Mail*. When he returned to France, he was required to go to Paris to speak to the newspaper *Le Matin*. This paper hung Blériot's plane outside of its Paris offices so that individuals passing by would be able to look at it. Blériot's flight also motivated many businessmen to buy the Blériot XI and led him to be named a Knight of the Legion of Honor.

Set Speed record in Reims

Later that year, the Gordon Bennett speed races were held in Reims, France. Airplanes were now very fashionable and this international event was attended by more than 20,000 people, including the president of France and former American president Teddy Roosevelt. There were far more French pilots than any other nationality, and since the Wright brothers were not in attendance, they showed French dominance in aviation at the time.

The competition was multi-dimensional and held over several days at the end of August. Latham won the height contest, flying at 508 ft, far higher than was typical at the time. Henri Farman flew a record 112 miles before he ran out of fuel, the furthest anyone had flown at the time. There were two different speed races for which Blériot, fresh off of his flight across the Channel, was the favorite. Unfortunately he fell to American Glenn Curtiss by six seconds in the first race and Blériot's plane crashed and burst into flames during the second. In spite of that, Blériot walked away with a speed record for the fastest lap at 47.75 miles/hour.

Manufactured Planes for the War

Blériot continued to work in aviation for the rest of his life, though he flew less frequently because of concerns that his wife had for his health. With the beginning of World War I, Blériot began to manufacture fighter airplanes for the military. They largely used the Blériot XI, first in France and Italy in 1910 and then later in England. Blériot made a few small design changes including replacing the engine with an Anzani engine with a 50 horsepower Gnome rotary engine. Eventually all of the Allied forces would be flying Blériot S.P.A.D. planes.

On July 25, 1929, Blériot made his final flight on the twentieth anniversary of his flight across the Channel. In 1934, Blériot came to Washington, DC as a delegate to the 34th congress of the Fédération Aéronautique Internationale, the Universal Aeronautical Federation. Blériot participated throughout the ceremony, but he had to skip a trip to Kitty Hawk, North Carolina, the home of the Wright Brothers, as his doctor had grounded him. His wife left a wreath there on his behalf. Blériot died on August 2, 1936.

Books

Dick, Ron and Dan Patterson, *Aviation Century: The Golden Age*, Boston Mills Press, 2004.

DISCovering Science, Gale, 2002

Flight: 100 Years of Aviation, edited by David Summers, DK Publishing, 2002.

Harris, Sherwood, *The First to Fly: Aviation's Pioneer Days*, Simon and Schuster, 1970

Periodicals

Science and Times, April, 16, 2002

Tech Directions, November, 2002

Washington Post, August, 2, 1936 □

Baruch Blumberg

The American medical researcher Baruch Blumberg (1925–2011) was the discoverer of the hepatitis B virus and helped to create a vaccine that prevented it. It was the first vaccine that prevented any form of cancer in humans.

laborers from around the world to work on the region's sugar plantations, Suriname's population was and remains unusually diverse, with groups from India, the Indonesian island of Java, various parts of Africa, China, and indigenous as well as Jewish groups. Blumberg as well as other observers noticed that members of different ethnic groups were susceptible to specific diseases in varying degrees. He wondered why, and he published an early paper on the range of immunity to the parasite that causes the disease elephantiasis. "Nature operates in a bold and dramatic manner in the tropics," Blumberg wrote in a biographical essay written when he received the Nobel Prize. "Biological effects are profound and tragic. The manifestations of important variables may often readily be seen and measured, and the rewards to health in terms of prevention or treatment of disease can be great."

Motivated by Hospital Scenes

Back in New York, Blumberg was struck by the plight of his patients, "including many formerly middle class people impoverished by the expenses of chronic illness. In his autobiography, he wrote that "the wards were crowded, often with beds in the halls. Scenes on the wards were sometimes reminiscent of Hogarth's woodcuts of the public institutions of 18th century London." Motivated in part by the Jewish precept that if one saves a single life, one saves the whole world, he began to think in terms of medical research with worldwide lifesaving potential. Blumberg completed his education with a Ph.D. at Oxford University in England in 1957. In 1954 he married Jean Liebesman, and the couple raised four children, Anne, George, Jane, and Noah.

Employed by the National Institutes of Health (1957–1964) and then by the Institute for Cancer Research in Philadelphia, Pennsylvania (later the Fox Chase Cancer Center), Blumberg set out to build a worldwide collection of blood samples that he could test for antigens, or substances that trigger an immune response when they enter the body. His first research trip was to Nigeria in 1957, and his adventures, recounted in his book *Hepatitis B: The Hunt for a Killer Virus,* included a near plane crash on the way to Africa. Blumberg used the new gel method of electrophoresis (separating proteins by applying an electric field to them and, essentially, straining them through a gel) to investigate the contents of these samples. Lacking the tools of modern molecular biology, he used the blood of hemophiliacs to look for reactions generated by his collection of blood samples—hemophiliacs, who receive frequent transfusions, thus produce immune responses to a large variety of antigens.

In 1963 Blumberg isolated a protein in a blood sample he had taken from an Australian aborigine and found that it caused an immune response in that of an American hemophiliac. Later he found other patients who had previously tested negative for antibodies to this protein but then showed a positive response and later developed the serious blood disease hepatitis B, whose cause was unknown at the time. Blumberg dubbed the protein the Australia antigen, and correctly hypothesized that it was part of the virus that caused hepatitis B. By the mid-1960s he and his colleagues

B lumberg's career was unconventional, marked by forays into diverse areas of inquiry that led later on to discoveries in new fields. Because he was not a virologist but a medical anthropologist (a researcher who studies disease and medicine in diverse cultures), his hepatitis B discoveries were at first ignored by the medical community. Blumberg's work was hands-on in nature, motivated by a desire to alleviate human suffering. The projects he devised required him to travel all over the world, a prospect he greeted with enthusiasm. Blumberg received a Nobel Prize in Physiology or Medicine in 1976 for his work, at a time when much of his professional career was still ahead of him.

Attended Jewish Schools

Baruch Samuel Blumberg, known to friends as Barry, was born in New York on July 28, 1925. He attended Jewish religious schools, mastered the Hebrew language, and studied the rigorous arguments of the Talmud (a key text of Judaism). After he won several science awards while a student at Far Rockaway High School (whose alumni roster boasts two other Nobel Prize winners), he enlisted in the United States Navy. Serving as a deck officer, he was able to attend college with the help of military programs. Blumberg graduated from Union College in Schenectady, New York, majoring in physics. Then he enrolled in a graduate program in mathematics at Columbia but soon switched to medicine, taking courses at Columbia's College of Physicians and Surgeons.

Blumberg graduated from Columbia in 1951 and served as an intern at New York's Bellevue Hospital from 1951 to 1953. His experiences during these years shaped the course of his entire career. Most formative was a trip to Suriname (then the colony of Dutch Guiana) between his third and fourth years of medical school. Due to the importation of had discovered a way to test for the presence of hepatitis B in donated blood, a common medium for its transmission.

Ignored by Medical Mainstream

Despite the importance of this discovery, Blumberg, whose research background was in biochemistry, was at first ignored by mainstream virologists, and a 1967 paper describing his results was turned down by the *Annals of Internal Medicine.* "We were outsiders not known to the main body of hepatitis investigators, some of whom had been pursuing their field of interest for decades," he recalled, as quoted in the London *Daily Telegraph,* and the members of his team "were surprised by the hostility engendered among our new colleagues." But as Blumberg's results were replicated by other investigators, his work gained wider recognition.

Blumberg immediately set about finding practical applications for his research, and in 1969 he and fellow Institute for Cancer Research investigator Irving Millman succeeded in creating a vaccine that, when refined, was over 90 percent effective in preventing hepatitis B, without serious side effects. Since hepatitis B is a frequent precursor to liver cancer, Blumberg's vaccine is regarded as having been the first one to act as a preventative for any form of cancer. Once again, he faced resistance from the medical establishment; in the early 1970s not all researchers were yet convinced that his research on hepatitis B was correct, and, he noted dryly in his Nobel Prize autobiography, "Vaccines are not an attractive product for pharmaceutical companies in that they are often used once or only a few times and they ordinarily do not generate as much income as a medication for a chronic disease that must be used for many years." Nevertheless, in 1976, the Merck pharmaceutical firm agreed to produce the vaccine, using a new method Blumberg himself had designed. Blumberg was awarded the Nobel Prize in Physiology or Medicine in that year, sharing the prize with infectious-disease specialist D. Carleton Gadjusek.

In Blumberg's case, the Nobel marked not the culmination of a life's work, but in some respects just a beginning. He continued to track and contribute to new hepatitis research, noting that by 2003, 79 percent of the members of the World Health Organization had hepatitis B vaccine programs in place, resulting in a drop in the prevalence of virus carriers in China from 16.3 to 1.4 percent, and a two-thirds reduction in the rate of liver cancer in Taiwan after a decade of vaccination. But he also sought new challenges, taking on teaching posts at several institutions. He returned to Oxford in 1989, not as a student this time but as Master (chief administrator) of the university's Balliol College. Blumberg was the first American and the first scientist (with the possible exception of an alchemist in the fourteenth century) to hold the post, and he introduced innovations such as an American-style development office aimed at stimulating private support in an era of declining government subsidies.

In 1999, after attending several workshops at the National Aeronautics and Space Administration, Blumberg was named founding director of the new NASA Astrobiology Institute, taking up residence near the institute's headquarters in California's Santa Cruz Mountains. Among his contributions to the organization was a suggestion that it focus research efforts on terrestrial organisms that can

survive in extreme environments. He remained with NASA until 2004, leaving the following year to take a post as president of the American Philosophical Society, an organization of learned individuals dating back to the days of Benjamin Franklin. In the midst of these tasks, Blumberg found time to write *Hepatitis B: The Hunt for a Killer Virus,* published by Princeton University Press in 2002. Peppered with nonscientific references, the book was aimed at general readers. The book's epigraph quoted the poem "The Quest," by W.H. Auden: "Suppose he'd listened to the erudite committee / He only would have found where not to look." Blumberg was also the author of more than 500 scientific papers.

Blumberg enjoyed outdoor sports, and he could frequently be seen running middle distances on Philadelphia streets. He was also part owner of a Maryland cattle farm and liked to unwind from scientific work by doing farm tasks, including shoveling manure. He remained active until the very end of his life, climbing Maine's sizable Bald Mountain in his last year. After delivering a lecture at NASA's Ames Research Center, he was felled by a heart attack and died at Moffett Field, California, on April 5, 2011, at the age of 85.

Books

Blumberg, Baruch, *Hepatitis B: The Hunt for a Killer Virus,* Princeton, 2002.

Periodicals

Daily Telegraph (London, England), April 7, 2011.
Independent (London, England), April 11, 2011.
New York Times, April 7, 2011.
Philadelphia Inquirer, April 6, 2011.
Times (London, England), April 8, 2011.

Online

"The Nobel Prize in Physiology or Medicine 1976," *Nobel Prize,* http:// www.nobelprize.org/nobel_prizes/medicine/ laureates/1976/blumberg-autobio.html (October 5, 2011).□

Max Ernst Bodenstein

German physical chemist Max Ernst Bodenstein (1871-1942) was a pioneer in chemical kinetics. His research on chain reactions and explosions would later be applied to the creation of the atom bomb.

M ax Ernst Bodenstein became well known for his pioneering research. Indeed, several firsts are attached to his work. He was noted for studying the decomposition of hydrohalic acids and their formation, but he was also the first to postulate a chain reaction mechanism and that explosions are branched chain reactions. His research would later be applied to the development of the atomic bomb.

die Zersetzung des Jodwasserstoffgases in der Hitze (which translated into English is *Degradation of hydrogen iodide in hot temperature.*)

The doctorate degree, and the thesis (as its title indicates), involved his research related to the thermal decomposition of hydrogen iodide. In gaining the degree, Bodenstein was mentored by Viktor Meyer (1848-1897), a renowned chemist (organic and inorganic) who was noted for advancing the field of stereochemistry. Also, Bodenstein impressed the scientific research community with the exactness that he demonstrated in conducting his experiments. Through the years, his thesis conclusions underwent revision by later researchers; however, his paper is regarded as a major milestone in the area of reaction kinetics.

Entered Academia

Bodenstein continued to research gas phase reactions after he earned his degree. He even funded some projects with his own money. Eventually, he accepted a position as the director of the Institute for Physical Chemistry, located in Berlin, Germany. He was a strict taskmaster, as he required all students to build their own laboratory equipment—as he had done when he conducted his boyhood experiments.

During this period of his life, Bodenstein began studying kinetics, and his efforts were bolstered by the improved approaches and methodology in this area. His work was substantially influenced by the writings on chemical kinetics that were produced by Jacobus Henricus van't Hoff (1852-1911) in the 1880s. (Hoff was awarded the Nobel Prize in Chemistry in 1901 for his work related to the laws of chemical dynamics and osmotic pressure in solutions.) Hoff clarified that reaction rates were a function of temperature. Bodenstein felt compelled to study reactions in the gas phase, as molecules are not as densely packed as in solutions—meaning that the fewer interactions (aside from the target reaction) needed to be explained.

In his own research of gas phase reactions, Bodenstein discovered that chemical reactions might create radicals (molecules with an odd number of electrons). The radicals, virtually unhindered, quickly react with other molecules. Further, radical-based creations create even more radicals. Again, these radicals quickly and easily react with other molecules, thus creating even more radicals. Chain reactions present with radicals, as Bodenstein observed, have an increased speed rate.

As a result of his research, Bodenstein pushed forward the study of polymolecular reactions in kinetic field; still, his work did not offer better understanding of unimolecular reactions, which proved a puzzle for his contemporary colleagues. However, the fellow researchers who would help solve the riddle based their own work on Bodenstein's efforts. In particular, William C. M. Lewis, the first researcher to meld quantum methodology to the study of reaction rate studies, helped confirm Bodenstein's discoveries.

An Educator and Experimenter

During the most productive and active phase of his career, Bodenstein would be both a researcher and educator. In 1896, after a year of military service, he went back to

Bodenstein was also the first to explain kinetics and mechanisms of heterogeneous reactions. In addition, he also studied catalysis in flowing systems, and he discovered diffusion controlled catalytic reactions. Further, he demonstrated the importance of termolecular collisions—a reaction which involves three molecular entities—in kinetics, and he studied photochemical reactions.

An Unlikely Chemist

Bodenstein was born on July 15, 1871 in Magdeburg, Germany, into a well-to-do family that gained its wealth in the brewery business. Interestingly, as a young boy, Bodenstein initially found chemistry to be boring. But he eventually comprehended the value of gas phase studies, and he later gained fame for his research involving kinetic reactions in the gas phase (he came to be recognized as the top researcher in this area).

Once he got over his initial negative feelings about chemistry, Bodenstein started his own chemical research as a boy, working in a makeshift laboratory in the basement of his father's shop. Bodenstein liked to tinker; he would build his own research equipment. When he was not toiling with his own self-developed tools and designed experiments, he enjoyed mountain climbing. The regional landscape in which he was raised offered him the kind of terrain that allowed him to indulge in this activity.

A Precocious Student

Bodenstein entered Heidelberg University, in Germany when he was only seventeen years old, with chemistry as his educational focus. Following graduation, which occurred after only six semesters, Bodenstein entered graduate school, eventually earning a PhD in chemistry. On October 25, 1893, he garnered the degree with a thesis entitled *Über*

Heidelberg University to teach. In that year, he married Marie Nebel (1862-1944). In 1899, he published a paper on reaction kinetics that solidified his stature as a scientific researcher.

His studies on the equilibria of gaseous reactions, particularly those of hydrogen and iodine, came to be considered classic research. He developed a technique that mixed hydrogen and iodine in a sealed tube. He placed the tube in a thermostat and held it at a constant high temperature. The reaction eventually reached equilibrium: the rate of formation of hydrogen iodide proved equal to the rate of decomposition to the original reactants ($H_2 + I_2 \equiv 2HI$). Bodenstein ''froze'' the equilibrium mixture of H_2, I_2, and HI with rapid cooling. This enabled the amount of hydrogen iodide to be effectively analyzed. In this way, and using different amounts of initial reactants, Bodenstein could vary the amounts present at equilibrium. Thus, he was able to verify the law of chemical equilibrium that was advanced in 1863 by Norwegian chemists Cato Maximillian Guldberg (1836-1902) and Peter Waage (1833-1900).

From 1900 to 1906, Bodenstein worked in Leipzig, where he studied the kinetics of catalytic processes. In 1904, he became honorary professor at the physicochemical institute at the University of Leipzig. Wilhelm Ostward, a Nobel Prize recipient (chemistry, 1909) was instrumental in securing the appointment. Bodenstein would then collaborate in research with Ostwald.

In 1906, Bodenstein became an extraordinary professor and department head at the University of Berlin. Two years later, he accepted a position as professor at the Technische Hochschule in Hannover. Eventually, he went back to the University of Berlin, an academic institution that, at the time, boasted a faculty that included Albert Einstein and Max Karl Ernst Ludwig Planck.

As he advanced in academia, he continued his research. In 1916, Bodenstein explained the speed of certain chemical reactions by demonstrating that they were chain reactions. He studied the photochemical chlorine hydrogen reaction. His experiments revealed the cause of a chain reaction and why photochemical reactions run counter to Einstein's law of equivalents. His revelations of chain reaction proved fundamental to the creation of the atomic bomb during World War II.

In 1923, Bodenstein was appointed director of the Institute of Physical Chemistry at the University of Berlin, a position he held until 1936. One of his students was Gertrud Kornfeld (1891-1955), who became the first female scientist to receive an academic appointment in chemistry at the University of Berlin. She obtained the ''venia legendi'' to lecture in physical chemistry at the university. Also, she was the first woman to lecture on chemistry at any German university. When Bodenstein became a professor at the University of Berlin in 1923, Kornfeld worked with him as an assistant at the university's Institute for Physical Chemistry. In 1928, she became a lecturer in physical chemistry at the University of Berlin. Under Bodenstein's direction, she became an advisor to several doctoral candidates.

Bodenstein also worked in the field of photochemistry. He died on September 3, 1942 in Berlin. Part of his outstanding legacy is being the first researcher to demonstrate how the large yield per quantum for the reaction of hydrogen and chlorine could be explained by a chain reaction. In 1925, he was made a fellow in the Berlin Academy of Sciences. In 1942, he was named a fellow in the Bavarian Academy of Sciences. He was seventy-one years old when he passed away.

Books

''Ernst Bodenstein,'' *World of Chemistry*. Thomson Gale, 2006.

Online

scs.illinois.edu,.http://www.scs.illinois.edu/~mainzv/Web_Genealogy/Info/bodensteinmea.pdf (December 5, 2011).

''Ernst Bodenstein Biography,'' *Bookrags.com,* http://www.bookrags.com/biography/ernst-bodenstein-woc/ (December 5, 2011).

''Max Bodenstein,'' *How Stuff Works,* http://science.howstuffworks.com/dictionary/famous-scientists/chemists/max-bodenstein-info.htm (December 5, 2011).

''Max Bodenstein,'' *Nernst.de,* http://www.nernst.de/bodenstein/bodenstein.htm (December 5, 2011).□

Poggio Bracciolini

Italian classicist Poggius Bracciolini (1380–1459) was a prolific author and pivotal figure in the Italian Renaissance. A respected private secretary to several popes, Bracciolini was also a renowned book collector who hunted down long-lost copies of ancient Greek and Roman manuscripts. His rediscovery of a lengthy prose poem from first-century BCE Roman writer Lucretius, *On the Nature of Things,* has been cited by historians as a watershed moment in European history.

In his day, Bracciolini was known as Poggio Florentinus (Poggio of Florence). He was born Gian Francesco Poggio Bracciolini on February 11, 1380, in a town called Terranuova located in the Val d'Arno region. Tax rolls list his father, Guccio Bracciolini, as a pharmacist and show the family moved from Terranuova to the larger town of Arezzo around 1388, when Bracciolini would have been eight years old. Bracciolini's mother, Iacoba Frutti, was the daughter of a notary, a respectable profession in late medieval Europe. In a society where literacy rates were quite low and many ordinary folk knew only how to sign their own names, notaries provided a trusted means of certifying the validity of property transfers, last wills and testaments, and other vital documents.

Worked as Copyist

Bracciolini received a solid education in Arezzo and in 1400, the year he turned 20, he moved to Florence to train as a notary. A signature of his notary grandfather survives, and Bracciolini apparently inherited a fantastic talent for penmanship from his Frutti forebears that helped him land

a job as a scribe in Florence. Scribes made copies of official documents, correspondence, and books by hand in the era before Johannes Gutenberg invented the printing press.

In Florence, Bracciolini was drawn into a prominent intellectual circle of Humanist scholars, among them Leonardo Bruni, a protégé of Florence's powerful chancellor. Through that connection Bracciolini was recommended for a job in Rome in 1403 in the office of the Bishop of Bari, Cardinal Landolfo Maramaldo. After a short time Bracciolini moved on to a much more prized post, as one of about a hundred men who served as official scriptors, or scribes, inside the Papal Curia, the actual administrative offices of the Christian Church in the West.

Sent to Lake Constance

Bracciolini entered these ranks in the final months of the stewardship of Pope Boniface IX, who died in 1404. At the time, however, the Church was in turmoil over what was known as the Western Schism, with a rival pope in Avignon, France, claiming to be the legitimate heir to the throne of St. Peter. In 1408 several cardinals removed themselves from Rome and set up a third papal court, this one in Pisa. Bracciolini went with them and became secretary to the latest papal claimant, Alexander V. After Alexander's death in 1410, the Pisan cardinals elected Baldassare Cossa as Pope John XXIII. Cossa promoted Bracciolini as his Apostolic Secretary, a position of enormous privilege. Bracciolini essentially served as the pope's secretary of record and personal correspondent.

The papal muddle was resolved at the 1414–18 Council of Constance, which met in the southern German city of the same name. Bracciolini was sent as John XXIII's emissary, but in between formal sessions of the Council, Bracciolini went in search of rare manuscripts in monasteries in the region.

Bracciolini and other Florentine Humanists had a keen interest in ancient texts from Greek and Roman antiquity. They were following the dictates of Petrarch, an Italian scholar who died in 1374 and is considered one of the founding figures of the Italian Renaissance. It was Petrarch who coined the term "Dark Ages" to describe Europe after the fall of Rome in 410 CE, when literacy rates declined sharply and the Christian Church emerged as the dominant power. Petrarch wrote that the philosophers, poets, and scholars of ancient Greece and Rome had helped those civilizations to build advanced, powerful empires, but those gains had been reversed and in some cases eradicated entirely as Europe descended into a feudal, agrarian society controlled by the Church. Scholarship was dictated and defined by religious authorities, who looked with suspicion on any historical remnants of the pagan past and thwarted scientific curiosity as a pursuit at odds with the laws of God.

Unearthed Gems of Classical Scholarship

En route to the city of Constance lay the monastery of St. Gallen. Founded around 720 CE, the Abbey was home to Benedictine monks who had, with the support of French kings like Charlemagne, created one of the best libraries in Europe. Its scriptors copied priceless church documents for posterity and also preserved texts from antiquity. Bracciolini stopped at St. Gallen with two Florentine Humanist scholars, Cencio de' Rustici and Bartolomeo da Montepulciano, to search for manuscripts from the classical era. It was Bracciolini who found at St. Gallen an important work of a Roman scholar named Marcus Fabius Quintilianus, dead some 13 centuries by then. This was the *Institutio Oratoria,* and Bracciolini's "salvaging of the complete text of the rhetorician Quintilian changed the curriculum of law schools and universities throughout Europe," wrote Stephen Greenblatt in the *New Yorker.*

Bracciolini also unearthed at St. Gallen a copy of *De architectura* (On Architecture), a multivolume work written during the reign of Caesar Augustus by a civil engineer named Marcus Vitruvius Pollio, better known as Vitruvius. The massive text laid out basic principles of urban planning in the world's first great city, including details about the proper construction and maintenance of the aqueducts, which carried fresh drinking water to Rome and were also deployed in the countryside to irrigate crops. The publication of *On Architecture* in Florence ignited tremendous interest in the building arts, and later in the century a printed edition of Vitruvius's opus was translated into several languages and influenced some of Europe's greatest architects.

De Rerum Natura Prompted "Swerve"

Greenblatt and other scholars are uncertain where Bracciolini actually discovered the copy of the famous poem by Lucretius; it may have been at St. Gallen or at another Benedictine monastery in Fulda, Germany, or a third site in Murbach, in the Franco-German Alsace region. In any case, the poem was a rich artifact of a radical movement known as Epicureanism. Named for the Greek philosopher Epicurus, who died in 270 BCE, the ideology asserted that the gods play no role in human life, and because there is no afterlife, humans should cherish their time on earth and avoid conflict. Epicurus also theorized that all living beings in the universe—from the snail to man to the trees and even beyond to the planets that moved in the night sky—were composed of the same infinitesimal "seeds" of matter. Two centuries after his death, Epicurus and his teachings were revived by a group of Roman philosophers, among them a poet named Titus Lucretius Carus.

Very little is known about Lucretius. St. Jerome, one of the Fathers of the Christian Church, wrote derisively about the poet, noting that he was born in 94 BCE, was driven mad by some type of aphrodisiac substance, and committed suicide at age 44. Jerome, however, and other early-Christian scholars looked askance at Epicureanism, viewing its adherents as indolent hedonists who were highly unlikely to take up arms for any cause.

Lucretius' *De Rerum Natura* (On the Nature of Things) expounds on the Epicureans' philosophy. Its 7,400 lines of hexameter were probably written around 50 BCE, and copies of it survived the fall of Rome and turned up in Carolingian monasteries in the early Middle Ages. It was last copied in the ninth century, and forgotten until Bracciolini read it in 1417, had a copy made, and took it back to Florence, where his wealthy friend Niccolò Niccoli underwrote the costs of making several more copies.

On the Nature of Things caused a minor sensation in Florence and beyond. It awakened Renaissance minds to the possibilities of atomism, first espoused by the ancient Greeks. "Every page reflected a core scientific vision—a vision of atoms randomly moving in an infinite universe—imbued with a poet's sense of wonder," wrote Greenblatt in the *New Yorker* article, which appeared in advance of his 2011 book. "Wonder did not depend on the dream of an afterlife; in Lucretius it welled up out of a recognition that we are made of the same matter as the stars and the oceans and all things else. And this recognition was the basis for the way he thought we should live—not in fear of the gods but in pursuit of pleasure, in avoidance of pain." In 2011 Greenblatt, a Harvard University professor and Renaissance specialist, devoted an entire book to Bracciolini's discovery and diffusion of the Lucretius work, titling it *The Swerve: How the World Became Modern.* "To people haunted by images of the bleeding Christ, gripped by a terror of Hell, and obsessed with escaping the purgatorial fires of the afterlife, Lucretius offered a vision of divine indifference," Greenblatt declared. "There was no afterlife, no system of rewards and punishments meted out from on high." These ideas, Greenblatt asserted, were not so much part of a distinct shift in thought but rather a swerve that had far-ranging repercussions in the sciences and humanities.

Employed by Bishop of Winchester

The Council of Constance had also resulted in a demotion back to scriptor for Bracciolini after the delegates agreed to remove all three popes and elected Oddo Colonna as Pope Martin V. An English cardinal whom Bracciolini met at Constance, Henry Beaufort, invited Bracciolini to come to England and work in his scriptorium in Winchester, the famous cathedral city. He stayed there nearly four years,

before finally securing the slot as Martin's Apostolic Secretary. He retained the title when the pope was succeeded by Eugenius IV in 1431, and when Nicholas V was consecrated Bishop of Rome in 1447.

Bracciolini continued to travel on official business during these years, and conducted a prolific correspondence. He also began writing his own essays and dialogues on various subjects in the late 1420s, beginning with *De avaritia* (On Greed). In 1436, at the age of 55, he penned *An seni sit uxor ducenda* (Should an Old Man Marry?), weighing the reasons for his decision to marry an 18-year-old named Vaggia de' Buondelmonti. The opinion of his longtime mistress Lucia Panelli, with whom he already had 14 children, on this matter is not known, but he had six more children by Buondelmonti.

Pope Nicholas sent Bracciolini to the 1439 Council of Florence, a trip that inspired his 1448 essay *De varietate fortunae* (On the Vicissitudes of Fortune). It recounts tales from some delegates he met in Florence, "including a Venetian merchant home from India, a northern Indian (understood through an Armenian interpreter), and some Ethiopians, who reported the existence of peoples beyond the limits of the world recognized by Ptolemy," wrote Alison Brown in *The Return of Lucretius to Renaissance Florence.*

Collected Jokes

Bracciolini's final, lasting contribution to the Renaissance sits at the intersection of scholarship and popular culture. The *Liber Facetiarum,* or "Book of Trifling Jests," was published in 1451 when Bracciolini was 70 years old. It is thought to be the first collection of humor published in at least a thousand years, following after a work from fourth-century BCE Greece, the *Philolegos* (Laughter-Lover). Bracciolini drew his material from informal gatherings of Curia copyists in a break room they called the *Bugiale,* or "Lie Factory." To relieve the stress and tedium of their jobs, they regaled one another with bawdy stories; priests and monks were often the targets of their jibes, even the pope himself.

Bracciolini spent his final years writing a history of Florence from a home he had bought in Terranuova, his birthplace. He died there on October 30, 1459, and was given one of the great resting places of honor in Florence, the Church of Santa Croce. No less an artist than Donatello was commissioned to create his marble tomb and a separate funerary statue.

Books

Brown, Alison, *The Return of Lucretius to Renaissance Florence,* Harvard University Press, 2010.

Greenblatt, Stephen, *The Swerve: How the World Became Modern,* W.W. Norton, 2011.

Schuchman, Anne M., "Bracciolini, Gian Francesco Poggio (1380–1459)," in *The Late Medieval Age of Crisis and Renewal, 1300–1500: A Biographical Dictionary,* edited by Clayton J. Drees, Greenwood Press, 2001.

Periodicals

New Yorker, April 19, 2004; August 8, 2011. □

Donna Brazile

American political strategist Donna Brazile (born 1959) became the first African American woman to manage a presidential campaign for a major party candidate when she headed the Al Gore campaign in 2000.

American political strategist Donna Brazile became the first African American woman to manage a major presidential candidate's campaign when Democratic candidate Al Gore named her to that post in 1999. This appointment culminated a nearly twenty-year career in Democratic politics that had seen Brazile help organize grassroots efforts to have the birthday of civil rights leader Dr. Martin Luther King, Jr. named a national holiday and taken her into every Democratic presidential campaign between 1976 and 2000. Known for her forthright personality and strong organizing instincts, Brazile acted as a superdelegate in the hotly contested 2008 Democratic presidential primary and, three years later, briefly served as interim director of the party's national committee.

The third of nine children, Brazile was born on December 15, 1959, at a charity hospital in New Orleans, Louisiana. Her father, Lionel Brazile, was a Korean War veteran who worked as a janitor after a job site accident injured his back and kept him from working again in construction. Her mother, Jean, was a domestic servant in a white household despite her middle-class background and the fact that she had attended college. Brazile grew up in the New Orleans suburb of Kenner, so poor that "my family didn't just live on the proverbial 'other side of the tracks,'" Brazile commented wryly in her autobiography, *Cooking with Grease.* "No, we lived behind *two* sets of tracks." The household included Brazile's paternal grandmother, who helped the family make do despite their financial difficulties. Throughout her later political career, Brazile often referred to her childhood poverty as an incentive for her to support Democratic politics, which typically favors social programs.

Hardship did not prevent Brazile from showing her mettle, however, and she got her first taste of political action when she was in the third grade. Shaken by the assassination of Dr. Martin Luther King, Jr., the young girl became increasingly aware of the changes that were building to reshape race relations in the United States. Hoping to support the cause of civil rights—and get a local candidate elected who promised to build a new playground in Kenner—Brazile organized her friends to go door-to-door speaking to African American adults about voter registration efforts. "I felt that this was the most fun, the most exciting thing anybody could do," she said in her autobiography. To make matters better, the candidate won.

By the time she finished high school, Brazile had again become active in political action, this time through a friend whose mother was working on statewide campaigns. In 1976, she volunteered locally with Democratic candidate Jimmy Carter's successful president campaign. She decided to attend Louisiana State University (LSU) in the state capital

of Baton Rouge, believing this location would enable her to gain valuable political experience. While at LSU, Brazile worked to increase minority representation on student governance committees and was active with the U.S. Student Association. After graduating in 1981, she joined the National Student Education Fund as a lobbyist. Soon, she was hired by Coretta Scott King—widow of Dr. Martin Luther King, Jr.—to work on efforts to commemorate the slain civil rights leader. In 1984, she worked on the presidential campaigns of both the Reverend Jesse Jackson and eventual Democratic nominee Walter Mondale.

In 1987, Brazile signed on as National Field Director with the presidential campaign of U.S. Senator Dick Gephardt. She was widely praised for her work helping the senator win an important victory at the Iowa caucuses, but the nomination ultimately went to Massachusetts Governor Michael Dukakis. His campaign hired Brazile to oversee operations taking place at the local level throughout the country, but Brazile remained unenthusiastic about Dukakis's candidacy. Dukakis seemed reluctant to speak about civil rights, and the press began questioning his dedication to the African American community. The opposing campaign of then-Vice President George H.W. Bush also pushed racial issues in its attacks on Dukakis, bringing up the story of Willie Horton, an African American convict in Massachusetts who had committed rape and murder while on a furlough approved by Dukakis. Frustrated and angry by what she felt were ceaseless racial attacks on Dukakis's campaign, Brazile snapped at a group of reporters that they should be asking about Bush's personal life, suggesting that he had a mistress. Knowing immediately that she had crossed a line, Brazile decided to simply speak her mind about what she believed were unfair racial overtones in the campaign and politics in general. But it was the accusation that Bush was unfaithful to his wife that made headlines.

The media firestorm that following her comments cost Brazile her job with the Dukakis campaign and branded her as a political loose cannon. Her difficulties were not yet over, however. Her mother, who had no health insurance, died several weeks later, and Brazile used her last check from the Dukakis campaign to pay for her funeral. The disgraced political staffer took a job with a homeless advocate, living for several months in a homeless shelter in 1989. The following year, she took a job as chief of staff for Eleanor Holmes Norton, who had recently been elected as the non-voting delegate to the U.S. House of Representatives from Washington, D.C. Brazile remained with Norton through much of the 1990s, occasionally taking time off to work on Democratic political campaigns, including the Clinton re-election effort of 1996 and as the head of a Democratic get-out-the-vote effort during the 1998 Congressional elections.

Despite her difficulties with the Dukasis campaign some years earlier, Brazile was named to the Democratic National Committee as an at-large member representing the District of Columbia in 1998. She had reservations about joining the party's leadership, but felt that it was her duty to take on the additional responsibilities that came with the job. Then-Vice President Al Gore soon reached out to Brazile to act in his interests with the committee, and she agreed after assuring that he supported her own goals of helping further women and minority involvement in politics. In the spring of 1999, Brazile signed on with Gore's presidential campaign as national political director and deputy campaign manager under overall campaign head Craig Smith. The campaign encountered stumbling blocks as it entered fall, however, and Gore decided to make sweeping changes. Among those changes were the elevation of Brazile to campaign manager and moving of the campaign's headquarters from Washington to Nashville. Writing in the *New York Times*, Melinda Henneberger noted that "if it's a shake-up Mr. Gore wants, then Ms. Brazile seems well suited," referencing her history of overcoming adversity in both life and politics. Her appointment was not without controversy, however, as the press revived discussion of her time with Dukakis and criticized some of her off-the-cuff comments as racially insensitive.

Quickly, Brazile set about restoring the campaign's fiscal discipline, cutting campaign staff and rooting out wasteful spending. She helped Gore triumph over his closest competition, former U.S. Senator Bill Bradley, in early primary states, and the vice-president eventually became the first candidate to carry every major caucus and primary in a contested election. After Gore formally took the nomination at the Democratic convention, Brazile focused on funneling resources in close-fought battleground states and on appealing to the liberal voters who might choose to vote for perennial presidential candidate Ralph Nader. Nader, running on the Green Party ticket, was campaigning to receive five percent of the overall vote and thus win federal funding for the third party in 2004. By the time Election Day rolled around, Brazile knew that the race would be a close one. She grew concerned by reports of voters being turned away at the polls and of other voting irregularities. Nevertheless, early in the evening she believed that her candidate had won. When reports came in that Florida was too close to call and a recount would ensue, an emotional roller coaster began that ended in a Supreme Court decision to end the Florida recount. Gore had lost.

Bush's defeat of Gore ushered in a long era of Republican dominance of the White House and the U.S. political conversation. Brazile remained active in Democratic politics, however, becoming the director of the party's Voting Rights Institute and working on the successful 2002 re-election campaign of Democratic U.S. Senator Mary Landrieu of Louisiana. Although not directly involved with the campaign of presidential candidate John Kerry in 2004, Brazile appeared around the country speaking on behalf of the Democratic Party and was sorely disappointed when he ultimately lost the election. This defeat encouraged her to renew her efforts to work for election reform and to reach out to potential Democratic voters. She founded her own consulting firm, Brazile and Associates, to help set up grassroots efforts and encourage citizen participation in the political process.

The following year, Brazile was named to the board of directors of the Louisiana Recovery Authority. In this role, she worked to rebuild the state following the devastation of Hurricane Katrina, and, three years later, Hurricane Ike. In 2008, Brazile served as one of the Democratic Party's unelected superdelegates during the party's presidential nomination process. Unlike regular delegates, superdelegates have the option to vote for any candidate they wish for the nomination; during the hard-fought primary campaign between Barack Obama and Hillary Rodham Clinton, speculation on the potentially decisive role of those superdelegates emerged. Brazile, however, focused more on her duties as a party ambassador than a decision maker. Speaking to S. Tia Brown of *Black Enterprise*, she explained, "as party activists, we network and spread the word about what's going on. We…are here to encourage voter participation, registration, and inform citizens about the candidates." She did, however, strongly support the party's decision to refuse to seat elected delegates from Michigan and Florida because of those states' decision to move up the dates of their primaries. The ultimate election of Obama to the presidency delighted Brazile, who attributed his success in part to the support of the young voters who turned out in unusually high numbers.

In 2009, Brazile was named the Democratic National Committee's vice chair of voter registration and participation. Two years later, she served briefly as the head of the party during the period between the resignation of former Virginia governor Tim Kaine and the assumption of office by his successor, Florida Representative Debbie Wasserman Schultz. The strategist Brazile was also a regular political commentator for CNN and ABC, in addition to contributing to print and online publications such as *O* and *Roll Call*. Widely acknowledged as one of the most powerful women working behind the scenes in Washington, Brazile argued strongly that the solution to many of the nation's political problems was the increased inclusion of women as leaders. "If we had more women in politics, this country would be farther ahead," she was quoted as stating by Carla Marinucci of the *San Francisco Chronicle*, "because women are not afraid to ask for directions when they're lost."

Books

Brazile, Donna, *Cooking with Grease: Stirring the Pots in America,* Simon and Schuster, 2005.

Oblender, David G., ed., *Contemporary Black Biography,* Gale, 2000.

Periodicals

Black Enterprise, September 2008.
New York Times, October 11, 1999.
San Francisco Chronicle, August 4, 2011.

Online

''About,'' Brazile & Associates LLC, http://www.brazileassociates. com/page.cfm?id=2 (September 15, 2011).

''Donna Brazile,'' Democratic National Committee, http://www. democrats.org/about/bio/donna_brazile (November 20, 2011). □

Pierre Paul Broca

Pierre Paul Broca (1824-1880) was a French surgeon and anthropologist. Broca is best remembered for his contributions to localizing the speech center of the brain, an area now referred to as Broca's area. In addition, Broca was the founder of the Société d'Anthropologie, the Anthropological Soceity of Paris and did extensive work on rehabilitating those with brain injuries that impaired their speech.

P ierre Paul Broca was born on June 29, 1824 at Sainte-Foy-la-Grande, near Bordeaux, France. He was born to protestant parents, and his father was a doctor. Broca was educated in Bordeaux and Paris, and he achieved his medical degree in 1848 in Paris. His early research was on cancer cells and how they can be spread by blood. He would later go on to study muscular dystrophy and rickets. As his research progressed, Broca found that he wanted to combine clinical findings with the information that he found in the lab.

Broca became a professor of surgery, as well as surgeon, at the Bicêntre in Paris. In 1859 Broca founded the Société d'Anthropologie, the Anthropological Society of Paris, and served as its secretary. Among other topics, the group discussed human groupings, intelligence, and the brain. Broca himself enjoyed studying Cro-Magnon man and Neolithic trephination, the burrowing of a hole in the skull to relieve head injuries. Eventually Broca would found his own institute of anthropology.

Localization of Speech

In the early 19th century, the location of speech centers in the brain was a hotly debated topic. Franz Joseph Gall placed the memory of words in the frontal lobes, based upon skull shape in the early 19th century. Another scientist, Jean Baptiste Bouillaud also placed it in the frontal

region of the brain. In 1836, Marc Dax proposed that speech problems were due to lesions on the left hemisphere. He wrote a memoir purporting this theory, but he died a year later. This information was not made public until his son, Gustave Dax, presented his father's findings in 1863 and published them in 1865. This would cause a small scandal later in Broca's career when he came to a similar conclusion years after Marc Dax but only slightly before Gustave Dax would present his father's findings.

Broca's investigation of the localization of speech began with a patient named Monsieur Leborgne. Leborgne was a 51-year old man who had lost the power of speech at the age of 31 and had developed epilepsy. He later became paralyzed on his right side, with accompanyng loss of sensitivity. Leborgne could only make indeterminate noises and utter one word: 'tan.' This earned him the nickname ''Tan,'' and he is often referred to by this nickname even in contemporary literature.

In April of 1861, Leborgne was admitted to Broca for surgery related to cellulitis and gangrene on his right leg. Broca also invited Ernest Auburtin, Bouillaud's son-in-law, to examine him, as he was also studying cerebral localization.

Only days later, Leborgne died. The day after Leborgne's death, Broca presented his autopsy findings before the Anthropological Society of Paris. During his autopsy, Broca found a softening of Tan's brain in the third left frontal convolution and chronic softening near the rolandic fissue of the left hemisphere. Broca assumed that because this was the most damaged portion of Tan's brain, that this was the problematic section. He used this inference to argue for localization of speech within the frontal cortical area of the brain. This region became known as Broca's area. Broca would come to be posthumously chided for his examination technique and inferences. Broca did not section Leborgne's brain; instead he kept it intact and presented his findings that August to the Anatomical Society of Paris. After this fascinating case, Broca became dedicated to cortical location and became the movement's champion.

In November of 1861, Broca presented a second case with similar symptoms and a lesion in the left third frontal convolution. Monsieur Lelong was admitted to the Bicêntre eight years previously when he was 76 years old for senile debility. In April 1860, he had lost consciousness and while he had partially recovered, he remained aphasic, unable to communicate. In October of 1861, Lelong fell and fractured his femur. He was brought to Broca for surgery. He died 12 days later. Broca found a lesion in Lelong's second and third frontal convolution during his autopsy, which reinforced Broca's idea about cerebral localization. Broca named Lelong's speech impairment "aphemia," which would be renamed by Armand Trousseau as "aphasia." Broca was against the renaming of this impairment as aphasia. He saw four separate types of language impairments: alogia, verbal amnesia, aphemia, and mechanical alalia. Alogia is the loss of speech because of the loss of intelligence. Verbal amnesia is the inability to remember words, later renamed as Wernicke's aphasia. Aphemia is the loss of speech because of a change in one's ability to articulate language. Finally, mechanical alalia is a loss of speech because of the loss of the physical ability to speak.

In 1863, Broca described several patients with aphasia who has lesions on their left hemisphere and a pathologic involvement of the third left frontal convolution. In spite of having presented as many as eight cases, he still felt the need to find and diagnose more cases in order to argue for the localization of speech in the left hemisphere. In 1865 Broca published his definitive position on left hemispheric dominance for language in an article in the *Bulletin of the Anthropological Society*. He also went on to expand upon his theories. He described a 47-year-old woman who had been epileptic since her childhood, who likely had a congenital atrophy of her left inferior frontal gyrus and adjacent cortex. In spite of these lesions, which would normally result in Broca's aphasia, she could communicate clearly. This led Broca to consider whether or not a child would suffer the same language deficits that an adult would with the same injuries; he thought perhaps not. Broca believed that her healthy right hemisphere was compensating for her unhealthy left hemisphere. These findings led him to believe that adults with speech problems could, perhaps, learn to speak again; maybe they would not be able to compensate as well as a child, but they could still regain some kind of speech. Other patients, though, might not have the intellectual capacity to regain their speech. He put forth the steps for re-learning, much like those of how a child learns: first sounds, then words, then phrases, and eventually sentences. In Broca's tests, his patients did well up to syllables, but they had a hard time constructing words.

Broca also believed that there might be an innate predisposition to handedness. Broca argued that while training might be important in some activities like writing or playing a musical instrument, some activities had an innate handedness preference, like throwing a ball. He believed that even if you tried to train that preferenece out of them, people would persist in attempting to use their dominant hand. This made it possible for Broca to argue for functional asymmetry as applied to language; if some people are left handed, perhaps some people are right hemisphere dominant for language as well, though whether or not a person was right or left handed had no bearing on where their language dominance resided.

Broca also found that while those who had left hemisphere lesions could not talk, they could understand speech. This showed Broca that it is not possible that all functions of speech could be localized to this area. Comprehension, he believed, might exist in both hemispheres.

Surgical Implications

In 1864, Broca began discussing the surgical implications for clinical-anatomical correlations relating to traumatic types of aphasia. In 1865, Broca was elected president of the Paris Surgical Society. In 1867, Broca was given an Incan skull with crosshatching cuts across it. He realized that the cuts had been performed on a living person who had survived the operation. This realization led him to become interested in trepanation, when a hole is drilled into the skull to treat intracranial diseases. He was able to find Neolithic skulls with the same markings. Broca theorized that this procedure was used to treat internal maladies, perhaps illnesses such as childhood epilepsy.

In 1868, Broca began to work on a technique for cerebral topography, mapping the areas of the brain to the skull using different landmarks. Broca had been measuring the hemispheres of a variety of patients for comparative data for many years at this point, so he had quite a bit of data to determine localization of different areas of the brain based upon the skull.

In 1871, Broca treated a man who was kicked in the head by a horse and who had suffered only a scalp wound. Eventually the patient had developed a nonfluent aphasia about a month after the injury. Based upon his symptoms, Broca believed that the patient had developed an abscess in the posterior aspect of the third left frontal gyrus. Broca performed a craniotomy based only upon cerebral localization and he was able to successfully drain an abscess. This is the first incidence of anyone using the clinical-anatomical correlation that Broca had described in 1864. It was only because of his understanding of the relationship between the articulate language and the brain and between the brain and the skull that he was able to diagnose and drain the abscess. In spite of his ability to find and drain the abscess, the patient died a few days later. During his autopsy it was found that the patient had a left-sided predominantly frontal purulent meningoencephalitis, a particularly dangerous infection.

In 1877, Broca gave his last talks about speech and the brain. Throughout his life he had performed other tasks and had other interests. He published what is considered a classic text on aneurysms. He also published a comparative study of the mammalian brain. He did significant work on the limbic system and had had his name attached to the diagonal band of Broca. In 1880, Broca died at the age of 56; he had been elected to the French Senate only a month before as a representative of science and medicine.

Many years later Broca's work would be challenged because of how limited his examination of Lebourgne's brain was, but his contribution to medicine, regardless of the flaws in his research methods, was considerable and lasting.

Books

Nadel, Lynn, ed., *Encyclopedia of Cognitive Science,* Wiley, 2005

Schiller, Francis, *Broca: Founder of French Anthropology, Explorere of the Brain,* University of California Press, 1979

Periodicals

Archives of Neurology, June, 1986

Archives of Pathology & Laboratory Medicine, March, 2002☐

Romaine Brooks

American painter Romaine Brooks (1874–1970) was among the first female portraitists to earn serious critical attention in the art world. Brooks lived a rather storied life in France and other parts of Europe in the first decades of the twentieth century, and her social circle included several notable women writers and other figures of the era, many of whom sat for her in the studio. "Brooks's portraits embody the traits of courage and dignity, resourcefulness, and forbearance that she prized in her own life," wrote Whitney Chadwick in the book *Amazons in the Drawing Room: The Art of Romaine Brooks.* "Her subjects gaze outward without flinching, the simplified dark shapes of their bodies dominating the canvas."

B eatrice Romaine Goddard Brooks was born into wealth and privilege, and also into a terrifyingly dysfunctional family. Born on May 1, 1874, in Rome, she was descended from a prominent Rhode Island furniture-making family on her father's side that had Mayflower connections. She was the last of three children born to Ella Waterman Goddard, the soon-to-be ex-wife of Major Harry Goddard. Brooks's mother hailed from a Philadelphia family that had made a fortune in the Utah mines, but the marriage had disintegrated precipitously by the time Brooks was born. Ella suffered from a variety of personality disorders and moved frequently with Beatrice, her elder daughter Maya, and Brooks's brother, St. Mar, along with a retinue of servants. Prone to outbursts of rage, Ella favored her son, who suffered from some severe mental health issues. He was violent toward Brooks, and her mother finally devised a solution in which the six-year-old girl was sent to live with a foster family in a New York City tenement. Her Waterman relatives eventually discovered her whereabouts and deposited her at St. Mary's Hall, a boarding school in New Jersey.

Classes in Paris, Summers on Capri

The rest of Brooks's education was filled in by stints at a Roman Catholic institution in Italy and a finishing school in Switzerland. In 1893, at the age of 19, she convinced her mother to provide her with a small monthly stipend to enable her to live on her own in Paris. She took voice lessons and sang in cabarets before moving on to Rome to take art classes at the Scuola Nazionale, where she was the sole female student in some of her classes. She first visited the Italian island of Capri in the summer of 1899, when she rented rooms in a poor quarter and sold drawings to earn extra income. The Mediterranean isle had been an elite summer destination since the time of the Roman emperors, who built villas there, but in the late nineteenth century had become a favorite haunt of artists, including John Singer Sargent. Capri was also remote and relaxed enough to have gained a quasi-underground reputation as a haven for gays and lesbians during this period.

Encouraged by artists she met on Capri, Brooks went back to Paris and enrolled at the Académie Colarossi, but struggled financially during these years. In 1901 she read the newspaper obituary of her mad brother, and went back to the United States to care for her distraught mother, who hired spiritualists to attempt to contact St. Mar from beyond the grave. The drama ended in 1902, when Ella Waterman Goddard died of complications from diabetes. With that, Brooks and her sister, Maya (born Mary Aimée), each inherited small fortunes from the Waterman trust, enabling Brooks to live independently and pursue her career.

Left Bisexual Husband

Throughout her life Brooks had affairs with both men and women. Her romantic history included a brief marriage to John Ellingham Brooks, an English intellectual and musician whom she had met on Capri. Her future husband, also bisexual, had affairs with the writers W. Somerset Maugham and, later, E.F. Benson of *Mapp and Lucia* fame, and was known to have financial difficulties. Soon after their 1903 marriage in London he proved himself to be more conventional than his new bride had assumed: feeling freed by her marriage license to behave as she pleased, the new Mrs. Brooks visited a tailor and ordered some custom suits for herself, which she preferred to the long, voluminous skirts and corset-fitted bodices women of her class were expected to wear. Her husband asserted that he refused to be seen in public with her in such garb, and she abandoned him. The couple divorced in 1905 and her ex-husband spent the remainder of his life on Capri, where he died in 1929.

After leaving her husband, Brooks roamed all the way to the southwest corner of England in 1904, where she isolated herself in a studio on the Cornish peninsula and trained herself to remove most traces of bold color from her palette of oil paints. From this point forward her work would be marked by somber shades of gray, blue, and black.

In 1905, at the age of 31, a freshly divorced Brooks moved to Paris and settled in an apartment in the affluent 16th arrondissement. The city was rapidly modernizing and becoming the center of exciting new artistic currents, but Brooks remained distant from the circle of rising new painters who were breaking new ground in color and perspective, among them Pablo Picasso and Henri Matisse. Instead she concentrated on the lucrative field of portraiture. One of her early notable works from this period was a portrait of a Basque-Chilean society figure and influential interior decorator in Paris, Eugenia Errázuriz.

Involved with Proto-Fascist D'Annunzio

The Galleries Durand-Ruel in Paris hosted Brooks's first solo exhibition in 1910. She showed 13 pieces, including two nude studies, which was a daring move for a female artist of the era. Her profile rose considerably with the success of the show, and new portrait commissions flooded in. That same year she ended what had been a three-year-long romance with Lord Alfred "Bosie" Douglas, whose name had been attached to an infamous scandal of the 1890s over his affair with the writer Oscar Wilde. Douglas's father was the Marquess of Queensberry, who harassed Wilde because of the relationship, and in turn Wilde had the Marquess arrested on criminal libel charges. The court case was salacious and one of the first same-sex tabloid scandals of the modern era of journalism, but ultimately resulted in countercharges that Wilde had paid male prostitutes, for which he was arrested, convicted, and imprisoned.

Another lover of Brooks's was Winnaretta Singer, heiress to the Singer sewing machine fortune. Singer became the Princesse de Polignac after marrying a much older gay French aristocrat, but had numerous affairs with prominent women in Paris and London. Around 1909 Brooks met Gabriele D'Annunzio, the Italian political figure and poet, and had an affair with him. D'Annunzio, in turn, collaborated with composer Claude Debussy on a scandalous stage work titled *Le martyre de Saint Sébastien* for Russian ballerina Ida Rubinstein. Brooks became romantically involved with the dancer and used her as a model on several occasions, including the nude *Le Trajet* (The Crossing, c. 1911), a work of blues and whites and strong horizontal lines in which Rubinstein appears almost corpse-like.

Rubinstein is also thought to have been the model for one of Brooks's best-known paintings, *La France Croisée* (The Cross of France). Painted at the onset of World War I and published with a poem by D'Annunzio, the image was subsequently used on the cover of a booklet sold to raise funds for the International Red Cross organization. "Cloaked in black with her head bound in flowing white and the insignia of the red cross," wrote Chadwick, "the figure is resolutely posed against an image of Ypres burning, her shadowed face displaying a magnificent and somber determination. Brooks's painting presents a symbolic image of a valiant France, while D'Annunzio's poem calls for courage, strength, and endurance, linking the theme of Christ's suffering on the cross with that of a nation at war." In 1920 Brooks was awarded a Legion of Honor medal from the French government for this contribution to the war effort.

Romance with Barney Inspired Book

The longest relationship Brooks would have was with another expatriate with American roots, the writer Natalie Clifford Barney. They met around 1915 and would remain in each others' lives until Brooks's death in 1970. Yet Barney was non-monogamous and conducted affairs with scores of other women over the years, which Brooks tolerated because of her own desire for independence. Their story even became the subject of a 2005 book, *Wild Girls: Paris, Sappho and Art: The Lives and Loves of Natalie Barney and Romaine Brooks,* by Diana Souhami.

Barney had a long-running literary salon at her home in Paris, but Brooks maintained a separate household, in an apartment on rue Raynouard. Brooks depicted Barney in a 1920 work as *L'Amazone,* and painted several other women from their social circle. These included Elisabeth de Gramont, a titled French aristocrat, and Elizabeth Eyre de Lanux, whom Brooks painted as *Chasseresse* (The Huntress, also titled *Boréal*). Eyre was among the first women to work in interior design as a profession, along with the much more famous Elsie de Wolfe, whose portrait Brooks also painted.

Brooks's and Barney's circle also included a lover with whom Brooks took up, the pianist Renata Borgatti, shown in the meditative *Renata Borgatti au Piano* from 1920. The sculptor Una Troubridge also sat for a portrait by Brooks. Troubridge was a British aristocrat who was the longtime lover of novelist Radclyffe Hall. Brooks painted Troubridge wearing a men's jacket, stiff collar and monocle, posing with her two dachshunds. Troubridge and Hall lived openly as a couple in London, a somewhat scandalous situation for the time, and Hall's 1928 novel *The Well of Loneliness* was one of the first serious works of literature to address lesbianism. An earlier work of hers, *The Forge,* featured a minor character thought to be a stand-in for Brooks.

Abruptly Ended Career

One of Brooks's best-known works is a *Self-Portrait* from 1923. She wore a riding coat, top hat, and gloves, along with her Legion of Honor medal. Two years later, she had several gallery exhibitions, including one in Paris, another in London, and a New York debut at the Wildenstein Galleries. Curiously, she seemed to have lost interest in art after 1925, with just a few portraits and drawings to follow. In the early 1930s she began a memoir with the working title of *No Pleasant Memories* that recounted her unhappy childhood, but it went unfinished and unpublished. In the late 1930s she spent some time in New York, where she rented a studio above Carnegie Hall. During this period she painted two more portraits, one of the writer Carl Van Vechten and another of society figure Muriel Draper. In 1961 Brooks painted one final work, a somber portrait of an Italian aristocrat, Duke Uberto Strozzi, whom she had known from a wartime sojourn outside Florence during World War II, the only time she and Barney ever lived together. Strozzi's portrait was done in 1961, when Brooks was 87 years old. It resides in the Smithsonian American Art Museum, to which Brooks had begun donating her archives in her later years.

Brooks grew increasingly reclusive after moving to Nice, France, in 1967, and feared that her household staff members were trying to poison her or steal her drawings. In the end, she refused to see even Barney, who begged to visit but was turned away. Brooks died on December 7, 1970, in Nice. By that point there were already plans for exhibitions of her work, championed in part by art historian Adelyn Breeskin, an expert on the paintings of another American woman painter of an earlier era, Mary Cassatt. Breeskin assembled a 1971 retrospective of Brooks's works for the Smithsonian. There was also a Whitney Museum of American Art show that same year. Writing about the posthumous interest in Brooks's career, the art critic Hilton Kramer wrote in the *New York Times* that "there is in Romaine Brooks's painting a force, even a vehemence, that can only be described as masculine. There is also a coldness—a severity at once esthetic and psychological—that strikes the viewer not as evidence of any lack of feeling, but as a clear-eyed instrument for divining an essential truth."

Books

Chadwick, Whitney, *Amazons in the Drawing Room: The Art of Romaine Brooks,* University of California Press, 2000.

Corinne, Tee A., "Romaine Brooks," in *Encyclopedia of Lesbian, Gay, Bisexual and Transgendered History in America,* edited by Marc Stein, Charles Scribner's Sons, 2004.

Periodicals

New York Times, April 25, 1971.

Online

"Romaine Brooks," Smithsonian American Art Museum, http://www.americanart.si.edu/search/artist_bio.cfm?ID=599 (November 23, 2011). □

C

James Thomas Cannon

American sports writer James Thomas "Jimmy" Cannon (1910-1973) was a highly innovative sports columnist, as well as a versatile and sometimes controversial sports writer. He gained a reputation as one of the best sports journalists.

In the era of great journalists, James "Jimmy" Cannon—who gained a reputation as one of the best sportswriters—was the quintessential newspaperman. He got his start by doing the grunt work, working as a copy boy and, later, toiling as a reporter assigned to producing stories from police blotters. Later, his employers placed him on the city street beat, an environment where Cannon developed his art and craft: He combined fact with poetry, a mixture that served him well when he was later assigned to a sports beat.

He liked to hang out in bars, but he considered this as an extension of his workplace, as that environment provided him with his best story leads. Later, when Cannon found it necessary to quit drinking (for health reasons) this versatile newspaper reporter still found the places that garnered him the best stories. Indeed, he was both resolute and resourceful when it came to finding the best sports story.

He was far more than a press-box mainstay who churned out daily copy from a manual typewriter. It was not enough for Cannon to just provide readers with a basic recount of a game. He took readers beyond the playing field and the stadium and into the very minds of the athletes he covered. In the process, he got into the minds of his readers. He developed a style that combined the basic fact—a newspaper necessity— with the word crafting artistry of a magazine feature writer, or even a novelist.

Though Cannon's education was cut short, he gained a deep appreciation of literature. Novelist Ernest Hemingway and newspaper columnist and playwright Damon Runyon were among his heroes. Those two men reciprocated Cannon's praise with their high estimation of this New York City sportswriter. Hemingway applauded Cannon's prose, and was a regular reader. A Nobel Prize-winning author, Hemingway—who laced his own literature with accounts of bullfighting, boxing, deep-sea fishing and big-game hunting—was a fan and described Cannon as "an excellent sportswriter," as quoted in the *Dictionary of American Biography*. But he added an important point: that Cannon was "also a very good writer aside from sports." In other words, Cannon knew how to churn out a good phrase and elevate a daily newspaper dispatch or column. In this way, Cannon helped revolutionize sports reporting. Reportage was more than just facts and stats; there was a story behind the numbers, and Cannon became a poet laureate of sports reportage.

Born and Raised in New York City

Jimmy Cannon came into the world as James Thomas Cannon on April 10, 1910, the first of three sons of Thomas J. Cannon and Loretta (Monahan) Cannon. He was born in New York City, specifically the Greenwich Village section. His father played a minor role in a major political machine: Thomas Cannon was a municipal clerk who served in the city's Tammany Hall, which was rife with patronage and bribery.

Young Jimmy Cannon became a street-smart kid, but this did not harden him; rather it imbued him with a compassion coupled with toughness—and this mixture would later help him appreciate people who had to work hard for a living. He developed an empathy that would

later inform his sports writing. Cannon did not just write about the superstars of sports. For instance, he would also write about the struggling boxer who was mismanaged by a manager. True, he would write about Joe Dimaggio's famous 56-game hitting streak, but it was just as important for Cannon to write about an outfielder who struggled to support both a career and a family. The underappreciated became better appreciated in his stories and columns.

Started Working As a Teenager

Cannon was self educated, as he cut short his own formal education. He dropped out of Regis High School when he was only fourteen years old, but one of his favorite places was the public library, where he developed his noted appreciation of literature.

After quitting school, the ambitious Cannon entered the newspaper business. First, he acquired a job at the *New York Evening World*, where he worked in the classified advertising department. Less than two years later, in 1926, Cannon took a job at the *New York Daily News*, toiling as a copy boy on the newspaper's graveyard shift. These were hard, demanding jobs. But Cannon did not mind the low pay or the odd hours. He would later comment (from his entry in *Dictionary of American Biography*, "I was sorry for anybody else who didn't work those hours because I thought it was the best of all possible lives."

Further, such early jobs provided Cannon with his informal apprenticeship. Given a chance to write a story for the *News*, Cannon made the most of the opportunity and earned himself a position as a general assignment reporter. During this early period, he covered crime but also produced a radio column for the International News Service, covering the Washington D.C. political scene.

Shifted into Sports Writing

His sports writing career truly began in 1936 when he joined the staff of the *New York American*, where he would work until 1939. Runyon, one of Cannon's heroes, admired how Cannon reported the Lindbergh baby kidnapping story (aviator Charles Lindbergh's son had been abducted in 1932 and later killed), and helped the young journalist gain the sports reporting position at the newspaper.

Cannon's civilian newspaper career was interrupted when he was drafted into the army during World War II. During his service, however, he continued his journalism activities, as he wrote as a combat correspondent for the army's newspaper *Stars and Stripes* (from 1942 to 1945). Many of his stories were about General George Patton.

After his military service, Cannon was hired by the *New York Post*. He worked for the newspaper from 1946 to 1959, although he did return to military service during the Korean War. He wrote about that conflict for the *Post*.

In 1959, he began working for the *New York Journal-American*, and he would eventually become the highest-paid sports columnist in the United States, a tribute to his experience and his talent. By this time, Cannon's writings were syndicated, meaning that his prose was savored by readers from coast to coast. Also, by this time, Cannon was influencing other sportswriters, just as he had once been influenced by Hemingway and Runyon. During a period when newspapers were either folding or consolidating, the *Journal-American* merged with the *New York Herald-Tribune* and the *World-Telegram and Sun*. This created the *World Journal Tribune*. That newspaper printed Cannon's columns until the periodical folded in 1967. Afterward, his writings would be distributed by the Hearst Headline Service (until 1972).

Columns Became a Favorite of Readers

One of his most popular columns was called "Nobody Asked Me, But . . ." He used it as a forum to string together short, punchy, and often powerful, observations. Barry Horn from the *Dallas Morning News* quoted one of these observations: "[He]is a credit to his race—the human race."

His perception could also result in witty, even self-deprecating remarks. In another widely quoted statement (recorded in the *New York Post Editorial*, he said, "I don't like Boston because all of the men look like me."

Cannon has been described as short and chunky, not at all athletic. His exercise was walking the streets of his Manhattan beat. He may have not liked Boston, but he loved New York City. During his career, he became a "man about town," frequenting famous nightclubs such as Lindy's, the Stork Club and El Morocco, and developing friendships with people such as Frank Sinatra, comedian Joe E. Lewis, nightclub owner Toots Shor and New York Yankees outfielder Joe DiMaggio. He enjoyed the nightlife, and the drinking, but a stomach operation in the 1940s curtailed his carousing. But that in no way affected the relationships he had developed, or his work, or basic lifestyle.

Cannon was an insomniac, so strolling through the city streets suited him well. He also did much of his writing at night, staying up at all hours editing his own work until he was satisfied. Cannon never married, as writing was his main passion. However, he was often seen with some of Broadway's leading actresses, such as Carol Channing. But the way he pursued his profession with single-minded purpose simply would not have been conducive to the survival of a long-term relationship. Quoted in a 2007 *New York Post* op-ed piece ("Thank You, Jimmy Cannon!"), W.C. Heinz—who once worked for the *New York Sun*—said "[Cannon's] column was his whole life. He has no family, no games he plays, no other activities. When he writes, it's the concentration of his whole being. He goes through the emotional wringer."

Indeed, Cannon brought a great deal of emotion into his pieces. He could be tough, highly opinionated, and even maudlin, and he would influence the so-called "new journalists" who became well known in the 1960s and 1970s: writers such as Jimmy Breslin, Pete Hamill, Gay Talese and Tom Wolfe.

Cannon covered baseball, producing memorable stories about DiMaggio and Mickey Mantle, but he seemed to prefer boxing, even though he thought the sport barbaric and filled with "low lifes." His sympathies clearly resided with the struggling fighters. His passage about a typical fight manager, quoted by *Sports Illustrated*'s Jonathan Yardley, indicates the power he could bring to a column: "The fight manager," he wrote, "wouldn't fight to defend his mother. He has never participated in a crime of violence but he lives by the code of the underworld. He is cranky and profane when he talks to the kids he manages but he is servile when addressing the gangster whom he considers his benefactor. He has cheated many people but he describes himself as a legitimate guy at every opportunity."

Died in New York City

As with his writing, Cannon approached life with great passion. But this also meant he developed some bad habits—too many cigarettes and too much coffee, hanging out all hours—and these likely contributed to the stroke he suffered in May 1971, which confined him to a wheelchair. A year later, he was rehired by the *New York Post*. In October 1973, his health took a downturn, and he died in New York City. He was sixty-three years old.

Cannon's sports columns were collected in three books: *Nobody Asked Me* (1951), *Who Struck John?* (1956), and *Nobody asked Me But. . .:The World of Jimmy Cannon* (1978), which was a compilation of columns put together by brothers Jack and Tom.

Through the years, he is still considered as one of the greatest sports writers of all time, ranking with the pantheon that includes Ring Lardner, Dick Young, and Red Smith. Appropriately, he was a recipient of the Associated Press's Red Smith Award, which honors outstanding contributions to sports journalism. However, Cannon received the award posthumously, in 2004. The award was initiated in 1981, almost a decade after Cannon's death. In an article published in the *Dallas Morning News* about Cannon's award, writer Barry Horn quoted Jerry Izenberg, who won

the award in 2000. "With [Red Smith] it was the phrases you remembered," said Izenberg. "With Jimmy, you remembered the characters he wrote about." Further, Izenberg described Cannon as a "blue-collar writer with a white-collar vocabulary."

"He was the biggest influence on how I wanted to communicate people's feelings," he said. "He taught young writers how to listen. He captured what sports people said and who they were better than anyone."

As quoted in the 2007 *Post* column, Hemingway said of Cannon, "I don't know anybody who takes his job more seriously or with more confidence."

Books

Contemporary Authors Online, Gale, 2011.
"James Thomas Cannon,"*Dictionary of American Biography, Supplement 9: 1971-1975,* Charles Scribner's Sons 1994.

Periodicals

Dallas Morning News, June, 2004.
New York Post, May 8, 2007.
Sports Illustrated, August 14, 1978.

Online

"Jimmy Cannon,"*Baseball Library.com,* http://www.baseballlibrary. com/ballplayers/player.php?name=Jimmy_Cannon. (December 15, 2011.)□

Solanus Casey

Solanus Casey (1870–1957) was a Roman Catholic priest whose piety and works of charity helped set him on a posthumous path to sainthood in his church. The humble friar of the Capuchin Brothers religious order ran a soup kitchen in Detroit, Michigan, that served meals to thousands during the Great Depression, and his influence and example earned him a devoted core of admirers among the city's faithful. In 1995, the appellation "Venerable" was added to Casey's name by Pope John Paul II, and Roman Catholics anticipate Father Solanus, as he is called, will become the first American-born male to achieve sainted status.

Bernard Francis Casey was the sixth of 16 children born to Irish immigrants on a farm in Oak Grove, Wisconsin. His parents had fled the potato famine that ravaged Ireland in the mid-nineteenth century, and produced nine other sons and six daughters before and after Casey's birth on November 25, 1870, in their log cabin home. A childhood bout with diphtheria—a disease that felled two of his siblings—left his vocal chords permanently damaged and his voice had a wispy, low-decibel timbre. At the age of 17, "Barney," as his family called him, left home for Stillwater, Minnesota, on the St. Croix River, where he found work in a lumber mill. He spent the next few years working in various jobs in Minnesota and back over the state border in Wisconsin, including that of prison guard, hospital orderly, and streetcar conductor. It was while on the last job in Superior, Wisconsin, that Casey witnessed a scene in which a drunken man had just stabbed a woman to death in a rage. The look on the man's face deeply moved Casey, and he realized there was much suffering and violence in the world and he wanted to do something to alleviate it.

Entered Seminary

Casey was 21 years old when he entered the St. Francis de Sales Seminary in Milwaukee, Wisconsin, in 1892. Initially he hoped to become a standard diocesan priest, the type that serve in neighborhood parish churches, but he struggled with the academic requirements, which required fluency in both German and Latin. After four years he was rejected for the priesthood, but decided to try to enter a religious order recently founded in Detroit, Michigan.

Unlike diocesan priests, men who enter Roman Catholic religious orders typically live together in a monastery or a mission house and serve the community through various occupations. Casey was drawn to the Capuchin Franciscan order, more formally known as the Order of Friars Minor Capuchin. Founded in Italy in the sixteenth century, its members wear the distinctive brown robes of the Franciscan order with a *cappuccio,* or hood that lends the Capuchins their name. Unlike other religious orders devoted to teaching or missionary work, the Franciscans were a mendicant order, which means that they relied solely on charitable donations to feed themselves and work to serve others, following the rule of St. Francis of Assisi.

Two Swiss Capuchins established the order in the United States in the 1850s, coming first to Milwaukee, which had a large German-speaking population. The American monastery was founded in 1882 in Detroit, which also had a sizable German-émigré and Roman Catholic population. This was the St. Bonaventure Capuchin Franciscan Monastery at which Casey arrived in December of 1896. On January 14, 1897, he was invested as a Capuchin novice and took the name Solanus after St. Francis Solanus, a Franciscan missionary priest who died in Lima, Peru, in 1610. Casey took his vows on July 21, 1898. Six years later, on July 24, 1904, he was ordained a priest at St. Francis of Assisi Church in Milwaukee.

Served in New York

Casey spent several years in the New York City area, serving as a sacristan or porter at Capuchin houses there. A sacristan is the priest responsible for the vestments and vessels used during Mass. He first went to the Sacred Heart Friary in Yonkers in 1904, and in 1918 was assigned to Our Lady of Sorrows in Lower Manhattan, a Capuchin church near the Williamsburg Bridge. From 1921 to 1924 he served Our Lady Queen of Angels in what was then a predominantly Hispanic section of Manhattan now known as East Harlem.

Casey was a popular friar with the predominantly immigrant parishioners in New York, known as a good listener and virtuous spiritual guide. He became particularly adept in signing up new enrollees in the Capuchins' Seraphic Mass Association, which collected funds for missionary work abroad. "His advice to those who came to him for help was simple," noted his entry in the *New Catholic Encyclopedia.* "After encouraging them to make a sacrifice for the foreign missions, that is, be enrolled in the Seraphic Mass Association, he would tell them to thank God ahead of time for granting the favor they requested."

"Thank God Ahead of Time" would become the title of one of Casey's numerous, posthumously published biographies. He began to gain a reputation as a particularly effective intercessor, as parishioners returned and told him that their prayers had had their desired effect. In 1923, the head of the Capuchins in America, Father Benno Aichinger, asked Casey to start keeping a record of these events.

Moved to Detroit

In 1924 Casey was sent to St. Bonaventure Monastery in Detroit to serve as assistant porter. By then the friars' home had become a local institution, serving the Roman Catholic population on the east side as it expanded along with the city's automotive manufacturing industry. As entire neighborhoods were built out of the swampy lands along the Detroit River in the early decades of the twentieth century, the faithful raised funds to build their parish churches, but there was a shortage of available priests. Catholics in Detroit relied on the Capuchin Franciscans to baptize, marry, and bury Roman Catholics according to the religion's tenets. By the time Casey arrived, the Monastery was a place of retreat for the semi-cloistered monks, but as the porter it was his duty to answer the front door, whose bell the poor regularly rang in search of food or other aid. Just as they had in New York City, the faithful came to him for help. One of the authorities on Casey's life and deeds is a Milwaukee priest, Rev. Michael Crosby, who explained to *New York Times* religion writer Gustav Niebuhr that "there is a thin line between the gift of prophecy, which Solanus had in abundance, and intuition. He had this uncanny ability to listen. He would look right at you, and he would take as much time with you as you would want."

Lay Catholics in Detroit had established a tertiary, or Third Order, at St. Bonaventure, during World War I. In November of 1930, a full year after the Wall Street stock market crash of 1929 that launched the Great Depression, the Third Order members started a soup kitchen to feed Detroit's poor. Casey ran it by securing donations from local food-providers and farmers, and even participated in day-long jaunts to farms willing to donate surplus harvest.

Casey spent a little over two decades in Detroit. In the mid-1940s he went back to New York City, working out of St. Michael's Friary in Brooklyn, and went into semi-retirement a year later, moving to St. Felix Friary in Huntington, Indiana. In 1956, he came back to Detroit and St. Bonaventure's, but his health was failing. At St. John Hospital, a massive, newly built edifice that served Detroit's enormous population of Roman Catholics on the east side, Casey died at the age of 86 from skin cancer and a chronic skin disease on

July 31, 1957. He was already a revered figure among the city's Roman Catholics, but the fact that the date and hour of his death coincided exactly with the date and hour of the first Mass he ever said, 53 years before, was to them a portent of spiritual honor. Thousands came to pay their respects when his body was laid out at St. Bonaventure Monastery in preparation for burial.

Considered for Sainthood

The Father Solanus Guild formed in 1960 to promote the late friar's life and good deeds and advocate for sainthood. The process of sainthood in the contemporary Roman Catholic church involves several stages, the first of which is to be declared a "Servant of God," which occurs no sooner than five years after death. In 1966 an office of vice postulator was approved for Casey. This was a church official who gathered information on Casey's life and impact on the lives of others. The Archbishop of Detroit, John Cardinal Dearden, formally submitted papers on Casey's record as a priest to the Vatican's Office of Congregation for Causes of Saints in 1981, and a year later the formal inquiry process crucial to the sainthood process was opened. Diocese officials "interviewed nearly 60 people who had known the priest," Niebuhr wrote in the New York Times. "The interviewers worked from 29 single-spaced pages of questions. The resulting testimony, 800 pages long, makes up one of the volumes of the document." Those documents, after being reviewed by Vatican officials, led to Casey being designated a Servant of God on November 7, 1986.

Received Designation of 'Venerated'

In one of the more macabre elements of Roman Catholicism's fixation on the corporal body, a canonical exhumation had to be conducted on Casey's grave in 1987 and supervised by the Archbishop and other church officials. The fact that his corpse had not significantly decayed was declared another sign of his special status. On July 11, 1995, Pope John Paul II issued a Decree of Heroic Virtue for Casey, placing his name on the list of "Venerable" Roman Catholics, the next step on the path to sainthood. He was the first American-born male ever to receive the designation of Venerable. The next step was to be beatified, which required at least one miraculous cure to have been attributed to prayers to Casey. An Office of the Vice Postulator for the Cause of Venerable Solanus Casey reviews such events. As of yet, there are no native-born male saints in the Roman Catholic canon. Elizabeth Ann Seton, the founder of the religious order American Sisters of Charity, was canonized in 1975. Two years later the church recognized the late Bishop of Philadelphia, John Nepomucene Neumann. He was the first American man to be deemed a saint, but he was born overseas, as were several other notable figures in the history of Roman Catholicism in the United States to achieve sainthood.

Casey's body was reinterred at a resplendent pilgrimage center at the St. Bonaventure Monastery, which still ministers to the poor in a part of Detroit so badly blighted that by the early twenty-first century entire blocks were reverting back into farmland. The Capuchin Soup Kitchen is still active and serves hundreds of meals daily at two locations, operates a bakery called On the Rise, and runs an agricultural venture, Earthworks Urban Farm. "Father Solanus had an ability to see potential and beauty in people and situations where others saw only human refuse and devastation," wrote David Nantais in the Roman Catholic magazine America in 2009 about Detroit's most celebrated Franciscan friar. "The city of Detroit itself is much in need of realizing the potential it holds beneath its grimy exterior, and Father Solanus would make an especially appropriate patron saint."

Books

Armstrong, R. J., "Solanus Casey," in New Catholic Encyclopedia, Gale, 2003.

Periodicals

America, June 22, 2009.

Michigan Historical Review, Spring 2001.

New York Times, August 5, 1995.

Online

"Doorway to Solanus Casey," SolanusCasey.org, http://www.solanuscasey.org/ (November 27, 2011).□

Catherine of Braganza

The Portuguese princess Catherine of Braganza (1638–1705) was one of several foreign-born royal women who ascended to the British throne through marriage. The daughter of the king of Portugal, she wed England's King Charles II in 1662, but her failure to produce an heir to the throne sparked a succession crisis in the years after her husband's death in 1685. It was through her marriage that the British gained a foothold on the Indian subcontinent in the form of a sleepy fishing port on India's western coastline that grew into the city of Mumbai.

Catherine of Braganza was born Catarina Henriqueta de Bragança on November 25, 1638, at her family's estate at Vila Viçosa. The House of Braganza was a significant Portuguese royal dynasty with ties to the ruling House of Aviz, which itself was descended from the French rulers of Burgundy. Dona Catarina de Bragança, as she was formally known, was named for her famous great-grandmother, the Duchess of Braganza, whose move to claim the Portuguese throne in 1580 prompted a brief war with Spain. King Philip II of Spain united the two Iberian nations and Spanish rule over Portugal lasted for the next six decades.

moderately sympathetic to Roman Catholicism, the dominant religion throughout France, Spain, Italy, and parts of the Austro-Hungarian Empire. Though England remained steadfastly Protestant, religious tensions between the two camps would play out through Catherine's three decades as queen consort.

Married in Portsmouth

The marriage treaty between Portugal and England was signed on June 23, 1661. Its terms included a provision that England would lend military aid to Portugal against Spain, if necessary, and that Catherine would be permitted to practice her Roman Catholic religion in England. Interestingly, Catherine was not married by proxy before she set off for England—a common convention at the time for European royal brides, with a stand-in for the groom during the church ceremony. This meant that the bride would be permitted to embark upon her journey with all the safeguarding and privileges normally accorded to the wife of a reigning monarch. In Catherine's case it was bypassed by her mother because a Roman Catholic ceremony for Charles would require papal dispensation, and the reigning pope had strong ties to the Spanish monarchy, which did not yet recognize the legitimacy of the Portuguese throne.

Catherine left Portugal on April 13, 1662, but her ship did not reach Portsmouth until four weeks later. On May 21, 1662, Charles arrived at the port city and the two were wed by Anglican rite at Domus Dei church in Portsmouth, also called the Royal Garrison Church. It was later revealed they also had a secret Roman Catholic ceremony. Catherine did not speak English, and Charles did not speak Portuguese. The two communicated with one another in a third language, Spanish, and though Catherine was tutored in English for many years she never became fully conversant.

At the time of her marriage, Catherine was 23 years old and had led a sheltered life. Contemporary accounts hint that she seemed quite thrilled with her handsome, dashing spouse. Charles, however, was a notorious rake who had put off marriage as long as he possibly could. A famous bon vivant and patron of the arts, he frequented the London theaters newly reopened by his authorization, which the previous regime had deemed dens of licentious behavior. Charles's enthusiastic support for the theater ushered in the era of Restoration drama in English literature, a period notable for the appearance of women on stage for the first time as professional actors; theses actresses were also the first women in Western civilization to achieve celebrity status in the performing arts. Among them was Nell Gwyn, who was the mistress of Charles.

Suffered Several Miscarriages

Charles had several mistresses, and his dalliances were widely known in London and at court. Another paramour was Barbara Villiers, who was pregnant with her second child by Charles when Catherine arrived at the royal palace at Hampton Court on May 29, 1662. Catherine had come to England with a retinue of older Portuguese noblewomen to serve as her ladies-in-waiting and a group of trusted priests and friars. In the summer of 1662 Charles sent some

Mother Arranged Marriage

Catherine's father became King João IV when the Portuguese throne was finally restored in 1640. Her mother was Luisa de Guzmán, a Spanish noble whose family was descended from St. Francis Borgia, a prince who renounced his royal titles to enter the priesthood and went on to lead the Jesuit religious order, or Society of Jesus. Catherine was raised in a devout atmosphere and educated by nuns. She had several siblings: Teodósio, born in 1634 and heir to his father's title, became Portugal's first Prince of Brazil when the South American land was seized by João from Spanish hands. But Teodósio died at age 19, at which point his titles passed to 13-year-old Afonso, who became King Afonso VI after the death of his father in 1656.

Catherine's older sister was the Infanta Joana, who died at the age of 18. Catherine inherited Joana's title as Princess of Beira in 1653. Another brother eventually succeeded Afonso to become King Pedro II of Portugal. Luisa, who had proved a skilled leader as regent for Afonso in the late 1650s, considered several well-placed matches for her only surviving daughter: one was the king of France, Louis XIV, who instead married Maria Theresa, a daughter of Spain's powerful Hapsburg dynasty. Another potential husband for Catherine was Maria Theresa's brother, John of Austria, who would prove an influential military and diplomatic force on the European continent. But these Roman Catholic prospects paled in comparison to the ultimate match for Portuguese global ambitions—a union with England via Catherine's marriage to its newly restored king, Charles II.

The restoration of the English throne in 1660 was a pivotal event in the history of the British Isles. Charles II was the son of the doomed Charles I, who was beheaded during the English Civil War in 1649. These House of Stuart monarchs had ties to the French dynasties and were of her maids back to Portugal and appointed Villiers to serve as Lady of the Bedchamber.

Villiers, who was later made the Duchess of Cleveland, would have five children in all by Charles. Catherine was decidedly less fortunate. She suffered several miscarriages, the first of which may have occurred in October of 1663; there was another in February 1666, and at least two more in 1668 and 1669. Senior officials at court begged Charles to divorce her and choose a new, younger spouse who could produce the necessary heir, but he refused. Instead he eventually acknowledged Villiers' children as his and arranged for his brother James, the Duke of York, to succeed him.

Catherine was drawn into a few salacious palace intrigues at court. There was the 1678 murder of the magistrate Sir Edmund Godfrey, who was one of a group of well-placed figures who had learned that Charles signed a secret treaty with France eight years earlier, the Treaty of Dover, that aligned England with France and, more significantly, called for Charles to convert to Roman Catholicism. One of Catherine's attendants was accused of Godfrey's murder, and anti-Catholic sentiment increased. This spiraled into the so-called Popish Plot during Charles's final decade on the throne. In that scheme, an Anglican cleric named Titus Oates fabricated a claim that Catherine was part of a plot to poison Charles with the aid of Jesuit priests.

England Divided over Future

Veteran diarist Samuel Pepys and others close to court considered Catherine largely blameless and a stoic bearer of her husband's widely known infidelities, and the king's unwillingness to divorce her seems to demonstrate a close bond between the two. He had at least a dozen children by several women, including the five born to Villiers and two with Gwyn. A French-born mistress, Louise de Kérouaille, produced a son and was given the title of the Duchess of Portsmouth. But the king's failure to produce a legitimate heir prompted the Exclusion Crisis of 1678–81, named after the Exclusion Bill introduced in Parliament that would prevent the king's brother James Stuart, the Roman Catholic king of Scotland, from succeeding to the throne after Charles. The movement to prevent James from ascension, as Charles had designated, was linked to strong anti-Catholic currents and ultimately failed, but two lasting factions arose in Parliament during the crisis. The Petitioners supported the Exclusion Bill and became known as the Whigs; Charles's supporters were called the "Abhorrers" and eventually evolved into the Tories, or Conservative Party.

Catherine remained a devout Catholic despite attempts to remove her ecclesiastical coterie and loyal Portuguese staffers. She had her own chapel at St. James Palace in London and patronized musicians from Italy to compose and perform music for Mass and private occasions, marking a change from the preference for French music. The queen also had a lasting impact on British culinary habits through her introduction of tea, a beverage that came to Portugal via its new trade routes to Asia. It became a fad among the Portuguese elite, and migrated with Catherine to England, where it became a deeply embedded national culinary tradition.

Charles fell ill in 1685 and converted to Roman Catholicism on his deathbed. The throne passed to his brother the Duke of York, who became King James II. Catherine remained in England, living at another royal palace, Somerset House, as Queen Dowager. Another illegitimate son of Charles's, James Scott, had been made the 1st Duke of Monmouth by his father and served as commander-in-chief of the English Army. After his father's death, this son led the so-called Monmouth Rebellion to seize the throne, which had some support from the most ardent of anti-Catholics in Parliament. Catherine apparently interceded when Monmouth and his forces were defeated, pleading with King James to spare his life, but the duke was beheaded.

Returned to Portugal

In 1688 Catherine was invited to become godmother to the newborn Prince of Wales, who was King James's first legitimately born son with his wife, Mary of Modena. There were rumors that the infant was stillborn or that the entire pregnancy had been a ruse, but Catherine gave testimony to the lords of the Privy Council that the infant, James Francis Edward Stuart, was indeed legitimate. A few months later, Mary and her infant son left England for France, fearing for their safety in a tide of growing anti-Catholic sentiment. These events led to the ouster of James II from the throne in what was known as the Glorious Revolution of 1688. A Dutch prince, William of Orange, had married Princess Mary, a daughter of James II. They ruled jointly as King William III and Queen Mary II.

Catherine's role as Queen Dowager diminished after this. She returned to Lisbon in 1693 after a 30-year absence. Her youngest brother, Pedro II, had become King of Portugal in 1683 and would reign until his death in 1706. She served as regent for him twice, in 1701 and again 1704–05. She died on December 31, 1705, at Bemposta Palace in Lisbon.

Gave England "Bom Baim"

Catherine's most enduring contribution to British history was an inadvertent one: the marriage treaty with Charles called for the Portuguese to hand over two foreign ports as part of her dowry. The first was the Moroccan city of Tangier, which the English held until 1681. The second was a faraway port on the Arabian Sea called "Bom Baim" (Good Harbor) by the Portuguese. Under British rule it was expanded and became known by its Anglicized name, Bombay. For decades it was home to the headquarters of the British East India Company, which helped the British gain a significant foothold in Asia. Bombay was later renamed Mumbai and grew into one of the world's largest cities.

The late Diana, Princess of Wales, was descended from Charles Lennox, de Kérouaille's son, and also through one of Villiers's sons. Diana's 1981 marriage to the son of England's reigning monarch produced two heirs to the throne. The first of them, Prince William, will thus become the first descendant of Charles II to wear the British crown in several hundred years. In 2011 he married a commoner, Catherine Middleton, who became the Duchess of Cambridge. When her husband eventually ascends to the throne, she will become Queen Catherine, a title not used since Catherine of Braganza.

Books

Corp, Edward, "Catherine of Braganza and Cultural Politics," *Queenship in Britain, 1660-1837: Royal Patronage, Court Culture, and Dynastic Politics,* edited by Clarissa Campbell Orr, Manchester University Press, 2002, pp. 53–73.

Hunt, Percival, *Samuel Pepys in the Diary,* University of Pittsburgh Press, 1958, pp. 136–141.

Periodicals

New York Times January 9, 1998. □

Olof Celsius

Swedish botanist Olof Celsius (1670–1756) spent his career at the University of Uppsala and was an important early mentor to Carl Linnaeus, the scientist who devised the system of modern taxonomy. In some sources he is called Olof Celsius the Elder to distinguish him from his historian son, who penned biographies of Swedish kings. Another member of the Celsius clan, Anders, would develop the temperature scale that bears the family name.

Olof Celsius the Elder was born July 19, 1670, probably in Uppsala, the seat of the Christian church in Sweden at the time. Located about 40 miles north of Stockholm, the city boasted a famous Northern Gothic cathedral built in the 1430s and the first university in any of the Scandinavian lands. In the late Middle Ages Sweden had emerged as a prosperous, expanding empire, and its kings followed England's break with the powerful Church in Rome. By the 1590s, Lutheranism, named after the Protestant reformer and German theologian Martin Luther, had become Sweden's official religion.

Born into Family of Scholars

Celsius's father, Magnus, taught math at the University of Uppsala but was a native of Helsingland, a more northerly province in Sweden. Magnus left his imprint on academia as the decoder of some mysterious rock carvings found in Helsingland called the Helsingland stones. The rune stones contained a variant of the Runic alphabet, the first written form of the Germanic languages, but Magnus died in 1679 and it was left to his sons to ensure that their father's work was completed and published posthumously. Celsius had an older brother named Nils, who was born in 1658. Nils succeeded their father as a professor of mathematics at the University of Uppsala. "A few closely intermarried clans dominated Uppsala—such as the Celsius, Aurivillius, and later Afzelius," wrote Lisbet Koerner in *Linnaeus: Nature and Nation.* "They modeled their academic posts on their ancestral Lutheran parsonages, and used them in turn to establish dynasties within the higher clergy."

Undertook an Adventuresome Sojourn in Italy

Scant English-language sources exist that give clues to Celsius's early years, or even a marriage and family. What is known is that after several years of advanced study in theology and classical languages he embarked on a journey that he hoped would take him all the way to the Middle East. His trek began in 1697 and was chronicled in a travel journal he maintained. "Celsius belonged to the new brotherhood of travelers, going from destination to destination in what was slowly institutionalized as the Grand Tour," wrote Orvar Löfgren in a 1999 work, *On Holiday: A History of Vacationing.* "This journey was meant to finish off their education and it produced a wealth of travel books and guides, sketches and bad poetry." In entries dated December of 1697, Celsius wrote of his stay in Florence, the leading city of the Italian Renaissance, where he discovered an unusually frigid spell that let him display his ice-skating skills on a frozen pond.

Celsius was apparently a bit more sober and studious than some of his fellow Scandinavians who were abroad for the first time. He wrote in his journal that other Swedes at his lodgings in Florence had behaved appallingly; even at this early stage of bourgeois travel, the sunnier lands were viewed as a place where northerners could behave with hedonistic excess. Celsius went on to Rome where, "after having been mistakenly suspected of trying to persuade a resident Swede in Rome who had converted to Catholicism to become a Lutheran again," wrote René Gothóni in *Pilgrims and Travellers in Search of the Holy,* Celsius "bought a dagger and locked himself in his room for a couple of days. After a while he overcame the panic. He brought quite a few Oriental manuscripts back to Uppsala from Rome, but it is also clear that he had no high opinion of Roman Catholicism."

Modern-day scholars like Gothóni and Löfgren used a 1909 Swedish language edition of Celsius's travelogue as their source, *Olof Celsius d. äs diarium öfver sin resa i Italien åren 1697 och 1698.* Both note that he never reached his destination of the Holy Land, probably because of the series of wars that disrupted Mediterranean travel in these years. According to Gothóni, he did visit the Adriatic coastal city of Loreto, where the Basilica della Santa Casa, or Shrine of the Holy House, was a popular pilgrimage site for Roman Catholics. The church supposedly housed the original home of Mary, the mother of Jesus, which according to fable had been brought by angels out of the Muslim-dominated Holy Land to safety in this part of northern Italy. In his accounts, Celsius "dismissed their expressions of devoutness in Santa Casa in the form of kneeling on the floor and kissing the images as outrageous proof of superstition," according to Gothóni.

Began Catalogue of Biblical Plants

After returning to Sweden, Celsius took up a teaching post at the University of Uppsala, eventually becoming a professor of theology and teaching Greek and other classical languages at the school. He also held the office of provost at Uppsala's famous cathedral. Over the years he became more interested in botany, which was likely the result of the University's unusual herbarium, or collection of dried plant specimens. The trove had been handed over to the University in the 1660s and had originally been seized as the spoils of one of Sweden's series of successful wars that century. At the time, Uppsala's most renowned scientist was Olof Rudbeck the Elder, a professor of medicine who founded the University's botanical garden in 1655, the first of its kind in Sweden. Botanical gardens were an offshoot of the ancient Greek and Roman gardens kept by physicians and other medical professionals as a source of therapeutic potions, salves, and other remedies.

But by the early 1700s Celsius's Uppsala was lagging behind other great centers of learning in Europe. During this period, Koerner wrote, "North Baltic universities were sleepy hamlets. They taught the rudiments of Lutheran orthodoxy to the future parsons and civil servants of the Swedish state, a Spartan war machine that was now, after the defeats of the Great Northern Wars (1700–1718), without purpose." The school's original botanical garden had been decimated by a terrible fire in 1702 that damaged many of the city's major landmarks, including the castle and cathedral. Olof Rudbeck the Younger took over supervision of the garden as the University of Uppsala's chair in medical botany, but he deputized Celsius to take over the duties of the job in order to work on another project, a massive dictionary with the working title *Thesaurus...harmonicus,* which would prove that the Hebrew language was the common tongue of many peoples, with links even to the indigenous Sami of northernmost Scandinavia and Russia.

Celsius was fascinated by the botanical garden and dreamed of his own magnum opus, which evolved into the *Hierobotanicon sive de plantis sacrae scripturae* of 1745–47. This was a compendium of all the plants mentioned in the Bible, and his effort was not the first scholarly attempt to sort out all the plants mentioned in the Bible and their modern names, but Celsius's proficiency in Greek and Latin aided his research immensely, and his work would be judged as the most complete to date. "As Celsius explained in the preface to his *Hierobotanicon,* his 'Biblical Botanica' had required the philological study of Arab, Greek, and Latin texts," noted Koerner. "It 'also demanded some knowledge of Botany in general, so that many years ago I felt called upon assiduously to hunt the plants and trees growing around the academy.'"

Sheltered a Young, Impoverished Linnaeus

Celsius was working on the *Hierobotanicon* when he first met a young Carl Linnaeus. Born into a devout Lutheran family with deep ties to the land, Linnaeus had planned to study medicine but had developed a deep interest in botany and plant collecting. He spent a year at the University of Lund before arriving in Uppsala in the summer of 1728, where a man he described in his autobiography as a "decent old graybeard," according to Koerner, found him wandering through the Uppsala botanic garden in the spring of the following year. The older professor was the 58-year-old Celsius, who was impressed by the young

man's interest in the plants of the garden and gave him an impromptu quiz. Linnaeus replied using terms devised by Joseph Pitton de Tournefort, a French scholar who died in 1708. Tournefort had first proposed a system of classification for plants that used the term *genus* to show a common set of characteristics between various examples of trees, shrubs, grasses, and flowers.

Celsius was impressed by Linnaeus's knowledge of the work of Tournefort and another highly regarded figure, English naturalist John Ray, who had died in 1705. Celsius invited Linnaeus to board at his home and paid Linnaeus to collect plants for *Hierobotanicon.* "To classify this material, Celsius used Tournefort's method," wrote Koerner, while "adding his own modifications and mixing in the systemics of Ray....He also surrounded this local flora with a biblical commentary—searching Sweden's conifer forests for clues to Sinai's desert shrubs."

Linnaeus was fascinated by the reproductive mysteries of plant life. Some scientists believed there was possibly a "male" and "female" component to plant biology, and Linnaeus came across the work of Sébastien Vaillant, a French botanist. In 1729 Linnaeus wrote a pamphlet summarizing Vaillant's research, titled *Praeludia sponsaliorum plantarum* (Preludes to the Betrothals of Plants). "This he gave on New Year's Day of 1730 to his patron, Olof Celsius, instead of the laudatory poem which was the customary gift on that day," wrote Koerner. "He also read it aloud in the Uppsala Science Society. It so impressed the professors in the audience that they appointed him to the post of curator of the University of Uppsala's botanic garden."

Aided New Era in Swedish Science

Celsius did much to further what would be a stellar career of his protégé Linnaeus. He recommended him to the Royal Swedish Academy of Sciences, which sent Linnaeus to the Arctic region to collect plants for the 1732 publication *Florula Lapponica* (Brief Lapland Flora), which became Linnaeus's first published book. In 1741 Linnaeus took over the directorship of the University's botanical garden. The younger Swede's efforts to improve its collection were chronicled in a 1748 work, *Hortus Upsaliensis,* and during this period he was also aiding Celsius in the completion of the *Hierobotanicon,* which was published between 1745 and 1747.

Celsius died on June 24, 1756, in Uppsala. His older brother Nils had died many years earlier, in 1724. Nils's son Anders Celsius, born in 1701, also went on to hold an esteemed position at the University of Uppsala, this one as an astronomer. The nephew's initial experiments with a centigrade thermometer—one in which 0 degrees on a scale represents the temperature that water freezes, while 100 degrees is the temperature that water boils—would later lead the international scientific community to formally name this the Celsius scale in 1948.

Celsius's own son, known as Olof Celsius the Younger, was born in 1716 and grew up to become the bishop of Lund. He wrote several works, including *The Ecclesiastical History of the Kingdom of Sweden* and biographies of the sixteenth-century kings Gustav I, also known as Gustavus Vasa, and Eric XIV.

Books

Gothóni, René, *Pilgrims and Travellers in Search of the Holy,* Peter Lang, 2010, pp. 62–63.

Koerner, Lisbet, *Linnaeus: Nature and Nation,* Harvard University Press, 1999, pp. 21, 34–35, 37, 38.

Löfgren, Orvar, *On Holiday: A History of Vacationing,* (Vol. 6, *California Studies in Critical Human Geography*), University of California Press, 1999, reprint, 2002, p. 158.□

Patrick Chamoiseau

The Martinican author Patrick Chamoiseau (born 1953) has become one of the most celebrated literary figures of the modern Caribbean region.

In Chamoiseau's work, fiction, theory, and autobiography came together to form an innovative whole. Chamoiseau was one of the young writers of the French-speaking Caribbean who, beginning in the late 1980s, promoted the idea of *créolité*—creoleness—as a cultural and artistic identity characteristic of the region. He has written large amounts of literary criticism and several volumes of autobiography. Chamoiseau's novels both delve into the culture of his native Martinique and experiment with language, mixing French and Antillean Creole, the language of the Martinican streets. The recipient of France's most prestigious literary award, the Prix Goncourt, Chamoiseau gained considerable popularity in the English-speaking world in spite of the considerable difficulty of translating his imaginative linguistic blends.

Heard Creole Language at Markets

Patrick Chamoiseau was born on March 12, 1953, in Fort-de-France, Martinique, which was and remains a part of France. His father, George Chamoiseau, was a postal worker, his mother was a cook. Much of the information about his life comes from his three volumes of autobiography, *Antan d'enfance* (Childhood of the past, translated as *Childhood,* 1990), Chemin d'école (School Road, translated as *School Days,* 1994), and *About d'enfance* (The End of Childhood, 2005). Chamoiseau grew up in a working class family, and he recalled soaking up the Creole language—a mixture of French, African, Native American, and other influences—while going to traditional street markets with his mother.

At school the situation was different: the use of Creole was forbidden. By using it among themselves, Chamoiseau and his classmates engaged in a kind of rebellion, and the language they grew up with was rebellious, quick, and filled with the frustrations of urban youth. At the same time, Chamoiseau did well enough in his French language classes to get into law school in Martinique, and he then went on to further studies in France. He earned a degree from the University of Sceaux in suburban Paris and was licensed to practice *droit privé* or judicial law. Back in Fort-de-France he found a post as a juvenile probation officer and continued to do that work during his stretch of celebrity.

Chamoiseau married, and he and his wife, Ghislaine, raised one son.

Chamoiseau's first novel, *Chronique des sept misès* (translated as *Chronicle of the Seven Sorrows,* 1999), was published in 1986. In both the English and French Caribbean, the use of local dialects had a history several decades long, but Chamoiseau immediately went past previous efforts. The novel told the story of Pipi Soleil, a wheelbarrow-pushing "djobber" (jobber or salesperson) in one of Fort-de-France's markets. As the novel depicts changes in Martinique and explores the stories of its various characters, the language shifts between classical French and Creole. It also features direct narration by the author himself, in the words of *New York Times* reviewer Alberto Manguel, "interweaving the voice of a marketplace storyteller with those of the scribes of France."

Used Detective Format to Comment on Culture

Chamoiseau followed that up in 1988 with *Solibo Magnfique* (translated as *Solibo Magnificent*). The central character of the book was a Creole storyteller who mysteriously begins to choke on his own words, falls silent while performing before a crowd in Fort-de-France, and then dies. The novel is framed as a sort of philosophico-linguistic murder mystery, with the French-speaking Martinican police trying to unravel the reasons for the storyteller's death. Among the suspects is Chamoiseau himself, appearing as a character in the novel. The rich language of *Solibo Magnifique* included coinages of new French words that pose problems for the novel's English translator.

These two novels got considerable critical attention in France as well as in Martinique, but it was in the field of literary theory that Chamoiseau began to make a major impact. In 1989 he joined with two other young Creole-speaking writers, Jean Bernabe and Raphael Confiant, to write the manifesto *Eloge de la créolité* (In Praise of Creoleness). In contrast to earlier African-descended writers, both in the Caribbean and beyond, who had tied the cultures of blacks in the Americas directly to their roots in Africa, Chamoiseau and his co-authors argued that the Creole artistic identity was distinctive. Chamoiseau and Confiant followed that essay up in 1991 with *Lettres créoles* (Creole Literature), a history of literature in Haiti, Guyana, Guadeloupe, and Martinique. Chamoiseau also edited a collection of Creole stories translated into English as *Creole Folktales* in 1994.

Chamoiseau remains perhaps best known for his novel *Texaco,* which appeared in 1991 and was published in English in 1996. The novel told much of the history of a small Martinican town, beginning in the early nineteenth century, through the words of a storyteller named Marie-Sophie Laborieux, who is convinced that the upcoming expansion of a Texaco oil refinery will mean the town's end: a character known as the Urban Planner has arrived to discuss the resettlement of the town's residents. Vast in scope, *Texaco* once again employed many layers of the French and Creole languages, mixing in historical description, poetry, song, and folktales. "A teeming jungle of a book," wrote *Publishers Weekly, Texaco* "brilliantly mixes historical events, Creole fables, snatches of poetry and satiric arias . . . into a polyphonous Caribbean epic."

Won Prix Goncourt

Texaco earned Chamoiseau the Prix Goncourt in 1992, catapulting him into the top rank of the French literary world, and sales of half a million copies of the novel were reported. The prize did not come without controversy—the Czech-French novelist Milan Kundera, a friend of Chamoiseau's, was accused of trying to influence the Goncourt jury by throwing a party at his house to which several jury members were invited. Kundera had also written a long, favorable review of the novel in the magazine *Lire* in advance of the jury's decision. Chamoiseau's defenders rejoined that the review had been written more than a year earlier, and that many observers felt Kundera's party would actually damage Chamoiseau's chances. In any event, the prize catapulted Chamoiseau to international recognition, and English translations of his work began to appear in the mid-1990s.

However, there seemed to be an impediment to Chamoiseau's general popularity: his works were devilishly difficult to translate. The relationship between Creole and French had analogues in English-speaking Caribbean countries, but the specific cultural references of Martinican Creole were difficult to render in English. The translation of *Texaco* by Rose-Myriam Rejouis and Val Vinokurov, who did not speak Caribbean English, earned some praise but was criticized by Paula Burnett of the London *Independent.* "If only a fluent Creole and Caribbean English speaker had translated it—a St. Lucian, for instance," she lamented. The language of St. Lucia poet Derek Walcott, Burnett argued, "shows what could have been done."

Nevertheless, English translations of other Chamoiseau writings began to appear, and Chamoiseau gained a strong readership in the United States. Kundera's essay was translated and published in the *New York Review of Books,* and Chamoiseau, a fluent English speaker who assisted in the translation of some of his writings, undertook a book tour of the East Coast to promote the English version of *Texaco,* during which he met the soon-to-be-successful Haitian-American writer Edwidge Danticat. "I have success as a writer but for the wrong reasons," Chamoiseau observed to *New York Times* writer Peter Watrous during that tour. "People go back for memories and souvenirs, which isn't what I want to accomplish by writing. Cultural identity is more complex than just a return to sources and roots. I want to show how complex the present cultural identity is."

Yet Chamoiseau remained a writer identified with the idea of cultural memory. Indeed, Maeve McCusker noted in her full-length study of Chamoiseau's work, *Patrick Chamoiseau: Recovering Memory,* that "Chamoiseau is one of the contemporary writers who exhibits the most explicit and far-reaching concern with memory, a term which permeates his writing and which looms large even in his titles." In the English-speaking world, general press citations of Chamoiseau's work declined sharply after about 2002, but scholarly investigation of his writings accelerated. Chamoiseau continued to write, issuing several small volumes in which he collaborated with photographers. He published a new novel, *Les sept consciences de Malfini* (The Seven Consciences of Malfini), in 2009.

Books

Contemporary Literary Criticism, volume 268, Gale, 2009.

McCusker, Maeve, *Patrick Chamoiseau: Recovering Memory,* Liverpool University Press, 2007.

Periodicals

Americas, July 1999.
Independent (London, England), March 8, 1997.
New York Times, May 27, 1997; March 23, 1998.
New York Times Book Review, January 16, 2000.
National Review, May 5, 1997.
Observer (London, England), February 28, 1999.
Publishers Weekly, December 9, 1996.
Seattle Post-Intelligencer, March 30, 1998.
Sunday Times (London, England), April 6, 1997.
Times (London, England), December 22, 1992.

Online

"Patrick Chamoiseau," *Contemporary Authors Online,* Detroit: Gale, 2005 (September 5, 2011).□

Ednah Dow Cheney

American author and reformer Ednah Dow Cheney (1824–1904) was one of the most active members of the reform movements centered in New England during the late 1900s.

American author and social reformer Ednah Dow Littlehale Cheney was one of the leading New England activists of the late nineteenth century. As part of her efforts supporting causes such as abolition, women's rights, and education, Cheney helped found several important institutions and organizations. These included the Boston School of Design for Women and the New England Hospital for Women and Children, of which she acted as both secretary and president. Cheney was also a popular public speaker and prolific writer who published essays, memoirs, and fictional works. Her best-known writing was a biography of Louisa May Alcott that stood as one of the most authoritative works on that author's life into the twenty-first century. Although little remembered today, Cheney commanded a great deal of respect during her lifetime and her work helped set the stage for the social advances of the twentieth century.

Early Life and Works

Born on June 27, 1824, in Boston, Massachusetts, Cheney was the third child of grocer Sargent Smith Littlehale and his wife, Ednah Parker (Dow) Littlehale. Cheney's family had deep roots in New England, although she readily admitted to lacking a particularly distinguished genealogy. Growing up in Boston, she attended local private schools, where she received a good education despite being a somewhat indifferent student; writing in *Reminiscences of Ednah Dow Cheney (born Littehale),* Cheney later recalled of one school that "I did not get the kind of intellectual training in thoroughness and accuracy that I needed.... I was in constant antagonism to constituted authority, which was a lesson not particularly needed." Yet these experiences helped shape her independent-minded spirit, as did her family's social views. Writing in *American National Biography Online,* Lawrence W. Snyder described Cheney's religious education as "unorthodox if not unusual for the times," with her father belonging to the reformist Universalist religious sect. The familial patriarch was also a supporter of voting rights for women and other liberal ideas of the day. This atmosphere surely contributed to Cheney's early interest in Transcendentalism, an intellectual movement that focused on the power of spiritual insight over reason and the unity of all creation.

The most important Transcendental influence in Cheney's early life was Boston feminist, journalist, and thinker Margaret Fuller. Because the laws of the day barred women from lecturing publically, Fuller began inviting intellectuals to her home for private discussions about issues and ideas. Through these meetings, Cheney first became acquainted with the ideas leading Transcendentalists such as Ralph Waldo Emerson and developed close friendships with members of the Transcendental movement including Fuller, James Freeman Clarke, and Elizabeth Palmer Peabody. Cheney worked as a nurse and tutor for the daughter of Unitarian preacher Theodore Parker, and in this way also became affiliated with that religious movement. These affiliations brought her into contact with numerous reform efforts and, later, made her a key member of the Free Religious Association.

In May of 1853, Cheney married a painter, Seth Wells Cheney. The newlyweds spent the summer visiting family and friends around New England before setting up their own household in Boston. By this time, Cheney had helped found the Boston School of Design for Women, and her husband occasionally served as an informal instructor for its students. The death of Seth Wells Cheney's mother that fall followed by the artist's own declining health the next spring cast a damper on the happiness of the household, however. The August after their marriage, the Cheneys traveled to Europe, where they visited England, Belgium, Switzerland, and France. In Paris, Cheney was greatly attracted to the works of French painter Jean-François Millet, and her husband enjoyed sketching and copying the works they saw. The winter of 1854–1855 proved a difficult one, however, with both Cheneys falling ill with various viruses and one of their traveling companions dying after contracting typhoid fever. Pregnant with the couple's child, Cheney returned with her husband to the United States in the early summer of 1855. The couple spent the summer in Manchester, New Hampshire, remaining there after Cheney gave birth to daughter Margaret Swan on September 8, 1855. Her husband's health remained poor; writing in *Memoir of Seth W. Cheney, Artist,* Cheney recalled him declaring, "When I was so ill before, I felt that I could not die, but now that I have every joy I could ask for in life, I feel that I can leave it," as he gazed at the infant. This statement proved prescient. Seth Wells Cheney succumbed to his poor health several months later, leaving his widow and daughter to return to Boston on their own in 1856. Cheney never remarried.

Became Social Reformer

The death of her husband marked the beginning of a new, higher level of involvement in social reform causes for the widow. During the late 1850s and indeed for much of her life Cheney was closely affiliated with the New England Hospital for Women and Children, a medical and educational facility which she helped found. She served for a time as the organization's secretary and, between 1887 and 1902, as its president. Like the Boston School of Design, the New England Hospital for Women and Children strove to provide women with career training and skills to help them succeed outside the home. "Although she supported the push for full political and economic rights of women," Snyder explained, "Cheney believed that such gains would be useless without the necessary educational and vocational experience to enjoy them." To this same end, Cheney was later one of the founders of Boston's Horticultural School for Women. Her daughter also helped open the doors of the city's Institute of Technology—now the Massachusetts Institute of Technology—to women before dying at the age of 22 from tuberculosis.

Through the last four decades of the nineteenth century, Cheney was involved with numerous other women's rights efforts. She was an active member of the New England Women's Club and an active supporter of voting rights for women. Cheney helped form the Massachusetts Women's School Suffrage Association and worked with the American Association for the Advancement of Women. This activism made Cheney a popular public speaker on issues ranging from dress reform to art and suffrage. She spoke at the State Agricultural Society, the Concord School of Philosophy, and—over the objections of some members of the faculty—became the first woman to lecture at Harvard's School of Divinity.

Cheney was also a fervent abolitionist who worked to support the transition of former African American slaves into free life after the close of the Civil War. She was a good friend of former slave and author Harriet Jacobs, who wrote the influential exposé *Incidents in the Life of a Slave Girl,* and knew the famed Underground Railroad conductor Harriet Tubman. Like most Americans of the era, Cheney followed the progress of the Civil War closely; she also served on a committee that provided packages of goods such as tobacco and cooking stoves to soldiers who did not receive them as part of their billet. Both before and after the conflict, Cheney took part in the activities of the New England Freedman's Aid Society, which bought the freedom of enslaved persons and, after emancipation, supported the efforts of the federal Freedmen's Bureau. Cheney was herself the secretary of that agency's Teachers' Commission during the Reconstruction era, and as a result of that role traveled throughout the South in 1869. There, she received a generally warm welcome because of her notoriety as the signatory on each teacher's certificate issued by the Freedmen's Bureau.

Published Biography of Louisa May Alcott

Along with her reform work, Cheney undertook a long and prolific career as a writer in the latter part of the nineteenth century. She published on a wide variety of topics ranging from variations on solitaire games to memoirs of her contemporaries to discussions of art. Cheney also dabbled in fiction with such works as *Sally Williams, The Mountain Girl* (1873) and *Nora's Return: A Sequel to The Doll's House* (1890). Published in 1889, Cheney's *Louisa May Alcott: Her Life, Letters and Journals* stands as her best-known and most important literary contribution. This first biography of the noted author of *Little Women* appeared soon after Alcott's death, and interspersed Cheney's prose with lengthy excerpts from Alcott's diaries and correspondence. In her introduction to the biography, Cheney argued, "Of no author can it be more truly said than of Louisa Alcott that her works are a revelation of herself. She rarely sought for the material of her stories in old chronicles, or foreign adventures. Her capital was her own life and experiences and those of others directly about her . . . It is therefore impossible to understand Miss Alcott's works fully without a knowledge of her own life and experiences." Later scholars largely agreed with this interpretation, and Cheney's biography has retained its value as not only a secondary source on the author's life, but also as a primary source for some of Alcott's otherwise lost personal writings.

By the beginning of the twentieth century, declining health had forced Cheney to give up most of her activities. The author's final major work, *Reminiscences of Ednah Dow Cheney (born Littlehale),* was published in 1902. This autobiography chronicled Cheney's long association with New England's intellectual and social reform movements

and, along with her biography of Alcott, became one of Cheney's few works to enjoy publication well after her death. Cheney died at her home in the Jamaica Plain neighborhood of Boston on November 19, 1904, at the age of 80. Her passage attracted notice in Boston, where Cheney commanded a great deal of respect and admiration from her intellectual peers. After her death, the New England Women's Club published a brief volume collecting the speeches given and tributes read at a special meeting memorializing Cheney that was held on February 20, 1905. According to this volume, Julia Howe praised Cheney for "her sound, temperate judgment and . . . the charm of her sympathetic presence," even as noted abolitionist William Lloyd Garrison hailed her "benevolence, culture, and unstudied social tact, genial, and radiating! A simple speech from her," Garrison continued, "impressed the hearer with a sense of her unusual quality and character, transcending mere brilliancy or accomplishments."

The social changes of the years following Cheney's death reflected the legacy of the efforts that she and her nineteenth-century contemporaries had made. Women at last won the right to vote nationally with the ratification of the Nineteenth Amendment to the U.S. Constitution in 1920, and African Americans gained important civil rights during the 1950s and 1960s. Later literary critics acknowledged the enduring qualities of Cheney's writings. In *American Women Writers: A Critical Reference Guide from Colonial Times to the Present,* Evelyn Shakir assessed Cheney's writing as "consistently lucid, unpretentious, and humane." Other scholars have noted Cheney's works' faults, however, with Snyder pointing out that her biographical sketches "lacked the critical edge of modern scholarship." Such changes in historical practice and preference have made most of Cheney's writings rarely read by the general public in the twenty-first century. Although the passing decades have left Cheney somewhat less well-known than some of her contemporaries, however, historians continue to recognize her importance as the epitome of a certain type of New England intellectual of the late nineteenth century and as a biographer and chronicler of that era.

Books

Bendow-Pfalzgraf, Taryn, ed., *American Women Writers: A Critical Reference Guide from Colonial Times to the Present,* St. James Press, 2000.

Cheney, Ednah D., *Louisa May Alcott: Her Life, Letters and Journals,* Roberts Brothers, 1892.

Cheney, Ednah D., *Memoir of Seth W. Cheney, Artist,* Lee and Shepard, 1881.

Cheney, Ednah D., *Reminiscences of Ednah Dow Cheney (born Littlehale),* Lee and Shepard, 2002.

Contemporary Authors, Gale, 2003.

New England Women's Club, *Ednah Dow Cheney, 1824–1904: Memorial Meeting,* New England Women's Club, 1905.

Online

"Cheney, Ednah Dow Littlehale," American National Biography Online, http://www.anb.org (November 20, 2011). □

Charlie Christian

The African-American jazz guitarist Charlie Christian (1916–1942) virtually invented the jazz vocabulary for the electric guitar and was a brilliant innovator who influenced players of many other instruments as well.

C hristian's career was tragically short, cut off by the tuberculosis that killed him in the spring of 1942. Yet his accomplishments over his barely two years of activity at the highest levels of the jazz world were ground-breaking. As a member of the Benny Goodman sextet, Christian took an instrument that had previously been used only in exotic forms of jazz and made it into a full-fledged solo vehicle. He was a member of the group of pioneering jazz musicians who gathered at Minton's jazz club in Harlem in the early 1940s, contributing to the harmonic and rhythmic experiments that divorced jazz solos from their harmonic and rhythmic underpinnings in popular song and laid the groundwork for bebop and all the many forms of modern jazz that descended from it. Christian's ability to innovate came from his absolute technical command of the language of jazz, and many of the observers who experienced his playing during his brief moment in the spotlight noticed that he seemed to arrive on the New York scene with his style having been fully formed in far-off Oklahoma City.

Made Guitar from Cigar Box

Charles Henry "Charlie" Christian was born in the small town of Bonham, in northeast Texas, on July 29, 1916. His family moved to Oklahoma City two years later. Christian's father, who was blind, his mother, and his older brothers all played music, and, despite their desperate poverty, managed to make a living doing so, performing on the streets or providing the accompaniment for silent movies. When Charlie was old enough, he joined them on the trumpet, his first instrument, on which he could play the classic blues of the day. In a shop class he made a guitar out of a cigar box, and soon he was given a real one. Sometimes the family would stroll through white neighborhoods in Oklahoma City, taking requests for songs or even classical compositions.

Christian's musical education deepened on several fronts during his teenage years. In the jazz clubs of Oklahoma City's Northeast Second Street, known as Deep Deuce, he heard the touring so-called territory bands of the Midwestern states and was especially impressed by saxophonist Lester Young, a bold soloist who seemed to stretch the possibilities of what a basic jazz tune might entail, both melodically and rhythmically. Attending high school at the Frederick Douglass School, where his classmate was novelist Ralph Ellison, Christian came under the influence of educator Zelia Breaux, who insisted on a rigorous music curriculum that included four years of harmony and music appreciation classes. She did not teach jazz, but neither did she discourage it, for she was involved in the operation of several Oklahoma City jazz venues.

By the mid-1930s Christian was ready to go on the road himself, joining the Alphonso Trent Band as a bassist and traveling around the upper Midwest. His travels brought him into contact with more musicians, and around 1937 he became fascinated by the electric guitar, an instrument that was then in its infancy. Texas country-swing musicians such as Leon McAuliffe and Bob Dunn had played an amplified steel guitar, and Christian met composer and arranger Eddie Durham, who taught him more about the instrument. Christian quickly developed a style that removed the guitar from its accompanimental roots, delivering clean, melodic solos that resembled and soon exceeded those of the usual solo instruments in the jazz band of the day.

Discovered by John Hammond

Word of Christian's talents began to spread, and one of the musicians who heard him was probably the pianist Mary Lou Williams. Whether through her or others, Christian came to the attention of the Columbia label's legendary talent scout, John Hammond, who stopped off in Oklahoma City on his way to a Los Angeles recording session in order to hear Christian play at the Ritz club. Hammond immediately contacted clarinetist Benny Goodman, the leader of perhaps the most successful big band of the time, to suggest that he audition Christian, who traveled to Los Angeles in August of 1939.

Goodman was not impressed by the young unknown, who showed up in a garish outfit and played an instrument that few jazz musicians were at all familiar with. He dismissed Christian after a brief audition, at which the guitarist was not even allowed to plug in his amplifier. But Hammond persisted, demanding that Christian be allowed on stage at Goodman's gig on the evening of August 16, 1939, at the Victor Hugo restaurant in Beverly Hills. The bandleader was finally won over when he called for "Rose

Room,'' a tune he thought Christian would not know, and Christian responded by engaging Goodman's fascinated musicians in a 47-minute improvisation.

That marked the beginning of a two-year Christian stint with the Benny Goodman Sextet. He also played occasionally with Goodman's larger swing orchestra, and he is thought to have originated some of Goodman's most famous pieces, including "Seven Come Eleven," "Solo Flight" (which Christian recorded with Goodman in 1941), and "A Smoo-o-o-th One." Goodman and his arranger Jimmy Mundy were often credited as co-writers on these compositions, however. Christian's recording career began in September of 1939 with a date involving an all-star band led by vibraphonist Lionel Hampton. His total recorded output is not large (it will fit on four compact discs), but nearly all of his recordings have been prized by jazz fans and collectors.

Influenced Future Jazz Guitarists

Christian's liquid, rhythmically flexible playing was unlike that of any other guitarist of the time, although it had clear roots in the music of Young and other wind players. Despite the inherently percussive nature of the guitar, Christian rarely played chords; his solos were primarily melodic. Jazz historian Mark Gridley, as quoted by Horace Porter in the *Antioch Review*, described Christian's style this way: "His long, swinging, single-note-at-a-time lines gave solo guitar the stature of a jazz horn. Some of his phrasing had the fluid swing and the freshness of tenor saxophonist Lester Young." Christian's own playing would influence that of other jazz guitarists for decades.

But Christian's influence extended beyond the sphere of the guitar. Driving himself at a furious pace, he often joined the jam sessions that had sprung up in 1940 at Minton's Playhouse, a jazz club on 118th Street in New York's Harlem neighborhood. These sessions began after Christian had finished his regular night's work with Goodman and stretched deep into the night. The house band at Minton's, which included trumpeter John Birks "Dizzy" Gillespie, saxophonist Charlie Parker, and pianist Thelonious Monk. This band was recognized as a crucible of what became the bebop jazz style, and Christian, with his exhaustive and harmonically sophisticated improvisations, is regarded as one of the style's key progenitors.

This brutal schedule eventually took its toll on Christian's health. Diagnosed in 1940 with tuberculosis, which may have had its genesis years earlier in the unhealthy conditions in which he grew up, Christian only intensified his activities in the first part of the following year. Abuse of alcohol and marijuana may have worsened his condition. By the end of a Midwestern tour in the summer of 1941 he was unable to continue and checked into Seaview Sanitarium on Staten Island. Despite reports of some improvement in his condition, he developed pneumonia and died there on March 2, 1942.

"It would be 25 years before jazz guitarists finally moved beyond Charlie Christian," wrote Scott Yanow on the *AllMusic* site. Christian's influence was fundamental in the work of guitarist Wes Montgomery, the instrument's foremost exponent in the 1960s, and even in the playing of jazz-funk guitarist George Benson. Critical appreciation

of Christian was fostered by his old classmate Ellison, whose 1958 essay "The Charlie Christian Story" (later reprinted in the collection *Shadow and Act*) was widely read and exemplified Ellison's conception of the richness that could flourish in African-American culture even in the midst of severe race-based repression. Christian's collected recordings were issued in 2002 by the Columbia Legacy label under the title *Charlie Christian: The Genius of the Electric Guitar.*

Books

Contemporary Musicians, volume 11, Gale, 1994.
Ellison, Ralph, *Shadow and Act,* Random House, 1964.
Goins, Wayne E., and Craig R. McKinney, *A Biography of Charlie Christian, Jazz Guitar's King of Swing,* Mellen, 2005.
Lyons, Len, and Don Perlo, *Jazz Portraits,* Quill, 1989.

Periodicals

Antioch Review, Summer 1999.
New York Times, October 20, 2002.

Online

"Charlie Christian," *AllMusic,* http://allmusic.com/artist/charlie-christian-p6276/biography (January 2, 2012).
"Charlie Christian Biography," *All About Jazz,* http://www.allaboutjazz.com/php/musician.php?id=5699 (January 2, 2012).
"Christian, Charles Henry," *Encyclopedia of Oklahoma History and Culture,* http://digital.library.okstate.edu/encyclopedia/entries/C/CH060.html (January 2, 2012). □

Manuel Chrysoloras

Byzantine scholar and diplomat Manuel Chrysoloras (c. 1349–1415) gave instruction in the Greek language to an eager generation of young scholars in Italy during the formative years of the Renaissance. A specialist in the teaching of ancient Greek, Chrysoloras lived in Florence for several years and amassed an impressive roster of students who went on to translate the forgotten texts of Greek antiquity. Those works were an integral part of the development of humanism, a philosophical reawakening during the Italian Renaissance that helped reverse centuries of religious-based skepticism and led, in the end, to the Protestant Reformation in Europe and then the Enlightenment.

Almost nothing is known about the early life of Manuel Chrysoloras, save for a few facts: he came from the Greek-heritage aristocracy in Constantinople, was probably born around 1349, and by the 1380s was renowned as a scholar and teacher of ancient Greek to students in Constantinople. He also shared a first name with a friend who went on to become the Byzantine emperor in

1391, Manuel II Palaiologus. Byzantium's new ruler was descended from a murderous royal house whose internecine battles for power helped weaken the empire in the East, which was the successor state to a province of the old Roman Empire.

The two realms had been divided into east and west since 395 CE, and as Rome lessened its grip over Europe and the Mediterranean regions, a series of Greek rulers in Constantinople rose to power as new imperial actors. East and west were further divided over doctrinal issues, which forced the establishment of two separate Christian churches, the Eastern Orthodox rite and its Latin—later called Roman Catholic—counterpart. In time, Byzantium itself fell into a period of decline. The Crusades had destabilized the region, bringing armies of mercenary soldiers from Western Europe through Byzantium on their mission to retake Jerusalem from Muslim rule. By Chrysoloras's lifetime, the Greeks' centuries-long dominance over southeastern Europe, Eurasia, and swaths of the Middle East was in an abrupt freefall.

Sent to Italy as Envoy

In 1391 Manuel II made Chrysoloras his envoy and sent him to the wealthy city-state of Venice to ask its doge-rulers for military aid in Byzantium's war with the Turks, a Muslim people who were rising to power under their new Ottoman dynasty. An expanding Ottoman empire represented a threat to the Venetians, too, who were enthusiastic mariners and had come to dominate the commerce between Europe and Asia. But relations between Venice and Constantinople had deteriorated considerably after a wave of Crusaders massacred Venetian merchants in the city in 1182.

Chrysoloras traveled to Venice in the company of Demetrius Kydones, a senior minister for several Palaiologus emperors who was best known for embracing the Latin rite and urging his Byzantine masters to reunite with Rome in order to combat the threat of Islam. Kydones was moderately well known in the West for these efforts, and was a rare figure of the era who was fluent in both his native Greek and in Latin, which he had taught himself on his path to conversion from the Orthodox rite. Latin was the language of the Roman church and of the entire scholarly world of Western Europe at the time; the classical language of ancient Rome had a codified grammar and instruction process, plus a wealth of literary output from the Roman Empire's peak cultural era. Classical Greek, by contrast, was taught only in the elite schools of Constantinople, which had become the center of Greek scholarship and learning several centuries earlier.

Visited by Florentine Scholars

News of the presence of Kydones and Chrysoloras in Venice reached Florence, one of northern Italy's powerful city-states. A pair of Florentine scholars determined to master the Greek language decided to travel to Venice to meet the envoys and plead their case. These were Roberto de' Rossi and Jacopo Angeli da Scarperia, who were both part of a circle of intellectuals in Florence devoted to humanism and the teachings of Petrarch, an Italian writer who died in 1374. Petrarch had written exultantly about the bygone civilizations of ancient Greece and Rome, and asserted that Europe had descended into a "dark age" since the fall of Rome in the sixth century. Petrarch urged scholars to turn to the texts of Cicero, Plato, and other political philosophers from the classical era, whose ideas had helped shape more advanced societies. The ancient Greeks, for example, enshrined the idea of a *demokratia*, or "rule by the common people," as preferable to an *aristokratia*, the term for "rule by the elite." Those Greek texts—along with plays, poetry, and other literary efforts—remained impenetrable to late medieval-era scholars in Florence and elsewhere because the Greek language was virtually unknown in Italy and the rest of Western Europe by Chrysoloras's lifetime. There were a few isolated pockets of centuries-old Greek settlements in southern Italy, but classical Greek had not been formally taught in Italy for 700 years.

Rossi and Angeli were closely associated with the wealthy, powerful, and progressive-minded chancellor of Florence, Coluccio Salutati. An ardent humanist, Salutati held firm against attempts by Rome to dominate the debate over the worthiness of classical philosophy, which the Church deemed pagan in origin and therefore inconsequential. Rossi and Angeli were among the Florentine humanists who were desperate to master Greek in order to delve into the writings of Plato, Socrates, Homer, and other legendary writers of Greek antiquity. They came to Venice to learn Greek from Kydones and Chrysoloras, and ask them to consider setting up a language academy in Italy. Rossi was tutored by Chrysoloras and returned to Florence with high praise for Chrysoloras's teaching methods.

Moved to Florence

In 1395 Angeli traveled to Constantinople to persuade Chrysoloras to return to Florence as an instructor in ancient Greek. The influential Salutati had arranged for an appealingly generous salary of 150 gold florins, and Chrysoloras agreed.

He arrived in Tuscany in February of 1397 after a four-month journey from Constantinople. His salary would later be raised to a final amount of 250 gold florins, an enormous sum.

Chrysoloras proved a particularly adept language instructor. He formulated several key concepts of Greek grammar and translation methods, which became part of the standard course for instruction in classical Greek for decades to follow in Western Europe. His students in Florence went on to prominent careers as translators, among them Angeli and Rossi along with Pier Paolo Vergerio, a canon lawyer and writer who translated Greek texts and wrote plays, and Leonardo Bruni, an important writer who pieced together the origins of the Florentine Republic and is sometimes described as the modern world's first historian. "These men not only set the cultural tone of their own city but were able eventually to make their influence felt all over Italy," wrote Ian Thomson in a 1966 article on Chrysoloras that originally appeared in the journal *Greek, Roman, and Byzantine Studies* and was reprinted in the book *Renaissance Thought: A Reader*. Before Chrysoloras, Thomson continued, "scholars paid lip service to Greek as an interesting and harmless bagatelle, but the majority of professors and students were simply not interested or were actively averse."

Chrysoloras's grammar exercises, in a catechism or question-and-answer format, was called the *Erotemata* and was still being used as late as the 1580s. A 1471 edition, created in Venice by a new invention from Germany, was the first Greek-language book ever printed by a printing press. Two important northern European scholars, Thomas Linacre and Desiderius Erasmus, used the *Erotemata* to teach successive generations of students of antiquity. Linacre was one of England's first professors of Greek at Oxford University, and Erasmus, more commonly known as Erasmus of Rotterdam, was a leading figure in Renaissance humanism, authoring several important works on philosophy that helped lay the foundation for the Protestant Reformation.

Curious Link to Christopher Columbus

In March of 1400, Chrysoloras went to Pavia to teach at the court of Giangaleazzo Visconti, the Duke of Milan. From there he journeyed to Milan itself and met up with the Emperor Manuel II, who had come West looking for financial support to rescue Byzantium from Muslim invaders. Chrysoloras stayed in Lombardy teaching while Manuel II went all the way to England to request military help in defeating the Turkish threat. On the return leg of Manuel's journey Chrysoloras accompanied the emperor back to Constantinople. Chrysoloras established his own school there, aided by his nephew John Chrysoloras. One of his most devoted students was Guarino da Verona, thought to be one of the first Italians of note to visit Constantinople in order to study ancient Greek. Chrysoloras's nephew probably taught Guarino, who went on to a notable career at the University of Ferrara. It was Guarino who translated a 17-volume work on geography written in the first century CE by the Greek writer Strabo. The Latin version of Strabo's text, available in Italy in the 1450s, was cited by the son of Christopher Columbus as having provided the explorer with the idea of reaching India by sailing west from the Iberian peninsula.

Chrysoloras spent the last decade of his life as an envoy. He returned to Venice in 1404 and again in 1406 as Byzantium's chief diplomat to the Latin West, and at some point followed Kydones's lead and converted to Roman Catholicism. A letter Chrysoloras wrote to Pope Innocent VII in 1405 requested permission for ordination as a priest and to celebrate the Latin rite in the Greek language. Nothing seems to have come of either proposal, though he did leave behind a translation of the Latin Mass into Greek. He served as Manuel II's emissary to the courts of northern Europe in 1408, meeting with heads of state in France, England, and Spain. Through Bruni, his former student, he was connected to Pope Gregory XII, for Bruni was papal secretary during a turbulent period in a long-running saga known as the Western Schism. Chrysoloras allied with the pope in Rome, not the rival pope then living in the southern French city of Avignon, and as an envoy worked to secure the cooperation of several European leaders to summon a new council to resolve the Schism. This became the Council of Constance, held in Konstanz, Germany, on the picturesque Lake Bodensee in 1414.

Died in Baden-Württemberg

Chrysoloras lived in Bologna in 1410, where the papal court was briefly situated, and returned with it to Rome in 1411. He penned some notable letters that compared the "old" Rome with its "new" counterpart in Byzantium, which had been established as a new imperial capital for the old Roman Empire in its waning days more than a millennium earlier. His *Epistolae tres de comparatione veteris et novae Romae* (Three Letters Comparing Ancient and Modern Rome) was widely distributed by Guarino da Varona, likely in a dual bid to pay tribute to Chrysoloras and advance the cause for better diplomatic ties between East and West.

Chrysoloras traveled to Konstanz with the papal entourage, but fell ill from a fever and died either in the city or its outskirts on April 15, 1414. The Council of Constance lasted until 1418 and finally resolved the Western Schism. Unfortunately Chrysoloras's original intent in traveling to Italy back in 1391—to build a firmer alliance between Italy and Constantinople on behalf of Manuel II—failed to materialize. In 1453, Ottoman forces "overran Constantinople" and demolished its dominance as a center of Greek scholarship, wrote Michael D. Reeve in the *English Historical Review*, "but Chrysoloras taught Greek to such effect that when it lost the East it was well on the way to conquering the West."

Books

Ciccolella, Federica, *Donati Graeci: Learning Greek in the Renaissance*, Koninklijke Brill NV, 2008.

"Manuel Chrysoloras," in *Encyclopedia of the Renaissance*, edited by Paul F. Grendler, Charles Scribner's Sons, 2000.

Thomson, Ian, "Manuel Chrysoloras and the Early Italian Renaissance," in *Renaissance Thought: A Reader*, edited by Robert Black, Routledge, 2001, pp. 97, 98, 99. Essay originally published in *Greek, Roman, and Byzantine Studies*: 7 (1966).

Periodicals

English Historical Review, February 1996.□

Steven Chu

The American scientist Steven Chu (born 1948) won the Nobel Prize for Physics in 1997 for his work on the measurement and manipulation of atomic particles. He came to the public eye as Secretary of Energy in the administration of United States president Barack Obama.

Those were only two of the inexhaustibly curious Chu's scientific accomplishments. He made several breakthroughs in the field of atomic physics, including a demonstration of the first atomic fountain, a laser-impelled shower of atoms. After he won the Nobel Prize, Chu applied the techniques he had developed to the field of biophysics, finding new ways to manipulate DNA molecules and using atomic-based microscopy to study living molecules. Disturbed by the problem of climate change, Chu switched to energy research and was named director of the Lawrence Berkeley National Laboratory in 2004. As Energy Secretary he spearheaded new initiatives designed to lead the United States toward energy independence but also faced scrutiny due to the failure of the Solyndra firm, a solar cell parts manufacturer that Chu's department had backed with loan guarantees.

Strong Familial Education Emphasis

Steven Chu was born in St. Louis, Missouri, on February 28, 1948. His parents had both come to the United States in the 1940s to pursue university educations and decided to stay on as conditions in China worsened. They settled in the New York City suburb of Garden City, New York, where there were only two other Chinese families. But the community had a strong public school system, and, Chu wrote in an autobiographical essay appearing on the Nobel Prize website, "Education in my family was not merely emphasized, it was our raison d'être." Almost all of Chu's aunts and uncles had advanced degrees—more than one in several cases.

Chu, in fact, termed himself the black sheep of the family because, although he managed an A average in high school, he performed less well than his older brother, who had the highest grade point average in the school's history. Chu preferred becoming absorbed in a specific project to broad-based studying, and the teacher who inspired him most, physics instructor Thomas Miner, was one who focused on general problem-solving rather than the recitation of facts. Chu and his friends enjoyed building model airplanes and rockets, and they turned their enthusiasm for chemistry into a neighborhood business that tested lawns for acidity and nutrient balance.

With his solid but unspectacular grades, Chu was rejected by Ivy League schools but was admitted to the University of Rochester. He declared a double major in mathematics and physics but was drawn to the latter by a teacher who used *The Feynman Lectures in Physics,* a collection of talks by famed theoretical physicist Richard Feynman, as a textbook. Chu was admitted to several top graduate schools and enrolled at the University of California

at Berkeley in 1970. At first drawn to theoretical physics himself, he devised an experiment to measure the tuning of musical instruments that convinced both him and his instructors that he was better suited to experimental physics. Chu earned a PhD from Berkeley in 1976 and stayed on for a postdoctoral fellowship in 1977 and 1978.

Worked at Bell Labs

At that point, anxious for new perspectives, Chu took a job as a researcher at AT&T Bell Laboratories, where he was told he had complete carte blanche to explore any field of research he wished. Then, however, he was informed that the shareholders of the telephone monopoly would frown on expensive pure physics research without practical results. "This was a devastating experience for me," Chu recalled (according to Paul Livingston of *R&D* magazine, which named Chu its scientist of the year in 2011). "On the one hand you have someone telling me to do whatever I wanted to do. On the other hand, I'm told not to do what I've been doing." Chu made the best of this situation, however, exploring common interests with other researchers in search of new projects.

One of those researchers was physicist Allen Mills, an expert in laser measurements, and Chu's work with Mills put him on the path that led him to the Nobel Prize. The pair began to work on using lasers to measure the behavior of subatomic particles, and after he moved to another Bell Labs facility in Holmdel, New Jersey, in 1983, he began another fruitful collaboration, this one with researcher Art Ashkin. Ashkin had suggested that lasers, dubbed optical tweezers, could be used to trap atomic particles but had had little success. "The conventional wisdom at that time was first you hold the atom with [laser] light and then you make it cold so you can do what you want with it," Chu was quoted as saying by Livingston. "My idea was to reverse this by cooling the atom first, then grabbing it with light."

Taking a job as professor of physics at Stanford University, Chu continued his work with laser manipulations in particle physics. He scored several breakthroughs, including the development of the first atomic fountain. The work for which he received the Nobel Prize involved his design for a so-called atomic box that trapped atomic particles with a configuration of three pairs of laser beams. This resulted in the slowing of atoms in the box to a speed of about 30 centimeters per second (glacial for an atom) and in a temperature of 240 millionths of a degree above absolute zero. Further developments of the experiment generated a unique form of matter called a Bose-Einstein condensate, which had been theoretically predicted by Albert Einstein and Indian physicist Satyendra Nath Bose in the 1920s, though never actually realized.

Won Nobel Prize

Chu received the 1997 Nobel Prize for this research, sharing it with two other researchers, the American William D. Phillips and France's Claude Cohen-Tannoudji, who had achieved related results. About 30 of the students in his Stanford labs have become professors themselves. By the time he won the award, Chu had already changed the focus of his research interests, delving into polymer physics and biology. He began to use the optical tweezers to try to examine individual DNA molecules, the building blocks of life. "By 1990," he wrote in his Nobel Prize essay, "we could see an image of a single, fluorescently labeled DNA molecule in real time as we stretched it out in water. My students improved upon our first attempts after they discovered our initial protocol demanded luck as a major ingredient. Using our new ability to simultaneously visualize and manipulate individual molecules of DNA, my group began to answer polymer dynamics questions that have persisted for decades."

In the early 2000s, Chu changed direction once again. His motivation was his increasing alarm over the problem of anthropogenic (human-caused) climate change. In 2004 Chu became director of the United States Department of Energy's Lawrence Berkeley National Laboratory, a facility devoted to energy research. "I did so because, in spite of the magnitude of the problem, I remain optimistic that science can offer us better choices than we can imagine today," he was quoted as saying in a 2009 *Times* article. Overseeing an annual budget of more than half a billion dollars, Chu was the first American of Asian descent named to head a United States national laboratory. He replaced Charles Shank, who had been his supervisor at Bell Labs from 1983 to 1987.

Chu's work at Lawrence Berkeley led directly to his appointment as Secretary of Energy when Barack Obama assumed the U.S. presidency in January of 2009. He was the first Nobel Prize winner and the first physicist to hold the post. As energy secretary, Chu has emphasized the idea that energy research is essential to U.S. economic competitiveness. While underscoring the role of private investment, Chu and his Energy Department provided financing and loan guarantees to small projects, such as a $20 million grant in 2010 to finance research and development at seven geothermal-energy facilities around the country.

One of those loan guarantees became the focus of controversy and U.S. congressional investigations after the company involved, solar panel parts maker Solyndra, went bankrupt after receiving a loan guarantee of $535 million. Chu was questioned by congressional committees about oversight on the project and about whether poltics were involved in the process; one of Solyndra's major backers was Oklahoma oil magnate George Kaiser, a major Obama campaign contributor. Chu stoutly defended his role, maintaining that he had been unaware of some decisions made by his staff and telling U.S. Representative Fred Upton (as quoted by Amy Harder of *NationalJournal.com*), "It is extremely unfortunate what has happened with Solyndra, but if you go back and look at the time the decision was being made, [and ask] was there incompetence, was there any influence of a political nature, . . . I would have to say no." Congressional investigations continued as of early 2012.

In addition to his Nobel Prize, Chu has received numerous other awards, including the Broida Prize for Laser Spectroscopy of the American Physical Society (1987), the King Faisal International Prize for Science (1993), and the William F. Meggers Award for Spectroscopy of the Optical Society of America (1994). He is married to Jean Chu, an Oxford-trained physicist who has served as Dean of Admissions at Stanford; he also has two sons, Geoffrey and Michael, by a previous marriage. In Taiwan, Chu has been reported to have attained a level of celebrity exceeded only by that of actor Leonardo DiCaprio. He has remained active as a scientist despite his top-level governmental post, publishing several papers during his tenure as energy secretary.

Books

World of Invention, Gale, 2006.

Periodicals

Discover, January-February 2011.

Public Utilities Fortnightly, November 2010.

Nationaljournal.com, November 16, 2011; November 17, 2011.

R & D, December 2011.

San Francisco Chronicle, June 18, 2004.

San Jose Mercury News, April 5, 2010.

Times (London, England), May 26, 2009.

Online

"Secretary of Energy Dr. Steven Chu," *United States Department of Energy,* http://energy.gov/contributors/secretary-energy-dr-steven-chu (January 14, 2012).

"Steven Chu," *The Nobel Prize in Physics 1997,* http://www.nobelprize.org/nobel_prizes/physics/laureates/1997/chu.html (January 14, 2012).

"Steven Chu," *Stanford University,* http://www.stanford.edu/dept/physics/people/faculty/chu_steven.html (January 14, 2012). □

Frances Folsom Cleveland

In 1886 Frances Folsom Cleveland (1864–1947) became the youngest woman to assume the duties of First Lady in U.S. presidential history. The new bride of President Grover Cleveland was just 21 years old when she moved into the White House, and her youth and natural charm turned her into a celebrity overnight. She handled the incessant press frenzy with characteristic grace, even when her husband lost his 1888 reelection bid, and returned to the White House four years later when he won the 1892 contest.

Frances Clara Folsom was named "Frank Clara" after an uncle, shortly after her birth on July 21, 1864, in Buffalo, New York. Years later, she would legally change her name to "Frances" but family and friends called her "Frank" in private, and the media dubbed her "Frankie" after she became First Lady, a nickname she was said to loathe. Her mother, Emma Harmon Folsom, came from a prominent New York State family with a town named after them, while her father's Folsom ancestors were among the founding families of Exeter, New Hampshire.

Lost Father to Accident

Cleveland's future husband was the law partner of her father, Oscar. An oft-repeated story notes that Grover Cleveland purchased a pram as a gift for her when she was born. He was close to the family and would become even more so when Oscar died after a carriage accident on July 23, 1875. Cleveland had just celebrated her eleventh birthday at the time and was visiting her mother's relatives in Medina, New York, when the tragedy occurred.

Oscar Folsom left no will but sizable assets, and Grover Cleveland was appointed administrator of the estate and guarded the widow and daughter's financial affairs with the same scrupulousness that had prompted friends in Buffalo to urge him to run for public office. He served first as sheriff of Erie County and then spent ten months as mayor of Buffalo before being elected governor of New York in 1882.

Proposal from President

Cleveland attended a co-ed academy in Medina and graduated from Buffalo's Central High School in 1882. At Wells College in Aurora, New York, she studied foreign languages and music and graduated a year early, in 1885. Two months later, the man who had been her unofficial guardian since her father's death wrote her a letter that included his marriage proposal. His interest in Cleveland, who had grown into an attractive, accomplished, and serene young woman, had not surprised those inside their circle of friends and family, and the politician had once again comported himself blamelessly, asking permission from Emma Folsom to write to her when she was in college.

Grover Cleveland was a 49-year-old bachelor, and president of the United States, when he proposed. He had beaten Maine Republican James G. Blaine in the 1884 presidential election, and there was tremendous public interest in his personal life and the potential that he would marry while in the White House. During the election his Republican foes had resurrected the curious case of a child born in Buffalo in September of 1874 to a widowed department store clerk named Maria Halpin. The child was likely the result of Halpin's relations with Oscar Folsom, though there were other Buffalo men in their circle who had dallied with her, but Grover Cleveland accepted paternity when she filed a child-support lawsuit, simply because he was the only unmarried one among the friends. The notoriety prompted Halpin's life to further spiral out of control, and she drank heavily. When it became obvious she was unable to care for the boy, Grover Cleveland arranged for him to be adopted. His Republican foes would continually resurrect the story for decades, though it is unclear whether Oscar Folsom (who died ten months after the boy's birth) or the future president was actually the biological parent.

Hounded by Press

Cleveland and her mother had visited their longtime friend at the White House during his first weeks in office in the spring of 1885. That event prompted a flurry of speculation that President Cleveland would marry the widow of his late law partner. After Cleveland accepted his marriage proposal—which she also did by letter—she and her mother spent several months in Europe with one of her male cousins. When they returned in May of 1886 the press were eager to uncover any evidence of a possible marriage for the president, and the Folsom party eluded journalists with the help of a U.S. Customs tugboat that ferried them from the ocean liner to a less obvious spot in New York's harbor. Cleveland and her mother were staying at the Gilsey House Hotel on May 28 when the White House announced President Cleveland's engagement to Frank Folsom, and the press seized upon all available details about "Frankie," whom they also dubbed "Yum-Yum" after a character in *The Mikado,* a popular new opera from Gilbert & Sullivan.

The pair were married on June 2, 1886, in a 7 p.m. ceremony held in the Blue Room of the White House. He was 49, and she was a few weeks away from her 22nd birthday. John Philip Sousa and the Marine Band played, and Cleveland wore an ivory satin gown with a 15-foot train. They immediately set off by private train for a picturesque mountain resort, Deer Park, in western Maryland. The press followed them there and harassed them constantly, which prompted them to return to the White House. The president even sent a letter to the *New York Evening Post* in which he rebuked journalists and their employers' "colossal impertinence" in what he viewed as an invasion of privacy, reported historian Carl Sferrazza Anthony in *First Ladies: The Saga of the Presidents' Wives and Their Power.* The editors of the *Washington Post* responded with an uncannily enduring defense, asserting that "privacy about a private matter does not suit the American people who, since the advent of modern journalism, have no private matters."

Prior to the marriage, the duties of First Lady at the Cleveland White House had been handled by the president's sister, Rose Elizabeth "Libbie" Cleveland, a teacher and literary essayist. "My new sister is a woman capable of great development; a much stronger character than appears on the surface," the rather formidable Rose told the press, according to Alyn Brodsky's biography of the president, *Grover Cleveland: A Study in Character.* "She is a superior person."

"Frankie" Covers Sold Magazines

Cleveland's youth and newlywed status incited intense public interest that was stoked by constant media scrutiny. Her personal style was endlessly analyzed, and her hairstyle—a low bun, with a shaved neck in the back, to make the bun stand out more dramatically—was dubbed "à la Cleveland" and widely copied. "Although she had not granted her consent, Mrs. Cleveland's image began to appear on a mind-boggling array of products from liver pills to women's undergarments," according to *New York Times* journalist Ginia Bellafante. "Her preference for shoulder-baring clothes managed to arouse the ire of the Woman's Christian Temperance Union, which petitioned her to dress more conservatively, saying that her style posed a threat to the chastity of young American women."

Cleveland refused to bow to such pressure. She also stood firm on another matter: the new twice-weekly receptions she introduced at the White House. Though her husband had initially been worried about her inexperience in such a high-pressure role, once he witnessed her adeptness at meeting and greeting the crowds that streamed through at her first event, he exuberantly said to an aide, "She'll do! She'll do!," according to *First Ladies.* Cleveland had added a Saturday afternoon reception event, which meant that young working women of the city could attend, for it was their only time off (Sunday worship strictures remained in place; even Cleveland reportedly refused to let the president out of the White House to go fishing on the Sabbath). Washington society doyennes and protocol advisors disdained the weekend crowds as "a great rabble of shop-girls. And of course a White House afternoon is not intended for them," Cleveland was told, according to Brodsky's biography. At that, she declared the schedule was to remain in place, "so long as there were any store clerks, or other self-supporting women and girls who wished to come to the White House."

Democrats Recognized Her Campaign Appeal

Cleveland's popularity made her a target for her husband's political enemies. The issue of the Halpin son in Buffalo was regularly resurrected, and more scurrilous rumor-mongers circulated unsubstantiated claims that he was physically abusive to his young bride. In reality the pair had an obvious mutual affection and bond, despite the age difference. At the 1888 Democratic National Convention her name was brought up in one of the speeches, marking the first time a First Lady was mentioned at a nominating event. The speaker earned thunderous applause, and some regional campaign managers ordered banners and other election material with her image, without her husband's permission. It was a brutal contest, with Republican supporters even spreading rumors of her infidelity. But there were much deeper economic issues at stake that election year, and Cleveland's husband became one of just a handful of incumbent presidents to lose his bid to remain in the White House.

When Grover Cleveland won his first term back in 1884, he had been the first Democrat in the White House since Andrew Johnson, and the first elected Democrat since James Buchanan in 1856. He lost to an Indiana Republican, Benjamin Harrison, and Cleveland was dejected at the result. On March 4, 1889, the day of Harrison's inauguration, as she supervised the last of the couple's personal possessions being packed up, she told White House staffer Jerry Smith, "I want you to take good care of all the furniture and ornaments in the house for I want to find everything just as it is now when we come back again," according to *First Ladies,* adding, "We are coming back just four years from today."

Cleveland and her husband moved to New York City and settled into a Fifth Avenue hotel, later acquiring a house at 816 Madison Avenue. Cleveland delivered the first of their five children, a daughter named Ruth, at home on October 3, 1891. The new father made another run for the White House in 1892, and won by a large margin. The Clevelands became the first—and only—presidential family to move into the White House on two separate occasions.

Throngs Came to White House

Cleveland was pregnant with her second child on Inauguration Day of 1893, and her daughter Esther was born inside the White House on September 9, 1893, another first for the presidential residence. The young daughters were the focus of even more prying media interest, though the president refused to let them be photographed, and Cleveland was forced to have the gates to the White House shut permanently when a crowd of curiosity seekers excitedly swarmed around Ruth in her carriage when she was out with a nursemaid, who was unable to prevent the crowd from picking up the infant and excitedly passing her around. The family, which grew to include a third daughter, Marion, born at the Cleveland summer home in Buzzards Bay, Massachusetts, in 1895, preferred to spend a solid portion of the year either at the seashore or at a country house the president rented in a suburban part of Washington that would later become known as Cleveland Park. Two sons followed, after Cleveland's husband finished his second term in office: Richard, born in 1897, and Francis in 1903. The Cleveland children were not immune to the deadly outbreaks of childhood infectious diseases in the pre-vaccination era: twelve-year-old Ruth died of diphtheria on January 7, 1904.

The Clevelands settled in Princeton, New Jersey, after moving out of the White House a second time in 1897. Grover Cleveland died on June 24, 1908, at the age of 71. Five years later Cleveland remarried, to a Princeton University archaeology professor named Thomas Jex Preston. She was the first widowed First Lady ever to remarry, and remained so until Jacqueline Kennedy married Greek shipping tycoon Aristotle Onassis in 1968. Cleveland lived well into the twentieth century, spending her final years at the home of her son Richard in Baltimore, where she died on October 29, 1947. In addition to being the only First Lady to deliver a child inside the White House, Cleveland remains the only bride ever to marry a sitting president at that historic residence.

Books

Angelo, Bonnie, *First Families: The Impact of the White House on Their Lives,* William Morrow, 2005.

Anthony, Carl Sferrazza, *America's First Families: An Inside View of 200 Years of Private Life in the White House,* Simon & Schuster, 2000.

Anthony, Carl Sferrazza, *First Ladies: The Saga of the Presidents' Wives and Their Power,* William Morrow, 1990.

Brodsky, Alyn, *Grover Cleveland: A Study in Character,* Macmillan, 2000.

Dunlap, Annette, *Frank: The Story of Frances Folsom Cleveland, America's Youngest First Lady,* SUNY Press, 2009.

Periodicals

New York Times, December 25, 1887; August 3, 2004.

Online

"Frances Folsom Cleveland," The White House, http://www.whitehouse.gov/about/first-ladies/francescleveland-0 (October 13, 2011). ☐

Leonard Cohen

Canadian singer, songwriter, and poet Leonard Cohen (born 1934) was one of the most respected and influential musical artists of the mid-twentieth century among his peers.

Canadian singer-songwriter Leonard Cohen has garnered numerous critical accolades for his broody, lyrical folk rock over the course of his lengthy career. After beginning his career as a poet and novelist in the late 1950s, Cohen shifted fields to become a songwriter and recording artist, releasing his debut album in late 1967 at the age of 33. Despite this late start, he quickly became one of the era's most influential—if not its best-known or most commercially successful—artists. Often compared to Bob Dylan, Cohen drew on his literary experience to write songs that probed the emotional depths of love, loss, religion, and modern life. Recording new material well into his golden years, Cohen continued to command critical respect in the twenty-first century, receiving a Grammy Lifetime Award in 2010 and winning induction in the Rock and Roll Hall of Fame in 2008.

The second child of Nathan Cohen and his wife Masha (Klinitsky) Cohen, the songwriter was born on September 21, 1934, in Montreal, Quebec, Canada. The family was well-off thanks to its ownership of a successful clothing manufacturing concern, but Nathan Cohen was frequently depressed and somewhat detached from his children. Nevertheless, his death greatly affected his son, who was just nine years old at the time of his father's passing. Writing in *Leonard Cohen,* David Sheppard described the event as leaving "a psychological scar that was to influence and characterize much of the writer's nascent outpourings." In what has been considered a gesture emblematic of Cohen's melancholic artistry, after his father's funeral, the young boy wrote a few poetic lines, wrapped them in the deceased man's bow tie, and buried them in the family's back garden. Indeed, the theme of loss proved to be a recurring one in Cohen's work, often noted for its depressing lyrics and dark sound.

Growing up, Cohen showed early affinities for both music and writing. He learned to play the piano and clarinet at a young age, and developed an interest in literature while attending Westmount High School. As a teenager, he discovered the works of Spanish poet Federico Garcia Lorca while browsing at a local secondhand bookstore. The poems instantly attracted him, and Cohen soon began writing poetry of his own. By the time he enrolled at Montreal's McGill University in 1951, Cohen had also learned to play guitar, forming a country music group called the Buckskin Boys. Although music, alcohol, and women occupied much of the student's time, his primary passion remained poetry. The literary journal *CIV/n* first published Cohen's work, "A Halloween Poem to Delight My Younger Friends," while he was attending McGill. More poems soon followed in various literary and student publications.

Shortly after Cohen graduated from McGill in 1955, the university's new poetry imprint published his debut volume of collected poetic works, *Let Us Compare Mythologies.* Cohen began appearing at Montreal clubs where he recited his poems, often with musical accompaniment, but still wrestled with the idea of pursuing literature as a profession. He moved to New York City to undertake graduate studies at Columbia University. Although Cohen was not a particularly dedicated student, he enjoyed the thriving coffeehouse culture of beat-era Manhattan during his year in the city. He then returned to Montreal where he worked various jobs while writing the poems that formed the 1961 collection *The Spice-Box of Earth.*

A government grant enabled Cohen to travel to Europe, and he took up residence in London in late 1959. Over the next several months, he wrote his first significant work of prose, the heavily autobiographical *The Favorite Game.* With the initial draft of this work completed, Cohen left London for the Greek island of Hydra in the spring of 1960. Cohen was taken with the bohemian atmosphere of the island, purchasing a house there and entering into a long-running domestic partnership with a Norwegian former model, Marianne Ihlen, by late 1960. He did not remain on Hydra exclusively, however, hopping repeatedly from Greece to Montreal to Havana to London and other European points over the next several years as his literary career grew. The favorable reception of *The Spice-Box of Earth* in 1961 and *The Favorite Game* in 1962 helped make Cohen a star in his native Canada, and he became a regular on the literary circuit there. By the time of the release of the Canadian documentary *Ladies & Gentlemen...Mr. Leonard Cohen* in 1965, the writer had returned to Hydra to write his second novel, *Beautiful Losers.* Published in 1966, the work received mixed reviews, as did that year's poetry collection, *Parasites of Heaven.*

Shifted from Literature to Music

The mid-1960s marked a significant turning point in Cohen's career. A respected if not wildly successful literary writer, he decided to pursue a different creative outlet: songwriting. Cohen returned to New York and moved into the famed Chelsea Hotel, which served as inspiration for the song of the same name. A fellow resident of the Chelsea Hotel, the German model and sometimes-singer Nico, introduced Cohen to Andy Warhol and members of his Factory art scene, including the group Velvet Underground.

Through these connections Cohen met several influential members of the New York music community. A meeting with pop singer Judy Collins proved to be the spark Cohen needed to set his nascent music career into action; she recorded Cohen's "Suzanne" for the 1966 release *In My Life,* and three Cohen compositions for the following year's *Wildflower.* At a New York performance that spring, Collins invited Cohen to come onstage to perform "Suzanne," and this appearance helped Cohen land a recording contract with Columbia. His resulting debut, *Songs of Leonard Cohen,* appeared at the end of 1967. Although it failed to generate much excitement among U.S. record buyers, the album performed well in Europe, reaching number 13 on the British charts.

The following year, Cohen—having marked the end of his relationship with Ihlen with the song "So Long, Marianne"—and new girlfriend Suzanne Elrod left New York for Nashville, Tennessee. There, Cohen recorded with producer Bob Johnston, who had worked on notable albums including Bob Dylan's *Blonde on Blonde* and Johnny Cash's *Fulsom Prison.* The resulting *Songs From a Room,* which featured one of Cohen's best-known songs, "Bird on a Wire," appeared to moderate success in 1969. Like its predecessor, Cohen's sophomore album performed better with European than U.S. audiences. The singer crisscrossed the Continent the following year in support of the album, playing before audiences of thousands at London's Royal Albert Hall and the seminal Isle of Wight festival. Despite the publication of a poetry retrospective in 1969, Cohen's transformation from a primarily literary to a primarily musical figure was by then essentially complete.

Back in Nashville, Cohen recorded his third album, 1971's *Songs of Love and Hate.* Characterized by Sheppard as "the album that established Cohen's enduring reputation as the suicide's serenade," *Songs of Love and Hate* contained songs that have become folk standards, including "Famous Blue Raincoat" and "Joan of Arc." The following year, Elrod gave birth to the couple's first child, Adam, and Cohen moved his family to his native Montreal; a second child, Lorca, followed before the relationship fizzled. Touring and live releases occupied much of the performer's time over the next several years, with just one album of new material, 1974's *New Skin for the Old Ceremony.* Largely centered on Europe, these performances also took Cohen to the Israel-Egypt border where he performed for troops in the Israeli army during the Yom Kippur War. Cohen's next studio effort, *Death of a Ladies' Man,* paired him with an unlikely collaborator: producer Phil Spector, best known for his trademark "wall of sound," a production technique that involved dense layers of sound. The unusual pairing of approaches led to an album that was largely dismissed at the time, and Cohen's 1979 follow-up *Recent Songs* saw him return to a more pared-down style.

In about 1982, Cohen began work on the libretto for an opera, *Night Music,* which was later turned into a film. In 1984, he released both a book of religious-influenced poetry entitled *The Book of Mercy* and an album of new material, *Various Positions.* This album contained what would become one of Cohen's most recognizable songs, the spiritually-inflected "Hallelujah." The following year, he conceptualized and participated in the production of a respected short art film, *I Am a Hotel,* which featured several of Cohen's songs as the backdrop to the action. *Famous Blue Raincoat,* an album of Cohen's songs sung by longtime friend and *Various Positions* collaborator Jennifer Warnes, appeared to unexpected success in 1987. A year later, Cohen returned with a new studio album entitled *I'm Your Man.* Incorporating electronic sounds and featuring Cohen's dry wit, the album was termed "a stunningly sophisticated leap into modern musical textures" by Jason Ankeny of Allmusic.

Already propelled by the popular success of *Famous Blue Raincoat,* Cohen's work again began reaching new audiences in the early 1990s, as younger artists reinterpreted his songs. The 1991 tribute collection *I'm Your Fan* and 1995 tribute album *Tower of Song* included performances of Cohen's works by artists ranging from indie rockers The Pixies to superstars Bono and Elton John. In 1992, Cohen released an album of new work, *The Future,* and undertook what would be his last major tour for several years. Long interested in the practices of Zen Buddhism, Cohen largely disappeared from the public eye in the mid- to late-1990s as he spent increasing amounts of time at the Mount Baldy Zen Center near Los Angeles, California; in time, he became a Buddhist monk. Cohen's work was not entirely absent during this period, however. Singer Jeff Buckley's death in 1997 revived interest in his recording of "Hallelujah." That same year, Columbia released the retrospective *More Best of Leonard Cohen.*

After leaving Mount Baldy in 1999, Cohen began work transforming the poems that he had written there into songs with the help of former backup singer Sharon Robinson. These collaborations became the 2001 release *Ten New Songs.* That same year, a version of "Hallelujah" was included in the blockbuster film *Shrek,* setting off a new spate of covers of the tracks by such diverse artists as British indie group Starsailor and Canadian singer-songwriter Allison Crowe. In *Leonard Cohen: Hallelujah,* Tim Footman quoted Andrew Mueller as noting that the song "has turned into the singer's equivalent of something like *Hamlet* or *Macbeth;* everybody wants to have a lash at it if they want to be taken seriously."

In 2004, Cohen released another album of new material, *Dear Heather.* Called "one of the most controversial albums of his career" by Bruce Eder of Allmusic, *Dear Heather* unusually contained a number of songs with music, but not lyrics, penned by Cohen. The following year, a new documentary entitled *Leonard Cohen: I'm Your Man* was released, featuring both contemporary and archival interviews and performances. That same year also saw Cohen thrust into the news when he sued his former business manager and romantic partner, Kelley Lynch. In the suit, Cohen alleged that Lynch had stolen some $5 million from him, mostly while he had been living at Mt. Baldy retreat. A judge awarded Cohen damages of $9 million in 2006, but Lynch ignored the judgment and did not pay the damages. Facing financial struggles, Cohen continued to create new works. In 2006, he released a print collection entitled *Book of Longing* that became the basis for a 2007 double album of the same name that featured music by composer Philip Glass. The following

year, Cohen embarked on his first world tour in 15 years. Portions of these performances were recorded and released as the 2009 collection *Live from London* and the following year's *Songs from the Road.* In 2011, Cohen recorded a new studio album, *Old Ideas,* that was set for release the following year.

Despite a career spanning more than 50 years, Cohen commented in an article written by Martin Roberts of Reuters that he still found creative work a challenge. "You know, when you're writing, you're always an absolute beginner," Cohen explained. "Each time you take up your guitar or sit by a blank page, you start from scratch. It's a struggle."

Books

Contemporary Canadian Biography, Gale, 1997.
Contemporary Musicians, Gale, 2005.
Footman, Tim, *Leonard Cohen: Hallelujah,* Chrome Dreams, 2009.
Sheppard, David. *Leonard Cohen,*Thunder's Mouth Press, 2000.

Periodicals

America, May 17, 2010.
Maclean's, January 19, 2009.

Online

"I'm Your Man," Allmusic, http://www.allmusic.com/album/im-your-man-r96061 (November 19, 2011).
"Leonard Cohen," Allmusic, http://www.allmusic.com/artist/leonard-cohen-p1948/biography (November 19, 2011).
"Leonard Cohen Biography," Leonard Cohen Official Website, http://www.leonardcohen.com/bio.html (September 15, 2011).
"Singer, poet Leonard Cohen to release new album," Reuters, http://www.reuters.com/article/2011/10/19/us-spain-cohen-idUSTRE79I70C20111019 (November 19, 2011).□

Mildred Cohn

American biochemist Mildred Cohn (1913-2009) engaged in scientific research that greatly contributed to the understanding of the mechanisms of enzymatic reactions and represented major advances in biochemistry. Further, it contributed to the development of magnetic resonance imaging. In becoming a leader in her field, she also overcame gender and religious discrimination.

By the end of the twentieth century, magnetic resonance imaging (commonly known as MRI) became one of the most prevalent and widely used radiologic techniques. This imaging technology can create images of internal body tissues and has been widely applied to diagnoses (particularly related to the heart, the brain and, most particularly, musculoskeletal disorders). Its development was revolutionary, and its application has been profound as far as treatment.

Mildred Cohn helped lay the groundwork for this medical advance, specifically by helping develop the most

sophisticated methodologies and instruments that measure how enzymes and proteins interact within the human body. In her research, Cohn deployed magnetic forces (e.g., examination of the atomic nucleus to study molecular shapes and better compound identification). Indeed, she was among the first researchers to utilize electronic spin and nuclear magnetic resonance in studies related to the body's metabolism.

Researchers who came later applied their own variations to her approach. As such, her impact has been substantial. Cohn authored numerous papers that came to be considered classics—and for her work, she received significant honors.

However, Cohn worked in a period (the early- to midtwentieth century) when her field was considered the property of men. This initially forestalled her advancement. She also had a second strike against her: She was Jewish. Despite this, Cohn overcame gender and religious barriers to exercise an enormous influence on biochemistry and biophysics.

Born to Immigrant Parents

Mildred Cohn was born on July 12, 1913 in New York City, to Isidore M. and Bertha (Klein) Cohn. She was the second of their two children. Her parents were Russian/Jewish immigrants. Her father, a businessman toiling in the tailor trade, developed a machine that more accurately cut cloth. His daughter appeared to have inherited his knack for innovation.

Mildred Cohn attended New York City public schools, where she excelled (no doubt inspired by her father's example). During her early education, Cohn's interests included mathematics and chemistry. An advanced student, she graduated from high school when she was fourteen years old. From there, she enrolled in Hunter College (in 1928). Her areas of study in the all-women's institution included chemistry (her major) and physics (her minor). She graduated in 1931 when she was only seventeen years old, receiving a cum laude bachelor's of art degree. She was intent on pursuing graduate education in the physical sciences. But she then became aware of the barriers placed upon women: One of her teachers advised that she forget about being a research chemist—it was not "ladylike," she was told. The educator counseled that she instead become a chemistry teacher.

Earned a Master's Degree

Undeterred—and ignoring the advice offered— Cohn pursued her own perceived educational path. She enrolled in a doctoral program at Columbia University in New York City. At the time she was barred from becoming a teaching assistant, as such positions were only offered to males.

Still, she stood out: Before she was nineteen years old, Cohn earned a master's degree in chemistry at Columbia. Meanwhile, she earned money as a babysitter. This was a mundane occupation when one considers that she was engaged in an educational regimen that encompassed classical mechanics, molecular spectroscopy, physical chemistry and thermodynamics. Nevertheless, babysitting helped fund her education.

In 1932, after receiving her master's degree, Cohn took a position in the laboratory at the National Advisory Committee for Aeronautics at Langley Field, in Virginia. This organization was the predecessor of NASA (the National Aeronautics and Space Administration). Her initial assignment was computational work. Later, she assumed a research position in the engine division. She engaged in a project to develop a fuel-injection, spark-ignition airplane engine that operated on a diesel cycle. Despite the "men's club" nature of the industry, Cohn became the only woman allowed to work on a project that included seventy male aeronautic engineers. Her efforts helped develop the engine. Still, she faced even more gender discrimination: She had published two important papers (one as senior author) but she was given to understand that—as a woman—she would not be promoted. Thus informed, she left the organization.

Returned to Academic Research

Perhaps embittered but certainly unencumbered, Cohn would later work with Nobel laureates. Realizing that her opportunities at Langley Field were effectively stymied by a prevailing, male-dominated corporate structure, Cohn went back to Columbia University to earn her PhD (in chemistry). Beginning in 1934, she worked with Harold Clayton Urey (1893-1981), a Nobel Prize-winning (1934) American physical chemist. Under Urey, Cohn worked on separating stable isotopes. The effort was unsuccessful, but the research experience gained her better understanding of experimental and theoretical methods. The experience would prove valuable in her later career.

By 1937, Cohn wrote her PhD dissertation, published along with Urey, that was titled "Oxygen Exchange Reactions of Organic Compounds and Water." Around this time, Cohn experienced another career barrier: religion. She had hoped to enter the industrial arena, and many graduates involved in similar research easily made the transition into the professional world. But Cohn couldn't garner interviews with major corporations–not just because of her gender, but because of her Jewish heritage. Corporate enterprises ignoring Cohn included DuPont and Standard Oil.

Became a Professor

Ever resilient, Cohn shifted her career path. She accepted a professorial position at George Washington University Medical School, located in Washington, D.C. Again, this wasn't a direction typically open to women at the time. But it enabled Cohn to work with Vincent du Vigneaud (1901-1978), another Nobel laureate and a biochemistry professor at the university. Urey helped secure the position for Cohn. At the time, du Vigneaud sought to introduce isotopic tracers into his research on sulfur-amino acid metabolism. Isotopic tracers, which are forms of chemical elements, are readily observable through their progression via metabolic pathway, due to their nuclear structure.

Working with du Vigneaud, Cohn helped establish effective methods of tracing isotopes as they progressed through the human body's complex physiological processes. By tracing an isotope path, Cohn added to the understanding of the mechanisms that are involved in the chemical reactions in animals, particularly mammals. Her work in tracing methods provided opportunities for much more broad and complex medical research at the molecular level. By this time, her pronounced talents were allowing her to cross gender obstacles.

Married a Colleague

During this period in her career (specifically May 31, 1938) Cohn married physicist Henry Primakoff. In 1946, her husband accepted a position in the physics department at Washington University in St. Louis. Cohn followed her husband where he was bound and took a position in the biochemistry department, where she worked with the Nobel Prize-winning husband and wife team of Gerty T. Cori and Carl Ferdinand Cori. It was a great opportunity for Cohn, as she worked with world-leading researchers. The Coris shared the Nobel Prize in Medicine in 1947 for their discovery of the catalytic conversion of glycogen.

One of Cohn's major objectives at the St. Louis-based university was to study the mechanisms of enzyme-catalyzed reactions. In her research, she used an isotope of oxygen, which helped her clarify the enzyme-catalyzed reactions of organic phosphates. In the 1950s, she moved forward. In 1958, Cohn began work with nuclear magnetic resonance toward the same purpose. During the decade, she helped advance identification of the adenosine triphosphate (ATP) structure. ATP is a molecule that stores energy for cellular functions and is recognized as the universal unit of energy in living cells.

Continued Her Research at the University of Pennsylvania

Cohn again accompanied her husband when he assumed a new position, this time at the University of Pennsylvania. In 1960, he was named the first Donner Professor of Science at the University of Pennsylvania. Cohn worked in the biophysics department and became a full professor in 1961.

The decade of the 1960s was revolutionary in thought. For Cohn, that meant opportunities for new accomplishments and, in turn, new accolades. In that vibrant period, gender no longer seemed to matter. In 1964, she was chosen by the American Heart Association to be a career investigator, the first woman to assume the role. She held the position for fourteen years.

While at the University of Pennsylvania, Cohn continued her research on transduction in cells, and in cellular reactions. Experiments involved ATP and nuclear magnetic resonance utilization. Continued research led Cohn deeper into to the human body, and that meant deeper into the structure and function of enzymes (via study of manganese-enzyme-substrate complexes).

She was on a *Fantastic Voyage,* to reference the title from a 1966 film. It was a new world she perceived, however microscopic or microcosmic, and Cohn was opening it up for the scientific community and the world. Her work at Washington University and at University of Pennsylvania furthered the understanding of ATP structure, and this had a substantial impact on the fields of neuroscience and biotechnology.

In her ongoing research, Cohn deployed every feasible aspect of magnetic resonance. Further, she collaborated with colleagues in studies that involved nuclear magnetic resonance of transfer ribonucleic acid, a key chemical in cellular protein synthesis. Cohn's work with nuclear magnetic resonance of various types of molecules, structures, and reactions proved to be a significant contribution to science and medicine. Medical companies integrated developments into their products, and customers who purchase the latest iterations of imaging technology (such as university research centers, hospitals and standalone imaging facilities) may not know Cohn's name, but they owe her a debt.

Later Career

From 1978 to 1979, Cohn served as president of the American Society of Biological Chemistry. In 1982, Cohn retired from the University of Pennsylvania as the Benjamin Rush Professor Emerita in Biochemistry and Biophysics. From 1982 to 1985, she held the role of a senior scientist at the Fox Chase Cancer Center in Philadelphia, Pennsylvania— which was a highly appropriate position, as her earlier work proved a great influence on development of cancer-fighting agents.

While Cohn was stationed at Fox Chase, her husband died (in 1983). Cohn retired in 1985, but she still performed research in her laboratory at the University of Pennsylvania.

During this late period in her career, Cohn received numerous awards. In 1982, she was awarded the National Medal of Science. In 1987, she received the Distinguished Award of the College of Physicians. In addition, she was elected as a member to important organizations: National Academy of Sciences, the American Academy of Arts and Sciences, and the American Philosophical Society.

As it turned out, her gender would not hold her back. During her career, she became the first woman appointed to the editorial board of *The Journal of Biological Chemistry* and the first woman to become president of the American Society for Biochemistry and Molecular Biology.

Moreover, as modern researchers moved forward, they would not let philosophic and/or religious beliefs—whether these be atheistic, agnostic or attached to a specific religion or creed—disallow a talented individual such as Cohn from contributing to science and the world's body of knowledge.

Cohn died on October 12, 2009 at the Penn Presbyterian Medical Center in Philadelphia. She suffered respiratory failure related to pneumonia at ninety-six years old. She was survived by three children: two daughters and one son. Throughout her life, her interests—beyond her professional activities—included hiking, writing, reading, and the theater.

On the day before she died, Cohn was inducted into the National Women's Hall of Fame. While it was a gender-related honor, Cohn demonstrated that an individual could transcend gender. Along with her significant accomplishments, it is a major part of her enduring legacy.

Books

"Cohn, Mildred" *Encyclopaedia Judaica,* Macmillan Reference USA, 2007.
"Mildred Cohn," *Notable Scientists: From 1900 to the Present,* Gale, 2001.
"Mildred Cohn," *World of Chemistry,* Thomas Gale, 2006.

Periodicals

Los Angeles Times, October 31, 2009.
The New York Times November 11, 2009.
Washington Post, October 23, 2009.

Online

"Mildred Cohn (1913-2009)," *ACS.org,* http://portal.acs.org/portal/acs/ (November 29, 2011). □

Glenna Collett Vare

The most successful amateur female golfer the United States has ever produced, Glenna Collett Vare (1903-1989) dominated the game during the 1920s. Over the course of her career, Vare swung her way to a record-setting six U.S. Women's Amateur Championships, and she also won both the French and Canadian Ladies Open championships. In addition, Vare wrote books and articles on golfing, becoming an early advocate for women in sports.

Glenna Collett Vare was born June 20, 1903, in New Haven, Connecticut, though she grew up in Providence, Rhode Island. Her father, George Collett, was a versatile athlete who missed her birth because he was racing his bike in France the day she was

born. George Collett won the U.S. amateur cycling championship in 1899. Vare inherited her father's athleticism. She started swimming and diving around the age of nine and fell in love with baseball. With her strong, accurate arm, Vare could out-throw any boy on the block and quickly became the starting third baseman on her brother's team. Vare's mother, Ada, worried about her daughter's infatuation with baseball, believing the sport was inappropriate for a young lady. Instead, Ada Collett encouraged her daughter to play tennis—at the time more socially acceptable for girls. Vare took her mother's advice and tried tennis, though she gave it up after a short trial even though she had no trouble winning matches.

Discovered Golf as a Teen

Vare took an interest in golf around the age of 14 after tagging along to watch her father play an exhibition round with up-and-coming stars Alexa Sterling, Perry Adair, and Bobby Jones. At the time, Sterling was the reigning U.S. female amateur champion. After watching the exhibition, Vare begged to play. In 1917, she played her first game on a regulation course at the Metacomet Country Club in Providence, Rhode Island, demonstrating beautiful tee shots by driving the ball right down the middle of the fairway. Vare's father noted her potential and hired the best instructor he could find. That turned out to be Scottish golf champ Alex Smith, a two-time U.S. Open winner who made his living as a golf pro in the United States. Smith had Vare practicing daily. "He, Alex, was a go-getter," Vare told *Golf Journal's* James Dodson in an article reprinted on the USGA Museum website. "He insisted I practice all the time. Without him I might never have gone very far at all."

One activity Vare did not excel in was school. As a teen she attended the Lincoln School, an all-girls Quaker school in Providence. She got into trouble, however, for concentrating on her golf game more than her studies. When officials asked her to pick one, Vare chose to drop out of school so she could focus on golf. The gamble paid off. In 1919, just two years after Vare took up the sport, she competed in the U.S. Women's Amateur Championship and won her first-round match before being ousted in a later round. In 1920, Vare won the Shennecosset Country Club championship, held in Groton, Connecticut, and established herself as an up-and-coming competitor in the sport.

With a couple victories under her belt, Vare began to attract attention. Under Smith's care, Vare developed her famous compact swing. In her prime, Vare stood just five-foot-six and weighed 125 pounds. The fact that she could drive a ball 300 yards astounded onlookers. Vare set a record by hitting the 300-yard mark; no woman had ever driven the ball that far. Even in the 21st century—with improved technology, such as graphite clubs and high-compression balls—the top male pro golfers averaged about 300 yards per drive. *Golf World* writer Bill Fields noted that Vare possessed an "eye-catching" swing. "It was brisk and powerful, with a full backswing marked by a distinctive up-and-down twirl of her left foot and an impact position at which she was up on both toes throwing all of her 125 pounds into the hit."

Won U.S., Canadian, and French Championships

At 19, Vare competed in the U.S. Women's Amateur Championship held in White Sulphur Springs, West Virginia, in September 1922. Vare made it to the final, where she faced a seasoned Englishwoman, Margaret Gavin. Gavin had played in the final twice before but had yet to win the U.S. championship. At the time, the amateur championship was a tournament that consisted of match play, which meant the golfers competed hole-by-hole and the golfer who won the most holes won the match. Vare won the championship match with a score of five up and four to play—meaning Vare won five more holes than Gavin and the game ended with four holes left to play because even if Gavin had won those holes, she could still not win the match. No one expected the undeveloped teenager to win. The *St. Louis Post-Dispatch* summed up the competition this way: "Miss Collett played more steadily, moved with more ease, [and] fought with less show of 'nerves' after the first few holes than did her rival."

During the time Vare played, there was no professional women's tour, which meant the best female golfers in the world all played the amateur circuit. Through the 1920s, Vare dominated the sport. In 1923 she won the Canadian Ladies Open. In 1924, she was nearly unbeatable. That year, Vare competed in 60 matches and lost only one. Unfortunately, the match she lost was a semifinal at the U.S. Women's Amateur when, on the 19th hole, her opponent's ball struck her ball, then promptly rolled into the cup. Despite the gut-wrenching loss at the U.S. championship, Vare did win a championship that year—the Canadian Ladies Open. In 1925, Vare won her second U.S. Women's Amateur Championship in a competition held in St. Louis. She also won the French Ladies Open.

One championship that eluded Vare was the British Open. During the 1920s, Joyce Wethered dominated golf

in Europe and is widely considered the best British female player of all time. In 1925, Vare and Wethered faced off in the British Open, with Wethered coming out on top. Four years later, in 1929, Vare announced she would travel back to England to take another shot at winning the British Open. Wethered had since given up the game but came out of retirement to play. As predicted, Vare and Wethered ended up in the championship final. Golf historians consider this match to be the greatest women's golf match of all time. After a fierce, breath-taking, knuckle-biting match, Wethered won the title for her fourth British Open championship. According to Patricia Davies of the *London Times,* Wethered said her matchups with Vare were "the fiercest battles I have ever been engaged in." The two never faced off on Vare's home turf because Wethered did not travel to the United States to compete, which was common for European golfers at the time because the trip across the Atlantic Ocean took a week by boat.

During the course of Vare's career it was not just Vare's game, but also her outfits that attracted attention. Vare was known to wear pearls during competition. She was highly superstitious and had certain hats she favored for different tournament situations. Sometimes Vare would wear the same hat, skirt, and red fingernail polish through a five-day tournament. While reporters often remarked on Vare's style, they also made note of her gracious yet highly competitive nature, which changed the course of the game for women. Prior to Vare's entry into the women's golf world, most female golfers played a conservative "lady-like" game. Women did not play for power or accuracy. Vare "taught us a new game," British golf champ Dorothy Hurd Campbell told *Golf World*. "Before Glenna, we ladies used to aim just for the green. Glenna showed us that ladies can play for the flag."

Along the way, Vare took up writing and in 1926 published *Golf for Young Players.* In 1928, she followed with *Ladies in the Rough,* a book that chronicled her rise through the golf ranks and also relayed tips and inspiration to other female golfers. Vare also wrote articles for the *Saturday Evening Post* and *Liberty Magazine,* advocating for support for women in athletics. Later, she served as an associate editor of *American Golfer* magazine.

Married, Discovered Skeet Shooting

In 1931 Vare married Edwin H. Vare Jr., a wealthy construction engineer and son of Pennsylvania Republican state senator Edwin H. Vare Sr. They settled in Philadelphia, the location of the family business, Vare Brothers. Edwin Vare Jr. was a sportsman who enjoyed golf and polo. Together, Vare and her husband competed in skeet shooting and also bred and trained hunting dogs. They also had two children, Ned and Glenna. During the first few years Vare was married, golf took a back seat to family life. Busy with her children and husband, Vare did not play as regularly. Vare's son went on to become captain of the Yale golf team. Daughter Glenna played tennis, field hockey, and lacrosse and also swam.

By 1935 Vare was eager to get her game back. That year, she made it to the finals at the U.S. Women's Amateur, held at the Interlachen Country Club near Minneapolis. This time, Vare—a 32-year-old mother of two—faced 17-year-old American Patty Berg, an emerging star on the golf circuit. The matchup, and Vare's return to form, drew thousands of spectators for the final day of the competition in which Vare emerged the victor on the 34th hole, capturing a record-setting sixth U.S. Amateur title. The record still stood in 2012.

An avid competitor, Vare also enjoyed skeet shooting. In 1937 she won the Tri-State women's skeet championship. Skeet shooting involves shooting at clay targets as they travel through the air. In 1938 Vare won the Belair Skeet Championship, a competition that included both men and women. "She was a great sportswoman," writer Pam Emory told the *Philadelphia Inquirer*'s Charlie Frush. "She'd pick up a sport like trapshooting and practically break records the first time she did anything. She was a great bridge player, a great tennis player."

Another contribution Vare made on behalf of female golfers was helping re-establish the Curtis Cup competition, a biannual matchup between the best female amateurs of the United States versus the best female amateurs of the United Kingdom. The Curtis Cup competition consisted of singles matches and foursome competitions. From 1932 to 1950, Vare played or captained the team six times. During the inaugural 1932 matchup, Vare helped lead the United States to victory. One sore spot, however, was that Vare faced Wethered for the third and final time in competitive match play and lost.

Still Golfing at 80

Even as Vare grew older and expanded her athletic hobbies, she continued golfing. In 1957, Vare—then a 54-year-old grandmother—won the Rhode Island state title, which she had first claimed in 1921. In 1961, she was the runner-up at the Senior Women's National Golf Tournament. The next year she was again the runner-up. Vare continued competing into her 80s. In 1987 she played her 62nd straight Point Judith Invitational golf tournament, held in Narragansett, Rhode Island.

For Vare, playing the game was the ultimate reward. She was not one to rehash her victories or lament her losses, or complain about the fact that if she had been born later and able to play in the Ladies Professional Golf Association tour, her career would have been worth an unfathomable amount of money. Instead, as an amateur, she played for trophies and prestige, not money. "Golf, when she wasn't playing or getting ready to play—it was over," Ned Vare told *Golf World*. "When a round was over, it was over. She didn't want to talk about her shots or hear about yours. My father and I would talk endlessly at dinner about how we played, and she would be bored sick. For Mom, it was enough to do it."

Vare died February 3, 1989, in Gulf Stream, Florida, after a battle with lymphoma. Her name lives on, memorialized in an award given by the Ladies Professional Golf Association. Each year the Vare Trophy goes to the player on the pro tour with the lowest scoring average.

Periodicals

Golf World, November 28, 1997.
Hartford Courant (CT), October 24, 2007.
Philadelphia Daily News, February 6, 1989.
Philadelphia Inquirer, February 6, 1989.
St. Louis Post-Dispatch, October 1, 1922.
Times (London), February 17, 1989.

Online

"From the Golf Journal Archives: A Lively Legend—and Her Tomato Soup," USGA Museum, http://www.usgamuseum.com/about_museum/news_events/news_article.aspx?newsid=140 (November 30, 2011).
"Glenna Collett Vare," *SI Vault,* http://sportsillustrated.cnn.com/vault/article/magazine/MAG1133398/index.htm (November 30, 2011).
"Glenna C. Vare, Top Woman's Golfer in the 1920s," *Sun Sentinel* (Fort Lauderdale, FL), http://articles.sun-sentinel.com/1989-02-07/news/8901070858_1_curtis-cup-glenna-collett-vare-american-golf (November 30, 2011).
"World Golf Hall of Fame Profile: Glenna Collett Vare," World Golf Hall of Fame, http://www.worldgolfhalloffame.org/hof/member.php?member=1119 (November 30, 2011). □

Concino Concini

Concino Concini (1575–1617) was an Italian adventurer who rose to a position of enormous influence at the French royal court in the early seventeenth century. The husband of a lady-in-waiting to Queen Marie de' Medici, Concini was able to amass both political power and an immense personal fortune before he was shot to death in an apparent assassination in 1617 by guards loyal to King Louis XIII. "The Concinis exerted a curious influence over the Queen Regent, enriching and foolishly flaunting themselves," wrote Alistair Horne in *La Belle France: A Short History.* "They soon became the scapegoat for all the real or imagined shortcomings of the regime."

Born in 1575, Concino Concini was a native of Florence, where his grandfather Bartolommeo had risen from notary to secretary to Cosimo de' Medici, the great patron of Italian Renaissance art. Bartolommeo's son was Giovanni Battista Concini, who served as an auditor to Cosimo's son, Francesco de' Medici, the Grand Duke of Tuscany. François de Bassompierre, a French diplomat who later penned an immense 1665 *Mémoires* giving an account of this period of French history, mentioned that he and Concini had known one another in Florence—when Bassompierre was a student in Italy for several months over 1596 and 1597—and that many years later Concini had reflected back on that period, of "my low estate," according to an 1843 English language source, *The Biographical Dictionary of the Society for the Diffusion of Useful Knowledge.* Concini described his earlier life as "debauched, sometimes in prison, sometimes banished, most frequently without money, always in irregularities and a lawless life."

Concini's fortunes changed in 1600 when his father's connections helped secure him a position in the bridal party entourage of Francesco's daughter Marie, who was engaged to marry France's King Henri IV. Marie's closest friend was Leonora Galigaï, who had been cared for by the same wet nurse during her and Marie's infancies. Galigaï—also known by the named Leonora Dori—was also part of the entourage as Marie's maid and confidant.

Marie was actually the second wife of Henri IV, one of the most popular kings of French history. Henri was especially esteemed for forging a peace agreement via his Edict of Nantes, which mandated religious tolerance in France and ended the kingdom's ruinous Wars of Religion. The king was also known for his amorous appetites and had numerous mistresses, a few of whom rose to positions of influence at court and plotted intrigues with other courtiers, but his first marriage had produced no children, and thus no male Dauphin, as the first son of the French king and heir to the throne is called. On September 27, 1601, Marie gave birth to her first son by Henri, a boy they named Louis.

Pursued the Hapless Galigaï

Concini, meanwhile, had worked to ingratiate himself with the new queen. The Italian-born Marie was unpopular and endlessly compared to her saintly predecessor, Margot. The French derided the slightly overweight Marie as "the fat banker," a reference to the marriage deal struck by her father, to whom France owed enormous sums that were forgiven in the marriage contract.

Concini had come to France bearing a letter of introduction from Francesco de' Medici. "He belongs to a family that is very well regarded by Their Highnesses," wrote the Grand Duke to Henri, according to Paul Lombard's *Vice and Virtue: Men of History, Great Crooks for the Greater Good.* "He would like to settle in France and will serve there with

fidelity and diligence to gain the good graces of His Majesty." Yet Henri remained suspicious of the foreigner, though he did appreciate Concini's efforts to placate a jealous, angry Marie when the queen was taunted by one of the king's mistresses.

Concini schemed to woo the rather homely, dour Leonora Galigaï, whom historians believe may have suffered from epilepsy and depression. Despite these disabilities she remained a favorite of Marie's, and in France was appointed as the queen's lady-in-waiting. Because of Galigaï's personal proximity to the queen, Concini's marriage proposal was considered a security matter and required Henri's permission, which the king initially refused to grant. But with Marie's intercession Concini and Galigaï were wed on July 12, 1601. A son, whom they named Henri in honor of the king, was born in 1603. The queen herself was one of the child's godparents.

Conspired with Queen

Concini was able to secure a position as superintendent of Marie's royal household, where he first began collecting kickbacks in return for highly coveted jobs. Marie, reviled by the rabble and nobles alike during her lifetime, was said to have been involved in this, receiving her own cut on the deals, which financed her own luxurious spending habits.

One facet of Concini's rise to power—and ignoble fall—came indirectly, via Henri's pursuit of a well-born young woman named Charlotte de Montmorency. The attractive 15-year-old daughter of the Constable of France and governor of Languedoc, Charlotte was engaged to marry another well-born scion of a elite family, Henri II de Bourbon, the prince de Condé. The king had arranged the 1609 match with the hope that the prince would be an acquiescent husband, but instead Condé fled with Charlotte to Brussels. Henri sent word demanding their return, but the pair defied the king and instead sought the protection of the Spanish monarch, one of France's most formidable enemies. Henri readied troops for a possible war in Flanders, which was a Spanish-held area with an enormous standing army at the ready.

Before leaving for battle, Henri had signed an order giving Marie power to rule in his absence. She also persuaded him to crown her Queen Consort, and the ceremony was held at the august Cathedral of Saint-Denis on May 13, 1610. A day later, the king was riding in his carriage on the Rue de la Ferronnerie when another carriage a few paces ahead overturned, and traffic on the narrow street came to a standstill. A Roman Catholic fanatic named François Ravaillac was waiting for the king to pass on the route and jumped into the royal carriage, stabbing the king several times.

Named Himself First Minister

Paris erupted in grief at the regicide, and many believed it was actually a clever plot by foreign interlopers to gain access to the throne. At the time, Marie and Henri's son Louis was just eight years old. He became King Louis XIII, but French law prevented a minor from ruling until the age of majority, which in this case was the thirteenth birthday. Marie was named regent for her son, a turn of events that placed Concini in a position of enormous influence. In July of 1610 the queen gave him a seat on her ruling council, and also permission to draw promissory notes out of Treasury. She loaned him funds to purchase a French title of nobility, the marquisat d'Ancre, an affront to French aristocrats whose titles went back several generations.

In February of 1611 Marie appointed Concini the lieutenant general of Picardy, and he went on to secure more titles to other territories over the next few years in Péronne, Roye, and Montdidier. Marie dismissed the unpopular *surintendant des finances*, Maximilien de Béthune, Duc de Sully, and placed Concini in the post, which gave both him and Leonora free access to millions of livres. They spent lavishly, amassing an enormous entourage of 200 lackeys, and sometimes paraded in their latest fashions before the windows of Louis's apartments in the Palais du Louvre. As *surintendant* Concini had control over the Dauphin's household expenses, and kept him on a strict budget. When Louis complained of this, Concini would offer the boy-king a loan.

France roiled at the power of an Italian of relatively common birth so near to the throne. There were rumors that Concini and Marie were lovers, for he would fuss with his garments after leaving private meetings with her and she granted him a choice parcel of land next to her palace. He created a new title for himself, that of first minister, and packed Marie's regency council with sympathizers, including a 31-year-old priest named Armand-Jean du Plessis de Richelieu, whom he placed in charge of foreign affairs.

Loathed by French Elite

In 1613 Marie approved an order that made Concini a marshal of France, an honor reserved for top-ranking generals, usually after bravery in battle. Concini had absolutely no military experience. At this, Condé—a potential rival for the throne itself—led an uprising of nobles against Concini and Marie. Several prominent figures removed themselves from the court in Paris in early 1614, and Condé authored a manifesto deriding Marie's regency as corrupt and illegitimate.

After a few military skirmishes in the spring of 1614, Concini and Marie offered the rebellious nobles the favorable terms of the Treaty of Sainte-Menehould. It parceled out massive sums to each of the nobles who had led individual armies against Marie's regency—essentially buying their loyalty—and in return she agreed to call an Estates General later that year. The Estates General was an assembly of representative members of the clergy, the nobility, and the people.

Louis reached the age of majority on September 27, 1614, but was unable to wrest full control of the reins of government from his mother and Concini. When the Estates General met a month later, Marie agreed to some reforms, which were never implemented. In the fall of 1615 Condé led another rebellion, but this time Concini commanded a force and actually managed to seize Condé's estate in Clermont-in-Beauvais. Condé was summoned to meet with Marie in September of 1616 at the Louvre, where Concini ordered him arrested. The prince and his wife Charlotte were imprisoned in the Parisian fortress of Bastille for the next three years.

King Feared Taking Action

Concini, widely reviled in pamphlets of the day under the name of his offensive purchased title, the Maréchal d'Ancre, was viewed as a grievous usurper to Louis' power. The poor of Paris, in particular, resented his displays of wealth, and the Concini palace on the rue Tournon was continually defaced with offensive graffiti denouncing them as satanic interlopers. In October of 1616, Concini began a legal process that would elevate him to the status of duke and peer, which enraged the nobles once again. Finally, Louis was spurred to act against Concini and Marie's power, which she refused to concede to her son, by one of his trusted advisors, his longtime falconer Charles d'Albert de Luynes. Concini retreated to the Normandy to amass a force, and on January 17, 1617, Louis ordered all rebels to surrender their arms. Louis summoned Concini to Louvre, where another close ally of his, Louis de L'Hôpital, baron de Vitry, was charged with the task of arresting him. The plan was to detain him on grounds of abuse of authority by the king's warrant, and try him before the Parlement de Paris.

On April 24, 1617, Concini entered the east gate of the Louvre with an entourage of about 50, many of them armed. Vitry, known for his fearlessness, "sprang out and took the right arm of Concini, announcing: 'The King has commanded me to seize your person,' " wrote Horne in *La Belle France*. Concini shouted for "À moi!" (To me!) which was interpreted as a call for help and technically resisting arrest. At that, Vitry and his men fired five fatal shots.

Once again, Paris erupted, but this time there was an unleashing of fury against the foreign courtier and his wife. Concini's grave at the cemetery of Saint-Germain-l'Auxerrois was robbed and a mob hacked off limbs and other body parts. Leonora was tried on charges of practicing sorcery, found guilty, and was burned at the stake at the Place de Grève on July 8, 1617. Their son Henri was forced to flee France, and died in Florence in 1631. Louis XIII reigned until 1643, and retained the services of Cardinal Richelieu as his own first minister. Richelieu was the force behind several initiatives that served to entrench the French monarchy as absolutist in scope. This curtailing of the nobles' power led, eventually, to the unrest that finally brought down the French monarchy in the 1789 Revolution.

Books

"Ancre, Le Maréchal d'," in *The Biographical Dictionary of the Society for the Diffusion of Useful Knowledge*, Volume 2, Part 2, Longman, Brown, Green, and Longmans, 1843, pp. 135–136.

Horne, Alistair, *La Belle France: A Short History*, Alfred A. Knopf, 2005.

Lombard, Paul, *Vice and Virtue: Men of History, Great Crooks for the Greater Good*, Algora Publishing, 2000; translated from the original French, *Le Vice et la Vertu*, Editions Grasset et Fasquelle, 1999.

Pardoe, Julia, *The Life of Marie de Medicis, Queen of France*, Cambridge University Press, 2010. Originally published by Colburn & Co., 1852. □

Eric Allin Cornell

American physicist Eric Cornell (born 1961) was the co-recipient of the 2001 Nobel Prize for Physics for his work involving the Bose-Einstein condensate, or BEC.

In 2001, the Royal Swedish Academy of Sciences awarded its Nobel Prize in Physics to three scientists, one of which included Eric Cornell. The others included Wolfgang Ketterle and Carl E. Weiman. They garnered the honor for their research related to the Bose-Einstein condensation (BEC).

Essentially, the three scientists—Cornell and Weiman collaborated, while Ketterle worked independently—transformed an idea into reality. In describing the achievement in the press release quoted on the official website, the Academy explained (helping to place it in laymen's terms), "A laser beam differs from the light from an ordinary light bulb in several ways. In the laser the light particles all have the same energy and oscillate together. To cause matter also to behave in this controlled way has long been a challenge for researchers."

Cornell, Ketterle and Weiman addressed that challenge. The 2001 physics Nobel Laureates, the Academy described, caused atoms to "sing in unison," which led to the discovery of a new state of matter: the Bose-Einstein condensate, or BEC.

The roots of the 2001 Nobel physics award, and the co-winners' achievement, date back to 1924, when Indian physicist and mathematician Satyendra Nath Bose came up with intriguing theoretical calculations about light particles. He then consulted with the famous German-born theoretical physicist Albert Einstein, who further advanced the theory, extending the idea to a certain type of atom. As the Academy relates, Einstein then made a provocative prediction: If a gas of these atoms were cooled to a very low temperature, all of the atoms would suddenly gather in the lowest possible energy state. "The process is similar to when drops of liquid form from a gas, hence the term condensation," the Academy described in the press release.

The idea remained as theory for seven decades. Then, in 1995, the three Nobel Laureates achieved this proposed extreme state of matter. According to the Academy, Cornell and Wieman then produced a pure condensate of about 2000 rubidium atoms at 20 nK (nanokelvin) –that is, 0.000 000 02 degrees above absolute zero. Working independently, Ketterle performed corresponding experiments with sodium atoms. Condensates he produced contained more atoms: thus, this enabled further investigation of the phenomenon. But this all raised a question: How could this new information become practically applied? In fields such as precision measurement and nanotechnology, the Academy replied, adding a caveat that this remained in the realm of speculation.

Raised in Fertile Educational Environments

In a Boulder, Colorado laboratory the scientific proposition became a matter of reality. Cornell, one of the three men who solidified the concept of BEC, was born in Palo Alto,

California on December 19, 1961. He was one of three children. When Cornell was born, his parents were completing their graduate degrees at Stanford University, in California. Two years later, the family moved to Cambridge, Massachusetts. According to his Nobel Prize autobiography, Cornell still considers Cambridge as his "home town." There, his father was a professor of civil engineering at the Massachusetts Institute of Technology (commonly referred to as MIT), and his mother was a high school English teacher.

Although his parents' educational and professional activities entailed a necessary amount of travel, the young Cornell didn't mind. "[These travels—to places such as Berkeley, California and Lisbon, Portugal] were wonderful experiences for me and no doubt they are in part to blame for my lifelong love of travel," he recalled in his autobiography found on the Nobel website.

In addition, his parents turned his youthful insomnia into a positive learning experience. As Cornell recalled when he received his Nobel Prize, "Some nights... I had trouble falling asleep at my appointed bedtime." While some parents would have read a bedtime story to their child in the hopes of helping them to drift off to sleep, Cornell remembered his father taking a different angle. "[O]n occasion my father would come in and suggest to me a 'problem' to think about. Stewing over these problems was supposed to help me go to sleep. It never did that, but it did get me in the lifelong habit of thinking about technical issues at all sorts of random moments in my daily life, and not only (or even primarily) during scheduled 'thinking time.' "

Among other early youthful interests, Cornell engaged in model rocket building (he preferred his own designs over what was offered in hobby stores), as well as chess, math, and computer programming. Because he had taught himself basic programming while just a freshman in high school, he eventually felt that computers were somewhat tedious. He admitted that while the activity proved initially captivating, he eventually became disenchanted, despite his ability to create and invent his own projects above and beyond the manuals he had read through.

When he eventually had the opportunity to establish his own lab, he recalled, one of his first acts as a young principal investigator was to write a program to output a precisely timed sequence of electronic pulses to control the lasers and magnetic fields. This would become the first successful Bose-Einstein condensation apparatus. Appropriately, Cornell wrote the program in 'Basic.'

By the time he reached his senior year in high school, he had moved with his mother and siblings to San Francisco, where he attended Lowell High School, which he describes as a "magnet school" developed to draw academically inclined and accelerated students from the region.

Following high school graduation, Cornell entered Stanford University. He majored in physics. As a freshman, he took on a student job to earn some spending money. It was also his first job related to physics: He served as a "scanner" at the Stanford Linear Accelerator Center. It was tedious work, and Cornell found it so "mind-numbing" that he quit after three days. His second student job turned out to be more satisfying: he worked in one of his professor's labs, building data acquisition electronics for a scanning magnetometer. For the rest of his time at Stanford, Cornell worked with low-temperature physics groups. "I really enjoyed this experience," he recalled in his Nobel Prize autobiography, "and it was these jobs, more than anything else, that persuaded me to pursue a career in scientific research."

A Career Detour

His career would not be a straightforward path, however. A thought deeply troubled Cornell: "Roughly halfway through my undergraduate years, I began to worry that my future was choosing me, instead of the other way around," he captured in his autobiography.

As such, Cornell decided that he would not head directly into a science career. He had also been studying Mandarin Chinese, and he had a great interest in books and politics. He became involved in a Stanford program called Volunteers in Asia, and he went to Taichung, Taiwan, where he taught conversational English at a YMCA. From there, he went to Hong Kong and then to China, where he spent three more months studying Chinese and trying to find direction.

Eventually, Cornell decided to return to Stanford, to continue pursuing science, as he realized his place was in a physics lab.

When he graduated from Stanford, he enrolled at the Massachusetts Institute of Technology (MIT) to earn his doctorate. While working toward his doctorate, Cornell engaged in a single-ion cyclotron resonance experiment in the fall of 1985. The purpose, Cornell described, "was to trap a single ion in a Penning trap, measure its cyclotron frequency to great accuracy, then swap in a different species of ion and do a comparison measurement. The ratio of cyclotron frequencies should be just the inverse of the ratio of masses."

Collaborated with Weiman in Colorado

After three years, he and his collaborators met with success. Finally, after five years of post-graduate work and earning his doctorate, Cornell accepted an offer from Weiman to work with him at the University of Colorado.

He moved to Boulder, Colorado, in October of 1990. By this time, he was beginning to think seriously about the Bose-Einstein condensation. In 1992, Cornell joined the National Institute of Standards and Technology (NIST) in Boulder, and became a physics professor at the University of Colorado. Eventually, he became a fellow at the Joint Institute for Laboratory Astrophysics (JILA). For his Nobel autobiography, he described the pleasure of working with Weiman, his co-Nobel Prize recipient: "I found working with Carl to be a very congenial experience. Carl and I share very similar tastes in what makes for an interesting physics experiment, and I was happy to assimilate a fraction of his seemingly endless bag of technological ideas."

Einstein had taken Bose's theoretical calculations about light particles and developed a theory that included particles of matter. Einstein predicted that when certain types of atoms produced a gas, cooled to very low temperatures, all of the atoms would gather in the lowest possible energy state. The subsequent matter waves (comprised of thousands of individual atoms) would merge into one wave, producing a "super atom." From this would be formed BEC, a new state of matter. In their research, Cornell and Wieman cooled rubidium atoms to less than 170 billionths of a degree above "absolute zero" (the theoretical temperature at which atoms have the least possible energy). Cornell solved the final problem that prevented condensation by creating the quadruple atom trap, which has been described as a magnetic field shaped like a snow cone. Cornell's trap became known as the "time-average orbiting-potential trap," or TOP. This trap draws the coldest, slowest atoms toward the top of the cone. There, fields fall to zero. The coldest atoms ultimately form a dense mass and then undergo condensation.

Awarded for Work

In October 2001, The Royal Swedish Academy of Sciences announced that it awarded the Nobel Prize in Physics jointly to Cornell, Wiemen, and Ketterle (who was doing independent similar research at MIT), "for the achievement of Bose-Einstein condensation in dilute gases of alkali atoms, and for early fundamental studies of the properties of the condensates," as quoted on the press release on the Academy's website.

Cornell has also received numerous awards and honors, including the the Fritz London Prize in Low Temperature Physics in 1996; the I.I. Rabi Prize, the King Faisal International Prize in Science, and the National Science Foundation Alan T. Waterman Award, (all in 1997); the Lorentz Medal, of the Royal Netherlands Academy of Arts and Sciences, 1998; and the Benjamin Franklin Medal in Physics, 1999. In 2000, Cornell was elected to the National Academy of Sciences. In April 2005, Cornell was elected a fellow of the American Academy of Arts and Sciences, an honor that recognizes individuals who are leaders in their fields.

In January 1995, Cornell married Celeste Landry. They have two daughters.

Books

Almanac of Famous People,, 10th edition, Gale 2011.

American Men & Women of Science, Gale 2008.

Biography Resource Center, Gale 2011.

Online

"Eric A. Cornell-Autobiography," *Nobelprize.org,* http://www.nobelprize.org/nobel_prizes/physics/laureates/2001/cornell.html (December 10, 2011). Gale 2008.

"Press Release-The Nobel Prize in Physics 2001," *Nobelprize.org,* http://www.nobelprize.org/nobel_prizes/physics/laureates/2001/press.html (December 10, 2011). Gale 2008.

"The Nobel Prize in Physics 2001," *Nobelprize.org,* http://www.nobelprize.org/nobel_prizes/physics/laureates/2001/ (December 10, 2011). Gale 2008.☐

D

Viola Desmond

Viola Desmond (1914–1965) is often cited as the Canadian precursor to Rosa Parks, the African-American seamstress who took a daring stand against segregation in Montgomery, Alabama, in 1955. Nine years earlier, Desmond was a 32-year-old hairdresser from Halifax, Nova Scotia, when she was arrested after refusing to sit in a segregated section of a movie theater. She took her case to the Nova Scotia Supreme Court in 1947, which upheld the conviction, but her plight stirred intense media debate across Canada.

Viola Desmond was born Viola Davis on July 6, 1914, in Halifax, the capital of Nova Scotia. Her father was James Albert Davis, a member of the city's longstanding black community. Her mother Gwendolin came from a mixed-race family that had moved to Nova Scotia from Connecticut some years earlier. Nova Scotia had a sizable black population, the largest in Canada for generations, thanks to a wave of African-descent Loyalist soldiers who settled there after the American Revolutionary War of 1775–83. These men had been slaves in the British Empire and fought on the British side in exchange for their freedom. When the war ended in the American colonies' favor, many of the black Loyalists relocated to the maritime provinces of British-held Canada.

Desmond attended Sir Joseph Howe Elementary School, one of the port city's public schools, and then Bloomfield Common School. Elsewhere in Nova Scotia, segregated schools were permitted under provincial law,

but these two schools in the downtown area were open to black and white students. After graduation, she took a job as a teacher at black schools in other parts of Halifax, Preston, and Hammonds Plains, then used her savings to enroll at a cosmetology college in Montreal, Quebec, in 1936.

A determined and practical young woman, Desmond had recognized that recent advances in hair-straightening processes and other new products and techniques were going to yield a potentially lucrative new service industry open to black women entrepreneurs. She enrolled at Montreal's Field Beauty Culture School because the cosmetology schools in Halifax had all turned her down as an applicant, then spent time in New York City and Atlantic City for additional training.

Established Salon, School, and Product Line

Desmond had married a Halifax man, John Gordon (Jack) Desmond, a descendant of the 1783 Loyalist settlers and the first black man to be licensed as a barber in Nova Scotia. He had a successful shop on Gottingen Street, in Halifax's North End, next door to which Desmond established Vi's Studio of Beauty Culture. Her business thrived, and Desmond eventually launched her own line of hair-care products, which she sold to salons across the province. With a Dodge sedan she had purchased, she served as her own sales representative and was frequently on the road to sell her products and give demonstrations to other black hairdressers.

On Friday, November 8, 1946, Desmond was traveling to the city of Sydney on the east coast of Cape Breton Island when her car broke down in the town of New Glasgow, on Nova Scotia's north coast. She found a mechanic but was told the repair would take several hours

and require her to stay overnight. To pass the evening hours, she bought a ticket for the 7 p.m. movie at the grand Roseland Theatre, New Glasgow's most ornate film theater. She told the ticket seller, "One down, please," meaning one ticket for lower-level seating, according to Constance Backhouse's *Colour-Coded: A Legal History of Racism in Canada, 1900–1950.*

Desmond later explained she was unaware that movie theaters outside Halifax had unofficial segregated seating policies, and did not notice that the cashier handed her a ticket for the balcony section. After giving her ticket to the usher, she went to take a seat on the main floor, but the usher informed her that she had an "upstairs ticket" and directed her to the balcony. Thinking that the cashier had made a mistake, Desmond went back to the box office to resolve the issue. According to Backhouse's research, the cashier told her "I'm sorry, but I'm not permitted to sell downstairs tickets to you people."

Dragged Through Lobby

Desmond returned to the main floor and walked past the usher, who called after her. When she ignored the usher's warning, the usher approached her and said, "I told you to go upstairs," according to court testimony recounted in *Colour-Coded*. Desmond refused, and the usher summoned owner-manager Henry MacNeil, who explained the seating policy. Desmond said she was nearsighted and would not be able to see the movie clearly from the balcony height, and offered to pay the ten-cent difference in price for the main floor seat. MacNeil rebuffed this offer and, in mounting frustration with Desmond, told her he was within his rights to eject her from his business on grounds of disorderly conduct. Remaining calm, Desmond insisted she was not being disorderly. At that, MacNeil went out into the street to fetch a police officer, who came in, assessed the situation, and told Desmond that she

indeed could be removed from the premises. "I told him that I was not doing anything and that I did not think he would do that," Desmond later said, according to Backhouse's account. "He then took me by the shoulders and dragged me as far as the lobby."

Writing in *The Beaver: Exploring Canada's History,* historian Dean Jobb reported that the officer used such force that Desmond's "legs and hip were bruised. She almost lost one of her shoes and a bystander had to retrieve her purse. It was an ugly scene: a stylishly dressed woman weighing less than a hundred pounds and just under five feet tall roughed up by a police officer likely twice her size. In the lobby, MacNeil grabbed her legs and the two men carried her to a waiting car." The car was a taxicab that deposited her at the New Glasgow police station. MacNeil soon turned up, met with the city's chief of police Elmo C. Langille, and Langille served Desmond with a warrant for her arrest. She was held overnight, with the usual Friday-night drunks, in a holding cell that was not segregated, either by color or by gender. She spent the entire night sitting upright on a bench, and the next day was brought before a magistrate.

Charged with Tax Evasion

The charge against Desmond was for a violation of the Nova Scotia Theatres, Cinemagraphs, and Amusements Act of 1915. As Jobb explained in *The Beaver* article, "Desmond had been sold a thirty-cent upstairs ticket, which included a two-cent tax, but the downstairs seat she insisted on taking cost forty cents and included a tax of three cents. Desmond stood accused of evading a penny in tax." She pled not guilty, and Magistrate Roderick Geddes MacKay heard testimony from the cashier, the usher, and MacNeil. After each, MacKay asked her if she had any questions, and she replied no. She did not know this meant she could cross-examine the witnesses; she thought the judge was simply trying to ensure she understood the process. Nor was she made aware that she had a right to her own lawyer, and that she could move to adjourn proceedings in order to request bail. When she was allowed to take the stand to present her defense, Desmond told the judge that she had offered to buy the more expensive ticket—a fact that none of the prosecution witnesses had mentioned and one that should have voided any charge that she was trying to evade paying a tax.

But MacKay ruled against her, levying a fine of $20 or 30 days in jail. Desmond paid the fine, collected her car, and drove back to Halifax. "She came home and said, 'Twelve hours I spent in jail.'" her sister Wanda Robson told Toronto *Globe & Mail* writer Oliver Moore years later, adding that this was an appalling situation for the family, who were exemplary citizens, Canadian patriots, and devout Baptists; Desmond's parents were so conservative that she had never even told them that she worked briefly in a Harlem nightclub as a cigarette girl during her time in New York.

Fought to Overturn Conviction

Desmond's bruises prompted her to see a physician whose practice was near her salon, and when she told him what had happened in New Glasgow, he suggested she talk to a lawyer. She went to Frederick W. Bissett, an attorney and member of the Progressive-Conservative Party who would later win election to the Nova Scotia Supreme Court. Bissett first moved to file a civil suit on her behalf, requesting damages from MacNeil and the Roseland Theatre for assault, malicious prosecution, false arrest, and false imprisonment.

Some members of Desmond's family, including her husband, were skittish about a lawsuit and the attendant publicity. But Desmond was determined to clear her name, and many blacks in Halifax and elsewhere in Nova Scotia rallied to her side. The Nova Scotia Association for the Advancement of Colored People (NSAACP), founded just a year earlier, offered to pay her legal fees. The province's first black-owned and edited newspaper, the *Clarion,* also kept the story on its front pages for several months.

In retrospect Desmond's case was poorly handled by Bissett, though the attorney was proceeding with the best of intentions. For whatever reason, he dropped the civil case, let the chance for an appeal run out, then filed a writ of certiorari with the Nova Scotia Supreme Court requesting that her conviction be overturned. A judge on the Nova Scotia Supreme Court chastised him for letting the appeal deadline pass, and after that a panel of Nova Scotia Supreme Court judges met to review the case. They ruled in May of 1947 that their provincial high court did not have the power to rule on the matter, and let Desmond's conviction stand.

Case Prompted Media Outcry

Canadians were characteristically, politely aghast at this news. *Saturday Night,* one of the country's most widely read weekly magazines, railed that the public segregation practices enshrined by law in several southern U.S. states had no place in Canada. An editorial that ran in *Maclean's,* a newsweekly with similarly high circulation figures, also sided with Desmond. Civil rights groups like the NSAACP went into action, pressuring municipalities and provinces to enact anti-discrimination measures. Segregated schools, permitted in Nova Scotia and Ontario, were outlawed in the early 1950s. By 1970 most provincial legislatures had enacted Bill of Rights laws that barred discrimination on the basis of race or religion; in 1977 the federal parliament enacted a sweeping Canadian Human Rights Act.

Desmond did not live to witness most of these changes. She died while in New York on business on February 7, 1965, at the age of 50. A brief footnote in Canadian history for many years, Desmond's courageous stand was kept alive by her sister Wanda Robson, who was present at Province House at a session of the Nova Scotia legislature in April of 2010 when the province's premier issued Desmond a posthumous free pardon. This is a type of clemency that recognizes there were no grounds for prosecution in the first place, and in Desmond's case is believed to have been the first to be granted posthumously in Canadian history. "This injustice has impacted not just Mrs. Desmond," asserted Nova Scotia Premier Darrell Dexter, according to a *Toronto Star* report, "but other African-Nova Scotians and all Nova Scotians who found and continue to find this event in Nova Scotia's history offensive and intolerable. On behalf of the province of Nova Scotia, I am sorry."

Had she lived to witness the day at Province House, Desmond would have been 95 years old. Her sister was 83 in 2010 and pronounced herself "numb with joy," Robson was quoted as saying by CBC News. "She's just one of many of us who have suffered. And when I say suffered I don't mean that you just couldn't do anything anymore. But it was a momentary sting of racism and then you pick yourself up, you dust yourself off and get on with life."

Books

Backhouse, Constance, *Colour-Coded: A Legal History of Racism in Canada, 1900–1950,* University of Toronto Press, 1999.

Lander, Dorothy A., "Performativity," in *Encyclopedia of Activism and Social Justice,* edited by Gary L. Anderson and Kathryn G. Herr, Volume 3, Sage Reference, 2007.

Periodicals

The Beaver: Exploring Canada's History, April–May 2009.

Globe & Mail (Toronto, Canada), October 4, 2007; April 16, 2010; May 22, 2010.

Toronto Star, April 16, 2010.

Online

"Rights Icon Desmond Gets N.S. Apology," Canadian Broadcasting Corporation News, April 15, 2010, http://www.cbc.ca/news/canada/nova-scotia/story/2010/04/15/ns-desmond-apology-dexter.html (February 3, 2012). □

William Dieterle

German-born film director William Dieterle (1893–1972) worked in Hollywood during the Golden Age of American cinema in the 1930s and '40s. His best-known works are adaptations of the literary classics *A Midsummer Night's Dream, The Hunchback of Notre Dame,* and *The Devil and Daniel Webster.* He also made several sober biopics for the Warner Brothers studio, including *The Life of Emile Zola,* which won Best Picture honors in 1938 at the 10th annual presentation of the Academy Awards.

Born Wilhelm Dieterle on July 15, 1893, in Ludwigshafen, the future director grew up as the last of nine children in a financially struggling family. In his teens he did carpentry work, which led to a job with a traveling theater troupe. Dieterle had shown a dramatic flair at an early age, staging barn productions for family and friends, and eventually he made his stage debut with the company. His first film appearance was in the 1913 costume drama *Fiesko.* World War I interrupted his career, but in 1918 he resumed acting and was discovered by Max Reinhardt, creative director of the Deutsches Theater in Berlin for more than two decades. Reinhardt was known for the

ambitious, avant-garde productions that made Berlin an exciting new center of the European arts in the 1920s.

Starred in Silent Films

Dieterle spent much of the 1920s appearing on stage and in scores of German movies, beginning with *Die Ver-mummten* in 1920. Handsome and appropriately emotive for film's silent era, he built a successful career as one of German cinema's most popular male romantic leads. Yet he was also eager to make his mark in Germany's thriving movie industry behind the camera. He made his directorial debut in 1923 with *Der Mensch am Wege* (The Man by the Roadside), a film he and some friends funded themselves with a screenplay based on a Leo Tolstoy short story. The silent film featured a young Marlene Dietrich in one of her first film roles.

Dieterle starred in a 1924 trilogy of stories *Das Wachs-figurenkabinett* with Conrad Veidt and Emil Jannings, and had a supporting role in one of the masterpieces of German Expressionist film, F.W. Murnau's *Faust* of 1926. Works by Murnau, Reinhardt, and others would later be assessed as significant artifacts of Germany's Weimar era, named for the city where a new postwar constitution had been signed. The dark, moody dramas of German Expressionist stage and screen were made by creative professionals and technicians who were either lured to Hollywood in the 1920s or fled a rising right wing movement in Germany in the early 1930s. Dieterle and Reinhardt belonged to those respective categories, and the influence of so many artistic visionaries had a profound impact on Hollywood cinematic standards.

Moved to Hollywood

In 1927 Dieterle and his wife, Charlotte Hagenbruch—a stage and screen actor who moved on to screenwriting—formed their own film production company, Charrha-Film. One of

their notable finished projects was *Geschlecht in Fesseln* (Fettered Sexuality, sometimes translated as *Sex in Chains*), a 1928 work directed by Dieterle in which he also starred. It had a somewhat provocative subject matter, dealing with what was considered at the time to be a human rights issue: whether prison inmates should be permitted conjugal visitation rights with their spouses.

In 1930 Dieterle and Hagenbruch moved to the United States when the Warner Brothers studio offered him a contract to appear in German-language versions of some planned projects. Only a few were made, among them *Dämon des Meeres,* a 1931 adventure film whose English-language counterpart was *Moby Dick* with John Barrymore in the Captain Ahab role that Dieterle played in the German version.

Dieterle made his English-language directorial debut in the summer of 1931 with *The Last Flight,* which starred a few promising young names whose careers failed to progress. The story followed the travails of a quartet of American men, who were among the first generation of wartime pilots during World War I, now aimlessly carousing through Paris after the war's end. A *New York Times* review by Mordaunt Hall found some flaws in the movie, but deemed it "in many respects a gifted production, the sum and substance of which frequently brings to mind Ernest Hemingway's novel, 'The Sun Also Rises.' "

Dieterle soon changed his first name from "Wilhelm" to "William" and struggled with the projects Warner Brothers assigned him to direct. He made a comedy with W.C. Fields, and then a 1932 movie about the 1929 stock market crash on Wall Street—an unpopular theme with audiences struggling in the worst years of the Great Depression. Solidly escapist fare was the formula for box office success, and Dieterle had his first genuine critical and commercial success with *Six Hours to Live,* his sixth movie for Warner Brothers. A drama with a science fiction twist, its plot centered around the murder of a diplomat, who is revived by a ray machine built by an aging scientist-inventor. The reanimated man, played by Warner Baxter, knows he only has six hours to solve the murder before the ray's properties give out, but in the end refuses to tell police detectives who strangled him, though he does seek out and confront his assailant and destroy the scientist's life-giving machine on moral grounds. In a review in the *New York Times,* Hall asserted that "Dieterle's gifted direction and the capable performances of the principals cause it to be an unusually compelling piece of work."

Reunited with Reinhardt

Dieterle churned out quickly forgotten fare as a director under contract to Warner Brothers. Among them was his fifteenth film in Hollywood, *Fog Over Frisco,* a 1934 drama starring a young Bette Davis. He made the costume drama *Madame Du Barry* that same year, which featured Delores del Rio. But he was soon to become involved in one of the most epic projects in Hollywood, a screen adaptation of William Shakespeare's *A Midsummer Night's Dream.* This was technically in the hands of Reinhardt, whose Jewish background had finally forced him to flee Germany, now under the control of a right-wing, anti-Semitic Nazi Party.

But Reinhardt did not speak English, and Dieterle was contracted as his assistant.

The film was based on an immensely successful stage production that Reinhardt had presented at the Hollywood Bowl in the late summer of 1934. It was a major cultural event in Los Angeles that year, the first time that one of the founders of the Salzburg Music Festival staged a production in Southern California, and 15,000 ticket holders turned out nightly at the outdoor amphitheater for the eight-night run. The film version also had an all-star cast, with James Cagney, Olivia de Havilland, Dick Powell, and a very young Mickey Rooney as Shakespeare's Puck. It marked a rare occasion when a major mass market Hollywood studio attempted to adapt Shakespeare for the screen, and the critics generally hated it. Even decades later, judgment was divided over whether it was an ambitious classic or an ill-conceived trainwreck. "The Warner Bros. stock company declaims the poetry of England's greatest dramatist with the subtlety of a vaudeville patter song," wrote Scott MacQueen in a lengthy essay on the movie for the scholarly journal *Moving Image*. "*A Midsummer Night's Dream* is absolutely bereft of taste, starved for respectability. Nevertheless, there are those who find every blessed, demented frame an utter delight."

Nominated for Oscar

MacQueen's article discussed Dieterle's role in the doomed production, noting that he engaged in a press war with his studio bosses over the final director's credit for the movie. Warner executives made an attempt to appease him by pairing him with another European émigré, Paul Muni, for a new, more serious project. This was *The Story of Louis Pasteur*, and under Dieterle's direction the 1936 movie won Muni the Academy Award for Best Actor. The two went on to make *The Life of Emile Zola* a year later, which was the long-shot winner for the Best Picture Oscar, beating out *Stage Door*, *A Star Is Born*, and *The Good Earth*, among others at that year's Academy Awards. For *Zola*, Dieterle was even nominated in the Best Director category, but this would be the only such nomination of his career.

Prior to filming a third biopic with Muni, 1939's *Juarez*, about Mexican revolutionary figure Benito Juárez, Dieterle made a film about the ongoing Spanish Civil War. This was *Blockade* with Henry Fonda, but its clear leftist sympathies riled producers, and the Grauman's Chinese Theater premiere was cancelled. Dieterle followed it with what would become one of his best-known films, the moving *Hunchback of Notre Dame*. Adapted from the classic Victor Hugo tale about the disabled bellringer of the famous Paris cathedral and his love for a Gypsy (Romany) woman, the film debuted during the last week in December of 1939, with Charles Laughton and Maureen O'Hara in the leads.

Made Memorable *Hunchback*

Dieterle's *Hunchback* is considered one of the deftest adaptations of a Hugo novel to reach the screen, even following Lon Chaney's impressive turn in a 1923 silent

version. For the director—who had become a naturalized U.S. citizen in 1937—the pitiable protagonist seemed to stand in for a beleaguered, threatened Europe. "Strongly influenced by the rise of right wing extremism in Europe and the outbreak of World War II, the filmmakers altered the relationship of Quasimodo and his mentor by cranking up the fascistic qualities of the worldly Frollo and turning the bellringer into more of a Christ-like martyr," wrote Martin F. Norden in *The Cinema of Isolation: A History of Physical Disability in the Movies*. "Dieterle viewed Quasimodo as one of innumerable victims of tyranny."

Dieterle made two biopics with actor Edward G. Robinson in 1940, *Dr. Ehrlich's Magic Bullet*, about the scientist who found a cure for syphilis, and *A Dispatch from Reuter's*, which chronicled the origins of the news agency. In the summer of 1940 Dieterle and Warner Brothers parted ways, and RKO hired him to direct Walter Huston in *The Devil and Daniel Webster*, a 1941 adaptation of a contemporary short story from Stephen Vincent Benét based on the mythical German tale of *Faust*. He worked steadily through the World War II years, and teamed with independent producer David O. Selznick for a few projects. Selznick was in the midst of a messy affair with a screen newcomer, Jennifer Jones, whom he would later marry. Dieterle first worked with Jones in the wartime romance *Love Letters* in 1945, then took over from Hollywood legend King Vidor during the shooting of *Duel in the Sun*, a 1946 Western. Selznick assigned Dieterle to direct Jones in what would be one of the director's last great works, *Portrait of Jennie*, released in 1948.

Retired in Germany

Dieterle's 1938 movie *Blockade* came back to haunt him in the late 1940s and early '50s, when the U.S. House of Representatives' Committee on Un-American Activities began targeting Hollywood writers and directors with known sympathies toward the political left. Though Dieterle's name did not appear on the secret "blacklist" of professionals the major studios agreed to freeze out, offers of work became scarcer. When Paramount hired him to direct *The Elephant Walk*, which starred Elizabeth Taylor, he had trouble obtaining clearance to travel to Sri Lanka, where the movie was being shot. After that, he made a 1955 biopic of German composer Richard Wagner, *Magic Fire*, and a little-seen 1957 release about the medieval Persian poet *Omar Khayyam*.

In 1958 Dieterle returned to Germany, where he made a handful of German language movies, most of them for television, over the next decade. He lived in Munich and died in a suburb of the southern German city on December 9, 1972, at the age of 79. In an interview from the early 1950s, he once credited the Hollywood "backlot"—where a variety of exterior scenes could be filmed, creating a range of historical periods—for "its unique and considerable contribution to the celluloid art," he said, according to Philip Kiszely's *Hollywood Through Private Eyes: The Screen Adaptation of the "Hard-Boiled" Private Detective Novel in the Studio Era*. "Here are the real geniuses, technical craftsmen unsurpassed in ability and constantly on the alert to improve their skills. They provide the bulwark the director enjoys nowhere else in the world.''

Books

Kiszely, Philip, *Hollywood Through Private Eyes: The Screen Adaptation of the ''Hard-Boiled'' Private Detective Novel in the Studio Era,* Peter Lang, 2006, p. 188.

Norden, Martin F., *The Cinema of Isolation: A History of Physical Disability in the Movies,* Rutgers University Press, 1994, p. 140.

Periodicals

Independent (London, England), October 15, 1998.

Moving Image, Fall 2009.

New York Times, August 30, 1931; October 30, 1932; December 16, 1972.

Online

''William Dieterle,'' IMDB.com, http://www.imdb.com/name/nm0226189/ (December 5, 2011). □

Rudolph Dirks

During the infancy of the newspaper comic strip, cartoonist Rudolph Dirks created one of the best loved strips of all time *The Katzenjammer Kids.*

Built around a simple premise, Rudolph Dirks's popular comic strip featured two mischievous boys named Hans and Fritz who played pranks on the adults—primarily their mother's star boarder the Captain. In an era when corporal punishment was the accepted remedy for childhood misbehavior, Hans and Fritz—whether they were provoked or not—were usually spanked for their misdeeds, much to the reader's delight. Among the first comic strips to feature a regular cast of characters, effectively sequence panels to tell a story, and refine the use of word balloons, *The Katzenjammer Kids* employed wild, knockabout comedic action while portraying characters who spoke English dialogue with heavy German accents. The result was a clever, innovative strip that spawned many imitations—including a competing version by another artist—side products and animated cartoons. At its peak, *The Katzenjammer Kids* a.k.a *Hans Und Fritz* and later *The Captain and the Kids* appeared in hundreds of newspapers nationwide. Moreover, various incarnations of the comic have remained popular enough to last as a Sunday feature well into the present era.

Born February 26, 1877 in Heide, Germany in the Schleswig-Holstein Province, Rudolph Dirks was one of nine children raised by woodcarver Johannes Dirks and wife Margareatha. In 1884, the Dirks family moved to the railroad and lumber district of Chicago, Illinois. Young Rudolph quickly mastered a form of broken English, a skill that would serve him well in the future, while selling discarded newspapers for a small profit and developing a knack for drawing.

When older brother Gus moved to New York and began finding work as an illustrator, the seventeen year-old Rudolph followed and began selling cartoons to various New York based publications including *Judge* and *Life*.

At age 20, Dirks was employed fulltime by the William Randolph Hearst owned newspaper, *The New York Journal* in 1897. Editor Rudolf Block, then looking for a way to compete with R.F. Outcault's phenomenally successful strip *The Yellow Kid* in Joseph Pulitizer's *New York World*, commissioned Dirks to draw a continuing feature in the style of William Busch's humorous picture book *Max und Moritz.* Busch's work, which had been popular in Germany for over 40 years, had already been licensed by Hearst, But translating German language humor for an American audience was no easy task. Dirks stayed true to Busch's visual spirit while crafting a strip about two mischievous boys who cannot help but get into trouble, *The Katzenjammer Kids.*

''Katzenjammer''— which came via editor Block— literally means a ''cat's cry'' or ''contrition after loss,'' but to many German-Americans it was a slang term referring to a ''hangover'' from excessive alcohol consumption. As a result, the implied joke behind the name of *The Katzenjammer Kids* became ''the hangover kids.'' Debuting as a full color Sunday page on December 12, 1897, the strip featuring mischief-making blonde-haired Hans and brown-haired Fritz became an immediate hit with readers. Subsequently, the feature was syndicated to the rest of Hearst's vast nationwide newspaper chain.

Mixing visual slapstick with zany dialogue, Dirks's creation often reflected the humor of the times and featured racial stereotypes and gags considered to be in poor taste by modern readers. However it is worth noting that the era's vaudeville comedians could always raise a laugh by employing a fake German accent and *The Katzenjammer Kids* proved especially popular in urban centers that boasted a strong German immigrant population.

Early strips actually featured the father of Hans and Fritz, who acted more like a bemused bystander than a parent. The strip also showed the cast traveling via steamship to various exotic locales, including South Africa and the mythical Squee-Jee Islands. As the storylines gelled, however, Dirks settled the characters in a lush island just off the coast of East Africa and the father was eased out. In 1902, the Captain became their mother's star boarder and chief straight man for the kids. A comedic predecessor to 1920s and '30s character actor Edgar Kennedy, the Captain's slow burns and over-the-top reactions made him the perfect foil for the irrepressible lead characters. Later, in 1905, the Captain was aided in his battles with Hans and Fritz by Der Inspector, an often-thwarted local truant officer. Through it all, only the boy's Momma believed the Kids were just innocent, misunderstood children.

Two Competing Versions

Initially *The Katzenjammer Kids* was simply drawn yet could be appreciated on two levels. Rich in sight gags— such as the use of sawing wood as shorthand for snoring or seeing stars as a symbol for pain—it could still be enjoyed by fans who couldn't read. The strip was also packed with colorful wordplay expressed in pidgin German. Dirks also refined the use of successive panel layouts to tell his story while honing the use of word balloons for his often frantic characters. Typical was a September 3, 1911 strip as reproduced in *The Smithsonian Collection of Newspaper Comics*. Seeking revenge after being kicked by the ship's irritable cook, Hans and Fritz attach a rope to his peg leg and pull it into a hole in a cabin wall. Then after bopping the cook's head with a Punch and Judy doll, the boys attach a concertina to his wooden leg. Captured by the Captain and spanked, the boys enjoy the last laugh as the cook's leg makes an accordion sound with every step he takes.

The advent of R.F. Outcault's wildly popular *Buster Brown* strip resulted in Dirks's editor asking him to tone down the wild slapstick in *The Katzenjammer Kids*. Dirks, who believed that the Buster Brown character behaved worse than Hans and Fritz and dressed to match his behavior, made one attempt to give his editors what they wanted. Quoted in a 1950 interview with Jane McMaster that is republished on the *StrippersGuide.blogspot* Dirks recalled drawing "one page showing two nice little boys and a nice little mother. It was terrible. Not funny at all. I had to get rough again."

With the exception of a brief stint as a corporal in the Army during the Spanish-American war, Dirks enjoyed an uninterrupted 15-year run as one of William Randolph Hearst's top comic strip artists. That would come to an end in 1912. The comic stripper wanted to take time off to become a serious painter in Europe, which provoked a rift with both his publisher and editor, who took the strip away from Dirks. After a year-long legal battle, a court ruled that Hearst's paper owned the title *The Katzenjammer Kids* but that Dirks owned the rights to his characters. As a result, two versions of the comic strip were seen nationwide each Sunday. The Hearst papers hired Harold H. Knerr, who had been doing the Katzenjammer knock-off titled *Der Fineheimer Twins* (1903-1914), to do an exact recreation of Dirks's work. Meanwhile, the strip's original creator moved to Joseph Pulitzer's *New York World* syndicate, where he had retitled his strip *Hans und Fritz*. (Briefly, a daily strip ran in the Hearst papers, but neither Dirks nor Knerr had any connection to it.) Despite subtle differences in the respective strips—Knerr's work contained more visual slapstick and Dirks's featured cleverer dialogue—the public at large accepted both versions. By virtue of the established connection with Hearst however, the copycat appeared in more newspapers. Knerr would draw the feature and its topper/companion strip *Dinglehoofer und His Dog* until his death in 1949.

World War Caused Strip's Decline in Popularity

Successful on its own merits, Dirks's work spawned a string of merchandising spin-offs including dolls, games, puzzles, and comic books. As early as 1898, the strip was remade into a series of live action films by the American Muto Scope Company and Biograph Studios. From 1910 until 1918, live action versions of the kids' adventures were produced by the Selig Polyscope studios and starred Guy Mohler as Hans, Emil Nuchberg as Fritz, Chauncey Herbert as the Captain, and Lillian Leighton as Momma Katzenjammer. Further, Dirks's original strip inspired a 1903 stage play and a 1920 musical revival.

The advent of World War I provoked strong anti-German sentiment around the world and suddenly the popularity of the strip fell. Subsequently, Knerr changed the title of his strip to *The Shenanigan Kids* and had Hans and Fritz swear to a cartoon judge that they were Dutch. Dirks renamed his characters *Mike and Aleck*. After the war ended, Knerr's strip reverted to its original title and Dirks' creation was redubbed *The Captain and the Kids*. The new title more accurately described the feature's appeal and eventually led to a series of 15 animated shorts produced by MGM studios between 1938 and 1939.

Son Followed in His Footsteps

Dirks continued to draw the strip until his first stab at retirement in 1932. United Features Syndicate replaced him with his assistant, Bernard Dibble, while the strip's creator concentrated on painting with oils and experimenting with engraving techniques. An enthusiastic member of a New England art colony in Ongunquit, Maine, Dirks created seascapes using a palette knife on a small board and still life paintings that were shown at prominent Manhattan art exhibitions. Further, the artist was a trophy-winning amateur golfer, but he could not stay retired and returned to *The Captain and the Kids* in 1940.

Dirks and his wife Helen raised their two children John and Barbara to have an appreciation of the arts, and oil painting in particular. However, son John enjoyed comic illustration and, after serving as a Captain in the U.S. Army, joined his father in 1947, assisting him on the newspaper strip and drawing *The Captain and the Kids* comic books series for Standard and Harvey Comics, respectively.

The elder Dirks was a strict taskmaster who would throw out his son's layouts if he did not like them. Yet the younger Dirks persevered, learned to render the strip exactly as his father had and, by 1958, was given sole responsibility for the feature. By that time, *The Captain and the Kids* was a nostalgic anachronism that appeared in only 100 papers. By contrast, the competing *Katzenjammer Kids* was seen in 300 papers, both a far cry from the circulation they enjoyed during their earlier incarnations.

Rudolph Dirks—called "Rudi" by his friends—died on April 20, 1968 in New York City, but his comic strip creation has lived on in one form or another. John Dirks drew *The Captain and the Kids* until United Features abruptly terminated it in 1979. During his watch, the animated hijinks of Hans and Fritz could be seen on television as part of *The ABC Saturday Superstar Movie* and later as part of NBC's *Fabulous Funnies*, where Hans and Fritz were both voiced by June Foray of *Rocky & Bullwinkle* fame. Like his father before him, the younger Dirks was seldom idle. A renowned sculptor, he specialized in metal fountains which were shown and installed all over the world. John Dirks died on January 29, 2010. A smaller, less artfully chaotic version of *The Katzenjammer Kids*, drawn by Hy Eisman who also inks the current version of *Popeye*, is still syndicated by King Features.

Although the passing years have rendered the artist's work politically incorrect, Dirks's influence can still be seen in such visually expressive comic strips as *Beetle Bailey* and *Garfield*. To commemorate the impact of the original comic strip artists, Dirks's *The Katzenjammer Kids* was issued as a postage stamp by the U.S. Postal Service in 1995, alongside other classics such as George McManus's *Bringing Up Father,* Chester Gould's *Dick Tracy* and Hal Foster's *Prince Valient.* In 2009, *An Anthology of the Captain and the Kids* was published through CreateSpace, "The Katzenjammer Kids" *Early Comic Anthology* followed in 2010.

Books

Blackbeard, Bill; Crain, Dale & Vance, James, *100 Years of Comic Strips,* Barnes and Noble Books, 1995.
Blackbeard, Bill and Williams, Martin, *The Smithsonian Collection of Newspaper Comics,* Smithsonian Institution Press/Harry N. Abrams, Inc., 1977.

Periodicals

New York Times, Feb. 4, 2010.
Time, Mar. 4, 1957, May 9, 1932.

Online

"Archives of American Art Journal, Vol. 14, No. 2," *The Smithsonian Institution,* http://www.jstor.org/stable/1557032, (September, 10, 2011).
"The Katzenjammer Kids," *Dumboozle.com,* http://www.dumboozle.com/dumboozle/katzies/katdex.html, (November 4, 2011).
"The Katzenjammer Kids," *eNotes.com,* http://www.enotes.com/topic.The_Katzenjammer_Kids?print=1, (September 18, 2011).
"The Katzenjammer Kids," *Don Markstein's Toonopedia,* http://www.toonopedia.com/katzen.htm, (November 4, 2011).
"Mit Dose Kids, Society Is Nix!," *Steve Stiles.com,* http://www.stevestiles.com/katzen.htm, (October 19, 2011).
"News of Yore: Rudolph and John Dirks Profiled," *Stripper's Guide,* http://www.strippersguide.blogspot.com/2007/news-of-yore-rudolph-and-john-dirks.html, (October 19, 2011).
"Rudolph Dirks," *Internet Movie Database,* http://www.imdb.com/name/nm/ 0228216, (October 19, 2011).□

Anatoly Dobrynin

Russian diplomat Anatoly Dobrynin (1919–2010) enjoyed an extraordinarily long tenure as his country's ambassador to the United States. Dobrynin arrived on the job in 1962, a few months before the dramatic Cuban Missile Crisis that brought the United States and Soviet Union ominously close to war. He stayed through six presidential administrations, finally returning to Moscow in 1986 to help Mikhail Gorbachev forge ahead with new foreign policy initiatives. "To a generation of Washington officials in a perilous nuclear age," noted *New York Times* journalist Robert D. McFadden, "Dobrynin was the pre-eminent channel for Soviet-American relations: a tough, nuanced, charming ambassador who was, as admirers and detractors put it, no more duplicitous than he had to be."

Anatoly Fyodorovich Dobrynin was born on November 16, 1919, near Moscow, just two years after the Soviet Union came into tenuous existence following the ouster of the Romanov dynasty and triumph of the Bolshevik faction of the Communist Party in the waning months of World War I. A member of his family, Pyotr Grigorievich Dobrynin, had died in the 1917 revolutionary struggle as a commander of a Bolshevik militia unit in Moscow, and would later be commemorated by the renaming of a station of Moscow's underground Metro transit system.

Earned History Degree

Dobrynin's father has alternately been described as a locksmith or a plumber, and his mother worked as a theater usher. As a young man Dobrynin attended the Moscow Aviation Institute, graduating in 1942 at the height of the Soviet Union's involvement in World War II. He worked as an aircraft designer before he was selected to train at the elite Higher Diplomatic School of the Soviet Ministry of Foreign Affairs. In 1945, the year the war ended, he joined the Communist Party of the Soviet Union (CPSU) while working on a graduate degree in history; his master's thesis examined the 1905 Portsmouth Treaty that ended a war between the former Russian Empire and neighboring Japan.

In 1946 Dobrynin began working for the foreign ministry as a trade representative. Some of his early years were mentioned in a 1995 memoir, *In Confidence: Moscow's Ambassador to Six Cold War Presidents.* But as a review of the book in the journal *Foreign Affairs* noted, Dobrynin's unlikely transition from aircraft designer to diplomat was tied to a major purge conducted by Soviet leader Josef Stalin in the 1930s. In the years following the 1917 revolution, the Soviet Foreign Office was staffed by predictably urbane professionals who, Stalin came to believe, were insufficiently devoted to the Soviet cause. According to the article, "Dobrynin's class, which stepped into the not-yet-cold shoes of this vanished group, was selected precisely to be a new breed—not self-important experts but obedient executors of a rigidly centralized foreign policy."

Part of U.N. Mission

Dobrynin rose rapidly through the ranks of the Foreign Office after he was noticed by Andrey Vyshinsky, a former prosecutor at the Nuremburg Trials who became Stalin's Foreign Minister in 1949 and had Dobrynin sent to the United States in 1952 as a counselor at the Soviet Embassy. Within a short time Dobrynin rose to the No. 2 diplomatic spot at the embassy. Returning to Moscow in 1955, he served as an assistant to two of Vyshinsky's successors. In 1957 he was sent abroad once again, this time to New York City to join the Soviet Union's mission to the United Nations. A year later he was named Undersecretary General for Political and Security Council Affairs at the United Nations. In this job he worked directly under United Nations Secretary-General Dag Hammarskjöld in a vital role that called for high level negotiations on several matters of international security, including the stalemate over a Germany divided into pro-Soviet and pro-Western halves.

In 1960 Dobrynin was recalled to Moscow to take charge of the Department of American Countries at the Ministry of Foreign Affairs. This time, his boss was Andrei Gromyko, who would serve as the Soviet Union's Minister for Foreign Affairs for a record 28 years. In late December of 1961 it was announced that Dobrynin would be replacing Mikhail A. Menshikov, the Soviet ambassador to the United States. He arrived on March 14, 1962, on a flight from Paris to New York City, then traveled by train to Washington with his wife, Irina. Newspaper reports and editorials noted that because of his previous service postings in America, he spoke fluent English and that his familiarity with the United States seemed to signal that Soviet premier Nikita Khrushchev and other senior Soviet officials were warming to the idea of improved relations between the world's two superpowers.

"Gregarious and Amiable"

Two weeks later Dobrynin visited the White House to formally present his credentials to U.S. President John F. Kennedy, and both assembled for the press corps after their Oval Office meeting. "The 42-year-old Ambassador appeared to be affable, urbane and good-humored," reported the *New York Times*. "Speaking in English with hardly a trace of an accent, he said that his meeting with the President had been 'very pleasant.'" A few months later, the *New York Times'* former Moscow correspondent, Max Frankel, described the new ambassador as "gregarious and amiable, more interested in learning about the United States and its people than in preaching about the Soviet Union."

Frankel also reported that Dobrynin knew U.S. Secretary of State Dean Rusk from his previous stint in the United States, when he was at the United Nations and Rusk was a foundation executive. Kennedy tapped Rusk for his cabinet, and in Washington Dobrynin and Rusk apparently indulged in the American custom of an early evening cocktail at the end of the workday. Dobrynin also liked to play chess with Robert McNamara, who was Kennedy's U.S. Secretary of Defense.

Dobrynin's finest hours as Soviet ambassador played out behind the scenes during the Cuban Missile Crisis that began in mid-October 1962. A Communist revolution had brought Fidel Castro to power in 1959, and the presence of a Communist nation so close to the mainland United States unnerved many Americans. Twice, the Central Intelligence Agency had attempted to foment a counterrevolution after Kennedy took office in 1961, to the point of arming and aiding Cuban exiles in a disastrously botched invasion at the Bay of Pigs. Castro relied on generous Soviet aid to bolster national security, and Khrushchev's government authorized the deployment of intermediate-range nuclear missiles in Cuba in a top-secret plan. U.S. spy planes discovered the missiles, but the Soviet and Cuban governments asserted they were ordinary defensive missiles, not nuclear weapons that had strike potential to take out much of the U.S. eastern seaboard.

Met Clandestinely with RFK

Kennedy responded with a naval blockade to prevent further missile shipments from the Soviet Union, and the threat of a large-scale invasion of Cuba loomed in what became known as the Cuban Missile Crisis; in the Soviet Union the standoff was referred to as the "Caribbean Crisis." The possibility of a nuclear strike by either side put both nations on high alert, and the president assigned his brother, U.S. Attorney General Robert F. Kennedy, to meet with Dobrynin in secret as the stalemate continued over the following two weeks. The Attorney General met once with Dobrynin at the Soviet embassy on October 23, then twice more at Kennedy's Department of Justice office. After each meeting, Dobrynin would cable Khrushchev. In the end, a compromise was hammered out that was acceptable to both sides: the missiles were to be removed from Cuba, the United States promised not to invade the island, and Jupiter nuclear missiles that the United States had recently installed in Turkey were to be dismantled.

Dobrynin earned the admiration of Robert Kennedy for negotiating the Soviet side so adroitly. He maintained a similarly even-keeled pragmatism on other occasions, including the Soviet invasion of Czechoslovakia in August of 1968, and his superiors in Moscow were sufficiently pleased with his job that he stayed on in Washington a stunning 24 years, when previous ambassadors had generally been rotated out every four or five years. He was closely allied with Gromyko, the Foreign Minister who served under Khrushchev and then Alexei Kosygin, Leonid Brezhnev, Yuri Andropov, Konstantin Chernenko, and finally Mikhail Gorbachev. Dobrynin's years in Washington coincided with an equally lengthy list of occupants of the White House following Kennedy's assassination in 1963. He smoothed U.S.-Soviet relations with Kennedy's successor, Lyndon B. Johnson, and proved particularly adept at mending frayed foreign affairs during the first administration of Richard M. Nixon. Dobrynin's status in the Soviet sphere was cemented in 1971 when he was elevated to the Central Committee of the Communist Party, a rare achievement for a mere ambassador.

Worked Closely with Kissinger

Dobrynin was a key player in an era of détente, or the relaxing of formerly tense relations between the two super-powers. He worked to arrange a summit between Brezhnev and Nixon in 1969 that eventually yielded the historic Strategic Arms Limitation Treaty, or SALT. SALT I required both nations to reduce their intercontinental ballistic missiles (ICBMs). Much of the groundwork for these historic treaties was done behind the scenes with Henry Kissinger, Nixon's Secretary of State after 1973.

Kissinger even went so far as to permit Dobrynin's official ambassadorial limousine to use the State Department garage, where the Soviet diplomat had access to a private elevator that whisked him to Kissinger's office quarters. Dobrynin continued to finesse arrangements for a second SALT treaty during the White House administrations of Gerald R. Ford, Nixon's successor, and Jimmy Carter, elected in 1976. But détente policies rankled some hardline conservatives in the United States, who continued to regard the Soviet Union, its authoritarian regime, and its potentially deadly military might as the most pressing threat to international security.

Around Washington, Dobrynin was known as "Doby" and hobnobbed with diplomats, politicians of a moderate stripe, and even business tycoons who offered their private jets for his vacation use. He attended the Kentucky Derby and enjoyed fishing off the waters of Islamorada, a pricey area in the Florida Keys. When Carter lost his reelection bid to conservative ideology standard-bearer Ronald Reagan in 1980, the diplomatic climate cooled considerably. The Soviet section of the U.S. State Department, which ran the U.S. Embassy in Moscow, had long resented Dobrynin's cozy relations in Washington and access to power channels, which put American Embassy diplomats in Moscow at a disadvantage. Several days after Reagan's inauguration in January of 1981, Dobrynin's limousine was refused entrance to the State Department garage on orders of the new Secretary of State, Alexander Haig. Relations deteriorated over the next half-decade, and in early 1986 Dobrynin was recalled to Moscow.

Advised Gorbachev

Gorbachev had come to power a year earlier and quickly began implementing significant domestic reforms that resulted in the end of decades of one-party Communist rule and, ultimately, the collapse of the Soviet Union. Dobrynin spent the final years of his career as one of Gorbachev's chief foreign policy advisors and held a seat on the Secretariat of the Communist Party. He participated in the historic Malta Summit in December of 1989, when Gorbachev and Reagan's former vice president and successor in the White House, George H.W. Bush, declared an official end to the cold war.

Dobrynin's wife Irina was also a popular figure on the Washington social circuit during her husband's years as ambassador. They had one daughter, Yelena, who was a teenager when her parents moved to Washington in 1962 and stayed behind to complete her education. Dobrynin's granddaughter made visits to the United States, however, where she and her famous grandparent enjoyed riding bicycles in the nation's capital.

Dobrynin died on April 6, 2010, at the age of 90, in Moscow. His historic role in conveying the most sensitive foreign policy communiqués between American and Soviet officials during the tensest periods of the cold war was commended on both sides. Russian news sources quoted from a letter that Dmitry Medvedev, president of the Russian Federation, sent to Dobrynin's widow, daughter, and granddaughter. "It is impossible to overestimate Anatoly Fyodorovich's personal contribution to the solution of the Caribbean crisis and the normalisation of Soviet-US relations," Medvedev said, according to a BBC News report. In the *New York Times,* McFadden's tribute to Dobrynin commended his remarkable presence as the Kremlin's representative in Washington. "Even in the dark days of the cold war," McFadden wrote, "embassy guests found it hard to imagine hostility in the portly, gregarious man with the hearty, infectious laugh."

Books

Kennedy, Robert F., *Thirteen Days: A Memoir of the Cuban Missile Crisis* W. W. Norton & Company, 1969, reprinted with foreword by Arthur Schlesinger Jr., 1999.

Periodicals

Foreign Affairs, September–October 1995.
Independent (London, England), April 12, 2010.
New York Times, March 15, 1962; April 24, 1962; July 29, 1962; April 8, 2010.
New York Times Magazine, May 13, 1984.
Sunday Times (London, England), June 22, 1986.

Online

"Russia Honours 'Legendary' Diplomat Anatoly Dobrynin," BBC News, April 9, 2010, http://www.news.bbc.co.uk/go/pr/fr/-/2/hi/europe/8610992.stm (November 10, 2011). □

Antal Dorati

The Hungarian conductor Antal Dorati (1906–1988) was one of the key builders of the classical music scene in the United States after World War II.

Dorati's recordings, many of them released as part of the Mercury record label's technically advanced Living Presence series, were in many cases best sellers. As conductor of symphony orchestras in Dallas, Minneapolis, and Detroit, he brought high standards to ensembles geographically far removed from classical music's traditional strongholds on the East Coast. Dorati retained close ties with Hungarian musicians despite the waves of fascist and then Communist dictatorship that

overran his native country. With a group of them he made a complete set of recordings of the symphonies of Franz Joseph Haydn, exposing the record-buying public to many of those works for the first time.

Had Bartók and Kodály as Family Friends

Antal Doráti was born in Budapest, Hungary, on April 9, 1906. With a music-teacher mother and a father who was a Budapest Philharmonic Orchestra violinist, it was no surprise that he soon became interested in music. Dorati attended Budapest's venerable Franz Liszt Academy, becoming its youngest graduate ever in 1924 at the age of 18. Dorati's parents were already acquainted with the heavyweights of Hungarian music, including composers Béla Bartók, and Zoltán Kodály. He was hired by the Budapest Opera as a rehearsal director and soon became its conductor—once again the youngest one the company had ever had.

For the first part of his career, Dorati remained an opera conductor. After four years at the Budapest Opera, Dorati landed a post as assistant to famed conductor Fritz Busch at Germany's Dresden Opera, moving on in 1929 to the conductorship of the Múnster Opera in Germany's Westphalia state. From his base there, he began to build a reputation around central Europe as a guest conductor. Dorati, who was of partly Jewish ancestry, remained there until 1933 but concluded after the rise to power that year of Adolf Hitler's Nazi party that his opportunities in Germany would be limited at best. He took a job with a Monaco ballet company, the Ballets Russes de Monte Carlo, and became chief conductor of its offshoot, the de Basil Company, in 1938.

With one eye on European political developments, Dorati tested the waters in the United States with a guest conducting gig at the National Symphony Orchestra in Washington, D.C., in 1937. After the outbreak of full-scale war in 1941 he decided to move to the United States for good—fortunately, for several of his colleagues in Monaco's arts scene died in German concentration camps. During World War II he served as music director of the American Ballet Theatre, at that time a brand-new organization, and the New Opera Company in New York. In 1947 Dorati became an American citizen. "From the first day I set foot on American soil," he observed in his autobiography, *Notes on Seven Decades,* "I felt a great affection for that extravagant country....The moment in its history when I arrived, the Rooseveltian New Deal era, the magnificent effort of rehabilitation after the recession years, was, especially, one of overpowering impact."

Moved to Texas

After World War II, Dorati switched to symphonic music, although he continued to conduct opera and ballet on occasion in a guest capacity. He received feelers from several orchestras, but was especially intrigued by one from a group in Dallas, where there was no symphony orchestra in operation. Flying to Texas and sketching out a budget on a sheet of paper on the plane, Dorati was met by a group of business executives and a journalist who, he recalled in *Notes on Seven Decades,* was the only one who knew what a symphony orchestra was. After a conversation at the airport bar "conducted in a broad Texan drawl counterpointed by my Hungarian-flavored semi-English," Dorati was hired, promising that if the new orchestra was not first-rate, "I hang myself." Dorati built the new ensemble from scratch and put it on a path toward becoming one of America's A-list orchestras. He moved to Minneapolis to become music director (a position combining the responsibilities of conductor and builder of an organization's overall artistic direction) of the Minneapolis Symphony in 1949. The group was later renamed the Minnesota Orchestra.

Dorati remained in Minnesota for 11 years, a period during which he made many of his central contributions to classical music in America. His rise as a conductor coincided with the advent of the long-play (LP) record, a format that allowed an entire classical composition lasting perhaps 45 minutes to be recorded on a single piece of vinyl instead of a bulky album of breakable 78 rpm discs. Many of his recordings were made for the Living Presence series issued by the Mercury label; with some of the most advanced engineering available at the time. These albums made possible such effects as the recording of Peter Tchaikovsky's *1812 Overture* with its intended fusillades of cannon fire and peals of carillon bells. Dorati was perhaps the first conductor to perform the piece as written; it has since become a staple of outdoor patriotic concerts in the United States. Dorati made some 100 albums for Mercury alone; it has sometimes been claimed that he is the most often recorded of all classical conductors, but an accurate reckoning of this statistic is difficult. Beginning in 1936 he made more than 600 recordings in all.

Not in dispute was Dorati's general popularity, which was matched by an outsized personality on the podium. Stories of the conductor's temper, to which he freely admitted, were legendary among Minneapolis Symphony veterans. Recalling the aftermath of a mistake he made during a performance of Claude Debussy's *La Mer,* trumpeter Ron Hasselman recalled the conductor's reaction in an article by Michael Anthony in the Minneapolis *Star Tribune*: "Dorati, it was like his teeth grew six inches, and his hair just flew. He glared at me and conducted the rest of the piece with his fist." Dorati threw chairs, stalked out of rehearsals, and once dashed a player's tambourine against the floor. None of this was personal, however, and he might take the offending player out to dinner the day after one of his outbursts.

Recorded Haydn's Complete Symphonies

Even at the height of his American popularity, Dorati never relinquished his European ties. After the Soviet Union's invasion of Hungary in 1956, a group of Hungarian musicians fled to Vienna and organized the expatriate Philharmonia Hungarica. Dorati hatched a plan to help the musicians by using them in a project he had been contemplating: a complete recording of all 104 symphonies by Franz Joseph Haydn. The project was daring; only a few of Haydn's symphonies were regularly performed by orchestras at the time, and Dorati had to put pressure on his label, Decca, to get the go-ahead. In 1971 the project went forward. Dorati's instincts were vindicated when the Haydn recordings became durable successes, notching sales of an estimated half-million copies collectively and remaining standard readings of many of the individual works for years to come. The influential British critic Norman Lebrecht placed Dorati's Haydn set at number 28 on his list of 100 definitive classical CD recordings.

Unlike most conductors active in the United States in the middle of the twentieth century (with Leonard Bernstein a major exception), Dorati was a composer as well as a conductor. Dorati's Concerto for cello and orchestra was premiered by the Minneapolis Symphony in 1957. "It's not a great work," opined Michael Anthony of the Minneapolis *Star Tribune.* "It owes much to Dorati's teachers, Bartók and Kodály, though there are weird moments, such as in the finale, where the music suddenly sounds like Elmer Bernstein's famous score for 'The Magnificent Seven.'"

By the 1960s Dorati was something of a superstar of the conducting world. Critics regarded other conductors as more capable of profound insight into classical works, but Dorati had few peers when it came to inspiring musicians to produce crisp, lively, appealing readings. Much in demand among orchestras on both sides of the Atlantic after leaving Minnesota, he became music director of the BBC Symphony in 1963, the Stockholm Philharmonic in 1966, the National Symphony in Washington in 1970, the Royal Philharmonic Orchestra in London in 1975, and the Detroit Symphony in 1977. At his death he held the position of conductor laureate (conductor-for-life) of the last three of these ensembles, and he continued to make guest appearances with many of the orchestras he had conducted over his long career.

Beginning in the 1960s Dorati maintained a home in Switzerland, traveling frequently to pick up awards such as a quartet of honorary doctoral degrees and designation as Chevalier of the Order of Vasa of Sweden. Queen Elizabeth II made him an honorary Knight of the British Empire in 1983. A significant honor he did not live to hear was a tribute

concert mounted by the Minnesota Orchestra in 2007. *Notes of Seven Decades* appeared in 1975, and Dorati revised it for publication in Detroit in 1981. He wrote a second book, *For Inner and Outer Peace,* drew, and painted. Dorati died in Gerzensee, near Bern, Switzerland, on November 13, 1988. He was survived by his wife, the pianist Ilse von Alpenheim, and by a son and daughter by his first wife, Klári.

Books

Doráti, Antal, *Notes of Seven Decades,* rev. ed., Wayne State University Press, 1981.

Periodicals

American Record Guide, May-June 1997.
Evening Standard (London, England), March 9, 2005.
New York Times, November 15, 1988.
Star Tribune (Minneapolis, MN), January 7, 2007; January 12, 2007.
Times (London, England), November 16, 1988.

Online

"Antal Dorati," *Naxos Records,* http://www.naxos.com/person/Antal_Dorati_27343/27343.htm (September 6, 2011).
"Biography," *Antal Dorati Official Website,* http://www.antaldorati.com (September 6, 2011). □

Jimmy Durante

One of the best-loved entertainers of his era, Jimmy Durante's (1893-1980) career encompassed vaudeville, early talking pictures, radio, television, and musical recordings. Best remembered for his jazz-inflected catch-phrase "Hot cha cha cha," the comic exclamation "I've got a million of 'em," and the exasperated cry "Everybody wants to get into the act," his was one of the most imitated voices of the early television era.

Born James Francis Durante on February 10, 1893 in New York City to Bartolomeo Durante, a barber and his wife Rosa. One of four children—including Michael, Albert, and sister Lillian—the youngster was raised on the rough and tumble lower east side of New York City. From the start, the boy was well-liked but teased about the size of his nose so often that he rarely attended school, dropping out in the seventh grade. His father, who played operatic recordings on a Victrola in his barber shop, exchanged free haircuts for a piano so his then 11-year-old son could play classical music. Although he quickly mastered the basics of classical and pop music, the youngest Durante fell under the influence of the hottest musical trend of that era—ragtime. After sneaking into local honky tonks and barrooms to hear pianists pound the ivories ragtime style, he would run back home and practice for

hours, trying to duplicate what he heard. According to Durante, his father was so disappointed that the boy forsook classical music that he refused to watch his son perform until he was 81 years old.

Began Professional Career in Dance and Beer Halls

Durante began playing local dances, nightclubs, social gatherings and the occasional house of ill-repute when he was 17 years old. Working at Diamond Tony's, a Coney Island beer hall, the young pianist, billed as "Ragtime Jimmy" sharpened his musical skills while learning to play his nose and off-beat looks for laughs. (His nickname "Schnozzola" came via a chance remark from Jack Duffy of the vaudeville team of Bernard and Duffy.) One of his better early Coney Island gigs featured another future star, Eddie Cantor, at the time a singing waiter. Expected to play and sing requests—when not shilling customers along the Boardwalk—the duo would simply make up songs, much to audience amusement. Performing before hard-drinking crowds often consisting of gangsters and prostitutes, Durante quickly learned how to diffuse potentially dangerous situations with self-deprecating humor and jazz-drenched hubris. According to *Inka Dinka Doo—The Life of Jimmy Durante*, when Cantor noted the pianist's natural comic skills and suggested that he tell a few jokes onstage Durante responded, "Gee Eddie, I can't do that. I'd be afraid they'd start laughing."

Formed Jazz Band

In 1918, while playing the Alamo club in Harlem, Durante and his friend Johnny Stein assembled a group of New Orleans-style jazz players for a band alternately called Durante's Jazz and Novelty Band, New Orleans Jazz Band, and the Original New Orleans Jazz Band. The band recorded sporadically for the Okeh and Gennett labels without much success, but Durante's frenetic piano style drew other musicians to him. During the early 1920s, he recorded with several jazz outfits, including the Original Memphis Five, Ladd's Black Aces, Bailey's Lucky Seven and Lanin's Serenaders. Further, he worked with African-American songwriter Chris Smith to write "Let's Agree to Disagree" and "Daddy, Your Mama is Lonesome for You" for the first blues artist to be commercially recorded, Mamie Smith.

Concurrently, the pianist/bandleader was coerced into part ownership of a Broadway area speakeasy called Club Durant. Frequented by the likes of gangster Legs Diamond, producer Billy Rose, writer Damon Runyon, boxing great Jack Dempsey and columnist and future TV variety show host Ed Sullivan, the nightspot set the stage for Durante's early partnership with Eddie Jackson and Lou Clayton.

Started Nightclub Act

Throughout his early career childhood friend Eddie Jackson worked some of the same rough joints that Durante did, first as a singing waiter, then as a singer and occasional straight man. Jackson and his song-and-dance partner Harry Harris were equal partners in Durante's share of the club. When Harris wanted out of the failing business, tap and soft-shoe dancer Lou Clayton bought out Harris's share. Subsequently, Clayton used his show-biz expertise to build an act with Durante and Jackson that became the talk of Broadway. A classic nightclub floor show, it featured Jackson singing from one side of the stage, Clayton dancing into view from the other and both playing off Durante's newfound skill as a comedian and master of ceremonies. The trio sang, told jokes and playfully roused delighted audience members sitting at ringside. Further, Durante himself was a whirlwind of energy, manhandling his piano, tearing up his sheet music, and making up new lyrics to old tunes on the spot, all punctuated with his jazz age cry, "Hot Cha Cha Cha!" During this time, Durante wrote songs that would become staples of his act for years to come, such as "Jimmy the Well-Dressed Man," "I Ups to Him and He Ups to Me," "I Can Do Without Broadway, But Can Broadway Do Without Me," and "Everybody Wants to Get Into the Act."

Nicknamed "The Three Sawdust Bums" by *Variety* editor Sime Silverman, nightclub audiences enjoyed the improvisational feel and the camaraderie of the act, knowing that each night's performance would play out substantially different than the last. Moreover, Clayton—born Louis Finkelstein—proved a canny manager. Once prohibition enforcement agents forced the closing of Club Durant and another jointly owned venture, the Dover club, he successfully moved the trio into such legitimate vaudeville and nightclub venues as Leow's State, and the Palace Theatre. When not playing New York nightspots—where they gave future Broadway star Ethel Merman her first major showcase—they toured the country playing vaudeville's Keith-Albee circuit of theatres and made a comedic splash in the 1929 musical *Show Girl*. Clayton, Jackson, and Durante were now an inexhaustible established act whose fame was rapidly spreading outside of the New York area. However, most of the critical attention was lavished on the comic exploits of "the Great Schnozzola" and soon Hollywood came calling.

Broke Into Films

Clayton, Jackson, and Durante were paid fifty thousand dollars to appear in Paramount Pictures' 1930 feature *Roadhouse Nights*. The trio's only filmed appearance did not feature their raucous stage act and only Durante was noticed by audiences. Despite the stock market crash and subsequent closing of many theatres, Clayton, Jackson, and Durante remained a major nightclub draw while simultaneously appearing in the Broadway musical *The New Yorkers*. In 1931, MGM offered Durante a five-year contract which netted him thirty-five thousand dollar per picture. Neither Jackson nor Clayton were part of the deal, nonetheless, the ever loyal Durante paid each of his partners a third of his movie salary to keep the act together. As Durante's Hollywood career began to stretch out, Jackson grew tired of the enforced idleness and left the act to start his own solo career while Clayton became Durante's full-time manager.

Made Films with Buster Keaton

Most of the comedian's film roles were simply conceived extensions of his own personality utilized as comedic relief in dramatic pictures such as *The Wet Parade* and *Hell Below* or as the star of b-movie comedies like *Blondie of the Follies* and *Cuban Love Song*. Durante overshadowed Broadway legend George M. Cohan in the 1932 feature *Phantom President* but, according to his biographers, most of Durante's early films were critical and box office failures. However, the three films he made with Buster Keaton: *The Passionate Plumber*, *Speak Easily*, and *What! No Beer?* were solid moneymakers, although they represented a career nadir for Keaton. One of the greats of the silent screen, Keaton was stung by the loss of creative control over his pictures, and Durante's non-stop rat-a-tat style of acting obliterated his attempts at anything subtle. Despite the financial success of their pictures together, Keaton eventually drank himself off the MGM roster and Durante soon became dissatisfied with the roles he was offered.

Returned to Broadway

In between film assignments, Durante earned critical praise on Broadway in such musical comedy revues as *Jumbo* (featuring Durante bouncing jokes off an elephant), *Red, Hot and Blue* (co-starring Bob Hope and Ethel Merman), *Star in Your Eyes,* and *Keep off the Grass*. Meanwhile, films were helping advance his secondary career as a singer-songwriter. In 1934, MGM loaned Durante out to United Artists, where he appeared as Knobby Walsh in the film version of the comic strip *Palooka Joe*. Simply titled *Palooka*, the film is notable for introducing Durante's best-known song, "Inka Dinka Do," the Brunswick recording of which hit number four on the Billboard pop charts. The 1944 MGM film *Music for Millions* introduced another self-composed hit, the number twenty four charting Decca release "Umbriago." Durante gave one of his best supporting performances in Warner Brothers' 1941 adaptation of the hit play *The Man Who Came to Dinner*. Singing his own composition "Did You Ever Have the Feeling?" he

steals attention away from stars Monty Wooley and Bette Davis simply by being himself.

Despite the lack of a breakout starring vehicle, movies helped make Durante one of the best-known faces of his time and he was caricatured numerous times in animated cartoons throughout his career. Further, his gruff voice and unique performance style made him easy for other comedians to mimic. Yet, none of Durante's imitators could capture the simple folksy decency and quixotic attitude that made him one of comedy's best-loved stars. It was not until a new medium grabbed a foothold on American audiences that Durante's talents could be seen in full bloom.

Became a Star on Radio and Television

Durante's first wife Jeanne was frequently ill during the late 1930s and early 40s, which caused the comedian to only take jobs that allowed him to stay with her. She died in 1943. That same year, with his career on the wane, he accepted an offer to co-host NBC radio's *The Camel Comedy Caravan* while Lou Costello of Abbott and Costello recovered from an attack of rheumatic fever. Teamed with young comic/master of ceremonies Garry Moore, Durante's blend of goofy wisdom sprinkled with outrageous malapropisms was an instant hit and given a regular spot on the CBS show. Moore, whose humor was more cerebral than Durante's, was used more as a partner than a straight man and their relaxed chemistry proved effective. The pairing lasted until 1947, when Moore departed for a solo career that resulted in his hosting such prime-time television programs as *The Garry Moore Show* and *I've Got a Secret* on CBS. Durante, who brought in future sitcom star Alan Young as Moore's replacement, continued on the show until network radio was overtaken by television in 1950.

According to Gene Fowler's colorful biography, Lou Clayton's final wish before his death was to have Durante regularly appear on network television, then in its infancy. Durante fulfilled that request when he began starring on NBC's *Colgate Comedy Hour*. One of four revolving hosts—Abbott & Costello, Martin & Lewis, and Eddie Cantor also took turns hosting—Durante made the Colgate hour his greatest showcase yet. Using his self-penned theme song "Start Off Each Day with A Song" as an opener, he would trot out old gags with a fresh twist, feign vanity over his large nose, fracture the English language, and ad-lib like mad during sketches with important guest stars like opera singer Helen Traubel and pop sensation Frank Sinatra. Then, exhibiting a bit of old-time show-biz panache, he would offer the wistful sign-off, "Goodnight Mrs. Calabash, wherever you are." (Despite numerous attempts to unearth her real-life counterpart, the fictional Mrs. Calabash remains shrouded in mystery.)

Durante's award-winning run with Colgate lasted until 1955 when he began a two-year stint hosting the weekly *Jimmy Durante Show*. From that point onward he was a constant presence on network television, hosting specials, making dozens of variety show guest appearances, and emceeing such programs as *The Hollywood Palace,* and *Sunday Showcase*. In addition, the aging comic reprised his role as the elephant trainer in the 1962 film version of *Billy Rose's Jumbo* and Stanley Kramer's 1963 all-star comic caper *It's a Mad Mad Mad Mad World*. Further, his recordings of sentimental standards for Warner Bros. records yielded several fine albums rife with poignant dramatics and a number 51 charting rendition of ''September Song.'' However, he was most welcome on television and in 1969, ABC hired him to co-star on the short-lived variety hour *Jimmy Durante Presents the Lennon Sisters.*

Still working into the early 1970s when he voiced the narration for the animated seasonal classic *Frosty the Snowman,* Durante suffered from a stroke and retired in 1972. By then he had been married to Margie Little, a former Copacabana hatcheck girl since 1960—they dated for 16 years—and treasured their adopted daughter Cecilia. Awarded and feted by his peers, the man known as ''the Great Schnozzola'' died on January 9, 1980.

Books

Fowler, Gene, *Schnozzola—The Life of Jimmy Durante,* Viking Press, 1952.
Robbins, Jhan, *Inka Dinka Doo—The Life of Jimmy Durante,* Paragon House, 1991.

Whitburn, Joel, *Joel Whitburn's Pop Memories 1890—1954,* Record Research, 1986.

Periodicals

Time, January 24, 1944.

Online

''Jimmy Durante,''*All About Jazz,* http://www.allaboutjazz.com/php/musician.php?id=16595, (October, 23, 2011).
''Jimmy Durante'' *All Music,* http://www.allmusic.com/artist/jimmy-durante-p24263/biography, (October 23, 2011).
''Jimmy Durante,'' *Internet Broadway database,* http://www.ibdb.com/person/php?id=67393&print=1, (October 21, 2011).
''Jimmy Durante,'' *Internet Movie Database,* http://www.imdb.com/name/nm/0002051/bio, (October 23, 2011).
''Jimmy 'Schnozzola' Durante,'' *Red Hot Jazz,* http://www.redhotjazz.com/jdurante.html, (October 23, 2011). □

E

Emma Edmonds

Canadian-born Emma Edmonds (1841–1889) was living under an assumed male identity in the United States when she enlisted in the Union Army in 1861. She spent two years as a battlefield nurse and, she claimed in her sensational 1864 memoir, as a spy behind Confederate Army lines. In 1884, she was granted a veteran's pension for her military service.

Sarah Emma Evelyn Edmondson was born in December of 1841 in a rural part of New Brunswick, Canada, near Lake Magaguadavic. She chose early on to be called by one of her middle names, and at some point altered the spelling of her family name. The last of four daughters born into an unhappy marriage, Edmonds recalled her Scottish-descent father Isaac as prone to fits of rage and violence against her long-suffering mother and equally pitiable brother, Thomas, who was an epileptic. The hard chores of the farm fell to Edmonds and her sisters, and she became a fearless tomboy as she grew into adolescence. Yet she also loved the one-room church-run school near Harvey, New Brunswick, her mother insisted the children attend and dreamed of becoming a foreign missionary.

Dreamed of Escape

Around the age of 13, a traveling salesperson appeared at the Edmondson farmhouse late one night, and her mother offered the man dinner and a bed for the night. When he departed the next morning, he gave the young Edmonds a novel as a parting gift, the first she had ever read. She eagerly devoured the book, an 1845 story of *Fanny Campbell, or the Female Pirate Captain,* written by a Boston journalist and based on some actual accounts of women who passed themselves off as men aboard privateer ships during the heyday of piracy. The impressionable youngster immediately began imagining what life would be like if she, too, cut off all her hair and donned boys' clothing.

When Edmonds was 16, her father arranged a marriage for her to a much older man who was also a farmer, and the drudgery of her future prompted her to act. Her mother helped her fashion an alternate plan, asking an old friend who was a milliner in the town of Salisbury to take her on as an apprentice. The woman agreed, and Edmonds sneaked away from home. Just before she departed, a childhood friend named Linus Seeley gave her some items of his own in case she needed to disguise herself should her father pursue her. Edmonds mastered some millinery skills and went into business with another hatmaker in Moncton, but one day, the New Brunswick woman known as Emma Edmonds simply vanished.

Edmonds had answered a job ad in a newspaper calling for traveling book salesmen who offered book subscription deals, a nineteenth-century form of print-on-demand. She had written to the company using the name Franklin Thompson, and after the sales materials arrived she cut her hair, put on a man's suit, and tried out her new disguise. When she made her first sales call at a farmhouse, the owners treated her cordially, and she realized that strangers readily accepted her as a man.

Moved to United States

Dressing as a man was one of the most daring acts a nineteenth-century woman might do: in most states and countries, it was actually illegal to wear the clothing of the **107** other gender. But women had done so for hundreds of years, and the transgressive deed even became a common plot device in fiction and drama. Edmonds proved so successful at her bookselling job in New Brunswick and New England that she earned a small fortune in commissions and was able to buy a horse and carriage. At one point she even went back to visit her family when she knew her father was not at home. Family members immediately recognized her once they realized the farm animals had not stirred at the presence of a stranger, as they usually did.

Edmonds eventually landed in Hartford, Connecticut, and was hired by the American Publishing Company, which also sold books by subscription. She was well-liked by her male colleagues, while her refined manners attracted attention from young women, and Edmonds went through the social ritual of dating but avoided situations where any intimacy was possible. The company sent her "out West" to the lumber town of Flint, Michigan, in December of 1860. The nation was on the eve of the Civil War, and Edmonds's sympathies were with both her adopted homeland and with the Union side. Slavery was the root cause of the war, and Edmonds opposed the practice on moral grounds. Some of her new male friends in Flint were members of a local militia, but once war was declared in April of 1861 there was an intense recruiting drive for all able-bodied men.

Edmonds had no desire to fight, but patriotism prompted her decision to enlist. At the time, most recruiting offices processed men into military service without any formal physical exam, and Edmonds was inducted into the Second Michigan Volunteer Infantry on May 14, 1861, as Franklin Thompson. She spent several weeks in basic training at the Detroit fairgrounds and was fortunate to be assigned for training as a battlefield nurse. At training camp she served alongside her male friends from Flint, who continued to tease "Frank" about his diminutive shoe size.

Took Part in Peninsula Campaign

Edmonds headed south with her unit and worked in the new tent hospitals set up near the battle sites. The first carnage she witnessed came in the First Battle of Bull Run in Manassas, Virginia, in July of 1861. It was a victory for the Confederate Army, with more than 800 dead and three times that number wounded. The war that both sides assumed would be quickly over dragged into a second year. Edmonds was present at the massive Battle of Williamsburg in May of 1862 in Virginia, and wrote of it in her memoir, recalling the horrific sight of more than two thousand war dead. "All night long we toiled," she wrote in her book *Nurse and Spy*. "When morning came still there were hundreds found upon the field. Those of the enemy were found in heaps, both dead and wounded piled together in ravines, among the felled timber, and in rifle pits half covered with mud."

Historians believe Edmonds significantly embellished her adventures as a spy in her memoir. She claimed that she volunteered for an espionage assignment after a Union Army comrade was unmasked in a Confederate city and hanged for it. After securing a recommendation from her

superior officers, "I was examined with regard to my knowledge of the use of firearms," she wrote of the vetting process for such a trusted assignment. "Then…came a phrenological examination, and finding that my organs of secretiveness, combativeness, etc., were largely developed, the oath of allegiance was administered, and I was dismissed with a few complimentary remarks."

Edmonds claimed to have carried out eleven missions behind enemy lines. For the first, she disguised herself as a black laborer by using silver nitrate to darken her skin. She managed to get a kitchen job in a Confederate camp and gleaned important information simply from eavesdropping, then stole away in the middle of the night back to her Union camp. On another occasion she posed as an Irish woman peddler, and in one instance as a black woman laundress. Later in 1862 her unit was transferred to Kentucky, one of the crucial border states. Kentucky was officially on the Union side but internally, its populace was divided in their loyalties. Edmonds purportedly lived in Louisville as a man and infiltrated a group of Confederate sympathizers among the city's elite.

Forced to Desert

Edmonds had contracted malaria during the Peninsula Campaign in Virginia in 1862. In the spring of 1863, with the second anniversary of the war nearing, Edmonds began falling ill from recurring fevers. She realized she would have to desert in order to be treated and not unmasked as a woman in a military hospital, and sneaked off once again, this time leaving behind her male disguise forever. Her plan was to return to her regiment once she recovered, but then she saw the name "Private Franklin Thompson" on "Wanted" posters of known Union Army deserters. When her health improved, she moved to Washington, D.C., and found work as a nurse in a military hospital there.

Edmonds wrote a memoir of her adventures that was published in 1864 while the Civil War was still raging, though she did not divulge the alias under which she had served. Titled *Unsexed; or, The Female Soldier. The Thrilling Adventures, Experiences and Escapes of a Woman as Nurse, Spy and Scout, in Hospitals, Camps and Battlefields,* it was first issued by the Philadelphia Publishing Company. Two years later it was reissued under the more sober title of *Nurse and Spy in the Union Army.* The work was a bestseller, and its author donated all profits from its sale to veterans' relief organizations. At the time of its publication, Edmonds's book—though her exploits may have been significantly embroidered—offered a fresh perspective on the standard paeans to the gentleman soldier of the Civil War, men who were ennobled by their commitment to military service and willingness to die for their beliefs, whichever the side. Away from polite society and their wives and mothers, men were epic swearers and drinkers, women like Edmonds discovered, and she also witnessed many acts of personal cowardice and avarice.

Edmonds was one of an estimated 400 women who served on both Union and Confederate sides in the Civil War. Many were unmasked, but a few successfully maintained their ruse for the duration of their military service. *Nurse and Spy* remains a rare first-person account of such audacity, and Edmonds hoped to show that women were equally capable in defending their county in combat situations. At the time, deeply entrenched gender biases made such equality unthinkable. The horrors of war, moreover, were considered to have a brutalizing effect on the men who served. Edmonds also addressed this topic in her memoir. "Although the outer man appears rough, and much drunkenness and other evils exist in the army, yet there is much that is pure, lovely, and of good report in the character of both officers and men," she reflected. "It is true many have backslidden since they left home; but is equally true that *very* many have been reformed, and are now better men than when they enlisted."

Granted Veteran's Pension

Edmonds returned to see her family in New Brunswick after the war and met up with Linus Seeley. The two were married in 1867 and she once again was compelled to adjust the name to her liking, altering the spelling to "Seeyle." They lived in Ohio for a time, then went to Missouri and Kansas. Edmonds gave birth to three sons, none of whom survived to adulthood. Her own health was severely compromised by the lingering effects of her malaria. At one point, the couple lived in Louisiana and ran an orphanage for African-American children, and in 1883 they adopted two sons. When Edmonds visited her former comrades from Flint as a woman and revealed her former identity, they were stunned. They also convinced her to apply for a veteran's pension, and provided testimony to her service that permitted the desertion charge to be expunged from "Franklin Thompson"'s record. She was reportedly the first woman ever given a veteran's pension for wartime service, and was also the first woman member of the Union Army veterans' organization the Grand Army of the Republic. She died in La Porte, Texas, on September 5, 1889, and was buried in the military section of Glenwood Cemetery in Houston, Texas.

Books

Edmonds, Sarah Emma, *Memoirs of a Soldier, Nurse, and Spy: A Woman's Adventures in the Union Army,* edited, with an introduction, by Elizabeth Leonard, Northern Illinois University Press, 1999.

Gansler, Laura Leedy, *The Mysterious Private Thompson: The Double Life of Sarah Emma Edmonds, Civil War Soldier,* University of Nebraska Press, 2007.

Edmonds, S. Emma E., *Nurse and Spy in the Union Army: Comprising the Adventures and Experiences of a Woman in Hospitals, Camps and Battle-fields,* W. S. Williams & Co., 1865, pp. 82, 83, 106, 128.

Marquis, Greg, *In Armageddon's Shadow: The Civil War and Canada's Maritime Provinces,* McGill-Queen's Press, 2000.

Periodicals

Historian, Fall 2001.

New York Times, May 30, 1886.

War, Literature & The Arts, January 2008. □

Theodor Eimer

The German zoologist Theodor Eimer (1843–1898) was one of the leading theorists in the field of evolutionary biology in the late 19th century.

For several decades after the English naturalist Charles Darwin published his groundbreaking book *The Origin of Species* in 1859, Darwin's ideas were far from being generally accepted. And even among scientists who concurred with Darwin's basic ideas of evolution and natural selection there were questions as to exactly how these mechanisms worked: was there a specific set of principles that governed the evolution of species and the relationships among individual organisms, species, and higher classifications of living things? Theodor Eimer attempted to answer these questions, applying an existing concept called orthogenesis (in German *Orthogenese*) and popularizing it widely. Orthogenesis means directed or directional evolution.

Born into Political Refugee Family

Theodor Gustav Heinrich Eimer was born on February 22, 1843, in Stéfa, Switzerland, near Zurich. His father, a physician, had been on the wrong side of an abortive coup attempt against the Federal Assembly of the German Confederation in Frankfurt and had been forced to flee across the Swiss border. He practiced medicine there for a time, and then the family returned to southwestern Germany, settling in the town of Lahr near the Black Forest. They moved from city to city several times as Theodor was growing up, and he was educated at first by private tutors.

Later Eimer attended *Gymnasium* high schools in Bruchsal and Freiburg; the term indicated not a gymnasium in the modern sense but a school that offered a classical education and a path into Germany's exclusive university system. Deciding to study medicine like his father, Eimer entered the University of Tübingen in 1862. Over the next few years he attended lectures at several different universities, including those in Freiburg and Heidelberg; this was not unusual at the time, for many university classes were open to anyone who could pay the fee, and a celebrity scientist might draw large numbers of students. From 1866 to 1868 Eimer worked in the laboratory of the physician and anthropologist Rudolf Virchow at the University of Berlin. Although a pioneer in the field of social medicine, Virchow was an early opponent of Darwin's theories and gave lectures in which he argued against them. He convinced Eimer to switch from anthropological and medical studies to zoology.

Eimer passed his medical exams in 1868 in the city of Karlsruhe and then studied zoology for a year with the important evolutionary biologist August Weismann at the University of Freiburg. He became a professor of comparative anatomy at the University of Würzburg in 1869 and received a doctoral degree from that institution. At this point Eimer was mostly a histologist, a specialist in tissues, working on the mechanisms by which the intestines absorb fat. The year 1870 was a busy one for Eimer; he married Anna Lutteroth and the following day was "habilitated"—officially recognized as qualified to teach in the German university system—in the fields of zoology and comparative anatomy.

Served in Franco-Prussian War

At this point Eimer's career was interrupted by service in the Franco-Prussian War, for which he volunteered his services as a surgeon. He was sent to the front as German troops besieged the city of Strasbourg, where his wife, a nurse, worked beside him. Eimer received military honors but was forced to leave his post as he battled a long illness. The work for which he became best known began on the island of Capri, off the southern Italian coast, where Eimer and his wife had traveled during his convalescence in 1871.

While he was there, Eimer became interested in the jellyfish swimming in the Bay of Naples and in the island's isolated population of distinctive lizards. He made four more trips to Capri during the 1870s, filling notebooks with observations each time. Some of his work dealt with the nervous system of jellyfish, parts of which he mapped out by systematically amputating parts of the creature and then observing how rhythmic pulsations through its body behaved. He discovered that a type of jellyfish called a medusa could reorganize and regenerate parts of its nervous system in case of damage. Eimer also continued his work on intestinal tissue, but his work at the microscopic level is considered less important than the species observations he carried out with the naked eye.

Many of those involved a wall lizard he spotted in the Faraglioni cliffs region of Capri. He noticed that these lizards had more of a dark blue coloration than other similar lizards on the island, and he attempted to determine why. His answer, refined through later studies of butterflies, birds, and other animals, was that new species, such as his new lizards on Capri, resulted from a variety of factors—inborn traits of organisms themselves, natural selection in the Darwinian sense (whereby organisms better adapted to their environment survive and reproduce more effectively), and environmental factors all played a role. In an extended work, *Organic Evolution as the Result of the Inheritance of Acquired Characters According to the Laws of Organic Growth*, published in 1888, Eimer argued that there were four principles governing the evolution: 1) that an evolutionary process is preceded by changes in the growth of individual organisms, 2) that new characteristics appear in mature males and are passed on as inherited traits, 3) that such new characteristics tend to appear on an animal's back end or underside, and 4) that individual species are the result of stages that develop in a certain direction. The last of these principles, to which Eimer believed all the others contributed, is what is known as orthogenesis or directed evolution.

Became Popular Lecturer

Eimer combined erudition and original theories that were worked out to a detailed level. As a result, he was in demand as a lecturer and scholar. He moved to the University of Tübingen as a full professor in 1875 and became the director of Hamburg's Natural History Museum in 1888, continuing to teach full-time at Tübingen; his lectures were popular among students, many of whom (in the words of a *Dictionary of Scientific Biography* sketch) were "loyal, even adulatory," and between 1875 and 1898, despite periods of ill health, he took only one semester off from teaching.

In the later part of his career Eimer de-emphasized the importance of natural selection in evolution and turned sharply against Darwinian ideas. This put him at odds with his former teacher, August Weismann, and the two engaged in a scholarly feud. As quoted by Stephen Jay Gould in his book *The Structure of Evolutionary Theory*, Eimer wrote, "The evolution—the growth—of one species from another proceeds onward as though following a plan drawn out beforehand." Eimer's 1897 book *Orthogenesis of Butterflies: A Proof of Definitely Directed Development and the Weakness of Natural Selection in the Origin of Species* stressed the role of the internal design of organisms in their evolution.

That idea had a long history in German thought stretching back to the natural science writings of poet Johann Wolfgang von Goethe, and Eimer's writings gained wide currency. They were translated into English and became, in Gould's words, "the major English language source for the theory of orthogenesis." Gould's book traces the interplay between Eimer's ideas and those of other evolutionary theorists of the late 19th century. Aspects of Eimer's ideas retained their appeal well into the 20th century but eventually were found to have less explanatory power than Darwin's theory of natural selection.

Eimer and his wife were enthusiastic world travelers, at one point sailing up the Nile River in Egypt as far as present-day northern Sudan. His trips were always working vacations, for he recorded biological observations wherever he went. Toward the end of his life Eimer bought a small villa on Lake Konstanz in southern Germany, hoping to continue his work there. He began to suffer increasingly severe intestinal symptoms in early 1898 but continued to teach until May, when he underwent surgery. He died in Tübingen at age 45 on May 29, 1898. His wife, two sons, and two daughters survived him.

Books

Complete Dictionary of Scientific Biography, Scribner's, 1998.

Gould, Stephen Jay, *The Structure of Evolutionary Theory,* Harvard, 2002.

Periodicals

Journal of the History of Medicine and Allied Sciences, 1979.

Online

"Theodor Eimer: Defender of Orthogenesis," *Suite101,* http://mark-ulett.suite101.com/theodor-eimer-defender-of-orthogenesis-a362966 (September 7, 2011). □

Amos Elon

The Israeli writer Amos Elon (1926–2009) was one of his country's most prominent literary figures, writing nonfiction works concerned with Israeli affairs and with the history of the Jewish people.

Ethan Bronner of the *New York Times* called Elon "for many years [Israel's] most renowned public intellectual. A journalist active with the Israeli daily newspaper *Haaretz* for many years, Elon was one of the first Israeli commentators to focus on the perspectives of Israel's historical enemies, first the Egyptians and later the Palestinian people living in lands occupied by Israel. Fluent in German, Hebrew, and English, he wrote in all three languages. Several of his books dealt with the history of European Jewry and its effects on the Zionist movement (the belief in Jewish self-determination) that led to Israel's founding. Later in life, Elon often served as an eye on Israel for outside observers, writing essays for various international publications. Never uncritical toward the Jewish state, he became increasingly disillusioned with Israel in later years and eventually left his adopted country for a new home in Italy.

Family Fled Austria

Amos Elon was born on July 4, 1926, in Vienna, Austria. His father, Max Elon, was a businessman. In 1933 the Elon family, aware of the probable effects of the Nazi takeover in Germany, reluctantly left Vienna for Tel Aviv, then part of British-controlled Palestine. Elon grew up speaking German and continued to use the language with his family, who were admirers of German culture, after moving to the Middle East. But he also learned Hebrew and became a member of the city's young Jewish intelligentsia, whose efforts aided the formation of Israel as an independent state in 1948. Elon studied law at Tel Aviv University from 1944 to 1946. He was a member of the Haganah, the Jewish paramilitary organization that resisted British rule in the late 1940s, and in 1948 and 1949 he served in the new nation's army, reaching the rank of first lieutenant.

In 1950 Elon enrolled at Hebrew University in Jerusalem, studying history there until 1952. He won a British Council scholarship to study at Cambridge University in England in 1953 and 1954. By that time he had already begun to write for the Israeli daily newspaper *Haaretz,* and in the mid-1950s he joined the newspaper's full-time staff. With his broad knowledge of languages and history, he was an ideal candidate for the paper's staff of foreign correspondents, and he spent time in France, Germany, and Poland. At home, he gained notice for a series of articles on the problems faced by Israeli immigrants from around the Middle East and North Africa, who long suffered from poverty and second-class status compared with the nation's primarily European founders.

After stints in Europe, Elon spent several years as a correspondent in the United States, where he met Beth Drexler, an editor. The two married in 1961 and had one daughter, Danae Elon, who became a cinematographer. He returned to Israel and joined *Haaretz's* editorial board in 1965. Elon remained connected with the paper for much of his life, although his increasing success as a writer led him to depart for periods of purely freelance activity. His first book, written in German and published in 1967 in English as *Journey Through a Haunted Land: The New Germany,* showed his tendency to choose a controversial topic but to treat it in an evenhanded way, soliciting opinions from all parties involved; the book examined the effect of the Holocaust on the German populace 20 years after World War II, paying particular attention to the reactions of young people who had had nothing to do with the slaughter of Europe's Jews but bore the burden of historical guilt. The book shocked Israelis with its complex portrayal of a country that they had grown up seeing as the face of unmitigated evil.

Recognized Roots of Arab-Israeli Conflict

The book for which Elon remains perhaps best known, *The Israelis: Fathers and Sons,* appeared in English in 1971. A detailed and penetrating study of Israel's modern history, the book was critical of the nation's founders and leadership on several counts. Jews in British Palestine, he pointed out, had been so absorbed in the Zionist project that they failed in some respects to aid European Jews during the events that led to the Holocaust. The most controversial of Elon's contentions was that Israel's early leaders failed to take into account the aspirations of the 750,000 Arabs living in Palestine, thus setting in motion the decades of Palestinian-Israeli conflict that have in fact occurred. Elon was among the first Israeli writers to consider Palestinian perspectives. With an Egyptian official, Sana Hassan, he issued *Between Enemies: A Compassionate Dialogue Between an Israeli and an Arab* in 1974.

In 1975 Elon began a series of writings about the European roots of Israel's founding with *Herzl,* a biography of the intellectual leader of Zionism, Theodor Herzl (1860–1904). Herzl remains an Israeli national hero, but Elon presented a nuanced picture of the man, showing the roots of his beliefs in his experiences of anti-Semitism, but also delving into ambivalent aspects of his life and personality. In Elon's obituary in *Haaretz*, writer Tom Segev called *Herzl* "arguably the best biography ever written of the founding father of Zionism," and other writers noted that despite its level of detail and documentation, the book had a dramatic quality. Indeed, Elon and Dore Schary turned the book into a three-act play, *Herzl*, that was produced on Broadway in 1976.

A pair of Elon books appeared in English in 1981. *Flight into Egypt* dealt with the relationship between Israel and Egypt in the 1970s, a turbulent period that involved both renewed war in 1973 and the signing of a historic peace accord between the two countries in 1979. Elon traveled to Egypt and interviewed a wide range of political and cultural figures there. Elon's *Timetable: The Story of Joel Brand* occupied a space between nonfiction and fiction, based on the efforts of Hungarian businessman Brand's efforts to save Jews from Nazi Germany's death camps. Once again, Elon probed the murky circumstances surrounding some of the concentration camp internments, using literary techniques to imagine courses of action by the Allied powers that might have resulted in the saving of Jewish lives.

Surveyed Conflict in Jerusalem

Elon continued to write about both Israel and European Jewry, issuing *Jerusalem: City of Mirrors* in 1989 and *Founder: A Portrait of the First Rothschild and His Time* in 1996. The former was updated in 1995 as *Jerusalem: Battlegrounds of Memory*, as religious strife continued to worsen in the city that Jews, Muslims, and Christians all claimed as a holy center. In what Lawrence Joffe of the London *Guardian* called "an affectionate yet ultimately sorrowful book," Elon traced the rise of violence carried out by both Muslims and Jews in Jerusalem, linking that violence to wider forces in the world.

By the 1990s, Elon had gained a reputation as one of the senior observers of Israel's political and cultural scene. He found himself in demand as a commentator for international broadcast and print media. In the United States he contributed numerous essays to the *New Yorker*, *New York Times Magazine*, and *New York Review of Books*; many of these essays were collected in a book, *The Blood-Dimmed Tide: Dispatches from the Middle East* (1997).

Elon's last book, *The Pity of It All: The History of Jews in Germany, 1743–1933*, was a vast survey of Jewish life in Germany and of the contributions of Jews to what is thought of as German culture. "Most readers know that the '1933' in Elon's subtitle refers to Hitler's accession to power, but few will recognize the significance of 1743," noted Daniel Lazare in a *Harper's* review of *The Pity of It All*. "It's the year that a fourteen-year-old Talmudic student named Moses Mendelssohn entered Berlin through the city gate reserved for Jews, cattle, and pigs. The boy must have been a sad sight--hunchbacked, ragged, nearly penniless, and, Elon surmises, probably barefoot as well, despite having just walked across a hundred miles of hilly countryside." Mendelssohn,

a major philosopher, was one of the founders of modern Reform Judaism and the grandfather of composer Felix Mendelssohn. *The Pity of It All* won the Wingate literary prize in 2004.

Elon, who had fought for the establishment of the state of Israel and whose entire career had focused in one way or another on its development, found himself increasingly disillusioned with Israeli life in the 1990s and 2000s. A supporter of Palestinian statehood, Elon warned repeatedly that frustration of Palestinian aspirations would lead to steadily increasing tensions. He wrote (as quoted by the London *Independent* that "The Arabs bore no responsibility for the centuries-long suffering of Jews in Europe. Whatever their subsequent follies and outrages might be, the punishment of the Arabs for the sins of Europe must burden the conscience of Israelis for a long time to come." Dismayed by what he saw as increasing religiosity and militarism in Israel, he purchased a villa in Italy's Tuscany region and left Israel for good. "The move smacked of a man saying, in effect, 'I am withdrawing to civilized Tuscany,'" Israeli author Amnon Rubinstein told Bronner. Elon died at his Italian home on May 25, 2009.

Periodicals

Bookseller, May 7, 2004.
Globe & Mail (Toronto, Ontario, Canada), May 27, 2009.
Guardian (London, England), June 4, 2009.
Harper's, April 2003.
Independent (London, England), May 28, 2009.
New York Times, May 26, 2009.
Publishers Weekly, September 2, 1996; April 14, 1997.

Online

Contemporary Authors Online, Gale Biography in Context (October 5, 2011).
"Veteran Haaretz Journalist Amos Elon Dies Aged 84," *Haaretz*, http://www.haaretz.com/print-edition/news/veteran-haaretz-journalist-amos-elon-dies-aged-84-1.276679 (October 5, 20110.□

Dorothy Harrison Eustis

The American philanthropist and executive Dorothy Harrison Eustis (1886–1946) was the founder of The Seeing Eye, a nonprofit organization that has trained thousands of service dogs for the blind.

Many English-speakers use the phrase "seeing-eye dog" to mean a guide dog generally, but in fact "Seeing Eye" is a trademark that was coined by Eustis, who was the first American to organize the training of dogs for the blind, and among the first individuals anywhere to implement it on a large scale. Inspired by close observations of dog breeding and of animals in general, Eustis was inspired to raise service dogs herself after writing an article for the *Saturday Evening Post* about a German

dog-training program and then receiving a request for a trained dog from a blind young American. The Seeing Eye was incorporated in 1929 and remains in operation today.

Met President McKinley

Born Dorothy Leib Harrison on May 30, 1886, in Philadelphia, Pennsylvania, Eustis grew up as the youngest of six children in affluence. Her parents, who owned five carriages and frequently traveled abroad, were both members of old American families; her father was a sugar company executive and later provost at the University of Pennsylvania. The family spent summers at a large mansion in the small farm town of St. David, and her enthusiasm for animals, and dogs in particular, likely began during these vacations. At the age of 12, Eustis met President William McKinley when he came to dinner at the Harrison home. She attended the Agnes Irwin School in Philadelphia and went on for a further year of study at the Rathgowrie School in Eastbourne, England.

In 1906 Eustis married Walter Abbott Wood, a New York state senator and the president of a farm equipment firm. At first she was disoriented by her move with her husband from posh Philadelphia to the small upstate community of Hoosick Falls, New York. But she soon took an interest in an experimental farm her husband operated, where selective breeding of cattle increased milk output. She also acquired a German shepherd, named Hans, that was apparently of exceptional intelligence. Eustis and her first husband had two sons. In 1915 she was widowed after Walter Wood contracted typhoid fever.

Returning to the Philadelphia area, Eustis made plans to move to Switzerland, where she acquired a large estate near Vevey that she called Fortunate Fields. Arriving in Switzerland in 1922, she married George Morris Eustis the following year. With the assistance of an American horse trainer she undertook a large-scale German shepherd breeding program that was successful enough that some of her dogs were placed with Switzerland's army and with European police departments.

Impressed by German Guide Dogs

Still, Eustis was skeptical when she traveled to Potsdam, Germany, in the mid-1920s to observe a dog-training school operated by the German government, the Shepherd Dog Club of Germany, and an association of German soldiers blinded in combat. Eustis had seen many trained dogs that failed to perform consistently, but this time she was amazed by what she saw when she followed one of the school's blind clients through heavy traffic across the city and through busy Potsdamer Platz. The dog not only guided its owner expertly through pedestrian traffic but also stopped unfailingly at curbs and even resisted dangerous orders to proceed across a street if it meant stepping into traffic. Besides the dogs themselves, Eustis was impressed by the improved psychological well-being of the veterans who received them and moved from near-total dependence on relatives or friends to free agents who could go where they wanted to in the city, sit in sidewalk cafes, and look for work they were capable of doing.

A key step toward the development of The Seeing Eye was taken when Eustis published a 3,000-word article in the *Saturday Evening Post* about her experiences. The article was titled "The Seeing Eye," a phrase Eustis took from the biblical Book of Proverbs ("The hearing ear and the seeing eye, the Lord has made both of them") and appeared on November 5, 1927. Eustis described in detail not only the training of the German guide dogs but also the steps by which often depressed blind recipients became acclimated to working with them. "The proud young scholar [the dog] now turns teacher and through the same streets which have so lately served as schoolrooms, with the help of his own instructor, he teaches his new master the technic of a lead dog and shows him how he can guide him safely and surely," she wrote.

Among the article's readers was 20-year-old Nashville, Tennessee, resident Morris Frank, who had been blinded as a teen and was intensely frustrated by the new restrictions on his activities. Frank wrote to Eustis in Switzerland, asking her to train a dog for him, and volunteering in return to publicize guide dogs in the United States. He departed for Switzerland in 1928, and Eustis, applying the methods she had seen in Potsdam, trained one of her German shepherds, named Buddy, as Frank's guide. Frank held up his end of the bargain, calling a press conference upon his return to the United States and demonstrating Buddy's ability to lead him across a busy New York City Street.

Formed The Seeing Eye

The Seeing Eye was officially formed by Eustis in Morristown, New Jersey, and incorporated in 1929 in Nashville. It was international in scope from the beginning, with the Nashville office soon producing two dog graduates, Tartar and Gala, in Tennessee, and with Eustis as chief executive training dogs and eventually opening her own school

(L'Oeil qui Voit, or The Seeing Eye) in Switzerland. She was divorced from George Eustis in 1928 and around that time converted from Episcopalianism to the First Church of Christ, Scientist. Frank met with President Herbert Hoover in 1930. The Seeing Eye formed an association with the Canadian Institute for the Blind in 1936 and continued to expand its activities internationally, helped along by Eustis's fundraising acumen. The fee to a blind person was set at $150 for a first dog and $50 for subsequent dogs (many Seeing Eye dog owners remain as part of the program even after the deaths of their first companion animals). The fee as of this writing has never increased, but neither was it eliminated, even after The Seeing Eye became financially self-sufficient in 1958. Eustis had always argued that an investment in the dog by the student would add to his or her sense of responsibility.

By 1939 the Seeing Eye was serving 150 students a year, who received transportation, room, and board for their sessions at the organization's new headquarters in Whippany, New Jersey. Most of the dogs were female; several other breeds, including Labrador retrievers, were later used in addition to German shepherds. As The Seeing Eye grew and other similar organizations sprang up, Eustis devoted much of her energy to overcoming barriers to the blind in public accommodations. Some of the exceptions for guide dogs that are made to dog prohibitions in public accommodations and public transportation stemmed from her initial work.

Eustis received a gold medal from the National Institute of Social Sciences in 1936. She stepped down as president of The Seeing Eye in 1940 but remained active in the organization. By the time of her death she could look back on a record of more than 1,300 dogs trained by The Seeing Eye, and she had trained a substantial number herself. Her fundraising efforts were so successful that the organization not only could continue to sustain itself from investments, but also made periodic contributions to research into veterinary medicine, the causes of blindness, and independent living. She also donated large amounts from her own considerable personal fortune to the organization. Eustis died from cancer in New York on September 8, 1946. The story of Buddy, the first Seeing Eye dog, has been told in several children's books.

Books

Ascarelli, Miriam, *Independent Vision: Dorothy Harrison Eustis and the Story of the Seeing Eye,* Purdue, 2010.

Periodicals

New York Times, January 19, 1929; October 18, 1942; September 10, 1946.

Saturday Evening Post, November 5, 1927.

Online

"Our Mission & History," *The Seeing Eye,* http://www.seeing eye.org/aboutus/default.aspx?M_ID=88 (October 24, 2011).□

F

Lucille Fletcher

American writer Lucille Fletcher (1912–2000) wrote two of radio's most famous suspense stories, *The Hitchhiker* and *Sorry, Wrong Number.*

American radio scriptwriter and novelist Lucille Fletcher achieved widespread recognition as the author of such chilling radio stories as *Sorry, Wrong Number,* and *The Hitchhiker.* During her long career, Fletcher—a regular contributor to the radio program *Suspense,* penned more than 20 produced radio plays along with a number of suspense novels. Some of these works found their way to film and television through screen adaptations starring major performers of the twentieth century, from Cary Grant to Elizabeth Taylor to Rock Hudson; *Sorry, Wrong Number* alone became the basis for a novel, an Academy Award-nominated film, and two operas. Critics generally applauded Fletcher's tightly woven psychological thrillers for their spare yet compelling depictions of fear and sharply plotted storylines. Fletcher continued working for more than fifty years, with her final work, a novel entitled *Mirror Image,* reaching bookshelves in 1988.

Became Radio Writer

Born Violet Lucille Fletcher on March 28, 1912, in Brooklyn, New York, the future scriptwriter was the daughter of marine draftsman Matthew Emerson Fletcher and his wife, Violet (Anderson) Fletcher. Growing up, Fletcher attended Brooklyn public schools, where she nursed an early ambition of becoming a writer. Fletcher was a good student who was president of her high school's honor society and served as editor of the school magazine. After graduating from Bay Ridge High School, she won a scholarship to attend Vassar College. There, she continued her development as a writer, competing in numerous literary competitions and hoping to launch a career as a music critic. After graduation from Vassar with a bachelor's degree in English in 1933, Fletcher landed a job with the Columbia Broadcast System (CBS).

Fletcher's job as a receptionist for the head of music clearance at CBS afforded her not only her entry into the world of radio, but also the chance to meet the man who would become her first husband, the composer Bernard Herrmann. The couple had first met casually on the subway shortly after Herrmann's work made its radio debut on the program *Music in the Modern Manner.* Fletcher had recognized the composer and complimented his piece, and the pair had then continued talking as they walked to the CBS building. Fletcher was immediately taken by Herrmann's intelligence and force of personality. "I was so struck by his knowledge and talent and excitement that I really was exhausted. It was like Minerva walking out of Jove's head and giving him a terrible headache," Herrmann biographer Steven C. Smith quoted Fletcher as stating in his *A Heart at Fire's Center: The Life and Music of Bernard Hermann.* The couple then met regularly at CBS, where Fletcher took on increasingly responsible roles, including music librarian and publicity writer. Despite her family's opposition to Hermann because of his Jewish faith and her own apparent reluctance to wed, Fletcher married the composer in 1939 after he demanded that she either formalize their relationship or end it altogether.

The year after her marriage, Fletcher decided to make the leap from typist of radio plays to creator. By that time, she had written a handful of stories and articles for publications such as *Movie Mirror,* the *New Yorker,* and the *Detroit Free Press.* Her first radio effort was an adaptation of a short story that she had penned earlier called *My Cousin Curley.*

115

Written in conjunction with experienced radio author Norman Corwin, the light-hearted tale featured a singing and dancing caterpillar who becomes famous.

Before long, however, Fletcher transitioned from comedy to drama. During 1940, Fletcher and her husband travelled frequently between New York and Los Angeles, where Herrmann was working on the score for Orson Welles's film *Citizen Kane*. During one trip via automobile, an unusual event struck Fletcher: she noticed a hitchhiker walking on the Brooklyn Bridge, and then saw someone who appeared to be the same man again several miles away on the Pulaski Skyway. "I didn't quite know what to do with the idea until a year later," Smith quoted Fletcher as recalling, "when...I conceived the idea of doing it as a ghost story." The resulting tale followed a man who sees the same odd-looking hitchhiker at various geographic points during a cross-country trip—much to his growing distress—only to discover that he himself died in a car accident some days before. The mysterious hitchhiker represents Death, calmly awaiting the protagonist to fully grasp his fate and take him along on his final ride. First broadcast with Welles in the main role, *The Hitchhiker* was made more ominous by the addition of Herrmann's dark score and the clever use of various sound effects to convey and highlight main points in the action, a relatively new approach to radio storytelling at the time. The program initially aired on the *Campbell Theater* and was hailed as one of the show's finest episodes of 1941.

That same year, Fletcher gave birth to her first daughter with Herrmann, Dorothy. Another daughter, Wendy, followed in 1945. The Herrmanns divorced in 1948 amidst the stresses of their careers, but later reconciled and remained friends until Herrmann's death in 1977. A year after her divorce, Fletcher remarried to writer Douglas Wallop, best known as the author of *The Year the Yankees Lost the Pennant*, which was adapted as the musical *Damn Yankees*. This marriage lasted until Wallop's death in 1985.

Plays Conveyed Fear and Anxiety

Fletcher wrote more than 20 radio screenplays in all, with many of these appearing on leading drama programs of the day, including *Suspense*, the *Mercury Theater on the Air*, *Lights Out*, and the *Chrysler Theater*. Many of her stories hinged on the psychological development of fear and suspense rather than on the details of a plot, building an increasing mood of terror by emphasizing the central character's growing isolation or anxiety. Perhaps as a result of this psychological focus, Fletcher's storylines typically followed a fairly predictable pattern. The *St. James Guide to Crime & Mystery Writers* explained that the "hallmark of Fletcher's mark is that the solution of the mystery is only the first part of a twofold conclusion. The second climax of each story provides an unexpected twist—a new murder is committed, a disguise penetrated, a motive revealed." This technique helped keep Fletcher's stories engaging for listeners, who typically found these twists fresh and surprising.

Just such a twist appeared in Fletcher's best-known radio play, *Sorry, Wrong Number*, first broadcast on *Suspense*

in May of 1943. Written as what Fletcher's daughter Dorothy Herrmann told Lawrence Van Gelder of the *New York Times* was "an act of revenge" against a particularly rude, seemingly well-off woman that had refused to let Fletcher go ahead of her in line at a supermarket when the writer was buying an item for a sick child, the drama focused on the events surrounding a bedridden woman who accidently overhears plans to commit a murder. Over the course of the story, the woman repeatedly attempts to get help from telephone operators or the police, who dismiss her increasingly hysterical claims that someone is about to be murdered as the ravings of a bored, lonely woman. By the end of the play, however, the murder—which has been revealed to be of the central character herself—goes ahead as planned, covered by the sound of a nearby train. The intense performance of actress Agnes Moorehead contributed to the taut thrill of the story. Despite a missed cue by the actor portraying the killer that made the resolution of the play somewhat unclear, *Sorry, Wrong Number*, was deemed an unqualified success. Writing in the *On the Air: Encyclopedia of Old-Time Radio*, John Dunning declared that "*Sorry* transcended *Suspense* and widely perceived to be the most effective radio show ever." Famed entertainer Orson Welles praised the program, and listeners made it so popular that *Suspense* recreated the performance seven times over the course of the next several years—a feat made possible in part by the popularity of the story itself, which helped *Suspense* pick up a sponsor and thus continue to broadcast.

Sorry, Wrong Number became the basis for Fletcher's first novel, an adaption of the story co-written with Allan Ullman. The collaborators teamed up again for the 1951 novel *Night Man*. Afterwards, Fletcher exclusively worked alone, producing seven more suspense novels between 1958 and 1988. These included *The Daughters of Jasper Clay* (1958), *Blindfold* (1960), *And Presumed Dead* (1963), *The Strange Blue Yawl* (1964), *The Girl in Cabin B4* (1968), *Eighty Dollars to Stamford* (1975), and *Mirror Image* (1988). Like her radio plays, Fletcher's novels relied on what the *St. James Guide to Mystery & Crime Writers* termed a "predictable pattern... Nevertheless, they are generally satisfying examples of this variation of the genre."

Works Adapted for Film and Television

During the course of her long career, Fletcher saw many of her radio plays and novels translated onto the large and small screens. Co-writer Corwin adapted Fletcher's *My Cousin Curley* into a 1944 movie starring actor Cary Grant that was renamed *Once Upon a Time*. The author's 1941 thriller debut *The Hitchhiker* was reinterpreted for television as an episode of *The Twilight Zone*, and *Blindfold* became a 1965 film starring Rock Hudson. In 1972, *Night Watch* was staged as a Broadway play; the following year, it also graced the silver screen with Elizabeth Taylor as its star. Ten years later, Fletcher's novel *Eighty Dollars to Stamford* came to movie screens as the retitled *Hit and Run*.

Unsurprisingly, Fletcher's most famous work was also the most frequently revived in various forms. *Sorry, Wrong*

Number was translated into 15 languages—including Zulu, a nod to the story's wide appeal—and became the basis for two operas and two films. In 1948, Barbara Stanwyck starred in the main role of the silver screen version of *Sorry, Wrong Number.* Her performance earned Stanwyck an Academy Award nomination, even as Fletcher garnered nominations for both an Edgar and a Writers Guild of America award for screenwriting. More than 50 years later, actress Loni Anderson reprised this central role in a cable television remake.

Some of these adaptations of Fletcher's works were more successful than others. Writing in 1944, the *New York Times*'s Bosley Crowther gently praised *My Cousin Curley* for its "whimsy" and "charming twist." Crowther offered a measured assessment of *Sorry, Wrong Number,* complaining of its reliance on coincidence and overly complex plot structure. "As a sheer exercise in melodrama and in cumulative suspense," he admitted, however, "this film has some highly vivid episodes and a grimly exciting final reel." Decades later, theater critic Walter Goodman skewered a 1986 revival of *Night Watch* in the *New York Times,* complaining that "The writing is wretched...and the cast lives down to it. This mystery is full of bad actors."

After the publication of *Mirror Image,* Fletcher retired from both writing and the public eye. She spent most her final years in Oxford, Maryland, a small town on the state's Eastern Shore. In her later years, the writer dedicated time to community involvement and was active as an organist in a local Methodist church. Fletcher died on August 31, 2000, in Langhorne, Pennsylvania. She was survived by her two daughters and two grandsons, as well as by her body of written and recorded work. Even decades after their first appearances, Fletcher's stories continued to attract recognition, and the writer herself was hailed by the online journal *Dagger of the Mind* as "Radio's First Queen of Screams."

Books

Dunning, John, *On the Air: The Encyclopedia of Old-Time Radio,* Oxford University Press, 1998.

Smith, Steven C., *A Heart at Fire's Center: the Life and Music of Bernard Herrmann* University of California Press, 1991.

St. James Guide to Mystery & Crime Writers, Gale, 1996.

Periodicals

Economist, September 16, 2000.

Journal of American Studies, Volume 44, Issue 1.

New York Times, May 18, 1919; June 30, 1944; September 2, 1948; December 9, 1986; September 6, 2000.

Online

"Fletcher, Lucille," American National Biography Online, http://www.anb.org (November 20, 2011).

"Lucille Fletcher: Radio's First Queen of Screams," *Dagger of the Mind,* http://web.archive.org/web/20091027132313/http://geocities.com/Vienna/Stage/1045/Features/Fletcher.html (September 15, 2011). □

Errol Flynn

Errol Flynn's vivid off-screen life rivaled the adventurous roles he played in big-budget Technicolor epics of the 1930s and '40s. The Australian-born actor swaggered through some of Hollywood's most expensive costume dramas and gritty war sagas as a contract player with Warner Brothers, but his substance abuse issues, romances, and arrests habitually landed him in the gossip columns and tabloid headlines of the day. Eventually Flynn's lifestyle took its toll on his health, and his career languished as he entered middle age. "Don't worry about me," his second ex-wife recalled him saying a few months before his death at age 50, according to *Hollywood's Original Rat Pack: The Bards of Bundy Drive.* "I have lived twice."

Errol Leslie Flynn was born on June 20, 1909, in Hobart, the capital city of Australia's island state of Tasmania. He claimed his mother, Marelle, was descended from one of the mutineers of the H.M.S. *Bounty,* who scattered throughout the South Pacific after the 1789 event, but his lineage almost certainly included settlers from a less romanticized era of Australian immigration, when convicts and indentured servants were shipped halfway around the world by British authorities to Tasmania's penal colonies.

Lived a Rogue's Life

Flynn's father was a respected professor of biology at the University of Tasmania, but his son was ill-suited to the regimen of formal schooling, and was expelled from several institutions for general insolence or various disciplinary infractions. The family moved to Sydney, Australia's largest city, in 1920, and for a time Flynn was sent to a boarding school in England, which he also disliked. Returning to the Antipodes, he was finally ejected from Sydney Church of England Grammar School in 1926 and went to work as a mail clerk. The job afforded him ample time for tennis, amateur boxing, and socializing with the opposite sex; even as a 17-year-old Flynn had gained a reputation in both Hobart and Sydney as a rakishly attractive charmer of women.

Flynn's thirst for adventure took him to New Guinea, where he carried on drinking and dallying with women while involved in a series of scattershot entrepreneurial schemes. For a time he ran a tobacco farm, then mined for gold, and finally bought a share in a yacht, the *Sirocco.* In mid-1932 he was cast by chance in an Australian movie based on the *Bounty* story, *In the Wake of the Bounty,* in the lead role of Fletcher Christian. He earned some good reviews, and within a year had made his way to England to pursue an acting career there. Along the way he made stops in Hong Kong and Thailand to visit brothels, where he allegedly contracted a venereal disease. He had already

come down with malaria in New Guinea, and these chronic conditions would be the first in a string of health problems for Flynn that belied his robust appearance.

Signed by Warner Brothers

In late 1933 Flynn joined the Northampton Repertory Players, and quickly became the most exciting new resident of this English Midlands city. Young women, entranced by his good looks and competence on the stage, waited outside the stage door at the close of performances. Flynn's charm soon took him to London, where he was cast in a 1934 thriller, *Murder at Monte Carlo,* made by Warner Brothers at their Teddington Studios in suburban London. Within a few months the head of the Hollywood studio, Jack Warner, had signed Flynn to a contract and paid his passage on a ship bound for New York City. On board, Flynn met an already moderately successful French film star, Lili Damita, who became his first wife.

Flynn fabricated many details of his biography for the benefit of the Warner Brothers publicity department. He claimed to be an Olympic-caliber boxer and had fended off a cannibal attack in New Guinea, in addition to his more demonstrable skills as a sailor. Betting heavily on his potential box office appeal, the studio cast him in the lead of a 1935 period drama called *Captain Blood,* a swashbuckler set in the seventeenth-century Caribbean that co-starred him with Olivia de Havilland. The movie earned decent reviews, and made Flynn a star virtually overnight.

Warner Brothers paired Flynn again and again with de Havilland, usually under the guidance of tough Hungarian émigré director Michael Curtiz, in epic action-adventure films. These included a Crimean War epic from 1936, *The Charge of the Light Brigade,* followed by *The Prince and the Pauper,* a costume drama based on the Mark Twain novel. One of Flynn's most memorable roles came as the lead in *The Adventures of Robin Hood,* an expensive

Technicolor film that became the second highest-grossing U.S. studio release of 1938 and was nominated for an Academy Award for Best Picture. Flynn sported green tights and ably slashed, rode, and romanced his way through medieval Sherwood Forest, with de Havilland as his Maid Marian. Writing in the *Los Angeles Times* decades later, film critic Susan King hailed Curtiz's epic as the best among all of the Robin Hood versions ever to appear on screen. "Dripping with sexuality, good humor, panache and swagger, Flynn's Robin of Locksley captures not only the derring-do of the character, but also the more dramatic side of his fight for injustice, uttering such delectable lines as...'It's injustice I hate, not the Normans.'"

Earned Bette Davis's Wrath

In a 25-year career, Flynn appeared in more than 50 movies, but he worked at a breakneck pace during his first decade. In addition to the *Robin Hood* project, he appeared in three other 1938 releases: *The Dawn Patrol,* a war saga; the romantic comedy *Four's a Crowd*; and *The Sisters,* a melodrama that co-starred him with Bette Davis. A year later, he romanced Davis again on screen in a costume drama about England's Tudor queen, *The Private Lives of Elizabeth and Essex,* but this coupling was not as successful as the visible on-screen chemistry between Flynn and de Havilland. A profile on Flynn for the Turner Classic Movies Web site called it "an oil-and-water mix, Flynn the arrogant upstart who made no pretense at art, Davis the intrepid artiste, later recounting how Flynn, upon their screen-kisses, would tongue-kiss her—a taboo in film then—with the taste of the previous night's bender in his mouth. In one scene that called for her to fake-slap him, Davis walloped Flynn, prompting a genuine near-violent reaction still evident in the film."

In 1940 Flynn made one of his best-loved films, *The Sea Hawk,* as an English pirate loosely based on the story of Sir Francis Drake and England's vanquishing of the mighty Spanish Armada. Its epic sword duel between Flynn and another actor took a stunning eight days to film under Curtiz's direction, while Flynn's penchant for drinking and womanizing started to take its toll on his physical health.

With the outbreak of World War II, Flynn pronounced himself ready to fight off-screen. He became a naturalized U.S. citizen in 1942, but draft boards declared him unfit for service due to his accumulating health issues. He suffered from an enlarged heart, a heart murmur, recurring episodes of malaria, jaundice, and tuberculosis, as well as at least one sexually transmitted disease and ongoing trouble with his back, which he medicated with morphine and then heroin. There was some public criticism for his failure to serve, but Warner Brothers resisted revealing any details about his health, lest it detract from the seemingly robust star's box office appeal.

Charged with Statutory Rape

Flynn's alcohol use and womanizing was also an issue for the studio. He was divorced from Damita in 1942, but a year earlier had taken the *Sirocco* out for a sail to Santa Catalina Island with friends and three young women. In

October 1942 the Los Angeles County District Attorney's office arrested Flynn on statutory rape charges for assaulting one of the women on the boat, Peggy Satterlee, who was 15 years old at the time. Prosecutors also had found another young woman, 17-year-old Betty Hansen, who claimed that Flynn had sexually assaulted her at a party at a private home in Bel Air in September of 1942.

The Flynn case made headlines as it went to trial in early 1943. Flynn's team of attorneys demolished the young women's reputations on the stand. A studio messenger testified that Hansen had engaged in sexual acts with him prior to the Bel Air party, and at the time of the trial the then-17-year-old Satterlee was living with her boyfriend. The jury, consisting of nine women and three men, voted for acquittal on both counts. "My confidence in American justice is completely justified," Flynn said at the end of the trial, according to film historian Jeannine Basinger's 2007 book *The Star Machine*. "I am sincerely grateful to all those whose confidence in me encouraged me to go through this ordeal."

With the criminal charges behind him, Flynn returned to an arduous workload. He made two war films directed by Raoul Walsh, *Uncertain Glory* and *Objective, Burma!* In 1946 he took a rare turn in a romantic comedy, *Never Say Goodbye* opposite Eleanor Parker. He returned to action hero form in another Technicolor epic, 1948's *Adventures of Don Juan,* but his career began to falter after that. For much of the 1950s he was cast in little-seen films that failed to make a dent at the box office. His single choice role came in the 1957 screen adaptation of Ernest Hemingway's novel *The Sun Also Rises.*

Died in Vancouver

Flynn's 1944 marriage to actress Nora Eddington produced two daughters, Deirdre and Rory, and he already had a son, Sean, from his first marriage. In 1950 he married for a third time, this time to Patrice Wymore, another actress. But his marital infidelities continued, and the scandalous 1943 trial had done little to dampen his dalliances with significantly younger women. In 1957 he met a 15-year-old dancer on a Warner Brothers movie set named Beverly Aadland, and threw her a 16th birthday party in Jamaica, where he owned property. Improbably, he cast her in a semi-documentary film he made in 1959 called *Cuban Rebel Girls,* about the Cuban revolution under Fidel Castro that had taken over the Caribbean island nation. The couple also met with director Stanley Kubrick, who was planning a controversial adaptation of Vladimir Nabokov's novel *Lolita,* whose plot centered around a middle-aged man's fascination with a pre-adolescent girl.

Aadland was with Flynn when he traveled to Vancouver, British Columbia, in October of 1959 to meet with a Canadian tycoon named George Caldough, who was interested in purchasing Flynn's yacht, the *Zaca.* Caldough was driving the couple to the airport when Flynn became ill, and Caldough drove him instead to the home of a physician friend, Dr. Grant Gould. Flynn seemed to recover at the apartment, and another round of drinking commenced. He then excused himself to take a nap, telling his audience "I shall return," while Aadland telephoned to reschedule their

flight. She returned to check on him an hour later and found him unconscious. Flynn had died of a heart attack at age 50.

Flynn's legacy as one of Hollywood's most legendary rakes endured for decades after his death, spawning several books that added salacious details to his already bawdy biography. The first of these was his bestselling memoir, *My Wicked, Wicked Ways,* published posthumously. Aadland's mother wrote a tell-all tome, as did his former stuntman and his daughter Rory. But the most scandalous of the recaps was Charles Higham's 1980 sensational *Errol Flynn: The Untold Story,* which alleged that Flynn was bisexual and had also engaged in espionage activities on behalf of Nazi Germany. These charges were both rebutted and bolstered in subsequent biographies.

Even Flynn's residence was the subject of its own book, *Errol Flynn Slept Here: The Flynns, the Hamblens, Rick Nelson, and the Most Notorious House in Hollywood.* The property at 3100 Torreyson Place off Mulholland Drive, which he built in the early 1940s, allegedly contained secret passageways, peepholes, and two-way mirrors. Pop star Rick Nelson of *Ozzie and Harriet* television fame later bought it, and his daughter Tracy claimed it was haunted. The house was torn down in 1988, and the new one constructed at the address was later bought by singer-actor Justin Timberlake. Even Flynn's son, Sean, led a storied life with details that seem scripted out of a Hollywood action thriller: he worked as a photojournalist for *Time* magazine during the Vietnam War and disappeared on assignment in Cambodia in 1970.

Books

Basinger, Jeannine, *The Star Machine,* Alfred A. Knopf, 2007.
Jordan, Stephen C., *Hollywood's Original Rat Pack: The Bards of Bundy Drive,* Scarecrow Press, 2007, p. 21.
McNulty, Thomas, *Errol Flynn: The Life and Career,* McFarland, 2004.

Periodicals

Entertainment Weekly, October 15, 1993.
Los Angeles Times, May 12, 2010.
New York Times, December 27, 1935; October 15, 1959; January 3, 1960.

Online

"Errol Flynn," Turner Classic Movies, http://www.tcm.com/tcmdb/person/63336|48996/Errol-Flynn/ (October 12, 2011). □

Gustav Theodor Fritsch

German scientist Gustav Theodor Fritsch (1838-1927) advanced knowledge about the human brain's motor functions, specifically in the regions of the cerebral cortex and cerebrum. The scientific and research discipline that most interested him included anthropology, anatomy, physiology, psychology, and zoology.

German scientist Gustav Theodor Fritsch advanced knowledge about brain function. In collaboration with Eduard Hitzig (1839-1907), the noted Berlin-born neurologist and neuropsychiatrist, Fritsch harnessed electricity to pinpoint the brain's motor areas. This so-called cortical localization research significantly enhanced understanding about the brain-body connection.

In a research activity that might be considered controversial in the twenty-first century, Fritsch and Hitzig opened up the head of a dog, exposing the animal's brain, and then probing the grey matter—specifically, the cerebral cortex—they applied electrical stimulation. What they learned, and later demonstrated to the scientific community, was that electrical provocation of different parts of the cerebrum caused involuntary muscular contractions in a dog's body. In other words, and applying these findings beyond an animal, touch one part of the brain and watch one part of the anatomical body react.

This was a crucial event in the development of modern neuroscience, wrote Charles G. Gross, Ph.D, in a 2007 article published in the *Journal of the History of the Neurosciences* ("The Discovery of the Motor Cortex and its Background"). It was the first good experimental evidence, Gross explained, for the cerebral cortex involvement in motor function, the electrical excitability of the cortex, the topographic (or mapping) representation in the brain, and the localization of different regions of the cerebral cortex.

Studied Under the Best Educators

Fritsch was born on March 5, 1838, in Cottbus, a city just south of Berlin in Germany. The son of a building inspector, he received his early education, or gymnasium education, in Breslau. Fritsch became interested in anthropology and physiology, and he studied these subjects at several academic institutions including the universities in Breslau, Berlin, and Heidelberg. There he expanded his knowledge in both disciplines and medicine. During his college years, Fritsch studied under renowned teachers such as Johannes Muller (1801-1858), a German anatomist and physiologist. Fritsch's other educators included Hermann von Helmholtz (1821-1894), a physician, physicist, and science philosopher; Ludwig Traube (1818-1876), a physician; Friedrich von Frerichs (1818-1885), a pathologist, and Bernard von Langenbeck (1810-1887), a surgeon. As such, Fritsch received the best education, as these men were recognized leaders in their areas. Fritsch earned his M.D. on August 9, 1862 with a thesis on the central nervous system, specifically the structure of the spinal cord.

Conducted Field Research in South Africa

The following year, Fritsch received his medical license. His subsequent career would entail a great deal of travel to conduct research as an ethnographer. In 1863, he traveled to South Africa, where he spent three years studying the anatomy and culture of various African groups (e.g., the Bushmen), as well as the region's geography. As a result of this, Fritsch became noted for his excellent field research methods.

When he returned to Germany in 1866, Fritsch accepted a position at the Institute of Anatomy in Berlin. There he worked as an assistant to Karl Bogislaus Reichert (1811-1883), an anatomist renowned for his research in embryology, cell theory, the brain and the inner ear. Fritsch's academic activities did not curtail his field research, however. He partook in several significant expeditions. In 1867, he traveled to Aden, where he could best observe a total solar eclipse.

Later he traveled to Upper Egypt, on a trip directed by German Egyptologist Johannes Dümichen (1833-1994). On this journey, Fritsch conducted substantial anthropological and ethnographical research. He would also travel to Syria and Persia (which later became known as Iran).

Fritsch remained at the Institute of Anatomy from 1867 to 1900. Also, he became head of the Physiological Institute. In 1871, Fritsch married the daughter of the University of Breslau's publisher, Ferdinand Hirt. The marriage would provide him with the financial independence to conduct his field research.

Fritsch served for a period during the Franco-Prussian War, which lasted from 1870 to 1871, and he received the Iron Cross. In 1874, he was appointed as extraordinary professor of comparative anatomy, working under Reichert. But he left to become part of the Prussian Venus expedition, which took him to Isfahan, Persia. He would also travel to Smyrna, where he conducted a comparative study of the fish brain. He went on to publish this work in 1878.

He also worked at the Institute of Pathology. Emil du Bois-Reymond (1818-1896), a German physician and physiologist, created a position for him (chief of histology and photography) in the department of physiology. Working with du Bois-Reymond revitalized Fritsch's curiosity about electric fishes (which led to another expedition, this time to Africa). When du Bois-Reymond retired, Fritsch worked with his successor, Theodor Wilhelm Engelmann (1843-1909), a German botanist, physiologist and microbiologist. By this time, Fritsch's main interests were in anthropology, an area where he demonstrated his skills as a photographer. He applied these skills on his trips to places such as Egypt, but he also attached his skills to photomicrography and stereoscopy in miscroscopic anatomy (he is considered a pioneer in applying photography to science and anthropology).

Worked with Eduard Hitzig

Despite all the early accomplishments, Fritsch is best known for the research that came out of his collaboration with fellow countryman and colleague Eduard Hitzig (1839-1907), the German neurologist and neuropsychologist. They were interested in unlocking the secrets about the electrophysiology of the brain. Their partnership would provide one of the major milestones in the history and science of physiology. This resulted from their shared interest in the brain's motor functions and cortical localization. Their work would become the standard in this area of study.

It began in 1870 when, taking time out from his extensive travels, Fritsch returned to Germany to pursue the electrical excitability of cerebral hemispheres with Hitzig. Their experimental subjects were dogs, and the two researchers probed the brains of canines. The basis of their research came from the observation that a portion of the cerebral hemispheres demonstrated motor function.

Gross described their research as the birth of modern neurophysiology. Their discovery—that electrical stimulation of the cerebral cortex produces movement—was important for several reasons, averred Gross: "First, it was the first clear experimental demonstration of a region of the cerebral cortex involved in motor function. Second, it was the first evidence that the cortex was electrically excitable. Third, it was the first experimental evidence of a topographically organized representation of the body in the brain. Finally, it was the first strong experimental evidence for localization of function in the cerebral cortex."

Fritsch and Hitzig conducted their research in makeshift home laboratories, on a dressing table, as university laboratories did not have the kind of space to accommodate their research. Gross provided details about the research, as quoted in the *Journal of the History of Neurosciences,* which might prove disturbing to modern sensibilities: "Fritsch and Hitzig strapped their dogs down on Frau Hitzig's dressing table, as there were no animal facilities at the institute. In their early experiments they used no anesthesia or analgesic, although ether surgical anesthesia had been introduced in 1846 and morphine analgesia in 1803. Later they did use 'morphine narcosis.' They began by removing the cranium and cutting the dura, the dog showing 'vivid pain.' They stimulated the cortex with platinum wires with 'galvanic stimulation': brief pulses of monophasic direct current from a battery at the minimum current that evoked a sensation on their tongue."

The procedure might suggest the cruelty of H.G. Wells' fictional "Dr. Moreau," but Fritsch and Hitzig weren't mad vivisectionists engaged in a scientifically dubious enterprise. Rather, their investigation revealed that, in the canine brain, motor functions were located at the front of the cerebral hemispheres and the non-motor areas were located in the back. They discovered the electrical stimulation in the motor area of each hemisphere resulted in muscle contractions.

The research advanced the motor-sensory association ideas advanced by researchers' previous work. Fritsch and Hitzig published the results of their research in 1870, *On the Electrical Excitability of the Brain,* which established the existence of functional localization in the cerebral cortex of the animal subject. This work provided the basis for future physiological experiments.

Other scientists had advanced similar ideas during the early part of the nineteenth century (including Jean-Baptiste Bouillaud, Pierre-Paul Broca, and J. Hughlings Jackson) but the work by Fritsch and Hitzig provided the evidence. Specifically, Fritsch and Hitzig stimulated with electricity small regions on the exposed surface of dogs, who were awake during the experimental procedure. Stimulation of some areas, the partners observed, produced muscle contractions in the head and neck, and stimulation of other distinct brain areas produced contractions of the forelegs or hind legs. The findings created new ways for brain mapping.

Pursued other Research Interests

While Fritsch and Hitzig helped pioneer the emerging field of cerebral physiology, their research would be the only time the two men would collaborate. Hitzig continued on in this area of study, but Fritsch went on to pursue his own interests, which were focused on anthropology. Hitzig became a famous psychiatrist, but Fritsch went back to his travels and field research.

Fritsch's interest in field research compelled him, in 1874, to resign from his post as the chair of psychology at the University of Berlin. Still, his work with electric fish (eels) further contributed to the world's increasing understanding of electrophysiology. In 1881 and 1882, he ventured to Egypt and eastern Mediterranean countries to study electric sea life. His trips were funded by the Academy of Economic Sciences in Berlin.

As Edwin Clarke related in the *Complete Dictionary of Scientific Biography* (2008), Fritsch possessed a many-sided character, which led to multiple scientific interests, as well as interests residing outside the field of science. "He had the characteristic tendency to collect data omnivorously and multisensorily but also a strong dislike of systematized and nonempirical methods," Clarke wrote. "Philosophical and metaphysical subjects were avoided, and he preferred to deal with practical rather than theoretical issues. Fritsch's energy was immense, and he was happy only when active."

In 1908, when he was seventy years old and still possessing vibrant curiosity, he published a fascinating work on the comparative racial morphology of the human retina. He enhanced the text with plates produced from his own photomicrographs. For Fritsch, photography was a life-long interest. Thus it was ironic that his failing vision led to his retirement in 1921. He died on June 12, 1927, leaving behind a profound research legacy, which has complemented understanding of humans and the world they inhabit.

Along with being a pioneering scientist and photographer, Fritsch was a prolific writer.

Books

"Fritsch, Gustav Theodor,"*Complete Dictionary of Scientific Biography,* Charles Scribner's Sons, 2008.

Periodicals

Journal of the History of Neurosciences, July 11, 2007.

Online

"Brain Maps: The Study of Brain Function in the Nineteenth Century,"*Cerebromente.org,* http://www.cerebromente.org.br/n01/frenolog/frenloc.htm.(December 15, 2011)

"Dr. G.T. Fritsch,"*People in Psychology,* http://elvers.us/hop/ (December 15, 2011)

"Fritsch, Gustav Theodor,"*Encyclopedia.com,* http://www.encyclopedia.com/doc/1G2-2830901535.html (December 15, 2011)

"Gustav Fritsch,"*Nature.com,* http://www.nature.com/nature/journal/v141/n3566/abs/141403c0.html.(December 15, 2011)

"Gustav Theodor Fritsch Biography,"*PageRank Studio.com,* http://pagerankstudio.com/Blog/2011/05/gustav-theodor-fritsch-biography/. (December 15, 2011)□

G

Abram Petrovich Gannibal

More than 200 years after his death in 1781, the story of Russian military officer Abram Petrovich Gannibal (c. 1696–1781) remains one of the most intriguing tales ever to come out of imperial Russia. Immortalized in an unfinished novel by his great-grandson Alexander Pushkin as _The Negro of Peter the Great,_ the Cameroon native was sold into slavery in his youth but then wound up, through a fortuitous set of circumstances, at the court of Russia's great modernizing emperor, Peter I.

An innate gift for languages likely propelled Abram Petrovich Gannibal on his fabled trajectory. Though Ethiopians claimed him as one of their own, a Beninese scholar named Dieudonné Gnammankou pursued the question in the 1990s and established that Gannibal actually came from the heart of Africa, a place called Logone-Birni in the extreme north of Cameroon, near the border with Chad.

"Fortune Has Changed My Life Entirely"

Historians had long been intrigued by the documents Gannibal submitted to tsarist officials in 1742 when the Empress Elizabeth elevated his civilian rank to the landowning class. Gannibal proposed a crest with the letters "FVMMO," ostensibly a Latin acronym for the sentence _Fortuna Vitam Meam Mutavit Oppido_ (Fortune Has Changed My Life Entirely). Yet _fummo_ also means "homeland" in the Kotoko language of Central Africa, which is particular to the region near Lake Chad. In his documents Gannibal had cited his place of birth as Lagon, which for

many years was interpreted as a place on Mareb River in present-day Eritrea. Scores of sources that traced the story of Pushkin's African ancestor repeated the claim that Gannibal was of Abyssinian origin, but Gnammankou's research proved he was instead a Kotoko chief's son.

Gannibal is thought to have been born around 1696. He was about seven years old when he turned up in Constantinople in 1703 at the court of the Ottoman Empire. Gnammankou theorized that Gannibal and his brother were kidnapped by a rival chief, and taken to the Indian Ocean coast—a journey of some 2,000 miles—and shipped to Constantinople as a part of a tribute payment to the Ottoman sultan Mustafa II. At some point Gannibal adopted Islam and used the name Ibrahim. Another biographer, Hugh Barnes, posits that Gannibal became a page to Mustafa's brother Ahmed, who was actually caged to prevent his political ambitions.

Gannibal's journey to the court of Tsar Peter I in St. Petersburg began when the Russian ruler sent a request to his ambassador in Constantinople—a diverse, multicultural metropolis—to find and send some African youths to serve as pages at the Petrine court. Peter, often hailed as the one of Russia's greatest political figures, came to the throne at the age of ten in 1682 and set about turning his homeland from an isolated, feudal backwater into a modern state on par with France, England, and Germany. The tsar traveled widely, imported legions of artisans and other professionals from across Europe to help build a new Russia, and showcased all of it in a glittering new city on the Gulf of Finland, Russia's door to Europe at its northwest frontier.

Dubbed "Arap"

A man named Sava Vladislavich Raguzhinsky, the deputy Russian ambassador in Constantinople, apparently paid a ransom to the sultan or simply kidnapped Gannibal, his brother, and another African boy. The third youth died en route to St. Petersburg, possibly from smallpox. Gannibal's older brother became an oboe player for a Russian military regiment. Gannibal had a much bolder personality and apparently made a great impression on the tsar, who had a similarly exuberant and temperamental disposition. The African was baptized into the Russian Orthodox faith at St. Paraskeva Church in Vilnius in 1705, with Peter as his godfather, and the tsar also formally adopted him. Gannibal's new name was Abram Petrovich, though the tsar called him "Arap"—a Russian misspelling of Arab—and he was known in St. Petersburg court circles as "the Tsar's Moor."

Gannibal received an excellent education, and was so multilingually literate that he became Peter's private secretary. During these years the tsar actively participated in a series of full-scale wars against the Ottomans and the Swedish kingdom to secure Russia's regional dominance, and Gannibal was part of these campaigns. In 1717, Peter made his second trip to Western Europe and took Gannibal along, who stayed on for five more years. Gannibal studied mathematics and the engineering of military fortifications, served in the French army from 1719 to 1721, and was among the first wave of students to enter a new royal artillery academy at La Fère, France. Some of the more fanciful accounts of Gannibal's time in France claim that he engaged in at least one love affair with a well-born woman who gave birth to a biracial child; the resulting scandal forced Gannibal back to St. Petersburg in 1722. It is known that Gannibal met and impressed two of the leading French intellectuals of the day, the writer-philosopher Voltaire and the encyclopedist Denis Diderot.

In 1724 Gannibal became an engineer-lieutenant with the Preobrazhensky Regiment and was sent to the newly conquered Baltic lands to build fortifications. He was living in Riga when Peter died in 1725, then returned to St. Petersburg. There he served as tutor to the late tsar's grandson during the rule of Catherine I, Peter's widow. She died in 1727 and rival factions competed for power; Gannibal took the wrong side and was effectively exiled when he was assigned to build new fortifications in a remote part of Siberia near Russia's border with China. It was during this period of his life he adopted the symbolically ominous surname of "Gannibal" after the great African general Hannibal of Carthage, who challenged Rome's dominance in the 17-year-long Second Punic War of 218–201 BCE. The Carthaginian commander famously marched on Rome from North Africa, taking an enormous army that included elephants over the Pyrenees and then the Alps. In Russian, there is no letter "H," so "Gannibal" was used instead.

Married Twice

Gannibal was restored to a more respectable position by the Empress Anna Ivanovna, Peter the Great's niece. She reassigned him as a captain-engineer at Pernov, a Baltic Sea installation now located in the Estonian county of Pärnu. Before leaving for Pernov, however, Gannibal entered into a marriage with a Greek woman named Evdokia or Eudoxia Dioper, which was reportedly arranged by her father, a sea captain who had heeded Peter the Great's call for immigrants. Dioper was unhappy about the situation, and

Gannibal claimed she had an extramarital affair. Their divorce took 21 years to wend its way through the Russian courts. "The legal documents included allegations that Gannibal set up a private torture chamber in his home to force his wife into testifying as he wished and that, for her part, Evdokia engaged in multiple infidelities and even plotted with one of her lovers to poison her husband," wrote Catharine Theimer Nepomnyashchy and Ludmilla A. Trigos in the introduction to *Under the Sky of My Africa: Alexander Pushkin and Blackness.* A Russian court finally granted him a divorce from Dioper in 1753, which included a dire life sentence for his ex-wife in a Russian Orthodox nunnery.

While stationed in Pernov, Gannibal met another captain's daughter, this one of aristocratic Scandinavian descent. He and Christina Regina von Schöberg lived together after 1734 on a parcel of farmland he bought near Reval, the present-day Estonian capital of Tallinn, and had seven children together. He was able to retire from the military for several years, but took up a new commission in 1741 as a lieutenant colonel and, a year later, was singled out for some premium perks by the newly installed Empress Elizabeth, Peter's daughter. She promoted him to major-general and superintendent of the installation at Reval, which he held from 1742 to 1752. She also elevated him to a more secure financial status by bestowing a 6,000-acre estate called Mikhailovskoe in nearby Pskov Oblast, which Gannibal rented out to a German aristocrat.

In the 1750s Gannibal was able to marry von Schöberg, which legitimatized their offspring as his legal heirs, and returned to the St. Petersburg region. Promoted to the rank of full general in 1759, he also wore the medals of the Order of St. Andrew and the Order of St. Alexander Nevsky for his military service. His empress-patroness died in early 1762 and was succeeded on the throne by his former pupil, now Peter III. That tsar had a notably brief reign of just six months. Catherine II, his widow, succeeded him, and after this point Gannibal settled on another estate he had acquired, this one at Suida, in what were known as the Ingermanlands near St. Petersburg, which Peter I had seized from Sweden in 1708. Gannibal died there 19 years later, on May 14, 1781, at the age of 85. He and Christina died within six months of one another.

Heirs Produced Russian Star

Gannibal and Christina's oldest son, Ivan Abramovich Gannibal, followed his father into military service and had an illustrious career in the Russian navy during Catherine II's long reign. Another son was Osip Abramovich Gannibal, whose daughter Nadezhda Osipovna Gannibal married into the illustrious Pushkin family. In 1799 her son Alexander was born. That Pushkin, Gannibal's great-grandson, emerged in the 1820s as one of Russia's greatest literary voices. He spent time on the Mikhailovskoe estate his mother had inherited. Before his death in 1837 Pushkin had attempted to write his ancestor's story in novel form, but abandoned the manuscript he titled *The Negro of Peter the Great.* Pushkin's daughter married a German prince, and her granddaughter in turn married into the Battenberg royal family, which changed its name to Mountbatten in the twentieth century. That descendant was Nadejda Mountbatten, the

Marchioness of Milford Haven, and through her husband was the aunt of Prince Philip, the Duke of Edinburgh and husband of England's Queen Elizabeth II.

The forts whose construction Gannibal oversaw were still in use nearly 200 years later when Russia was battered by a powerful German military during World War II. He once wrote his memoir, as all accomplished men and military leaders of his day were expected to do, but grew fearful of Catherine's secret police in his later years and burned the manuscript. One of his daughters married a man named Adam K. Rotkirkh, who wrote a German-language biography later deemed to be rigorously embellished.

Dieudonné Gnammankou's research was published in Russian for the 200th anniversary year celebrations of Pushkin's birth in 1999. The most complete English-language source of information on Gannibal is Hugh Barnes' *Gannibal: The Moor of Petersburg,* which earned a slew of favorable reviews when it was published in Britain in 2005. Writing in the London *Observer,* book critic Peter Conrad assessed Gannibal's curious story and role as an exotic emissary in France at a time when Russia was considered a barbaric hinterland: "Gannibal's ursine feudal captors were the true savages. Polylingual, cultured and mathematically skilled, he did his best to educate them. Perhaps he was the first representative of a socially indeterminate elite for which Russia in [the] next century invented a word."

Books

Barnes, Hugh, *Gannibal: The Moor of Petersburg,* Profile Books, 2005.

Nepomnyashchy, Catharine Theimer, Nicole Svobodny, and Ludmilla A. Trigos, editors, *Under the Sky of My Africa: Alexander Pushkin and Blackness,* Northwestern University Press, 2006.

Periodicals

Independent (London, England), August 26, 2005.
New Statesman, August 8, 2005.
New York Times, November 13, 2010.
Observer (London, England), August 14, 2005.
Sunday Times (London, England), August 7, 2005. □

Lucretia Rudolph Garfield

American First Lady Lucretia Rudolph Garfield (1832–1918) captured the heart of the nation despite serving the second-shortest stint as First Lady in U.S. history.

First Lady Lucretia Garfield resided in the White House for only six months during the presidency of her husband James Garfield before his administration was cut short by his death from complications of an assassin's bullet. An educated woman who treasured middle-class respectability, Garfield earned the affection of the nation during her brief tenure as First Lady, particularly for her

dedicated care of her wounded husband. She lived out her widowhood quietly after seeing to efforts to honor her husband's memory, retaining a preference for privacy and family life throughout her long life.

The eldest of the four children of farmer and carpenter Zebulon Rudolph and his wife Arabella Mason Rudolph, Garfield was born on April 19, 1832, in the rural northeastern Ohio community of Garrettsville. From childhood, she bore the nickname "Crete," a shortened form of her given name, Lucretia. The Rudolph family was a pious one who numbered themselves as members of the Disciples of Christ. Garfield's father assisted in the founding of Western Reserve Eclectic Institute, a college affiliated with the Disciples, and the family's lifestyle was a financially comfortable, if emotionally reserved one. The young Garfield received an unusually good education for a young woman of her time, first attending school at the Christian Geauga Seminary in Chester, Ohio, and later studying at the Western Reserve Eclectic Institute closer to home. A series of childhood illnesses also helped shape the young woman's serious, scholarly personality by affording her a great deal of opportunity to read as she recovered in bed.

Married James Garfield

The initial meetings between the future First Lady and President Garfield came when both were students at the Geauga Seminary. Later, they renewed their acquaintance at the Eclectic Institute. James Garfield, the son of a poor farmer and a former dissolute wanderer along the Ohio Canal, had nevertheless emerged as one of the brightest students at the school. This intellectual cachet helped him bridge the social gap between his own humble beginnings and his future wife's more middle-class roots. During the early months of their revived friendship, the two had little romantic interest in each other as each nursed separate infatuations. These eventually ended, and in November of

1853, the pair began exchanging letters that evolved from scholarly discussions of ancient languages to ones of a more personal nature. Although Garfield's reticent personality prevented her from making the sorts of passionate written declarations that her suitor hoped for, the couple's courtship continued mostly via letter, especially after James Garfield left Ohio to pursue further studies at Williams College in Massachusetts. This long-distance relationship proved to be generally a happier one than their in-person encounters, which often resulted in bickering and hard feelings. Despite their quarrels, the couple became engaged to marry in early 1854.

The wedding was not immediately forthcoming, however, and Garfield taught school around northern Ohio while her fiancé continued his education in New England. During this time, he developed the first of several romantic attachments to women other than his intended spouse. The relationship went through such a low period in 1856 and 1857 that Garfield left Hiram to teach in Cleveland, where the specter of her betrothed's infidelities was not a constant presence. The pair at last married on November 11, 1858, at the home of the bride's family. This event seems to have stemmed more from a sense of duty than from any strong affection between the Garfields, and the early period of their marriage was, perhaps unsurprisingly, a difficult one. James Garfield's growing career in politics and service in the Civil War meant that the couple spent just 20 weeks of their first five years of marriage together, and his extramarital interests continued. The death of the couple's oldest child, Eliza, in 1863 helped draw them together in sorrow, however, and in 1864 Garfield took the then-unusual step of joining her husband in Washington, D.C., where he was serving in Congress.

This time, physical proximity resulted in a new affection between the Garfields, aided by their growing family. A second son, Harry, had appeared in 1863, and he was joined by James Rudolph in 1865, Mary in 1867, Irvin in 1870, Abram in 1872, and Edward in 1874. This last son did not survive to see his second birthday, but the remainder of the children formed the heart of the family home. Garfield dedicated herself to motherhood and kept a low profile, preferring the reading of poetry and popular literature to holding elaborate political gatherings. She was forced into a new role, however, after her husband was nominated for the presidency as a compromise candidate of two warring Republican factions in the election of 1880.

Served as First Lady

Although Garfield seems to have mixed feelings about her husband's nomination, she lent her support to his campaign. Because candidates did not then travel the country on the campaign trail, Garfield conducted a front-porch campaign that saw supporters seek him out at the family home in Ohio, Lawnfield. The prospective First Lady refused to be formally photographed as part of the campaign, but her hospitality to those who visited the family at their home certainly helped her husband's candidacy. Garfield carried the election, and the following March was inaugurated in the nation's highest office. The new First

Lady had little experience as a high-level political hostess and lacked much interest in formal social affairs; thus, she relied on the advice of the wife of Garfield's Secretary of State, James Blaine, to make decisions. These included the reintroduction of alcoholic beverages to White House dinners, a practice banned under the tenure of her predecessor, Lucy Hayes. Garfield also began gathering information about the physical status of the White House with the intention of asking Congress for money to refurbish the aging presidential mansion.

Illness, however, interrupted Garfield's burgeoning plans. In early May, she became ill and was soon diagnosed with malaria. Suffering from an extremely high fever and other worrisome symptoms, Garfield became the focus of attention both within the White House and across the nation. The President disregarded his duties to care for his wife, and newspapers around the United States followed his intense devotion and her fragile health. Within a couple of weeks, Garfield had begun to recover, and at the end of the month doctors deemed her cured. The First Lady remained weak, however, and several more days passed before she resumed some regular activities; on June 18, she left Washington for Long Branch, New Jersey, where she planned to recuperate further. Her delicate appearance and obvious affection for her husband temporarily delayed the plans of Charles Guiteau, who had come to the capital's train station with the intent of assassinating the President; writing in *Lucretia*, John Shaw quoted Guiteau as later writing, "Mrs. Garfield looked so thin and clung so tenderly to the President's arm, my heart failed me to part them."

Before long, however, Guiteau—a mentally disturbed man who believed that Garfield owed him a government job—followed through with his decision to assassinate the President, shooting him twice as he prepared to board a train in Washington. The fallen Garfield immediately told onlookers to send his love to his wife and ask for her to return to the capital, and she quickly did so, bringing her own nurse to help care for him. Disregarding her own poor health, the First Lady set about attending her husband, assuring him that she would keep him from dying of his wounds. But the President's condition worsened over the next several weeks. Although modern medical techniques would have rendered Garfield's injuries minor ones—with twentieth-century techniques, "he would have gone home in a matter of two or three days," surgery professor Ira Rutkow told Amanda Schaffer of the *New York Times* in 2006—the doctors of the day were unable to locate the bullet that had lodged in the President's back. With his condition complicated by unsanitary medical practices and harmful treatments, Garfield was beyond the help of his dedicated wife. After lingering for 80 days, the President at last died.

Retired from Public View

The death of her husband essentially ended the widow Garfield's brief time in the public eye. After overseeing preparations for the fallen president's public funeral and initiating the construction of his tomb at Lake View Cemetery in Cleveland, Garfield largely returned to focusing on raising her children and, later, grandchildren. She also dedicated part of her time to furthering her husband's memory by overseeing the historical preservation of his papers and providing information to a Garfield biographer. A substantial trust fund to support the widow created through popular subscription, along with some public financial assistance, helped her live out the remainder of her life comfortably in both Ohio and, after a bout of tuberculosis around the turn of the century, in the more favorable climate of South Pasadena, California. She lived to see her children become successful in their own rights, with son James serving in Theodore Roosevelt's Cabinet and son Harry rising to act as president of Williams College. In the twentieth century, Garfield was active in World War I-era Red Cross efforts and broke with the Republican Party to lend her support to successful Democratic presidential candidate Woodrow Wilson in 1916. Garfield never remarried, and vehemently rejected speculation that she might do so. Nevertheless, she remained active socially; writing in a 1916 letter quoted by Shaw, Mollie Garfield described her mother by saying, "She sits on the front porch like a lady the whole afternoon and receives callers there, is read to, visits when the spirit moves her, and is altogether a charming dear little grandmother...She is a veritable queen holding court."

Garfield died from complications of pneumonia on March 13, 1918, in South Pasadena, California, at the age of 85. She was interred shortly thereafter at the Garfield tomb in Cleveland where her husband had been laid to rest. After the former First Lady had spent so many years out of the public spotlight, her passing inspired the Cleveland *Plain-Dealer* to comment that readers might be surprised to discover that she had, in fact, still been alive. An educated woman in a time when middle-class women lived largely within the private sphere of the home, and a First Lady who had little chance to make her mark on the nation's leading home, Garfield remains something of a footnote to the history of the institution she so briefly served. Today, scholars generally agree that Garfield's legacy was greatly curtailed by the assassination of her husband. "Her career...was richer with possibilities than with accomplishments—a dramatic and tragic interlude in the story of First Ladies," assessed Allan Peskin in *American First Ladies: Their Lives and Their Legacy*. Yet, her dedication to her husband and quiet respectability undoubtedly garnered her the affection of Americans of her time, and her efforts as a parent helped shape men who went on to the kind of public lives denied to their mother.

Books

Encyclopedia of Women and Politics, Facts on File, 2008.

Gould, Lewis L., ed. *American First Ladies: Their Lives and Legacies,* Routledge, 2001.

Schneider, Dorothy and Carl J. Schneider, *First Ladies: A Biographical Dictionary,* Facts on File, 2005.

Shaw, John, *Lucretia,* Nova History Publications, 2004.

Periodicals

New York Times, July 25, 2006.

Online

"Lucretia Randolph Garfield," White House, http://www.white house.gov/about/first-ladies/lucretiagarfield (November 7, 2011).□

Roland Garros

The French aviator Roland Garros (1888–1918) was a key pioneer in the field of aerial combat.

Garros's name is known today primarily as that of the stadium where the French Open tennis tournament is played. The stadium was named in his honor and recognized his largely forgotten accomplishments. Foremost among these was his development and subsequent successful deployment of an aircraft propeller design that allowed him to fire his weapon at an enemy plane in midair. Although a few aerial dogfights had taken place previously, Garros essentially inaugurated the era of air warfare, and the term "flying ace" was coined to describe his exploits. Garros also became the first pilot to fly across the Mediterranean Sea, set several altitude records, and was among the first stunt pilots, popularizing airplane flight with a series of demonstrations in both Europe and the United States.

Studied Music

Roland Adrien Georges Garros was born in Saint-Denis, an industrial suburb of Paris, on October 6, 1888. His early life has not been well documented, but he studied music and apparently hoped for a career as a concert pianist. In 1909 Garros attended an air show in the city of Reims and was fascinated. He took flying lessons and received his pilot's license (number 147) on July 19, 1910. Garros quickly emerged as one of the most talented of the small band of demonstration flyers in action at the time.

Garros made several appearances in the United States and Mexico. Flying an early two-cylinder French plane, the *Demoiselle,* Garros appeared in aviation tournaments at New York's Belmont Park racetrack and in Chattanooga, Tennessee, in late 1910; in the latter event Garros appeared in races against local automobile drivers. In March of 1911 Garros participated in a demonstration of the airplane's military capabilities for the benefit of Mexican dictator Porfirio Díaz: a group of troops hid in some nearby hills, but Garros had no trouble spotting them from the air. A handsome man with a large, bushy dark moustache, Garros was one of the charismatic figures of early aviation.

Back in France, Garros entered a Paris-to-Rome air race in 1911 and placed second. In 1911 and 1912 he set various aviation records, including a world altitude record of 16,240 feet at Houlgate, France, on September 6, 1912, eclipsing the previous record by nearly 2,500 feet. The thin air caused the engine of Garros's monoplane to fail, but he successfully glided back to earth. In April of 1913 Garros won his first race, the International Air Rally in Monaco. The first in a long series of famous aviation water crossings

occurred when Garros successfully flew from France to Tunisia on September 23, 1913, marking history's first nonstop trans-Mediterranean flight and logging a distance of about 800 kilometers. Garros then took a job as a military aviation instructor in Germany.

With the outbreak of World War I in August of 1914, Garros had to sneak out of Germany. He returned to France by way of neutral Switzerland, flying at night. He enlisted in the French air corps and was given the rank of lieutenant, joining an elite squadron called the Storks. In the early days of the war, aircraft were used mostly for reconnaissance. A few pilots had experimented with engaging enemy planes, but were hampered by the inability of the pilot himself to fire forward; if he hit his own propeller blades, he ran a strong risk of shooting down his own plane. Sometimes a passenger was brought aboard to carry out firearms duty, but Garros was convinced that a better method was possible. Late in 1914 he was granted leave from his squadron to join a research team at the Morane-Saulnier aircraft company.

Added Plates to Propeller Blades

The idea of enabling the pilot to participate in an aerial dogfight had been under consideration since about 1912, and several firms had experimented with using the plane's engine itself as a firing mechanism in order to coordinate gun and propeller blade. Garros and factory owner Raymond Saulnier devised a simpler idea: they reinforced a plane's propeller blades with steel plates. Over a period of several months, Garros added deflector plates to the propeller apparatus, angling them in various directions and adding small steel wedges. He broke numerous propeller blades and also lost many bullets, which, he found, had to be made of either copper or lead-jacketed steel in order not to shatter on impact.

By March of 1915 Garros and Saulnier had received French patent number 477, 530 for their new design, and Garros was ready to return to the skies. "He was all the

keener to demonstrate the efficacy of the new deflectors," noted Richard Townshend Bickers in *The First Great Air War*, "because General Headquarters had shown its total indifference to this great innovation by cancelling an order for several Moranes to be modified with it." Instead, he outfitted his own plane with his deflector apparatus and a front-mounted Hotchkiss machine gun.

The results were dramatic. On April 1, 1915, Garros encountered a group of four German Albatros B-II planes, and instead of retreating he confronted one directly. "Almost certainly the German pilot was stunned when the French aircraft attacked him head-on," noted the *Fighter Pilot University* website, and the other three German planes fled in confusion. The encounter ended with the crash of Garros's direct adversary.

Garros followed up that victory with several more aerial triumphs over the next three weeks; the number was variously reported as three and five. Whatever the actual number, Garros's exploits made headlines as far away as the United States, where a newspaper dubbed Garros a flying "ace," a term that eventually became used for any skilled combat pilot. Garros's streak came to an end on April 18 when he flew too low over a German brigade, and one Private Schlenstedt hit his gas tank with a bullet and brought down his plane.

Tried to Keep Technology from Germans

Garros followed military protocol by trying to burn the aircraft before German troops reached him on the ground several hours later, but he was unsuccessful due to damp weather. As a result, Dutch aircraft pioneer Anthony Fokker was able to reverse engineer and then improve upon Garros's innovations, and supremacy in the increasingly important air war shifted from France to Germany. What became known as the Fokker Scourge was based on Garros's innovations, while Garros himself was respected by the Germans for his technical prowess and was held in a comfortable camp for elite prisoners of war. He spent three years in the camp, managing to escape in February of 1918 and return to France by way of the Netherlands.

A crash landing and several years of captivity did not deter Garros from military service; he immediately rejoined the French Air Force and emerged victorious in several more dogfights in mid-1918. He was shot down again, this time fatally, near Vouziers in the Ardennes region of northeastern France, on October 5, 1918, one day before his 30th birthday and just weeks before the end of the war. Reportedly he was chasing a German zeppelin that was preparing a lethal bombing attack on the city of Nancy. He was buried in Vouziers.

Garros and a friend from school, Emile Lesieur, had been members of a sports club called the Stade Franais, where Garros apparently never played tennis but was an enthusiastic rugby player. When the Stade Franais joined in sponsoring the Internationaux de France (later the French Open) tennis tournament in 1925, the popularity of tennis in France was about to grow dramatically, and the club decided to construct a new stadium. Lesieur campaigned successfully for the naming of the stadium in honor of Roland Garros.

Books

Bickers, Richard Townshend, *The First Great Air War,* Hodder & Stoughton, 1988.

Campbell, Christopher, *Aces and Aircraft of World War I,* Blandford, 1981.

Morrow, John H., *The Great War in the Air: Military Aviation from 1909 to 1921,* Smithsonian Institution Press, 1993.

Oughton, Frederick, *The Aces,* Putnam's, 1960.

Periodicals

Scotsman (Edinburgh, Scotland), May 29, 2010.

Online

"Roland Garros: Biography," *The Early Birds of Aviation,* http://www.earlyaviators.com/egarros1.htm(September 10, 2011).

"Roland Garros (1888–1918)," *Air Racing History,* http://www.air-racing-history.com/PILOTS/Roland%20Garros.htm (September 10, 2011).

"Roland Garros," france.com, http://www.web.france.com/story/events/2004/05/roland_garros (September 10, 2011).

"Roland Garros—FU Hero," *Fighter Pilot University,* http://www.fighterpilotuniversity.com/history/fu-heroes/roland-garros-fu-hero/ (September 10, 2011).

"Roland Garros," *Warfare and Wargaming,* http://www.warandgamesmw.com/blog/465992-roland-garros/ (September 10, 2011).

"Who's Who—Roland Garros," *firstworldwar.com,* http://www.firstworldwar.com/bio/garros.htm (September 10, 2011). □

Thomas Sovereign Gates

American educator and businessperson Thomas Sovereign Gates (1873–1948) served as the first president of the University of Pennsylvania.

University administrator and banker Thomas Sovereign Gates became the first president of the University of Pennsylvania in 1930, inaugurating the post after certain responsibilities were split off from those of the office of provost, which dated back to about the time of the institution's founding by Benjamin Franklin in the mid-1700s. Prior to his assumption of the university presidency, Gates had worked as a lawyer and, later, as an executive with some of Philadelphia's leading investment banks. He served on the board of directors of several major corporations including the Baldwin Locomotive Works and the Public Service Corporation of New Jersey, and participated in numerous community organizations. Long a trustee of the university, Gates embraced the challenge of leading the institution amid the difficult years of the Great Depression and into the World War II era. He retired from office in 1944, but remained active in university affairs until his death four years later.

Became Lawyer and Businessperson

A native of the Germantown section of Philadelphia, Pennsylvania, Gates was born on March 21, 1873. He was the younger of the two sons of Jabez Gates, a merchant who eventually became the president of the Mutual Fire Insurance Company of Germantown, and his wife; historical records alternately record her name as Isabel Sovereign and Rebecca Toy Sovereign. As a youth, Gates attended the Germantown Academy. In 1889, he enrolled at Haverford College near Philadelphia. Two years later, he transferred to the city's University of Pennsylvania. There, he took courses with the Wharton School of Finance, completing an undergraduate degree in 1893. Gates then continued his education at the University of Pennsylvania's law school. For a time, he also held a part-time job with the law office of George Wharton Pepper, who later served as a Republican U.S. Senator from Pennsylvania. After completing his law degree in 1896, Gates began practicing locally under lawyer John G. Johnson, and continued in this profession for about the next decade. In 1905, he married for the first of three times, to Marie Rogers; he was left a widower the following year when she died giving birth to their son, Thomas Sovereign Gates, Jr.

At about this time, Gates also underwent a professional change when he left the law to begin a career in business. He took a job as a trust officer with the Pennsylvania Company for Insurance Lives and Granting Annuities which involved the settlement of estates. Speaking to Lawrence Davies of the *New York Times* several years later, Gates recalled this job caused him to "[leave] law to go into banking without knowing it." He remarried to Mary Emma Gibson in early 1910, and the couple went on to have a son, Jay Gibson, and a daughter Virginia Ewing, before Gibson died in 1925. In time, he rose to become a vice-president of the firm, but left in 1912 to become the president of the Philadelphia Trust Company. This work brought Gates into contact with investment banking firms, and in 1918 he became a partner of Drexel and Company, a local affiliate of the banking giant J.P. Morgan. Three years later, Gates also signed on as a partner with the latter institution. During the boom years of the 1920s, he helped sell bonds and provided business and financial advice to large companies. He also served as a trustee of his alma mater, the University of Pennsylvania, and was a member of numerous Philadelphia clubs. Gates married for the third and final time in 1929 to a local widow, Emma Barton (Brewster) Waller.

Gates's involvement with the University of Pennsylvania brought him to a new endeavor in 1930. Throughout the 1920s, he had been actively involved in fundraising and strategic planning efforts for the school, and had eventually been named the chairman of the executive board of university trustees. This position carried a great deal of responsibility for overseeing the university's 12 schools, 16,000 students, and numerous affiliated institutions including a museum, two hospitals, and two medical research institutes. "As the duties of chairman preyed more and more on my time, I became increasingly interested in the work of the university as a whole," he explained to Davies of his road to the presidency, "and therefore the development of the matter was perfectly logical. The provost and trustees were good enough to ask me whether I would take more active part in the affairs of the institution." This active role was the new job of president, which Gates, intrigued by the work he had been doing, eagerly accepted with a few stipulations: that he not receive any pay, that he have time to manage his existing business interests, that he be freed from management of details that would continually tie him to the campus, and that he have the help of fellow trustee, the engineer Charles Day. The agreement was finalized and Gates became president in the fall of 1930.

Served as University President

Gates faced immediate difficulties in his new role brought on by the dismal financial climate of the Great Depression. The crash of the stock market one year earlier had marked the beginning of a series of economic problems; by the end of 1930, more than 2,000 banks had failed and the unemployment rate had more than doubled from one year previously. "Few administrators with a difficult financial problem to solve have entered office in more unpromising times than those in which Mr. Gates took up his duties as President Gates," assessed Edward P. Cheyney in his *History of the University of Pennsylvania, 1740–1940*. "The University was subject to the same storms as were breaking on other institutions. It suffered many harsh effects: reduced appropriations for books and research, restriction on what seemed necessary purchases and expenditures, painfully rigid economies, a slowing down of the normal course of appointments and promotions," he continued. Gates embraced these problems with vigor, bringing his financial expertise to bear on the institution's troubled situation.

The challenges of his position attracted Gates, in fact, and he worked diligently to improve the institution. "I find this work more enjoyable, more constructive and more alive than either law or banking," Gates was quoted as

saying in his *New York Times* obituary. "As I walk through the campus, in and out among old stately buildings, I experience a sense of romance and high adventure in directing the growth of this old institution," he continued. Among his most notable successes was the reorganization of the school's athletic program as a department under the authority of the university administration rather than the alumni association. Gates also emphasized arts education and oversaw the creation of a "Cultural Olympics" in fields such as music, crafts, literature, drama, and dance. In 1937, he launched a major campaign to grow the university's endowment by over $12 million both to shore up the existing school's finances and to potentially create a small, experimental campus in nearby Valley Forge.

World War II interrupted plans to execute this expansion, however, and Gates himself dedicated much of his attention to the conflict. In October of 1940, he created a University Committee on National Defense, and the university's engineering school inaugurated a defense training program soon after. After the United States entered the conflict, the university encouraged students fighting overseas to take correspondence courses and housed several wartime training programs. In 1944, Gates retired from the presidency; he was succeeded by sitting University of Pennsylvania provost George William McClelland. Even after his retirement, however, Gates remained a force in university affairs. He served as chairman of the university from 1944 until 1945. When he stepped down from that role, Gates took on the newly created position of chairman of the board of university trustees. This job allowed Gates to forego the day-to-day management of the university while still having influence in the formulation and execution of high-level policies.

Family Life and Legacy

Gates experienced some personal concerns during his tenure with the University of Pennsylvania. In August of 1934, his 22-year-old daughter Virginia disappeared while hitchhiking in the West; the Department of Justice became involved in the search for the young woman, who did not communicate with her father until after being found by police about a month later. "I was not compelled to sleep in the open and did not go hungry," she declared in an Associated Press article printed in the *New York Times*. She had, however, spent all of her money—and gotten married in the intervening period to a former taxi driver, mechanic, and wrestler from California whom she had met while traveling. Gates gave his blessing to the whirlwind romance and provided a monthly allowance to the young couple. The drama continued, however, when the newlyweds were in a serious car accident in northern California just days later. Despite being critically injured, both Gates's daughter and her new husband fully recovered. Yet the accident resulted in the death of one of the passengers of the other vehicle, and the court levied a judgment of more than $45,000 in damages against the McCaffertys the following year. The couple remained in California, but divorced in 1939 "after [McCafferty] blacked both my eyes and threw an ash tray at me," Gates's daughter was quoted as stating in a separate *New York Times* article.

Another of Gates's children was even more news-worthy, albeit in a less melodramatic way. A Republican like his father, Thomas Sovereign Gates, Jr., served in the U.S. government during the Eisenhower administration of the 1950s. In 1953, Eisenhower named the younger Gates Undersecretary of the Navy; four years later, he advanced to become Secretary of the Navy. When incumbent Secretary of Defense Neil H. McElroy stepped down in 1959, Gates advanced to this position. He remained in that role until the end of the Eisenhower administration in January of 1961.

In 1946, Gates finally completed the doctorate degree in philosophy that he had begun nearly five decades previously. He remained active until his death from what some historians have suggested was a cerebral hemorrhage at his summer home in Osterville, Massachusetts, on April 8, 1948. After his death, Gates was interred at the Church of the Redeemer in Bryn Mawr, Pennsylvania. During his lifetime, Gates was well-respected by his peers for both his personal abilities and his dedication. "I know of no one who had greater capacity than Dr. Gates," wrote H. Birchard Taylor in *Charles Day: Symbol of American Genius.* "He had untiring energy, a tremendous acquaintance, a constructive imagination, and great personal charm.... One of the secrets of his great capacity to serve in many things, was his ability to secure effect help. It was considered an honor to be asked by Dr. Gates to help, for those whom he asked knew that he is activities well worth while and they served enthusiastically without any thought of a tangible reward for themselves." Although the University of Pennsylvania had existed for some two centuries before Gates became its inaugural president, he nevertheless had an important role in shaping the modern institution. His fundraising efforts helped guide the university through one of the darkest financial periods in U.S. history, and his administration left a legacy of reformed and improved university academics, research, and athletics.

Books

Cheyney, Edward Potts, *History of the University of Pennsylvania, 1740–1940,* University of Pennsylvania Press, 1940.

Dictionary of American Biography, Scribner's, 1974.

Taylor, H. Birchard, *Charles Day (1879–1931): Symbol of American Industrial Genius,* Newcomen Society in North America, 1953.

Periodicals

New York Times, August 3, 1930; September 17, 1934; September 24, 1934; December 2, 1939; October 23, 1945; March 20, 1976.

Time, June 23, 1930; October 25, 1937.

Online

"History of Institutional Planning at the University of Pennsylvania: Thomas Sovereign Gates, President (1930–1944), University of Pennsylvania, http://www.archives.upenn.edu/histy/features/uplans/gates.html (September 21, 2011).□

Edwin Gaustad

One of the most distinguished historians of religion in the United States, Edwin Gaustad (1923–2011) focused especially on dissenters and freethinkers in colonial times.

Gaustad's work on religious liberty led him to make contributions outside the academic realm. He wrote several well-reviewed works of popular history, and entered contemporary controversies relating to the separation of church and state with a longer view of the subject than almost anyone else. Yet Gaustad is best remembered for his academic writings, which include several standard works and an atlas of American religion that remains an indispensable tool for both historians and journalists. A scholar of broad curiosity, Gaustad wrote about many of the major figures of colonial America, situating their careers and beliefs in the broad story of American religion.

Served in Army Air Corps

The youngest of three sons, Edwin Scott Gaustad was born to Sverre and Norma Gaustad (the name rhymes with "ousted") on November 14, 1923, in Rowley, Iowa. Both there and in Houston, Texas, where the family moved when he was young, he was raised in the Baptist church, with which he remained affiliated for all his life. Despite the political activism that developed later in the twentieth century among some Baptist groups, the Baptist denomination was historically devoted to the principle of separation between church and state, and that heritage left an impression on Gaustad. He served in the U.S. Army Air Corps during World War II from 1943 to 1945, was stationed in Italy, and earned an Air Medal.

Returning to Texas after the war, Gaustad enrolled at Baylor University in Waco, majoring in history and English. He married Virginia Morgan in December of 1946. Graduating from Baylor the following year, he went on for graduate work at Brown University to study the history of religion under one of the foremost general American historians of the day, Edmund S. Morgan. He received a master's degree in 1948 and a PhD in 1951 for a dissertation titled *The Great Awakening in New England.* After a year as an instructor at Brown, he became a professor of religion and philosophy at Shorter College (now Shorter University) in Rome, Georgia, a school associated with the Baptist church.

Gaustad remained at Shorter until 1957, the year he finished revising his dissertation into a book of the same title. It was published not by an academic press but by the mainstream publisher Harper. *The Great Awakening in New England* examined a widespread strain of religious revivalism that spread rapidly in New England in the 1740s—one of a series of such flowerings of religious fervor that have characterized American history. Gaustad argued that the effects of the movement known as the Great Awakening were broader than had been generally supposed, affecting American culture beyond the purely religious sphere, and beyond the lower and lower middle class layers of society with which evangelical movements have sometimes been associated. On the strength of this publication, Gaustad was offered and accepted a post as associate professor (a tenured position) at the University of Redlands, another Baptist school, in southern California.

Published Atlas of Religion

At Redlands, Gaustad worked on perhaps his most widely used book, *Historical Atlas of Religion in America,* which was published by Harper in 1962. The book detailed the geography of American religious belief down to the county level—and surprised its author. "I thought we would be a much more homogeneous country religiously," Gaustad was quoted as saying in the *Los Angeles Times.* "We aren't." The book was revised in 1976 and again in 2001, each time with new attention to the diversity of faith in America, including Native American and African-American traditions. The most recent edition contained 260 full-color maps as well as a large variety of maps and charts.

In 1965 Gaustad moved to the growing University of California at Riverside, where he established a religious studies program. He remained at Riverside for the rest of his career. In 1966 Gaustad authored the textbook *A Religious History of America,* another book that was successful and lasting enough to be reissued in revised form; the 2002 edition, co-written with Leigh Schmidt, was titled *The Religious History of America.* Gaustad made contributions as editor or as section author to several other general works on American and world religions, including *Religious Issues in American Culture* (with R.A. Spivey and R.F. Allen, 1972) and *Religious Issues in World Cultures* (with Spivey and Allen, 1976).

After these general works, Gaustad devoted himself to more specific topics for much of the rest of his career. After issuing *Dissent in American Religion,* another standard work in the religious history field, in 1973, Gaustad penned studies of individual figures. He was a recognized authority on Roger Williams, the dissenter who helped pave the way for the founding of the colony of Rhode Island. Gaustad wrote two books on Williams, *Liberty of Conscience: Roger Williams in America* (1991) and a general biography, *Roger Williams* (2005). In an interview that year (quoted in the *New York Times*), he said that "Williams advocated the scariest political heresy of his day: namely, that a civil institution could survive without the supporting arm of the church. He was alone in this view in all New England, alone in most of the other colonies, and certainly alone in his own homeland of England."

Wrote Jefferson Biography

Gaustad also wrote books about Thomas Jefferson (*Sworn on the Altar of God: A Religious Biography of Thomas Jefferson,* 1996) and about another Rhode Island resident, the Irish philosopher and American Anglican leader George Berkeley (*George Berkeley in America,* 1979). Gaustad was the author of several books devoted more closely to the history of the Baptist church in America, including *Baptist Piety: The Last Will and Testament of Obadiah Holmes* (1978), and he wrote a history of the rise

of Seventh-Day Adventism. In addition to Harper, his books were issued by various publishers: the university presses of Chicago, Yale, and Oxford, and the religious publisher Eerdmans, among others.

Mistrustful of the power of religious conservatives in American politics, Gaustad wrote (as quoted by Associated Baptist Press) that for the religious right "the American past is idealized into a Christian hegemony that never was; the American future is envisioned in terms of a Christian establishment that cannot constitutionally be." In 2002 Gaustad served as an expert witness called by the American Civil Liberties Union in a successful lawsuit brought against Alabama judge Roy Moore, who had refused to remove a display of the biblical Ten Commandments in his courtroom; Gaustad told the court that Thomas Jefferson's statement that liberties are God-given referred to God as manifested in the natural world rather than the God of the Bible.

Gaustad retired from UC Riverside in 1989 but remained active as a visiting professor and writer. He received Distinguished Alumni Awards at both Baylor and Brown Universities, as well as the Distinguished Teaching Award at UC Riverside and the Alumni Religious Liberty Award from Baylor. He and his wife raised three children, Susan, Scott, and Peggy, to whom *Dissent in American Religion* was dedicated. He said that they and the student counterculture of which they were part had taught him more about dissent than he really wanted to know. In 2005 he published a short biography of scientist, publisher, and diplomat Benjamin Franklin. Gaustad moved to Santa Fe, New Mexico, late in life and died there on March 25, 2011. Plans were already underway to honor him with a Festschrift, a celebratory book consisting of essays by the many younger scholars and writers touched by the work of this important academic figure.

Periodicals

Books & Culture, January-February 2003.
Church & State, May 2011.
Los Angeles Times, April 5, 2011.
New York Times, April 4, 2011.
Publishers Weekly, December 11, 2000.
Santa Fe New Mexican, October 3, 2004.

Online

"Edwin Scott Gaustand, a Witness for Conscience," *Associated Baptist Press,* http://www.abpnews.com/content/view/6268/9/(October 28, 2011). □

David Gelernter

The American computer scientist and author David Gelernter (born 1955) has been unusually accurate in forecasting new developments in computing. He has also become a writer with an uncommonly wide variety of interests and areas of expertise, ranging from Judaism to American history, conservative political thought, and the nature of creativity.

Gelernter may be best known to the general public as a victim of Theodore Kaczynski, the so-called Unabomber: in 1993, Gelernter opened a package on his desk at Yale University, and it exploded, leaving him with lifelong injuries. Despite the trauma of that event, Gelernter resumed his activities as a writer and even branched out into a wider variety of fields than he had explored previously. Prior to Kaczynski's attack, Gelernter had already predicted the emergence of what is now known as the Internet; he returned in 2000 with a widely read essay, "The Second Coming—A Manifesto," that anticipated the rise of cloud computing. By 2011 Gelernter, through his essays in the *Weekly Standard* magazine, had become an important spokesman for American conservative thinking, and his creative activities ranged from painting to fiction writing.

Showed Artistic Talent

David Hillel Gelernter was born in 1955 and grew up on Long Island outside of New York City. His father, Herbert Gelernter, was a professor of computer science at the State University of New York at Stony Brook. In contrast to Gelernter's political philosophy as an adult, the family was generally liberal; his own mind was changed, he later said, by the chaotic scenes that accompanied the retreat of the United States after its defeat in the Vietnam War. Gelernter showed artistic ability as a child, and won a drawing contest. For a time he contemplated a career as an artist, and he took art and music classes and studied Hebrew at Yale University. He later switched his interests to the field of computer science.

He never viewed the switch as an abandonment of his creativity, however. "I am rotten at everything that is not art; have succeeded in computer science only by forcing software

into a strictly aesthetic mold, making it a design issue like architecture or painting," Gelernter wrote in his memoir, *Drawing Life: Surviving the Unabomber.* "I hate machines except insofar as they are beautiful (as the best are)." Gelernter began a PhD program in Judaic studies at Yale, moved to New York to study the Talmud (a central text of Judaism) at Yeshiva University, and finally returned to Stony Brook, where he earned his PhD in 1982 for a dissertation titled *An Integrated Microcomputer Network for Experiments in Distributed Programming.* In the early 1980s he joined the faculty at Yale University in New Haven, Connecticut. He married, and he and his wife, Jane, raised two sons.

Created New Programming Language

The topic of that dissertation pointed to the field that would occupy Gelernter for much of the first part of his career: "distributed" computing is the harnessing of multiple computers in a network in order to make them work with a common purpose. Even before receiving his doctorate, Gelernter (with fellow graduate student Nicholas Carriero) had created a new programming language called Linda that enabled the efficient linking of computers, or parts of the same computer, in order to facilitate what is known as parallel processing. The Linda language supplanted one called Ada that had been named for Ada Augusta Lovelace, the daughter of the poet Lord Byron. Gelernter named his new language after a different Lovelace: pornographic film star Linda Lovelace. "I was a graduate student at the time," he confessed to John Markoff of the *New York Times.*

Gelernter's innovations had great commercial significance, for they enabled institutional computer buyers, by programming their machines more efficiently, to manage with smaller units than they would previously have needed. The Linda program established Gelernter as a rising star in the computer field, and he and Carriero collaborated on a textbook, *How to Write Parallel Programs: A First Course,* published by MIT Press in 1990. He also contributed to another textbook and edited a series of essays devoted to parallel computing. From the beginning, however, Gelernter was more interested in the theoretical and visionary aspects of getting computers to work together than in the purely practical applications of the field. His thinking culminated in the 1991 book *Mirror Worlds, or, The Day Software Puts the Universe in a Shoebox: How It Will Happen and What It Will Mean,* published by Oxford University Press.

Mirror Worlds became recognized as a classic text in computer science. In Markoff's words, Gelernter imagined "that virtually all information would be captured in digital form and that it would be available instantly." "Mirror worlds" were all of the computing applications that would today be described with the terms virtual or virtual reality, from online models of physical sites or processes to computer games of previously unimaginable detail. Furthermore, Gelernter suggested that small desktop computers, instead of being independent entities, would be connected to each other in a large electronic web. Gelernter did not invent the basic machinery of the Internet or network computing, but his ideas are credited with anticipating and laying the groundwork for the rapid growth of the Internet in the early and mid-1990s.

On the morning of July 24, 1993, Gelernter opened a package in his cluttered Yale office. He heard a hiss, saw a flash, and was staggered by an explosion large enough to embed the nails of the bomb in metal file cabinets. The package had been mailed by Theodore "Ted" Kaczynski, an anti-technology terrorist known as the Unabomber, whose bombs killed three people and injured 23 before his arrest in 1996. Gelernter managed to walk to the Yale Health Center; when he arrived, his blood pressure was zero. Doctors and ambulance crews struggled to stop him from bleeding to death. During a six-week hospitalization, Gelernter underwent skin grafts and reconstructive surgery on his shattered dominant right hand, which eventually restored it to partial function. Among Gelernter's thoughts following the bombing was that there were many paintings he would never be able to execute, but he was eventually able to resume painting. He later underwent a cornea transplant that gave him partial vision in his damaged right eye.

Pondered Computers and Creativity

Two years after the bombing, but before his arrest, Kaczynski sent Gelernter a letter that read in part (as quoted by Evan R. Goldstein in the *Chronicle of Higher Education*): "If you'd had any brains you would have realized that there are a lot of people out there who resent bitterly the way techno-nerds like you are changing the world." In fact, Gelernter had always been ambivalent about computing, and had written articles arguing that schools should place less emphasis on computer usage. He was interested in creativity itself and in the possibilities of creative thinking by computers, and while recovering from the bomb blast he wrote *The Muse in the Machine Computerizing the Poetry of Human Thought* (1994). The book distinguished between high-focus (or rational) thought and low-focus thought, in which the human brain is free to make new, creative associations. Gelernter argued that true artificial intelligence would be impossible unless computers could be made capable of low-focus thinking. He wrote several books about beauty in computing, including *Machine Beauty: Elegance and the Heart of Computing* (1997) and *The Aesthetics of Computing* (1998).

In 2000 Gelernter issued another widely read document that has been seen as a prophetic statement of the Internet age: his essay "The Second Coming—A Manifesto" was published in Germany's *Frankfurter Allgemeine* newspaper and later appeared on the website *The Edge*. Cast as a series of 58 aphorisms, "The Second Coming" envisioned a near future in which "computing transcends computers. Information travels through a sea of anonymous, interchangeable computers like a breeze through tall grass. A desktop computer is a scooped-out hole in the beach where information from the Cybersphere wells up like seawater." What Gelernter called the Cybersphere bore many resemblances to what over the next decade became known as cloud computing, in which individual devices worked as parts of often invisible and automatic networks.

Gelernter's activities as a writer in the years after the Unabomber's attack broadened far beyond computing; it was as if his near-death experience compelled him to express an opinion on a wide variety of topics. Several of his books dealt with what he considered the status of the United States as a uniquely great country; this line of thought found expression in *1939: The World of the Fair* (1995), a book that traced the technological impact and vision of the 1939 New York World's Fair. Gelernter summed up his ideas in *Americanism: The Fourth Great Western Religion* (2007), in which he argued that American freedoms have resulted in a morally superior belief system. Beginning in the late 1990s, Gelernter penned numerous opinion pieces for the magazines *Commentary* and later *The Weekly Standard,* arguing positions that made him, by his own testimony, an extreme right-winger. Among them was a series of attacks on feminism in general and advocacy of the idea that women should not work outside the home. In the summer of 2011, Gelernter championed conservative economic proposals being advanced by Republicans in the U.S. House of Representatives.

Gelernter returned to his religious roots with *Judaism: A Way of Being,* published by Yale University Press in 2009. He continued to be closely involved with new computing initiatives, and the continuing vitality of his ideas was shown in 2010 when Mirror Worlds LLC, a company he founded, was awarded $625.5 million after a federal jury in Texas found that Apple, Inc., had infringed on three of the company's patents. The patents involved three of the most widely publicized innovations of Apple's computer operating system during the 2000s decade (Cover Flow, Spotlight, and Time Machine). Although the cash judgment was reversed by a U.S. federal judge in 2011, Gelernter's patents were ruled valid.

Books

Gelernter, David, *Drawing Life: Surviving the Unabomber,* Simon & Schuster, 1997.

Henderson, Harry, *A to Z of Computer Scientists,* Facts of File, 2003.

Periodicals

Daily News (Los Angeles, CA), December 7, 1997.

New York Times, January 19, 1992; July 31, 1994; January 23, 1998.

Record (Bergen County, NJ), April 21, 1996; July 28, 2005.

St. Louis Post-Dispatch, July 29, 2007; October 6, 2010.

Weekly Standard, June 20, 2011.

Online

"Apple Wins: Judge Reverses $625.5 Million Patent Judgment Previously Awarded to Mirror Worlds," *Edible Apple,* (September 22, 2011).

"David Hillel Gelernter," *Contemporary Authors Online,* Detroit: Gale, 2006. Gale Biography In Context (September 22, 2011).

"The Images Dancing in David Gelernter's Head," *Chronicle of Higher Education,* http://www.chronicle.com/article/The-Images-Dancing-in-David/49252/ (September 22, 2011).

"The Second Coming—A Manifesto," *The Edge,* http://www.edge.org/3rd_culture/gelernter/gelernter_index.html (September 22, 2011). □

George Gey

American doctor and scientist George Gey (1899–1970) cultivated the world's first immortal human cell line.

American doctor and scientist George Gey is best remembered as the collector and propagator of the so-called "immortal cells" of the HeLa cell strain. A cancer researcher whose dedication bordered on obsession, Gey spent his career working to find ways to stop the growth of deadly cancerous cells in human beings. As part of his work at Baltimore, Maryland's Johns Hopkins in the mid-twentieth century, the scientist collected cell samples from the hospital's patients and then attempted to get those cells to survive outside of their living host. His efforts met with failure until he began working with cancerous cells taken from a particularly aggressive tumor that was sickening a local woman, Henrietta Lacks. This cell sample not only grew in the laboratory, it thrived, and researchers around the world began using the strain in a wide variety of research applications. Gey also developed other advances in the practice of cell culture, such as the usage of the roller-tube technique.

Became Medical Researcher

A native of Pittsburgh, Pennsylvania, Gey—pronounced like the word *guy*—was born to German immigrant parents on July 6, 1899. His upbringing was a somewhat hardscrabble one; the Gey family survived on the food his mother could cultivate in their back garden, and as a boy Gey collected coal from a small mine he had constructed in a nearby hillside to provide heating and cooking fuel. Such resourcefulness persisted throughout his career. After graduating from high school, Gey served in the U.S. Army during World War I. He then found work as a carpenter and mason in order to earn money to put himself through college. He studied biology at the University of Pittsburgh, where he first developed his lifelong interest in cancer research. Writing in *Pitt* magazine, Rebecca Skloot noted that Gey "spent countless hours in Pittsburgh hospitals where...he came to understand the gravity of cancer. There was no chemotherapy, no treatment of any kind, no hope. In the early 1920s cancer meant certain death. Gey saw this, and resolved to find its cause and cure."

To pursue this goal, Gey enrolled in medical school at the Johns Hopkins University in Baltimore, Maryland, after finishing his undergraduate degree in 1921. Over the next several years, he continued his studies off and on, taking breaks into order to work to earn money to pay for his schooling. From the beginning, however, Gey was fascinated by cell growth and propagation. He employed the make-do attitude of his childhood to create contraptions that combined junkyard finds and other repurposed parts to help him record and study this process. In *The Immortal Life of Henrietta Lacks,* Skloot recounted one such invention, devised by Gey during his second year at Johns Hopkins: "he rigged a microscope with a time-lapse motion picture camera to capture live cells on film. It was a Frankensteinish mishmash of microscope parts, glass, and 16-millimeter camera equipment...plus metal scraps, and old motors from Shapiro's junkyard. He built it in a hole he'd blasted in the foundation of Hopkins, right below the morgue, its base entirely underground and surrounded by a thick wall of cork to keep it from jiggling when street cars passed." While completing his medical training, Gey married the women who would become his lifelong research partner, Margaret (Koudelka) Gey. The couple later had a son, George, and a daughter, Frances.

By the time that Gey completed his medical degree in 1933, he had already been named the director of Johns Hopkins' tissue culture lab. Along with his wife, Gey worked diligently to develop the first "immortal" human cell line. Typically, cells kept in the artificial conditions of a laboratory divided between 20 and 50 times before dying. Immortal cell lines, however, continue to draw on the culture material and divide indefinitely. Scientists had had success with creating such a cell line with animal samples, but Gey wanted to produce a human cell line that could better serve medical research. To this end, he developed a roller drum machine that slowly and steadily rotated cell samples in order to provide optimal conditions for their growth and continued development. Because he wished to use them simply to further his own research, Gey did not publish papers on or patent his inventions. Instead, researchers came to his laboratory to observe his creations and methods, and knowledge about them spread. In later years, Gey's roller drum device, for example, was used to grow the polio virus in certain types of cells and then to develop the vaccine against that disease.

Collected HeLa Cell Strain

Little evidence exists to suggest that Gey ever met the woman who provided the cells that defined much of his career. When Henrietta Lacks first arrived at Johns Hopkins in 1951, she was a 31-year-old mother of five who had moved to Baltimore from rural Virginia some years previously with her husband, who worked in the city's steel industry. The family had little money, and Lacks came to Johns Hopkins after discovering a lump on her cervix because the hospital offered free medical care to the area's African American community. A gynecologist there, Dr. Howard Jones, visually confirmed the existence of the lump and quickly diagnosed it as a cancerous growth. "I can see that lesion today because it was not like an ordinary cancer," he recalled to Glenda Cooper of the *Independent*. This was different...I'd never seen anything look like it." Doctors began aggressive treatment, but Lacks's cancer proved more powerful than medical knowledge. Over the next several months, the cancer metastasized throughout her body, and Lacks died from the disease in October of 1951.

As part of the early diagnosis and treatment for the cancer, doctors collected two samples from Lacks's cervix. One of these samples contained healthy tissue, and the other held cancerous cells. Such cell collection was standard procedure at the hospital; so was providing these samples to Gey, who hoped to use them to develop his immortal cell line. Although he had consistently failed to do this, Gey remained confident that his efforts would pay off. His assistant, Mary Kubicek, was less confident, and was thus less than delighted when the arrival of Lacks's cells interrupted her lunch one day in 1951. Nevertheless, she transferred both samples to the Gey Culture Medium— a combination of chicken plasma, human umbilical cord blood, and a host of other biological matter—to a roller drum machine. Within days, Kubicek was surprised to discover that the cancerous cervical cell sample taken from Lacks had not only survived, but had begun growing rapidly, filling the test tubes without any sign of slowing their division. Gey was initially hesitant to pass judgment, but it soon became clear that his lab had succeeded in doing what it had never done before: cultivate an immortal human cell line. Following the conventions of the lab, it was called HeLa for *He*nrietta *La*cks. Despite the significance of this discovery, Gey did not tell Lacks's surviving family members of the cells' collection or usage in this era before the institution of informed consent. Decades later, their ignorance became a source of controversy.

By 1952, Gey had begun providing samples of HeLa cells to fellow researchers. The National Foundation for Infantile Paralysis approached him about using some of his cells in polio research, and Gey readily agreed. The cells traveled to the Tuskegee Institute, where they were used to prove the efficacy of Jonas Salk's new polio vaccine. From there, HeLa cells were sold to numerous other medical research facilities. Although biomedical corporations made vast amounts of money from the cells over the years, Gey did not share in this financial windfall. As Skloot wrote in *The Immortal Life of Henrietta Lacks,* Gey "was relieved that companies had taken over HeLa distribution so that he didn't have to do it himself, but he didn't like the fact that HeLa was now completely out of his control." In keeping with his focus on his research to the exclusion of all else, Gey did not even publish a paper on his finding until the mid-1950s. The Pan American Cancer Cytology Congress did recognize his work, however, with the 1956 Leonard Wien award for what Gey's *New York Times* biography called "brilliant work in the tissue culture field." Gey and his laboratory continued to work on cell cultivation throughout the 1960s, exploring other possible immortal cell lines and refining medical techniques.

A Living Legacy

After spending most of his life working to cure cancer, Gey fell victim to the disease himself when he was diagnosed with pancreatic cancer in the summer of 1970. In August of that year, he underwent surgery to attempt to remove the tumor. Before entering the operating room, Gey instructed the surgeons to remove a sample of the growth that he hoped would, in time, become its own human cell line suitable for research. However, doctors discovered while Gey was on the operating table that the cancer had spread throughout his abdomen and invaded his stomach, spleen, intestines, and liver. Concerned that attempting to remove even parts of the growth would immediately kill the patient, surgeons instead decided to leave them in place and intact. The researcher's hoped-for GeGe cell line was not to be, much to his personal frustration and anger. Yet

he refused to simply wait for death quietly. Gey offered to serve as a research subject for any doctor conducting studies into pancreatic cancer, and took part in several separate experimental drug therapies over the remaining months of his life. The treatments caused him a great deal of physical discomfort and confined him to a wheelchair, but Gey perservered in the hopes of furthering his life's work. He died as a result of the disease on November 8, 1970, in Baltimore.

Gey's death did not end the continuation of his work, however. Researchers continued to conduct studies using the HeLa cell line, discussion of which enjoyed a brief revival in the medical press as a result of Gey's passage. By 1973, one writer estimated the combined weight of all of the HeLa cells worldwide outweighed that of their original human donor; more than thirty-five years later, that estimated total had grown to outweigh the Empire State Building, and the length of the cells placed end-to-end was suggested to be substantial enough to encircle Earth three times. Those who knew and worked with the doctor personally spoke of his great dedication to improving human health. In Gey's obituary in *Cancer Research,* John Hopkins staffers John H. Hanks and Frederick B. Bang stated, "to those [investigators] and to many others with whom his activities brought him into daily contact there will always remain the warm recollection of an inspiring and humane friend." Gey's efforts continued to receive recognition well into the twenty-first century, especially as interest in HeLa cell donor Henrietta Lacks arose. "In the end, he did not leave a towering stack of published papers or patented inventions, wrote Lacks biographer Skloot of Gey's work in *Pitt,* continuing, "he left a legacy of understanding, and a foundation upon which cancer research and cell culture have grown."

Books

Skloot, Rebecca, *The Immortal Life of Henrietta Lacks,* Crown, 2010.

Periodicals

Cancer Research, Volume 31, 1971.
Independent (London, England), March 14, 1997.
Johns Hopkins Magazine, April 2000.
New York Times, November 9, 1970.
Pitt, March 2001.

Online

"The George O. Gey Collection," Medical Archives of the Johns Hopkins Medical Institutions, http://www.medicalarchives. jhmi.edu/papers/gey.html (September 27, 2011). □

Josh Gibson

American baseball player Josh Gibson (1911-1947) was one of the greatest power hitter in the Negro Leagues, a much-mythologized figure who could hit home runs farther than anyone else. Some called

him the "black Babe Ruth," comparing him to the famous home run champion. Plagued by poor health, Gibson died just months before the major leagues were integrated.

"Josh was the greatest hitter I ever pitched to, and I pitched to everybody," Satchel Paige, the Hall of Fame pitcher who played in the Negro Leagues and the major leagues, once said (as quoted by Dave Anderson in the *New York Times*). "I had to throw sidearm curves to Josh, break it on the outside corner and pray. Break it inside, he'd just rip it."

Youth in Pittsburgh

Gibson was born in Buena Vista, Georgia, on December 21, 1911, the oldest of three children. He and his family became part of the Great Migration, in which millions of black Americans moved from southern to northern states in the 1910s and 1920s in search of better jobs and relative freedom from segregation and persecution. His father, Mark Gibson, a sharecropper, moved from Georgia to Pittsburgh, Pennsylvania, in 1921 to take a job at the Carnegie-Illinois Steel plant there. His family joined him in 1924 in Pleasant Valley, a neighborhood on Pittsburgh's north side. The city would be Gibson's home for most of his life.

Gibson went to the Allegheny Pre-Vocational School, where he studied to become an electrician. But his athletic skills quickly blossomed. A few weeks after moving to Pittsburgh, at age 12, he got his first pair of roller skates and sped up and down his neighborhood's streets. He won awards in track competitions and became a skilled swimmer in meets at city pools. He also embraced baseball, a game he had played occasionally in Georgia, and quickly began hitting the ball hard.

Pittsburgh was a good place for a young, athletic black teen to embrace baseball. The Homestead Grays, Pennsylvania's best black baseball team (named after a small town east of Pittsburgh), was attracting top players and inspiring young fans in the stands at the city's Forbes Field. In 1927, Gibson began playing baseball in sandlot teams as a catcher. By the next year, he was playing for the Crawford Colored Giants, a semi-professional boys' team. By 1930, Gibson's frequent home runs for the Crawford team were attracting coverage from Pittsburgh's black newspaper, the *Courier*. The Homestead Grays noticed him too. Cumberland Posey, the Grays' owner and manager, wrote to Gibson and told him to be ready to join the Grays whenever the team had an opening for him.

Made Debut as Power Hitter

Like much of Gibson's career, his debut for the Grays is obscured by legend. A popular story claims that Posey called Gibson out of the stands in the middle of a game in 1930 after regular Grays catcher Buck Ewing split a finger. Gibson biographer William Brashler identified his first game as July 25, 1930, and says Gibson was brought over from the Crawford Giants' ballpark mid-game after Ewing's finger injury. Other accounts have Gibson playing one game for the Grays a year earlier, in 1929.

Gibson remained on the Grays for the rest of the 1930 season, alternating between backup catcher behind Ewing and starting in the outfield, batting sixth or seventh in the lineup. He struggled at first to catch balls thrown by the Grays' pitchers, but quickly established himself as a strong hitter. Writers for black newspapers began celebrating and mythologizing Gibson's performance as a hitter as well as his off-field appetite for food, including quarts of vanilla ice cream.

The Grays, a strong team in 1930, played an unofficial ten-game playoff that fall against the New York Lincoln Giants. In one game at Yankee Stadium, Gibson is said to have hit a home run into the left-field bullpen, an amazing 500 feet away from home plate. The Grays beat the Giants, winning six games out of ten. Though Negro League statistics were unreliable, some sources credit Gibson with either a .441 or .461 batting average in 1930 with the Grays.

Gibson's accomplishments that year were shadowed by loss. Earlier that year, the 18-year-old Gibson had married his 17-year-old girlfriend, Helen Mason, after she had become pregnant. The young couple moved in with her parents. But in August, Helen suffered complications while giving birth to twins, Helen and Josh Jr. She fell into a coma and soon died of a heart attack. The tragedy struck just weeks after Gibson's debut with the Grays. Since Gibson was often traveling with the team, Helen's parents raised the twins, while his relationship with them was distant.

Eager to make a living as a professional baseball player, in the fall of 1930 Gibson joined the first of many cross-country exhibition tours in which all-black teams played against white major-league players. He also traveled to South America to play at the end of the year. In 1931, he rejoined the Grays, replacing the retired Ewing as the full-time catcher. That season, the Grays assembled one of the most talented rosters in the history of the Negro Leagues, yet

Gibson still stood out as a star. One source credits him with a .367 batting average and an amazing 75 home runs. The Grays won a second championship that year.

Joined the Pittsburgh Crawfords

In 1932, Gibson left the Grays to join the Pittsburgh Crawfords, owned by the free-spending Gus Greenlee, who was paying top salaries to attract some of the best talent in black baseball. The Crawfords dominated the Negro Leagues during the 1930s and became the best team in black baseball history and perhaps one of the best baseball teams ever. Gibson averaged .380 and hit 34 home runs in 1932 and went on to hit above .400 for three of the next four years. He developed a reputation as the Negro Leagues' best hitter, a natural talent, a slugger who could hit the ball farther than any player, white or black.

"He had perfected his batting style to the point where it became flawless," wrote Brashler in his book *Josh Gibson: A Life in the Negro Leagues.* "Josh's power came almost completely from strength above his waist: arms, shoulders, and back muscles so awesome that he didn't need the coiled power of his legs or the whiplike action of his wrists. With his upper-body power, he could thrash a ball with a motion much like that of beating a rug."

Between Negro League seasons, Gibson, like many black ballplayers, traveled south to play in leagues in Puerto Rico, Mexico, and South America. There, salaries were often better than in the U.S. and the players rarely experienced racial discrimination. The warm welcome from fans in Puerto Rico, where Gibson won several most valuable player awards, was said to have meant more to him than his accomplishments with Pittsburgh's teams.

In 1937, after Gibson briefly rejoined the Grays, he and several other Negro League stars, including Satchel Paige, left the United States to play for the Trujillo All-Stars, organized by the president of the Dominican Republic, Rafael Trujillo. Gibson led the Dominican league with a .453 average during a short season, then returned to the Grays, who won the Negro National League pennant. In 1938 and 1939, according to at least one account, Gibson racked up batting averages of .433 and .440. His slugging percentage was above 1.000 both years.

Attracted by a better salary, Gibson spent 1940 and 1941 playing in Latin American leagues. He played for a team in Venezuela until it folded, then switched to Veracruz in the Mexican League. Though he only played a quarter of the season for Veracruz, he finished one home run behind the league's top home-run hitter. In 1941, he hit .374 for Veracruz and hit 33 home runs, the most of any Mexican League hitter. He led the league in runs batted in and helped Veracruz win the Mexican League pennant. Gibson made a $6,000 salary in Mexico, but when Cumberland Posey filed a $10,000 lawsuit to force Gibson to return to the United States and play for the Grays, the move no longer seemed worth it. Gibson and Posey reached a settlement, and Gibson rejoined the Grays in 1942.

In 1942, Gibson's first year back with the Grays, he hit .344 and helped the team win another Negro National League title. The season ended with the first Negro World Series in 15 years, in which the Grays played the Kansas City Monarchs. The expected competition between Gibson and Paige, the Negro Leagues' best batter and best pitcher, was anticlimactic. Gibson batted less than .200, and Kansas City swept the series.

Fell Into a Coma

Gibson's health was eroding. He had gained weight and lost speed running the bases. His knees ached. Sometimes, chasing foul pop-ups, he would become dizzy and disoriented. After the 1942 season, doctors told Gibson to take time off from baseball. He refused, playing in postseason games.

On New Years' Day 1943, Gibson lost consciousness, fell into a coma, and was hospitalized. His ailment was publicly described as a nervous breakdown. But his sister, Annie, later said he had been diagnosed with a brain tumor and had refused to let doctors operate on him, afraid that the surgery would destroy his mental function. Gibson also drank heavily, and may have taken heroin with a girlfriend, Grace Fournier. While traveling, he would alarm his teammates with increasingly erratic behavior. Some accounts say he spent time in mental hospitals between games.

Still, Gibson continued to perform well on the field most of the time. In 1943, he hit for an incredible average, either .474 or .526 (sources differ), and he was the starting catcher in the Negro Leagues' all-star game at Chicago's Comiskey Park. He hit a 460-foot home run in Washington, D.C.'s Griffith Stadium that year, one of many examples of him hitting longer home runs in major-league ballparks than the major leaguers of the time. During the 1943 season, when the Grays split their home games between Pittsburgh and Washington, Clark Griffith, owner of the Washington Senators, asked for a meeting with Gibson and teammate Buck Leonard and asked if they were interested in playing in the major leagues. But he never made them an offer, and the major leagues remained segregated until 1947.

Returned to Negro World Series

In 1943, when the Grays returned to the Negro World Series, Gibson was again exhausted and played poorly, not contributing much to his team's series victory over the Birmingham Black Barons. But in the 1944 season, Gibson became more of a singles hitter than a slugger, averaging .345 during the regular season. He hit .400 with one home run in the Negro World Series as the Grays beat Birmingham again.

In 1945, Gibson started the season poorly but went on a hitting spree to close the year. He batted .393 and won the league batting title. The Grays went to the Negro World Series again, though they lost to the Cleveland Buckeyes.

By then, Gibson's health had deteriorated so much that younger players, returning from fighting in World War II, were struck by the change in him. He could still hit, but his skills as a catcher had suffered greatly. He had gained weight and could no longer get into a catcher's crouch. Instead, he would stand behind home plate and catch pitches while stooping down. Toward the end of the 1946 season, he was hurt and frequently out of the lineup.

But even while very ill, he averaged .361 at bat and is said to have hit a 550-foot home run.

In late 1946, Gibson was living with his mother in Pittsburgh, drinking heavily in bars, losing weight rapidly, and suffering from knee pain, headaches, and dizziness. Some have sentimentally claimed that the news of Jackie Robinson's impending debut with the major-league Brooklyn Dodgers broke Gibson's heart, driving him into despair at a lost opportunity. But it is more likely that his failing health simply left him depressed.

On the night of January 19, 1947, Gibson suffered a stroke at a movie theater. He died early the next morning, on January 20, 1947, at age 35. He died just months before Robinson became the first black major-league baseball player in the 20th century.

In 1972, Gibson was named to baseball's Hall of Fame. His plaque there calls him the greatest slugger in the Negro Leagues and credits him with hitting almost 800 home runs (though other sources say he hit 600 home runs or less). Gibson was the second Negro League player inducted into the Hall of Fame, after only Paige.

Books

Brashler, William, *Josh Gibson: A Life in the Negro Leagues,* Ivan R. Dee, 2000.

Ribowsky, Mark, *Josh Gibson: The Power and the Darkness,* University of Illinois Press, 2004.

Periodicals

New York Times, February 6, 1972.

Online

"Personal Profiles: Josh Gibson," Negro Leagues Baseball eMuseum, http://coe.ksu.edu/nlbemuseum/history/players/gibsonj.html (November 24, 2011).

Schwartz, Larry, "No joshing about Gibson's talents," ESPN.com, http://espn.go.com/sportscentury/features/00016050.html (November 24, 2011). □

Cammi Granato

The American hockey player Cammi Granato (born 1971) was a pioneer among female players of the sport.

Granato was a founding member of the United States women's national ice hockey team, which she helped lead to an impressive string of victories on the world stage—especially impressive in a country where there was only a small formal infrastructure for women's hockey. Granato's biggest victory of all was the gold medal earned by Team USA in the 1998 Winter Olympics in Nagano, Japan. Granato became the first woman inducted into the International Ice Hockey Federation Hall of Fame, and she was part of the first group of female players to join the larger Hockey Hall of Fame in

Toronto, Ontario, Canada. "Man or woman," fellow Olympian and Detroit Red Wings star Chris Chelios was quoted as saying on the *Greatest Hockey Legends* website, "Cammi Granato is one of the most impressive hockey leaders I've ever come across."

Snuck Away from Figure Skating Lessons

Catherine Michelle Granato was born on March 25, 1971, in Downers Grove, Illinois, a suburb of Chicago,. Her father, Don, was a beer distributor. Granato was the second youngest of six children, and all four of her brothers played ice hockey. Her mother, Marie, hoped to interest her daughter in figure skating, but even at the age of four she would leave the figure skating rink to watch her brothers playing hockey nearby. Her mother insisted that she take a year of figure skating lessons, but after that, Granato switched to the Downers Grove Huskies club and remained there from kindergarten through junior high school. Her brothers tried to steer her toward playing goalie, but she was clear that she wanted to take a shotmaking position.

Granato rarely encountered another female player and participated in all-boys' leagues until her junior year in high school. By that point she was smaller than the boys she played against, and at a disadvantage in the physical blocking technique known as bodychecking; her adult height and weight were about five-foot seven inches and 140 pounds. In high school she played boys' baseball (batting fourth, or "cleanup"), girls' basketball and soccer, and handball, a sport where she showed talent. "I always loved team sports," she told Steve Trivett of Denver's *Rocky Mountain News.* "Maybe it was because, at our house, all we played were team sports. But I did learn a lot by playing all sports. I think it's a mistake to commit young kids to one sport so early." But she remained most interested in hockey, and when she was offered a hockey scholarship from Providence College in Rhode Island, one of the few schools in the United States to emphasize women's hockey, she jumped at the chance. Her first game at Providence in 1989 marked the first time she had played against other girls. Granato was a four-year starter and three-time Eastern College Athletic Conference Women's Hockey Player of the Year at Providence.

She had already made up her mind to enter international competition after traveling to Calgary, Alberta, Canada, for the 1988 Winter Olympic Games and witnessing the games' opening parade. In 1990, with the number of registered female hockey players in the United States in the low five figures (by 1997 it was 21,555), Granato became a member of the first U.S. national women's hockey team. Despite having to buy their own gear bags and sweatsuits, the squad notched a startling silver medal in the 1990 world championships, losing only to Canada. Granato returned to the U.S. team in 1991, 1992, 1994, 1995, 1996, and 1997, by which time they had arch-rival Canada in their sights for the 1998 Winter Olympics gold medal.

Earned Master's Degree in Canada

Despite these accomplishments, Granato felt unsure of her own abilities. By the time she graduated from Providence in 1993, her brother Tony Granato already had several years under his belt at the position of left winger with the New York Rangers and the Los Angeles Kings of the National Hockey League. "At times at Providence she felt guilty getting all the attention," Granato's roommate, Michelle Johansson, told Michael Farber of *Sports Illustrated*. "She thought it was because she was Tony's sister and it made a cute story. I had to tell her, 'Tony didn't score all those goals for you.'" Those doubts began to evaporate when Granato joined the hockey team at Concordia University in Montreal, Quebec, Canada, where she earned a master's degree in sports administration in 1997. She was part of a Concordia team that won three Quebec Intercollegiate Hockey League titles, and in 123 games there she scored 178 goals and 148 assists.

Her path in international play was anything but smooth. In the 1995 Pacific Rim tournament, she took a tough hit from a Chinese player and came up unable to walk. Fearing the loss of her knee, she was instead diagnosed with a broken fibula. Heavily taped, Granato played four more games in the tournament. "Sure, the pain killed me," she admitted to Farber, "but it was a non-weight-bearing bone." Unlike male players in major sports, Granato lived a spartan life in Montreal, living with her hockey player boyfriend in a Montreal apartment on a graduate stipend of about $15,000 a year.

All the struggles of Granato's early years turned out to be worth it when she made the 1998 U.S. women's hockey team that competed in the Nagano, Japan, Winter Olympics; the event was the inaugural of the Olympic women's ice hockey competition. Granato was following in the footsteps of her brother Tony, who played on the 1988 Olympic team. Playing center, Granato paced the U.S. team to two victories over heavily favored Canada, including a 3-1 victory in the finals to take the gold medal. Impressed by the fairytale win of the U.S. men's hockey team in the 1980 Olympics, Granato had dreamed of the moment. "It's

funny thinking back on it now," she told Trivett. "But I didn't know until then that you got to keep the medals. I felt like that kid I had in me that had watched 1980 was in me again." Granato was chosen to carry the U.S. flag in the Olympics' closing ceremonies.

Invited by Islanders for Tryout

The victory raised the profile of U.S. women's hockey in general and Granato in particular. She was invited to try out for the New York Islanders National Hockey League team, and gave the offer serious consideration, ultimately deciding that there was no way a 140-pound player, male or female, was going to succeed in the NHL and that the offer had aspects of a press gimmick. Faced with the necessity of making a living in the absence of a professional sports league that would reward her for her talents, Granato took a job with the Los Angeles Kings as a broadcast commentator. She longed for more playing time, however, and left the Kings after one season, returning to the U.S. national team and playing in the world championships between 1999 and 2001.

In 2002 Granato served as captain of the U.S. Olympic team that fell in a closely contested final against Canada in Salt Lake City, Utah. She continued to play for the U.S. national team, scoring one more world championship in 2005. Granato played for a time in Canada's National Women's Hockey League, which limits the number of foreign players, and she argued in favor of the creation of a post-collegiate professional league in the United States.

In 2006 Granato hoped for a shot at a third Olympic medal, but was cut from the team by coach Ben Smith, who believed that her best playing days were over. Granato said in an interview quoted on the *Greatest Hockey Legends* site that she felt "an overwhelming sadness. I'm not an angry person. I have a big loving family and a roster full of former teammates that I love and respect. But I'm so heartbroken right now. I could never fathom this is how my hockey career would end."

Even without the 2006 Olympics, Granato left the game as the top scorer in international women's hockey. She was the first woman inducted into the U.S. Hockey Hall of Fame and the International Ice Hockey Federation Hall of Fame in 2008, and one of the first group of women to join the Hockey Hall of Fame in Toronto in 2010. Married to former NHL player Ray Ferraro, Granato settled in Vancouver, British Columbia, Canada, and had two sons, Riley and Reese. She is a partner in a girls' hockey equipment business.

Books

Notable Sports Figures, Gale, 2004.

Periodicals

Denver Post, November 11, 2007.
Globe & Mail (Toronto), November 6, 2010.
Hamilton Spectator (Hamilton, Ontario, Canada), November 9, 2010.

Rocky Mountain News (Denver, CO), January 2, 2004.
San Jose Mercury News, January 17, 2006.
Sports Illustrated, June 20, 2005; July 14, 2008.

Online

"Cammi Granato," *Greatest Hockey Legends,* http://womens
hockeylegends.blogspot.com/2008/07/cammi-granato.html
(October 1, 2011).
"Cammi Granato," *Hockey Hall of Fame,* http://www.hhof.com/
htmlInduct/ind10Granato.shtml (October 1, 2011).
Farber, Michael, "The Ice Queen," *Sports Illustrated,* http://
sportsillustrated.cnn.com/features/1997/womenmag/icequeen.
html (October 1, 2011).□

Ella T. Grasso

American politician Ella T. Grasso (1919–1981) was the first woman elected governor of a U.S. state without running on the record of a husband.

American politician Ella Grasso became the first woman elected governor of a U.S. state without having been married to a preceding governor when Connecticut voters chose her for the state's top job in 1974. Beginning in the 1940s, Grasso dedicated her career to government service, combining support for social spending and inherent fiscal frugality that allowed her to appeal to a broad base of voters. She won her first elective office at the state level in 1952, and went on to serve as Connecticut's Secretary of State and one of its U.S. Representatives in Congress. Grasso's popularity carried her to a landslide victory in her first gubernatorial run, and despite breaking numerous campaign promises due to the state's financial challenges she managed to end her first term on a high note. Midway into her second term, Grasso was diagnosed with ovarian cancer, and her failing health forced her to resign several months later. Although she died soon after, Grasso's political legacy laid the groundwork for other women to achieve the top job in states around the nation in the coming years and helped inspire a new generation of women to public service.

Launched State-Level Career

Born Ella Rosa Giovanna Tambussi on May 10, 1919, in Windsor Locks, Connecticut, Grasso was the only daughter of Italian immigrants who had come separately to the United States seeking economic opportunity some years earlier. Her father, Giacomo Tambussi, was a baker, and her mother, Maria Oliva, worked in a General Electric factory before marrying and giving birth. Although Tambussi's bakery succeeded and the family earned a comfortable income, Grasso's parents valued frugality and simplicity, two ideals that later shaped the adult politician's actions in government. A dedicated student, Grasso attended a local Catholic school before winning a scholarship to the prestigious Chaffee School. After graduating

from that institution, she attended Mount Holyoke in Massachusetts, where she became interested in labor relations and economics. She completed her bachelor's degree in 1940, and continued with graduate studies at Mount Holyoke in economics. The year 1942 marked two significant milestones for Grasso as she both finished her master's degree and married longtime boyfriend Thomas Grasso. The couple settled in Grasso's hometown, buying a house just across the street from her parents.

After her marriage, Grasso spent three years working with the Federal War Manpower Commission in nearby Hartford. World War II wound to an end, however, and Grasso chose to stay home to care for her growing family after the agency was dispersed. She gave birth to a daughter, Susanne, in 1948, and a son, Jim, in 1951. Before long, Grasso sought to return to government service. She became active in the local Democratic Party, and won one of Windsor Lock's two seats in a competitive race for the state General Assembly in 1952. Building on her image as a "housewife politician" and her own economics and labor experience, Grasso focused on legislative efforts such as calling for the addition of expiration dates to milk bottle caps while fiercely striving to reduce inefficiency by eliminating county government. Her natural political savvy brought the new legislator into the political circle of state Democratic chair and party boss John Moran Bailey, and with his support she became the national Democratic committee woman in 1956. During the mid-1950s, Grasso helped author the state Democratic political platforms and worked on the successful campaign of Abraham Ribicoff, Connecticut's first Jewish governor.

In 1958, she ran a successful campaign for Secretary of State, taking office amidst a general Democratic ascendency in Connecticut politics. Grasso's new role placed her in charge of overseeing elections, enforcing voting regulations, and encouraging voter turnout—all largely non-partisan functions that typically made the Secretary's job an uncontroversial and not especially notable one. Grasso, who had long displayed a knack for keeping herself in the media eye, managed to attract notice for such matters as her refusal to purchase the new car typically demanded by incoming officeholders and her decision to visit local election officials personally in order to discuss statewide election rules. This latter effort helped her raise her profile statewide. As Susan Bysiewicz observed in *Ella: A Biography of Governor Ella Grasso*, the "innovative new policy represented a deliberate effort not only to expand the office of the Secretary of State but also to enhance her own influence and broaden her power base." Grasso's popularity grew, and she won re-election as Secretary of State by over 80,000 votes in 1962.

Became a Leader in Connecticut Politics

Over the next several years, Grasso maintained a high level of popular support even as she worked to help strengthen the Democratic party in Connecticut and throughout the nation. She managed the reapportionment process of the mid-1960s with care to ensure that the small towns that had offered her much of her early support retained a measure of political authority, and drafted new amendments to the state constitution to encourage education and civil rights advances. Grasso broke with the national Democratic party on Vietnam by strongly supporting a peace measure at the 1968 Democratic National Convention. Some state strategists encouraged Grasso to run for U.S. Congress that year, but she declined because she was unwilling to leave her family behind to legislate from Washington, D.C.

Two years later, however, the opportunity for Grasso to make the jump to the national level again arose when one of the state's U.S. Congress seats offered an open contest. Grasso won the seat by a small margin, and entered the U.S. House of Representatives in 1971. She received appointments to the committees servicing Veterans' Affairs and Education and Labor, but grew frustrated at the limited influence that new lawmakers could exercise in the national Congressional system. Unable to exert much authority or lead the sorts of initiatives she was accustomed to, Grasso began considering ways to return to state-level politics even as she won re-election to her Congressional seat in 1972.

By 1973, Democratic party strategists had begun to suggest Grasso as a possible candidate for governor in the following year's elections. She announced her intention to run early the following year, and began working to consolidate her support around the state. Grasso's two decades of involvement in Connecticut politics paid off as her diverse areas of interest generated broad-based support. "Labor, liberal, and education groups eagerly climbed aboard the Grasso bandwagon," Bysiewicz reported. Grasso's nomination as the Democratic candidate for governor was by no means secure, however. Her primary challenger, Attorney General Robert Killian, was also a popular politician who had won his office in a strong Republican year. An early Grasso victory in Hartford squelched Killian's campaign, and he instead signed on to run as Lieutenant Governor on Grasso's ticket.

Grasso faced Republican opponent Robert Steele, Jr., who also served in the U.S. House of Representatives in the general election, which played out against the backdrop of

the Watergate controversy plaguing the Republican Nixon White House and the shifting social currents of women's rights. Grasso's historic candidacy propelled the Connecticut race to national news, and she focused her campaign on her populist appeal. When the election results were returned in November of 1974, Grasso had carried the governorship by a measure of more than 200,000 votes—the second-largest margin of victory for that office in Connecticut history.

Served as Governor of Connecticut

A series of challenges to Grasso's combination of social liberalism and fiscal conservatism presented itself even before her inauguration. Connecticut faced a budget deficit in excess of two million dollars, and the outgoing governor happily passed along the chore of restoring the state to solvency to his successor. Grasso undertook the task by restructuring state government, decreasing promised aid to cities, and slashing spending budgets to achieve significant savings without inaugurating the state income tax that Connecticut residents had long resisted. A moral opponent of abortion, Grasso eliminated funding to pregnant women on welfare to obtain the procedure. She cut state government jobs and failed to live up to most of her campaign promises. These measures hurt Grasso's popularity, but other events counterbalanced their effect. Rumors spread that Grasso was being considered as a potential vice-presidential candidate on the national Democratic ticket in 1976. By the following year, the state's budget was again in the black. Grasso began efforts to renew support among her traditional loyalists, and generated a great deal of public goodwill for her handling of a major blizzard that struck the state in the winter of 1978 that included personal efforts to aid state residents. "The public now believed that it had not just a politician but a pro-active, caring, compassionate woman as governor," explained Grasso's biography on the Connecticut State Library website. "Mother Ella," as Grasso became known, rode to an easy victory in November of that year in what proved to be her final elective contest. In over 25 years in Connecticut politics, Grasso never lost a race.

The improved fiscal climate of Grasso's second term initially allowed her to begin fulfilling some of the 1974 campaign promises to up spending to help senior citizens, the poor, and others. She lowered the state speed limit and spearheaded efforts to improve support and job training for the urban poor. Grasso carefully managed the gas crisis of 1979 by implementing a system of rationing based on the final digit of a vehicle's license plate, and took part in a series of talks about the energy crisis held at Camp David. She encouraged business development through tax incentives and other programs. Yet problems remained as energy costs and unemployment pressured the state budget, forcing her to propose a hefty increase to the state sales tax in 1980.

The governor also faced a serious personal challenge. In March of 1980, doctors diagnosed Grasso with ovarian cancer. She began treatment, having her ovaries removed and undergoing radiation therapy. But the disease continued to spread, and Grasso's health worsened. As the months progressed, Grasso decided to resign from office. She announced her resignation on December 4, and served her final day in office on December 31, 1980. Sitting Lieutenant

Governor William A. O'Neill then ascended to the state's top executive seat. Grasso died from her cancer short weeks later on February 5, 1981. "We in Connecticut have been most fortunate to have known, worked with and been the beneficiaries of all her good works, throughout her lifetime," said O'Neill in a statement quoted by Matthew L. Wald in the *New York Times*. "She will not be replaced, because she is irreplaceable," O'Neill continued, "nor will she ever be forgotten. My own personal heart is breaking." After lying in state at the Capitol, Grasso was buried in St. Mary's Cemetery in Windsor Locks, Connecticut.

Grasso's legacy lives on in Connecticut and throughout the United States. After her death, she became the first woman honored with a statue in the state's Capitol, and numerous public buildings and roads in the state bear her name. Grasso's groundbreaking election as governor helped pave the way for women to hold more and higher offices at the state and national levels; in the decades following Grasso's governorship, women won election to that office in states from Vermont to Alaska to Texas to Hawaii. In a 2002 preface to her biography of Grasso, Bysiewicz noted that several women had gained important offices in Connecticut including Secretary of State, State Treasurer, and Speaker of the House. "I believe that these 'firsts' would not have been possible without Ella Grasso's trailblazing tenure as Governor," she contended. Although Grasso's own time in office was cut short, her role of influence and inspiration continued.

Books

Bysiewicz, Susan, *Ella: A Biography of Government Ella Grasso*, The Connecticut Consortium for Law and Citizenship Education, 1984.

Periodicals

Hog River Journal, August/September/October 2004.
New York Times, February 6, 1981.

Online

"Ella Giovanna Oliva (Tambussi) Grasso," Connecticut State Library, http://www.cslib.org/gov/grassoe.htm (September 27, 2011).
"Ella Tambussi Grasso," Women in Congress, U.S. House of Representatives, http://womenincongress.house.gov/member-profiles/profile.html?intID=90 (September 27, 2011).
"Grasso, Ella Tambussi," American National Biography Online, http://www.anb.org (November 20, 2011).□

Ellie Greenwich

Ellie Greenwich (1940-2009) was a songwriter, record producer and singer who exerted enormous influence upon the pop music scene during the 1960s. With her ex-husband Jeff Barry, she wrote some of the most famous and popular songs of that decade, including *The Leader of the Pack*, a pop anthem.

I n the mid-1960s, Ellie Greenwich displayed a headful of dyed blonde hair darkened by black roots. This made her look like a street-toughened New York City girl. In reality, she was a poet blessed with a creative soul: one of the great pop-song composers in one of the music industry's most vibrant decades. In the 1960s, and with then-husband Jeff Barry, she wrote some of the era's most memorable songs.

Typically, and historically, the best songwriting teams were male partnerships—the Gershwin brothers, Rodgers and Hammerstein, Lennon and McCartney, Jagger and Richards—but Greenwich worked in the fertile environment (the Brill Building in New York City), where gender did not seem to matter much. Indeed, that's where another husband/wife team (Gerry Goffin and Carole King) matched Barry/Greenwich in terms of productivity and song popularity.

The Barry/Greenwich songbook includes some of the most famous music ever recorded: songs such as *And Then He Kissed Me*, *Be My Baby*, *Chapel of Love*, *Do Wah Diddy*, *Hanky Panky*, *Maybe I Know*, and the monumental *The Leader of the Pack*.

Grew up in New York

Ellie Greenwich was born October 23, 1940 in Brooklyn, New York. When she was eleven years old, she moved with her family to the suburbs of Levittown, New York on Long Island. As a young girl, she demonstrated talent and creativity. Youthful activities included dancing, singing, and poetry writing (one of the poems she penned won a local newspaper's poetry contest). Also, she played the accordion and taught herself how to play the piano. By the time she was thirteen years old, she was already writing songs.

While attending high school during the 1950s, Greenwich formed a singing group with two friends. As the Jivettes, this trio of friends performed at area high schools, hospitals and charity events. Around this time, Greenwich's supportive mother arranged a meeting with a man named Archie Bleyer, who was president of a company called Cadence Records and who had helped advance the careers of the Everly Brothers and the Chordettes. Bleyer appreciated Greenwich's talent, but he advised her to complete her education. At the same time, he encouraged her to keep writing. But Greenwich did record one 45 rpm single (the record's label identified her as "Ellie Gaye"); however, sales were only local and meager. Greater success, however, would eventually come.

Greenwich attended Hofstra University, earning a bachelor's degree in English literature and graduating with high honors. While attending college she met Jeff Barry, who would become her husband and her songwriting partner. Their eventual collaboration would result in some of the most famous rock and roll records.

Chose Music over Education

After graduation, Greenwich followed up on her educational path and became a high school English teacher. This lasted for only about a month, however. She wanted to be a full-time songwriter. In 1962, she entered the music business, and she was fortunate to find a place in the offices of famed songwriters Jerry Leiber and Mike Stoller. The Leiber/Stoller songwriting collaboration proved just as important to pop music development as Lennon/McCartney. Songs they wrote include *Jailhouse Rock, Poison Ivy,* and *Charlie Brown.*

Artists that recorded their compositions included Elvis Presley, the Drifters, the Coasters, and the Shangri-Las (who recorded the Barry/Greenwich penned *The Leader of the Pack.*

Leiber and Stoller were part of the famed Brill Building scene, which included the best songwriters of the era, including Carole King and Neil Sedaka, and another famed male/female songwriting team: Barry Mann and Cynthia Weil (who wrote *You've Lost that Lovin' Feelin',* a considered classic recorded by the Righteous Brothers and produced by the legendary record-producing master Phil Spector, whose roots are also attached to the Brill Building). Along with Lennon and McCartney, the Brill Building songwriters were pivotal in shaping the direction of pop music. Their compositions were recorded by "British Invasion" bands such as the Animals and the Searchers, and American groups such as Paul Revere and the Raiders and the Monkees. One of the Brill Building songwriters included a young Carole Bayer Sager, who would later collaborate with one of America's best songwriters, Burt Bacharach. Early in her career, Sager co-wrote *A Groovy Kind of Love,* a composition recorded by the Mindbenders.

Along with Barry, Greenwich wrote songs with other famed writers such as Doc Pomus and Tony Powers. Also, with Barry, she formed a group called the Raindrops, who recorded a string of hits that met with regional, if not national success. *The Kind of Boy you Can't Forget* is the best remembered.

Composed Teen Symphonies

The Barry/Greenwich songwriting team firmly attached itself to Spector, the legendary record producer who developed what became known as the "wall of sound." This "wall" was comprised of heavy orchestration and symphonic arrangements, and Greenwich, Barry, and Spector churned out hit records on a regular basis, including girl-group smashes such as *Be My Baby* and *Da Doo Ron Ron.* Violins and horns were as much a part of the sound as electric guitars and drums. Greenwich also co-wrote *Hanky Panky,* a song that introduced the public to Tommy James and the Shondells, and *River Deep, Mountain High,* which was recorded by Ike and Tina Turner.

Flew to the Red Bird Record Label

Greenwich's career and fortunes would follow those of Leiber and Stoller's. In 1964, the two men left Brill Building to establish the Red Bird Records label, along with producer George "Shadow" Morton, and they recruited Greenwich and Barry. The label's main claim to fame was the girl group, the Shangri-Las, fronted by blonde, pouty-faced, leather vested, spike-heel booted lead singer Mary Weiss. Her image made her appear much more worldly wise than a fifteen-year-old girl deserved to be, and that visual element compelled people to take notice. But Red Bird matched the compelling image with great songs. The Shangri-Las made a strong impression with their first single *Remember (Walking in the Sand).* This recording, which was released in the summer of 1964, amidst the boyish exuberance of the so-called "British Invasion" was a dark counterpart to the Spector groups and their celebratory chorus of love that rang with orchestration. It haunted. But the best was yet to come, thanks to a Barry/Greenwich composition (written along with producer Morton) that depicted the death of a motorcycle-riding rebel.

It was titled *The Leader of the Pack,* and it raised adolescent drama to a Shakespearean level. Production levels were also high: Red Bird's output was characterized by sophisticated orchestration and sound effects (the Shangri-La's first record was enhanced by the sound of chirping sea gulls). "Leader" featured sound effects that included the sound of spinning wheels and smashing glass. The overall effect diverted the United States' attention away from the seemingly endless string of Beatles singles that dominated the record charts. This is the song for which Greenwich and Barry are best remembered, and deservedly so.

Diamonds and Divorce

During this productive period, Greenwich continued with her singing activities. A talented vocalist, she lent her voice as a background singer for records released by artists such as Bobby Darin, Ella Fitzgerald, Lesley Gore, Frank Sinatra and Dusty Springfield. She also worked as an arranger and producer. In that capacity, she advanced the career of Neil Diamond. In the mid-1960s, Diamond, a singer and songwriter, made an impression with an early single, *Solitary Man* (1966). Greenwich helped him on his way to becoming an industry superstar, as she produced some of his early and better-known hits such as *Cherry Cherry, I Got the Feeling, Thank the Lord for the Night Time, Kentucky Woman* and *Shiloh.* For Diamond, Greenwich also co-wrote songs and provided background vocal support on his early hits.

But a year previous to Greenwich's association with Diamond, in 1965, she and Barry recorded a single, *Our Love Can Still be Saved.* There was irony in the title. The record underscored personal problems. By this time, the Greenwich/Barry marriage was falling apart. They divorced at the end of the year. Greenwich and Barry would continue to collaborate for several more years, but eventually the inevitable happened: They would no longer work together. This did not mean an end to Greenwich's career, however.

Started Writing Jingles

As her marriage was breaking up, Greenwich was expanding her horizons. She continued producing records and branched into commercial jingle writing, which proved lucrative. During the late 1960s and early 1970s, she composed both commercial jingles and theme songs for television shows, and even established a jingle production company (clients included Cheerios, Clairol, Ford, and Sassoon).

In 1971, Brill Building colleague Carole King, who had divorced from her own husband and songwriting partner Gerry Goffin, released an album of her own compositions. This record, *Tapestry,* became one of the best selling records ever. Success compelled Greenwich to consider making her own album. The result was *Let it be Written, Let it be Sung,* but Greenwich suffered stage fright. During a tour to support the album's release, she resorted to lip synching. As such, the work came nowhere close to matching King's masterwork and its subsequent commercial success. Failure, Greenwich admitted, was also compounded by what she described as a nervous breakdown.

Greenwich recovered and continued thriving, though, thanks to commercial activities and associations she developed with fellow singers and musicians such as Desmond Child, Nona Hendryx, Cyndi Lauper, and Paul Shaffer.

Achieved Success on Broadway

One of the most famous songs that came out of the Brill Building era was *On Broadway,* written by Mann and Weil (with help from Leiber and Stoller), and on Broadway is where Greenwich would later shine. Even though her first album didn't match the success of King's solo *Tapestry* achievement, Greenwich achieved significant success with a show about her life and the songs she wrote. Titled *The Leader of the Pack,* after her most famous song, the show debuted in 1984 at the Bottom Line, in New York City's Greenwich Village. Initial success led to Broadway: In 1985, the evolving show opened at the Ambassador Theater and ran for five months, despite a bad review from *The New York Times.*

"The songs meld into one long screech," wrote reviewer Frank Rich in a *New York Times* article. "They're delivered by mostly charmless performers whose primary responsibility is to model an extravagant assortment of hideous costumes and grotesquely campy beehive wigs. Even the band arrangements are garish: If the legendary 60's rock-record producer Phil Spector erected a 'wall of sound,' this show drops a shroud of noise."

Despite that negative review, people who still loved the Greenwich/Barry songs thronged to the show, which earned a Tony Award Nomination for Best Musical and a Grammy nomination for Best Cast Album. The production won the New York Music Award for Best Broadway Musical.

A Legacy Recognized

With Barry, Greenwich was inducted into the Songwriters Hall of Fame in 1991. In 2004, *Rolling Stone* magazine ranked six of the Greenwich/Barry songs among the 500 best-ever rock songs (including, of course, the teen epic *The Leader of the Pack*). During this period, Greenwich remained quite active.

Her life was cut short by a heart attack, however. She died on August 26, 2009, at the age of 68 years old.

She produced an amazing legacy of music, as her songs were recorded by a diverse list of performers that include Mariah Carey, the Rolling Stones, John Lennon, Elton John, Melissa Etheridge, Meatloaf, Cher, Bette Midler, Celine Dion, U2 and Twisted Sister. Her songs garnered more than 25 gold and platinum records. Recordings she was involved in represented sales in the tens of millions of dollars.

If Greenwich died young, she died rich—maybe not in terms of money, but definitely in terms of influence. Most people may not know her name, but they know her music.

Books

The Heart of Rock & Soul: The 1001 Great Singles Ever Made, Dave Marsh. New American Library, 1989.

Tucker, Ken and Geoffrey Stokes, eds., *Rock of Ages: The Rolling Stone History of Rock & Roll,* Rolling Stone Press/Summit Books New York, 1986.

Periodicals

New York Times, April 19, 1985.

Online

"Ellie Greenwich," *Biography.com,* http://www.biography.com/people/ellie-greenwich-17172158 (November 15, 2011).

"Ellie Greenwich," *Ellie Greenwich.com,* http://www.elliegreenwich.com/musicography.htm (November 15, 2011).

"Ellie Greenwich Biography," *Songwriters Hall of Fame,* http://www.songwritershalloffame.org/exhibits/bio/C126 (November 15, 2011).

"The Ellie Greenwich Story," *The Ellie Greenwich Web Site,* http://www.elliegreenwich.com/bio.html (November 15, 2011).□

Allvar Gullstrand

The Swedish ophthalmologist Allvar Gullstrand (1862–1930) invented or devised the modern forms of key instruments—the slit lamp and the reflexless ophthalmoscope—still used in ophthalmological offices today.

An unusually deep and systematic thinker who rigorously examined the basic physical phenomena involved in his field, Gullstrand was awarded the Nobel Prize for Physiology or Medicine in 1911. While other ophthalmologists have won for work in other fields, and nonspecialists have won for ophthalmological discoveries, Gullstrand remains the only ophthalmologist to receive the prize for work in ophthalmology. It was for his theoretical writings, not his practical ophthalmological inventions, that he was awarded the prize. Gullstrand's writings were terse and difficult to understand, making an assumption that points that were clear to him would be clear to others. And his own personality, driven and somewhat egotistical, was another hurdle for those seeking to understand his work. But both his theoretical and practical discoveries have continued to yield benefits in the field of ophthalmology to the present day.

Stimulated by College-Level Courses

Born on June 5, 1862, in the small town of Landskrona in southern Sweden, Allvar Gullstrand was the son of physician and town medical officer Alfred Gullstrand and his wife, Sofia Mathilda Korsell Gullstrand. A gifted but restless student, he admitted that he preferred playing pranks on the streets to going to school. His family, sensing his talent but guessing that it would never be nurtured in Landskrona, moved to the larger town of Jönköping, and the move paid off: a math teacher there held Gullstrand's attention by challenging him with university-level mathematics. Other than that episode, Gullstrand was largely self-taught in mathematics. He at first wanted to become an engineer, but decided to major in medicine at the University of Uppsala after his father gave him a summer job as a medical assistant.

Gullstrand spent a year in the mid-1880s in Vienna, studying instruments for examining the eyes, ears, and throat; the technology in Austria was superior at the time to anything available in Sweden. Although he must have mastered German during this time, he wrote mostly in Swedish, which hampered international understanding of the significance of his work. Gullstrand married Signe Christine Breitholz in 1885, and the pair had a daughter, Esther, in 1886. In 1888 the child died of diphtheria.

Gullstrand received his medical degree in Uppsala that same year and moved on to a residency at Stockholm's Seraphim Hospital. Gifted with unusual stamina, he worked on his PhD dissertation at the same time, completing A Contribution to the Theory of Astigmatism in 1890 and receiving the highest possible grade for it.

In 1891 Gullstrand was appointed as lecturer in ophthalmology at Stockholm's Karolinska Institute, also opening a private clinic and serving on Sweden's National Board of Health and Welfare. In 1894 he was invited—without applying—to become the first professor and chair in ophthalmology at Uppsala. From the start, he had responsibilities as a teacher and administrator that competed for his time with his first love, research. Moreover, he created in Uppsala an ophthalmological clinic, the town's first. Gullstrand responded to these demands on his time by setting aside the hours of 10 p.m. to 2 a.m., as well as holidays, for pure research endeavors. His normal work day began at 8 a.m. and ended well after midnight, seven days a week. In the 1890s he began to publish papers on eye disorders and on the mechanics of the eye; two of them won awards from the Swedish Medical Association in 1892 ("The Objective Differential Diagnosis and Photographic Illustration of Disabilities of the Eye Muscles") and 1896 ("Photographic-Ophthalmometric and Clinical Investigations of Corneal Refractions").

Won Nobel Prize

A third major Gullstrand paper, "The Pigments of the Central Macula of the Retina," won the Uppsala Faculty of Medicine's Brörkén Prize in 1905. These papers, although devoted to specific issues in ophthalmology, relied on Gullstrand's sophisticated understanding of mathematics and physics, and they outlined a profound understanding of the workings of the eye. It was for his insights into dioptrics—the refraction of light in the eye—contained in his published work that Gullstrand was awarded the Nobel Prize in 1911.

At around that time, Gullstrand began to put his technical knowledge to work in the creation of new and improved devices for examining the eye. The year 1911 saw one of his most successful inventions: the slit lamp, which produces a sharply focused beam of light that allows an examiner to see into the interior of a patient's eye. There were slit lamps before Gullstrand, and the device reached its modern form when German ophthalmologists fitted it out with other optical instruments, but the crucial step toward the strong beam that is part of every eye exam was Gullstrand's. In 1911 Gullstrand also perfected a reflex-free ophthalmoscope, an eye-examining device that minimized reflections from different parts of the eye. He worked with the precision optics firm of Zeiss in Jena, Germany, to produce these and other devices.

After he was awarded the Nobel Prize, Uppsala's academic senate asked the Swedish parliament to create a special chair that would allow Gullstrand to devote himself to research full-time. This request was granted in 1914, and Gullstrand responded by intensifying his research efforts. He refused various prestigious academic positions so that he could devote himself to research. Gullstrand did, however, join the Nobel Physics Committee of the Swedish Academy of Sciences—the body that bestows the Nobel Prizes. In the 1910s and early 1920s he resisted the awarding of the physics prize to Albert Einstein because he considered Einstein's Theory of Relativity unproven, but he was persuaded to relent, and Einstein was awarded the 1922 prize.

Estimated Own Abilities Highly

The episode was typical of Gullstrand's high opinion of his own abilities. When he turned down an invitation to return to the Karolinska Institute in an administrative post, and the job went to another Swedish ophthalmologist, Gullstrand remarked that the loss to science was less than if he himself had taken the job. As a colleague and administrator Gullstrand could be brutal. According to biographers Berndt Ehinger and Andrzej Grzybowski, writing in *Acta Ophthalmologica,* "Gullstrand often judged his colleagues by their willingness to accept his proposals. He made it clear that once he had spoken he regarded further comments as a waste of time."

His saving grace was that, as his colleagues recognized, he was usually right. Ehinger and Grzybowski pointed out that "Gullstrand's contributions to optics are sometimes compared with those of [Isaac] Newton, [Christiaan] Huygens, and [Hermann von] Helmholtz," and that he might have been even better known had he not written much of his work in Swedish and German. His works were not translated into English until 1922, and then only a selection of them. Gullstrand remained productive later in life, writing treatises on general principles of optics that scholars are still trying to unpack almost a century later.

Another measure of Gullstrand's influence is the number of eponymous items, or things named for him, that have appeared. These include the aspherical Gullstrand lens produced by Zeiss beginning in 1911; the Gullstrand schematic eye, a drawing of the eye based on Gullstrand's own precise measurements; the Gullstrand reflexless ophthalmoscope (a stationary model); the Gullstrand handheld ophthalmoscope; and the Gullstrand condition, a quality of eyeglasses that have a certain relationship to the apparent rotation center of the eye.

During his last year, Gullstrand did take time away from the laboratory to attend various international conferences, receiving a fresh round of honors. He traveled to the United States in 1922, where, according to Ehinger and Grzybowski, the president of the American Society of Ophthalmology Congress said that after the invention of Gullstrand's slit lamp, medicine had not only a "Lady with the Lamp" (nurse Florence Nightingale) but also a "Gentleman with the Lamp." Gullstrand retired in 1927 but continued to do scientific work. He died from the effects of a stroke in Stockholm on July 28, 1930.

Periodicals

Acta Ophthalmologica, 2011 (vol. 89).

Online

"Allvar Gullstrand," *Nobel Prize,* http://www.nobelprize.org/nobel_prizes/medicine/laureates/1911/gullstrand-bio.html (November 4, 2011).

"Who Was Allvar Gullstrand?" *Pearls in Ophthalmology,* http://www.medrounds.org/ophthalmology-pearls/2009/06/who-was-allvar-gullstrand.html (November 4, 2011). □

H

Lasse Hallström

The Swedish film director Lasse Hallström (born 1946) made his mark in both Europe and the United States with appealing yet unsentimental feature films populated by offeat characters navigating difficult situations.

Hallström first made an impression internationally with *My Life as a Dog* in 1985, and that coming-of-age story remains his most famous film. Yet Hallström's entire career has been notable, from the long series of music videos he made for the pop group ABBA in the 1970s to arthouse hits like *Chocolat* in the 2000s. Hallström remains one of the few European directors who has succeeded in reconciling the demands of big-budget Hollywood cinema with his own sensibilities. Whether working with unknown Swedes or American stars of the magnitude of Julia Roberts, he has remained steadfast in his cinematic vision. Hallström told Ed Potton of the London *Times,* "The key thing for me is to create things that are true. It's better for actors to capture the irrationality of human behaviour, because irrational behaviour rings absolutely true."

Created Music Videos for ABBA

Lasse Hallström (pronounced LUSS-eh HULL-strum) was born on June 2, 1946, in Stockholm Sweden. His father was a dentist and an enthusiastic amateur filmmaker. Unlike other young people who have to struggle to realize their dreams of a career in the arts, Hallström was almost pressured into it. "It was not [spoken] aloud, but it was implied in our home that I might someday pick up on what my father had

not the chance to pick up: that is, a life devoted to movie making," he said in his website biography. At the age of ten he had already directed a short documentary about Sweden's Gotland Island and a short thriller.

He continued his development in high school with a well-executed documentary about a group of his classmates who formed a rock band. The film was good enough to be shown on Swedish television, and Hallström then began to study television production in earnest. Beginning with 1969's *Shall We Dance?* he directed a number of made-for-television films in Sweden, gaining increasing respect in the Swedish entertainment industry for such films as *Shall We Go to My or to Your Place or Each Go Home Alone?* (1970). His 1972 television film *The Love Seeker* was chosen as Sweden's entry at the Montreux Television Festival in 1972.

After that honor, Hallström was ready to begin making feature films, and he released *En Kille och en Tjej* (A Guy and a Gal) in 1975. But for several years his energy was primarily directed toward promotional films he made for the internationally popular Swedish pop group ABBA. His association with the group began in 1974, when group members asked him to create promotional films to be used in pitching ABBA songs to radio stations. At the time, music videos did not exist as such, but Hallström can lay a reasonable claim to being one of their creators, for his promotional films quickly outgrew their original purpose and were widely shown. ABBA members have credited Hallström's films for popularizing the songs "Mamma Mia" and "I Do, I Do, I Do, I Do, I Do" and for creating a mania for the group's songs when they were shown in Australia. Hallström was a key contributor to the band's all-important visual image. Until the group began to decline in popularity around 1982 and turned to new projects such as the musical *Chess,* Hallström directed most of their promotional films.

My Life As a Dog

Hallström directed *ABBA: The Movie* in 1977. As with most of his films, he served as both director and screenwriter for that release. Hallström returned to non-ABBA-related feature filmmaking with 1979's *Father-To-Be,* 1981's *The Rooster,* and 1983's *Happy We.* He was gaining a reputation in Sweden as a reliable creator of successful romantic comedies, but nothing prepared industry observers either in Sweden or internationally for Hallström's next film, *Mitt Liv som Hund* (My Life as a Dog), released in 1985.

That film traced the story of a boy named Ingemar (named for Swedish boxer Ingemar Johansson) whose mother is dying and who is sent to live with relatives. Without diminishing the pain of the boy's situation, Hallström depicted it without sentimentality, showing his state of mind mostly in a series of awkward situations with which he has difficulty coping. Among them is a blossoming relationship with a young woman who has ambitions to become a boxer, and whose attitude toward Ingemar is alternately hostile and flirtatious. The film's warm-hearted plot made it a hit internationally despite the lack of established stars, and Hallström earned Academy Award nominations for Best Director and Best Adapted Screenplay and won several top prizes from critics' associations.

At that point, Hallström could probably have signed a lucrative contract to direct films in the United States, but instead he stayed in Sweden, directing the children's films *The Children of Bullerby Village* (1986) and *More About the Children of Bullerby Villlage* (1987). "For me, going to America is a representation of following our temptations and sensual impulses," he explained to Potton. "Staying in Sweden is probably the puritan choice."

Another reason for staying in Sweden may have been Hallström's developing relationship with Swedish actress Lena Olin. "I knew that he had his eyes on me a little bit because he kept saying hello when I was shooting another movie. He kept saying hello, and I would say hello to him, and then he said hello again," Olin was quoted as saying on Hallström's website. After Olin returned to Sweden from a stint working in the United States, the two began dating. They married in 1994 and had a daughter, Tora, in 1995; Hallström also had one son from the marriage to his first wife, Malou, and the couple later adopted Olin's son, August.

Worked in America

Hallström and Olin continued to live in Sweden after their marriage, finally moving to Los Angeles in 1997. By that time, however, Hallström had already become well established in Hollywood, commuting at first from Stockholm. His American debut was *Once Around* (1991), for which he also wrote the screenplay. The film starred Richard Dreyfuss as a classic Hallström character, a somewhat rude salesman who comically tries to ingratiate himself with the family of his new wife (played by Holly Hunter).

Hallström's next film, *What's Eating Gilbert Grape?* (1993), was probably the most successful of his Hollywood releases. The film earned positive reviews, although the evaluation of influential critic Roger Ebert (quoted by Potton) was mixed: "Did it bore me? Not for a moment. Is it a good film? Not in any conventional way." Mixing elements of comedy and drama, the film starred Johnny Depp as a small-town teen struggling to cope with an extremely unorthodox family. His problems are compounded by the fact that the small-town grocery where he works is under threat from national corporate chains. With such stars as Leonardo DiCaprio, Juliette Lewis, and Mary Steenburgen in lead roles, and with its creative and original concept, the film marked Hallström's coming of age as an American director who could score both critical and popular success.

Despite the presence of star Julia Roberts, Hallström stumbled both critically and commercially with his next film, the 1995 infidelity comedy-drama *Something to Talk About.* He bounced back in 1999 with his film of the John Irving novel *The Cider House Rules,* another film with a youthful protagonist. Hallström returned to Europe and to the arthouse audience with *Chocolat* (2000), the story of a chocolate maker who upends the normal rhythms of life in a small French town. The film marked the first time Olin had appeared in one of Hallström's films.

In Hallström's films of the 2000s, he continued to pursue his interests in intelligent novel adaptations and unusual characters, rather than subsuming his art in the quest for a blockbuster. *The Shipping News* (2001), *An Unfinished Life* (2005), *The Hoax* (2009, based on the true story of a writer who falsely claimed to possess the memoirs of aviator tycoon Howard Hughes), and the war story *Dear John* (2010) were all adaptations of prominent books. *Casanova* (2005) was a biographical film based on the life of the legendary Italian seducer Giacomo Casanova, while *Hachi: A Dog's Tale* (2008) starred Richard Gere as a professor who forms a bond with an Akita dog. As of 2011, Hallström's most recent release was the little-known satire *Salmon Fishing in the Yemen.*

Books

International Dictionary of Films and Filmmakers, Gale, 2000.

Periodicals

Film Journal International, April 2007.
New York Times, March 24, 1987.
Times (London, England), March 3, 2001.
Variety, September 19, 2011.
WWD, January 2, 2001.

Online

"Biography," *Lasse Hallstroöm Official Website,* http://www.
lassehallstrom.com/bio.php (December 5, 2011).
"Lasse Hallström," *Rovi,* http://www.allrovi.com/name/lasse-
hallstr%C3%B6m-p93205 (December 5, 2011).□

James Harrison

Australia's James Harrison (born 1936) set a world's record for most blood donated by a single individual. As of early 2012 he had donated blood more than 1,000 times.

Harrison had a specific reason for donating so much blood: it contained a rare antibody that has been shown to prevent a tragic condition, Rhesus disease, when it is given to pregnant women. Women with Rhesus disease may find that their own immune systems attack their unborn children in the womb, causing brain damage or worse; a therapy called Anti-D can remove the danger. Anti-D is found in Harrison's blood and that of only a few dozen other Australians. Estimates of the lives Harrison has saved with his donations run as high as two million, and he has been dubbed the Man with the Golden Arm. But Harrison, who has resolutely refused to classify himself as a hero, has focused as well on the contributions ordinary blood donors can make. "Only 3 percent of our population donates blood, and I will do anything I can to encourage more," he pointed out to Terry Collins of Australia's *Central Coast Express Advocate.*

Required 13 Liters of Blood in Transfusion

A resident of Umina in Australia's New South Wales state, James Christopher Harrison was born around 1936. In interviews he has talked very little about his life apart from his blood donation activities. The crucial event in his early life came when he was 14 or 15, when he underwent a three-month hospital stay as a bronchial ailment required chest surgery and transfusions that required 13 liters of donated blood. Harrison's father had been a regular blood donor. "It may have been a throwaway line," Harrison confessed to a Radio Netherlands interviewer (and quoted from their website), but the teenager promised to become a blood donor himself once his ordeal was over and he was legally old enough.

When he was 18 Harrison made his first donation, and since then he has continued to donate as often as once a week. "I just catch the train down to Sydney from the Central Coast as often as I can, read a good book, donate, and come back," he was quoted as saying by Richard Noone of the Sydney *Daily Telegraph.* He has been able to donate so frequently because he donates only plasma, a process in which blood is drawn, the plasma is removed, and the blood returned to the donor; donors of whole blood must wait longer before repeating their donations. Since he began donating blood, he told Radio Netherlands, "I haven't had a day of sickness."

When Harrison began donating blood, neither he nor anyone else had any idea of how important his donations would turn out to be. The classification of human blood as either Rhesus-positive (Rh-positive) or Rhesus-negative had been accomplished in 1940. (The terminology came from the original research, in which blood from Rhesus macaques were injected into rabbits.) But it would still be some time before the connection was made between Rhesus blood type and Rhesus disease, also known as hemolytic disease of the newborn, or HDN. The disease could occur when a pregnant woman who was Rh-negative was bearing an Rh-positive fetus. Babies born were termed blue babies and required large blood transfusions to survive.

Blood Used in Anti-D Vaccine

Shortly after he began to donate, Harrison was found to have an antibody in his blood that could prevent Rh-negative women from developing antibodies that would attack their own fetuses (and cause their newborns to have antibodies that would attack their own cells). In 1966, Australian medical authorities began work on a medicine or vaccine called Anti-D that would allow women to give birth normally even if they suffered from the Rh mismatch. Large amounts of Harrison's blood were used in the production of Anti-D ("There is a little bit of me" in all the babies whose mothers were given the vaccine, he pointed out to Miranda Wood, as quoted in the *Sydney Morning Herald*), and his blood itself was insured for either one hundred thousand or one million Australian dollars (he has cited both figures in interviews). Part of the agreement was that Harrison's wife, Barbara, herself a frequent blood donor, would be compensated in the event that anything happened to Harrison.

One of the beneficiaries of Harrison's donations was his own daughter, Tracey, who was born in 1967. She required Anti-D injections in connection with the birth of both her sons. She was given the antidote after the birth of her first son, Jarrod, to counteract the effects of the antibodies that had been released in her own body, and she was injected while she was pregnant with her second son, Scott. Both children (and their mother) remained healthy. Tracey was far from alone; between 10 and 17 percent of women are at risk of a pregnancy involving Rhesus disease.

Both in Australia and elsewhere there were others who carried the beneficial antibodies, and some of them donated blood. None, however, approached Harrison's donation record, which by 2011 he estimated to have exceeded two 44-gallon drums of blood. He was called the Man with the Golden Arm or the Man in Two Million, referring to the number of babies who received Anti-D made from Harrison's blood. Harrison first came to public attention when he received the Medal of the Order of Australia in 1999.

Set World Record

A fresh round of news articles followed in 2003, when the Australian Red Cross announced that Harrison had set a world record as the individual who had donated the most blood over a lifetime. As of 2011 *Guinness World Records* did not list that exact category; most of its records involved the donation of whole blood. A South African, Maurice Creswick, had donated blood since 1944 and held the record for most blood donated over consecutive years. Still, Harrison's contribution was clearly unique, and fresh milestones brought him new press coverage both in Australia and abroad. In 2010 Harrison received a nomination for the honor of New South Wales Australian of the Year. In the mid-2000s Harrison wrote an article for the *Australian* newspaper arguing against the opening of Australian plasma production to foreign companies.

One new round of coverage occurred in 2011, when Harrison approached and then passed the 1,000-donation milestone. He had no immediate plans to stop donating and urged others to do the same, pointing out that although only 3 percent of Australians donate blood, 8 percent would need a transfusion at some point in their lives. He had been informed by doctors that he would have to stop donating when he reached the age of 81. "When I'm retired," he told Radio Netherlands, "I'll say the slate is now clean."

Periodicals

Advertiser (Adelaide, Australia), August 15, 2003.

Australian, July 8, 2003.

Brisbane Times, May 21, 2009.

Central Coast Express Advocate (New South Wales, Australia), November 12, 2010; June 15, 2011.

Daily Mail (London, England), March 23, 2010.

Mercury (Hobart, Tasmania, Australia), July 8, 2003.

Sydney Morning Herald, December 13, 2003.

Online

"HARRISON, James Christopher," *It's an Honour,* http://www.itsanhonour.gov.au/honours/honour_roll/search.cfm?aus_award_id=878145&search_type=advanced&showInd=true (January 3, 2012).

"James Harrison: Australian Man with Special Blood Type Saves 2 Million Babies," *Huffington Post,* http://www.huffingtonpost.com/2010/03/24/james-harrison-australian_n_512112.html (January 3, 2012).

"James Harrison: FTA Threatens Blood Donor System," *The Australian,* http://www.theaustralian.com.au/news/opinion/james-harrison-fta-threatens-blood-donor-system/story-e6frg6zo-1111112853758 (January 2, 2012).

"James Harrison OAM," *Australian of the Year,* http://www.australianoftheyear.org.au/recipients/?m=james-harrison-2011 (January 3, 2012).

Other

Interview, Radio Netherlands, October 26, 2011 (http://download.radionetherlands.nl/rnw/smac/cms/en_tswi_man_with_golden_arm_20111022_64_44_2.mp3).□

Cyrus Harvey

American entrepreneur Cyrus Harvey (1925–2011) created two radically different companies, but each was tied to his passion for all things European. As the co-founder of Janus Films in the 1950s, he introduced foreign films to U.S. audiences, packaging them as cinematic works of art from daring new directors like Federico Fellini, Ingmar Bergman, and François Truffaut. In the 1970s, Harvey and his wife founded the phenomenally successful Crabtree & Evelyn, a retailer of botanical-based soaps and other toiletries.

Harvey was a native of Cambridge, Massachusetts, where he was born Cyrus Isadore Harvey Jr. on October 14, 1925. His father, a Lithuanian immigrant, ran a company that sold children's furniture and toys. His mother died when he was still quite young. She, too, was a Jewish immigrant from Poland—an area that had been annexed by the Russian Empire, like the Baltic homeland of his father.

Became Fulbright Scholar

During World War II Harvey served in the U.S. Army Air Forces as a navigator, then entered Harvard University. He studied history and literature, graduating in 1947, then won one of the new Fulbright scholarship grants enabling American college graduates to study abroad. Choosing Paris and the Sorbonne, Harvey discovered Henri Langlois's Cinémathèque Française, a landmark destination for cinephiles at the time. Langlois showed both new films and historic curiosities from his vast personal trove, and the Cinémathèque became a gathering point for a new generation of young French filmmakers in the years after the war.

When Harvey returned to Cambridge, he teamed with a part-time actor and Harvard Law School dropout named Bryant Haliday, who was part-owner of the Brattle Theatre. This was an 1890s structure located at 40 Brattle Street that had been home to a series of amateur theater companies over the decades. Harvey and Haliday wanted to introduce Cambridge residents to art-house movies, the kind Harvey had discovered in Paris, and they acquired a screen and rear-projection system, in which the projector and the equipment sat behind the screen, instead of at the rear of the theater. The Brattle opened as one of America's first art-house theaters in February of 1953 with a screening of *The Captain from Koepenick,* a satirical look at imperial Germany.

In the first years of the Brattle's operation, Harvey traveled to Europe frequently to find films to screen in Cambridge. One surprise success was *Skanderbeg,* a 1954 Cannes Film Festival prizewinner about a medieval Balkans war hero. Another profitable event was the annual Humphrey Bogart film festival that coincided with spring exam week at Harvard. The festival grew out of an idea to honor the American actor shortly after his death in January of 1957. "At some point, we thought that we ought to bring in some of the American films that hadn't been shown that much," Harvey told Aljean Harmetz in a *New York Times* article, adding that he and his business partner "both thought that the Bogarts were vastly underrated. I think 'Casablanca' was the first one we played. . . .The audience began to chant the lines. It was more than just going to the movies. It was sort of partaking in a ritual." The annual Bogart week became a spring tradition for Harvard undergraduates, and served to revive critical interest in Bogart's films. Harvey and Brattle even opened a coffeehouse adjacent to the Brattle they named "the Casablanca."

Founded Janus Films

By then Harvey was fully immersed in art-house cinema, widely hailed as one of the first visionaries to bring foreign films to U.S. audiences. Not long after the Brattle venture proved successful, he and Haliday acquired the 55th Street Playhouse in New York City, one of the first venues in that city to show new classics from a dazzling wave of postwar European directors, among them Jean-Luc Godard, François Truffaut, Federico Fellini, and Michelangelo Antonioni. These films were expensive to import, and required sound dubbing or translated subtitles. In March of 1956, Harvey and Haliday founded Janus Films, a distribution company. Named after the Roman god of doorways (*januae*) and archways (*jani*) who is also honored with the first month of the calendar year, Harvey and Haliday came up with a logo based on the traditional imagery of Janus: "one face looking towards commerce and the other face looking toward art," Harvey told Andrea Shea of National Public Radio's *All Things Considered.*

One of the most successful deals Harvey brokered on behalf of Janus was to show the full, uncut version of a somewhat racy Swedish film from 1953 called *Sommaren med Monika* (Summer with Monika) that featured a daring amount of nudity. Janus then cut a deal with the director, Ingmar Bergman, to roll out his next several films to U.S. audiences, which incited a minor Bergman craze among foreign film fans. The films included two from 1957, *Det sjunde inseglet* (The Seventh Seal) and *Smultronstället* (Wild Strawberries), which gained Bergman an ardent following in the United States. *Time* magazine film critic Richard Corliss wrote about seeing the former at a Philadelphia cinema, which he described as a life-changing moment. "*The Seventh Seal* sparked a generation of young people to make foreign-language films their urgent research project, their obsession, their religion," Corliss asserted.

When Bergman's 1960 drama *Jungfrukällan* (The Virgin Spring) won the Academy Award for Best Foreign Film in April of 1961, Harvey went to Los Angeles to accept it on behalf of the director. The Brattle continued its historic run as a Cambridge landmark. It showed *I Vitelloni,* an early work by Federico Fellini that cemented his career as one of Italian neorealist cinema's newest auteurs, and Part II of Sergei Eisenstein's *Ivan the Terrible,* completed in 1946, two years after Part I premiered. The saga of the late-medieval Russian tsar was a bloody one, and Soviet leader Josef Stalin was displeased with the second part of the planned trilogy; film historians had assumed all prints had been burned by Soviet censors, but the 1963 Eisenstein Festival at the Brattle featured a rare surviving copy of the masterpiece.

Exited the Movie Business

The early 1960s were the peak of Janus' success as a film distributor. Within a few short years Bergman, Fellini, and other European star filmmakers began signing deals with Hollywood studios eager for a cut of the art-house cinema market. Harvey and Haliday sold Janus in 1966 to two documentary film producers, Saul J. Turell and William Becker, who kept the business afloat for a few years by leasing innocuous foreign films like the 34-minute French classic *The Red Balloon* to schools. "I'll tell you a big secret," Harvey confessed in the *All Things Considered* interview. "I barely came out of there with a dollar. I mean, we broke even after 12 years of work."

Harvey and Haliday continued to hold the lease on the Brattle Theatre until 1976, though Haliday had moved to Europe to work as an actor, appearing in works like the cult classic *Tower of Evil,* also known as *Horror on Snape Island.* Its rear-projection system became one of the last ones still in use in the United States. Harvey, meanwhile, found great success with another venture underneath the Brattle, where he converted unused space into a retail arcade called the Truc that became a thriving counterculture magnet in the late 1960s. Its name came from the French slang word for "gadget" or "knack," and the Truc boutiques sold an array of hard-to-find imported items, such as vintage posters, Swiss-made dinnerware, and specialty soaps perfumed with genuine botanical oils and essences. Harvey and his second wife, Rebecca Miller, ran the emporium. "We thought we'd put in small boutiques, specializing in certain things, but do it for the kids and do it right," he told *New York Times* journalist Marylin Bender in a 1969 article about the popularity of the arcade. "People in Cambridge don't have as much money as they do in New York, but we don't want to sell them junky things."

One of the stalls at the Truc was called The Soap Box and inspired the founding of Crabtree & Evelyn. Few companies made toiletries using genuine aromatic oils at the time, because cheaper synthetic scents had become the standard. Harvey was a fan of Caswell - Massey, a Rhode Island firm founded in 1751 that had a devoted following. He made an offer to buy the privately held company, but its owners were not ready to sell. He decided to create a faux British knockoff instead.

Created Luxury-Niche Brand

Harvey teamed with a British graphic artist, Peter Windett, who came up with the "Crabtree & Evelyn" name, paying homage to the beloved crabapple tree of England and British scholar John Evelyn, whose 1693 tome *Terra; The Compleat Gardener,* was a landmark in horticulture. The brand was launched in 1972, with Harvey and Miller initially selling repackaged soaps manufactured at factories in France and Switzerland at the Truc and by mail order out of their home in Woodstock, Connecticut.

Windett's packaging was designed to look authentically vintage Georgian-era British. The extravagantly fragranced soaps soon became popular sellers in both London and New York. Crabtree & Evelyn products were sold at upscale retailers like Harrods and Bloomingdale's, but by 1976 there was a small store on London's famed Savile Row, also home to venerable custom menswear tailors. The first Crabtree & Evelyn retail store in the United States opened in Philadelphia in 1977, and Harvey began a retail expansion in earnest in the 1980s. The product lines were refined, and he set up manufacturing operations in both Britain and the United States. "That was the time," he told Stafford Cliff in the book *50 Trade Secrets of Great Design Packaging,* "when we looked at marketing around the world and decided we'd have to go vertical— to design the product, make it, distribute it and be in control of the retail outlet."

Popular Crabtree & Evelyn scents included Goatmilk, Jojoba Oil, Nantucket Briar, and West Indian Lime. The standalone stores were located at upscale malls like Water Tower Place in Chicago or Southern California's Sherman Oaks Galleria. By the late 1980s the company was enormously successful, and new product lines like LaSource and Gardeners were rolled out to become top sellers.

In 1996, Harvey sold Crabtree & Evelyn to a Malaysian conglomerate, Kuala Lumpur Kepong Berhad, which owned vast palm oil plantations in Asia. He and Miller retired, dividing their time between their Connecticut home and a manor house in the picturesque Cotswold region in England. They were avid gardeners and owners of several Welsh corgi dogs, considered one of the quintessential British breeds. Harvey suffered a stroke on April 10, 2011, and died four days later at the age of 85. Survivors include his wife, Rebecca, and daughters Natasha, Tanya, and Viviane. His longtime friend from childhood was George Wein, who founded the Newport Jazz Festival and was born eleven days before Harvey. "They made a world thing out of soap," Wein told the *New York Times.* "It was amazing. I've tried to do the same thing out of jazz, but I haven't done as well."

Books

Balio, Tino, *The Foreign Film Renaissance on American Screens, 1946–1973,* University of Wisconsin Press, 2010.
Cliff, Stafford, *50 Trade Secrets of Great Design Packaging,* Rockport Publishers, 2002, p. 139.

Periodicals

Harvard Crimson, November 21, 2002.
New York Times, March 20, 1956; April 18, 1961; October 18, 1969; November 29, 1992; August 1, 2007; April 16, 2011.
Time, November 10, 2006.
Variety, April 16, 2011.

Online

Shea, Andrea, "Janus Films, the Face of Art and Foreign Film," *All Things Considered,* National Public Radio, November 3, 2006, http://www.npr.org/templates/transcript/transcript.php?storyId=6430428 (July 5, 2011).□

Francesco Hayez

Italian painter and printmaker Francesco Hayez (1791–1882) was one of the leading Romantic artists of nineteenth-century Italy.

Italian painter and printmaker Francesco Hayez became one of the leading artists of the Romantic movement prominent in nineteenth-century Europe after beginning his career in the Neoclassical style. Today known largely for his historical works and portraiture, Hayez often placed contemporary cultural and political figures into historical settings. Later in his career, he focused on allegorical works that conveyed political themes, a particularly timely topic as Italy moved towards unification. Working mostly in Rome and Milan, the artist achieved great success in his lifetime and, later in his career, served as an instructor at Milan's respected Brera Academy; he was also notable for his friendship with the composer Verdi, who relied on Hayez for advice on the staging of many of his famous operas. Many of his historical works fell out of favor with art historians for nearly a century after his death, however. Beginning in the 1970s, scholars began to reconsider his work with a more positive eye, and by the twenty-first century Hayez's paintings could be viewed at museums and galleries in diverse places across Europe including Italy, Great Britain, Austria, and Germany.

Studied in Venice and Rome

Born on February 11, 1791, in Venice, Italy, Hayez was the son of a fisherman who originally came from Valenciennes, France. As a child, Hayez was sent to live in the household of a Venetian antiquarian and art collector uncle, Giovanni Binasco. Binasco planned to instruct the young boy in the skill of painting restoration, and Hayez's obvious talent as an artist instead earned him a place studying painting with the artist Francesco Maggiotto, who was locally known for his historical and allegorical works. Additional training came from the study of classical and Renaissance works at Venetian galleries as a youth, along with visits to area cathedrals with his uncle. Hayez pursued formal lessons in life drawing at the city's Accademia di Pittura e Scultura (Academy of Painting and Sculpture) and training in color theory under the painter Lattanzio Querena, who was then working in Venice. By 1807, the teenaged artist had progressed enough to paint a *Portrait of the Artist's Family*, and the following year he gained admission to the freshly reopened Accademia di Bella Arti di Venezia (Academy of Fine Arts of Venice). There, he worked under the tutelage of the Neo-Classical painter Teodoro Matteini and the arts scholar Count Leopoldo Cicognara, who had recently been named head of the institution and had set about improving and expanding its educational offerings.

More than styles of art instruction were changing in the Venice of the late eighteenth and early nineteenth centuries, however. The once-independent Republic of Venice fell first under the control of the French army of Napoleon Bonaparte and, over the next several years, was shuffled between French and Austrian control as Napoleon's power waxed and waned. This politically charged climate helped shape the young artist's awareness of the world. As Margaret Plant wrote in *Venice: Fragile City, 1797–1997*, "Hayez understood the relevance and emotional power of certain episodes of Italian history within a climate of embryonic nationalism."

The Academy of Fine Arts awarded Hayez a scholarship to continue his artistic studies in Rome, and in 1809 Hayez set off for that city. The artist's Roman sojourn proved to be a greatly formative one. He met numerous other Italian and foreign artists working there, and spent much time at the workshop of the renowned sculptor and fellow Venetian Antonio Canova, who was an important influence and mentor for the young Hayez. After two years developing his early Neoclassical style in Rome, Hayez left the city for Naples to try to win entrance to an arts competition held by that city's Accademia. His entry was unsuccessful, but the trip gave Hayez the chance to spend several months studying the classical and Renaissance works on display there. Hayez's next attempt at an art competition was more fruitful. After returning to Rome in 1812, he entered a painting entitled *Laokoon* in a competition sponsored by the Accademia di Brera (Brera Academy) in Milan. This work was not only accepted for judging, but shared the first prize. Hayez declined to enter the competition again to focus on what scholar Fernando Mazzocca argued in Grove Art Online was "the greatest work of [Hayez's] Neoclassical period," *Rinaldo and Armida*. Inspired by a story by the sixteenth-century Italian poet Torquato Tasso, the painting depicts the titular lovers—the sorcerer Armida and warrior Rinaldo—in a semi-nude state as one of Rinaldo's fellow Christian Crusaders looks on.

Hayez returned to Naples, spending a couple of years in the southern city before again returning to Rome. There, Canova gave the young artist a job decorating part of the Vatican Museums with frescos celebrating the repatriation of Italian artworks from France, but Hayez's slow progress cost him the position. He spent time in Venice and Padua decorating grand palaces, including the Venetian Ducal Palace, and exploring the works of Venetian painters of the fifteenth century. Inspired by these pieces, Hayez painted the pivotal 1820 work *Pietro Rossi*. Depicting a historical scene of a fourteenth-century Venetian saying goodbye to his family before traveling to battle, *Pietro Rossi* kickstarted a new era of historical painting for Hayez and first indicated his shift from the Neoclassical to Romantic style. The work failed to excite Venetian audiences, but fared well in Milan at the 1820 annual exhibition.

Settled in Milan

A few years later, Hayez moved to the city that embraced his new Romantic style. He taught at the Brera Academy and, over the next several years, became one of Milan's foremost historical and portrait painters. The artist was friends with the Italian writer and patriot Alessandro Manzoni, and Italian themes soon began to infuse his historical works, replacing the mythological ideas favored by the Neoclassicists. Hayez portrayed contemporary Italian figures in historical settings as well as historical persons embraced by the nationalist movement such as the fourteenth-century popular hero Vittore Pisani. These works often drew on the recorded history of Venice, but channeled contemporary themes of resistance against the perceived repressive Austrian authority. As Plant explained, "the choice of a subject from the past could allude to a contemporary situation but skirt censorship. Such subjects held intense interest because of the then current trial of [Italian writer] Silvio Pellico for subversive activity'' against the Austrian government. Thus, both the political nature and artistic style of Hayez's paintings generated growing discussion and notoriety for him in Milan, and the artist became quite renowned by the early 1830s. In 1833, Hayez started on a massive work that occupied part of his time for nearly the following two decades. Eventually supported by King Charles Albert of the Italian kingdom of Sardinia, *Thirst Suffered by the First Crusaders beneath the Walls of Jerusalem* was installed in the Royal Palace in Turin in 1850.

Hayez's great success at portraiture and printmaking also contributed to his growing esteem. His involvement with Milanese artistic and literary circles brought him into contact with people from across the city's arts and political communities, and individuals ranging from the ballerina Carlotta Chabert to the exiled princess Cristina Belgiojoso sat for portraits with Hayez. He also experimented with the printmaking technique of lithography, interpreting the same historical and political themes from his more traditional works to the newer process in such works as *Lombards in the First Crusade* and a group of illustrations depicting scenes from the 1819 Sir Walter Scott novel *Ivanhoe*.

Painted Political Allegories

The Revolutions of 1848 that swept through Europe reshaped both the Italian landscape and Hayez's artistic outlook. Revolts against Austrian rule broke out in northern Italy, and before many years had passed Italian nationalists began agitating to bring about the unification of the peninsula's various small, independent political units into one joined Italian state. This surge of patriotic activity also marked a shift in Hayez's work toward the political. After 1848, the artist largely abandoned traditional historical themes in favor of more political allegory and portraiture. Among the most important and well-received paintings of this latter stage of Hayez's career are three related works with Venetian themes: the 1848 *Secret Accusation,* 1851 *Plotting Revenge,* and 1853 *Women of Venice.* Together, these three paintings explore themes of love, betrayal, and revenge. Later in the decade, Hayez painted what has become his best-known work, *Il Bacio* (*The Kiss*), an allegorical nod to the reunification of Italy. The artist also created portraits of notable figures such as the Count of Cavour and the composer Rossini. Yet historical themes were not entirely absent from Hayez's work. In 1867, the artist produced one of at least five depictions of the fourteenth-century Venetian political figure Marino Faliero, this time showing the disgraced doge preparing for his beheading. Another painting of the same year depicted the historical destruction of the Jewish temple at Jerusalem. Teaching also occupied part of the artist's time during the latter third of his life. In 1820, he became a professor at the Brera Academy; ten years later, he was named director there.

Advancing age also did not prevent Hayez from continuing to paint. His last major work, *Vase of Flowers at the Window of the Harem,* was first exhibited at the National Exhibition in Milan in 1881, when the artist was 90 years old. Mazzocca noted in Grove Art Online that this painting, unlike other works from Hayez's late period, was ''a simple and joyful homage to the art of painting.'' The following year, Hayez died in Milan, and his remains were later entombed at the city's Cimitero Monumentale (Monumental Cemetery). For about two decades before his death, Hayez had worked on the dictation of his memoirs. Ranging from his recollections of the fall of Venice during his early childhood to contemporary assessments of his art, these personal stories were eventually published in Milan in 1890 under the title *Le mie memorie* (*My Memories*) and remained an important source of information about the artist and the Italy of his time for decades to follow.

Hayez's primary legacy, however, was his body of work. Acclaimed by David Rodgers in the *Oxford Companion to Western Art* as ''a pivotal figure in the transition from Neoclassicism to Romanticism in Italian painting,'' Hayez created pieces that depicted many of the most important figures and themes of his day. In the twenty-first century, the most significant collection of the artist's output, including the famed *Il Bacio* and a selection of important portraits, remained in Hayez's adopted home of Milan at the museum attached the Brera Academy. Other works were displayed in the collections of the National Gallery in London, England; the Liechtenstein Museum in Vienna, Austria; and at numerous galleries in major Italian cities including Milan, Venice, Florence, Rome, and Naples. Hayez's fame remains greatest in his native Italy, where his life and work were the subject of monographs more than a century after his death.

Books

Plant, Margaret, *Venice: Fragile City, 1797–1997,* Yale University Press, 2002.

Online

''Francesco Hayez,'' National Gallery, http://www.national gallery.org.uk/artists/francesco-hayez (September 27, 2011).

''Hayez, Francesco,'' Grove Art Online, http://www.oxford artonline.com (September 27, 2011).

''Hayez, Francesco, *Oxford Companion to Western Art,* Oxford Art Online, http://www.oxfordartonline.com (September 27, 2011).□

John Heartfield

German artist John Heartfield (1891–1968) was a pioneer in the art of political photomontage. His subversive images appeared in the left-leaning publications of Weimar Germany and, then, from outside the country once Adolf Hitler and the Nazi Party rose to power in 1933. Jost Hermand wrote in *Unmasking Hitler: Cultural Representations of Hitler from the Weimar Republic to the Present:* ''Heartfield's most famous anti-Hitler images depict

Hitler as a hypocritical loudmouth, a ham actor, or an obedient follower of the...same circles already making plans for a second World War.''

John Heartfield was so revolted by a rising tide of German nationalism and xenophobia during World War I that he Anglicized his name, Helmut Herzfelde, to John Heartfield as a young man. He was born on June 19, 1891, in the Schmargendorf section of southwest Berlin. His father Franz was a writer who incurred the wrath of imperial Germany's censors for his writings, and in 1895 the family was forced to move to Switzerland. They later lived in Austria, but Heartfield was able to return and study graphic design at schools in Munich and Berlin as a young man. He was 23 years old when World War I erupted in the late summer of 1914. Drafted into Kaiser Wilhelm II's army, he served in the trenches before successfully faking a nervous breakdown and earning his discharge.

During the war years Heartfield befriended a fellow Berliner, George Grosz, who was a terrific illustrator and master caricaturist. When they began collaborating on satirical works that mocked the German bourgeoisie and cult of militarism, Heartfield was so intimidated by Grosz's artistic gifts that he abandoned line drawing altogether. He turned instead to photomontage, the cutting and pasting of photographs and typography to create a vivid, slightly surreal image with a clear message. Both he and Grosz worked with Heartfield's younger brother Wieland, who ran a small publishing house.

Swept into Dada Art Movement

The Herzfelde brothers and Grosz became swept up in the Dadaist movement that emerged during the war years and was especially active in Berlin at the time. Dadaism announced itself as the anti-art movement, a rejection of the materialism of the modern age and commercialization of the creative process. Like others involved, Heartfield avoided calling himself an artist, preferring instead the term *monteur,* a term used for film editing. Heartfield and Grosz were among the organizers of the First International Dada Fair in Berlin in 1920.

Heartfield gravitated toward the far left of the political spectrum, inspired in part by the sweeping changes that had rocked Germany's wartime foe, imperial Russia, in the last year of the war. There, reformists had forced the tsar to abdicate and then a group of dedicated Socialists established the world's first Communist state. Germany itself teetered on the brink of collapse in the months following the abdication of the Kaiser, and Communism very nearly prevailed there, too. But instead the Social Democrats seized power with the assistance of a special militia force called the Freikorps (Free Corps), and a new Weimar Republic of Germany was proclaimed. Named after the city in which the new postwar constitution was signed, the parliamentary democracy abolished much of the old order, but not enough for some. Heartfield and Grosz continued to use the printing press as their medium, creating posters and more short-lived satirical magazines that mocked President Friedrich Ebert's authority and other aspects of the Weimar government. Despite new laws prohibiting censorship, their publications were confiscated by authorities on various sham pretexts. ''The agenda was to expose the ruling social democrats under Friedrich Ebert as a counterrevolutionary clique employing the right-wing Free Corps and remnants of the Reichswehr to suppress uprisings by the suppressed and suffering working class,'' wrote Hermand in *Unmasking Hitler.*

Heartfield was part of a circle of left-wing artists in Berlin that included the playwright Bertolt Brecht and painter Otto Dix, both of whom savagely critiqued modern Weimar society and imperial Germany's role in World War I. One of the figures of opprobrium was Field Marshal Paul von Hindenburg, a revered figure among conservative Germans embittered over their nation's defeat in 1918 and the harsh reparations imposed by the victorious Allied nations. ''On the tenth anniversary of the war's outbreak'' in 1924, wrote *Times* of London journalist Richard Cork, ''Heartfield displayed a gruesome image in a Berlin bookshop window. Dominated by a row of skeletons, posed as if for an army medical inspection, a procession of helmeted boy soldiers march towards the foreground. They are the sons whose fathers were slaughtered, and the corpulent Hindenburg appears as a grandfatherly figure leading them to extinction.'' A year later, Hindenburg replaced Ebert as Weimar Germany's second elected president.

Teamed with Popular Biweekly

The outcome of the 1925 election inspired leftists to step up their campaign against the Weimar system, which was viewed as politically impotent and corrupt. By then Heartfield's photomontages were appearing in *Die Rote Fahne* (The Red Flag), the Communist Party newspaper in Germany, and he also produced a dramatic election poster for the party in 1928 showing an outstretched hand; its caption read, "The Hand Has Five Fingers. With These Five Grasp the Enemy!" His brother Wieland came up with many of the compelling slogans that appeared under Heartfield's photomontages, most notably for scores that ran in a new biweekly, the *Arbeiter-Illustrierte-Zeitung*, or "Workers' Illustrated Magazine." Heartfield became one of a long list of prominent contributors to *AIZ*, as it was known by its German-language acronym.

Heartfield's photomontages for *AIZ* offer a dramatic glimpse of the end of Weimar democracy and the swift rise to power of the National Socialist (Nazi) Party under Adolf Hitler. The Nazis were a rabidly anti-Communist, right-wing group that shared some similarities with the Italian Fascists under Benito Mussolini. Even before the October 1929 stock market crash on Wall Street, Germany was beset by serious economic problems, many of them related to the draconian reparations payments demanded by the treaty that concluded World War I. Inflation and unemployment skyrocketed in Germany when the Great Depression began in earnest. Both the Communist Party and its right-wing enemy, Adolf Hitler's National Socialist Party, attempted to sway the masses to their side by playing upon longstanding rifts and biases.

Created "Millions Stand Behind Me"

The first image that Heartfield created for *AIZ* showed a man whose head seems to have been wrapped entirely in the front pages of two popular newspapers of the day. The caption on the 1930 work reads: "Whoever Reads Bourgeois Newspapers Becomes Blind and Deaf: Away with These Stultifying Bandages!" He spent several months in 1931–32 on an extended visit to the Soviet Union, where he taught photomontage and helped lay out images for a new magazine, *USSR in Construction*. The peak period of his work came when he returned to Berlin in 1932 as the hobbled Weimar government headed toward collapse. Elections were held in July of 1932 and again in November, but the Reichstag, or parliament, was so dramatically divided that it was impossible for any party or coalition to form a working government.

For the July 17, 1932, issue of *AIZ* Heartfield created one of his best-known mockeries of Hitler, superimposing the leader's head, mouth open in mid-word, over a chest x-ray that revealed a gullet full of gold coins. The caption read, "Adolf The Superman: Swallows Gold and Spouts Junk." Scores more followed over the next few months, most of them sharply critical of Hitler and the Nazis' use of intimidation and violence, and many were used for the front cover of the top-selling *AIZ*. The most famous of his anti-Hitler propaganda montages appeared in the October 16, 1932, issue of *AIZ* and was widely reprinted. It shows Hitler in profile, with his right arm upraised in the customary response he used at rallies when supporters raised their right arms in the *Heil Hitler* salute. Behind Hitler stands an enormous shadowy tycoon, handing over 1,000-mark banknotes. "Millions Stand Behind Me. The Meaning of the Hitler Salute" read the caption. "It stands as one of the most memorable works of 20th-century propaganda," noted Tom Lubbock in the London *Independent*. "The capitalist fills almost half the picture, an embodiment of massive, immovable,

anonymous might. His head is cropped out of frame. His body is a slow, dark curve, like the silhouette of an artillery shell."

Forced into Exile, Interned

On January 30, 1933, President Hindenburg appointed Hitler as chancellor of Germany. The Nazis rapidly began consolidating power and harassing political rivals, and Heartfield walked across the border into Czechoslovakia. *AIZ* had been forced to relocate to Prague, where it continued to publish and Heartfield remained a contributor. Another of his most memorable images for *AIZ* appeared on December 19, 1935. It shows a German family at their dinner table happily consuming various metal objects, including bicycle parts and guns, as their meal; even the dog gnaws at a large bolt. The English-language translation of its caption is "Hurray, The Butter Is Gone!" This was a reference to a speech from a senior Nazi official, Hermann Göring, about recent food shortages. "Iron has always made a nation strong," Göring asserted, while "butter and lard have only made the people fat."

Heartfield was honored with a show of his work at the preeminent Gallery Mánes in Prague in 1934. The German ambassador to Czechoslovakia had some success in pressuring Mánes curators to remove seven of the 35 prints. "Heartfield's response," wrote Arthur Coleman Danto in the *Nation*, "was a masterful montage in *AIZ* that depicts the exhibition, in which a good many of his most biting images are shown, while, in the blank spaces left by the removed ones, the viewer sees the walls of a prison and a man with head wounds lying bleeding in the street. The caption reads, 'The more pictures they remove, the more visible reality becomes.'"

Three years later Heartfield was feted with another exhibition at Gallery Mánes, and this time Czechoslovak cultural authorities caved entirely to political pressure. Germany even demanded his extradition, and Heartfield departed Czechoslovakia on October 7, 1938, joining Wieland in London. He worked briefly as a photomontagist there, but once World War II erupted in earnest he was detained as an enemy alien and sent to an internment camp—a galling turn of events for an artist who had been assaulted on the streets of Berlin by Nazi thugs for his political art.

Forgotten by West

Released midway through the war, Heartfield was able to find work as a book designer in England. When the Nazis were defeated in the spring of 1945, Soviet military authorities governed an eastern section of Germany and a quadrant of Berlin; both of those territories became, respectively, the German Democratic Republic and East Berlin, the capital of a communist East Germany. Heartfield returned in 1950, living first in Leipzig and then in East Berlin, where he designed theater sets and posters; his surrealist-influenced graphic art influenced a generation of commercial artists in the Soviet bloc, where artistic expression was tightly controlled by the state. He continued to create propagandistic art, but much of it followed Communist ideology so faithfully that he lost much of his artistic credibility in the West. Finally, in 1967 he was feted with a retrospective at the Moderna Museet in Stockholm, which he hung himself. He later traveled to London to arrange a planned 1969 exhibition at the Institute of Contemporary Arts (ICA), but died in East Berlin on April 26, 1968.

Heartfield's artistic reputation languished for years, until the fall of Communism permitted art historians access to a trove of original images held by the German Academy of Arts in the former East Berlin. A major retrospective of his work toured museums in several cities in the early 1990s. "Heartfield showed that the artist could develop a visual language by using familiar images in new contexts, images that would be understood by a mass audience," asserted contemporary photomontagist and Royal College of Art professor Peter Kennard in the London *Guardian*. "By using the most sophisticated methods of photomontage and reproduction available, his work was reproduced on posters, leaflets, book jackets, and magazines and reached far beyond the confines of the art gallery."

Books

Hermand, Jost, "John Heartfield or The Art of Cutting Out Hitler," in *Unmasking Hitler: Cultural Representations of Hitler from the Weimar Republic to the Present,* edited by Klaus L. Berghahn and Jost Hermand, Peter Lang, 2005, pp. 59–80.

Periodicals

Art Journal, Winter 1993.
ArtUS, Spring 2008.
Guardian (London, England), March 26, 1991.
Independent (London, England), May 4, 2007.
Nation, June 28, 1993.
New York Times, April 16, 1993.
Sunday Times (London, England), August 9, 1992.
Times (London, England), September 16, 1967; August 21, 1992.□

Beth Heiden

Multisport American athlete Beth Heiden (born 1959) won top honors as a speedskater, cyclist, and cross-country skier. Heiden skated her way to a World Championship in 1979, then capped off her speed skating career with an Olympic bronze in 1980. Six months later, she won the World Road Cycling Championship in Sallanches, France, before taking up skiing and winning the NCAA individual cross-country championship in 1983.

Raised by Active Parents

Elizabeth Lee Heiden was born September 27, 1959, in Madison, Wisconsin, to Jack and Nancy Heiden. That Heiden ended up an athlete was no surprise, given her parents' history. Heiden's mother, the daughter of a hockey coach, excelled at tennis and was a state-ranked

player. Heiden's father, an orthopedic surgeon, grew up a skilled fencer, then turned to cycling as an adult, becoming a state senior champion. The Heidens spread their love of physical activity to their children. "My memories of growing up won't be so much of talking together, but that we were always *doing* something together," Heiden told the *Washington Post*'s Thomas Boswell. "Skiing, backpacking or taking canoe trips with our grandparents."

Heiden grew up alongside an older brother, Eric, who was born about 15 months before her. The Heiden children began recreational skating early on, toted to the area lakes by their parents when the lakes froze over during the winter. Both kids took to skating, with Beth Heiden pursuing figure skating and Eric Heiden playing hockey. Along the way, they both became interested in speed skating and joined a local speed skating club, competing for fun. Beth Heiden excelled at several sports; she played tennis and soccer at Madison West High School. She also ran track, once setting a national girls record for the mile run at 5 minutes, 1.7 seconds.

Dedicated to Speed Skating

In 1972, Beth and Eric Heiden's lives changed forever when the brother-sister duo began focusing on speed skating in earnest. That was the year Dianne Holum moved to Madison. A speed skater, Holum won gold and set an Olympic record at the 1972 games in the 1,500 meter event. She also won a silver in the 3,000 meters. Afterward, Holum retired from competition and moved to Madison to attend college. Holum, still passionate about speed skating, hooked up with the local club and began coaching. Beth Heiden was 13; brother Eric was 14.

Around this time speed skating was just taking off in the United States and the Heidens joined several other kids at the club in a training regimen under Holum's direction. "They trained hard and made a big jump the first year,"

Holum told *Sports Illustrated*'s E.M. Swift. "But that second year when they didn't make that big jump again, they had to learn patience. That was the big thing. A lot of the kids quit, but Beth and Eric stayed with it, even when they couldn't see the improvement."

Holum's training regimen included extensive hours on the ice, as well as bicycling, weight lifting, running, and duck-walking—an extreme deep-squat walk used by skaters to strengthen their legs. The grueling workouts paid off and in 1976 both Eric and Beth Heiden made the U.S. speed skating team and traveled to Innsbruck, Austria, to compete in the Olympics. Beth Heiden, just 16, came in eleventh in the 3,000 meters, while Eric Heiden finished seventh in the 1,500 meters.

Over the next few years, the Heidens continued their arduous workouts, hoping to improve their speed. Holum provided a lot of variety in the training regimen for the up-and-coming speed skaters. By now, both siblings were completing two workouts a day with segments that included weight-lifting, sprint-running, hill-running, distance running, circuit training, speed-lifting, track skating, and bike sprints. Other segments included slide-boarding, a workout where Heiden would wear wool socks, then slide across a Formica board simulating her skating style. There was also dry skating, which constituted getting into the skating position, then jumping from one leg to the other. Holum also required the Heidens to enter bike races.

Around this time an Olympic-sized rink opened in West Allis, Wisconsin, some 70-plus miles from Madison. Eager to train at a rink the appropriate size, the Heidens began driving there every day, leaving Madison at noon and skating from 2 to 6:30 p.m. While the rink was the appropriate size, the conditions were not exactly world class. Speaking to the *Washington Post*'s Boswell, Eric Heiden described their rink. "These are the worst conditions of any training site in the world. We breathe fumes from factories and cars that are close enough to hit with a snowball. The wind's so bad it knocks you off your feet in the turns, because our [windbreak] fences are pathetic. And, oh yeah, our ice is rather slow. You see, it has cement in it. Wind blows particles from the cement plant next door."

Won World Championship, Olympic Bronze

In 1978, Beth Heiden dominated the World Junior Speed Skating Championships held in Montreal. The competition included races at the following distances: 500 meters, 1,000 meters, 1,500 meters, and 3,000 meters. Heiden won them all, sweeping the meet. At the time, she was enrolled at the University of Wisconsin, studying civil engineering.

Beth Heiden continued her dominance in February 1979 while skating at the World Championships at The Hague, Netherlands, winning gold at all four distances—the 500, 1,000, 1,500, and 3,000 meters. Heiden won the 500 in 44.49 seconds and the 1,500 with a time of 2:13:79. For the first time since 1936, an American woman was the reigning speed skating world champion. A week later, Eric Heiden won the men's world championship, also sweeping all four of the distance events. By now, Beth Heiden was also competing in cycling races during the off-season, having grown to love the sport through her workouts. In

August 1979, Heiden finished first at the National Time Trial Championships in Wautoma, Wisconsin. She finished second in the National Road Race Championships, also held in August.

As the 1980 Winter Olympics approached, the media pounced on the Heiden siblings who would be competing in the U.S.-hosted games at Lake Placid, New York. Beth Heiden was favored to win the 1,500- and 3,000-meter races, while her brother was favored to win all five men's events. All told, the brother-sister duo had a shot at bringing home nine gold medals if they repeated their performances from the 1979 World Championships.

Magazines and newspapers across the United States splashed the siblings across their pages. Writing in the *Washington Post*, Boswell called them "sibling champions as opposite as fire and ice." Boswell described the 6-foot-1, 190-pound Eric as "a swashbuckler" who is "proudly self-evident." He called Beth Heiden a "5-foot-1, 105-pound ectomorph who seems like a hank of nerves, skin, bone, brain and long blowing hair."

The siblings skated with different styles as well. Eric Heiden used his tall, muscular frame to dig around the rink, whereas Beth Heiden, with her slight build, skated with swift, mechanical, efficient precision. Speaking to *Sports Illustrated*, Coach Holum praised Beth Heiden's grit. "Other people may be built better, and may be stronger, too. But Beth is more efficient. And she is a fighter. She feels that she has to make up for her size."

Once the Olympics arrived in February 1980, Beth Heiden struggled to live up to the hype. "I was just too nervous to do well in Lake Placid," she told the *Milwaukee Sentinel*'s Paul Peterson, noting she put too much pressure on herself. "Nerves got the best of me." Despite being hampered by an ankle injury, Beth Heiden managed to eke out a bronze in the 3,000 meters, while her brother stole the spotlight, winning five gold medals.

Turned to Cycling, Skiing

After the games, Beth Heiden decided to give up the sport and turned her attention to cycling. Though Heiden had competed in cycling events before, she had a break-out year in 1980. In August 1980 Heiden won first place at the national road championships in Bisbee, Arizona, sponsored by the United States Cycling Federation and a few weeks later competed in the world road cycling championships in Sallanches, France. Heiden won the event, becoming the second American woman to win a world cycling championship. That same year, Heiden also won the Coors International Bicycle Classic, at the time the premier stage race for women.

In 1981, racing the Mount Washington Hill Climb, one of the more demanding U.S. races, Heiden set a women's record, finishing the eight-mile course in 1 hour, 16 minutes and 30 seconds. Because of her performance, the media began to suggest Heiden might be the United States' next big hope for cycling gold in 1984. Heiden gave some thought to pursuing another Olympic berth, but decided she wanted to focus on school.

Heiden transferred to the University of Vermont (UVM) and joined the cross-country ski team, competing for the first time during the winter of 1981. Each weekend, she raced an individual event and also skied the middle leg of a three-member relay. Heiden rose to the top of the sport after only two years on skis, in 1983 capturing an NCAA individual championship. Heiden showed so much promise her name began to circulate as part of the U.S. ski team's talent pool.

Settled into Obscurity

Despite showing promise as a probable Olympic cyclist and/or skier, Heiden decided to settle down. She studied mathematics and physics at UVM and graduated in 1983. She married Russell Reid and changed her name to Beth Heiden Reid. The couple settled near Houghton, Michigan, after Russell Reid accepted a job teaching mathematics at Michigan Tech. The couple had three children, Garrett, Carl, and Joanne. Heiden Reid also gave birth to an infant daughter who died in 1991 of heart and kidney failure less than a month after her birth.

Once Heiden Reid had children, they became the focus of her life. "I never imagined me being a housewife even when I was pregnant with my first one," she told Rob Schultz of the *Capital Times*. "But then I realized I didn't want to leave him with anybody else. I don't think you can pay someone to do the job you could do." Not one to give up sports and competition completely, Heiden Reid coached hockey and soccer for her kids.

In 2000 the family moved to Palo Alto, California, and began weekend skiing trips to Truckee, California. Heiden Reid helped her children train, drove them to races, and worked the stopwatch. As Heiden Reid watched her children develop on their skis, she caught the racing bug again. In 2010, Heiden Reid competed in the U.S. Cross Country Ski Championships in Anchorage. She placed sixth of 125 in the freestyle sprint, beating women one-third her age. She took eighth place in the 10-kilometer and 17th place in the 20-kilometer event. During the competition, Heiden Reid skied alongside her 17-year-old daughter, Joanne. Joanne Reid took 24th in the freestyle event. Of the top-40 10-K finishers, Joanne Reid was the youngest. She made the 2010 world junior team and finished in the top 20. In January 2011, Joanne Reid won the 5K junior freestyle U.S. cross-country championship.

"I guess I was pretty young to stop competing," Heiden Reid told Nick Zaccardi in an article on the U.S. Speed Skating website. "I had been on two Olympic teams, and I had been to the world championships in a couple sports. I had lots of interests. There are so many great things to do in this world. I probably spent my top athletic years being a coach and a mom instead of racing." But in the end, Heiden Reid had no misgivings about calling off her career early and was busy writing workouts for her daughter and training alongside her. "I don't regret it at all," she said of her decision to quit competing in her 20s.

Periodicals

Capital Times (Madison, WI), June 6, 1991.
Christian Science Monitor, February 3, 1983.
Milwaukee Sentinel, January 19, 1994.
Newsweek, March 5, 1979.
New York Times, August 18, 1980; September 14, 1981.
Sports Illustrated, February 26, 1979.
Washington Post, February 10, 1980, p. 18; February 13, 1980.
Wisconsin State Journal, June 2, 1991; June 7, 1991.

Online

"Call Him Kid Cool," *Sports Illustrated Vault,* http://sports illustrated.cnn.com/vault/article/magazine/MAG1093171/index.htm (November 18, 2011).
"Speed Skater Beth Heiden-Reid Reflects on Time," U.S. Speed Skating, http://speedskating.teamusa.org/news/2010/02/07/speed-skater-beth-heiden-reid-reflects-on-time/31548 (November 18, 2011).□

Piet Hein

The Danish writer and designer Piet Hein (1905–1996) was a Renaissance man active in many fields from poetry to game design to city planning. He is best known for short humorous poems called grooks, which subtly communicated attitudes of resistance among Danes to Nazi German authority during World War II.

Studied Math, Art, Physics

Piet Hein was born in the Danish capital of Copenhagen on December 16, 1905, to Hjalmar Hein, an engineer, and Estrid Octavius Hein, an ophthalmologist who was related to author Karen Blixen (also known as Isak Dinesen). On his father's side he was descended from a Dutch naval hero, also named Piet Hein. He attended one of Denmark's top private high schools, the Metropolitanskolen, concentrating in mathematics and graduating in 1924. After taking some private art lessons, he went to Stockholm to study at the Royal Swedish School of Fine Arts. There he also studied with a Swedish cartoonist named Albert Engstrom. Hein left Sweden before graduating and returned to Copenhagen in 1927. There he took courses at the University of Copenhagen, the Technical University of Denmark, and the Niels Bohr Institute, where he studied with the famed atomic physicist whose name the institute carried. He never received a degree from any of these schools.

In a world that divided intellectual activity into arts and sciences, Hein perceived the two as indissolubly linked. He managed to partially resolve this conundrum by entering the field of industrial design, to which he made contributions for most of his career. Hein invented various games, some of which, like Tangrams, are still in use today. His first puzzle, the Soma Cube, appeared in 1936 and was said to have been invented while Hein was listening to a lecture by physicist Werner Heisenberg. His 1942 board game Hex (also known as Polygon) fascinated physicist Albert Einstein, who kept a copy on hand in his office.

In the 1930s Hein wrote several short poems that were published in Danish newspapers. His writing career began in earnest after German troops overran Denmark in April of 1940. Hein, who had a lifelong suspicion of political ideologies, was head of Denmark's Anti-Nazi Union at the time. "That was not the best thing to be on April 9, 1940," he recalled to Jim Hicks of *Life*. "I had to go underground. It was a great strain not being able to say anything. Then I found a way, those small poems. I grasped the word grook out of empty air." The grooks (*gruk* in Danish) began appearing in newspapers in 1940 and immediately became very popular.

Embedded Anti-Nazi Messages in Poems

Seemingly innocent, the grooks were readily approved by German censors. Yet one of the first ones became famous among Danes for its clear double meaning, warning against the moral consequences of collaborating with the Germans. *Consolation Grook* was translated into English this way: "Losing one glove / is certainly painful / but nothing / compared to the pain / of losing one / throwing away the other / and finding / the first one again." Danes understood it to mean that although they had lost their freedom, it would be doubly difficult for them if they lost their self-respect as well after freedom was restored. Hein's earlier grooks were published under the pen name Kumbel Kumbell, an elaborate Danish and Old Norse pun on his own name.

Hein continued to produce grooks for many years after the war, and not all of them had explicitly political intent. But all had a distinctive combination of everyday simplicity with often profound thinking. "Problems worthy / of attack / prove their worth / by hitting back," Hein wrote. In the center of a drawing for the highly original but seemingly simple super ellipse design he created later in life, Hein wrote this grook: "There is one art / no more, no less: / to do all things / with art- / lessness." In their original form the grooks had a distinctive graphic appearance on the page and always used the Helvetica font. In published collections they were often accompanied by small cartoons.

The grooks were enormously successful. Hein's grooks, estimated at between 7,000 and 10,000 poems in all, were integrated into Danish society and freely quoted in speeches and journalistic writings, much as Shakespeare's plays are used in English. Grooks appeared in advertisements, trade brochures, holiday cards, and even with kitchen equipment. Hein served as a Danish representative to the international writers' association PEN, and later became almost an official literary voice of Denmark, writing a slogan for Denmark's display at the 1967 Expo World's Fair in Montreal, Canada. In 1970 he wrote the script for a documentary about Danish industry.

Saw "Grooks" Published Worldwide

Hein translated many of his grooks into English himself, and also wrote some as English originals. Five collections of English grooks were published in Britain (where Hein lived for several years in the late 1960s and early 1970s),

the United States, and Canada. The grooks were also published in other languages as diverse as Chinese, Japanese, Indonesian, and Farsi. Hein also wrote a good deal of poetry in more conventional forms; a play, *Spirit Is to Remain,* was produced at Copenhagen's Royal Theatre in 1968, and he also penned radio and television scripts.

Motivating Hein's writing was a general commitment to world peace, a goal he shared with his one-time physics colleagues Einstein and Bohr. A proponent of globalism, he worked to spread the constructed global language Esperanto, and translated some of his grooks into that language. He believed in science as a force for good and idealistically viewed international groupings of scientists as a positive force for peace. One of his grooks was adopted as a motto of anti–Vietnam War protests in the 1960s: "The noble art of losing face / may one day save the human race / and turn into eternal merit / what weaker minds / would call disgrace."

The major accomplishment of Hein's later years was his creation of the super-ellipse, a shape that combined aspects of a square, a circle, and an oval. Contrary to what has sometimes been stated, Hein did not invent the super-ellipse, but he popularized it and identified a wide range of applications for it. Hein's super-ellipse was created in 1959 for a traffic pattern to be used in the construction of Stockholm's Sergel's Square, but it eventually appeared in furniture design, building architecture, and even an office anti-stress toy called the Super Egg.

In later life, Hein also wrote works of pure philosophy. He was perhaps more widely honored than any other contemporary Dane, receiving a long series of Danish and foreign awards beginning with the Alexander Graham Silver Bell from Boston University in 1968. He received an honorary doctorate from Yale University in 1972. In 1966 Hein was profiled in the *Life* magazine article "Poet with a Slide Rule." The most striking indication of the affection in which he was held by ordinary Danes was the fact that in a nation of some five million people, two and a half million copies of his books were sold in Denmark.

Hein married Gunver Holck in 1937. After that marriage ended in divorce, he married Gerda Ruth Conheim in 1942; that marriage produced two sons, Juan Alvaro Hein and Andrés Humberto Hein, both born in 1943. Hein's marriage to Anne Cathrina Krøyer Pedersen resulted in one son, Lars Hein, born in 1950. Finally, in 1956, he married Gerd Ericsson, by whom he had two more sons, Jotun Hein, born in 1956, and Hugo Piet Hein, born in 1963.

Hein died in rural Middelfart, Denmark, on Funen Island, on April 17 (or 18) 1996. Although several writings about Hein exist in Danish, his life and work have been poorly documented in English.

Books

Stecher-Hansen, Marianne, ed., *Twentieth-Century Danish Writers* (Dictionary of Literary Biography, Vol. 214), Gale, 1999.

Periodicals

Guardian (London, England), May 4, 1996.
Independent (London, England), April 22, 1996.
Life, October 14, 1966.

Online

"Biography of Piet Hein," *PoemHunter,* http://www.poem hunter.com/piet-hein/biography/(November 4, 2011).

"Piet Hein: The Rational Idealist," http://www.piethein.com (November 4, 2011).□

John Arnold Heydler

A very influential baseball figure, John Heydler (1869-1956) served as the National League president, first in 1909 and then from 1918 to 1934. He helped establish baseball's Hall of Fame, and he advanced the idea that eventually became Major League Baseball's "designated hitter" rule.

John Heydler was one of Major League baseball's most influential executives. While his name might not be as well known as early baseball executives such as Kenesaw "Mountain" Landis (the sport's first commissioner, who was brought in to clean up after the Black Sox scandal), Heydler helped transform the sport into its twentieth- and twenty-first century incarnations. Indeed, he was a catalyst in professional baseball's evolution.

His impact was significant: Not only did Heydler serve as National League president during a turbulent period (from 1918 to 1934), he also helped establish baseball's Hall of Fame, and he advanced the idea of compiling players' statistics. Anyone who ever enjoyed analyzing the numbers placed on the back of baseball cards or in the entries in *The Baseball Encyclopedia* should tip their cap to Heydler.

Baseball was an Early Passion

The future baseball executive was born as John Arnold Heydler on July 10, 1869 in La Fargeville, New York. By the time he was fourteen years old, he started working as a printer's apprentice for a newspaper published in Rochester, New York. All the while, he engaged in his one true passion: baseball. Most of his free time was directed toward sandlot baseball.

As he grew older, work and baseball remained intertwined. In Washington, D.C., he secured a job as a government printer, but he also played baseball and often umpired college and semi-pro baseball games. Appropriately, Heydler later found work as a newspaper sports writer, covering the sport he loved best.

Became a Statistician

His passion for the sport led to a professional appointment: For a period in the late 1890s, he worked as an umpire in professional baseball's National League. The Heydler legend has it that this came about by chance. When an umpiring official failed to show up for a game that Heydler was attending, Heydler was asked to fill in.

After that, he returned to sports writing (1899), and he compiled the batting and fielding averages of baseball players, a concept based upon nineteenth-century baseball writer Henry Chadwick's system of scorekeeping, which included development of the box score, which became a sports page mainstay.

In 1903, Heydler entered the ranks of professional baseball's executive branch, first as a low-level administrator. Harry Pulliam, who was the National League president, hired the young Heydler to be his secretary. From there, Heydler would remain in professional baseball for the rest of his life.

Heydler then became the National League's secretary-treasurer. In this new position, he continued compiling the statistics of league players. Further, he perceived new ways to mathematically measure a player's on-field accomplishments and, in turn, calculate a player's value to a team. To his mind, runs-batted-in (RBI) was a strong indicator of a batter's worth. In addition, Heydler advanced the concept of a pitcher's earned run average (ERA). Heydler came up with his numerical ideas when he was working as a sportswriter, and he helped advance statistical measures as something that could be sold to other newspapers.

Helped Initiate Other Changes

When Pulliam died (he committed suicide in 1909), Heydler served for a year as the National League's interim president. During this period, he made another major change that helped define professional baseball as it came to be known: He limited a team's roster to twenty-five players, which remains a modern standard.

Thomas J. Lynch was eventually selected as Pulliam's replacement, and, in 1914, Heydler returned to his previous position as league secretary-treasurer.

Then in 1918, Heydler was appointed National League president once again. This time, the appointment was not temporary. Replacing John Tener (who resigned), Heydler would serve as league president for sixteen years (until 1934). Ever the proponent of math related to on-field performance, in 1919, he hired the Elias brothers (Al and Walter) to keep track of player statistics. Earlier, in 1913, the brothers formed the Al Munro Elias Bureau in New York City (this would later evolve into the Elias Sports Bureau, which today provides historic research and statistic services for professional sports). Modern-day statisticians—such as Bill James (who advanced the algebra and geometry of baseball numbers, and then translated that data into digestible information)—owe a debt to Heydler.

Led During a Troubled Era

When Heydler assumed the presidency, baseball was still a rough-and-tumble sport. At the time, baseball moguls (like Charles Comiskey, owner of the Chicago White Sox) exploited their players, offering only low salaries and ostracizing those who objected to what was essentially a feudal arrangement. Some baseball players responded by associating with gamblers and gangsters, to earn what they felt was their piece of the pie (professional baseball, by this time, was a profitable industry).

The situation led to the so-called "Black Sox" scandal that involved the 1919 World Series (Comiskey's White Sox team versus the Cincinnati Reds). Gambling on baseball was quite common, and a potential payoff proved luring to ballplayers.

That year, the White Sox were regarded as the best in baseball, and the team made it to the World Series. Its loss in the championship series aroused suspicion. The team's ranks included "Shoeless" Joe Jackson, who could regularly post a .400 batting average, and pitcher Eddie Cicotte, who had previously posted a 30-game winning season on the mound. There were other stars on the team, but Comiskey was a frugal owner and he was stingy when it came to compensation.

This did not sit well with some team members. One of the White Sox stars, first baseman Charles "Chick" Gandil conspired with gambler Joseph Sullivan to "throw" the World Series, which would enable other gamblers to realize a big pay day (odds makers heavily favored the White Sox over the Reds)—and also line his pockets with the kind of money that Comiskey was unwilling to give up. Into this narrative came big-time New York City gambler/gangster Arnold Rothstein, and other White Sox players including Cicotte, Claude "Lefty" Williams (a pitcher who won twenty-three games during the regular 1919 season), talented shortstop Charles "Swede" Risberg, infielder Fred McMullin, and centerfielder Oscar "Happy" Felsch.

Thanks to his involvement with the shadier personages, Risberg was paid $15,000 for his involvement in the "fix," a figure that amounted to more than four times his regular season salary.

As a result of the fix, the underdog Reds beat the White Sox. Meanwhile, other players on other teams were colluding with gamblers. Rumors abounded about how members of the Boston Braves, Cleveland Indians, Chicago Cubs, New York Yankees and the New York Giants threw games.

This led to an investigation that spotlighted the 1919 World Series.

Heydler was part of the investigating body, the National Commission, a three-man entity that also included American League President Byron Bancroft "Ban" Johnson and Cincinnati Reds owner August Hermann (the commission's chairman). In the wake of the gambling scandals, the commission decided to appoint a single commissioner who would have the power to fine and suspend players for activities such as gambling. Indeed, it was Heydler who suggested the idea of a single commissioner, and he supported the appointment of Kenesaw "Mountain" Landis, who was a federal judge.

Landis was a resolute individual who would govern the sport with an iron fist. In one of his first rulings, he banned eight White Sox players from the game. These players, who would later become known as the "eight men out," included Gandil, Cicotte, Williams, Risberg, McMullin, and Felsh, as well as third baseman George "Buck" Weaver and Jackson. Weaver and Jackson were not proven to be directly involved in the "fix," but their "sin" was that they were aware of what was going on. Landis banned them because they did not report their knowledge. Their ouster from baseball has come to be regarded as one of baseball's mythic tragedies. Landis' ruling was controversial, but it helped restore the reputation of professional baseball.

Helped Developed the "Designated Hitter" Rule

Heydler would continue as National League president for sixteen years, a tenure that was longer than the combined years that the previous league presidents served. But longevity was not the defining element of Heydler's administration; rather, it was the man's innovative ideas. For instance, well before the major leagues adopted the idea of the designated hitter, Heydler advanced the notion of the "10th hitter," an idea he first advanced in 1928. This tenth hitter, he proposed, would step to the plate in place of the starting pitcher.

Heydler presented this notion during the major league meetings that took place in Chicago in December 1929. As related in the book, *The Big Bam,* Heydler felt it would re-energize the sport and, further, extend the career of George Herman "Babe" Ruth, whose career was winding down, even though he could still knock the ball out of the stadium. This "10th man" would bat in place of the starting pitcher, placing a permanent pinch-hitter on a team's roster who would never have to play in the field. The purpose was obvious; Heydler wanted to spark offensive fireworks.

Heydler's idea did not immediately catch on. Most baseball professionals found the idea laughable. National League owners were open to the idea, however, but the American League owners rejected the concept. This is ironic, as in 1973 it was the American League that adopted the designated hitter rule, and the National League considered it an abomination. The only time the National League uses the designated hitter rule is during the World Series and in interleague games played in American League parks, and many members were—and continue to be—outspoken against it.

In spite of opposition to the designated hitter institution, adoption of the rule would prolong the careers of one-dimensional or aging players such as Reggie Jackson.

Pushed for a Hall of Fame

Before he retired as National League president in 1934 (due to health reasons), Heydler offered at least one more intriguing notion: He advanced the idea of a baseball Hall of Fame, and he played an important role in the establishment of the Cooperstown institution. Even after his retirement, Heydler remained involved in baseball. He was appointed as chairman of the National League Board of Directors, a position he held until his death.

Heydler's health continued weakening, and he died in Mercy Hospital in San Diego, California, on April 18, 1956. He was eighty-six years old. He was survived by his wife, Nancy. He had no children.

Heydler left behind a strong legacy. Baseball historians recognize his influence, even if the average baseball fan does not even know his name. Ironically, this man, who had substantial impact on a sport he loved, is not enshrined in the institution he helped create: the National Baseball Hall of Fame and Museum.

Books

Montville, Leigh, *The Big Bam*, Anchor, 2007.

Porter, David L., *Biographical Dictionary of American Sports*, Greenwood Publishing Group, 2000.

Periodicals

The New York Times, April 19, 1956.

Online

"John Heydler," *The Baseball Page.com*, http://www.thebaseball page.com/history/john-heydler (December 1, 2011.)

"John Heydler," *Baseball-Reference.com*, http://www.baseball-reference.com/bullpen/John_Heydler (December 1, 2011.)

"John Heydler," *Find a Grave*, http://www.findagrave.com/cgi-bin/fg.cgi?page=gr&GRid=14584268 (December 1, 2011.)

"John Heydler," *Sports E-cyclopedia.com*, http://www.sports ecyclopedia.com/mlb/nl/heydler.html (December 1, 2011.)□

Kinue Hitomi

Kinue Hitomi (1907–1931) became the first Japanese woman, and apparently the first woman of color, to win an Olympic medal when she took home the silver medal in the 800-meter track and field event at the 1928 Olympics in Amsterdam, the Netherlands. She also set several world records during her short career, truncated by a fatal illness.

What made Hitomi's accomplishments all the more remarkable was that they took place in the infancy of modern women's sports in Japan. Traditional gender roles began to break down during the Meiji era (beginning in 1868), but the country's sports infrastructure, especially for women, was just beginning to develop in the 1920s. One of Hitomi's few role models was the actress and golfer Sunado Komako, known as the Japanese Gloria Swanson.

Played Tennis at First

Hitomi was born in the small farming village of Fukuhama-mura, Mitsu-gun, in Okayama Prefecture in western Japan, on January 1, 1907. Her father, Isaku Hitomi, was a rice farmer, and from the start she enjoyed outdoor activities. The family farm prospered, and it was decided that Kinue, who showed both physical and intellectual gifts, should be given the best education possible. After scoring in the top 25 percent on the entrance exam, she was admitted to the Okayama Girls' School. Her first sport was tennis, at which she was a fierce competitor, but at one meet she filled in as a long jumper, and the school's principal noticed her talent. He convinced Hitomi's father that she should be given the chance to attend a college where she would have the chance to develop her athletic abilities.

By the time she graduated in 1924, Hitomi had already set what was thought to be a Japanese record in the long jump, with a jump of 4.67 meters. Some of her claimed national and world records have not gained official recognition from international sanctioning bodies, perhaps because record-keeping and event standardization techniques were still developing in Japan at the time. But when Hitomi enrolled at the Nikaido School of Athletes in Tokyo (now known as the Japan Women's College of Physical Education), it was clear that she was emerging as Japan's top female track and field athlete. At a meet in her home Okayama Prefecture, she notched a triple jump of 10.33 meters that was claimed as a world record.

Graduating from the women's college, Hitomi took a job teaching at the First Kyoto Girls' High School. She switched professions, however, when she landed a sports-writing position at the *Mainichi Shimbun* newspaper in Osaka in the spring of 1926. Not only was the paper one of Japan's top publications, but it frequently sponsored sports events. A fine writer who penned two books on track and field as well as an autobiography during her short life, Hitomi may have sensed that she would be able to combine her talents by taking the newspaper job.

Traveled to Sweden by Train

Indeed, that was how the situation developed. Entering the Japanese national track and field championships in May of 1926, she excelled in events ranging from the 100-meter dash to the shot put. Hitomi was chosen to represent Japan at the International Women's Games held in Göteburg, Sweden, in August. She took the Trans-Siberian Railroad to Moscow alone, meeting a *Mainichi Shimbun* correspondent who then rode with her to Sweden. Swedish stadium staff let her train on a local track despite the lack of an official facility for the ragtag Japanese team. Despite the rigors of the trip, Hitomi won two events, took runner-up in another, and finished third in yet another. One of her winning events was the long jump, in which she improved on her high school mark with a jump of 5.5 meters. She was picked as the games' outstanding athlete after Japan came in fifth in the competition with 23 points—all scored by Hitomi.

Setting her sights on the 1928 Amsterdam Olympics, Hitomi trained hard and gradually began to improve her already stellar times and distances. She set several world records over the summer of 1928, including a long jump of 5.98 meters that stood until 1939. These accomplishments raised Hitomi's profile in the international press, and she headed for Amsterdam in anticipation of testing herself against the world's best. Unfortunately, the women's program of events at the Olympics was much shorter than it later became, and only one of Hitomi's top events, the 100-meter dash, was included. She won her first heat at 100 meters, becoming the first Asian woman to compete at the Olympics in any sport, but in the semifinal round she finished fourth.

Apparently quoting Hitomi's Japanese-language autobiography, the *Treasure Box: Discovering Japan* web site reported her thoughts this way: "I can never return to Japan with such a [miserable] result! Am I such a person who does that? I have to fight to clear my own name and fulfill my responsibility...My last chance is 800 meters...I do not have energy enough to spare for running in 800 meters, but I have to try as hard as I can till I fall down." Hitomi had little experience at 800 meters but finished second, less than a second behind German runner Lina Radke, and earned the silver medal for Japan. Her time remained an Asian record for two decades. The *New York Post* (as quoted on the *Treasure Box* site) editorialized that Hitomi had "changed our philosophy of Japanese women." The International Olympic Committee was less impressed; several of the other competitors in the 800-meter race collapsed at its end, and the event was banned until the 1960 games.

Competed Despite Illness

At a Japan-Germany dual meet held in Seoul, Korea (then under Japanese occupation), in 1929, Hitomi achieved a world-record time of 24.7 seconds in the 200-meter race and a staggering 6.075 meters in the long jump, but both marks were disallowed because they were considered wind assisted. In 1930 she headed for Europe on the Trans-Siberian train once again to take part in the International Women's Games, this time held in Prague, Czechoslovakia (now Czech Republic). She had herself trained the other five athletes on the team and spearheaded fundraising for their trip. She arrived in Prague running a fever but insisted on competing in driving rainstorms, taking first place in the long jump, second in the triathlon, and third in the 60-meter dash and javelin. Hitomi's performance was honored by the city of Prague with the construction of a stone monument.

After the Women's Games, the Japanese team embarked on a grueling schedule of dual meets in various European capitals. Suffering from exhaustion and under care from physicians almost every day, Hitomi insisted on keeping to a planned schedule of 20 events in one week in

Warsaw, Berlin, and Paris. In Brussels, Belgium she felt too weak to participate but then took to the track in the 800-meter race to prevent a Japanese loss, finishing second.

After this ordeal, Hitomi returned to Japan by sea, from Marseilles to Kobe. Despite her father's urgings that she take a break, Hitomi plunged into a full work schedule and also held coaching seminars on the side as a service to Japan's national sports federation. By the spring of 1931 she was showing symptoms of an illness variously reported as pleurisy, pneumonia, and tuberculosis. She died at Osaka Imperial University Hospital on August 2, 1931, at the age of 24. Observers believed that a showdown between Hitomi and American triple medal winner Mildred "Babe" Didrikson at the 1932 Olympics would have resulted in close races.

Although her story is not well known in the West, Hitomi is widely remembered for her accomplishments in Japan and has been recognized for contributions to Japanese athletics beyond the list of those she achieved in the stadium. These included reforms in coaching and spirit-building rituals in high school sports matches. Her Olympic silver medal, thought to have been melted down during World War II, was discovered in 2000 among a group of her belongings kept at her family home. A statue of Hitomi was erected in Tokyo in 2001.

Books

Christensen, Karen, et al., *International Encyclopedia of Women and Sports,* Macmillan, 2001.

Periodicals

Journal of Olympic History, September 2000.s
Mainichi Daily News, August 23, 2000.

Online

"Kinue Hitomi (1907–1931)," *Treasure Box: Discovery of Japan,* http://www.jpn-miyabi.com/Vol.39/hitomi-1.html(September 30, 2011).
"1st Woman of Color to Win," *Alic Coachman Track & Field Foundation,* http://www.alicecoachman.org/lost1woc.html (September 30, 2011).□

Eduard Hitzig

The German neurophysiologist Eduard Hitzig (1838–1907) was one of the most important of the early researchers who established and mapped localized function in the brain.

For much the history of physiology up to the nineteenth century, the brain was thought to be a single organ that acted as a whole in producing the entire range of human physical and mental phenomena. Even after researchers began to notice that damage to specific

parts of the brain resulted in specific forms of physical incapacity, many of them believed that the brain acted holistically, with its various parts working in concert to enable motion and thought. Hitzig's experiments, painstaking and detailed, began to demonstrate the brain's complexity and the degree to which small areas of the brain controlled individual organs and specific human and animal actions.

Raised in Academically Successful Family

Born in Berlin on February 6, 1838, Julius Eduard Hitzig came from a German Jewish family with a record of overachievement made more impressive by the fact that they were never wealthy. He was named for his grandfather Julius Eduard Hitzig (1780–1849), who was a writer, bookstore owner, and criminal law attorney. The former Friedrich Hitzig Strasse in Berlin was named after Hitzig's father, and the Nobel Prize–winning chemist Adolf von Baeyer was his cousin. Hitzig himself set out to study law but soon switched to medicine and took classes in Berlin and Wüzburg. He had the good fortune to encounter some of Germany's top teachers, including the pioneer of social medicine Rudolf Virchow. In 1862 he received an M.D. degree and set up an internal medicine practice in Berlin.

Hitzig served as a medic in the Franco-Prussian War in 1870, and for a time it was assumed that his interest in physiology stemmed from his wartime experiences. His important writings, however, began to appear several months before war broke out, and it was clear that he had been following contemporary developments in brain physiology for several years. He may have made some initial observations during the Prussian-Danish war of 1864. The theory of brain function localization was quite controversial in the 1860s, but several researchers had taken important steps: the British investigator John Hughlings Jackson had closely observed the brains of epileptics and determined that

seizures were tied to specific brain locations, and Roberts Bartolow, a professor at the Medical College of Ohio (then in Cincinnati), was soon (in 1874) to carry out electrical brain stimulation experiments on a human patient who was grateful for Bartolow's care and agreed to let him attach electrodes to her exposed brain during surgery.

This was controversial at the time, and Bartolow was forced to leave Cincinnati and take a job teaching elsewhere. Hitzig, for his part, was often unable to obtain funding for his research, and he was denied lab space at Berlin's Physiological Institute. As a result, he and his colleague, Theodor Fritsch, were forced to carry out their experiments at Hitzig's house, reportedly in the bedroom on the dressing table of his wife, Etta. Far from objecting, she became an enthusiastic participant in her husband's scientific endeavors, and the two worked together on a book about food catering in neuropsychiatric hospitals. They had no children.

Performed Detailed Brain Experiments on Dogs

Working on dogs, Hitzig and Fritsch found that the cerebrum (the forward part of the brain) would produce specific results when stimulated electrically in specific places, and they set about to establish the cerebrum's precise topology. Although Fritsch was the senior researcher at the time, he soon left the field, while Hitzig continued to develop his ideas; the primary impetus behind their experiments is thought to have come from Hitzig. Their experiments were extremely detailed, showing, for example, not just that the removal of part of the brain impeded the motion of a dog's paw but specifically establishing how the paw's coordination and lateral motion might be affected.

Hitzig and Fritsch summarized their findings in their 1870 paper, titled "Über die elektrische Erregbarkeit des Grosshirns" (On the Electrical Excitability of the Brain). The *Dictionary of Scientific Biography* termed it "a classic of physiology," and despite the controversial nature of Hitzig's investigations, the paper was soon translated into English and widely distributed. The paper gave the then-unknown Hitzig credibility in the profession, and in 1872 he wrote a *Habilitationsschrift*, a dissertation-like document that, when accepted, qualified him to teach in the German university system. Working without Fritsch this time, he carried out and published further brain localization investigations in 1874, this time experimenting on the visual cortex and its relation to blindness.

In 1875 Hitzig was invited to become the director of the Burghölzli mental asylum near Zurich, Switzerland (now the psychiatric hospital of the University of Zurich). This was a prestigious appointment for a psychiatric investigator of the time, for it offered the rare opportunity to put ideas in mental health treatment directly into practice. Hitzig made earnest attempts to professionalize the environment at the asylum, and he notched several accomplishments, including the establishment of a Provident Society for the Mentally Afflicted—a fund that helped discharged inmates reintegrate into outside society. But Hitzig was frustrated by the cronyism of its internal culture and clashed repeatedly with other administrators.

He faced formidable obstacles in cleaning up the asylum. The asylum steward, a man named Schnurrenberger, was apparently quite corrupt; Hitzig arrived to find that Schnurrenberger had leased a building on the edge of the asylum grounds to a local tavern owner who turned it into a house of prostitution that served asylum workers. Matters were not helped by Hitzig's own autocratic personality, which was attributed by ethnically prejudiced observers of the time to either his Jewish or his Prussian background. After four years, Hitzig resigned his post and took a job as professor of psychiatry at the University of Halle in northern Germany. When the university opened a new psychiatric clinic in 1885, Hitzig became its director.

Influential in Field of Psychiatry

Hitzig's work as a psychiatric practitioner during the later part of his career is highly regarded, although it was overshadowed by the revolutionary developments in the field that occurred in Vienna in the early twentieth century. In the words of Albert Kuntz, writing in *Founders of Neurology,* it was through Hitzig's influence that "psychiatrists became increasingly aware that the brain is the instrument of the mind and that the treatment of mental patients must be placed on a more scientific basis. He also brought to public attention the need for more adequate provisions for the care of mental patients." Hitzig continued to work on brain localization and wrote several books. He became a senior figure in the field of brain physiology, delivering the prestigious Hughlings Jackson lecture in London in 1900; this, too, was adapted into a book the following year.

Many of Hitzig's later writings and public appearances were concerned with arguing a specific position. Even after the theory of localized brain function began to supplant earlier so-called holistic approaches, many physiologists believed that specific parts of the brain worked together to manifest themselves in phenomena of the body and mind, a position known as the aggregation theory and favored by the researcher and key Hitzig rival Hermann Munk. Hitzig, by contrast, favored a close correspondence between single areas of the brain and specific manifestations. He focused on closely mapping the cerebral cortex and trying to determine its role in thought. In these efforts some of his ideas turned out to be erroneous, but his basic ideas about the localization of brain function were sound. Hitzig trained younger investigators and was reportedly a supportive and fatherly figure. But he relished intellectual debate with his opponents and could be quite cutting in his written and spoken commentary.

It was with great reluctance that Hitzig was forced by poor health to cut back his activities in the early years of the new century. Suffering from gout and diabetes-induced blindness, he retired from the Halle psychiatric clinic in the fall of 1903. He died in the town of Luisenheim zu St. Blasien in southern Germany on August 20, 1907, and one of his successors, G. Anton, summed up his accomplishments (according to Caoimhghin S. Breathnach, writing in *History of Psychiatry*) by saying that "narrow compartmentalization of knowledge had been forsaken as a result of the sound foundations laid by Hitzig and his fellow workers, who had shown that psychiatry was a vital link between clinical medicine and physiological psychology." Every brain surgeon is in his debt.

Books

Gillispie, Charles Coulston, ed. in chief, *Dictionary of Scientific Biography,* Scribner's, 1972.

Haymaker, Webb, and Francis Schiller, compilers, *The Founders of Neurology: One Hundred and Forty-Six Biographical Studies by Eighty-Eight Authors,* 2nd ed., Charles C. Thomas, 1970.

Periodicals

History of Psychiatry, issue 3, 1992. □

Betty Holberton

A pioneer in the field of computer science, American mathematician Betty Holberton (1917-2001) used her mental prowess to program the world's first electronic computer. Known as ENIAC, the machine was built by the U.S. military during World War II to compute artillery firing tables. After the war, Holberton continued to work in this newly emerging tech field and went on to assist in developing the computing languages known as COBOL and FORTRAN, which enjoyed widespread use as some of the first user-friendly standard programming languages to emerge.

Showed Early Penchant for Mathematics

Holberton was born Frances Elizabeth Snyder on March 7, 1917, in Philadelphia, Pennsylvania, to a family of scientists and teachers who specialized in mathematics, physics, and astronomy. She was one of eight children in a family of four boys and four girls. Growing up, Holberton attended the George School, a co-educational Quaker boarding school in Newtown, Pennsylvania. She credited the school with teaching her how to think critically and problem-solve.

Simple mathematical machines captured Holberton's interest early on. Her family owned a Marchant, a handcranked, wheel-and-gear-driven calculator. One day when Holberton was about 15, she and her 13-year-old brother decided the machine was not dividing properly. They opted to take it apart. Holberton labeled and diagrammed every part, carefully laying it out on the table for easy reassembly. They put the machine back together properly but failed to fix the issue. This mechanical ability proved helpful later on when Holberton worked on ENIAC. Programming this first primitive computer involved manually setting switches and cables inside the machine to direct the flow of calculations.

Holberton earned a scholarship to the University of Pennsylvania and decided to study mathematics. Her first course, analytic geometry, was taught by a Russian professor named J.A. Shohat. Shohat did not think women belonged in college and consequently, he treated them poorly. In an interview with James Ross of the Charles Babbage Institute, Holberton recalled that professor Shohat came into class every day and told the women they should be home raising children. Shohat's behavior led Holberton to drop mathematics. "Well after you have four months of that every day, and you go and you find out the next semester in mathematics is taught by the same fellow with no alternatives, I just gave up and decided I'd get an education."

Entered the Field of Journalism

After abandoning mathematics, Holberton studied English and journalism. After graduating, Holberton landed a job with the *Farm Journal* and was happy to receive assignments that required her math skills. At the publication, Holberton worked in the economics department, compiling statistics and information on such things as consumer spending. Once again, the mathematical machinery caught her eye. To compile statistics, the *Farm Journal* relied on Remington Rand tabulating machines, which used a punch-card system to tabulate data. When a punch-card was inserted into the machine, it would advance a counter dial.

As Holberton studied the results of one survey, she realized something was off and discovered many of the cards were being punched incorrectly before they were tabulated because the punch-system was not user-friendly. Holberton went to her boss and persuaded him to ditch the results and start over. Holberton saw the situation as an equipment problem—not a human problem—because, as she told Ross, "the equipment wouldn't do what the human wanted it to do." This experience had a tremendous impact on Holberton. Later, when she was working on writing computer programming languages, she was careful to ensure they were easy to use in an effort to reduce unintentional errors.

Recruited by Army

After the December 1941 attack on Pearl Harbor, the United States entered World War II and Holberton's relatives joined in the war effort. Two of Holberton's sisters signed on with WAVES—a division of women who served in the U.S. Naval Reserves. WAVES was an acronym for Women Accepted for Volunteer Emergency Service. Because she was cross-eyed, Holberton was not able to join WAVES, though she wanted to serve in some way. Soon, Holberton saw a newspaper ad that said the U.S. military was looking for some "girls" who could do mathematics because they were short on male mathematicians with so many men overseas fighting the war. Holberton applied and was hired.

Holberton reported for duty in the summer of 1942, stationed at the University of Pennsylvania's Moore School of Electrical Engineering. Holberton spent her first three months in training, learning calculus and brushing up on her math skills in a crash course that required her to study eight hours a day, six days a week. Afterward, she and the other women—there were about 80—were given the tedious job of calculating ballistics trajectories for different weapons. There was so much work to be done the women worked in two shifts, with the first group completing calculations from 8 a.m. to 4 p.m. and the second group sliding into the desks at 4 p.m. and working until 1 a.m. Holberton worked on trajectory tables for the 155mm Howitzer, among other weapons.

The women were classified as "computers." At the time, a computer was not a machine but a person who did computations. Kay Mauchly Antonelli was one of the women who worked with Holberton. In an interview with K.L. Heyman of the *Electronic Engineering Times,* Mauchly Antonelli explained the arduous task of compiling the trajectory tables. "We had to calculate where the bullet would be every tenth of a second, and just to find out where it was after a tenth of a second required over six multiplications, a couple of square roots and a couple of divisions and subtractions." As such, it took several months to produce a complete firing table. As D-Day approached in June 1944, the women were under increasing pressure to finish trajectories, particularly for the guns mounted on the support aircraft that would fly over as Allied troops landed on the shores of Normandy, France.

Tapped to Program First Computer

By early 1945, the U.S. Army was recruiting some of the women to work on programming the Electronic Numerical Integrator and Computer. Better known as ENIAC, it was the first general-purpose electronic computer ever built. The army had decided to build a digital machine capable of automating the trajectory calculations the women had been compiling. Holberton volunteered and ended up as one of six women on the team.

The ENIAC was a top-secret project and a completely newfangled piece of equipment. No computer had ever been programmed, so the women were left to figure it out on their own. Instead of receiving a manual, the women were given electrical block diagrams and blueprints of the internal circuitry of the mammoth, 30-ton machine that took up some 1,800 square feet of space and included 18,000 vacuum tubes, 1,500 relays, and hundreds of thousands of resistors, capacitors, and inductors.

There were no computer languages, so "programming" the computer involved routing data and electronic impulses through the machine and timing the various calculations to occur at the correct moment. To do this, the women had to set switches and insert plugs by hand. "There were no manuals," Mauchly Antonelli told *Computerworld's* Kathleen Melymuka. "They gave us all the blueprints, and we could ask the engineers anything. We had to learn how the machine was built, what each tube did. We had to study how the machine worked and figure out how to do a job on it."

Another ENIAC programmer, Jean J. Bartik, told the *New York Times'* Steve Lohr that Holberton was instrumental in figuring out how to route the calculations through the machine. "Betty had an amazing logical mind, and she solved more problems in her sleep than other people did awake." Once the women got the machine up and running, it was able to complete in 15 seconds calculations that used to take 30 hours to compute by hand. The machine even performed calculations for the Manhattan Project, which resulted in the development of the atomic bomb.

Contributions Overshadowed by Male Counterparts

Recognition for the six women of ENIAC was decades in the making. A 1975 ENIAC commemoration failed to mention their contributions. During the 1990s, computer programmer, lawyer, and documentary-maker Kathryn A. Kleiman delved into the history of ENIAC and brought the women's stories to light. After Kleiman released her research, the six female programmers were inducted into the Women in Technology International Hall of Fame. In addition, Holberton was awarded the Augusta Ada Lovelace Award, one of the highest honors a female computer programmer can earn. She was the only one of the six female programmers to receive the honor.

From the beginning, the women's contributions were downplayed. The most famous ENIAC publicity photo shows the women messing with plugs and switches while a male stands back, looking like a supervisor. Writing in the *Electronic Engineering Times,* Heyman noted that the women look like mere "switchboard operators" and that the image "contributed to the misconception that they were little more than low-level technicians who set up the machine according to the instructions of others."

In addition, when ENIAC developer Lt. Col. Herman H. Goldstine wrote his 1980 book on computer history—titled *The Computer From Pascal to von Neumann*—he discussed ENIAC but mentioned the women only in relation to the men they met and married while working on the project. Holberton met her husband, John Vaughan Holberton, while working on the project. They were married 51 years before her death and had two daughters.

Contributed to Emerging Computer Field

In 1946, Holberton joined the Eckert-Mauchly Computer Corp., which was founded by John Presper Eckert and John Mauchly, two of the ENIAC engineers. After the war, the men founded their own company to build computers for both commercial and military use and they were happy to have Holberton on board. At Eckert-Mauchly, Holberton helped develop the UNIVAC I, which stood for Universal Automatic Computer I. Holberton was involved with both software and hardware considerations for UNIVAC, which was unveiled in 1951. One of her most noted contributions to the project was an application she wrote called the Sort Merge Generator, a data-sorting program that was used in computers going forward. The UNIVAC revolutionized the business world with its ability to be programmed to help with payroll and inventory.

The U.S. government utilized the UNIVAC for the 1950 census. Holberton wrote a statistical analysis package to tabulate the census. While working at Eckert-Mauchly, Holberton also wrote an instruction code called C-10 that enabled the user to program the computer through keyboard commands instead of setting dials and switches. Holberton left Eckert-Mauchly in 1953 to work for the Navy's Applied Math Lab at the David Taylor Model Basin in Maryland. She worked as a supervisor of advanced programming until 1966, when she joined the National Bureau of Standards, where she stayed until retiring in 1983.

Over the course of her lifetime, Holberton made many contributions to the computing world. In 1959, she joined the committee that developed the computer language COBOL, which stands for COmmon Business Oriented Language. The language was unveiled in 1960 and remained the dominant language for business applications for the next 50 years. Holberton later helped write the standards for FORTRAN, another early computer language.

In all of her work, Holberton was concerned with making the computer easy to use. She figured computer use would take off only if the machines were simple to operate. Holberton came up with the idea of using alphanumerics in computer-programming codes so users could remember commands. For example, the use of "a" for add and "b" for bring. Holberton also insisted that control panels include a numeric keypad next to the keyboard. She also asked engineers to use gray-beige instead of black for the UNIVAC's exterior color. This became a standard computer color for decades to come.

Holberton died on December 8, 2001, in Rockville, Maryland. "Betty Holberton was a real software pioneer," Stanford University computer science professor emeritus Donald E. Knuth told the *New York Times* shortly after her death. Thanks to recognition by Knuth and Kleiman, Holberton's legacy lives on, serving as a role model for future generations of women in technology.

Periodicals

Computerworld, November 16, 1998.
Electronic Engineering Times, March 17, 1997.
New York Times, December 17, 2001.
Pittsburgh Post-Gazette, December 16, 2001.
Washington Post, December 11, 2001; May 10, 2003.

Online

"Computer Oral History Collection, 1969-1973, 1977," Smithsonian National Museum of American History, http://invention.smithsonian.org/downloads/fa_cohe_tr_bart730427.pdf (September 5, 2011).
"Frances E. Holberton Interview," Charles Babbage Institute, http://conservancy.umn.edu/bitstream/107363/1/oh050feh.pdf (September 5, 2011).□

Bertha Marian Holt

During the 1950s, American activist Bertha Marian Holt (1904-2000) helped revolutionize the manner of international adoption in the United States. With her husband Harry Holt, she established an Oregon-based adoption agency that found homes for thousands of children.

She became known as "Grandma" Holt, a nickname given with the greatest of affection, for Bertha Marian Holt demonstrated maternal care that helped connect homeless children from around the world with families seeking to adopt. Together with husband Harry Holt, she helped changed laws related to international adoption.

Her initial purpose was not to change perceptions and stigma related to adoption (even though that turned out to be one of her substantial accomplishments). Rather she wanted to bring more children into her large family (via adoption). The Holts had six of their own biological children but they wanted to bring eight more children (South Korean orphans) into their family. The Holts were compelled by a film that depicted the plight of American-Asian children who were conceived during the Korean War and then left abandoned. The couple believed Americans should be responsible for the care of the children, but they faced legal barriers. Eventually, they helped change American adoption laws, as well as public perception related to international adoption. Their efforts led to a congressional bill that made it easier to facilitate foreign adoptions. This bill was passed in 1955. A year later, the Holts would establish the Holt International Children's Services, based in Eugene, Oregon. Their enduring non-profit agency provides a broad range of child welfare services in many countries, and the Holt's efforts eventually helped more than 50,000 international orphans find a safe and secure place in American homes.

In 1999, the year before Bertha Holt died, the Oregon Legislative Assembly officially recognized her efforts. The Assembly passed a resolution to commend the ninety-five year old Holt for pioneering international adoption work. The resolution also noted Bertha Holt's skills as a photographer, researcher (she wrote four books) and athlete (in 1996, she set a world time record for her age group in the 400-meter dash). In their resolution, (as quoted on the official website), the Assembly wrote, "[We] pay tribute to this renowned woman and express our sincere gratitude to Bertha Marian Holt, on the occasion of her 95th birthday, for her continuing commitment to the welfare of children in Oregon and worldwide."

Born into a Large Family

Bertha Marian Holt was born in Des Moines, Iowa, on February 5, 1904. She was the fourth of nine children born to parents Clifford and Eva Holt. As theirs was a large family, the Holts had to work hard to make ends meet. When Clifford Holt was not teaching school, he worked as a mail carrier. To add to the income, the family also sold produce grown on their land.

In her hometown, Bertha Holt attended East High School and then she enrolled in the University of Iowa. A versatile individual, she studied nursing, liberal arts, and education. She received her nursing degree in 1926.

Married Harry Holt

The next year (on December 31) Bertha Holt married cousin Harry Holt, who worked as a wheat farmer in South Dakota. The couple settled near Firesteel, South Dakota, where they engaged in "custom farming," an activity where farmers work land owned by others in exchange for a portion of the crops. This only provided a meager income and, as such, the early years of their marriage were harsh. The hours were long and the work was hard. As the couple possessed no land, they lived in something called a "cook shack," essentially a very small house on wheels. During this period, the couple shared all of the hard work. At one point, while Bertha Holt was seven months pregnant she helped load wheat sacks onto a truck.

Thankfully, the hard work paid off. The couple was able to eventually purchase land. But they still faced a hard existence. Harry Holt had to build the house that they would live in. There, the couple raised their first four children. And conditions would become even severe during the Great Depression, which began with the stock market crash on October 29, 1929 and continued until the years preceding World War II. For farmers in the Midwest, the international economic calamity was accompanied by drought and resulting dust storms that devastated many farmers' crop production.

During this period, many farms went under, but Harry Holt sustained the family by purchasing flour mill equipment to bolster income. In addition, he used his farming equipment to mine lignite coal. Bertha Holt contributed to the family's income by becoming a midwife. And ever ready to do what was needed to be done to ensure his family's survival, Harry Holt engaged in midwifery, too (tutored by his wife).

When customers could no longer afford to buy the coal that Harry mined, the family decided to move on to a region that might offer better income opportunity. That took them to Oregon, specifically the Willamette River Valley, which offered a less harsh climate and more fertile soil. The Holts made the move in 1937, and this entailed allowing their house and farm to go to the state to help pay for owed taxes.

The Holts made their new home near Creswell, Oregon. Fortunately, they had family members in the area, and these relatives helped Harry and Bertha get back on their feet. Swallowing his pride, Harry borrowed $1,200 to buy a new house. Borrowing money was something he was loathe to do, but through sheer will and determination, he was able to pay back the loan with a year. In this new location, Harry deployed his farming equipment, and his old sawmill parts, to start a lumber business. It soon thrived, and he was able to hire a workforce that included more than fifty people.

Meanwhile, Bertha Holt gave birth to two more children; now the family included five daughters and one son. As Harry Holt's business grew, the parents of this large brood built a new and larger house, and Harry Holt expanded his business activities into new areas—including farming and commercial fishing (which entailed the purchase of a boat that would take them on business ventures as far north as Alaska).

Health Problems Invigorated Spiritual Values

The hard work and success did not come without a devastating personal price, however. After all of the worry, pressure and physical labor, Harry Holt suffered a heart attack.

Indeed, the attack was so severe that death seemed inevitable. As a degreed nurse, Bertha Holt understood the seriousness of the situation. In response to this health crisis, the couple turned to religious faith and prayer.

Both of their families had been religious, but with all of the hard work and worries that they endured, Bertha and Harry had allowed their spiritual values to lapse. But now they found a renewed commitment. As part of that, they recognized a personal mission. They found it in addressing the circumstances of orphans.

They perceived their mission in 1954, after they viewed a film about the Ameriasian children placed in Korean orphanages following America's involvement in the Korean War. The film was screened in a high school auditorium in Eugene, Oregon. Later, in one of her books about adoption, *The Seeds From the East*, Bertha Holt wrote: "We had never heard of such poverty and despair. We had never seen such emaciated arms and legs, such bloated starvation-stomachs and such wistful little faces searching for someone to care."

Initially, the Holts contributed money to the orphaned children's cause, which helped provide food and clothing, but they felt they needed to do more. The children, the couple believed, needed to be taken in by families. At the time, Bertha and Harry were more than fifty years old, and they had already had six of their own children. Still, they wanted to adopt eight Korean children, but federal law prevented families from adopting more than two foreign-born children. Then, in 1955, after the Holt's advocacy efforts, both houses of Congress passed the Bill for Relief of Certain War Orphans (this bill was also known as the "Holt bill"). This allowed the Holts to adopt four boys and four girls (with ages ranging from infancy to about four years old). Harry Holt had gone to Korea; meanwhile back home, Bertha Holt campaigned through letter writing, all the while taking care of the farm. In October 1955, Harry Holt returned to the United States with eight Korean adoptees.

One of the problems that the Holts faced was a prevailing attitude among the social work community: It had discouraged inter-country adoption. Traditionally, children were matched by color and ethnicity, in order to better conceal adoption. The Holts found that practice ludicrous. If a child needed a home, who cared who they were or where they came from, and what would it matter the adopting parent's nationality and race? Indeed, the Holts' adoption revolution would forever erase this attitude from the process. Moving forward, Harry Holt returned to South Korea to find children in need, and Bertha Holt worked to find families willing to take in children.

Expanding Commitment

As their commitment strengthened, the Holts wanted to do more than just change outdated laws and adopt their own children. Their perceived mission led them to establish the International Children's Services in 1956 (the organization has come to be known more simply as the Holt Agency). The Korean-American children were the first such large group to benefit. Later, the agency would serve all orphaned children throughout the world. The organization evolved into one that includes a network of "partner agencies" in many countries. It has benefited children and families in many countries including: Bangladesh, Belarus, Bolivia, Brazil, Cambodia, China, Colombia, Costa Rica, Ecuador, El Salvador, Guatemala, Honduras, Hong Kong, India, Korea, Mexico, Nicaragua, Peru, Philippines, Romania, Russia, Taiwan, Thailand, Ukraine, United States, and Vietnam.

Enduring Enterprise

Though Bertha and Harry Holt have passed away, their organization endures. Harry Holt died in April 1964 while in South Korea, still heavily engaged in his humanitarian activities. He suffered another heart attack, this one fatal. Some people thought that his death would bring an end to the agency he created with his wife. That proved not true. Bertha carried on, continuing to expand the agency's efforts.

Bertha Holt died on July 24, 2000. She was ninety-six years old. She was tireless up until her death. Indeed, her energy was underscored by her athletic activities. She was not only known as "Grandma Holt" but also as the "jogging Grandma." She ran a mile nearly every day. In 1996 she even set the world record for the 400-meter run in her age category. At the moment she died, she was engaged in her daily exercise regimen.

She remained mentally and physically active in late life. Her daily schedule included agency activities as well as prayer, Bible reading and exercise.

The Holts are remembered as a couple that willingly assumed liability for the children fathered by those who shirked responsibility, at first in Korea. Bertha Holt helped destroy the boundaries that attached stigma to adoption. When "Grandma Holt" died, former First Lady Hillary Rodham Clinton commented (as quoted from her *New York Times* obituary), "She championed the idea that love and a safe, permanent home could transcend differences of nationality, race and ethnic background."

Books

"Bertha Marian Holt," *Almanac of Famous People,* 10 edition, Gale Group, 2011.

"Bertha Marian Holt," *Biography Resource Center,* Gale Group, 2001.

Periodicals

The New York Times, August 2, 2000.

Online

"A Brief Historical Overview of the Life and Times of Harry and Bertha Holt and the Origin of International Adoption," *Transracialeyes.com,* http://transracialeyes.com/2011/08/11/a-brief-historical-overview-of-the-life-and-times-of-harry-and-bertha-holt-and-the-origin-of-international-adoption/ (November 25, 2011).

70th Oregon Legislative Assembly-1999 Regular Session, http://www.leg.state.or.us/99reg/measures/hcr1.dir/hcr0002.a.htm (November 25, 2011).

"Bertha Marian Holt," *Britannica Online Encyclopedia,* http://www.britannica.com/EBchecked/topic/712572/Bertha-Marian-Holt (November 25, 2011).

"The Legacy of Bertha 'Grandma' Holt," *HoltInternational.org,* http://www.holtinternational.org/historybg.shtml (November 25, 2011).□

Marilyn Horne

The American opera singer Marilyn Horne (born 1934) is considered one of the greatest mezzo soprano singers of the twentieth century.

Horne, wrote Terence McNally in the foreword to Horne's memoir, *The Song Continues,* "could sing anything. Not only could she sing anything, she could sing it well." Horne's range was enormous, and she often sang soprano roles in addition to those in the lower mezzo soprano range. And she was extremely versatile. Unlike most singers of her day, she enthusiastically performed operas of the Baroque era (from the early 1700s) and also commissioned new modern music. Immensely influential, Horne revived an entire type of singing, known as bel canto, performing operas that had fallen into obscurity as she began her career. Horne combined these accomplishments with an independence of spirit and strength of personality—she was, perhaps, a positive diva—that made her a beloved star wherever operas were staged.

Appeared at Rally at Age Four

Marilyn Berneice Horne was born in Bradford, Pennsylvania, on January 16, 1934. " Horne wrote in her book *The Song Continues,* "Our household was, with few exceptions, American Normal." It also might have been described as borderline poor; Horne was born during the heart of the Great Depression, and the extra income her father, Bentz Horne, made singing in local churches and a Jewish temple helped balance the family books. Horne's parents were both small-town political officials. They both loved music and encouraged their daughter's gifts. Horne sang recognizably at age two, made a public appearance at four at a campaign rally for President Franklin D. Roosevelt, and soon was accompanying her father at money-making gigs in Pennsylvania social halls and the like.

It was an appreciation of Horne's talent, combined with lack of money, that induced her family to attach a trailer to their aging Plymouth and head for Long Beach, California, in 1945. The Golden State, in those days, was renowned for its system of free public education, accessible to all. Horne graduated from Long Beach Polytechnic High School and gained experience in musicals and in local choruses, although she was turned down for a school chorus because her voice was too loud. Horne attended the University of Southern California (USC), a private school, and took several voice master classes with the German soprano Lotte Lehmann at the University of California at

Santa Barbara and the California Institute of Technology in Pasadena. After a rocky start in which Horne was publicly dressed down by Lehmann, the German singer became Horne's mentor.

In 1954 Horne made her operatic debut in a production of *The Bartered Bride,* a comedy by Czech composer Bedrich Smetana. The same year, her voice was dubbed over the screen singing of African-American actress Dorothy Dandridge in the film adaptation of the opera-musical fusion *Carmen Jones.* Wanting to get her feet wet in opera's European homeland, Horne spent three years as part of the resident company at the Gelsenkirchen Municipal Opera house in Germany. Among her roles there was that of Marie in the violent modern opera *Wozzeck,* and it was in that opera that Horne made her major-company American debut, with the San Francisco Opera, in 1960. She followed that up with an appearance at the Lyric Opera of Chicago in 1961, and her path to a top-flight operatic career seemed clear.

Broke Through as Last-Minute Sub

That year, a fortuitous event put Horne on a new path, one that perhaps turned her from a good singer into a great one. After a cancellation, Horne was tapped to sing the mezzo-soprano role of Agnese in a production of Vincenzo Bellini's opera *Beatrice di Tenda* at the American Opera Society in New York, opposite Australian soprano Joan Sutherland. *Beatrice di Tenda* was part of what is known as the bel canto (meaning "beautiful singing" in Italian) repertory, and at the time such operas had largely fallen out of fashion, supplanted by dramatically heftier fare by the likes of Giuseppe Verdi and Richard Wagner. But bel canto seemed tailor made for Horne's voice, enabling her to show off her clear, brilliant high notes in sparkling ornaments, her rich middle range, and her powerful lower register. For much of her career, Horne would be identified with the bel canto operatic repertory, especially with the operas of Gioacchino Rossini.

Horne scored a series of major triumphs around the operatic world in the 1960s. She appeared with Sutherland in a production of Rossini's *Semiramide* at the Covent Garden opera house in London, England, in 1967, and in 1969 she appeared in Rossini's *The Siege of Corinth,* an opera long thought essentially unsingable due to its difficulty, at the great citadel of Italian opera, the Teatro alla Scala in Milan, Italy. Horne rejoined Sutherland to make her debut at the Metropolitan Opera in New York in Bellini's *Norma* in 1970. She remained a lead singer with the Met until her retirement in 1996. Horne credited her vocal longevity to the fact that her father had warned her against trying to tackle difficult roles too quickly when she was young.

Horne notched these accomplishments in spite of an aspect of her personal life that caused controversy and indeed for the first part of her career was illegal in many parts of the United States: her husband, Henry Lewis, whom she met at USC and married in 1960, was African American. The couple raised one daughter, Angela. They divorced in 1976 but remained close. Lewis, a double bass player and conductor, was the first African-American member of a major symphony orchestra and also conducted the New Jersey Symphony Orchestra, becoming the first African-American conductor of a major American orchestra.

Performed Handel Operas

Although she was associated with bel canto roles, Horne fully exploited the range of her magnificent voice over the course of her career. In the early 1960s she was part of a circle of performers that revived the exotic Renaissance-era Italian madrigals of composer Carlo Gesualdo. She performed the Baroque-era operas of German-Italian-British composer George Frideric Handel as well as mainstream roles like that of Amneris in Verdi's *Aida*. She sang works of the late nineteenth century that required real vocal heft, such as Bizet's *Carmen* and the orchestral songs of Gustav Mahler. In 1991 she commissioned a new cycle of songs to texts by women poets by the contemporary American composer William Bolcom. In general, although opera has been a notoriously conservative art form, Horne was never afraid to perform new music. She retained an affection for the popular music with which she had grown up, and later in life she often performed Broadway standards and incorporated the Irish-American standard "Danny Boy" into her song recitals.

Horne's career corresponded with a productive period in the recording of opera, after the advent of the LP record made possible recordings of entire operas but before sales of major-label classical albums declined. Beginning with

an album called *The Age of Bel Canto* that she and Sutherland recorded in 1964 for the London label, her art was well documented on recordings. Her solo recital debut, *Presenting Marilyn Horne,* appeared the following year. Other highlights of her career included a pair of recordings made with Sutherland and tenor Luciano Pavarotti, one of Verdi's *Requiem* mass (1968) and one of his opera *Il Trovatore* (1977).

As she approached her retirement, which she announced in 1996, Horne began to look toward the future of classical singing. In 1994 she established the Marilyn Horne Foundation, which in 2010 became part of New-York's Carnegie Hall. The aim of the foundation was to help preserve the vocal recital, and in its first 15 years of existence it presented young singers in concerts that reached audiences numbering more than 100,000. Horne's foundation entered the Internet age with its "On Wings of Song" webcasts that introduced emerging singers.

Horne was also active as a teacher. She has directed the voice program at the University of the West in Santa Barbara, California, since 1997, and has given numerous master classes. Horne was diagnosed with pancreatic cancer in 2003 but successfully battled the disease and by 2009 had been fully cured. In 2008 Horne made a brief appearance in a concert presentation of the musical *Show Boat* in New York to benefit Carnegie Hall. Among her numerous awards were Kennedy Center Honors bestowed by U.S. President Bill Clinton in 1995. "Her voice," noted her Kennedy Center biography, "has been compared to [Vladimir] Horowitz's piano and [Jascha] Heifetz's violin, as well as to the most powerful forces in nature."

Books

Horne, Marilyn, and Jane Scovell, *Marilyn Horne: The Song Continues,* Baskerville, 2004.

International Dictionary of Opera, 1993.

Periodicals

National Review, November 1, 2008.

New York Times, March 24, 1991; March 16, 1997; January 18, 2009.

Ovation, July 1983.

Online

"Marilyn Horne," *Columbia Artists Management,* http://www.cami.com/?webid=224(November 21, 2011).

"Marilyn Horne," *Kennedy Center,* http://www.kennedy-center.org/explorer/artists/?entity_id=3744&source_type=A (November 21, 2011).□

J

Murray Jarvik

The American medical researcher and educator Murray Jarvik (1923–2008) was the co-inventor and primary force behind the development of the nicotine patch, a device that has helped many smokers defeat tobacco addiction.

Jarvik had a strong instinct for fields of medical research with wide public applicability, and prior to his work on the patch he made important discoveries in other areas. He was among the first scientists to formally demonstrate that cigarettes were indeed addictive, and that nicotine was the primary substance contributing to their addictive quality. Prior to that work, Jarvik became one of the first American scientists to investigate the hallucinogenic drug LSD. According to his University of California at Los Angeles obituary, Jarvik was "often called the 'dean of psychopharmacology' by students and colleagues alike." But it was the patch, for which Jarvik and his associates were granted a patent in 1990, that put the results of his investigations into pharmacies around the United States and the world.

Suffered Cardiac Impairment as Child

Murray Elias Jarvik was born in the New York City borough of the Bronx on June 1, 1923. He grew up in near poverty as the son of an upholsterer, Jacob Jarvik, but scientific originality clearly ran in the family. Jarvik's brother Daniel became a medical researcher and key collaborator; Robert Jarvik, the inventor of the artificial heart, was Jarvik's nephew; and Jarvik's son Jeffrey became a professor of neuroradiology at the University of Washington. Jarvik

himself won the Westinghouse science contest at George Washington High School; working with another student, he developed a wooden model of an iron lung. His achievement was all the more remarkable in that he had battled back from a case of rheumatic fever; contracted when he was 12, the disease left Jarvik with a lifelong heart murmur.

Jarvik earned a bachelor's degree at City College of New York in 1944, taking night classes and working his way through school with a job as a research assistant. Attracted by the West Coast, he moved to the University of California at Los Angeles for a master's degree the following year. At the University of California's main campus in Berkeley he pursued a dual MD-and-PhD degree in the late 1940s, a combination that was rare at the time. He was granted the PhD in 1952, taking medical classes at the University of California at San Francisco. Once again he financed his education with a series of lab jobs in California and, from 1951 to 1953, at Yerkes Labs in Florida. He again triumphed over illness; at the age of 28 he was diagnosed with polio.

After receiving his degree, Jarvik returned to New York to take dual jobs as a researcher at Mount Sinai Hospital and as a lecturer in physiological psychology at Columbia University. He was already interested in the links between the brain and physical manifestations of its chemical makeup, and his gifts as a researcher and conceptual thinker led him into a hot area of research: at Mount Sinai he worked on d-lysergic acid, a chemical closely related to lysergic acid diethylamide, or LSD. Discovered by a Swiss scientist in the 1940s, LSD had hallucinogenic qualities. Unbeknownst to Jarvik himself, the U.S. Central Intelligence Agency (CIA) had funded his research, hoping that the drug might serve as a truth serum that could be administered to spies captured from the Communist world.

Recruited LSD Test Volunteers

Jarvik placed ads in alternative newspapers, seeking volunteers for experiments, and "hippies would volunteer to be subjects. I gave them LSD and various psychological tests I had worked out," he wrote in a report for the National Institute on Drug Abuse, as quoted in his *New York Times* obituary. He also took LSD himself on occasion, although he was reluctant to discuss his usage of the drug in later life. LSD turned out not to have the psychotropic qualities the CIA was searching for, but Jarvik contributed to some of the first research papers documenting the drug's well-known psychedelic effects. Jarvik became an assistant professor of psychopharmacology at the Albert Einstein College of Medicine in the Bronx in 1955.

Jarvik's time at Mount Sinai was important in another way, both personally and professionally. It was there that he met intern Lissy Feingold; the two married in 1954 and had two sons. Although Jarvik never smoked and was strongly against smoking before that was a common position, Lissy was a heavy cigarette smoker who was unsuccessful in many attempts to quit. With his training in the then-young field of psychopharmacology, Jarvik was intellectually interested in his wife's addiction. "Murray was always asking, 'Why do people smoke?'" according to UCLA psychiatry researcher Richard Olmstead in *UCLA Newsroom*. Beginning at Albert Einstein College of Medicine, Jarvik set out to investigate the mechanics of tobacco addiction, becoming one of the first researchers to do so.

His method was straightforward: he taught monkeys to smoke. Jarvik and a colleague offered a cigarette smoke–like substance to monkeys through tubes on which they could suck, and within a few days the monkeys were smoking heavily. Observing them, Jarvik developed a paper, published in 1970, that ranked among the first solid scientific assertions of the addictive nature of cigarette smoking and of the role nicotine played in the process. The U.S. Surgeon General had already warned against the health dangers of smoking in a 1964 report, and the habit-forming qualities of tobacco usage were anecdotally known (the 1950s hit "Smoke! Smoke! Smoke!" observed that "nicotine slaves are all the same"), but Jarvik was a pioneer in subjecting smoking to rigorous scientific investigation.

Noted Illnesses Among Nonsmoking Farmworkers

In 1969 Jarvik became a full professor at Albert Einstein, but he was lured back to UCLA in 1972 by the offer of a post as professor of psychiatry and pharmacology. Bringing his research monkeys West, he spent the rest of his life at UCLA, and Lissy Jarvik also became a professor of psychiatry there. In 1977 he wrote the introduction to a National Institute on Drug Abuse tobacco study, noting (according to the *New York Times* obituary), "It is strange that people should go to such lengths to burn and then inhale some vegetable matter." Having made strides in understanding tobacco addiction, Jarvik began searching for a way to treat it. He worked closely with his brother Daniel and for a time with graduate student Jed Rose. The three noted that tobacco farm workers who harvested the crop sometimes suffered from a disease called "green tobacco sickness," even when they themselves did not smoke, and showed certain symptoms also characteristic of those experienced by cigarette smokers. The researchers hypothesized that the farm workers were absorbing nicotine through the skin.

This time Jarvik and his fellow researchers used themselves as guinea pigs, placing tobacco against their bodies and measuring the physiological effects. (They had been barred from carrying out human trials on others.) "Our heart rates increased," Jarvik was quoted as saying in the London *Independent*. "Adrenaline began pumping, all the things that happen to smokers." By 1990 Jarvik had developed a transdermal (skin-crossing) nicotine delivery system, dubbed the nicotine patch, for which he registered a patent through the University of California in 1990. The university licensed the device to the Swiss pharmaceutical firm Ciba-Geigy (now Novartis) in 1992, and in 1996 the patch became available via retail sales without a prescription.

Jarvik's only regret was that the patch, while helpful, was not universally successful in helping smokers to quit. He never fully succeeded, but made great strides in his stated goal of understanding why people become addicted to tobacco, and he was a pioneering figure who was inspiring to the students and colleagues who have carried his work forward. His natural spirit of good-humored curiosity was remarked upon by friends. Jarvik edited psychopharmacology publications, was a member of numerous professional organizations, and served as chief of psychopharmacology at the West Los Angeles Veterans Administration Medical Center. In 1992 Jarvik was diagnosed with lung cancer; the lifelong nonsmoker speculated that the disease had resulted from poor air quality in Los Angeles. With the help and care of his wife, he recovered. He died of complications from congestive heart failure in Santa Monica, California, on May 8, 2008, having told his friend, UCLA professor Samuel Barondes, that his accomplishments had greatly exceeded his own expectations.

Books

American Men & Women of Science, Gale, 2008.

Periodicals

Independent (London, England), May 17, 2008.

New York Times, May 13, 2008; May 16, 2008; May 22, 2008.

Seattle Post-Intelligencer, May 12, 2008.

Online

"Health Blog Obit: Murray Jarvik Studied LSD, Developed Nicotine Patch," *Wall Street Journal,* http://www.blogs.wsj.com/health/2008/05/13/(September 22, 2011).

"Obituary: Murray E. Jarvik, 1923–2008," *Nature,* http://www.nature.com/npp/journal/v33/n13/full/npp2008168a.html (September 22, 2011).

"Obituary: Murray E. Jarvik, 84," *UCLA Newsroom,* http://www.newsroom.ucla.edu/portal/ucla/obituary-murray-e-jarvik-85-ucla-50218.aspx (September 22, 2011).□

K

Oscar Kambona

Oscar Kambona (1928–1997) was a leading figure in the African liberation movement of the 1950s and served as Tanzania's minister for foreign affairs as the southern African nation took its place on the world stage in the early 1960s. Later that decade he and Tanzanian president Julius Nyerere became locked in an ideological power struggle as Nyerere moved to establish a uniquely African version of socialism, and Kambona was forced into exile.

Son of Anglican Minister

Oscar Salathiel Kambona was born on August 13, 1928, in a village called Kwambe on the shores of Lake Nyasa, one of the three main bodies of water that border the southern African nation that adopted the name "Tanzania" in 1965. On its western border is Lake Tanganyika, and neighbors Kenya and Uganda share access to Lake Victoria in the north. At the time of his birth, his homeland was the British Trust Territory of Tanganyika and had come into British hands after the end of World War I, when a defeated Germany was forced to hand over its East African colonies.

Kambona came from a family of schoolteachers of the Luo ethnic group, and his father David was one of the first ordained black Anglican clerics in the Anglican Church of Tanganyika. Kambona attended St. Barnabas Middle School in Liuli and went on to the Alliance Secondary School the larger city of Dodoma. As a teenager he won a spot at the elite Tabora Boys' Senior Government School, a British-run institution designed to train young men for careers as civil servants in Tanganyika and other parts of British East Africa. Its students were culled largely from the children of local "headmen," or village chieftains. Kambona's father had been a headman in Kwambe, and the school had also provided an education for Julius Nyerere, whose father had been a Zanaki chief in a northern province.

Nyerere was six years older than Kambona and already working as a teacher in Tabora when the two met. Both became involved in an emerging nationalist movement established by young men like themselves who had benefited from phenomenal educational opportunities in British-ruled Kenya, Uganda, and Tanganyika. Kambona, Nyerere, and their counterparts in Eastern Africa chafed at the preferential treatment British colonial authorities gave to Indian and Arab residents of the region, which had been a multicultural trading hub for centuries.

Married in London

Kambona was active in the Tanganyika African Association, which Nyerere headed after 1953. Nyerere politicized the organization into the beginnings of a genuine political party, the Tanganyika African National Union (TANU), and its membership ranks swelled over the next few years. A confluence of fortuitous factors helped Tanganyika achieve independence from Britain without war or any bloodshed. The first step toward self-rule was the 1958–59 general election, followed by another round of balloting in August of 1960. Nyerere became chief minister after TANU candidates once again outpolled the other parties in the 1960 contest. Following terms of the deal hammered out with Britain, Tanganyika achieved independence on December 9, 1961, with Nyerere becoming the first prime minister of the newly independent nation.

175

Kambona was the first minister for education in Tanganyika's new post-colonial era, and then Nyerere's minister of home affairs. Considered to be Nyerere's most trusted confidante at home, he was also well known in the wider liberation movement across the continent. His minor celebrity even reached Britain, when in November of 1960, three months after the general election, Kambona appeared in the society pages of the August *Times* of London. The occasion was his wedding to Flora Moriyo, a 20-year-old Tanganyikan studying in Britain, and they were the first black couple ever to be married at St. Paul's Cathedral, the London landmark.

Tanganyika became the Republic of Tanganyika in December of 1962, a year after independence, and Nyerere was elected its president. Kambona served in Tanganyika's National Assembly from a seat assigned to a representative of the Morogoro East constituency in south-central Tanganyika. During these years Nyerere reorganized the TANU party and began promoting his new policy of *ujamaa*, a Swahili word that means familyhood.

Because the transfer of power in Tanganyika had been so comparatively uneventful, many British stayed on, along with Asian and Arab residents, who made up the majority of the merchant and civil service sectors. Tensions emerged, however, as a new black leadership asserted its legitimacy and standing in the new order. In 1962, when Kambona was home affairs minister, Nyerere's government began issuing 24-hour deportation notices. One of the first notable ones was imposed upon a British manager of a hotel in Dar es Salaam, the capital city, who had complained about a group of patrons in the hotel bar. Among the noisemakers was the new black mayor of Dar es Salaam. A year later, in 1963, Kambona was ushering the president of Guinea, Sékou Touré, through a hotel in Arusha, a major city in Tanganyika's north. Within hours the

hotel was ordered to close indefinitely. "When we came into the hotel, an attitude of mind showed up, and we thought it was time we showed an example," Kambona told *New Yorker* writer William Edgett Smith in a 1971 article. "One thing an African will never stand for is this lack of dignity accorded him as a human being."

Headed OAU Liberation Committee

President Nyerere was one of the leading figures at an important conference in Addis Ababa, Ethiopia, that resulted in the formation of the Organization of African Unity, or OAU, in May of 1963. A few months later, Kambona—now the country's minister of external affairs and defense—became the first chair of the OAU's Liberation Committee. Its mission was to bring majority rule to all nations on the continent. At the time, Portugal still clung to its overseas territories of Mozambique and Angola, and the British had established a timetable for independence for its holdouts in Rhodesia, Nyasaland, Gambia, and some sections on the border of South Africa.

In July of 1963 Kambona spoke to the press in Dar es Salaam following the inaugural meeting of the OAU Liberation Committee, confidently telling reporters that the British timetable was unacceptable and the OAU's Liberation Committee would consider deploying "all the means at its disposal" to move forward, according to a *Times* of London article. When asked by reporters if that meant the use of military might, Kambona replied, "When the British failed to reason with Hitler what did they do?"

Calmed Nation and Avoided Coup

Kambona was involved in a curious event that occurred in January of 1964. On the night of January 19–20, the First Battalion of the Tanganyika Rifles mutinied at Colito Barracks in Dar es Salaam. Formerly known as the King's African Rifles during the colonial era, the regiment consisted of African soldiers serving under British officers; the soldiers demanded higher wages and an acceleration of the Africanization process for black candidate officers. Nyerere and the vice president, Rashidi Kawawa, went into hiding, and it was left to Kambona to negotiate with mutineers, who at one point threatened to shoot him.

Over the next few hours Kambona arranged for British officers and their families to be evacuated safely, then delivered a radio broadcast on Monday. "This is your Minister of External Affairs and Defense," he told the nation, according to the *New Yorker* article. "There has been some misunderstanding between the Africans and the British officers in the Tanganyika Rifles. At my intervention, the soldiers have now returned to Colito Barracks." "It was the greatest rupture of public order in Dar es Salaam's history," wrote James R. Brennan in an article for the scholarly journal *Africa* many years later. "As Nyerere re-emerged and began negotiations with the mutineers, rumours swirled that the Police Field Force Unit was set to mutiny as well. Facing a complete security breakdown, Kambona and Nyerere agreed to call in British military assistance to restore law and order," Brennan continued. "Several shops were looted the following day, and in total some fifty people, many of them Arab shopkeepers, were killed in popular violence.''

In the days that followed, one British newspaper, the *Daily Mirror,* ran alarmist stories about Kambona's role, hinting he may have instigated the coup himself. Kambona filed a libel suit against the newspaper and its publisher in May of 1964. ''The article described him as Moscow's Boss in East Africa,'' reported the *Times* of London, ''and suggested that he was a communist agent...and that he was attempting to undermine the position of Mr. Nyerere.'' Though Nyerere had commended Kambona for his bravery, he removed him from the post of Defense Minister that same month, returning to him the portfolios of home affairs and education.

Broke with Nyerere

Kambona turned up in international news again in November of 1964 when he held a press conference asserting that the United States and Portugal were planning a joint attack on Tanzania, which had moved to unite with the Indian Ocean island nation of Zanzibar earlier that year. In December of 1965 Nyerere's government boldly broke off diplomatic ties with Britain for the latter's failure to act over the stalemate in Rhodesia, which had made a Unilateral Declaration affirming both independence from Britain and white-minority rule, copying South Africa's odious policy of denying the African majority their political rights.

After these events Nyerere moved closer to China, a hard-line Communist state, and in February of 1967 made his dramatic Arusha Declaration. This formally turned Tanzania into a one-party, TANU-ruled state; it also called for the nationalization of all industries and proposed a rapid shift to the agricultural cooperatives. Another crucial element of the Arusha Declaration was the imposition of strict party discipline on all members of government, who were given a timetable to divest themselves of any other sources of income; they were expected to live on a modest government salary as a way to forestall corruption and graft.

Kambona resisted the Arusha Declaration as too sudden a swerve toward socialism, fearing it would lead to social unrest and, ultimately, foreign intervention. In a June 1967 cabinet reshuffle, he was demoted to minister of local government and rural development, a post he held for just two days before tendering his resignation from Nyerere's cabinet. He was also forced to step down from his post as TANU's secretary-general.

Fled to England

In late July of 1967 Kambona drove across the border to Kenya with his wife and three children, then boarded a London-bound plane in Nairobi. Nyerere's government claimed he had sent thousands of dollars overseas during an 18-month period between June of 1965 and December of 1966, hinting that Kambona may have had access to funds donated by other African states in his role as chair of the OAU's Liberation Committee. From London, Kambona became one of Nyerere's most vocal critics. In 1970 he was charged in absentia with treason for a 1969 plot to assassinate Nyerere and return to power in a coup.

Nyerere remained in power for many years, and though his vision of ujamaa did little to improve Tanzania's economy, it did result in notable gains in literacy and health care. But the president stayed in office and was firmly resistant to political opposition. In February of 1982 a group of Tanzanian militants hijacked a flight that originated in Dar es Salaam and was bound for London. Members of the Tanzanian Revolutionary Youth Movement held 83 passengers hostage at Stansted Airport—Essex and requested that Kambona negotiate on their behalf. He persuaded the four hijackers to release the hostages and turn themselves in. Though he disagreed with the use of terrorism, Kambona told the media that Nyerere's anti-democratic regime forced such actions. ''The only way open to draw world attention to the plight of our people, who have suffered at the hands of a cruel dictator for a long time,'' he told *Times* of London journalist David Cross. Nyerere finally stepped down in 1985.

Kambona returned to Tanzania in 1993 on a special passport issued by the United Nations in a bid to resurrect his political career, which was unsuccessful. He returned to London, where he died in July of 1997.

Periodicals

Africa, Spring 2006.
New York Times, November 20, 1960.
New Yorker, October 23, 1971; October 30, 1971.
Times (London, England), November 21, 1960; December 9, 1961; July 6, 1963; May 15, 1964; January 5, 1968; March 5, 1982.□

Tamara Karsavina

Russian dancer Tamara Karsavina (1885–1978) was one of ballet's leading lights in pre-revolutionary Russia. The prima ballerina of St. Petersburg's Imperial Ballet, she went on to an esteemed career with Serge Diaghilev's famously daring Ballets Russes in Paris in the years just before World War I. Karsavina rode out the tumult of the 1917 revolutions for a few months before escaping to England, where she lent her expertise to the dance company that would become the Royal Ballet. Her 1978 *New York Times* obituary deemed her ''the first modern ballerina,'' wrote dance critic Anna Kisselgoff. ''She was the first Firebird, the first Ballerina-Doll in 'Petrouchka' [and] cast a spell over the public with the expressiveness of every movement.''

Tamara Platonovna Karsavina was born into a world of minor privilege and modest affluence in St. Petersburg on March 10, 1885. Her father, Platon Karsavin, was a professional mime and principal dancer with the Imperial Ballet, formed more than a century before in the cultural capital of Russia. By the time of Karsavina's

birth, the royal dance company, housed inside the grandly baroque Imperial Maryinsky Theatre, was world-famous and attracted some of the leading artists of Europe to its stage and affiliated academy. Her father eventually retired and became a master at that school.

Because he knew firsthand the rigors a career in dance demanded, Karsavina's father was reluctant to let his daughter take lessons as a child. But he eventually took over her instruction in the family's home, which was in the fifth-floor apartment of a building overlooking one of St. Petersburg's numerous canals. Karsavina grew up with a gifted brother named Lev who went on to an esteemed career in academia. Both were under the care of the family's longtime servant, a Russian peasant woman named Douniasha.

Accepted into Elite School

Karsavina later wrote a memoir of her life before the 1917 revolution, *Theatre Street: The Reminiscences of Tamara Karsavina*, which yields fascinating details about the Imperial Ballet and its famously tough school. She was nine when she was first accepted as a pupil in 1894, and ten when she began at its even more demanding boarding school, where a rigid discipline ruled every aspect of the youths' lives. The students marched in formation to meals, recited Russian Orthodox prayers before bed, and refrained from ever questioning the perfectionism demanded of them by their ballet masters. Early on, Karsavina was singled out as one of the more exceptionally talented students, and was even chosen to perform at the 1896 coronation of Tsar Nicholas II.

Debuted in 1902

The Imperial Ballet was full of intrigues and professional backstabbing. Karsavina's father had turned up on the enemies list of the school's formidable director, Marius Petipa, and was forced out. Karsavina's mother pushed for her

daughter to be allowed to graduate a year early and turn professional, as the family now needed a source of income. On May 1, 1902, Karsavina made her professional debut on the stage of the Maryinsky a few weeks before her graduation. She was allowed the special honor of dancing a *pas de deux* in the final act of the Camille Saint-Saëns ballet *Javotte* on the closing night of the ballet season. Her teacher, she recalled in *Theatre Street*, "made the sign of the Cross over me at the first notes of introduction and hurried to watch me from there. My parents and Lev were in the audience. Douniasha came with them, but had to be led out on account of her loud sobbing when she saw me."

Karsavina was fortunate to enter the second, higher-salaried rank of the Imperial Ballet, the coryphée dancers, and in her memoir recounted the dramas and intrigues surrounding the publication of the *Journal of Orders*, which listed new role assignments and even fines levied against dancers for various infractions. Her first lead came as *Giselle*, one of the best-loved ballets of the era, and she soon emerged as one of the two star ballerinas of the Imperial Theater along with Anna Pavlova. As a form of entertainment, the ballet had few rivals among St. Petersburg's elite. Season tickets for the premier boxes were virtually impossible to obtain, while the pit and gallery seats of the theater were filled with young men with a stalker-level interest in the ethereal, attractive dancers. They waited outside the stage doors, or sent endless gifts to their homes, but the cosseted atmosphere of ballet school had, in Karsavina's case, succeeded in instilling in her a deep fear of any moral transgression that would blight her name. Not all of the school's graduates followed suit: many became the mistresses of wealthy and powerful noblemen. During Karsavina's first years as an Imperial Ballet dancer, the *prima ballerina assoluta* was the famous Mathilde Kschessinska, who had been the mistress of the tsar before his marriage.

Tsarist Russia's first stirrings of unrest came in early 1905, in the aftermath of the disastrous Russo-Japanese War. There was tremendous resentment in the Empire against Nicholas's absolutist rule and a growing clamor for political reform. The entire year was marked by a series of strikes and unrest, and even the dancers at the Imperial Ballet walked off the job. Karsavina was among the committee of twelve elevated by the striking dancers to serve as delegates to the tsar to request some management reforms. But she confronted a more formidable authority first when her mother learned of her participation in the strike. "So you are in arms against the Emperor who gave you an education, position, means of livelihood," Karsavina recalled her mother fuming, in *Theatre Street*.

Joined Ballets Russes

Once order was restored across Russia, several of the dancers suffered professional repercussions, and at this point a few stars began defecting to ballet companies in Europe or even lucrative solo engagements across the globe. Karsavina was close to one of the top Russian male dancers, Michel Fokine, who began choreographing independent productions for her and for Pavlova. This led to her involvement in the legendary Ballets Russes, which had its formal premiere in Paris in May of 1909. The new company was the genesis of several currents in St. Petersburg artistic circles, and aimed to create a new form of Russian national ballet that blended folk elements with modern stage sets, costumes, and choreography. Its mastermind was Serge Diaghilev, who had served as assistant to the director of the Imperial Ballet for several years. Fokine was involved, as was Pavlova and Vaslav Nijinsky, one of the most exciting and athletic male stars to come out of the Imperial Ballet School.

Karsavina recounted the excitement of preparing for the debut performance of the Ballets Russes in Paris on May 19, 1909. The opening night program at the Théâtre du Châtelet featured selections from the opera *Prince Igor* and two original ballets by Fokine, *Pavilion d'Armide* and *Le Festin*. In *Festin* Karsavina danced a newly choreographed version of the *Bluebird Pas de Deux* from *Sleeping Beauty* with Nijinsky, remembering, "It seemed to me that the hitherto quietly admiring mood of the public burst into enthusiasm when a pas de trois with Nijinsky, his sister and myself was about halfway through," she wrote in *Theatre Street*. There was one particular moment when Nijinsky finished a part and should have exited the stage to return for a solo, but instead he leapt away. "No one of the audience could see him land; to all eyes he floated up and vanished. A storm of applause broke; the orchestra had to stop." A little while later the orchestra would have to temporarily halt again after an explosion of applause for Karsavina's solo.

Karsavina awoke the next morning as a celebrity in Paris. The next five years were the apex of her career, and she enjoyed *premiere danseuse* (prima ballerina) status at the Imperial Ballet after 1910 and stardom abroad as one of the top three dancers with the Ballets Russes under Diaghilev. In her 1911 debut at London's Covent Garden opera house with the Ballets Russes, England's King George V and Queen Mary were present in the royal box.

Witnessed Revolution

Fokine originated several roles for Karsavina, among them the Doll in *Petrushka,* a ballet with music by Igor Stravinsky, and another Stravinsky epic, *L'Oiseau de Feu* (The Firebird), considered one of the classics of this period of the Russian-Paris avant-garde axis. With other Ballets Russes members she moved in elite circles among the titled aristocracy and literary demimonde of London and Paris. She married a Russian named Vassily Moukhin, who worked for the Imperial Ministry of Finance, but fell in love with Henry James Bruce, a British diplomat posted to St. Petersburg, and married him in 1915 after divorcing Moukhin. Their son Nikita was born a year later during the worst years of World War I, when the Tsar's blundering decisions in both battle and on the home front of the war against Germany eventually forced the end of centuries of Romanov dynasty rule.

Preceding that event, however, was the murder of a favored but uncouth Russian Orthodox monk named Grigori Rasputin, who had enormous influence over the hapless tsar's wife, the Empress Alexandra. Rasputin, who had peasant origins, greatly revolted some members of the

Russian imperial court and they plotted to murder him. The slaying took place at the Moika Palace, which at the time was the home of the powerful Yusupov family. Karsavina had socialized many times with Prince Felix Felixovich Yusupov, the ringleader of the assassination plot, and first heard word of Rasputin's death via the maid Douniasha, who had been informed by the milkman early in the morning. Karsavina was devastated when Douniasha was struck and killed by a car in front of their home a few months later.

Karsavina was performing in Kiev when she learned of the February 1917 revolution and the abdication of Nicholas. She wrote in her memoir that she returned to St. Petersburg and watched as flames consumed several key buildings over the following nights, also noting that in the first days of the tumult only a few private homes had been looted, Mathilde Kchessinska's among them. Vladimir I. Lenin would later proclaim the new Soviet regime from Kchessinska's balcony during the second revolution later in 1917, commonly referred to as the October Revolution.

Karsavina was elected president of the newly formed workers' committee at the Maryinsky, where she tried to balance rehearsals with a stream of paperwork. When her brother Lev was arrested and detained, he was asked why he had been corresponding with foreigners. He replied that the letters had been to his sister when she was in Europe for performances. "'*You* are the brother of Karsavina!'," his questioner exclaimed, she wrote in *Theatre Street*. "The Commissar veered round in his revolving chair. '*Giselle* is her best part, don't you think?'"

Worked with Royal Ballet

Karsavina was fortunate to have married Bruce, for his diplomatic contacts helped her leave the country. The journey was perilous and took several weeks, but she was able to return to the London stage in 1919 in revivals of famed Ballets Russes works, *Carnaval* and *Schéhérazade*. She made her American debut in 1924 at Carnegie Hall and was involved with the Ballets Russes again in the late 1920s, though its era of creative brilliance ended with the death of Diaghilev in 1929.

A year later Karsavina teamed with a new group of dancers and choreographers in London that called themselves the Ballet Club. It was later known as the Ballet Rambert and then secured royal patronage to become the Royal Ballet. Karsavina spent many years working with its dancers and as a founding member of the Royal Academy of Dance; she trained both Margot Fonteyn and Rudolf Nureyev, among other twentieth-century greats, and was revered as the direct link back to the glory of both the Imperial Ballet and Diaghilev's Ballets Russes. On her eightieth birthday in 1965, the British Broadcasting Corporation honored her with a television special. She died thirteen years later at the age of ninety-three in Beaconsfield, Buckinghamshire, England. Like a generation of Russian émigrés, she never returned to Russia. Her brother Lev managed to settle in Lithuania and continued his career as a professor, but the Baltic republic later came under Soviet control and he died in a Siberian prison camp in 1952.

Books

Garafola, Lynn, *Diaghilev's Ballets Russes,* Oxford University Press, 1989.
Karsavina, Tamara, *Theatre Street: The Reminiscences of Tamara Karsavina,* with a foreword by J.M. Barrie, E. P. Dutton, 1931, pp. 141, 191, 240, 330.
"Tamara Karsavina," in *International Dictionary of Ballet,* Gale, 1993.

Periodicals

New York Times, November 2, 1924; May 27, 1978; May 28, 1978.
Times (London, England), June 24, 1912; June 5, 1919; March 10, 1965. □

Carole King

American singer-songwriter Carole King (born 1942) is known as one of the most successful females ever to work in the music industry. She has written dozens of number one singles, won numerous Grammy Awards, and her album, *Tapestry* is among the highest selling recordings of all time.

Carole King was born Carol Klein on February 9, 1942, in Manhattan, New York. Her father, Sidney Klein, was a former firefighter turned insurance salesman and her mother was a school teacher. Soon after her birth, the family moved to Brooklyn, where they would live throughout her childhood. Carol began taking piano lessons when she was four years old. Her talent and love of music were immediately obvious and she spent many hours at the family piano playing Russian classics and popular show tunes.

Changed Her Name

King's childhood was both challenging and loving. Her younger brother, Richard, was born deaf and severely mentally disabled. Her parents were unable to care for him and he was sent to live in an institution. The strain of this situation caused her parents to divorce when she was barely a teenager, something that rarely happened in the 1950s. Despite these circumstances, her parents were loving and supportive. They encouraged her to play music and develop her talents. When she was fourteen, she decided that her surname, Klein, was too ethnic-sounding for a career in the spotlight. According to Sheila Weller, author of *Girls Like Us,* she wanted to change it to something that still began with the letter K and was still only one syllable. She and a girlfriend went through the phone book until they found something that met those criteria and was ethnically generic. "King" fit the bill. Around the same time, Carol decided to add an 'E' to the end of her first name to make it more unique. Thus, Carol Klein became Carole King.

King wrote songs throughout her adolescence. She started her first band, the Co-sines, in high school. By the time she graduated, she was a regular on the Tin Pan Alley scene—an area of Manhattan where songwriters worked. In 1958, she began attending Queens College. There she met Gerry Goffin, a chemistry student who became her songwriting partner. The two married in 1960 and had two daughters together. Soon after they met, they joined the Aldon Music Company. It did not take long before they had their first number one hit, *Will You Still Love Me Tomorrow,* which was performed by the Shirelles. *The Encyclopedia Judaica* reported that a string of hits followed including *He's a Rebel* for the Chiffons, *The Locomotion* for Little Eva, *Go Away Little Girl* for Steve Lawrence, *Up on the Roof* for the Drifters, *Take Good Care of My Baby* for Bobby Vee, *I'm Into Something Good* for Herman's Hermits, *Natural Woman* for Aretha Franklin, and *Pleasant Valley Sunday* for the Monkees. King and Goffin also wrote *It Might As Well Rain Until September* during this time period, which King herself recorded. It broke the top twenty on the pop charts. In all, the songwriting duo of Goffin and King wrote over one hundred hits.

King and Goffin were among the most sought songwriters of the 1960s. According to Rachel Louise Snyder in a *Salon.com* article, "Goffin and King came from an era when performers rarely wrote their own material, but relied heavily on songwriters to provide them with hit singles." She goes on to quote Jon Landau who wrote in *Rolling Stone,* "The Songs of Goffin and King are superb examples of the songwriting craft of the '60s. Finely honed to meet the demands of the clients who commissioned them, and written with the requirements of AM radio always firmly in mind, they still managed to express themselves in a rich way." As a result of their undeniable talent, they became an inspiration to many up and coming artists who wanted to not only sing hit songs but write them, too. The *St. James Encyclopedia of Popular Culture* wrote, "Goffin and King made standard pop formulas seem fresh and alive. Though they wrote in a small office around the corner from the Brill

Building, their melodies and lyrics were expansive: simple but original, memorable and timeless... In 1963 John Lennon and Paul McCartney stated their ambition to be the British Goffin and King."

Divorced Goffin

In the late 1960s, King and Goffin divorced. Recognizing that more and more recording artists were beginning to write their own songs, King moved to the Laurel Canyon area of Los Angeles, California with her two daughters. Once there she immersed herself in the music scene which was dominated by singer-songwriters such as James Taylor, Joni Mitchell, Bob Dylan, and the Eagles. Taylor later wrote of that time, as quoted by Snyder, "Those were remarkable days in Laurel Canyon. Exceptional was commonplace. The record industry was a labor of love in the service of music. It was a hoot." Soon after arriving in California, King met Charles Larkey, a bassist who would become her second husband and the father of her third daughter and only son. Together with Danny "Kootch" Kortchmar, they formed a band called the City. Their only album, *Now That Everything's Been Said,* was unsuccessful, but served as a catalyst for King's solo career.

Released First Solo Album

In 1970, King released her first solo album, *Writer,* produced by Lou Adler for the Ode label. It was only moderately successful, but laid the foundation for what would become one of the best-selling albums of all time, *Tapestry.* In her book, *She's a Rebel: the History of Women in Rock and Roll,* Gillian G. Gaar stated, "*Writer,* in addition to featuring new material, also had King digging back into her own songbook, as she would do on her subsequent albums, including a version of *Goin' Back,* previously recorded by the Byrds, and *Up on the Roof,* recorded by the Drifters. The album made little impression on the charts, but the stage had been set for *Tapestry,* which King recorded with many of the same musicians who had played on *Writer* and with Lou Adler again serving as producer."

Released Successful Album *Tapestry*

Tapestry was released in 1971, at the same time King began touring as an opening act for James Taylor. Notorious for giving in to fits of stage fright—one of the reasons for *Now That Everything's Been Said*'s lackluster success was King's inability to tour—King worked hard to overcome her fears. It paid off. Noting the album's phenomenal success, Snyder writes, "*Tapestry,* released in February 1971, spent 15 weeks in the No. 1 spot on Billboard's chart and stayed in the top 100 for six years. By the end of 1971, *Tapestry* was still selling 150,000 copies per week and had scored four top 10 hits; while a complete accounting of its sales has never been made, it remains one of the biggest-selling albums of all time." Snyder goes on to write, "Upon the record's release, *Rolling Stone* critic Landau wrote: 'It is an album of surpassing personal intimacy and musical accomplishment. Every note reminds you that *Tapestry* is not the work of pop star hacks diddling around in the studio to relieve

their own boredom. Carole King is thoroughly involved in her music; she reaches out towards us and gives everything she has.''

A critical and commercial success, *Tapestry* earned four Grammys. The album itself won for Album of the Year, the song *It's Too Late* won for Record of the Year, *You've Got a Friend* won for Song of the Year, and King was awarded Best Pop Female Vocalist. She did not attend the award ceremony, an act many attribute to her problem with stage fright. After *Tapestry,* King released six more albums on the Ode label. Several of them earned Gold Records and one of them, *Wrap Around Joy,* included the song *Jazzman* which went to No. 1 on the charts. None of them were met with nearly the same success as *Tapestry,* however.

Left Record Label

This was a turbulent time for King both professionally and personally. In 1976, she divorced Charles Larkey. That same year she met Rick Evers, a drifter with very little going for himself. None of her peers approved of the relationship, but Carole fell deeply in love with Evers, which influenced her career choices. Weller comments on the effects of King's relationship with Evers when she writes, "It was obviously awkward for Carole's colleagues and friends to so strongly dislike someone she was clearly madly in love with, and her need to be out of their view may have led to what, in December 1976, the *Los Angeles Times* called a 'surprise move': Carole left Lou Adler's Ode label and signed with Capitol Records." Evers became King's musical partner in addition to her third husband.

Lost Third Husband to Overdose

The couple moved to Idaho and began living a communal lifestyle with several other people. Despite regularly traveling back to LA to continue their musical endeavors, King and Evers saw very little success. Frustrated, Evers became increasingly dependent on drugs and was often witnessed behaving violently towards King and others. In March 1978, while King was in Hawaii, he was found dead of a drug overdose. King was devastated and returned to Idaho, where she would live for several years.

Continued to Make Music

King was not entirely reclusive during this time, though. She met and married her fourth husband, Richard Sorensen. She embraced environmental causes, concentrated on raising her two youngest children, and continued to make music. She released several albums, did a brief stint in an off-Broadway play, and made a few television appearances. In 1987 she and Gerry Goffin were given a Lifetime Achievement Award by the National Academy of Songwriters. In 1990 they were inducted in the Rock and Roll Hall of Fame. In 2004 the National Academy of Recording Arts and Sciences honored them with the Grammy Trustees Award. King received an Oscar nomination for her song, *Now and Forever* which was written for the 1992 film *A League of Their Own.* In 1994, she played the lead in the

Broadway play *Blood Brothers.* In 2010, King joined her longtime friend James Taylor on the Troubadour Reunion Tour. It was hugely successful, selling out venues across the United States. They also released a companion CD *Live at the Troubadour* which earned a Gold Record.

A reluctant star, King's career is nonetheless a remarkable showcase of her musical talent. Snyder summed up the impact of King's success when she wrote, "Even today, mention Carole King to a teenager—someone born long after *Tapestry*—and the name may not be familiar. But sing a line or two, and she'll sashay down the street, humming the familiar tune like it's as true and timeless as the earth itself."

Books

Beloff, Ruth, *Encyclopedia Judaica,* Keter Publishing House, 2007.

Gaar, Gillian, *She's a Rebel: The History of Women in Rock and Roll,* St. James Press, 2000.

Pendergrast, Sara, and Pendergrast, Tom *St. James Encyclopedia of Popular Culture,* Atria Books, 2008.

Weller, Sheila, *Girls Like Us,* Atria Books, 2008.

Periodicals

Contemporary Musicians, December, 18, 1991.

Online

Snyder, Rachel Louise "Will you still love me tomorrow," http://salon.com/people/feature/199/06/19/king/index.html (June 5, 2011). □

King Curtis

American saxophonist King Curtis (1934–1971) was one of the most influential horn players and studio musicians of the 1950s and 1960s.

American saxophone player Curtis "King" Ousley, better known by his stage name of King Curtis, was one of the most popular session musicians of the 1950s and 1960s. His saxophone playing was featured on songs including The Coasters' "Yakety Yak" and Aretha Franklin's "Respect," as well as on his own solo tracks such as "Soul Twist," "Soul Serenade," and "Games People Play," for which he won a Grammy Award in 1969. Over the course of his career, Curtis played at some of the leading jazz venues in the United States and appeared at the respected Swiss Montreaux Jazz Festival. He also recorded commercial and novelty music, and wrote the theme song for the New York City public television program *Soul.* By the time of his murder in 1971, Curtis—long respected by his musical peers—had also begun to attract popular audiences who had long heard the sounds of his saxophone without necessarily knowing who the artist was. He remained a well-regarded musician long after his death, and was inducted into the Rock and Roll Hall of Fame in 2000.

Played on Numerous Popular Songs

Born Curtis Ousley on February 7, 1934, in Fort Worth, Texas, Curtis was the adopted son of guitarist William Ousley and his wife, Ethel. Growing up in Mansfield, Texas, Curtis developed an early interest in jazz saxophone music after hearing a performance by musician Louis Jordan on the radio. The young boy was also drawn to the sounds of players like Lester Young and Red Connor. Curtis's parents gave their son his first alto saxophone as a gift for his eleventh birthday, and before long the budding musician had also began picking up skills on the tenor saxophone. Although Curtis began dabbling in the baritone saxophone during his time playing the school band at I.M. Terrell High Scholl in Fort Worth, the tenor saxophone became his preferred instrument. Inspired by the "honkers and screamers" of the Texas jazz music scene, Curtis honed his skills across the popular genres of the day, delving into jazz, R&B, pop, and the emerging rock and roll format.

Even as a teenager, Curtis displayed both a high level of talent and a drive to make a living as a musician. He started his first band at about the age of 15, and soon began leading the group in performances at Fort Worth's Paradise Inn. Soon, the musician was also playing at parties and dances around town, and as high school wound to a close he received scholarship offers from Bishop College and Wyley College. When he was 18 years old, a visit to family in New York City gave Curtis the chance to enter amateur music competitions at Harlem's famed Apollo Theater. By then beginning to use the name "King Curtis," he took the top spot on two occasions and cut some recordings with the Doc Pomus All Stars and the Doc Kent Band. Back in Texas, Curtis attracted the attention of renowned jazz bandleader and vibraphonist Lionel Hampton, who invited the young saxophonist to play with his orchestra. Curtis signed on and toured with the outfit for less than a year before Hampton and Curtis parted ways. Settling in New York City, Curtis began studying with jazz player Garvin Bushell and performing at various jazz and R&B gigs around town.

Curtis's music career took flight in New York as he established his own jazz trio, allowing him to indulge his interest in long-form experimental musical pieces. He soon realized that the appeal of this style of jazz was limited to a relatively small audience, however, and decided to make the shift to the more popular rock and rhythm and blues sounds of the time. As a result, his saxophone playing developed into what Howard Rye termed "an intense, full-toned, muscular style" in Curtis's *American National Biography Online* entry. This intensity combined with the sharply syncopated beats of the musician's playing—and a general uptick in the popularity of the saxophone solo as a central component of rock and roll tunes—made him a highly sought-after studio musician as the 1950s wore on. He appeared on studio cuts of tracks such as "A Lover's Question" by Clyde McPhatter and "What Am I Living For" by Chuck Willis. The best-known of Curtis's musical contributions of this era, however, was certainly the bouncing saxophone solo of the Coasters's 1958 hit "Yakety Yak." The song cruised to the top of both the *Billboard* R&B and pop charts in the summer of that year, helping bring Curtis's playing to millions of avid listeners' ears.

Cut Solo Recordings

By the late 1950s, Curtis's live performances in New York City had helped him win the attention of record producer Bobby Robinson, who helped the saxophonist hone his own solo tracks. The musician first found significant solo success with the 1962 instrumental single "Soul Twist." Featuring the saxophonist backed by his group, the Noble Knights—later known as the Kingpins—the track climbed to the top of the *Billboard* R&B charts and hit number 17 on the mainstream pop listings. This success of this track helped the musician gain more high-profile slots, including a stint on tour with rhythm and blues singer Sam Cooke, and helped him land a recording deal with Capitol Records. Over the following months, Curtis released a few albums, the most successful of which was the 1964 *Soul Serenade*. Led by a single of the same name, that LP enjoyed moderate success on the *Billboard* R&B charts. Curtis, however, was unhappy with Capitol and made the jump to Atlantic Records a year following *Soul Serenade*'s release.

Atlantic proved a happier home for the saxophonist, who had begun exploring the new sounds of soul music. He played with some of the era's finest soul performers, including Aretha Franklin, Donny Hathaway, Don Covay, and Roberta Flack. As a solo artist, Curtis recorded the 1966 single "Memphis Soul Stew" and the 1967 track "Ode to Billie Joe," both of which achieved some success with R&B audiences. In 1965, Curtis and his group opened for the Beatles at their famous Shea Stadium show. Around this time, Curtis began singing and playing guitar on his recordings; he also took up playing the saxello, an instrument closely related to the soprano saxophone. Yet his distinctive tenor saxophone wail remained his signature.

Speaking to John S. Wilson of the *New York Times* in 1969, Curtis explained that he emulated the style of a vocalist in his instrumental performances. "I can take a record by a singer, and I can play the identical vocal version on my horn, with the little passing thing—the passing notes—that singers do. Listening to the singer, I get the soul feelings. But in playing the songs, I still play me," he added. "It turns out to be something that people think is different."

During the late 1960s and early 1970s, Curtis's career continued to thrive. In 1969, he won a Grammy award in the Best R&B Instrumental Performance category for the song "Games People Play," which appeared on that year's album *Instant Groove*. Along with the Kingpins, he played at clubs around New York, and on his own formed a lucrative music publishing business. He became Franklin's musical director and led the Kingpins as her studio backing band. In 1971, he toured with Franklin in Europe; on this trip, he played and recorded at the annual Montreaux Jazz Festival in Switzerland. Back in the United States later that summer, he recorded some solo saxophone pieces for John Lennon's *Imagine* album, worked as the musical director for the public television program *Soul*, polished tracks for his planned studio album *Everybody's Talkin'*, and continued producing artists for Atlantic.

Career Interrupted by Murder

This rise came to a sharp end when Curtis met an unexpected and violent end at the height of his career. On the hot night of August 13, 1971, the musician was taking an air conditioning unit to an apartment building where he lived on Manhattan's West Side. When he arrived, Curtis discovered some men on the steps of the building; some sources suggest that the men may have been using drugs at the time. An altercation arose between the musician and one of the men, Juan Montanez, although the exact cause remains unclear. In the course of the fight, Montanez produced a knife and stabbed Curtis in the chest. Curtis managed to remove the knife and stab Montanez four times before collapsing from his wound. Montanez left the scene by the time police arrived, and Curtis was taken to Roosevelt Hospital. He died there soon after from his injuries. While police were investigating the attack, they discovered that another man had been admitted to the same hospital at about the same time with stab wounds; that led them to Montanez, who was also severely injured. Unlike Curtis, however, Montanez recovered from his wounds. He later stood trial and was convicted for the crime.

The saxophonist's death generated an immediate response from musicians and music listeners alike. New York radio stations began playing retrospectives of Curtis's work almost immediately upon the news of his death. "King Curtis," observed Murray Schumach in the musician's *New York Times* obituary, "was even more highly regarded by his fellow musicians than by his large public following." Indeed, numerous musical luminaries formed part of the estimated 2,000 mourners who paid their respects to the saxophonist's memory at Curtis's New York City funeral, held at St. Peter's Lutheran Church a few days after his death. The Kingpins performed several variations of the Curtis hit "Soul Serenade," and both Franklin and Stevie Wonder sang as part of the service. The musician was later interred at Pinelawn Memorial Park in Long Island, New York. He was survived by his long-estranged wife, Ethelynn, and an eleven-year-old son.

Curtis's death did not, however, end his music career. His final new album, *Live At Fillmore West*, had been released just a week before his murder. Called "a brilliant confirmation of the saxophonist's place in popular music" by Jim Smith of the *Allmusic Guide*, the album climbed to the number three position on the *Billboard* Jazz Albums chart and broke the top ten of the organization's R&B Albums charts in the wake of the performer's murder. Reissues of his albums and new compilations appeared decades after his death. Among these, critics generally consider *Instant Soul: The Legendary King Curtis* to be the most definitive and interesting collection of his solo songs. In 2000, Curtis received a major posthumous accolade when he was inducted into the Rock and Roll Hall of Fame. Although Curtis's notoriety faded somewhat over time, he retained a loyal fan base among jazz fans and musicians who flocked to his skillful playing and distinctive interpretation of rock and R&B sounds, and critics have attributed his influence to the sounds of famous muscians such as The Band and Bruce Springsteen.

Books

Contemporary Black Biography, Gale, 2011.
Contemporary Musicians, Gale, 1996.

Periodicals

New York Times, February 5, 1969; August 15, 1971; August 19, 1971.

Online

"Curtis, King," *American National Biography Online,* http://www.anb.org, (November 20, 2011).

"King Curtis Biography," *Rock and Roll Hall of Fame and Museum,* http://rockhall.com/inductees/king-curtis/bio/ (October 4, 2011).

"King Curtis: King of the Yakety Sax," *Texas Heritage Music Foundation,* http://www.texasheritagemusic.org/special_stories/Texas_Stories/King%20Curtis.pdf (October 4, 2011).

"Live at Fillmore West," *Allmusic Guide,* http://www.allmusic.com/album/live-at-fillmore-west-r42295 (December 1, 2011). □

Andrei Kolmogorov

The Soviet Russian mathematician and educator Andrei Kolmogorov (1903–1987) made groundbreaking discoveries in many areas of mathematics during a long career lasting through the middle years of the twentieth century.

At the top of Kolmogorov's accomplishments was his work in the field of probability theory, which he largely organized into its modern form. "He was one of the very greatest mathematicians," New York University professor Peter Lax told James Gleick of the *New York Times.* "He was to probability theory what Euclid was to geometry." But Kolmogorov's work was notable for its breadth as well as its depth; he made important discoveries in almost every area of mathematical inquiry and solved several longstanding problems in the field. After decades, his name is still attached to numerous mathematical theorems and processes.

Spotted Mathematical Pattern at Five

Andrei (or Andrey) Nikolaevich Kolmogorov was born in Tambov, in central Russia, on April 25, 1903. His parents were not married; his mother, Mariya Yakovlevna Kolmogorova, was passing through Tambov when he was born, and died in childbirth. Kolmogorov was raised by his mother's sister, Vera Yakovlevna Kolmogorova, who was said to have instilled in him a habit of independent thinking. Not much is known of his father, Nikolai Kataev, except that he was an agricultural scientist who was killed in World War I. Vera Kolmogorova and another sister were schoolteachers, and Kolmogorov received a good education at their school. His unusual talents were first noticed at age five, when he pointed out a pattern involving sums of ascending series of odd numbers (such as 1+3+5+7) that generate a series of whole numbers that are square roots of those sums.

The Kolmogorov family had some land holdings, but after the Russian Revolution of 1917, Kolmogorov had few resources and took a job as a train conductor. He also wrote a paper about Isaac Newton and read a book called *New Ideas in Mathematics,* gaining enough knowledge of the field to win admission to Moscow University in the fall of 1920. Conditions after several years of chaos in Russia were primitive, and Kolmogorov and other students attended class in unheated classrooms and subsisted on a semester's ration of 16 kilograms of baked bread and one kilogram of fat. He did not immediately decide to major in mathematics, making significant discoveries in the field of early Russian history while still in his first years as an undergraduate.

By his sophomore year, however, Kolmogorov had already made independent discoveries in his mathematics classes and had attracted the attention of the university's mathematics faculty, which at the time included several famous figures. Among them was Nikolai Luzin, whose followers were dubbed Luzitania. Under Luzin's direction, Kolmogorov made a discovery in the field of Fourier analysis (a branch of trigonometry) that attracted international attention and was one of the first major achievements of Soviet mathematics. By the time he graduated in 1925, Kolmogorov had already published papers and discovered an operation in mathematical logic that continues to be known as the Kolmogorov function.

Published Groundbreaking Probability Treatise

Kolmogorov managed to stay on at the university in research posts until 1929, and by that time he had completed the draft of one of his most influential pieces of writing, the German-language *Grundbegriffe der Wahrscheinlichkeitsrechnung* (Foundations of Probability Calculation). That book, once dubbed the New Testament of Mathematics by one of Kolmogorov's colleagues, was published in Berlin in 1933. Kolmogorov was named professor at Moscow University in 1931, and from 1937 onward he held a special chair in probability theory. Between 1930 and 1940, he published some 60 papers in that field, laying out its basic modern precepts in a systematic and fundamental way.

Contrary to stereotypes of mathematicians as pale, office-bound scholars, Kolmogorov was always active outdoors. His long and productive collaboration with mathematician Pavel Alexandrov began (after Kolmogorov took some courses with the older scholar as an undergraduate) with an 800-mile boat trip the two took on the Volga River in a rented boat in 1929, bringing a folding writing desk with them for mathematical work en route. The two later acquired a large country house in Komarkova, turning it into a kind of informal mathematical research center that was open to colleagues and students. Mornings at this *dacha* would begin with a walk as long as 30 miles, but later in the day alcoholic drinks were copiously provided by Kolmogorov himself. Kolmogorov married Anna Dmitrievna Egorova in 1942; the pair had no children.

Kolmogorov was inducted into the Soviet Academy of Sciences in 1939 and explored an astonishing variety of mathematical questions over the next two and a half decades. Some of it consisted of showing ways that his discoveries in probability theory could be applied to practical scientific and engineering problems. During World War II, he contributed to the Soviet resistance against Germany's invasion by calculating the maximally effective deployment of barrage balloons (balloons intended to damage bombers by colliding with them and thus defend a city against aerial attack) and by applying statistical methods to artillery fire. His probability theories have also been applied to the study of epidemics.

In 1900, German mathematician David Hilbert listed a set of twenty-three unsolved problems in mathematics. Some still remain unsolved, but Kolmogorov made substantial contributions to solving two of them. The probability axioms introduced in his 1933 *Grundbegriffe* were relevant to the Sixth Problem, which dealt with the reducibility of physical phenomena to axioms. And in 1957, Kolmogorov took the most important step in solving the 13th, which dealt with the solution of seventh-degree equations; he showed that Hilbert was incorrect in postulating that a certain proof pertaining to the functions and variables involved was required. Later mathematicians have elaborated on Kolmogorov's work, which he considered the most important he did as a mathematician.

Worked in Many Fields

Probability theory and the issue of Hilbert's 13th Problem by no means marked the extent of Kolmogorov's mathematical endeavors. He made important contributions to mathematical logic, topology, set theory, functional analysis, and many other fields—virtually every branch of mathematics except for number theory. His work on fluid dynamics had wide general applicability, and the Kolmogorov-Arnold-Moser theorem pertaining to stability in physical systems has had wide use in astronomy and physics. A colleague said that to those around Kolmogorov it seemed as though his brain was in constant intensive operation. It was said that any single sentence from his writings could become the basis for a PhD dissertation, and indeed the students Kolmogorov trained, and their students in turn, kept the Soviet Union in the forefront of mathematical research until the country ceased to exist in 1991.

Despite his unusually long and fertile career, Kolmogorov believed that it was impossible for a mathematician to do significant research after age 60, and in 1963 he retired from active mathematical research. For the next 20 years he taught high school at a mathematical boarding school at the University of Moscow known as the Kolmogorov School, also lecturing on literature and other arts. He was active on Soviet boards and commissions working to set national mathematics curricula, and he wrote geometry, algebra, and analysis textbooks for high school students. He continued to teach at the college level at the University of Moscow as well, and beginning in 1983 he was the editor of the journal *Russian Mathematical Surveys*.

Adding to the magnitude of Kolmogorov's accomplishments was the fact that many of them were made during periods when Soviet scholars were largely cut off from their colleagues in the West. In later life, however, he began to receive international recognition. He won the International Bolzano Prize in 1963, contributing much of the prize money to a Moscow statistics library. In 1959, during a thaw in Soviet-American relations, he was inducted into the American Academy of Arts and Sciences in Boston, and he subsequently received honorary degrees and joined prominent scholarly societies in the United States and western Europe. He won the Lenin Prize in 1965 and earned other top Soviet civilian honors. After his death in Moscow on October 20, 1987, one of his obituaries was signed by Mikhail S. Gorbachev, the Soviet leader.

Books

Notable Mathematicians, Gale, 2008.

Periodicals

New York Times, October 23, 1987.
Times (London, England), October 26, 1987.

Online

"Andrey Nikolaevich Kolmogorov," *History of Mathematics* (University of St. Andrews, Scotland), http://www-history.mcs.st-andrews.ac.uk/Biographies/Kolmogorov.html (November 4, 2011).

"A Short Biography of A.N. Kolmogorov," *Centrum Wiskunde & Informatica* (Netherlands), http://www.homepages.cwi.nl/~paulv/KOLMOGOROV.BIOGRAPHY.html (November 4, 2011). □

Stanley Kramer

American filmmaker Stanley Kramer (1913-2001) produced and directed memorable motion pictures characterized by their socially conscious themes. His films were described as having a strong "message," and he tackled subjects such as race relations.

Filmmaker Stanley Kramer developed a reputation as someone not afraid to tackle emotionally charged and controversial issues. Race relations were a recurring theme in the films he either produced or directed in the 1940s, 1950s, and 1960s. His body of work also dealt with nuclear devastation, juvenile delinquency, religious intolerance, and the threat of fascism.

In Kramer's obituary published in *The New York Times* in 2001, Rick Lyman wrote, "[Kramer] began as a passionate Wunderkind, an independent producer eager to shake up the status quo with a string of socially conscious films in the early 1950's that raised many of the issues... that mainstream film companies were often too timid to explore."

Kramer's films helped move important issues to the forefront of the collective American consciousness, but film critics often complained of Kramer's heavy handed, and simplistic treatment. He was viewed as a "message filmmaker," but Kramer preferred to think of himself as just a storyteller—and some of his "stories" were the most powerful placed on celluloid. For instance, *The Defiant Ones* (1958) is considered one of the most provocative indictments of racial prejudice. Still, Kramer would concede that his characteristic approach came with a sacrifice. "Looking back," he once commented, as quoted in *Authors and Artists for Young Children,* "I think most [of my films] were too ambitious to qualify as true art."

In other words, his works were cinematic equivalents of pamphlets. To communicate a message, Kramer often found it necessary to compromise aesthetics for the sake of story, but that doesn't mean his work excluded powerful symbolism. One of the most potent images in film history occurred when Sidney Poitier's black hand reached out to grab Tony Curtis' white hand in *The Defiant Ones.* It is an unforgettable scene. Further, Kramer also knew how to underscore his visual imagery with music. In *On the Beach* (1959), he orchestrated an Australian bush song ("Waltzing Matilda") to forceful effect. People would never hear that old song the same way again.

Critics may have often been harsh, but the public certainly loved his films. Despite critical complaints—and the occasional box office flop—Kramer's body of work garnered significant recognition. He produced and/or directed thirty-five films, and the best of these were nominated for eighty-five Academy Awards and won fifteen. Even though Kramer never received an Academy Award for best director, in 1962 he received the Academy of Motion Picture Arts and Sciences' Irving G. Thalberg Award, which honors filmmakers and actors for consistent high quality of work.

Abandoned by Father

Stanley Kramer's film work displayed a high level of compassion, which most likely resulted from his youth. He was born on September 29, 1913, in New York City, in a section known as Manhattan's "Hell's Kitchen." His father abandoned the family before Kramer ever had a chance to know him, a situation that solidified his relationship with his mother, Mildred Kramer, and his maternal grandparents. This extended, but male-deprived, family resided in close quarters: a one-bedroom apartment. A daughter of poor immigrants, Kramer's mother secured a job at Paramount Pictures' branch in New York City, a job that helped Mildred create a warm and loving home life.

While times were hard, Mildred Kramer still managed to instill positive values in her son. A New York City boy, Stanley Kramer became involved in street gangs, which was a simple matter of survival. The experience taught him about racism, however, and the young Kramer wondered why there was a problem with transgressing racial barriers—an attitude that would inform his later film work.

Rapid Rise through Educational Ranks

As Kramer's family was poor, his mother instilled in him the value of education, and Kramer rapidly rose through the city's educational system. Indeed, the system fostered fast advancement, allowing the best students to skip grades and quickly graduate. Kramer was only fifteen years old when he left DeWitt Clinton High School and entered New York University (NYU). He studied business administration and graduated when he was nineteen years old. While this rapid rise is admirable, Kramer felt it robbed him of his youth. But this didn't embitter him. Rather, he translated his experience, both street and schooling, into his later film work.

Kramer graduated from NYU in 1933 with a business degree, but his scholastic activities included writing for the school's literary magazine (*Medley*), which turned his face toward the wind—and to career possibilities not typically available to a street kid. Kramer wanted to apply his writing talents to film, so he traveled to Hollywood. He was still only nineteen years old.

His early screenplays were rejected, and he worked at low-level jobs such as set construction at Twentieth Century-Fox. But his intellectual gifts and efforts were rewarded with a research job at Metro-Goldwyn-Mayer (MGM), the studio regarded as the best in Hollywood. This then led into a position as an apprentice writer. The busy and ambitious Kramer would then assume roles as a senior script editor, film editor, and staff writer for radio programs (he contributed material to programs such as "Lux Radio Theater" and the "Rudy Vallee Show"). He also wrote screenplays for Columbia and Republic Pictures, which at the time were considered "B" or lower level studios.

His ambition did not go unrewarded: In 1942, MGM brought him back to work as an executive assistant for producer David L. Loew on a film called *The Moon and Sixpence,* based on the novel by W. Somerset Maugham. It was a plum assignment, but Kramer's career was interrupted by the untimely World War II.

Became an Independent Producer

The war did not prove to be a career detour, however. Because of his civilian experience, Kramer was placed in the U.S Army Signals Corps, the military branch involved in communications. He helped make training and propaganda films. This army experience added to his resume, as it taught him how to quickly make small films on a limited budget.

In 1945, Kramer returned to civilian life and Hollywood, as a producer. In 1947, he started Screen Play Incorporated, an independent film company. Kramer's first two films were based on stories written by Ring Lardner (which he purchased) and included *So This is New York* (1948) and *Champion* (1949), which starred a young Kirk Douglas. The latter was a brutal and powerful drama about professional boxing, and it was a hit with both the critics and audiences. The film earned an Academy Award for editing. Kramer followed up in the same year with *The Home of the Brave,* which was a film with an ironic title, as it dealt with racism in the United States military. This film, too, was both a critical and commercial success.

Fast-forwarded into the 1950s

The 1950s would be a strong decade for Kramer, and he started off with *The Men* (1950), which depicted the lives of soldiers who were crippled in battle. It starred Marlon Brando, and it was one of that famous actor's early film roles. That same year, Kramer married actress Ann Pearce (they would have two children before divorcing in 1962).

In 1951, Kramer gave up running his own company to join Columbia Pictures, a move that would provide him with bigger budgets and better projects. Films made during this period included *Death of a Salesman* (1951), a film adaptation of Arthur Miller's famous play; *The Sniper* (1952), a minor but vivid drama that predated later films about serial killers, and *The Member of the Wedding* (1952), another film based on a successful play (and written by Carson McCullers).

In his arrangement with Columbia Pictures, Kramer would produce several of his most notable films, including *High Noon* (1952), the famous western starring Gary Cooper as a sheriff who single-handedly engaged in a street fight with a band of outlaws. The film is now considered a classic, and Cooper won an Academy Award for best actor. At the time, the film generated some controversy, as some people (including actor John Wayne) viewed it as a negative allegory about McCarthyism.

In 1954, Kramer made another movie that generated criticism and controversy, *The Wild One,* starring Brando as the leader of a motorcycle gang that terrorized a small town. It was the first-ever "biker" movie, which would become a popular film genre in the 1960s and early 1970s. Also that year, Kramer made *The Caine Mutiny,* which provided Humphrey Bogart with one of his best film roles (as "Captain Queeg," a neurotic naval officer whose idiosyncratic behavior provoked a mutiny and subsequent military trial that resulted in a surprising conclusion).

Started Directing Films

By the middle of the decade, Kramer would start directing as well as producing movies. His first two directed films were a pair of his lesser known efforts: *Not as a Stranger* (1955), a soap opera-ish hospital melodrama starring Robert Mitchum and Frank Sinatra and *The Pride and the Passion* (1957), a film about the movement of a large cannon across rugged terrain during the Napoleonic-Era wars. The narrative would seem to have lent itself well to cinematic treatment, but despite big name stars (Cary Grant, Sinatra, and Sophia Loren) and an ample budget, it was major failure with critics and moviegoers alike.

Kramer responded to that artistic disaster by making one of his most successful and best known films in 1958. *The Defiant Ones,* another cinematic essay about racial prejudice, told the story of two escaped convicts, one black and one white (portrayed by Poitier and Curtis), who are chained together at the wrist. For Kramer, it was his personal favorite of all the films he made. Poitier was nominated for an Academy Award.

Kramer followed this with an equally powerful film that dealt with an entirely different subject: the end of civilization resulting from nuclear fallout. *On the Beach* (released in 1959 and based on Nevil Shute's novel) is a haunting film, as it depicts a world that comes to an end not with a bang but with a whimper. Unlike Stanley Kubrick's later—and equally disturbing— *Dr. Strangelove* (1964), Kramer's film does not conclude with explosions of mushroom clouds. Rather, it depicts the last remnants of human society, gasping a last breath as nuclear fallout chokes out life, and gathering in Australia, a last sanctuary before modern apocalypse sets in. The main characters face the inevitable, but what helps make this film so powerful is that some characters seriously consider, and even commit, suicide rather than waiting for the world's end.

The way the subject matter is handled is as haunting as Kramer's usage of the Australian folk song "Waltzing Matilda." At one point in the film, the song is represented as a barroom anthem (sung by beer drinking and boisterous soldiers who know that they are soon going to die); later, it serves as a heavily orchestrated background theme that underscores the fatal relationship of the film's stars (Gregory Peck and Ava Gardner). Indeed, the song provides the film with an audio motif—in the movie, it is never heard the same way twice—that matches the film's somber, black-and-white cinematography. One complaint that critics had is that Kramer ended the film with a bold "message": a final scene that shows a banner, after all humanity is presumably dead, that reads "There is still time, brother" —an endpoint punctuated by a loud and brassy musical coda. Subtlety, which characterized the film, was suddenly tossed out of the window. Critics may have felt that Kramer concluded the film with his typically heavy hand, but United States government officials were disquieted. They felt that Kramer had alarmed the public (which, of course, was Kramer's intention).

Into the '60s and Into Decline

Kramer entered the 1960s with two more highly regarded films. The first, *Inherit the Wind* (1960), was an adaptation of the 1955 Jerome Lawrence/Robert Edwin Lee play that fictionalized the 1925 Scopes "Monkey" Trial, which involved the teaching of evolution in public schools. It was another Kramer "message" film, and it starred Spencer Tracy (as a lawyer based on Clarence Darrow), Fredric March (as a politician/lawyer based on William Jennings Bryan), and Gene Kelly (portraying a journalist based on H.L. Mencken). The second film, *Judgment at Nuremburg*

(1961), depicted the Nazi war crime trials, and it featured an all-star cast including Tracy, Maximilian Schell, Marlene Dietrich, Burt Lancaster, Judy Garland, Richard Widmark, and Montgomery Clift. Anyone who was anybody in the film world wanted to play a role, no matter how small, in this film. But Kramer had only so many roles he could accommodate.

In his next major work, however, a rare foray into comedy titled *It's a Mad, Mad, Mad, Mad World,* Kramer had enough room for anyone who wanted to get involved. Stars included Tracy, Sid Caesar, Edie Adams, Phil Silvers, Milton Berle, Buddy Hackett, Ethel Merman, Dick Shawn, Terry Thomas, Mickey Rooney, Jonathan Winters, Dorothy Provine, and Jim Backus. But one of the things that makes the film so remarkable—and so enjoyable for film buffs—is that Kramer loaded the movie with supporting and cameo appearances by a roster of Hollywood's most beloved funnymen and funny women, including Joe E. Brown, Andy Devine, Selma Diamond, Leo Gorcey (of the Dead End Kids, the East Side Kids, and the Bowery Boys), the Three Stooges, Jimmy Durante, Buster Keaton, Zasu Pitts, Jack Benny, Jerry Lewis, and Don Knotts. Indeed, one of the most enjoyable elements of the film is recognizing the familiar faces as they crop up in various scenes. Also, for this 1963 release, Kramer utilized the new Cinerama technology (which would prove too unwieldy for most movie theaters to adopt).

In 1962, the Academy of Arts and Sciences presented Kramer with the Irving G. Thalberg Award for "consistently high quality in filmmaking." Kramer's next, and last, major work was *Ship of Fools* (1965), an adaptation of Katherine Anne Porter's novel, another film that featured a large cast. It took place right before World War II, and the plot involved a luxury liner headed to Germany with a passenger list that included both Jews and Nazi sympathizers. But it was downhill from there. He did direct *Guess Who's Coming to Dinner,* and this 1967 film (which starred Tracy, Poitier, and Katherine Hepburn) proved popular, but critics complained that Kramer handled a serious theme—interracial marriage— in preachy, simplistic fashion. Meanwhile, in 1966, Kramer married Karen Sharpe four years after his divorce from his first wife. The couple had two daughters.

Before his retirement, Kramer made a series of unsuccessful films including *The Secret of Santa Vittoria* (1969), *RPM* (1970), and *Bless the Beast and the Children* (1971). The latter included all of the cornball platitudes that characterized "social conscious" pictures that came to the fore in the 1970s. It was a pop soda polemic designed for a pop-culture audience, and the gulf between this movie and something like *The Defiant Ones* was immeasurable. The best of a bad lot of later films was *Oklahoma Crude* (1973), which starred George C. Scott and Faye Dunaway. This was then followed by two more critical and commercial disasters: *The Domino Principle* (1976) and *The Runner Stumbles* (1979), which is regarded as an unmitigated disaster.

Became an Educator and Writer

In 1980, Kramer retired from filmmaking and moved to Seattle, Washington, where he kept himself busy teaching, writing a newspaper column, and working on his autobiography (which was eventually released in 1997 and titled *A Mad, Mad, Mad, Mad World: A Life in Hollywood.*

Despite the failure of later films, Kramer remained well-regarded. In 1991, he received the Producers Guild's David O. Selznick Award and the Lifetime Achievement Award from the American Foundation for the Performing Arts.

During the 1990s, Kramer's health declined. He suffered from diabetes and spent his last years in Motion Picture and Television Actors Hospital in Woodland Hills, California, a long-term care facility. There, he died on February 19, 2001, due to complications related to pneumonia. He was eighty-seven years old.

During his career, he was nominated for nine Academy Awards (six as a producer and three as a director) but he never won one. Still, he was fondly remembered by the actors he worked with, and audiences flocked to most of his movies.

Books

"Kramer, Stanley Earl" *The Scribner Encyclopedia of American Lives,* Vol. 6: 2000-2002. New York: Charles Scribner's Sons, 2004.

"Kramer, Stanley E.," *Encyclopedia Judaica.* Michael Berenbaum and Fred Skolnik, eds. 2nd ed. 22 vols. Macmillan Reference USA, 2007.

"Stanley Kramer," *Authors and Artists for Young Adults, Volume 86,* Thomson Gale, 2006.

"Stanley Kramer," *International Dictionary of Films and Filmmakers, Volume 2: Directors* 4th edition, St. James Press, 2000.

Periodicals

The New York Times, February 1, 2001.

Online

Official Website & Library of Stanley Kramer, http://www.stanleykramer.com/ (December 1, 2011.

"Stanley Kramer," *TCM.com* http://www.tcm.com/tcmdb/person/105309%7C141975/Stanley-Kramer/ (December 1, 2011.□

Ellen Kuras

American cinematographer and director Ellen Kuras (born 1959) has shot films with some of the late twentieth and early twenty-first centuries' leading directors, including Martin Scorsese, Spike Lee, and Michel Gondry.

Ellen Kuras was one of the few women working as directors of photography in the late twentieth and early twenty-first centuries. A busy cinematographer who shot numerous documentaries and feature films after entering the field in the 1980s, Kuras was an Academy Award nominee and an Emmy Award winner for her directorial debut, the 2008 documentary *The Betrayal.* Kuras's cinematography helped define the looks of films including

Michel Gondry's *Eternal Sunshine of the Spotless Mind,* Spike Lee's *Summer of Sam* and *Bamboozled,* and Martin Scorsese's Rolling Stones documentary *Shine a Light.* In 1999, Kuras became a member of the American Society of Cinematographers; less than a decade later, she was featured in the documentary *Women Behind the Camera.*

Drawn to Creative Activities

A native of New Jersey, Kuras was born on July 10, 1959. Although her family did not have a particularly artistic bent, other than an aunt who dabbled in amateur photography, Kuras was drawn to certain creative ventures. She acted in local theater productions and dreamed of becoming a sculptor. "I never really thought about it until recently," she told Bob Fisher in an interview posted on the International Cinematographers Guild website, "when someone had asked what I had wanted to be when I was a kid, and I realized that I had always dreamed of working with my hands, of wanting to shape something textural, luminous." She went on to connect this idea to her adult work. "For me, when you're lighting someone, or lighting the space, the ideas revolve in part around sculptural forms. It's about three-dimensionality." Kuras was also active in team sports such as softball, basketball, and field hockey, which helped shape her leadership abilities and develop the teamwork skills needed to work with a crew.

After graduating from high school, Kuras enrolled at Brown University in Providence, Rhode Island, to study Egyptology. Although the subject matter fascinated Kuras, she disliked the prospect of spending the rest of her life doing research in a library. On a whim, she took a photography class at the city's Rhode Island School of Design and, instantly attracted to form, decided to instead pursue the visual arts. In 1979, she traveled to France to spend a year studying at the University of Paris. There, she delved into the connections among symbolism, post-modernism, psychology, and film in her intensive coursework, and worked at a photography gallery on the side. Back in the United States, she changed her major to semiotics—the study of symbols—and social anthropology, eventually earning her bachelor's degree in those subjects in 1981. Kuras remained in Providence for a time after graduation, working as an intern at the Roger Williams Park Museum and continuing to pursue photography. About a year later, she entered the Visual Studies Workshop at Rochester, New York, on a fellowship. That program focused more on building arts skills than technical mastery, and thus introduced Kuras to new ideas about approaching her craft. She then received a Fullbright Fellowship to study in Eastern Europe, but political problems in the region prevented her from following through. Instead, she moved to New York City, where she began taking classes in the usage of Super 8 film.

Kuras's first true experience in the film industry came not long after when she got a job as an associate producer on a documentary. She decided that she wanted to go into cinematography, and after taking some classes in the field at New York University, landed a job as a camera assistant. Over the next several years, she honed her skills while working on various documentaries and independent films.

Became Cinematographer

In 1987, Kuras received her first opportunity to shoot footage on a documentary about a war in El Salvador. The experience encouraged her drive to make films that conveyed a message rather than simply those that entertained, and her next project reflected this goal. Filmmaker Ellen Bruno planned to shoot a documentary about Cambodia, an area that had long interested Kuras. Bruno asked her to suggest someone to travel with her to shoot the documentary, but a scheduling conflict prevented Kuras's recommendation from being able to take the job. Instead, Kuras herself—despite having few technical skills and no experience shooting an entire documentary film—convinced Bruno to let her take on the challenge. The resulting *Samsara: Death and Rebirth in Cambodia* won worldwide accolades and transformed Kuras from camera assistant to cinematographer, and she soon began shooting commercials and television documentaries. In 1992, her work on the drama *Swoon* garnered the budding cinematographer her first Sundance award for cinematography.

During the 1990s, Kuras continued to work on respected documentaries and feature films. She shot the 1993 film *Coffee and Cigarettes: Somewhere in California* for director Jim Jarmusch, and the next year received her first Emmy nomination for *A Century of Women*. In 1995, Kuras picked up her second nod at Sundance for her work on the Rebecca Miller film *Angela*, and served as cinematographer on the fashion industry documentary *Unzipped*. Another pop culture outing *I Shot Andy Warhol* followed in 1996, with Kuras serving as cinematographer on the fictionalized story of would-be Warhol assassin Valerie Solanas. The cinematographer continued shooting features as the twentieth century gave way to the twenty-first, including Spike Lee's 1997 documentary *Four Little Girls*, about the 1963 church bombing in Birmingham, Alabama; his

1999 period film *Summer of Sam;* and the 2000 satire *Bamboozled.* Kuras also shot the stylish 1999 action caper *The Mod Squad* and the 2002 Johnny Depp vehicle *Blow.*

In 2002, Kuras again worked with director Rebecca Miller on the art house drama *Personal Velocity.* In *The Village Voice,* Anthony Kaufman proclaimed that Kuras had "accomplished the near impossible on...*Personal Velocity:* she made digital video look good." Her sensitive application of cinematography techniques on the film earned Kuras a third Sundance award for best cinematography and an Independent Spirit nomination. Two big-budget productions followed as Kuras stepped behind the camera for the 2002 Robert De Niro-Billy Crystal comedy *Analyze That* and the offbeat 2004 drama *Eternal Sunshine of the Spotless Mind,* directed by French filmmaker Michel Gondry. The director wanted to meld what John Pavlus, in the *American Cinematographer,* called "location-shoot authenticity with unpredictable flashes of whimsy" and turned to Kuras to bring her combination of documentary sensibilities with raw emotion. Gondry's insistence on the usage of natural light sources rather than traditional film lights and the somewhat spontaneous nature of the shoots frustrated the cinematographer at times, but she employed her ingenuity to meet Gondry's vision. "We had different assortments of lightbulbs—refrigerator bulbs, or small bulbs on hand dimmers—that we'd hide behind furniture or lampshades in order to give ourselves some stop," she recalled to Pavlus. "It was a game of hide-and-seek, determining how and where we could hide our little kit of light bulbs," continued Kuras.

After wrapping *Eternal Sunshine of the Spotless Mind,* Kuras reteamed with Miller to make the dramatic film *Ballad of Jack and Rose.* She then worked on a number of documentaries, including Martin Scorsese's 2005 film *No Direction Home: Bob Dylan* and Jonathan Demme's 2006 rock documentary *Neil Young: Heart of Gold.* Kuras also worked again with Gondry, along with comedian Dave Chappelle, to film the 2005 documentary *Block Party.* The cinematographer continued her involvement with classic rock documentaries by shooting the 2006 Lou Reed concert film *Berlin* and serving as a camera operator on the 2008 Scorsese effort *Shine a Light.* That same year, Kuras's next collaboration with Gondry, the comedy *Be Kind Rewind,* was released widely.

Made Directorial Debut

In 2008, Kuras's own directorial debut, *The Betrayal,* appeared on the film festival circuit. Made in conjunction with Thavisouk Phrasavath, the documentary followed Phrasavath and his Laotian family over the course of 23 years as they sought to rebuild their lives in New York state after escaping from their war-stricken homeland. The patriarch of the Phrasavath family had worked with the United States during the conflict in Southeast Asia in the late 1960s and 1970s, and was sentenced to perform hard labor under the new Communist regime. His wife and most of the children—two sisters were left behind—fled to the United States. Kuras's interest in the subject dated back even before her entrance into the world of filmmaking. "When I was a senior at Brown University, I...came to know many of the refugees recently resettled in the area....The enigma of their situation in the States—the fact that they had fought a war for the U.S. and yet were unrecognized here because the war was a secret air war that was only unofficially recognized—intrigued me," she explained in an interview posted on the International Documentary Association website. Her long involvement with the family allowed her to build a deeply personal story that captured an unusually emotional layer. "Kuras shoots the film not in straightforward documentary style but as a kind of agonized tone poem," noted Ty Burr of the *Boston Globe*. Over the course of shooting, Thavisouk Phrasavath also became involved in filming certain scenes and eventually served as the film's editor.

The Betrayal generated a great deal of positive response. "It is quiet, contemplative and impressionistic, which makes the story it has to tell all the more powerful," stated A.O. Scott in the *New York Times*. Writing in *Variety*, Scott Foundas commented that despite an occasional lack of focus, *The Betrayal* was "resolutely gripping." The film was screened at the 2008 Sundance Film Festival, where it was nominated for the Grand Jury Prize; later, it also received nominations for best documentary at both the Academy Awards and the Independent Spirit Awards. Public television series *P.O.V.* gave the film its primary U.S. release, and Kuras won an Emmy for the production.

Following the release of *The Betrayal*, Kuras returned to cinematography. She served as director of photography on the 2009 Sam Mendes-helmed comedy *Away We Go* starring John Krasinski and Maya Rudolph. According to Steve Weintraub of the website Collider, the film "has everything going for it—from a great script...to beautiful cinematography by Ellen Kuras, and a great set of songs[.]" Next up was the 2010 HBO documentary *Public Speaking*, for which Kuras again acted as director of photography. Kuras then shot the New York scenes of the 2011 drama *Tree of Life* and worked on another HBO documentary, *George Harrison: Living in the Material World*. As someone who has worked on film and television crews for most of her adult life, Kuras has commented that being on set is like being at home for her. Cinematography also provided a stable basis throughout her hectic life, and she showed little interest in giving up the craft in favor of other artistic endeavors. "I consider myself a cinematographer who is a filmmaker," she told Fisher. "A cinematographer has to take all elements of the story into consideration when you create images. It's about making a composite picture in the service of the story, so you have to constantly think about how you are going to help tell the story with images."

Periodicals

American Cinematographer, April 2004.

Boston Globe, April 10, 2009.

Globe & Mail (Toronto, Canada), January 24, 2008.

New York, November 16, 2008.

New York Times, June 8, 2008; November 21, 2008.

Variety, November 29, 2006; February 4, 2008.

Village Voice, November 20–November 26, 2002.

Online

"Ellen Kuras, ASC," *International Cinematographers Guild*, https://www.cameraguild.com/AboutUs/memberspotlightcustom/member-spotlight-ellen-kuras.aspx (December 4, 2011).

"Ellen Kuras," Yahoo! Movies, http://movies.yahoo.com/movie/contributor/1800019610/bio (September 27, 2011).

"Meet the Academy Award Nominees: Ellen Kuras—'The Betrayal (Nerakhoon),'" *International Documentary Association*, http://www.documentary.org/content/meet-academy-award-nominees-ellen-kuras-betrayal-nerakhoon (September 27, 2011).

"Sam Mendes Exclusive Video Interview AWAY WE GO," *Collider*, http://collider.com/sam-mendes-exclusive-video-interview-away-we-go/1652/ (December 4, 2011).□

Harvey Kurtzman

American cartoonist Harvey Kurtzman (1924–1993) created *Mad* in 1952, one of the best-loved humor magazines of the twentieth century and beyond. Kurtzman's irreverent voice and pen shaped the illustrated monthly's tone and look, but he walked away from the job in 1956 and the magazine continued on without him—though it was said *Mad* never regained its original, vicious bite. "Kurtzman's *Mad* was the first comic enterprise that got its effects almost entirely from parodying other kinds of popular entertainment," asserted Adam Gopnik in the *New Yorker* in 1993. "Almost all American satire today follows a formula that Harvey Kurtzman thought up."

Like many notable humorists of his era, Harvey Kurtzman came from a Jewish family in New York City. He was born on October 3, 1924, as the second of three sons in a household headed by his father David, a jeweler's assistant who died from a bleeding ulcer at the age of 36 when Kurtzman was four. "Kurtzman's mother, Edith, a firebrand who took her family's hardships as evidence of the inequity of capitalism, subscribed to the *Daily Worker* and sent her sons to the red-diaper Camp Kinderland in the Catskills for at least one summer," wrote David Hadju in *The Ten-Cent Plague: The Great Comic-Book Scare and How It Changed America*.

Drew for *Yank, the Army Weekly*

Kurtzman grew up in Brooklyn and the Bronx. On the latter borough's sidewalks he drew his first comic strip, a tale called "Ikey and Mikey," with pieces of plaster he pulled from buildings as a substitute for chalk. By his teens he emerged as a talented artist and won a spot at New York's High School of Music and Art. There he met several other students who would go on to collaborative careers with him at *Mad* and elsewhere, including Will Elder (born Wolf William Eisenberg), Harry Chester, Al Jaffee, and John Severin.

For urban youth of the pre-television era, comic books were the cultural currency, and Kurtzman read all of them with a critical eye. He entered cartoon contests and eventually landed his first job with the *Classics Illustrated* series in 1942, drawing an adaptation of Herman Melville's novel *Moby-Dick.* During this period he also took courses at the prestigious Cooper Union School of Art, but was soon drafted into the U.S. Army at the height of World War II. He worked as an illustrator for *Yank, the Army Weekly,* a counterpart to the more staid *Stars & Stripes* daily newspaper.

After returning to civilian life and New York City in 1946, Kurtzman freelanced for the forerunner of Marvel Comics, drawing one-page fillers for various titles. In 1948, he sold an original strip to the *New York Herald Tribune,* but "Silver Linings" ran for just three months before it was dropped. In 1949, he went to work for E.C. Comics, which stood for "Educational Comics." The Manhattan company, however, was in the process of a second-generation shakeup and began putting out standard pulp-comic fare. The first title he ever drew for the company was *Lucky Fights It Through,* a straightforward educational story about the dangers of venereal disease.

Edited War-Themed Comics

In 1950, Kurtzman was put in charge of two new titles at E.C., *Frontline Combat* and *Two-Fisted Tales,* but his scrupulous attention to detail maddened his colleagues. He devoted hours of research to ensure that even the smallest details in a panel were correct, to the point of the specific arrangement of a regulation Army medic kit. Furthermore, with the United States enmeshed in another overseas war on the Korean peninsula that began in 1950, Kurtzman avoided boilerplate patriotism-laden tales. "On Kurtzman's battlefields, the gallant American knights who marched through most war comics gave way to jittery, ambivalent GIs, sympathetic enemies who felt pain when they were shot, devastating losses, and pointless victories," wrote Hadju in *The Ten-Cent Plague.* Years later Steven Heller, writing in the *New York Times Book Review,* would also single out these titles, asserting "they prefigure recent novels and films that demythologize warfare. In 'Corpse on the Imjin!,' a six-page story he created for 'Two-Fisted Tales,' war is embodied in a solitary G.I. watching an enemy corpse float downriver—the drawing of the half-submerged form is heartbreaking."

E.C. Comics had made the transition from "Educational" to "Entertainment" Comics under William M. "Bill" Gaines, the son of the man who had done much to create the entire comic-book industry in the 1930s. The younger Gaines sought to publish higher-quality comics and was open to new ideas, including using the medium as a commentary on social issues of the day. E.C.'s horror and crime titles explored the fear of the outsider and hypocrisy of the justice system, just as its war titles and Western-themed comics offered a different version of the American hero. Kurtzman also drew comics for two other lucrative E.C. titles, *Tales from the Crypt* and *Weird Science,* and worked with Elder and Severin, along with two more notable figures in the field, Jack Davis and Wally Wood.

Mad Emerged as Nonconformist Voice

When Kurtzman learned that another E.C. editor, Al Feldstein, earned more money than he did, he complained to Gaines, who retorted that Feldstein produced more pages. Kurtzman offered to helm a new title, a humor publication, and out of this came the first issue of *Mad* in August of 1952. It started out as one of E.C.'s ten-cent comics, and Kurtzman created it as a parody of all the other E.C. comics, a dig at the prolific Feldstein. The first issue's science fiction story, "Blobs!" mocked the postwar suburban landscape as visitors from the future examine life in America in 1952. One caption as quoted from Hajdu, read: "Friends would drive over to other friends' houses in automobiles. . . and instead of talking to the friends, they would look at television machines for a few hours, and then they would ride home!"

Mad took a few issues to start earning a profit, but the real threat to its existence came in the form of alarmists who campaigned for some form of censorship in the industry. As other titles from E.C. and its competitors became enormously successful, parents, teachers, and other authority figures regularly confiscated the pulpy, lurid comics from kids' bedrooms, desks, and bookbags. A 1954 book titled *Seduction of the Innocent: The Influence of Comic Books on Today's Youth,* resulted in a special U.S. Senate Subcommittee on Juvenile Delinquency hearings and an industry effort to regulate itself, lest federal, state, or local governments impose their own laws. The Comics Magazine Association of America adopted a code that banned certain themes, and in response Gaines moved to make *Mad* a 25-cent magazine, which meant it was exempt from the new rules of the Comics Code Authority. The first issue in this new format appeared in July of 1955, along with its new cover mascot, the fictional Alfred E. Neuman. The odd man-boy face, with oversized ears and a missing front tooth, was a stock photo of uncertain provenance, once used in a high school biology textbook showing an example of a person with an iodine deficiency. Kurtzman liked it for its mischievous appearance and added a signature motto for Neuman, "What, me worry?" that would appear alongside the figure on every issue after the July 1955 reformatting.

Kurtzman's gift for razor-sharp satire had struck a nerve with readers in the 1950s, not just the teen age group it originally targeted. "We began. . .by doing parodies of every comic book in sight. And when we ran out of comics, we started to do parodies of everything else: movies, TV, sports, politics, families, cars, teenagers, you name it," he explained in his 1988 autobiography, *My Life as a Cartoonist.* Every issue was a trove of visual commentary and caricature of public figures, but Kurtzman was deft at dropping the *non sequitur,* a Latin phrase used in literature and philosophy which translates as "it does not follow." On the pages of *Mad,* these were words or sentences that had no comic payoff elsewhere in the narrative, and the non sequiturs mystified readers but also invited them to delve deeper into the text. Veteran music writer Greil Marcus, who became a contributing editor at *Artforum International,* discussed *Mad'*s use of them in a 2005 essay. "The non sequitur as the foundation of Kurtzman's assault on postwar mass culture," Marcus wrote, "was an argument about brainwashing, passivity, entertainment reduced to mindless consumption, and any other fear-of-mass-culture shibboleth current in the '50s."

Bankrolled by *Playboy* Empire

By the spring of 1956, with *Mad* sales soaring and his nemesis Feldstein gone, Kurtzman went to Gaines and asked for a 51 percent share in the magazine. Gaines declined, and Kurtzman walked away in protest. Gaines then hired Feldstein to replace Kurtzman as *Mad*'s editor. The magazine continued to hold a strong place in American pop culture—and helped bring about the creation of such counterculture gems as *National Lampoon* magazine and *Saturday Night Live*—but chroniclers of currents in American humor argued it lost a certain intellectual edge when Kurtzman departed that it never regained.

Kurtzman's career faltered after leaving *Mad,* though there were a few promising breaks. Hugh Hefner, the publisher of *Playboy,* offered to fund a new magazine, but *Trump* lasted just two issues in 1957 before folding. Kurtzman then formed an artists' collective with Will Elder, Jack Davis, Al Jaffee, and Arnold Roth to launch *Humbug* that same year, but it, too, folded after eleven issues. Finally, in 1962, Kurtzman resigned himself to a deal offered by Hefner to create a regular comic strip for *Playboy*. "Little Annie Fanny," co-authored with Elder, was of course a send-up of the proliferation of buxom blondes in *Playboy* and adolescent spirit that drove the entire men's-magazine genre.

Provided Base for Emerging Counterculture Artists

Kurtzman's last great career achievement was *Help!*, which put out 26 issues between 1960 and 1965. Working with Elder once again, he created a terrific illustrated humor magazine that attracted a roster of important contributors, including Ray Bradbury, Arthur C. Clarke, and Gloria Steinem. Robert Crumb was an early illustrator, and Terry Gilliam, a California artist who later moved to England and formed Monty Python's Flying Circus, met fellow Python founder John Cleese while an assistant editor at *Help!*

Kurtzman and *Help!* became enmeshed in an expensive legal battle when Archie Comics sued it for copyright violation of the popular Archie series. Kurtzman and Elder had created a devastating parody that ran in the February 1962 issue, with their naïve Goodman Beaver returning to the Archie and Friends world after some time away, but perplexed by the adult behavior of suddenly adult pals like Betty, Veronica, and even Jughead. "Looking at the panels now, nearly half a century later, little has changed," wrote Marcus in *Artforum International*. "The Playboy kids with their expensive restaurants and their Lancias...are just the day before yesterday's yuppies and today's food fanatics. Goodman Beaver wants to know how the football team is doing. 'You've been away too long,' Archie says. 'Nowadays, the gang is interested mainly in hipness—awareness.'" As Marcus dryly commented, "Welcome to the New Age."

Kurtzman worked as a freelance illustrator for years and taught cartooning at the School of Visual Arts in New York City. He died of liver cancer on February 21, 1993, at the age of 68. In 2009, writers Denis Kitchen and Paul Buhle put out a definitive survey of Kurtzman's career for Abrams. "If not for *Mad* magazine, there might never have been (in no particular order) 1960s youth culture, underground comics,...'Saturday Night Live,' R. Crumb, Art Spiegelman or an age of irony, period," asserted Heller in the *New York Times Book Review*. "Kurtzman was the spiritual father of postwar American satire and the godfather of late-20th-century alternative humor."

Books

Hajdu, David, *The Ten-Cent Plague: The Great Comic-Book Scare and How It Changed America,* Macmillan, 2009.
Kurtzman, Harvey, with Howard Zimmerman, *My Life as a Cartoonist,* Pocket Books, 1988.

Periodicals

Artforum International, November 2005; April 2009.
New York Times Book Review, August 9, 2009.
New Yorker, March 29, 1993.
Shofar, Winter 2011.
Sunday Telegraph (London, England), July 5, 2009. □

L

La Malinche

An indigenous woman called La Malinche (c.1505–1551) holds a controversial place in the history of Mexico. Also known by the name Malinalli Teneépal, the Nahuatl language-speaker served as translator for Spanish conquistador Hernán Cortés during his conquest of Mexico and had a son by him in the early 1520s. The woman the Spanish dubbed Doñna Marina was later scorned by Mexicans of subsequent generations for her role in the subjugation of the Aztec Empire.

La Malinche is believed to have been born in 1505 in what was then called Coatzacoalcos, a territorial designation for part of the modern-day province of Veracruz, Mexico. Her father was the *cacique*, or chief, of Coatzacoalcos, one of the Nahuatl-speaking regions allied with a larger empire in present-day Mexico City. The Nahua are also known as the Aztec people, though they did not use this term, instead using "Mexìcâ" to refer to themselves. The word Aztec comes from Lake Aztlan, a mythical source of their origin. The empire's capital was Tenochtitlán, an enormous and magnificent city built at Lake Texcoco in the Valley of Mexico.

Sold into Slavery

La Malinche's father died when she was still young, and her mother, named Cimatl, remarried another cacique and had a son. Because Aztec society did not prevent noble-born women like La Malinche from inheriting property, she was destined to receive her late father's patrimony, but

Cimatl favored her new son and sold her young daughter off to slave traders in the area. Cimatl claimed that La Malinche had died and used the recently deceased daughter of one of their household servants to bolster her claims; the corpse was buried with proper funerary honors for a child of noble rank.

The slave traders were from the town of Xicalango and spoke Mayan, the language of another indigenous group. The Mayans lived on the Yucatán Peninsula and further south into present-day Central America, and were the descendants of a much earlier empire. Like the Aztecs, the Mayans created a complex political, economic, and cultural civilization, but their empire fell into decline and gave way to Nahuan dominance by 1000 CE.

Presented as Gift to Spanish

The Xicalango traders sold La Malinche to the Tabascans, a populace who lived further along the Yucatán Peninsula. They spoke a language known as Chontal Mayan, and she became fluent in this, along with her native Nahuatl. Using her purported birthdate of 1505, La Malinche was 13 or 14 years old when a contingent of Spanish forces, led by Hernán Cortés, arrived in the region in March of 1519. Cortés was from Castile and had already spent 15 years as a colonial official on the first lands to be conquered and claimed by the Spanish Empire: the island of Hispaniola (present-day Haiti and the Dominican Republic) and then Cuba, where he rose to the position of chief magistrate of Santiago, the main city. The Spanish had heard there was a large land mass to the east, and Cortés sailed for it with a contingent of about 600 men in the early months of 1519. They landed first on Cozumel Island, then proceeded onward to the Yucatán Peninsula.

Cortés learned that two Spanish men, en route to Hispaniola from another Spanish settlement in present-day

Panama, had been kidnapped by Mayans after a 1511 shipwreck. One of them was a priest named Gerónimo Alonso de Aguilar, who had become fluent in Mayan and was granted permission to join Cortés' expedition by the cacique in whose jurisdiction Aguilar lived. The Spaniards fought briefly with some Tabascans, and while the invaders were regrouping on the island of San Juan de Ulúa, the Tabascans came with a peace offering for the Europeans. Among the gifts they presented was a contingent of 20 slaves, La Malinche among them. Enslaved women were designated for use as corn grinders in military expeditions, responsible for food preparation for caciques and their soldiers.

One of the first sources of information about La Malinche was written by a Spanish soldier who had served under Cortés, Bernal Díaz del Castillo. Díaz wrote about the Spanish conquest of Mexico many years later, in a 1568 work he titled *Historia Verdadera de la Conquista de la Nueva España* (True Story of the Conquest of New Spain). He said the woman they came to know as "Doñna Marina" was of exceptional beauty and immediately noticed by the Spaniards, who were told she was an Aztec of noble rank sold into slavery by her family. Díaz wrote favorably of her, emphasizing she was vital to the success of Cortés's conquest of the Mexìcâ.

Revealed Plot to Slay Spaniards

Cortés accepted the 20 slaves and had them baptized into the Christian faith on March 20, 1519. La Malinche took the name Marina after some basic catechism instruction from Aguilar, the priest, and made preparations for the journey to the main city of Tenochtitlán. Tabascans and other Mayan-speakers resented the regional dominance of the Aztec Empire, which extended a powerful influence over the region and demanded a heavy annual tribute tax, which included sacrificial victims to appease Huitzilopochtli, the

Aztec god of war. The Aztecs also believed that another important deity, Quetzalcoatl, the god of peace, would return to earth, and he would come from the east in the year they designated *Ce Acatl* (One Reed) in their calendar, or 1519.

The Aztec emperor Moctezuma II had learned that "floating mountains" of foreigners had arrived on the coastline of the Gulf of Mexico and were heading inland. The emperor sent representatives to meet them at Veracruz, but the Mayan-speaking Aguilar was unable to comprehend their greetings. "It was at this moment that Doña Marina interceded and surprised everyone when she began to speak to the Aztec ambassadors in their own Nahua language, thereby making communication possible," wrote Adelaida R. Del Castillo in an essay that appeared in the 1999 volume *Latina Issues: Fragments of Historia(ella) (herstory)*.

Cortés and his party made their way inland and engaged in skirmishes with various groups, who were either subdued or opted to join the Spanish in their mission to conquer the land on behalf of King Carlos V of Spain. In September of 1519, Cortés' forces and independent city-state Tlaxcala allied, and marched toward Tenochtitlán. There were fears about the holy city of Chohula, the second-largest urban area of Nahua-speakers in the Valley of Mexico. La Malinche was said to have learned from the wife of one of the Chohulan nobles that there was a plot to kill the Spanish while they slept. She informed Cortés of the plot, and he arranged an ostensibly peaceful meeting with Chohula's leaders in which the men were massacred. The thousand-strong Tlaxcaltecan militia then burned the city and killed hundreds in retaliation for past grievances against the Chohulans and Moctezuma.

Rescued from Tenochtitlán

La Malinche was part of the official delegation that arrived at Tenochtitlán on November 8, 1519, and was present when the conquistador and Moctezuma held their first summit. The emperor spoke Nahuatl to her, which she then translated into Chontal Mayan to Aguilar, who then translated into Spanish for Cortés. When Cortés spoke, the process was reversed. Moctezuma gave Cortés the use of his late father's palace, Axayáctal, and initially seemed acquiescent to Spanish demands, including swearing fealty to King Carlos V and handing over pieces of gold, the true mission behind the Spanish incursion. To ensure Aztec loyalty, Cortés decided that Moctezuma needed to be taken into protective custody at Axayáctal, which the emperor initially resisted, realizing that this would be viewed as a humiliating capitulation to the foreigners. Díaz wrote of the tense meeting between Moctezuma and Cortés' retinue, some of whom argued for the immediate assassination of the emperor. La Malinche told Moctezuma "to go at once to their quarters without any disturbance at all, for I know that they will pay you much honour as a great Prince such as you are, otherwise you will remain here a dead man," she said, according to Díaz in the volume *The Discovery and Conquest of Mexico: 1517–1521*.

Moctezuma was eventually killed, and a major war broke out between the Aztecs and a combined Spanish-Tlaxcaltecan force. At one point, La Malinche had to be spirited out of Tenochtitlán to safety during an 11-week siege. The city fell and most of its inhabitants died, either from starvation, warfare, or a smallpox epidemic. The capitulation of the Aztecs in August of 1521 marked a decisive turning point for the Spanish conquest of the Americas.

Married in Veracruz Church

La Malinche traveled with Cortés and his entourage for at least two more years. Around 1522, a son was born to her, named Martín in honor of the conquistador's father. Martín Cortés was one of first mestizos—those of mixed European and indigenous American heritage—on record, and it took a papal bull for the child to be declared Cortés' legitimate child. Cortés had a house built for them in Coyoacán, on the outskirts of a destroyed Tenochtitlán, where they lived for a time, but in 1523 a marriage was arranged between La Malinche and another Spaniard, Juan de Jaramillo, a wealthy and trusted ally of Cortés'.

Díaz writes that he was present in 1524 on a journey south to Honduras, when they stopped near La Malinche's Coatzacoalcos homeland. Cimatl was summoned to see the now-grown daughter she had sold into slavery, along with La Malinche's half-brother, who had become cacique. The pair, wrote Díaz, "were in great fear of Doña Marina, for they thought she had sent for them to put them to death, and they were weeping." Instead she gave them gifts "and told them to return to their town, and said that God had been very gracious to her in freeing her from the worship of idols," Díaz reported.

After this La Malinche disappears from the historical record. Her son was raised by Cortés and eventually returned to Spain with his father, where he was knighted and married a Spanish woman. La Malinche is known to have had a daughter with Jaramillo, named María, who married a Spaniard, Luis López de Quesada. Her death date is unknown. Jaramillo remarried in 1531, spurring some to believe that he was widowed by then, but other sources say she was the "doña Marina" mentioned in colonial records as late as 1551.

House Still Stands

La Malinche is the first female figure to appear in the culture of post-Columbian Mexico. Because she had a child with the ruthless Cortés, one of the most reviled figures in the history of the Spanish conquest of the Americas, she has been alternately referred to as either the mother of the nation or an opportunistic prostitute. The term "malinchista" is a derogatory term for Mexicans who readily adopt the habits of European or American culture. Parts of the original house where she lived with Cortés still stands at 57 Higuera Street, now part of Mexico City proper. *New York Times* journalist Clifford Krauss visited it in 1997 for an article bearing the headline, "After 500 Years, Cortés's Girlfriend Is Not Forgiven."

Krauss's article recounted a disastrous attempt to erect a fountain and statue of La Malinche and her son in the Coyoacán neighborhood, which was met with fierce protest, and called her "a symbol of a nation that is still not entirely comfortable with either its European or Indian roots. Some Mexican feminists have said she is even at the root of much of the disdain Mexican men display toward Mexican women, expressed in the country's high rates of infidelity and domestic violence." Others have appraised her role in the founding of the nation more favorably. "Doñna Marina is significant in that she embodies effective, decisive action in the feminine form, and most important, because her own actions syncretized two conflicting worlds causing the emergence of a new one—our own," Del Castillo wrote in *Latina Issues*. "Here, woman acts not as a goddess in some mythology, but as an actual force in the making of history."

Books

Cypess, Sandra Messinger, *La Malinche in Mexican Literature from History to Myth,* University of Texas Press, 1991.

Del Castillo, Adelaida R., "Malintzin Teneépal: A Preliminary Look into a New Perspective," in *Latina Issues: Fragments of Historia (ella) (herstory),* edited by Antoinette Sedillo López, Taylor & Francis, 1999.

Díaz del Castillo, Bernal, *The Discovery and Conquest of Mexico: 1517–1521,* translated by Alfred Percival Maudslay, Da Capo Press, 2004.

"La Malinche (Malinalli Tenepal) (1505–1551)," in *Latinas in the United States: A Historical Encyclopedia,* edited by Vicki L. Ruiz and Virginia Sanchez Korrol, Volume 2, Indiana University Press, 2006.

Mirandé, Alfredo, *La Chicana: The Mexican-American Woman,* University of Chicago Press, 1979.

Periodicals

Independent (London, England), August 18, 2006.

New York Times, March 26, 1997. □

Anne Lamott

American author Anne Lamott (born 1954) became widely hailed for her novels and memoirs employing honesty and humor to depict such topics as faith, family, and substance abuse in modern life.

American author Anne Lamott rose to nationwide bestselling status as a non-fiction writer during the 1990s with the publication of her memoir of the first days of motherhood, *Operating Instructions: A Journal of My Son's First Year*. Sometimes hailed as a study in contradictions, Lamott is both a strong political liberal and a devout born-again Christian. Her beliefs and experiences as a former alcoholic have informed both her fiction and non-fiction writing, with memoirs exploring writing, faith, and family forming the heart of her oeuvre. Along with *Operating Instructions,* Lamott's best-known works include 1994's writing instructional guide *Bird by Bird: Some Instructions on Writing and Life* and 1999's spiritual exploration *Traveling Mercies: Some Thoughts of Faith*. Critics and fans alike hailed these books and others for their author's signature blend of honesty, humor, and insight.

Battled Personal Problems in Early Life

Born on April 10, 1954, Lamott is a native of San Francisco, California who grew up mostly in the nearby coastal town of Bolinas. Her father, Kenneth Lamott, was a writer, and her mother, Dorothy Lamott, was a former journalist and homemaker who later became a lawyer. Lamott's parents were unhappy in their marriage, and even as a child the future author recognized the difficult atmosphere. "I didn't grow up in a close family," she recalled to Pamela Feinsilver of *Publishers Weekly* in a 1993 interview. "I grew up in a traditional American family where no one talked about their emotions... I was a very tense little kid," she added. Growing up, she frequently felt like an outsider. She excelled in tennis, however, and won a scholarship to play the sport at Goucher College in Baltimore, Maryland. There, Lamott studied English, religion, and philosophy, but she dropped out before completing her degree.

Back in California by 1974, she got a job as a journalist with the publication *WomenSports* and began writing short stories based on her life and observations in coastal California in her spare time. Through her father's connections, Lamott was able to have many of these early efforts reviewed—and rejected. After her father was diagnosed with a brain tumor, however, Lamott's work took a new turn and found a better reception. Soon, several of her short stories interested a publisher, and these pieces became several chapters of her first novel, *Hard Laughter*. Drawing on her own experiences, Lamott wrote about a family dealing with the effects of its patriarch developing a brain tumor. Although Lamott's own father did not live to see the publication of the book in 1980, he was pleased to know that his daughter had begun to walk her own literary path. A second novel, *Rosie,* followed in 1983. In this work, Lamott told the story of a girl growing up in the wake of her father's death in a car accident and her mother's struggles with grief and quiet alcoholism. The central

characters of this novel appeared in later Lamott novels, including 1997's *Crooked Little Heart* and 2010's *Imperfect Birds.*

Lamott's third novel, *Joe Jones,* appeared in 1985 and drew on the author's experiences working at a Petaluma restaurant. Negative reviews and a lukewarm reception pushed Lamott to increase her already occasionally heavy alcohol consumption so much that she began regularly blacking out. Finally, a very public incident brought her to a sharp realization that she had become too dependent on substances. "One hundred and fifty people had paid $20 to come to a fund-raiser and hear me speak," she later recalled to Ruth Reichl in the *New York Times.* "I hadn't written the speech, I can't remember why, and I'd had a whole lot to drink. I was stoned, too. I ordered another bottle, the guy poured it and I came to 15 minutes later from a blackout. I was in the middle of the speech and I didn't know what I was saying," she concluded. She initially disliked being sober, but in time discovered that working helped her adjust to her new state. "When I started writing again after I got sober, I tiptoed into it, but it felt really natural," she commented in the same interview with Reichl. The resulting novel, *All New People,* received the kind of positive reception that its predecessor missed out on, and the author herself counted it among her favorite works.

Embraced Christianity

About a year after she stopped drinking, Lamott again took a life-shaping move by getting baptized. Although she had long had an on-and-off relationship with religion and spirituality, her decision to formally accept Christianity was a significant one for her. Before she had quit drinking, Lamott had had her first brush with what she felt was the physical presence of Jesus Christ; however, "some people dismissed the experience because she was hungover," reported Agnieszka Tennant in *Christianity Today.* The author's next spiritual encounter of this sort came several years later, well after she had stopped drinking and embraced faith. While traveling on an airplane, Lamott visited the restroom. "I started hearing this song, 'Just As I Am,'" she told Tennant in the same interview. "I sat on the toilet, with my knees pulled up, and I started to sing it. And I absolutely, as clearly as I hear your voice now, felt Jesus. I opened my eyes and he didn't go away. I didn't see him like I'm seeing photographs on the wall, but I saw him with my spiritual eyes," she continued.

This metaphysical closeness with Jesus Christ informed many of the author's best-known memoirs. In 1999's *Traveling Mercies: Some Thoughts on Faith,* Lamott discussed her spiritual journey and her relationship with Christianity. Although the author diverged greatly from much of the stereotypical contemporary born-again Christian community due to her liberal political beliefs, history of substance abuse, and willingness to accept non-believers into her personal life, *Traveling Mercies* won much praise from Christian reviewers—and from secular ones. "What turns me on about her story is that she sees God at work all along the paths of her life and not only at the point of conversion," commented a reviewer for the *Presbyterian Record,*-while *Kirkus Reviews* termed it "an anguishing account that also heals.'' Lamott later returned to the question of faith in her 2005 memoir, *Plan B: Further Thoughts on Faith* and again in a 2007 non-fiction follow-up, *Grace (Eventually): Thoughts on Faith.*

Christian themes also influenced the author's fiction. In 2002's *Blue Shoe,* Lamott's devoutly Christian heroine tries to deal with the temptations of real-world sin and the frustrations of day-to-day life in the wake of her divorce. She continues a sexual relationship with her remarried ex-husband, and develops another relationship with a married man, all the while dealing with her children and ailing mother. ''Though readers might dislike the kitchen-sink aspect of Lamott's storytelling ...this is real life she's depicting, with all its tedium, misery, absurdity, occasional flashes of enlightenment and moments of joy,'' observed Charlotte Innes of *The Nation.*

Wrote About Family

Another defining life change came a couple of years following her conversion to Christianity: Lamott became a mother. Although the father wished her to terminate the pregnancy, Lamott—who had had an abortion some years earlier—decided to have the child. The father left, leaving Lamott as a working single mother to a new son, Sam. Her struggles to adapt to motherhood and realizations about the difficulties of raising a child alone were fodder for what proved to be her major breakthrough, *Operating Instructions.* Lamott's humor and honesty provided a rare look at the times that new mothers were perhaps less than certain about their new role as she offered depictions of her on-the-ground experiences making sure that baby Sam was fed, diapered, and loved even throughout her own emotional turmoil; not long after Sam's birth, Lamott lost her best friend to cancer. Kirkus Reviews applauded ''Lamott's wry efforts to get a grip on her ever-wavering self-esteem and her unwillingness to engage in any truth-varnishing when it comes to the ever-so-bumpy road of mothering,'' and readers helped the book enjoy two weeks on the *New York Times* bestseller list.

Over the next several years, Lamott published mostly non-fiction. Among the most respected of these works was 1994's *Bird by Bird: Some Instructions on Writing and Life.* A primer on the craft of writing, the book was widely hailed as one of the finest manuals on writing technique of its day. Lamott asserted that writers must risk being bad and dedicate time daily to writing, just as her father once told her brother to get through a school report about birds by taking it ''bird by bird.'' Writing in the *New York Times,* Carol Muske Dukes hailed the book as ''good writing about writing, object lessons in the craft and art, by a tough-minded veteran...Setting euphemism firmly aside in breaking down the writing process, Ms. Lamott calls a bird a bird and a bad first draft what it deserves to be called.'' Later in the decade, Lamott became a regular columnist for the online magazine *Slate* along with continuing her long-form work. In this role, she often discussed her liberal political ideals and, later, frustrations with the administration of Republican President George W. Bush.

In 2010, Lamott published her first fiction in almost a decade, *Imperfect Birds.* Revisiting the protagonists of earlier novels *Rosie* and *Crooked Little Heart,* Lamott explored the complex relationship between teens and parents by recounting the contrast between the public face of academic achievement and the private life of drug abuse that the novel's central teenaged character presented to her parents and the world. Characterized as a ''a stark illustration of deception, denial and parents' desperate desire to stay loved'' by Mary Pols of *Time,* the novel received generally strong critical notices for its unflinching depiction of dependency and family. That same year, the California Hall of Fame recognized the author's achievements by inducting her into its ranks alongside such famed names as Betty White and James Cameron. Lamott accepted the award with pride, but noted that her true accolades came from her readers. ''I have this huge love for the people that read me. I have more love from an audience than anyone else I know... [A]s God is my witness, the love and loyalty of my readers is so far beyond any award,'' she told Kevin Young in an interview with the San Francisco-focused section of the website City's Best.

In the spring of 2012, Lamott returned with a new book of memoirs, *Some Assembly Required: A Journal of My Son's First Son.* Written in conjunction with her son, the book describes Lamott's experiences as a grandmother, her son's experiences as a teenage father, and the growth and development of new grandson Jax. In some ways a companion piece to the author's 1993 *Operating Instructions,* the memoir seemed likely to continue to satisfy Lamott's dedicated fans—a remarkably disparate group of readers united at times only by their respect for her work. As Lauren F. Winner observed in the *New York Times,* ''Lamott is one of the handful of contemporary Christian writers beloved by people who usually agree about very little. [L]ots of different people love Anne Lamott, because she's funny and she tells the truth, and truth and laughter are two things we need more of.''

Books

Contemporary Authors Online, Gale, 2010.

Periodicals

Christianity Today, January 2003.

Kirkus Reviews, May 1, 1993; February 1, 1999.

New York Times, December 1, 1994; March 5, 1995; May 1, 2005.

Presbyterian Record, October 1999.

Publishers Weekly, May 31, 1993.

The Nation, November 18, 2002.

Time, April 12, 2010.

Writer's Digest, June 1996.

Online

''Anne Lamott,'' *California Hall of Fame,* http://www.california museum.org/exhibits/halloffame/inductee/new-inductee-3 (November 21, 2011).

''Up Close with S.F. Author Anne Lamott,'' *City's Best,* http://www.citysbest.com/san-francisco/news/2010/12/20/up-close-with-s-f-author-anne-lamott/ (November 21, 2011).□

Allie B. Latimer

American lawyer and civil rights activist Allie B. Latimer (born 1929) helped form the women's rights group Federally Employed Women (FEW) and served as the first African American woman general counsel of a major federal agency.

American lawyer and civil rights activist Allie Latimer became both the first African American and the first woman to serve as general counsel of a major federal agency in 1977 when she joined the General Services Administration (GSA) in that role. Latimer was also one of the primary founders and the inaugural president of the group Federally Employed Women (FEW), which was begun in the late 1960s to help encourage gender equality and discourage discrimination against women working with or for the federal government. Over the next few decades, that organization grew to include some 200 chapters nationwide. Involved with humanitarian and civil rights efforts throughout her career, Latimer received numerous awards for her efforts including two Presidential Rank Awards in the 1980s and the Ollie May Cooper Award from the Washington, D.C. Bar Association in 1998. In 2009, the National Women's Hall of Fame inducted Latimer in recognition of her efforts to advance the role of women in government.

Came from Education Background

The youngest of four children, Latimer was born in the early 1930s in the Pittsburgh suburb of Coraopolis, Pennsylvania to Lonnie S. Latimer and Bennie (Comer) Latimer. Her exact date of birth went unrecorded, and Latimer herself was uncertain of the specifics even as an adult. "I was hatched, not born," she joked to Racine Tucker Hamilton in an oral history interview posted on the History-Makers website. Latimer's ancestry included white plantation owners and Native Americans along with enslaved African Americans; her maternal grandfather had successfully escaped slavery, and her paternal grandfather had become such a respected farmer that he was invited to teach agricultural methods at the Tuskegee Institute. Both of Latimer's parents received good educations. Her father, a Georgia native, became a builder, and her Alabama-born mother worked as a schoolteacher. When Latimer was small, the family returned to the South, and so she grew up mostly in Montgomery, Alabama. There, she became close to her maternal grandmother, who helped raise the young girl until her death when Latimer was about seven. Growing up, Latimer attended the Alabama State Laboratory School and the public Booker T. Washington School, where she was a good, if not particularly diligent student.

After graduating from high school in the mid-1940s, Latimer enrolled for a year at Barber-Scotia College in Concord, North Carolina, and then transferred to the Hampton Institute in Hampton, Virginia. By that time, she had become interested in social work and the law, but her mother wanted her to pursue teaching. Latimer thus took course work in that subject, although she resisted actually entering the field. In the same series of interviews with Tucker Hamilton, Latimer recalled, "this lady that was in charge of placement, she kept sending for me. . .to interview with all of these principals and so when I turned everything down she finally said. . .'Well, what's the problem?' I said, 'Well I don't want to teach.'" And. . .that was almost unheard of. . . .she almost said something like well what are you gonna do, domestic work. . .? Those were the only two things available to blacks," she continued.

Latimer, however, was determined to plot her own course after completing her bachelor's degree. She worked as a volunteer at a New Jersey women's prison through a program run by the Quakers for a time hoping to earn credit towards a graduate degree in social work, and later received a fellowship to travel to Europe as part of the Quaker International Voluntary Service. The continent was recovering from the still-recent trauma of World War II, and Latimer worked on community improvement projects in France and Switzerland. In the early 1950s, she returned to the United States and soon took a job with the Justice Department that placed her in a federal women's prison in Alderson, West Virginia. After a year, Latimer left this position to attend law school at Howard University in Washington, D.C. She completed her law degree at that institution in 1953, but the state of North Carolina delayed her taking the bar exam there until 1955 and postponed granting her a legal license until 1956. For the remainder of the decade, Latimer instead continued studies in various fields, earning a master's in legal letters from the Catholic University's Columbus School of Law, along with a master's of divinity and a doctor of ministry from Howard's School of Divinity.

Helped Found FEW

While Latimer was still attending graduate school, she decided to seek a job in the federal government. She applied with several different agencies—including a failed attempt to become an FBI agent—and eventually was hired on with the General Services Administration, the agency that provides broad-based administrative and office management services to other federal entities. This position led her to help found the organization Federally Employed Women (FEW) in 1968. The group's history dated back to earlier in the decade, however. In 1964, Congress had passed a major Civil Rights Act that barred discrimination based on race and gender. The legislation did not, however, bar gender discrimination within the federal government; Latimer later argued that the prohibition had been included mostly as a deterrent to passage of the bill, not as a true intended protection of women's rights. Angered by the shortcomings of the Civil Rights Act, a number of female federal employees who had been nominated for the Federal Women's Award—a prestigious government honor—decided to take active steps towards requiring the federal government to enact gender equality measures. As part of their prize, the award recipients visited the White House. In 1967, the group arrived there with a draft of an executive order that prohibited gender discrimination both within the U.S. federal government and in the businesses of those firms that received federal contracts. Then-President Lyndon B. Johnson soon signed the executive order, and as part of its execution the federal Civil Service Commission instructed each federal agency to establish an internal federal women's program.

Latimer's years of service with the General Services Administration had brought her to what was essentially the organization's advancement ceiling for women. After starting out at the pay grade of GS-7 when she joined the agency in the late 1950s, Latimer had steadily risen to the pay grade of GS-15. This made her the highest-paid woman in the agency and, thus, the natural candidate to become the chairwoman on the new women's program that the agency was required to institute. As part of the duties of this new position, Latimer began exploring the activities of other agencies in implementing the order in the hopes of finding a model after which to pattern the General Services Administration's group. In doing this, she discovered that several agencies were essentially unaware of the effort, and that little coordinated effort was underway to execute it. Latimer and other committee members decided to form their own group to ensure that the program went forward as planned. When the resulting Federally Employed Women organization officially formed in 1968, Latimer became its first president. "From the beginning FEW was envisioned as a three-tier structure—the organization itself, individual chapters, and finally regions," explained the organization's website. Latimer's tenure as the group's head was thus largely dedicated to setting up the organization and ensuring that it had a sound structure that would enable the construction of those levels.

Coming in the changing social climate of the 1960s, the establishment of FEW was widely seen as a positive step for working women in the United States. "There are a great many new forces moving in the direction of securing equality of employment opportunity for the black woman," wrote Sonia Pressman in a contemporary issue of *The Crisis,* referencing the formation of FEW along with the work of other groups such as the National Organization for Women (NOW) and the Women's Equity Action League (WEAL). "It is now up to the black woman to use the available means to secure her rights, and up to the rest of the country to cooperate and assist her in her struggle for equality," Pressman concluded.

Appointed to Historical Post

Although Latimer's tenure as president of FEW ended in 1969, her efforts to further the status of women did not cease. She advanced to become the assistant general counsel of the General Services Administration in 1971, remaining in that post for five years. Then, a new director of Equal Employment Opportunity joined the National Aeronautics and Space Agency (NASA). Upon learning that NASA had no African Americans in its general counsel office, the director pursued Latimer, who was well-respected within the federal government as both an attorney and a women's rights advocate. Although Latimer was reluctant to leave the GSA after nearly two decades with the agency, NASA won her over with a special pay rise. Latimer was with that organization for only a brief time, however, before

returning to the General Services Administration, this time as general counsel. This appointment made her the first African American and the first woman to hold this position at any major federal agency. Latimer, however, did not see the accomplishment as the culmination of her efforts. Speaking to Tucker Hamilton, she explained, "my emphasis has always been on service, what I can do to help somebody else....I don't know that I've ever had a goal of just trying to get...a job or a position or something like that because success is measured different for me."

Latimer's tenure as general counsel lasted until 1987, when she downshifted to become a special counsel with the GSA. During her time as general counsel, she worked to bring more women and African Americans in the agency at large as well as into her own office. Latimer was also active in several professional and civil rights organizations, including the National Bar, the National Association for the Advancement of Colored People (NAACP), and the Northeastern Presbyterian Church, which had named her an elder in 1969. Latimer retired from the federal government in 1997.

Latimer's career and efforts to expand women's rights garnered her numerous accolades. In 1971, the General Services Administration granted her its Public Service Award; each year between 1976 and 1979, that organization recognized her with its Exceptional Service Award, and in 1984 granted her its Distinguished Service Award. The Sigma Delta Tau Legal Fraternity granted Latimer a Humanitarian Award in 1978, the same year that the Kiwanis Club of Washington, D.C. recognized her work. Latimer also received the prestigious Presidential Rank Award in 1983 and 1995, as well as the Ollie May Cooper Award in 1998. She was twice inducted into organizational halls of fame. In 1999, the National Bar Association—an organization of African American lawyers and judges—named her to the ranks of its hall, and a decade later the National Women's Hall of Fame inducted her as well. Latimer also received nods from the Veteran Feminists of America and the National Black Presbyterian Women. Despite this outpouring of respect, Latimer remained humble about her efforts. "It's not all about me, it's all about us," she was quoted as stating upon accepted the National Black Presbyterian Women's Lucy Craft Laney award in 2009 on the Presbyterian Church website. "It's about the common road," she concluded.

Books

Who's Who Among African Americans, Gale, 2010.

Periodicals

The Crisis, March 1970.

Online

"Allie B. Latimer," *National Women's Hall of Fame,* https://www.greatwomen.org/women-of-the-hall/search-the-hall/details/2/231-Latimer (September 29, 2011).

"Allie Latimer," *The HistoryMakers,* http://www.idvl.org/the historymakers/ (November 28, 2011).

"History," *Federally Employed Women,* http://www.few.org/history.asp (September 29, 2011).

"Tremendous Legacy," *Presbyterian Church* (U.S.A.), http://www.pcusa.org/news/2009/8/4/tremendous-legacy/ (November 28, 2011).□

Tom Lea

The works of the American artist and author Tom Lea (1907–2001) have become recognized as icons of the southwestern United States.

Lea's work had both public and private sides. His murals, regarded as some of the finest produced in the United States, appear in public buildings in his native Texas and around the country. He was an accomplished portraitist who painted some of the best-known figures of the twentieth century, but much of his work was executed for friends and acquaintances, and until the end of his long life, he was never represented by a gallery or agent. Some of the work of which Lea was most proud included a series of war illustrations he executed for *Life* magazine while embedded with U.S. troops in the Pacific theater during World War II. As an author, Lea wrote and illustrated several best-selling novels and penned nonfiction books on subjects ranging from horse training in New Spain to the giant King Ranch in Texas. Not well known beyond Texas for much of his life, Lea gained renewed attention in old age partly as a result of being championed by U.S. President George W. Bush, a personal friend.

Threatened by Pancho Villa

Thomas Calloway Lea III was born on July 11, 1907, in El Paso, Texas. His father, Tom Lea Sr., was an attorney and a veteran of the Spanish-American War who became El Paso's mayor in 1915. The Mexican revolutionary leader Pancho Villa was active in the border area during this period, and at one point the elder Lea jailed Villa's wife on gun smuggling charges and threatened Villa himself with arrest. Villa responded by putting a price on the mayor's head, and the Lea family received kidnapping threats directed toward Tom Lea Jr. and his younger brother, Joe. The two boys were placed under armed guard but were apparently not traumatized: "For the Lea boys it was a high-toned adventure," Lea recalled (according to Lynwood Abram of the *Houston Chronicle*).

Lea had obvious artistic talent, displayed early when he made a painting of a woman in a fashionable short skirt. That painting was destroyed by Lea's religiously devout mother, but an art teacher at El Paso High School and a librarian at the El Paso Public Library recognized his skill, gave him art books, and encouraged him to apply to the Chicago Art Institute. Lea enrolled at age 17, studying with the muralist John Norton. He put himself through school largely by doing whatever paid illustration work he could find, including drawing portraits for a weekly lecture series and painting a talcum powder advertising sign. Lea maintained that all these activities helped him develop his craft.

For a time Lea served as Norton's formal apprentice, and after graduating from the Institute in 1926, he stayed on in Chicago and continued to do commercial art work and occasional murals. He married another art student, Nancy Taylor, and by 1930 the pair had scraped together enough money to take Norton's suggestion that they travel to Europe. Sailing third class in ship's steerage, they arrived in Paris to find an exhibition of the monumental paintings of French artist Eugène Delacroix on display at the Louvre Museum. Lea studied Delacroix's murals at the church of St. Sulpice in Paris and then moved on to Florence and Rome, Italy, and absorbed the great murals of the Renaissance-era churches in those cities.

Made Anthropological Drawings at Lab

Back in the United States in 1933, Lea decided to fulfill a childhood dream by moving to New Mexico. Arriving in a 1926 Dodge sedan that he had bought for $75, with a broken back window he could not afford to replace, Lea found magazine illustration work and, after initial reluctance to take what he considered charity, executed paintings for Works Progress Administration projects; some of these are still owned by the New Mexico Fine Arts Museum. Lea further honed his skills by working in an anthropological laboratory where he had to make detailed drawings of objects such as Navajo rugs, and he began to make contact with other southwestern artists. Lea's time in New Mexico was cut short after his wife suffered an infection when equipment used in an emergency appendectomy was inadequately sterilized. The couple returned to El Paso, where Nancy Lea died on April 1, 1936. "I've chosen to blank out that part of my life," Lea recalled in an oral history quoted on his official website. From then on he lived in El Paso.

In 1938, he married Sarah Dighton after a first date in which he asked her if she wanted to see a mural he had painted. On their second date he proposed. By that time, Lea had completed several large projects, including the Texas Centennial murals at the Hall of State at the Texas State Fairgrounds in Dallas, and a now-lost mural at a post office in Washington, D.C. He garnered several more commissions between 1938 and 1940, including one for a mural at the railroad station in Lacrosse, Wisconsin. In 1940, he provided the illustrations for the book *The Longhorns,* by Texas's premier historian, J. Frank Dobie. Lea's career was clearly ascending, and in 1941 he was awarded the prestigious Rosenwald Fellowship.

Lea had to turn the fellowship down, however, for he received what he considered a better offer: *Life* magazine proposed that he be embedded with U.S. troops as a war artist. Lea joined battalions in Iceland, Africa, and China, but perhaps his most harrowing series of works was accomplished as American forces fought their way across the South Pacific, encountering entrenched Japanese forces on each island. Lea made sketches on the battlefield, later turning them into finished oil paintings that were reproduced in *Life.*

Embedded with Marines During Pacific Battle

In September of 1944, Lea was present at the Battle of Peleliu in what is now the nation of Pulau, observing fighting in which about 1,200 U.S. Marines lost their lives. "All I carried was a musette bag with a nine-by-twelve sketchbook, pencils, and a couple of fountain pens. I made a few sketches, but it was impossible to attempt any real drawings ashore. I wasn't holding the pencil too steadily; I was too busy trying to keep alive," he recalled to *Texas Monthly.* In one painting, "First Wave, Going In, Peleliu," Lea depicted a young Marine gazing at the island's beach, his face set in a mixture of fear and resolution. Throughout the considerable danger he himself experienced, Lea carried a snapshot of his wife, Sarah, and in 1947 he turned it into a simple painting, "Sarah in the Summertime." He considered it his personal favorite among all his paintings and kept it for the rest of his life in his living room.

Generally, however, Lea's gaze as a painter looked outward to the wide world. "We have the privilege of living in this life in this marvelous place," he said, as quoted by gallery owner Adair Margo in a memorial address reproduced on Lea's official website. "And writing and painting to me don't have anything to do with who I am and what I do, but with what is so wonderful about what's out there." Stylistically Lea's art was difficult to categorize as either modern or traditional. His training during the age of twentieth-century modernism showed in the geometric forms that appeared in his southwestern landscapes, but his portraits and especially his representations of soldiers at war relied on unvarnished realism and psychological insight.

Lea converted some of his Peleliu images into a 1945 book, *Peleliu Landing,* which he wrote and illustrated himself. As the golden age of American mural painting came to

an end after World War II, Lea turned increasingly to writing, although he continued to paint prolifically in his studio in the hills overlooking El Paso and Ciudad Juarez, Mexico. He became interested in the history of bullfighting in the Americas while working on a *Life* article, and wrote his first novel, *The Brave Bulls* (1949), on the theme of bullfighting. His 1952 novel *The Wonderful Country* depicted the U.S.-Mexican border area where he lived. Both those novels were made into successful films; Lea himself had a bit part as a barber in the film of *The Wonderful Country.* Along with several other works of fiction, Lea earned acclaim for the two-volume work *The King Ranch* (1957), a history of a south Texas ranch covering parts of six counties and nearly 1,300 square miles. That book, as well as most of Lea's other writings, included his own illustrations.

Although he rarely accepted specific commissions for small paintings, he did execute a portrait of Madame Chiang Kai-shek, wife of the Chinese nationalist leader, at the behest of *Time* publisher Henry Luce. He painted the portrait of Texas U.S. Representative Sam Rayburn that hangs in the Rayburn House Office Building in Washington, D.C. He continued to paint into the 1990s, but was finally slowed by vision problems. In 1996, the El Paso Museum of Art opened a gallery dedicated to Lea's work. Lea's public profile was raised in 2000 by the election of George W. Bush, an admirer of his work. Bush quoted Lea's book *A Picture Gallery* in his acceptance speech at the 2000 Republican Convention. Lea's painting "Rio Grande" hung in the White House during Bush's presidency, and after Lea's death in El Paso on January 29, 2001, the first official trip made by First Lady Laura Bush was to attend his funeral.

Books

Antone, Evan Haywood, *Tom Lea: His Life and Work,* Western, 1988.
Lea, Tom, et al., *Tom Lea: An Oral History,* Western, 1995.

Periodicals

Austin American-Statesman, January 14, 2001.
Houston Chronicle, January 31, 2001.
New York Times, August 16, 2000.
PR Newswire, October 18, 2006.
Texas Monthly, August 1994.

Online

"Tom Lea Biography," *Tom Lea Official Website,* http://www.tomlea.net (September 30, 2011). □

Richard Leacock

British filmmaker Richard Leacock (1921–2011) was among the most influential documentary directors of the mid-twentieth century. His gritty, unadorned style helped shape the *cinéma vérité* movement, in which filmmakers simply let the camera roll to

provide as close to a "truthful"—the *vérité* of the French term—experience as possible for the audience. Leacock's contemporaries and collaborators include brothers Albert Maysles and David Maysles and D.A. Pennebaker. Even among his peers, Leacock stood out as "a liberator and iconoclast," noted a writer for the *Economist*. "Those outside the profession who may never have heard his name will see the influence of his camerawork whenever they turn on the news."

Richard Leacock came from an affluent British family that would also produce a second filmmaker, his older brother Philip. Born in London on July 18, 1921, "Ricky," as he was called, spent his early years on a banana plantation owned by their father in the Canary Islands, an archipelago off the northwest coast of the African continent. That idyll ended at age eight, when he was shipped off to Bedales, a boarding school in Hampshire, England. Leacock went on to Dartington Hall, a progressive, arts-centered preparatory school in Devon.

As a youngster, Leacock was fascinated by photography and built his own darkroom to develop film. That interest evolved into filmmaking after he saw the silent film *Turk-Sib,* a 1929 documentary from the Soviet Union about the construction of the Turkestan-Siberian railroad. Inspired, Leacock procured a 16-millimeter movie camera and made his own documentary, *Canary Island Bananas,* around 1935. It was a short work, around twelve minutes in length, but told the story of how bananas were picked, packed, and shipped off to British consumers from his father's Canary Island plantation.

One of the documentary genre's pioneers was the American adventurer Robert J. Flaherty, whose epic *Nanook of the North* was shot in the Canadian Arctic in the early 1920s and caused an international sensation. *Nanook* would later be deemed one of the most important milestones in film, for it was the first full-length movie to portray a real story, without actors, and in this case showed the vanishing culture of an Inuit hunter and his family. Flaherty eventually settled in Britain with his family, and two of his daughters were at Dartington at the same time as Leacock. The school's headmaster screened *Canary Island Bananas* for Flaherty, and Flaherty contacted Leacock and promised him a job when he finished his education.

Majored in Physics at Harvard

While at Dartington Hall, Leacock won a plum assignment to accompany the school's biology teacher, ornithologist David Lack, to the remote Galapagos Islands off the coast of Ecuador. Lack was an expert in finches, and the 1938–39 expedition yielded important clues about the evolutionary history of the species. With the outbreak of World War II in Europe in the late summer of 1939, Leacock chose to remain abroad and entered Harvard University as a physics major. He should have graduated with the Class of 1943, but took time off to work on a 1941 documentary film, *To

Hear Your Banjo Play, which showcased an American folk music festival in Virginia. He served as cameraperson and assistant editor on the project, which was one of the first documentary films to feature live sound.

Leacock's education was also interrupted by his enlistment in the U.S. Army in 1942, shortly after his marriage to a Radcliffe College student named Eleanor Burke. With his technical experience, Leacock was assigned to work as a combat photographer in Myanmar and China. After his Army discharge, he went to New York City—where his wife was finishing her studies—to meet Flaherty. The veteran documentarian had not made a film since 1934's *Man of Aran,* which depicted life on a hardscrabble piece of land in the Irish Sea, but kept his word and hired Leacock to work as a camera operator on a new project to be called *Louisiana Story.*

Louisiana Story, released in 1948, was not technically a documentary film. Like *Nanook,* it was funded by a company—in this case Standard Oil—and as with *Man of Aran,* Flaherty staged certain scenes for narrative effect. Leacock worked with Flaherty to film the story of a Cajun family, descendants of French "Acadian" settlers in Nova Scotia and other parts of Canada's Maritime Provinces, who had fled British rule in the 1760s and settled in Louisiana. The work followed Joseph Boudreaux, a youngster who roams the Louisiana bayou—an area whose isolation helped preserve Cajun culture for generations—with his pet raccoon, hunts down the enormous alligator believed to have snatched the raccoon, and witnesses the positive changes brought to the family when his grandfather finally acquiesces and allows an oil company to drill on their land.

Realized Equipment Hindered the Story

The making of *Louisiana Story* shaped the direction of Leacock's career. As he recalled in an interview with P. J. O'Connell that appeared in the book *Robert Drew and the Development of Cinema Verite in America,* there were two types of cameras used in the filming. "When we were using small cameras, we had tremendous flexibility," he told O'Connell. That diminished immediately, he continued, "the moment we had to shoot dialogue, lip-sync—everything had to be locked down, the whole nature of the film changed...We had heavy disk recorders, and the camera that, instead of weighing six pounds, weighed two hundred pounds, a sort of monster." It was Leacock himself who would come up with the technological advance a few years later that ended this laborious process.

In the interim, Leacock worked on projects for the new medium of television. One was the acclaimed *Omnibus* series that first aired on CBS in the early 1950s. This was a landmark cultural program, and one of Leacock's contributions was *Toby and the Tall Corn,* about a Missouri tent theater. His freelance work for the *Omnibus* series included *How the F100 Got Its Tail* and a journey with the New York Philharmonic under its musical director Leonard Bernstein through Europe and the Soviet Union.

Leacock's major breakthrough as a filmmaker came in 1958 in the technical realm, when he tinkered with the method by which the sound-recording equipment worked with the portable cameras in use at the time. He came up with a wireless control, using a part from a Bulova wristwatch, that synchronized the camera and a separate sound recorder. The device was used well into the 1990s. His achievement brought him to the attention of Robert Drew, a photo editor at the Time-Life media empire. *Life* magazine had virtually created the field of photojournalism, and Drew wanted to trigger the same transformation for documentary news footage. He formed Robert Drew Associates and hired Leacock to work for him. Several other young filmmakers also worked for Drew during this period, including brothers Albert Maysles and David Maysles, who would later achieve fame with the cult classic documentary *Grey Gardens.*

Shot *Primary*

Leacock worked with Albert Maysles and another film buff, D.A. Pennebaker, to make the landmark political documentary *Primary* in 1960. They had unprecedented access to the Democratic Party nomination process, tracking the two frontrunners, both of them U.S senators: John F. Kennedy from Massachusetts and Minnesota's Hubert H. Humphrey. The film focused on the candidates' battle to secure delegates from a crucial state, Wisconsin, which Kennedy ultimately won and then went on to secure the 1960 Democratic Party nomination. *Primary,* wrote William Grimes in the *New York Times* years later, "offered deadpan, highly revealing scenes of two candidates in the throes of American-style campaigning, in all its tedium and exhaustive repetition. This was something new in journalistic filmmaking. For the first time, audiences were given a sustained cinematic look behind the curtain of politics and an unvarnished portrait of two candidates going all-out for the brass ring."

Primary is customarily deemed a turning point in documentary filmmaking, in news coverage of political campaigns, and as one of the building blocks of reality television. "What are now clichés—behind-the-scenes shots of a political campaign—were then startling, fresh and unprecedentedly intimate," noted Brian Winston, a journalist with London's *Independent* newspaper. Leacock was not credited as director of *Primary*—Robert Drew was—but he was the cinematographer who "famously filmed Kennedy pacing his hotel room listening to the election results with an unobtrusive camera resting on the arm of his chair," wrote Winston. "There were no extra lights, no tripod, no personal microphones; and, it would seem, no awareness of the camera on the part of the people being filmed."

Leacock and Pennebaker left Drew Associates to form their own production company in 1963. Together they made *Crisis: Behind a Presidential Commitment* about the Kennedy administration's efforts to enforce new federal civil rights legislation in the South. One of Leacock's first directorial credits since *Canary Island Bananas* also came in 1963 with *Happy Mother's Day,* a 26-minute tale of the first set of American quintuplets to survive birth and early infancy. Leacock's camera followed the story of the family in Aberdeen, South Dakota, and the fanfare that accompanied the event. "There is a great deal of gentle irony at the expense of the townsfolk," noted a *Times* of London

correspondent, "but what emerges from the film is the warmth and sincerity of Mrs. Fisher and her bewilderment of what is happening to her."

Taught at MIT

Leacock and Pennebaker's company were responsible for two vital pieces of rock cinema in the 1960s: the Bob Dylan documentary *Don't Look Back* in 1967 and *Monterey Pop,* filmed at California's Monterey Pop Festival that same year. Both concert films are considered precursors to the modern music video. In the late 1960s, Leacock and Pennebaker also worked briefly with legendary French filmmaker Jean-Luc Godard, a pioneer of the postwar *Nouvelle Vague* (New Wave) cinema who was exploring the documentary medium.

Leacock's career took a major shift when he accepted an invitation from the Massachusetts Institute of Technology (MIT) to set up its film department with Ed Pincus, who had made several influential documentaries during the height of the civil rights movement in America. Leacock taught at MIT for years and made fewer films, but among them was 1984's *Lulu in Berlin,* an interview with Louise Brooks, the reclusive retired film star of Weimar Germany during the 1920s and '30s.

By 1990, Leacock was retired from MIT and living in Paris. His marriage to Burke produced four children, but the couple divorced; a second marriage that produced a second son also dissolved. In the early 1990s, Leacock resumed filmmaking with Valérie Lalonde, his longtime partner. They had a home near the famed Mont St. Michel fortress in Normandy, but Leacock died at their Paris home on March 23, 2011. His son by Burke, Robert Leacock, served as director of photography on 1991's *Madonna: Truth or Dare.* By marriage, Leacock was the uncle of singer-songwriter Harry Chapin, whose mother was Eleanor Burke's sister.

Before his death, Leacock worked on a memoir, *Richard Leacock: The Feeling of Being There,* that was published in both standard print format and as a digital video book in 2011. The title is borrowed from one of his best-known turns of phrase in which he asserted that what he wanted in his documentaries was simply "the feeling of being there." As he explained to O'Connell, he realized early on that any advance notice of a documentary project would excite everyone involved, a feeling heightened by the presence of large cameras, boom microphones, and other imposing technical wizardry. "It was all so organized that we took all the life out of it," he remarked. "I've often said that we spent enormous amounts of effort going out into the real world and destroying the very thing we set out to record."

Books

O'Connell, P. J., "Other Voices: Richard Leacock," in *Robert Drew and the Development of Cinema Verite in America,* Southern Illinois University Press, 1992.

"Richard Leacock," in *International Dictionary of Films and Filmmakers,* Volume 2, Gale, 2000.

Periodicals

Economist, October 6, 2001.

Independent (London, England), April 1, 2008.

New York Times, February 11, 1972; November 13, 1997; March 24, 2011.

Times (London, England), February 29, 1964.

Online

"Innovator of Journalism, Film Dies," *All Things Considered,* National Public Radio, March 25, 2011, http://www.npr.org/2011/03/25/134862145/Innovator-of-Journalism-Film-Dies (October 28, 2011).

"Richard Leacock," *IMDB.com,* http://www.imdb.com/name/nm0494886/ (October 28, 2011). □

Lilly Ledbetter

American women's rights advocate Lilly Ledbetter (born 1938) was the plaintiff in a landmark Supreme Court case on equal pay and the inspiration for the Lilly Ledbetter Fair Pay Act of 2009.

American women's equality advocate Lilly Ledbetter began a pivotal lawsuit over gender-based pay differences that went all the way to the U.S. Supreme Court in 2007. Although the Court ruled against her in *Ledbetter v. Goodyear Tire & Rubber Co.* and thus barred Ledbetter's own claims for financial recompense for decades of discriminatory pay, the U.S. Congress took up the matter by passing the Lilly Ledbetter Fair Pay Act. This law, which amended the Civil Rights Act of 1964 to permit a much longer statute of limitations for legal claims relating to pay inequality, became the first major bill signed into law by newly inaugurated President Barack Obama in January of 2009. Although into her retirement years, Ledbetter remained a voice for greater equality in the United States even after the passage of the law named for her. "She's a special lady, a working class lady, and a fighter," First Lady Michelle Obama declared of Ledbetter on CNN's *Larry King Live,* according to a *Time* piece by Kate Pickert. The National Women's Hall of Fame agreed, and inducted Ledbetter into its ranks in 2011.

Became Supervisor at Goodyear Tire

Born Lilly McDaniel on April 18, 1938, in the rural town of Jacksonville, Alabama, Ledbetter was perhaps an unexpected figure to institute a national discussion on gender and pay equality. The daughter of mechanic J.C. McDaniel and his wife, homemaker Edna (Smith) McDaniel, Ledbetter grew up an only child in the Alabama countryside. As a girl, she worked in her grandfather's cotton fields and attended local schools. The hard labor of her childhood pushed Ledbetter to pursue a more middle-class adult life. "That direction made me the strong individual I am today," Ledbetter told Heidi Brown in a 2009 *Forbes* story. "My mother told me I could be and do anything I wanted, but I had to get educated." Ledbetter graduated from Jacksonville High School in 1956, and as an adult took college-level classes and put in volunteer hours that enabled her to eventually earn the equivalent of a degree.

Ledbetter spent much of her adult life working and raising her family, however. Soon after graduating from high school, she married U.S. Army officer, Charles J. Ledbetter; the couple went on to have two children—son Phillip and daughter Vickie— and remained together until Charles Ledbetter's death in December of 2008. Over the next two decades, Ledbetter held various positions, including work as a manager of various area branches of tax preparation firm H & R Block and as an assistant financial aid officer at the local educational institution, Jacksonville State University. In 1979, she successfully applied for a position with the Goodyear Tire & Rubber Company in Gadsen, Alabama, not far from her home in Jacksonville. At first, Ledbetter served as an overnight line supervisor on the 7 p.m. to 7 a.m. rotation. Before long, she advanced to become an area manager, a role she held until her retirement in 1998.

Ledbetter's relative competence at her job during this period proved an important talking point in her later court case. According to Ledbetter, she had ranked among the top performers of her 150-person group during a management training course, and Goodyear granted her a Top Performer award in 1996. Despite these positive indicators, Ledbetter received consistently lower pay than the other managers in equivalent positions, all of whom were male. Later research revealed that this pattern of pay disparity was common throughout the Goodyear plant. Some female managers were paid less than the male employees they supervised, and Ledbetter was denied at least one pay increase by a male supervisor widely known to be against the advancement of women in the workplace in general. In another instance in the early 1980s, a supervisor requested that Ledbetter provide sexual favors in return for a positive job performance review. This instance of sexual harassment was not isolated, but it was so significant that Ledbetter filed a complaint with the Equal Employment Opportunity Commission. Although this claim resulted in the removal of that manager from contact with Ledbetter, she later stated that she felt it led to isolation and increased discrimination by co-workers. Despite having worked tirelessly for years to gain the respect of her peers, Ledbetter became known as a troublemaker and was increasingly isolated from her co-workers.

Filed *Ledbetter v. Goodyear Tire* & *Rubber Co.*

At least one other Goodyear employee believed that Ledbetter had been treated unfairly, however. Shortly before she was set to retire in the late 1990s, Ledbetter found an anonymous note in her locker that listed the salaries of three male co-workers in equivalent positions with roughly equal levels of seniority. At that time, Ledbetter earned $3,727 each month—the annual equivalent of about $44,725. Her male co-workers earned between about $51,500 and $63,000 annually, and had consistently outearned her throughout the course of her career. "I would never have dreamed I was getting paid less," Ledbetter told Brown. Ledbetter filed another claim with the Equal Employment Opportunity Commission over the differences in her pay under the Equal Pay Act and Title VII of the Civil Rights Act of 1964, which specifically bars discriminatory employment practices. Soon after, Goodyear assigned her a new job: inspecting tires for the massive Hummer SUV. The 60-year-old Ledbetter spent the next ten months performing the laborious tasks of lifting and studying the 80-pound tires before her doctor warned her that the task would quickly leave her disabled. In November of 1998, Ledbetter retired earlier than planned to avoid these health consequences.

A few months later, she hired Jon Goldfarb, an attorney from Birmingham, Alabama, who agreed to take her case on contingency. Goldfarb filed a claim for wage discrimination under the Equal Pay Act and Title VII, among others, with the U.S. District Court in northern Alabama. Over the next several years, Ledbetter's case progressed through the court system. The U.S. District Court disregarded the Equal Pay Act because Ledbetter's performance evaluation had been lower than that of her male counterparts, which legally allowed her to receive lower pay; Ledbetter, however, argued that this disparity resulted from her gender rather than from her actual performance, pointing to her 1996 award. The court did permit Ledbetter's other claims to proceed to trial, and the jury found in her favor to the tune of $3.3 million. Goodyear quickly filed an appeal with the U.S. Court of Appeals, and the damages were reduced to $360,000. The case then moved on to the U.S. Supreme Court.

The Court heard Ledbetter's case in 2007 and narrowly ruled in Goodyear's favor. According to the majority opinion, Ledbetter's claim had simply come too late; according to the statutes of the Civil Rights Act, claims for pay discrimination were required to be filed within 180

days of the issuance of the unfair paycheck. Ledbetter, who argued that she had been paid unfairly throughout her tenure with Goodyear, had filed more than 7,000 days after the first act of discrimination. Members of the Court, however, broke sharply on the decision. "A worker knows immediately if she is denied a promotion or transfer, if she is fired or refused employment. And promotions, transfers, hirings, and firings are generally public events, known to co-workers," wrote Supreme Court Justice Ruth Bader Ginsberg in the minority dissenting opinion for the Court. "When an employer makes a decision of such open and definitive character, an employee can immediately seek out an explanation and evaluate it for pretext. Compensation disparities, in contrast, are often hidden from sight," she pointed out. On these grounds, the minority opinion argued that Ledbetter's claim was a valid one because she had no practical way of knowing about the discriminatory pay within the period of the statute of limitations, particularly because Ledbetter's employment contract barred her from discussing such matters with co-workers.

The decision reversed the earlier rulings, thus stripping Ledbetter of the previously ordered damages, although the Court did not contest that discrimination had taken place. Although the Court suggested that the length of time that had passed made the matter simply an unfortunate happening of the past, Ledbetter argued that the pay differential continued to affect her because of lowered pensions and Social Security payments based on her consistently lower wages.

Served as Advocate for Lilly Ledbetter Fair Pay Act

The Supreme Court decision galvanized advocates for women's rights. Democrats in the U.S. Congress quickly began efforts to introduce a new law named the Lilly Ledbetter Fair Pay Act. Under this law, the existing 180-day statute of limitations was reset each time a worker received a discriminatory paycheck. Had this provision been in effect at the time of the Supreme Court ruling, the decision would most likely have gone in Ledbetter's favor because she had filed her original case within the required six-month period. Democrats and Republicans largely split along partisan lines over the bill, and it became an issue in the 2008 presidential election. Democratic candidate Barack Obama came out in support of the measure, and Ledbetter was a speaker at that year's Democratic National convention. In contrast, Republican candidate John McCain opposed the bill. With the entrance of a new Congress in January of 2009, the Lilly Ledbetter Fair Pay Act won passage, and was soon signed in law by the newly inaugurated President Obama.

Ledbetter then began efforts to secure the passage of another equal pay measure, the Paycheck Fairness Act. This bill proposed changes to existing laws that would have allowed employees who had been discriminated against to receive unlimited damages and secured employees' rights to learn what others in similar positions within their companies earned, among other provisions. Although a version of the bill passed the House in January of 2010, it languished in the Senate. The rightward shift of the House of Representatives following the midterm elections later that year further stymied efforts to pass the bill. Challenges also emerged to the Lilly Ledbetter Fair Pay Act. By March of 2011, for example, a Texas state-level challenge to the application of the law to claims leveled under the state's Commission on Human Rights Act had resulted in competing interpretations by a district-level court and the court of appeals. The case then proceeded to the Texas Supreme Court, where it remained unresolved several months later.

Ledbetter, however, continued to speak in favor of the act and of pay equity in general—and to gain recognition for her efforts as an unlikely civil rights leader. In 2011, the National Women's Hall of Fame inducted her into its ranks. "If I can change just one of your lives for the betterment of the future, my trip here was worth it," Ledbetter told a group of high school and college students shortly thereafter, according to Sarah Moses of the Syracuse, New York *Post-Standard.* The following year, Ledbetter published her memoirs, *Grace and Grit: My Fight for Equal Pay and Fairness at Goodyear and Beyond.*

Periodicals

Business Insurance, November 22, 2010.
HRMagazine, March 2011.
New Yorker, September 15, 2008.
Post-Standard (Syracuse, NY), October 1, 2011.

Online

"Equal Payback for Lilly Ledbetter," *Forbes,* http://www.forbes.com/2009/04/28/equal-pay-discrimination-forbes-woman-leadership-wages.html (September 29, 2011).
"For Women, What a Difference a Year Almost Made," *Huffington Post,* http://www.huffingtonpost.com/lilly-ledbetter/for-women-what-a-differen_b_436113.html (September 29, 2011).
"Lilly Ledbetter," *Encyclopedia of Alabama,* http://www.encyclopediaofalabama.org/face/Article.jsp?id=h-3130 (November 30, 2011).
"Lilly Ledbetter," *National Women's Hall of Fame,* http://www.greatwomen.org/women-of-the-hall/search-the-hall/details/2/248-Ledbetter (November 30, 2011).
"Lilly Ledbetter," *Time,* http://www.time.com/time/nation/article/0,8599,1874954,00.html (September 29, 2011).
"Lilly M. Ledbetter, Petitioner v. The Goodyear Tire & Rubber Company," *Supreme Court of the United States,* Legal Information Institute, Cornell University, http://www.law.cornell.edu/supct/pdf/05-1074P.ZD (November 30, 2011).□

Peggy Lee

American singer Peggy Lee (1920–2002) is widely considered one of the finest female jazz vocalists of the twentieth century.

American singer Peggy Lee has been widely acknowledged as one of the leading jazz singers of the twentieth century. Her intentionally low-key singing style, breathy delivery, and sultry tones combined to give the vocalist a distinctive sound that continues to influence performers in the twenty-first century. After getting her start in supper clubs and radio shows, Lee broke through to national acclaim as the singer with the Benny Goodman Orchestra in the early 1940s. She went on to be a prolific recording artist and songwriter in her own right, as well as an Academy Award-nominated actress. Among her best-known performances were "Why Don't You Do Right?", the sultry "Fever," and the world-weary "Is That All There Is?", for which Lee received a Grammy Award.

The sixth of seven children, Lee was born Norma Deloris Egstrom on May 27, 1920, in the small town of Jamestown, North Dakota, to Marvin Egstrom and Selma (Anderson) Egstrom. Trouble plagued Lee's childhood. Her father was an alcoholic who was demoted from his job as a railroad superintendent shortly after her birth due to his drinking. Her mother died a few months after giving birth to the final Egstrom child when the future singer was just four years old. Not long afterward, the family home burned down. This litany of woes was compounded for the young Lee after her father remarried to Min Schaumberg, a former nurse in the household of one of Lee's much older married sisters. Lee's stepmother abused her physically and emotionally, beating her for small infractions and regularly criticizing her appearance. "All of the kindness was gone," Lee remembered in her autobiography, *Miss Peggy Lee.* One beating with a razor strap capped with a metal end left a scar on the singer's face that remained visible decades later.

As a child, Lee attended school and helped tend house. She got her first job at the age of eleven, working on a farm for a nearby family. Later, she managed the railroad depot in Wimbledon, where her father was transferred when she was fourteen, when his drinking incapacitated him. But she dreamed of music and singing, listening regularly to radio broadcasts from far-distant Fargo. Lee sang with her high school glee club, and as a teenager landed a job singing with a local orchestra led by bandleader Doc Haines. She appeared on local radio station KOVC, and before long was hired on as a singer at Fargo station WDAY. This job marked not only the true launch of her professional career, but also the creation of her stage name by the WDAY station manager.

Launched Career with Benny Goodman

When Lee was 17, she left North Dakota to join a friend who had moved to Los Angeles. The Great Depression lingered on, and work was scarce; Lee found short-term work as a waitress and, later, working as a carnival barker. Some acquaintances heard her sing and suggested she audition at the Jade Room, a small club in Hollywood. She landed a job as a singer with the club, but was forced to return to North Dakota after contracting tonsillitis and fainting during a performance. Back in North Dakota, Lee underwent a difficult tonsillectomy that contributed to the distinctive throatiness of her singing voice. After she recovered, Lee worked as a singer on Fargo radio and in a local hotel before moving east to Minneapolis to sing with a band there. Soon, she attracted the attention of bandleader Will Osborne, who hired her for his national touring orchestra. This job did not last long, however; short weeks later, Lee felt a lump on her throat and immediately visited a doctor to request an excision. He suggested surgery, and Lee came in the next day. While she was under anesthesia, the hospital staff accidentally dropped her on the floor, and she landed on her face. By the time Lee recovered from her injuries, Osborne's band had broken up. Undaunted, Lee returned to California and soon was singing in the thriving resort town of Palm Springs. There, a Chicago hotel manager spotted her and offered her a job back in Illinois.

Lee's acceptance proved fateful; it was in this spot that famed bandleader Benny Goodman spotted the budding performer in August of 1941. His band's previous singer had recently quit, and Goodman decided to hire Lee—then a total unknown—after seeing the twenty-one-year-old sing just one time. She signed on and made her debut the following day. Her limited experience had not prepared her for the types of performances mounted by Goodman's world-renowned jazz orchestra. Lee was terrified, but Goodman refused to let her quit. Lee stuck it out, and before long was putting her emerging vocal stamp on the band's live performances and recordings alike. "Befitting the style of the time, most of the song was instrumental," wrote Peter Richmond of the 1941 recording of Goodman's version of the standard "Let's Do It" in *Fever: The Life and Music of Miss Peggy Lee.* "But when it was over, it was a Peggy Lee song—the first Benny tune claimed by its young singer." Lee's natural sense of timing helped her channel the energy of Goodman's jazz standards, and her sparse, minimalistic singing technique gave her a distinctiveness unusual for the "canaries" of the big band era. She began receiving positive critical notices, and scored a genuine hit singing on the 1942 Goodman recording of "Why Don't You Do Right?" The following year, Lee's tenure with Goodman came to an end when she decided to quit the band and marry one of its former musicians, Dave Barbour.

Recorded Nationwide Hit Songs

By this time a famed singer at the national level, Lee received many offers. She initially turned them down to focus on her husband and, later in 1943, their baby daughter, Nicki. Lee began writing songs with Barbour, though, and before long she was back in the studio to record two standards for Capitol Records. These songs helped land Lee and Barbour a recording contract with that label, and the couple scored a hit in 1944 with "You Was Right, Baby." Lee began appearing regularly on popular radio shows hosted by Bing Crosby and Jimmy Durante, and her co-written "Mañana (Is Good Enough for Me)" sold over two million units in 1948. But troubles were on the horizon even as Lee's career flourished. Her husband struggled with alcohol dependency, and by the late 1940s could no longer perform on the road. The couple's marriage was faltering, and in 1951 Barbour asked Lee for a divorce, telling her that he did not want their daughter to deal with the effects of his alcoholism. Over the next several years, Lee remarried three more times: to actors Brad Dexter and Dewey Martin in the 1950s, and briefly to bandleader Jack del Rio in 1964. Barbour remained her acknowledged true love, however, and the couple's plans to remarry in 1965 after Barbour had stopped drinking were halted only by his death.

During the 1950s, Lee built her career through radio, television, and film as well as live performances. She co-starred in the 1953 film *The Jazz Singer,* and her portrayal of an alcoholic singer in the 1955 film *Pete Kelly's Blues* garnered her an Academy Award nomination for best supporting actress. Lee wrote and performed several songs for the animated Disney film *Lady and the Tramp,* earning a fee of just $3,500 for her work. *Pete Kelly's Blues* proved to be her final film effort, however, in part because her management wished to pursue more lucrative singing work, and perhaps, in part because many people assumed that the character Lee portrayed was a direct representation of herself. Her career thrived late in the decade with the release of the iconic track "Fever" and her booking of a series of running performances at New York City's Basin Street East supper club. These shows regularly packed the house, with such famous names as Judy Garland and Cary Grant turning out to see Lee. "*Newsweek* credited me with 'single-handedly reviving the supper club business,'" the singer proudly reported in her memoirs. She continued to perform at the club off and on for some time to great success.

An adaptable performer, Lee experimented with the sounds of rock and roll during the 1960s to mixed results. Her 1963 album *I'm a Woman* took tentative steps towards the emerging rock sounds of the decade; Richmond argued that "despite its flaws, [*I'm a Woman*] was arguably Peggy's best album for more than a decade." The album marked the first collaboration between Lee and the songwriting duo of Leiber and Stoller, who had penned hits for acts such as Elvis Presley. In 1968, the duo sent an unusual song they had written to Lee for consideration. Mostly comprised of spoken verses, the track had only a few sung lines in the chorus. Lee agreed to record "Is That All There

Is?'' The song became an unexpected hit, topping the *Bill-board* Adult Contemporary chart and nearly cracking into the top ten in an era dominated by psychedelic rock. It also garnered Lee her only Grammy Award.

Health Faded in Later Years

Throughout the 1970s and 1980s, Lee continued to tour and record, although none of these later efforts garnered the same kind of critical or popular attention as had her earlier career. Ever a perfectionist, the singer continued to perform in glamorous gowns with sharply trained musicians throughout, bringing an echo of her bygone heyday into the contemporary world. She helped create a short-lived Broadway musical autobiography, *Peg,* in 1983, and published her memoirs in 1989.

In 1988, Lee sued Disney for compensation from the proposed video sales of *Lady and the Tramp;* unsurprisingly, her 1955 contract for work on the film had not included payment for its release in a medium not yet imagined. A lengthy court battle ensued, with Lee ultimately being awarded more than $2 million. Other difficulties plagued the singer, however; the combination of her diabetes, double-bypass surgery, and a fall left her in poor health that essentially ended Lee's ability to perform publicly. Instead, she filled her time with such activities as helping her daughter manage an art gallery, painting, and listening to old jazz records. In 1992, she sang at a nightclub attached to the New York Hilton Hotel, inspiring *New York Times* reviewer Stephen Holden to praise ''her will power, musicality and professionalism,'' and to note that despite some vocal feebleness that Lee could still ''project a fair degree of the old magic.'' Soon after, she recorded her final album, *Moments Like These.* The following year, the singer appeared at the Concord Jazz Festival in California, and in 1995, she delivered her swan song at the Hollywood Bowl. The Grammy committee honored her that year with a Lifetime Achievement Award. Three years later, she suffered a major stroke that left her bedridden and mostly mute. But Lee lingered for some time, helped by a respirator and other medical devices. She died on January 21, 2002, at her home in Los Angeles, California, as the result of a heart attack.

Lee's musical legacy, however, endures. Widely recognized as one of the finest jazz singers of the twentieth century, Lee inspired later singers such as diverse as Madonna, k.d. lang, and Diana Krall. During her career, Lee recorded more than 700 songs and over sixty albums that have been enjoyed by millions of music listeners around the world. Those fans have worked to ensure that the singer remains in the spotlight. In 2010, efforts began to commemorate the singer's life through an interpretive center housed in the railroad depot that her father had once managed in Wimbledon, North Dakota. That same year, actress Reese Witherspoon secured the rights to Lee's life story from her estate with the intention of developing a biopic about the singer. As long as people listen to jazz, it seems certain that they will continue to remember the breathy, effortless singing voice of Miss Peggy Lee.

Books

Contemporary Musicians, Gale, 1992.

Lee, Peggy, *Miss Peggy Lee: An Autobiography,* Donald I. Fine, 1989.

Richmond, Peter, *Fever: The Life and Music of Miss Peggy Lee,* Holt, 2006.

Periodicals

New York Times, August 3, 1992; January 22, 2002.

Online

''Peggy Lee's Legacy in Music,'' *BBC News,* http://news.bbc.co.uk/2/hi/entertainment/1775077.stm (November 19, 2011).

''Witherspoon in Tune with Peggy Lee,'' *Variety,* http://www.variety.com/article/VR1118022766?refCatId=13 (November 19, 2011).□

Jerry Leiber and Mike Stoller

Jerry Leiber (1933-2011) and Mike Stoller (born 1933) were the most important and successful songwriting team of the early rock'n'roll era. Best remembered for writing a string of hits for megastars like the Coasters and Elvis Presley as well as supplying hit material to the likes of Wilbert Harrison, Dion, Peggy Lee, Lavern Baker, Jay and the Americans and the Clovers, the men also co-wrote and produced a string of memorable hits for the Drifters during the late 1950s and early 1960s. After founding a record label, later in their career, their funniest, most streetwise songs were used as the basis for a 1994 Broadway show, *Smokey Joe's Café.*

Born April 25, 1933, in Baltimore, Maryland, Jerome Leiber was a white Jewish kid who grew up on the outskirts of a Polish, Italian, and black community. His father, a milkman, died of a cerebral hemorrhage when he was just five years old, so his mother Mayna Lerner Leiber supported the youngster and his two older sisters by running a small grocery store. Young Jerome's first language was Yiddish and he was often taunted and bullied by other boys in the neighborhood, but found that he was welcome in the area's black neighborhoods where he delivered groceries. Intrigued by the sounds of boogie woogie and jump blues, he took piano lessons from a boarder at his Uncle Dave's house until the disapproving relative abruptly brought them to an end. Eventually, his mother started a more lucrative business that sold pots and pans, and this turn of fortune enabled both her and Jerome to follow her daughters out to Los Angeles, California just as World War II was ending. It was there that Leiber would meet his lifelong friend and partner.

Born March 13, 1933, in Belle Harbor, in the Queens section of New York, Mike Stoller is the son of Abe Stoller, an engineer and draftsman, and Adelyn Endore, a former model and actress. Young Michael and his sister benefitted from the musical traditions that ran through their mother's side of the family. Starting at the age of five, Stoller took piano lessons from his aunt, a concert pianist and, after rejecting her strict ways, a local itinerant teacher. Initially, the youngster loved the works of such classical composers as Bach and Richard Strauss. After attending an interracial summer camp with a friend named Al Levitt, however, he discovered the works of Louis Armstrong, Fats Waller, Jelly Roll Morton, and Baby Dodds, and his outlook changed. This newfound connection to jazz led the youngster to the great boogie woogie pianists Albert Ammons and Meade Lux Lewis, along with personal instruction by the great stride pianist James P. Johnson. Although their lessons together only lasted a few months, the gentle and encouraging Johnson helped the aspiring pianist understand the structure of the blues. The lessons ended in 1949, when he was sixteen years old and Stoller's father moved the family out to California.

While Leiber attended Fairfax High and Stoller studied at Belmont High, both were learning the ins and outs of the local music scene. Listening to disc jockey Hunter Hancock's radio show, Leiber heard Jimmy Witherspoon singing "Ain't Nobody's Business" and he grew determined to become a lyric writer. In 1950, encouraged by Lester Sill, the man in charge of sales and promotion for Modern Records, Leiber began looking for a partner who could write music for a lead sheet. Meanwhile, Stoller played rancheros with a small group and tried his hand at composing symphonies while maintaining his love of jazz and blues. A drummer named Jerry Horowitz recommended Leiber get in touch with Stoller, whom he had seen playing at a local dance. At first, the pianist was uninterested in working with the young lyricist, but once he realized that Leiber wanted to write blues, they joined forces.

Through Lester Sill, they got their first song "That's What the Good Book Says" recorded by the Robins. Afterwards, Jimmy Witherspoon recorded their "Real Ugly Woman" and the inimitable Charles Brown cut "Hard Times." The duo's working method was simple: Stoller would improvise on the piano and the ever fertile Leiber would spill out ideas at a rapid pace, then Stoller would occasionally offer a counter idea. In the process, the two learned that creativity was a constant tug-of-war that included arguments, redrafting, and polishing. Among their early efforts was a song titled "Kansas City," recorded as "K.C. Lovin'" by Little Willie Littlefield. Leiber thought the song's music sounded inauthentic, but when it was recorded with its original title by Wilbert Harrison in 1959, the song became a number one pop record.

Wrote for Big Mama Thornton

Despite placing songs with artists on such influential independent labels as Aladdin, Modern, Kent, Federal, Specialty, and Swingtime, they did not enjoy their first national hit until they received a call from local bandleader/producer Johnny Otis. Asked to bring a song to a Big Mama Thornton session, Leiber and Stoller created "Hound Dog," a snarling repudiation of a gigolo. "She was a wonderful blues singer," Stoller told *Rolling Stone* in 1990, "with a great moaning style. But it was as much her appearance as her blues style that influenced the writing of 'Hound Dog' and the idea that we wanted her to growl it. Which she rejected at first. Her thing was 'Don't you tell me how to sing no song!'" Released on Don Robey's Peacock label, Thornton's rendition of "Hound Dog" became a number one R&B record for seven weeks during the spring of 1953.

Royalty disputes with Don Robey—he wrote them a check that he stopped payment on—led to the team starting their own label, Spark. Partnering with Sill, the company lasted two years, in the process recording such acts as Gil Bernal, Ernie Andrews, the Honeybears, and the Robins. The latter recorded two songs that would figure prominently in Leiber and Stoller's catalog, "There's a Riot Going On" and "Smokey Joe's Café." Hamstrung by poor distribution, Spark folded after two years. A chance meeting with Neshui Ertegun led to his brother Ahmet signing the duo to Atlantic Records' first writer-producer freelance agreement. When not composing hits for other artists like "Black Denim Trousers" for the Cheers—later covered by French singer Edith Piaf as "L'Homme a la Moto"—they wrote songs for Ruth Brown, Big Joe Turner, and the Drifters.

Wrote Hits for Elvis Presley and the Coasters

By 1956, Leiber and Stoller were content making R&B music that occasionally sold to white teens, but after Elvis Presley made his cleaned up version of "Hound Dog" and "Don't Be Cruel," the biggest selling single of all time, they suddenly found themselves part of the burgeoning rock'n'roll market. Presley had recorded Freddie Bell's version of the song and the writers liked neither the lyric change nor the playful hard rockin' approach, but they did like the big jump in their royalty statements. Subsequently, they ended up writing 20 songs that the King of Rock'n'roll recorded, including material for the soundtracks for the films *Loving You*, *Jailhouse Rock* (in which Stoller had a bit part as the star's piano player), and *King Creole*. At Presley's request, the duo worked with the singer in the studio, demonstrating songs and helping him work up production ideas. They came to scoff but quickly learned that Presley shared their encyclopedic knowledge of blues and was a hard worker in the studio.

Ever prolific, the songwriters crafted the tongue-in-cheek hard rocker "Jailhouse Rock," the sensual ballad "Don't," and the snarling blues threats "Trouble" and "Santa Claus is Back in Town" for Presley, and he turned everything into enormous hit records. Unfortunately, dealing with Presley also meant dealing with his overbearing manager, Col. Tom Parker. After they made suggestions to the singer about possible film projects, Parker began to put restrictions on what Leiber and Stoller could do with Presley, and when they could do it. The final straw came when Parker sent the songwriters a blank contract for their services saying he would fill the details in later. With the exception of "She's Not You," which was co-written with Doc Pomus, Leiber and Stoller stopped writing specifically for Presley, although the rocker-turned-movie-star did cherry pick several of their songs recorded by other artists, including "Bosa Nova Baby," "Fools Fall in Love," "Saved," "Little Egypt" and "Girls, Girls, Girls." Losing Presley would have been a major blow to most careers, but Leiber and Stoller had another hot act waiting in the wings: the Coasters.

Featuring Carl Gardner, Bobby Nunn of the Robins, Billy Guy, and Leon Hughes, the Coasters proved the perfect exponent of the two-minute and thirty second playlet song that Leiber and Stoller had been experimenting with at Spark Records. Recording R&B with a comic vaudeville edge and King Curtis on sax, the group scored a string of hit records that appealed to American teens, including "Searchin'," "Young Blood," "Yakety Yak," "Charlie Brown," "Poison Ivy," and "Along Came Jones." Dubbed the clown princes of rock'n'roll, they also put a comedic spin on the black experience in such lesser hits as "Run Red Run," "Shopping for Clothes," and biting the hand that fed them, so to speak, "That is Rock'n'Roll." Their sly comic handling of the songwriter's razor sharp material resulted in their 1987 induction into the Rock and Roll Hall of Fame.

Working out of the Brill Building for Atlantic Records during the early 1960s, Leiber and Stoller began recording a new kind of R&B that featured string arrangements, Brazillian baion rhythms, allusions to Debussy and Ravel, and more mainstream adult lyrics. Working with a new line-up of the Drifters, they produced and occasionally co-wrote such enduring hits as "On Broadway," "Dance with Me," "Save the Last Dance for Me," and "There Goes My Baby." Working with Ben E. King after he left the Drifters, they continued the trend with "Spanish Harlem" and "Stand By Me." On the former, they gave a young Phil Spector a break, collaborating on the song and co-producing with him. Later, Spector, who played guitar on some sessions, would take

credit for producing the Drifters' big hits, but Leiber and Stoller have flatly denied these claims.

Founded Red Bird Records

Squabbles between Leiber and Stoller and Atlantic president Jerry Wexler provoked the duo into wiping the Drifters off "Only in America" and replacing them with Jay and the Americans. When the release became a Top 40 hit, Wexler made it difficult for the team to work with Atlantic's acts again. Subsequently, they began to spend more time producing for United Artists, Wand, Scepter, Kapp, and Big Top. After cutting hits with Jay and the Americans, the Exciters and Mike Clifford, they decided to helm their own label again.

Commissioning Red Bird and three subsidiaries, Tiger, Daisy, and Blue Cat, Leiber and Stoller began to hemorrhage cash. They knew how to make records but not how to sell them. In a bind, they hired producer George Goldner. Boasting a track record nearly as enviable as theirs, Goldner had produced hits for Gee, Rama, Gone, End, and Roulette Records. An inveterate gambler, he had lost his ownership stake in every label he had worked for, but he knew how to pick and produce hits. Offered a full partnership if the first record he produced became a hit, he took home a stack of acetates. "He was in early the next morning, his eyeballs hanging out of his head, very excited and enthusiastic," Leiber recalled in the liner notes to *The Red Bird Story*. "He held up this one acetate and said 'This is it—I'll bet my life on it.' It was 'Chapel of Love,' a record I hated with a real passion. It sold something like 1.2 million copies and that more or less determined the character of the company."

Red Bird also housed the songwriting team of Jeff Barry and Ellie Greenwich, who wrote "Chapel of Love" and the label's biggest hit "Leader of the Pack" by the Shangri-Las. One of the toughest looking of the girl groups, the Shangri-Las were produced by George "Shadow" Morton, who with Leiber and Stoller's help imbued their records— "Remember (Walking in the Sand)," "I Can Never Go Home Anymore", and "Give Him A Great Big Kiss"—with stomping drums, squealing tires, the sound of the surf, and unquenchable teenage angst. Red Bird and its subsidiaries recorded 20 chart records, some very big hits, but Leiber and Stoller were unhappy with Goldner's mainstream pop philosophy. Worse, their partner had gambled his share of their company away, making them partners with the New York mob. Selling Goldner their shares for one dollar, they abandoned the label and just concentrated on writing and producing once again.

After the Red Bird experience, the team sought ways to cultivate an older audience, which led to several failed attempts to mount an original Broadway musical. Showing a new maturity, they wrote the 1969 hit, "Is That All There Is?" Recorded by Peggy Lee and arranged by a young Randy Newman, the ironic fatalistic song became a number one Adult Contemporary hit, earning its singer a Grammy in the process.

Working on their publishing interests through most of the 1970s, Leiber and Stoller occasionally reappeared to produce albums by Peggy Lee, Procol Harum, Stealers

Wheel, and T-Bone Walker. During the 1980s, appreciation for their early works mounted, and musicals based around their songs *Only in America* and *Yakety Yak* appeared in Great Britain. In 1994, the duo enjoyed a great popular success with the staging of *Smokey Joe's Café—The Songs of Leiber and Stoller,* which ran for over 2000 performances on Broadway.

In 2009, Simon & Schuster released *Hound Dog—The Leiber and Stoller Autobiography.* At that time, the songwriters claimed their decades-long partnership was intact and that they had been collaborating with writer Michael Bywater on material for a Ken Hughes production of *The Trials of Oscar Wilde.* With songs left uncompleted, however, Jerry Leiber died of cardiopulmonary failure on August 22, 2011. He left behind three sons, two granddaughters, and a wealth of memorable songs. On behalf of the team, Mike Stoller accepted the American Celebration Lifetime Achievement in the Arts Award in November of that year.

Books

Bronson, Fred, *The Billboard Book of Number One Hits,* Billboard, 1997.

Feldman, Christopher G., *The Billboard Book of Number Two Hits,* Billboard, 2000.

Hyatt, Wesley *The Billboard Book of Number One Adult Contemporary Hits,* Billboard, 1999.

Leiber, Jerry; Stoller, Mike w/ Ritz, David, *Hound Dog—The Leiber and Stoller Biography,* Simon & Schuster, 2009.

Neely, Tim, ed., *Goldmine Roots of Rock Digest,* Krause Publications, 1999.

Periodicals

Variety, August 22, 2011.

Rolling Stone, April 19, 1990.

Online

"Leiber and Stoller,"*All Music,* http://www.allmmusic.com/artist/leiber-stoller-p13501/biography, (January 26, 2012).

"Leiber and Stoller" *BFI.Com,* http://www.bfi.org.uk/features/interviews/leiberstoller.html, (January 26, 2012).

"Jerry Leiber," *Internet Broadway Database,* http://www.ibdb.com/person (January 26, 2012).

"Jerry Leiber," *Internet Movie Database,* http://www.imdb.com/name/nm0500023/bio#trivia, (January 26, 2012).

"Mike Stoller," *Internet Movie Database,* http://www.imdb.com/name/nm0005469/bio, (January 26, 2012).

"Leiber and Stoller," *Songwriters Hall of Fame,* http://www.songwritershalloffame.org/index.php/ehxibits/bio/C20, (January 26, 2012).

"Mike Stoller Awarded American Celebration Lifetime Achievement in the Arts," *Broadway World.Com,* http://www.losangeles.broadwayworld.com.php?id=290929, (October 23, 2011).

Other

Liner notes for *The Red Bird Story,* Charly Records, 2011.□

Elmore John Leonard

American novelist Elmore Leonard (born 1925) established himself in the 1970s and 1980s as one of the nation's leading writers of crime fiction. His sharp dialogue, colorful characters, and complex plots make his novels highly entertaining, and several have been made into movies.

Leonard was born Elmore John Leonard Jr. in New Orleans, Louisiana on October 11, 1925, to Elmore Leonard Sr., who worked for the dealership network of General Motors, and Flora Rivé Leonard. When Leonard was very young, the job took the family across the country, to Dallas, Texas, Oklahoma City, Oklahoma, Memphis, Tennessee, and finally Detroit, Michigan. Leonard attended Detroit University High School, where he acquired the nickname Dutch, after the baseball player Dutch Leonard, a pitcher for the Washington Senators.

After graduating from high school in 1943, Leonard was drafted into the Navy. He served in a construction battalion in the Pacific, near New Guinea, during World War II. Upon returning to Detroit in 1946, he started college at the University of Detroit. He married Beverly Cline in 1949. In 1950, he graduated from college and began working for the Campbell-Ewald advertising agency.

Wrote Western Stories

While at Campbell-Ewald, Leonard began to write fiction. He chose Westerns as a genre for both artistic and commercial reasons, his childhood love of Western films such as *Stagecoach* and the fact that pulp magazines featuring Western stories were popular at the time. He developed a disciplined schedule, writing for two hours each morning before work, and also stole writing time away from the job. His first published short story, "Trail of the Apache," was published in the men's magazine *Argosy* in 1951. The story's vivid details about the Apache tribe caught the attention of literary agent Marguerite Harper, who contacted Leonard and became his agent. By the end of 1951, she had sold his story "Road to Desperation" to *Zane Grey's Western Magazine.* Meanwhile, Leonard, convinced that authentic detail greatly improved fiction, was researching his works by reading magazines and library books on the Southwest and the Apache tribe.

For the rest of the 1950s, Leonard balanced his writing and advertising careers. "My agent and editors would discourage me from trying to write full time," Leonard recalled to Ben Yagoda of the *New York Times.* "They said, 'Don't *have* to write. You'll become a hack, writing under a bunch of different names. Do it at your leisure, and do it right.'" He left Campbell-Ewald, where he had been a low-level office worker, and joined a smaller agency to learn more about the business, then returned to Campbell-Ewald fifteen months later in a more prestigious position, as a copywriter for Chevrolet ads. Meanwhile, he wrote four Western novels. Several of his stories were made into Hollywood films, including the movies

3:10 to Yuma and *The Tall T,* the latter based on his story "The Captives."

Made Industrial Films

Taking a risk, Leonard resigned from Campbell-Ewald in 1961, intending to write a book while living off a profit-sharing check. But with five children to provide for, he instead spent the next five years as a freelance ad copy writer and made several industrial and educational movies, some for Encyclopedia Britannica Films. The experience gave him valuable confidence in writing screenplays. In 1965, Twentieth Century Fox bought the film rights to his novel *Hombre,* which he had written roughly five years earlier. The $10,000 sale convinced Leonard to return to writing and devote himself to it full-time. From the mid-1960s on, he wrote at his desk five days a week from 9:30 to 6.

By then, the Western pulp magazines were dying or dead, their readers lured away by Western television shows. Switching to a new genre, Leonard wrote a crime novel based in Michigan, *The Big Bounce.* It featured a working-class Detroiter named Jack Ryan who comes up with a money-making scam and commits acts of vandalism in lakeside resorts with an 18-year-old bad influence named Nancy Hayes. Harper passed the novel to Hollywood agent H. N. Swanson, who sold both the book and the film rights.

Movie studios soon bought the rights to another Leonard novel, *Valdez Is Coming,* and his idea for a screenplay about Kentucky bootleggers, *The Moonshine War.* The sales, for $45,000 and $50,000, convinced Leonard to always keep in mind a story's potential as a film. Leonard wrote *The Moonshine War* as both a novel and as his first screenplay. During the late 1960s and early 1970s, Leonard wrote several screenplays that were not made into films. But Hollywood did release several movies based on Leonard stories: *Hombre,* starring Paul Newman, in 1967;

The Big Bounce, in 1969, with Ryan O'Neal; *The Moonshine War* in 1970; *Valdez is Coming,* starring Burt Lancaster, in 1971; and *Joe Kidd,* starring Clint Eastwood, in 1972.

Moved to Crime Fiction

Soon, Leonard took a major step in his career, writing the first of several books that would establish his reputation as one of America's best crime novelists. Influenced by the crime writer George V. Higgins, Leonard wrote his 1974 novel *52 Pick-Up,* set in downtown Detroit and its suburbs. The novel introduced some of the signature elements of Leonard's later fiction, including mentally disturbed characters and complicated heists or plots involving large amounts of cash (the 52 in the title is $52,000). The novel also included one of Leonard's first important black characters, pimp and robber Bobby Shy, who spoke in a laid-back black English.

The new novel also featured breakthroughs in Leonard's writing style. "He jumped about more, moving into scenes confidently, letting his characters' speech make clear to the reader who was talking and what was going on," wrote James E. Devlin in his biography, *Elmore Leonard.* "He writes best — albeit with mordant humor — of a dark, multiracial America," Devlin also wrote, "a country of gloomy or sun-baked cities where values are minimal and psychotics lurk at every turn, where betrayal and dysfunction are norms, where the violent prey on the weak, and crime is one way of making a living."

Divorced From First Wife

The 1970s were a transitional period in Leonard's writing career and personal life. He wrote two more novels set in Detroit, *Unknown Man #89* and *The Switch,* and his final Western, *Gunsights.* He traveled to Israel in 1974 after a film company there bought the rights to *52 Pick-Up,* and the trip inspired a novel set in Israel, *The Hunted.* His intense social life and heavy drinking may have contributed to the breakup of his marriage; he and Beverly, mother of his five children, separated in 1974 and divorced in 1977. He joined Alcoholics Anonymous in 1974, but did not give up drinking for good until 1977.

The next year, Leonard's investment in the crime novel genre deepened. The *Detroit News* asked him to write an article about the Detroit police. So he spent months at the city's police headquarters and accompanying cops on the streets, establishing relationships with several officers who gave him valuable information about police procedure for years after. The experience led to his moody 1980 novel *City Primeval.*

During the 1980s, Leonard took his characters from Detroit to south Florida and the Dominican Republic, and the flashes of humor in his writing became more frequent. The publisher Arbor House began publishing Leonard's novels after the head of the company promised to personally contact influential reviewers and build a new reputation for him. Sure enough, critical recognition of Leonard's work, which had been slowly building, expanded in response to his 1983 novels *Stick* and *LaBrava.* The latter book, set in Los Angeles in the mid-twentieth century, attracted rave reviews from *Newsweek* and the *New York Times*, and won Leonard the Edgar Award as crime novel of the year. *New York Times* critic Herbert Mitgang declared that Leonard should no longer be typecast as a novelist in the mystery or suspense genre, but instead be considered a serious novelist.

His next book, *Glitz,* set in Atlantic City and Puerto Rico, attracted intense praise and attention from nationally known writers. It became Leonard's first book to top the *New York Times* bestseller list. His next books, including *Freaky Deaky* and *Killshot,* attracted $1.5 million advances.

Gained Critical Respect and Popularity

Some reviewers compared Leonard to the writer Dashiell Hammett, the founder of hard-boiled detective fiction and an inspiration for film noir. Leonard grumpily resisted the association. He told Yagoda, writing for the *New York Times,* that he had not read Hammett in 40 years, and he described how a magazine photographer had tried to get him to conform to a mystery story stereotype. "He wanted to use a smoke machine," Leonard told Yagoda. "I talked him out of that, but he still brought a trench coat for me to wear. Luckily, it didn't have epaulets or a belt."

More incisive critics pointed to the dialogue in Leonard's books. Leonard paid attention to people's dialects and turns of phrase—for instance, taking notes while watching a television documentary about West Virginia coal miners. He often credited Ernest Hemingway as a major influence on his dialogue. In his book *Elmore Leonard's 10 Rules of Writing,* he advised writers to "avoid detailed descriptions of characters." Hemingway included only one line of physical description in his short story "Hills Like White Elephants," Leonard noted, "Yet we see the couple and know them by their tones of voice."

The 1990s found Leonard reaching an even higher level of recognition. Two more of his novels were made into movies, introducing his storytelling to a younger generation. His 1990 novel *Get Shorty,* about a loan shark named Chili Palmer who wants to break into movies, was made into a 1995 film starring John Travolta as Palmer. *Rum Punch,* a 1992 book, became the film Jackie Brown, directed by Quentin Tarantino. Leonard continued to stretch his talents by writing characters such as Karen Sisco in the novel *Out of Sight,* a tough law-enforcement agent inspired by a newspaper photograph of a shotgun-toting U.S. Marshal. The character later became the basis for a television show. He also defied his audience's expectations with *Cuba Libre,* a historical novel set during the Spanish-American War.

In the 2000s, Leonard continued his prolific writing, publishing several new novels. *New York Times* critic Bruce DeSilva, reviewing his 2000 book *Pagan Babies,* argued that Leonard was straying from his strengths by trying too hard to be funny, perhaps because the film version of *Get Shorty* had played up the book's subtle humor. DeSilva called the book "a dead-end descent into parody and a departure from his strength as a wry observer of humanity." But in 2002, when Leonard released a collection of short stories, *When the Women Came Out to Dance,* another *New York Times* critic, Charles Taylor, called it one of his most satisfying recent books and praised

his "unfailingly accurate dialogue." His work for the screen continued with the television series *Justified,* based on his novella *Fire in the Hole.*

Provided Tips to Young Writers

Leonard explained his minimalist style succinctly in a 2001 essay, published six years later as an illustrated book, *Elmore Leonard's 10 Rules of Writing.* The ten rules "help me remain invisible when I'm writing a book," he explained. Leonard advised writers to "Never open a book with weather," since readers would rather read about people. He warned them never to use any word except "said" to describe dialogue and never to add an adverb to "said." Finally, he warned them to "leave out the part that readers tend to skip," by which he meant long paragraphs of description. "I'll bet you don't skip dialogue," he wrote.

Books

Devlin, James E., *Elmore Leonard,* Twayne Publishers, 1999.
Leonard, Elmore, *Elmore Leonard's 10 Rules of Writing,* William Morrow, 2007.

Periodicals

New York Times, December 30, 1984; September 17, 2000; July 16, 2001; December 29, 2002. □

Julie De Lespinasse

Julie de Lespinasse (1732–1776) hosted one of the leading salons in Paris at the height of the French Enlightenment. She was close to a number of prominent writers, philosophers, and intellectual giants of the era, including Jean Le Rond d'Alembert, a mathematician and co-editor of the great *Encyclopédie,* and Nicolas de Condorcet, an influential political theorist. Though never married, Lespinasse led an emotionally turbulent private life she documented in a storied trove of letters published posthumously. "She was the soul of conversation, and thus she never made herself its object," remarked one of her admirers, the comte de Guibert, according to *The Republic of Letters: A Cultural History of the French Enlightenment.* "Her great art was to show to advantage the minds of others, and she enjoyed doing that more than revealing her own."

Descended from Old French Nobility

Born on November 9, 1732, in Lyon, Julie-Jeanne-Éléonore de Lespinasse was assumed to be the product of an extramarital affair between her mother, Julie-Claude-Hilaire d'Albon, and the man who would later marry Lespinasse's older sister. D'Albon came from an old aristocratic family and possessed several titles, including princesse d'Yvetot, marquise de Saint-Forgeux, and comtesse d'Albon. At sixteen, Lespinasse's mother had married one of her d'Albon cousins, which produced two legitimate heirs: a sister named Marie-Camille-Diane who was about sixteen years old at the time of Lespinasse's birth and known as Diane, and brother Camille, about eight years older than Lespinasse. Their father, Claude d'Albon, was separated from his wife when she bore a third child, Lespinasse, whose birth was registered in Lyon in a document that claimed she was the daughter of Julie Navarre and Claude de Lespinasse, two fictitious names. The ''de Lespinasse'' surname was taken from one of the d'Albon family's extensive property holdings. A few years later, her half-sister, Diane, married Gaspard de Vichy, comte de Champrond, the man believed to have been Lespinasse's biological father.

Julie d'Albon explained the arrival of an infant in her house by claiming she had adopted an illegitimate child. The house was a château in Avauges, between Lyon and Tarare, and Lespinasse was raised there and spent some time in a convent school run by French nuns. Her mother's death in 1748 placed Lespinasse in a precarious position, for the family was aware she was not a legitimate heir, but technically she had been born during her mother's marriage and thus considered a d'Albon by law. Her mother attempted to remedy this in her will, leaving Lespinasse a dowry of 6,000 livres and an annual pension of 300 livres. Lespinasse either loaned or gave this money to her brother, who then refused to return it.

Moved to Paris

For a few years a penniless Lespinasse served as governess at the household of her half-sister, Diane, to Diane's children with Gaspard de Vichy. It was during this period that she learned that the comte de Champrond was actually her real father, which was a tremendous emotional blow to her. Fortunately, Vichy's well-known and highly literate sister took pity on the young woman and offered to support her. This was Marie Anne de Vichy-Champrond, marquise du Deffand, who was in her late fifties by then. In 1754, Madame du Deffand returned to her former quarters in Paris and reestablished the salon that had attracted some of the leading figures of the era, including the writer Voltaire and Montesquieu, the political philosopher.

Du Deffand's eyesight was failing and she required a reader-companion, a role Lespinasse agreed to fulfill in return for room and board. They lived in a house built for the Convent of Saint-Joseph in the rue Saint-Dominique, where du Deffand's nightly salon attracted scores of important literary names of the Enlightenment. Among them was Denis Diderot, a philosopher and writer who created the massive *Encyclopédie*, published between 1751 and 1772. Another was Diderot's co-editor, Jean Le Rond d'Alembert, an expert on the mathematical sciences and physics. D'Alembert took a special interest in Lespinasse, whose attractiveness, intelligence, and social charm were mentioned in letters and other documents written by her contemporaries.

Broke with du Deffand

Lespinasse spent a decade co-hosting salons at du Deffand's, but the relationship between niece and aunt deteriorated. An insomniac, du Deffand demanded that Lespinasse read to her long into the night, and is thought to have hindered a potential marriage between her charge and a salon visitor named Taaffe, scion of the titled Irish landowning family that boasted tight connections to the Hapsburgs dynasty. Distraught, Lespinasse allegedly attempted suicide via an overdose of opium, but survived. The final split between the two women came in 1764 when du Deffand discovered that salon attendees were quietly meeting an hour earlier in Lespinasse's quarters. Du Deffand ordered her to move out, and Lespinasse's prominent and generous sympathizers helped her relocate to nearby quarters in the rue de Belle-Chasse. Among them were the Marèchal de Luxembourg and his wife, Madame de Luxembourg, who had been one of du Deffand's oldest friends but was better known as the patron of philosopher-writer Jean-Jacques Rousseau.

D'Alembert was among Lespinasse's staunchest supporters and played a key role in helping organize Lespinasse's nightly salon in the rue de Belle-Chasse, which lasted an impressive twelve years. From six to ten p.m. she greeted longstanding guests and newcomers who came to discuss the latest topics in current events and the arts. Authors read excerpts from their newest works, and Lespinasse encouraged engaged debates on important issues of the day. An invitation to her salon was one of the most coveted in Paris, along with those hosted in the homes of Madame Marie Thérèse Rodet Geoffrin and Suzanne Necker, wife of Swiss-French political figure Jacques Necker, the French finance minister. Du Deffand, however, continued to malign Lespinasse to others for years following the rupture of their friendship.

Lespinasse was rumored to have been romantically involved with d'Alembert, who quietly moved into rooms on another floor of the house in rue de Belle-Chasse around 1765. Historians of the *salonnière* era surmise that he may have been in love with her, but the passion was not reciprocated. In any case, they were close friends for many years and their living arrangements allowed them to economize on household expenses.

Fell in Love with Spanish Noble

Lespinasse's two great loves were well documented in her letters. The first was Don José Pignatelli y Gonzaga, Marques de Mora, whose father was the Spanish ambassador to Paris. He was significantly younger, just twenty-two years old when he met the thirty-four-year-old Lespinasse in 1766, and came from an exceedingly well-connected and wealthy family; through the Pignatelli line he was connected to Spain's royal house of Aragon. Their affair probably began in earnest in 1768, and he hoped to propose marriage; his family objected strenuously, however, and eventually ordered him to return to Spain around 1772. He and Lespinasse corresponded after that date, and a longed-for reunion was continually postponed by his tuberculosis. Pining for Lespinasse, Mora eventually began his journey back to her in Paris, but died en route in Bordeaux in May of 1774. Lespinasse, awaiting his return, was devastated when she received the news.

By that point, however, Lespinasse was also deeply enmeshed in another doomed romantic entanglement. In mid-1772, she made a visit to the famed house and gardens at Moulin-Joli, home of a wealthy financier and pioneering landscape architect named Claude-Henri Watelet, who was a friend of d'Alembert's. There she met Comte Jacques-Antoine-Hippolyte de Guibert, a dashing army commander and war hero of the recent struggle with the Corsicans. Guibert was at least a decade her junior as well as suitably intense and erudite; that same year he had written a controversial military strategy manual that was said to have influenced American colonial rebel army leader George Washington. Guibert became a regular visitor at Lespinasse's salon, where he read from his other works in progress, including historical plays. At the time, he was involved with a woman named Jeanne Thiroux de Montsauge, and at first Guibert and Lespinasse confided their respective romantic and financial woes to one another.

Took Up with Another Correspondent

When Guibert traveled to Germany and Prussia in 1773 on a mission to glean information on the well-disciplined armies of Frederick the Great for a new book, he and Lespinasse carried on an extensive correspondence. By this point she had developed strong romantic feelings for him, and was torn by the emotional infidelity she experienced because she and Mora were still writing to one another with customary ardor. Her relationship with Guibert evolved into a physical one probably in early 1774, and she was wracked with guilt over this even before Mora's death.

Guibert, it seems, did not respond to Lespinasse's letters with the same fervor, and this agitated her already-fragile mental state. "I have seen, I believe, forty persons today, and I only wanted one, whose thoughts surely did not turn to me," she wrote him in one letter, according to Benedetta Craveri in *The Age of Conversation*. Lespinasse stayed up late into the night furtively writing these letters, and this compromised her health further. She had likely developed a form of tuberculosis as early as 1771, and her addiction to opium continued, too. Grains of opium, she once wrote, "calm me as Medusa's head once calmed. I am petrified, incapable of motion, and lost to the use of all my faculties," one letter read, according to *Julie de Lespinasse*, a biography by Pierre Marie Maurice Henri, the marquis de Ségur. "Oh, but it is a strange thing—thus to be dead while still alive!"

Said to Have Died of Heartbreak

Depressed and continually anxious, Lespinasse regretted her involvement with Guibert, for she had full knowledge of his own precarious financial position. His circumstances, both knew, would require him to marry for money. She was devastated when he wed a seventeen-year-old from a wealthy family, Alexandrine Louise Boutinon des Hays de Courcelles, on June 1, 1775. Though Guibert had asserted to Lespinasse his marriage was one of convenience, not romance, she initially refused to see him but rebuked him in frequent, heartwrenching letters. Under these conditions her health declined within a matter of months, and the following spring her face became partially paralyzed, possibly from an infection of the central nervous system. After this she

refused to see Guibert at all, and d'Alembert cared for her until the end, which came on May 22, 1776. She was just forty-four years old and buried without fanfare, as she requested, on the grounds of Paris's grand Saint-Sulpice church.

D'Alembert had remained a faithful companion and friend to Lespinasse over the years and she asked him to burn her correspondence with Mora after she died; he was shocked to realize she had been passionately in love with not one but two men, for he had often claimed she was incapable of love. More than a quarter-century after Lespinasse's death, the comtesse de Guibert—Alexandrine de Courcelles, the seventeen-year-old bride—edited and published a volume of 180 letters from Lespinasse to her late husband, who had died in 1790. *Lettres de Mademoiselle de Lespinasse* caused a minor literary sensation in France in 1809 and sparked scholarly interest in Lespinasse's life as a salonnière and prolific letter writer. Since then, her writings have riveted critics and historians as among the earliest examples of a distinctive female voice in French literature. Katharine Ann Jensen's book, *Writing Love: Letters, Women, and the Novel in France, 1605–1776*, delved extensively into this topic, and quoted one of Lespinasse's most cutting remarks to Guibert. "Two things make me believe in fatality," she told him. "I had to live to see you, and I had to die from it."

Books

Craveri, Benedetta, *The Age of Conversation,* New York Review of Books, 2006, p. 323.

Dalton, Susan, *Engendering the Republic of Letters: Reconnecting Public and Private Spheres in Eighteenth-Century Europe,* McGill-Queen's Press, 2003.

Goodman, Dena, *The Republic of Letters: A Cultural History of the French Enlightenment,* Cornell University Press, 1996, p. 103.

Jensen, Katharine Ann, *Writing Love: Letters, Women, and the Novel in France, 1605–1776,* Southern Illinois University Press, 1995, p. 144.

Pierre Marie Maurice Henri Ségur (marquis de), *Julie de Lespinasse,* translated by Philip Henry Lee-Warner, Henry Holt & Company, 1907, p. 389.

Sturzer, Felicia B. "Julie-Jeanne-Eleonore de Lespinasse," in *Dictionary of Literary Biography,* Vol. 313, *Writers of the French Enlightenment I,* edited by Samia I. Spencer, Gale, 2005.□

Almena Lomax

Almena Lomax (1915–2011) was a pioneer of crusading African-American journalism in the twentieth century, both as founder and longtime editor of the *Los Angeles Tribune* and as a writer on the ground during the epic civil rights struggles of the 1960s.

Although she was not the century's best-known African-American journalist, Lomax was one of the few women in the field. Beyond that, her voice was distinct. She was sharp, combative, and often funny. Rather than adopting a stance of moral uplift or approaching the problem of discrimination in general terms, she confronted

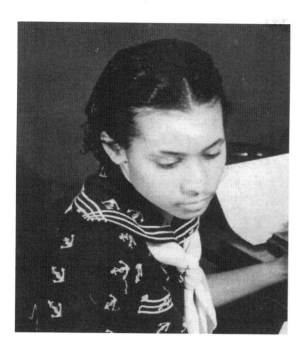

the conditions faced by African Americans head-on, launching investigative projects and demanding fairer treatment from white journalists. Lomax abandoned her home and her marriage to leave relatively egalitarian California for the Deep South in the late 1950s so that she could experience the civil rights movement first-hand, a move that resulted in a fresh crop of acclaimed articles.

Unable to Land Journalism Job

Born on July 23, 1915, Lomax was a native of Galveston, Texas, and the middle of three children. Her birth name was Hattie Almena Davis, and her father was a postal worker. Her mother contributed to the family income with sewing. When Lomax was two, the family joined the first wave of the Great Migration north to Chicago. Later they moved to Los Angeles, and Lomax attended Jordan High School in the south Los Angeles neighborhood. She majored in journalism at Los Angeles City College, but found newspapers in fast-growing California unwilling to hire her after she received her degree. "They were taking them [other students] out of there as fast as they learned who, what, when, where, and how," Lomax recalled in an oral history project recorded for California State University at Fullerton, and quoted in an obituary on the CBS Los Angeles website.

After several fruitless attempts, Lomax accepted a position with a black-oriented weekly newspaper, the Los Angeles *Eagle.* She also hosted a radio news program for a time, making her among the first African-American radio hosts in the country. In 1941, finding the doors of daily newspapers still closed to her, she decided to start one of her own. Lucius W. Lomax Sr., the owner of the famed Dunbar Hotel and one of the most colorful figures in the African-American business district along south L.A.'s Central Avenue, offered to lend Lomax $100 to buy out a small publication called the *Interfaith Churchman.* From that modest investment grew the *Los Angeles Tribune,* a publication that lasted nearly two decades

and reached a peak circulation of 25,000. Almena Lomax later recalled how the neighborhood's elegantly dressed clubgoers would park their Lincoln and Cadillac cars outside her office and check in on her as she worked late at night on the paper.

Lomax was much more than simply a managing editor and often wrote much of the paper herself. Lucius Lomax was deputized to walk to the local police station and ask for crime news. "She wrote seven days a week, 12 hours a day, " her son Michael Lomax recalled to Michael Taylor of the California Media Workers Guild, in his mother's obituary there. She soon began to make a name for herself with controversial articles such as one that took issue with the stereotype of sexual expertise among African-American men; that article won the inaugural Wendell L. Willkie Award for Negro Journalism in a *Washington Post*–sponsored contest. In addition to numerous African-American writers, Lomax hired Hisaye Yamamoto and Wakako Yamauchi, who had been victims of the internment of Japanese Americans during World War II; both went on to successful writing careers.

Organized Film Boycotts

Becoming a leader herself in the Los Angeles African-American community, Lomax served as a delegate to the 1952 Democratic convention. Objecting to the depictions of African-American life in the hit Hollywood films *Porgy and Bess* and *Imitation of Life,* she organized boycotts of those films. And she continued to expose discrimination, becoming one of the first writers to take on the topic of racism within the Los Angeles Police Department. "She was a terrific writer...the only one of all the black newspapers at the time who was really fearless about exposing things as they were," civil rights attorney Leo Branton Jr. told Elaine Woo of the *Los Angeles Times.* "She didn't soft-pedal anything." Yet her sense of humor, which could manifest itself in headline writing, was once described as impish by poet Langston Hughes, a regular reader.

As the civil rights movement began to gather steam in the 1950s, Lomax resolved to see it firsthand. Still running the *Tribune* on minimal funds, she could not afford a trip to the Deep South and decided to solicit funds from the paper's readership. The effort was successful, and in 1956 she made a one-week trip to Montgomery, Alabama, to cover the bus boycott led by the Rev. Martin Luther King Jr. During the trip she met King and his wife, Coretta, and had dinner at King's Montgomery home.

Lomax was newly energized, but the trip caused strains in her marriage, for her husband was not on board with her activism. "Montgomery meant nothing to my husband," Lomax wrote, as quoted by Leslie Pitterson in *Clutch Magazine.* "He hadn't heard the signal to rise. 'The brother' meant nothing to him. He didn't feel the emotion pulsing rhythmically under his skin when the halting, crippled words of a front-line fighter like Moses Wright, the ancient uncle of [murdered African-American teen] Emmett Till, were lined out like a hymn at a mass meeting: 'I said to myself, if a man's got to die, he might as well go out the right way.'" Almena and Lucius Lomax divorced in 1959.

Boarded Bus After Car Breakdown

The following year, Lomax shuttered the *Los Angeles Tribune,* loaded her six children and many of her belongings into a decaying Lincoln automobile and set out for Alabama, where she intended to fight on the front lines for civil rights herself. Friends, including future Los Angeles mayor Tom Bradley, warned her against making the trip, which got off to an unpromising start: the car failed an hour outside Los Angeles. Undaunted, Lomax took the family to the Greyhound bus station and boarded a bus for Alabama. They had their first taste of Southern segregation when they were refused service in a bus station dining room in Big Spring, Texas. Lomax's children later spoke of being traumatized by such events; she simultaneously regretted putting them through those experiences and retained her determination to work directly for civil rights.

Living in Tuskegee, Alabama, and sometimes returning to Los Angeles, Lomax filed freelance dispatches that appeared in such magazines as *Harper's* and *The Nation,* which published her piece "Journey to the Beginning." In that article she described her family's direct encounters with segregation. Lomax became radicalized for a time and was barred from the offices of the Southern Christian Leadership Conference for advocating violent activities. Lomax eventually returned to California, spending several years living in Berkeley and then working as a reporter for the *San Francisco Examiner* from 1970 to 1976. Her assignments included the kidnapping of heiress Patty Hearst, the activities of the Black Panther Party, and the search for fugitive black activist Angela Davis.

Lomax died March 25, 2011, in Pasadena, California, having outlived several of her children. Her offspring were an accomplished group: daughter Michele Lomax, who died in 1987, was an *Examiner* film critic; another daughter, Melanie, was an attorney who at one time headed the Los Angeles Police Commission; and son Michael Lomax became president and chief executive officer of the United Negro College Fund. An oral history recorded by Lomax is housed at California State University at Fullerton. According to Michael Lomax, she left a large body of unpublished writing at her death, including a novel titled *The Ten Most Wanted White Men* and an account of her own family, called *The Women of Montgomery.* "This was a woman who was a writer to her bone," Michael Lomax told Taylor.

Periodicals

Los Angeles Times, April 1, 2011.
New York Times, April 9, 2011.
UPI NewsTrack, April 2, 2011.

Online

"Noted Black Journalist Almena Lomax Dies at 95," *CBS Los Angeles,* http://www.losangeles.cbslocal.com/2011/04/01/noted-black-journalist-almena-lomax-dies-at-95/ (September 29, 2011).s

Pitterson, Leslie, "Legendary Civil Rights Journalist Almena Lomax Passes Away," *Clutch Magazine,* http://www.clutchmagonline.com/2011/04/legendary-civil-rights-journalist-almena-lomax-passes-away/(September 29, 2011).

Roderick, Kevin, "Conversations with Almena Lomax, Journalist," *LA Observed,* http://www.laobserved.com/archive/2011/04/conversations_with_almena.php (September 29, 2011).

Taylor, Michael, "Former Examiner Reporter Almena Lomax, editor of LA Tribune, Dead at 95," *Media Workers Guild,* http://www.mediaworkers.org/index.php?ID=7945 (September 29, 2011)□

Bette Bao Lord

The Chinese-born American author and activist Bette Bao Lord (1938–) has, in her novels, nonfiction writings, and a children's book, become a key interpreter of modern Chinese history and of the Chinese-American immigrant experience for American readers. Whatever their genre, Lord's writings focus not on facts and figures but on the personal stories of Chinese people.

Lord also had an interesting story of her own to draw on. Coming to the United States with her family at the age of eight, she assimilated to American life but also became keenly aware of her Chinese heritage as her life in China receded from the realm of the possible for her Nationalist Chinese family. Married to American diplomat Winston Lord, she returned to China intermittently during the 1970s and 1980s—one of the most turbulent times in its long history. There she learned about the experiences of family members and friends who had lived through repression and complete societal upheaval. Lord's experiences awakened her impulses both as a writer and as an activist on behalf of human rights.

Family Settled in United States

Bette Bao was born on November 3, 1938, in Shanghai, China. Her father, Sandys Bao, was an engineer who had studied in Europe and spoke English and German in addition to Mandarin Chinese. He served in the Chinese army during World War II and gained experience working on a power plant in Hunan Province, where Chinese forces resisted Japanese control for much of the war. After the war ended, he took his wife and two older daughters to the United States on a government mission to buy construction equipment for China's rebuilding; his hope was that Bette would spend six months to a year in the United States learning English, and then return to China. But the family decided to stay on in the United States after the Nationalist Chinese government was defeated by Mao Zedong's Communist army and retreated to the island of Taiwan. The youngest Bao daughter, Sansan, was an infant at the time and had been left with relatives in China.

Landing in Brooklyn, New York, and settling in suburban Teaneck, New Jersey, the Bao family sent their daughter to local schools. Bette adapted well and was even elected secretary of her high school student council. But, Lord told Bruce Cole of the National Endowment for the Humanities, her parents did not subscribe to the melting-pot theory of American culture. She recalled that "they

never said that you are not going to be Chinese because you became an American. You can be both and you can decide which part of each culture that is right for you, that you want to believe in." After Lord had learned English well, her parents began to emphasize the Chinese language, which she was beginning to forget.

When Lord enrolled at Tufts University near Boston, she planned to study chemistry at her parents' behest. Most immigrant Chinese, she explained to Cole, believe that science is "the golden ticket in America or any society: 'Science, that's wonderful.'...My talents, if I had any, were certainly not in that field because I like to fidget with things and science is so exacting. My parents were open enough to know that when I cried, 'I can't do this,' they said, 'Okay. You can't do this. Go ahead and do what you want.'" Lord majored in history and political science, graduating in 1959 and earning a master's degree from Tufts in 1960.

Reunified with Sister

Lord spent the 1961-62 academic year as assistant to the director of the East-West Cultural Center at the University of Hawaii, moving on to the Fulbright Exchange Program in Washington, D.C., as a program officer. There she became reacquainted with diplomat Winston Lord, whom she had known as a master's student at Tufts. The two married in 1962, and that year also brought another important reunification in her life: her mother, claiming serious illness, persuaded Chinese authorities to let Sansan Bao cross the border into Hong Kong (then under British control) to visit her. The pair escaped to the United States, where Lord learned about what it was like for her sister to grow up in China.

That gave Lord the idea of writing a book about her sister's life, and she left her job to have more time to interview Sansan systematically (and to prepare for the birth of her first child, Elizabeth Pillsbury Lord). She still lacked self-confidence as a writer, but a friend pushed her to take a

chance. While the two were waiting in a line at the American Booksellers Association convention, Lord recalled to Cole, "My friend said to this elderly man...'Bette has a book she wants to write.' I went with him to the corner and he said, 'I'll give you five minutes. If you can sell me on the story, I'll publish it.'" The elderly man was Harper & Row publishing head Cass Canfield. "Now today it would be impossible," Lord continued. "In those days there was still a publisher who could say, 'I have a feeling about this book. I'll publish it.' That's how I became a writer."

Eighth Moon: The Story of a Young Girl's Life in Communist China appeared in 1964 and was successful from the beginning, appearing in the popular *Reader's Digest* Condensed Book series and finding a place on many school reading lists. It has been translated into 15 languages. Bao and her husband were posted to Switzerland in 1965, where Lord began to explore another of her many interests, modern dance. She had a second child, Winston Bao Lord, in 1967. Her reconnection with mainland China began the following year when her husband began to travel there as an aide to Henry Kissinger, foreign policy adviser and later Secretary of State in the administration of President Richard Nixon.

Feared for Friends' Safety in China

After Winston Lord made several trips to China alone, Bette was allowed to go with him in 1973, as Nixon's policy of detente with China took hold. She took numerous photographs during this trip; they were published in photo-essay form in the *Washington Post,* for which she earned a National Graphic Arts Prize in 1974. She was contracted by Harper & Row to write a nonfiction account of her experiences in China, but with the hard-line repression of the Cultural Revolution still in full force, a situation in which even contact with Westerners was criminalized, she worried that to do so would endanger friends and family members still in China. Thus she adapted her work into a novel, *Spring Moon,* which appeared in 1981. The book spent nearly a year on the *New York Times* bestseller list and was nominated for a National Book Award.

Spring Moon, which was translated into 18 languages, was a saga covering five generations of an aristocratic family as it experienced the changes that wracked China in the twentieth century. Lord followed her own experiences more closely with *In the Year of the Boar and Jackie Robinson* (1984), a children's book whose central character was a Chinese girl who arrives in the United States with her family in 1947. In the words of *School Library Journal,* "Bette Bao Lord's wonderfully humorous story shows what it means to be an American from the eyes of a spunky young immigrant."

When Winston Lord was appointed ambassador to China in 1985, his wife accompanied him. She organized a performance in Chinese of a play based on the Herman Wouk novel *The Caine Mutiny* and recruited actor Charlton Heston to direct it, guessing that Chinese audiences would apply the play's examination of authoritarianism to their own situation. She also took the opportunity to delve more deeply into the experiences of Chinese citizens from all walks of life. She collected some 600 oral histories on tape, some from her own relatives, others from strangers. As dissent in China grew in 1989, the Lords' term in China ended and they returned to the United States. Shortly after their return, the Chinese government used violence to disband protesters in Beijing's Tiananmen Square and clamped down on the country's growing pro-democracy movement. Lord then felt that it was all the more important to publish her interviews, many of which shed light on the ordeals of those branded as rightists during the Cultural Revolution, and drew parallels to the country's contemporary situation. *Legacies: A Chinese Mosaic* was published in 1990 by Knopf and blended the oral histories with accounts of Lord's own experiences in China. She served as a commentator for CBS News in the wake of the Tiananmen Square events, and wrote newspaper articles about large and small themes pertaining to Chinese life.

Lord's most recent book as of this writing is *The Middle Heart,* a novel following three friends of different social backgrounds through the war years and the rise of Communism, and ending with the Tiananmen Square crackdown. She served in the 1990s as the chairwoman of Freedom House, a Washington-based organization that promotes democracy around the world. Lord has received numerous awards, including a Literary Lion citation from the New York Public Library and a host of honorary doctoral degrees. She and her husband live in New York, and she has remained active as a guest lecturer and has expressed a desire to write a book about the experiences of elderly Americans. In 2011, she was a guest at a White House state dinner honoring Chinese president Hu Jintao.

Books

Fox, Mary Virginia, *Bette Bao Lord: Novelist and Chinese Voice for Change,* Children's Press, 1993.

Notable Asian Americans, Gale, 1995.

Periodicals

Denver Post, March 17, 1996.

Globe & Mail (Toronto, Ontario, Canada), September 21, 1988.

Houston Chronicle, February 25, 1996.

New Republic, July 30, 1990.

New York Times, June 4, 1989; March 28, 1990; January 20, 2011.

School Library Journal, July 2008.

Online

"Bette Bao Lord," *Contemporary Authors Online,* Gale, 2007.

"Bridging Two Worlds: A Conversation with Bette Bao Lord," *National Endowment for the Humanities,* http://www.neh.gov/news/humanities/2005-11/bridging.html (October 2, 2011).

"Chinese American Philanthropist Bette Bao Lord," *Asian Week,* http://www.asianweek.com/2009/07/23/chinese-american-philanthropist-bette-bao-lord/ (October 2, 2011). □

Francisco Antonio Lorenzana

The Spanish ecclesiastical leader Francisco Antonio Lorenzana (1722–1804) left a strong imprint on Mexican life during his six years as archbishop of Mexico, from 1766 to 1772. A conscientious writer and researcher on many topics, he is remembered in the Western hemisphere primarily as the author one of the earliest detailed histories of Spain's New World colonies.

Lorenzana was an important church administrator over much of his long life, and the Spanish landscape of today, as well as that of Mexico, bears numerous imprints of his activities. His work as a musical researcher was notable, as was his promotion of charitable institutions in both the Old World and the New. But perhaps his most distinctive creation was the *Historía de Nueva España* (History of New Spain), which was published in 1770. Cast as a reissue of some of the letters of explorer Hernando Cortez, the lavishly illustrated volume contained detailed information on ecclesiastical history, Spanish settlement, and the indigenous cultures of Mexico at a time when few Spanish observers concerned themselves with the cultures they had conquered.

Groomed for Religious Life

Francisco Antonio de Lorenzana y Buitrón was born (or at least baptized) in the Spanish city of Léon on September 22, 1722. The third son of the city's ruler, Jacinto de Lorenzana y Varela, he was the godson and nephew by marriage of Athanasius de Lorenzana, a canon, or priest, at Léon Cathedral, and after his father's death when he was nine, he was groomed for religious life. He was enrolled at a grammar school in Léon operated by the Jesuit order, and he later studied at a Benedictine priory school in the nearby Bierzo region. He received the tonsure, a mark of religious preparation often indicated by the partial shaving of the head, in 1734, and in 1739 he earned a bachelor's degree at the University of Santa Catalina de Burgo de Osma.

After passing several exams, Lorenzana embarked on a long course of legal and administrative studies that led him into the central circles of the Spanish ecclesiastical power elite. In 1744, he entered the Gimnasio Canónigo-Civil de Santo Tomás in Valladolid, a law school where he was mentored by the future vicar-general of the large Toledo Cathedral, Juan Antonio Sáenz de Santa María. In 1748, he moved to Salamaca for further legal studies, making friends there among powerful figures such as José Nicolás de Azara, Spain's future ambassador to Rome. These studies culminated in Lorenzana's ascension to the post of canon at Sigüenza Cathedral in 1751.

There, and at the larger Toledo Cathedral where Lorenzana moved in 1755, he distinguished himself as a scholar. At Sigüenza, he inventoried the cathedral's collection of books, old manuscripts, and valuable objects, and in Toledo, where he advanced to the positions of vicar-general, vice-treasurer, and dean, he did pathbreaking historical research. He wrote a history of the cathedral's early councils, did linguistic studies, and founded an academy of church history. Most important, he edited a volume of so-called Mozarabic chant, a species of medieval plainchant, related to Gregorian chant, that was specific to Spain. Although Mozarabic chant was largely displaced by the standardized Gregorian chant, it continues, as a result of Lorenzana's work, to be sung at some churches in the Toledo area, and it offers scholars insight into the musical world of the early Catholic church. Lorenzana's edition of the Mozarabic missal was published in Los Angeles, Alta California, in 1770, after Lorenzana's move to Mexico.

Chosen as Mexican Archbishop

In Toledo, Lorenzana hobnobbed with top Spanish church leaders such as José Javier Rodriguez de Arellano and Juan Saenz de Buruaga, and he was clearly headed for a position of responsibility himself. In 1765, Spain's King Charles III named Lorenzana bishop of Plascencia, but he spent only a few months in that post before being elected the 24th archbishop of Mexico. He arrived in New Spain on July 23, 1766, having crossed the Atlantic in the company of the colony's new secular leader, the Marques de Croix. The churchman, who had previously headed only a cathedral in a provincial Spanish city, found himself the leader of a thousand priests in New Spain, which stretched from the present-day Oregon-California border south through Guatemala, and of 300,000 Catholic worshipers.

During his six years as archbishop, Lorenzana faced numerous controversies and upheavals. The first of these, the expulsion of the Jesuits from Mexico, was not even his own doing but was the result of conflicts between the Jesuit order and secular and church authorities across Europe, resulting in part from connections between the order and the rising forces of democracy and reform in European society. Much of Lorenzana's energy during his first years as archbishop was consumed with tasks related to the Jesuit expulsion, which required the appointment of large numbers of new priests and missionaries in the northern parts of New Spain. The move also opened Lorenaza up to criticism from the Jesuits' supporters, and a number of satirical drawings of him appeared in Mexican publications.

More specific to Mexico was Lorenzana's conflict with Mexican nuns, one of a long series of clashes between nuns and their male superiors that have marked Catholic history. With the backing of Charles III, Lorenzana attempted to implement what was known as the *vida común* or communal life in Catholic convents. Margaret Chowning, in *Rebellious Nuns: The Troubled History of a Catholic Convent, 1752–1863,* quoted Lorenzana as saying, ''The female convents are full of servants and secular persons, to the extent that they resemble disorderly villages more than communities of nuns in peaceful retirement from the world.'' Lorenzana ordered that the number of maids and servants in convents be reduced and that nuns live simply, mostly taking care of their own needs. The move cut nuns off from their communities and produced sharp resistance; nuns organized and besieged

Charles III with letters and petitions, with the result that nuns who had already taken vows under the old system were allowed to vote on whether to retain it. The controversy dragged on until after Lorenzana left Mexico.

Convened Mexican Religious Council

Lorenzana put in place various other reforms in Mexican churches. He mandated that church bells be rung throughout the day, and regulated the gatherings of the poor at cathedral entrances. In exchange for the latter regulations he founded a new orphans' home and hospital for the indigent. Working with the priest José Antonio de Alzate, he made a new atlas of Mexican parishes and reorganized their boundaries. In 1771, he convened the Fourth Mexican Provincial Council, the first such meeting of the Mexican church hierarchy in almost two centuries (the first three were held in 155, 1565, and 1585).

Perhaps Lorenzana's greatest accomplishment as archbishop of Mexico was the *Historía de Nueva España,* published in 1770. More than 400 pages long, including a detailed index, the book bore the modest full title of *Historía de Nueva Españ: Escrito para el esclarecido conquistador Hernán Corés, aumentada con otros documentos y notas por el illustrísimo Señor Don Francisco Antonio Lorenzana, Arzobispo de México* (History of New Spain: Written by the Radiant Conquistador Hernando Cortez, Augmented with Other Documents and Notes by the Illustrious Lord Don Francisco Antonio Lorenzana, Archbishop of Mexico). It did include some of the letters Cortez wrote to the Spanish ruler and Habsburg emperor Charles V, but more significant for modern historians were Lorenzana's own ''notes''—478 in all—that covered nearly every aspect of Mexican history and life. Lorenzana included military history, accounts of earlier church conclaves, and notes on Spanish attempts to evangelize Mexico's Native population. The final topic led him into the culture of Mexico's indigenous peoples, and among his many illustrations he included one that dated back to pre-colonial times, showing tributes paid to the Aztec emperor Moctezuma II. He remarked in his *Historía* that the Nahuatl language was ''very elegant…sweet, and with an abundance of phrases and forms of composition'' sufficient to allow Native peoples to grasp Christian teachings in their own language.

The later parts of Lorenzana's tenure in Mexico coincided with the beginning of a sustained program of mission-building that has left its mark on Mexico and the American state of California down to the present day. Lorenzana was recalled to Spain in 1772 to take up the important post of archbishop of Toledo, and there he continued to exercise his talents as a construction administrator, founding several hospitals, renovating an old palace into the Royal House of Charity, and constructing additions to the cathedral. He employed top architects for these tasks, one of whom designed a handsome space for the archbishop's library and large collection of old manuscripts and curiosities of natural history. Lorenzana used frozen Jesuit funds for the palace construction projects.

In old age, Lorenzana ascended to the top of the Catholic hierarchy. He was made a cardinal by Pope Pius VI in 1789, moved to Italy in 1797, and lived for the rest of his life in Venice and Rome, where he founded a new Catholic academy. His last will left his personal fortune of 25,000 scudi to the poor, however. Lorenzana died in Rome on April 17, 1804 (the year 1803 has also been given, but the *New Catholic Encyclopedia* lists the 1804 date). He was buried in the Basilica of the Holy Cross in Jerusalem, a famed Roman church. In 1956, he was disinterred, and his remains were moved to the Crypt of the Archbishops at the Mexico City Metropolitan Cathedral.

Books

Chowning, Margaret, *Rebellious Nuns: The Troubled History of a Mexican Convent, 1752–1863,* Oxford, 2006.

Lorenzana, Francisco Antonio, *Historia de Nueva Espña Escrita por su esclarecido conquistador Hernán Cortes, zaumentada con otros documentos, y notas, por... Don Francisco Antonio Lorenzana, Arzobispo de México,* Joseph Antonio de Hogal, 1770.

Periodicals

Bulletin of the American Geographical Society, volume 47 (1915).

Online

"Francisco Antonio de Lorenzana," *New Advent,* http://www.newadvent.org/cathen/09357b.htm (October 24, 2011).

"FRANCISCO ANTONIO LORENZANA. Historia de Nueva Espña Escrita por su esclarecido conquistador Hernán Cortes, zaumentada con otros documentos, y notas, por... Don Francisco Antonio Lorenzana, Arzobispo de México," *California at the Los Angeles Public Library,* http://www.lapl.org/central/californiana.html (October 24, 2011).

"Lorenzana y Buitrón, Francisco Antonio de (1722–1803)," *La web de biografís,* http://www.mcnbiografias.com/app-bio/do/show?key=lorenzana-y-buitron-francisco-antonio-de (October 24, 2011). □

Rowland H. Macy

Retailer Rowland H. Macy (1822–1877) founded the first Macy's department store in New York City in 1858.

American retailer and businessman R.H. Macy founded the department store R.H. Macy & Company in New York City in 1858 after several false starts in the merchandising industry. Macy's store rose to become one of the first major department stores in the United States, thanks largely to its proprietor's combination of innovative selling techniques, such as the requirement of cash rather than credit for purchases, the use of visually striking advertising, and the setting of low fixed prices for goods. Within a few years of its establishment, Macy's New York store had expanded to include a mail-order business; by 1870, its sales exceeded $1 million each year. After Macy's death in 1877, the store remained under family control but was sold to business associates by the end of the nineteenth century. It then grew in both size and scope to become a national retailer that remained one of the United States' major department store chains into the twenty-first century.

Early Career in Massachusetts

Rowland Hussey Macy was born on August 30, 1822, on Nantucket Island, Massachusetts, as the fourth of the six children of ship captain and retail merchant John Macy and his wife, Elisa Myrick Barnard Macy. Through his father, Macy was a descendent of one of the first white European settlers of Nantucket Island, Thomas Macy, who came to the island in 1659 after a run-in with Puritan authorities at Salisbury, Massachusetts, over his hospitality to a small group of Quakers traveling through the area. The Macys—who in time also became Quakers—were one of the best-known of Nantucket's seafaring families, and the future retailer followed in the family tradition by joining the crew of a whaling ship named the *Emily Morgan* when he was 15 years old. He spent the next four years traveling, returning to Massachusetts with the sum of $550 dollars in payment for his efforts as a junior crew member. The five-pointed red star that he had had tattooed onto the backs of his hands—a visual reference to the points of the compass—later became the logo for his most successful retail venture.

Whaling failed to capture the young man's interest as a lifelong career, however, and Macy did not ship back out again. Instead, he left Nantucket in 1842 for the Massachusetts capital of Boston, accompanied by a brother, Robert. There, he found work as a printer's apprentice, but short months later left that position to start his own dry goods store. Macy's first two stores failed. Through his efforts, however, he met Louisa Houghton, the sister of local retailer George Houghton. Macy and Houghton married in 1844; the couple later had one son, Rowland H. Macy, Jr., and one daughter, Florence.

Estimates of Macy's successes in Boston vary, with his *New York Times* obituary hailing the young merchant's perceived "foresight and discrimination" but more modern historians gauging his efforts much more poorly. By about 1850, Macy's business ventures had reached enough of an impasse that he decided to try his hand in the booming gold country of California. Along with another brother, George, Macy undertook the months-long overseas journey to San Francisco. Their hopes to strike it rich through prospecting quickly evaporated, and Macy soon returned to retailing. Along with yet another brother, Charles, he opened a dry goods store in Marysville, California, then a fast-growing mining town. The store failed, but Macy earned a substantial

223

sum through real estate investment. Back in Massachusetts in 1851, he founded another dry goods store in Haverhill, an emerging industrial town. Like his previous ventures, this store, called the Granite, ultimately failed. However, this enterprise marked the first time that Macy introduced a number of innovative retail practices. He established low fixed prices for his goods and required consumers to pay for their purchases in cash, in contrast to the then-standard usage of negotiation and store credit in selling. Macy also put his skills gained as a printer's apprentice to work by using creative print advertising to brand and market his store. The store initially thrived, but Macy expanded too quickly in the town's highly competitive market and was forced into bankruptcy in about 1855.

Founded Macy's in New York City

Over the next few years, Macy engaged in a number of mostly unsuccessful business ventures, including a stint as a Boston stock broker and a return to real estate speculation, this time in Wisconsin. A poor economic climate ended the latter effort, and in 1858 Macy moved his family to New York City to again try his hand at retailing. He rented a relatively small, inexpensive storefront at the corner of Sixth Avenue and Fourteenth Street in Lower Manhattan, and opened a dry goods store there in a space measuring as little as 17 feet by 40 feet. By the time of this store's opening, Macy's challenges had become significant. As Edward L. Lach, Jr. noted in his entry on Macy for American National Biography Online, the retailer "was an outsider in the highly competitive Manhattan marketplace, his credit history was made suspect by virtue of his previous business failures, and his store was both modest in appearance . . . and situated well north of the city's established retail district." Indeed, the location had generally been an ill-fated one, as several earlier merchants had tried and failed to establish successful stores there. Nevertheless, Macy was willing to make an attempt, believing that the city's growing mass transit system would allow shoppers to reach his store with sufficient ease.

Drawing on the lessons of his previous failures, Macy began selling "fancy" goods such as gloves, feathers, ribbons, and other goods. Initial sales of just over eleven dollars failed to deter the optimistic entrepreneur. He began heavily advertising his store shortly after its opening, using interesting typesetting styles and repetition, among other techniques to draw readers' attention. Macy undercut his competitors by an average of six percent, and promoted these low prices by printing them in his advertisements, another departure from standard practices of the era. He also revived his cash-only policy, requiring all customers to pay cash for their goods and himself buying most of his wholesale stock outright. Macy's willingness to try new things extended beyond his purchasing regulations. In 1866, he promoted a female family member whom he had hired some years earlier, Margaret Getchell, to the position of store superintendent, making her the first woman to hold such a high position in the U.S. retail industry. Getchell managed the store well and helped choose items to stock. With Getchell's assistance, the store further developed its appeal to female shoppers. Before long, the store had expanded physically and financially, drawing in ever-higher profits and initiating efforts including a mail-order business and an annual clearance sale. By 1870, Macy had grown his sales from just $80,000 to over $1 million each year. The store had expanded into neighboring locations and offered more than 15 departments. Macy's selection had surpassed that of a typical dry goods enterprise to include such diverse offerings as costume jewelry, household linens, and hats.

Although Getchell provided valuable contributions to the store, not all of Macy's family members proved so helpful. His son had little interest in retailing and involved himself in a variety of escapades. During the Civil War, the teenaged Macy joined the Union Army under an assumed name only to desert days later, and throughout his young adulthood drank alcohol excessively enough to concern his father. A positive outcome of the young man's mishap with the military did arise, however, when the elder Macy met Abiel T. LaForge, an older officer who became a friend and mentor to the brash youth. After the war ended, LaForge came to New York, and Macy persuaded him to take a job with the store. LaForge first became a buyer, but—after meeting and marrying Getchell—rose to become a partner in the business in 1872. Macy's son, however, remained a disappointment to his father. The patriarch's attempt to bring him into the family business failed when the young man was rude to a customer while working in the store, and Macy essentially wrote him out of the enterprise in favor of LaForge and a nephew, Robert M. Valentine, who became a partner in 1873.

Later Years and Legacy

That same year, Macy embarked on another innovative business venture. He leased a portion of the store's basement to Lazarus Straus and his sons to sell china, silver, and glassware. Straus was a German immigrant who had operated a dry goods business in Georgia before coming to New York in the late 1860s. The arrangement proved a mutually profitable one, with china quickly becoming the single most successful department in the Macy's store, with about ten percent of overall sales. The Straus family went on to have a long involvement with the retailer's business.

Despite being only in his 50s, Macy had begun to experience health problems by the mid-1870s. Doctors eventually diagnosed him with Bright's disease, a catch-all term for kidney disorders often caused by other root problems, and suggested that Macy travel to Europe on a rest cure. This voyage failed to help much, however, and Macy died in Paris, France on March 29, 1877. His body was later returned to the United States, and he was interred in Woodlawn Cemetery in the Bronx. The execution of Macy's will the following May caused something of a stir, with the *New York Times* characterizing it at the time as a "peculiar document." None of the retailer's estate save a yearly annuity was transferred to his eldest son, with his wife instead retaining a life interest in the family home and personal property, and his daughter inheriting a large sum; the remainder was split between the two women. According to the same *New York Times* article, Macy explained this decision thus: "my experience has been such with my son . . . that I cannot intrust (sic) him with the care or management of his property. . . . His passion for strong drink has not hitherto been controlled by him."

The ownership of Macy's retail enterprise passed to LaForge and Valentine. Macy's thus remained in the family for several more years until being sold entirely to the Strauses, the proprietors of the store's china division. The success of the existing business discouraged the brothers from changing the store's name, and Macy's as a business enterprise independent of the Macy family began. It was under the ownership of the Straus brothers that Macy's constructed its famed flagship store in New York's Herald Square, began its involvement with the city's Thanksgiving Day Parade, and commenced expansion in other U.S. cities. The legacy of the store's founder remained evident in the company's name and in some of its business practices, however, such as its long reliance on cash, rather than credit, transactions, which persisted well into the twentieth century. Well over a century after the elder Macy's death, the chain he had founded remained a retail presence around the United States.

Books

Barmash, Isadore, *Macy's for Sale: The Leveraged Buyout of the World's Largest Store,* Weidenfeld & Nicolson, 1989.

Hast, Adele, ed., *International Directory of Company Histories,* St. James Press, 1992.

Periodicals

New York Times, March 31, 1877; May 1, 1877.

Online

"Macy, R.H.," *American National Biography Online,* http://www.anb.org (November 19, 2011).

Other

Additional information from the A & E Biography episode *R.H. Macy: Merchant Prince.*□

Shozo Makino

Japanese director Shozo Makino (1878–1929) is widely regarded as the "father of Japanese cinema."

Japanese director Shozo Makino has been largely hailed as the "father of Japanese cinema." Widely credited with essentially inventing the Japanese film style of *jidaigeki,* or period drama, and hailed as the first true director in Japan, Makino made an estimated 300 films during his nearly two decade-long career. He innovated several camera techniques that added to the expressiveness of the silent era, and discovered an actor who became one of the nation's most popular film stars of all time, Matsunosuke Onoe. Makino also formed his own film studio, Makino Film Productions, in 1921. The director's best-known films include *Jitsuroku Chushingura* (alternately translated as *Chushingura: The Truth, The True Story of the 47 Loyal Samurai,* or *The True Story of the Loyal Retainers,* (1928) and the posthumous *Raiden* (1928). Both of these latter films featured another of Makino's major contributions to the history of Japanese film: his son, Masahiro Makino, who became a prominent film director in his own right. Several more of Makino's descendents also went on to contribute to the art form.

Became First Japanese Director

Born on September 22, 1878, in Kyoto prefecture, Japan, Makino was the son of a soldier father and a theater owner mother. Makino's father had fought on the losing side of the 1877 Satsuma rebellion in Kyushu against the reformist Meiji government; writing in *The Japanese Film: Art and Industry,* Joseph L. Anderson and Donald Richie argued that "Makino, like his father, was deeply affected by rebel prejudices, particularly against those involving 'restoration and Westernization[.]'" His mother's life also exerted an influence on Makino's life. During his early career, the young man was involved with kabuki theater. That involvement changed, however, after the arrival of motion pictures in Japan.

Film developed rapidly after the Lumière brothers first displayed their cinematograph—an early film camera—in France in 1895. Within several months, the cinematograph, Edison's kinetoscope player, and the popular Vitascope player had all reached Japan. U.S. films of Japanese subjects such as dancing geishas were shown in Japan in 1898, and the following year a Tokyo theater played the first domestically produced film. In 1903—the same year that U.S. audiences were watching the groundbreaking *Great Train Robbery*—Japan's first true movie theater opened in Asakusa, Tokyo. The first major film studios did not appear in Japan until two years later, when the Yokota Shokai company established one in Kyoto. Soon after, the businessperson Shokichi Umeya established the M. Pathe Company, which also produced many early Japanese silent films.

Yet Japanese film developments lagged somewhat behind those of other nations in North America and Europe. In 1908, there were some 8,000 nickelodeons—movie houses that charged customers an entrance fee of a nickel—operating in the United States. These theaters showed about three different programs each week, and approximately 20 U.S. movie studios had arisen to fill that high demand. In contrast, Japanese studios produced just 54 films in 1908. The year marked two important developments in the development of the industry there, however; in Tokyo, a film studio created the first glassed-in set in Japan, and in Kyoto, Makino shot his first short film.

By that year, Makino had established himself in Kyoto as the leader of a kabuki theater troupe. The Yokota Shokai company asked him to film one of the live performances of this troupe, and Makino agreed. In his first attempt at filmmaking, the budding director rented a Kyoto temple and there staged a production of the kabuki play *Honnoji gassen* (*The Battle of Honnoji*.) The event proved a fateful one. The process of filming the kabuki play intrigued Makino, and before long he had begun creating silent films at a fast clip; during the early period of his film career in 1908, Makino produced a new film roughly every three days.

Although practically all of these early pieces are lost, film historians believe that they probably employed the traditional kabuki theater practice of *kuchidate*. Under this style, Makino, as head of the kabuki troupe, recited lines to his actors while the camera filmed; because motion pictures then had no sound, these lines did not form a component of the finished production. The actors—Japanese films did not feature female actresses until the 1920s—then used these oral directions to carry out the performance. Throughout his filmmaking, career, however, Makino built his films on a triad of essential qualities. Writing in *Patterns of Time: Mizoguchi and the 1930s*, Donald Kirihara noted that "Makino's fabled three dicta for film production respected the need for principles of clarity and story logic: 'First, a visibly clear print; second, a clear story line; third, liveliness of action.'"

Discovered Japan's First Superstar

In 1909, Makino discovered the actor Matsunosuke Onoe, who was then also working in the kabuki form. By then in his mid-30s, Onoe had been acting since he was just five years old, and had roughly two decades of professional experience performing with a traveling kabuki troupe under his belt. Writing in the *Journal of Film Preservation*, Yoshiro Irie described the actor as "a small man, and a skillful kabuki actor known for his mastery of extravagant stage tricks." Makino saw Onoe's potential as a film actor and quickly convinced him to appear in a film that Makino was shooting for Yokota Shokai, *Goban Tadanobu (Tadanobu the Fox)*. The collaboration proved a fruitful one. Over the next several years, Makino directed Onoe in as many as 60 to 80 films annually. Over the course of his career, ended by his death in 1926, Onoe was reputed to have starred in as many as 1,000 cinematic productions; more than half of these were directed by Makino. Very few of this vast output of films have survived, however.

In these early motion pictures, Makino employed the style known as *kyugeki*, literally meaning "old drama." *Kyugeki* films incorporated traditional kabuki theatrical practices with popular stories and new filmic techniques such as the usage of trick photography. The director's nods to standard Japanese theater included his use of a single, wide shot that displayed the entire scene without camera movement, and the filming of scenes as one long take with few cuts, creating a tableau not unlike that seen by an audience member at a live performance. Irie argued that "Onoe adapted his particular skills to the *kyugeki* style, establishing a new, dynamically kinetic swashbuckling genre." Indeed, many of the films that Makino made with the actor saw him perform as a ninja or samurai, interpreting some of Japan's historical heroes for the contemporary audiences. Yet it was Onoe himself who was the true popular hero of the day. Although film historians have noted that other kabuki actors were more talented, better-looking, or more seemingly marketable than Onoe, he became the nation's undisputed king of cinema and its first superstar. The director and actor continued to work together extensively until 1921.

Filmed sometime between 1910 and 1912, the film *Chushingura (The Loyal Forty-Seven Ronin)*, survived to the present day and can thus serve as an exemplar of the style that Makino and Onoe popularized. The film tells the story of a group of famed semi-legendary Japanese samurai, or ronin, who plan and take revenge on a court official who forces their lord to commit ritual suicide. Because of their crime, the group of samurai warriors then commit ritual suicide themselves. Based on a series of actual events of the early eighteenth century, the story was one that Makino retold repeatedly throughout his career. For the early 1910s production, the episodes of the film were filmed and released separately over a period of time, and later strung together to create one long film. Onoe portrayed not one, but three main characters, a reflection of the traditional kabuki practice in which the same actor filled several roles as well as a nod to the Japanese public's seemingly insatiable desire for motion pictures starring the performer.

Founded Makino Studios

After years of making films for Yokota Shokai and its successor, Nikkatsu, Makino launched his own studio, Makino Film Productions, in 1921; Onoe replaced the director as the leading figure of the Kyoto efforts of Nikkatsu and from then on starred mostly in films directed by Tomiyasu Ikeda. The Makino production company, conversely, existed solely to release the works that Makino directed. Although this setup bears little resemblance to the modern studio structure, the practice of one director creating films for a company exclusively dedicated to them was not uncommon in the Japanese film industry of the time. Writing in *A Critical Handbook of Japanese Film Directors From the Silent Era to the Present Day*, Alexander Jacoby argued that Makino's studio "was responsible for some of the more innovative *jidai-gaeki* (or period drama) of the twenties."

Although most of the director's films with Onoe followed principles similar to those of the films they had made together during the preceding decade, film historians have pointed to Makino's films with the younger star Tsumasaburo Bando as more daring. The 1927 film *Hyakumanryo hibun (Mystery of a Million Ryo)*, for example, saw Makino rely on faster cuts and more sophisticated mobile camera techniques. A new generation of followers, however, had by this time begun to upstage Makino with more modern approaches to filmmaking. Nevertheless, some of Makino's best-known films date from this latter period of his career. In 1928, he directed a new version of *Chushingura* that was released as the director turned 50 years old. Even Makino's death from heart failure on July 25, 1929 did not interrupt his output, with his final major film, *Raiden* appearing after his death.

Even decades after the director's passing, his films remained of interest to fans and scholars alike. A 1941 remake of *Chushingura* by Kenji Mizoguchi brought the story into the world of sound. In 1990, director Kazuo Kiroki made *Ronin Gai,* another updated version of Makino's classic samurai tale as an homage to the initiator of the period drama. The film received another reboot in 2012 as the Keanu Reeves vehicle *47 Ronin,* directed by Carl Rinsch.

By the twenty-first century, film restoration techniques had also salvaged a handful of Makino's classic films. Makino's legacy continued not only in the lasting influence of his own work, but also in his fostering of the acting and directorial talents of his family. Most notable was Makino's son Masahiro Makino, who himself became one of Japan's leading directors with a career reaching from the silent era to the 1970s and encompassing more than 200 films.

Books

Anderson, Joseph L. and Donald Richie, *The Japanese Film: Art and Industry,* Princeton University Press, 1982.

Jacoby, Alexander, *A Critical Handbook of Japanese Film Directors From the Silent Era to the Present Day,* Stone Bridge Press, 2008.

Kirihara, Donald, *Patterns of Time: Mizoguchi and the 1930s,* University of Wisconsin Press, 1992.

Richie, Donald, *A Hundred Years of Japanese Film,* Kodansha International, 2005.

Periodicals

Journal of Film Preservation, November 2006.

Online

"Timeline of Japanese Silent Films," Matsuda Film Productions, http://www.matsudafilm.com/matsuda/c_pages/c_be.html (December 4, 2011). □

Ilyas Malayev

Ilyas Malayev (1936–2008) was one of the leading cultural figures in his Central Asian homeland of Uzbekistan during the Soviet era. The musician, singer, comedian, and poet was renowned for his expertise in *shashmaqam*, a vanishing form of classical music associated for centuries with the ethnic culture of Bukharin Jews like himself. After resettling in the United States in the early 1990s, Malayev rebuilt his audience among the Jewish émigré community in the New York City area.

Born into Stalinist Empire

Ilyas Malayev was born on January 12, 1936, in the city of Mary, sometimes called Merv, a desert oasis in Turkmenistan. His hometown had been one of the important stops on the Silk Road, the centuries-old route used by traders from Europe and the Middle East into China and other parts of Asia. At the time of Malayev's birth, however, Turkmenistan was known as the Turkmen Soviet Socialist Republic and was one of the Central Asian republics that had come under Russian control in the nineteenth century.

Malayev's family belonged to a deeply entrenched community of Bukharin Jews who had lived in this part of Central Asia for centuries. The Bukharin Jewish presence in Uzbekistan, Turkmenistan, and nearby states remains somewhat of a mystery; historians surmise they may have arrived after the 6th century BCE, when thousands of Israelites were forced from the Kingdom of Judah during a war and held in captivity in Babylon by the enemy. Babylon—the term used for a vanished empire located in what is present-day Iraq—eventually fell and was succeeded by a mightier Persian power in the region, whose rulers permitted Jews to return to their original homeland in the Levant. Some of them opted instead to venture further east and then north, settling into what became known as Bukhara Province. In the modern era, Bukharin Jews speak a dialect of Tajik-Persian that retains some ties to the ancient Hebrew language.

Over the next several centuries Bukharin Jews emerged as significant players in the social, economic, and cultural scene in Transoxania. This was the name given to the region after the advances of Alexander the Great, a Macedonian Greek general whose armies conquered vast swaths of territories in Central and Southwest Asia in the fourth century BCE. Transoxania retained its Hellenistic culture for several more centuries, and the stable Greek presence opened up the trade routes with the east for the rest of Europe. The city of Merv—located about the midway point on an overland route between the ports of the Mediterranean and Calcutta, India—flourished as a stop on the Silk Road. Bukharin Jews were known as expert fabric dyers, and they also prospered as merchants in the region. In the seventh century CE the main cities of Bukhara and Samarkand came under Arab and Muslim control, as did other parts of Central Asia. Both sites emerged as centers of Islamic scholarship and culture, retaining their reputations well into the Middle Ages. In the 13th century, the area was conquered by Genghis Khan.

Adopted Musical Traditions

Against these sweeping changes Bukharin Jews retained much of their culture, language, and religious practices, though they were occasionally persecuted and forced to conduct religious observances in secret. Their numbers were periodically enlarged when Jews from other parts of the diaspora—from Iran, or the Middle East, and even the remnants of Moorish Spain—joined their community. Over the centuries, a form of Central Asian classical music emerged that had roots in Sufi Islamic traditions. Known as *shashmaqam*, it is considered the classical music of the Uzbek and Tajik peoples, for it was developed at the royal court of the khans, or rulers. For centuries Bukharin Jews held a cultural monopoly over the form, having long before established themselves as the favored performers at court.

By the early twentieth century Bukharin Jews had become prominent musicians and performers in vaudeville-style venues that kept the shashmaqam form alive in the modern era. But the advent of Soviet socialism was particularly repressive for ethnic groups across the Soviet realm after the Russian Revolution of 1917. Malayev was born at a time when Soviet leader Josef Stalin had ordered the closing of Jewish theaters in Bukhara, Samarkand, and other main cities in Central Asia with large Jewish populations.

Malayev emerged as a talented musician at an early age on the traditional Uzbek instruments. He played the *tar,* a handheld stringed instrument of ancient Persia that has ties to both the sitar of classical Indian music and the guitar familiar to Western culture. In 1951, at the age of 15, he moved to Tashkent, the capital of what was then the Uzbekistan Soviet Socialist Republic. From 1952 to 1960 he performed with the Ensemble of Song and Dance, a folk music performing arts troupe that was run under the auspices of the state-sponsored Uzbek Philharmonia. After 1956 he performed with the Folk and Variety Orchestras of Uzbekistan Radio, and beginning in 1962 had a long association with the Symphonic Variety Orchestra of Uzbekistan Radio. When former U.S. vice president Richard Nixon visited the Soviet Union in early 1967, Malayev was among the musicians who performed for the future U.S. president.

Became Uzbekistan's Biggest Star

In the 1970s Malayev's solo career blossomed despite the repressive nature of life in the Soviet sphere. As one of his contemporaries recalled, there were arena events in which "25,000 people would squeeze into bleachers to hear him croon, tell jokes, and show his hilarious imitations of drunks and his carefully calculated satires of public figures," a fellow Uzbek musician told Theodore Levin about Malayev in *The Hundred Thousand Fools of God: Musical Travels in Central Asia (and Queens, New York).* Malayev even performed for Soviet leader Leonid I. Brezhnev on Brezhnev's official visits to the city of Tashkent, which was leveled by a serious earthquake in 1966 and was the focus of a massive rebuilding effort to turn it into one of the Soviet Union's showcase cities.

Malayev's success was partly attributable to the support of a top-ranking government official in Uzbekistan named Sharaf Rashidov, who headed the Uzbekistan Communist Party from 1959 until an apparent suicide in 1983. Rashidov's death was tied to an emerging scandal involving revelations that Uzbekistan's cotton production output numbers had been inflated on a near-farcical scale for years. Uzbekistan fields had been the center of cotton production for the Soviet Union and even the Russian Empire that preceded it, and cotton had proved a profitable export for the Soviets on the international market for decades. Rashidov was among those who "devised an elaborate fraud in which they managed to bill the central Government in Moscow for the costs of producing large amounts of cotton which in fact did not exist," reported *New York Times* journalist Stephen Kinzer. "The scam thrived until the mid-1980's, when aides to the Soviet leader Yuri V. Andropov realized from satellite photographs that land supposedly producing cotton was in fact

lying fallow." Revelations of corruption on such a large scale helped undermine faith in the Soviet system, which collapsed entirely in 1991. Kinzer wrote of Rashidov, "Reviled in death as a corrupt thief by the Soviets, he is now widely viewed here as a clever Uzbek who managed to outwit the supposedly more sophisticated Russians."

Malayev's career was inextricably tied to Rashidov's power, and the latter reportedly killed himself rather than face a trial and death sentence. "He wasn't a nationalist," Malayev told Levin in *The Hundred Thousand Fools of God.* "He was a very decent person." Malayev, who was one of Uzbekistan's most widely recognized performing arts figures for years, explained how the system worked. "Frequently the Ministry of Culture would write a letter to the radio requesting that we be given to them for a performance. We were in the highest pay category. The Ministry established a tariff rate for us— how much we'd get paid for a performance.... At the end, they gave us double pay: twenty-nine rubles. In those days, you could buy six or seven kilograms of meat or good shoes with that money. When we performed in stadiums, so many people came that there were casualties."

Immigrated to United States

When the Rashidov scandal erupted, Malayev lost his top ally. There was a shakeup at the Ministry of Culture, and Malayev's wife, Muhabbat Shamayeva, a singer who had attained the rank of "People's Artist" in the Soviet system, was marginalized. Jews living under the Soviet regime, however, had the support of international human rights groups and were able to secure exit visas to move to Israel or the United States beginning in the 1970s. Those who chose the latter settled in New York City's outer boroughs, and Bukharin Jews set up their particular émigré enclave in the Forest Hills section of Queens. Malayev, Shamayeva, and several of their grown children moved there in 1992, a year after the collapse of the Soviet Union. While working on his book, Levin interviewed Malayev in New York, though he had met him years earlier on visits to Tashkent. Malayev seemed hopeful about his new life in America. "In the capitalist world you can do everything," he enthused. "No one asks, 'What's your nationality?'"

Both Forest Hills and neighboring Rego Park had strong Bukharin Jewish émigré populations, and Malayev was able to form a new ensemble called Maqam-I-Nawa that played traditional shashmaqam music for weddings and other celebratory events. In January of 1996, for his 60th birthday, some 1,300 former Soviet Jews turned up to celebrate at the official party. For the Shanachie label he recorded a 1997 disc, *At the Bazaar of Love,* with other members of the Ilyas Malayev Ensemble. He became a naturalized U.S. citizen in 2001. At the time, he was trying to spur a revival of classical Uzbek-Persian poetry. "For a person born in a totalitarian system to come to a capitalistic world and adapt is very difficult," he told *New York Times* writer Celia W. Dugger later in 2001. "I thought I would come here and a Bukharan millionaire would offer to pay to publish my poetry. Unfortunately, my expectations blew up like a soap bubble." Quoting an old proverb, he added, "as a chicken becomes fatter, she stops laying eggs. So it seems that the richer people become, the stingier they become."

Participated in *Silk Road* Project

In 2002 Malayev was among an esteemed group of invitees to perform at Carnegie Hall in an event dubbed the *Silk Road* concert project by its founder, the renowned cellist Yo-Yo Ma. Ma wanted to showcase classical music from non-Western sources and show the links between the West and East. Among the Carnegie Hall performers was an Azerbaijani vocalist who, wrote Alex Ross in the *New Yorker,* "demonstrated his passionate assimilation of the *mugham,* the Azerbaijani version of the monumental Islamic art-music genre the *maqam.*" Ross wrote effusively of Malayev and his Ensemble, who "performed their own delicately ornamented variation on the *maqam* while wearing the brilliant garb of Muslim court entertainers. Certain modal patterns, especially that of the lowered second, were common to all this music, suggesting that some Jews and Muslims once sang alike."

Malayev died from pancreatic cancer on May 2, 2008, in Queens, New York, at the age of 72. Among his survivors were his wife, two sons, three daughters, and four great-grandchildren, nearly all of whom lived in the Forest Hills/Rego Park area. "While other Central Asian émigré musicians plugged in and sang pop songs in the hope of appealing to a younger crowd, Malayev never abandoned his belief in the power of traditional music and poetry to stir the spirit," Levin told *New York Times* obituary writer William Grimes. "A listener didn't need to understand Uzbek or Tajik to feel the power of his songs and poetry."

Books

Levin, Theodore, *The Hundred Thousand Fools of God: Musical Travels in Central Asia (and Queens, New York),* Indiana University Press, 1996, pp. 261, 268, 269.

Periodicals

New York Times, February 20, 1997; November 20, 1997; November 16, 2001; May 7, 2008.
New Yorker, May 27, 2002.

Online

"About Ilyas Malayev," http://www.ilyasmalayev.com/about.htm (December 26, 2011). □

Effa Manley

Effa Manley (1900-1981) was an African-American sports figure and civil rights activist. A former owner of the Negro National League's Newark Eagles, she was the first woman inducted into the National Baseball Hall of Fame.

Effa Manley was born near the turn of the century in Philadelphia, Pennsylvania. The date of her birth is inconsistently reported as either March 27, 1897 or March 27, 1900. There are also multiple contradictory statements regarding her race, with many sources claiming

she was white and others identifying her as having a black mother. Some reports go as far as saying she was a white woman who simply preferred the company of blacks. The confusion is exacerbated by the fact that Manley herself would often claim to be either white or black depending on what social situation she found herself. In a 2006 *Essence* magazine article, Manley's niece, Connie Brooks, stated, "Effa Manley was not white. I don't understand reporters saying that she just liked Black people. What kind of ignorance is that?"

It is most likely that Manley was the product of an extramarital affair between Bertha Ford Brooks, a black seamstress, and John Bishop, a white businessman. Bob Luke noted in his Manley biography, *The Most Famous Woman in Baseball,* that as a result of this affair, Bertha's husband sued Bishop for alienation of affection and was awarded $10,000. He then divorced Bertha, who later remarried a black man named Benjamin Cole.

Despite this inauspicious beginning, Manley had a happy childhood with several brothers and sisters. She took vocational classes at William Penn High School and graduated in 1916. Upon graduation, she moved to Harlem and began what would become a lifelong pattern of deceiving others in regard to her race. According to Luke, she immediately found employment as a seamstress in a shop that only hired white employees. She remained in this position for about 16 years and had a brief marriage that ended in divorce.

Became Involved in Baseball

While living in New York, Manley became a huge baseball fan. According to a *Biography in Context* article, Manley once stated, "Babe Ruth made a baseball fan of me. I used to go to Yankee Stadium just to see him come to bat." While attending a 1932 World Series game between the New York Yankees and Chicago Cubs, she met Abe Manley. They were married the following year. Abe was over 20 years older, but they had a lot in common, and he respected her opinion on important issues of the day and their favorite sport.

Soon after their wedding, the Manleys were presented with a unique opportunity. In addition to being Yankees fans, both Abe and Effa had enjoyed following the teams of the Negro National League (NNL), which had been around since 1920. The Great Depression of 1929 had resulted in a huge decrease in attendance at NNL games and as a result the league was dying. According to Gai Ingham Berlage in the book *Women in Baseball: The Forgotten History,* Abe, who had made quite a bit of money on the gambling circuit, saw this as a chance to finally pursue a legitimate business opportunity. By 1935, he and several other black numbers runners bought teams and successfully revitalized the NNL.

Moved Team to Newark

The Manleys were co-owners of the Brooklyn Eagles. It was immediately decided that Effa would handle the business side of the team, allowing Abe to focus on player development. It was an arrangement that both found agreeable; however, despite the hard work they each put forth, the Eagles finished their first year with a disappointing 30-29 record. Effa, in particular, hated to lose. According to Berlage, when the Eagles lost their first game to the Homestead Grays, she later stated "I never saw so many home runs in my life...I went home in the third inning and had my first drink of whiskey." After one year in Brooklyn, the Manleys realized they were unable to compete for fans with the much-loved Brooklyn Dodgers so, in 1936, they moved the team to Newark, New Jersey, where it would remain for the duration of the NNL.

Because she was a woman, Manley's involvement with the team and the league was met with hostility from some players, coaches, and the press. Players resented her demands for discipline both on and off the field. In his book, *Effa Manley and the Newark Eagles,* James Overmyer quoted former player James Walker who stated, "Mrs. Manley was the disciplinarian of the team. She would call you in and tell you how to dress, what to do, who to associate with. When you had your problems, if they were personal, you went to Mrs. Manley, and she was very understanding, as long as you toed the line."

Not used to dealing with female bosses, the Eagles' coaches were also often at odds with Manley, though occasionally this was warranted. According to Berlage, "Two Newark managers, Willie Wells and Biz Mackey, said they had difficulty working with her. One favorite story about her meddling ways is the time she supposedly sent a message down to the Eagles' manager to pitch Terris McDuffie, her favorite pitcher. She wanted her girlfriends to see how handsome he was."

Manley's outspoken style also found her vilified in the press. According to Berlage, her habit of criticizing other team's owners at league meetings resulted in an article in the *Amsterdam New York Star News* that stated, "Effa Manley has long been a sore spot in the N.N.L. setup...the rough and tumble gentleman comprising its inner sanction have complained often and loudly that "baseball ain't no place for no woman.'"

Advocated for Players' Rights

Despite the criticism she faced at all levels of the NNL, Manley thrived in her role as the Eagles' business manager. She became an advocate for the players and demanded better treatment on their behalf. According to the Negro League Baseball Players Association (NLBPA) website, she continuously pushed for better schedules, improved travel conditions and increased salaries. She practiced what she preached by providing the Eagles with an air-conditioned bus for traveling to away games—the first in the NNL. Concerned for their players' financial well-being in the offseason, she and her husband sponsored a team in the Puerto Rican winter league. She also encouraged other team owners to take these measures.

Eventually her advocacy earned Manley the players' respect despite their dislike of her rules. Berlage noted that many of the players became like family to Manley—she served as a godparent to one player's child, loaned another several thousand dollars for a down payment on a house, and helped another open a tavern after he retired from baseball. That player was Lenny Pearson and he stated, "After I quit playing, she started me out in business. She interceded for me and spoke to people and helped me. She financed the first tavern I ever had. A beautiful, beautiful person in all ways."

Early on Manley recognized the importance of developing a strong commitment to public relations. She firmly believed that the Eagles and the Newark community could and would have a mutually beneficial relationship. In the book, *100 Trailblazers: Great Women Athletes Who Opened the Door for Future Generations,* William A. Sutton wrote, "The one thing that set Manley apart from many of her contemporaries was her ability to see the value of long-term marketing initiatives—those initiatives with more of a future impact on financial fortunes rather than an immediate return. Sponsoring youth baseball teams in order to teach young people about the game and to create an ongoing relationship between the youth and the game was a viable long-term growth strategy—growing and developing a market to ensure the long-term stability of the team."

Manley was a strong activist for black rights both inside and outside of baseball. She became treasurer of the New Jersey NAACP. In 1935 she helped establish the Citizen's League for Fair Play (CLFP), a civic group dedicated to improving the lives of blacks. As Berlage noted, the group organized a boycott of Harlem stores on 125th Street that refused to hire black employees. Using the slogan, "Don't shop where you can't work," the CLFP picketed for six weeks. At that point the shop owners gave in to their demands. Within one year, there were over 300 black employees on 125th Street. Manley's stance against racism filtered into baseball as well. She hosted Anti-Lynching Day at one of the Eagles' home games, an event Dan Rogosin, a sports writer of the day quoted in Berlage's book, called, "Probably the most remarkable special day in Negro baseball history."

Throughout all of these endeavors, the Newark Eagles remained Manley's primary focus. After the move to New Jersey, the team consistently made the playoffs and was considered to be worthy opponents by everyone in the NNL. In 1946, they advanced to the World Series, where they beat the Kansas City Monarchs. World War II brought an increased interest in Negro baseball, with many blacks arguing that if a man was good enough to serve in the military, he was good enough to play in Major League Baseball. Jackie Robinson finally broke the color barrier by signing with the Triple A Montreal Royals team in 1946 and becoming a Brooklyn Dodger in 1947.

For Manley, integration was both something to celebrate and something to mourn. As a longtime advocate for black rights, she was, of course, pleased to see blacks accepted. However, this turn of events meant that many of the best players in the NNL, including those that played for the Eagles, left the league in order to play in the majors. Fans followed their favorite players and attendance at NNL games began to decline rapidly. The Eagles were disbanded in 1948 and the entire NNL soon followed suit.

Continued Advocacy for Former Players

Manley devoted the remainder of her life to making sure the NNL was not forgotten. She wrote a book about Negro Baseball. She continued to advocate on behalf of black players, arguing for their admission into the Baseball Hall of Fame. She participated in oral histories and film documentaries about the Negro Leagues. She celebrated in the 1970s when 11 former players from the Negro Leagues were admitted into the National Baseball Hall of Fame, but wrote letters urging the inclusion of several more.

Effa Manley died on April 16, 1981. She was the last surviving owner from the NNL. In 2006, she became the first woman admitted into the National Baseball Hall of Fame. *Biography in Context* noted that at that time, a Major League Baseball website writer stated, "'Effa Manley was ahead of her time.' He described her as 'aggressive and progressive, glamorous and magnanimous,' and noted that she made her mark as one of the most fascinating and significant figures in Negro League history." Appropriately, Manley's gravestone bears a simple but undeniably true statement about her life. It reads, "She loved baseball."

Books

Berlage, Gai Ingham, *Women in Baseball: the Forgotten History,* Praeger, 1994

Lapchick, Richard, *100 Trailblazers: Great Women Athletes,* Fitness Information Technology, 2009

Luke, Bob, *The Most Famous Woman in Baseball: Effa Manley and the Negro Leagues,* Potomac Books, Inc., 2011

Overmyer, James, *Effa Manley and the Newark Eagles,* The Scarecrow Press, Inc., 1993

Periodicals

Essence, October, 2006

Online

Biography in Context, "Effa Manley," http://www.gale.cengage.com/InContext/bio.htm (June 5, 2011)

Negro League Baseball Players Association, "Effa Manley," http://www.nlbpa.com/manley_effa.html (June 5, 2011) ☐

Manteo

The Algonquian chieftain Manteo, who lived at the end of the sixteenth century, was among the Native Americans who assisted the early English settlers of North America, hoping for friendly relations between the English and Native American worlds.

We know of Manteo only through what was written about him during the period in the 1580s when his life intersected with those of English explorers, but even these limited sources offer fascinating windows into the early relationships between Native Americans and the English, when some members of both groups believed that they could live in peace on the North American continent. Manteo traveled to England twice, learned to speak English and taught an English linguist Algonquian, and became the first Native American to be baptized as an Anglican and accorded an English noble title. He was at least nearby when the so-called Lost Colony of settlers was established on Roanoke Island. The colony later mysteriously disappeared. Much about his background and motivations, however, remain a mystery.

Likely a Chieftain

Beyond the fact that he was described as "lustie" when he first joined the English (according to Giles Milton, writing in *Big Chief Elizabeth: The Adventures and Fate of the First English Colonists in America*) and thus was presumably fairly young, there is no evidence showing when Manteo was born. He may have come from the southern end of Croatoan Island (now Hatteras Island), and he was clearly a member of the Croatoan (or Croatan) tribe, an Algonquian-speaking people living in the area of what is now North Carolina's Outer Banks. Judging from his connections to powerful members of the tribe, revealed when he accompanied English colonists back to his homeland, it is likely that he was a chieftain of some sort himself.

On July 4, 1584, an English exploratory party headed by Philip Amadas and Arthur Barlowe, under directions from Sir Walter Raleigh, arrived in the Outer Banks area and soon laid claim to one of the barrier islands in the name of Queen Elizabeth I. Finding a generally friendly reception from the local Native Americans, they engaged in small-scale trade and explored villages on Roanoke Island with a view toward reporting back to Raleigh on the area's suitability for settlement. By around the month of August they had left for England, and Manteo and another Native American, Wanchese, were with them.

How Manteo met the English settlers, and why he decided to go with them, remain matters of speculation. Possible reasons include the traditional Algonquian belief that the world was filled with godlike beings called *Mantoac* that the English, with their exotic technology, seemed to resemble. He may simply have been afraid of English firepower, and he may have been influenced by the fact that the some of the earliest waves of English explorers operated under instructions to avoid conflict with Native American groups.

Manteo and Wanchese, who from the beginning was less cooperative with the English than Manteo, were housed at Raleigh's elaborate Durham House residence on the Thames. At first, according to a German visitor, they wore "no shirts, only a piece of fur to cover the pudenda and the skins of wild animals to cover their shoulders." Later they were given taffeta blouses and made to resemble English gentleman. Raleigh, who was keenly interested in the information Manteo and Wanchese could provide, took pains to keep them from being exhibited as curiosities. But to get the information he needed, more than a rudimentary sign language was necessary.

Taught Scientist Algonquian Language

Raleigh turned to Thomas Harriot, a mathematician and scientist who was regarded as one of the most learned men of the time (and who invented the mathematical symbols for "less than" and "greater than"). Harriot and Manteo (and to a lesser extent Wanchese) undertook a full-time effort to communicate, with the result that by Christmas of 1584 they could carry on simple conversations in Algonquian, and Manteo's knowledge of English was expanding rapidly. Harriot compiled an alphabet for writing Algonquian, a difficult task that required 36 letters (Roman, Greek, and invented) for the representation of the unfamiliar sounds of Native American languages. He began a dictionary and a phrase book, but these materials were lost with the Roanoke Island colony or in the Great Fire of London in 1585. Raleigh may have brought Manteo with him when he visited the Houses of Parliament to promote further American ventures.

Raleigh's promotional efforts were successful, and when an expedition led by Ralph Lane departed for the Outer Banks in 1585, Manteo and Wanchese were with them. Upon landing, Wanchese almost immediately disappeared, and he later took up arms against the English. But Manteo became a key member of the expedition. In the words of historian Michael L. Oberg, in his article "Between 'Savage Man' and 'Most Faithful Englishman': Manteo and the Early Anglo-Indian Exchange, 1584-1590," "No evidence exists to suggest that Manteo ever wavered in his cooperation, and his absolute identification with the English. His motives for doing so cannot be reconstructed with absolute certainty. It seems at least plausible that he found opportunity, advantage, status, and security through what he recognized as the more powerful English."

As relations between the English and the local Native Americans deterioriated under what were probably food-supply pressures, Manteo aided English groups in armed conflicts with tribes farther into the Carolina interior, sometimes making use of his superior ability to detect when a Native American attack was about to be launched. He certainly rendered the English great services as an interpreter and diplomat, and he left for England when Lane gave up his effort in June of 1586. Not much is known of Manteo's second sojourn in London, but he is likely to have studied the Anglican religion there and to have participated in planning for the launch of a permanent colony in the Chesapeake Bay area in 1587.

Baptized and Made English Lord

That mission bogged down when it reached Roanoke Island, as exhausted crew members refused to travel any farther. Some of them, led by Edward Stafford, attacked members of the Croatoan tribe, who at first did not recognize the anglicized Manteo. After he spoke to them in Algonquian, he managed to prevent an escalation of hostilities. On August 13, 1587, Manteo, at Raleigh's direction, (as quoted by Oberg) was "christened in Roanoak and called Lord thereof, and of Dasmongueponke [a nearby village], in reward of his faithful service." He was the first Native American to be baptized, and the first to receive an English noble title.

Nothing certain is known of Manteo's activities after these events, but speculation abounds. A small group of colonists was left behind on Roanoke Island, presumably to await a second ship under the command of Governor John White that would bring supplies and bring them to the Chesapeake. White recorded the birth of a child, Virginia Dare, to one woman in this group; she was the first child born to English parents in North America. But due to the British conflict with the Spanish Armada in 1588, White was unable to return to Roanoke until 1590. At that time he found the colony abandoned.

Manteo's possible part in this story stems from the fact that the word "Croatoan" was found carved into a post on the site, referring to the island on which he was born and likely wielded considerable influence. The colonists had agreed on a Maltese Cross as a distress signal, but no such cross was found. It seems plausible, therefore, that the colonists sought Manteo's protection, and perhaps were gradually assimilated into his tribe. The theory received some support from ongoing rumors that some Native Americans in the area had white ancestry, but no hard evidence to confirm it has ever emerged.

Books

Kupperman, Karen Ordahl, *Indians and English: Facing Off in Early America,* Cornell, 2000.

La Vere, David, *The Lost Rocks: The Dare Stones and the Unsolved Mystery of Sir Walter Raleigh's Lost Colony,* Burnt Mill, 2011.

Mancall, Peter, *Hakluyt's Promise: An Elizabethan's Obsession for an English America,* Yale, 2007.

Milton, Giles, *Big Chief Elizabeth: The Adventures and Fate of the First English Colonists in America,* Sceptre, 2011.

Online

"Biography of Manteo, Algonquian Indian," *NCGenWeb,* http://www.ncgenweb.us/dare/photosbios/indianmanteo.html (December 12, 2011).

Obert, Michael Leroy, "Between Savage Man and 'Most Faithful Englishman': Manteo and the Early Anglo-Indian Exchange, 1584–1590," http://www.homepages.rootsweb.ancestry.com/~jmack/algonqin/oberg1.htm, reproduction of *Itinerario: Europea Journal of Overseas History,* 24/2 (December 12, 2011).□

Sergio Marchionne

The Italian-Canadian auto executive Sergio Marchionne (born 1952) has been one of the corporate world's most prominent turnaround artists of the twenty-first century, reviving the venerable but moribund Fiat and Chrysler automotive brands.

In both cases Marchionne's efforts were at first derided as implausible. In a field dominated by executives with years of experience in automotive operations, he had no management background in the industry whatsoever when he was named to head Fiat in 2003. Although he had a broad background in corporate finance, he was not an accounting wizard. Nor did Marchionne follow executives in many other fields by gutting the companies he took over—his successes at Fiat were accomplished largely without conflict with Italy's combative labor unions, and at Chrysler, within a few years of taking over, he was already announcing expansions in the company's workforce. Marchionne seemed to achieve results through sheer hard work: his hallmarks as an executive were desks overrun with communications devices, middle-of-the-night phone calls to talk business with subordinates, and nonstop commutes by Ferrari over the Alps and by jet over the Atlantic, flying at night so as not to lose valuable work hours.

Moved to Toronto with Family

Sergio Marchionne (mar-kee-OHN-nay) was born in the small city of Chieti, Italy, northeast of Rome, on June 17, 1952. His father, Concezio, was a member of the *carabinieri,* Italy's national police force. The family lived frugally, and when Concezio Marchionne was 50 he was able to retire and move to Toronto, Canada, where Sergio and his sister Luciana would have a better chance to attend college. At first Marchionne was disoriented by life in a new country. "Trying to get friendly with girls with whom you cannot communicate was a problem," he recalled to Eric Reguly of the Toronto *Globe & Mail.* But eventually Marchionne, who holds dual Italian and Canadian citizenship, would begin to think in English rather than Italian.

A lifelong lover of the arts and humanities, especially opera, Marchionne majored in philosophy at the University of Toronto, receiving a BA in 1978. He then switched to business-related programs, earning a second bachelor's degree at the University of Windsor in 1979 and an MBA from the same school in 1980. That year, Luciana Marchionne died of cancer. Marchionne became certified as an accountant and then entered Osgoode Hall Law School at Toronto's York University, receiving his degree in 1983.

Marchionne worked in corporate finance for the first decade of his career, rising quickly in part because of his ability to move easily between North American and European worlds. His first job was at the large accounting firm Deloitte & Touche, in Toronto, from 1983 to 1985. Then he moved to the Toronto packaging company Lawson Mardon, beginning as group controller and then becoming director of corporate development. His boss there remembered him for his intelligence, his messy office, and his tobacco habit. In 1989 and 1990 he was executive vice president of Glenex Industries, a conglomerate whose activities ranged from film and video to mining and oil and gas extraction. Marchionne moved to the accounting firm Acklands as chief financial officer in 1990 and then returned to Lawson Mardon in 1992, this time as vice president of legal and corporate development.

In 1994 Marchionne moved to Switzerland to take an executive vice president position at Algroup (Alusuisse-Lonza Holdings, Ltd.), a packaging firm that had acquired Lawson Mardon earlier that year. Marchionne and his wife, Orie, made Switzerland their permanent home, raising two sons, Alessio and Tyler. By 1997 Marchionne was Algroup's CEO. In two years he blew by his five-year goal of doubling the company's business. The company was itself sold in 2000, and the Lonza division, which made drug ingredients, was spun off with Marchionne as chief executive. He added chairman to his portfolio in 2002 but left later that year to become chief executive at SGS (Société Genéral Surveillance), a venerable testing and certification firm, based in Switzerland with a worldwide reach.

Named Fiat CEO

Italy's Agnelli family, direct descendants of Fiat founder Giovanni Agnelli, were part-owners of SGS at the time. A succession of deaths in the family had interrupted management continuity and displaced Fiat from its 1990s roost as Europe's largest automaker. After the death of the aging Umberto Agnelli, grandson of Giovanni, in 2003, the company was hemorrhaging money and lacking an obvious candidate to become CEO. Marchionne was added to the company's board of directors, which then, in Reguly's words, "looked around the room and gambled on Marchionne, the outsider who spoke Italian and English, had plenty of international experience and a reputation for toughness. He was made CEO in 2004 and was given carte blanche to do what was needed to fix Fiat, which was then on the verge of bankruptcy."

At the time, Marchionne described himself as a car buff who liked fast cars. As of 2007 he owned three Ferraris (Ferrari is a Fiat brand), including a 12-cylinder Enzo racing model, and used them in lightning commutes from his home in Switzerland to Fiat headquarters in Turin, Italy (under real time pressure he sometimes took a helicopter). He did not have a day of experience as an auto executive. In fact, Marchionne pointed out to Luca Ciferro of *Automotive News Europe,* ''I've never had any experience in any industry I've been in, but I still turned things around.'' Indeed, he read the automotive landscape like a lifelong observer. Rather than confront Italy's powerful labor unions by announcing factory closings, he attacked Fiat's layers of ineffectual middle management, eventually shedding more than 2,000 positions. With this process in motion, Marchionne used a provision of Italian law to reduce shop-floor wages and furlough rather than eliminating assembly-line jobs outright.

Marchionne was not shy about describing the magnitude of his accomplishment. ''We spit blood to clean up and restart Fiat,'' he was quoted as saying by Tom Bawden of the London *Times.* ''When I took over, there was a smell of death here.'' Marchionne's triumph was not merely one of corporate and labor restructuring; he demanded that the company reduce its disorganized set of 19 car platforms (basic chassis and mounting points, components, and engineering shared across various models) and its unwieldy set of 18 different heating and air conditioning systems to six and five, respectively. By 2006 Fiat had turned its first profit in five years; costs had been reduced by 500 million Euros; and the new Fiat Bravo small car had gone from sketches to production in 18 months—half the usual time.

Proposed Chrysler Deal

With the global auto industry in free fall during the recession that began in 2007 and 2008, most executives were in retrenchment mode, if not struggling for their companies' survival. Marchionne instead embarked on a bold growth strategy. In 2009 he offered a lifeline (in the form of an alliance with Fiat) to the bankrupt Chrysler corporation in the United States in return for a 20 percent stake in the company, rising to 51 percent after the achievement of certain performance benchmarks. (By late 2011 Marchionne was passing benchmarks so fast that Fiat's share of Chrysler had grown to 58.5 percent.) Although the deal involved no direct cash investment on Fiat's part, Chrysler was given little chance of survival even with Fiat's help; auto analyst Eric-Alain Michelis told Reguly that the deal could mark Fiat's ''Vietnam.'' Owned by the venture capital firm Cerberus Capital Management for several years (until the company's bailout by the administration of U.S. president Barack Obama), Chrysler had few new products in the pipeline.

Nevertheless, the speed of the turnaround Marchionne engineered at Chrysler was striking. This time, in tandem with an industry-wide restructuring of wages in the United States, Marchionne did shutter seven American assembly plants. But once again he spread the pain equally, reducing the company's American dealer network by nearly 800 stores. With large infusions of cash from American and Canadian governments, Chrysler was well positioned to benefit as consumers returned to showrooms in 2009 and 2010. New Jeep Cherokee and Chrysler 300 models performed well, and Marchionne laid plans for an integration of Chrysler and Fiat platforms that would duplicate his European success.

By 2012, although the new Fiat 500 subcompact had been slow to get off the ground in North America, the turnaround was in full swing. Marchionne had plans in place to add thousands of new Chrysler assembly-line jobs in unionized plants in Toledo, Ohio, and Detroit, earning him a reservoir of good will among the company's blue-collar workers despite wage and health care cuts. A new Dodge Dart, based on a Fiat platform, was unveiled at the 2012 Detroit auto show. And the executive in his trademark black sweaters (Marchionne donned a suit only to meet the Pope in 2007) had become the best-known corporate leader of Italian descent since Lee Iacocca.

Periodicals

Automotive News Europe, June 14, 2004.
Blade (Toledo, OH), August 14, 2011; November 16, 2011.
Financial Times, February 15, 1999.
Globe & Mail (Toronto, Ontario, Canada), July 21, 2007; November 27, 2009.
Times (London, England), May 5, 2009.
Toronto Star, January 29, 2007; April 12, 2009.

Online

''Fiat Boosts Stake in Chrysler to 58.5% After Reaching Its Efficiency Goal,'' *Bloomberg News,* http://www.bloomberg.com/news/2012-01-05/ (January 7, 2012).□

Maria the Jewess

Maria the Jewess (born and died c. first or second century CE) is commonly cited as one of the first women writers on the subject of alchemy, the forerunner science of modern chemistry. She was Jewish, possibly from Syria, and lived in Alexandria, Egypt, during that city's flourishing period under Greek rule. Thus she is often described as a Hellenic Jew, and though little concrete information on her has survived the ages, she was mentioned by other writers in later centuries in texts that make reference to her achievements. Several chemical laboratory instruments were either invented or improved upon by Maria, or at least turned up as the first mention in a scholarly text under her pen. The *bain-marie,* used in both chemistry and the food arts, is thought to have been named after her.

Maria is known as the Jewess, the Prophetess, and in some sources as ''the Sister of Moses,'' though of course she lived several centuries after the biblical prophet of the Old Testament. The most probable dates for her life are either in the first century or second century CE. The first surviving reference to her comes from Zosimos of Panopolis, a renowned alchemist who lived in what is today the Egyptian city of Akhmim. Zosimos is the first Greek writer on alchemy whose works are available to contemporary scholars. Around 300 CE he published a 28-volume encyclopedia of chemistry called the *Cheirokmeta* that mentions Maria and another alchemist who called herself "Cleopatra" after the late queen of Hellenic Egypt.

Alchemy was less a science at the time than a loosely organized set of ideas about the nature of life and the universe based on observations of the curious properties of natural elements. Alchemists felt that the world was composed of not just plants and animals but various minerals and essences, too. They experimented with base metals and heat to produce new compounds, or sought what they believed was the elixir, or potion, that gave life to all creatures.

The Light of the West

The city of Alexandria was the epicenter of alchemy and several other scholarly pursuits for a few exciting centuries, including Maria's lifetime. Founded by the famous Macedonian Greek conqueror Alexander the Great in 332 BCE at the mouth of the Nile River, the city had ambitions to become the greatest city of the Western world, in both population and technological advances, under the Ptolemaic rulers and their successors. The cosmopolitan city grew to an enormous size, thanks to access to grains grown in the fertile Nile Delta region, which could support a large urban populace, and served as a key trade port between Europe, Asia, and Africa.

Alexandria's civic ambition to become the epicenter of scholarship was anchored by the Great Library of Alexandria, which was for several centuries the largest repository of texts of its kind in the West. Any ship that entered Alexandria's harbor—with its magnificent island lighthouse lit by a flame that could be seen 70 miles away—had to turn over its scrolls. Copyists would make a facsimile to return, keeping the original for the Library. Alexandria was also one of the most diverse urban communities of the first millennium CE, with its mix of Greek, Egyptian, and Jewish peoples. It was, more notably, one of the first cities in history with a significant Jewish population. Alexandria's Jewish scholars achieved some impressive feats, including a translation of the original five books of the Torah into a Greek version for Alexandrian Jews who were unable to read the written Hebrew language any longer. This translation into Greek was of course an invaluable aid to the inclusion of the Old Testament in later versions of the Christian Bible.

The Library of Alexandria may have burned by the time Maria lived; the exact date of its destruction by fire is uncertain, but older sources generally date it to 48 BCE, when Julius Caesar, the Roman emperor who greatly expanded his empire, made a move to seize the majestic city. Alexandria remained under Roman jurisdiction for five more centuries, and after the founding of Christianity in the first century CE became a center of the Coptic sect of the faith. Coptic Christians were largely native-born Egyptians who embraced the new faith. The Roman emperors finally converted, too, in the early fourth century CE. The Greeks, however, continued to hold what were viewed as "pagan" views, and became the target of persecution, as did the Jews.

Left Instructions for *Tribikos*

Zosimos, who was either Greek or Egyptian, was the first writer to mention Maria and make reference to her major work on alchemy, the *Maria Practica*. Her original manuscript does not survive, but he discussed several of the advances she made in chemistry and laboratory equipment in his *Cheirokmeta,* and quoted from the *Practica.* One of her devices was the three-armed distillation chamber, called a *tribikos.* "Maria's description included instructions for making the copper tubing from sheet metal, and she compared the thickness of the metal to that of a 'pastrycook's copper frying-pan,'" wrote Margaret Alic in *Hypatia's Heritage: A History of Women in Science from Antiquity through the Nineteenth Century.* "Flour paste was recommended for sealing the joints." Alic gave a further description of the tribikos and its use, noting that "it consisted of an earthenware vessel for holding the liquid to be distilled, a still-head for condensing the vapour (the *ambix* or *alembic*), three copper delivery spouts fitted into the still-head, and glass receiving flasks. A gutter or rim on the inside of the still-head collected the distillate and carried it to the delivery spouts."

The title of Alic's book refers to another important woman scholar in Alexandria, Hypatia, who was particularly gifted in mathematics and the theories of the ancient Greek philosophers Plato and Aristotle. Hypatia lived after Maria and was killed by a mob in 415 CE during a wave of religious persecutions. Referring to the alchemist named after the famous queen, Alic asserted that "Maria and Cleopatra mark both the beginning and the end of alchemy as a true experimental science. The third-century Roman Emperor Diocletian initiated the systematic persecution of the Alexandrian alchemists and burned their texts," Alic wrote in *Hypatia's Heritage.*

Wrote about the *Kerotakis*

Another modern-day writer, Raphael Patai, wrote about Maria for the 1995 work *The Jewish Alchemists: A History and Source Book.* Using sources from Zosimos and beyond, Patai and Alic surmise that Maria probably carried out experiments on arsenic, mercury, and other chemical elements, researching what happened when they came into contact with silver, gold, or alloys like bronze. She did some of this with the help of the kerotakis, another lab instrument often mentioned in reports of her work. "The Greek name of the still, *kerotakis,* was derived from the name of the palette on which the ancient Greek painters mixed their four basic pigments—white, black, yellow, and red—with wax (*keros*)," Patai wrote. "The triangular or rectangular metal plate which served as the kerotakis had to be kept warm in order to prevent the wax from hardening."

Maria also investigated various methods of maintaining a steady, even temperature in her experiments. It is known that she discussed the *thermospodion,* or hot-ash bath, and tried out a dung bed for heating various concoctions at a steady temperature without burning. There were also forays into phosphorescent gemstones, using chemicals that would glow in the dark. "Maria advises that mixtures of certain organic substances, such as the gall of fish and tortoises, the juice of jellyfish, oils of plants, resins, and so on—all of which are readily oxidized in the air—should be added in 'the proper proportion' to the 'tints and varnishes''' to create glow-in-the-dark stones, wrote Patai.

Some scholars attribute *The Letter of the Crown and the Nature of the Creation by Mary the Copt of Egypt* to Maria, but it is unclear if she was the Copt mentioned, for she referred to herself as "the Jewess." The letter "was found in a volume of Arabic alchemical manuscripts, translated from Greek," noted an essay on Maria in *Notable Women Scientists*. "This work summarized the major theories of Alexandrian alchemy and described the manufacture of colored glass, as well as other chemical processes."

Wrote on Mystical Properties of Metals

Alexandria's scholars left behind such an impressive body of knowledge that a few contemporary theorists believe they possessed enough technical know-how to create significant mechanical advances like steam power, which drove the Industrial Revolution 16 centuries after Maria's lifetime. The reign of Diocletian, mentioned above, marked the beginning of the end for alchemists, who came to be viewed with a degree of suspicion for their interest in the seemingly supernatural or magical events that occurred when chemical elements were combined. "Maria believed that metals were living males and females and that the products of her laboratory experiments were the result of sexual generation," noted the essay in *Notable Women Scientists*. "The early alchemists believed that the base metals were evolving toward the perfect metal—gold. They clearly distinguished between gilding or forming alloys of base metals to simulate gold and silver, and true transmutation. By transferring the 'spirit' or vapor of gold to a base metal, as measured by the transfer of color, alchemists saw themselves as encouraging a natural process."

After the fourth century CE, Alexandria's exalted place as a center of scholarship began to decline precipitously. One of the last philosophers in the city from the Neoplatonist school—the continuation of the teachings of Plato, who lived in Athens nearly a thousand years earlier—was Olympiodorus the Younger of Alexandria, who mentioned Maria's work in his sixth-century CE writings. In 642 CE, Egypt was invaded by armies from the Arabian peninsula who firmly established Islam in Alexandria, in Egypt, and across much of North Africa. Arab scholars kept Maria's writings, and also maintained copies of some of the great works of ancient Greece and Rome, which would be rediscovered by the West several centuries later. Alchemy, in the Middle Ages of Western Europe, was deemed a type of sorcery, and there were some unscrupulous practitioners who attempted to pass off cheaper alloys as gold or other precious metals.

Maria's most enduring contribution to science came more than a millennium after her death. Zosimos mentioned her use of what is essentially a double boiler, where a pot of water is heated steadily and a second pot placed inside it, so that the element or ingredient in the second will be heated consistently. A well-known Spanish professor of the sciences, Arnaldus de Villa Nova, was fluent in Arabic and taught medicine in France before his death in 1311. He may have translated some of the surviving fragments of Maria's *Practica* or worked from other sources to describe the double boiler as the *balneum mariae,* Latin for "Maria's bath." Recipes requiring a modicum of technical ability usually specify a *bain-marie* to melt chocolate or keep dairy-based sauces from separating.

Books

Alic, Margaret, *Hypatia's Heritage: A History of Women in Science from Antiquity through the Nineteenth Century,* Beacon Press, 1986, pp. 37–41.

"Maria the Jewess," *Notable Women Scientists,* Gale, 2000.

"Maria the Jewess," *World of Chemistry,* Gale, 2006.

Patai, Raphael, *The Jewish Alchemists: A History and Source Book,* Princeton University Press, 1995, pp. 61, 65.

Periodicals

New Yorker, May 8, 2000. □

Roger Maris

American Major League Baseball player Roger Maris (1934-1985) was best known for breaking Babe Ruth's long-standing single-season home run record. His career lasted twelve years. An outfielder, he gained his greatest fame with the New York Yankees, but he also played for the Cleveland Indians, the Kansas City Athletics and the St. Louis Cardinals. His home run record stood until 1998.

R oger Maris will be forever remembered as the man who broke Babe Ruth's once seemingly insurmountable single-season record of sixty home runs. Unfortunately, this accomplishment created only misery for Maris, as sports writers and New York fans resented his restructuring of baseball's record books. For them, he not only broke tradition but displayed an alienating personality. The story is one of baseball's most dramatic narratives, as Maris—a shy man and consummate professional—found himself thrust into one of his sport's most high-pressured situations.

The future Major League baseball star was born Roger Eugene Maras in Hibbing, Minnesota on September 10, 1934. In 1955, a year after he became a professional baseball player, he officially changed the spelling of his name (replacing the "a" with an "i") to avoid being teased, as he had been when he was younger. The original spelling had provoked vulgar and vocal plays on his name. This name change represented a defensiveness that Roger Maris would exhibit throughout his life. Later, his family also took on the spelling change.

Excelled in Multiple Sports

The man who would become a heel to many and a hero to others was the younger of two sons born to Rudolph Maras, Sr., a mechanics supervisor for the Great Northern Railroad and a former semiprofessional hockey player, and Anne

Corinne (Sturbitz), a housewife. His family moved to Grand Forks, North Dakota, when he was still an infant. The family later settled in Fargo, in the same state.

In Fargo, Roger attended Bishop Shanley High School with older brother Rudy and was an outstanding athlete for all seasons, doing well in football, basketball and track. During his senior year, he set a national high school football record by scoring four touchdowns in one game.

As for baseball, his high school had no team—in North Dakota, spring was still far too cold to even consider basesball—so Maris participated in that sport with American Legion teams in summer months. And he stood out: The organization named him its most valuable player in 1950.

Chose Baseball over College

When he graduated from high school in 1952, Maris was offered an athletic scholarship with the University of Oklahoma. By this time, he was six feet tall and weighed 200 solid pounds that was topped by blond hair that he later sculpted into a crew cut in his Yankee years. However, Maris did not relish the thought of being confined in classrooms. Instead, he looked to professional baseball. The Chicago Cubs and Cleveland Indians were interested in acquiring his considerable skills. Maris tried out with the Indians and impressed the organization's general manager, Hank Greenberg, who was one of baseball's greatest players. Cleveland offered him $5,000 and promised Maris another $10,000 if he made it to the major leagues in five years.

Maris would rise swiftly through the Indian farm system; however, he also displayed a defiant attitude, something that would bedevil him throughout his career. For instance, he demanded to be assigned to the Class C Northern League, so that he could play on the Fargo/Moorehead team, which was close to his hometown. Also, he once walked off the field when he didn't like the way he

was being treated by a manager. That points to another problem: Maris, an intelligent man, did not suffer fools well; and he felt professional baseball had its share.

Otherwise, Maris' minor league years were positive and productive. In 1953, in his first year, he was named the C league's rookie of the year. He was promoted to Class B the following year. In 1956, he was promoted to the Class AA farm team in Indianapolis. He was a standout in that year's minor league Little World Series. Also that year, on October 13, Maris married his high school sweetheart, Patricia Ann Carvell. They would have six children.

Maris earned his $10,000 bonus, beating the five-year deadline when he made it to the Cleveland Indians' major league team in 1957. In this rookie season, Maris recorded a mediocre .235 batting average, but he hit 14 home runs. He only played one full season with the team: In June 1958, he was traded to the Kansas City Athletics. By this time, Maris and his wife settled in the Midwest, in Raytown, Missouri, and he would have liked to have remained with Kansas City. However, on December 11, 1959, he was traded once again, this time to the team where he would achieve his greatest fame and make baseball history: the New York Yankees. But while the move led to personal glory, it also led to personal nightmare.

Became a "Bronx Bomber"

In the trade, Kansas city offered Maris, Joe DeMaestri, and Kent Hadley, while the Yankees moved Hank Bauer, Norm Siebern, and Marv Throneberry, as well as pitcher Don Larsen.

Larsen's career resembled Maris's in one respect. Both men, while playing for the Yankees, made sports history. Larsen pitched a perfect game for the Yankees in the 1956 World Series. Maris, of course, broke Babe Ruth's home run record six years later. Both men saw their careers defined by their singular historic achievements, with Maris having the more complete overall resumé.

Maris was the major element in the Yankees-Athletics trade. The Yankee organization was attracted by Maris' well-rounded set of skills: He displayed excellent defense, speed on the basepaths, and batting power.

Maris did not disappoint. Playing right field, he became a star on a team filled with stars, including the great Yankee centerfielder Mickey Mantle, his good friend and perceived rival for home run supremacy in 1961. He was impressive in that first year. In 1960, in his debut game in Yankee pinstripes, Maris hit a single, a double, and two home runs. For the season, he compiled a .283 batting average, slammed 39 homes and led the American League in runs batted in (112) and slugging percentage (.581). He helped his team win that year's pennant, and he received the league's Most Valuable Player (MVP) award. He also won the Gold Glove award. Starting in 1960, the Yankees won five straight pennants, and Maris was a crucial component.

Maris and Mantle would become known as the "M&M" boys, as they were a fearsome one-two power punch. When Maris won the MVP award in 1960, he edged out Mantle by only three votes (225 to 222). That same year, when Mantle won the American League's home run crown with 40, he hit only one more than Maris. The next year, they would both chase Babe Ruth's single-season home run record of 60 home runs (set in 1927).

Hit 61 in '61

In the baseball world, 1961 will always be remembered as the season when Roger Maris broke Babe Ruth's home run record. It was an accomplishment that should have been lauded. Instead it provoked consternation among fans, sportswriters, and even the Yankee organization. The attitude among all was that Roger Maris did not deserve to breach a seemingly unattainable level. New York never really took to Maris, and Maris did not particularly like New York. Sports writer Joe Durso, who penned Maris' obituary for *The New York Times*, in 1985, wrote: "[Maris] was considered an upstart in the House That Ruth Built, and the house that Mantle dominated. He was dour, aloof, sometimes arch, and in no way the flamboyant bear portrayed by Babe Ruth."

And that points to the problem: If the home-run record would be broken, people felt, then it should be broken by Mickey Mantle, a player that had endeared himself to Yankee fan's hearts and minds. After all, Mantle had been with the team since the early 1950s, and he assumed the "mantle" that had been left empty by the trading of Babe Ruth, the health problems suffered by Lou Gehrig, and the retirement of Joe DiMaggio. Maris was considered an out-of-town interloper separate from Yankee tradition. Ironically, Mantle had gone through his own trouble winning over Yankee fans, and only acheived complete acceptance as a counterpoint to Maris.

It is surprising, the vehemence that Maris' presence and accomplishments generated. After all, he was only doing the job he was paid to do, and he did his job well. For the 1961 season, he scored 142 runs and compiled 132 runs batted in (the highest in the American League)—which means, home runs aside, that he was an extremely productive player that contributed to his team's fortunes.

Those who knew about such things provided him the appropriate recognition: For the second straight year, he was voted the league's MVP. Also, he was named the *Sporting News* Player of the Year, *Sports Illustrated* Sportsman of the Year, *Sport* magazine Man of the Year, and Associated Press Professional Athlete of the Year, as he helped lead the Yankees to another pennant and World Series.

Still, what should have been a memorable season turned out a miserable one for Maris. He was neither embraced by the New York sports writing press or by the New York sports-going public. As Mantle and Maris pursued Babe Ruth's home run record, Maris suffered abuse from the fans (they threw objects at him from the stands), and the New York sportswriters were harsh. They reported a feud between Maris and Mantle, which did not exist. The truth was that Mantle and Maris were good friends, shared an apartment during the season, and they laughed at what the media reported.

But, really, it was no laughing matter, and Maris did not help his own cause. He could never overcome an innate shyness, nor an incapacity to suffer fools well—and he considered the sports writing ranks to be populated by fools. Everyone asked him the same questions, over and over again. Eventually, he retreated into himself, which sportswriters reported as a negative. "The sportswriters portrayed him as a moody, sullen, nasty, selfish player who didn't deserve to

break Ruth's record," wrote actor Robert Wuhl, a lifelong Yankee fan who contributed an essay about Maris for the book *Cult Baseball Players*, (edited by Danny Peary) and who embraced Maris as a hero.

The pressure had a physical effect on Maris: He lost weight along with clumps of hair.

Throughout most of the season Maris and Mantle matched home run for home run, and it appeared that the race for the record would come down to a season-ending photo finish. Indeed, the chase remained close until September, when Mantle suffered a hip injury and was placed on the disabled list for the last three weeks of the season. Mantle was stymied at 54 home runs. Maris would now pursue the record alone. And it came down to the end of the season. After 159 games in a 162-game schedule, Maris had tied Ruth's record. Finally in the last game of the season, and facing Boston Red Sox pitcher Tracy Stallard, the 27-year-old Maris hit a fourth-inning solo home run that broke the record. The shot was appropriate in several ways: it was Maris' 61st home run in the 1961 season, and the home run was the only run scored in the Yankees' win, and it was hit in Yankee Stadium.

Despite the poetry of the circumstances, Maris' feat was tarnished by the infamous "asterisk," perpetrated by then-baseball commissioner Ford Frick, who essentially said that a new home run record would be meaningless if it could not be accomplished in 154 games instead of 162 games. Due to expansion, the 1961 season was the first in which the regular season consisted of 162 games. During Ruth's career, the season generally consisted of 154 games. But it was a meaningless proclamation, as both Ruth and Maris had a similar number of total at-bats. For the record, this is how it played out: Maris hit 59 home runs in the first 154 games of the 1961 season and hit his 61st home run on the last day (and 162nd game) of the season, on October 1. So, Frick's ruling tarnished the achievement.

The entire experience made Maris bitter. After he hit the record-breaking home run, he was reluctant to leave the dugout to tip his hat to the home crowd that was now wildly cheering him. But team members encouraged him to embrace the moment. Eventually, Maris emerged from the dugout and took his bow.

As the cheers indicated, many people considered Maris a hero. After all, he was handsome and accomplished—and for some, his silence and surliness translated into cool charisma. As Wuhl related in his essay, the home run was a "moment" with a capital "M"—a 1960s moment similar to the Kennedy assassination, the Beatles' appearance on the "Ed Sullivan Show" and the US landing on the moon. "It was one of those 'where were you then' moments," reported Wuhl, adding the essential question: "Where were you when Roger Maris hit his 61st home run?"

Endured Injuries and Contract Disputes

Subsequent years in a Yankee uniform were proved even unhappier for Maris. The one big question everyone asked: How could he follow up? The answer, in short, was that he did it quite well. In the following year, Maris hit 33 home runs and helped lead the Yankees to yet another pennant.

But, before the season, he entered into contentious contract negotiations that distanced the slugger from the team. Further, he suffered leg injuries and back pain. These were legitimate maladies, but both the front office and the fans considered him a malingerer—an unfair assessment.

His 1961 season earned him about $40,000 and a subsequent salary dispute almost raised the figure twice. The contract dispute, however, unfairly marked Maris as a contentious individual. The press portrayed him as a whiner. He headed into the 1962 season with no contract but eventually accepted $72,500.

That year, Maris had what would be considered a fine season for anyone else. Along with his 33 home runs, he drove in 100 runs. His defensive skills were also consistently excellent: In the World Series, he made a play in right field that proved pivotal to the Yankees' world championship. But all of this wasn't enough. Sport writers and fans considered his 1962 season a disappointment, as his numbers (specifically his home run total) did not match those of his '61 season.

Things went from bad to worse. In 1963, still enduring leg and back pain, Maris would only play in 90 games. His home run total dropped to twenty-three (which is still a respectable amount, especially considering his reduced number of games). In 1964, he hit 26 home runs. But it would be his last good offensive season with the Yankees (he batted .281 with 144 hits). During the season, Maris was "benched," a humiliating circumstance that newspapers reported with glee. Also, it would be the last year that the Yankees won an American League pennant until the George Steinbrenner era that began in the 1970s.

In 1965, Maris suffered a serious right-hand injury while sliding into home plate. A chipped bone caused him severe pain, and the injury eventually required surgery. He never did regain full strength in the hand, though, and experienced numbness in several fingers. He would only play in 46 games, to the consternation of Yankee management, who felt he should have remained in the team's lineup.

Traded to St. Louis Cardinals

Maris remained with the Yankees through the 1966 season. Still hampered by pain and injury, he played in 119 games, recording a .233 batting average and hitting only 13 home runs. Maris expressed a desire to retire from baseball, but on December 8, 1966 the Yankees traded Maris to the St. Louis Cardinals, a National League team.

Maris still owned a house in the Midwest—in Raytown, Missouri—so the trade was like coming home. He decided to delay his retirement. He would play for the Cardinals for two seasons (1967 and 1968) and, just as he did with the Yankees, he helped the Cardinal team win two league pennants and play in two World Series. The situation was completely different from New York. Although Maris could no longer post the big power numbers, St. Louis—the team and the fans—were happy to have him. And Maris was happy to be there. The team—which included players such as Hall of Fame pitcher Bob Gibson, catcher Tim McCarver, first baseman Orlando Cepeda, base-stealer Lou Brock, talented outfielder Curt Flood, excellent shortstop Julian Javier, and up-and-coming pitching superstar Steve Carlton—was like a family.

And Maris fit right in. Everyone—the team's management, the players, the fans, and the sportwriters—appreciated Maris' professionalism, experience, enthusiasm and work ethic.

After he helped lead his new team to the 1967 World Series, he turned in an outstanding performance in the "fall classic," in which the Cardinals beat the Boston Red Sox in seven games. During the series, Maris recorded a .385 batting average and knocked in seven of his team's 25 runs scored.

After this satisfying season, Maris again expressed his wish to retire. However, team owner August Busch (who also owned the hugely successful Anheuser-Busch company—the brewery that produced Budweiser beer) wanted Maris to stick around for at least one more season. To entice Maris, Busch offered him a beer distributorship. Maris agreed, and he helped the Cardinals win another National League pennant. After the Cardinal's lost the 1968 World Series to the Detroit Tigers, Maris felt that retirement time had at last come.

Became a Successful Businessman

Busch's deal was that Maris could choose anywhere in the country to work his offered beer distributorship. Maris chose Gainesville, Florida. There, he took his family and brought members into a business enterprise that proved enormously successful. Older brother Rudy Maris became a partner.

Meanwhile, Maris claimed he would never again set foot in Yankee Stadium after the treatment he received from management, sports writers and fans. After the team came under new ownership, however—George Steinbrenner purchased the Yankees in 1973—Maris was more open to a reconciliation.

He agreed to appear at Yankee Stadium in 1978, to honor the raising of the 1977 American League pennant that the team had won. (In the 1977 World Series, the Yankees beat the Los Angeles Dodgers, bolstered by a game-six, three home-run performance by Reggie Jackson, the new Yankees superstar.)

During an Old Timers' Day celebration in 1984, the Yankees honored Maris by retiring his jersey number (9). The Yankee organization also placed a bronze plaque in the memorial section of the stadium's center field, alongside other Yankee greats, including the man whose record Maris broke: Babe Ruth.

Died from Cancer

By this time, Maris had been diagnosed with lymphatic cancer (in 1983). In 1984, he was undergoing chemotherapy treatment. After a short remission, the disease came back in 1985. Maris opted for experimental treatment, but he died on December 14, 1985 at the M.D. Anderson Tumor Institute in Houston, Texas. He was 51 years old.

He was buried at Holy Cross Cemetery in Fargo, North Dakota. A funeral mass, conducted by John Cardinal O'Connor, was held at Saint Patrick's Cathedral in New York City.

In 1991, then Commissioner Fay Vincent announced that the asterisk next to Maris' 61 home run achievement would be permanently deleted from baseball's record books.

Maris' record stood until September 8, 1998, when St. Louis Cardinals' Mark McGwire punched out his 62nd home run. Just as Maris' accomplishment once was anticipated, this occasion was a foregone conclusion, and five of Maris' six children were present. Since then, McGwire's record has been broken by Barry Bonds. But all of these recent home-run accomplishments have been darkened by the controversy surrounding steroid use by baseball players in the late 1990s and early 2000s.

The Ongoing Hall of Fame Question

Likewise, controversy continues to follow the Maris career, even after death. Each year, when Hall of Fame voting comes around, a question arises: Does Roger Maris deserve inclusion in Major League Baseball's Hall of Fame? For years, he has been denied entrance, primarily because his lifetime totals do not appear to measure up to the Hall's standards. Maris only played for twelve years. He compiled a .260 lifetime batting average and accumulated only 275 career home runs, which doesn't place him in the home-run hitter's pantheon. But advocates point to his appearance in seven All-Star games and seven World Series. And, of course, there is that 61-home run season.

Famed sportscaster Bob Costas once made a comment that supports Maris' inclusion in the Hall. His career statistics may be short, he said, but his historical importance is huge.

But there are contrarian viewpoints. Highly respected sports writer and book author Allen Barra, who reported Costas' comments in an article for a 2011 issue of *The Village Voice*, wrote that Maris does not belong in the Hall of Fame: ''It isn't just that his career performance did not merit the honor...[h]e didn't have a long career (just 12 full seasons), he didn't hit for a high average (.260), and unlike some great players who didn't hit for average (Mike Schmidt for instance), he didn't have a particularly high on-base percentage (.348). He only hit 275 runs in his career and drove in over 100 runs just three times.''

Further, Barra noted that Maris only hit more than 40 home runs in only one season—1961, the year that he broke the record. Compare that to career statistics of players like Willie Mays, Mantle and Henry Aaron, who were far more consistent.

Despite all this, Maris was well liked among his peers, for his humility and honesty and professionalism. It turns out that Maris' career statistics reveal him to be a journeyman player who shined in one glorious season, and most likely he wouldn't want anyone to think otherwise. As Barra wrote: ''Roger Maris would have been the first to tell you that he didn't quite deserve to be in the Hall of Fame.''

Still, Maris's career—and his personality—still holds the imagination. Perhaps that is why numerous books have been written about Maris and his signature accomplishment. Maris may not be honored by Hall of Fame induction, but a plethora of literature exists about the man. These include *Roger Maris at Bat*, published in 1962 and describing Maris' own story as told to writer Jim Ogle; *Roger Maris: A Man for All Seasons*, written by sportswriter Maury Allen, and *Roger Maris: A Title to Fame*, written by Harvey Rosenfeld and published in 1991.

If one thing could be said about Roger Maris, it is this: He has been forgiven for breaking Babe Ruth's record, and he is appreciated for his own accomplishments. His career numbers might fall short, but Maris remains one of Major League Baseball's most fascinating figures.

Books

Jackson, Kenneth T., ed., *The Scribner Encyclopedia of American Lives Thematic Series: Sport Figures*, New York: Charles Scribner's Sons, 2002.

O'Neill, William L. and Kenneth T. Jackson, eds., *The Scribner Encyclopedia of American Lives Thematic Series: The 1960s*, New York: Charles Scribner's Sons, 2003.

Notable Sports Figures, Gale, 2004.

Peary, Danny, ed., *Cult Baseball Players*, New York: Simon and Schuster, 1990.

St. James Encyclopedia of Popular Culture, St. James Press, 2000.

The Scribner Encyclopedia of American Lives, Volume 1: 1981-1985, Charles Scribner's Sons, 1998.

Periodicals

New York Times, December 15, 1985.

New York Times, October 1, 1961.

Village Voice, May 4, 2001.

Online

''Roger Maris,'' *Historic Baseball*, www.historicbaseball.com/players/m/maris_roger.html (November 15, 2011).□

Marjorie Swank Matthews

American United Methodist Church minister Marjorie Swank Matthews (1916-1986) penetrated the close-knit, male-only club of bishops when she was elected to the position in 1980. Matthews' elevation to the post made her the first female bishop to serve in any mainline Christian church, opening the way for more women to follow in both the United Methodist Church and other denominations.

Matthews was born in July 1916 in Onaway, a small northern Michigan town less than 20 miles from the shores of Lake Huron. It is believed she was born on or about July 11. Matthews was the fifth of six children born to Jess A. and Mae (Chapman) Swank. Her father was a barrel maker and the family suffered terribly through the Depression. Matthews' parents stayed educated about current events, and often, the dinner table conversation turned to religion and politics and the world at large. Such discussions prompted the young Matthews to think she might like to grow up and become a missionary teacher in either Japan or India.

Matthews graduated third from the top of her high school class in Alma, Michigan, then attended secretarial school and got married. During World War II, she followed her husband to different Army posts and gave birth to a son, William Jesse Matthews. By the time the war ended, Matthews' marriage was over and she moved back to Alma with her son. In 1946 she landed a job as a secretary to the president of the Lobdell-Emery Manufacturing Co., which made auto parts. She also served as assistant treasurer.

Matthews felt content with the job, but eventually began to think there might be more she could do with her life. In an interview with Kenneth A. Briggs of the *New York Times,* Matthews discussed her a-ha moment: "I looked out on the busy street one day and I knew I could stay another 17 years and retire and never get out of this place. I thought there must be something else to do with my life, I was grateful to God for having gotten me through difficulty and I wanted to do something in return."

Tried Ministry as Second Career

Matthews decided she wanted to further her education and enrolled at nearby Central Michigan University, located some 20 miles from Alma in Mount Pleasant. Around this same time, she began to feel a pull toward the ministry. It had been only a few years since the Methodist Church had approved the ordination of women, and at the time, entering the ministry was still a relatively novel idea for a woman. Nonetheless, Matthews decided to pursue that path and obtained two part-time pastorates, worth a total of $50 a week. One of the churches she served early on as a lay preacher was the Pleasant Valley Methodist Church. Her church ministry position, coupled with a university job, paid enough money to allow Matthews to work her way through college.

In the early 1960s, Matthews was ordained as a minister of the United Methodist Church. In 1967, she graduated summa cum laude with her bachelor of arts degree from Central Michigan University. She was 51. It had taken her eight years to finish the degree. Next, Matthews earned her bachelor of divinity from New York's Colgate Rochester Divinity School in 1970, followed by a doctorate in philosophy/humanities in 1976 from Florida State University. She served churches in Michigan, New York, and Florida while earning her degrees. The churches ranged in size from 80 members to 1,700.

Matthews' doctoral dissertation was titled, "Issues and Answers in the Book of Job and Joban Issues and Answers in Three Twentieth Century Writers: Carl Jung, Robert Frost and Archibald MacLeish." In her dissertation, Matthews explored the theme of suffering, a topic she felt drawn to after a life of struggle—first as a child of the Depression, then as a single, divorced parent, and later, overcoming the prejudice against female clergy that prevailed at the time. Matthews was drawn to the story of Job because it was a story of human suffering.

Endured Struggle as Female Minister

Being a female minister in the United States during the 1970s was not an easy task. Society was not used to seeing women in leadership roles. The women's movement had made some gains in promoting equality for women, yet failed to garner enough support to get the Equal Rights Amendment to the Constitution ratified. By the late 1970s,

as a new wave of conservatism swept across the United States, people began to distance themselves from the movement and it faltered.

It was during this climate that Matthews built her ministry, at times facing an uphill battle from those who believed a woman should not be a minister. "I was sometimes surprised by opposition from people from other churches," Matthews told the *New York Times'* Briggs. "They would tell people in my church they were going to hell for having a woman minister. Or they would call on people and urge them to be baptized by a male, as if [the] baptism I had given was no good. I would assure them I had the proper credentials."

Besides serving her own church, Matthews contributed to the Methodist Church ministry by training pastors to serve American Indian communities. She also helped prepare new ministers at the Garrett Theological Seminary in Evanston, Illinois, where she served as a trustee. Matthews impressed her peers and in 1976 was named the district superintendent of the United Methodist Church's Western Michigan Conference, becoming the second woman to serve as a district superintendent.

Dubbed *Most Electable* by Colleagues

In January 1979, 600 United Methodist Church clergy and laywomen met at the Clergywomen's Consultation in Dallas, Texas. The women discussed the upcoming 1980 bishop elections, wondering if it would be possible to elect a female. As one clergywoman noted, according to Patricia Broughton of the *Flyer,* a publication of the Methodist Church, "We asked who of all of us [clergywomen] would be the most electable? It was clearly Marge."

After much wrangling, Matthews made the ballot as a potential bishop and during the months leading up to the election, she received several endorsements from delegates. In April 1980, at the Methodist General Conference, Matthews was elected to chair a prominent legislative committee. Serving in this position expanded her exposure among the Methodists, but also brought increased scrutiny. "The first week was just plain violent for Marge and for many women in leadership in the church," the Rev. Sharon Rader told the *Flyer.* "Everything about Marge was being challenged—her age, health, leadership style. People didn't like that fact that she was barely five feet tall, that she didn't command attention by her very presence. They said, 'She doesn't look like a bishop....'"

Made History as 1st Female Bishop

In July 1980, Matthews found herself at the United Methodist Church's North Central Jurisdictional Conference, held in Dayton, Ohio. Delegates to the conference were voting to elect new bishops. There were 16 candidates, including Matthews, for three spots. The female delegates to the conference wore yellow ribbons in support of Matthews, as well as buttons with her image.

On the first ballot, Matthews received 135 votes but she needed 306 votes to secure the two-thirds majority needed for election. On the next eleven ballots, she received between 135 and 149 votes. After these first 12 ballots, no candidate had received the 306 votes necessary to become a bishop. More balloting ensued and eventually, the Rev. Chuck Jordan, an African-American clergyman from Cincinnati, withdrew his name figuring that would help Matthews' cause. Jordan realized the delegates were unlikely to choose both a female and a black bishop at the same time. After Jordan withdrew, Matthews began receiving more votes each round, but she still did not receive enough to overcome the deadlock between her and the Rev. Emerson Colaw. A record 29 ballots had been cast and not one bishop elected.

Finally, a delegate made a motion from the floor, moving that the assembly suspend its rules and elect both Colaw and Matthews by acclamation. The motion carried and at 6:08 p.m., on July 17, 1980, in the waning hours of the conference, Matthews became the first female bishop elected to serve any mainline Protestant or Anglican church. The Service of Consecration took place within hours. According to Judith Craig, author of *The Leading Women,* when the Episcopal stole was placed around Matthews' neck, she quipped, "Don't give me a crozier. It will make me look like Little Bo Peep." The Episcopal stole, made before the election to fit a six-foot male, curled around her feet as Matthews stood just barely five feet tall.

Matthews' election as the first female bishop of the Methodist Church made the news—even if the stories were buried. The *New York Times* mentioned Matthews' election on page six. One newspaper headline proclaimed, "The Bishop Is A Woman" and others noted a "64-year-old grandmother" had been elected. According to the Lorain, Ohio, *Chronicle-Telegram,* Matthews announced after her election, "There are no models for me. I'll have to make my own way." Making her own way proved a hard journey for Matthews. After her election she received mail both in support of her election and against it. Naysayers continued to question how a woman could serve as a bishop.

According to the *Flyer,* one male letter writer urged Matthews to not mention her gender. "Divorce yourself from sexual language," the writer said. "Why must you sully this historic action with political sexism? Disregard the fact that you are a woman. Never mention you are a woman. Lead others to forget your sex." Such letters dampened Matthews' spirit. "My first reaction is one of dismay," she told the *Flyer.* "Those who know me know I do not make an issue of my sex. I am glad to be a minister of the gospel. But then, it is quite obvious that I am a woman. Every time I look in a mirror I know that."

Felt "Isolated" on Bishop Council

Matthews was assigned bishop of the Wisconsin area, giving her dominion over 135,000 Methodists, eight district superintendents, 339 ministers, and 522 churches. She joined about 45 other bishops on the Council of Bishops. As the only female on the council, Matthews struggled to find her voice. Writing in *The Leading Women,* Craig acknowledged that Matthews' time on the Council of Bishops was lonely. "She spoke of the isolation she felt at mealtimes and in social times. She was single and female. The Council really didn't know what to do with this diminutive powerhouse of a woman. She had to push against so much as a 'first' that

she chose not to push hard at the Council, and simply endured her isolation."

Matthews served just one four-year term as bishop, retiring in 1984. Known as a biblical scholar, Matthews turned to education after retiring and landed a position teaching a course on the Old Testament at Florida Southern College in Lakeland, Florida. The placement did not last long, however, because Matthews became ill with cancer and moved back to Michigan to be near family.

Matthews died on June 30, 1986, at the M.J. Clark Memorial Home in Grand Rapids, Michigan. She was buried at the Riverside Cemetery in Alma. After Matthews' death, the Rev. Richard Tholin summed up her life this way: "She was a remarkable combination of things and with great courage and persistence found her calling," Tholin told the *Chicago Sun-Times'* Philip Franchine. "Her story is the story of women's struggle to adapt to new roles in the church."

Books

Craig, Judith, *The Leading Women: Stories of the First Women Bishops of the United Methodist Church,* Abingdon Press, 2004.

Periodicals

Chicago Sun-Times, July 3, 1986.
Chronicle-Telegram (Lorain, Ohio), July 18, 1980.
Flyer, August 31, 1980.
New York Times, July 18, 1980; September 8, 1980.
Wisconsin State Journal, October 14, 1984.

Online

"Marjorie Swank Matthews," Michigan Women's Hall of Fame, http://hall.michiganwomen.org/ (November 1, 2011).
"Pioneer Marjorie Matthews 'Knew the Call,'" *Worldwide Faith News,* http://www.wfn.org/2000/12/msg00031.html (November 1, 2011).□

Victoria Earle Matthews

A prominent leader in the struggle for the rights of black women, African American journalist and social reformer Victoria Earle Matthews (1861-1907) dedicated herself to improving the lives of black Americans in the decades following the Civil War. One of her largest contributions included founding the White Rose Mission in 1897. Based in New York City, the mission offered classes to young black Americans aimed at helping them gain skills to find better employment. The organization also fed, sheltered, and mentored young black women as they migrated to New York City looking for work, which they struggled to find in the South.

Victoria Earle Matthews was born Victoria Smith on May 27, 1861, in Fort Valley, Georgia, shortly after the start of the Civil War. Her mother, a slave named Caroline Smith, fled to New York—without her children—shortly after Matthews was born. As for Matthews' father, family lore held that he was a white slave master, although Matthews' marriage certificate listed William Smith, a slave, as her father.

Sometime after President Abraham Lincoln signed the Emancipation Proclamation in 1863, which granted freedom to slaves, Caroline Smith returned to Georgia and went through the court system to claim her children. Of her nine children, Caroline Smith received custody of four, including Matthews. Some accounts suggest the children were being raised as Caucasians by their former master. Matthews may have been about eight years old before she was reunited with her mother. After Caroline Smith regained custody of her children, she moved the family to Virginia. In 1873, they settled in New York City; Matthews was about 12 years old.

Matthews attended grammar school for a while, but her education was cut short when she was forced to take a job to help support the family. Matthews, however, possessed a deep desire for knowledge and continued her studies on her own. She attended lectures and tried to surround herself with people who were skilled or trained in various vocations. Matthews mostly worked as a servant and at one house, and gained permission to read books from her employer's extensive library. In 1879 she married William E. Matthews; she was 18 years old. They had one son, Lamartine, who died in 1895 at the age of 16.

Worked as Journalist

During the 1880s, Matthews worked as a journalist, often under the pen name Victoria Earle. She wrote for T. Thomas Fortune, editor and publisher of the *New York Globe* and founder of the *New York Age,* the most influential black newspaper in the United States. Matthews also served as an editor for *Woman's Era,* the first national newspaper published by and for African American women. In addition, she worked as a correspondent for the *Southern Christian Recorder* and the *Washington Bee;* both publications were aimed at a black audience. Matthews proved herself to be a capable, dependable journalist and earned assignments for white newspapers as well, including the *New York Times* and *New York Herald.* She also wrote for the *Sunday Mercury, Phonographic World, Detroit Plain-Dealer,* and the *A.M.E. Church Review.*

While Matthews was best known for her journalism, she also published short fiction. Her most famous literary work, *Aunt Lindy: A Story Founded on Real Life,* appeared in 1893. Set in Matthews' birthplace of Fort Valley, Georgia, *Aunt Lindy* told the tale of a former-slave-turned-nurse who ends up treating a fire victim only to discover the patient is her former master—the man who sold off her children. With their roles reversed and the former slave holding all of the power, the nurse considers letting the man die in retaliation for all he put her through. In the end, the nurse helped the man and ended up healing her own bitter self in the process.

By the late 1880s, Matthews had moved from reporter to columnist and wrote a regular political affairs column for the *National Leader,* a black newspaper edited by Magnus Robinson and Frederick Douglass Jr., son of the famed abolitionist Frederick Douglass. Matthews used her column to call for an end to discrimination, lynching, and disenfranchisement. She wrote fiery pieces urging the government's Republican administration to hire African Americans and she criticized the Democratic South for the way it treated African Americans. Matthews also wrote about black political clubs, such as the Empire Women's Republican Club of New York City, hoping to raise awareness and bring support to such organizations. During the Spanish-American War in 1898, she complained about the mistreatment of black soldiers, who were often looked upon as second-class citizens. Matthews helped establish medical facilities for them.

Helped Establish Women's Clubs

Matthews did more than just write about the issues facing African Americans—she became an activist intent on doing something about the problems they faced. In 1892 Matthews helped establish the Woman's Loyal Union, becoming the organization's first president. The Woman's Loyal Union (WLU) attacked racial discrimination on both the local and national levels. One big undertaking by the WLU included raising money to support fellow journalist Ida B. Wells and her anti-lynching campaign. The WLU held a fund-raiser to help Wells publish *Southern Horrors: Lynch Law in All Its Phases. Southern Horrors* was a pamphlet Wells published after researching accounts of several lynchings that had taken place in the South. In 1894 the WLU presented several petitions to the U.S. government calling for a congressional inquiry into lynching in the South.

During the late 19th century, the women's club movement spread across the United States as women of different classes and races formed their own clubs to fight for such things as women's suffrage and self-improvement, social justice, and political activism. By the 1890s regional black women's clubs existed, but Matthews envisioned a national black women's club, believing a larger, united organization would be more effective in influencing change. In 1895, Matthews helped found the National Federation of Afro-American Women.

In an effort to reach more people, Matthews took up public speaking and delivered a number of inspiring and forceful lectures on social responsibility. During the first meeting of the National Federation of Afro-American Women, Matthews gave one of her most-noted orations, a talk titled "The Value of Race Literature." In the address Matthews noted that through literature, African Americans could circulate positive images of black women, offering an alternative image to the racial stereotypes presented by white writers. Matthews urged her sisters to write their stories.

According to Shirley Wilson Logan's With Pen and Voice, Matthews called for "thoughtful, well-defined and intelligently placed efforts . . . to serve as counter-irritants" to the way many white writers portrayed African Americans in literature. In 1897, Matthews delivered "The Awakening of the Afro-American Woman" at the annual conference of the Society of Christian Endeavor. During this oration calling for social reformation, Matthews urged conference-goers to work for an end to laws that prohibited marriage between races and for an end to segregated train cars.

In 1896, the National Association of Colored Women (NACW) was founded as a result of a merger between the National Federation of Afro-American Women and the National League of Colored Women of Washington, D.C., as well as several other smaller black women's clubs. While Matthews was not a principal player in the merger, she offered behind-the-scenes support to the NACW and served as the group's national organizer.

Investigated Plight of African Americans

During the mid-1890s, Matthews traveled through the South investigating the living conditions and working conditions of black women on plantations and in the cities. She was disturbed to find that employment agencies were luring young black women to the North, or to Southern cities, promising good jobs but ultimately shipping them off to red light districts. Able to pass as a white woman, Matthews entered segregated establishments and gained an eye-opening, firsthand look at the prejudice and mistreatment black women faced.

Matthews began working for reform in the South but was called back north by a New York minister named H.G. Miller of Mount Tabor Presbyterian Church. Miller contacted Matthews and informed her that her fellow African Americans were struggling in the North and needed assistance. At the time, African Americans in New York faced dwindling job opportunities, poor housing, and prejudice.

As white European immigrants settled in the city, jobs that were once available to African Americans became scarcer as white employers began hiring white immigrant workers. This forced many African Americans to work as unskilled laborers in jobs that paid poorly. This created problems with living conditions because with their meager wages, they could only afford shabby housing, which was often overpriced.

Founded White Rose Mission

Matthews returned to New York and began conducting home visits to African American families on the Upper East Side. Matthews offered tips to the families on how to take better, more efficient care of themselves. Despite the squalid living conditions of their run-down apartments, Matthews promoted better hygiene and showed mothers how to prepare healthy meals.

In Hallie Q. Brown's Homespun Heroines and Other Women of Distinction, Matthews recalled her work from that time. "Then I began to hold mothers' meetings at the various homes where I visited . . . but one day at one of these meetings we prayed especially for a permanent home where we might train the boys and girls and make a social center for them where the only influence would be good and true and pure." Shortly thereafter, a white apartment house owner offered a flat for free for a three-month trial and the White Rose Mission Industrial Association opened in February 1897.

As founder and director of the White Rose Mission, Matthews looked for ways the organization could improve the lives of the black men, women, and children in the area. With the help of volunteers, the mission trained young black women for domestic work, offering classes on sewing, dress-making, and millinery. The cooking class included salad making, larding and boning, and instruction on how to garnish a dish and prepare an entrée. Some of the young women reported their wages improved after taking the cooking classes.

The mission also offered singing and mandolin classes, lectures on health and hygiene and woodcarving and other skills for young men. In addition, the mission hosted dances and offered its parlors as a safe hangout spot where young men and women could gather. Volunteers took young children on outings to the circus and beach and Matthews offered classes and lectures on African American history and literature using prose and poetry from Phyllis Wheatley and Booker T. Washington.

Around 1900, the mission expanded its work and began organizing volunteers to meet incoming young black women at the docks as they arrived in the city seeking employment. Matthews organized the escorts after she had a bad experience on the docks. In 1900, a friend of Matthews asked her to meet a young girl at the docks. Before Matthews could locate the girl, she was lured away by a man promising work and was taken advantage of. Wishing no other young, innocent women would face the same fate, Matthews organized escorts and opened a boarding house to help the young women.

Matthews died on March 10, 1907. She had been ill with tuberculosis for years. Matthews' greatest legacy, perhaps, was not just that she worked to improve the lives of African Americans, but that she served as a catalyst for others. Through her outreach work, her writing, and her speeches, Matthews brought attention to the issues facing African Americans, prompting other agencies to step in and offer help. By 1915, there were at least a dozen social agencies offering help to black Americans in New York

City. The Hope Day Nursery opened in 1902, offering care for African American children. In 1906, a black educator named William L. Bulkley began offering night courses to help African Americans improve their education and skills. The list goes on, filled with countless others inspired by Matthews to step out and step up in the quest for social reform.

Books

Brown, Hallie Q., *Homespun Heroines and Other Women of Distinction,* Oxford University Press, 1988.

Foner, Philip S. and Robert James Branham, eds., *Lift Every Voice: African American Oratory, 1787-1900,* University of Alabama Press, 1998.

Harris, Sharon M., Jacobs, Heidi L.M., and Jennifer Putzi, eds., *Dictionary of Literary Biography, Vol. 221: American Women Prose Writers, 1870-1920,* Gale Group, 2000.

Logan, Shirley Wilson, ed., *With Pen and Voice: A Critical Anthology of Nineteenth-Century African-American Women,* Southern Illinois University Press, 1995.

Periodicals

Journal of African American History, Summer 2006.

Libraries & the Cultural Record, Winter 2006.□

Frank McCourt

Writer Frank McCourt (1930–2009) turned his Irish family's desolate history into the 1996 bestseller *Angela's Ashes: A Memoir,* which won him the Pulitzer Prize for biography.

Born in New York City, Frank McCourt moved to Limerick, Ireland, with his parents after they abandoned their hopes for a better life in America. His memoir, named in honor of his late mother, recounted grim details of the hovels in which he and his perpetually malnourished siblings lived, yet its "clear-eyed look at childhood misery, its incongruously lilting, buoyant prose and its heartfelt urgency struck a remarkable chord with readers and critics," wrote *New York Times* journalist William Grimes. The McCourt parents immortalized by their son in print were Malachy and Angela, who met in New York City in late 1929, were married the following March, and became parents to Francis, shortened to "Frank," on August 19, 1930. His brother, also named Malachy, was born 13 months later, followed in 1932 by twin boys, Oliver and Eugene. The family lived in a tenement flat in Brooklyn's Bedford-Stuyvesant neighborhood, and McCourt Sr. habitually drank away his week's wages, drifting from one job to another. Both parents were devastated when the family's first daughter, Margaret, died in infancy.

Settled in Slums of Limerick

At the height of the Great Depression Malachy Sr. was unable to find work, and finally Brooklyn-émigré relatives of Angela's, appalled by the conditions in which the family lived, arranged for them to sail back to Ireland. They settled in Angela's hometown of Limerick, but once again the shiftless McCourt father had trouble keeping a job. They survived with the help of a charity organization, St. Vincent de Paul, and unemployment benefits that amounted to about four dollars a week. Their changing addresses were in a rough part of Limerick near Dock Road, in decrepit housing that had neither running water nor electricity. One of McCourt's beloved toddler-twin brothers died not long after their arrival. McCourt recalled in *Angela's Ashes* that his father took him out that night begging, "asking for food or anything they can give to a family that has two children dead in a year, one in America, one in Limerick, and in danger of losing three more for the want of food and drink." Their rounds ended in a pub, where sympathetic men bought Malachy Sr. pints for his sorrows until the bartender ejected both father and son.

McCourt and his brothers starved that first week when their father spent the 19 shillings of "dole" benefits. The next week, Angela went with him to collect the funds, and McCourt and Malachy Jr. were installed at a local school, Leamy's, where they were immediately attacked for their American accents. "There are seven masters in Leamy's National School and they all have leather straps, canes, blackthorn sticks," McCourt recalled in *Angela's Ashes.* "They hit you if you're late, if you have a leaky nib on your pen, if you laugh, if you talk, and if you don't know things." Six months after Oliver died, his twin Eugene did, too. This time McCourt's parents did not rush to the doctor or hospital with a sick infant, as they had with the previous two: sadly, McCourt and his brother simply awoke one morning to find the toddler dead next to them in bed.

Left School at 13

At one place the McCourts lived, their home was next door to a public lavatory where 11 families on the street came to empty their chamber pots several times a day. At age ten, McCourt contracted typhoid fever and remembers waking up in a hospital as the priest was performing the Roman Catholic sacrament of Last Rites, but he recovered and spent several weeks enjoying the relatively comfortable surroundings. His hospital stay was memorable for the pair of books another patient loaned him, one on the history of England, and another which contained the first Shakespeare he ever encountered, plus the epic poem *The Highwayman.*

World War II had erupted by that point, and McCourt's father took a job in a munitions factory in England, but rarely sent any of his earnings home to his family. Angela considered putting McCourt and his brothers—the deceased twins were supplanted by Michael, born in 1936, and Alphonsus four years later—in an orphanage, but applied for welfare relief and eked by on that. At 13, his mother sought a place for him in a high school for boys run by a Roman Catholic order, armed with a recommendation from his headmaster at Leamy's, but was told there was no chance. McCourt was eager to find full-time work anyway, and was hired by the post office as a telegram delivery person. When he turned up for work on his first day, the clerks and other delivery boys openly jeered at him, for by that point McCourt had been staying with relatives, stealing food, and was plagued by terrible bouts of conjunctivitis. An aunt bought him a new set of clothes and at the end of the first week he received his wages—a single pound note, the first he ever owned.

McCourt worked in Limerick until he was 19 and had saved the 55-pound price that bought him passage on a ship bound for America. His father, always having regretted the return to Ireland, had urged him to stay in school and get out of Ireland. "Some day I'll go back to America and get an inside job where I'll be sitting at a desk with two fountain pens in my pocket, one red and one blue, making decisions. I'll be in out of the rain and I'll have a suit and shoes and a warm place to live," McCourt wrote in *Angela's Ashes.* His father reminded him "you can do anything in America, it's the land of opportunity. You can be a fisherman in Maine or a farmer in California. America is not like Limerick, a gray place with a river that kills."

Taught High School English

McCourt's first job in the United States was at the palatial Biltmore Hotel in New York City, secured with the help of a priest he had met on board the ship. Because he was born in the United States, he was eligible for the military draft and was called up in 1951 during the Korean War, but spent the better part of his two-year stint on a U.S. Army base in West Germany. With his G.I. Bill benefits he was able to enter New York University—though the admissions office initially gave him a conditional acceptance, because he lacked a high school diploma—and worked the night shift as a dockworker while earning a degree in English education in 1957. By then he had sent money to his

brother Malachy to join him in New York, and Malachy in turn helped brothers Mike and Alphie emigrate.

In 1959 McCourt began teaching at McKee Vocational and Technical High School on Staten Island, and spent the next 28 years as one of the most popular English teachers in the New York City public school system. He married in 1961, returned to school and earned a graduate degree in English from Brooklyn College in 1967, and was recruited to teach at a magnet school in Manhattan, Peter Stuyvesant High School, in the early 1970s. His brother Malachy became a film and television actor and ran his own bar in New York City for many years. The pair were known as terrific raconteurs and storytellers at a handful of New York taverns frequented by journalists and writers; in 1977 the duo wrote and performed a two-man Off-Broadway play called *A Couple of Blaguards,* borrowing a vintage term for a rogue or scoundrel.

McCourt's inspiration for setting down his life story on paper came from the creative writing classes he taught in the New York public school system. He had always been riveted by some of his students' tales of immense hardship in new immigrant families, and urged them to write their family's stories. "I'd say: 'If you write, I'll write.' So I did. Little remembrances," he told Robert Sullivan in an interview for the *New York Times Magazine* in 1996. "And they said: 'Oh, Mr. McCourt. You should write a book. You had such an interesting childhood.'"

Penned Surprise Bestseller

In 1987 McCourt retired from teaching and began work on his memoir in earnest. He was a friend to many writers, including veteran journalists Jimmy Breslin and Pete Hamill, and was part of a drinking circle that met every Friday at a bar called Eamonn Doran's. A friend from there had some publishing-industry experience and passed on the incomplete manuscript to a literary agent, who signed McCourt and then sold the book to Scribner. *Angela's Ashes: A Memoir* was published in September of 1996, just after McCourt's 66th birthday, and the first reviews that rolled in were effusive. *Publishers Weekly* commended the skill with which he conjured, in a first-person child's viewpoint, "so persuasively the voices and images of a ragged and hungry Irish childhood. . . . The sights, the stinks, the savage comedy of survival in the slums of 1930s and 1940s Limerick are mesmerizing."

Angela's Ashes sold four million copies in hardcover and was still on the *New York Times* hardcover nonfiction bestseller list a full two years after its publication. It also collected a slew of awards, including the Pulitzer Prize for biography and a National Book Critics Circle Award. The only detractors seemed to be citizens of Limerick, who were dejected that the city's slums were resurrected so vividly in print. McCourt admitted he was surprised at the positive reaction, he told Sullivan in the *New York Times Magazine* profile. "I thought it was a modest book, modestly written, and that it might have a modest reception. I've often said that poverty is rarely portrayed well, and I tried to portray the stink of poverty."

Many reviewers hoped that the cliffhanging end of *Angela's Ashes*—when McCourt arrives in New York in 1949—foreshadowed the possibility of a sequel. McCourt followed through with *'Tis: A Memoir,* published in 1999, and *Teacher Man* in 2005. *Angela's Ashes* was made into a feature film with Emily Watson and Robert Carlyle as McCourt's brooding, dysfunctional parents. His mother died in 1981, but his hard-drinking father managed to hang on until 1985, dying at the age of 84. McCourt passed away from metastatic melanoma on July 19, 2009, in New York, at the age of 78. Survivors included Malachy, Mike, Alphie, a daughter from his first marriage, and third wife Ellen Frey. ''For some reason, I had a responsibility to my family and the people who lived around me,'' he once told interviewer Terry Gross, host of National Public Radio's *Fresh Air.* ''I felt that I had to convey their dignity—the way they dealt with adversity and poverty—and their good humor.''

Books

McCourt, Frank, *Angela's Ashes: A Memoir,* Touchstone/Simon & Schuster, 1999.

Periodicals

New York, September 27, 1999.
New York Times, September 15, 1996; July 20, 2009.
New York Times Magazine, September 1, 1996.
Publishers Weekly, July 1, 1996.

Online

''Frank McCourt: A Responsibility to Write,'' *Fresh Air,* National Public Radio, July 20, 2009, http://www.npr.org/templates/story/story.php?storyId=106799343 (January 30, 2012). □

Jim McKay

American television sportscaster Jim McKay (1921-2008) is best known for his work as commentator for the American Broadcasting Company's popular show ''Wide World of Sports'' and his coverage of Olympic Games. His work garnered him numerous awards.

The face, the name, and most especially the voice became a broadcasting icon. Jim McKay is one of the most famous sportscasters in television history. His distinctive intonations opened each episode of the American Broadcasting Company's television show ''Wide World of Sports'': ''The thrill of victory . . . the agony of defeat.''

As host of the show, he took on assignments that placed him across the globe and introduced the American viewing audience to sports not typically covered. As the show demonstrated, and as McKay so insightfully explained, sports drama did not just entail what took place on a baseball diamond or between a football field's sidelines, or on the paint of a basketball court. The thrill and agony also took place in environments that included an indoor diving board, a weightlifting stage, and the circuitous arena of a demolition derby. But no matter the venue, no matter the sport (and

especially no matter the obscurity of the sport), McKay made viewers aware of the drama: the agony and ecstasy of competition.

Sports activity generates human drama, and McKay could get right at the core of the story, without hyperbole and with perception that always pleased. That was because he was more than merely a commentator who reported what viewers already witnessed with their own eyes (he worked in the day when Olympic Games were televised live). He knew when to speak, and he also knew when to just let powerful images speak for themselves. Indeed, his television work combined the power of great sports photography with great sports writing.

McKay was also a journalist, and his skills were best demonstrated during the 1972 Olympic Games, when he reported on an ongoing situation (terrorists had captured Israeli athletes) and its devastating outcome (the captured athletes were killed in a bungled rescue attempt).

Born in Philadelphia

The future sportscaster was born on September 24, 1921 in Philadelphia, Pennsylvania as James Kenneth McManus. As with many who worked in high-profile jobs, he would later change his name.

His father, Joseph Francis McManus, worked in real estate, and his mother, Florence (Gallagher) McManus, was a housewife. His personal history includes an irony: His first job, as a paperboy, indicated his life's direction, but when customers went delinquent on payments, the shy McKay depended on his sister to call payments due—a far less than aggressive approach than journalism would require.

In his early teens, McKay moved with his family to Baltimore, Maryland. He later attended Loyola College, where he received a bachelor's degree in 1943. During his college years, he became president of the school's drama club and a member of the debating team. These activities would later help advance his career. Following graduation, McKay entered the United States Navy during World War II (he served from 1943 to 1946). He became a lieutenant and took the helm of a minesweeper.

Became a News Reporter

After McKay was discharged, the former paperboy took a job as a news reporter for the *Baltimore Sun,* working the police beat. Two years later (in 1948) he married Margaret Dempsey, who was also a reporter.

In the meantime, in 1947, the newspaper became involved in an emerging communications medium: television. At a Baltimore television station (WMAR-TV), McKay became an on-air personality. But his duties also included producing, directing, writing, and serving as a news and sports reporter. As the host of a daily afternoon program, he even sang, as he was gifted with a mellifluous voice.

In 1950, McKay's hard work led to a job as a host of a New York City-based variety show on the Columbia Broadcasting System, commonly known as CBS. This new job opportunity placed him in the United States' largest media market, where he hosted a daily ninety-minute variety show on WCBS-TV. The program was titled "The Real McKay," and he changed his name from McManus to McKay.

Throughout the decade, McKay also covered sports assignments for the CBS network, including the reports for the network's "Morning Show" (hosted by famed news anchor Walter Cronkite) and coverage of the Master's Golf tournaments and the 1960 Olympic Games in Rome. Again, his hard work and demonstrated skill led to yet another opportunity, one that would make him a national sports broadcasting figure.

"The Thrill of Victory"

In 1960, television sports producer Roone Arledge was developing a sports anthology program to be called "Wide World of Sports." Arledge had worked for the National Broadcasting Company (commonly known as NBC) and became the head of the American Broadcasting Company's (ABC) sports department. Arledge wanted to do something different in sports coverage, and his program would be the vehicle. But he needed the appropriate on-air host, and he was impressed by McKay's work and style. Arledge asked McKay to join his team.

Arledge was an innovative producer. He later created the American television institution "Monday Night Football," and for sports coverage, he would deploy new satellite technology to provide live coverage. He also advanced the use of instance replay and slow motion replay. His "Wide World of Sports" concept was revolutionary: Arledge wanted to introduce the American viewing audience to sports not typically covered.

The show was initially conceived as a limited, one-season presentation, but it was so well-received that it became an ongoing program. Indeed, it became one of the longest running sports programs in television history (it lasted for thirty-seven years), and McKay became a central figure in its success. Arledge initially offered a deal that would make McKay the host of a twenty-week summer replacement program. As it turned out, McKay hosted the program from 1961 to 1998.

The show premiered on Saturday, April 29, 1961 and opened with McKay's narration over a visual montage of vivid sports scenes: "Spanning the globe to bring you the constant variety of sports...the thrill of victory and the agony of defeat...This is ABC's Wide World of Sports." This was not hyperbole. The comprehensive program provided a showcase for sports that were once considered obscure or odd: surfing, rodeo competition, softball, badminton, motor car racing, figure skating, skiing, gymnastics, competitive diving and swimming, track and field events, cycling, soccer, arm wrestling, amateur wrestling, weightlifting, sledding, and much more. No matter the sport, the show revealed the drama of competition in a fashion that garnered it numerous awards. And, as host and main reporter, McKay did indeed travel the world to provide his insightful coverage. The variety of sports later covered in daily sports pages and on broadcasting outlets such as ESPN is attributable to the show. The show helped make stars of broadcaster Howard Cosell and boxer Cassius Clay (who later renamed himself Muhammad Ali). For McKay, his name became indelibly attached to the program.

Covered Olympic Games

McKay's name also became synonymous with Olympic coverage. His voice and commentary were as much a part of the spectacle as the competition and the athletes. He would cover ten Olympics for ABC, and he covered his last Olympic event in 2002 (for NBC). "[Olympians] were McKay's athletes," wrote Christine Brennan in *USA Today,* "and he told their stories better than anyone else ever did. They became quite a team: McKay, and those charming Olympic Games."

But the Olympic Games weren't always charming and innocent, and McKay covered the events during periods of controversy; for instance, describing the significance of the "Black Power" salute that United States track medalists John Carlos and Tommy Smith demonstrated during the playing of the National Anthem in a medal ceremony in 1968 summer games in Mexico City. McKay's most memorable coverage, which combined his superior journalistic and broadcasting skills, also involved tragic circumstances: the hostage crisis in the 1972 Summer Olympic Games in Munich, Germany that resulted in the deaths of eleven Israeli team members (athletes and coaches). The remaining innocence of the games was forever lost.

At the "Olympic Village," where athletes were housed during the games, Palestinian (Black September) terrorists invaded the compound and took hostage the Israeli team members. The televised coverage unfolded live, and the world was riveted to the television screen.

Before the crisis, McKay had been delivering his typical and comprehensive coverage. Taking a day off, enjoying a restful sauna and about to take a swim at his hotel, McKay was informed about the situation. "You're on the air in 45 minutes," he was told, according to the article from *USA Today.* Quickly throwing on some clothes, but still wearing his damp swimming trunks, McKay rushed to the ABC Olympic studio. Then, for the next sixteen hours, he served as anchor for the news coverage (colleagues Peter Jennings and Cosell provided field reports). For the anxious world, McKay was the information intermediary. Thanks to satellite technology, he reported the events in real time. His coverage included updates about hostage negotiations and then the subsequent failed rescue attempt. All hostages were killed. McKay memorably reported the aftermath with a sad statement. "They're all gone," he said, looking directly at the camera.

McKay won two Emmy Awards for his work at the 1972 games, one for sports coverage and the other for his news reporting about the crisis. The same year, he received the George Polk Memorial Award for Journalism, given each year to a journalist whose work represents the best reportage. McKay's coverage also earned him the Officer's Cross of the Legion of Merit, bestowed by the former West German Federal Republic.

He earned many awards during his career, including thirteen Emmy Awards. Other honors that McKay received include the Peabody Award (1989) and membership in the Olympic Order (1998), which is the highest honor given by the International Olympic Committee. He was also inducted into the Sportscasters and Sportswriters Hall of Fame in 1987 and the Television Academy Hall of Fame in 1995. In addition to his on-air accomplishments, McKay is also an author. He has written two books based on his life and experiences in sports: *My Wide World* (1973) and *The Real McKay: My Wide World of Sports* (1998).

Curtailed his Broadcasting Activities

In the late 1980s, McKay started reducing his amount of work. He left the anchor position with "Wide World of Sports," but he continued covering major sport events for ABC. In 1993 McKay and his wife bought a minority share of the Baltimore Orioles baseball team. McKay also spent more time on his book writing.

During his later years, McKay lived in a nineteenth-century farmhouse in Monkton, Maryland, in a rural area just north of Baltimore. He also owned a winter home in Key Largo, Florida. He passed away on his Maryland estate on June 7, 2008, at the age of eighty-six years old. He was survived by his wife, Margaret, and their two children, Mary and Sean.

In McKay's *New York Times* obituary, writers Frank Litsky and Richard Sandomir quote McKay's colleague, Bob Costas: "Jim McKay had a very important quality. You never felt what he expressed wasn't genuine. You never felt his reaction was, 'What's called for here is a tear.' You never had a sense that he professed to be moved and when they went to a commercial he blew his nose."

Books

"McKay, James McManus ('Jim')," *The Scribner Encyclopedia of American Lives Thematic Series: Sports Figures,* Charles Scribner's Sons, 2002.

"McKay, James McManus ('Jim')," *World of Sports Science,* Thomson Gale, 2007.

Periodicals

The New York Times, June 8, 2008.
USA Today, December 30, 2005.
USA Today, June 12, 2008.

Online

"Jim McKay," *Biography.com,*http://www.biography.com/print/profile/jim-mckay-259486 (December 20, 2011).
"McKay, Jim," *The Museum of Broadcast Communications,* http://www.museum.tv/eotvsection.php?entrycode=mckayjim (December 20, 2011.☐

Malcolm McLaren

Malcolm McLaren (1946–2010) was the brash and cunning British impresario who turned a grotty quartet of Londoners into the Sex Pistols. Indelibly associated with the explosion of the punk rock movement in Britain in 1976, McLaren was a provocateur and in a short time accrued a long list of enemies, including the band itself, who sued to extricate themselves from their management contract with him. Music writer Jon Savage, who chronicled the cultural moment in his 1991 book *England's Dreaming: Anarchy, Sex Pistols, Punk Rock, and Beyond,* paid tribute in the London *Guardian* a few days after McLaren's 2010 death. "McLaren made a huge difference. He had a vision and he pursued it to extraordinary effect," Savage declared, further describing him as "an artist who used humans—including himself—and the media as his canvas. McLaren was one of those rare individuals who have had a profound impact on our national life."

Malcolm Robert Andrew McLaren was born on January 22, 1946, in London, England. He never knew his father, an engineer from Scotland, and was primarily raised by his maternal grandmother, Rose Corré, who had Portuguese Sephardic Jewish roots. He attended school only intermittently and developed some behavioral issues in his teens, particularly after his mother's remarriage. Though he did not get along with his stepfather, McLaren did learn some of the ropes of the wholesale apparel business through the East London dress factory his mother and stepfather owned.

Kicked Out of Art School

McLaren spent much of the 1960s enrolled at various art schools, including Central St. Martin's College of Art, and Harrow Art College, and was particularly drawn to new currents in performance art and theater. Along the way he met a fashion school dropout named Vivienne Westwood, and the couple had a son, Joseph Corré, in 1967. They were part of a small subset of the London scene who were revolted by the predominant hippie counterculture of the era and searched for something fresher and, in their view, more authentic.

McLaren wound up selling records at a store called Paradise Garage located at the end of Kings Road in London's Chelsea neighborhood. When the leaseholder walked away

in late 1971, McLaren and Westwood took over the shop and renamed it Let It Rock. They also worked as costume designers for film and stage productions, outfitting the casts of forgotten rock movies like *That'll Be the Day*, a 1973 Ringo Starr-David Essex project. That same year they changed the name of their store, calling it Too Fast To Live, Too Young To Die, the slogan of fans of the late actor James Dean.

Descended On New York

McLaren had already heard of a gritty American band that had a cult following for their stage look, which involved women's clothing and heavy makeup. The New York Dolls were also known for their excessive drug use, and were on the brink of stardom in 1973 when their drummer died. By 1975 they had been dropped by their label when McLaren turned up in New York and offered to manage them. McLaren wanted to imprint his artistic vision onto a rock band, using manufactured controversy to stir up interest. "He had us dressing up in matching red leather suits and playing in front of a giant communist flag," the Dolls' second drummer, Jerry Nolan, said in *Please Kill Me: The Uncensored Oral History of Punk*. "It was so stupid! Malcolm caught us at a very vulnerable moment. The limos were long gone. Then Malcolm booked this horrible string of gigs for us in Florida . . . we weren't happy about it." The Dolls essentially disbanded mid-tour, and McLaren returned to London.

By then McLaren and Westwood had renamed the store once again, dubbing it SEX in the spring of 1974. The Kings Road window featured headless, clothing-less mannequins, with a curtain hiding the rest of the store from view. Inside they sold latex and leather fetish gear along with their own line of apparel. "We designed our own military trousers," McLaren recalled in "Elements of Anti-Style," an article he wrote for a 1997 issue of the *New Yorker*. "I tracked down the shiny, heavy black fabric,

which used to be worn by British Rail porters, to an old factory in Manchester," he continued, and the slim-fitting pants featured "a strap between the legs . . . and a zipper than went straight down the crotch and wound its way up."

Created Sex Pistols

McLaren and Westwood's SEX store inevitably attracted throngs of disaffected youth in London. Among them were members of a band called "The Strand," after the Roxy Music song, and McLaren became their manager. He wanted to bring the gritty authenticity he had found in the music scene centered around New York's Lower East Side, and bands like the Dolls and the Ramones, to British teens yearning for something different. He took the Strand's drummer, Paul Cook, plus guitarist Steve Jones and bass player Glen Matlock, and began trying to secure a singer from New York—either the Dolls' Sylvain Sylvain or Richard Hell, who had formed the seminal New York City band called Television. Neither was interested, but McLaren found a new lead singer closer to home when John Lydon turned up at the store one day. Lydon sported green hair, a Pink Floyd concert T-shirt, over which he had scrawled the words "I HATE," and a ready snarl. McLaren dubbed him "Johnny Rotten" for, it was said, the abominable state of Lydon's teeth.

The Sex Pistols' first live performance was at St. Martin's School of Art in London on November 6, 1975 and, predictably, was an utter disaster. They were jeered off stage after two songs and then a fight broke out between them and another act on the bill. Despite the inauspicious start, the Pistols rapidly garnered a small but devoted cult following over the next few months, with fans adopting the same grubby, alarming look that was available for purchase at the Kings Road store. The new punk uniform usually consisted of leather, McLaren's aforementioned bondage pants, studded accessories, spiked hair and, occasionally, a safety pin through a nostril. By the summer of 1976 two new bands had emerged out of their fan base: the Damned and the Clash, with scores more to follow.

In the fall of 1976, after generating immense promotional buzz for the band, McLaren negotiated a stupendous deal with EMI Records, which handed over £40,000 to them to record their debut album. Their first single, "Anarchy in the U.K.," prompted a flurry of outrage upon its release in November of 1976. On December 1, 1976, the band agreed to appear as a last-minute fill-in for ITV's *Today* show to discuss the new phenomenon. The show went out live and the band brought along their entourage, one of whom sported an armband adorned with a Nazi swastika. Toward the end, the notoriously inflammatory Lydon let loose with a string of profanities, and the broadcast prompted widespread outrage across Britain the next day. "THE FILTH AND THE FURY" blared the infamous headline in the *Daily Mirror* tabloid the next day. EMI backed out of the deal, but let the band keep the advance money thanks to McLaren's negotiating skills. He then cut a more lucrative deal for the band with A&M Records for £75,000, orchestrating a signing with Buckingham Palace as the backdrop. That label, too, reneged on the deal and once again, the Pistols became one of the wealthiest rock bands before they had even released their debut album.

Arrested for Publicity Stunt

McLaren's flair for promotional opportunities reached its peak in the summer of 1977, as England was swept up in Queen Elizabeth II's Silver Jubilee fever. The Sex Pistols' second single, "God Save the Queen," was released on Virgin Records just in time for the festivities and duly banned by the British Broadcasting Corporation. McLaren was even arrested as part of another publicity stunt he arranged, which involved having the band play the song from a boat in front of the Houses of Parliament. Virgin released the debut album, *Never Mind the Bollocks, Here's the Sex Pistols,* in October of 1977 and it immediately shot to number one in Britain.

McLaren planned to conquer the United States next, but the tour was disastrous. By this point Matlock had been replaced on bass by another denizen of the SEX store—now renamed Seditionaries—named John Simon Ritchie, whom McLaren dubbed Sid Vicious. Just as the Pistols were emerging as stars of Britain's emergent punk scene, an American named Nancy Spungen turned up at the store looking for Jerry Nolan. She met Vicious that same night and, by most accounts, introduced him to heroin, the drug that had brought down the Dolls.

The U.S. tour ended abruptly in January of 1978 when Lydon walked off the stage of the Winterland Ballroom in San Francisco. McLaren asserted that it had been his intention all along to create a band that would self-destruct, but he became enmeshed in an enormous legal quagmire when the band, together with the Virgin label, filed a lawsuit against him accusing him of misuse of funds. As that trial neared, Nancy Spungen was found stabbed to death in the Chelsea Hotel room she shared with Vicious in October of 1978. McLaren flew to New York City to extricate Vicious from the Riker's Island detention center and made plans to bring the newly sober singer to the Las Vegas stage. Vicious died of a heroin overdose on February 2, 1979.

Moved on to "Hip-Hopera"

McLaren sensed his court case in London was not going to turn out well, and on the last day of the trial he skipped the country, withdrawing £40,000 and flying to Paris; the legal wrangling over rights, royalties, and management fees was finally settled in 1986. Nothing McLaren ever produced after the Sex Pistols came close to inciting actual anarchy, but he managed to remain in the headlines for years. He returned to the music scene in 1981 with a band called Bow Wow Wow, fronted by a 14-year-old named Annabella Lwin, and two years later put out *Duck Rock* as his first solo project. He had some success with that record, bringing the scratching and stutter-stops of the New York urban underground music scene to Britain. In 1984 he released the ambitious *Fans,* which merged opera arias with hip-hop. At the end of the 1980s he made *Waltz Darling,* following up five years later with the album *Paris.* He was involved in various art and music projects, while his son with Westwood—who went on to have an enormously successful career as a fashion designer—founded the lingerie line Agent Provocateur.

In 2009 McLaren was diagnosed with mesothelioma, a cancer of the tissue linings linked to asbestos exposure. He died six months later, on April 8, 2010, in Switzerland at the age of 64. Family members believe the renovations he undertook at the numerous incarnations of his and Westwood's Kings Road store in the 1970s were the likely culprit.

The story of McLaren and the Sex Pistols was told in two films: *The Great Rock 'n' Roll Swindle,* made in 1979, and *The Filth and the Fury* in 2000, both directed by Julian Temple. The filmmaker paid tribute to McLaren in the London *Observer* a few days after his death, describing him as "an incredible catalyst." Temple added that McLaren's "assault on the last bastions of Victorian morality completed the process that began in the 50s and 60s and liberated us all. He made ugly beautiful and revealed how bloated, complacent and out of touch the music industry had become. But his impact was not limited to music alone. Right across the creative spectrum Malcolm made young people—artists, designers, writers, film-makers—aware that they had a distinctive voice and encouraged them to use it right there and then."

Books

McNeil, Legs, and Gillian McCain, *Please Kill Me: The Uncensored Oral History of Punk,* Grove Press, 1996.

Periodicals

Guardian (London, England), April 9, 2010; April 10, 2010.
New Yorker, September 22, 1997.
Observer (London, England), April 11, 2010.
Times (London, England), April 9, 2010.□

Rachel Louise McManus

A pioneer in the field of nursing education, American college professor Louise McManus (1896-1993) spent 36 years on the faculty of Columbia University's Teachers College. She was instrumental in establishing a nationwide testing service for the nursing profession, which led to a national standardization of nurse licensing exams. Throughout her career, McManus worked to strengthen the professional standing of nurses, both in the United States and abroad, and in 1963 received the Florence Nightingale International Red Cross Society Citation and Medal in recognition of her work.

The daughter of John and Hattie Metcalfe, Rachel Louise McManus was born March 4, 1896, in the rural farming community of North Smithfield, Rhode Island. Growing up, she went by the name Louise. In 1916, McManus graduated from the Institutional Management Program at Pratt Institute, a private-arts college in Brooklyn, New York. Four years later, she finished her nursing degree at the Massachusetts General Hospital School of Nursing in Boston. In 1920, McManus joined the Waterbury Hospital School of Nursing in Waterbury, Connecticut. She decided to continue her education and enrolled at New York City's Columbia University, earning her bachelor's degree in 1923. In 1925, McManus earned her master's degree and joined the faculty of the Teachers College of Columbia University.

Accepted Job in Nursing Research

McManus started pursuing her doctorate but put it on hold after marrying John H. McManus on June 22, 1929. John McManus was a widower with six children. Louise and John McManus had a daughter of their own, Joan, before John McManus died in 1934, leaving Louise McManus to raise seven children and care for her elderly mother-in-law.

After her husband died, Louise McManus took a position as a research assistant for a curriculum study that was being conducted by the National League for Nursing Education (NLNE). In 1917, the NLNE had released the first Standard Curriculum for Schools of Nursing. As a research assistant for the NLNE, McManus joined others who were evaluating the instructional outcomes at several nursing programs. The researchers were particularly interested in learning if the nursing graduates had mastered the curriculum standards set forth in the NLNE's curriculum guidelines.

As McManus began working with standardized testing, she became interested in how a standardized test might help with nursing admissions. In 1940, McManus was appointed chairwoman of the NLNE's Committee on Nursing Tests, which later became the Committee on Measurement and Guidance. A year later, the NLNE launched its Pre-Nursing and Guidance Test Service to help nursing programs select qualified students and also guide their course of study. McManus was instrumental in setting up the testing service, which operated from her office at Columbia.

Developed State Licensing Exam

Once the United States became involved in World War II, the military needed nurses. Enrollment in nursing schools had increased but state boards were unable to keep up with licensing new graduates and the military would not take them until they were licensed. Soon, the American Medical Association requested assistance from McManus's Committee on Measurement and Guidance in speeding up the licensing process. The AMA wanted McManus to develop a comprehensive, standardized, machine-scorable test that could be used by state boards to license nurses in a quick, efficient manner.

The first State Board Test Pool Examination was used by New York in January 1944. McManus's committee provided the New York State Board of Nurse Examiners with tabulated test results for the entire group and also offered a report card for each test-taker, which indicated scores in each test area. The board was also given a manual to help members interpret results and clarify the lowest acceptable raw score for licensing in that state. Some states were reluctant to use the test at first but within two years, every U.S. state was using the State Board Test Pool Service.

McManus's work in this area caught the attention of the U.S. military, which greatly appreciated the speedier process of licensing nurses. In recognition of McManus's

abilities, General George Marshall invited her to join the Defense Advisory Committee on Women in the Services. McManus served on the committee for six years, beginning in 1949.

Pursued Doctorate Degree

As McManus worked with the Committee on Measurement and Guidance, she became interested in nursing education research and decided to finish her doctorate. McManus completed her PhD in educational research in 1947, becoming the first professional nurse to earn a doctorate. That same year, McManus became director of the Division of Nursing Education at Teachers College, a position she held until her retirement in 1961.

As director of the nursing education division, McManus initiated many reforms in nursing education and nursing research. Her interest in research and the idea to improve nursing education dated back to her dissertation, *The Effect of Experience on Nursing Achievement,* which was published in 1949. For her dissertation, McManus prepared an exam called the "Test of Basic Nursing and Judgment." Some questions on the test involved simple recall, while others required the test-taker to employ higher-level reasoning and judgment skills.

What McManus hoped to determine from the test was if professional experience helped nurses develop higher mental processes, thus enabling them to make competent decisions about patient care. McManus wondered if schools were educating nurses, or merely training them. She surmised that if schools were educating nurses, their skills and reasoning would improve with experience; however, if schools were merely training nurses—by having them memorize facts and act according to a set pattern of standardized solutions—they would not be resourceful enough to handle new or unusual situations.

For her test pool, McManus needed inexperienced and experienced nurses. She looked to several U.S. Army hospitals to find senior cadets in their final term of nurse training. These became her "inexperienced" nurses and they represented 70 schools of nursing in eight states. The "experienced" nurses in the pool included nurses who had completed their training, had met requirements for licensing, and been admitted to the U.S. Army Nurse Corps with some prior professional experience. Those polled represented 58 schools of nursing in 16 states.

The results surprised McManus, as she wrote in her dissertation: "The assumption that the scores of the experienced and inexperienced groups on tests of higher complexity would differ increasingly was not upheld." What McManus determined was that to produce the best nurses, schools needed to teach reasoning skills to nursing students. "The school that fosters the establishment in each student of habits of intellectual inquiry and of analyzing and reasoning through nursing problems of her patient insures [sic] for the student not only enduring zest for her professional work but, through the functioning of habit, the continued development of her higher mental abilities." McManus concluded her dissertation by noting that if students were taught reasoning and then continued their education after leaving school, it would lead to "a much finer quality of professional nursing service."

Strengthened Professional Standing of Nurses

During the time McManus served as an administrator for the nursing division, it was rare to find women in college leadership roles. When the Teachers College set up a committee—comprising the dean, provost, controller, and heads of each instructional division—to offer advice on policies, programs, and budgets, McManus was disinvited to meetings even though she was the head of the nursing division.

McManus related the story to Gwendolyn Safier in her book *Contemporary American Leaders in Nursing.* McManus told Safier that when she objected to being left out, Dean Hollis L. Caswell told her, "Well, I don't know that you will particularly like it. We may sit with our feet on the table and we're not used to having a woman around. Some of our language . . ." McManus proclaimed herself a full-fledged member of the committee even though she was not wanted.

Once McManus began participating in the committee, she quickly realized that the salaries and promotion rates of the faculty in the nursing division lagged behind other departments. McManus proposed that the situation be rectified and the salaries were eventually adjusted. In addition, McManus fought for educational leave for nursing faculty members so they could conduct research or further their studies. This was common practice in other divisions. "Within a decade," McManus told Safier, "the nursing faculty had come to be recognized as a graduate faculty in every sense of the word."

Created First Research Institute for Nursing

By the early 1950s, McManus saw a need for a division to conduct research in nursing. She envisioned a research institute housed at Columbia. McManus developed a plan, a list of objectives, and a budget for a five-year trial of a new research unit. She included a list of issues facing nurses and nursing education that could be investigated—and improved—by a research unit. McManus wanted Columbia University to help with administrative costs; she proposed that the rest of the funding come from grants.

Both the Teachers College dean and president liked McManus's plan and gave her permission to seek funds to launch a research institute. McManus worked tirelessly, approaching foundations, government agencies, and individuals in her quest for funding. Though she was turned down many times McManus did not give up, she told Safier, because she had been warned the task might be hard. "A professional fund raiser for universities had once told me that a good batting average was one success out of twenty tries and that the seeker had to face refusal nineteen times to earn the right to success once. Encouraged by this thought, I kept on trying."

Finally, McManus secured a grant from the Rockefeller Foundation and the Institute of Research and Service in Nursing Education opened in 1953. McManus served as director. One of the Institute's first field service projects included developing a nursing program at the University of Istanbul in Turkey. McManus was instrumental in helping to establish the overseas program. After conducting research on the cost of graduate nursing programs and realizing such programs were underfunded, the Institute helped establish the National Fund for Graduate Nurse Education in 1961.

Another program McManus helped launch at Teachers College was the Cooperative Project for Junior College Nursing Education. During the 1950s, as the junior and community college movement grew, McManus pushed for the development of a two-year, associate's degree in nursing to help alleviate a nursing shortage in the United States. While Mildred Montag oversaw the project to develop the two-year program and test if it was sufficient, McManus offered support and spoke in favor of the program, thus helping it succeed.

Spent Retirement Traveling, Consulting

Despite the many accomplishments of her career, McManus told Safier she was actually "very disorganized" and had a tendency to procrastinate. "I find it hard to do things I don't like to do. If I have a job to do, I put it off. Then I can find a *dozen* things to do that interest me more than what I have to do."

After retiring in 1961, McManus continued her consulting work. She traveled to Kenya to prepare a training program for nurses there. She enjoyed traveling—for work and pleasure—often inviting her granddaughters to join her. McManus had 23 grandchildren and 37 great-grandchildren. McManus believed in continuing her education and frequently enrolled in evening adult education classes. She took courses in tailoring, furniture refinishing, and cake decorating. McManus died May 29, 1993, at a nursing home in Natick, Massachusetts. She was 97. In an effort to recognize McManus's achievements, the National Council of State Boards of Nursing (NCSBN) established the R. Louise McManus Award given to individuals who make important contributions toward the mission of the NCSBN.

Books

McManus, R. Louise, *The Effect of Experience on Nursing Achievement,* Bureau of Publications, Teachers College, Columbia University, 1949.

Safier, Gwendolyn, *Contemporary American Leaders in Nursing: An Oral History,* McGraw-Hill Book Co., 1977.

Periodicals

New York Times, December 24, 1951; June 4, 1993.

Online

"Louise McManus," National Women's Hall of Fame, http://www.greatwomen.org/women-of-the-hall/search-the-hall-results/details/2/107-McManus (October 27, 2011). □

Ved Mehta

The Indian-born American writer Ved Mehta (born 1934) has communicated vivid impressions of two realms largely unknown to the citizens of his adopted country: life in India and the life of the blind. Many of Mehta's writings are autobiographical, rooted in one of the most unusual lives of any twentieth-century writer.

Mehta once said that he was a mixture of five cultures: Indian, British, American, blind, and the *New Yorker,* the magazine where Mehta was a staff writer from 1961 until 1994 and produced some of his best work. He wrote about each of those five cultures, touching on his family's life in British-controlled India, his own struggles as a blind person, his education in the southern United States, the politics and society of contemporary India, and the *New Yorker* editor who served as his mentor, William Shawn. Many of Mehta's books contained such detailed visual descriptions that he was accused of exaggerating his blindness, but his difficult childhood in India left no doubt as to his veracity. The culmination of Mehta's achievement has been a cycle of 11 connected works of autobiography, collectively entitled Continents of Exile.

Blinded at an Early Age

Ved Mehta was born on March 21, 1934, in Lahore, which is now in Pakistan but was then part of the undivided British-controlled Indian subcontinent. His father, Amolak Ram Mehta, was a noted physician who was active in India's Red Cross Society and spearheaded anti-tuberculosis campaigns. After India's independence from Britain in 1947, Amolak Mehta served as the country's deputy director-general of health services. Mehta was blinded at age four by cerebrospinal meningitis. Faith healers suggested (among other solutions) that his mother, Shanti, touch two raw eggs to his eyes and then place them at a crossroads. When such measures failed, Mehta was sent to the Dadar American Mission School for the Blind in Bombay (now Mumbai).

Over the course of three years at the school, which Mehta said resembled an orphanage in many respects, he contracted malaria, typhoid fever, bronchitis, and ringworm. Classes were conducted in the Marathi language, which Mehta did not speak. His ability to cope with the world developed to a greater degree after he returned home and challenged himself to develop his senses other than sight. Mehta followed his sister to school, learning to pick out her voice in a crowd and to locate it precisely. He rode a bicycle, occasionally suffering crashes but acquiring keen facial vision, which he described on his official website as "an ability that the blind develop to sense objects and terrain by the feel of the air and by differences in sound." By the time he left India, Mehta had begun to acquire the uncanny abilities he later displayed as a writer—he could form detailed impressions of his surroundings even though he could not see them.

After numerous rejected applications, Mehta was accepted for admission at the Arkansas State School for the Blind in Little Rock, leaving India after his Hindu family had already fled a deteriorating situation for Hindus in the new Muslim-majority nation of Pakistan. He arrived in Little Rock in 1949. The American South presented a new set of challenges for Mehta, but for the first time he was able to reap the benefits of a formal education. Although his English was shaky at first, his talent as a writer was soon recognized, and he completed the school's 12-year curriculum in three years. As a strange aside, while holding down a job at an ice-cream factory on the side, Mehta fell into an open manhole while taking a shortcut. Mehta graduated from the Arkansas State School and was admitted to Pomona College, where he was elected to the Phi Beta Kappa honors society during his junior year. He received a BA degree from Pomona in 1956, went to Oxford University in England for a second bachelor's degree (in history) from 1956 to 1959, and returned to the United States for an MA at Harvard, which he earned in 1961.

Focused on Writing

During this period Mehta was aiming toward an academic career, but he soon decided that writing was where his true interests lay. He was already a published author, having written *Face to Face: An Autobiography* while he was still at Pomona and saw it published by the major Little, Brown house in 1957. In 1960 he published a second book, *Walking the Indian Streets*, about his return to India. A piece of writing related to that book had been published in the *New Yorker*, and that led to a 1959 meeting between Mehta and the magazine's legendary editor, William Shawn, an encounter that marked a turning point for the young Indian writer. Mehta was hired as a staff writer at the magazine in 1961.

At first Mehta was intimidated. "I began sitting anxiously by the phone waiting for Mr. Shawn's call, as if I were in love," he recalled (as quoted in the *Spectator*). But, as he did for so many other writers, the *New Yorker* editor helped Mehta develop his own style and voice. He did not simply have Mehta write for India, although the majority of Mehta's writings for the magazine would touch on the culture of his native country (and Mehta himself would be hailed by Shawn as the most important windows on India published in America). Shawn also drew on Mehta's rigorous academic background and his general ability to explain complex topics clearly for a general audience.

For example, *Fly and the Fly-Bottle: Encounters with British Intellectuals* (1962) collected a group of interviews Mehta conducted with leading British philosophers. Mehta's own tone of amusement at some of the more arcane details of his subjects' thinking clearly showed through in the interviews, causing some consternation in Britain but helping establish Mehta as a highly readable author at home with a large variety of topics. *The New Theologians* (1965) repeated the interview format, showing Mehta in conversation with influential religious thinkers such as Reinhold Niebuhr and Paul Tillich. Those two books, as well as other early Mehta volumes, were based directly on his articles for the *New Yorker*.

Often Mehta would include visual details about scenes he described in India or about his interview subjects, describing the Indian writer R.K. Narayan as peering out from behind thick glasses, for example. Some of the details involved things he could not possibly have seen, but Mehta was extremely adept at divining his surrroundings through his facial vision, and at integrating what he knew with what he learned in conversation with those around him. Mehta worked with an amanuensis, or helper, who read to him from books and set down Mehta's writings, which he dictated—he was unable to write in longhand. Despite the slowness of the process, Mehta was an exacting self-editor, revising some of his works up to 150 times. Except in writings where he specifically addressed the experience of being blind, he declined to have himself identified as blind in promotional material associated with his books.

In 1971 Mehta received a pair of prestigious financial stipends, a Guggenheim Fellowship and a five-year grant from the Ford Foundation. He also entered psychoanalysis at around the same time. After he became an American citizen in 1975, he received more awards, including a Mac-Arthur Foundation Fellowship in 1982. While he continued to write for the *New Yorker* until 1994, he now had the latitude to pursue more personal writing projects. In 1972 he embarked on a massive autobiographical cycle of 11 books, entitled *Continents of Exile*. The first book in the series was *Daddyji*, an account of the life and career of Mehta's own father; the second, *Mamaji* (1979) was about his traditionally raised mother and her family.

In most of the *Continents of Exile* books, Mehta put his own life under the microscope. *Vedi* (1982) dealt with his years at the Dadar School for the blind, while *The Ledge Between the Streams* (1984) described his family's experiences during the partition of India and Pakistan. *Sound Shadows of the New World* (1985) recounted Mehta's experiences as a student in Arkansas, and *Stolen Light* (1989) and *Up at Oxford* (1993) continued the story of Mehta's education, focusing respectively upon his years as the first Indian student at Pomona College and his experiences at Oxford.

The eighth volume of *Continents of Exile* was a fond memoir of Mehta's employer: *Remembering Mr. Shawn's New Yorker: The Invisible Art of Editing* appeared in 1998. The most personal book in the series was *All for Love* (2001), in which Mehta reflected on his own difficult romantic life as a blind person. Those difficulties had already come to an end by that time: in 1983 Mehta married Linn Cary, a great-great-great-granddaughter of author James Fenimore Cooper. The pair had two daughters, Alexandra and Natasha.

Mehta's experiences in building a house on an island off the Maine coast formed the subject of the tenth book in the series, *Dark Harbor: Building House and Home on an Enchanted Island* (2003). He returned to Indian ground for the final book, *The Red Letters: My Father's Enchanted Period*, based on Mehta's discovery that his father had carried on an extramarital affair. In between these books, Mehta managed to write several others, including *Rajiv Gandhi and Rama's Kingdom* (1994), on Indian politics. He wrote one novel, *Delinquent Chacha*. Many of his shorter pieces were collected in *Ved Mehta: The Art of the Essay* (1998). Mehta, who has issued 23 books as of this writing, has served as a visiting professor at top American schools including Williams College, Vassar College, and New York University.

Books

Alam, Fakrul, ed., *South Asian Writers in English* (*Dictionary of Literary Biography*, vol. 323), Gale, 2006.
Mehta, Ved, *Face to Face: An Autobiography*, Little, Brown, 1957.

Periodicals

American Scholar, Winter 2010.
Financial Express, November 8, 2009.
New York Times, May 22, 2003.
New York Times Magazine, June 10, 1984.
Smithsonian, August 1984.
Spectator, January 22, 2005.

Online

"About Ved Mehta," *Ved Mehta Official Website,*; http://www.vedmehta.com (January 2, 2012).☐

Alice Thompson Meynell

Alice Meynell (1847-1922) was an influential British woman poet. The first woman to ever be considered for poet laureate of England, she was an influential force in the revival of Catholic poetry and an advocate for women's emancipation.

Alice Christiana Gertrude Thompson was born in 1847 in Barnes, England. She was the daughter of Thomas James Thompson and Christiana Weller. Thomas James was a wealthy widower. His grandfather, Dr. Thomas Pepper Thompson of Liverpool had immigrated to Jamaica where he had acquired sugar plantations in the mid-18th century. Thomas Pepper Thompson's son, James, had a Creole mistress of mixed parentage who produced Thomas James Thompson as James's illegitimate son. When James died in Jamaica, Thomas Pepper Thompson left his fortune to his grandson, Thomas James Thompson. Before he married Christiana, Thompson had married previously, but his wife had died in 1844. Shortly thereafter he remarried to Christiana Weller, a concert pianist with a promising career that she left behind for Thompson. Thompson's friend, the prominent author Charles Dickens, was a witness at Thomas and Christiana's wedding. Meynell had one sister, Elizabeth Thompson, who would one day be an accomplished painter known as Lady Butler.

In part because of her father's financial freedom, the family spent much of their time traveling around Europe. By the age of one, Meynell was fluent in both French and English. The Thompson family spent much of their time in Italy, particularly on the Ligurian coast, alternating between living in Italy and returning to England.

Thomas James Thompson educated his daughters himself. Meynell became grounded particularly in novelists contemporary to her time including the Brontës, Dickens, Scott, Trollope, Austen, George Eliot, and Hawthorn as well as in other great authors such as Wordsworth, Tennyson, and Shelley. Meynell wrote her first poem at the age of seven, and by 13 she was keeping a journal entitled First Endeavors by A.C.T.

Early Adulthood

In 1864, the Thompson family returned to England. Once they arrived, Meynell was restless. She felt disadvantaged and frustrated because of the limitations that were placed upon her as a woman. This feeling would motivate her to become an advocate for women's rights in England.

In 1868, Meynell converted to Catholicism from Anglicanism while she was living in Malvern. Her mother converted with her. Father Dignam, a Jesuit priest, was particularly influential in both her conversion and her early poetry. He was an advocate and a critic, praised and evaluated her work. Meynell moved to London and Italy, but the two of them maintained correspondence. Evidence shows that Meynell may have grown too fond of Father Dignam and when she returned, he requested that he be posted elsewhere. His request was granted. Meynell took the news harshly, and she wrote a poem about this loss that was included in her work *Preludes* called "Renouncement." Still, her newfound Catholic faith would eventually make her an important contributor to the Catholic revival in poetry.

In 1870, she moved to South Kensington, London where she wrote poetry and book reviews. In 1874 her sister, Lady Butler, painted a very successful painting with a war theme called *Roll Call*, which was eventually bought by the Queen. This kind of notoriety forced the family into high society. It was at one of these high society gatherings that Alice Meynell met Aubrey de Vere. De Vere would be one of Meynell's greatest advocates and would introduce her to many other important literary figures including John Ruskin and Alfred Lord Tennyson. De Vere encouraged Meynell to publish her first volume of poetry, which she did in 1875.

Published by Henry S. Kin, *Preludes* was Meynell's first published collection of poetry. In this work, illustrated by her sister, Meynell showed very strong emotions. This collection contained many famous poems by Meynell including "The Garden" and a poem about her conversion, "The Young Neophyte". This collection gained praise by writers such as George Eliot, Francis Thompson, John Ruskin, and Coventry Patmore.

In 1876, Meynell met a young journalist, Wilfrid Meynell. Wilfrid Meynell was a Catholic convert from a Quaker family in Newcastle. He admired Meynell's poetry and contrived a way to meet her. In 1877, the two married. Between 1879 and 1891 they would have eight children, one of whom would die in infancy. They named all of their children from Shakespeare, particularly from *Twelfth Night*. Her children were a great inspiration to Meynell, and motherhood was a consistent theme in Meynell's later work.

In 1880, the Meynells attempted to start their own independent publication: *Pen: A Journal of Literature,* which lasted only seven issues. In 1881, Wilfrid Meynell was giving the editorship of the *Weekly Register* by Cardinal Manning. This would be the family's steady work for eighteen years. At the time Alice also wrote for the *Spectator*, the *National Observer*, and the *Saturday Review*. She had two of her poems printed in *Sonnets of Three Centuries*.

In 1883, Wilfrid Meynell launched *Merry England*, a monthly about literature and the arts, with publisher Burns and Oates, eventually taking the publication on himself. In 1887, Francis Thompson would contribute to *Merry England* and a year later Wilfrid Meynell would meet him. Wilfrid Meynell took Thompson in, revived him from destitution and laudanum addiction and encouraged him to write. Wilfrid Meynell would remain Thompson's financial and emotional support for the rest of his life. Thompson greatly admired and was inspired by Alice Meynell's work.

Meynell's most important literary contribution of this time was her "Rhythm of Life" column. She also had some of her essays collected and printed in 1890. With her new family, the 1880s and 1890s were a hectic time in the Meynell family, so Alice produced very few works during this time.

The Palace Court

The Meynells' home quickly became known as the Palace Court. Each Sunday they would open their home to a variety of literary, artistic, and religious individuals from across England. Visitors would include such literary figures as Coventry Patmore, W.B. Yeats, Oscar Wilde, Aubrey Beardsley, George Meredith, Katherine Tynan, and Lionel Johnson.

In 1873, Aubrey de Vere introduced Meynell's poetry to Coventry Patmore. It was not until 1892 that a true friendship evolved between Patmore and Meynell. They carried on a platonic relationship for about three years. Meynell believed that Patmore was a poetic genius, and Patmore greatly respected Meynell and her work. She made frequent visits to him in Lymington, sometimes bringing her children along with her. Patmore, though, became more and more possessive and demanding of her and she broke off their relationship. Patmore died in 1896.

Shortly after Patmore's death, which devastated Meynell, she met George Meredith. He was very attracted to Meynell's prose. They would remain close friends until his death in 1909. Meredith would mentor Meynell when she began to write regularly again.

New Works and World Travel

In 1896, Meynell privately printed her volume entitled *Other Poems* with ten new poems. It would eventually become her most popular anthology. That same year *The Colour of Life, and Other Essays on Things Seen and Heard* was published. This was a popular column called ''Ware of Autolycus'' that Meynell wrote for *Pall Mall*. She published *The Children*, a collection of poems, in 1897. Finally, in 1899, the *Weekly Register* was sold, freeing some time for Meynell.

In 1900, the Meynell family visited Italy for the first time since Alice and Wilfrid Meynell married. The next year Alice Meynell did a lecture tour in the United States and Mexico at the invitation of her friend Agnes Tobin. She left on September 7, 1901 for New York City and would wind her way across the country to San Francisco. She wanted to be home for Christmas, but Tobin convinced her to stay until the spring. This time away from her family was particularly painful for Meynell. She returned to England in April 1902. *Later Poems* had been published earlier that year.

From 1903 to 1911 Meynell wrote introductions to Blackwell's editions of other writers, including volumes on Wordsworth, Keats, Coleridge, Herrick, Christina Rosetti, and Blake. From 1904 to 1914 she would also continue to travel abroad every year except one. In 1906, she was lucky enough to have a semi-private audience with Pope Pius X. Unfortunately, the next few years would be marred by the deaths of close friends and family, with Francis Thompson dying in 1907, George Meredith in 1909, and Meynell's mother, Christiana Thompson, dying in 1910.

In 1911, the Meynell family bought eighty acres of land at Greatham in Sussex, England. In 1914, Meynell was elected to the Royal Society of Literature and her work *Essays* was published.

When World War I broke out, it caused many problems and much heartache in the Meynell household. Alice and Wilfrid Meynell's son-in-law was killed in the war. Everard Meynell enlisted in the army. Francis Meynell adopted a pacifist position with which Alice Meynell adamantly disagreed. Alice Meynell's health had been at issue before this, plagued by overwork and migraines, but her health noticeably and permanently weakened during this time.

Meynell continued writing. She reviewed for the *Dublin Review*, translated a European novel, and wrote a book on Mary, Jesus' mother. For the second time she was on the short-list to be named poet laureate. The first time had been in 1895, at Patmore's recommendation. At the time, though, Meynell's body of work was to grow greatly. Then in 1913 she and Rudyard Kipling led the race for poet laureate in a popular poll. Though she was never selected, she was the first woman ever to be considered for this honor.

Meynell then published several works in quick succession. First came *Shepherdess and Other Verses* in 1914. Then in 1915 she published *Ten Poems*. In 1916 came *Poems on War*. Finally, in 1917 she published *A Father of Women and Other Poems*.

In 1916, Meynell began correspondence with a trusted spiritual advisor in America, a nun named Mother St. Ignatius. She would correspond with her until Meynell's death. In 1918, Meynell became seriously ill, but recovered. Meynell began work on a children's anthology, but did not live to complete it. On November 27, 1922, Meynell died after seven weeks of illness.

Books

Badeni, June, *The Slender Tree: A Life of Alice Meynell,* T.J. Press, 1981

Beum, Robert Lawrence, ed., *Modern British Essayists: First Series,* Gale, 1990.

Contemporary Authors Online, Gale, 2003

Flesch, William, *The Facts on File Companion to British Poetry: 19th Century,* Facts on File, 2010

Sage, Lorna, Germaine Greer, and Elaine Showalter, eds., *Cambridge Guide to Women's Writings in English,* Cambridge, 1999

Standford, Donald E., ed., *British Poets, 1880-1914,* Gale, 1983

Periodicals

Guide to Literary Masters and Their Works, January, 2007☐

Minsky Brothers

American theater owners the Minsky Brothers owned more than half of Manhattan's burlesque theaters at the height of the form's popularity.

American theater owners and producers the Minsky Brothers—Abe (1882–1948), Billy (1887–1932), Herbert (1891–1959), and Morton (1902–1987)—helped popularize burlesque performances during the 1910s and 1920s through their famed New York City theaters. Beginning with the opening of the National Winter Garden in the 1910s, the Minskys pushed the boundaries of contemporary ideas of public decency through live shows that they proudly declared were not family-friendly. Even as the eyes of moralists and the police focused on the Minskys, however, so did the feet of a growing flock of patrons. By the mid-1920s, regular police raids cleared burlesque patrons, and in 1931, the Minskys took their show uptown to Broadway. At the height of their career, the brothers operated over 15 theaters in New York City as well as shows at points around the nation. The election of reformer Fiorello la Guardia as mayor of New York brought the era of burlesque to an end, however, and the Minskys' last theater closed down in 1942. The family's story later served as inspiration for the book *The Night They Raided Minsky's,* which in turn gave rise to the 1968 film of the same name.

Operated First Theaters

Persecution of Jews in Russia and Eastern Europe drove the Minskys to immigrate to the United States in the 1880s. The family patriarch, Louis Minsky, had married Esther Linkski in Russia in 1881; the following year, the first Minsky brother, Abraham—commonly called Abe throughout his life—was born in that country. Louis Minsky came to the United States first to earn money to move his family, and began working in New York City's Lower East Side as a street peddler. Within a few years, he had opened a dry goods store and the Minskys were rejoined. The Minsky family grew in both size and influence over the next several years; Louis Minsky's business thrived, and he was elected to local government in the Tammany Hall government of Big Tim Sullivan in 1895. More children also followed, including Michael William "Billy" in 1887, Herbert in 1891, and youngest brother Morton "Mort" in 1902. Together, these four siblings became the heart of the Minsky burlesque business. Show business, however, was not necessarily any of the young men's top career pick. Billy Minsky wrote for the society pages of the *World Telegram,* Herbert attended law school at Columbia, and Mort went to New York University.

Abe Minsky seemed most likely to make a go in the entertainment industry. In about 1908, he and a friend purchased a former Lutheran church in the Lower East Side and opened a nickelodeon movie house—so called because admission cost a nickel—that quickly became a success. At least part of this success was thanks to the somewhat risqué films they played. Louis Minsky shut down the operation when he found out the content of the nickelodeon's shows. Before long, however, the brothers had reinstated a theater on the sixth floor of the building. Rather than being a movie house, this theater, called the National Winter Garden, was suited for live performance. At first, the Minskys leased one of the complete traveling burlesque live shows, but the freight elevator leading to their sixth floor theater could not accommodate the necessary equipment. The brothers then decided to build on the success of their lurid movie house by staging ongoing, fixed-set shows that fell between the lowbrow circuit shows and the upscale Broadway shows like the Ziegfeld Follies.

Popularized the Striptease

During the late 1910s, these shows typically leaned more toward those of traditional vaudeville than the ribald material that would define the brothers' career. Shows alternated among broad comic sketches, popular and comic songs, and dance acts. The brothers kept the naysayers at bay by keeping the theaters free of drinking, smoking, and swearing, and invited respectable middle-aged women to attend. Before long, however, the tenor of the programming changed. Morton Minksy later claimed that it was an enthusiastic audience response to one performer removing her collar and cuffs to send off for laundering as she left the stage that marked the beginning of striptease. At that time, on stage nudity was legal as long as the performers remained still; this allowed producers such as Florenz

Ziegfeld to display "living tableaus" of topless women at his famous Follies, but prevented burlesque performers from showing actual skin. Instead, performers wore skin-tight, one-piece union suits.

The accidental appearance of bare skin on the National Winter Garden stage marked a turning point. In *Minsky's Burlesque,* Mort Minsky recalled his brother Herbert describing the scene. "They clapped like crazy.... Between the heat and the applause, Mae lost her head, went back for a short chorus, and unbuttoned her bodice as she left the stage again." The house manager at first fined the performer and threatened to clear the audience. When Billy Minsky saw the effect of the show on the crowd, however, he refunded the fine, gave the performer a raise, and decided to brave the law. "If people want it, we'll give it to him," Minsky recounted his brother as declaring. "When a court finds that I've broken some law, I'll stop. Until then, we'll sell tickets."

Although numerous historians have challenged the idea that this was the first instance of a striptease taking place, it certainly began the practice at Minsky's. Soon after, the theater owners created a warning light system to alert stage personnel and performers of a police presence. When the backstage lights were switched to red, the performers changed to the clean version of their show. Although this plan surely prevented some police raids from taking place, the brothers nevertheless had their theater cleared often after they began staging more lurid shows. The most famous of these raids took place in 1927, when the planned evacuation of the audience devolved into a riot. Police arrested 12 theater-goers and served Abe Minsky with a summons for smoking a cigar backstage. Decades later, this raid was immortalized in a Hollywood film, although Mort Minsky dismissed it as but one among many of the run-ins between the theater and the police.

Such incidents kept the Minskys in the news, however, and often led to an effect quite different from the intended one. The brothers claimed that their shows were based on the artistic French Folies-Bergères, and employed techniques inspired by the shows such as a lit runway on which performers could walk out into the audience to give them an eyeful of bare leg. Despite the condemnation of moral groups and the law, the Minskys hit the pinnacle of their theater career in the early 1930s. A renovation of the National Winter Garden and changes in public tastes had made them a popular haunt for socialites and upper-class businessmen on a downtown adventure. In 1931, Billy Minsky oversaw the opening of a new burlesque theater on Broadway, at last bringing popular entertainment uptown. "It is practically impossible to overestimate the impact of Minsky's taking over the Republic," argued Rachel Shteir in *Striptease: The Untold History of the Girlie Show.* The Minskys' elevated burlesque attracted a broad clientele, who came to see performers such as Gypsy Rose Lee, Abbott and Costello, and Red Buttons. More burlesque houses flocked to the district, and the cheap thrills of the form played well to audiences increasingly seeking inexpensive entertainment in the gloomy economic days of the early Depression.

Reformers Closed Down Business

Legal problems soon presented serious challenges to the brothers, however. Billy Minsky re-applied for the theater's operating license in 1932 only to find that government reformers had decided to allow citizens' groups a chance to essentially block the proposal. Minsky promised to end the striptease elements of the show and won the renewal, but died soon after. Because Billy Minsky had long been the driving force behind the operation, his death left a serious hole for the brothers to fill. Rather than drawing closer together, however, the remaining three brothers began to go their separate ways. The National Winter Garden closed the same year as Billy Minsky's death. Abe Minsky dedicated his time mostly to the Gaiety Theater and, in 1933, opened his own New Gotham theater in Harlem. Herbert and Mort continued running the surviving Minsky operations, including a new midtown location, the Central. Burlesque became more ribald, and the authorities in turn became more interested in shutting it down. "It is easy to imagine that if Billy Minsky had lived after 1932, old-fashioned burlesque striptease might have lived longer in New York," commented Shteir. "None of the other brothers could conjure up his flair, his panache, his silver-tongued success at placating the authorities." By the late 1930s, new government restrictions forced the theaters to tone down their acts, and burlesque business began drying up.

The final Minsky burlesque house, the Gaiety Theater, was closed down in 1942; the *New York Times* later described it as "the last of the city's burlesque houses featuring strip-tease dancers and baggy-pants comedians." Herbert Minsky fell out of the news by the 1940s and died on December 21, 1959, after battling heart disease for several months. Of the surviving Minskys, only Abe Minsky and his adopted son Harold remained involved in the entertainment business throughout their lifetimes. The elder Minsky ran night clubs and revues in Miami and New York City until his death from a cerebral hemorrhage on September 5, 1949. Harold Minsky continued the family business. In 1957, he moved to Las Vegas, where he inaugurated a new "Follies" production at the then recently-opened Dunes Hotel and casino. The show ran for six years at that location, and Minsky later operated shows at other Las Vegas hotels including the Silver Slipper, the Thunderbird, and the Aladdin. He died in Las Vegas in 1977. In contrast, Mort Minsky left show business proper in 1938 to become involved in marketing and, later, real estate. He worked as an executive with the Diamond Sales Corporation for many years, and became a senior vice president in charge of movie theater sales and leasing with the firm Daniel A. Brener Inc., in 1967.

The Minskys' story, however, did not end with the closure of New York's burlesque houses. In 1960, author Rowland Barber penned what he called a "fanciful" history of the family's development of the burlesque business up to the night of the famed raid in 1927. Writing in the *New York Times,* Gilbert Millstein hailed the book as "a loving and greatly energetic reconstruction, free of any intellectual fiddle-faddle, loud-mouthed, raw and direct[.]" Later in the decade, the book served as the basis for a light-hearted fictionalized comedy of the same name, with Elliott Gould portraying Billy Minsky. Nearly two decades later, Mort Minsky—by that time the only surviving member of

the original burlesque clan—co-authored a book on the rise and fall of the family's entertainment empire entitled *Minsky's Burlesque: A Fast and Funny Look at America's Bawdiest Era.* Although the ribald styles of the 1920s and early 1930s seem unlikely to enjoy a serious revival, the Minskys' involvement with the creation of that new form of entertainment, their colorful interactions with the authorities and the press, and their provision of a launch pad for the careers of some of the century's top show business names seem equally unlikely to be entirely forgotten.

Books

Minsky, Morton and Milt Machlin, *Minsky's Burlesque: A Fast and Funny Look at America's Bawdiest Era,* Arbor House, 1986.
Shteir, Rachel, *Striptease: The Untold History of the Girlie Show,* Oxford University Press, 2004.

Periodicals

New York Times, September 5, 1949; June 12, 1960; December 26, 1977; March 30, 1986; March 24, 1987.
Time, May 2, 1932.

Online

"Minsky's Burlesque," Online Nevada Encyclopedia, http://www.onlinenevada.org/minsky_s_burlesque (December 3, 2011). □

Joaquim Miranda

The Portuguese politician and economist Joaquim Miranda (1950–2006) was Portugal's longest-serving member of the European Parliament and a longtime leader of its left-wing bloc.

A member of the Portuguese Communist Party, Miranda worked his way up in the country's political hierarchy, beginning with local posts in his home city of Portalegre. An economist by training, his local background in Portugal was in agricultural economics. In the European Parliament, however, his interests were primarily international in nature. Like former United States president Jimmy Carter, Miranda was a frequent participant in international observer teams designed to foster the spread of free and democratic elections around the world. He was especially interested in emerging democracies, and he was also active in support of the rights of migrant workers in Europe. In the parliament itself he emerged as a leader of a coalition of various far-left and environmentally oriented parties.

Worked in Agriculture Ministry

Joaquim Miranda da Silva was born in the small town of Portalegre in eastern Portugal on September 7, 1950. As a university student he studied economics, but even then he seems to have had a political career in mind; after his graduation in 1973 he worked for a single year as a secondary school teacher before taking a position as executive officer in Portugal's ministry of agriculture in 1975. He remained with the ministry until 1977, staying on as an adviser on agricultural cooperatives in 1978 and 1979. By that time Miranda had already begun his career as an elected official, winning a spot on the Portalegre town council in 1977. Around that time he joined the Communist Party of Portugal, eventually becoming a member of its Central Committee. From 1979 to 1985 he was Portalegre's deputy mayor.

In 1980 Miranda was elected to the Portalegre Municipal Assembly, a regional body covering an area of more than 400 square kilometers. He remained in that post until 1994, also holding a seat in the Assembly of the Republic, Portugal's national parliament, from 1980 to 1986. During this period, bodies governing the increasingly close relationships among European countries were evolving. Miranda joined the transnational Interparliamentary Union in 1980. He then emerged as a candidate to represent Portugal in the operations of the European Economic Community (EEC) as the country approached a decision in favor of membership in the early 1980s, and he served on the Interparliamentary Assembly of the Council of Europe from 1983 to 1985.

These and other bodies had existed for some time, yet were inadequate to oversee the increasingly complex relationships among European countries—and the budgets for the institutions that oversaw those relationships. In 1979 the European Parliament held its first direct elections for members (known as MEPs), of which there are currently 736. Portugal became a member of the European Community on January 1, 1986, and held elections the following year. Miranda was put forward as a Communist candidate and was elected, joining the Parliament on July 19, 1987.

Headed Left Bloc

Miranda quickly emerged in leadership positions. In 1989 he became a founding member of the parliament's Left Unity bloc, known by its French initials, CG. This group was initially oriented toward pure Communist ideology and had ties to the government of the Soviet Union, but after the fall of Soviet Communism in 1991, Miranda became more sympathetic to western European democratic institutions. From 1989 to 1993 Miranda served as the CG group's vice-chair, and he became its chairman in 1994 shortly before its dissolution. In 1994 he became vice-chair of its replacement, the European United Left/Nordic Green Left group known by the intitials GUE/NGL, an assortment of old-line Communist parties, newer leftist groups, and an environmentalist bloc.

The European Parliament, among other things, held jurisdiction over food and drink brand names and appellations, and in 1992 Miranda waded into a dispute over the Torres wine denomination claimed by both Portuguese and Spanish makers. With the launch of the common euro currency in 1999, Miranda became one of a group of MEPs who introduced measures aiming to bring greater transparency to the notoriously byzantine European Community bureaucracy headquartered in Brussels, Belgium. Most of his work, however, came in the international arena. In 1997 he helped shepherd aid for East Timor, which was still under Indonesian occupation but approaching independence, through the parliament; the region had formerly been a Portuguese colony but had suffered through two decades of repression by the Indonesian military, and the aid had to be funneled through non-governmental organizations.

Miranda's other activities included fact-finding tours connected with development initiatives in some of the world's poorest countries. He traveled to Bangladesh in 2000 to meet with officials and inspect European Community–financed projects, and in 2002 he worked to provide 125 million euros in aid to Angola, another former Portuguese colony whose infrastructure was devastated by several decades of war. In 2001, Miranda condemned the UNITA group led by guerrilla fighter Jonas Savimbi as a terrorist organization. In 2002 Miranda visited Palestinian Authority leader Yasir Arafat, helping to put in motion some of the aid that brought new prosperity to Palestinian lands in the 2000s decade.

Active in Election-Monitoring Delegations

Many of Miranda's international efforts involved the monitoring of elections in emerging democracies. In 2001 he served as Chief Election Observer and head of the European Union Core Team overseeing elections in Bangladesh, a process marked by unrest that caused more than 500 injuries. Miranda oversaw a team of 32 long-term observers and more than 40 short-term observers in 14 locations across the densely populated country. In 2002 Miranda headed a 43-member European Union observer mission that oversaw elections in the Republic of Congo, resulting in only minor irregularities and no violence.

Married with one daughter, Miranda retired from the European Parliament in January of 2004 due to health problems. At the time, he was the continent's longest-serving representative in a European institution. In his last years he was active in Communist Party organizing in Portugal's Alentejo region. Suffering from a chronic illness, Miranda was hospitalized in his last days, and he died in his home city of Portalegre on June 17, 2006. Portugal's Left Bloc party (as quoted on the website of Portuguese radio and Television) called him "a particularly active and determined voice in the fight of the European left against racism and xenophobia and for a European immigration policy based on respect for political and social rights of migrant workers." Covered with the Portuguese Communist Party flag, his body was taken to a crematorium in Alentejo.

Books

Who's Who in International Affairs, Europa, 1996.

Periodicals

Africa News, March 13, 2002; March 14, 2002; June 17, 2003.
BBC Monitoring International Reports, October 10, 1997; September 25, 2001; February 20, 2002; November 4, 2002; November 16, 2002.
BBC Summary of World Broadcasts, November 16, 2002.
Christian Science Monitor, January 13, 1999.

Guardian (London, England), October 13, 1992.

Independent (London, England), September 14, 2000; August 28, 2001; August 30, 2001.

Xinhua, August 30, 2001.

Online

"Joaquim Miranda, Portugal," *European Parliament,* http://www.europarl.europa.eu/meps/en/1356/Joaquim_MIRANDA.html (January 24, 2012).

"Morte de Joaquim Miranda deixa democracia mais pobre" (Death of Joaquim Miranda Leaves Democracy Poorer), *Portuguese Radio and Television,* http://rtp.pt/noticias (January 24, 2012). ☐

María Montez

Dominican-born María Montez (1912–1951) had a short but dazzling career in Hollywood in the 1940s as the "Queen of Technicolor." She starred in a string of campy, preposterous fables made by Universal Studios with a new color film process, and was one of Hollywood's first Latina screen stars. In the years after her 1951 death, those movies became the focus of a particular subculture of gay iconography for their sheer spectacle and her obvious determination to rise above the B-movie schlock into which she had been slotted. "Almost no one was more fun to watch than Maria Montez," asserted Jeanine Basinger in *The Star Machine.* "She was so willing to be passionately sincere about nonsense."

The film star adopted the name "Montez" when she began her career in Hollywood in homage to Lola Montez, a famous entertainer and political figure in nineteenth-century Europe. She was born María África Antonia Gracia Vidal de Santo Silas on June 6, 1912, in Barahona, a city on the southern coast of La Hispaniola, the island that is home to both Haiti and the Dominican Republic. Her father was originally from Spain and had served as Spain's honorary vice consul to the Caribbean nation. He ran a successful textile export business and had ten children with Montez's Dominican-born mother, Regia Teresa Vidal.

Began as Pin-Up Model

Montez's father was actually from the Canary Islands, an archipelago in the Atlantic Ocean off the coast of Morocco that had been under European domination since the early fifteenth century, and young Maria was sent to a convent school there. In November of 1932, at the age of 20, she married William G. Macfeeters, a native of Ireland who had served with the British Army. They lived in Belfast and Liverpool before Montez arrived in New York City around 1939 or 1940. She quickly landed work as a model for a well-known commercial artist named McClelland Barclay, who had a high-profile career as a pin-up illustrator, and the success of those billboard images prompted her to move to Hollywood to launch her career in film.

Montez was signed by Universal Pictures and made her movie debut in a 1940 western, *Boss of Bullion City.* She had another bit part in *The Invisible Woman* that same year, but quickly ascertained that moving from obscurity to stardom required a set of savvy self-promotion skills. Befriending press photographers, she regularly gave them comically glamorous shots that appeared in the tabloid press and movie magazines of the day. "It isn't the nice little demure people who get places" in Hollywood, she asserted to United Press International reporter Frederick C. Othman for a story that ran in the *St. Petersburg Times.* "It is the people who always tell all the other people how wonderful they are. That is what I tell people about me."

Universal put Montez in several smaller roles in four movies released in 1941—*Lucky Devils, Moonlight in Hawaii, That Night in Rio,* and *Raiders of the Desert*—before giving her a starring role in the adventure tale *South of Tahiti,* released in October of 1941. Set on a mysterious island discovered by castaways from a shipwreck, *South of Tahiti* co-starred Montez with Brian Donlevy and Broderick Crawford and marked the start of a film career where her acting talents seemed of less importance than her ability to look seductive in skimpy, exotic outfits.

Dubbed "The Caribbean Cyclone"

Montez had a supporting role in an airliner-set thriller from 1942, *Bombay Clipper,* and turned up in period costume in an adaptation of an Edgar Allan Poe tale, *The Mystery of Marie Roget.* Studio executives at Universal soon realized her appeal was best showcased in outlandish adventure fables filmed with the Technicolor process. The color technology allowed wardrobe and set designers to indulge in garishly hued tableaux that dazzled audiences long accustomed to the sedate tones of black-and-white film. The first of Montez's Technicolor epics was *Arabian Nights,* released on Christmas Day of 1942. It co-starred her with Jon Hall, with whom she would go on to make several more films, and the plot was a predictably pulpy version of the famous Islamic folktale *One Thousand and One Nights.* Montez played Scheherazade, the clever prisoner of a king's harem who saves her life by keeping the jealous despot entertained with her storytelling.

Montez was under contract to a studio that had few serious stars on its roster but was enormously profitable. Universal Pictures churned out B-movies that were box office hits, and had perfected the horror film in the 1930s with the *Dracula* and *Frankenstein* franchises. It was also the studio home of comedians Abbott & Costello. In *Arabian Nights,* one of Montez's co-stars was Shemp Howard (of the future Three Stooges), along with the leopards that guarded her harem-prison. She longed to move into more serious roles, as she told Othman, complaining that she was making just $250 a week. "When I wear clothes and make $150,000 per picture I will call myself a success," she said.

Montez would make a few more Technicolor epics for Universal and producer Walter Wanger, most of which were drubbed by critics but did well at the box office. They included *Ali Baba and the Forty Thieves* and *Cobra Woman,* both released in 1944. The latter was a particularly campy tale in which she played the villainous priestess of a snake-centered religion whose practices included human sacrifices to a volcano. The set included a massive S-shaped snakeskin throne for her. Historians of the B-movie genre later noted that she seemed deadly serious in her movies, which added to their camp appeal. Film writer Jerry Vermilye interviewed the director of *Cobra Woman,* Robert Siodmak, for a 1978 issue of *Nostalgia Monthly,* in which Siodmak described the movie as "silly but fun. . . . Montez couldn't act from here to there, but she was a great personality and she believed completely in her roles."

Married French Movie Star

Montez made several movies that had a 1944 release date. There was *Gypsy Wildcat,* which required some equestrian skills, and a more conventional drama in *Bowery to Broadway.* Costume dramas like *Sudan* and *Tangier* followed in 1945 and 1946, respectively. These sketchily plotted stories were fodder for a theater-going public weary of World War II, which coincided with the peak years of Montez's career. This was also the era in which another Latina star, Brazilian singer-dancer Carmen Miranda, became a household name through her roles in similarly exotic comedies and musicals. "Montez and Miranda were important escape fantasies of World War II," wrote Basinger. "While they were on top, and while the world needed them, they were sensational, stars of the moment in an era that needed their humor, their color, and their considerable pizzazz."

Montez's career prospects seemed to brighten when she wed French actor Jean-Pierre Aumont in July of 1943 after a brief courtship. Aumont had come to Hollywood after achieving some notable success in French stage and cinema, and wrote in his 1976 autobiography that he first saw Montez in the lobby of the famed Beverly Wilshire Hotel, "covered

with gold and topaz like some Byzantine idol," he recalled in *Sun and Shadow.* He soon moved into her Beverly Hills home, which he described as "a strange house. You didn't answer the telephone or read the mail; the doors were always open. Diamonds were left around in ashtrays. *Lives of the Saints* lay between two issues of movie magazines. An astrologer, a physical culture expert, a priest, a Chinese cook, and two Hungarian masseurs were part of the furnishing." During one of the massage sessions, Aumont proposed marriage, for he was about to ship out and join the Free French Forces in North Africa, and Montez agreed, after first consulting with her astrologer about the date.

Aumont survived World War II and returned to Hollywood, where by this time several of Montez's siblings had joined her in America. One brother appeared as a bit player in several films, while her sister Lucita (Luz) was introduced to her future husband, Jean Roy, via Aumont. Montez gave birth to a daughter, Maria Christina, in February of 1946. Her career took some sharp skids after that: she made *The Exile* for respected German director Max Ophüls in 1947, a swashbuckler that also starred Douglas Fairbanks Jr. But her contract with Universal was set to expire, and she was unhappy with the terms of a new one they offered. Furthermore, the studio had found a younger version of her exotic-bombshell screen persona in the form of Yvonne DeCarlo, and its publicists were fomenting a friction between the two women to keep both names in the gossip columns. In an appalling move, Universal first considered Montez for the lead in a 1947 musical starring Aumont, then cast DeCarlo in *Song of Scheherazade* instead.

Died in Salt Bath

Montez and Aumont decided to move to France after he took her there on their long-delayed honeymoon. He bought her a house in Suresnes, a suburb of Paris, and worked on a play that was produced in Paris in 1947. They made a single film together, 1949's *L'Atlantide* (also known as *Siren of Atlantis*), in which Montez played the queen of a lost kingdom and her husband was cast as one of a string of unlucky explorers to have discovered it. The predecessors that found the land ruled by this "Siren" were seduced by her, then embalmed and plated in gold for posterity. The movie earned terrible reviews, and Montez sued its producer, Seymour Nebenzal, who had pledged a $100,000 salary for her starring role, then paid her just $62,000. A Los Angeles Superior Court jury agreed with Montez and ordered Nebenzal to pay her the remaining $38,000.

Montez's career faltered after she exited her contract with Universal. She had a role in a 1949 French thriller, *Portrait d'un assassin,* the 1950 costume epic *The Thief of Venice,* and what would turn out to be her final film, *Revenge of the Pirates* in 1951. She died on September 7, 1951, in her bathtub at Suresnes, while two of her sisters were waiting to have lunch with her, Aumont was filming a French movie nearby, and their five-year-old daughter was with Aumont's brother and his family. Montez had always been fanatical about her weight, and favored a hot temperature soak in a bath stoked with reducing salts. On that day she suffered a heart attack in the bath, but the cause of death was drowning. Her young daughter went on to follow both parents into a film career, and appeared as Tina Aumont in Italian cinema of the 1960s and '70s; she died in 2006, five years after the death of her father.

Inspired Avant-Garde Cinema

Montez had a curious afterlife as a gay icon. Just a few short years after her death, a New York artist and filmmaker named Jack Smith began making 16-millimeter color movies that paid homage to some of her best-known Technicolor spectacles. Smith was a collector of Hollywood studio props and costumes and would invite his friends over for parties in which he dressed them in outlandish get-ups and filmed the plotless art projects. These experiments quickly gained underground cult status in New York, and inspired artist Andy Warhol to begin making similar movies in the 1960s. Warhol worked with avant-garde filmmaker Jonas Mekas, who was the editor of the journal *Film Culture.* Smith's most oft-cited work was an article he wrote about Montez for the Winter 1962 issue of *Film Culture,* titled "The Perfect Filmic Appositeness of Maria Montez." Usually described as a manifesto, Smith's treatise "laid out Smith's vision for a new Queer cinema," noted the London *Guardian* years later in a review of a Jack Smith cult film retrospective. "In so doing, he created the Underground conduit that led from classical Hollywood camp to the transgressive trash of the 1970s and 1980s that, in turn, kickstarted the indie rebellion against corporate studio blockbusterism."

Books

Aumont, Jean-Pierre, *Sun and Shadow,* with foreword by François Truffaut, translated from the original French edition *Le Soleil et Les Ombres,* by Bruce Benderson, W.W. Norton, 1977.

Basinger, Jeanine, *The Star Machine,* Alfred A. Knopf, 2007.

Periodicals

New York Times, January 3, 1951; September 8, 1951; April 11, 2007.

Nostalgia Monthly, September 1978.

St. Petersburg Times, October 1, 1942; November 8, 1942.

Online

guardian.co.uk, No title provided, original URL: http://www.guardian.co.uk/film/filmblog/2011/sep/23/jack-smith-muse-maria-montez?INTCMP=SRCH.

"Maria Montez," IMDB.com, http://www.imdb.com/name/nm0599688/ (October 28, 2011).

"Maria Montez: A Dominican Star," MariaMontez.com, http://www.mariamontez.org/bio.html (October 29, 2011).□

Clelia Duel Mosher

Dr. Clelia Duel Mosher (1863–1940) conducted important research on women's health in the first decades of twentieth-century America. A physician and educator at Stanford University in California, Mosher did much to debunk the myth that women of childbearing age were physically and psychologically hindered by their reproductive cycles, but she also conducted a decades-long poll in which she asked married women about their private lives. That study remained buried in the Stanford University archives for decades after Mosher's death, but became a focal point for feminist scholarship in the 1970s and beyond. In academic circles her questionnaire is considered the first sex survey of American women by a qualified professional.

Clelia Duel Mosher was born on December 16, 1863, in Albany, New York, where her father, Cornelius, was a prominent local physician and civic leader. At one point he served as police surgeon in the city and also sat on the Albany Board of Education, where he fought for the establishment of evening classes for working students. Both Mosher and her sister, Esther, suffered from health problems, and Mosher endured a bout with tuberculosis as a child. In 1881 she graduated from the Albany Female Academy, but was dismayed when her parents rejected the idea of college. To appease her and slake her thirst for advanced study, her father turned their home's greenhouse into a makeshift classroom for her, hiring a local professor of botany to tutor her. Her horticultural skills evolved to the point where she started running a successful florist business out of the home, and eight years later announced to her parents that she had saved the $2,000 (about $48,000 in 2011 currency) and was on her way to Wellesley College in Massachusetts, one of the leading women's schools in the United States.

Mosher's first few years were hard on her, both physically and mentally. She felt underprepared for her courses, and her health suffered as a result. At one point she withdrew for medical reasons, then transferred to the University of Wisconsin in Madison. This was a progressive school at the time and emphasized academic research and self-study, following a European university model over the traditional American curriculum. She transferred one more time, following one of her instructors from Wellesley to Stanford University.

Debunked "Costal" Breathing Theory

At the time, Leland Stanford Junior University was a new school, founded in a pleasant part of northern California in 1891 by a railroad tycoon in honor of his late son and namesake. Stanford University was singular in this era for encouraging qualified women to apply, and had an unusually balanced ratio of male-to-female-students. Mosher earned her undergraduate degree in zoology from Stanford in 1893 and spent two years as a hygiene assistant at the school. The job required her to take measurements of incoming classes, in this case the female students, and the work played a key role in helping her settle on a thesis topic for her master's degree in physiology. At the time, medical professionals asserted that women breathed costally, using the muscles of their upper chest and their ribs, while men breathed with their diaphragm, a thin sheet of muscle located below the two lungs. Women breathed differently, it was argued, because of the presence of reproductive organs below the diaphragm, and because diaphragmatic breathing was more efficient and thus preferable, it bolstered the argument that men were physically superior to women.

Mosher set out to debunk this idea, asserting that the garments women wore were actually restricting their breathing. Corsets, which gave an hourglass form to the figure and in some cases required the assistance of another person to properly lace up, prevented diaphragmatic breathing, she argued. She surveyed Stanford students as well as young women who were living in Pacific Rescue Home, an institution for unwed mothers. She created an apparatus to measure their breathing and was the first professional to conduct a study of women's respiratory functions when the women were undressed. Her thesis debunked the idea that there were physiological differences between men's and women's respiratory systems, and she earned her master's degree with it in 1894. Two years later, a Harvard University professor published a similar study that reported the same findings.

Surveyed Women about Menstrual Cycles

Women of Mosher's era regularly excused themselves from customary activities once a month when they menstruated. Many felt debilitated for a day or two, and the lack of reliable sanitary products on the consumer market also played a role in this custom, which had antecedents dating all the way back to the earliest civilizations, when menstruating women were considered "unclean" and retreated from public view. In arguments against women pursuing higher education or careers, medical professionals argued that because women were regularly debilitated by their menstrual cycle, which began at puberty and lasted all the way to menopause, they were indeed the weaker sex and not expected to be able to fully contribute to the world in the same way that men did.

Mosher set out to debunk this, too. At the time, most of the scientific research on women and menstruation was based on anecdotal reports of doctors. But this represented a skewed sample, culled for the large part from women who sought advice from their doctors about painful or unusually heavy periods, a condition known as dysmenorrhea. Mosher came up with a survey that queried a few hundred women about their menstrual cycles, but soon realized she needed much more rigorous training. In 1896, she enrolled at the Johns Hopkins School of Medicine in Baltimore, Maryland.

Mosher was one of 13 women to earn medical degrees out of a class of 41 at Johns Hopkins in 1900. She stayed on for a year after receiving an offer of an externship, but was discouraged by male mentors from pursuing a specialization in gynecological surgery. Nevertheless, she secured her professional scientific credentials with a paper published in the April–May–June 1901 issue of the *Johns Hopkins Hospital Bulletin*. It was titled "Normal Menstruation and Some of the Factors Modifying It," and in it Mosher summarized the results of her survey data. "These records represented the first collection of written reports about menstruation made by normally healthy women over time," noted Elizabeth Griego in a chapter on Mosher in *Lone Voyagers: Academic Women in Coeducational Universities, 1870–1937*. "Backed by the

evidence from her data, Mosher felt confident enough to refute publicly the prevailing belief that menstruation was an incapacitating disease that caused women to become chronic periodic invalids, disqualified from regular work and advanced study. She argued not only that women could be active during their menstrual periods, but that they should be."

Returned to Stanford

With her medical degree and published credentials, Mosher applied for research grants to study women's cycles at several institutions, but was rejected by all of them. She returned to Palo Alto, the home of Stanford University, and established a private medical practice. In 1910 Stanford University hired her as assistant professor of personal hygiene, medical advisor for women, and director of the Roble Gymnasium. She was responsible for physical hygiene classes for women, a sort of combined gym and health class. Some of the students joined her continuing study about women's menstrual cycles, and all were taught the "Mosher" exercises to alleviate dysmenorrhea, or normal cramps. This was a deep-breathing technique done while lying prone, knees up, with one hand on the abdomen, and designed to improve circulation and strengthen the core muscles. Mosher suggested they be done twice a day, and during the menstrual cycle, too. She also urged her students to be physically active, drink plenty of water, incorporate fruit and fiber into their diet, and shun the restrictive garments dictated by fashion.

In 1915 Mosher was invited to speak at a national convention of officers of Young Women's Christian Associations, or YWCAs, held that year at the Asilomar Conference Center on California's Monterey Peninsula. These YWCA officers were among the staunchest advocates of physical exercise for women as part of a healthy lifestyle, and the National YWCA Board liked Mosher's speech so much that it was transcribed into a 1916 booklet, *Health and the Woman Movement*, for national publication. In it, Mosher spoke about her ongoing research on women's menstrual cycles, and asserted that "if every young girl were taught that menstruation is not normally a 'bad time' and that pain or incapacity at that period is as discreditable and unnecessary as bad breath due to decaying teeth, we might almost look for a revolution in the physical life of women."

Mosher lived and worked in an era when women had made great strides in professional and academic achievement, but faced tremendous discrimination and bias; in 1915 American women, for example, were still campaigning for the right to vote in national elections. One argument against this was that women were too ruled by emotion to be expected to make rational choices at the ballot box. "The day of the type of woman who is all spirit, a burning flame, consuming her misused body, is passing," Mosher said in her YWCA speech. "What we need are women no less fine and womanly, but with beautiful perfect bodies, a suitable receptacle for their equally beautiful souls, who look sanely out on life with steady nerves and clear vision. These are the women to whom, in spite of any encroaching demands of the woman movement, we may safely leave the future of the race."

Joined the Red Cross

Mosher demonstrated her own capacity for toughness when she joined the Red Cross after America's entry into World War I in 1917. She worked as associate medical director of its Bureau of Refugees and Relief in France, supervising the evacuation of children from Paris and other cities. Traveling through landscapes wrecked by the war, she was nevertheless gratified to see French wives, mothers, and even war widows carrying on in the absence of men on farms and in various industries. This became the basis for another booklet, *Strength of Women*, in which she argued that females possessed the same physical capacities as males, but had been socially conditioned to keep their bodies underdeveloped. That was published in 1920 by the Women's Press, and Mosher wrote a similar work three years later with Stanford colleague Ernest Martin, titled *Woman's Physical Freedom*.

Mosher was promoted to associate professor and finally professor of personal hygiene at Stanford. She was one of just three women to achieve a full professorship since the school was founded more than four decades earlier. She retired in 1929, in her mid-sixties, and spent her last years in a home she designed for herself on the Palo Alto campus. She died on December 21, 1940, five days after her 77th birthday. Her research papers languished in the Stanford archives until a professor of American history, Carl Degler, came across an unusual study that Mosher had apparently started while still a student at the University of Wisconsin. She had been asked to deliver a speech to a group of faculty wives in Madison, and began a survey of married women and their attitudes toward sexual activity. Over the years she expanded the survey to include patients in her private practice and women she met at Stanford. Most of these women were her own age, or younger, and until this point no researcher had ever attempted to conduct a systematic study of women's sexuality via a direct, standardized survey.

Degler was astonished at the cache and wrote an article for a 1974 issue of the *American Historical Review*. That ignited the interest of feminist scholars, and Mosher's summaries were finally published decades after her death in a 1980 volume, *The Mosher Survey: Sexual Attitudes of 45 Victorian Women*. Her work is considered pioneering, for she posed some of the first-ever questions about women's attitudes toward sexuality in America. Her subjects' responses and added comments reveal surprisingly modern thoughts about intercourse and even the use of contraception for the era. As Kathryn Allamong Jacob wrote in a 1981 article for *American Heritage*, "Mosher demonstrated in her small, pioneering survey that despite the conflicting warnings of the marriage manuals of the Victorian age, most of the women she studied engaged in sex with neither reluctance nor distaste."

Books

Bullough, Vern L., *Science in the Bedroom: A History of Sex Research*, Basic Books, 1994.

"Clelia Duel Mosher," in *Encyclopedia of the American West*, edited by Charles Phillips and Alan Axelrod, Macmillan Reference USA, 1996.

Griego, Elizabeth, "The Making of a 'Misfit': Clelia Duel Mosher, 1863–1940," in *Lone Voyagers: Academic Women in Coeducational Universities, 1870–1937*, edited by Geraldine Jonçich Clifford, Feminist Press, 1989, pp. 149–182.

Mosher, Clelia Duel, *Health and the Woman Movement*, National Board of the Young Women's Christian Associations, 1916.

Periodicals

American Heritage, June-July 1981.

New York Times, December 24, 1940.

Stanford Magazine, March–April 2010.

Online

"Guide to the Clelia D. Mosher Papers, 1886-1938," Online Archive of California, http://www.oac.cdlib.org/ (November 21, 2011). □

Samuel Alexander Mudd

American physician Samuel Alexander Mudd (1833-1883) was convicted and imprisoned for aiding and abetting John Wilkes Booth after the actor and assassin shot United States President Abraham Lincoln in 1865. Mudd has been considered an innocent man caught up in difficult circumstances, but his involvement in the assassination remains a point of controversy. While pardoned by United States President Andrew Johnson in 1869, his name has been sullied by connection to the murder. The nature, and extent, of his involvement in the assassination remains a question in the minds of many people.

The story of Doctor Samuel Alexander Mudd, as related through the years, is a compelling one. Supposedly, he was a country doctor who found himself in the wrong place at the wrong time. Here are the basic details (which form an American legend): During the early morning hours of April 15, 1865, a man urgently knocked on the door at Mudd's farmhouse/doctor's office, seeking treatment for a broken leg. According to one version of the narrative, Mudd failed to realize that he was treating John Wilkes Booth, who hours before had fatally shot United States President Abraham Lincoln. But historic records and court testimony appear to indicate that Mudd was not quite the innocent doctor that legend would have us believe.

Mudd proved to be his own worst enemy, as his narrative of that fateful night's events stretched the limits of military investigators' credulity. Indeed, his prevarications made it hard for him to be taken at his word. He was later tried and convicted, but not for just administering treatment; he was perceived as part of a larger conspiracy that had successfully accomplished the assassination of an American president.

People like to believe that Mudd's story is a true and tragic part of American mythology, involving an innocent man who became caught up in the upheaval that involved the death of a controversial commander-in-chief during the United States' most turbulent period (which involved the Civil War and Reconstruction). Evidence from official records, as well as historical research, however, indicates that Mudd was not exactly an innocent doctor adhering to the Hippocratic Oath (a concept that means that physicians are required to administer health care non-discriminately, ethically, and effectively—in other words, all who need care must be treated, and with the utmost consideration).

Son of a Slaveowner

Doctor Mudd's story presents a troubling dichotomy: myth clashing with fact. For one thing, Mudd was the son of a slave owner residing in Maryland, a state positioned between the North and the South during the Civil War. The Mudd family sided with the states wishing to secede from the Union. In this home environment, Mudd developed attitudes toward blacks that were, if not outright racist, at least racially insensitive. Slavery, his family felt, was necessary to sustain the regional economy, and if this required human servitude, then so be it. This was the world in which Mudd was raised.

Mudd was born in Charles County, Maryland, on December 20, 1833. His parents were Henry Lowe Mudd and Sarah Ann (Reeves) Mudd. He was the fourth of their ten children. Mudd was born on his father's tobacco plantation, "Oak Hill," located about thirty miles from Washington, D.C. Here Samuel Mudd received his early education from the family's governess. Meanwhile, African-American slaves toiled his father's fields.

Expulsion Led to Medical Career

In 1849, Mudd was sent to a boarding school at St. John's College in Frederick, Maryland, to receive further education. Two years later, he enrolled at Georgetown College near Washington, D.C. (the academic institution eventually became Georgetown University). In 1852, however, after only a year at Georgetown, Mudd was expelled with several others for protesting what they felt was the too harsh discipline of another student.

Back home, Mudd considered his educational and career options. He decided to take up medicine. A relative, Dr. George Dyer Mudd, became his mentor. In 1854, Samuel Mudd entered the University of Maryland, where he received his formal medical education. He graduated in 1856 with a medical degree.

Mudd then returned to Charles County to practice medicine. In 1857, he married his childhood sweetheart, Sarah Francis Dyer. He was twenty-three years old; his wife was twenty-two. They would have nine children.

Mudd purchased a 218-acre farm in a rural area near Bryantown, Maryland, where he not only practiced medicine but also raised wheat, corn, and tobacco on his expansive property. Like his father, he was also a slave owner. His wife's family had also owned slaves for several generations. Historical records show that Mudd acquired at least nine slaves between 1859 and 1864, and later court testimony indicated that Mudd harbored harsh attitudes about the darker-skinned humans that he owned. A highly opinionated supporter of slavery, he was a Confederate sympathizer during the Civil War, and he frequently expressed his antipathy toward then-United States President Abraham Lincoln. Mudd was prone to make comments about how Lincoln's death would best serve the nation, and these statements would later come back to haunt him when he stood before the court in the national conspiracy trial. It was here on his Bryantown farm that the event occurred that would forever change his life.

Infamous Visitor Came Calling in the Night

The Samuel Mudd story that became generally accepted legend was that on April 15, 1865, at around four in the morning, a man came to Mudd's house seeking treatment for a broken leg. Mudd administered the medical care, supposedly not knowing that he was helping John Wilkes Booth, who had assassinated President Lincoln on the night of April 14 at the Ford's Theater in Washington, D.C., as Lincoln was watching a play entitled *Our American Cousin*. Booth (who was able to intrude into the unsecured theater balcony box) shot him in the back of his head with a pistol. Booth then jumped from the theater box and onto the stage, fracturing his leg in the process.

According to the narrative that depicts Mudd in a sympathetic light, Booth escaped from the theater and managed to make it into Maryland, where he sought treatment. Mudd would provide the medical solace. But through the years, details emerged that strongly suggest that Mudd was not the unwitting helper of a president's assassin, for he had established relationships with dangerous people.

Mudd was not just visited by one man on that tragic night. The door knock came from both Booth and co-conspirator David Herold. It has been established that Mudd did more than just treat Booth's leg injury. He provided the two men lodging and breakfast. Within the sanctuary that Mudd provided, John Wilkes Booth shaved off his identifiable mustache. Mudd would later provide the two men with directions to Virginia, pointing out a safe passage that would circumvent confrontation with a full-force military that had sables raised and guns loaded.

Just as Booth knew where to head, federal agents immediately moved toward Mudd's farm, and these circumstances call into question Mudd's innocence. When interrogated by Lieutenant Alexander Lovett, a military investigator pursuing Booth, Mudd denied knowing anything about the man he treated. This would later prove to be a lie; and Mudd subsequently admitted it. He did indeed know Booth, he would later reveal. At the time, military investigators already suspected as much. After subsequent questioning, which resulted from Mudd's previous evasiveness and prevarications, the country doctor was arrested.

On April 26, Booth was eventually surrounded in a Virginia farm and was shot and killed after he refused to surrender. Following Booth's death, Mudd was charged with being a co-conspirator in the Lincoln Assassination. On May 1, 1865, the newly placed President Andrew Johnson formed a nine-man military commission to try the conspirators. Along with Mudd, these included Samuel Arnold, George Atzerodt, Herold, Michael O'Laughlin, Lewis Powell, Edman Spangler, and Mary Surratt. Trials began on May 10 of that year. A conspiracy was perceived, and Mudd came to be considered a part of the plan.

Stood Trial

During Mudd's trial, information came out that he had more than an incidental or accidental acquaintance with Booth. Testimony indicated that he had lied to investigators about not knowing Booth. Several witnesses claimed they saw Mudd and Booth together on November 13, 1864, when Mudd allegedly helped Booth buy a horse. About a month later, according to testimony, Mudd and Booth were seen walking together near the National Hotel in Washington, D.C. Louis Weichmann, one of the government's main witnesses, testified that he then saw Mudd, Booth, and John Surratt engage in a private conversation. (Surratt, the son of Mary Surratt, had been introduced to Booth by Mudd. John Surratt was later tried in a separate trial, which ended with a hung jury which led to dropped charges.)

Other witnesses described John Surratt and other conspirators visiting Mudd's farm in the months leading up to the assassination. Further, a minister, William Evans, said that he saw Mudd enter Mary Surratt's boarding home in March, 1865 (Mary Surratt, John Surratt's mother, would eventually be executed [by hanging] for her alleged part in the assassination.) Also, Lieutenant Lovett testified to the commission that Mudd appeared nervous when first questioned. Indeed, Mudd's obvious anxiety aroused Lovett's suspicions.

Further, logic demands that Booth's appearance at Mudd's farm—under the cover of night's darkness—was more than just coincidence.

Mudd did not help his case with inconsistencies in his story. His attorneys argued that he had only but one brief encounter with Booth. Testimonies about a previous meeting were filled with fabrications, they said. But, to the prosecutors' minds, that didn't satisfactorily explain how and why Mudd did not recognize Booth when the assassin came to his farm. Indeed, Mudd's descriptions about that fateful night exceeded the bounds of believability.

During his trial, Mudd was confronted with inflammatory statements he made about Lincoln, as well as about slaves. Prosecutors made their case by portraying Mudd as a disagreeable man. At the same time, Mudd's attorney Thomas Ewing essentially brought the Hippocratic Oath into play: He argued that it was a doctor's job to treat a broken leg, even if the patient was an assassin and even if the doctor knew the patient was an assassin. Ewing also argued that prosecutors needed more proof that Mudd was actually part of the conspiracy. The prosecutors countered by pointing out that Mudd also went beyond the requirements of the Oath and provided Booth and Herold with the directions to their escape route.

Sentenced and Imprisoned

On June 29, 1865, the military commission found Mudd guilty of conspiracy to murder Lincoln. But, unlike the other convicted conspirators, Mudd was spared the death penalty, and by a margin of just one vote. Instead, he was sentenced to life in prison and sent to the Fort Jefferson military prison, located in the Dry Tortugas off the Florida Gulf coast.

True, much of the evidence that convicted Mudd was circumstantial. As such, even today, historians have differing views about Mudd's alleged complicity. For instance, Dr. Edward Steers, a Lincoln scholar, published a book in October 1997, *His Name is Still Mudd*, that argued a case for Mudd's guilt. The work was noted for including substantial incriminating evidence that the general public did not know about. Many assassination experts reside on Steers' side of the fence. Other historians make a case on Mudd's behalf, however. For example, in 2004, assassination expert Michael Kauffman made a convincing argument for Mudd's innocence in *American Brutus: John Wilkes Booth and the Lincoln Conspiracies.*

Still, even a casual perusal of all available literature related to the case of Dr. Mudd (and these include the books as well as official records) raise troubling questions in regard to innocence. And these questions haunt: Was Mudd an unsuspecting country doctor suddenly tossed into circumstances upon which he had no control? Apparently not, if one is to believe historic records: While being taken to prison, Mudd reportedly told his military escort, Captain George W. Dutton, that he indeed did know Booth but lied to protect himself and his family. Mudd even admitted to Dutton that he met Booth in Washington D.C. in March 1865. Further, convicted conspirator Atzerodt, right before he was executed, said Mudd played a significant role in a plan to kidnap Lincoln (the failed plan was to take Lincoln into Confederate territory in Richmond, Virginia).

Treated Prisoners for Yellow Fever

After his sentencing Mudd, along with Arnold, O'Laughin, Samuel Arnold, and Spangler were transported to Fort Jefferson. Conditions at the prison were horrid, and Mudd tried to escape on a prison supply ship. After this failed effort, Mudd was placed in irons and held in solitary confinement.

Subsequently, in 1867, an outbreak of yellow fever occurred at the prison, and the circumstances placed Mudd's reputation in a more positive light. When the prison doctor died, Mudd assumed the position and effectively treated those stricken. For Mudd supporters, these circumstances underscored their beliefs: that Mudd was a gallant doctor unjustly convicted.

Granted a Pardon

In part because of his prison medical efforts, Mudd was pardoned by President Andrew Johnson on February 8, 1869. A month later (on March 8), Mudd was released from prison. Understandably, his wife was his main advocate.

Following his release, Mudd returned home to Maryland. He resumed his medical practice, but he was also engaged in public affairs. In 1877, he ran as a democratic candidate for the Maryland House of Delegates, but his campaign was unsuccessful. Subsequently, he led a quiet life. In the last year of his life, he contracted pneumonia, a disease that proved fatal. He died on January 10, 1883. He was forty-nine years old. He was buried at the Saint Mary's Catholic Church cemetery in Byrantown, Maryland.

Doctor Mudd's story continued to intrigue, though. He was the subject of a sympathetic film, *The Prisoner of Shark Island* (1936), directed by legendary filmmaker John Ford. Typical of films of that era, however, the movie was filled with inaccuracies and fabrications. Still, it helped promote the scenario that Mudd was an innocent and conscientious doctor who got caught up in a bad situation. The film made no mention that Mudd already knew Booth before he treated the assassin's broken leg, and it strongly focused on his efforts in treating yellow fever at the Fort Jefferson prison. In 1980, a made-for-television movie, *The Ordeal of Dr. Mudd*, essentially offered the same viewpoint: that Mudd was a courageous doctor innocent of any complicity in Lincoln's murder. In the first film, Mudd was portrayed by Warner Baxter; in the second, Mudd was portrayed by Dennis Weaver.

The pardon, as well as the sympathetic film depictions, were not enough for Mudd's family. Nothing but complete exoneration would satisfy them. In particular, Mudd's grandson, Doctor Richard Dyer Mudd, was quite vehement in the matter of Samuel Mudd's innocence.

Family efforts were not without positive results. In October 1959, then-US President Dwight Eisenhower authorized the placing of a plaque at Fort Jefferson to honor Mudd and his medical efforts. Other US presidents (including Jimmy Carter and Ronald Reagan) expressed their beliefs that Mudd was innocent.

Historical records indicate that their beliefs may be misguided, however. Indeed, the jury is still out, so to speak, on the matter of Doctor Mudd's innocence. The definitive argument that truly exonerates or convincingly condemns the Maryland doctor has yet to be made.

Online

"Dr. Samuel A. Mudd," *Historynet.com,* http://www.historynet.com/dr-samuel-a-mudd.htm (November 15, 2011).

"Dr. Samuel A. Mudd," *Lincoln Conspiracy Assassination Trial,* http://law2.umkc.edu/faculty/projects/ftrials/lincolnconspiracy/mudd.html (November 15, 2011).

"Samuel A. Mudd," *Dr. Samuel A, Mudd Research Site,* http://sites.google.com/site/drsamudd/(November 15, 2011).

"Samuel Alexander Mudd," *Find a Grave,* http://www.findagrave.com (November 15, 2011).

"Samuel Mudd," *Spiritus-Temporis.com,* http://www.spiritus-temporis.com/samuel-mudd/ (November 15, 2011).

"Six Degrees of Separation—or Less," *The Smithsonian Associates Civil War E-mail Newsletter, Volume 5, Number 2,* http://civilwarstudies.org/articles/Vol_5/louise-mudd.shtm (November 15, 2011).□

Paul Muni

Paul Muni (1895-1967) is considered one of the world's great actors. Born in Austria, he became an American citizen and enjoyed great success on stage and screen. Today, he is best remembered for his film roles, particularly those in the 1930s. In 1936, he received the Academy Award for Best Actor for his performance in *The Story of Louis Pasteur*.

In a film era (Hollywood's so-called "Golden Age") that demanded classical handsomeness in leading men, Paul Muni possessed facial features that could be considered inelegant. But that helped audiences better relate to his screen persona. Like his contemporary, Edward G. Robinson, Muni transcended the appearance strictures that Hollywood placed upon "leading" males. And like Robinson, Muni was a most unlikely candidate to become a star, but stardom he achieved. His was an ordinary face, but it was also a rubber face, well fitted to the roles he was assigned. He was a character actor who assumed starring roles, and he was a method actor before that term ever came into common parlance.

Audiences knew who Paul Muni was, even if his face was buried beneath a makeup-artist's beard and wig. He portrayed Emile Zola, Louis Pasteur, and Benito Juarez. And in an era ruled by matinee idols such as Clark Gable, Muni possessed a chameleon countenance that shifted colors with each role he portrayed and that mirrored the facial profile of the common man.

Muni's influence continues even to today, with actors not content to play the same role twice. There was never a Muni screen persona. Rather, Muni buried himself in a role, perfectly content to surrender his own identity, an approach that won him the 1936 Academy Award for *The Story of Louis Pasteur*. Actress Bette Davis, who worked

with Muni, commented that "Mr. Muni seemed so intent on submerging himself so completely that he disappeared."

Muni's film reputation is enormous, even though he only made twenty-three movies. But that meager amount is not too surprising, when one takes into account that Muni never perceived himself as a "movie star." Rather, he considered himself an actor, and he found his greatest professional satisfaction on stage and not in front of the camera. He also worked on television, during that medium's early years (the 1950s), when it was still innovative and presented prestigious dramatic productions on a regular basis.

Raised in the Yiddish Theater

"Paul Muni" was the famed actor's stage name, as the future Academy Award-winner was born as Mehilem Meier Weisenfreund on September 22, 1895 in Lemberg, Austria. His parents were Nachum Favel Weisenfreund and his wife, Salche. Both were involved in the Yiddish theater. They acted, sang, and danced. This would prove a major influence on Muni's own career. When he was four years old, his family moved to London, England, where his father performed small parts in a Yiddish theater in the city's Whitechapel section, which was essentially an urban ghetto, where the infamous serial killer "Jack the Ripper" once murdered prostitutes between 1888 and 1891.

In 1901, the family (which now included mother, father, and three sons) immigrated to America, first settling in the Lower East Side section of New York City. There Muni attended public school while his parents performed in Yiddish theater companies. But the work became too meager and, in 1904, Muni's father moved his family to Cleveland. While attending the Case-Woodland Elementary School, Muni made his stage debut at the Perry Theater in 1908. Muni was only eleven years old, but he portrayed an elderly man in a play called *Two Corpses at the Breakfast Table.* The young actor made a strong impression.

Despite his success in the role, Muni's parents were not all that pleased. They preferred that their children become musicians instead of actors (Muni learned to play the violin and, later in his film career, he would play the instrument between the filming of scenes—an activity that helped foster his reputation as an eccentric). But given a taste of the stage, Muni wanted to remain an actor. He was only thirteen years old when he affirmed his career direction.

At that time, his family moved again, this time to Chicago, where Muni's parents started their own theater. The venture collapsed in 1913, however, with the death of Muni's father. Muni then took on conventional occupations to support himself while he continued performing in Yiddish theatrical companies. During World War I, he performed in Boston, Philadelphia, and New York City.

After the First World War (circa 1919), a theatrical producer named Maurice Schwartz, who established the Yiddish Art Theater in New York City—and who recognized Muni's stage skills—convinced the young actor to join his company. Muni agreed and developed a reputation as a talented and convincing character actor. Soon, he became a major figure in the Yiddish theater. During this period, he met actress Bella Finkel, who would become his wife. They married on May 8, 1921. Two years later, Muni attained American citizenship.

Until 1926, Muni remained a member of the Yiddish-speaking theater. That year he transitioned to the English-speaking theater, when he replaced Edward G. Robinson in *We Americans.* At this point, he was known as Muni Weisenfreund, and his entrance to this new theatrical realm came at an opportune time: the Yiddish theatrical tradition was coming to its end. In 1927, and still billed as Muni Weisenfreund, he scored a major success in the role of an ex-convict in *Four Walls.*

Transitioned From Stage to Screen

By this time, stage actors were in great demand in Hollywood, as the movie industry was transitioning from silent to sound films. Producers were now looking for actors that were not only physically expressive but also possessed recordable voices. Muni, who was stage-trained—his voice was rich and resonant—and willing to mask his face in makeup, scored well on both counts. In 1929, and now officially billed as Paul Muni, the ambitious actor signed with the Fox Film Corporation (which later evolved into 20th Century Fox) and appeared in the film *The Valiant.* It was a personal triumph: He received the first of his six Academy Award nominations for Best Actor. The film was a financial failure, though, as was his second film *Seven Faces,* wherein he portrayed a character (the curator of a wax museum) much older than his years (a typical Muni role). But Muni was establishing a screen presence.

Still, he was not satisfied with his film accomplishments, and he returned to the stage, the forum where he experienced his most profound satisfaction. While critics lauded his stage performances, the public stayed away: productions flopped. Muni decided to give Hollywood another try. This led to a role that solidified his stature as a screen star.

Starred in *Scarface*

In the early 1930s, when Muni was struggling on Broadway, the nation was riveted by newspaper accounts of gangster Al Capone, who rose to "underworld" power during America's ill-fated Prohibition era. Hollywood capitalized on this fascination with films such as *Little Caesar* (1930), starring Robinson, and *The Public Enemy* (1931), which made James Cagney a major movie star. These films were loosely based on Capone's criminal career and both proved enormously successful at the box office. These gave rise to the "gangster film" genre that flourished in the late 1930s and early 1940s. But perhaps the most riveting, and disturbing, early-period gangster film was *Scarface* (1932), another thinly disguised and highly fictionalized account of Capone's underworld ascension.

Rife with violence and sexual innuendo (a hint of incest), the film related the story of "Tony Camonte," a role assumed by Muni. While this vivid characterization helped cement Muni's reputation, the actor was initially reluctant. He did not want to portray that kind of individual. But Howard Hawks, the film's director, was able to persuade Muni to take on the role. The result is one of the most memorable portrayals in early Hollywood history.

The film was controversial. The industry's appointed censors felt it glorified a criminal (despite the fact that the print media had already portrayed Capone as something of a folk hero), and the depicted relationship that the overprotective "Camonte" had with his sister "Cesca" (portrayed by Ann Dvorak) made them squirm in their seats. The criticism compelled the studio, Universal, to attach a subtitle: "The Shame of a Nation." Despite the censors' discomfort, the film was a box-office hit, and it led to Muni signing a contract with Warner Brothers, a professional agreement that allowed him to continue his stage activities between film assignments.

Became a "Fugitive"

From 1931 to 1933, Muni appeared on Broadway in the Elmer Rice play *Counsellor-at-Law,* an uncompromising depiction of the legal profession. In between, in 1932, he starred in *I Am a Fugitive From a Chain Gang,* a powerful, frightening film which still impresses modern film lovers with its relentless intensity. It was based on an autobiographical novel written by Robert Elliot Burns, who was convicted of a petty robbery and sentenced to serve on a chain gang in Georgia.

The movie scored high with both critics and the public. Muni portrayed the Burns character (named "James Allen" in the movie). Directed by Mervyn LeRoy, the film depicted the harsh treatment of chain gang prisoners, and the narrative related the lead character's conviction, incarceration, escape, capture, re-incarceration, and second escape. The film's final scene haunted audiences. "How do you live," Allen's lover asks the fugitive (portrayed by an unshaven Muni). "I steal," he answers as he backs away into the shadows of the night. There, the film ends, slipping into the fadeout without a happy ending. Indeed, the film became noted for this black ending, which did not offer the satisfaction of a "happily ever after" conclusion.

Even decades after its release, it sticks in a viewer's mind. No one who has ever watched it can forget it. The film garnered three Academy Award nominations (best picture, best actor [Muni], and best sound). Although it lost in all categories, it is interesting to note that the film that did win the Best Picture Oscar that year (*Cavalcade*) is virtually forgotten. Meanwhile, the story of the "Fugitive" lingers like a recurring nightmare. Indeed, *I Am a Fugitive From a Chain Gang* is regarded as a great American film. In 1991, it was selected for preservation in the United States National Film Registry by the Library of Congress for its historical, cultural, and aesthetic significance. When released, the film was banned in Georgia (where chain gangs were prevalent), but it led to reforms in America's penal system. Muni's face and acting helped produce its power.

Starred in Warner Brothers "Biography" Films

Muni's "Fugitive"-era contract with the Warner Brothers studios was a three-picture deal. After the chain gang film, he starred in *The World Changes* (1933) and *Hi Nellie* (1934). Even though those two films did not measure up to the impact of the "Fugitive" film, Muni then signed a longer-term contract that gave him final approval on film projects, a situation that was rare during the era of the Hollywood studio system, wherein movie executives wielded great power over their stars.

In 1935, he starred in *Bordertown* and *Black Fury,* but these are now remembered only by "film buffs," as was his next film, *Dr. Socrates,*, a gangster film. But then he starred in a series of prestigious "biography" films which cemented his stardom. These included *The Story of Louis Pasteur* (1936), which earned him an Academy Award, *The Life of Emile Zola* (1937), which was an even better film, and *Juarez* (1939). Muni's "Zola" role garnered him another Academy Award nomination for best actor. Though he didn't win another Oscar, he did win the New York Film Critics' best actor award. His work led to a cover story in *Time* magazine (August 16, 1937), a laudatory profile that described him as the "first actor of the American screen."

For such roles, Muni did months of research about the historic figure he portrayed. When filming began, Muni (who by now had developed a reputation as a perfectionist) submerged his own personality beneath the role, essentially becoming the person he was portraying. He remained in character during filming and afterward.

During this period, he also played in *The Good Earth* (1937), another "prestige" picture (it was based on Pearl Buck's novel), but this one produced by Metro-Goldwyn-Mayer; and *The Woman I Love,* also released in 1937.

Curtailed Film Activity

Muni's last movie for Warner Brothers would be *We Are Not Alone,* a romantic melodrama released in 1939. That same year, he returned to the stage, appearing in the Maxwell Anderson play *Key Largo,* which was filmed in 1948 by Warner Brothers, but without Muni. Muni ended his relationship with Warner Brothers in 1940, when he turned down the offer to play the lead role in *High Sierra.*

The part eventually went to Humphrey Bogart, and it was one of the films that established Bogart as a major star.

After ending his relationship with Warner Brothers, Muni would only make eight more films, and none of these matched the artistic, critical, and popular success of his previous work. During the 1940s, he appeared in *Hudsons' Bay* (1941), a historical drama released by 20th Century Fox; *The Commandos Strike at Dawn* (1942), a wartime drama produced at Columbia; *Stage Door Canteen* (1943), wherein he made a cameo appearance as himself; *A Song to Remember* (1945), also for Columbia; *Counter Attack* (1945), another wartime drama released by Columbia, and *Angel on My Shoulder* (1946), an independent production that combined comedy and fantasy with the gangster genre (it was considered by many to be the best of his post-Warner Brothers pictures).

Also during the decade, Muni worked both in radio and on stage. In 1949, he starred in a Broadway revival of Sidney Howard's *They Knew What They Wanted*. That same year, he portrayed "Willy Loman" in a London production of Arthur Miller's *Death of a Salesman*.

In 1952, Muni appeared in an obscure Italian film *Stranger on the Prowl*. This was followed by several years of inactivity, until Muni came back strong in 1955, when he portrayed "Henry Drummond" (a character based on lawyer Clarence Darrow) in *Inherit the Wind*, the highly regarded play co-written by Jerome Lawrence and Robert Edwin Lee that fictionalized the 1925 Scopes "Monkey Trial" (which placed the teaching of evolution in the courtroom). For his performance, Muni won every major Broadway acting award, including the Antoinette Perry (Tony) Award, Donaldson Award, Variety Critics Poll, Outer Circle Award, and Newspaper Guild Page One Award.

During the 1950s, Muni also acted on television. In 1958, his performance in *Last Clear Chance*, presented on "Playhouse 90," resulted in an Emmy nomination. That same year, Muni made his last film, *The Last Angry Man*. The performance earned him yet one more Academy Award nomination.

Died in California

By the mid-1950s, Muni's health was failing (in 1955, his left had to be removed because of a tumor), and he would essentially retire from performing by the end of the decade. He lived out his remaining years with his wife, in Montecito, California. There, he died at home on August 25, 1967 from heart illness. He was 71 years old. The couple had no children, but Muni left behind an acting legacy that, fortunately, remains readily available, thanks to broadcasting outlets such as Turner Classic Movies and new video technology, such as DVD, which makes America's historic film heritage easily accessible.

Books

"Paul Muni," *Dictionary of American Biography Supplement 8: 1966-1970,* American Council of Learned Societies, 1988.

"Muni, Paul," *Encyclopaedia Judaica,* Michael Berenbaum and Fred Skolnik, eds. 2nd ed. 22 vols. Macmillan Reference USA, 2007.

"Paul Muni," *International Dictionary of Films and Filmakers Volume 3: Actors and Actresses,* St. James Press, 2000.

"Paul Muni," *St. James Encyclopedia of Popular Culture,* St. James Press, 2000.

The Great Movie Stars: The Golden Years, David Shipman, Bonanza Books, New York, 1970.

Online

"Filmsite Movie Review: I Am A Fugitive From A Chain Gang (1932)," *Filmsite.org.,* http://www.filmsite.org/iama.html (November 15, 2011).

"Paul Muni," *Biography.com,* http://www.biography.com/people/paul-muni-9418148 (November 15, 2011).

"Paul Muni," *Encyclopedia Britannica,* http://www.britannica.com/EBchecked/topic/397497/Paul-Muni (November 15, 2011).

"Paul Muni Profile," *Turner Classic Movies,* http://www.tcm.com/this-month/article/253048%7C0/Paul-Muni-Profile.html (November 15, 2011).□

N

Claude Navier

The French engineer Claude Navier (1785–1836) helped establish a scientific and mathematical basis for the practice of engineering.

When Navier began his career, many aspects of civil engineering were investigated by purely empirical means. Engineers designed and built structures out of various substances, testing them simply by repeated trials to discover their elasticity and strength. Navier built on the works of his predecessors to systematize the field of engineering and to find the basic scientific principles underlying engineering phenomena. The Navier-Stokes equations, governing fluid dynamics, are still regarded as fundamental to engineering today. Known in his day for a spectacular bridge failure for which he was hardly responsible, Navier has been remembered instead as one of the pioneers of modern engineering. Several marks of his career are still visible as parts of the Parisian landscape.

Raised and Tutored by Engineer Uncle

Claude-Louis-Marie-Henri Navier was born in Dijon, France, on February 10, 1785. His father, a lawyer who served the new French Legislative Assembly during the revolutionary period, died in 1793, whereupon his mother returned to her hometown and left him in the care of a successful relative, her uncle Emiland Gauthey. Gauthey was an engineer employed by the goverment's Office of Bridges and Roads. Widely known among French engineers, he wrote down in systematic form much of what was known about civil engineering at the time. He tutored Navier himself.

At first Navier was apparently an unenthusiastic student, scoring barely well enough to be admitted to the Ecole Polytechnique, a major technical university, in 1802. He may, in fact, have had to rely on his uncle's influence with the admissions committee. But he immediately turned his habits around during his first year, and his diligence had two lasting results. First, he was among a group of students selected to work on site at projects in the seaside city of Boulogne during his second year. And second, he was able to enter the class of the famed Jean Baptiste Joseph Fourier, a mathematician and scientist who had served Napoleon Bonaparte as governor of Egypt and who is thought to have been one of the first scientists to recognize the greenhouse effect.

Fourier became the young man's mentor and patron, and Navier's educational career shifted into high gear. He entered an advanced engineering school, the Ecole des Ponts et Chaussées (School of Bridges and Roads) in 1804, graduating with top grades in 1806. After a few months of work in the French provinces, he accepted an offer to return to Paris to edit the writings of Gauthey, who had become France's best-known engineer by the time he died in 1806. Living in modest quarters in the St.-German-des-Prés neighborhood, Navier married Marie Charlot around 1812. He had few financial resources and never became wealthy.

Revised Existing Books

Navier's engineering innovations began when he revised Gauthey's works, adding conclusions based on his own initial research into the theoretical bases of mechanics. To the first volume of Gauthey's writings, which he issued in 1809, he added very little. But between 1809 and 1812 he carried out detailed studies of the science underlying the strength of various materials, and his second volume of Gauthey's works was almost like a new book in itself.

The same was true of Navier's revision of another book, Bernard Forest de Bélidor's *Science of Engineering*, which appeared in 1813.

In the words of John David Anderson, writing in *A History of Aerodynamics and Its Impact on Flying Machines,* Navier "introduced the basic principles of engineering science to a field that previously had been almost completely empirical." Traditionally, French engineers had relied on empirical data relating to the strength of materials, conceived of as rigid objects. The founding of the Ecole Polytechnique had led to the growth of analytical approaches that conceived of materials as elastic, subject to bending according to mathematical laws. Taking a fresh approach to the study of the properties of iron, a key material for building bridges, Navier integrated these two approaches into a wealth of practical teachings that he compiled in his publications and dispensed to other French engineers.

Navier applied his new ideas himself in his career as a civil engineer with the Seine *Département,* the regional government whose territory included the city of Paris. He built the Choisy, Asnières, and Argenteuil bridges, the last two of which still exist, over the Seine River. Between 1821 and 1823, Navier visited England to study that country's rapidly growing network of railways and roads. Upon his return, he was invited to join the mechanical section of the French Academy of Sciences.

Navier maintained a busy writing schedule during these years as well, continuing to expand earlier works and to bring them up to date with original research. In the course of his work on Bélidor's *Architecture hydraulique* (Hydraulic Architecture), carried out between 1814 and 1818, he sought to make the material useful to general technical school graduates, and thus undertook a thorough review of the physics of liquids and the forces acting on them. He formulated what became known as the Navier-Stokes equations, which governed the behavior of fluids subjected to force. The equations came in two sets, one (in 1821) for incompressible and another (in 1822) for viscous fluids. The Navier-Stokes equations remain important in fluid dynamics today. The Irish physicist George Gabriel Stokes (1819–1903) refined the ideas that Navier suggested in incomplete form without full awareness of their implications.

Taught Mechanics

For much of his career, Navier made a living as an educator. Beginning as an assistant at the school, he was named professor of applied mechanics at the Ecole des Ponts et Chaussées in 1819. In 1831, he became professor of analysis and mechanics at the Ecole Polytechnique. Navier published numerous short papers on such diverse topics as the equilibrium of elastic solid bodies and the behavior of liquids in pipes. Throughout his career he divided his research between theoretical and practical questions, and he wrote operations analyses for the planned Paris-to-Le Havre railway line.

One of Navier's areas of expertise was the building of suspension bridges, and during the 1820s he planned something of a magnum opus in that field: a new suspension bridge that would cross the Seine near the splendid collection of military monuments known as Les Invalides

(on the site of today's Pont Alexandre III). As the bridge neared completion, a water main (or sewer) break at one end broke and flooded one of the landings, causing the bridge to tip to one side. Bridge engineers tried to reassure officials that the alignment problem could easily be repaired, but the Paris Municipal Council, some of whose members had opposed the construction of the bridge from the start, seized the chance to halt it for good. Despite his many other accomplishments, the bridge fiasco became the story for which Navier was best known; it was chronicled in amused tones by the top French novelist of the day, Honoré de Balzac.

Politically, Navier was a follower of the ideas of Claude Henri de Rouvray, Count of Saint-Simon, who believed that technology had the potential to usher in a socialistic utopia. Navier embraced the ideals of the Revolution, offering his services to the new government and writing reports on roads and France's still-embryonic railway system, for which he was named head inspector in 1835. He was inducted into the French Academy of Sciences, a sort of scientific hall of fame, in 1824, and was made Chevalier of the Legion of Honor, a French equivalent to knighthood, in 1831. He was depressed by the bridge failure, however, and he died in Paris on August 21, 1836, with recognition of his accomplishments still mostly in the future.

Books

Anderson, John David, *A History of Aerodynamics,* (Cambridge, 1997).

Gillispie, Charles Coulston, ed., *Dictionary of Scientific Biography,* Scribner's, 1970–1980.

Online

"Claude Louis Marie Henri Navier," *MacTutor* (St. Andrews University, Scotland), http://www.gap-system.org/~history/Biographies/Navier.html (October 28, 2011).

"NAVIER, Claude," *Planete TP,* http://www.planete-tp.com/en/navier-claude-a271.html (October 28, 2011).□

Ernesto Nazareth

The Brazilian composer and pianist Ernesto Nazareth (1863–1934) was a key figure in the development of South American music, creating models for a tradition that was neither popular nor strictly classical, but contained elements of both.

Sometimes compared to the African-American ragtime composer Scott Joplin, Nazareth was an immensely popular figure in Brazil in his day, drawing large crowds on concert tours and writing more than 200 short compositions, many of which have been played ever since by Brazilian pianists in both the classical and popular fields. He profoundly influenced the dean of twentieth-century Brazilian composition, Heitor Villa-Lobos, who (according to Joseph Stevenson of the *All Music Guide*) called Nazareth "the truest incarnation of the Brazilian musical soul." Nazareth played a key role in popularizing the tango in the late nineteenth century, and later composers such as the Argentine tango master Astor Piazzolla followed Nazareth's example directly or indirectly. Yet his career remains poorly documented, especially in English-language media.

Ernesto Júlio de Nazareth (whose last name was also sometimes spelled Nazaré) was born in Rio de Janeiro, Brazil, on March 20, 1863, and he remained a resident of Rio for his entire life. His father, Vasco Lourenço da Silva Nazareth, was a customs officer. Nazareth's mother played the piano and recognized her son's talent after some lessons; following her death, he went on to study with Eduardo Madeira and the New Orleans–born African-American composer Lucien Lambert, who had lived in France and introduced him to the short but intricate piano dance pieces of Fryderyk Chopin. Another probable influence was the composer and touring pianist Louis Moreau Gottschalk, whose music incorporated African-derived New World rhythms; Gottschalk died of malaria in Rio in 1869, but he had appeared frequently in Brazil, and his music remained popular there. Other than his childhood lessons, Nazareth was essentially self-taught in music.

By the age of fourteen, Nazareth had already published his first composition, a polka called *Você bem sabe* (You Well Know). With several more successful compositions under his belt in his teens, Nazareth began performing with other groups in the salons and clubs of well-off European-oriented Brazilians. At the same time he was drawn to Brazilian roots music, and for a time he performed with a band of street musicians called *chorinhos*. Chorinho ensembles developed a style of music called *chôro* that had a nostalgic but rhythmically vital mood, sometimes described as bluesy.

As Nazareth's catalogue of compositions grew and he mixed European and native Brazilian rhythms, the genre designations he used for them did not always have clear boundaries. Like Scott Joplin, Nazareth hungered for recognition from the classical establishment; he rejected the chôro label and its street connotations in spite of the fact that the syncopated rhythms of the chôro were unmistakable in his music, some of which sounds quite similar to Joplin's ragtime. Later in his career he did write music based on the characteristically Brazilian samba rhythm, and finally accepted the chôro designation in the work *Apanhei-te Cavaquinho*, a piece popular enough that it was arranged for numerous small ensembles.

Nazareth wrote polkas and other European dances like quadrilles and schottisches, often giving them a New World kick and designating them *marchas brasileiras* (Brazilian marches) and the like. His most characteristically European compositions were his waltzes, which were generally longer than his other works and showed Chopin's influence. The largest single group of his compositions were tangos, based on a form that had emerged in Argentina and Uruguay and then exploded in popularity across the Americas and even in Europe. Nazareth's *Tangos brasileiros* included rhythmic elements borrowed from other dances like the Brazilian maxixe (a sort of African-influenced polka) and the Cuban habanera.

In the 1880s and 1890s, Nazareth experienced steadily increasing success and made a living as a musician, not a common thing for someone of modest background in the late nineteenth century. One of his most popular works, the tango *Brejeiro* (Naughty), was published in 1893. By that time, Nazareth was married and had started a family that grew to include four children. Anxious for ready money, he sold the rights to the piece and was unable to profit from the considerable royalties it brought in later. He never got the recognition he hoped for from the classical world, but he had admirers in that sphere: some of them tried to include his music on a recital program at Brazil's National School of Music, but they were attacked by partisans of pure European styles; the controversy grew into a melee that required police intervention.

Nazareth supplemented his publishing income by giving private piano lessons, and he never gave up performing in any venue where music was needed and he could play it for profit. When motion pictures came to Brazil, he took a job playing piano in the waiting room of the Odeon movie theater, a situation that inspired his hit tango *Odeon*. These film preludes grew so popular that musicians from around Brazil would come to the theater just to hear them, and the management permitted Nazareth to expand his music-making to include the theater's in-house orchestra. Villa-Lobos played the cello for a time in the same orchestra, but sources differ as to whether the two knew each other at that time. However, Villa-Lobos certainly became acquainted with Nazareth's music.

In 1919, after the death of his daughter Maria de Lourdes in the influenza pandemic of the previous year, Nazareth took a regular job as a pianist-demonstrator in the salesroom of the Carlos Gomes music publishing house. When customers asked to try out his own compositions, he would reportedly critique their performances. Meanwhile Nazareth's own fame as a performer was growing, and he was able to take time off from his cinema and publishing house jobs to tour the Brazilian regions of Rio de Janeiro and São Paulo in 1921, and during the 1920s he undertook several other tours of Brazil.

In the late 1920s, Nazareth began to suffer from hearing loss, and his depression over that development was intensified by the death of his wife in 1929. He was able to tour as late as 1931, but eventually became completely deaf. His mental health deteriorated; he completely lost his hearing in one ear, and in 1933 he was institutionalized in Rio. On February 4, 1934, he was found dead in some nearby woods, apparently having become lost after an escape attempt. The circumstances of his death remain murky, with some accounts saying that he died of a self-inflicted wound.

During his own lifetime, Nazareth attained substantial popularity both within and beyond Brazil. According to Larry Rohter of the *New York Times*, the French composer Darius Milhaud said, "It was when I heard Nazareth that I understood the essence of the Brazilian soul," and it was likely through Nazareth that Milhaud absorbed the Brazilian rhythms that began to appear in his own music—his *Saudades do Brazil* (Nostalgia for Brazil) incorporated some of Nazareth's melodies. In Brazil itself, Nazareth's music was selected to inaugurate the programming of station Radio Sociedade in 1930. After his death, though, Nazareth's music fell into obscurity, as music split into more mutually exclusive popular and classical camps. His pieces continued to be played by student pianists in Brazil, however.

Toward the end of the twentieth century, however, Nazareth's music was rediscovered as modern Latin American composers reawakened to the region's popular music roots. Among its champions were Brazilian pianists Marcelo Bratke and Arthur Moreira Lima, as well as the Uruguayan-Dutch player Jessie de Bellis. "Catchy and unmistakable, his music is instantly recognizable, though it falls short of the demands of art music," wrote John Bell Young in the *American Record Guide.* "Nazareth's music is repetitive, structurally simplistic, and wants for variety and compositional sophistication. But no matter; it's also nostalgic, charming, and irresistible. To know it is to love it." Nazareth's colorful career awaits a full-length account in English.

Books

Sadie, Stanley, ed., *The New Grove Dictionary of Music and Musicians,* 2nd ed., Macmillan, 2001.

Slonimsky, Nicolas, ed. emeritus, *Baker's Biographical Dictionary of Musicians,* Schirmer, 2001.

Periodicals

American Record Guide, November-December 1994; July-August 1998; May-June 2005.

New York Times, September 25, 2004.

Online

"Ernesto Nazareth," *AllBrazilianMusic,* http://www.allbrazilian music.com/artistas/ver/ernesto-nazareth(September 22, 2011).

"Ernesto Nazareth," *All Music Guide,* http://www.allmusic.com/ artist/ernesto-nazareth-q7770/biography (September 22, 2011).□

Sergei Nechaev

Sergei Nechaev (1847–1882) was one of nineteenth-century Russia's most infamous revolutionaries. An extremist who advocated both regicide and wholesale terror, he stirred up trouble in Moscow and abroad before authorities arrested and successfully prosecuted him for the murder of a fellow activist. Nechaev's extremist views served as the basis for those voiced by the character Verkhovensky in Fyodor Dostoevsky's 1872 novel *Demons*.

Sergei Gennadyevich Nechaev was born on September 20, 1847 (Old Style; October 2, 1847, according to the New Style, or Gregorian calendar), in Ivanovno, a center of imperial Russia's textile-manufacturing industry. The city was home to a robust new middle class, and Nechaev initially tried to follow his father into a lucrative career as a banquet waiter at inns in Ivanovno, but loathed the nouveau riche clientele. Nechaev's father also worked as either a sign or house painter, according to conflicting reports.

Influenced by Fictional Rakhmetov

In 1865, an eighteen-year-old Nechaev moved to Moscow to continue his education. A year later, he turned up in St. Petersburg, the Russian Empire's grand capital, and was able to pass a teaching examination that qualified him to teach at a Russian Orthodox-run school called St. Sergius. He had come to St. Petersburg just after a significant event in Russian history: the first attempt by an ordinary person to assassinate the reigning tsar. The gunshot narrowly missed Tsar Alexander II, but Dmitry Karakozov's daring act— members of the ruling Romanov dynasty were anointed as divine by the patriarchs of the Russian Orthodox church— sparked a new wave of political opposition among Russians dissatisfied with the country's gross social and economic iniquities.

Karakozov was said to have been inspired by an 1863 novel, *Shto delat?* (What Is to Be Done?) by an influential populist writer, Nikolai Chernyshevsky. Chernyshevsky had actually written it and had it published while jailed at the notorious Peter and Paul Fortress, the original fort of the St. Petersburg settlement that had become a forbidding prison for enemies of the tsar. *What Is to Be Done?* was an important influence on a young generation of Russians like Karakozov and Nechaev, who was said to have followed the privations of the novel's hero, Rakhmetov, by subsisting on a diet of black bread and sleeping on a board.

Nechaev audited courses at St. Petersburg University in the late 1860s and fell in with revolutionary-minded students there during a period of intense unrest on campus. He allied with a young extremist who had already spent time inside the Peter and Paul Fortress, Petr Tkachev, and together they wrote a pamphlet they titled "Program of Revolutionary Action." They and a few others were quickly moving to the fringes of the St. Petersburg student movement known as the Nihilists, who advocated a complete overthrow of the imperial regime by the underclass. They urged swift change through a program of terror modeled on the Jacobin faction of the French Revolution, which held power through a vicious program of informants and summary executions from 1793 to 1794.

Escaped to Switzerland

Nechaev's extremist ideas alienated him from others in the student movement in St. Petersburg, and he began to consider going into exile. He met a young woman named Vera Ivanovna Zasulich, and had hoped she would flee into exile with him after asking if she knew any French or German. She declined, but fell under the sway of his revolution tirades. In January of 1869, he managed to send word to her that he had been arrested but had escaped from Peter and Paul Fortress. In reality he had made it aboard an English ship, then arrived in Belgium several weeks later and traveled on to Geneva, Switzerland. This was the home of

Mikhail Bakunin, a famous Russian exile who had been the founding architect of collective anarchism. Bakunin had nearly died inside Peter and Paul Fortress and had managed a release only through family connections, but he was a well-connected figure in European political circles for his theory of collective anarchism, which argued for the dissolution of the state and the abolition of private property. Only by seizing and controlling the means of production, Bakunin and others argued, could a truly egalitarian society emerge.

Nechaev told Bakunin he had escaped from Peter and Paul Fortress, and that there was a large secret network of anti-tsarist resisters inside Russia. This group, he boasted, had sent him to Switzerland to find Bakunin and another key theorist, Alexander Herzen, to provide financial backing for their cause. Bakunin by then had been somewhat marginalized by the leaders of the First International, a coalition of left wing groups originally formed as the International Workingmen's Association in 1864. Despite his German name, Herzen was a Russian by birth and one of the great figures of Russian socialist theory. He also controlled a large endowment left in his care by a former Russian landowner named Pavel Aleksandrovich Bakhmetev, who had sold his serfs and lands and attempted to establish a commune in the Portuguese islands of the Azores. Bakhmetev knew Chernyshevsky and was said to have been the inspiration for the Rakhmetov character.

Launched Propaganda Campaign

Bakunin quickly adopted Nechaev as his newest protégé. He introduced him to Herzen, and then to another leading theorist of the left, Karl Marx. Herzen disliked Nechaev, and sensed that much of what Nechaev was claiming about a resistance movement was pure fabrication. Marx, too, was suspicious of the young man Bakunin referred to as his "Tiger Cub." Bakunin, working with another Russian exile, the poet Nikolai Ogarev, persuaded Herzen to hand over some of the Bakhmetev rubles to fund a propaganda flood they planned for Russia. Bakunin, Ogarev, and Nechaev created leaflets with incendiary revolution proclamations and slogans, urging the assassination of the tsar and the wholesale massacre of all landowners and nobles, and mailed them to hundreds of names in Russia. As expected, postal inspectors and the tsar's police intercepted the mailings, and several inside Russia were arrested, including Zasulich. Some of the parcels included the first Russian translation of Marx's *Communist Manifesto,* which Bakunin had translated.

Among the pamphlets Nechaev wrote and sent during that spring of 1869 was his own infamous tract, *Catechism of a Revolutionary,* which can be found in its entirety on the web site *Marxists.org.* "The revolutionary is a doomed man," he asserted in its opening paragraphs. "He has no personal interests, no business affairs, no emotions, no attachments, no property, and no name. Everything in him is wholly absorbed in the single thought and the single passion for revolution." In the second paragraph, he noted that "the revolutionary...has broken all the bonds which tie him to the social order and the civilized world with all its laws, moralities, and customs, and with all its generally accepted conventions. He is their implacable enemy, and if he continues to live with them it is only in order to destroy them more speedily."

Further on, Nechaev described one of the first events of a revolution, which requires its fomenters to devise a list of "those who must be condemned to death without delay.... Those who are especially inimical to the revolutionary organization must be destroyed; their violent and sudden deaths will produce the utmost panic in the government." According to Edvard Radzinsky, author of *Alexander II: The Last Great Tsar,* Nechaev was once "asked which of the royal family should be killed," Radzinsky wrote. "He laughed and replied, the whole *ektinya* (the prayer for the tsar's family listing all the members). Young Ulyanov-Lenin would later be particularly fond of this phrase, and able to execute Nechaev's dream." Radzinsky was referring to Vladimir I. Lenin, the leader of the Russian Revolution of 1917.

Formed "Fighting Fives" Cells

Nechaev's alliance with Bakunin did not endure, but he did manage to convince Bakunin to authorize a document asserting that Nechaev was the representative for Russia of the World Revolutionary Alliance. With this in hand, Nechaev stole back into Russia, and settled into the underground community in Moscow, where few potentially recruitable students knew of his earlier plots and schemes in St. Petersburg. Forming a secret society he called *Narodnaya Rasprava,* or "People's Reprisal" (sometimes translated as "People's Retribution"), he asserted it had been in existence for decades and had many cells throughout Russia. He organized a few small cells in Moscow, but soon had a falling out with a recruit named Ivan Ivanovich Ivanov. Nechaev convinced others that Ivanov was plotting against them, and organized an attack on Ivanov that was carried out with ferocity but concluded sloppily on November 21, 1869. Ivanov was told to turn up at a nighttime hour at a grotto in the park of the Petrov Academy, where a highly coveted printing press was buried by sympathizers. Instead, Nechaev and three or possibly four others jumped Ivanov, beat him, and Nechaev tried to strangle him. When Ivanov bit Nechaev on the hand, Nechaev pulled out a pistol and shot his victim. The conspirators then pushed the body through a hole in the ice of the park's frozen lake. The body, improperly weighted with rocks, soon surfaced and within a short time the police suspected leftists at the agricultural college for the Ivanov murder.

Miraculously, Nechaev once again evaded authorities. He fled first to St. Petersburg, and by mid-December was back in Geneva. Bakunin was initially happy to see him again, but soon learned of his protégé's role in the Ivanov murder from Petr Lavrov, a well-credentialed former tsarist officer and professor of math with strong leftist sympathies. Lavrov's son-in-law was one of several dozen Moscow students implicated in the crime, which had caused a sensation in the Russian newspapers. Lavrov urged Bakunin to distance himself from Nechaev, and Bakunin did so.

Tsar Decreed "Forever"

Increasingly marginalized, Nechaev began to steal letters and documents from others, including Bakunin. In September of 1870, Nechaev went to London, then made his way to Zurich via Paris. Finally, he was tracked down at a Zurich café on August 14, 1872, and arrested. After being transported back to Russia under guard, he was tried for Ivanov's murder and found guilty on January 8, 1873. The sentence the court handed down was twenty years of hard labor, but Tsar Alexander II, who had gone over trial transcripts every day, overruled that, as his authority permitted. Instead, reported Radzinsky, the tsar "crossed out the sentence, and wrote instead: 'the fortress forever,' underlining 'forever.'"

The tsar was referring to the dreadful Peter and Paul Fortress, where the highest security detainees were kept. Even there Nechaev managed to scheme, telling his uneducated, superstitious guards there was actually an ultra-Orthodox conspiracy to remove Alexander from the throne because he was the Antichrist, and that the tsar's own son was part of the secret organization. Nechaev convinced his guards that he had been jailed because he was a part of the plot, and because of this Nechaev managed to smuggle out letters to the group *Narodnaya Volya,* or "The People's Will." This terrorist organization successfully carried out its plot to kill Tsar Alexander II in 1881. A few years later, a young revolutionary named Alexander Ulyanov was sentenced to death for his role in a plot to assassinate Alexander III, the next Romanov to rule Russia. Ulyanov's younger brother Vladimir Lenin would go on to lead the 1917 Bolshevik Revolution; several months after the abdication of the last Romanov tsar, Nicholas II, Lenin deemed it politically expedient to assassinate the former tsar, his wife, and their five children.

Inspired Dostoevsky's Novel

Nechaev died in prison in 1882, and became a footnote to Russia history. But two more stories, one real and the other fictional, emerged from his short, mostly reviled personal and political life. The first involved Vera Zasulich, who heard in 1878 that a prisoner was flogged inside Peter and Paul Fortress. Assuming it was Nechaev, she turned up at the St. Petersburg police headquarters and fired a shot from a revolver at police chief Fyodor Trepov, who survived. Zasulich was acquitted and fled the country, and was a well-known figure in revolutionary circles until her death in 1919. The other story involves the writer Fyodor Dostoevsky, who was so aghast at the Ivanov murder that he used it as the basis for one of his last novels, *Demons,* also known as *The Possessed.* The radical Verkhovensky is said to be the literary stand-in for Nechaev, predicting a future police state: "Everyone belongs to all the others, and the others belong to each one," Verkhovensky exults, according to *The Dostoevsky Encyclopedia.* "They're all slaves and equal in their slavery."

Books

Lantz, Kenneth A., *The Dostoevsky Encyclopedia,* Greenwood Publishing Group, 2004, p. 87.

McClellan, Woodford, *Revolutionary Exiles: The Russians in the First International and the Paris Commune,* Psychology Press, 1979, pp. 32–44.

"Nechayev, Sergei," *Terrorism Reference Library,* edited by Matthew May, James L. Outman, and Elisabeth M. Outman, Vol. 3: Primary Sources, UXL, 2003, pp. 37–45.

Radzinsky, Edvard, *Alexander II: The Last Great Tsar,* translated by Antonina W. Bouis, Simon and Schuster, 2005, pp. 217, 227.

Online

The Revolutionary Catechism, Marxists.org, http://www.marxists.org/subject/anarchism/nechayev/catechism.htm (October 18, 2011).□

Wallace Neff

American architect Wallace Neff (1895–1982) was one of the defining designers of the California style of the early twentieth century.

American architect Wallace Neff was one of the pioneers of the California style of the early twentieth century. Influenced by romantic Italian and Spanish styles, Neff rose to great popularity as a designer of large, extravagant homes in the heady days of 1920s Los Angeles. He worked with major Hollywood stars Mary Pickford and Douglas Fairbanks on their estate, Pickfair, for nearly a decade, and created homes for director King Vidor and other entertainment notables. Later in his career, Neff designed the unusual bubble house, a semi-circular concrete structure that he hoped could offer sturdy housing at a low price. Although primarily remembered for the Southern California homes that remained in demand by celebrities in the twenty-first century, Neff's bubble houses brought his work to such far-flung destinations as West Africa and South America.

Began Career as Architect

A native of the Southern California town of La Mirada, the architect was born Edwin Wallace Neff on January 28, 1895. His parents had come to California less than a year before his birth to live on a ranch owned by Neff's maternal grandfather Andrew McNally, a mapmaker and founder of publishing firm Rand McNally. In the late nineteenth century, much of Southern California was undeveloped; despite being just twenty miles from central Los Angeles, the area surrounding La Mirada—which McNally developed himself—was sufficiently wild to permit the existence of the 700-acre lemon and olive fields of the family ranch. La Mirada grew slowly, and Neff and his siblings mostly attended school in Altadena, near the community of Pasadena. As a teenager, Neff went with his family to live in Switzerland and Germany while a younger sister underwent treatment for a heart defect. This European sojourn helped shape the young Neff's ideas about architecture and design. While traveling throughout the continent from England to Italy, Neff observed and sketched buildings and artworks that appealed to him. He also studied landscape painting and drawing.

With the outbreak of World War I in 1914, the Neff family returned to Southern California. By then of age to begin university studies, Neff found that his somewhat informal education up to that point presented an obstacle to pursuing higher learning; the Throop College of Pasadena (now the California Institute of Technology) declined to admit him in 1915, much to Neff's dismay. He later won admission to the architecture program at the Massachusetts Institute of Technology (MIT) on the basis of the strength of his sketches and his first-hand knowledge of European architecture and design. At MIT, Neff studied under Ralph Adams Cram, one of the leading architects of the day, and continued to impress instructors and classmates with his drawing skills. War again interrupted Neff's life, however, and he left the school to return to California after the United States entered World War I in 1917. As Alson Clark explained in the introduction to *Wallace Neff: Architect of California's Golden Age,* Neff was "never intensely political and almost never belligerent, [so] he did not rush to get into the service. He had lived in Germany and had friends there with whom he corresponded." Instead, Neff found work with the Fulton Shipbuilding Company in Wilmington, California, to help construct wooden cargo ships. He also continued his education by studying naval architecture at the University of Southern California.

The end of the war in 1919 allowed Neff's architectural career to at last begin in earnest. His mother commissioned him to design a small cottage in Santa Barbara, and Neff set about devising a functional home influenced by the historical buildings he had examined in Europe. After completing this project, he worked for a time with the Hollywood office of the Frank Meline Company, a housing developer. Shortly after receiving his architect's license in 1921, Neff opened his own office in Pasadena, and soon received commissions for traditional colonial-style houses. Before long, however, Neff began designing the Spanish- and Italian-influenced homes that became the hallmark of the California style. The growing popularity of that form helped bring Neff to national notice among architectural circles, and his number of commissions rose so quickly throughout the decade that he undertook only large and expensive buildings by the end of the decade. The decade also marked a time of personal change for the young architect, who married a local woman, Louise Up de Graff, in 1923. The couple had two sons and one daughter between 1926 and 1932 before separating in 1935.

Built Lavish Hollywood Homes

Among Neff's clients during these pre-Depression years were some of the leading figures of the entertainment industry centered in Hollywood. In 1923, he undertook a commission to design a sprawling estate for movie cowboy Fred Thomson and his wife, screenwriter Frances Marion. The pair had originally hired a different architect for the project, but he recommended Neff as a replacement when he left the area. The completed ranch contained multiple structures including stables, an aviary, terraces, and a massive pool, all decorated with fanciful grandeur. The project attracted a great deal of attention both nationally and locally, and Marion introduced Neff to silent film star Mary Pickford. Pickford and her husband Douglas Fairbanks owned several acres of land in Beverly Hills that had come with a house, but the couple were not satisfied with the dwelling. Between 1926 and 1934, Neff oversaw the renovation of the main house along with the design and construction of several new buildings for the property, including a guest house, a stable, and a garage. Although the resulting estate was not fully a Neff original, the immense fame of the property's owners made Pickfair the project most closely associated with his name. He also designed homes for director King Vidor, MCA studio founder Jules Stein, and later, actress Claudette Colbert.

Neff believed that the homes he designed should reflect the lifestyles and needs of the people who lived there. He worked to channel what he saw as the essence of his clients into physical form, striving to create buildings that matched the outlooks of their inhabitants. For his silver screen clients, Neff often included slightly oversized details that some observers have argued reflected their inhabitants' own larger-than-life status. Speaking to Amy M. Spindler of the *New York Times,* real estate agent Barry Sloane explained that Neff "had this wonderful theatrical flair. . . . The frivolity, the touches he did. He was a master of scale proportion."

Developed the Bubble House

During the 1940s, Neff created the building that would define the second half of his career: the bubble house, also known as the "Airform" house. Conceived as a way to construct durable housing at a low cost, the house was originally intended as a way to provide inexpensive, adequate shelter for people unable to afford a traditional free-standing home; thus, Neff saw the venture as both a potential source of profit and a humanitarian effort. Indeed, his plan did allow for the construction of cheap houses around the world. To create a bubble house, Neff first secured a Goodyear rubber balloon to a stable concrete slab. Then, he covered the bubble shape formed by the balloon with layers of concrete and insulation. The resulting structure was both durable and somewhat larger than might be expected; the sole surviving bubble house in the United States—built for Neff's brother and later home to the architect himself—boasts roughly 1,000 square feet of floor space, two bedrooms, and a maximum ceiling height of 12 feet at its central apex. Although this was tiny compared to the sprawling mansions that Neff had designed for celebrities, it was not out of line with the contemporary suburban dwellings that home builders began developing after World War II. The typical Levittown two-bedroom ranch, for example, spanned just 800 square feet. "We opened the front door and it was like we were stepping into the New York World Fair's House of Tomorrow," recalled Steve Roden, who with his wife purchased Neff's Pasadena bubble house in 1998, to Tina Daunt of the *Los Angeles Times*.

Despite its innovative qualities and relatively low construction costs, the bubble house never generated much excitement in the United States. Consumers lacked interest, and local governments were reluctant to grant the architect permission to build the unusual structures. This concern was not entirely unwarranted; the bubble house that Neff built for his brother collapsed twice before being successfully executed. "I always thought people would come rushing in by the thousands to buy houses," Neff was quoted as saying at a 1977 Pasadena Historical Society meeting in the same article by Daunt. "But it never happened," Neff concluded. Foreign governments were somewhat more welcoming, however, particularly those in developing countries. During the 1940s and 1950s, Neff constructed bubble houses in Central and South America, the Middle East, and West Africa, where entire villages were erected using the simple structure. Of the small number of U.S. bubble houses, only the Neff home in Pasadena survived into the twenty-first century.

Architectural trends shifted after World War II, with modernist styles becoming more popular than the traditional California forms that Neff had designed before the Depression. Despite his bubble houses, the majority of Neff's work through the 1950s and 1960s only nodded to modern forms, and architectural magazines and critics ceased to pay much attention to his work. "What this did to the morale of Neff...is difficult to analyze," Clark acknowledged, "but it was surely not beneficial to [his] confidence in [himself] as [a designer]. So it is no wonder that much of the work of the fifties lacked the excitement and the sensibility of the prewar oeuvre." Neff remained

reasonably popular, however, with his office typically overseeing the design and construction of five to ten buildings at any given point. Among the more important of his homes during this period were the 1962 Roy Eaton House and the 1969 Robert K. Straus House, both in Santa Barbara, along with the 1970 Henry Singleton House in Holmby Hills.

Neff continued to work into his 70s, giving design and construction direction via telephone after declining health made him unable to drive to job sites. He spent his final years in retirement in a home that he had designed in the mid-1940s for a family member in Pasadena. Neff died from complications of pneumonia in Pasadena on June 8, 1982. He was interred soon after at Mountain View Cemetery and Mausoleum in Altadena.

Neff's greatest memorials, however, remain standing through the Los Angeles region: his houses. Decades after the architect's death, Hollywood celebrities several generations removed from Neff's original star clients continued to seek out the historic homes. Celebrity couple Brad Pitt and Jennifer Aniston famously lived in a Neff home during their marriage, and other high-powered fans of the twenty-first century included Madonna and Diane Keaton. But not all of Neff's famed homes survived changing times and tastes, including Pickfair, which was torn down in the 1980s. "As wonderful as these are, they were built for a different time," real estate agent Loren Judd told David Keeps of the *Los Angeles Times*. "Kitchens were small working rooms, not the heart of the house. If you wanted something to eat, you'd call the cook to prepare it. Unfortunately, we've lost a lot of the great estates because people didn't have the vision to respect the architecture." Yet the attention given to Neff a century after his peak stands in testament to the power of his creative legacy.

Books

Neff, Wallace, Jr., ed., *Wallace Neff: Architect of California's Golden Age,* Capra Press, 1986.

Periodicals

Los Angeles Times, March 18, 2004; March 18, 2004.
New York Times, June 11, 1982; October 7, 2001.

Online

"Wallace Neff—Airform Dome Pioneer," *Mortarsprayer.com,* http://www.mortarsprayer.com/thin-shell-construction/wallace-neff/ (October 4, 2011).□

O

Barack Obama

The American political leader Barack Obama (born 1961) made history in 2008 when he became the 44th President of the United States and the first African American to hold that office.

Elected by a convincing margin in 2008, Obama rode into office on a wave of national euphoria. Yet his presidency has proven one of the most contentious of modern times, marked by grueling legislative struggles, a major electoral setback in 2010, and continuing threats of a government shutdown the following year as Obama and members of his Republican Party congressional opposition wrangled over tax and budgetary questions. In spite of major legislative accomplishments involving health-care reform and other issues, as well as notable foreign policy successes, he faced questions from voters regarding his handling of the American economy as the 2012 general elections approached and the country struggled to recover from its deepest economic recession in decades.

Product of Kenyan-American Marriage

Barack Hussein Obama Jr. was born at Kapi'olani Medical Center in Honolulu, Hawaii, on August 4, 1961. His family background was unusually complicated; reflecting on it, singer-songwriter Bob Dylan told Obama biographer David Remnick, writing in *The Bridge: The Life and Rise of Barack Obama,* that "he's like a fictional character, but he's real." Obama's father, Barack Obama Sr., was a Kenyan exchange student whose father, a member of the Luo tribe, was a goat herder. The elder Barack Obama met the future president's mother, Kansas-born white American Ann Dunham, when

both were students at the University of Hawaii; Dunham was later active as an anthropologist. The marriage between Obama's parents dissolved in 1964, and three years later Ann Dunham married another foreign graduate student, Indonesian graduate student Lolo Soetoro. Obama has a half-sister, Maya Soetoro-Ng.

The family moved to Jakarta, Indonesia, settling in a modest neighborhood where Obama attended a Catholic school, St. Francis of Assisi. As their situation improved, they moved to the prosperous Menteng neighborhood in South Jakarta and enrolled Barack in the public but elite Menteng State Elementary School 01, then called Model Primary School Menteng 1. The student body there was predominantly Muslim, but Obama recalled that he did not take religious instruction at either school very seriously. He learned to speak Indonesian fairly well, however, and Jakarta resident Elizabeth Bryant told Janny Scott of the *New York Times* that Obama had been marked by Indonesian ways: "He has the manners of Asians and the ways of Americans—being *halus* [polite, refined], being patient, calm, a good listener." When Obama was ten, he was sent to Hawaii to live with his maternal grandparents in Honolulu, where he attended the Punahou prep school. Obama, known at the time as Barry, struggled with his mixed-race identity and experimented with drugs. Even so, he excelled at basketball and graduated with honors from Punahou in 1979.

Obama attended Occidental College in Los Angeles for one year, but after a visit to his mother in Indonesia he transferred to Columbia University in New York. He hoped to find, and did find, a more diverse environment there, but he also became more aware of the American racial divide than he had been in laid-back, multicultural Hawaii. "I began to grasp the almost mathematical precision with which America's race and class problems, joined; the depth, the ferocity, of resulting tribal wars; the bile that flowed

freely not just out on the streets but in the stalls of Columbia's bathrooms as well, where, no matter how many times the administration tried to paint them over, the walls remained scratched with blunt correspondence" between blacks and Jews, Obama recalled in his autobiography, *Dreams from My Father.* He graduated from Columbia in 1983 with a political science major and a concentration in international relations.

Worked as Community Organizer

After working for a year for an internationally oriented business publisher, Obama decided to become a community organizer. "There wasn't much detail to the idea; I didn't know anyone making a living that way," he wrote in *Dreams from My Father.* "When classmates in college asked me just what it was that a community organizer did, I couldn't answer them directly." Obama moved from New York to Chicago, working with the Developing Communities Project on job-training and student-tutoring programs. It was during this period that Obama began to identify himself more closely with African-American culture as he explored life on Chicago's South Side and realized that, no matter what the intricacies of his background might be, American society would always view him as black. Large sections of *Dreams from My Father* describe Obama's introduction to life in Chicago and his thoughts on the ways the lives of poor African Americans might be improved. Eventually he rejected (according to Remnick) the "suspicion of politics" that ran through the traditions of community organizing in which he was working. He began to think of a political future for himself, and for an unknown young African American without major financial resources, that meant law school was the next step.

Elected President of *Harvard Law Review*

At Harvard Law School, Obama's academic gifts bloomed fully for the first time. He was elected by his peers to the presidency of the *Harvard Law Review* publication, a prestigious post that he was the first African American to hold. He earned a JD degree *magna cum laude* from Harvard in 1991. During this period he spent two summers as an intern at Chicago's Sidley Austin law firm, where Princeton-trained attorney Michelle Robinson, a native of Chicago's South Side, was his assigned mentor. The two fell in love, marrried in 1992, and had two children, Malia (born in 1998) and Natasha, known as Sasha (born in 2001).

By the mid-1990s Obama's political potential was becoming clear, and the publisher Crown signed him to write the book that became *Dreams from My Father.* In the middle and late 1990s he taught courses in constitutional law at the University of Chicago and was offered a tenure-track position there. With his eye on a political career, he turned it down. Obama was elected to the Illinois state senate from his South Side Hyde Park neighborhood in 1996. In 2000, he declared his candidacy for the U.S. House of Representatives but suffered his only loss to date when he was trounced by veteran South Side politician Bobby Rush. "I was completely mortified and humiliated, and felt terrible," he told Remnick. "The biggest problem in politics is the fear of loss. It's a very public thing, which most people don't have to go through."

Elected to Senate

The House run did expose Obama to a wider range of politically oriented Chicagoans, and he developed a strong following among progressive voters impressed by his early and unequivocal opposition to the Iraq War. In 2004, he bounced back with a victory in the Democratic primary for one of Illinois U.S. Senate seats, defeating longtime Chicago politician Thomas Hynes and millionaire Blair Hull. Obama's eloquent speech at the 2004 Democratic convention in Boston, hailed as one of the best convention speeches in history, put him on the national political radar, and his resounding victory over Republican candidate Alan Keyes continued to fuel talk of higher office. In 2006, Obama published the book *The Audacity of Hope,* using it as a springboard for the presidential campaign he launched in February of 2007.

Obama was sufficiently different from any previous presidential candidate that it was difficult to evaluate his chances against two more conventional candidates, New York senator (and former First Lady) Hillary Rodham Clinton and North Carolina senator John Edwards. Obama's victory in the delegate-selection caucuses held in the overwhelmingly white state of Iowa gave an indication of what was coming, but the nomination contest between Obama and Clinton that followed was hard-fought, with the lead changing hands several times. Obama had to fend off controversy resulting from racially charged comments made by his Chicago pastor, the Rev. Jeremiah Wright, whom he eventually repudiated. By early June of 2008, Obama had clinched the Democratic nomination. He selected Delaware senator Joseph Biden as his vice-presidential running mate.

In the 2008 general election, backers of Republican candidate and Vietnam War hero John McCain attempted to paint Obama as insufficiently experienced for the presidency, with some suggesting that he harbored concealed radical positions based on his affiliation with Wright and his activities in Chicago prior to entering politics. Obama countered with strong performances in a series of debates with McCain and with a widely viewed half-hour television infomercial aired a week before the election. On November 4, 2008, he defeated McCain by a substantial margin of 365 to 173 in the electoral college, amassing almost ten million more votes than his opponent. He was inaugurated as President of the United States on January 20, 2009.

Obama's election was internationally recognized as a historic event, but it was particularly significant for African Americans who had experienced the violent regime of American racial segregation. Georgia U.S. Representative John Lewis, whose skull had been fractured by Alabama state police during a civil rights demonstration in 1965, told the *New Yorker* at the inauguration that "Barack has lifted people. Old people, young people, children, black and white. Look out on the Mall here. You can see it in their walk, can't you?"

Promoted Stimulus Package

The usual honeymoon of good will accorded to newly elected presidents was intense but short in Obama's case. In spite of the fact that his Democratic Party had an almost filibuster-proof majority in both houses of Congress, his initiatives encountered strong opposition almost from the start. The economy, which had begun a sharp contraction at the end of the administration of Obama's predecessor, George W. Bush, plummeted in 2009, and the bleeding was stanched but not stopped by a $787 billion economic stimulus package that Obama shepherded with difficulty through Congress. Obama enjoyed stronger support in passing a bailout package for bankrupt auto manufacturers General Motors and Chrysler (which Bush had also aided financially), but that plan too drew Republican opposition from, among others, 2012 Republican presidential candidate Mitt Romney.

Perhaps the most contentious issue of Obama's first term was his attempt to deliver on his promise of universal health care, a goal that had eluded his Democratic predecessors. His administration rolled out his health-care reform proposals in the spring and summer of 2009, basing them on an idea—health insurance exchanges that would control costs by negotiating with care providers—that in the past had been advocated by both Democrats and Republicans. Trying to gain Republican votes and hold those of moderate and conservative Democrats, Obama infuriated liberal supporters by dropping a publicly funded option from the final bill. Obama signed the Patient Protection and Affordable Care Act into law on March 23, 2010, but as of 2012 it faced a court challenge over its requirement that all consumers carry health insurance. The court battle was expected to reach the U.S. Supreme Court.

With controversy over the health care law festering and the economy in tatters, Obama's Democrats suffered major setbacks in the 2010 midterm elections, losing their House of Representatives majority. The year 2011 was marked by repeated conflicts between Obama and congressional Republicans, who delayed approval of normally routine fiscal measures in order to extract deficit-cutting concessions from Obama, bringing the government to the brink of a shutdown. Obama faced less criticism on the foreign policy front as he supervised a successful operation on May 1, 2011, that killed Osama bin Laden, the mastermind of the September 11, 2001, terrorist attacks in New York and Washington, D.C., at his compound in Abbottabad, Pakistan. Even with incremental improvements in the economy in late 2011 and early 2012, however, Obama faced a close re-election battle against his Republican opponent.

Books

Contemporary Black Biography, vol. 74, Gale, 2009.

Obama, Barack, *Dreams from My Father: A Story of Race and Inheritance,* Crown, 1995.

Remnick, David, *The Bridge: The Life and Rise of Barack Obama,* Knopf, 2010.

Periodicals

Ebony, November 2004; November 2005.

Los Angeles Times, February 5, 2012.

New York Times, April 4, 2011; April 24, 2011.

New Yorker, May 31, 2004; February 2, 2009.

Washington Post, May 1, 2011.

Online

"Barack Obama: President of the United States," *Washington Post,* http://www.washingtonpost.com/politics/barack-obama/gIQAp4524O_topic.html (February 1, 2012).

"Obama's Indonesian Childhood: Facts vs. Myths," *Jakarta Globe* (March 23, 2010), http://www.thejakartaglobe.com/home/obamas-indonesian-childhood-facts-vs-myths/365325 (February 1, 2012). □

Red Hugh O'Donnell

The Irish chieftain Red Hugh O'Donnell (1572–1602) was a key leader of Irish forces during the Nine Years War fought by Celtic tribes against the armies of England's Queen Elizabeth I.

O'Donnell may have been a casualty of the war, dying under mysterious circumstances during a trip to Spain to seek help from England's historical enemy. He lived for only thirty years, but his life was the stuff of legend. Imprisoned by the English as a teen, he escaped and was given a high title in the Celtic hereditary world, The O'Donnell, Prince of Tir-Connaill, in 1593. Embittered by the growing power of Ireland's English overlords, he helped cement a league of Gaelic princes that drove Elizabeth's armies out of Ireland for several years.

Son of Irish Chieftain

Red Hugh O'Donnell, also known as Hugh Roe O'Donnell, was born in late October of 1572, in the Irish chieftancy of Tir Connaill, covering much of present-day County Donegal in the northern part of the Irish Republic. His Irish name was Aodh Rua Ó Dónaill. He was the oldest of four sons and at least three daughters born to Tir Connaill's chief, Hugh McManus O'Donnell and his wife, Ineen Dubh, also known as Fionnghuala McDonnell. The political situation in which he grew up was complex, with Irish chieftains jockeying for influence among themselves while trying to resist English encroachment. In parts of Ireland where English influence was already strong, some Irish leaders contended for administrative posts or reached diplomatic arrangements with the invaders. O'Donnell's mother, backed by her own contingent of Scottish mercenaries, known as redshanks, was no helpless onlooker but a formidable power in her own right.

Not much is known of O'Donnell's childhood. As a member of an Irish chieftain's family he would have been taught horsemanship and the arts of war beginning at a very early age. He would also have had academic tutors. He spoke Irish Gaelic; despite his father's attempts to make peace with the English, he never learned to speak the English language well, but it was said that as an adult he could understand it. One of O'Donnell's half-sisters (his father had numerous illegitimate children) was married off in an attempt to form a political alliance with a rival prince, and O'Donnell himself was used as a political tool by his parents: he was sent to live in the houses of other princes in a kind of exchange of foster care arrangements. As the elder O'Donnell's web of alliances shifted, O'Donnell moved from place to place several times. While back at home, his mother strove to encourage a prophecy that he would be the leader who drove the English out of Ireland.

The formative event of O'Donnell's young life occurred in September of 1587, as relations deteriorated between the Irish clans and the English administration. Queen Elizabeth's Lord Deputy, Sir John Perrot, possibly acting with the direct approval of the Queen, decided to teach the Irish a lesson. He hired a Dublin merchant ship, loaded it with Spanish wines and luxury goods, and concealed a brigade of soldiers aboard. The ship was sent to northern Ireland, which at the time was still under the control of Gaelic clans, under the pretext that Irish leaders were to be offered the merchandise. Red Hugh O'Donnell, along with the sons of two other princes, were invited aboard to sample the merchandise, whereupon their bodyguards were subdued and they were seized.

Held Hostage in Tower

O'Donnell spent the next four years as a prisoner in a tower at Dublin Castle, with Perrot warning the O'Donnell clan that he would remain unharmed only as long as the situation in northern Ireland was peaceful. The Ulster region soon faced larger concerns: the English in 1588 went to war with and then defeated the 130-ship Spanish Armada that had been meant to pave the way for a Spanish invasion of England. Thousands of Spanish soldiers made their way to the Irish coast and were pursued by both the English and the Irish, throwing the region into disarray. Hugh McManus O'Donnell seized a Spanish contingent and wanted to trade the men for his son, but another chieftain, Hugh O'Neill, convinced him that the Irish might need Spanish help against the English in the future, and O'Donnell remained in his cell, his hatred for the English growing.

In January of 1591, O'Donnell and several comrades rappelled down the side of the castle, landing on a bridge, and managed to flee Dublin. O'Donnell made it as far as the home of a sympathetic Irishman, Phelim O'Toole, but he was cut off from Irish territory by a flooded river and was soon recaptured. He tried again on January 6, 1592, known in Ireland as Little Christmas. This time his escape attempt succeeded, because the castle constable lay dying, and possibly also because English officials had been bribed. O'Donnell was better prepared with heavy clothing this time than on the first attempt, but he and fellow escapee Art O'Neill ran into cold weather as they fled into the Wicklow Mountains. O'Donnell survived by using the body of the lifeless O'Neill as a blanket but had to have both of his big toes amputated after his shoes froze to his feet.

O'Donnell returned to Ireland a hero, and his aging father abdicated in his favor, making his son The O'Donnell— the leader of Clan O'Donnell, a status O'Donnell assumed as he stood on the ancestral Rock of Doone in May of 1593. At the same time, the O'Donnells' rival, Hugh O'Neill, renounced his English title of Earl of Tyrone and became The O'Neill. Alarmed English forces attacked a fort belonging to the chief known as The Maguire, who had brought O'Donnell back to Ireland, and The Maguire asked O'Donnell for help. When O'Donnell complied by attacking the English, the Nine Years War began.

Led Victory over English

The first years of the war resulted in a nearly unbroken series of Irish victories. Some were due to the contributions of Hugh O'Neill, who had received English military training and could guess the tactics that might be used by their commanders. At the head of an army of 7,000 foot soldiers and 1,000 cavalry riders, O'Donnell, Maguire, and O'Neill moved toward a key crossing point on the Callan River known as the Yellow Ford. The English army suffered a massive defeat in the Battle of Yellow Ford on August 14, 1598, and all of Ireland seemed to be within the reach of the clan leaders. Elizabeth responded by dispatching a 25,000-man army under the Earl of Essex to halt the Irish advance.

At first the situation went from bad to worse for the English, as their advance forces were picked off by Irish fighters hiding in the Wicklow Mountains. O'Donnell defeated an English contingent at Curlew Pass in County Roscommon, where a statue in his honor still stands today. Essex, who was laying plans for a rebellion against Elizabeth, offered O'Neill and O'Donnell a truce, left the army, and returned to London. An outraged Elizabeth imprisoned him in the Tower of London and ordered an execution that turned gruesome when an inexperienced executioner required six blows to cut his head off.

The Irish victory seemed complete, but O'Donnell and O'Neill were not the only leaders of the time to underestimate Elizabeth. She dispatched Charles Blount,

Lord Mountjoy, who made several successful sea landing and then implemented an early version of scorched-earth tactics, engaging in large-scale destruction of crops and causing widespread hunger. O'Donnell asked for Spanish assistance, a move that could very well have worked; in the words of historian Darren McGettigan, writing in *Red Hugh O'Donnell and the Nine Years War,* "What marks O'Donnell out as a truly remarkable leader was his Spanish alliance." A battalion of 4,000 Spanish soldiers arrived in Ireland, but Mountjoy succeeded in cutting them off from the main Irish force. At the battle of Kinsale in 1601, O'Donnell led a cavalry charge against an English force but was frustrated by the novel technique of trench warfare used by the English. The battle ended in a disastrous defeat for the Irish, made worse by a long retreat through famine-stricken lands.

With Elizabeth in poor health, O'Donnell still hoped to outlast the English and set off for Spain to ask for additional help from King Philip III. At Simancas Castle, on September 10, 1602, he suddenly became ill and died. Historians have disagreed over whether he was poisoned, and his grave, at a Franciscan monastery in Spain's Valladolid region, has disappeared. He was memorialized in the song "O'Donnell Abu," which almost became the Irish national anthem when independence was achieved more than three centuries later, and which remains the official song of America's Ancient Order of Hibernians.

Books

McGettigan, Darren, *Red Hugh O'Donnell and the Nine Years War,* Four Courts, 2005.
New Catholic Encyclopedia, Gale, 2003.

Periodicals

Irish History, September 2009.

Online

"O'Donnell," *The Internet Heraldry Store,* http://www.araltas.com/features/odonnell/ (October 12, 2011).
"*Story of Ireland,* by A.M. Sullivan," *Library Ireland,* http://www.libraryireland.com/Atlas/XXXIX-Red-Hugh-ODonnell.php (October 12, 2011). □

Fritz Von Opel

German engineer Fritz von Opel (1899–1971) made aviation history in 1929 in a rocket-propelled aircraft he flew above a Frankfurt airfield. A grandson of the founder of the automotive dynasty that carries the family name, von Opel placed his life in peril for this event and many times over, in his quest to create the world's first rocket-powered planes and race cars. "It is marvelous to fly like this," he wrote in an article that ran in the *New York Times* on October 1, 1929, a day after his historic flight. "When we are able to make full use of this gas we shall be able to fly around the world in under five hours."

Fritz von Opel was born on May 4, 1899, in Rüsselsheim, Germany. His grandfather Adam Opel was one of the country's first manufacturers of sewing machines, and in the last decades of the nineteenth century Adam's five sons helped the company make the transition into a successful bicycle manufacturing enterprise. The second son, Wilhelm, was the father of Fritz, and he played a key role in moving the company into the nascent automobile industry at its massive plant in Dessau, Germany. In 1912, on the fiftieth anniversary of the founding of Adam Opel's sewing machine company, the Grand Duke of Hesse ennobled the family, which permitted them to add the "von" to the Opel surname.

Studied Engineering in Darmstadt

Von Opel had a younger sister, Eleonore, and was fifteen years old when World War I erupted. He enlisted in the imperial German army, and after the war's end in 1918 entered the technical university in Darmstadt to study engineering. He joined the family firm at an exciting time in the early 1920s, when significant technological and aerodynamic advances spurred designers and engineers to build much faster cars. As director of testing for Opel, he personally demonstrated the safety of its products at racing events. When a new test track was completed outside Berlin in 1921, he won the first-ever car racing event held at the Avus Speedway. This was a 12-mile-long straightaway with a hairpin loop at the northern end. Its name was an acronym for the Automobil-Verkehrs- und Übungs-Strasse (Automobile Traffic and Practice Road), and it later became part of the country's highway system after its hairpin turn was eliminated. The automaker Opel eventually built its own test track near the company's headquarters in Rüsselsheim.

Germans of von Opel's generation were swept up in der Raketenrummel, or mania for new rocket-powered technology. Hermann von Oberth, a Transylvanian German physicist, published an influential book in 1923 titled *Die Rakete zu den Planetenräumen* (The Rocket into Planetary Space). Von Oberth posited that space travel would become a genuine possibility through the principles of rocket propulsion, which relied on an intense discharge of energy, ignited by explosion, to give an object astonishing thrust power. A few eager experimenters founded Germany's *Verein für Raumschiffahrt (VfR)* or Spaceflight Society, to work toward the goals of French author Jules Verne's landmark science-fiction novel of 1865, *From the Earth to the Moon*.

Max Valier was one of the founders of the VfR. He was a few years older than von Opel and had studied at the university in Innsbruck, Austria, before World War I. Valier was conducting experiments on the differences between solid-fuel and liquid-fuel rockets when von Opel, already a well-known daredevil on the automotive and boat racing circuit, began funding Valier's efforts with the hope of creating the world's first rocket-propelled vehicle. Valier brought on board Friedrich Wilhelm Sander, an entrepreneur whose company used gunpowder to make signal flares, an early type of rocket technology.

Used Fortune to Fund Rocket Vehicles

Von Opel did not test drive the first rocket car, the RAK.1, at the Rüsselsheim track on March 15, 1928. An Opel employee and racer named Kurt Volckhart drove it—despite von Opel's eagerness to test it himself—and Volckhart managed to get the RAK.1 up to just 47 miles per hour in a cloud of smoke in a 35-second run. But on May 23, 1928, von Opel took the wheel of an Opel racer refitted with Sander's powerful blast rockets for a demonstration at a well-publicized event at the Avus track. Von Opel had drummed up significant publicity, including a national radio broadcast and several high-profile invitees, among them the president of the German Weimar Republic, famed military hero General Paul von Hindenburg, and senior government officials.

Von Opel gunned the RAK.2 to 143 miles per hour after pressing the pedal that fired the rocket engine perfected by Valier and Sander. "There was a loud hissing sound and then a deafening roar," reported a *Times* of London correspondent. "Some of the more nervous spectators made a dive for safety, and the craning heads were quickly withdrawn as a black object with a flaming tail several feet long hurtled past." A cloud of heavy black smoke descended, and nervous laughter broke the stunned silence of the onlookers as they waited for Opel and his rocket-racer to return. "There was a momentary glimpse of the driver with his hair streaming straight out behind him," reported the correspondent.

There were three significant milestones in von Opel's rocketry career. The first was the RAK.2 test run on May 23, 1928. Another came nineteen days later on June 11 when he, along with Valier and Sander, visited an unusually shaped plateau in Hessen's Rhön Mountains called the Wasserkuppe. The elevation had been the site of several experiments in glider flight, and it was there that they had met an

aviation engineer named Alexander Lippisch, who was testing a tail-less aircraft a few months earlier. On June 11, a Lippisch-built glider called the *Ente* (German for "duck") made a test flight after it had been specially outfitted with twin rockets by von Opel, Valier, and Sander. The Ente made one test flight with a single rocket, but a second attempt later that day resulted in a mid-air explosion that might have ended the life of a less experienced pilot than Fritz Stamer, who managed to bring the damaged craft back to the ground. Despite the failure, this was the first successful flight of a rocket-powered aircraft in aviation history.

Spent 75 Seconds Aloft over Frankfurt

After some failures with the rocket-fueled car, von Opel returned to his dream of building a rocket plane. He teamed with a German aircraft designer, Julius Hatry, and unveiled another RAK.1 model, as his car had also been called. This aircraft is also referred to as the Opel-Hatry RAK.1 or the Opel-Sander RAK.1. Von Opel's third major achievement in rocket science came on September 30, 1929, when he flew the plane at the Rebstock airfield near Frankfurt, Germany.

The RAK.1 was put on a trolley on a railway track, and its first set of rockets were fired. Von Opel and the car were shot down the end of the track, where a buffer—a shock absorber used to keep train cars from crashing into one another—was positioned. At that point, von Opel switched on the plane's rockets, which lifted him airborne. He wrote about the experience in the *New York Times* article the next day. "I feel the machine racing forward. It tries to rear like a horse. I feel amidst the hissing of the charge that the wings may break under the immense pressure," he recalled, adding that he physically experienced a distinct change in air pressure from the force of the rocket blast. Once the plane gained some altitude, "the suffocating pressure eases and I can breath[e] again....I ignite and force the machine upward. It mounts if driven by a giant force. At the great speed I can hear only an even roar. The landscape races beneath me."

Von Opel managed to make a controlled crash landing after flying just under one mile in 75 seconds, at an altitude of about 50 feet. Among the crowd awaiting his safe return was his fiancé, Margot, one of first German women to earn a pilot's license. Von Opel seemed to have abandoned his interest in aviation and automotive rocketry around 1930, the same year that Max Valier was killed in his Berlin workshop while testing combinations of liquid rocket fuel. This was also the same period when von Opel lost his executive position at the family firm, after U.S. automotive giant General Motors acquired an 80 percent stake in the company in March of 1929. The von Opel heirs became enormously wealthy, and von Opel retired to Switzerland to conduct balloon experiments from his mountain aerie in St. Moritz. German photographer-filmmaker Leni Riefenstahl was a friend of Margot's and recalled a balloon trip she made with von Opel once near Dessau. "We drifted through utter silence," she wrote in *Leni Riefenstahl: A Memoir*. "Often we hovered only a few yards over the forests and now and then we heard the barking of dogs," she wrote of the moonlit outing. "Sometimes, when the bottom of our gondola grazed the treetops, Fritz von Opel tossed down a sack of sand."

Emigrated to United States

Riefenstahl made several propaganda films for Adolf Hitler and his Nazi Party after it came to power in Germany in 1933. Hitler's government funded rocketry experiments that the previous Weimar government had been uninterested in underwriting. In the spring of 1940, von Opel and his wife fled Europe, now enmeshed in a devastating world war sparked by Hitler's plan to conquer the continent through force. They obtained passports issued by the tiny principality of Liechtenstein, which permitted them to board a liner bound for New York City. British authorities detained him in the Spanish port of Gibraltar, but the von Opels were permitted to continue on to the United States. It is known that he lived in Palm Beach, Florida, where he was arrested in February of 1942 under the Alien Enemies Act that permitted detention of foreign nationals from countries with whom the United States was at war.

Von Opel spent the remainder of World War II in an internment camp in New Jersey. He entered into a long legal battle after the end of the war in 1945 over his shares in a Swiss holding company, Überzee Finanz-Korporation A.G. His fortune was linked to a gift of Opel stock his parents had given him back in 1935, which he later sold to General Motors. With the proceeds of that transaction he bought a brewery in Lowell, Massachusetts, and a Nashville-based gasoline station operator called Spur Distributing. Von Opel's assets were seized when he was arrested in 1942, and he fought for financial compensation for many years. In 1951, the U.S. Court of Appeals ruled against him, and in 1957 von Opel's attorneys petitioned the U.S. Supreme Court to adjudicate the matter, but the High Court declined to hear the case. Some of von Opel's troubles were also related to legal woes involving his divorce from Margot after he became involved with the daughter of a Colombian diplomat. A New York court ordered von Opel to pay his ex-wife a stunning $60,000 a year in alimony.

Von Opel had two children with his second wife, Emita Herrán Olozaga. Their son Frederick, called Rikky, went on to drive Formula One race cars in the 1970s. Daughter Marie Christine, known as ''Putzi,'' led a jet-set but troubled life that included a highly publicized arrest and stint in French prison for hashish possession. Putzi had inherited her father's fortune after his death on April 8, 1971, in Samedan, Switzerland, four years after Emita's passing. The family's web of tragedy and misfortune is a storied one: von Opel's sister Eleonore married Wilhelm Sachs, a German ball bearing tycoon who committed suicide in 1958. Their son Ernst died in a 1977 avalanche in the French Alps; another son, Gunter, was once married to Brigitte Bardot, and killed himself in 2011. Putzi von Opel died in an automobile accident in Spain in 2006.

Books

Riefenstahl, Leni, *Leni Riefenstahl: A Memoir,* Macmillan, 1995, p. 218.

Periodicals

New York Times, May 5, 1929; October 1, 1929; February 28, 1942; February 9, 1951; January 2, 1969; April 12, 1971.

Times (London, England), May 23, 1928; June 25, 1928; October 1, 1929; May 4, 1945.

Online

''Fritz von Opel Flies First Jet in 1929,'' *YouTube.com,* http://www.youtube.com/watch?v=oEyf1KFgE-o (November 3, 2011). □

Opothleyahola

The Native American tribal leader Opothleyahola (c. 1798–1863) was an indefatigable fighter on behalf of the Upper Creek people, whom he served as chief in the middle of the nineteenth century and into the United States Civil War.

K nown (according to a Kansas Humanities Council web site) as ''the Abraham Lincoln of the Upper Creek Muskogee,'' Opothleyahola shaped the course of Native American history with several eloquent speeches. He was a skilled military leader as well, fending off Confederate troops at several Civil War battles in the Oklahoma territory before succumbing to a brutal defeat. His life spanned much of the tragic history of Native Americans in the nineteenth century, from expulsion from their ancestral homelands in the eastern United States to the beginnings of total military domination by invading whites, and he met each new challenge with insight and resolution.

Fought Against Andrew Jackson

Opothleyahola was born around 1798 in the Creek Nation town of Tuckabatchee, now in Elmore County, Alabama. The town was the site of the tribe's council house and the home of its chief, known as Big Warrior. During the early nineteenth century, the expansion of American settlement led in some cases to alliances between Native American tribes determined to resist white encroachment, but also to dissension between and within tribes as they disagreed over whether to try to reach an accommodation with the invaders. The Creek Nation was split in two: the Upper Creeks and their Red Stick militia hoped to drive out the Americans and return the tribe to its traditional way of life, while the Lower Creeks favored negotiations. When the War of 1812 broke out, an atmosphere of instability led to a Creek civil war as well. Opothleyahola is believed to have fought with the Red Sticks against the Lower Creeks and later against American forces led by General Andrew Jackson.

After the Upper Creeks were defeated by Jackson's forces at the Battle of Horseshoe Bend on March 27, 1814, Opothleyahola was forced to take an oath of allegiance stating that he would not take up arms against the United States again. Jackson had enjoyed some support from Lower Creeks, but this did them no good during the war's aftermath; Upper and Lower Creeks alike were expelled from large parts of southern Alabama and Georgia over the next several years, with local and state American authorities, as elsewhere in the country, disregarding one treaty after another. It was during this period that Opothleyahola emerged as the principal speaker for the Upper Creeks.

When a Lower Creek group led by William McIntosh, relying on promises of new lands farther to the west, signed a treaty ceding the remaining Creek lands in Georgia to the United States on February 12, 1825, the split between the Upper and Lower Creeks became permanent. The first major speech by Opothleyahola on record warned McIntosh against signing the treaty. After he signed it nevertheless, he was executed by a group of 100 Upper Creeks. Opothleyahola set out for Washington, D.C., to plead the case before President John Quincy Adams that the treaty agreed to by McIntosh was invalid. Adams was convinced, and he and Opothleyahola signed a treaty on January 24, 1826, that preserved some Creek lands. This treaty, however, lasted no longer than earlier agreements, as Georgia and Alabama authorities began to expel remaining Creek groups. Many Lower Creeks moved voluntarily to lands in Mississippi; Opothleyahola continued to lead resistance, but eventually bowed to the inevitable and signed the Treaty of Cusseta in March of 1832. This treaty gave Creeks the option of submitting to Alabama state law or moving to new lands in the West over the next five years.

Led People Along Trail of Tears

Opothleyahola, by this time chief of the entire Creek tribe, at this point began an attempt to work within the system, hoping to carve out a sphere of maximum autonomy for the Creek people. He traveled to Nacogdoches, Texas, in 1834, hoping to purchase a new homeland for the tribe. He arrived in the middle of Texas's revolution against Mexico, resulting in the formation of the Republic of Texas in 1836. Although he made a down payment of $20,000, he yielded to pressure from the various governments involved and abandoned the scheme. In 1836, he led a Creek band that joined with U.S. forces during the long Second Seminole War in Florida, receiving the rank of colonel. The following year, under Opothleyahola's leadership, the remaining Creeks in Alabama joined with the Cherokees along the so-called Trail of Tears leading to the Indian Territory, present-day Oklahoma.

Although the division between the Upper and Lower Creeks continued to fester, Opothleyahola's first years in Indian Territory were calm. He joined the Baptist church, gained wealth from trading, and acquired a 2,000-acre plantation with a number of African-American slaves. He became known as Old Gouge. In a famous oration delivered in 1859 and reproduced in the *Chronicles of Oklahoma*, Opothleyahola urged Creeks to seek out education for the tribe's young people, recalling an island in the Chattahoochee River that he had known when he was young. The island had been eroded and nearly washed away by river floods, but Opothleyahola had learned that if a certain kind of grass had been planted along its banks, the island might have been preserved.

"My brothers," he said, "we Indians are like that island in the middle of the river. The white man comes upon us as a flood. We crumble and fall, even as the sandy banks of that beautiful island in the Chattahoochee." As the island might have been saved by the planting of the special grass, "so let us save our people by educating our boys and girls and young men and young women in the ways of the white man. Then they may be planted and deeply rooted about us and our people may stand unmoved in the flood of the white man."

Rejected Confederate Alliance

Although some of the tribes that had been pushed westward urged neutrality, the outbreak of the U.S. Civil War often exacerbated existing tribal tensions. In 1861, Opothleyahola wrote to President Abraham Lincoln, reminding him of his loyalty to the federal government and asking for protection from an alliance of Confederate troops and their Lower Creek sympathizers, who were already menacing Upper Creek lands in Oklahoma. Lincoln replied in the affirmative, instructing Opothleyahola to lead his band of several thousand Creeks, Cherokees, and Seminoles (numbers from 2,500 to 9,000 have been recorded) to Fort Row in Wilson County, Kansas. Inasmuch as he himself was a slaveholder, it is unlikely that Opothleyahola opposed the Confederate secession on abolitionist grounds.

Confederate general Douglas H. Cooper, a Mexican War veteran, was sympathetic to the cause of Native Americans in Oklahoma in general, and at first he was open to negotiations with Opothleyahola. But some of the Creek leader's historical enemies, including two of William McIntosh's sons, convinced Cooper that the Creek chief represented a threat to the Confederacy, and on November 15, 1861, Cooper demanded that Opothleyahola and his followers either join the Confederate cause or be driven out of Oklahoma. The Battle of Round Mountain on November 19, 1861, was the first Civil War engagement in Indian Territory. It ended in defeat for Cooper and his freshly minted group of Texas cavalrymen, as Opothleyahola's forces conducted an aggressive retreat, setting prairie fires and trapping the Confederates and their Indian allies in a horseshoe-shaped field.

Opothleyahola fought Confederate reinforcements to a stalemate at the Battle of Chusto-Talasah on December 9, but with his supplies depleted and federal help failing to materialize, was routed in the Battle of Chustenahlah on December 26. His decimated following walked through winter blizzards to Fort Row, a miserable odyssey that later became known as the Trail of Blood on the Ice. Despite Lincoln's personal assurances, Opothleyahola found that Fort Row lacked the facilities to house and treat the exhausted band of Creeks, most of whom had little more than the clothes on their backs. Many, including Opothleyahola's daughter, died, and some, including Opothleyahola, continued on to other refugee camps in Kansas. Ill and without hope for his people, Opothleyahola died in one of those camps near Quenemo, Kansas, on March 22, 1863.

Books

Downing, David C., *A South Divided: Portraits of Dissent in the Confederacy*, Cumberland House, 2007.

White, Christine Schulz, and Benton R. White, *Now the Wolf Has Come: The Creek Nation in the Civil War*, Texas A&M, 1996.

Online

"Chief Opothleyahola," *Chronicles of Oklahoma,* December 1931, http://www.digital.library.okstate.edu/Chronicles/v009/v009p439.html (October 27, 2011).s

"On This Date in Civil War History: December 9, 1861—The Battle of Chusto-Talasah," http://www.thisweekinthecivilwar.com/2011/12/10/on-this-date-in-civil-war-history-december-9-1861-the-battle-of-chusto-talasah-150th-anniversary/ (October 27, 2011).

"On This Date in Civil War History: November 19, 1861—Battle of Round Mountain (150th Anniversary)," *This Week in the Civil War,* http://www.thisweekinthecivilwar.com/2011/12/16/on-this-date-in-civil-war-history-november-19-1861-battle-of-round-mountain-150th-anniversary (October 27, 2011).

"Pothleyahola (c.1780–1863)," *Encyclopedia of Oklahoma History and Culture,* http://www.digital.library.okstate.edu/encyclopedia/entries/O/OP003.html (October 27, 2011).

"The Story of Opothleyahola," *Kansas Humanities Council,* http://www.kansashumanities.org/site/programs/165-7-the-story-of-opothleyahola.html (October 27, 2011).□

Mary Ewing Outerbridge

Mary Ewing Outerbridge (1852–1886) introduced the sport of lawn tennis to the United States in the 1870s. While visiting relatives in Bermuda, she discovered Royal Navy personnel playing a newly created version of the racquet sport, and brought a set of the equipment back with her when she sailed for home in early 1874. A few months later she supervised the construction of an hourglass-shaped court at the Staten Island Cricket and Baseball Club, which six years later hosted the first lawn tennis championship match ever played in the United States.

Almost nothing is known about Outerbridge aside from these few details. A wealth of information, however, survives about the Outerbridge family. They were among the first settlers of Bermuda, the Atlantic Ocean archipelago located about 600 miles off the coast of North Carolina. A part of the British Empire since 1609, Bermuda became a vital port in the transatlantic trade in the centuries that followed. Seventeenth-century settlers and their descendants mined available timber, built notably swift and seaworthy ships, and established a profitable trade in salt between three continents. The first Outerbridge in Bermuda was a Yorkshire man who arrived in 1619, ten years after the colony's formal founding. His descendants prospered thanks to their ties to the Virginia tobacco trade, maritime interests in Newfoundland, and other lucrative pursuits. "The First Families of Bermuda are more or less affectionately known as the Forty Thieves, because so many island fortunes were founded on privateering, blockade-running in the Civil War, and similar activities," remarked Brendan Gill and Gordon Cotler for a *New Yorker* piece in 1953, who noted Mary Outerbridge's

contribution to the history of racquet sports, then added, "Bermuda has been defined as a group of coral islands connected by Outerbridges."

Bermudians had large families, with infants and children thriving in the lush climate with its distinctive pink-sand beaches. Outerbridge was one of ten children produced from a marriage between two wealthy Bermuda clans. Her father was Alexander Ewing Outerbridge, born in 1816 in Bermuda. Outerbridge's mother, Laura Catherine Harvey, was the daughter of a physician, Augustus Harvey, and hailed from a Newfoundland branch that had longstanding ties to Bermuda. Their fortune was tied in part to the saltfish, or dried cod, trade managed by Harvey & Company, a Newfoundland venture that grew out of the original Bermuda Trading Company.

Seventh of Ten Children

Outerbridge was born in Philadelphia, Pennsylvania, on February 16, 1852. She had several siblings, some of whom were born in Bermuda. Albert, the oldest child, became a lawyer in Philadelphia; her brother Joseph joined the Harvey firm in St. John's, Newfoundland, and eventually established himself in politics and was knighted by King George V in 1913. Outerbridge's third brother was Augustus, who married a daughter of the prominent Roosevelt family of New York. After Augustus came two older sisters: Catharine, whose husband served as British vice-consul in Key West, and Harriet. They were followed by another brother, Alexander II, who became a leading metallurgist and worked for the U.S. Mint. Mary was the seventh Outerbridge child, sandwiched between Alexander II and a younger sister named Laura. After that came the two youngest brothers, Adolphus and Eugenius.

Outerbridge went to visit family in Bermuda in the winter of 1873–74, just before her 22nd birthday. She spent time at a villa on Harbour Road called Clermont, the home of the Chief Justice of Bermuda, Sir Brownlow Gray. Clermont was reportedly the first private residence on the island to install a court for lawn tennis, a new sport adapted from some older handball and racquet pastimes by a British Army officer named Major Walter Clopton Wingfield.

A form of tennis had been popularized by fifteenth-century French aristocrats on indoor courts and migrated to England, where King Henry VIII had an indoor court built at his Hampton Court palace. Wingfield's achievement was to devise a new form of the sport that could be played out of doors. He came up with new racquets and rules and drew upon ancient Greek to name the game *sphairistike,* which translates as "skill at playing at ball." This version was first demonstrated at a party on Wingfield's estate, Nantclwyd, in Llanelidan, Wales, in December of 1873. But by then Wingfield had also taught it to other officers, who were then posted to British naval installations overseas—including a sizable one at Hamilton, Bermuda's main city.

Sphairistike Set Perplexed Customs Officials

There would be years of ardent debate in the late nineteenth and early twentieth century over who exactly brought the game of lawn tennis to the United States. Some claimed that Outerbridge could not have been the first to bring the equipment to U.S. shores and that she had actually visited the British colony in the winter of 1874–75, after the sport was introduced at a Massachusetts estate. One historian, however, tracked down a ship's manifest that listed Outerbridge and a brother as passengers on the *S.S. Canima,* a ship that made weekly runs between New York and Bermuda. She is listed among the passengers that debarked at New York Harbor on February 2, 1874.

An oft-told part of the tale is that U.S. Customs inspectors seized the unfamiliar sports equipment carried by Outerbridge, unsure about what kind of import duty to assign it, but she prevailed upon her brother Augustus, a shipping company executive with some connections to the Customs office, to have it released. Her youngest brother Eugenius confirmed that his sister had brought the equipment to the United States in a letter he sent to the U.S. Lawn Tennis Association in 1923 that was later quoted in a book commemorating the organization's 50th anniversary in 1931. The letter was also quoted in Roger W. Ohnsorg's book *Robert Lindley Murray: The Reluctant U. S. Tennis Champion: Includes the First Forty Years of American Tennis.* "To the best of my knowledge and belief," Eugenius wrote, "it was in the spring of 1874 that my sister, Mary Ewing Outerbridge, brought from Bermuda a lawn tennis net, rackets and balls which she had obtained from the regimental stores through the courtesy of the colonel or some or some of the officers with whom she had played the game there."

Outerbridge's briefly confiscated goods included an adapted fishing net that served as the focal point of the game, some square-shaped racquets strung with natural "gut"—usually made from a part of a cow intestine—and a canvas ball filled with horsehair that is slightly larger than the standard tennis ball. She also had a diagram of how to lay out the hourglass-shaped court as decreed by Wingfield, but probably not his official rule-book, which was still being written or typeset around the time of her stay in Bermuda. Wingfield later attempted to patent his game, but was unsuccessful. A different form of lawn tennis was apparently being played elsewhere in England as early as the 1870s, and swept across the country as a new sports fad called "sticky."

Laid Out Court at Cricket Club

Outerbridge instructed her brothers on how to play the game. At the time, her family home was located at 210–212 St. Paul's Avenue in the ritzy North Shore section of Staten Island. Her brother Augustus was a board member of the recently formed Staten Island Cricket and Baseball Club, which established itself on a decommissioned military site known in Outerbridge's era as Old Camp Washington. This is where Union Army regiments had mustered at the start of the Civil War.

Augustus Outerbridge secured the board's permission to let his sister set up a tennis court on the grounds of the Staten Island Cricket and Baseball Club, the first semi-public tennis court in the United States, in the spring of 1874. Six years later, that same court hosted the first national lawn tennis championship tournament ever

played on American soil. The event took place on September 1, 1880, and the turnout was significant, according to the *New York Times'* coverage. A player from England named O.E. Woodhouse won the silver trophy cup. In England, the sport was thriving, and several elite private clubs had been established in the decade since Wingfield and others reintroduced the sport. In 1877, the top players met at the All England Lawn Tennis and Croquet Club for the first English championship tournament, which became known as Wimbledon.

Early Death Went Unnoticed

One of Outerbridge's Harvey cousins played in the 1880 tournament on Staten Island. The New York City borough, however, competed with more elitist enclaves to claim the title of the birthplace of American tennis. Eleven months later, in August of 1881, a men's tournament was held in Newport, Rhode Island. A player named Richard Sears won that championship event, which eventually evolved into the U.S. Open. Sears had learned to play the game in the summer of 1874 in Nahant, Massachusetts, where a tennis court had been set up on the grounds of an estate owned by William Appleton. Appleton's nephew was James Dwight, who had also returned from abroad in early 1874 and brought back some tennis equipment. Dwight claimed credit for introducing tennis to America before Outerbridge did, and he went on to become one of the founders of the U.S. Lawn Tennis Association and served as its president for more than two decades. Women players, meanwhile, agitated for several years to be permitted to play in their own officially sanctioned tournaments; the first U.S. Ladies Singles Championship was held in Philadelphia in 1887.

Outerbridge never lived to see that game. She died at the age of thirty-four in the New Brighton section of Staten Island on May 3, 1886. The hourglass court she set up at the Old Camp Washington was demolished when the Staten Island Cricket Club moved in 1885 to make way for a new ferry terminal. Her youngest brother, Eugenius, became a prominent New York City leader and served as the first president of the Port Authority of New York and New Jersey. The Outerbridge Crossing, which connects Staten Island's southern end to Perth Amboy, New Jersey, was built in 1928 and named in his honor. Outerbridge descendants in Bermuda remain plentiful, and the Clermont address off Harbour Road, between Highwood Lane and Lovers' Lane, still stands. Google Earth satellite images from 2011 unmistakenly reveal an enormous tennis court on the vast lawn.

Books

Ohnsorg, Roger W., *Robert Lindley Murray: The Reluctant U. S. Tennis Champion: Includes the First Forty Years of American Tennis,* Trafford Publishing, 2011.

Whitman, Malcolm D., *Tennis: Origins and Mysteries,* Derrydale Press, 1932, reprinted by Dover Publications, 2004.

Periodicals

New York Times, September 4, 1880; April 28, 1931; July 22, 1949; August 16, 1974; August 21, 2010.

New Yorker, December 5, 1953. □

P

Seymour Papert

The South African–born computer scientist and mathematician Seymour Papert (born 1928) has been a visionary pioneer in the application of computers in the education of children.

Papert's career has gone through distinct phases, each of which provided the seed for a creative shift in direction. He began his career as a mathematician in his native South Africa. An encounter with Swiss child psychologist Jean Piaget led him into the study of how children learn, which in turn stimulated an interest in artificial intelligence. He is regarded as a pioneer in that field. He became interested in computers generally, and created a widely used programming language, Logo, that made computers accessible to children for the first time. In the 1980s and 1990s, Papert put all of these areas of expertise together, forming important ideas about new ways computers might be used in education. His 1980 book *Mindstorms: Children, Computers, and Powerful Ideas* is regarded as a classic that has influenced both educators and toymakers; the latter group has provided substantial financial backing for his research and has been rewarded with ideas leading to popular new products. Later in life, Papert explored the application of his ideas to the education of at-risk youth.

Active Against Apartheid

A native of Pretoria, South Africa, Seymour Papert was born on March 1, 1928. His father was an entomologist who thought nothing of taking the entire family on long treks through the wilderness in pursuit of tsetse fly samples. Papert grew up mostly among black South Africans, and early on he began to question the country's entrenched system of apartheid, or racial segregation. He attended South Africa's University of the Witwatersrand, majoring in mathematics and philosophy and receiving his BA degree in 1949. He went on for a PhD in mathematics at the University of the Witwatersrand, and received a second doctorate at Cambridge University in England, staying on at Cambridge through much of the mid-1950s as a post-doctoral research scholar. During this period he also spent substantial amounts of time working in Paris, which was a hot spot for mathematical research. But the city's vigorous intellectual scene brought Papert back to his interest in philosophy, and made him think about the connections between the world of ideas and the prospects for resistance to apartheid. As a young man in South Africa, Papert had already become active in the anti-apartheid movement.

"I was interested in philosophy of mind, partly coming out of my experience in South Africa," Papert explained to Geraldine Doogue of Australia's ABC radio. "One of the most fascinating things for me, since I was a teenager, was how people could possibly think the things I heard them thinking...that good, kind people could also be these racists. So this was a big thing for me to try and understand how the mind could possibly work, and so I was in Paris officially doing mathematics, but frequenting circles with people interested in questions of the mind." Those circles lead Papert to Piaget, who was looking for a mathematician to review his own research on how children master numbers. Impressed with Papert's belief that "it's really the same issues that underlie real mathematics and children's mathematics," Piaget brought Papert on board at the International Center of Genetic Epistemology at the University of Geneva in Switzerland from 1958 to 1963.

Newly married to psychologist Androula Christofides (the couple had one daughter, Artemis), Papert moved to

the Massachusetts Institute of Technology (MIT) in 1964. Owing to his anti-apartheid activities, he had difficulty obtaining a visa to enter the United States. Drawing on both his psychological work with Piaget and his training as a mathematician, Papert began to formulate original ideas in the field of artificial intelligence, at the time an almost entirely new discipline. At MIT, Papert and Marvin Minsky founded the school's influential Artificial Intelligence Laboratory. One of Papert's most significant early accomplishments was his creation, along with several other scientists, of the Logo programming language, which first appeared in 1967 and has remained in use for decades. The language enabled children, using a turtle-shaped on-screen cursor, to generate shapes and arrays, and also spawned a simple turtle-like robot. In 1970, Papert and Minsky wrote *Perceptrons*, a key text in early artificial intelligence efforts, although it was superseded by later ideas.

Won Guggenheim Fellowship

Papert spent the years from 1968 to 1980 as a professor of applied mathematics at MIT. In 1980 and 1981, he won prestigious Guggenheim and Marconi fellowships, and he spent the 1982–83 academic year as scientific director of the World Center for Computer Studies and Human Resources in Paris. In 1983, he returned to MIT as professor of mathematics and education in the Department of Arts and Media Technology. Divorced from Christofides, he married MIT sociology professor Sherry Turkle in 1977. The two were divorced in 1985, and in 1992 Papert married Russian literature scholar Suzanne Massie. Papert was a classic absent-minded professor. According to a legend among his colleagues, he was said to have once unintentionally left his wife (information as to which one has not been transmitted) behind in a New York airport when boarding a trans-Atlantic flight.

The research that led to Papert's new appointment at MIT involved new possibilities for the uses of computers by children. Some of Papert's work dealt with physical computers themselves; a collaboration with MIT scientist Alan Kay led to Kay's conceptualization of what became the laptop computer. But Papert was also interested in completely rethinking the ways computers could be incorporated into education. The major product of Papert's research during this period was the book *Mindstorms: Children, Computers, and Powerful Ideas,* originally published in 1980, issued by the large educational publisher Basic Books in 1982, and reprinted several times over a much longer lifespan than computer-related books have generally enjoyed. Papert himself indicated that he was unaware of how widely the book would be read among elementary-school educators.

In *Mindstorms*, Papert argued that children could be taught to use computers—could, in fact, master them on their own—and that the skills they developed in doing so could remake the nature of education itself. The Lego Mindstorms line of computer-enhanced construction toys was named after Papert's book, and the Lego firm donated money to the new MIT Media Lab that Papert founded in 1985, for a new endowed position, the Lego-Papert Chair of Learning Research. The video game maker Nintendo also funded Papert's research, which has continued to yield applications relevant to commercial products that engage children's imaginations. But Papert was less interested in commercial developments than in the applications of his work to education. He issued a second book on the subject, *The Children's Machine: Rethinking School in the Age of the Computer,* in 1993.

Urged Family Computing Activities

By the mid-1990s, Papert was a well-known figure to whom journalists often turned for commentary on the question of how to incorporate computers into child-rearing. Papert advocated an entire rethinking of school curricula with computers at the heart of the school experience, replacing the traditional focus on reading, writing, and arithmetic. He emphasized the importance of exploration, and dismissed software that merely told children whether they were giving right or wrong answers as "interpassive," not interactive, according to Laura Evenson in the *San Francisco Chronicle.* Papert had little use for the traditional education establishment, and recommended the abolition of the U.S. federal Department of Education. At home, Papert suggested that parents involve children in joint projects that induced children to think about how the computer could be used. The fruits of his thinking about computers and the family were summarized in his 1996 book *The Connected Family: Bridging the Digital Generation Gap.*

While many educators worried about the effects of video games on children, Papert told Evenson that "even with the most stupid video games, kids learn more about learning than they ever did before, because they want to learn codes and moves before other kids figure them out. They're motivated to seek out someone or search the Net for help. A student who makes a video game has to solve mathematical problems to make special effects happen on the screen." After retiring from MIT, Papert accepted a position at the University of Maine and established the Learning Barn and the Seymour Papert Institute in Blue Hill, Maine. These institutions also provided consulting services to communities and governments interested in new educational approaches. In Maine, Papert worked with troubled and at-risk youth to find ways in which a greater emphasis on computer-related creativity in education might help overcome their problems in school. In 2001, *Newsweek* magazine named Papert one of the top ten education innovators in the United States.

Beginning in the 1980s, Papert traveled frequently, both as a guest of foreign organizations and governments and for academic conferences. He worked with the government of Costa Rica to implement widespread computer distribution in that country's schools. But as he joined a group of more than 100 computer education researchers in Hanoi, Vietnam, in December of 2006, Papert was struck by a motorbike while attempting to cross six lanes of traffic to reach a conference site. He spent several days in a coma in Hanoi and was hospitalized in the United States for several months. As of this writing, he was reported to be gradually improving, walking with the aid of a walker and relearning the power of speech. According to Massie, as quoted in *Information Week,* he was "a constant learner."

Periodicals

Christian Science Monitor, April 21, 1997.

InformationWeek, July 15, 2008.

New Republic, November 3, 1997.

New York Times, December 26, 1990; October 23, 1999; December 8, 2006.

San Francisco Chronicle, February 2, 1997.

Online

"The History of Mr. Papert," Gary S. Stager, http://www.stager.org/ omaet2004/papertbio.html (October 14, 2011).

"Seymour Papert," *ICT in Education: Incremental Progress or Fundamental Change?,* http://www.fundamentalchange. carolstrohecker.info/delegates/delegateinfo/papert.htm (October 14, 2011).

"Seymour Papert" *Massachusetts Institute of Technology,* http:// www.web.mit.edu/~papert (October 14, 2011).

"Sunday Profile: Seymour Papert," *ABC Radio (Australia),* http:// www.abc.net.au/sundayprofile/stories/s1144341.htm (October 14, 2011).

"Works by Papert," *Seymour Papert Official Website,* http:// www.papert.org (October 14, 2011).□

Violeta Parra

The Chilean singer and songwriter Violeta Parra (1917–1967) was among the most influential Latin American musicians of the twentieth century. She is regarded as a major formative influence on the *nueva canción* (new song) movement of the 1960s and 1970s.

In English-speaking countries, Parra remains best known for her song "Grácias a la vida" (Thanks to Life), which was covered in the 1970s by American folk vocalist Joan Baez. In France, where she lived for many years, she became famous as one of the first musicians to introduce Latin American folk music to European audiences, and also as a visual artist. But it was in Latin America that Parra's influence loomed largest. Parra's own roots lay in the culture of rural Chile, and she became an enthusiastic and systematic investigator of her native country's folk music. She coupled the musical styles she learned with social and political lyrics that protested injustice and lampooned the rich and powerful. This combination directly inspired the most prominent female figure in the nueva canción movement, Argentina's Mercedes Sosa, and laid the groundwork for the music of many other Latin American singer-songwriters.

Descended from Mapuche Tribe

The defining event of Parra's childhood was a bout with smallpox, which she contracted in 1920. She survived the often fatal disease but bore its characteristic scars on her face for the rest of her life, and as she began to recover she was stricken with yellow fever and then diphtheria. The experience made her something of a social outcast among other children and gave her a quality of intense restlessness, of wanting to wring everything she could out of each moment of life. During her long convalescence, her mother taught her to make lace, and her father gave her a few singing lessons.

Parra often heard music in public spaces as a child, and she loved it from the beginning. As Nicanor's drinking problem worsened, the family's attitude toward music became ambivalent, and his guitar was often locked away. One day when she was seven, however, she found a hidden key to his guitar case and began to play; several years after that she started writing her own songs. After her father's death in 1929, Parra and her siblings contributed to the family income by singing on the street and later, when she moved to the Chilean capital of Santiago, in bars and clubs. Sometimes she and her sister Hilda performed as Las Hermanas Parra, the Parra Sisters.

Performed While Raising Children

In 1938, Parra married railroad engineer Luis Cereceda and tried to settle down. The couple raised two children, Ángel (who became well known as a singer under the name Ángel Parra) and Isabel. But Parra continued to sing and write, earning an honorable mention award in a poetry contest and appearing at a restaurant called No Me Olvides. As soon as her children were old enough, she incorporated them into a show she performed at a sweet shop called Casanova. Continually restless, Parra sought out new performance opportunities and joined a theater group. She and Cereceda divorced in 1948; she married Luis Arce that year and had two more daughters, Carmen Luisa in 1949 and Rosita Clara in 1952. But that marriage, too, did not last.

Violeta and Hilda Parra recorded as the Parra Sisters during this period. But Violeta earned a living largely by singing in circuses, a lifestyle she had first been exposed to years earlier. Accompanied by her brother Nicanor, who became a noted Chilean poet in his own right, Parra began to investigate Chilean folk traditions, aided by the growth of portable tape recording technology. She amassed a collection of some 3,000 songs and began to write new original material marked by a powerful folk simplicity. In 1953, she recorded two singles for the EMI-Odéon label, and these marked her commercial breakthrough. All four sides—"Que pena siente el alma" (What Pain I Feel in My Soul), "Verso por el fin del mundo" (Verse for the End of the World), "Casamiento de los negros" (Black Wedding), and "Verso por padacimiento" (Verse for Suffering)—became well-known Parra standards.

In 1954, Parra began a radio program, *Violeta Parra Sings*. The show was a success, but soon Parra had the chance to explore wider horizons: she was invited to a World Youth Festival in Poland and jumped at the chance, arriving in Warsaw in July of 1955 and subsequently moving into an apartment in the Latin Quarter neighborhood in Paris, France. During this trip she received word of the death of her daughter Rosita in Santiago; though strongly affected, she did not return to Chile.

Met Swiss Musicologist

Parra's motivation was a desire to spread the unique musical culture she had discovered in Chile. According to her friend Enrique Bello, as quoted on the *This Is Chile* website, "She didn't go to Paris like the ladies of the 19th century to learn about the latest fashion. She went there to impose Chilean song; that was her challenge. She wanted to submit herself to the test." Parra met a number of European scholars and intellectuals, and she became romantically involved with the Swiss musician and musicologist Gilbert Favré, a specialist in South American music. She would divide the rest of her life between Chile and Europe, later moving to Switzerland to live with Favré. In 1962, she embarked on a long European tour that took her from a festival in Helsinki, Finland, through the Soviet Union, Germany, Italy, and France.

Parra's music, often featuring only her own voice and her own accompaniment on a variety of Chilean stringed instruments (including a 25-string guitar), differed sharply from the romantic female vocals of popular song. Some of it closely followed song models from Parra's Mapuche heritage. Her relationship with Favré coincided with several scorching love songs, including "Corazón maldito" (Cursed Heart). But many of Parra's songs, such as "Qué dirá el Santo Padre?" (What Will the Holy Father Say?), involved social criticism. Some were banned in various South American countries as right-wing regimes took hold.

Beginning when she returned to Chile in 1956 and continuing through subsequent periods in Europe, Parra began to think in terms of a fusion of the arts. She contemplated a folk opera, and she herself took up painting and tapestry, considering the latter art form similar to a visual representation of music. Her artwork, which often used colors associated with the heavily Mapuche city of Arauco, tended to tell stories, sometimes of searchers (religious or otherwise). As a visual artist she was virtually self-taught, but that did not stop her from walking into the prestigious Louvre museum in Paris in 1964 with a group of her tapestries and asking the museum to exhibit her work. The resulting exhibition of 26 paintings, 22 tapestries, and several small wire sculptures covered with rice, lentils, and seeds was the first solo show in the Louvre's history to feature a Latin American artist. Parra's artworks have been widely exhibited since her death, and in 2011 a new Violeta Parra Museum was under construction on Santiago's Avenida Vicuña.

In the mid-1960s, Parra seemed to be riding high. Her reputation was international in scope, and in 1966 she entered the studio to record a group of songs that contained her most famous composition of all, the reverently celebratory "Grácias a la vida". These songs would be issued after her death as the album "Las últimas composiciones de Violeta Parra" (The Last Compositions of Violeta Parra). She told an interviewer in *This Is Chile* that "something is missing in me. I don't know what it is. I look for it and I never find it. Surely I will never come upon it." On February 5, 1967, in the Santiago suburb of La Reina, Parra took her guitar in hand and killed herself with a shotgun. Her fame expanded in the years after her death as her songs inspired younger artists who were part of the *nueva canción* movement, chief among them Argentina's Mercedes Sosa. American folk vocalist Joan Baez recorded "Grácias a la vida" as the title track of a 1974 album, and both Sosa and Baez, as well as many other artists, continued to perform the song in concert. Parra's children created the Violeta Parra Foundation in 1992, and a new exhibition of her visual art was mounted at the Louvre in 1997.

Books

Kerschen, Karen, *Violeta Parra: By the Whim of the Wind*, ABQ Press, 2010.

Periodicals

Santa Fe New Mexican, August 17, 2007.

Online

"Cronología de Violeta Parra" (Violeta Parra Chronology), *Violeta Parra Official Website*, http://www.violetaparra.cl (November 1, 2011).

''Spiritual Folklorist: Violeta Parra,'' *I Love Chile,* http://www.ilovechile.cl/2011/02/03/spiritual-folklorist-violeta-parra/16915 (November 1, 2011).

''Violeta Parra,'' *All Music Guide,* http://www.allmusic.com (November 1, 2011).

''Violeta Parra,'' *National Geographic World Music,* http://www.worldmusic.nationalgeographic.com/view/page.basic/artist/content.artist/violeta_parra/en_US (November 1, 2011).

''Violeta Parra: Grácias a la vida,'' *This Is Chile,* http://www.thisischile.cl/6928/2/violeta-parra/News.aspx (November 1, 2011).

''Violeta Parra's Visual Art,'' *Latino Art Adventure,* http://www.latinoartadventure.blogspot.com/2010/03/violeta-parras-visual-art.html (November 1, 2011). □

Raphael Patkanian

The Armenian poet Raphael Patkanian (1830–1892) expressed the national aspirations of his people, who for much of their history have been occupied by larger powers, Russia to the north and the Turkish Ottoman Empire to the west.

During Patkanian's life, the lands that made up the ancient kingdom of Armenia, culturally and linguistically coherent, were split between the Ottoman and Russian empires. Patkanian's poetry reflected the characteristics of the Armenian landscape, its people and history. Beyond that, it addressed to an unusual degree the political and military events of his lifetime. He wrote of the hopes Armenians experienced, and of their disappointments when moves on the chessboard of world politics dashed those hopes. In the words of Louise Nalbandian, writing in *The Armenian Revolutionary Movement,* Patkanian was a ''nationalist poet who encouraged rebellion through his writings.''

Raised by Defrocked Priest

The name Raphael Patkanian has been transliterated many ways from Armenian script; some of the common variants include Raphayel (or Rafael) Patkanian, Rapayel Patkanean, and Raphael Badganian. He was also known as Kamar Katiba. Patkanian was born in the heavily Armenian city of Nor Nakhichevan, now Nakhichevan-on-Don in southern Russia; the entire area, including eastern Armenia, was then part of Russia, while western Armenia was ruled by the Ottomans. Both his father and grandfather were writers. His father, Gabriel Patkanian, has been described as a priest, but according to Kevork B. Bardakjian, writing in *A Reference Guide to Modern Armenian Literature, 1500–1920,* he married, was defrocked, spent time in prison, and was finally banished to the Russian interior due to a claimed assassination plot. Raphael Patkanian attended the Lazarian Institute in Moscow (also known as the Lazarev Institute), a top school with a specialty in foreign languages; among his other studies, he learned English.

During one of his father's periods of freedom he took up residence in Tiflis (now Tblisi, Georgia) and started a literary magazine, *Ararat,* there. The younger Patkanian went to join him and had some of his first poems published in *Ararat.* Patkanian's father also directed the Tiflis Nersessian Seminary, and Patkanian worked there as a teacher for a time. He moved on to the University of Dorpat (now the University of Tartu, Estonia) in 1851, remaining there for one year until his funds ran low. Then he moved to Moscow and, although not enrolled in school, joined with other Armenian students in 1852 to form an Armenian literary club.

The club was named Kamar Katiba, a name formed by combining the first initials and last names of its three chief members, K. Kanayan, M. Timurian, and R. Badganian (Patkanian). Patkanian's writing accelerated as he took charge of the club's activities in connection with poetry. By 1855, Patkanian had gathered sufficient funds to resume his education, this time at the University of St. Petersburg. He received a degree in 1860 and continued to use the pen name Kamar Katiba after the members of his literary club went their separate ways. He stayed on for several years in St. Petersburg and founded a short-lived literary journal, *Hiusiss* (North). He formed a small Young Armenia movement that may have been inspired by an idealistic Young Russia group at Moscow University.

Worked as Educator

In 1866 or 1867, Patkanian returned to Nor Nakhichevan and took a post as a teacher. He published several books of poetry and prose under the name Kamar Katiba in the 1850s and 1860s, and many of his poems were issued in journals. His ascent to wide popularity among Armenians occurred mostly after he returned to Armenian lands, however. He traveled widely and was hailed as a great representative of Armenian culture among Armenians who had migrated around the Near East and Eastern Europe. By the time of his death in 1892, Patkanian had published nine books, and collections of his work continued to appear posthumously. In the words of the Armenian House website, he was ''the most popular of Armenian poets.'' He began writing in the dialect of his native region but later switched to the modern East Armenian language promoted by novelist Khachatur Abovian.

Patkanian wrote in many genres. He remains best known for his poetry but also wrote prose, children's stories, plays, tales of life in Armenian-speaking regions, and educational materials such as textbooks. In advance of most such activity in Europe, he collected and edited Armenian folklore. Other than his poetry, very few of Patkanian's works have been translated into English. He himself translated Daniel Defoe's novel *Robinson Crusoe,* as well as the Greek fables of Aesop, into Armenian. Some of his writing was satirical in the manner of Russian novelist and playwright Nikolai Gogol, but for the most part Patkanian was a stirring patriotic writer.

The number-one topic in Patkanian's poetry was Armenia itself. Even a topic such as Armenian womanhood, which he celebrated in ''The Armenian Girl'' (''Lo, beside Armenia's maiden / Dark and dim the bright moon is''), seemed to have nationalistic overtones in his hands. One of his most famous poems was ''The Tears of Araxes,'' referring to the Araxes (or Aras) River that runs from Armenia through Iran and empties into the Caspian Sea. Patkanian turned the river into a symbol of Armenia's frustrated hopes, writing ''Still, while my sons are exiled / Shall I be sad, as now / This is my heart's deep utterance / My deep and holy vow. / No more spake Mother Arax; / She foamed up mightily / And, coiling like a serpent, / Wound sorrowing toward the sea.''

Affected by Russo-Turkish War

A new surge in Patkanian's creativity occurred when historical crossroads began to affect Armenian lands anew in the 1870s. The Russo-Turkish War of 1877 and 1878 was ended by the Treaty of San Stefano, under which the Ottoman Empire initially ceded large amounts of modern-day Armenia to Russia, which was far more sympathetic to Armenian aspirations. Armenians dreamed of a free and independent country, only to be disappointed when the 1878 Treaty of Berlin carved out new Eastern European countries from Ottoman lands, but backed off on Armenian autonomy.

Patkanian's poetry faithfully reflected these events. In the poem ''Complaint to Europe,'' he reflected bitterly on Armenian sacrifices during the war, and on how little had come of them. ''Have you forgotten, Europe, how the dart / Of the fierce Persian pointed at your heart / Until, on that dread field of Avarair, / Armenian blood quenched his fanatic fire?'' he wrote. ''Two hundred years Armenia, bathed in blood, / Europe was safe, our living wall behind, / Until the enemy's huge strength declined.''

Even after this political setback, Patkanian continued to campaign in his writing for Armenian self-determination. He became a venerated figure in Armenian culture, and when he visited Constantinople (present-day Istanbul, which prior to the Armenian genocide of the 1910s and 1920s had a large Armenian population) in 1890, he was hailed as a hero. Patkanian died in Nor Nakhichevan on August 22, 1892. One contemporary eulogy said that he ''left nine children orphaned, four million brothers unconsoled, and a name that will never be forgotten as long as the Armenian language is spoken.''

Books

Bardakjian, Kevork B., *A Reference Guide to Modern Armenian Literature: 1500–1920,* Wayne State University Press, 2000.

Becka, Jiri, *Dictionary of Oriental Literatures,* Allen & Unwin, 1974.

Nalbandian, Louise, *The Armenian Revolutionary Movement,* University of California Press, 1963.

Online

''Raphael Patkanian,'' *AllPoetry,* http://www.allpoetry.com/ Raphael_Patkanian (October 24, 2011).

''Raphael Patkanian,'' *Armenian House,* http://www.armenianhouse. org/blackwell/armenian-poems/patkanian.html (October 24, 2011). □

Milorad Pavić

The Serbian writer Milorad Pavić (1929–2009), a major experimenter with the form of the novel, gained international renown for his book *Dictionary of the Khazars: A Lexicon Novel in 100,000 Words.*

O ften suggested as a candidate for the Nobel Prize in Literature but never a winner, Pavić became famous comparatively late in life. He wrote five novels, only three of which have been translated into English. Those three books are original in structure and technique, comparable only to the works of major twentieth-century literary innovators such as Argentina's Jorge Luis Borges or the American John Barth. Although almost all of his writing was done before the advent of the Internet, his writing, consisting of separate pieces of information that could be absorbed in any order, appeared to anticipate the rise of hypertext. The most original of all his books was *The Dictionary of the Khazars,* which as its title suggests was a story told in the format of a dictionary. Pavić worked for much of his life as a professor of literature in his native Belgrade, and he also wrote poetry, short stories, and nonfiction works on literary and historical subjects.

Survived World War II Bombings

Milorad Pavić was born in Belgrade, then part of the Kingdom of Yugoslavia, on October 15, 1929. His father, Zdenko Pavić, has often been described as a sculptor, but Pavić told Thanassis Lallas of the *Review of Contemporary Fiction* that he was a housebuilder who pursued sculpture and painting on the side. Pavić's mother, Vera, was a professor of philosophy. He often remarked that he came from a line of writers going back to the eighteenth century. In an autobiography appearing on his website, Pavić wrote, ''The first time bombs rained down on me I was twelve.'' He survived other bombings as a teen during World War II, learning German, French, English, and Russian from various occupying forces and fellow wartime refuge seekers.

Pavić earned an undergraduate degree at the University of Belgrade, beginning a translation of the works of Alexander Pushkin from Russian into his native Serbo-Croation while he was there. He moved to the University of Zagreb for a PhD in literary history. Pavić also studied violin and reached a near-virtuoso level of skill, but he decided not to pursue a musical career. For several years he worked as an editor at Radio Zagreb and at the Belgrade publishing house Prosveta. In the 1950s and 1960s, Yugoslavia charted a course independent from the Soviet Union and the other countries of the Communist East Bloc, and Pavić was able to leave the country and teach in Paris and Vienna for short periods. He later taught at universities in Freiburg, Switzerland, and Regensburg, Germany. The bulk of his academic career was spent at the University of Novi Sad (1974–1982) and then the University of Belgrade in Yugoslavia. Pavić married literary critic Jasmina Mihajlovic.

Pavić's first work of creative fiction was a book of poems, *Palimpsests,* that was published in 1966; he was in his late 30s, and he remarked to Lallas that it was not

until then that "the appropriate conditions were established that allowed me to publish my first book in my country." He wrote several histories of Serbian literature as well as studies of the poet Vojislav Ilic and even a history of the city of Belgrade. In 1973, Pavić published his first book of short stories, *Iron Curtain,* and he continued to pursue the short story form over his entire career, even after his novels became famous. Among his short story collections were two titled *Borzoi* and *Russian Wolfhound,* both of which appeared in 1979. Pavić and his wife raised borzoi dogs in their Belgrade home.

Published *Dictionary of the Khazars*

None of these works (with the exception of *A Short History of Belgrade*) has been translated into English, and Pavić by his own testimony was little known even in Yugoslavia. All that changed with the publication of Pavić's first novel, *Dictionary of the Khazars: A Lexicon Novel in 100,000 Words,* in 1984. The book gained recognition in Yugoslavia at first, winning the Nin Award for best Yugoslavian novel of the year. In 1988, it was translated into English by Christina Pribicevic-Zoric and issued by the publisher Knopf in the United States. It has since been translated into eighty languages, in countries as geographically remote as Indonesia. Despite its 1980s publication date, several critics dubbed *Dictionary of the Khazars* the first novel of the twenty-first century for its experimental approach.

The structure of the book was unique. It embodied a largely imaginary historical lexicon of a real group of people, the Khazars, who flourished in southern Russia in the seventh and eighth centuries C.E.; the dictionary covered major events in the history of the Khazars, who practiced religious tolerance among Jews, Muslims, and Christians. Interwoven into the story is a plot concerning scholars of the seventeenth and twentieth centuries (the later group a reincarnation of the earlier one), who are trying to locate

an earlier Khazar dictionary and derive from it information of great spiritual significance. Adding to the book's complexity was the fact that Pavić arranged for it to appear in two separate editions, designated as male and female, which differed by only seventeen lines but in fact recast many of the novel's important events in a new light.

Despite its complexity, *Dictionary of the Khazars* was entertaining, filled with puzzles, dreams, and a shifting boundary between dreams and reality that was reminiscent of the so-called magic realism of Colombian novelist Gabriel García Márquez. And the book seemed to anticipate a new development in writing: Mihajlovic was one of the literary critics who pointed out that the book resembled hypertext—linked text on a computer, although the Internet was in its infancy when Pavić wrote the book. Pavić himself agreed that *Dictionary of the Khazars* could be read in different orders: alphabetically, chronologically, or randomly. Hillel Halkin enthused in the *New Republic* that *Dictionary of the Khazars* was a "book about the labyrinths of historical scholarship, about illusion and reality, about the unreal nature of space and time, about people who dream each other's lives and deaths, about transpersonal identity, about reincarnation, about the search for God, about the parallels between language and the universe."

Judith Shulevitz of the *New York Times Book Review* quoted Pavić as saying that "we are tired of the old way of reading from beginning to end." Pavić set out to equal the originality of *Dictionary of the Khazars*—no small feat—and his second novel, *Landscape Painted with Tea,* appeared in Yugoslavia in 1988 and was translated into English in 1990. The book dealt with a failed architect who investigates his family's past in an attempt to understand himself, and is led back to the world of Belgrade during World War II.

Structured Book Like Crossword

The book was, in Pavić's words as well as those of others, structured like a crossword puzzle: it could be read Across (that is, in sequential order, although the chapters are not presented consecutively) or Down (non-chronologically), following individual characters. Once again, the book contained a large variety of subplots, dreams, and historical details, organized into two intersecting stories (or sets of words that cross). Pavić avoided a sophomore slump with *Landscape Painted with Tea,* which earned strong reviews. His next book, *The Inner Side of the Wind: A Novel of Hero and Leander* (1991) presented a pair of modern characters who reenacted the lives of the title characters, figures from Greek mythology. Pavić intended the novel's structure to resemble that of a clepsydra, a water clock. In his fourth novel, *Last Love in Constantinople: A Tarot Novel for Divination* (1998), he used the device of a deck of tarot cards to tell the story of two rival families.

Pavić continued to write prolifically through the first decade of the new century, but much of his output awaits translation from Serbo-Croatian. Several of his later books have appeared in editions formatted for portable electronic readers such as Amazon.com's Kindle; these later Pavić works included *Blue Book* and *Unique Item: Delta Novel,* both of which involved multiple endings from which a reader could choose. *Unique Item: Delta Novel* was billed as a detective story that diverges into one hundred branches. In 2011, his *Second Body* became one of the first works issued by the new Amazon Digital Services electronic publishing venture. Pavić died in Belgrade on November 30, 2009.

Periodicals

Independent (London, England), February 1, 2010.
New Republic, December 19, 1988.
New York Times Book Review, December 16, 1990.
Publishers Weekly, May 18, 1998.
Review of Contemporary Fiction, Summer 1998.

Online

"Autobiography," Milorad Pavić Official Website, http://khazars. com/en/biography (September 27, 2011).
Contemporary Authors Online, Gale, 2010 (September 27, 2011).
"In Memoriam: Brother Academic Milorad Pavic," *Regular Grand Lodge of Serbia (Freemason),* http://www.rglserbia. org/?p=66 (September 27, 2011).
"Milorad Pavic, (1929–2009)," *Books and Writers,* http://www. kirjasto.sci.fi/pavic.htm (September 27, 2011).□

Rebecca Talbot Perkins

American activist Rebecca Talbot Perkins (1866-1956) helped advance the concept of adoption. She was a successful business woman, but she is best remembered for her efforts in facilitating the bringing together of parentless children with couples that wanted to provide them a home.

Rebecca Clarendon Talbot Perkins was a successful businesswoman in a period (the late eighteenth century) when it was rare for a female to achieve success. That alone makes her remarkable. But, more importantly, she followed her humanitarian impulses to promote adoption of children when agencies posed significant barriers. Her efforts would lead to her induction into National Women's Hall of Fame.

Ran Father's Business Upon His Death

Rebecca Clarendon Talbot was born on February 14, 1866, in Brooklyn, New York. She was one of three daughters of Joseph Talbot and Eliza Clarendon. Her father came to the United States in 1855. Previously, he lived in Street, a small town located in Somerset in England. Her mother, it is believed, was born in Ireland.

When she was only twenty-four years old, her father succumbed to illness after an influenza epidemic ravaged the area where they lived. Before he passed away, he had established a successful real estate brokerage firm in Brooklyn. When he died, Rebecca assumed the reins of the four-year-old business, which helped her to support the emotionally and financially devastated family. Most likely, she was strongly influenced by her aunt, Caroline Talbot, an English citizen and the first postmistress in Street.

Rebecca Clarendon Talbot kept her late father's business afloat, which was remarkable, considering contemporary circumstances: During the late nineteenth century, few women engaged in business activities or even operated their own enterprises. But Talbot managed to succeed in Brooklyn, a tough neighborhood. Indeed, she was one of the first two women to possess a brokerage license in that New York borough.

Many businesses like to hang their first-earned dollar on the wall. But after five decades of success, she preferred to display a framed newspaper article dated March 9, 1891 (as quoted on the *Chy an Gof* website tribute to her) that read: "Rebecca C. Talbot, a daughter of the late Joseph Talbot, was this week appointed a Commissioner of Deeds by County Clerk Kaiser. Miss Talbot is the first lady appointed by the present County Clerk and the second lady to receive the distinction in the history of Kings County."

Established a Children's Service

Hers were substantial accomplishments, especially for a woman. But Talbot would soon become very active in both charitable and civic work. Indeed, Talbot would become best known for her philanthropy, especially as it related to the best interests of young children. She became known as a successful and compassionate woman. Today, the business she ran, and the success she realized, are overshadowed by the charitable organization that she helped establish: the Talbot Children's Services. Her fifty years of business success matched her half-century of philanthropic interests.

Indeed, after she became successful, it did not take long for her to establish a strong presence in the civic and charitable sector. She was an individual who took on many causes. For instance, in 1893, she became part of the Brooklyn Women's Suffrage Society, well before women campaigned for—and proved successful in—changing the Constitution, as far as women's rights. She advocated women's voting rights long before the nineteenth amendment to the United States was passed. Also, for many years, she was chairman of the Alliance of Women's Clubs of Brooklyn, and she served as president of the People's Political League of Kings County. She was vice-president of the Memorial Hospital for Women and Children and a director of the Welcome Home for Girls. In 1915, she became president of the Women's Suffrage Society New York.

Married Agar Perkins

Meanwhile, after operating the brokerage business for several years on her own, she partnered with Agar Ludlow Perkins, a family acquaintance from Iroquois, Dundas, Canada. His family had emigrated from Warwickshire, England in about 1630. Talbot and Perkins married on September 5, 1895, in Brooklyn. Once married, they continued to jointly operate the brokerage business.

In the early part of the 1920s—the exact date is indefinite according to records—Talbot, now known as Rebecca Talbot Perkins, was asked to help find an adoptive family for an out-of-wedlock child. She bought advertisement space in a local newspaper, announcing the need. She received many responses to the ad. This encouraged her to continue in this direction.

In 1927, she connected with a committee that was part of the Alliance of Women's Clubs of Brooklyn to form a membership corporation called the The Rebecca Talbot Perkins Adoption Society (it later became known as the Talbot Perkins Children's Services). This agency was incorporated on April 13 of that year. The incorporation document was prepared by her niece, Reba Talbot Swain, an attorney and the first female deputy attorney general for New York State, according to family history. Perkins' sister, Minnie, the mother of Reba Swain, was also on the board of the Adoption Society. At the time, few agencies existed that promoted adoption. Perkins's organization would later provide foster care, day care, and family support, as well as improved—and more compassionate—adoption services to many families throughout the United States that sought to bring parentless children into their homes and families.

This service became the focus of her community activities—indeed, her life—and she served as president from 1927 to 1949. She also held the position of honorary president until her death in 1956. The service was first located in Brooklyn Heights. Later it relocated to Manhattan, a move that helped the organization widen its activities and increase its offered social services.

Even as she aged, Perkins put in long daily and weekly hours. She embodied a great deal of energy. She would attribute this to her earlier work experience. "When I started in business, the hours for real estate offices were from eight o'clock in the morning until nine o'clock at night and no half-holiday on Saturday," she remembered (as recorded in the *Chy an Gof* website).

Though the daily work load would shrink, Perkins still devoted her time to her philanthropic efforts. Along with her adoption-related activities, Perkins strived to establish better schools, make reforms in the court system, battle for better pay for civil service workers, and expand social services for women and children. But throughout the years, her main focus was on adoption and the organization she helped establish.

Died in New York City

After many years of indefatigable public service, Perkins died on November 1, 1956, in Brooklyn, in New York City. She was ninety years old. Her husband preceded her in death, on August 31, 1948. Ironically, for a woman who strived to match adoptive parents with children, Perkins was childless. Her only survivor was her sister, Minnie, an Adoption Society board member.

After nearly eighty years of providing adoption services and foster care for numerous families in the United States, the organization that Perkins founded closed in April 2002, due to lack of government funding. Still, the impact that Perkins had on adoption services is profound.

Posthumously Inducted in Hall

In 2009, she was posthumously inducted into the National Women's Hall of Fame in America. In that year, she was part of a very select group of ten accomplished women including artist Louise Bourgeois, scientist Mildred Cohn, women's activist and lawyer Karen DeCrow, as well as Susan Kelly-Dreiss, who raised awareness about the plight of battered women and children; Allie B. Latimer, an attorney and civil rights activist who helped organize the Federally Employed Women in 1968; Emma Lazarus, a Jewish-American author who penned the phrase "Give me your tired, your poor/Your huddled masses yearning to breathe free"; Ruth Patrick, a pioneering scientist; Susan Solomon, who advanced theories about ozone holes, and Katherine Stoneman, the first woman admitted to practice law in New York State.

Perkins was in great company. She and the other women joined 226 previous inductees honored by the National Women's Hall of Fame, which recognizes and celebrates the accomplishments of American women. The not-for-profit Hall was founded in Seneca Falls, New York, site of the first Women's Rights Convention in 1848.

Periodicals

Brooklyn Eagle, January 19, 1950.

Online

"Rebecca Talbot Perkins," *Chy an Gof,* http://www.btinternet.com/~e.newbery/rebecca.htm (December 10, 2011).

"Rebecca Talbot Perkins," *National Women's Hall of Fame,* http://www.greatwomen.org/women-of-the-hall/search-the-hall/details/2/234-Perkins (December 10, 2011).

"Ten Phenomenal Women Named as Inductees to the National Womens Hall of Fame," *Academy of Natural Sciences,.* http://www.ansp.org/press/release/2009/NWHF_2009_Inductees.pdf (December 10, 2011).□

Sam Phillips

Known as the "father of rock 'n' roll," American record producer Sam Phillips (1923-2003) founded Sun Records in 1952 and subsequently launched the careers of several noted musicians. Johnny Cash, B.B. King, Jerry Lee Lewis, Roy Orbison, Elvis Presley, and Conway Twitty all passed through the doors of Phillips's legendary Memphis studio to record their first songs. Phillips was known for his contributions to the early sounds of rock and remains the only person ever inducted into the rock 'n' roll, country, blues, and rockabilly halls of fame.

The youngest of eight children, Samuel Cornelius Phillips was born January 5, 1923, in Florence, Alabama. His parents were poor tenant farmers who lived along the Tennessee River. As a child, Phillips picked cotton alongside black and white farm laborers and though the South remained segregated, he felt a kinship beyond skin color. Phillips was particularly intrigued with the soulful songs

the black workers sang. "There was a certain feeling I developed as a young person for black people," Phillips told Dave Hoekstra of the *Chicago Sun-Times*. "Somehow they were able to get pleasure out of things that I couldn't see them enjoying. I heard them sing a lot, and I didn't hear white folks going down the cotton rows singing that much." At Coffee High School, Phillips played drums and sousaphone and directed the school's marching band.

Hit the Airwaves as DJ

As an adolescent, Phillips dreamed of becoming a criminal defense attorney. He idolized Clarence Darrow, the country lawyer who defended John T. Scopes in the 1925 Scopes Trial over the teaching of evolution. That dream came to an end after Phillips's father died and he dropped out of high school to work two jobs to support his family. Instead of finishing his education, Phillips worked at a local grocery and at a funeral parlor.

Realizing he would never make it to law school, Phillips decided to focus on music and took some audio engineering classes, then landed a job as a disc jockey at WLAY, a 250-watt AM radio station in Muscle Shoals, Alabama. He moved to a station in Decatur, Alabama, then worked in Nashville. In 1945, Phillips relocated to Memphis to work as an announcer at WREC. At WREC, Phillips hosted *Songs of the West* and *Saturday Afternoon Tea Dance,* which he broadcast from the Skyway Room at the top of the Memphis Peabody Hotel. The program enjoyed a national audience through syndication with the CBS radio network.

Opened Studio

Phillips soon realized that Memphis lacked a studio where aspiring black musicians could record their music. Hoping to offer that service, Phillips leased an abandoned radiator shop at 706 Union Avenue in October 1949. With the help

of his assistant—Memphis radio celebrity Marion Keisker—Phillips renovated the space. In Peter Guralnick's *Last Train to Memphis,* Keisker described how the recording studio came to be. " He would talk about this idea that he had, this dream, I suppose, to have a facility where black people could come and play their own music, a place where they would feel free and relaxed to do it. One day we were riding along, and he saw that spot on Union, and he said, 'That's the spot I want.'"

In early 1950, Phillips opened the Memphis Recording Service out of his Union Street space. Phillips hoped to attract musicians, but also figured he could find work recording weddings, funerals, and other ceremonies. Phillips adopted the slogan, "We Record Anything, Anywhere, Anytime." Almost immediately, Phillips attracted local gospel and blues musicians who were eager to have their work recorded and heard outside the mid-South. Phillips recorded their performances, made a gramophone copy of the recording, then leased it to larger record labels who took care of pressing the records and distributing them.

During this time Phillips worked with Chicago-based Chess Records, RPM Records out of Los Angeles, and the local Duke Records. Making the gramophone records from the recordings took a lot of skill. To make the discs he offered to record labels, Phillips taped the artist's work, then used a recording lathe to cut a sound-modulated groove into the surface of a 16-inch blank acetate disc. Phillips had gained exposure to disc-making through his work as a DJ. At the time, most DJs recorded their programs, then duplicated them for other stations, thus giving them experience as recording engineers.

Produced Breakthrough Recordings

During those early years, Phillips recorded many bluesmen, including Bobby "Blue" Bland, James Cotton, B.B. King, Joe Hill Lewis, and Howlin' Wolf. In 1951, Phillips released a recording of Howlin' Wolf growling his raw-and-dirty blues on "How Many More Years/Moanin' At Midnight." It was the booming bluesman's first single. Wolf's success with Sun Records prompted him to move to Chicago, where he became an important contributor to the Windy City's blues scene.

In 1951, Phillips engineered a breakthrough with "Rocket 88" by Jackie Brenston, a member of Ike Turner's band. The song—which included a heavy backbeat and guitar distortion—offered praise for the Oldsmobile Rocket 88. The distortion effect was somewhat accidental but later became a rock standard. On the way to the studio, the band's amplifier fell off the car, damaging the cone. Phillips stuffed the cone full of newspaper to hold it in place, which distorted the sound. "Rocket 88" is often cited as an important milestone in the evolution of rock music; some music historians call it the first rock song ever recorded. The song topped the rhythm and blues chart, becoming Phillips' first big hit.

During this time life was stressful for Phillips as he maintained his radio job and tried to run his recording service on the side. In addition, he had a wife and two young boys. In 1942, prior to moving to Memphis, he had married Rebecca Burns. In an interview with Hoekstra, Phillips described that time. "I would get up around 5:30

and work at the radio station from 7 until 3. Then I'd work the P.A. system at the Peabody after that. And then I'd work with the unproven talent at Sun—which I loved the most. I dropped down to 125 pounds and almost had a nervous breakdown, so I had to decide whether I could stay on with the job that I loved at the radio station or go into recording.'' Phillips, in fact, was hospitalized at the age of 28 and underwent electroshock therapy.

Opened Sun Records

The success of ''Rocket 88'' convinced Phillips he could make it as a record producer. He quit his radio job and launched into producing full-time, founding Sun Records in 1952. Instead of giving his recordings to other labels for pressing and distribution, he decided to do it himself and enjoy the full profits of his work. Phillips created a distinctive yellow and brown sunburst logo, which he stamped on every record. Phillips used the name sun because he felt a new day was dawning—the use of the sun in both the name and logo reflected Phillips's optimism.

The first official release from Sun Records was ''Drivin' Slow,'' an instrumental by black teenage saxophonist Johnny London. Even in this early recording, Phillips showed his creativity in trying to capture a certain mood. On ''Drivin' Slow'' Phillips wanted to re-create the atmosphere of Beale Street so the song would sound like it was being played in the open alleyways, bouncing off the walls of the buildings. Phillips built a wooden contraption, which he placed over the bell of the saxophone before recording. This gave the horn a dense, muted quality, making it sound more like a sax on the street. In March 1953, Phillips recorded ''Bear Cat'' by sharecropper-turned-singer Rufus Thomas. The song topped the R&B chart, becoming the first number one hit released by Sun Records.

Discovered Elvis Presley

In 1953, a truck driver named Elvis Presley wandered into the studio to record a song for fun. Phillips ran a deal—for $3.98, anyone could use the studio to record a song, which Phillips would press into a keepsake single. Intrigued by the recording, Phillips signed Presley to a deal. In the summer of 1954, Phillips invited Presley in for a recording session. Presley considered himself a ballad singer and was intent on recording a ballad. Phillips did not like the way things were going, so he halted the session. During the break, Presley picked up his guitar and started messing around, strumming some blues and fooling around with his voice. Phillips liked the uptempo change of direction and they ended up recording ''That's All Right (Mama),'' an Arthur Crudup cover, and ''Blue Moon of Kentucky'' for the record's B-side. Phillips did not have a drummer on hand, so the bass player kept time. Phillips immediately delivered the record to a local DJ, who put it on the air and had his telephone lines jammed with callers eager to know more about the new artist.

Phillips continued working with Presley, but his biggest hit in 1955 came from country crooner Johnny Cash. Cash had visited Phillips in 1954 and auditioned singing gospel music. Phillips turned him away and Cash later returned with some rockabilly tunes, which Phillips liked. In 1955, Cash recorded ''Folsom Prison Blues'' at Sun Studios; it hit number one on the country singles chart and was a *Billboard* top 40 hit. In 1956, Sun Records released Cash's ''I Walk the Line,'' which spent more than 40 weeks on the country chart, hitting number one. At the end of 1955, Presley left Sun and moved to RCA Records after RCA negotiated a contract buyout worth $40,000, which was the most paid for a recording artist. By that time, Presley had recorded ten songs with Phillips.

Through the mid-1950s, Sun Records released a string of multi-chart hits. In December 1955, Carl Perkins recorded ''Blue Suede Shoes,'' which charted on both the country music and R&B charts, though Presley's later recording of the song is most remembered. Perkins's recording, however, sold well, becoming Sun Records's first million-seller. Phillips signed Roy Orbison in 1956, followed by Jerry Lee Lewis, who showed up on Phillips's doorstep after reading an article about Presley. Lewis's first single, ''Crazy Arms,'' was released in 1956. In 1957, Lewis released his famed rollicking piano hit, ''Great Balls of Fire,'' on the Sun label. The song charted on *Billboard*'s pop, country, and R&B charts. In 1957, Phillips put Bill Justis's rock instrumental ''Raunchy'' on three charts—the pop, R&B, and country. In 1958, Lewis hit all three charts with ''Breathless.'' Other noted musicians who passed through Sun Studios during those years included country singer Charlie Rich and rockabilly artists Sonny Burgess and Billy Lee Riley.

Noted for Stripped-Down Sound

Over the years, Sun Records earned a reputation for releasing simple, unadorned performances. Phillips preferred to capture passion over technique. He liked the stripped-down raw sounds of his hardscrabble youth and did not work to perfect his recordings. Phillips was also one of the first producers to record with ''slapback.'' What Phillips did was use a radio console to bounce the signal, with a small delay, to his tape machines, which were mounted on the wall. This made the songs sound richer and resembled what a person might hear out of a jukebox with the sound bouncing off a diner wall. This technique was a defining element of the Sun sound.

Los Angeles Times music critic Robert Hilburn praised Phillips's contributions to music and pop culture. ''Phillips was arguably the single most important figure in the birth of rock 'n' roll because he always saw it as a revolutionary force, not just a hit sound. From the beginning he saw that it was a vehicle for social and cultural expression that would be used by generations to come.''

By the mid-1960s, most of Phillips's stars had moved on to bigger labels. In addition, the music scene had evolved with the coming of the Beatles; long-playing, wall-of-sound albums were all the rage. Instead of adapting, Phillips decided to leave the business and sold Sun Records in 1969 for $1 million to Shelby Singleton, an executive with Mercury Records. Phillips took his money and invested in Holiday Inn. He spent the remainder of his life running radio stations and rarely granted interviews. Phillips died in Memphis on July 30, 2003, of respiratory failure.

Books

Guralnick, Peter, *Last Train to Memphis: The Rise of Elvis Presley,* Little, Brown and Company, 1994.
Petrusich, Amanda, *It Still Moves,* Faber and Faber, Inc., 2008

Periodicals

Los Angeles Times, July 31, 2003.
Mobile Register (AL), August 1, 2003.
New York Times, August 1, 2003.
Variety, August 4-10, 2003.

Online

"Recalling Sam Phillips/Sun Records," *Chicago Sun-Times,* http://blogs.suntimes.com/hoekstra/2008/10/recalling_sam_phillipssun_reco.html (December 23, 2011).
"Sam Phillips: The Sound and Legacy of Sun Records," *NPR,* http://www.npr.org/programs/morning/features/2001/nov/phillips/011128.sam.phillips.html (November 3, 2011).□

William D. Phillips

The American physicist William D. Phillips (born 1948) won the Nobel Prize for Physics in 1997 for his work on the laser cooling and trapping of atoms.

William Daniel Phillips was born Wilkes-Barre, Pennsylvania, on November 5, 1948. Both his parents were social workers who had little knowledge of science but supported their son's obvious interest and ability. Phillips's father, William Cornelius Phillips, was of Methodist background and could trace his family background in the United States to the American Revolution; his mother, Mary Catherine Savino (she later used the name Savine) was a Catholic, born in Italy. Phillips grew up doing science experiments with household cleaners and a small microscope. Before entering his teens, he was already convinced that he wanted to make science his life's work. Attending Camp Hill High School near Harrisburg, Pennsylvania, Phillips was placed in advanced classes. "I can see that the classes that emphasized language and writing skills were just as important for the development of my scientific career as were science and math," he observed in an autobiographical sketch written for the Nobel Prize observances.

In the summer after his junior year of high school, Phillips was able to work in a lab at the nearby University of Delaware, where he was impressed by a graduate student who told him that an experimental physicist was someone who got paid for pursuing his hobby. During his senior year, Phillips began dating Jane Van Wynen. The romance endured through Phillips's four years at Juniata College (which both his parents had attended) and Van Wynen's at Penn State University, ensuring that Phillips would not pursue a heavy social schedule at Juniata but instead focus on his physics studies. He was inspired by the filmed lectures of physicist Richard Feynman that were played in class by one of his professors. Phillips and Van Wynen were married in 1970 and raised two daughters, Catherine (Caitlin) and Christine.

After graduating *summa cum laude* from Juniata that year, Phillips entered graduate school at the Massachusetts Institute of Technology (MIT). It was during this period that he began to do the work that led to his Nobel Prize–winning discoveries. He was one of a group of researchers attempting to bring about a condition called a Bose-Einstein condensate, in which a group of supercooled atoms come to a nearly complete standstill and form an oddly regular configuration. The phenomenon had been theoretically described by Albert Einstein and Indian physicist Satyendra Nath Bose in the 1920s but never actually realized. Phillips's initial attempts were unsuccessful, but he gained valuable insights into the field of low-temperature physics and its possible applications.

Attempted to Realize Einstein's Prediction

Phillips's PhD thesis at MIT underwent several stages of evolution as he undertook to measure the behavior of protons in water molecules and learned more about the available precision instruments that could be brought to bear on the task. An adviser, Dan Kleppner, steered him toward experiments involving collisions of atoms that have been subjected to the impact of laser beams. Phillips received his doctorate from MIT in 1976 and remained at the university for two more years under a Chaim Weizmann fellowship, doing experiments related to the elusive Bose-Einstein condensate. In 1978, he accepted a position at the National Bureau of Standards, later renamed the National Institute of Standards and Technology (NIST), in Gaithersburg, Maryland. The NIST, a part of the U.S. Department of

Commerce, seeks to promote U.S. industrial competitiveness through research into precise measurements and measurement technology; as part of this effort the agency funds pure research.

Among the most visible public manifestations of NIST's work were the various atomic clocks that provide reference points for sensitive time measurements such as the astronomical observations of the U.S. Naval Observatory, and later the orbits of the group of satellites on which Global Positioning System (GPS) technology relies. Atomic clocks are calibrated to the frequencies of atoms and were, as Phillips began his prize-winning research, accurate to within one part in trillions. But in the world of precision time measurement, Phillips told a meeting of the American Scientific Affiliation organization, "we are greedy . . . and we want better accuracy." The way to obtain better accuracy was to slow atoms down so that their movement could be measured more precisely. As atoms began to move very slowly, they also became colder; the temperatures of the materials with which Phillips worked in his research approached absolute zero (-459.67 Fahrenheit).

Several scientists were working on aspects of the problem, and it became clear that lasers, of which Phillips was already an expert manipulator, were of central importance, for atoms reacted to laser beams by absorbing and giving off energy in unusual ways. A team led by Steven Chu, later Secretary of Energy in the administration of U.S. president Barack Obama, experimented with a group of six lasers that converged on a single point, creating a zone of what, according to *Science News,* the team called "optical molasses." Chu showed that sodium atoms introduced into this zone could be considerably slowed down.

Exceeded Theoretical Cooling Limit

The stage was set for Phillips's breakthrough, which occurred at NIST in 1988. Using Chu's method, Phillips and his team succeeded in cooling sodium atoms to 43 microkelvins, or -459.669923 degrees Fahrenheit, just slightly above absolute zero (the temperature at which all molecular motion stops). This was far lower than the limit of 240 microkelvins that had been theoretically predicted for laser cooling techniques, and Phillips claimed that it was the coldest three-dimensional gas ever observed up to that time. Shortly after Phillips's experiments, French physicist Claude Cohen-Tannoudji of the Ecole Normale Supérieure in Paris (where Phillips taught during the 1989-90 academic year, having mastered French as a college student), succeeded in refining Phillips's results still further, to a point where atoms reached a temperature of just 180 billionths of one degree above absolute zero and moved at only two centimeters per second.

On October 15, 1997, Phillips's wife, Jane, heard on the radio that her husband, along with Chu and Cohen-Tannoudji, had been awarded the 1997 Nobel Prize for Physics. Steve Rolston, a member of Phillips's research team at NIST, partly credited Phillips's attitude for his success, telling Arlo Wagner of the *Washington Times* that

"he's a great guy to work with, one of the most enthusiastic individuals I've ever known." Each of the three investigators won a cash prize of $1 million in addition to the honor that came with the Nobel; Phillips expressed confidence that, after receiving the prize, he would be able to finance his children's college educations.

Phillips also viewed his discoveries in spiritual terms. According to Wagner, Phillips told a news conference after he received the Nobel that "God has given us an incredibly fascinating world to live in and explore." Phillips and his family were comparatively rare among top-level scientists in their active adherence to Christianity. According to *American Scientific Affiliation,* he was dubbed the "religious Nobelist." Phillips has often lectured on the relationship between religion and science, arguing that there is no ultimate conflict between them; he believes that science illuminates God's design of the universe, and that religion deals with interpersonal matters that are beyond the reach of science. Phillips and his family attend Fairhaven Methodist Church in Darnestown, Maryland, where he teaches Sunday school and sings in a gospel choir he formed himself.

In the mid-1990s, Phillips had the satisfaction of seeing a group of Colorado researchers finally produce a Bose-Einstein condensate. His own group in Maryland extended the work of the Colorado team, learning to manipulate sodium atoms with lasers and make them move at desired speeds and in specific directions. In addition to his work at NIST, Phillips has held the position of distinguished professor of physics at the University of Maryland since 1992. He is the recipient of honorary degrees from Juniata, Williams College, and the University of Buenos Aires. Beyond their applications in atomic timekeeping, Phillips's discoveries occurred at a fundamental level where they held the possibility of inspiring as-yet unknown innovations.

Books

American Men & Women of Science, Gale, 2008.

Periodicals

Atlanta Journal-Constitution, March 14, 1999.
Morning Call (Allentown, PA), April 18, 2000.
Science News, October 25, 1997.
Washington Times, October 16, 1997.

Online

"Abbreviated Curriculum Vitae of William D. Phillips," *National Institute of Standards and Technology,* http://www.physics.nist.gov/News/Nobel/phillipscv.html (October 16, 2011).

"The Nobel Prize in Physics 1997," *Nobel Prize,* http://www.nobelprize.org/nobel_prizes/physics/laureates/1997/phillips (October 16, 2011).

"Nobelist William Phillips Addresses ASA99," *The American Scientific Affiliation: A Network of Christians in the Sciences,* http://www.asa3.org/ASA/newsletter/SEPOCT99.htm (October 16, 2011). □

R

Bessica Medlar Raiche

American aviator Bessica Medlar Raiche (1875–1932) was recognized in 1910 as the first woman to fly an airplane in the United States.

As with so many of the accomplishments in the world of early aviation, Raiche's priority has been contested. Another flight, by aviatrix Blanche Stuart Scott, preceded Raiche's flight by several weeks but was reported to be unintentional—Scott was practicing runway acceleration when a gust of wind lifted her plane off the ground. Aviators and aviation historians have disputed the sequence of events, but Raiche's accomplishments, which included flying virtually without instruction and surviving what is universally recognized as the country's first female-piloted plane crash, earned her a solid place in aviation history books.

Showed Artistic, Linguistic Talents

Raiche was born Bessica Medlar in April of 1875 near Beloit, Wisconsin. She or her family may have used the surname Medler as well, and for a time she used the name Faith Medlar; Faith may have been her middle name. Her spirit of adventure and determination apparently came from both sides of her family: her father was an inventor, and her mother's ancestry dated back to the Puritans of Massachusetts. She had one younger sister, Alice Medlar. As a young person her curiosity was wide-ranging: she showed talent in art and music, and she reportedly mastered several languages.

On top of all this, Raiche was one of very few women of her time who were equal to the rigors of obtaining a medical degree; she attended Tufts University and was awarded an M.D. degree in 1903. Raiche apparently practiced dentistry for a time in the town of New Hampton in central New Hampshire. The picture of Raiche that emerges from contemporary descriptions shows a young woman with a fearless love of the outdoors who thought nothing of engaging in typically masculine pursuits such as trap shooting and swimming.

It was a desire for artistic instruction that took her to Paris, France, in her late twenties. There she studied the technique of painting miniature watercolors on ivory and also took music lessons. Her Parisian trip was marked by several other important events in her life. First, she became interested in aviation. She saw the Wright Brothers, who came to France in 1908 to give flying demonstrations that aimed at (and in large part succeeded in) quieting the skepticism French writers expressed toward their pioneering accomplishments. She also was impressed by the exploits of the Baroness Raymonde de Laroche, who flew (as would Raiche a year later) with very little formal instruction in the fall of 1909 and became probably the world's first woman to be licensed as a pilot. Finally, Raiche was lucky enough to meet a man who shared her enthusiasm for flying: François Raiche, known as Frank after the couple returned to the United States, was an avid amateur aircraft designer.

Built Plane in Living Room

Both Frank and Bessica Raiche have been credited as the designer of the plane in which Bessica made her pioneering flight; probably they worked together. The couple built the plane jointly, making individual pieces in the living room of their Mineola, Long Island, New York home and doing large-scale assembly in the backyard when the plane outgrew the house. Following the older Wright brothers' designs rather than the newer Curtiss type, they nevertheless devised several important innovations in aircraft design, substituting silk for heavy cloth and piano wire for iron stove wire in the critical quest for lighter weight. They presented the finished plane to the Aeronautical Society of New York, whose members had observed Scott's flight on September 2, 1910, and determined that Scott had not flown intentionally. Although women pilots may have been regarded as a curiosity at the time, a number were given the chance to fly at aviation shows, where their presence drew enthusiastic crowds.

The date of Raiche's own flight has been variously reported as September 15, September 16 (the consensus choice, appearing in a Knoxville, Tennessee *Sentinel* account at the time, and noted on the Early Aviators website), and September 26, 1910. Raiche had never been at the controls of a plane or even ridden in one. She recalled, as quoted by Henry M. Holden and Captain Lori Griffith in *Ladybirds: The Untold Story of Women Pilots in America,* that her entire course of flying instruction began and ended when a mechanic showed her the steering apparatus and said, "Pull it this way to go up, and that way to go down."

Climbing into the cockpit of her plane on the morning of the appointed day at Mineola Aviation Grounds, Raiche had no problem becoming airborne after several preliminary attempts. Skimming the tops of the field's long grasses, she stayed aloft for about a mile before miscalculating a maneuver above a small depression in the ground and a subsequent rise. The nose of the plane hit the ground, ejecting Raiche from the cockpit. She hit the ground, and the plane landed on top of her. Perhaps thanks to the plane's unusually lightweight construction, she was able to crawl out from under the wreckage, limping slightly but hastening to shut down the plane's still-running engine. According to the *Aerofiles* website, Raiche "calmly said she was not injured to those who ran to her aid, and then she directed the men to drag the wrecked plane back to the shed." The *Sentinel* reported the event as the "First Smash-Up of Aeroplane by Woman in the USA."

Credited Rival with First Flight

At a dinner held October 13, 1910, the Aeronautical Society of America presented Raiche with a diamond-studded gold medal bearing the words "First Woman Aviator in America." The presenter was Hudson Maxim, the inventor of smokeless gunpowder. Blanche Scott's partisans later claimed that her flight had occurred earlier, but Raiche refused to be drawn into a rivalry and even backed Scott's claim, pointing to her own unorthodox pursuits as a magnet that had drawn media attention to herself. "Blanche deserved the recognition," she recalled, as quoted by Holden and Griffith, but I got more attention because of my lifestyle. I drove an automobile, was active in sports like shooting and swimming, and I even wore riding pants and knickers." Raiche recalled that some had looked down on such behavior, but she rejoined that "I enjoyed life, and just wanted to be myself."

After Raiche was honored, she and her husband formed the French-American Aeroplane Company. The new firm did not last long, but the couple refined some of their light aircraft ideas and are credited with several innovations. They did succeed in constructing and selling two more planes. Raiche herself made several more flights but retired from flying after dubious medical advice that she received following an illness warned that high-altitude air was bad for her lungs.

Around 1913, Raiche and her husband moved west to the Los Angeles area, where she resumed her medical career; Frank Raiche was active as an attorney. She opened what developed into an active practice in obstetrics and gynecology, becoming one of the first group of women active in that specialty. Raiche was named president of the Orange County Medical Association in 1923. She and her husband raised one daughter, Catherine E. Raiche.

Interviewed shortly before her death, Raiche said that it had been so long since she had been in the air that she would be afraid to fly again. She died in her sleep, apparently of heart disease, in Balboa, California, on April 11, 1932. Much of Raiche's life remains sparsely documented, but author Marge Bitetti is reportedly at work on a full-length biography of the aviator.

Books

Holden, Henry M., with Captain Lori Griffith, *Ladybirds: The Untold Story of Women Pilots in America,* Black Hawk, 1993.

Periodicals

New York Times, April 12, 1932.
Record (Bergen County, NJ), November 7, 2009.

Online

"Bessica Medlar Raiche, 1875–1932," *EarlyAviators.com,* http://www.earlyaviators.com/eraiche.htm (October 22, 2011).
"Bessica Raiche," *Smithsonian National Air and Space Museum,* http://www.nasm.si.edu/research/aero/women_aviators/bessica_raiche.htm (October 22, 2011).
"Bessie Raiche," *Aerofiles,* http://www.aerofiles.com/bio_r.html (October 22, 2011).
"Dr. Bessica Medlar Raiche, M1903," *Tufts Alumni Association,* http://www.tuftsalumni.org/who-we-are/alumni-recognition/tufts-notables/luminaries-2/#raiche (October 22, 2011). □

Ariel Ramírez

The Argentine composer Ariel Ramírez (1921–2010) created one of the most popular works of twentieth-century classical music with his *Misa Criolla,* a choral Mass that drew on folk materials of his native country.

Ramírez composed other music besides the *Misa Criolla,* and he was well known both in Argentina and abroad for his explorations of Argentine folk rhythms and instruments. Motivated by broadly humanitarian and democratic instincts, he wrote large vocal works celebrating figures from Argentine history. Yet it was for the *Misa Criolla* that he remains best known. A colorful, joyful celebration of the Mass, underlaid by traditional instruments, the work was a best seller when it first appeared,

and it has been performed countless times by artists ranging from opera stars to ordinary church choirs to folk vocalists.

Named After Education Essay Title

Ariel Ramírez was born on September 4, 1921, in Santa Fe in northeastern Argentina. The famed Argentine gaucho, or cowboy, Segundo Ramírez, was his father's stepbrother. His parents valued education and named him Ariel after the title of an essay by the progressive Uruguayan educator José Enrique Rodó (the name in turn came from Shakespeare''s *The Tempest*). His father was one of ten siblings who all became teachers. Ramírez was expected to enter the profession as well, and dutifully took education classes and earned a teaching certificate. But "in my first job as a fourth-grade teacher in Santa Fe I lasted two days. I couldn't say no to those schemers. I had discipline problems," he recalled to Caleb Bach of *Americas.*

The real issue was that Ramírez was more interested in music than in teaching, and he was fortunate enough to have a piano available to play—in a small museum housed in the school where his father was the chief administrator. Sharing the small hall with stuffed birds when the museum was closed, Ramírez learned to play the popular tangos of the day. But, at a time when the category of folk music hardly existed and few musicians outside of rural cultures were interested in keeping roots traditions alive in Argentina or anywhere else, Ramírez became interested in the range of music that existed in his native country. His father supported him to the extent of giving him traveling money to go the Villa Tulumba in central Argentina, where he lived with a friend for a time and met Atahualpa Yupanqui, one of the founders of folk music in Argentina, when both were performing at a party.

On hearing of the young musician''s interests, Yupanqui advised him to travel to the small towns of northern Argentina where folk traditions were strong. Ramírez objected that he lacked the money, and the next day he received a bus ticket to the town of Jujuy along with a hotel name and ten pesos. He had no trouble finding musicians to teach him in that area, and for several years he moved around northern Argentina from town to town, living in Tucuman, San Juan, and Mendoza. In 1943, Yupanqui invited Ramírez to the capital city of Buenos Aires to perform in a revue called *Voces de la tierra* (Voices of the Earth). The production bombed and closed after a week, and Ramírez took a job as a pianist at station Radio El Mundo.

That job, too, came to an end as the government of strongman Juan Perón began to demand loyalty oaths from employees of media organizations. As a political independent and the son of a radical father, Ramírez soon found himself out of work at the radio station. With tango crowding out other genres of Argentine music, Ramírez decided to try his luck in Europe. Buying a third-class ticket on a ship bound for Italy, and with only $100 in his pocket, he settled in Rome among a small group of expatriate Argentine creative figures. "We were a family," he recalled to Bach. "No one had a peso, but we led a beautiful life."

Met Nuns Who Aided Nazi Victims

The decision was a good one: Ramírez was able to travel around Europe performing and lecturing, and he picked up longer-lasting gigs along the way. In 1952, he spent several months teaching music at a school for novice nuns in southern Germany, with a Spanish-speaking nun serving as interpreter. Staying on for a meal one night, he mentioned the beauty of the area, which prompted the nuns to recall the wartime devastation that had been present just a few years earlier. Ramírez learned that there had been a nearby concentration camp holding a thousand Jewish prisoners, and that some of the nuns had carried out an eight-month campaign to help smuggle food packages into the camp, a campaign that ended only when the packages started to accumulate at the drop-off point.

The experience awakened Ramírez's greater ambitions as an artist. "I felt that I had to compose something deep and religious that would revere life and involve people beyond their creeds, race, color or origin,' he explained in an interview quoted by Adam Bernstein of the *Washington Post,* and he later traced the genesis of the *Misa Criolla* to that kitchen conversation. It was several years before his dream would be realized, however. Returning to Argentina in 1954, Ramírez found that the political situation remained difficult. He took to the road once more, traveling to Bolivia, Peru, and Uruguay, and soaking up local folk traditions.

Later in the 1950s, democratic reforms took place in Argentina, and Ramírez returned to Buenos Aires. He released several albums of his own compositions on the RCA label, taking courses at Argentina's National Conservatory of Music on the side and deepening his knowledge of classical composition. Also, Ramírez met a future collaborator, lawyer Felix Luna, as both were working on the campaign of soon-to-be Argentine president Arturo Frondizi, and decided to compose some music in support of the campaign. The pair also wrote a song that Luna used as part of a successful marriage proposal, and the lawyer's interests began to shift toward literary endeavors.

Set Spanish Text of Mass

Most of Ramírez's creative energy in the early 1960s, however, was devoted to the *Misa Criolla*, whose name meant Creole Mass. The term ''Criolla'' in a Latin American setting meant, roughly, ''native,'' and Ramírez's Mass was set for native Argentine instruments from the northern Andes region as well as choir, keyboard, percussion, and a solo tenor. The opening passage of the Mass showcased the variety of Andean instruments and was unlike anything previously heard on classical recordings. By the time the Mass was completed in 1964, the Second Vatican Council of the Roman Catholic Church had agreed to the celebration of Mass in vernacular (everyday) languages instead of Latin, and Ramírez set the words of the Mass in Spanish.

Shortly after it was completed, the *Misa Criolla* was released on an LP on the Philips label, with the folk vocal group Los Fronterizos, a Buenos Aires choir called the Cantoría de la Basílica del Socorro, and an ensemble of folk instrumentalists, with Ramírez conducting. The Mass was paired on the LP with a Christmas piece, *Navidad Nuestra*, with words by Luna and music by Ramírez. The label took a chance on Ramírez because it had recently had some success with a recording of a similar piece from the Congo, the *Missa Luba*, but few could have predicted how successful the album would eventually become: 2,000 copies were sold in its first week of release, 50,000 in its first year, and several million by the early 2000s. Oddly, it was recorded several years before its first live performance, which did not occur until a concert at the Rheinhalle in Düsseldorf, Germany, in March of 1967.

The *Misa Criolla* established Ramírez's reputation, both abroad and at home, where he conducted a triumphant performance in the fall of 1968. Over the next decades, Ramírez composed several hundred more works that straddled the borders between classical, popular and folk music. Most of them were vocal and composed in collaboration with Luna; these included the cantata *Mujeres Argentinas* (Argentine Women), the political dramatic work *Los Caudillos* (The Leaders), and the *Misa por la Paz y la Justicia* (Mass for Peace and Justice), which Ramírez composed in 1980 in response to popular demand for a new work in the vein of the *Misa Criolla*; Ramírez himself considered the new Mass a more ambitious work. In the early 1980s, however, Argentina once again came under military control, and the work was largely suppressed in Ramírez's home country.

It was the *Misa Criolla* for which Ramírez remained best known. Ramírez received little academic recognition and did not appear in the second edition of the *New Grove Dictionary of Music and Musicians*, classical music's standard reference work. But the *Misa Criolla* was beloved. It was recorded in new versions that featured well-known performers, from Spanish opera singer José Carreras to Argentine *nueva canció* (New Song) folk vocalist Mercedes Sosa as soloists; and beyond that it was performed countless times in churches larges and small, its joyous mood proving consistently pleasing to attendees. In his later years, Ramírez was a celebrated figure of Argentine classical music

and served as secretary-general of the Argentine Society of Authors and Composers. Married to Inées Cuello de Ramírez, the composer had two sons. He died in Buenos Aires on February 18, 2010, after a struggle with degenerative disease.

Periodicals

Americas, September-October 2003.
EFE World News Service, February 19, 2010.
Washington Post, February 21, 2010.

Online

''Ariel Ramírez,'' *All Music Guide*, http://www.allmusic.com/artist/ariel-ramrez-q7872/biography (September 23, 2011).□

Alice Huyler Ramsey

Automobilist Alice Huyler Ramsey (1886–1983) holds a singular spot in the history of the American road trip as the first woman to drive a car across the United States. She completed her New York-to-San Francisco trek in 1909 at a time when paved roads were virtually nonexistent except for a few stretches of major cities. Commended for her intrepid spirit as well as her mechanical and navigational skills, Ramsey was honored as the ''Woman Motorist of the Century'' by the American Automobile Association in 1960.

Alice Taylor Huyler Ramsey came from a family of Dutch immigrants who settled Bergen County, New Jersey, and had long civic and commercial ties to Hackensack, where she was born on November 11, 1886. Her paternal great-grandfather was a judge who was elected to Congress in the 1850s, and her father ran a thriving lumber business and encouraged her interest in tinkering and mechanics. She graduated from Hackensack High School in 1903 and spent a few years at Vassar College in Poughkeepsie, New York. She left the private women's liberal-arts college to marry a widowed Bergen County attorney and politician, John Rathbone Ramsey. Their first child, a son named John Jr., was born in 1907.

Entered Road Rallies

One day in 1908, the Ramsey family's horses were startled by an automobile—a persistent and potentially dangerous occurrence in the era when nature's original beasts of burden shared the road with the noisy new mechanical carriages. Ramsey's husband decided it best to have his wife make the switch, and bought her a zippy red roadster made by the Maxwell-Briscoe Motor Company. She quickly mastered the art of driving, and within months had put a few thousand miles onto her car's odometer as she raced along country roads in Bergen County. She was the founding president of the Women's Motoring Club of New Jersey and earned a perfect score for the Montauk Point Rally, a race from one end of Long Island to the other.

Ramsey's performance in the Montauk rally piqued the interest of a sales executive with Maxwell-Briscoe, who accurately sensed that the novelty of a woman driver could be a publicity tool to assure buyers that the automobile was a safe, reliable, and respectable form of transportation for both genders. The executive, Carl Kelsey, proposed a cross-country trip and after proving her road skills in a few more rallies Ramsey agreed to the all-expense-paid adventure. The idea of a woman traveling almost anywhere unaccompanied was a bit sensational, but Ramsey had two willing companions in the form of her husband's sisters, who were in their 40s and eager for some excitement, and a sixteen-year-old named Hermine Jahns, who had been involved in a road rally in the Philadelphia area and possessed some mechanical aptitude. Ramsey's husband also agreed to let her leave their son in the care of their dependable nurse-maid in their Hackensack home at 325 Union Street.

Internal-combustion, steam-powered, and even early electric vehicles had been frightening horses and pedestrians on the streets of several European and American cities since the mid-1880s. The first automobiles were complex pieces of machinery that required arduous hand-cranking to start a motor, featured a notable lack of precautionary safety measures, and were prone to frequent breakdowns. Maxwell-Briscoe, founded in 1904, produced cars out of its factory in Tarrytown, New York, and gained a reputation for making high-quality vehicles.

A Multiple-Terrain Vehicle

The first person to make a cross-country trip was a young physician from Vermont named Horatio Nelson Jackson. He accepted a bet in San Francisco in 1903, bought a used Winton automobile—made in Cleveland, Ohio—and hired a mechanic to accompany him back to Vermont. It took over two months for them to reach New York City. Like Jackson, Ramsey was not in a hurry to reach her destination of nearly four thousand miles, and there were several scheduled publicity stops along the way. Maxwell-Briscoe provided her with a four-cylinder, 30-horsepower "Maxwell 30" in a shade of forest green. Its standard 14-gallon gas tank was refitted with 20-gallon one; cars of this era did not even come with a fuel gauge—drivers checked the tank by inserting a dipstick. "It had a right-hand drive," Ramsey recalled in a newspaper article she wrote in 1964 that appeared in a Washington State paper, the *Tri-City Herald,* "but, because of the rubber bulb of the 'honk-honk' horn and extra spare tires on that side, I had to get in from the left."

Ramsey, Jahns, and sisters-in-law Margaret Atwood and Nettie Powell set out from the showroom of the Maxwell-Briscoe Motor Company at 1930 Broadway on the rainy Wednesday afternoon of June 9, 1909, amidst a fanfare of publicity. Treaded rubber tires were still in their infancy, so Ramsey's Maxwell had to be weighted down with chains trailing off the rear because of the slick road, one of a fractional 152 miles of paved surfaces her journey would enjoy.

The women spent their first night on the road in Poughkeepsie, the Vassar college town. Ramsey wrote that her sister-in-law Nettie helped navigate with the help of the *Blue Book,* the newish route guides published by the American Automobile Association (AAA). The books did not yet feature printed maps for all destinations, instead relying on turn-by-turn instructions using local landmarks. Their second night was spent in Auburn, New York, and after a tour of its model correctional facility the Maxwell failed to start. The car had to be towed and the women waited for a coil to be replaced. After that, they went through Buffalo, sailed through Cleveland, and arrived in Chicago a full two weeks after departure. "So far it has been perfectly lovely, and I feel certain that the remainder of the trip will be equally so," Ramsey told reporters, according to the *New York Times.*

Stranded by High Waters

That was an overly optimistic sentiment. The rest of the trip proved arduous and delayed by several breakdowns. It took just under two weeks to get across Iowa, not the widest of states, due to a combination of wet weather, impassable dirt roads, and rising riverbanks. At times, Ramsey and her passengers had to clamber out of the Maxwell so that a farmer's horse could tow the car out of a river of mud; on one occasion, they had to sleep in the car and wait for high waters to recede overnight. Ramsey changed several tires herself, endured a bedbug-infested hotel in Wyoming, and relied on ranches and farms to provide fuel and sustenance. There were no *Blue Book* guides for states west of the Mississippi, and so Ramsey relied on the old Pony Express routes and the telegraph poles to guide her to the coast. Maxwell-Briscoe also sent out advance teams, who traveled ahead by train, to arrange details for the women and drum up publicity in local newspapers.

Some of the route Ramsey drove formed part of the famous Lincoln Highway, the first coast-to-coast road built a few years later. "Roads in Wyoming were scarcely what we would designate as such," Ramsey later recalled, according to a commemorative tome by Drake Hokanson published in 1999, *The Lincoln Highway: Main Street across America.* "They were wagon trails, pure and simple; at times, mere horse trails. Where the conveyances had usually been drawn by a team, there would be just the two definite tracks—or maybe ruts—often grass-grown in between.... With no signboards and not too many telegraph poles, it was an easy matter to pick up a side train and find oneself arrived at the wrong destination."

For the final leg of the 3,800-mile trip, Ramsey and her passengers bumped along to Salt Lake City in Utah, then the frontier town of Reno, Nevada, before soldiering on through the formidable Sierra Nevada Mountains into California. Via Sacramento they reached Oakland, then took the ferry-boat to San Francisco; it would take nearly 25 more years before San Francisco Bay was spanned by a bridge solid enough to carry automobile traffic. They arrived on August 7, 1909, after 41 days of driving, and were duly feted in the city. Not surprisingly, they took a more comfortable train ride back East for the return trip.

"The Plucky Little Woman"

Both Ramsey and Maxwell-Briscoe enjoyed a brief burst of goodwill and celebrity. *Motor Print* magazine wrote of her feat in its September 1909 issue. "That the unavoidable hardships of so long a trip were endured and all difficulties conquered by a party of what we in the error of our masculine ways are accustomed to calling the weaker sex is all the more to the credit of the plucky little woman who piloted her car to success," its editors concluded, according to a *New York Times* article.

That *New York Times* piece came in 1959, on the 50th anniversary of Ramsey's epic road trip. A year later, the American Automobile Association gave her the "Woman Motorist of the Century" at the 1960 National Automobile Show in Detroit. In 1961, Ramsey penned her memoir of the trip, *Veil, Duster, and Tire Iron,* which was published by Castle Press of Pasadena, California. She had moved to California back in 1949, sixteen years after her husband passed away. Her daughter, also named Alice, was born in 1910. Her son John Rathbone Ramsey Jr. became an Episcopal minister in Massachusetts.

Car Lost to History

Ramsey died on September 10, 1983, at the age of 96. Her daughter Alice Valleau Ramsey Bruns was 90 years old when she traveled to Dearborn, Michigan, for her mother's posthumous induction into the Automotive Hall of Fame in 2000, and 98 years old in 2009 when a Seattle woman, Emily Anderson, retraced her trip for the hundredth anniversary. Anderson drove a hand-cranked 1909 Maxwell that her car-buff father had rebuilt. "She was not recognized at the time," Bruns told the Bergen *Record* about her mother's journey. "The car should have gone into the Smithsonian, but instead, Mother said it burned up in a garage in Passaic." The Maxwell-Briscoe Motor Company fell victim to overly enthusiastic expansion plans, took on a heavy debt, and was eventually folded into the Chrysler Corporation in the 1920s.

Ramsey drove cross-country another 30 times, the next time in 1919, using the magnificent Lincoln Highway, and the last time at the age of 89. She also drove in Europe, venturing through five of the six mountain passes of the Alps. In the *Tri-City Herald* article she wrote in 1964, she marveled at the state of the modern U.S. federal interstate system, created out of the spine of the Lincoln Highway, noting that the last time she drove cross-country was a year earlier. "Shortly before we set out, I hurt my arm in a slight fall but thought little of it," she wrote. "We made a leisurely trip, and I drove my 200 miles a day. On arrival I had my elbow X-rayed, and the film showed a break. Transcontinental driving is now so easy that you can even do it with a broken arm!"

Books

Hokanson, Drake *The Lincoln Highway: Main Street across America,* University of Iowa Press, 1999.

"Ramsey, Alice Huyler (1886–1983)," *Women in World History: A Biographical Encyclopedia,* edited by Anne Commire, Volume 13, Yorkin Publications, 2002.

Periodicals

Car & Driver, April 2000.

Lewiston Morning Tribune (Lewiston, ID), January 30, 1977.

New York Times, June 6, 1909; June 20, 1909; June 7, 1959; June 6, 1999.

Record (Bergen County, NJ), June 10, 2009.

Tri-City Herald (Washington State), September 27, 1964.

Online

"Guide to the Alice Huyler Ramsey Papers, 1905–1989," *Vassar College Libraries,* http://specialcollections.vassar.edu/findingaids/ramsey_alice_huyler.html (January 22, 2012).

Ruben, Marina Koestler, "Alice Ramsey's Historic Cross-Country Drive," *Smithsonian.com,* June 5, 2009, http://www.smithsonianmag.com/specialsections/womens-history/The-Centennial-of-Alice-Ramseys-Drive.html (January 22, 2012).

"Trailblazing Ride Made History," *Record* (Bergen, NJ), March 22, 2009, http://www.hackensacknow.org/index.php?topic=848.0 html (January 24, 2012).□

Johann Adam Reincken

The Dutch-born German composer and organist Johann Adam Reincken (1643–1722) was one of the key figures in the mighty North German organ music tradition that culminated in the works of Johann Sebastian Bach.

Although few of his works have survived, Reincken's influence is clear. Testimony and confirmation come from Bach himself, who copied out Reincken's music as a young man and made long journeys on foot to hear him play. Some of Bach's music appears to be based on themes by Reincken. Bach learned to improvise on the organ in Reincken's style, surprising the older man, who had thought that his improvisational art was dying out. Other contemporary observers attested to Reincken's influence as well, and the evidence of his music itself is also strong: surviving works by Reincken display an exhaustive, intellectually virtuosic quality that reminds the attentive listener of Bach's music.

Large Discrepancies in Reported Age

An eighteenth-century music historian, Johann Mattheson, stated that Johann Adam Reincken was born in 1623, in a place called Wilhuisen that might have been either Wilhausen in what his now France's Alscace region or Wildeshausen in southern Germany. If true, that date would have made Reincken almost 100 years old at his death in 1722. Reincken is now thought to have been born in Deventer, the Netherlands (the birthplace he himself claimed in a foreword to one of his compositions), on December 10, 1643. The reason for the large discrepancy is not clear; Reincken could have lied about his age when applying for a job in order to make himself appear older and more experienced than he actually was, or Mattheson, who was also a composer and competed for work with Reincken at one point, could have added to Reincken's age to make him seem out-of-date. Reincken's name has been spelled many ways; at birth it was probably Jan Reincken, and, following German custom, he took his father's name, Adam, as a middle name.

Reincken took music lessons in Deventer beginning in 1650 from local church organist Lucas van Lennick (another argument in favor of the later birthdate—27 would have been a very old age for beginning music studies at that time). A wealthy family paid for his lessons, and he responded by working diligently. In 1654, he was sent to Hamburg in northern Germany (then a free city-state) to study with one of the leading organists of the day, Heinrich Scheidemann. He worked with Scheidemann for three years and then returned home, accepting a post as town musician and church organist in Deventer in 1657. At the time, a town or city might have a single musical director, who would furnish music for both church services and civic events; in a large city, musicians' roles would have been more specialized.

The young composer seems to have had horizons wider than the small town of Deventer in mind, and he lasted only slightly more than a year in his job there. In 1658, he left for a post as Scheidemann's assistant at St. Catherine's Church in Hamburg, and after Scheidemann's death in 1663 he was appointed organist himself. He married one of Scheidemann's daughters in 1665 (a common pattern among successive generations of German organists), and they had one daughter, Margaretha-Maria. At first Reincken had duties as a church clerk as well, but by 1666 he felt sufficiently well established to demand that he be relieved of those duties. He also asked for and received a raise in his annual salary, although it might have been expected to decline since his job responsibilities had been reduced.

Supervised Organ Reconstruction

This may suggest that Reincken had already achieved fame as a musician. Another reason the church fathers might have wanted to keep him happy was that the church's great organ was in need of renovation, and Reincken had the skills to supervise the job. The entire organ was rebuilt, and Bach, hearing it several decades later, praised its high quality in an area where fine instruments were common. Reincken in his own day was rivaled only by Dietrich Buxtehude—another composer Bach admired—as an authority in the field of organ construction, and there exists an oil painting from 1674 showing the two composers together.

One of the most hotly debated issues in staunchly Lutheran Hamburg in the late seventeenth century was whether to allow an opera house to be established, and despite his church affiliation, Reincken was part of a group of influential citizens who successfully argued in favor of permitting it to open. In 1678, together with lawyer and politician Gerhard Schott, he founded the new Oper am Gänsemarket (Goose Market Opera). After 1685 he relinquished his role in the day-to-day management of the opera house, which was soon to help launch the career of Georg Friedrich Handel, but he remained involved and was eventually rewarded with a pair of lifetime passes.

Well paid for his work in prosperous Hamburg, Reincken seems to have had little interest in having his music

published in order to reap new profits from it. Partly as a result, although his output must have been substantial over his long career, not much of his music survives today. He did publish *Hortus Musicus* (The Garden of Music), a set of six sonatas and dance suites for two violins, viola, viola da gamba (an ancestor of the cello), and basso continuo (a chordal part that may be taken by any of several instruments, including a harpsichord) in Hamburg in 1688. In a preface to the publication, written in Latin, he wrote that he was trying to drive inferior composers out of the garden of music, using his own work as a medium for mirroring the insufficiencies of others'. This has prompted speculation that he intended the publication not as a money-making venture but as a response to unknown critics of his work. Outwardly entertaining, the pieces in the *Hortus Musicus* contain hidden mathematical proportions that may have carried allegorical meanings, a combination that likely appealed greatly to the young Bach, who arranged several sections of the *Hortus Musicus* for harpsichord.

Wrote Giant Chorale Fantasias

Even more ambitious were two chorale fantasias, or long, quasi-improvisatory pieces for organ that expanded musically upon a chorale, or Lutheran religious song. This must have been a form that Reincken cultivated frequently, and his two surviving examples hint at riches lost. One, *An den Wasser Flüssen Babylon* (By the Waters of Babylon), was conceived by the composer as a kind of musical self-portrait. In the words of an essayist writing on the Bach Cantatas website, the work "provides a compendium of most of his styles, techniques and figurations available to a German composer of the mid- to-late 17th century." The copy made of this piece in 1700 by the fifteen-year-old Bach is Bach's earliest known autograph, or manuscript in his own handwriting. *An den Wasser Flüssen Babylon* and Reincken's other surviving chorale fantasia, *Wass kan uns kommen an für Noth*, is the longest existing North German chorale fantasia, and both are large works that explore the musical language of Reincken's time in totalizing detail.

Several other works by Reincken exist. He wrote a group of eight suites (sets of French-style dances) for harpsichord, two toccatas (organ pieces in the style of free improvisation), several sets of variations for harpsichord, and a few short polyphonic (multi-line) organ pieces. He also penned several instructional books. Reincken's works were known mostly to scholars until the 1960s and 1970s, when modern editions of his work appeared. Now his works sometimes appear on programs of Baroque-era music, and a festival in his honor, the Reincken Festival of Early Music, has been established in his hometown of Deventer.

Reincken's most important admirer was undoubtedly Bach, who traveled, reportedly on foot, to Hamburg twice to hear Reincken in person. One trip, around 1700, was from Lüneburg, about 35 miles away, where Bach received much of his musical training. The second trip occurred in 1720, when Bach was a court composer in Küthen, about 200 miles from Hamburg. It was on that occasion that Reincken, according to the *Sojurn* web site, heard Bach improvise on *An den Wasser Flüssen Babylon* and remarked, "I thought this art was dead, but I see it still lives in you."

Reincken's first wife died in 1685; three years later he married Anna Wagener and he outlived her as well. His later years were marked by workplace controversy; one faction at St. Catherine's wanted to appoint Mattheson to replace Reincken in 1705, but he fended off the challenge. In 1718, he suggested that his student, Johann Heinrich Uthmöller, be named his successor; church officials agreed but then asked Reincken to pay Uthmöller's salary. Reincken responded by writing the church out of his will and leaving most of his considerable wealth to the niece of his second wife. Reincken died in Hamburg on November 24, 1722, and was buried at St. Catherine's on December 7.

Books

Sadie, Stanley, ed., *The New Grove Dictionary of Music and Musicians,* 2nd ed., Macmillan, 2001.

Online

"Jan Adams Reincken, 1643–1722," *Sojurn,* http://www.jan.ucc.nau.edu/~tas3/reincken.html (October 26, 2011).
"Johann Adam Reincken (Composer)," http://www.bach-cantatas.com/Lib/Reincken-Johann-Adam.htm (October 26, 2011).
"Who Was Reincken?" *Reincken Festival of Early Music, Deventer,* Reincken Festival of Early Music, Deventer (October 26, 2011). □

Joanna Russ

American author Joanna Russ (1937–2011) innovated in the genre of feminist science fiction in the 1970s.

Science fiction writer Joanna Russ became widely recognized as a pioneering author in the genre for her introduction of feminist themes to what had previously been an overtly masculine world. Her best-known novel, 1975's *The Female Man,* has been acknowledged as ushering in a new breed of feminist science fiction that went on to become both critically and commercially popular. An instructor and essayist as well as a fiction writer, Russ published nearly 20 books over the course of a four-decade career that spanned science fiction, literary criticism, and even children's fiction. She was the recipient of both of science fiction's most prestigious awards, winning a Nebula in 1974 for her story "When It Changed" and a Hugo in 1983 for the novella *Souls.* Russ also taught at the State University of New York, the University of Colorado, and the University of Washington.

Education and Early Writing Career

Born Joanna Ruth Russ on February 22, 1937, Russ was the daughter of teachers Everett I. and Bertha (Zinner) Russ. She grew up in the Bronx borough of New York City, where she enjoyed visiting the Bronx Zoo and the city's Botanical Gardens. From a young age, Russ showed an interest in writing, producing simple stories when she was as young as five years old. A good student who began high school

when she was just twelve, Russ was nevertheless challenged by both society's expectations and her own of herself during her preteen and adolescent years. "I was a tall, overly-bright and overly-self-assertive girl, too much so to fit anybody's notions of femininity (and too bookish and odd to fit other children's ideas of an acceptable human being)," she recalled in an autobiographical essay in *Magic Mommas, Trembling Sisters, Puritans & Perverts.* Russ also struggled with her sexuality, telling Victoria A. Brownworth in the *Lambda Book Report* that she "came out [as a lesbian] at 11 and went back in at 15 convinced that there wasn't another lesbian anywhere." She did, however, find respite in escapist science fiction stories. After graduating from high school, Russ enrolled at Cornell University. There, she studied the works of Vladimir Nabokov as part of her coursework in English, completing her bachelor's degree in 1957. She then continued her education with graduate work at Yale University's drama school, earning a master's degree in playwriting and dramatic literature from that institution in 1960.

By the time she completed her education, however, science fiction rather than the theater had already begun to shape Russ's career. She had published her first story, "Nor Custom Stale," in *Magazine of Fantasy & Science Fiction* in 1959, immediately becoming a rarity in that she—unlike the wide majority of other female science fiction writers of the era—published under her own name rather a male or gender-neutral pseudonym. Over the next several years, Russ contributed more stories to science fiction magazine while working as an instructor in speech and English at Queensborough Community College in New York and, later, at Cornell University. She married Albert Amateau in 1963, but the ill-fated married ended in 1967 without issue. That same year, Russ published her first novel, *Picnic on Paradise,* featuring the character of Alyx. A female protagonist who worked as a thief and assassin, Alyx survived by her brains and her wits, not her beauty. The character's stories, which served as a precursor to the author's more strongly feminist works, were later collected in *The Adventures of Alyx.*

Russ's fiction took a new turn after she attended a feminist colloquium at Cornell University, where she was then teaching, in 1969. Struck by the growing feminist ideas of the time, she decided to openly declare her own homosexuality and begin exploring these themes in her writing. Russ's entry in *Feminist Writers* argued that she "proved that science fiction was entirely compatible with feminism. Because science fiction by definition requires a 'different' world—different in one or many ways from the world of the author and reader—Russ could invent worlds from a feminist viewpoint." One of the author's first works to investigate this theme was the 1969 short story "When It Changed." In this story, Russ presented an all-female world in which men had been killed long ago in a plague, leaving women to procreate through artificial means. Within the society, however, women display both traditionally male and female behaviors, challenging the ideas of real-world contemporary gender roles. Innovative and daring for its day, the story was well received and earned Russ a Nebula award in 1973.

Broke New Ground with *The Female Man*

In 1975, Russ published what became her best-known novel, *The Female Man*. The story of four genetically connected women—all embodiments of Russ herself—living in different places, times, and histories, the novel melded alternate reality fiction with social commentary. One of the women, Jeannine, lives in an alternate United States in which World War II never took place, leaving the nation economically depressed and women's lives void of opportunity outside marriage; another, Jael, fights in a violent war against men to create the "Whileaway;" another, Janet, lives in the entirely female world created by Jael's conflict; and the last, Joanna, lives in the United States of the 1970s, in which she struggles to achieve true freedom as the "female man" amidst a climate not entirely friendly to feminism. The challenging nature of *The Female Man* can be readily seen in its path to bookshelves; although Russ had written the novel at about the same time that she publically declared her homosexuality, publishing delays kept it under wraps for several years.

Yet *The Female Man* became widely acknowledged as a seminal piece in the development of not only science fiction or even women's writing, but also in the larger feminist movement. "With that book...[Russ] helped inaugurate the now flourishing tradition of feminist science fiction," argued Margalit Fox in the *New York Times*. Writing in *The Guardian*, Christopher Priest agreed, proclaiming, "No consideration of the women's movement in the U.S. can be complete without acknowledging the importance of this novel, a weirdly effective blend of [humor] and anger."

Russ continued to write about gender relations and roles in both her fiction and non-fiction. The 1977 novel *We Who Are About To...* explored the dynamics within a group of tourists trapped on a deserted planet as the female protagonist fights against the group's plan to create civilization afresh, with her as its literal mother. In *The Two of Them*, published in 1978, Russ described the rescue of an adolescent girl from a male-dominated world by another strong female protagonist. In her Hugo-award winning novella *Souls*, published as part of the 1984 collection *Extra(-Ordinary) People*, Russ recounted the story of a medieval abbess who faced down a group of male invaders who wished to ravage her abbey and the surrounding lands. The author also wrote on topics of feminism, human sexuality, and gender in her essay collections. She was not afraid to take unpopular stands or court controversy. The 1985 *Magic Mommas, Trembling Sisters, Puritans & Perverts,* for example, told about Russ's own experiences dealing with her homosexuality, and discussed the pitfalls of the anti-pornography movement. "Why did some of those who wanted to ban pornography make light of the civil rights arguments? Why did some of them scoff at the idea that such could possibly be turned against feminist material?" she demanded in the book, raising—as was common in much of her work—more questions than answers.

Disease Hampered Later Life

Beginning in the late 1980s, Russ was forced to greatly curtail her career after being diagnosed with Chronic Fatigue Immune Deficiency Syndrome, a virus that affects the immune and central nervous system and causes intense, relentless exhaustion. Russ quit her teaching job and moved to Tucson, Arizona, hoping that the city's smaller size would make it easier for her to take part in day-to-day life. Her writing output also declined. "For two years I couldn't sit up enough to type, so I couldn't write," the author told Brownworth. With treatment, Russ was able to again begin writing, but she never regained the same capabilities that she had enjoyed before her illness. "I'm not going to say that I've gotten used to this disease, or that I've conquered it or even that I've learned to cope with it," she told Brownworth in the same interview. "But I have learned from it. Perhaps more than I ever wanted to know."

Despite these challenges, Russ managed to produce some major works in the last two decades of her life. She published the non-fiction essay collections *To Write Like a Woman* in 1995 and *What Are We Fighting For?: Sex, Race, Class, and the Future of Feminism* in 1997. Her final collection, *The Country You Have Never Seen,* was published in 2007. This book brought together numerous reviews and articles that the author had written during her long career, but contemporary critics found much to praise even about Russ's back catalogue. "Russ's talent as writer, critic, and activist is evident in every piece in this book. Anyone who writes book reviews or is interested in feminist history and politics will find something to delight, instruct, and amuse in Russ's works.... The wit and clarity with which she dissects the literary and ideological operations of texts means that even reading thirty-year-old book reviews is both pleasurable and instructive," declared Helen Merrick in *Feminist Collections: A Quarterly of Women's Studies Resources.*

Assessments of Russ's work have generally placed her high in the pantheon of science fiction. "Only Ursula La Guin rivals Russ in wedding stylistic virtuosity to thematic relevance, but not even she has challenged out gender assumptions—and the fictional norms through which these assumptions are usually reinforced—so often and so radically," argued Larry McCaffrey in *Across the Wounded Galaxies: Interviews with Contemporary American Science Fiction Writers.* Indeed, the author's ability to incorporate feminist ideas and social commentary into her work has been broadly considered among her strongest literary merits. Russ herself believed that these elements informed and propelled her fiction. As she wrote in her introduction to *To Write Like a Woman,* "If any theme runs through all my work, it is what Adrienne Rich once called 're-vision,' i.e., the re-perceiving of experience, not because our experience is complex or subtle or hard to understand (though it is sometimes all three) but because so much of what's presented to us as 'the real world' or 'the way it is' is so obviously untrue that a great deal of social energy must be mobilized to hide that gross and ghastly fact....Hence, my love for science fiction, which analyzes reality by changing it."

Russ died on April 29, 2011, in hospice care in Tucson from complications resulting from a stroke that she had suffered several weeks previously. She was 74 years old. Despite Russ's limited involvement in literary life during the latter portion of her life, her passing received international attention. The British newspaper the *Independent* hailed her as a "pioneering feminist," and Fox of the *New York Times* pointed out that "many praised her liquid prose style, intellectual ferocity and cheerfully unorthodox approach[.]" As one of the writers who made science fiction not only accessible to women but also about their concerns and goals, Russ's works seemed likely to continue to attract critical and popular notice for years to come.

Books

Contemporary Novelists, Gale, 2001.

Kester, Shelton, Pamela, ed., *Feminist Writers,* St. James Press, 1996.

McCaffrey, Larry, ed., *Across the Wounded Galaxies: Interviews with Contemporary American Science Fiction Writers,* University of Illinois Press, 1990.

Russ, Joanna, *Magic Mommas, Trembling Sisters, Puritans & Perverts: Feminist Essays,* The Crossing Press, 1985.

Russ, Joanna, *To Write Like a Woman: Essays in Feminism and Science Fiction,* Indiana University Press, 1995.

St. James Guide to Science Fiction Writers, St. James Press, 1996.

Periodicals

Feminist Collections: A Quarterly of Women's Studies Resources, Winter 2009.

Guardian (London, England), May 12, 2011.

Independent (London, England), July 27, 2011.

Lambda Book Report, November–December 1994.

New York Times, May 7, 2011.□

S

Rod Serling

American television writer Rod Serling (1924-1975), one of the great writers of television's early years, created one of the most groundbreaking and influential television shows of the 1960s, the dark, fantastical series *The Twilight Zone.*

Serling was born in Syracuse, New York, on December 25, 1924, and grew up in Binghamton, New York. Like many American boys of his time, he enjoyed early science fiction movies such as *Flash Gordon* and *Buck Rogers.* His two favorite radio shows, which would become major influences on his writing, were *Lights Out,* a ghost story series which introduced its tales to the sound of a creaking door, and *The Fall of the City,* a radio play by poet Archibald MacLeish that addressed the evils of fascism.

Served in World War II

In 1943, right after graduating from high school, Serling joined the United States Army. He became a paratrooper and fought in the Philippines during World War II, where he killed at least one enemy soldier and was wounded. While serving in the South Pacific, Serling wrote for radio for the first time, helping to create a partially scripted show performed live on Armed Forces Radio with comedian Jack Benny.

After the war, Serling studied English literature and drama at Antioch College in Ohio. He married fellow student Carol Kramer while still in college. He became manager of the campus radio station and formed a troupe of writers and actors that wrote and broadcast a weekly anthology of dramas. He found work-study jobs at several

local radio stations and New York City's public radio station, WNYC. Encouraged by his wife, Serling entered a scriptwriting contest held by the broadcast network ABC. He tied for second, winning $500.

Began Writing for Television

Upon graduating from Antioch in 1950, he went to work as an ad copy writer for the Cincinnati, Ohio radio station WLW. But he quickly realized that television, a new medium, offered more opportunity for a young writer and, at the time, more freedom. He quit WLW to write for *The Storm,* a weekly drama broadcast on Cincinnati TV station WKRC. He also created scripts for national television networks. Some drew on his experience as a combat veteran and portrayed war as more disturbing and morally wrenching than Hollywood movies did at the time. Drama shows such as *Lux Video Theatre* on CBS and *Hallmark Hall of Fame* on NBC began airing his teleplays in 1952.

Won His First Emmy

In 1954, Serling and his wife Carol moved to Westport, Connecticut, so that he could be closer to the TV and radio networks' headquarters in New York City. He quickly found that he could write for the eye, not just the ear. He became one of the star writers of television's golden age, the late 1940s through the mid-1950s, when the new medium broadcast many serious dramas, often performed live. His breakthrough came with his teleplay "Patterns," about a man in his 50s being forced out of a company he helped found. It was produced live on NBC in January of 1955 and won an Emmy Award.

Observers praised "Patterns" for its accurate portrayal of big business, but Serling noted in a commentary about the script (in the book *Patterns,* which collected four of his

313

teleplays) that it was simply a story about power. His observations read more poignantly today because of the ups and downs of his career. "It is the story of ambition and the price tag that hangs on success," Serling wrote. "Every human being has a minimum set of ethics.... When he refuses to compromise these ethics, his career must suffer; when he does compromise them, his conscience does the suffering."

In 1956, Serling wrote perhaps his most famous character, Mountain McClintock, the protagonist of "Requiem for a Heavyweight." The teleplay told the story of a boxer, played by Jack Palance, who has to give up boxing. Serling drew on his experience learning to box in the military at age 19, when he fought in several bouts and had his nose broken. The show was a triumph for both Sterling and Palance. After the broadcast, CBS head William S. Paley called the control room and declared (according to John J. O'Connor of the *New York Times*), "Tell everyone, especially Rod Serling, that tonight we put television ahead 10 years."

"Requiem for a Heavyweight" won Serling his second Emmy and a George Foster Peabody Award. In his commentary on the teleplay (in the book *Patterns*), Serling praised Palance's performance and provided insight into his conception of the character. "His was the incoherent, inarticulate yearning and hunger to belong to something he didn't understand," Serling wrote. "Here was the heart-rending picture of a misfit battered into a shapeless ugliness and yet possessing a simplicity, a humility and the kind of beauty that comes with decency."

The show made Serling a sought-after writer. He began writing for the drama anthology series *Playhouse 90*, helping to make it the most prestigious show on TV. Publisher Simon and Schuster published *Patterns*, which included a long introduction titled "About Writing For Television." In it, Serling daringly complained about the limitations on a TV writer's craft, such as commercials that interrupt the drama of a story and networks' and TV show sponsors' objections to potentially controversial plots.

"At their very worst, their interference is an often stultifying, often destructive and inexcusable by-product of our mass-media system," he wrote. "No dramatic art form should be dictated and controlled by men whose training, interest and instincts are cut of entirely different cloth. The fact remains that these gentlemen sell consumer goods, not an art form." Serling's comments made him an unofficial spokesman for the idea that television should have high artistic standards and serious messages, but it also began to build his reputation as an angry rebel.

Created *The Twilight Zone*

In the late 1950s, Serling and his agents sold the CBS network on an idea for a weekly anthology series, a mix of science fiction and fantastical stories, with merely the role of imagination uniting them. The show, *The Twilight Zone,* debuted in the fall of 1959 and appeared on CBS on Friday nights for five years. Serling was the creator, executive producer, artistic director, and main screenwriter. Serling wrote 92 of the 156 episodes of *The Twilight Zone,* enjoying a great degree of artistic freedom, won by his agents after difficult negotiations. Serling found that writing science-fiction stories allowed him to use allegory and metaphor to address topics that sponsors would have likely objected to in straightforward dramas. "I found that it was all right to have Martians saying things Democrats and Republicans could never say," he said (as quoted by O'Connor).

Serling introduced many episodes of the show himself, in a clipped yet resonant voice so distinctive that it was still widely imitated decades later. "There is a fifth dimension," he often said (as quoted by Peter M. Nichols in the *New York Times*). "It is the middle ground between light and shadow, between science and superstition, and it lies between the pit of man's fears and the summit of his knowledge."

Serling created *The Twilight Zone* with high expectations. "We want to tell stories that are different," he wrote in a 1959 article for *TV Guide* (reprinted in *As Timeless As Infinity: The Complete Twilight Zone Scripts of Rod Serling, Volume 1*). "The fresh and the untried can carry more infinite appeal than a palpable imitation of the already proven."

At a time when television was settling into convention, with many of its shows depicting an idealized home and family life, *The Twilight Zone* consistently challenged the audience with piercing, often dark insights into the human condition. The best, classic episodes of the show, wrote Douglas Brode and Carol Serling in *Rod Serling and The Twilight Zone,* " offered viewers a seemingly other worldly story only to comment on the hard truth of our existence, providing an electric shock to a shattered sensibility."

The Twilight Zone stretched viewers' imaginations. Its stories' plots sometimes involved travel through space or time and often ended with surprising twists. But only some of the episodes were voyages in outer space; many took place in everyday life, with a fantastical element added. In his *TV Guide* article, Serling promised that viewers would find themselves visiting an asteroid and watching a man fall in love with a robot, but also standing on the bridge of a doomed ship and walking a Western street with an aging gunslinger. Often, an episode's main character was a middle-class man with a strong conscience thrown into a morally challenging situation. "One especially recurrent character, drawn from the writer's own life, is the weary professional seeking consolation in evocations of an idealized past," observed O'Connor of the *New York Times*.

Fought for Artistic Integrity

Though *The Twilight Zone* is now considered Serling's finest work, he felt constrained by the show and was searching for his next project even before CBS cancelled the show in January of 1964. He wrote the screenplay for *Seven Days In May*, a film adaptation of a novel about members of the military plotting to overthrow the president. He also wrote scripts for episodes of the anthology show *Bob Hope Presents the Chrysler Theater* and created a newsreel about new president Lyndon Johnson for the U.S. Information Agency after John F. Kennedy's assassination. Elected president of the National Academy of Television Arts and Sciences in May of 1964, he used the position to argue that television programs should be considered an art form, as they had been in TV's golden age.

Serling attempted to jump from television to movies, but he did not enjoy the success he had a television writer. His greatest success in movie screenwriting, besides *Seven Days in May,* was probably the adaptation of the science-fiction novel *Planet of the Apes*. But even then, Serling's drafts proved too elaborate to film, and he had to share credit with another writer who simplified the script.

He returned to television with *The Loner,* a Western series he had conceived of years earlier about a Civil War veteran traveling through the American West. The show's 13 episodes were innovative in their cinematography, and Serling's ambitions to make a statement about the wounds of war often succeeded. But TV critics did not appreciate the show, and CBS executives pushed Serling to add more action to it. Serling aired his disagreements with the network in a newspaper interview, and CBS fired him and cancelled the show.

Serling briefly hosted a game show, *Rod Serling's Liar's Club,* in the late 1960s. He hosted *Night Gallery,* a thriller series on NBC, in the early 1970s, and wrote some strong scripts for it. But he grew disillusioned with the show as it embraced conventional horror formulas and his differences of opinion with its producer grew.

In his final years, Serling spent most of his time and energy on teaching dramatic writing at Ithaca College in upstate New York. He continued to complain that the commercial nature of TV hurt the art of storytelling. "How do you put on a meaningful drama or documentary that is adult, incisive, probing, when every 15 minutes proceedings are interrupted by 12 dancing rabbits with toilet paper?" he said in 1974 (according to Edward Hudson of the *New York Times*). Serling died in 1975 at age 50 from complications after open-heart surgery.

Books

Albarella, Tony, ed., *As Timeless as Infinity: The Complete Twilight Zone Scripts of Rod Serling: Volume 1,* Gauntlet Publications, 2004.
Brode, Douglas, and Carol Serling, *Rod Serling and The Twilight Zone,* Barricade Books, 2009.
Engel, Joel, *Rod Serling: The Dreams and Nightmares of Life in The Twilight Zone,* Contemporary Books, 1989.
Sander, Gordon F., *Serling: The Rise and Twilight of Television's Last Angry Man,* Dutton, 1992.
Serling, Rod, *Patterns,* Simon and Schuster, 1957.
Wolfe, Peter, *In the Zone: The Twilight World of Rod Serling,* Bowling Green State University Popular Press, 1997.

Periodicals

New York Times, June 29, 1975; November 29, 1995; December 6, 1998. □

May French-Sheldon

Author and London socialite May French-Sheldon (1847–1936) made an epic solo journey into sub-Saharan Africa in 1891. The exploits of this American-born amateur ethnologist were well chronicled in the newspapers on both sides of the Atlantic at the time, for she was believed to be the first non-African woman to explore this part of the continent without a white male escort. Instead she trekked with a bevy of Swahili porters from the Indian Ocean port city of Mombasa, Kenya, to the foot of Mount Kilimanjaro at Lake Chala, a distance of some 200 miles through hilly, dangerous terrain. Her adventures were detailed in an 1892 travelogue, *Sultan to Sultan: Adventures among the Masai and other Tribes of East Africa.*

F rench-Sheldon was born Mary French on May 10, 1847, in the town of Beaver, Pennsylvania, northeast of Pittsburgh. According to contemporary accounts, her father was "Colonel" Joseph French, a civil engineer, mathematician, and purported descendant of gifted English physicist Sir Isaac Newton. Her paternal grandfather was likely a cobbler in this region who grew wealthy from prudent land investments. French-Sheldon's mother, Elizabeth Poorman French, was from Mechanicsburg, Pennsylvania, and newspaper articles asserted she was a trained physician. Elizabeth French was likelier a holistic practitioner who, probably around 1853, took French-Sheldon and her two younger sisters to live in New York City, where she practiced as a medium. U.S. Census records list her mother living in a boarding house there with a man, Thomas Culbertson, who was probably Elizabeth's paramour and séance assistant. They operated out of an office on Broadway, but apparently ran into legal trouble for conning susceptible believers out of large sums, court documents show.

Obscured Tumultuous Childhood

French-Sheldon claimed she was well educated and well traveled, and had hunted game out West with her father, who in reality was probably Pittsburgh's superintendent of waterworks in the years following the U.S. Civil War. At some point in the 1860s, French-Sheldon was briefly married, and seemed to have lived in both Philadelphia and Boston with her mother, who had moved on from spiritualism to a new fad called "electronic" therapeutics. In 1870, French-Sheldon married Eli Lemon Sheldon, an attorney and investment banker from the American Midwest. The couple moved to London when Sheldon's employer, Jarvis-Conklin Mortgage Trust Company, put him in charge of its office there.

Befriended African Adventurers

French-Sheldon and her husband were avid bibliophiles and hosted a weekly salon at their London home that attracted some notable names. One of them was a Welsh-American who, like French-Sheldon, had obscured some details of his early life in his official biography. This was journalist Henry Morton Stanley, more famously known for trekking through Africa to find the missing Scottish missionary David Livingstone in Tanzania. It was Stanley who uttered the famous phrase, "Dr. Livingstone, I presume?" when he finally found the missing minister in 1871. Stanley wanted to build a railroad in East Africa, which at the time was the site of much colonial development by British and German entrepreneurs, and hoped Eli Sheldon could help him arrange financing.

The Sheldons were also friends of Henry Wellcome, another transplanted American. Wellcome was a pharmaceutical entrepreneur who founded the company that evolved into GlaxoSmithKline, and also had extensive experience in Africa. It took some years before French-Sheldon set her sights on exploring what was known as "the Dark Continent" herself, though, as her earlier ambitions were literary in scope. She and her husband set up a small publishing house, Saxon & Company, to publish titles like *Everybody's Cyclopedia of Things Worth Knowing* and their translation, from French into English, of Gustave Flaubert's 1862 novel *Salammbô*. The torrid novel of an ancient Carthaginian war appeared in English in 1885, but was largely forgotten by critics. French-Sheldon also wrote a novel, *Herbert Severance*, that was published in 1889 by Rand McNally.

French-Sheldon began making preparations for her solo trip to Africa, a trip with a $50,000 price tag that her husband funded. She styled herself an ethnographer seeking to learn more about African customs and cultures, different from the usually hyperbolical reports written by male explorers, who most commonly adopted a policy to display firepower first and ask questions later. There were a few wives of colonial officials living in British East Africa, as a large swath of Kenya and Uganda was known at the time; the area bordered Tanzania, a colonial property of imperial Germany. Nurses and missionary women were also present, but it was almost unthinkable for a white woman to declare her intention to visit Africa unchaperoned, relying entirely on Africans to guide her.

Brought Couture Gown, Tiara

Even Henry Stanley warned her to stay in Mombasa, but did write a letter of introduction to the Imperial British East Africa Company on her behalf. Wellcome helped her design a woven wood *palanquin*, or traveling carriage. Five and a half feet in diameter, it contained a bed, writing desk, and waterproof compartments for French-Sheldon's personal items, and was carried aloft by porters on each of its four poles. Her traveling attire included a single extravagant dress, a white satin number made by the House of Worth in Paris, which she donned when meeting with African chiefs or local officials.

Not surprisingly, French-Sheldon had difficulty in setting up her journey once she arrived in Mombasa via ship in February of 1891. British East Africa Company officials tried to discourage her and even prevent her from leaving Mombasa, fearing that she might get lost and an expensive search operation would have to be mounted. But French-Sheldon planned to use a fairly well-traveled caravan route favored by ivory traders to and from Mount Kilimanjaro, Africa's highest peak. Frustrated, French-Sheldon ventured to Zanzibar, the island home of the local Muslim sultanate that still nominally controlled this part of East Africa. Charmed by her nerve, the sultan ordered several dozen Swahili porters to be put at her disposal. These porters were part of a small but vital industry that enabled Europeans to travel through otherwise impenetrable regions, both in Africa and elsewhere in the British Empire. She had brought with her an enormous kit of goods to trade and barter, and each of the 138 men—some of whom even had their own enslaved porters to carry *their* possessions—carried a pack weighing about 55 pounds atop their heads.

French-Sheldon's formal attire also included a rhinestone tiara, blonde wig, pair of pistols in a hip holster, and ceremonial sword. She claimed to have carried a poison-tipped dagger for emergency measures, too. There was also a banner that proclaimed *Nolo mi tangere* (Latin for "touch me not"). "My crooked Alpine stock, with its blue pennant" bearing that phrase, she wrote in her travelogue *Sultan to Sultan* (as quoted in the book *White Queen: May French-Sheldon and the Imperial Origins of American Feminist Identity*), "was much admired and I fear coveted. They innocently deemed it to be a badge of high rank, never having seen one before, hence inferred that I must be of supreme importance and possessed of limitless power."

Wrote Sympathetic Account of Africans

French-Sheldon made it all the way to Lake Chala, a volcanic body of water at the northeastern slope of Mount Kilimanjaro that was thought to be dramatically inaccessible, ringed all around by steep cliffs. She managed to circumnavigate it, her one significant achievement as Africa's first solo female explorer, and would later extol the men who made it possible. Initially she had been nervous, she confessed, wondering whether she would "always be able to control them and make them subservient to my commands,'' she told a rapt audience at the 1893 Chicago World's Fair, also known as the World's Columbian Exposition. Her speech appeared in a 1894 volume titled *The Congress of Women: Held in the Woman's Building, World's Columbian Exposition, Chicago, USA, 1893.* ''However, after experience with them, when I had to trust my life to them, they proved faithful, uncomplaining, chivalrous, and marvels of patience, endurance, and consistent marching day after day.''

Aside from her trek around Lake Chala, French-Sheldon's more lasting contribution to global exploration was in visiting and recording her impressions of ordinary life in this part of sub-Saharan Africa. When women heard there was a white female on the route, they came out to meet her and often brought their children to show. She went inside the huts, called *bomas,* that sheltered families, and chronicled their daily routine, which usually included tending to cattle and crops, grinding meal, and cooking. The men hunted and, unusually, occupied themselves with decorative beadwork in their spare time. She went through some areas that were more affluent than others, and wrote that polygamy was practiced in these parts. ''A man accumulates more land or more cattle than his first wife can attend to without becoming a toilsome task,'' *The Congress of Women* volume quoted her as saying, and thus he ''takes another wife, and so on. The established wife or wives are far from being jealous of one another; to the contrary are delighted to welcome a new wife, and make great preparations for her homecoming, realizing that the work of all will be commeasurably lessened.''

Spoke at Chicago World's Fair

On her expedition French-Sheldon was dropped down a ravine twice by accident when her palanquin-bearers slipped, and also came down with dysentery. She proudly noted she lost just one porter, who was attacked and eaten by a lion, and other porters volunteered to join her trek to Lake Chala. She recuperated in part of German-controlled Egypt, where doctors pronounced her too ill to travel back to England, but she boarded a ship anyway and returned to London a minor celebrity in June of 1891. She spoke before a huge crowd at the British Association for the Advancement of Science and then embarked on a lecture tour. She also spent time in the United States writing *Sultan to Sultan,* and was feted at the Chicago World's Fair of 1893, which displayed her palanquin and collected artifacts in its groundbreaking Congress of Women hall. She and a globe-trotting British woman named Isabella Bird Bishop became the first of their gender admitted as fellows of the Royal Geographical Society in 1892.

Despite the triumph, that year also ended a chapter in French-Sheldon's life: her husband, Eli, died unexpectedly in 1892 while she was in the United States. As a result, her social status and income both suffered blows, and friends like Henry Wellcome helped her financially. She made a second trip to Africa, this one more than a year long and through French and Belgian Congo, in 1903 and 1904. This jaunt was sponsored by the Congo Reform Association and was conducted as a fact-finding mission to collect information that might discredit King Leopold II of Belgium, who

owned the colony outright and suppressed dissent with a paid personal army. Between 1905 and 1907 French-Sheldon attempted to raise money for her own model community, which she hoped to locate in the free nation of Liberia, but there was little interest.

During World War I French-Sheldon worked as a Red Cross volunteer in London, where she lived with a woman named Nellie Butler for many years. She retreated from public life in the 1920s as she approached her eightieth birthday, and lived to the age of 88. Her passing on February 10, 1936, was noted by most major newspapers in both London and America, which recognized her achievement as the first woman to venture unaccompanied into sub-Saharan Africa. ''I found the people and conditions very much what I aspired to make them, and certainly the natives are not so [ruthless] as painted,'' she asserted at the 1893 Columbian Exposition in Chicago, describing Africans as ''amenable to gentleness and kindness, and tractable through their vanity and love of power. They are all of one piece of a common humanity.''

Books

Boisseau, Tracey Jean, *White Queen: May French-Sheldon and the Imperial Origins of American Feminist Identity,* Indiana University Press, 2004.

Eagle, Mary Kavanaugh Oldham, editor, *The Congress of Women: Held in the Woman's Building, World's Columbian Exposition, Chicago, USA, 1893,* W.B. Conkey Company, 1894, pp. 131–134.

Periodicals

New York Times, December 14, 1890; March 22, 1892; December 18, 1904; January 16, 1915; February 11, 1936; February 15, 1936.

Online

''The Trajectory of An Opportunist, And The Writing Of History: The Real Life of Elizabeth J. French,'' The Emma Hardinge Britten Archive, E.H. Britten.org, http://www.ehbritten.org/papers/ej_french_biography.pdf (July 6, 2011).□

Catherine Filene Shouse

A contributor to the causes of education, politics, women's affairs, and the performing arts, Catherine Filene Shouse (1896-1994) devoted her life to public service and holds many records for women's firsts. Shouse was the first woman to receive a graduate degree in education from Harvard University and the first woman appointed to the Democratic National Committee. In addition, her donation of land and funds to the U.S. government made the Wolf Trap National Park for the Performing Arts, the only U.S. national park dedicated to the performing arts, a reality.

Catherine Filene Shouse was born Catherine Filene on June 9, 1896, in Boston, the daughter of Lincoln Filene and Therese Filene. Her Jewish-German grandfather, William Filene, was born in Posen, Prussia, but immigrated to Boston in the 1840s and founded the Filene Specialty Store, later known as Filene's Sons Co. Shouse, who was known as Kay during her childhood, grew up alongside a younger sister, Helen. The family divided its time between Boston and Weston, Massachusetts, where the Filenes owned a country house.

Enjoyed Comfortable Upbringing

Shouse grew up privileged in a wealthy, prosperous family. The Filenes found success in the United States operating their store. Lincoln Filene and his brother, Edward, were crafty businessmen who grew their father's small clothing shop and piece-goods store into one of the largest department stores in the United States. In 1912, the brothers opened a new flagship store in Boston, designed by famed Chicago architect Daniel Burnham. The department store was highly successful—partly due to the Filene philosophy of customer and employee satisfaction. As the business grew, more locations opened around New England. The store later became part of the Federated Department Stores.

Shouse grew up around music. Her mother, an accomplished amateur musician, established the Boston Music School Settlement, which served underprivileged children. Therese Filene's musician friends also frequented the house in Weston. Shouse took piano lessons, as required by her parents, but was never much of a musician because she did not care to practice.

Shouse's father valued education. Because Lincoln Filene quit school at fourteen to help with the family business, he wanted to make sure his daughters had a complete education. From 1911-13, Shouse attended Bradford Academy, located in Andover, Massachusetts. She spent the next year at Vassar College, then transferred to Wheaton College in Norton, Massachusetts, earning her bachelor's degree in 1918. While attending Wheaton, Shouse got involved with women's affairs and began organizing conferences to examine and promote job opportunities for educated women.

With her interest in women's employment, Shouse earned a job in 1917 working for the Women's Division of the U.S. Employment Service at the Department of Labor in Washington, D.C. It is interesting to note that Shouse's desire to promote careers for women was not related to her interest in the early women's movement. For Shouse, it was a practical concern. She believed that women should have the opportunity to support themselves if need be. Shouse's work in this area caught the attention of Houghton-Mifflin and the publishing company commissioned her to write and edit *Careers for Women: New Ideas, New Methods, New Opportunities to Fit a New World.* The book was published in 1920.

Took Interest in Politics

In 1919, Shouse began attending Radcliffe College to pursue a graduate degree. Around this time she was appointed to the Democratic National Committee to represent Massachusetts,

becoming the first woman to serve in that capacity. She transferred to Harvard and in 1923 became the first woman to earn a master's degree in education from the Ivy League school. Speaking to the *New York Times* in 1971, Shouse recalled the uproar she caused. ''I was the first woman given that degree, and the Harvard marshal at that time said he would resign if a woman ever put her foot on the Harvard platform. Well, he didn't have to resign because at the time they gave the degree I was having a baby and I couldn't step on his platform. They had to mail it to me.''

Shouse married Alvin Dodd, an economist, on December 10, 1921. They settled in Washington, D.C., to be close to Dodd's job with the U.S. Department of Commerce. They had one daughter, Joan. Dodd later became manager of the distribution department of the U.S. Chamber of Commerce. Around this time, Shouse became active in politics as she befriended Washington's movers and shakers. In 1925, Shouse and her friend, suffragette Daisy Harriman, founded the Women's National Democratic Club and began inviting influential Washingtonians to speak at club luncheons. From 1929-32, Shouse edited the club's newsletter, the *Bulletin.*

With her entrance into the political scene, Shouse received an appointment from President Calvin Coolidge. In 1926, Coolidge tapped Shouse to serve as the first board chairperson of the Federal Women's Prison for the Rehabilitation and Education of Women. Working in this capacity, Shouse helped establish a job-training program for female prisoners. Shouse also continued her work trying to open job opportunities for professional women. In 1929, she founded the Institute of Women's Professional Relations.

Shouse filed for divorce from Dodd in 1930. At the time, Dodd was working as an assistant to the president of Sears Roebuck & Co. After Dodd took the position in 1928, he moved to New York City; Shouse stayed in Washington. In her divorce petition, she charged Dodd with ''desertion.''

Purchased Wolf Trap Farm

During her separation from Dodd, Shouse bought a 52-acre farm with a rundown, 300-year-old farmhouse near Vienna, Virginia. She dubbed the place Wolf Trap, in keeping with its history. From the time the early colonists moved into the area in the 1630s, it had been overrun with wolves who posed such a menace the government offered rewards to those who set traps to capture the creatures. After her divorce, Shouse settled at Wolf Trap and began selling eggs and milk to supplement a monthly stipend provided by her father.

In 1932, Shouse married Jouett Shouse, a former newspaperman-turned-Congressman from Kansas. Jouett Shouse was an active member of the Democratic Party, serving as chairman of the Democratic National Committee in 1929. Jouett Shouse led the Association Against the Prohibition Amendment. As an influential Washington insider, he was featured in *Time* magazine in 1930. The couple met in Washington and married after Jouett Shouse divorced his wife of some 20 years.

Over the next three decades, the Shouses continued to renovate Wolf Trap and purchase additional parcels of land, eventually growing the property to more than 160 acres and setting up a working farm. They grew corn, wheat, and oats for the chickens, ducks, and turkeys. Angus steer, hogs, milk cows, and horses also populated the premises. Catherine Shouse also operated a kennel at Wolf Trap, breeding pedigreed Boxers. Located about fifteen miles west of Washington, Wolf Trap was an ideal destination, a place the Shouses used for entertaining by providing a quiet retreat for their city friends. Guests ate food raised on the farm and could spend their time hunting or riding horses. Catherine Shouse also hosted charity carnivals at Wolf Trap.

Dove into Public Service

After marrying Jouett Shouse, Catherine Shouse's focus turned from politics to civic and cultural affairs. She arranged candlelight concerts at her home to augment the salaries of the National Symphony Orchestra musicians. In 1942, she raised money for the Community War Fund. During the late 1940s and early 1950s, Catherine Shouse led fundraising efforts for the General Clay Fund for German Youth Activities. The program, run by the U.S. Armed Forces, promoted leadership skills among German youth during the post-World War II Allied occupation.

Catherine Shouse proved herself an effective and efficient fundraiser, prompting President Herbert Hoover to enlist her efforts to help with the Hungarian Relief Fund, which aided the Hungarians who fled the country following the Hungarian Uprising of 1956. Within a month, Catherine Shouse had raised $500,000 for the fund.

Eventually, Catherine Shouse began working with the arts. In 1949, she joined the board of the National Symphony Orchestra Association, serving as vice president from 1951-68. In 1957, President Dwight D. Eisenhower tapped her to chair the People-to-People Program of the President's Music Committee. She later served on the executive and building committees of the John F. Kennedy Center for the Performing Arts.

Donated Land, Funds for Arts Center

During the 1960s, the Shouses lost part of their Wolf Trap property when the government acquired a portion for the Dulles Airport access road. With her property divided by the road, Catherine Shouse decided to give a portion to the U.S. government for a performing arts park to be run by the National Park Service. Shouse believed such a park would help fill a gap. She reasoned there were plenty of parks for people who liked to fish and camp or hike, but none devoted solely to the arts. In 1966, she gave 100 acres for this purpose and promised to provide $2 million in funding to build an open-air amphitheater.

After Congress accepted her gift in 1966, Catherine Shouse began visiting theaters and auditoriums around the globe to get ideas for an outdoor amphitheater at Wolf Trap, which she planned to name the Filene Center in honor of her parents. Jouett Shouse died in 1968 and after her husband's death, Catherine Shouse threw herself into the project full force. She was heavily involved with the design and construction of the Filene Center. The groundbreaking took place in 1968. In March 1971, as construction of the amphitheater neared completion, tragedy struck when a fire destroyed most of the ten-story-tall structure. Catherine Shouse wanted to ensure the park's opening would not be delayed, so she paid the construction workers overtime and delivered sandwiches and coffee to them so they could keep working.

The Wolf Trap Farm Park for the Performing Arts opened in July 1971, with the fire delaying the first performance by only a month. Wolf Trap's inaugural performance consisted of a concert given by the National Symphony and famed American pianist Van Cliburn. The first season included performances by the New York City Opera, the Stuttgart Ballet, and the Cleveland Symphony. Shouse regularly traveled abroad to scout new talent and brought an acrobatic troupe from the People's Republic of China to perform at Wolf Trap during the 1970s. The National Folk Festival was held there as well.

Ran Wolf Trap Foundation

Once the facility opened, Catherine Shouse turned her attention to running the Wolf Trap Foundation, which managed the park, set up programming, and raised funds. To keep the performances accessible and reasonably priced, the foundation had to raise some $2 million a year. Shouse served on the foundation's board through the mid-1990s. While her contributions were invaluable, some suggest she was hard to work with. The Foundation went through eight executive directors in the first sixteen years.

In 1982, another fire ripped through the Filene Center, destroying the amphitheater. Once again, Catherine Shouse led the charge to rebuild. The new Filene Center, built of Douglas Fir and Southern Yellow Pine, included covered seating for about 4,000 with open sides looking out onto the rolling hills. The adjoining sloping lawn seating accommodated about 3,000. During the 1980s, Shouse helped expand programming by purchasing two early 18th-century Maine barns, which she had moved to the property to allow for indoor winter and autumn performances.

The Wolf Trap season typically ran from May through September, with some 90 performances encompassing pop, country, folk, dance, theater, and opera. Many popular performers flocked to play there because of the extraordinary acoustics provided by the wooden, open-air stage. Dolly Parton, Johnny Cash, Leonard Bernstein, Luciano Pavarotti, and Mikhail Baryshnikov performed at Wolf Trap. During the 1990s, attendance hit about 500,000 visitors per year.

For many years, Shouse was a fixture at Wolf Trap and enjoyed attending performances to witness what she had helped create. "I like to see the people coming up the hill and smiling," Shouse once told a reporter, according to the *Richmond Times-Dispatch*. "For a little while, they can forget the world and leave their troubles in the parking lot with the car."

Periodicals

Los Angeles Times, December 10, 1988.
New York Times, November 17, 1930; November 4, 1932; December 3, 1932; September 26, 1971; December 15, 1994.
Richmond Times-Dispatch (VA), December 15, 1994.
Washington Post, December 15, 1994.

Online

"Catherine Filene Shouse (1896-1994)," *Wolf Trap*, http://www. wolftrap.org/Learn_About_Wolf_Trap/Founder.aspx (November 1, 2011).

"Shouse, Catherine Filene. Papers, 1878-1998: A Finding Aid," *Harvard University Library*, http://oasis.lib.harvard.edu/oasis/ deliver/~sch00014 (November 1, 2011).

"Women Working, Catherine Filene Shouse (1896-1994)," *Harvard University Open Collections Program*, http://ocp.hul.harvard. edu/ww/shouse.html (November 1, 2011). □

Sonia Sotomayor

Sonia Sotomayor (born 1954) is the first American of Hispanic descent to sit on the U.S. Supreme Court. Nominated by President Barack Obama in 2009, the New York City-area federal judge became only the third woman ever to serve on the nation's high court and the 111th American jurist to receive the prestigious lifetime appointment. With her swearing-in ceremony on August 9, 2009, Sotomayor became the highest ranking person of Puerto Rican heritage in the United States government.

S onia Maria Sotomayor was born on June 25, 1954, to parents who had taken advantage of a unique World War I-era law that gave Puerto Ricans U.S. citizenship. Her mother Celina had enlisted in the Women's Army Corps during World War II, and later married Juan Sotomayor. The couple settled in New York City, home to a thriving Puerto Rican-émigré community, where Juan worked as a welder and Sotomayor's mother became a licensed practical nurse at a small hospital in the South Bronx.

Grew Up in Public Housing

In 1957, Sotomayor's younger brother Juan Jr. was born, and that same year the family moved out of their tenement apartment into a public housing unit at the Bronxdale Houses. Sotomayor and her brother attended Roman Catholic schools in southeast Bronx, and her mother "had almost a fanatical emphasis on education," Sotomayor once recalled in an interview with *New York Times* journalist Jan Hoffman. "We got encyclopedias, and she struggled to make those payments. She kept saying, 'I don't care what you do, but be the best at it.'"

Sotomayor's pleasant childhood was disrupted by two serious events: at the age of eight she was diagnosed with Type I diabetes, and began a lifelong dependence on daily insulin injections. A year later, her father died of a heart attack, though he was just 42 years old. Sotomayor's mother struggled to keep her two children in parochial school, and was able to move them into an even safer place, the enormous new Co-Op City in the northeast quadrant of the Bronx, in the late 1960s.

Earned Scholarship to Princeton

By then Sotomayor had entered Cardinal Spellman High School and had set her sights on a career in law. She earned top grades at the single-sex unit of the school—which became a co-educational institution at the start of her senior year in 1971—was a member of the debate team and the National Honor Society, and graduated as her class valedictorian. Her efforts yielded a full-ride scholarship to an Ivy League school, Princeton University, at a time when the New Jersey college was moving to diversify its student body. She majored in history while working in the college cafeteria, and became active in a Hispanic student group called Accion Puertorriquena that worked to urge Princeton officials to hire and promote more Hispanic-heritage faculty members. She graduated summa cum laude from Princeton in 1976, collecting a top academic prize for her grades along with Phi Beta Kappa distinction. Later that year she married Kevin E. Noonan, a classmate from her Cardinal Spellman days, who went on to become a molecular biologist, and also began classes at Yale Law School in New Haven, Connecticut.

After earning her law degree in 1979, Sotomayor went to work for the District Attorney's office in New York County under prosecutor Robert M. Morgenthau. She spent five years as an assistant district attorney at the famed 100 Centre Street building in Manhattan, at a time when violent crime rates in New York City were skyrocketing. Assistant district attorneys handled about 300 cases a year, collecting evidence and arguing the prosecution's side for conviction. The heavy caseloads handled by Morgenthau's office were the focus of a 1983 *New York Times Magazine* article by Jonathan Barzilay. "I had more problems during my first year in the office with the low-grade crimes," Sotomayor told Barzilay. "The shoplifting, the prostitution, the minor assault cases. In large measure, in those cases you were dealing with socioeconomic crimes, crimes that could be the product of the environment and of poverty."

Halted Fendi-Counterfeit Purse Scam

During this era, after the breakup of her marriage, Sotomayor lived in the Carroll Gardens section of Brooklyn long before it became a gentrified enclave. In 1984, she opted to go into private practice, choosing a Manhattan boutique firm. In her eight years with Pavia & Harcourt, she handled intellectual property cases for clients that included Ferrari and Fendi and was promoted to partner. In 1991, President George H. W. Bush nominated Sotomayor for a federal judgeship with the U.S. District Court for the Southern District of New York. Her selection had been championed by Daniel Patrick Moynihan, the U.S. senator from New York, and she was the first Puerto Rican ever to be nominated for the federal bench in New York. The Bush nomination sailed through the Senate, confirmed by unanimous vote in August of 1992.

Sotomayor was one of 58 judges on the high-profile federal bench of the Southern District of New York, which often landed the most sizzling cases involving organized crime figures—brought in under federal anti-racketeering statutes—and even Wall Street-related misdeeds, because banks and other major financial institutions were headquartered in this federal court's jurisdiction.

Rescued 1995 Baseball Season

Sotomayor, who grew up a New York Yankees fan, first turned up in national news headlines in the spring of 1995 when she made a firm ruling on an ongoing labor dispute between the Major League Baseball Players Association (MLBPA) and team owners. The athletes had walked off the job the previous August over proposed new salary rules in the league, and their walkout forced the cancellation of the rest of the 1994 season. The strike threatened to drag on into another year, and even Congress and President Bill Clinton were unable to bring the two sides to a compromise. When team owners began moving replacement players to training camps and then voted to begin the season with them, the case came onto Sotomayor's docket. Famously, she issued an injunction preventing team owners from hiring new teams. "Sotomayor chided baseball owners, saying they had no right to unilaterally eliminate the 20-year-old system of free agents and salary arbitration while bargaining continues," wrote *New York Times* journalist James C. McKinley Jr. Other newspaper headlines commended her as the woman who finally ended the seven-month-long baseball strike and saved the 1995 MLB season.

In June of 1997, Sotomayor was nominated for another federal judgeship, this one on the U.S. Court of Appeals for the Second Circuit. This is the New York City-based appellate court in between the federal courts—like the U.S. District Court for the Southern District of New York and five other district courts—and the U.S. Supreme Court. President Clinton nominated her for this, and the process once again included vetting by the Senate Judiciary Committee and confirmation by Senate vote. But conservative forces marshaled against Sotomayor, and Republicans in the Senate managed to delay the vote for months. Finally, after more than a year of political wrangling, the Senate confirmed her appointment on October 3, 1998. "Some

Republicans," wrote Neil A. Lewis in the *New York Times,* "did not want to consider the nomination because, they said, putting her on the appeals court would enhance her prospects for elevation to the Supreme Court."

Ruled Against New Haven Firefighters

Sotomayor spent the next eleven years on the federal appeals bench while also teaching courses at the New York University School of Law and Columbia University. One of her most closely watched rulings came in *Ricci v. DeStefano,* a so-called "reverse affirmative action" case brought by white firefighters in New Haven, Connecticut. To qualify for a promotion, the first-responders had to pass an annual examination, and one year no African-Americans firefighters in the department had earned a qualifying score on the test. New Haven officials decided to nullify the test results, which angered the non-minority candidates who had passed the exam. The city's legal team believed that had they not thrown out the scores from that year's exam, the city might be liable for another lawsuit, this one from minority firefighters claiming that the city of New Haven imposed enough barriers to job promotion to be construed as a form of discrimination. Sotomayor upheld a lower court's ruling, prompting controversy even among some of her federal appellate judges, and the case became mired in a myriad of legal procedural issues; eventually the U.S. Supreme Court agreed to review the case, and overturned Sotomayor's ruling.

By then Sotomayor had become a contender for a Supreme Court appointment. A little over three months after President Barack Obama took office, Supreme Court Associate Justice David Souter announced his retirement from the bench. Sotomayor turned up on the Obama administration's shortlist of four female finalists, and on May 26, 2009, the president announced she was his choice to become the 111th justice of the Supreme Court. "She's faced down barriers, overcome the odds, lived out the American dream that brought her parents here so long ago," the president said at a new conference announcing his choice, according to *USA Today.*

The "Wise Latina" Controversy

Conservative pundits immediately began discussing Sotomayor's ruling on the New Haven case, and also discovered a 2001 speech she gave at the University of California—Berkeley School of Law in an annual event for Latino law students and attorneys. In it, she reflected back on her own life and the importance of diversity in the legal-justice system. "I would hope that a wise Latina woman, with the richness of her experiences, would more often than not reach a better conclusion than a white male who hasn't lived that life," she said, a quote that was cited by conservative media sources as evidence of her pro-Hispanic bias. The *National Review* was one such publication, and Andrew C. McCarthy devoted 1,500 words to her remark, calling it "a lightning rod of a claim: Had a white man contended that the richness of his experience rendered him a better judge than a Latina woman, his career would be over."

Sotomayor was given a chance to address that remark by the Senate Judiciary Committee on the first day of her confirmation hearings in July. The televised proceedings showed Sotomayor hobbled by a broken ankle, which she had suffered while running to catch a plane at New York's LaGuardia airport in June. "I was trying to inspire them to believe that their life experiences would enrich the legal system, because different life experiences and backgrounds always do," she said, according to the *Washington Post.* Conceding that the eight-year-old speech had riled those who believed she was not impartial enough to serve on the Supreme Court, she told the Senate and the nation, "I want to state up front, unequivocally and without doubt, I do not believe that any ethnic, racial or gender group has an advantage in sound judging. I do believe that every person has an equal opportunity to be a good and wise judge regardless of their background or life experiences."

Sotomayor was confirmed by Senate vote on August 6, 2009, and sworn in as an Associate Justice by Supreme Court Chief Justice John G. Roberts Jr. on August 9. Her mother, Celina—remarried, retired, and visiting Washington from her home in Margate, Florida—held the Bible for the ceremony. One of the more intriguing bits of information that came out of Sotomayor's nomination process was from the financial disclosure forms she was required to submit. Back in 2008, Sotomayor had been visiting a Florida casino with her mother and walked away from a card table with more than $8,000 in winnings, which she then duly claimed on her federal tax return. Her former law clerks had described her to inquiring journalists as an enthusiastic Texas hold'em player.

Periodicals

National Review, June 22, 2009.
New York Times, September 25, 1992; April 1, 1995; October 3, 1998; May 28, 2009; July 10, 2009.
New York Times Magazine, November 27, 1983; July 12, 2009.
New Yorker, July 27, 2009; January 11, 2010; March 22, 2010.
USA Today, May 27, 2009.
Washington Post, July 14, 2009. □

F. N. Souza

The Indian artist F.N. Souza (1924–2002) was among the first modern artists from the Indian subcontinent to earn an international reputation.

Souza's works, mostly paintings, were satirical and often shocking, with a critical streak that applied equally to the West and to his own culture. Many were explicitly erotic, but he was also strongly influenced by his Roman Catholic religious heritage, by Expressionism and other modern European art generally, and by Pablo Picasso and Georges Rouault in particular. He fell into no specific school, and there was always a distinct Indian element in his work. The critic John Berger, quoted on the *Contemporary Indian Art* website, pointed out that Souza "straddles many traditions but serves none." Although he had a strong following in Britain as well as several key supporters in the United States, Souza's work was little known in his native India during his own lifetime. He exploded in popularity, in both India and the West, after his death in 2002.

Survived Smallpox

F.N. Souza was born Newton Souza on April 12, 1924, in Saligao, Goa, India, which at the time was controlled by Portugal. His father, an English teacher, died when he was three months old, and his only sister died shortly after that. Souza and his mother, Lily Mary, headed for the rapidly growing city of Bombay (now Mumbai), but their luck went from bad to worse: Souza contracted smallpox. Cared for by a grandmother in Goa, he survived and rejoined his mother, who had built a small dressmaking business into the Institute of Needle Craft and Domestic Science. Grateful for his recovery, she gave her son the first name Francis, in honor of Goa's patron saint, and urged him to pursue a career as a Jesuit priest.

Souza did consent to attend a Jesuit school in Bombay, but he was expelled after school administrators found pornographic drawings he had made on the bathroom walls. As he recalled in an autobiographical note quoted by Geeta Kapur in *Contemporary Indian Artists,* he would watch his mother bathe through a peephole he had drilled in the door: "I drew her on the walls and prudes thought I was rude. I can't see why, because so far as I can recollect, I have even painted murals on the walls of her womb." Souza made art prolifically beginning in childhood, and decided to become an artist while still in his teens. In 1940, he enrolled at the Jamshetjee Jeejebhoy School of Art, which had at least tenuous affiliations with the Royal Academy of Great Britain. He was expelled from that school as well, this time for participating in the Quit India independence movement, but by that time he had obtained a grasp of basic academic painting principles.

In the 1940s, Souza's art had a political flavor. He joined the Communist Party and painted scenes with titles that explicitly analyzed class struggles in Indian society. Despite this, he won first prize at the annual exhibition of the conservative Bombay Art Society in 1947, the year India became independent from Britain. That year he founded a Progressive Artists Group that also included another future star of Indian art, M.F. Husain, but the group soon fragmented because its members had differing political goals. In 1949, Souza decided to try his luck as an artist in London, England.

Gained Notice as Writer

At first, as a complete unknown, Souza had little luck in attracting interest to his work. His wife, Maria, was forced to do odd jobs, while Souza turned to freelance journalism. On the point of giving up and returning to India, he gained notice in England not as an artist but as a writer: his colorful autobiographical essay "Nirvana of a Maggot" caught the eye of poet Stephen Spender and was published in the journal *Encounter* in 1955. Around the same time, he met influential gallery owners in London and Paris, and a one-man show of his works mounted at London's Gallery One sold out. Suddenly Souza was a London sensation, with a sharp pen to match his daring paintings. He wrote much of the material for his catalogues himself and collected his critical writings into a short book, *Words & Lines*.

The style of Souza's mature works cannot be easily classified. His point of departure was the European Expressionist movement, with its rough, distorted figures that aimed to express an emotional state more than to depict the world realistically. But Souza added many ideas of his own to the style, including a humorous twist that drew viewers to his work. Like the German painter George Grosz, he sometimes distorted the shape of a subject's head in order to make a satirical point about the person's identity. And he was recognizably an Indian painter, setting landscapes in India and later in his career using subjects from Hindu mythology. The letters of his distinctive signature hung from a straight line, as in the scripts of many Indian languages.

Souza's paintings embraced several often contradictory themes. A large group drew on Christian themes. They were hardly reverent, but they did not attack religion either. One of Souza's most famous religious works was *Crucifixion* (1959), in which the crucified Jesus appears as a mysterious black figure with large teeth, pierced with thorns in various parts of his body. Souza was inspired in part by Expressionist religious paintings and the drawings of French artist Georges Rouault (1871–1958), but went even further than Rouault in his departures from traditional religious imagery.

Referred to Indian Erotic Art Tradition

Paradoxically, many of Souza's paintings were erotic. He drew numerous female nudes, and some of his paintings were explicitly sexual. Souza referred to the long tradition of erotic depictions in Indian art as a precedent for his own work, although the degree of visible Indian influence in these works waxed and waned over the course of his career. Souza apparently did not conceive of erotic art in the abstract. "The nudes were almost like his little black book of dalliances," gallery owner Uday Jain told the *Times of India*. "You could tell who he was with." Souza was married three times and was in a partnership with a fourth woman, Srimati Lal, at his death; he had five children, Shelley, Karen, Francesca, Anya, and Patrick.

In 1956 an American collector, Harold Kovner, offered to bankroll Souza's work in return for regular shipments of paintings. Souza responded to the commission with 200 works over several years, and he was able to live comfortably off the proceeds. He struggled with alcoholism in the late 1950s. In 1960, he received a British Council fellowship to work in Italy and from there traveled to India. This trip brought his addiction to a crisis point, and when he returned to London he checked into a rehab center and underwent a successful course of treatment. In the early 1960s he began to mount shows around the world, including in France, Germany, Japan, Sweden, Brazil, Argentina, Canada, and the United States.

In 1964, after London audiences were scandalized by Souza's marriage to a 17-year-old girl, he received the offer of a gallery show from the London Arts Group in Detroit. That was the springboard for Souza's move to New York, where he lived for the rest of his life, making increasingly frequent trips to India in the winter and filling his small apartment with hundreds of paintings. *Crucifixion* was acquired by the Tate Gallery in London, a prestigious museum that eventually dedicated an entire room to Souza's works. In India itself, Souza remained little known, but in the 1980s and 1990s New Delhi's Dhoomimal Art Gallery began to champion his work. Major retrospective shows of his work were held in New Delhi and Bombay in 1987 and 1996.

Souza died after suffering a heart attack in New Delhi on March 28, 2002. He was reported to be nearly bankrupt at the time, but after his death his popularity exploded, especially in India. Auctions of his work set new price records, and in the year 2009 alone he was the subject of thirteen separate gallery exhibitions. Souza seemed an artist for violent times. "At the heart of Souza's creativity," art historian Yashodhara Dalmia told the *Times of India*, "was the belief that society's destructive aspects shouldn't be suppressed, they should be aired and confronted."

Books

Kapur, Geeta, *Contemporary Indian Artists*, Vikas, 1978.
Tuli, Neville, *Contemporary Indian Painting*, Abrams, 1998.

Periodicals

Guardian (London, England), June 17, 2002.
New York Times, October 23, 1998.
Times of India, May 5, 2010.

Online

"Francis Newton Souza," *Contemporary Indian Art,* http://www.contemporaryindianart.com/francis_newton_souza.htm (October 18, 2011).
"Francis Newton Souza," *Francis Newton Souza Official Website,* http://www.fnsouza.com (October 18, 2011).
"Francis Newton Souza," *Saffronart,* http://www.saffronart.com/artist/ArtistBiography.aspx?artistid=71 (October 18, 2011).□

Frederick Stanley

Frederick Stanley, also known as Lord Stanley of Preston and the sixteenth Earl of Derby, is the figure for whom hockey's famed Stanley Cup is named. Stanley was serving as Governor General of Canada in the 1890s when several of his athletic sons took up the sport during their time in the Canadian capital city of Ottawa. According to the legend surrounding the championship trophy cup of the National Hockey League (NHL), Stanley never actually saw a hockey game, but did pay about $50 for the silver cup, which was originally known as the Dominion Hockey Challenge Cup and is the oldest sports championship prize in North America.

Lord Stanley hailed from a family whose service to the English throne dated back several centuries. He was born Frederick Arthur Stanley on January 15, 1841, in London, the second son of Edward George Geoffrey Stanley, the 14th Earl of Derby and a well-known figure in Conservative (Tory)

politics who went on to lead the party for several years. During the reign of Queen Victoria, Stanley's father served as prime minister for three separate terms, the first of which began in 1852. The Earl of Derby title dated back to 1139, and had been held by the Lancashire-landowning Stanley family after 1485 with the elevation of one ancestor to the House of Lords. An earlier family member had risen to prominence by subduing some of Ireland's infamously recalcitrant chieftains on behalf of King Richard II of England in the 1390s. Stanley's mother was Emma Caroline Bootle-Wilbraham, daughter of the 1st Baron Skelmersdale. Her family had ties to Lancaster and Newcastle in the north of England.

Served with Grenadier Guards

As the second son of the family, Stanley would not inherit the title and was expected to forge his own path in the world. A military career was one of the avenues open to him, and he entered the Royal Military College at Sandhurst after graduating from Eton College. He joined the Grenadier Guards of the British Army in 1858, and rose to the rank of captain in 1862. Two years later he wed Lady Constance Villiers, the daughter of the Earl of Clarendon, with whom he would have eight children.

Stanley retired from the Grenadier Guards in 1865 to enter politics, as his older brother Edward had done. In the 1865 general election, Stanley won a seat in the House of Commons from the district of Preston in Lancashire on the Tory ticket. This was the last election to be held before the Reform Act of 1867 went into effect, which effectively doubled the number of eligible voters in Britain; prior to this, only male adults who met certain income guidelines could vote in general elections. The 1868 general election featured a marked advance by the Liberal Party, but Stanley kept a seat in the House of Commons after switching over to run in the district of North Lancashire, which he would

hold for the next 17 years. In the 1885 general election—again, after significant reform measures were passed by Parliament—Stanley won a seat representing the coastal city of Blackpool.

Stanley held a variety of cabinet posts in Tory governments. In 1868 he served as Civil Lord of the Admiralty, and from 1874 to 1878 was Financial Secretary for Britain's War Office under Prime Minister Benjamin Disraeli. He spent a brief stint as Secretary to the Treasury before Disraeli named him War Secretary in 1878, a post he held for two years. William Gladstone's Liberal Party won the 1880 general election, and Stanley stepped down from his cabinet post. The Tories returned to power in 1885 and new prime minister Robert Gascoyne-Cecil appointed Stanley as Secretary of State for the Colonies. In 1886 Queen Victoria recognized his long record of public service by bestowing a hereditary peerage upon him, creating the title Baron Stanley of Preston. This elevated him to the House of Lords, the upper chamber of British Parliament, a seat he would hold until his death in 1908.

Appointed Governor General

On May 1, 1888, Queen Victoria appointed Stanley as the newest Governor General of Canada. This was a post held exclusively by members of the peerage until well into the twentieth century. The British Empire was a vast global entity by that point, but in 1867 Canadian subjects had successfully pushed for home rule. This gave them the right to govern their own affairs except for foreign policy, though the 1867 constitution technically gave the reigning king or queen of England the highest executive, legislative, and judicial powers in Canada. The resident Governor General was permitted to exercise those powers on behalf of the monarch. Governors General were generally appointed to five-year terms, though they could be recalled at will by the monarch. Their chief duty was to formally open parliament every year, and they also appointed members of the Senate, the upper chamber of Canada's Parliament.

Stanley and Constance had seven sons and one daughter. The first son was Edward, born in 1865, and five more boys came after him. Daughter Isobel was born in 1875, followed by their last child, Frederick, in 1878. The majority of the children seemed to have sailed for Canada with their parents, with Edward serving as his father's aide-de-camp after Lord Stanley took the oath of office in Ottawa on June 11, 1888. They moved into the palatial Rideau Hall, the Governor General's official residence. The sons were a famously athletic bunch and had already taken up the new fad for ice skating that swept through Britain and other European countries thanks to advances in refrigeration technology.

Field hockey, a sport in which two opposing sides wielded curved wooden sticks to move a ball past one another's defense lines, was common to many cultures around the world. Hockey was also related to hurling, an ancient Irish pastime, and was cousin to the netted-stick and ball games played by Native American populations that evolved into lacrosse. The Dutch were especially adept at ice skating, and the first form of ice hockey was thought to have originated there in the Middle Ages. Canada's northerly climate proved an ideal place for a skating rink version of field hockey to flourish on its numerous rivers and lakes. The first officially recognized hockey game was played at Montreal's McGill University in 1875.

Paterfamilias of "Seven Skating Stanleys"

Stanley's sons eagerly took to the new sport. The third son, Arthur, founded a hockey club called the Rideau Rebels, which played on the rink built on Rideau Hall parklands several years earlier by a previous Governor General, the Earl of Dufferin. But the Rideau ice was soon the site of clashes between pleasure skaters and hockey players, as was the case elsewhere on rinks both public and private in North America and Europe, and the Rebels were forced to move to a private rink. The team, led by Edward and Arthur, soon became the top outfit in Ottawa and began playing travel games with Montreal and Toronto clubs. These games became exciting spectator sport events and popularized the game immensely in the provinces of Ontario and Quebec.

On November 27, 1890, Stanley's son Arthur presided over a meeting in which attendees agreed to form an ice hockey association for Canada. This became the Ontario Hockey Association, a federation of leagues across the province. Lady Stanley was apparently an ardent supporter of the sport, though her husband's actual role in promoting the sport survives only in the story behind the silver championship cup that bears the family name: the brothers asked their father to donate a trophy, and he ordered his secretary, Captain Charles Colville of the Coldstream Guards, to locate a suitable object on his next visit to London. Colville picked up a gold-lined silver bowl for about ten guineas, the equivalent of $48.67.

Dubbed "Lord Stanley's Cup"

The Dominion Hockey Challenge Cup made its public debut at the Ottawa Athletic Association banquet on March 18, 1892. Stanley was not present, but another aide and Grenadier Guard, Viscount Kilcoursie (born Frederic Rudolph Lambart, and also known as the 10th Earl of Cavan), read aloud a letter from Stanley that accompanied the cup. "I have for some time been thinking that it would be a good thing if there were a challenge cup which should be held from year to year by the champion hockey team in the Dominion," it read, according to *The Ultimate Prize: The Stanley Cup,* a 2003 book by Dan Diamond. The first team to win the trophy was the Montreal Amateur Athletic Association in 1893, which kept it in the first-ever playoff series, in 1894, but lost it to the Montreal Victorias in 1895.

Stanley had by then returned to England permanently. His older brother died in April of 1893, and Stanley and his family sailed back to England in July. He became the 16th Earl of Derby, was appointed Lord Mayor of Liverpool, and served as chancellor of the University of Liverpool before his death in London at the age of 67 on June 14, 1908. His titles passed to his son Edward, who had done much to drum up interest in hockey in England. In the frigid

winter of 1894–95, the artificial lake at the royal residence in London, Buckingham Palace, froze over, and the Stanley brothers played a game on it with several members of the royal household, including the future King Edward VII.

Declined to Rule on Sectarian Controversy

Though Stanley's name is perhaps best known for its attachment to the oldest sporting trophy in North America, he served a tenure as Governor General of Canada that was notable for a few other events. He made an historic trip through western Canada in the fall of 1889 on the newly built Canadian Pacific Railway, and sought to rule judiciously on fisheries disputes between Canada and the United States off the coast of Newfoundland. He also declined to involve himself in a major controversy that was roiling in Canada for several months by the time he arrived to become Governor General. The Jesuit Estates Act of 1888 offered compensation for lands seized more than a century earlier when the British overpowered French interests in Quebec. The properties belonging to the Society of Jesuits, a Roman Catholic missionary order, were confiscated at that time, but in 1888 the provincial legislature of Quebec voted to award compensation to the order. The plan stirred major anti-Catholic sentiment in Canada, and as the Queen's representative in Canada, Stanley had the right to disallow the measure, preventing it from becoming law. The House of Commons in Ottawa sided with Protestants in Quebec and passed a motion requesting him to formally oppose it. He declined to do so, asserting that the Quebec legislature's measure was entirely constitutional.

Stanley's wife founded the Lady Stanley Institute for Trained Nurses in Ottawa, the first nursing school in the city. She died in 1922, 14 years after her husband. Their first son, Edward, served as Britain's Secretary of State for War during World War I and ambassador to France. Their second son, Victor, rose to the rank of admiral in the Royal Navy. The family's most enthusiastic hockey player, Arthur, served in Britain's House of Commons for many years, as did his brother George, the fifth son. A fourth son, Ferdinand Charles, became a British Army brigadier general and married into the famous Spencer-Churchill/Fellowes clan. The sixth son, Algernon, also served in World War I and died in 1962. Lord Stanley's only daughter, Isobel, died a year later at the age of 88. The youngest son, Frederick, died in 1942 at the age of 64.

Lord Stanley's Cup became a storied piece of sports legend, engraved with the names of players of the winning championship team of the National Hockey League (NHL) after its formation in 1917. The victors customarily skate holding it aloft after their post-season win and quaff champagne from it. In the 1960s, the original cup was replaced by a facsimile after it became too fragile to handle. The original cup brought from London by Captain Colville on Stanley's order sits inside a vault at the Hockey Hall of Fame in Toronto. Lord Stanley was inducted posthumously into the Hall of Fame in 1945. The Ontario Hockey Association (OHA), formed by his son Arthur in 1890, still endures and is a top source of farm team talent for NHL franchises in North America.

Books

Coward, Barry, *The Stanleys, Lords Stanley, and Earls of Derby, 1385-1672: The Origins, Wealth, and Power of a Landowning Family,* Manchester University Press, 1983.

Diamond, Dan, James Duplacey, and Eric Zweig, *The Ultimate Prize: The Stanley Cup,* Andrews McMeel Publishing, 2003.

Periodicals

New York Times, August 9, 1889.

Online

''Lord Stanley and Sons,'' *NHL.com,* http://www.nhl.com/ice/page.htm?id=25428 (October 14, 2011).

''Lord Stanley,'' *The Governor General of Canada,* http://www.gg.ca/document.aspx?id=55 (October 14, 2011). □

George Steinbrenner

American baseball executive George Steinbrenner (1930-2010) was the highly controversial owner of the New York Yankees from the early 1970s until his death. A shipbuilding tycoon who purchased the club in 1973, he resuscitated a once-grand baseball team that had become a moribund organization by the late 1960s. His career included a downside, however: Twice he was suspended from the sport for legal and ethical transgressions. Further, he wasn't well liked by those who worked with him and for him.

I t is appropriate that George Michael Steinbrenner III would come to own a team called the New York Yankees (and one of America's legendary sports organizations), as he was born on the Fourth of July. The shipping industry magnate helped turn around a team that had become merely a shadow of its former greatness.

He became known as ''The Boss'' for his aggressive leadership style, and New York fans either loved him or hated him. There was no middle ground. His relationship with his players, his coaches and managers, and the New York sportswriters was constantly contentious. His feuds with two of his players (Reggie Jackson and Dave Winfield) and at least one of his managers (Billy Martin) are legendary. However, fellow baseball executives granted him grudging respect for the turnaround he engineered through major trades and big-money contracts. Under Steinbrenner, the team won numerous championships (division, league, and World Series) and in the 1970s and early 1980s, he navigated the team into a new Yankee golden era.

Son of a Strict Shipbuilder

Steinbrenner was born in 1930 in Rocky River, Ohio, not far from Cleveland. He was one of three children (he had two sisters). His father was Henry Steinbrenner, who built a Great Lakes shipping enterprise. His mother, Rita (Haley) Steinbrenner, was a homemaker. The parents couldn't have been more different. George Steinbrenner described his father as a disciplinarian who expected much from his three children. Conversely, his Irish mother, a devout Christian Scientist, was a compassionate woman. This dichotomy helped shaped his personality. During his professional career Steinbrenner could be at once charitable and unforgiving.

While Steinbrenner was influenced by his mother's example, his father was the more dominate figure in his early life. Henry Steinbrenner was a track and field star in college, and he encouraged his son to engage in athletic competition. Like his father, George Steinbrenner participated in track and field events, and he did quite well. However, Henry Steinbrenner was a hard man to please. For instance, during one high school competition, the younger Steinbrenner participated in three events. He finished first in two and came in second in a third. The father was more focused on that second-place finish. In a 2010 obituary published in *The New York Times,* writer Richard Goldstein quoted Steinbrenner as saying, ''He was a tough taskmaster. If I ran four races in track, won three and lost one, he'd say, 'Now go sit down and study that one race and see why you lost it.'''

As a result, Steinbrenner would become a perfectionist, a personality trait that would contribute to his later success in both the industrial and baseball world. Meanwhile, he added in the same Goldstein article, ''It was my mom who gave me compassion for the underdog and for the people in need.''

Harry Steinbrenner was a Massachusetts Institute of Technology graduate, earning a degree in naval architecture and engineering. Following graduation, he took over his family's maritime shipping business. At the helm, he made the Kinsman Marine Transit Company an ongoing success, and he provided his family a comfortable, secure living. But he wouldn't allow his son to become complacent, nor did he offer an allowance. Harry instilled in George a strong work ethic and a will to succeed. As such, when he was nine years old, George Steinbrenner started the George Company, which he established with the chickens that his father provided. He went from door-to-door selling eggs, which provided him pocket money. This business thrived and became the S & J company when George gave it to his sisters, Susan and Judy, when he left home to attend military school.

Was an Average but Active Student

Steinbrenner attended the Culver Military Academy near South Bend, Indiana, where he became involved in sports—but, ironically, not baseball. Following graduation, he entered Williams College in Williamstown, Massachusetts. While he was only an average student, he was active in extracurricular activities. He became captain of the track and field team, played in the school's band and ran the glee club. Also, he served as the sports editor for the college's student newspaper. During summers at home, he worked in his father's shipping enterprise, learning the business from the ground up.

Steinbrenner earned his bachelor's degree in 1952. After he graduated, he entered the United States Air Force. He became a second lieutenant and was stationed at the Lockbourne Air Force Base, located near Columbus, Ohio. During his military duty, he managed several projects that demonstrated his growing leadership skills. He established a sports program and set up his own food service business, a coffee-cart concept that eventually served nearly 16,000 military and civilian personnel on the base.

Became a Football Coach

After his discharge in 1954, Steinbrenner engaged in post-graduate study in physical education at Ohio State University. There, he met his future wife, Elizabeth Joan Zieg, who he married on May 12, 1956. In the meantime, he became a high school football coach. This led to coaching positions at the collegiate level at Northwestern and Purdue universities.

Harry Steinbrenner was not too happy about his son's career direction. In 1957, he convinced George to come back into the family shipping business. From there, Steinbrenner took on an increasingly important role in the company, while he still maintained his interest in sports.

Bought a Basketball Team

In 1960—and again making his father unhappy—Steinbrenner joined a group of investors that purchased a basketball team, the Cleveland Pipers, which competed in the AAU in an industrial league. Steinbrenner became a highly visible and outspoken owner, foreshadowing his tenure with the New York Yankees. He verbally abused the team after losses and criticized newspaper editors who he felt provided too little coverage. After only two years, the team and the league folded, and Steinbrenner lost more than a quarter of a million dollars—essentially all of his personal savings.

Following this financial debacle, Steinbrenner was advised to file for bankruptcy. Instead, he chose to work off his debts. His father retired from the family shipping business, and Steinbrenner took over. At the helm, he turned around a declining company. By 1967, the business was again thriving. Success compelled Steinbrenner to form a partnership of investors. This group bought a third of the shares of the American Ship Building Company and elected Steinbrenner as president. As the business continued to flourish, Steinbrenner became a multimillionaire. He even brought his father out of retirement to help run the company. As sportwriter Dick Schaap, who co-wrote the biography *Steinbrenner!* wryly noted, Steinbrenner's imperious father was now working for him.

Invited Legal Trouble

Business success led to political influence. Indeed, Steinbrenner established strong business and political connections. He became chief fundraiser for the Democratic Congressional Campaign Committee. During a two-year period in the late 1960s, he helped raise nearly two million dollars. This was a period when Democratic presidential nominee Hubert Humphrey campaigned against Republican nominee Richard M. Nixon; Nixon soundly defeated Humphrey in the 1968 United States presidential election. Swimming with the tide, the pragmatic Steinbrenner shifted allegiance. In 1972, when Nixon ran for re-election, Steinbrenner contributed a significant amount of money to the two-term president's campaign.

This led to legal problems, however. Steinbrenner's donations violated several campaign finance laws. He used corporate funds and created false employee bonuses. He eventually pleaded guilty to all counts filed against him and was fined a total of $35,000.

Bought the New York Yankees

Steinbrenner's legal trouble occurred while he was re-entering the sports arena—as a Major League baseball team owner. In January of 1973, Steinbrenner and fellow investors purchased the New York Yankees for $10 million. The group bought the team from CBS, the commercial broadcasting giant.

CBS had purchased the Yankees following the 1964 season, when the team made the last of five straight World Series appearances (but lost to the St. Louis Cardinals in seven games). Up to that point, the team was perhaps the best-ever in baseball. It had won twenty-nine pennants and twenty world championships in forty-five years. In thirty-nine years, it had never experienced a losing season. But during the CBS era, the team became one of the worst in baseball. In 1965, the Yankees finished in the second division. In 1966, they finished in last place in the American League, which would have been previously unthinkable.

The 1967 though 1972 seasons also witnessed also-ran status for the franchise. With no pennants, no World Series, or even contention, attendance declined.

After Steinbrenner and his investor group purchased the team in 1973, an insistent Steinbrenner firmly asserted that he would stick to building ships. It was not long, however, before he became almost obsessed with rebuilding the Yankee tradition. He hired former Cleveland Indian's General Manager Gabe Paul to oversee the process.

Temporarily Banished From Baseball

But his legal troubles came back to haunt him. In 1974, Steinbrenner pled guilty to two felony counts related to the shady campaign contributions. While he suffered only a fine of $15,000, then-baseball commissioner Bowie Kuhn suspended Steinbrenner from the game for fifteen months. During Steinbrenner's exile, Gabe Paul made a number of trades and free-agent deals that would help restore the Yankee team to its former grandeur. One of these involved the acquisition of free-agent pitcher James "Catfish" Hunter. Hunter, whose previous boss, Oakland Athletics owner Charlie Finley, had violated the terms of Hunter's contract, was signed for a five-year contract valued at $3.35 million, which placed a player's salary at a new level. Also, in 1975, the Yankees hired Billy Martin to manage the team. Martin, while temperamental, would prove to play an important role in the Yankees' renaissance.

Steinbrenner's suspension ended in 1976, and he came back to a team with a talent-filled roster. During that season, the team, managed by Martin, won the American League East Division, won the league pennant, the franchise's first in twelve years, and met the Cincinnati Reds in the World Series. The Reds swept the Yankees in four games, but the Yankee resurgence had begun.

By this time, the free-agency era was in full swing, and Steinbrenner proved a generous bidder for the services of the best available players. He assembled a team filled with high-paid free agents, including Dave Collins, Oscar Gamble, Rich "Goose" Gossage, Ken Griffey, Tommy John, and Luis Tiant. But Steinbrenner's most famous deal involved signing the slugging outfielder Reggie Jackson, the former Oakland Athletics star who tested the free agent waters and became well paid. Jackson, with his clutch-hitting prowess and his home-run power, became the latest in a long line of Yankee superstars, following Babe Ruth, Lou Gehrig, Joe DiMaggio, Mickey Mantle, and Roger Maris.

Cultivated Success and Club Disharmony

Along with all of the star power and enormous salaries, however, came a clash of big egos. The team's clubhouse was a hostile atmosphere where owner clashed with manager, manager clashed with players (Martin had a pronounced dislike for Jackson), and players clashed with players. Yankee Stadium became known as "The Bronx Zoo."

Despite the internal problems, the team made it to a second World Series in a row. In 1977, the Yankees beat the Los Angeles Dodgers in six games. Steinbrenner made good on his promise to the New York press and the city's fans: that he would bring a world championship back to Yankee Stadium. The series was highlighted by Jackson's three home runs in the deciding game.

Despite Jackson's contributions, Martin disdained the slugger and did not want him on the team. Their volatile relationship was underscored by an incident that occurred during a nationally televised broadcast. Cameras focused in on the Yankee dugout, where Martin and Jackson almost engaged in a fistfight. Teammates had to restrain the two men. Martin accused Jackson of not hustling after a seemingly catchable fly ball and removed him from the field in the middle of the inning. The incident underscored New York baseball in the "Son of Sam" era.

Tensions continued into the 1978 season. In July, Martin, sitting at a bar with reporters, made a famous quote, saying that Jackson and Steinbrenner deserved each other, and insinuated that one was a born liar and the other convicted. The comment led to Martin being fired, but it was not the last of Martin's time with the Yankees, or with Steinbrenner. Ultimately, Steinbrenner would hire and fire Martin five times.

Despite turmoil, Yankee success continued. Steinbrenner hired Bob Lemon as manager, and the team won the East Division title after a dramatic and famous (infamous, if you are a Boston fan) one-game playoff with the Boston Red Sox. The Yankees entered into another World Series and, once again, defeated the Los Angeles Dodgers.

Made Numerous Managerial Changes

Steinbrenner brought Martin back to manage the team in 1979. The hard-drinking, tempestuous manager got fired once again, though, after getting into a barroom brawl. By this time, Steinbrenner became known for placing a "revolving door" on the managerial office. In between hiring and firing Martin, he hired Gene Michael, Dick Howser, and Lou Piniella. Each man endured Steinbrenner's constant interference, which was widely—and gleefully—depicted by the New York sportswriters.

Steinbrenner became known for calling the Yankee dugout to give a manager instructions during a game, entering the locker room after losses to berate the team, and to belittle a manager, coaches, and players in the press. He also humiliated players in highly publicized fashion. For instance, in 1981, when Jackson was having a poor season, Steinbrenner forced him to undergo a physical examination. He did the same to Doyle Alexander after the pitcher turned in several unsatisfactory mound performances. Steinbrenner claimed he did this because he was afraid some of his players would get hurt playing behind Alexander. This compelled fellow Yankees pitcher Gossage to comment, as quoted in Steinbrenner's Los Angeles Times obituary, "George says Doyle needs a physical? George needs a mental." Indeed, the Yankee team provided sportswriters with plenty of headline-making quotes and copy.

Suffered Additional Legal Trouble

In 1980, Steinbrenner signed future Hall-of-Famer Dave Winfield to a $23 million contract, which made the outfielder the highest paid player in baseball. Winfield played for the Yankees from 1981 to 1990, but it was a far from happy experience, as Steinbrenner and Winfield constantly feuded.

The feud culminated in legal troubles that seriously damaged Steinbrenner's reputation and got him banned from baseball a second time. A main issue of contention was the David M. Winfield Foundation, which the outfielder established to help poor children. The two men continually argued about how the Foundation's funds should be used, which led to a legal battle that was settled out of court. But Steinbrenner accused Winfield of misappropriating funds, more specifically, using the Foundation's dollars on personal perks.

In 1990, in an effort to dig up information that would soil Winfield's reputation, Steinbrenner associated himself with one of baseball's seedier individuals: Howard Spira. Steinbrenner paid $40,000 to Spira to come up with the dirt. Spira, though a former Foundation member, was also a gambler and a baseball hanger-on. The plan backfired on Steinbrenner when Spira tried to blackmail him about the deal.

Then-baseball commissioner Fay Vincent was appalled by the whole sordid mess, and he suspended Steinbrenner from the sport on July 30, 1990. Even worse, in 1991 Spira was convicted of extortion and sentenced to two-and-a-half years in prison.

During Steinbrenner's absence, team control was given to limited partner Robert Nederlander. The Steinbrenner-less Yankee management then began rebuilding the team's weakened minor league farm system and made some trades that would bolster the major league team. This would lead to a second Yankee renaissance during the Steinbrenner era. After appearing in the 1981 World Series (and losing to the Los Angeles Dodgers) the Yankees had again fallen into a period of decline during the 1980s, despite the presence of superstars such as Winfield, Don Mattingly, and Rickey Henderson. The decade was also marred by numerous managerial hirings and firings, contractual fights, and the neglect of the farm system. By 1990, the Yankees were again one of baseball's worst teams.

Returned to a Contender

After Spira's conviction, Commission Vincent announced that Steinbrenner could return to the sport in March 1993. By then, the team—thanks to the temporary upper management efforts—was once again a contender.

In 1996, Steinbrenner made one of his best-ever decisions when he hired Joe Torre to be the field manager for the Yankees. Under Torre's leadership, the team won the World Series in four of the next five years. In 1998, the team boasted the best record in American League history at 114-48. That record has since been eclipsed by the 2001 Seattle Mariners with 116 wins.

Rebuilding the "House that Ruth Built"

During this late period in his career, Steinbrenner now focused on the Yankee Stadium infrastructure. He asked city and state government to either help him build a new stadium or at least rebuild the old one. Steinbrenner got his wish. The new Yankee Stadium was completed in 2009—in April and just in time for a new baseball season—and it is located next to the old stadium, which was built in 1923, during the Babe Ruth era. The price tag for the new venue was $1.6 billion. Meanwhile, Steinbrenner kept opening his wallet to buy the best talent. By 2004, the Yankees had the highest payroll in baseball: $187.9 million.

Slowed by Health Problems

During the first decade of the twenty-first century, Steinbrenner appeared to have mellowed. He was no longer the blustery "Boss." This led to speculation that he had suffered a stroke, though the Yankee organization denied the rumors. Still, the George Steinbrenner era was nearing its end. On October 14, 2007, Steinbrenner handed daily control of the New York Yankees over to his sons, Hank and Hal.

Steinbrenner died on July 13, 2010, in Tampa, Florida, after suffering a heart attack at the age eighty years old. He was survived by his wife, his two sons, his daughter, and his two sisters. Despite the throngs who either love him or hate him, no one can deny that he effectively changed the Yankee organization and gave greatly to baseball as a whole.

Books

"George Steinbrenner," *Business Leaders Profiles for Students,* Gale Group, 2002.

"George Steinbrenner," *Encyclopedia of World Biography Supplement,* Volume 19, Gale Group, 1999.

"George Steinbrenner," *Notable Sports Figures,* Gale, 2004.

"George Steinbrenner," *St. James Enclyclopedia of Popular Culture,* St. James Press, 2000.

"Steinbrenner George Michael, III," *The Scribner Encyclopedia of American Lives Thematic Series: Sports Figures,* Charles Scribner's Sons, 2002.

Periodicals

Los Angeles Times, July 13, 2010.

The New York Post, July 18, 2010.

The New York Times, August 28, 1981.

USA Today, April 16, 2009.

Online

"A Steinbrenner Dilemma," *Forbes.com,* http://www.forbes.com/2007/07/11/brady-media-steinbrenner-oped-cx_jb_0712brady.html (December 31, 2011).

"George Steinbrenner Biography," *Baseball Almanac.com,* http://www.baseball-almanac.com/articles/george_steinbrenner_biography.shtml (December 31, 2011).

"Steinbrenner Relinquishes Control of Yankees," *MSNBC.com,* http://nbcsports.msnbc.com/id/21293470/ (December 31, 2011).□

Madge Syers

British figure skater Madge Syers (1881–1917) bears the distinction of being the first woman to win a world championship medal in her sport. Syers's historic win occurred at the 1902 World Figure Skating

Championships in London, when she narrowly lost to the reigning champion, Sweden's Ulrich Salchow. At the 1908 Olympic Games, she became the first woman to win a gold medal in the newly introduced sport. "Skating is an exercise particularly appropriate for women," she wrote in a chapter for a 1908 book she co-edited, *The Book of Winter Sports*. "It requires not so much strength as grace, combined with a fine balance, and the ability to move the feet rapidly. In these qualifications a woman has often the advantage, particularly in our country, as Englishmen are usually inclined to be rather slow and heavy skaters."

Born Florence Madeline Cave in London on September 16, 1881, Syers was one of fifteen children born to Edward Jarvis Cave and Elizabeth Ann Cave. Her father was a prosperous builder who erected blocks on Old Broad Street and Kensington High Street. The seventh daughter in the family, Syers displayed athletic gifts at an early age, as both a swimmer and equestrienne.

Joined Prince's Club

Skating was one of the fashionable new winter sports, like skiing, which emerged out of the resorts in the Swiss Alps. Advances in refrigeration technology made possible new artificial rinks that began opening elsewhere in Europe in the 1870s and '80s. In 1896, the Prince's Skating Club opened in the Knightsbridge area of London. This was a members-only artificial rink and named in honor of Queen Victoria's great-grandson, Prince Edward. In his youth he was a keen hockey player and helped introduce the sport to England, but would later achieve infamy for abdicating the throne in 1936 in order to marry a divorced American, Wallis Simpson.

Syers joined the Prince's Skating Club and soon emerged as one of its most talented competitors. At the time, figure skating was divided into two schools: the English style was bound by strict rules governing the movement of the arms, feet, and torso; the so-called "continental" or international style was less formal and its skaters displayed a more appealing fluidity, complete with jumps and graceful pirouettes. In 1899, Syers was part of the team that won first place in the National Skating Association's Challenge Shield event, a competition that adhered to English-style rules. That same year she met Edgar Syers, a skater and coach, who was nearly twenty years her senior. He urged her to switch to the more aesthetically pleasing international style, and she was among the first women skaters to successfully make the transition.

Syers and Edgar were married on June 23, 1900, at St. Saviour's Church on Warwick Avenue in London. They were among the first pairs skaters in England, a new branch of figure skating that had gained some popularity in Scandinavian and German lands. They placed second in a pairs competition in Berlin in 1900, and finished second again in Stockholm a year later. When the first World Championship in pairs skating was held in London in 1902, they won first place.

Entered World Championship Contest

That was the same year that Syers entered the World Figure Skating Championships, which had been held annually under the auspices of the International Skating Union (ISU) since 1896. In its six-year history until that point, all the competitors had been men, but Syers and her husband discovered that there was no specific wording barring women in the ISU rules book. Officials were thus forced to let Syers compete in that year's contest, which was held at a popular public rink at Niagara Hall in Westminster in February of 1902. England's reigning monarch, King Edward VII, was in attendance along with his wife, Queen Alexandra, and some of their adult children in the royal enclosure. "Announcements of what was about to take place were made from time to time by Mr. H. Grenander, a former champion skater, who, in frock coat and top hat, skated into the middle of the ice, faced the King, delivered his message, and glided away backwards after he had done so with perfect ease and aplomb," reported the *Times* of London. This was Henning Grenander, a Swede who won the third ISU world championship title in 1898.

Figure skating events in this era began with compulsory figures, a series of symmetrical patterns on the ice that skaters were expected to execute perfectly, followed by a "free skate" segment, which permitted more artistic displays. "Syers's performance was watched with specially sympathetic interest," the *Times* correspondent wrote. "Dressed in a neat black costume trimmed with astrakhan, the lady competitor went through her figures with charming grace." Syers dazzled the crowd, but the judges awarded her a silver medal for second place, perhaps uneasy with the prospect of allowing a woman skater to unseat the reigning world champion, Ulrich Salchow of Sweden. Salchow would collect ten world championships, and the arduous backward jump he invented and perfected was named in his honor.

Won First ISU Ladies' Event

When ISU officials met for their annual congress in 1903, they debated whether to allow women to compete, and voted to adopt a new rule barring them instead. Undaunted, Syers went on to win the first-ever British Figure Skating Championships in March of 1903, which was known as the Swedish Cup and run by a different organization, the National Skating Association. The second-place finisher was a male skater, Horatio Torromé, and she won the Cup again in 1904, this time with her husband taking second place. Finally, the 1905 ISU congress bowed to pressure and created a women's event, called the Ladies' Championship of the ISU. This was entirely separate from the men's competition, which was still known as the "World Championships." Years later, the ISU retroactively made Syers and subsequent winners of the Ladies' event co-champions. Nevertheless, the ISU's conciliatory gesture marked one of the first times in organized sports that men and women competed for titles on a relatively equal playing field.

The Ladies' Championship of the ISU was held on January 27, 1906, in Davos, Switzerland. Syers won first place, with Jenny Herz of Austria second, and Lily Kronberger, a Hungarian skater, third. The results were the same for the 1907 Ladies' ISU championship, with Syers winning the gold medal followed by Herz's silver and Kronberger's bronze. The event was hosted by Austrian figure skating clubs at an outdoor rink in Vienna. "The Championship of 1907 will long be remembered by those who took part in it owing to the suffering entailed on them by the intense cold which, accentuated by a bitter wind, was almost unbearable," Syers wrote in the "Skating for Ladies" chapter of *The Book of Winter Sports.* "Several times the benumbed skaters were forced to retire and restore the circulation to their hands and feet, and many of the competitors and judges were subsequently *hors de combat* [out of action] as the result of this trying experience."

Syers and her husband continued to win pairs events, notably in Berlin in 1904 and the 1906 European title, though pairs skating would not become an ISU-sanctioned event until 1908. But it was her prowess on the ice on her own which earned her a measure of celebrity. "The record that Mrs. Syers has achieved is wonderful; no lady, English or foreign, has ever come near equalling it," asserted a *Times* of London assessment of the current state of the sport in 1907. "Indeed, the number of men as good as she is can be counted on the fingers of one hand."

Earned Historic Olympic Gold

Figure skating became an enormously popular spectator attraction, and was included at the 1908 Olympic Games in London. These were technically "Summer" Games, but the ice events were held in October, three months after the other events, at the Prince's Skating Club, Syers's home rink. There were four skating contests: men's, women's, pairs, and special figures. Only five women competed: Syers, along with fellow Britons Dorothy Greenhough Smith and Gwendolyn Lycett, and Germany's Elsa Rendschmidt and Elna Montgomery of Sweden. Syers won the gold medal in the ladies' singles event, and she and her husband came in third for a bronze medal win in the pairs event.

At the next Olympics, held in Stockholm in 1912, there were no figure skating events at all, with the host country contending that the inclusion of winter sports would detract from the enormously successful Nordic Games, held every four years in Sweden. The 1916 Olympics, slated for Berlin, were cancelled after the outbreak of World War I. Skating returned as an Olympic sport at the 1920 Games, held in Antwerp, Belgium, and the event continued to prove so popular that the International Olympic Committee (IOC) finally created a separate Winter Olympics to showcase the world's best skaters, skiers, and hockey players. The French Alpine resort of Chamonix hosted the first Winter Games in 1924.

Syers did not live to witness the 1920 Antwerp Games. She suffered from acute endocarditis, an infection of the heart, and died of heart failure on September 9, 1917, at her home in Weybridge, England. She was just 35 years old. Her husband and skating partner outlived her by nearly thirty years, passing away in 1946 at the age of 82.

"Look As If You Enjoyed It"

Syers is one of very few British athletes to win an individual gold medal in a winter Olympic sport. It took nearly a half-century before another British woman won the ladies singles' event in Olympic figure skating; this was Jeannette Altwegg at the 1952 Oslo Games. Since then the medal rosters have been dominated by American and German skaters. Syers's gold medal victory at the Prince's Skating Club marked the first-ever ice event in Olympic history, and would be the only time an Olympic ice competition would be held in Britain.

Women figure skaters were among the first celebrity athletes to emerge in the twentieth century. In Syers's day, she and her fellow competitors battled antiquated and since-debunked medical claims that exercise was ruinous to a woman's health and potential reproductive capabilities. Tennis was another popular sport that produced pioneering women champions in the first decades of the century, but as with skating they were bound by dress codes that impeded their movement. Syers was particularly adamant about the danger of wearing a corset while skating, explaining in the "Skating for Ladies" chapter that restricting the back muscles in such a garment could actually turn a minor tumble into a crippling accident. She suggested loose clothing, and a slightly shorter skirt than standard Edwardian-era dresses, and weighted at its hem with fur or another trimming. She also gave "a word of advice to the beginner" in her chapter: "Do not assume an agonised or anxious expression when skating, look as if you enjoyed it, look up and about you, remember that the exhibition is not in the nature of a tragedy."

Books

Syers, Madge, "Skating for Ladies," in *The Book of Winter Sports,* edited by Edgar Syers and Madge Syers, Edward Arnold, 1908.

Periodicals

Globe & Mail (Toronto, Canada), October 15, 1994.

Times (London, England), February 14, 1902; March 29, 1907; April 1, 1907; October 24, 1908; October 29, 1908; July 22, 1982.

Online

"Madge Syers," *Sports-Reference.com,* http://www.sports-reference.com/olympics/athletes/sy/madge-syers-1.html (October 11, 2011). □

T

René Thom

René Thom (1923-2002) was a French mathematician and philosopher most notably responsible for developing catastrophe theory, a way to qualitatively explain how a system with predictable inputs would have unpredictable outcomes. In 1958 Thom also received the Field Medal for his work with cobordism in algebraic topography.

René Thom was born on September 2, 1923 in Montbéliard, France, near the Swiss border. His parents, Gustav Thom and Louise Ramel, were shopkeepers. He attended Collége Cuvier in Montbéliard and was very successful in both primary and secondary schools. It is said that he learned to visualize in four dimensions by the time he was 10 years old. In 1940, he received his baccalauréat in elementary mathematics in Besançon.

World War II disrupted Thom's studies. He and his brother were sent south when Germany threatened France's borders. On his way home, Thom detoured through Switzerland and then settled in Lyons, where in 1941 he received his baccalauréat in philosophy.

Thom then received a scholarship to attend the Lycée Saint-Louis in Paris, the only lycée in France at the time that had Classes Prépatoires. In 1943, Thom entered the Ecole Normale Supérieure in Paris. He received the equivalent of his Masters in Mathematics in 1946. He then spent several years as a CNRS fellow in Strasbourg in order to follow Henri Cartan, a prominent mathematician. When he returned to Paris, Thom defended his thesis, "Espaces fibrés en spheres et carrées de Steenrod" or "Fiber spaces in spheres and Steenrod squares" under Cartan in 1951 and received his doctorate.

In 1949, while he was completing his doctorate, Thom married Suzanne Heimlinger. They would go on to have three children: Françoise, Elizabeth, and Christian. He would regularly reminisce about and take his family to his hometown of Montebéliard, France.

Early Career

Shortly after delivering his thesis, Thom went to Princeton University where he had the opportunity to consult prominent mathematicians and scientists of the time including Albert Einstein and Hermann Weyl. From 1953-1954 Thom taught in Grenoble as an associate professor. After this, Thom returned to Strasbourg, where he taught first as an associate professor from 1954-1957, and then as a full professor from 1957-1964.

In the 1950s, Thom began to work with Hassler Whitney in differential topology. Differential topology deals with objects with smooth surfaces that can be understood through calculus. While this is not the work for which he would become famous, Thom made significant strides in this area. In 1958 Thom received the Fields Medal from the International Mathematical Union at the International Congress in Edinburgh. He received this honor for the invention of the theory of cobordism in algebraic topology. Cobordism roughly defined is a way of classifying objects that was not possible previously.

In a symposium in 1991, Thom would confess that he was not sure that he could continue to generate meaningful results in topology, so he decided to switch to more algebraic problems, specifically singularities of differentiable maps. This was, in part, because of Alexandre Grothendieck who created the modern theory of algebraic geometry, a unification of geometry, number theory, topology, and complex analysis. Later Thom would begin to work with a physicist on caustics in optical geometry as well.

Catastrophe Theory

In 1964, Thom was named a professor at the Institut des Etudes Scientifiques (IHES) at Bures-sur-Yvette; he would remain there for the rest of his career until 1988. Thom was exclusively focused on research and had no teaching duties. He started off his time there by arguing against the trend in education to remove geometry from the mathematics curriculum because of the value of studying singularities of function maps. It was this line of thought that brought him to form his theory of singularities.

As Thom's career continued, he started to move away from his mathematical roots, and he began to consider the philosophical and scientific education of his youth. In the 1960s Thom's interests shifted once more, this time to embryology rather than optical geometry. Thom wanted to apply his transversality theory to explain where natural forms came from.

In 1972, Thom published *Stabilité Structurelle et Morphogénése* or *Structural Stability and Morphogenesis*. It is from this book that catastrophe theory was derived. A branch of geometry, catastrophe theory explains predictable discontinuities within systems that have continuous inputs; why when one gives a regular stream of inputs, one can get predictably different results. This kind of mapping of variables and results cannot be done using differential calculus. The 'catastrophe' in the title refers to a sudden change in a system or a loss of stability in a system. A common example is a balloon. When an individual inflates a balloon, if he or she blows at a continuous rate, then the balloon inflates relatively uniformly. That is, until the balloon reaches critical mass, at which point it makes an abrupt predictable change in how it inflates right before it pops. Thom also proposed and mapped seven possible discontinuities or catastrophes in a system: fold, cusp, swallowtail, butterfly, hyperbolic umbilic, elliptic, umbilic, and parabolic umbilic.

There were other aspects of Thom's *Structural Stability and Morphogenesis* that did not receive as much attention and were much less mathematical. For example, Thom discusses how women are more spherical than men, relating to spheres being the strongest shape in the universe. He also discusses how animals do what we would call reading, in a sense; a tiger looks at a shape and can recognize that it is a gazelle hoof the same way that we would see a word and know its meaning. These more philosophical tangents are a part of a shift in Thom's interests, which was away from mathematics and into numerous other fields including philosophy and the social sciences.

The Rise and Fall of Catastrophe Theory

E. Christopher Zeeman at the University of Warwick was fascinated by Thom's theories in the 1970s. He took them and expanded them out of four-dimensional space-time and applied it to any locally Euclidean space. It was Zeeman who, while giving lectures and in an article for *Scientific American,* coined the phrase catastrophe theory.

Largely because of Zeeman's work, catastrophe theory had its heyday in the 1970s and 1980s. But because of its popularity, individuals began to use catastrophe theory to explain situations that catastrophe theory could not possibly explain. For example, some individuals used it to prove that the universe is deterministic, but the theory does not pretend to throw away the indeterminacy of areas such as nuclear physics. Also, others criticized it because it can lead to qualitative predictions, but not quantitative predictions. These issues led many individuals to consider it to be a fad or a metaphysical concept, rather than mathematical.

Thom spent much of the rest of his life discussing and defending catastrophe theory. When asked about it, he would respond that his intention was not to declare something that was true and false; he asserted that he would rather put forth a wrong theory that had the power to organize the universe in a meaningful way and bring us closer to a great truth, than to put forth a meaningless truth. He noted that there are many errors that have led to great truths, while there are many other meaningless truths in science.

That being said, catastrophe theory has been used in many fields including hydrodynamics, geology, particle physics, industrial relations, embryology, economics, linguistics, civil engineering, and medicine. Thom studied and defended catastrophe theory in all of these areas, leading him further from his mathematical roots.

In 1974, Thom was awarded the Grand Prix Scientifique de la Ville de Paris. In 1976 he became a member of the French Academy of Sciences and he was named a Chevalier de la Légion d'Honneur or a Knight of the Legion of Honor.

Later Life

In 1983 Thom published *Modèles mathématiques de la morphogénèse* or *Mathematical Models of Morphogenesis.* He studied a multitude of fields including biology, linguistics, philosophy, and the social sciences. In his spare time Thom enjoyed trains, as they fascinated him as intricate and organized systems.

Thom's ideas were very influential in the world even outside of the mathematical community. In 1983 Jean-Luc Godard shot a movie entitled *René* about Thom and his personality. Salvador Dali's last painting, *The Swallow's Tail—Series on Catastrophes,* is taken from Thom's four-dimensional graph of the swallow's tail discontinuity combined with that of the cusp discontinuity. Dali pairs it with the integral symbol in calculus and the curve of a cello. This came shortly after Dali painted *The Topological Abduction of Europe—Homage à René Thom,* which included Thom's formula for the swallow's tail. A composer, Pascal Dusapin, was also inspired by Thom when he wrote his piece *Loop.*

Thom retired in 1988. On October 25, 2002, Thom died in Bures-sur-Yvette France of vascular disease at 79 years old.

Books

Avery, Laura, ed., *Newsmakers,* Gale, 2004

C. Bartocci et al., eds., *Mathematical Lives,* Springer-Verlag, 2011

Narins, Brigham, ed., *Notable Scientists from 1900 to the Present,* Gale, 2008

Notable Mathematicians, Gale, 2008

Periodicals

Bulletin of the American Mathematical Society, 2004.

Economist, November, 16, 2002.

Irish Times, November 16, 2002. □

Howard Thurman

The African-American author, educator, and minister Howard Thurman (1899–1981) exerted a strong influence on the civil rights movement, made pioneering steps in the integration of American churches and universities, and was an original religious thinker in his own right.

The name of Howard Thurman is rarely listed among those of the African-American pioneers of the civil rights movement. Yet the Rev. Martin Luther King Jr. knew Thurman well and carried Thurman's writings with him wherever he went. On the day King was assassinated, he was carrying a copy of Thurman's book *Jesus and the Disinherited,* which inspired not only King but also several other civil rights leaders. Thurman's name has been obscure, partly because he was not a political activist but a thinker and spiritual leader. Yet his ideas, as expressed in his 21 books, as well as in the careers of students he mentored, have continued to prove productive in the years since his death in 1981, even after the immediate goals of the civil rights movement were achieved.

Inspired by Grandmother Who Survived Slavery

Thurman's birthday was November 18, but sources disagree as to whether he was born in 1899 or 1900. Thurman himself

gave no year in his autobiography, *With Head and Heart,* but the copyright materials of the book listed the 1899 date. Thurman was born and raised in racially segregated Daytona Beach, Florida. Baptized in the Halifax River, he was the son of railroad worker Saul Thurman and Alice Ambrose Thurman, a cook. Saul Thurman died of pneumonia while his son was very young. An important figure in his early life was his maternal grandmother, Nancy Ambrose, a former slave. "She couldn't read her name if it was as big as this chapel," Thurman said of her in a lecture quoted by Sharon Weightman of the *Florida Times Union.* "But she had stood inside of Jesus and looked out on the world through his eyes. And she knew by heart what I could never know." Ambrose often told Thurman of a preacher she had heard on her plantation, who told her and other workers that they were not slaves but children of God.

After completing eighth grade, Thurman had no high school to attend—there were only three African-American high schools in the entire state of Florida. Instead, Thurman enrolled at Florida Baptist Academy in Jacksonville, an African-American religious academy with a rigorous curriculum that included Latin and ancient Greek. Almost penniless, he had help from several people, including James N. Gamble of the Procter and Gamble Corporation. Gamble had made contributions to the enterprises of Daytona Beach educator Mary McLeod Bethune, so Thurman wrote him a letter asking him for financial assistance, and received in return five dollars a month for one academic year. Even with this assistance, Thurman collapsed during the run-up to the ceremony in which he graduated as valedictorian.

Recharging his dwindling funds with a stint in the shipping department of a Jacksonville bakery, Thurman enrolled at historically African-American Morehouse College in Atlanta, where one of his classmates was Martin Luther King Sr.; sometimes he had dinner with the King family. Majoring in economics at Morehouse, Thurman was reputed to have read every book in the school's library. He received his B.A. from Morehouse in 1923 and moved on for a B.D. degree at Colgate-Rochester Theological Seminary in upstate New York in 1926, and also married Katie Kelley in that year. Ordained as a Baptist minister, he returned to Atlanta and taught theology at Spelman College, a women's college associated with Morehouse, from 1929 to 1932. In 1932 he moved to Howard University in Washington as a theology professor and chair of the campus committee on religious life.

Met Mahatma Gandhi

In 1935 Thurman traveled to India, Burma, and present-day Sri Lanka. In India his meeting with Mohandas K. Gandhi, known as Mahatma Gandhi, likely inspired the study of Gandhi's nonviolent protest methods among the followers of the later civil rights movement. Thurman's encounter with Gandhi also led him to engage more closely with the teachings of Jesus Christ as opposed to Christian institutions. According to Larry Bellinger of *Sojourners,* Gandhi told Thurman that "the greatest enemy that the religion of Jesus has in India is Christianity in India." Thurman also distinguished between Jesus' ideas and institutional Christianity when asked about racial segregation in the predominantly Christian United States.

Thurman's trip to India had two tangible results. First, he began to lecture more widely after returning to Howard, and his ideas included a new and distinctly mystical strain, drawing connections between ethics and the attempt to find direct inner knowledge of God. Thurman believed that the source of social justice and racial reconciliation was the realization of the common ground humans shared through spiritual experiences. Second, in 1944 Thurman went to San Francisco to found the Church for the Fellowship of All Peoples, serving as co-pastor there for several years. The church is sometimes described as the first interracial congregation in the United States; it was preceded in that respect by Pentecostal groups and others, but it may have been the country's first interracial and interfaith church.

Beginning with *The Greatest of These* in 1941, Thurman remained productive as an author for the rest of his life. In the 1940s he wrote a pair of books about the African-American spiritual. Perhaps Thurman's best-known book, and the one that most deeply influenced King and other civil rights leaders, was *Jesus and the Disinherited* (1949), which had its genesis in a conversation Thurman had with an Indian Hindu who asked how Thurman could subscribe to the religion of a culture that had enslaved his people. Thurman's response was to distinguish between the thinking of Jesus and institutional Christianity, pointing out that Jesus himself was part of a minority group oppressed by a dominant colonial power. Many of Thurman's 21 books were issued by the large Harper & Row publishing house. His autobiography, *With Head and Heart: The Autobiography of Howard Thurman,* was published by Harcourt, Brace & Company and appeared in 1979.

Followed Mystical Disciplines

Indeed, Thurman's vision of the divine was not specifically Christian. "It is my belief," he wrote, as quoted in *Cross Currents* magazine, "that in the Presence of God there is neither male nor female, white nor black, Gentile nor Jew, Protestant nor Catholic, Hindu, Buddhist, nor Moslem, but a human spirit stripped to the literal substance of itself before God." His religious practices were often inwardly oriented, and he used the word meditation as well as prayer to describe them. But the ultimate goals of such practices were reconciliation with others and affirmation of the spiritual dignity of adversaries.

In 1953, the year *Life* magazine named him one of America's 12 most influential preachers, Thurman moved to Boston University, becoming a professor of spiritual resources and disciplines as well as dean of the school's Daniel L. Marsh Chapel. He was the first African American to teach full-time at the school. In 1965 he took the title of dean emeritus, retaining it until his death. In his later years, Thurman accepted a large number of guest lecturer engagements and professorships, including one at the University of Ibadan in Nigeria in 1963. Over his lifetime he gave lectures at more than 500 educational institutions around the United States and the world. In 1951 he founded the Howard Thurman Educational Trust, which worked to bring educational opportunities to disadvantaged students, and led it for the rest of his life.

Despite the immense effect of his writings on King, the Rev. Jesse Jackson, and other civil rights leaders, Thurman avoided becoming a visible symbol of the movement himself. With the rise of more confrontational African-American leadership in the late 1960s, Thurman's ideas were eclipsed somewhat, although he remained widely respected and continued to write voluminously and to preach sermons, many of which were collected and later housed at Morehouse College, along with Thurman's personal papers. Suffering from cancer in his later years, he returned to live in San Francisco. Thurman died there on April 10, 1981.

Books

Religious Leaders of America, Gale, 1999.

Thurman, Howard, *With Head and Heart: The Autobiography of Howard Thurman,* Harcourt, Brace & Company, 1979.

Periodicals

Albany Times Union, January 19, 2002.

Atlanta Journal-Constitution, January 13, 2007.

Cross Currents, December 2010.

Florida Times Union, April 4, 1997.

New York Times, April 14, 1981.

Sojourners, July 1999.

Online

"Who Was Howard Thurman?" *BU Today,* http://www.bu.edu/today/2011/who-was-howard-thurman/ (October 22, 2011).□

Primož Trubar

Primož Trubar (1508–1586) is a revered figure in the history of Slovenia. A Protestant reformer who is sometimes referred to as the Martin Luther of his Balkan nation, Trubar standardized the dialects of the peasant masses into the Slovene language and authored the first two books ever printed in that tongue. "Trubar and his followers," asserted Oto Luthar and the authors of *The Land Between: A History of Slovenia,* "anchored their native language on the cultural map of Europe in less than 50 years."

Slovenia celebrates a national holiday on Primož Trubar's birthday, deemed the eighth of June, though he may have been born on June 9, 1508. Likewise the contemporary spelling of his surname, "Trubar," differs from the one he used in his lifetime, which was "Truber." He came from a place called Rašica, which was later incorporated into the larger town of Velike Lašče, in the Duchy of Carniola.

Descended from Alpine Slavs

At the time of Trubar's birth, the duchy was under the rule of the Austrian Habsburg dynasty and would remain so until the end of World War I. Carniola is the center of the Slovene homelands, though the fertile, valleyed region had been inhabited by others. The Celts were the first known dwellers, followed by ancient Greeks. In the first century BCE, Roman legions overtook the territory and established it as part of the province of Pannonia. Lombard peoples moved in after the decline of the Roman Empire a few centuries later, but then waves of Slavic peoples from the east moved into the area, beginning around 480 CE. The Slavs had been displaced from Eastern Europe by Germanic tribes, who pushed in from Western Europe just as the Huns, who were probably a Turkic group from Central Asia, moved westward into Europe.

The Duchy of Carniola was a successor state to Carantania, a Slavic political territory founded in 630 CE. Carantania was the first state of the Alpine Slavs, the ancestors of the modern Slovene people. The Alpine Slavs inhabited a strategically tricky parcel of land: they lived on the eastern side of the mighty Alps, wedged between Italy and the Balkan Peninsula, with Hungary looming over on the northeast and the Germanic stronghold of Austria always above and moving southward. The Slovene lands were the gateway to vital Adriatic seaports, including Trieste and Venice. In the 600s, Carantania was visited by Irish missionary priests who used an ancient Roman road that connected Carantania to the northern Italian city of Aquileia. The Slovenes formally abandoned their pagan deities and practices for Christianity in 745, when a Carantanian duke entered into a security pact with an emerging southern German power in Bavaria; he was required to formally convert, and his subjects did, too. At the time, the Alpine Slavs were imperiled by Magyar and other invading armies from the east. Carantania became part of the Holy Roman Empire as the Duchy of Carinthia in 976 and was eventually subsumed into the Austrian House of Habsburg.

Overlords Abused Slovene Population

A German-speaking elite would rule in Slovenia for centuries. The alliance brought princely families from southern Germany and present-day Austria into the region, and they established feudal fiefdoms. Trubar wrote about one such dynasty, centered in the once-grand Roman city of Celje. "Their land does not last to the third heir, their folk and blood will soon cease to be," he wrote, according to *The Land Between: A History of Slovenia.* "[A]s for the Princes of Celje, no matter how many cloisters and curacies they erected, how many journeys they made to Rome, before they all met their end or were done to death, they forced themselves on their peasants' daughters, dishonored them and committed other injustices by force or fraud."

In Trubar's youth the Slovene language was spoken only by peasants in various dialects; German and Latin were taught in schools. In 1520, at the age of 12, Trubar moved to the Adriatic seaport of Sankt Veit am Pflaum—present-day Rijeka, Croatia—to begin his education. Two years later he made the journey to Salzburg, Austria, one of the major cities of the Habsburg Empire. There he met Johann von Staupitz, a Benedictine abbot who had played an important role in the early life of Martin Luther, the northern German priest whose protests against the questionable practices of the Church and its clergy set in motion the Protestant Reformation in 1517.

As a young man Trubar became fluent first in German, then Latin and Italian in addition to his native Slovene. In 1524 he went to Trieste for the final step in his religious studies toward the priesthood. There he fell into a circle of Italian Humanists centered around the city's influential bishop, Pietro Bonomo, and was ordained into the priesthood. In the spring of 1528 Trubar started studies at the University of Vienna, but was forced to leave when the city came under siege by Ottoman Turks a year later. He returned to Slovenia in 1530. The Turks remained a serious threat in the region for several more decades, and Western Europe feared a successful invasion and the imposition of Muslim rule would bring harsh retribution for the abuses committed during the Crusades to retake the Holy Land from Arab conquerors.

Rose to Fame in Ljubljana

The main city in the Duchy of Carniola was Ljubljana, which had been created as a new diocese in the 1460s. Its religious leaders were eager to establish their spiritual and cultural dominance, but as a young and forward-thinking priest "Trubar soon became renowned for his stark opposition to the widespread building of churches and worship of saints, which was enough to make him a Protestant in the eyes of many," Luthar noted. Martin Luther's teachings were gaining acceptance in German lands of the Holy Roman Empire, including Ljubljana, which had a heavy German presence. The religious reform movement initially swept up princes and the nobles, who resented Rome's intrusions into domestic affairs and were disinclined to raise armies for religious wars on behalf of the Papal States. In Carniola, followers of Luther—the first "Lutherans"—found themselves at odds with their overlords in Rome and in Graz, the seat of the Habsburg branch that ruled Inner Austria. Carniola, Carinthia, Styria, Trieste, and parts of Croatia were all part of the crown lands, or hereditary holdings, of the Graz-based Habsburg princes.

Trubar was close to the Bishop of Ljubljana, Franc Kacijanar, who held the post from 1536 to 1543 and appointed Trubar to serve as canon priest of Ljubljana in 1542. Kacijanar worked to quell rising tensions between Lutherans and those faithful to Rome—a division erupting into outright war in many places across Europe. But when Kacijanar was succeeded by a more conservative bishop in 1543, Trubar was targeted by anti-Lutheran church leaders and an arrest warrant was issued for statements he made in sermons about certain religious practices in the region, which in his view bordered on superstition and even idolatry. Forced to flee from Inner Austria, he made his way to the city of Rothenburg ob der Tauber in southern Germany, where Veit Dietrich, a friend of Martin Luther, recommended him for a preaching position in the Lutheran stronghold.

Devised Slovene Alphabet, Spelling

The earliest known written example of the Slovene language was found in the *Freising Manuscripts,* a collection of sermons and liturgical texts named for the Bavarian town where it was found. Dating back to the year 1000 or earlier, this is one of the first documented examples of any Slavic language at all. But five hundred years later, in Trubar's time, there were no other books or other printed material in the Slovene language.

From Germany, Trubar set about standardizing the Slovene dialects into a formal, written language, in order to spread the message of Luther's Reformation. The first two books ever written in the Slovene language were his *Catechismus,* a primer on the basic tenets of the Christian faith in question-and-answer form, and the *Abecedarium,* or alphabet book, both published in late 1550 by a printing house in Tübingen, a renowned university city in southern Germany. Over the next three decades he wrote or translated at least 25 more titles, including installments of the New Testament that were issued between 1555 and 1577, with a complete edition printed in 1582. He also produced a book of hymns, liturgical calendar, and translation of Luther's *Postils,* or Bible commentaries.

Some of these works were underwritten by a nobleman and former governor of Styria, Hans von Ungnad zu Sonneck. Von Ungnad funded the establishment of a bible institute Trubar set up in Bad Urach, Württemburg, the independent kingdom in southern Germany that, like Rothenburg, was outside the Hapsburg realm. Its printing press published Protestant texts in Slovene, Croatian, and Serbian. These books were then smuggled into Slovenia. "By bringing the biblical message closer to his contemporaries, Trubar helped ensure that Slovene thus became the chosen tool for salvation," wrote Luthar in *The Land Between.* Trubar's efforts "not only disproved the general belief that Slovene, like Hungarian, was unsuitable as a written language, but also nourished hopes that the translations of his writings into Croatian and Serbian would play a crucial role in converting the Turks to Christianity."

Preached Luther's Message

When religious conflicts abated for a time in Slovenia, Trubar was permitted to return in 1561 to Ljubljana, where he was named the official superintendent of the Protestant church in Slovenia. In this capacity he embarked on missionary work to nearby regions, in some parts riding a donkey in a display of Protestant humility—a dramatic contrast to the pomp and spectacle accorded visitors from Rome or Trieste. In Friuli, an isolated pocket of land between the Alps and the Adriatic, he addressed villagers in their native Italian, a rare event in that century of Lutheran preaching in that language. *The Land Between* references from a letter Trubar wrote to von Ungnad in December of 1563 in which Trubar asserted the publication of "Luther's *Church Postil* would strike a serious blow against the Pope in the Apennine Peninsula," wrote Luthar. "In Trubar 's opinion, the easiest way for Protestant beliefs to enter Italy, guarded by the Alps, was through Carniola and Gorizia."

Trubar was sent into exile once again after the 1564 publication of *Cerkovna ordninga* (Church Ordinance). It argued for the establishment of universal education throughout the lands of the Holy Roman Empire in order to compete with emerging—and more prosperous—powers in Europe. "Not a province, a city, or a common can survive without schools, scholars, and men of knowledge, and are even less able to attend to and pursue the cares of the world and of the spirit," Trubar asserted, according to Luthar. "This any man of common sense can understand."

In his final years Trubar was a mentor to Slovenian students studying at the University of Tübingen, and continued to serve as a preacher in nearby Derendingen. One of his protégés was Jurij Dalmatin, who was in his mid-thirties in 1584 when he finished the first complete Slovene translation of both the Old and New Testaments of the Bible, which was used in Slovenia for the next 200 years—even by Roman Catholics.

Trubar died in Derendingen on June 28, 1586. His efforts on behalf of his nation and the Slovene language remained important to Slovenian nationalists in generations to follow, despite the fact the region was successfully "Counter"-Reformed in the decades after Trubar's death and became a Roman Catholic stronghold. Austrian domination of Slovenia ended with World War I, and after the end of World War II it became one of the republics of Yugoslavia, whose name means "land of the southern Slavs." In 1991 Slovenia became an independent state and Trubar's image was used on its 10-*tolar* bank notes. Later Trubar was honored with a one-Euro coin after nations of the European Union adopted a single unit of currency. In June of 2008, on the 500th anniversary of his birth, the National Museum of Slovenia offered a special exhibit and several events hailing Trubar and his achievements.

Books

The Land Between: A History of Slovenia, edited by Oto Luthar, Peter Lang, 2008.

Online

"The Year of Trubar 2008," http://www.trubar2008.si/eng/ (January 24, 2012). □

Sophie Tucker

The American singer Sophie Tucker (1886–1966) was perhaps the preeminent female vocalist of the vaudeville era in the United States, with a humorous style and a mastery of African-American musical idioms that exerted a strong influence on later performers.

During her heyday in the 1910s and 1920s, Tucker was one of the most popular singers in America, introducing double-entendre numbers with crackling syncopated rhythms that had often been written specifically for her. Tucker's music drew on African-American ragtime but also on her own Jewish heritage, and she popularized one of the most enduring of all Jewish-American popular songs, "My Yiddishe Momme." Tucker's story was one of rags to riches, and above all she was notable as an entertainer who could forge a relationship with an audience; her popularity was only dented when the new media of movies and phonograph recordings added an intermediate layer between her and her listeners. Tucker's tough, sexy persona, summed up by the "Last of the Red Hot

Mamas" title under which she was billed during the last part of her career, paved the way for several generations of future female performers.

Born in Small Russian Town

Sonya Kalish was born in the then heavily Jewish town of Tulchin, now in Ukraine, probably on January 13, 1886. Her birth year has often been given as 1884, but her biographer Armond Fields gives the 1886 date, pointing out that her older brother, Philip, had been born in January of 1884. At the time the area was part of Russia, and Tucker's parents, Charles and Jennie Kalish, were being menaced by anti-Semitic activities on the part of Russia's Tsarist government. Shortly after their daughter's birth, the family made their way to Germany and set sail for the United States. Charles Kalish, for unknown reasons, began using the name Abuza during the crossing and immigrated to the United States under that name.

Jewish aid societies settled the Abuza family in Boston, where Tucker's father worked as a bartender. In 1895 they moved to Hartford, Connecticut, and opened Abuza's Restaurant, a kosher diner. From the age of ten, Tucker helped out in the kitchen, and then on the waitstaff. As a girl she enjoyed the popular songs of the day, and she was especially fascinated by the touring vaudeville performers who stopped in at the diner. After a debut performance in which she was asked by a teacher to sing a Christmas carol but instead broke into the popular song "Hello Ma Baby," she began to sing at the restaurant as well, and customers began to suggest that she pursue a musical career. She auditioned for and won a chance to perform on an amateur night at the local vaudeville hall, Poli's Theater.

A musical career was almost unheard-of for a young Jewish immigrant woman at the time, however. Even though Tucker had announced to her mother that she wanted something other than a life spent mostly at the stove and the kitchen sink, she began planning for a life of marriage and motherhood. In 1903 she married teamster (cart driver) Louis Tuck, a version of whose name she would use professionally, and a son, Burt, was born in 1906. But soon Tucker was restless, claiming that her husband lacked ambition. Armed with a hundred dollars and a letter of introduction to songwriter Harry Von Tilzer, she set out alone for New York, writing her parents a letter asking them to take care of her baby and telling them she would make good. They ignored her attempts to communicate.

Performed in Beer Garden

At first Tucker sang in venues where she was paid little more than a meal, but she graduated to a paying, recurring gig at the German Village beer garden on 40th Street and set about making her name known among the "song pluggers" or music salesmen who pitched songs to performers in the hope of launching the next big sheet music hit. After another amateur night audition, she was hired to perform at the 125th St. Theater in Harlem for $20 a week. The management there was impressed by her talent and even sent her out on tours of vaudeville stages around New England, but insisted that she sing in blackface—the burnt-cork makeup used by white performers of the time to satirize and degrade black culture. Tucker agreed at first, and was billed as a "coon shouter," but she disliked the makeup and devised a routine in which she would remove it during her set, revealing herself as white. In 1909 she stopped using it altogether.

Tucker's rising stature on the vaudeville circuit became evident when she was added to the cast of the major Ziegfeld Follies—and even more so when the company's star, Nora Bayes, complained that she was being upstaged and demanded that Tucker's role be reduced to one song. Soon Tucker was off the roster entirely, but by now she had found her distinctive voice and could draw crowds at such large theaters as the American Music Hall in New York, with suggestive numbers such as "There's Company in the Parlor, Girls, Come on Down" and "The Angle Worm Wiggle" replacing racially themed material. The latter song drew an indecency charge in Portland, Oregon, but a judge ordered the case dropped.

Tucker preferred performing live, but beginning in 1910 she made cylinder recordings for the Edison National Phonograph Company. These reveal a powerful alto voice comfortable with the syncopations (off-beat accents) and rhythmic flexibility of African-American music. Despite the derogatory racial imagery of her early music, Tucker was heavily influenced by African-American music. She sometimes took lessons from black singers, and one of her biggest hits, "Some of These Days" (1911), was written by African-American songwriter Shelton Brooks; Tucker purchased exclusive rights to the song from Brooks. In 2004 the song was added to the U.S. National Recording Registry.

Appeared at Tony Pastor's Palace

As Tucker's popularity grew, songs that she introduced and that fit her tough, independent image became major hits. Mostly she looked for songs with humor that leavened their liberated content, and songs like "A Good Man Is Hard to Find" and "I Ain't Takin' Orders from No One" were standards of the vaudeville era. In the 1910s and 1920s Tucker appeared at the king of all the vaudeville halls, Tony Pastor's Palace, and toured Europe, performing in England for King George V and Queen Mary at the London Palladium in 1926. Beginning in 1921, songwriter Ted Shapiro served as her musical director, keeping her well supplied with new material and serving as a straight man for Tucker's considerable reservoir of on-stage humor.

Parallel to the English-speaking world of songs and musicals in New York was a flourishing Yiddish-language theatrical culture. Tucker did not contribute much to that culture, but in 1928, after her own mother's death, she did record, in both Yiddish and English, the Jack Yellen composition "My Yiddishe Momme" ("My Yiddish Mama"). The recording became a top ten hit and was popular across Europe; the Nazi regime in Germany, fearful of the positive image of Jewish culture it presented, banned the record. "Even though I loved the song and it was a sensational hit every time I sang it, I was always careful to use it only when I knew the majority of the house would understand Yiddish," Tucker reflected, as quoted on the *Jewish Women's Archive* site. "However, you didn't have to be a Jew to be moved by 'My Yiddishe Momme.' 'Mother' in any language means the same thing."

As the vaudeville era began to decline under pressure from movies and recordings, Tucker's career proved unusually durable, and she performed regularly until shortly before her death. The "Last of the Red Hot Mamas" billing she received later in life marked the passing of the colorful theatrical personality she represented. Although not a fan of the movies, she was enough of an icon to appear in six features: *Honky Tonk* (1929), *Gay Love* (1934), *Broadway Melody of 1938, Thoroughbreds Don't Cry* (1937), and *Follow the Boys* and *Sensations of 1945* (1944). In *Broadway Melody of 1938,* the finale is designed as a tribute to Tucker; her name shows up in lights in the background even though she is singing in character.

True to the title of her hit song "I'm Living Alone and I Like It," Tucker was only intermittently devoted to the institution of marriage. Her marriages to Tuck, musician Frank Westphal, and manager Al Lackey all ended in divorce. Tucker's influence on such liberated performers as Mae West, Bette Midler, and Roseanne Barr was profound. She died in New York on February 9, 1966.

Books

Fields, Armond, *Sophie Tucker: First Lady of Show Business,* Macfarland, 2003.

Tucker, Sophie, *Some of These Days,* self-published, 1945.

Periodicals

New York Times, February 10, 1966; August 30, 2009.

Online

"My Yiddishe Momme," *Songfacts,* http://www.songfacts.com/detail.php?id=18211 (November 15, 2011).

"Sophie Tucker," *Jewish Women's Archive,* http://www.jwa.org/
discover/infocus/comedy/tucker.html (November 15, 2011).
"Sophie's Biography," *The Outrageous Sophie Tucker* (documentary
film), http://www.sophietucker.com/ (November 15, 2011). □

Mikhail Tukhachevsky

Mikhail Tukhachevsky (1893–1937) was among several high-ranking military officials who fell victim to Soviet leader Josef Stalin in the 1930s and met their death by firing squad. A famous war hero whose service to the Communist cause dated back to the Russian Revolution of 1917, Tukhachevsky was convicted on spurious charges of treason during a wave of terror, reprisals, and show trials instigated by Stalin to consolidate his power and crush all internal dissent.

Mikhail Nikolayevich Tukhachevsky hailed from a family of minor aristocratic lineage, a class that enjoyed enormous privileges under the tsarist regime. Born on February 16, 1893, in Smolensk Oblast, he came from a family that had suffered some recent financial hardships, a situation that left him with few options save for a military career. In 1911 he entered the Alexandrovskoye Military Academy, completed his schooling three years later, and was commissioned an officer in the elite Semyenovsky Regiment just in time for Russia's entrance into World War I. He was captured by German forces in 1915 and held as a prisoner of war at the Ingolstadt fortress prison in Bavaria, from which he was said to have escaped. Standard biographies of Tukhachevsky portray him as one of the many young officers of the tsar's army who were eager to see the end of the monarchy and enter the fight to establish the world's first socialist state.

Despite his bourgeois origins, Tukhachevsky was indeed a committed Bolshevik, and quickly proved that in battle. Promoted up through the Red Army ranks, he came to the attention of Leon Trotsky, the People's Commissar for Military Affairs, and advanced further to become one of the important military heroes of the Russian Civil War. This conflict, which erupted during the tumultuous 1917 Revolution, pitted Communist "Reds" against "White" Russians who were either loyal to the tsar or fiercely anti-Communist. By 1919 Tukhachevsky was put in charge of a major division, the 5th Army, and scored a decisive victory when he led his troops to retake Siberia from the Whites and former Russian Navy admiral Aleksandr Kolchak.

Clashed with Stalin

The roots of Stalin's distrust of Tukhachevsky were said to have dated back to this period, more specifically to the summer of 1920 during the Polish-Soviet War. This skirmish was not technically part of the Russian Civil War but posed a grave threat to the stability of the new Soviet state. A newly independent Polish republic had moved to retake long-disputed territory on its border with Soviet-held Ukraine. The

Red Army mounted a counterattack and pushed back Polish forces, then tried to capture Warsaw. At the time, Stalin was political commissar of the Southwest Front and was near the Ukrainian city of Lviv, about 200 miles from Warsaw. Stalin apparently disobeyed an order to send his cavalry troops to assist Tukhachevsky's forces. As a result, Tukhachevsky's army retreated, and there were heavy losses. The taking of the Polish capital was thought to have been an assured Soviet victory, and that failure was a stunning defeat for the Reds. Publicly and behind closed doors with Soviet leader Vladimir I. Lenin, Tukhachevsky and Stalin blamed one another for the failure.

Aside from the Warsaw setback, Tukhachevsky had a stunning record of military successes. After Siberia, he was sent to secure the Crimea from the Whites, and then put down the potentially disastrous Kronstadt mutiny in March of 1921, when a naval garrison near St. Petersburg rebelled against harsh Bolshevik policies. This eruption quickly gained popular support because of dire food shortages, and Tukhachevsky led his forces in a 12-day assault that became known for its particularly brutal fighting. The Kronstadt instigators and participants were rooted out, arrested, and either summarily executed or detained in prison camps. Later in the spring of 1921, Tukhachevsky was sent to suppress another uprising in the Tambov Oblast, about 300 miles south of Moscow. In this conflict Tukhachevsky deployed poison gas to annihilate peasants who had fled to the forests.

Lenin died in January of 1924. Predictably, Stalin and Trotsky vied for leadership, but Stalin had risen to become the general secretary of the Communist Party by then, and managed to neutralize Trotsky's power with the help of two other influential leaders, Lev Kamenev and Grigory Zinoviev. Stalin would later turn on both of these allies in the infamous Moscow Show Trial of 1936. But in the intervening years they helped Stalin consolidate power and eventually force Trotsky into exile.

Demoted in 1928

Tukhachevsky was one of the new Soviet Union's most famous war heroes and favored by Mikhail Frunze, whose Bolshevik roots dated back to the first years of the twentieth century and the failed 1905 revolution. Frunze held Trotsky's former post as People's Commissar for Military Affairs and was one of the so-called Old Guard who sat on the decision-making Central Committee of the Communist Party. But Frunze was also drawn into the shifting alliances and plots surrounding Stalin and his cadre, and died of an overdose of chloroform during surgery to mend an ulcer in October of 1925.

Frunze was succeeded as head of Commissar for Military Affairs by Kliment Voroshilov, a devoted ally of Stalin. Like Stalin, Voroshilov came from a much humbler background than Tukhachevsky, and though the 1917 revolution was designed to forever eradicate class enmities, they still existed inside the Soviet Union. Voroshilov was among the military leaders who distrusted Tukhachevsky. "Physically immensely strong and personally charismatic, at times insufferably arrogant, Tukhachevsky would have presented great difficulties to a commander who had earned his respect, let alone one as weak and insecure as Voroshilov," wrote military historian David R. Stone in a profile of Tukhachevsky for the journal *Europe-Asia Studies.*

Stone's research paper examined a three-year period when Tukhachevsky was demoted from the post of commander-in-chief of the Red Army in 1928 and given command of the Leningrad Military District instead. Tukhachevsky spent these years in the former St. Petersburg—renamed in Lenin's honor—which removed him from the power elite in Moscow and the Kremlin, the seat of government. Some of the antagonism toward him was linked to his efforts to modernize the Red Army. Tukhachevsky was the author of several lengthy, well researched, and enduring works on military strategy in the 1920s. In the 700-page *Future War,* published in 1928, he theorized what might happen if the Soviets went to war with China, Germany, or any one of its numerous allies. He advocated for a more mechanized force, replacing cavalry units with tank battalions, and weighed the arguments for and against a better equipped air force with strike capabilities.

Began Ambitious Reform

In 1931 Tukhachevsky was installed as Director of Armaments, which enabled him to return to Moscow and begin to implement his reforms. He urged Stalin and the Central Committee to authorize massive expenditures for new tanks and aircraft. "Tukhachevsky's bent for hordes of weaponry was fodder for jokes for the Central Committee," according to Stone. "Outlining the successes of the first five-year plan at the January 1933 plenum of the Central Committee and the Central Control Commission, Ordzhonikidze, People's Commissar of Heavy Industry, enumerated Soviet industry's achievements in military production. Stalin interjected: 'But to Tukhachevsky it's all very little,' provoking laughter."

Tukhachevsky wrote an influential work on military strategy, *Instructions on Deep Battle,* in which he reasoned that the most effective way to quash an enemy force was to attack it from the rear, destroying the supply lines that serviced the front. This tactic was adopted in the Red Army's official *Provisional Field Regulations of 1936,* and would be used later in World War II with much success, particularly in the long battle to keep the city of Stalingrad out of German hands.

In September of 1935, Tukhachevsky was named one of five Marshals of the Soviet Union. This is a rank equal to that of six-star generals, and seemed to affirm his status as one of the most respected military figures in the Soviet Union. In January of 1936 he was among the Soviet delegation at the funeral of England's King George V. The British monarch was succeeded by his son as Edward VIII, but Edward abdicated the throne late in 1936 when it became clear he would not be permitted to marry a twice-divorced American woman, Wallis Simpson. Edward's younger brother Albert assumed the throne, and Tukhachevsky was scheduled to attend the coronation in London on May 12, 1937.

Tortured into Confession

But the annual May Day military parade on May 1, 1937, revealed tensions among Tukhachevsky and the other marshals and generals, who were visibly frosty to one another. Tukhachevsky was informed of a plot against him uncovered by agents of the NKVD (*Narodnyy komissariat vnutrennikh del,* or People's Commissariat for Internal Affairs), and told he would not be permitted to leave the country for reasons of personal safety.

By this point Stalin's Great Purge was underway, though the full scale of the treachery would become known only years later. At the time, it was publicized as an effort to rid the Communist Party of those who were secretly disloyal and conspiring to overturn the achievements of the revolution either internally or with help from foreign enemies. In reality, it was Stalin's masterful plan to quell all dissent within the party, particularly those who had supported Trotsky. There were two major show trials in August of 1936 and January of 1937, in which top-ranking party officials were convicted of conspiracies against Stalin, the party, and the Soviet state itself. The evidence included confessions in which each suspect had implicated one another. Kamenev and Zinoviev were tried and executed, along with scores of other party figures. Both show trials, with their cleverly manufactured "evidence," riveted the Soviet Union and dominated the pages of *Pravda,* the Communist Party newspaper. Ordinary Russians were duly alarmed that there was such plotting at the highest levels of government.

Tukhachevsky was believed to be among the top military officials who may have harbored doubts about Stalin's zeal to root out dissent. This posed an actual threat to Stalin, for only the top Red Army brass could muster the necessary resources for a coup. The beginning of Tukhachevsky's downfall came on May 10, 1937, when he was reassigned and given charge of the Volga Military District. He was arrested 12 days later, taken to Moscow's infamous Lubyanka prison, and interrogated for days on end by the NKVD chief, Nikolai Yezhov. He was also tortured, as were other members of the military High Command. Finally, on May 29, he agreed with his interrogators that he had been recruited back in 1928 into a high-level plot to oust Stalin, and also admitted to being an agent of Nazi Germany.

Suffered "A Dog's Death"

Tukhachevsky and seven other top-ranking Soviet military officers were tried in secret on June 11, 1937, found guilty, and sentenced to death. He and his co-defendants were likely shot in the back of the head on the night of June 11–12 on the grounds of Lubyanka. The *Pravda* headline on June 12 announced, "For Dogs—A Dog's Death," reported the *Times* of London. "Nobody believes that the official account is the true version of what is happening, but what the truth is it is difficult to say," noted the *Times* correspondent, who also mentioned that Soviet encyclopedias still hailed Tukhachevsky as the youngest leader of any modern army.

Tukhachevsky's entire family was arrested and sent to remote prison camps. His wife, Nina, suffered a nervous breakdown and was incarcerated in a psychiatric hospital in the Urals, and was sentenced to death a few years later as an enemy of the people. Two of Tukhachevsky's ex-wives also spent time in the gulag, while his daughter Svetlana, 11 at the time of his death, was tried at the age of 17 and sentenced to five years in a labor camp. Tukhachevsky's sister, mother, and two brothers were all slain.

The very mention of Tukhachevsky's name or military strategies was risky for many years, but one of his advocates was Georgy Zhukov, the marshal who led the Red Army to victory in World War II using some of the deep battle techniques Tukhachevsky had suggested.

Books

Conquest, Robert, *The Great Terror: A Reassessment,* Oxford University Press, 1990, 40th anniversary edition, 2008.

Montefiore, Simon Sebag, *Stalin : The Court of the Red Tsar,* Alfred A. Knopf, 2004.

Rayfield, Donald, *Stalin and His Hangmen: The Tyrant and Those Who Killed for Him,* Random House, 2004.

Stoecker, Sally W., "Tukhachevsky, Mikhail Nikolayevich," *Encyclopedia of Russian History,* edited by James R. Millar, Volume 4, Macmillan Reference USA, 2004, pp. 1583–1584.

Periodicals

Europe-Asia Studies, December 1996.

Times (London, England), June 11, 1937; June 12, 1937; June 14, 1937.

Online

"Prominent Russians: Mikhail Tukhachevsky," Russiapedia, http://www.russiapedia.rt.com/prominent-russians/military/mikhail-tukhachevsky/ (August 14, 2011). □

U

Bob Uecker

American baseball announcer and actor Bob Uecker (born 1935) parlayed his sense of humor and his mediocre career as a baseball player into a second career as a national media figure. His skills as a comedian made him a fixture on national television in the 1970s and 1980s, while his upbeat personality and knowledge of baseball have made him a popular radio and TV announcer nationwide, and a beloved personality in his hometown of Milwaukee, Wisconsin.

Robert George Uecker was born in Milwaukee, Wisconsin, on January 26, 1935. He grew up and went to school in Milwaukee, where his constant joking provoked his teachers but entertained his friends. After graduating from high school, he served in the U.S. Army, then signed a contract with the Milwaukee Braves in 1956 to play minor-league baseball. After several seasons in the minor leagues, at Braves affiliates in towns such as Evansville, Indiana, and Eau Claire, Wisconsin, Uecker made it to the Braves in 1962, nine years after they had relocated from Boston to Milwaukee. "I was proud to be the first native Milwaukeean signed by the Braves," Uecker once said (as quoted by Tom Haudricourt of the *Milwaukee Journal Sentinel*). "And I was the first native Milwaukeean to be sent to the minors by the Braves. I was always proud of that."

Became a Journeyman Catcher

Uecker spent six seasons in the major leagues. Those years would later become the main subject of his comedy routines.

Uecker was a mediocre big-league player, with an even .200 career batting average. In 297 games, he never stole a base, hit only 14 home runs and had only 74 runs batted in. He was mostly a backup catcher, valued for his defensive skills. He went from Milwaukee to the St. Louis Cardinals and the Philadelphia Phillies, then returned to the Braves after their move to Atlanta.

Yet despite his underwhelming accomplishments as a hitter and his self-mocking humor, he was part of the St. Louis Cardinals team that won the 1964 World Series. "People don't know this, but I helped the Cardinals win the pennant," Uecker sometimes joked, as recalled by Sam Mellinger in *Baseball Digest*. "I came down with hepatitis. The trainer injected me with it." Actually, he sat on the bench for the entire series while starting catcher Tim McCarver batted over .400. Uecker's only performance during the series came during warmups before the first game, when he grabbed a tuba left on the field by a Dixieland band and started catching fly balls with it.

Uecker played with four future members of baseball's Hall of Fame: Hank Aaron, Eddie Mathews, Warren Spahn, and Bob Gibson. "In my heart of hearts, I believe my accomplishments were as great as theirs," he wrote in his book *Catcher in the Wry*. "Anybody with ability can play in the big leagues. To last as long as I did with the skills I had, with the numbers I produced, was a triumph of the human spirit."

In 1967, his last year playing, he set a major league record for the number of passed balls allowed by a catcher. That was probably not his fault, however. His special assignment was to catch for Atlanta pitcher Phil Niekro, who threw a knuckleball, a pitch that is difficult to catch. Uecker recalled the experience in a 2003 speech at the National Baseball Hall of Fame, as recorded on the Hall of Fame website. "I found the easy way out to catch a knuckleball," he said. "It was to wait until it stopped rolling and then pick it up."

Began Second Career as Broadcaster

Uecker is best known for his second career, after his playing days, in broadcasting and entertainment. In 1970, Milwaukee's new baseball team, the Brewers, hired Uecker as a scout. He was, according to former Brewers owner Bud Selig, the worst scout the team ever had. One day, team general manager Frank Lane angrily showed Selig one of Uecker's scouting reports. It had gravy and mashed potato stains on it. "Yeah, I did scouting, if you could call it that," Uecker told Richard Sandomir of the *New York Times.* "For every guy, I wrote, 'Fringe major leaguer,' so in case he made it nobody could say, 'How'd you miss that guy?'"

In 1971, Selig made Uecker the Brewers' radio announcer instead. Uecker still held the job 40 years later. He began as an analyst, but in 1972 he and the team discovered he had the talent to be the team's play-by-play announcer. It happened when his broadcast partners left him alone for an inning at Yankee Stadium. "I had my cough switch down and begged them to come back, but they wouldn't," Uecker told Sandomir. "The engineer said: 'You'd better start talking. There's one out.'" Uecker went on to provide commentary for ABC's *Monday Night Baseball* in the 1970s and NBC baseball broadcasts in the 1990s.

Entered Show Business

Even as he held down a regular job as the Brewers' announcer, Uecker also pursued a successful career in comedy. In Atlanta in 1969, he began doing comedy routines at a nightclub owned by a friend. His big break came when the club owner brought in jazz musician Al Hirt to perform, and Uecker did comedy in between Hirt's acts. Afterward, Hirt's agent, impressed, arranged to have Uecker appear on *The Tonight Show with Johnny Carson.* Uecker was a hit on the late-night talk show, one of television's best showcases for comedy. Carson called him "Mr. Baseball," a nickname that stuck. Uecker made about 100 appearances on The Tonight

Show over the years. The exposure led him to a career as a comic actor in TV shows, commercials, and films.

Uecker hosted two TV shows, *Bob Uecker's Wacky World of Sports* and *Bob Uecker's War of the Stars.* He also starred as the character George Owens in the ABC situation comedy *Mr. Belvedere,* which first aired in 1985 and lasted 122 episodes. But his most memorable television appearances may have been in several popular commercials for the beer Miller Lite. In one commercial, an usher threw Uecker out of choice seats in a baseball stadium. "I must be in the *front* row!" Uecker declared (as recalled by Mellinger of *Baseball Digest*). The next scene showed him in a far corner of the stadium. In honor of Uecker, the Milwaukee Brewers now sell $1 "Uecker seats," upper deck seats with views obstructed by posts.

Starred in *Major League* Trilogy

Uecker also appeared in the film *Major League* and its sequel, *Major League II,* as Harry Doyle, a whiskey-drinking radio announcer for a fictitious version of the Cleveland Indians. Many of Uecker's funniest lines in the movies were unscripted; the producer and director let him ad lib. "*Just* a bit outside," Doyle quipped in understatement after a wild pitch from Charlie Sheen's character flew past the catcher and hit the backstop (as recalled by Bob Wolfley in the *Milwaukee Journal Sentinel*) was one such memorable ad lib.

During the 1980s, Uecker also made two memorable appearances on professional wrestling's main event, WrestleMania. He was a guest announcer for the WrestleMania III match-up between two of the 1980s wrestling's biggest personalities, Hulk Hogan and Andre the Giant. A year later, while interviewing the 520-pound Andre the Giant at WrestleMania IV, his banter provoked the wrestler into placing Uecker in a choke hold. In commemoration of those two appearances, Uecker was inducted into pro wrestling's WWE Hall of Fame in 2010. "Everything I've done, no matter how weird or ignorant it seems, people like it," Uecker told Mellinger of *Baseball Digest.*

Uecker collected many of his funniest baseball stories in the 1982 book *Catcher in the Wry,* co-written with Mickey Herskowitz. "Sure, I had my critics, people who swore I would never make it," he wrote in the book. "They never bothered me. I always thought I was bigger than baseball and I think my record proves it."

Inducted into Baseball Hall of Fame

In 2003, the National Baseball Hall of Fame awarded Uecker the Ford C. Frick Award, which honors major contributions to baseball broadcasting. The award was ironic, since Uecker's comedy act once included a routine about being passed over for induction into the Hall of Fame as a player. "Sitting around all those years," Uecker said (as quoted by Drew Olson of the *Milwaukee Journal Sentinel*) "with your wife and kids, waiting for the phone, it finally got to the point where I had to say, 'Hey, I don't need it.' I can bronze my own glove and hang it on a nail in my garage and build a little grotto out there."

His acceptance speech was vintage Uecker, full of comic exaggerations about his life, and recorded on the official website. "During every player's career there comes a time when you know that your services are no longer required, that you might be moving on," he quipped. "I remember [manager] Gene Mauch doing things to me at Philadelphia. I'd be sitting there and he'd say, 'Grab a bat and stop this rally.' [He would] send me up there without a bat and tell me to try for a walk."

In Wisconsin, Uecker is closely identified with the Brewers, thanks to his 40 years as the team's radio announcer. Despite his comic reputation, Uecker calls a game with few jokes if the game is close. But he injects humor and old baseball stories into a broadcast if the Brewers are losing badly. "Uecker is in a league of his own when it comes to baseball play-by-play men," wrote Mark Yost of the *Wall Street Journal*. "Part comic, part encyclopedia, he can recall an amazing number of pertinent facts when the game is on the line, and have a heck of a lot of fun when it isn't."

Underwent Heart Surgeries

Many Milwaukeeans consider Uecker's voice so familiar, he reminds them of family. That thought especially struck many of them in 2010, when Uecker missed about half of the Brewers' season after undergoing two heart operations. But he returned to the broadcast booth in 2011, healthy again at age 76.

During a broadcast of a spring training game that year, a foul tip to a catcher inspired Uecker to talk for a half-inning, between pitches, about how catching had changed since he was a player. "I used to soak my mitts in a bucket of water for about two days. Then I'd put a couple of baseballs in the pocket and wrap it up with a rubber band," Uecker told the audience (as quoted by Yost of the *Wall Street Journal*). "Today you don't have to do that, because catchers' mitts are more like first baseman's gloves."

Uecker has often expressed his desire to keep broadcasting forever, or at least as long as he can do the job well. "I could have left there a long time ago," Uecker told Michael Hunt of the *Milwaukee Journal Sentinel* in 2003. "But no matter what I do, I'm staying. All the television stuff, the movies, the sitcoms, the commercials, that's all fun. All I wanted to do is come back to Milwaukee every spring to do baseball."

Books

Uecker, Bob, and Mickey Herskowitz, *Catcher in the Wry*, G. P. Putnam's Son, 1982.

Periodicals

Baseball Digest, September 2006.

Chicago Tribune, October 16, 1995.

Milwaukee Journal Sentinel, March 13, 2003; July 25, 2003; March 25, 2007; May 11, 2009; January 29, 2011.

New York Times, August 14, 2010.

Wall Street Journal, March 31, 2011.

Online

"Bob Uecker," Radio Hall of Fame, http://www.radiohof.org/sportscasters/bobuecker.html (November 2, 2011).

"Bob Uecker: Biography," Biography.com, http://www.biography.com/people/bob-uecker-224920 (November 2, 2011).

"Broadcasters: Bob Uecker," Milwaukee Brewers, http:// http://broadwayworld.com/printcolumn.php?id=197852 (December 1, 2011).

Dale, Michael, "Is Michael Riedel The New Bob Uecker?" Broadway World, http://milwaukee.brewers.mlb.com/team/broadcasters.jsp?c_id=mil(November 2, 2011).

"Deal or No Deal? Uecker Seats at Miller Park," Milwaukee Consumer, http://milwaukeeconsumer.com/deal-or-no-deal/deal-or-no-deal-uecker-seats-at-miller-park (December 1, 2011).

Tarnoff, Andy, "Milwaukee Talks: Bob Uecker," onmilwaukee.com, http://onmilwaukee.com/buzz/articles/uecker.html (November 2, 2011).

Uecker, Bob, "Text of Ford C. Frick Award Winner Bob Uecker's Speech, July 27, 2003," Baseball Hall of Fame, http://web.archive.org/web/20070614191140/http://www.baseballhallzoffame.org/hof_weekend/2003/speeches/uecker.htm (November 2, 2011).

"WWE: Bob Uecker," WWE, http://www.wwe.com/superstars/halloffame/inductees/bobuecker (November 2, 2011).☐

Saskia Van Uijlenburgh

Saskia van Uijlenburgh (1612–1642) appeared in several works of art painted by her husband, Rembrandt van Rijn, one of the greatest creative forces in seventeenth-century Dutch art's Golden Age. After bearing him four children—three of whom died in infancy—Rembrandt's muse died in 1642 at the age of just 29. Her nine-year marriage to one of the most enduringly popular of Western art's Old Masters has been scrutinized by historians for the financial decisions made during this period, for in the years following her death the widowed Rembrandt struggled with mounting debt despite the lucrative output from his studio.

S askia van Uijlenburgh van Rijn came from a prominent family in Leeuwarden, the largest city in the province of Friesland. Her father, Rombertus van Uijlenburgh, had played a key role in the formation of the Republic of the Seven United Netherlands in the early 1580s, when Friesland united with several other *neder* or "low" lands to form an independent Dutch state. Because Friesland is a separate language from standard Dutch, there are variations in the spelling of van Uijlenburgh's first and last names. In Friesian her given name is "Saske"; likewise with her mother, whose name variants are Sjuke Osinga and Sjoukje Ozinga.

Daughter of Leeuwarden Mayor

Van Uijlenburgh was the last of eight children in her family, born on August 2, 1612. Her father is listed as an *advokat* or lawyer in historical documents, and also served as Leeuwarden's burgomaster, or chief executive or magistrate. He died in 1624, when van Uijlenburgh was 12 years old, five years after her mother's passing. One oft-repeated assertion is that van Uijlenburgh was a wealthy young woman with a considerable inheritance she brought with her when she married Rembrandt, but more contemporary scholarship has determined that her assets were slim when she married the rising young star of affluent Amsterdam's new art scene.

It is known that van Uijlenburgh lived with her next-oldest sister, Hiskje, who in 1627 married Gerrit van Loo, a municipal official in a Frisian town called Het Bildt. She also spent time with a sister named Antje, who married a renowned professor of Protestant theology from Poland, Johannes Maccovius, and lived in the university town of Franeker. There was another connection to Poland in the person of van Uijlenburgh's cousin, an art dealer named Hendrick van Uijlenburgh. Hendrick had grown up in Kraków and become an art dealer in Gdansk before returning to the Netherlands in the 1620s. These far-ranging travels were not uncommon for the Dutch, who had actually gone to war in the 1430s to establish maritime trading rights in the Baltic region.

Like other art dealers of the era, Hendrick van Uijlenburgh worked in three areas: he bought and sold paintings between collectors, commissioned new ones from a talented stable of young artists working for him, and also had those painters copy the masterworks of the Italian Renaissance. His business on the Jodenbreestraat (Jewish Broad Street) in Amsterdam became one of the leading art galleries in the city in its first few years in business in the late 1620s. The street was actually the southern part of Sint-Anthoniesbreestraat and took its name from an influx of Sephardic Jews who settled there in the years that followed the new Dutch Republic's edict mandating religious tolerance.

Moved to Amsterdam

Van Uijlenburgh moved to Amsterdam in 1631. At the time, it was one of the most cosmopolitan and advanced cities in Europe. The Dutch Republic's artisan guilds produced some of the finest consumer goods in the world, and its trading prowess and savvy financial management had made it the wealthiest nation in Europe. More importantly, the wealth was not concentrated in the hands of powerful landowners or nobles, but instead spread across an emerging middle class, who ardently adopted all the trappings of the aristocratic elite. The historical record shows that Van Uijlenburgh came to the city with a pair of male chaperones, two young Leeuwarden painters named Govert Flinck and Jacob Backer. Flinck became an apprentice painter at the Hendrick van Uijlenburgh art factory, along with an artist from Leiden, a city in the province of South Holland. This was Rembrandt Harmenszoon van Rijn, whose family had a successful grain milling business.

Rembrandt was 25 years old in 1631 when he, too, arrived in Amsterdam. A year later his *Anatomy Lesson of Dr. Nicolaes Tulp,* which showed the dissection of a cadaver by a prominent surgeon, caused a minor sensation for its vivid anatomical detail. Van Uijlenburgh and Rembrandt probably met in the house or studio owned by her cousin Hendrick, and were engaged to be married in June of 1633. The exact date is known because of an inscription he added to a silver-point drawing he made of her on vellum, titled *Saskia in a Straw Hat, 8 June 1633.* "This is my wife made when she was 21 years old three days after our betrothal on 8 June 1633" according to David Bomford's 2006 volume *Art in the Making: Rembrandt.* Historian Simon Schama appraised it in an article for the *New Yorker.* "It is a little act of adoration," Schama declared. "Saskia's face and upper body are caught in a fresh early-summer light. . . .At the center is Saskia's heart-shaped face; the eyes show her to be amused, flattered, tolerating the examination with good humor."

The couple were married on June 22, 1634, in Het Bildt by one of her cousins, a Calvinist minister. They probably lived at Hendrick van Uijlenburgh's capacious quarters for the first year of their marriage before moving into a rented house on the Nieuwe Doelenstraat, one of Amsterdam's most expensive residential areas. Their home had a view of the Amstel River and the couple soon began a family.

Became Rembrandt's Model

Van Uijlenburgh appears in several paintings made during this phase of her husband's career. Like other artists of the era, Rembrandt looked to the Greek and Roman myths and biblical tales for inspiration. He painted her as the Roman goddess of war, *Bellona,* in 1633. She was also costumed as *Artemisia,* a Persian warrior-queen of the fifth century BCE, in 1634. For multiple sittings she appeared as Flora, the Roman goddess of flowers and spring, and her place of honor in his life was enshrined in a depiction of her as *Minerva,* a major Roman deity long feted as the patroness of the creative arts.

Van Uijlenburgh's blond tresses are also seen in a 1636 work, *Self-Portrait with Saskia (The Prodigal Son),* a version of the wedding portrait. In this case the couple are not shown in their home with their possessions, as was customary for this type of portrait, but instead in a tavern. He raises his wine glass in a toast as she sits on his lap, and while both turn behind to look at the viewer, her gaze is stern while his is exuberant. The work's subtitle—a reference to the biblical tale of a wayward son who is forgiven by his father—has some echoes to Rembrandt 's own life, for apparently none in his family attended his wedding to Saskia. "An anecdotal tradition grew up around the canvas," Schama wrote, "seeing it as an unapologetic celebration of Rembrandt and Saskia's notorious appetite for high-roller living—sex, wine, and peacock pie." Schama theorized that Rembrandt's biographers of later centuries latched on to it because "the painting's hedonism matched their need for an image of Rembrandt's shameless dissipation: the moment of hubris before his eventual fall into debt, widowerhood, and bankruptcy."

Died at 29

Van Uijlenburgh's presence in Rembrandt's life endured a little more than a decade, but it was marked by tragedies that were commonplace for the era: their first child was a son they named Rombertus after van Uijlenburgh's father. The infant was born in December of 1635 during a particularly virulent outbreak of the bubonic plague that winter and was buried two months later. A second child, named Cornelia after Rembrandt's grandmother, was born in July of 1638 and buried in August. The couple had a third child, another daughter they also named Cornelia, who was born in the summer July 1640 and was buried, like her namesake sister, within just a few weeks after her birth. Finally, their son Titus was born in September 1641 and survived his infancy, but van Uijlenburgh did not. She died less than a year later, on June 14, 1642, at the age of 29. The cause of death was likely tuberculosis and she was buried inside Amsterdam's Oude Kerk (Old Church), the resting spot of the city's elite. There are drawings and other works that show van Uijlenburgh ailing and confined to an elaborate "box-bed" in their home. These were carved and curtained enclosures off the main room and a standard element of Dutch domestic life of the era before central heating systems.

A legal trail provides a few other clues to van Uijlenburgh and her husband's marriage and its aftermath. At one point around 1638 her family raised complaints that the couple was spending too much of her inheritance—which scholars doubt she had much of to begin with—and Rembrandt responded with a libel action against them. In 1639 the couple bought a property at 4 Jodenbreestraat for 13,000 guilders. This was adjacent to his studio at No. 6, and he would later be forced to sell the house after a series of financial missteps.

Rembrandt Hamstrung by Will

Van Uijlenburgh made out a last will and testament on June 5, 1642, nine days before her death. She left her assets to Titus, but a clause in the will permitted Rembrandt to draw upon the inheritance so long as he remained unmarried. He did not remarry, but after a period of grieving in which he turned from the lucrative portraiture market to painting elegiac landscapes, he took up with a widow hired to care for Titus, named Geertje Dircx, who was in her late twenties or early thirties by then. Dircx apparently expected Rembrandt to marry her, which he was unlikely to do because it would mean his access to Titus's inheritance would come to an end. He gave Dircx some jewelry that had belonged to his late wife, but when he took up with a new employee in his household, a 23-year-old named Hendrickje Stoffels, he asked Dircx to make a will. This document is dated January 1648 and affirms that the items Rembrandt gave her would revert to Titus upon Dircx's death. In exchange for this promise, he agreed to pay Dircx 160 guilders a year.

Turned out of the famous artist's house for a younger woman, Dircx retaliated and reneged on the agreement. She pawned some of van Uijlenburgh's items and then filed a lawsuit against Rembrandt for breach of marriage contract. He denied any intimate relationship with Dircx when called before Amsterdam's board of Commissioners of Marital Affairs in 1649. They offered him a compromise deal in which he would not have to marry Dircx, but should pay her an increased alimony amount of 200 guilders a year. The case was scandalous but became even more distasteful when Rembrandt was able to convince some of Dircx's neighbors to testify she was mentally unstable and led an amoral lifestyle. This time, authorities sided with him and Dircx was sent to a dreadful workhouse-prison in the city of Gouda. Known as the Spinhuis, its inmates were expected to spin cloth as their penance, and the five years that Dircx spent there ruined her health. She died in late 1656.

Rembrandt had by then defaulted on the court-ordered payments to Dircx, and in an even greater scandal had a daughter by Stoffels, Cornelia, born in September of 1654. His financial situation was so grave by that point that he was forced to declare himself insolvent and had to sell off his paintings, a vast collection of artworks and antiques he had amassed, and the grand Jodenbreestraat house. In 1662, he even sold van Uijlenburgh's grave plot in the Oude Kerk. He spent the final decade of his life in smaller quarters on the Rozengracht. Stoffels died in 1663, and his son Titus died in 1668. Rembrandt died at the age of 63 in Amsterdam on October 4, 1669. The house on Jodenbreestraat later became a museum dedicated to his life and work, the Rembrandthuis.

Books

Alpers, Svetlana, *Rembrandt's Enterprise: The Studio and the Market,* University of Chicago Press, 1988.

Bomford, David, and National Gallery (London), *Art in the Making: Rembrandt,* Yale University Press, 2006.

Periodicals

American Artist, November 2007.

Apollo, September 2006.

Calliope, March 2006.

Guardian (London, England), March 11, 1992.

New York Times, June 18, 2006.

Online

"Salon (Sael)," Rembrandthuis.com, http://www.rembrandthuis. com/2004/tour_sael_02_en.html (November 5, 2011).☐

V

Alberto Vargas

The Peruvian-born artist Alberto Vargas (1896–1982) became famous for his distinctive and masterfully crafted magazine illustrations featuring young women in sexy poses—"pin-up girls," as they were generally known for much of the twentieth century.

Vargas's paintings were reproduced in large quantities and were so widely distributed that they became icons of the U.S. military during World War II. Yet Vargas was anything but a mass-production artist. He labored painstakingly over his paintings, suffered badly when forced to rush them, and maintained an attitude of respect toward his subjects that contrasted with the sometimes tawdry uses to which his works were put. An immigrant beset by waves of good and bad fortune during his career, Vargas created works that earned recognition after his death, in the form of gallery and museum exhibitions and most of all rising prices at auction.

Received European Education

The artist whose works became integral to American popular visual imagery was born in rural Peru. Joaquín Alberto Vargas y Chávez was a native of Arequipa in southern Peru, born on February 9, 1896. His father, Max Vargas, was a well-known photographer who could afford to send Vargas and his younger brother, Max Vargas II, to Europe for an education; the plan was that Alberto would apprentice himself at a well-established photography studio in Switzerland or London, while Max II would study banking.

The family arrived in Europe in 1911, traveling by way of Paris because the elder Vargas was scheduled to accept a photography award there. The visit changed the career plans of the 15-year-old Alberto Vargas, who was fascinated by the paintings he saw firsthand in Parisian museums—not only the detailed neo-classical canvases of Jean-August Dominique Ingres, but also by modern art and by classical Greek sculpture, with its detailed representations of the nude human form. Vargas went along with his father's wishes, enrolling in school in Geneva, Switzerland, and beginning a photography apprenticeship there, but his interests were beginning to pull him in new directions.

The rising danger World War I posed for ordinary citizens caused Vargas's ultimate break from his father's plans. In 1916 he left Europe on a ship bound for New York, intending to make his way from there to Peru. But when he arrived in New York in October of that year, he found himself captivated by the city, and specifically by its female population. "From every building came torrents of girls," he recalled, as quoted by Paul Chutkow of *Cigar Aficionado*. "I had never seen anything like it...Hundreds of girls with an air of self-assuredness and determination that said, 'Here I am, how do you like me?' This certainly was not the Spanish, Swiss, or French girl!" With no job and little money, Vargas decided to stay on in New York, and his financial prospects worsened after his father cut off parental support.

Met Showgirl

Soon Vargas's adulation toward American womanhood found a specific target in Tennessee-born showgirl Anna Mae Clift, whom he spotted on the street and followed to the Greenwich Village Follies stage show, where she was performing. Waiting for her outside the theater, Vargas suggested in his still-broken English that he paint her portrait, even though he had no money to pay her for modeling services. The attraction was evidently mutual,

for Clift agreed to pose. Heartened, he set about looking for part-time work and landed jobs at a photography studio and at the catalogue production studio of a sewing pattern maker. After selling a few drawings, Vargas confidently launched himself as a freelance artist and succeeded in placing several illustrations in New York magazines.

Vargas received his first big opportunity when theater impresario Florenz Ziegfeld spotted some of these illustrations and hired him to create portraits of his trademark chorus line "Ziegfeld girls" for use in advertising. The deal was sealed with a handshake, and over the course of the 1920s Vargas's position evolved to the point where he was the Ziegfeld organization's official portrait painter. This in turn stimulated demand for Vargas's work, and he created portraits for promotional materials and sometimes for private individuals. He also drew sheet music covers. With money coming in, Vargas and Clift finally felt ready to marry, and did so in 1930 after she proposed to him.

Vargas's work in New York slowed down with the dismal economic climate of the 1930s, as well as the decline in live theater as sound films became more popular. But he made a successful move to Hollywood in 1934, taking a job with the 20th Century Fox studio and creating portraits of the glamorous female stars of the era such as Greta Garbo, Paulette Godard, and Marlene Dietrich, as well as child star Shirley Temple. Vargas moved to the Warner Brothers studio in the late 1930s, but his career was upended again after he participated in a strike called by a studio artists' union. Accused of being a Communist, Vargas was banned by all of the major Hollywood studios in a move that anticipated the widespread 1950s blacklist of suspected Communists. For several months, the Vargases scraped by on income derived from renting out parts of their small west Los Angeles home.

Joined *Esquire* Staff

In 1939 Vargas became an American citizen, and the following year he seemingly bounced back from his stretch of unemployment with a new job at *Esquire* magazine, which paid him $75 a week to produce images that the magazine insisted on calling Varga Girls, dropping the final "s" of his name. Many of Vargas's paintings up to this point had been only subtly sexual, but the Varga Girls helped to define the classic image of the pin-up girl, an image cut or torn from a magazine and posted in the living quarters of mostly young men. Vargas's timing was perfect: with military mobilization underway in advance of the U.S. entry into World War II, *Esquire* notched sales of hundreds of thousands of Varga Girl calendars and posters, as well as copies of the magazine itself. The Varga Girl became a phenomenon, and even the sophisticated *New Yorker* magazine took notice, pointing out (as quoted by Chutkow) that Vargas "could make a girl look nude if she were rolled up in a rug." Vargas and his wife moved to Chicago to be nearer to *Esquire*'s offices.

The problem for Vargas was that his contract with *Esquire* required him to work at a superhuman pace of a full-size painting a week, at a salary that increased only slowly to $12,000 a year—a pittance for an artist who may have been the country's most famous illustrator during the war years, and who earned *Esquire* more than $1 million during the year 1945 alone. Vargas was a poor businessman who reputedly did not even read the contract he signed with the magazine. *Esquire* in turn failed to send a copy of the contract to Vargas's wife, who handled many of his financial arrangements.

With work piling up due to the demands of his bosses, Vargas became depressed, and the quality of his work declined. When his wife finally discovered what was in his *Esquire* contract, she realized that Vargas was being exploited, and the couple launched a long and ultimately unsuccessful lawsuit against the magazine, in spite of successfully having persuaded a jury at one point that they had been wronged. Their financial situation worsened, and only credit advanced by a friendly physician enabled Anna Vargas to undergo breast cancer surgery in 1950. Difficult financial straits apparently never damaged the couple's mutual affection. "I've never seen such compassion between two people...such ease or grace between a couple, such mutual respect," *Esquire* artist Reid Austin told Chutkow.

Paintings Appeared in *Playboy*

Once again, Vargas recovered and entered a successful new phase of his career. After two *Esquire* employees, Austin and advertising copywriter Hugh Hefner, also left *Esquire* (Hefner likewise over a financial dispute), Hefner launched *Playboy* and saw it quickly grow into a cultural phenomenon. Vargas met with Hefner in 1953, showed him a portfolio of drawings of nudes, and beginning in 1956 Vargas's artwork began appearing in the magazine occasionally. He distributed business cards billing himself as the "originator of the pin-up" (although other artists such as *Esquire*'s George Petty also contributed to the phenomenon), with a small Vargas Girl printed on the back. In 1960 Vargas Girls, with the final "s" of Vargas's name restored, became a monthly *Playboy* feature, and between 1960 and 1974 Vargas created 152 paintings for the magazine, with his fee rising from $500 to $1,500 per painting.

Vargas slowed down after his beloved Anna was incapacitated after a fall in 1974 and died from her injuries. He retired in 1976, collaborating with Austin on an autobiography two years later. Vargas died in Los Angeles on December 30, 1982. His estate was represented by a gallery called the San Francisco Art Exchange, whose sales of Vargas works testified to the increasing respect his work was receiving from art collectors. By the mid-1990s, after several exhibitions of Vargas works, prices for an original Vargas canvas had reached the $3,000 range. In 1997 a two-volume book of Vargas's *Esquire* work, *Alberto Vargas: The Esquire Years,* was published. Even ordinary Vargas items from the *Esquire* days carried a premium by the early 2000s. Syndicated collectibles columnist Leslie Hindman, writing in New Jersey's Bergen County *Record,* explained that "Vargas was a master of his craft, and so his work commands a higher price than the work of his contemporaries."

Books

Vargas, Alberto, and Michael Goldberg, *Alberto Vargas: The Esquire Years,* Collectors Press, 1997.
Vargas, Alberto, and Reid Stuart Austin, *Vargas,* Playboy, 1981.

Periodicals

Booklist, January 1, 1998.
Record (Bergen County, NJ), December 5, 2002; March 14, 2004.

Online

"Alberto Vargas," *Illustrators* (JVJ Publishing), http://www.bpib.com/illustra2/vargas.htm (September 30, 2011).
"History," *The Vargas Collection,* http://www.vargascollection.com/history/ (September 30, 2011).
"The Real Vargas," *Cigar Aficionado* (September 1, 1996), http://www.cigaraficionado.com/webfeatures/show/id/The-Real-Vargas_1599 (September 30, 2011). □

John Vassall

In 1962 British civil servant John Vassall (1924–1996) was exposed as a spy for the Soviet Union. Targeted while working at the British Embassy in Moscow several years earlier, Vassall was lured into a sexually compromising situation and then blackmailed by the Soviets with secretly taken photographs. He continued to pass information when he returned to London and worked at the British Admiralty. The revelation of his treachery rocked MI5, as Britain's security service is called, and "contributed to a growing impression of establishment incompetence and complacency which was to lead in 1964 to the end of 13 years of Tory

rule," wrote Richard Norton-Taylor in Vassall's obituary in the London *Guardian.* "To many, his name also became synonymous with homosexuality and made homosexuality synonymous with treason, before the liberating 1960s took hold."

Vassall was born William John Christopher Vassall on September 20, 1924, and used his middle name for much of his life. His father was a Church of England vicar and served as chaplain of St. Bartholomew's Hospital in London, and Vassall's mother had worked as a nurse. Educated at boarding schools in the Sussex region and in Wales, he was three weeks shy of his fifteenth birthday when England declared war on Nazi Germany in September 1939. In the early 1940s he worked as a bank clerk before his hiring as a temporary worker at the Admiralty Records Office. In 1943 he was called up for military service and spent the remaining two years of World War II as a photographer with the No. 137 Wing of the Royal Air Force (RAF). Discharged in 1947, he returned to civilian life and found a permanent position as a clerk at the Admiralty in 1948.

Blackmailed in Moscow

In early 1954 Vassall was posted to the British Embassy in Moscow as a staff member to Britain's naval attaché. At the time, the Soviet Union was a rigidly authoritarian state and blatantly distrustful of foreigners, especially those from the West. Embassy staffers lived in a virtual bubble, and contact with Russians was strongly discouraged by both their superiors and by the Soviets, whose internal police carefully monitored foreign residents. Vassall's colleagues at the Embassy were diplomats and other civil servants of the Foreign Office who were culled from elite establishment families or top universities. Vassall felt socially rejected by his co-workers and was admittedly lonely during his time in Moscow.

Vassall was also a gay man who came of age at a time when homosexual acts were subject to criminal prosecution, both in Britain and the Soviet Union. As a result, there was a serious risk, as well as deep shame, involved in any exposure. Vassall seems to have first been targeted by a Polish man named Mikhailsky, who worked at the British Embassy. They met for dinner on several occasions, then Mikhailsky introduced him to another man, who invited Vassall to a dinner party at a restaurant near the famed Bolshoi Theater. He was encouraged to drink prodigiously, and in one of the restaurant's private dining rooms an inebriated Vassall was secretly photographed while engaged in acts with at least two other men who were probably in the pay of the KGB, the Russian-language acronym for the Committee for State Security, the feared secret police and spy agency. Vassall was with one of these men at a later date when police officials entered the room, brandishing the incriminating photographs. Vassall was told that homosexuality was a criminal act, and that if the British Embassy officials were notified it might spark an international diplomatic incident. Terrified, Vassall agreed to provide what the agents described as "harmless" information to the KGB about the Embassy and its staffers.

The Soviets began paying Vassall for information later in 1955. Eventually he was transferred back to the Admiralty office in London, and when he notified his Moscow contact that he would be returning home, he hoped this would bring an end to their demands for information—but instead they supplied him with a miniature Minox camera, a superbly engineered device used by spies during the Cold War to surreptitiously photograph top secret documents.

Photographed Admiralty Files

Back in London, Vassall was assigned to the naval intelligence division of the Admiralty. In 1957 he became assistant private secretary to Baron Strathclyde, born Thomas Dunlop Galbraith and called "Tam." The Scottish peer was also an elected member of Parliament (MP) and a staunch Tory, or Conservative Party supporter. From 1957 to 1959 Galbraith served as Civil Lord of the Admiralty. Vassall's trusted position gave him access to Galbraith's files, as well as those in the office of Peter Carrington, another peer who held the title First Lord of the Admiralty, one of the top-ranked defense-related cabinet posts in Britain. Lord Carrington served British Prime Minister Harold Macmillan and was involved in high-level meetings of NATO, or the North Atlantic Treaty Organization. NATO was a joint effort between Britain, the United States, and several other nations of Western Europe to guard against the Soviet military threat.

Vassall apparently provided the Soviets with information from classified documents relating to British radar and weapons systems along with equipment used to track and halt Soviet submarines, some of which carried nuclear warheads. In late 1961, a high-level KGB official by the name of Anatoliy Golitsyn defected to the United States while posted in Helsinki, Finland. Golitsyn provided a wealth of information on KGB networks overseas, and

spoke of having seen Admiralty documents. The KGB, fearing Vassall would be discovered, told him to halt his activities for a time.

Later in 1962 another KBG agent, Yuri Nosenko, made contact with American intelligence officials in Switzerland. Nosenko claimed a gay man had been supplying information to the Soviets from inside the Admiralty, but when officials from MI5 questioned Galbraith, he vouched for Vassall's loyalty. Finally, agents from MI5 embarked on a covert operation, illegally entering Vassall's flat. They discovered a cache of ingeniously hidden espionage artifacts, including some incriminating rolls of film.

Lived in Luxury Apartment Block

British intelligence sources would later claim that Vassall brought suspicion upon himself for his extravagant lifestyle. His job at the Admiralty paid just £15 a week, or £780 a year, but Vassall lived in the luxury Dolphin Square apartment complex near the Thames Embankment. Home to scores of well-heeled politicians and celebrities, Dolphin Square had even been used during World War II as the headquarters of French general Charles DeGaulle and his Free French forces. A favorite of high-ranking Admiralty officials, Dolphin Square had a maritime theme and each of its eight buildings was named after a famous British naval hero. De Gaulle had lived at Grenville House, named after Sir Richard Grenville, who died fighting the Spanish Armada in 1591. Vassall lived in Hood House, named for Samuel Hood, who commanded Royal Navy vessels off the coastline of North America during the American Revolutionary War.

Vassall had usually claimed he had come into an inheritance when asked about his Dolphin Square address and how he could afford a flat with an annual rent of £400, which was more than half his Admiralty salary. MI5 agents had also found custom-made Savile Row suits and hand-lasted shoes in his meticulously kept closet, giving rise to the suspicion that the Soviets were paying him generously for the information he supplied.

Years later, Vassall wrote his memoir, *Vassall: The Autobiography of a Spy.* He recounted one ominous incident in which he arrived at his flat, and "opened the door to find three men dressed in white overalls and with a ladder. They wanted to check the kitchen on the excuse that someone had spilt acid down the sink above mine." He also recalled a day of being tailed, on September 12, 1962. "In spite of my premonitions, it was a complete surprise when, as I left the north-west door of the Admiralty in the Mall and went to cross the road, two men in mackintoshes came forward," he later recalled, according to the *Guardian,* who "flashed me a warrant and asked me to accompany them to a car waiting by the statue of Captain Cook....For hours I poured out what had been bottled up in my mind for years."

"Entrapped by His Lust"

Vassall claimed that he did not believe his espionage activities were that transgressive, or that any of the information he passed along was of serious significance. He assumed he would be transferred out of the Admiralty and into a less sensitive job in the civil service, but instead he was formally charged under Britain's Official Secrets Act. During an interrogation that lasted well into the next morning, Vassall had willingly told his arrestors where to search in his apartment—though they already knew the items were stashed inside a secret compartment in a bookcase. Among the evidence presented in court was a camera, 35-millimeter cassettes, and 140 images of 17 documents from the Admiralty that Vassall had not yet handed over to his London handler during their regular Monday meetings.

Details of Vassall's case and trial, which was heard at the Old Bailey *in camera*, or in a closed court session, were not revealed until the following day, October 23, 1962. The Crown's Attorney General, Sir John Hobson, refuted Vassall's assertions that he had felt lonely and isolated while in Moscow, and described him as a man "entrapped by his lust" into treasonous activities. The judge agreed and sentenced Vassall to 18 years' imprisonment.

Linked to the Cambridge Five

News of a spy inside Admiralty House stunned Britain, but Vassall was not the first such person charged with working for the Soviets. A decade earlier, two high-ranking British diplomats had suddenly vanished. Five years later, in 1956, Guy Burgess and Donald Maclean turned up at a Moscow press conference. The pair were part of a ring of Cambridge University graduates who had harbored secret Communist sympathies for two decades and passed on significant pieces of information to the Soviets. A third diplomat, Kim Philby, defected a few months after Vassall's trial. In 1979 a prominent art historian, Anthony Blunt, was also revealed to have been a member of the so-called "Cambridge Five," recruited to the Soviet foreign service as far back as their college days in the 1930s.

Though Vassall was not part of the elite Cambridge Five, he and some of its members were implicated in details provided by Golitsyn, the KGB defector. Vassall's exposure as a spy was a major embarrassment to Prime Minister Harold Macmillan's government, and questions were raised about MI5's competence. Vassall's former boss, Galbraith, resigned in early November 1962 as under-secretary of state for Scotland, but was cleared of any wrongdoing. A few months later, however, Macmillan's government fell when it was revealed that his Secretary of State for War, John Profumo, had had an extramarital affair with a woman named Christine Keeler in the summer of 1961. At the time, Keeler was also romantically involved with the Soviet naval attaché in London, Yevgeni Ivanov.

Vassall was freed from Maidstone Prison on October 24, 1972. Sidgwick & Jackson published his 1975 memoir, *Vassall: The Autobiography of a Spy*. He lived quietly under a new surname, Phillips, in the north London neighborhood of St. John's Wood, and worked as a clerk and archivist after his release. On November 18, 1996, he suffered a heart attack at the entrance to the Baker Street underground station, and died at the age of 72. Friends did not release news of his death until after his burial, fearing a disruption to the memorial service at Brompton Oratory.

Books

Andrew, Christopher M., *Defend the Realm: The Authorized History of MI5,* Alfred A. Knopf, 2009. Also published as *The Defence of the Realm: The Authorized History of MI5,* Allen Lane, 2009.

Periodicals

Daily Mail (London, England), December 6, 1996.
Guardian (London, England), December 6, 1996.
Independent on Sunday (London, England), December 8, 1996.
New York Times, December 6, 1996.
Times (London, England), October 23, 1962; January 23, 1975; December 6, 1996.

Online

"John William Vassall," Gay History, http://www.gayhistory.wikidot.com/john-william-vassall (August 14, 2011).□

Wilhelm Von Gloeden

German photographer Wilhelm von Gloeden (1856–1931) devoted most of his career to capturing the beauty of Sicily, the Mediterranean isle that became his adopted home. Though he photographed its rocky and idyllic landscapes for widely reproduced postcards, von Gloeden is perhaps best known among art critics and scholars of the history of erotica for the prolific number of male nude images he also shot. "Von Gloeden," asserted Thomas Waugh in the 1996 book *Hard to Imagine: Gay Male Eroticism in Photography and Film From Their Beginnings to Stonewall,* "has emerged from a half a century of subsequent obscurity to become enshrined as the most important gay visual artist of the pre-World War I era

Wilhelm von Gloeden was sometimes referred to as "Baron von Gloeden" in the literature of his day, though his legal claims to the title are tenuous. He came from a Prussian aristocratic family with an estate near Wismar, a Baltic Sea port in the German state of Mecklenburg-Vorpommern. Born at Schloss Volkshagen on September 16, 1856, he was the son of the local *forstmeister,* or head forester in charge of hunting lands preserved for the Mecklenburg royal family. His father, Hermann, died when he was quite young, and his mother, Charlotte Maassen, remarried in 1864. Her new husband, Baron Wilhelm von Hammerstein, would later gain infamy as the fiercely anti-Semitic head of Germany's Conservative Party and newspaper editor in the 1880s. In 1895 he was charged with forgery and embezzlement, and served a stint in prison. Von Gloeden's homosexuality and career would later prompt other members of the family to dispute his connection to the von Gloeden baronetcy.

As a young man von Gloeden studied art history at the University of Rostock, then went on to study under the painter Carl Gehrts at the Kunstakademie in Weimar after 1876. He was forced to halt his education after suffering a bout of some pulmonary illness, perhaps tuberculosis, and subsequently recuperated at a sanatorium on the Baltic Sea. Doctors advised him to relocate to a friendlier climate, and he made his way down the coast of Italy in 1877. He stopped in Naples to visit a cousin, Wilhelm (Guglielmo) von Plüschow, who was four years older than von Gloeden and already established as a photographer in the city. It was von Plüschow who introduced von Gloeden to the technical art of photography, and also apparently to the practice of photographing young male nudes.

Settled in Taormina

Von Gloeden's plan was to visit Sicily, the Mediterranean island that had been a stopping point for various mariners since the eleventh century BCE. Though it was technically part of the kingdom of Italy by that time, Sicily had a darker, more unsettled character than the more heterogeneous Italian mainland, whose inhabitants derided Sicilians as clannish and ungovernable. Von Gloeden knew that another Prussian artist, Otto Geleng, had settled in Sicily in the 1860s, forged a successful career as a landscape painter, and had even been elected mayor of the coastal stronghold of Taormina. Thanks to the success of Geleng's works on the art market, Europeans began making the trek to Sicily, which began to thrive as a tourist destination.

Von Gloeden liked Taormina so much he bought a piece of property there and eventually set up his own photography business. He had pursued it as a hobby, but after the troubles with his family and stepfather, he apparently needed some form of income. His evolution into a serious art photographer came in part through the patronage of Prince Friedrich Franz III, the Grand Duke of

Mecklenburg-Schwerin. Married to a grand duchess of the Russian Romanov dynasty, the duke was believed to have been gay and lived in Sicily for several years. The duke was said to have given von Gloeden a much-prized large-format plate camera.

Von Gloeden gained some early success through his landscape photography, which showed pastoral scenes of life in Taormina, a rustic and picturesque spot where few of the encroachments of the modern world had yet arrived. He began recruiting young Sicilian teenaged boys for nude portraits that rode a narrow line between art and pornography, though in the modern-day ethical sense these would be construed as child pornography, because most of his models were obviously underage—some of them barely in their teens. Around Taormina, however, there was little scandal attached to this practice, for von Gloeden paid his subjects a not insignificant sum for their work and even assigned royalties for later prints. One of his models was Pancrazio Buciunì, who worked as his assistant and was dubbed *Il Moro* (The Moor) for his similarities to North African peoples, many of whom had landed and stayed in Sicily over the centuries. For gay Europeans from devastatingly codified societies like late-nineteenth century Prussia or Victorian England—where same-sex relations were forbiddingly taboo—the southern Mediterranean countries represented a freedom from repressive statutes and social ostracism. Sicily seemed to be one of those places where elements of the pre-Christian acceptance of same-sex relations between adult males and developing males had not been entirely stamped out.

Collected by "Uranians"

In Victorian-era Britain there was a subculture of gay men who called themselves "the Uranians." They named themselves after Aphrodite Urania, a separate Greek deity as defined by passages in Plato's *Symposium*; this Aphrodite of "heavenly love" (*Urania*) was distinguished from Aphrodite Pandemos, the goddess of physical love. As one of the world's first elite and developed civilizations, the Greeks viewed same-sex relationships as an acceptable method of population control, and some even went as far as to deem male-to-male connections as more exalted than traditional heterosexual acts, which were conducted with the goal of procreation. The Irish playwright Oscar Wilde made mention of Uranian tendencies in his letters, and was a collector of von Gloeden's works. Wilde even visited Taormina in December of 1897.

Von Gloeden's nudes found a receptive audience in this subculture. The first major showing of his work was in London in 1893 at the Royal Photographic Society, and included several nudes. "They are instructive in a high degree, and it is not too much to say that such a series is now for the first time placed before the public at a photographic exhibition," noted a *Times* of London correspondent.

Von Gloeden posed his models out of doors, sometimes against whitewashed buildings or against one of the island's lush landscapes. The young males were often draped against enormous vases called amphoras that were a legacy of the long-ago Greek colonization of Sicily, or wore laurel wreaths upon their heads, another symbol of classical art. Von Gloeden used special filters to give the images a more painterly evenness, and also made a special concoction of milk, olive oil, and glycerin as body paint to cover up uneven shades of skin due to sun exposure. The pastoral landscape, wrote Waugh, "evokes the related iconographic tradition, often Christian in origin, of out-of-doors nudity as symbol for prelapsarian innocence, of primordial natural sexuality in a sun-dappled flower-decked Eden. The nude is heroicized as much as it is eroticized in this setting. Much has been written in the von Gloeden fan literature of the effect of sunlight on bronze skin, whose erotic connotation of warmth and sensual pleasure is indulged in by the pale and consumptive northern photographers."

Possibly Inspired 1923 Picasso Work

Nine years after Wilde's visit to Taormina an even more famous Englishman paid a visit to von Gloeden's studio while wintering on Sicily: the Prince of Wales, England's future King Edward VII—though his views on von Gloeden's artistic direction were likely significantly distant from those of Wilde. Another famous German, industrial magnate Friedrich Alfred Krupp, favored the Italian island of Capri—an even more tolerant place for closeted homosexuals of the era—and was said to have been a collector of von Gloeden's works. In 1902, a German political party publicly outed Krupp as a homosexual, and he committed suicide days later.

Galleries on both sides of the Atlantic mounted exhibitions of von Gloeden's photography in the first decade of the twentieth century. His first show in the United States was in Philadelphia in 1902, followed by exhibits in Marseilles and Nice in 1903, and Dresden in 1909. Art historians believe that one of Spanish artist Pablo Picasso's paintings from 1923, *Pipes of Pan,* was based on one of von Gloeden's images from 1901. Picasso's work showed two young males, wearing the briefest of coverings, posed against a backdrop that clearly evokes a sun-dappled Mediterranean climate.

Legacy Targeted by Fascists

Scholars of von Gloeden's work surmise he may have kept a special private collection of images that were shown only to trusted clients. The most productive period of his career ended with the onset of World War I, when he was forced to leave Sicily. He spent the war years in Germany, but returned to Taormina in 1918. After this date, there were no more new works, but he made prints from his vast repository of glass plate negatives and sold those on the art market. His archives contained at least 3,000 original images, and perhaps even twice that number. In the years before his death he willed his estate to Buciunì, who continued to make prints after von Gloeden's death in Taormina on February 16, 1931. Sicily had come under the rule of Italian Fascists by then, a powerful right-wing, anti-Communist political movement led by Benito Mussolini. After coming to power in 1922, Mussolini pushed through stringent new laws that the Roman Catholic Church and more conservative Italians eagerly welcomed, including prohibitions on birth control and pornography.

In the mid-1930s the Italian government authorities raided the von Gloeden archives, destroying an estimated 2,000 of the glass plate negatives, and arrested Buciunì. He was prosecuted on pornography distribution charges. For this reason, surviving and authenticated works by von Gloeden fetch high prices on the art market. Some original negatives are safeguarded by the Florence gallery Fratelli Alinari, while rare prints are either in private collections or in institutions like the J. Paul Getty Museum in Malibu, California. Von Gloeden's place in gay and lesbian culture remained largely forgotten, save for a mention in a 1949 work by French diplomat and novelist Roger Peyrefitte, *Les amours singulières,* in which Peyrefitte described Sicily as a welcoming place for gay men.

In the 1970s, von Gloeden's works were rediscovered by art history scholars focusing on gay artists and a closeted subculture of the past, who deemed his works to be the first critically accepted photographs of the male body. "As most male nude photographs up to his time had been 'academies'—studio studies of mature individuals that were intended for artists and that made no effort at naturalness—von Gloeden's work was a kind of treasure trove for artists," wrote Vicki Goldberg in the *New York Times.* "In his own time, he had an influence on. . .Maxfield Parrish, and after his death on Cecil Beaton, Andy Warhol, Robert Mapplethorpe and Bruce Weber." As late as 2007 works from von Gloeden caused a stir in Milan when an exhibit titled *Arte e Omosessualita: da von Gloeden a Pierre et Gilles* (Art and Homosexuality: From von Gloeden to Pierre and Gilles) was planned for the northern Italian city. The show was mounted instead at the Palazzina Reale in Florence.

Books

Ellenzweig, Allen, *Male Images from Durieu/Delacroix to Mapplethorpe,* Columbia University Press, 1992.
Waugh, Thomas, *Hard to Imagine: Gay Male Eroticism in Photography and Film From Their Beginnings to Stonewall,* Columbia University Press, 1996, pp. 72, 101.

Periodicals

New York Times, August 13, 2000.
Times (London, England), September 25, 1893; January 8, 1909. □

Carl Ferdinand von Graefe

The Polish-born German surgeon Carl Ferdinand von Graefe (1787–1840) is renowned among modern plastic surgeons as a key pioneer of rhinoplasty—the "nose job" in popular terminology. He was apparently the first person to use the term "plastic" (German: plastik) to describe cosmetic surgery.

V on Graefe's contributions to surgical technique went far beyond rhinoplasty, which at first was used to repair injuries or serious deformities rather than simply for aesthetic purposes. Serving Prussia in the Napoleonic Wars, he made major advances in the care of injured military personnel. Von Graefe introduced major refinements to several surgical procedures and described them in a set of widely read papers. In his own day he was something of a celebrity surgeon, with talents in demand among Europe's royal families. Above all, though, von Graefe's name lives on because of his 1818 pamphlet "Rhinoplastik oder die Kunst, den Verlust der Nase organisch zu ersetzen" (Rhinoplasty, or the Art of Organically Replacing the Lost Nose). According to Blair O. Rogers, writing in *Plastic and Reconstructive Surgery,* some historians consider von Graefe "the founder of *modern* plastic surgery because of the scope of his early contributions to this field—including articles on palatoplasty, rhinoplasty, blepharoplasty, etc."

Excelled in Studies and Career

Carl (or Karl) Ferdinand von Graefe was born in Warsaw, then part of the Polish-Lithuanian Commonwealth, on March 8, 1787. His father was a secretary to a nobleman, Count Moszynsky. He grew up mostly in the small town of Dolsk, where he was homeschooled by a tutor. When he was 14 he enrolled in a *Gynmasium* (a German high school oriented toward the teaching of the classics) and then in Dresden's City School. At these institutions he excelled in his studies of ancient Greek and Latin, and emerged bearing very strong letters of recommendation from his teachers.

Matriculating at the Collegium Medico-Chirurgicum in Dresden, he almost immediately showed promise as a surgeon. To complete his medical education, he had to dodge the first events of the Napoleonic Wars. He moved to the University of Halle in 1805, impressing his pathology professor so much that he put the still-teenaged von Graefe in charge of the city's hospital. When the university was temporarily shuttered after Napoleon's armies invaded the region, von Graefe moved again, graduating from the University of Leipzig with the title of Doctor of Medicine and Surgery in 1807, at the age of 20. His dissertation dealt with a type of lip mole that often turned cancerous because of inadequate treatment.

One of von Graefe's teachers recommended him for a plum post as physician to a nobleman, Duke Alexis of Anhalt-Bernburg. Von Graefe used this post as an opportunity to investigate the curative powers of a nearby spring that he dubbed the Alexisbad (Alexis Spa) after learning that its waters had high iron content. Although the health benefits of mineral springs eventually fell out of scientific regard, von Graefe's Alexisbad became one of Germany's most famous places to "take the waters," attracting visitors from all over Europe after he published a series of papers outlining the benefits of the spa water. These efforts spread von Graefe's name widely, and he received high-profile job offers to become professor of surgery at the University of Königsberg and again at the University of Halle. He turned those offers down in order to care for the ailing Duke Alexis, but in 1810 he accepted the post of full professor of surgery and director of the clinical-surgical-ophthalmologic institute at the University of Berlin.

Only 23, von Graefe was the very picture of a rising young medical star, admired by the Prussian public but hated by some of his rivals. His talent as a surgeon was clear: during one period he performed 13 amputations, losing not a single patient and seeing them all essentially healed within three weeks—an astonishing feat in the early nineteenth century. He published a book on amputation in 1812 and dedicated it to the Kaiser. In 1813, however, von Graefe gave up his professorship, leaving his comfortable post to volunteer his services to the Prussian military during the later phase of the Napoleonic Wars.

Von Graefe was made surgeon-general of an entire Prussian army division, becoming commander of all the military hospitals between the Rhine and Vistula rivers, encompassing a large part of present-day Germany and Poland, and of Prussian hospitals in the Netherlands as well. The hospitals under his command were recognized, by military leaders from friendly and hostile powers alike, as models of organization, and they reportedly rendered aid to 100,000 soldiers. Von Graefe published a series of practical guides that were invaluable for military surgeons, outlining state-of-the-art procedures for dealing with common battlefield medical issues such as Egyptian ophthalmia (a serious type of conjunctivitis).

These accomplishments made von Graefe one of the most famous surgeons in Europe by the end of the war in 1815. Honors flowed in, and his full title at the University of Berlin (where he returned as professor) is worth stating in full: he was (according to Rogers) "Royal (Privy) Councillor and Director General of the Army Medical Services; Co-Director of the Medical Surgical Academy and of the Friedrich-Wilhelm Institute of Berlin; Full Professor of Medicin and Surgery (at the same University); Full Member of the Imperial and Royal Academies of Paris, Padual, Naples, Moscow—as well as of the Universities of Pest (Hungary), Wilna, and Cracow; Commander (1st Class) and Knight of the Prussian, Russian, French, Swedish, Bavarian, Hanoverian, and Royal Hessian Orders (decorations), etc."

Advanced Rhinosplasty Procedure

Although von Graefe is most often identified with rhinoplasty, he did not originate the procedure, which dates back to ancient India. Surgeons in Italy and England had also outlined new methods of rhinoplasty in the years before von Graefe turned his attention to the field, and von Graefe's contribution lay mostly in improvements he made to the procedures followed by a sixteenth-century Italian surgeon named Tagliacozzi. Von Graefe's 1818 "Rhinoplastik" monograph, in fact, outlined several successful surgeries: one of Tagliacozzi's (who used arm skin), an Indian example (in which skin was cut from the forehead to make the new nose tissue), and his own, in which he immediately attached a flap of arm skin to the nose rather than waiting for it to thicken. His monograph was notable for its tone of sympathy with those afflicted by facial deformities. "We have compassion when we see people on crutches," von Graefe wrote (as quoted by Sander L. Gillman in *Making the Body Beautiful: A Cultural History of Aesthetic Surgery,* Princeton, 2000. "Being crippled does not stop them from being happy and pleasant in society...[But those] who have suffered a deformation of the face, even if it is partially disguised by a mask, create disgust in our imagination."

More significant was von Graefe's role in the history of surgery to repair a cleft palate, colloquially known as a harelip. Historians credit von Graefe as the first surgeon to undertake an operation to correct a cleft palate, in 1816. That operation failed, but by 1820 he had successfully completed a cleft palate operation—and so had several other surgeons in other countries, each of them clamoring for credit. Von Graefe also notched several less common surgical firsts, including the first successful partial resection (removal) of the lower jaw in 1821 and the first ligation (tying-together) of the innominate artery, the vessel that comes from the aortic arch, in 1822.

Von Graefe was also recognized as an excellent eye surgeon and performed many cataract-removal operations. Some medical historians consider his 1823 paper on Egyptian ophthalmia his most significant written work. In 1830 von Graefe attempted to escape the stress of his high-flying career by taking a vacation in southern Italy, but the trip was disrupted when he was wounded in the shoulder by an accidental musket shot originating from one of his friends.

He returned to Berlin, where he earned plaudits for his work in combatting a cholera outbreak in the city in 1831.

In 1840 von Graefe traveled to the city of Hanover to perform an operation on the crown prince of the small kingdom of which the city was a part. He died there suddenly on July 4, 1840. A lengthy memorial notice posted in the British medical journal *The Lancet* in November of that year pointed out that von Graefe died a wealthy man and that "his loss is universally deplored, and his fame immortal."

Books

Gillman, Sander L., *Making the Body Beautiful: A Cultural History of Aesthetic Surgery,* Princeton, 2000.

Maltz, Maxwell, *Evolution of Plastic Surgery,* Froben, 1946.

Periodicals

Lancet, 1840, vol. 1.

Plastic and Reconstructive Surgery, December 1970. □

Joseph Warioba

The Tanzanian political leader and attorney Joseph Warioba (born 1940) served his country as Prime Minister between 1985 and 1990. He has since become a respected elder statesman in the East African political sphere, active in both national and international affairs.

Warioba represented a new breed of East African political leader, educated abroad and dedicated to the rule of law and the ideal of transparency. His political patron was Tanzania's first president, Julius Nyerere, and he and Nyerere shared a similar ethnic background. But the mild-mannered Warioba was no fire-breathing African nationalist leader. After leaving the Tanzanian government in the early 1990s, he embarked on a second career as a leader in the generally successful effort to foster democracy in Africa. Warioba has been active in election monitoring with delegations from the U.S.-based Carter Center, led by former president Jimmy Carter, and he has been a relentless critic of corruption at home.

Majored in Law

Joseph Sinde Warioba was born on September 3, 1940, in Bunda (one source indicates Ikizu), in the Mara District on the shores of Lake Victoria in what was then British-controlled Tanzania. Like Nyerere, he is a member of the Zanaki ethnic group. Warioba attended the Sarawe and Ikizu primary schools and the Bwiru and Tabora secondary schools in his home area. In a *Tanzania Daily News* interview reproduced on *AllAfrica.com,* Warioba recalled the discrimination Africans experienced at the hands of white colonizers: "I went to Bwiru Secondary School and used to travel from Musoma to Mwanza by steamer. The steamer had three classes—First class, second class and third class. First class was for whites only, second class for Asians and third class for Africans. And, the third class was on the deck with various luggage and cargo. So we used to be grouped together with cargo. It was the same on trains." Warioba went on to Dar es Salaam University in the capital of newly independent Tanzania, majoring in law. He graduated in 1966 and immediately took a job in the young country's attorney general's office.

The young lawyer immediately attracted notice from his superiors and was sent to represent Tanzania at the United Nations Human Rights Conference in Tehran, Iran. From 1968 to 1970 Warioba served as a staff attorney for the Dar es Salaam city council. In 1970 he traveled to the Netherlands, earning a master's degree at the Academy of International Law in The Hague. He then returned to the national government as director of the legal and international organizations division of Tanzania's foreign affairs ministry from 1971 to 1975.

During that period, Warioba began his involvement with the conferences that led to the signing of the United Nations Law of the Sea treaty in 1982, advocating for the rights of developing countries in the management of the world's ocean resources. From 1976 to 1980 he held seminars on the Law of the Sea at the University of Dar es Salaam. After the treaty was signed, Warioba was elected chairman of the Law of the Sea Preparatory Commission, serving until 1987. At home Warioba served as Tanzania's assistant attorney general in 1975 and 1976, winning a promotion to attorney general in 1977. In that capacity he substantially rewrote many of the country's laws.

Became Prime Minister Under Mwinyi

In 1983 Warioba was appointed minister of justice—a cabinet-level post (attorney general was not). With the election of **357**

Tanzania's second president, Ali Hassan Mwinyi, in 1985, Warioba was elevated to prime minister, replacing a politician who was not allowed to serve because he and Mwinyi were both members of the same ethnic group. As prime minister, Warioba was Tanzania's chief executive, responsible for implementing Mwinyi's relaxation of Nyerere's socialist-oriented policies. He was also the secretary of Tanzania's defense and security committee, a powerful post.

Warioba aided in the reform of Tanzania's economy, which had suffered during the final years of Nyerere's rule. He presented a new five-year economic plan, called on the country's bickering political parties to cooperate, and exhorted Tanzania's workers to greater discipline and efficiency. By 1987 Warioba could point to a increase in the economic growth rate to 3.8 percent, up from 2.5 percent the previous year, and to a variety of other positive agricultural and economic indicators. He remained active in the foreign-policy realm as well, calling on the United Kingdom to pressure South Africa for a quick end to the apartheid system of racial segregation, and urging unity among South African anti-apartheid forces themselves.

In March of 1990 Mwinyi reappointed Warioba as prime minister. Warioba began his second term with a speech directed at Tanzanian journalists, urging them to cover the issues facing the country clearly during the upcoming general elections. In November of 1990, however, Warioba was removed as prime minister and replaced by John Malecela, who according to some observers was personally closer to Mwinyi. In 1991 Warioba was stripped of his parliamentary seat even though he had won election to it by a margin of 35,000 to 4,000 votes. Tanzania's electoral commission ruled that Warioba had improperly used the resources of his office in the campaign.

Exposed Corruption Problem

Whatever the truth behind these charges, the debacle only paved the way for a new phase of Warioba's career. He soon emerged as a severe critic of corruption in his own country, assuming the chairmanship of a presidential commission on corruption in 1996. Warioba did not try to sugarcoat Tanzania's corruption problem, even in conversation with foreign observers. "In my country, you have to pay a bribe for everything," he told Michael Switow of the *Christian Science Monitor*. Warioba returned to the International Tribunal for the Law of the Sea as a judge from 1996 to 1999.

He also became more active in a regional role in East Africa. In the 2000s Warioba served as a judge on the East African Court of Justice, a judicial body connected with the East African Community (a group of East African nations that cooperated economically). In 2003 he urged Ugandans to implement term limits for politicians during a keynote address at a regional conference on political succession, saying (as quoted by *Africa News*) that "[a] fixed term will facilitate a smooth succession. It's a system which will remove us from the 'traditional chief mindset' and also prevent ushering in dictators."

Warioba's most visible role in the new century was as an election observer, both on his own and as part of groups connected with the Carter Center. In the mid-2000s he led a group of election monitors sponsored by the Commonwealth group of nations in Nigeria and Malawi, and he also joined teams of international election observers in Zambia, Nigeria, and Ethiopia. In 2011 he joined Jimmy Carter, former United Nations Secretary General Kofi Annan, and several other international leaders at the head of a group of more than 100 observers to oversee the largely peaceful referendum that led to the independence of South Sudan, as of the end of 2011 the world's youngest independent country.

In his later years Warioba only intensified his campaign against corruption in Tanzania. "Corruption is an impediment in the country's development and shatters people's dreams for better lives," he said in a 2007 speech to a group of journalists (as quoted by *BBC Monitoring Africa*), saying that corruption was "skyrocketing" in Tanzania. Even the poor, known in Swahili as "wananchi," felt that they had to give bribes in order to obtain basic public services. "Corruption can only be got rid of by action, not by too much talking," he warned, adding that "[t]he country can only manage to flush out corruption if there is cultural and behavioral change among the public in general." He favored the strengthening of existing anti-corruption agencies within government rather than forming a sequence of new commissions and task forces.

By 2011 Warioba had become a revered elder figure in Tanzanian society. He lent his name to a campaign to raise 500 million Tanzanian shillings for his alma mater, the University of Dar es Salaam, and he delivered a commencement address at Mzumbe University that year. "Presently, it is very shocking to see that we have lost our ethics and the discipline left behind by the Father of the Nation," he said, according to an article in *The Citizen*, referring to Nyerere. "People seek leadership position to amass wealth and not to be servants of the people."

Books

Africa Who's Who, Africa Journal 1981.
International Tribunal for the Law of the Sea Yearbook, Nijhoff, 1999.
Peter, Chris Maina, and Fritz Kopsieker, *Political Succession in East Africa: In Search for a Limited Leadership,* Friedrich Ebert Stiftung, 2006.
Rake, Alan, *Who's Who in Africa: Leaders for the 1990s,* Scarecrow, 1992.

Periodicals

Africa News, July 12, 2003; April 10, 2007; August 20, 2008; July 18, 2011.
BBC Monitoring Africa—Political, September 28, 2007.
BBC Summary of World Broadcasts, November 13, 1985; September 9, 1986; May 12 1987; October 6, 1987; November 24, 1987; April 13, 1989; June 16 ,1989; March 15, 1990; July 21 1990; October 23, 1991.
Christian Science Monitor, October 15, 1997.
The Citizen (Dar es Salaam), October 11, 2011; November 17, 2011.

Online

"Jimmy Carter, Kofi Annan, Joseph Warioba, and John Hardman to Lead Carter Center Delegation to Observe Referendum on Self-Determination of Southern Sudan," *Carter Center,* http://www.cartercenter.org/news/pr/sudan-010311.html (January 10, 2012).
"Progress Cause of Many Challenges—Warioba," *AllAfrica.com* (November 28, 2011), http://allafrica.com/stories/20111130 1162.html (January 10, 2012). □

Martha Washington

American First Lady Martha Washington (1731–1802) became the surrogate mother of the new nation as wife of the first President, George Washington.

American First Lady Martha Washington helped establish precedents for future executive spouses as the nation's inaugural first lady. A mother figure for the country even before its formal existence, Washington served as her husband George Washington's "worthy partner" for over 40 years, offering support to the general and his soldiers during the American Revolution before becoming the new nation's top social hostess during Washington's two terms as president. Her gracious temperament made her a well-respected figure both during her lifetime and afterward. Washington's memory was honored in the centuries after her death, as she became the first woman to grace U.S. currency in the late 1800s, the first woman to appear on a U.S. postage stamp in 1902, and the namesake of a World War I-era transport ship.

Born June 2, 1731, in New Kent County, Virginia, Washington was the eldest child of planter and county clerk John Dandridge and his wife, Frances (Jones) Dandridge. On her mother's side, Washington traced her American lineage to at least 1664; her father had immigrated to the colonies from England as a teenager. Although respectable, the Dandridge family was not among the most prominent of the colony. The young Patsy, as Washington was known from birth, shared the family's six-room home with her parents and a growing number of younger siblings. Washington helped care for her seven younger siblings from the time of her own childhood. "No wonder motherliness was one of her distinguishing attributes as a woman," commented Patricia Brady in *Martha Washington: An American Life,* "or that she always enjoyed the company of young people." Although little evidence survives, historians assume that the young Washington received an education typical of a girl of her era and class, learning basic literacy, music, needlework, and perhaps plantation management from her parents or private tutors.

Became Wife and Wealthy Widow

Washington grew into an appealing young lady who won the admiration of the much older and wealthier Daniel Parke Custis while still in her teens. Custis's father initially opposed the match, wishing his heir to marry a woman of higher station who carried a higher dowry than the modest sum that Washington's family could provide. The young Washington, however, had a force of personality belied by her five-foot-tall frame; she seemed to have found a way to plead her and her nearly forty-year-old suitor's case to his domineering father. This boldness won the day. Soon after giving his blessing to the marriage, the elder Custis passed away, leaving much of his considerable fortune to his son. When Washington married at her parents' home on May 15, 1750, she entered the upper echelons of Virginia society. The newlyweds then settled into

their new home on the Custis plantation, named—oddly enough—White House.

By all indications, the marriage was a happy one, and the Custis household soon grew with the birth of Daniel Parke in 1751. A second son, John Parke, followed in 1754, along with daughters Frances Parke and Martha Parke in 1753 and 1756, respectively. This familial happiness proved short-lived, howeve; Daniel and Frances both died before reaching their fifth birthdays, and Custis himself passed away unexpectedly after a brief illness in the summer of 1757. His widow, then just 26 years old, found herself with control of some 17,500 acres of Virginia land and 300 enslaved Africans; like many Virginians of the time, she seems to have had no moral concerns over slavery, regarding the practice as one of economic necessity but also taking efforts to ensure the comfort and stability of her slaves' lives.

Custis had died intestate, leaving Washington to discharge his debts and handle other complex legal matters alongside her new duties as head of White House. Nothing in the young widow's life had prepared her to handle the financial and business management of such a large enterprise, but Washington seems to have stepped up to the task bravely. She acted as her own plantation manager, making business decisions and relying on a younger brother for legal advice. But it is unlikely that Washington expected to remain a widow for long. Along with the attraction of her great wealth and genial personality, the young woman seems to have been somewhat more physically pleasing than later portraits might suggest. A portrait of Washington created in 2009 using sophisticated age regression "depicts a slim, alluring and self-possessed woman ready to take on the world," assessed Kim A. O'Connell in an article for *American History.*

Married George Washington

Indeed, the young widow soon had a serious suitor in the person of George Washington. A fellow Virginian, Washington had trained as a surveyor and fought in the French and Indian War on the colonial frontier earlier in the decade. But he had not yet married, perhaps due to a long-standing but completely hopeless affection for an older married neighbor. In 1758, however, Washington determined to focus his attentions on the wealthy widow Custis. Probably, the two were already acquainted from Williamsburg social events; undoubtedly, their personalities and outlooks on life made them a compatible match. The widow saw in the young soldier a person worthy of entrusting her newfound fortune, and, more importantly, the care of her two young children. The Washingtons married at White House on January 6, 1759, and soon settled in at Mount Vernon, the Washington plantation. Although he fathered no children with his new wife, George Washington proved a dedicated stepfather to the Custis children, and the next several years passed in contented family life. Tragedy struck in 1773, however, when Washington's remaining daughter from her first marriage died suddenly, probably as a complication of lifelong epilepsy.

The onset of the American Revolution further disturbed the couple's comfortable existence. At the First Continental Congress in 1775, Washington was appointed head of the Continental Army; soon after, his wife left Mount Vernon at the general's urging to stay with extended family and, that fall, to join her husband at the army's winter quarters in Cambridge, Massachusetts. Along the way, she stopped off at Philadelphia, where she encountered both formal fussing over her as the wife of an important Patriot and a series of rumors claiming that she had Loyalist sympathies that had divided her from her husband. Washington's reunion with her husband was a happy one, however, and she soon began domestic activities at his winter camp, including forming a sewing circle to help single soldiers care for their clothing and to provide bandages for the military hospital. Soldiers and camp dwellers regarded Washington as a kindly matriarch, and she in turn seems to have held a special motherly regard for her husband's men. Although Washington returned to Virginia when the army resumed operations in the spring, she rejoined her husband each winter at camp, picking up her role as surrogate mother to the Continental Army. Yet camp life also brought personal tragedy. Washington's surviving son from her first marriage died in 1781 after accepting the general's invitation to join the family at Yorktown, the site of the final American victory over the British.

Following the close of the war, the Washingtons returned to Mount Vernon. However, this retirement did not last long; by 1787, the new U.S. government established under the Articles of Confederation had proven so problematic that a convention was called for its revision. George Washington attended and was named head of the convention, which soon abandoned efforts to simply revise the Articles in favor of writing an entirely new national constitution. That fall, Washington rejoined his wife at Mount Vernon, but this interlude again proved shorter than anticipated. In 1789, Washington—much to the dismay of both him and his wife—was unanimously elected the first president under the terms of the 1787 Constitution. He left the plantation for the national capital at New York City, where his wife joined him soon after.

Served as the Inaugural First Lady

With no precedents for their conduct, the Washingtons had to make their own way in public life. Ever a gregarious hostess, Washington disliked her husband's declaration that the couple would not dine in any private households. Writing in *American First Ladies: Their Lives and Their Legacy*, Brady reported that Washington complained, "I am more like a state prisoner than anything else, there is (sic) certain bounds set for me which I must depart from . . . " The Washingtons held weekly receptions at their home, where the First Lady, often seated alongside friend and fellow executive spouse Abigail Adams, generally garnered praise and affection for the genial welcome with which she received visitors. Although critics accused the Washingtons of behaving in too royal a fashion for a democratic republic, they took great pains to avoid putting on airs; after considering several options such as "Lady Washington" or "Madame President" as her title—the term "First Lady" was not used for several more decades—Washington determined that she should simply be known by the unassuming "Mrs. Washington."

In 1790, the Washingtons left New York to live in Philadelphia, which was to serve as a temporary capital while the new seat of government was built at the freshly-created District of Columbia. Then more cosmopolitan than New York, the city of Philadelphia proved more congenial to the First Lady. She enjoyed a greater variety of social engagements, as the president slowly began allowing the family to attend private functions, and filled her life with entertainments and conversation with her circle of extended family, friends, and young people working for her husband. Yet the president disliked the strains of his office, especially as political strife rose between factions headed by Alexander Hamilton and Thomas Jefferson. The leader wished to retire to private life at the end of his first term, but his announcement of his intentions to do so garnered urgent pleas to reconsider from several leading members of the government. Washington gave in and agreed to serve a second term, much to the dismay of his wife. These concerns were not unwarranted. Washington faced criticism from the press during his second term amidst the turmoil created by the Whiskey Rebellion in western Pennsylvania, the conflicts between Western settlers and Native Americans, and even the spreading influence of French Revolutionary ideas. Although the president retained solid support from the people, he firmly declined to run for a third term, setting a precedent that lasted until the administration of Franklin Delano Roosevelt.

The stresses of the presidency had worn on both Washingtons, and the couple found great relief in their retirement to Mount Vernon following the inauguration of Washington's successor John Adams in 1797. The former chief executive died in late 1799, however, cutting short this respite. The death of her husband of over four decades devastated Washington. She burned the letters that she and her husband had exchanged over the years, and otherwise occupied herself by receiving visitors who offered condolences and by responding to written requests for mementos of her fallen spouse. General Washington had left Mount Vernon in the control of his wife for the remainder of her lifetime, and several family members and their young children joined Washington there. Visitors, however, noted her flagging spirits, and before long

Washington's health began to fail. She died at Mount Vernon on May 22, 1802, following an illness; three days later, she was buried alongside her husband in the family tomb. "She was the worthy partner of the worthiest of men, and those who witnessed their conduct could not determine which excelled in their different characters, both were so well sustained on every occasion," proclaimed her obituary in the *Alexandria Advertiser and Commercial Intelligencer*. History has largely agreed with this assessment, noting the quiet but important supporting role that Washington played as the first First Lady.

Books

Brady, Patricia. *Martha Washington: An American Life,* Penguin, 2006.

Gould, Lewis L., ed. *American First Ladies: Their Lives and Legacies,* Routledge, 2001.

Schneider, Dorothy and Carl J. Schneider, *First Ladies: A Biographical Dictionary,* Facts on Files, 2005.

Periodicals

Alexandria Advertiser and Commercial Intelligencer, May 25, 1802.

Online

"First Lady Biography: Martha Washington," National First Ladies Library, http://www.firstladies.org/biographies/firstladies.aspx?biography=1 (September 14, 2011).

"Martha Dandridge Custis Washington," White House, http://www.whitehouse.gov/about/liveproduction/martha-dandridge-custis-washington (September 14, 2011).

"Martha Washington: A Life," Roy Rosenzweig Center for History and New Media/ Mount Vernon, http://marthawashington.us/exhibits/show/martha-washington--a-life/ (September 14, 2011).

"Washington, Martha Dandridge Custis," American National Biography, http://www.anb.org/articles/02/02-00333.html (September 14, 2011).□

Carl Wieman

American physicist Carl Wieman (born 1951) shared the 2001 Nobel Prize for Physics, honoring their creation of a Bose-Einstein condensate, a new form of matter theoretically predicted in the 1920s by Albert Einstein and Indian physicist Satyendra Nath Bose.

Wieman's career since he received his award has been as remarkable as the activities that led up to it. Rather than expanding on the ideas that won him the award or plunging into new areas of research, Wieman virtually ceased his activities as a research physicist and began work on a new project: the improvement of undergraduate physics instruction. He has pioneered new methods of teaching that rely less on traditional lectures and more on group work among students—a pattern that he

believed was responsible in part for his own scientific creativity. Wieman's work has led him to leave the University of Colorado, where he accomplished his Nobel Prize–winning research; he has established a new science education center at the University of British Columbia in Canada. In 2010 Wieman was named associate director for science in the White House Office of Science and Technology Policy by U.S. President Barack Obama.

Grew Up in Lumbering Community

Carl Edwin Wieman was born in Corvallis, Oregon, on March 26, 1951. His father was a lumber mill worker, and he grew up far from university centers of learning; the nearest store was several miles away by dirt road, and major shopping trips, which invariably included a trip to the public library, occurred only once a week. "At the time," Wieman wrote in his Nobel Prize autobiography, "I was quite envious that my friends had television while we did not, but in retrospect I am very grateful that I spent this time reading instead of watching TV." The family moved to Corvallis when Wieman was in the eighth grade, and his mother was active for a time as a social worker. As a high school student he was enthusiastic about literature, writing, chess, tennis, and improvised construction projects he undertook with his older brother, Howard.

Although he had no clear idea that he wanted to become a scientist, Wieman applied to the Massachusetts Institute of Technology (MIT) and was accepted—partly, he believed, because he had grown up in the forests of Oregon. As a freshman he devoted his attention not to science classes but to tennis and squash, even switching from his right arm to his left after injuring the former from overuse. When he injured his left arm as well, he plunged into physics with typical single-minded energy. Wieman became part of a research group led by famed MIT physicist Daniel Kleppner. He felt that he actually learned physics by working on independent research. He "quickly adopted a philosophy of taking as few courses as possible," he wrote in his Nobel autobiography, and when he found he needed to know some aspect of the standard physics curriculum, he studied it on his own. To those who asserted that this approach worked only because he was an exceptional student, Wieman responded that nothing in his early college career suggested that he had remarkable abilities as a scientist.

As an undergraduate, Wieman had already gained experience in using lasers to manipulate atomic structure, a new field at the time. After graduating from MIT, he attended graduate school at Stanford University in California, working with physicist Ted Hänsch on applications of tunable dye lasers and investigating what is known as parity violation in atoms, a condition in which atoms unexpectedly behave asymmetrically. Wieman received his PhD from Stanford in 1977. In that year he was hired as a research scientist at the University of Michigan, gaining a promotion to assistant professor in 1979.

Materials Moved into Hallway

Wieman's experiences at Michigan were not happy ones. He attempted to develop new experiments in laser manipulation, but, as he recalled to Dan Curry of the *Chronicle of Higher Education,* he "naively ran afoul of departmental politics" and "offended the large ego of a powerful and vindictive person in the department." After Wieman's lab was banished to a hallway to make room for graduate student offices, he resigned his position and moved to the University of Colorado as an associate professor in 1984. Wieman and fellow physicist Sarah Gilbert moved their belongings into their new Boulder home, and flew to Oregon for their wedding. By 1984, several other scientists, including future U.S. Energy Secretary Steven Chu, were at work on the idea of using lasers to study the behavior of atoms in supercold temperatures just a fraction of a degree above absolute zero (-459.67 Fahrenheit, the temperature at which all molecular motion ceases).

In the late 1980s and early 1990s Wieman began to work closely with Colorado post-doctoral researcher Eric Cornell, and the two began to think of themselves as kindred spirits. Working together in labs around a hallway corner from each other, the two began to generate a flurry of experiments that broke new ground in the understanding of how supercooled atoms behaved. Their ultimate grail was the Bose-Einstein condensate: a unique grid-like structure of sub-atomic particles that Bose and Einstein had considered theoretically possible, but not of great importance given the total impossibility, at the time, of realizing such a thing.

By 1995 Wieman and Cornell felt they were closing in on the creation of a Bose-Einstein condensate, as were several other researchers. In May and June of that year their team put in 17-hour days, trying to find better ways of viewing the laser-generated clouds of chilled rubidium atoms they were creating, and on June 5, 1995, at 10:54 a.m., a unique shape, like a cherry pit, appeared. Skeptical at first, Wieman and Cornell went on to verify their results, and Cornell delivered them to a stunned audience at a conference of physicists on the Italian island of Capri. "It was great fun," Cornell told Lisa Levitt Ryckman of Denver's *Rocky Mountain News.* "It was enormously fun. It was off-the-scale fun."

Wieman received a spate of awards in the late 1990s as other labs duplicated his results. Thus it was not a complete surprise when Wieman, Cornell, and MIT researcher Wolfgang Ketterle, who performed a similar experiment using sodium atoms four months later, shared the 2001 Nobel Prize for Physics. Wieman heard about the award from his brother Lynd, who had been expecting him to win. The three winners shared a cash prize of $943,000 from the Royal Swedish Academy of Sciences.

Contributed Prize Money to Start Center

From his share of $314,333, Wieman immediately contributed $250,000 as seed money to begin the next phase of his career: the creation of a science education foundation that he hoped to establish at Colorado. His plan was to attract a mix of public and private support to finance the foundation, but he was disappointed to find that support did not materialize. Disillusioned, Wieman accepted an offer from the University of British Columbia in Vancouver, Canada, to establish the center there, with initial financing of $10.6 million. He was also named professor of physics there. Wieman blamed the failure of his initiative at Colorado partly on a university culture that privileged athletics over academics. "If you want to have any sort of large-scale education initiative, where you're really focusing on education, you need people at the highest levels to put thought and attention into it," he told Jim Erickson of the *Rocky Mountain News.* "If our Board of Regents spent half the time on discussions of how to improve the education for students that they do on athletics, it would be a very different university." In Canada, Wieman later criticized funding cuts that occurred under the administration of Prime Minister Stephen Harper.

Taking up his position in British Columbia in January of 2007, Wieman led a team that within a few years generated dramatic and controversial results. His study involved a large undergraduate physics class that was divided into two halves beginning with the 12th week in a semester. One group of students received traditional lectures, while the second worked in collaborative teams under an instructor, working together to master material pertaining to electromagnetic waves. The second group's scores on an exam administered after the comparison period were twice as high as those of the traditional control group. Some experts cautioned that the use of members of Wieman's own research team as teachers in the study might have skewed the results, but Weiman responded that undergraduates in large lecture courses rarely form strong personal interactions with their instructors.

Wieman's study appeared in the spring of 2011 and seemed likely to prompt further research. By that time Wieman was serving as associate director of the White House Office of Science and Technology Policy in the Obama administration, a position in which he continued to discuss reform in American science education. In an era of controversies over science in general, the position brought a new set of challenges for one of America's most brilliant and outspoken scientists.

Periodicals

Chronicle of Higher Education, November 23, 2001; April 7, 2006.

Denver Post, March 22, 2006.

Globe & Mail (Toronto, Ontario, Canada), October 30, 2007; January 31, 2009.

New York Times, May 17, 2011.

Rocky Mountain News (Denver, CO), October 10, 2001; December 8, 2001; September 4, 2002; March 21, 2006.

States News Service, August 30, 2011.

Targeted News Service, May 13, 2011.

Toronto Star, May 13, 2011.

Online

"Carl Wieman: Autobiography," *Nobel Foundation,* http://www.nobelprize.org/nobel_prizes/physics/laureates/2001/wieman-autobio.html (October 27, 2011). □

Lois Wilson

American activist Lois Wilson (1891-1988) was the co-founder of Al-Anon, a support group focused on the family and friends of alcoholics. She was the wife of Bill Wilson, who co-founded Alcoholics Anonymous.

Lois Wilson has been called the "first lady of Al-Anon." She co-founded the international organization with her husband Bill Wilson, the man who had earlier co-founded Alcoholics Anonymous, which resulted from his own severe alcohol problem.

Though the two organizations are closely related, they are different in at least one substantial way. Alcoholics Anonymous focuses on helping the individual suffering from alcoholism. Al-Anon, which was started in 1951, also helps the addicted, but its main focus is to provide support for the family and friends of alcoholics. Such individuals confront many of their own emotional and psychological problems stemming from their relationships with the alcohol addicted—that is the governing principle of this organization that offers group meetings as well as help on a one-to-one basis.

As *New York Time's* Eric Pace wrote in Lois Wilson's obituary in 1988, Wilson never condemned alcohol. Rather, as Pace quoted her, Wilson opposed "only the disease of alcoholism and the damage it does to a family."

Through her marriage to Bill Wilson, Lois experienced first-hand the damage the disease could do.

The organization that she helped establish (which became known as Al-Anon Family Groups, a non-profit organization) proved very influential. At the time of Lois Wilson's death in 1988, it boasted 30,000 groups, which included several thousand groups for teenagers (Alateen, which was formed in 1957). More than 20,000 of the Al-Anon groups were in the United States and Canada. The rest were located in as many as a hundred other countries. Worldwide membership was estimated at 500,000.

Born into a Nurturing Family

The future activist was born Lois Burnham on March 4, 1891 in Brooklyn Heights, New York. Her parents were Clark Burnham, who was a physician, and Matilda (Spelman) Burnham.

Lois Burnham was the first of six children and her childhood was a happy one (contrasted with her early adult life). Her parents were loving people who provided their children the best education. The siblings attended the Pratt Institute in Brooklyn, one of the first schools in the United States to embrace the pre-school concept of kindergarten. Later, the Burnham children attended Quakers' Friends School.

The young Lois Burnham has been described as somewhat tomboyish and very adventuresome. She also had a very artistic nature, however, and developed an interest in the fine arts as well as interior decoration. She attended Packer Collegiate Institute in Brooklyn, where she concentrated on the fine arts. Later, she took drawing classes at the New York School of Fine and Applied Art.

Met and Fell in Love with Bill Wilson

Her family spent summers in Vermont. There, in 1913, Rogers Burnham, her younger brother, befriended a Vermont teenager named Bill Wilson. Lois' initial acquaintance with Wilson led to romance and, in turn, a secretive 1915 engagement. During the First World War, Bill Wilson entered the United States Army. Before he left for Europe, the couple married on January 24, 1918.

Meanwhile, Lois Wilson was able to make a living, thanks to her education and her independent nature. She worked at a YWCA, where she received several promotions. In 1917, she worked at a school that her aunt created in Short Hills, New Jersey. She left that school when she got married.

All seemed hopeful, but a dark cloud loomed large. While Bill Wilson was in the Army, Lois received a hint of trouble to come. When her husband was stationed in New Bedford, Massachusetts, she went to visit. While there, his Army friends related to her a story about how her husband one night drank himself into unconsciousness. He had to be carried back to the barracks.

A Happy Couple Beset with a Problem

It was a troublesome anecdote, but Lois Wilson chose to look the other way (later, alcohol counselors would call this "denial"). After all, the future appeared promising. Bill Wilson was an ambitious young man. When he returned from military duty, he began a career on Wall Street in the 1920s. Also, Bill was just as adventuresome as his wife, and the couple liked to take cross-country motorcycle trips.

Early married life was happy and affluent, and the couple eagerly looked forward to starting a family. But Lois suffered a series of miscarriages. Eventually, she was told by physicians that further attempts at pregnancy would be impossible and even dangerous to her health. The couple sadly gave up on their shared dreams about having children.

This led to efforts to adopt, but the Wilsons were always turned down. Eventually, Lois found out why. Adoption agencies conduct background checks of prospective parents, and in their routine investigation of the Wilsons, they learned about Bill Wilson's drinking habits (which became prodigious after he left the army).

The information shocked Lois Wilson, but she shouldn't have been surprised. During the early part of their marriage, Lois witnessed Bill's increased drinking. Eventually, alcohol ruined his promising career. The situation became so bad that the Wilsons had to move into Lois's parents' home.

Stood by her Husband

Bill Wilson's descent into alcoholism progressed through the 1920s and into the 1930s. Still, Lois remained loyal to her husband. She tried to help him stop drinking, and her love was unconditional, even through seventeen tortuous years. During that time Bill Wilson's health—both physical and mental—seriously declined. Insanity seemed imminent, if an early death didn't come first. During this period, he was in and out of sanitariums.

Then, with the help of an old drinking buddy and recovering alcoholic Edwin "Ebby" Thacher, Bill Wilson was pointed toward the path of recovery. Thacher introduced him to a new concept of "God," one that was better recognized as a higher power that embraced all religious backgrounds. Bill Wilson was intrigued by his old friend's ideas, but he suffered more relapses. Then something happened: reportedly, while again seeking medical treatment (in December 1934), Wilson underwent a deeply spiritual experience while hospitalized. He became determined never to drink again. His personal conversion led him into a relationship with another seriously afflicted alcoholic, Dr. Robert Holbrook Smith (commonly known to recovering alcoholics as "Doctor Bob").

In 1935, Bill Wilson and "Doctor Bob" Smith co-founded Alcoholics Anonymous. Often referred to as simply AA, the organization subsequently grew into an international program with membership in the millions.

Ongoing Problems

What Lois Wilson couldn't accomplish with her husband, Thacher and Smith managed to achieve. And Lois Wilson knew she should be happy that her husband had achieved sobriety. But Bill Wilson was a driven man, totally focused on AA and almost obsessive about maintaining his sobriety and helping others achieve their own. Lois Wilson began to feel detached from his life. This led her to a significant realization, alcoholism—even if it becomes managed by the suffering individual—takes a toll on relationships.

Pace, in penning Lois Wilson's *New York Times* obituary, described the Wilson narrative: "After [AA] was founded, Mrs. Wilson became discontented. 'It seemed I saw nothing of the man I had tried to help,' she later recalled."

In other words, she felt like a woman betrayed—after all, before Thacher and Smith entered the picture, she was

the one bearing the brunt of the suffering and forced to put forth all of the effort. Pace quoted Lois again: "He was always with his [AA] cronies" [who helped him to resist alcohol]. "I guess I was jealous and resentful that these strangers had done for him what I could not do."

A turning point came when Bill Wilson asked wife Lois to attend yet another of his many AA meetings. Her response was to throw a shoe at him, and as hard as she could. As a wife, she felt neglected. But she later realized that her reaction was irrational. This led to a more importation realization: a relationship with an alcoholic not only resulted in immediate and profound pain, but produced problems that could linger beyond rehabilitation. As a result, she understood that she, too, needed some therapy.

Formation of Al-Anon

She developed a personal regimen that involved the same self-help principles that her husband and AA colleagues used: the 12-steps (the foundation of AA). Further, she discovered that she was not alone in her feelings, and didn't need to suffer guilt about how she felt. Many relatives of alcoholics—whether they be the wife, the husband, a son or daughter—had their lives devastated, and in so many different ways, by the disease. Further, their lives were not immediately cured by a relative's rehabilitation. The effects lingered.

Lois Wilson wanted to connect with others. AA is all about sharing—indeed, one of the key phrases is "Thank you for sharing" —and Lois Wilson gathered individuals who shared her experience. This occurred first in informal meetings. The purpose was not specifically to discuss relationships with alcoholic relatives; rather, the informal meetings provided a forum where relatives could discuss the impact of the experiences and, hopefully, bring some sanity into their own lives.

This would lead to the establishment of the Al-Anon Family Groups, which Lois Wilson co-founded with her husband in 1951.

But something had happened in the meantime: In 1939, Lois and Bill Wilson were forced to leave her parents' home. Even though they had inherited the property, they couldn't make payments and eventually faced foreclosure. After that, they lived in friends' homes. During this period, Lois Wilson provided the main income: She worked in department stores as a decorator and wrote articles for magazines. Still, this unanchored life was hard on Lois, and she feared she and her husband would end up homeless.

But only two years later, a friend offered them the opportunity to purchase a home in Westchester County, New York. This allowed the Wilsons to move into their first real home. The abode was named Stepping Stones, and it was located in Bedford Hills, New York.

Lois Wilson enjoyed life in the rural Stepping Stones. She gardened and engaged in a lifelong interest of art. So when the creation of Al-Anon was suggested, she was reluctant. She was sixty years old and had endured a great deal of hardship. She was getting tired and just wanted to enjoy life. But in 1951, she succumbed to a strong sense of community service. By the end of that year, at an AA conference, she met with delegate wives and family groups at her beloved Stepping Stones property, fully prepared to move forward in establishing a formal organization that would serve people such as her. While once tired, she now became indefatigable.

A Leader Until Death

Lois Wilson took leadership in Al-Anon, despite the great personal sacrifice. She remained active in the organization until her death on October 5, 1988 at the Northern Westchester Hospital in Mount Kisco, New York (her husband died in 1971). Childless, she was ninety-seven years old. She just missed a personal goal: she wanted to live to be 100 years old.

Surprisingly, during her later years, despite her advanced age, she remained very active in the Al-Anon organization. She bequeathed her beloved Stepping Stones home to the Stepping Stones Foundation. The home was eventually placed on the National Register of Historic Places.

A Print and Film Legacy

Wilson's autobiography, *Lois Remembers: Memoirs of the Co-Founder of Al-Anon and Wife of the Co-Founder of Alcoholics Anonymous* was published in 1979. Her life was also depicted in the book *The Lois Wilson Story: When Love Is Not Enough,* which was written by William G. Borchert and released in 2005. Borchert's book was produced as a made-for-TV movie in 2010, with actress Winona Ryder portraying Lois Wilson. Both the book and film were relentless in depicting the suffering and abuse that Lois Wilson endured. At the same time, these works powerfully communicated her compassion for a deeply troubled man who appeared powerless to deal with a disease not easily understood by medical professionals and that confounded the sufferer.

Such works introduced the world to an important woman whose life had been overshadowed by that of her husband's. She could be justified in saying that that is what happens when you marry a talented alcoholic. But she was far too compassionate to make such a statement. As quoted on the Stepping Stones website, she observed, "I believe that people are good if you give them half a chance and that good is more powerful than evil."

She provided that very half a chance to a man suffering an insidious disease, and in the process she impacted the world in which she lived. In fact, her impact endured beyond her death.

Periodicals

The New York Times, October 6, 1988.

Online

"Al-Anon History," *Al-Anon Family Groups,* http://www.al-anon.alateen.org/al-anon-history (November 29, 2011).

"Bill's Story," *SteppingStones.org,* http://www.steppingstones.org/billsstory.html (November 29, 2011).

"Lois Wilson," *BeyondHumanAid.com,* http://www.beyondhumanaid.com/lois-wilson-and-al-anon.html (November 29, 2011).

"Lois Wilson and the 12 Steps-Women in Recovery," *A Celebration of Women,* http://acelebrationofwomen.org/?p=3255 (November 29, 2011).

"Lois Wilson Biography," *AA Bibliography,* http://www.aabibliography.com/lois_wilson_biography.html (November 29, 2011).

"Lois' Story," *SteppingStones.org,* http://www.steppingstones.org/loisstory.html (November 29, 2011).□

Philip K. Wrigley

The American business executive Philip K. Wrigley (1894–1977) is closely identified with two icons of American culture: Wrigley's Chewing Gum and the Chicago Cubs professional baseball franchise, whose longtime stadium bears the Wrigley family name.

It was Wrigley's father, William Wrigley, who founded the company and acquired the Cubs, but it was Philip Wrigley who made Wrigley's gum an internationally familiar product, and made the William Wrigley Jr. Co. into the world's largest producer of chewing gum. Wrigley's career as owner of the Cubs was eccentric and innovative rather than consistently successful on the field, although the team did win several National League pennants during the early years of his reign. Above all, rather than a great baseball strategist or even a shrewd businessman, Wrigley was one of twentieth-century America's great marketing geniuses. He created a demand for chewing gum and for baseball where none had existed, and he took a hands-on approach to the marketing of the products that bore his name, often writing advertising copy for Wrigley's gum brands himself and devising new developments in baseball, not in the cooperative atmosphere of a corporate boardroom but purely through the power of his own imagination.

Born in Hotel

Philip Knight Wrigley was born in Chicago, Illinois, on December 5, 1894. William Wrigley was one of the many Easterners who flocked to the fast-growing Midwestern metropolis to try his luck in small manufacturing in the late nineteenth century, founding a company that at first made soap. The elder Wrigley made his fortune when he branched into chewing gum, which was at first marketed as a healthful product. Philip Wrigley, known to his family as P.K., was born in the Plaza Hotel on Chicago's swank Near North Side. He attended Phillips Academy, an elite prep school in Massachusetts. His sport there was lacrosse.

A notable feature of Wrigley's early life was the control he exerted over his own education. He left Phillips before graduating, deciding that he would learn more by traveling around the world and taking lessons from a private tutor, who happened to be the son of the president of

the University of Chicago. After this adventure Wrigley was admitted to Yale and Stanford universities, but turned down both those prestigious schools in favor of a trip to Australia to establish a new Wrigley factory in Melbourne. Back in Chicago in 1916, he took chemistry courses at the University of Chicago as a non-degree student. Thus he gained management experience, relevant scientific background, and general practical knowledge, all without benefit of a college degree.

Wrigley enlisted in the United States Naval Reserve in 1917 and, as a commissioned officer with the rank of ensign and then lieutenant, became the commander of a school for aviation mechanics. In 1918 he married Helen Blanche Atwater, the daughter of one of his father's top executives. The couple had one son, William, and two daughters, Dorothy and Ada. In 1920, the same year ground was broken for the company's namesake skyscraper on Chicago's North Michigan Avenue, he joined the Wrigley firm as a vice president. He was chosen as the company president in 1925, and in 1932 he inherited the chairmanship, along with the Cubs and a real estate empire that included Santa Catalina Island off the southern California coast, upon his father's death.

Among American industrialists Wrigley was something of a rarity, in that he generally supported President Franklin Roosevelt's New Deal social welfare measures, and even stated that he had voted for Roosevelt once. During the depths of the Great Depression, the Wrigley firm paid dividends to its stockholders, gave employees raises, and put in place unemployment compensation and pension plans. When sales faltered, Wrigley countered with the first of his major advertising blitzes, expanding the market through ads in women's magazines and sponsoring radio appearances by Canadian-American bandleader Guy Lombardo.

The Cubs, meanwhile, were one of the National League's powerhouses, winning pennants in 1932, 1935, and 1938, although the World Series title continued to elude them (as it had since 1908, and continued to do into the twenty-first century). Wrigley approached the club as a marketing challenge rather than purely as a baseball strategist. He justified the expensive acquisition of aging veteran pitcher Jay Hanna "Dizzy" Dean in the late 1930s on the grounds that he would bring the franchise valuable publicity, and he was among the first to actively promote baseball viewing as a wholesome family activity.

Supplied Gum to Armed Forces

The World War II years brought Wrigley success on all fronts. The Cubs won another pennant in 1945, and Wrigley overcame wartime shortages that impeded chewing gum production through a series of moves that made gum into almost an icon of the American infantryman. He funded research showing that gum could reduce the urge to smoke in situations where access to tobacco might be difficult. The U.S. Army, in turn, worked out a deal with Wrigley to include gum in the "K-rations," or daily combat food rations, issued to individual soldiers. This enabled Wrigley to craft ads positioning Wrigley as a supporter of the war effort, and in general to build profound brand loyalty.

Another contributor to the eventual dominance of the Wrigley gum brand was a perception of its reliable high quality. This was largely Wrigley's own doing. During the war, with gum base from southeast Asia in short supply, the firm's managers wanted to dilute it with inferior substances. Wrigley briefly resigned in protest, was reinstated, and generally refused to compromise on the quality issue, even though the large-scale manufacturing of gum for the military brought the company little in the way of profits. He did agree to the production of a lower-cost, lower-quality gum called Orbit, but kept it out of Wrigley's advertising and discontinued it when the war ended. Wrigley placed long-term brand-building over short-term profits. "We are in a nickel business," he pointed out, according to the *Chicago Tribune.* "The hardest thing to do is to keep people up top here from turning the whole thing into a banking business."

One of Wrigley's most notable baseball innovations was the founding of the All-American Girls Professional Baseball League in 1943. At first he had the idea because he was worried that an influx of male players into the armed forces during the war might necessitate a hiatus in major league play, but the women's league outgrew his original plans and lasted 12 years, with ten teams across the Midwest and an annual attendance of about one million fans at its peak. The women who played earned from $45 to $85 a week— less than male players earned, but a reasonable salary for the 1940s. As the war neared its end, Wrigley turned over management of the league to others and occupied himself once again with the Cubs, which became one of the first major-league teams to have games appear on television. Wrigley, unlike some other team owners, immediately guessed that the reach and advertising potential of the new medium would more than make up for any loss of live attendance at games.

Created "College of Coaches"

Wrigley gave his baseball imagination full rein during the post–World War II era, attempting to replace the standard staffing of a single team manager with a so-called college of coaches who would rotate in head-coaching duties. He also emulated college sports in creating an athletic director position. None of these moves resulted in success on the field, and the Cubs began a long period in which they were perpetually mired in the National League cellar. Wrigley endeared himself to North Side Chicago residents, however, by resisting pressure to install lights at Wrigley Field, arguing that night baseball activity would be detrimental to the surrounding neighborhood. (He had actually planned to install lights during World War II, but the materials were redirected to the war effort, and he declined to revive the idea.) Wrigley Field remained the major leagues' sole daytime-only park for many years, until lights were added in 1988.

Wrigley was known as a civic-minded executive, not only in Chicago but in Southern California, where he established the Santa Catalina Island Conservancy and donated much of the island to the new body, keeping Santa Catalina in the largely wild state in which it remains today. He was an informal man who often dispensed with a jacket at work, and at the Wrigley Building was sometimes mistaken for a clerk. In his spare time he enjoyed building boats and working on antique cars in a home workshop. He died on April 12, 1977, at his summer home near Elkhorn, Wisconsin, after a gastrointestinal hemorrhage.

Books

American Decades, Gale, 1998.

Angle, Paul M., *Philip K. Wrigley: A Memoir of a Modest Man,* Rand McNally, 1975.

Periodicals

Chicago Tribune, April 13, 1977.

Cobblestone, April 2010.

Crain's Chicago Business, October 17, 2005.

Online

"Philip Wrigley," *The Baseball Biography Project,* http://www.bioproj.sabr.org (October 5, 2011).□

Y

Wakako Yamauchi

The daughter of Japanese immigrants, playwright Wakako Yamauchi (born 1924) grew up in California at a time when anti-Asian sentiment ran strong. During World War II, Yamauchi was sent to live in an internment camp with thousands of Japanese Americans after the United States declared war on Japan. Later in life, Yamauchi wrote award-winning plays and short stories colored by her experiences and gained notoriety for her ability to articulate the Asian-American experience.

The youngest of three, Wakako Yamauchi was born Wakako Nakamura in Westmoreland, California, in 1924 to a family of immigrant tenant farmers. Her parents had moved from Japan and settled in an agricultural area of Southern California known as the Imperial Valley. Due to the Alien Land Law of 1913—passed by the California legislature—the Nakamuras were unable to own land. Laws permitted them to lease land, but with restrictions that forced them to relocate every few years.

In Yamauchi's home, the family spoke only Japanese. Yamauchi did not learn English until she started attending Trifolium, a two-room school in Westmoreland where 90 percent of the students were Japanese. Yamauchi was taught by a white, American teacher who drilled her on the letter sounds R and L—two phonetic sounds that do not exist in the Japanese language. Yamauchi also attended a Buddhist church in nearby Brawley, California.

Aside from school, Yamauchi endured an isolated childhood. The desert farms of her youth were spread out along an irrigation canal. As such, there were no neighbors nearby. Once she learned to read, Yamauchi turned to books for company. One thing she remembered poring over again and again was *The Book of Knowledge,* a children's encyclopedia set that included literature and poetry. "My father could not resist a traveling salesman, and he bought the twenty volumes even before most of us could read," she recalled in a *MELUS* interview with William P. Osborn and Sylvia A. Watanabe.

Yamauchi also read old newspapers. Her father purchased bales of outdated newspapers to cover his seedlings from the frost. One publication Yamauchi discovered was the *Kashu Mainichi,* a daily English-Japanese newspaper. Yamauchi was particularly taken with a writer named Hisaye Yamamoto, who wrote a column detailing her experiences as an Asian American.

In 1940, a 6.9-magnitude earthquake struck the Imperial Valley, ruining the family's crop. The loss prompted Yamauchi's father to give up farming. The family moved to Oceanside, California, and opened a boarding house for transient farm laborers who traveled the coast following the harvest seasons. The boardinghouse was owned by a white landlord, but nonetheless, proved fairly fruitful.

Forced into Internment Camp

When Yamauchi was 17 and a senior in high school, World War II raged in Europe and the threat of a war with Japan loomed largely in the minds of the Japanese-American elders. One Sunday, Yamauchi went to the theater to see *Sergeant York,* a war hero story starring Gary Cooper. "I came home full of rah-rah," Yamauchi recalled in an article she wrote for the *Los Angeles Times.* "My mother met me in the yard. She whispered, 'America is at war with Japan.' Her face was white; my heart sank for her. On Dec. 7, we became the enemy."

Soon, Yamauchi's mother's fears came true. In February 1942, President Franklin D. Roosevelt signed Executive Order 9066, which granted the U.S. military the power to ban citizens from coastal areas along the Pacific coast in an effort to prevent espionage or sabotage. Exclusion orders forced Japanese Americans from areas along the West Coast and some 100,000 Japanese immigrants and their families were forced into internment camps.

In May 1942, Yamauchi's family was sent to the Poston War Relocation Center in dusty Southwestern Arizona. They lost most of their possessions because they were allowed to bring only what they could carry. The fenced camp included several rows of wood-and-tar-paper barracks, a mess hall, and lavatories and gun towers. At one point, some 10,000 people lived at Poston. "The bathrooms were in separate buildings," Yamauchi told the *Daily Breeze's* Debbi K. Swanson. "And there were no doors or privacy in them. People would wait until all hours to go to the bathroom. There were a half-dozen faucets to brush your teeth, and you tried not to get the one at the end, because you'd see everybody else's junk in the trough. And the sewers were always plugging up."

While interned, Yamauchi found an outlet for her creativity working as an artist at the *Poston Chronicle* creating cartoons and mastheads. At the *Chronicle* Yamauchi befriended Hisaye Yamamoto—the columnist she had discovered years earlier while reading her father's castoff newspapers. Yamamoto wrote for the *Poston Chronicle*. The camp had a small library with old books and magazines. Yamamoto rummaged through them and introduced Yamauchi to the work of Thomas Wolfe, Marcel Proust, and the *New Yorker*. The two friends spent a lot of their time reading and discussing different writers.

Aside from the poor living conditions, teenagers like Yamauchi—who had been born in the United States—felt betrayed and shocked. As Yamauchi told the *Daily Breeze*, "It was terrible for us, because we grew up thinking America was the land of the free and the melting pot—this really told us where we stood." The feelings stayed with Yamauchi. In an interview with King-Kok Cheung for *Words Matter*, Yamauchi discussed the affect the internment had on her psyche. "The worst is the colonization of the mind. You think you are less than what other people are because you are there."

Yamauchi spent about 18 months in the camp, then received permission to go to Chicago. While there, she worked in a candy factory. Yamauchi returned to Poston in the waning days of the war—called back because her father was ill. By the time she arrived, her father was dead. Yamauchi's father had suffered from an ulcer, which got worse after the United States bombed Hiroshima.

Turned to Art, Writing

After the camp disbanded, Yamauchi returned to California and found a job at a photofinishing factory. She also took art classes at the Otis Art Center in Los Angeles. In 1948, she married Chester Yamauchi, who was a friend of her brother. Next, she worked various day jobs to finance her husband's education at UCLA. In 1955, they had a daughter, Joy.

Yamauchi spent the next period of her life focused on raising her daughter. She did find a small amount of time for her artwork and in 1959 was asked to contribute some graphic-art work to *Rafu Shimpo*, a bilingual Japanese-English daily published in Los Angeles. The editor, Henry Mori, needed lots of artwork for the paper's holiday edition.

Yamauchi had also begun writing short stories, inspired by the idea of keeping her family's memory alive and recording her feelings regarding the dehumanizing experiences of her youth. Yamauchi's husband, Chester, suggested she tell the editor she would submit artwork if he would print one of her stories. Beginning in 1960, Yamauchi began contributing a story to *Rafu Shimpo* for the annual holiday edition.

One of the first fiction stories Yamauchi wrote was "And the Soul Shall Dance." Yamauchi sent it to mainstream magazines but received only rejection notices, so she gave it to *Rafu Shimpo*. In the 1970s, Yamauchi submitted the story for consideration in an anthology called *Aiiieeeee!* Published in 1974, the anthology included works by pioneering Asian-American writers, including Yamauchi's "And the Soul Shall Dance."

Penned Award-Winning Play

In 1975 Yamauchi began writing full time after divorcing her husband. Around this time, she was contacted by Mako, the artistic director and co-founder of the East West Players, the first Asian-American theater company in the United States. Mako had read the anthology and loved "And the Soul Shall Dance" so much he wanted Yamauchi to turn it into a play. Mako helped Yamauchi earn a Rockefeller playwright-in-residence grant so she could work on adapting the story for the stage.

"And the Soul Shall Dance" tells the story of two immigrant farm families living in California's Imperial Valley as they suffer though the Depression. One family is resilient and assimilates to life in the United States. This family consists of a mother, father, and 11-year-old daughter. Through good humor and discipline, they make their way, with the father often telling his daughter, as noted by Karen D'Souza in the *Sacramento Bee*, "When the winds blow, bamboo bends. You bend or you break."

Their neighbors, a man named Oka and his wife, Emiko, suffer terribly and erupt in violence toward each other, becoming victims of their circumstances. Emiko spends her time drunk on sake, dreaming of the past and a future when she might return to Japan. Emiko never wanted to come to the United States. Oka traveled to the states to look for a better life, then sent for his wife—Emiko's older sister. She had died, so the family sent Emiko in her place as a substitute wife. Theater critic Stephen Holden, writing in the *New York Times*, described the play as, "a psychological study of people struggling to adapt to the stringent traditions and laws of two worlds simultaneously: one they have left and one in which they are trying to forge a new identity." Yamauchi re-wrote the play six times before settling on a final version.

The play won critical acclaim after its 1977 debut in Los Angeles. Later, the Pan Asian Repertory Theater took the play on the road, touring California and later, New York City.

"And the Soul Shall Dance" was also produced by a Los Angeles PBS station and aired across the United States in 1977-78. The play won a Los Angeles Drama Critics Circle award for best new play.

Brought Asian-American Experience to Life

With this success, Yamauchi turned to writing in earnest, becoming one of the preeminent Asian voices of her generation and helping to change stereotypes about Asian Americans. Yamauchi wrote short stories, essays, and memoirs for anthologies and literary magazines and also continued her playwriting. In 1987, the Yale Repertory Theater staged *Memento,* Yamauchi's play about two women who fall in love with the same man. The man dies and his wife brings an ancient Noh mask of his to his former girlfriend as a memento. When she places the mask on her face she is transported to a dreamy, fantasy world, a setting that afforded Yamauchi the opportunity to explore Japanese tradition.

In 1992 Yamauchi's play *12-1-A* hit the stage at UCLA, becoming the first Asian play featured on the campus' main stage, though it originally debuted with the East West Players. *12-1-A* was based on Yamauchi's experiences in the Poston internment camp. The numbers represent her address—block 12, barracks 1, apartment A. Yamauchi continued writing into her 80s. In 2011, Yamauchi released *Rosebud and Other Stories,* a collective volume filled with tales about marriage, motherhood, and heartbreak as told through the eyes of farmers, factory workers, housewives, con artists, and dreamers struggling to make their way.

In the introduction for Yamauchi's 1994 book *Songs My Mother Taught Me,* Yamauchi's first volume of collected works, University of Wisconsin Asian American Studies director Amy Ling described the importance of Yamauchi's work. "Yamauchi's themes—love unconsummated, opportunities missed, 'songs of longing' and resignation...of despair and renewal of hope—are handled with consummate skill, presented with beauty and grace." Ling commended Yamauchi for her ability to write stories with a cheery twist, not making the characters into victims. Ling said Yamauchi's stories serve as "moving testaments to human endurance, survival, and strength." Ling noted that although Yamauchi's stories predominantly relate the experiences of Japanese Americans during the 1930s "their resonance and significance extend—as with all lasting literature—to all people, everywhere."

Books

Cheung, King-Kok, ed., *Words Matter: Conversations with Asian America Writers,* University of Hawaii Press, 2000.
Yamauchi, Wakako, *Songs My Mother Taught Me: Stories, Plays and Memoir,* The Feminist Press, 1994.

Periodicals

Daily Breeze (Torrance, CA), November 6, 1992.
Los Angeles Times, February 8, 1986; March 8, 1991; November 8, 1992.
MELUS, Summer 1998.
New York Times, March 25, 1990.
Sacramento Bee, January 10, 2000.

Online

"Author Wakako Yamauchi to Discuss New Works at JANM," *Rafu Shimpo,* http://rafu.com/news/2011/04 (November 14, 2011).□

Freddie Young

The British cinematographer Freddie Young (1902–1998) was among the most respected practitioners of his craft, with a career that began during the silent film era and spanned much of the history of cinema itself.

Young worked with a variety of directors, both British and American, over 161 films stretching from the 1920s to the 1980s. Many cinematic classics bore his stamp, revealing resourceful solutions to technical problems posed by directors who knew what they wanted but had no idea how to achieve it. But the high-water mark of Young's achievement was likely the series of films he made with British director David Lean in the 1960s, more than two decades after the pair had started out on the wrong foot during an initial clash of personalities. In such films as *Lawrence of Arabia* (1962) and *Doctor Zhivago* (1965), Young was largely responsible for the realization of some of the most famous and distinctive shots in the entire history of film.

Touted Brownie Camera as Qualification

Frederick Archibald Young was born in London on October 9, 1902. At the age of 14, due to family financial hardships, he had to leave school and take a job in an arms factory, drilling holes in the tops of hand grenades. He loved films from the beginning, and in 1917, hoping to find a job he liked more, he knocked on the door of a greenhouse-like film studio called Gaumont that was opposite a swimming pool he and his brother liked to visit in London's Shepherd's Bush neighborhood. The only qualification he could offer was an enthusiasm for his Brownie camera. To his surprise, with many British men of employment age away at the World War I front, he was hired and given a job in the film developing lab. After a year, and with further studio losses to the British military, Young became the lab's manager, free to experiment with chemicals and film stock.

Young learned the craft of camera operation when Gaumont expanded after the war and promoted him to assistant cameraman. This was a less specialized post than the name implied—Young learned the entire workings of the studio, shooting photographic stills, driving the studio car, and even on one occasion filling in for a stuntman in a scene that required him to fall off a 40-foot wall. Good-looking in his youth, Young even served as a body double for British matinee idol Ivor Novello on a location shoot in Paris for the film *Triumph of the Rat,* and he got his first taste of desert work during the filming of *Fires of Fate*

(1923). He was on the scene when the tomb of the young King Tut was discovered by archaeologist Howard Carter in 1922.

In 1927 Young left Gaumont to take a post as lead cinematographer on a silent World War I adventure called *Victory,* marking the beginning of six decades of cinematography credits. During the first part of his career he often billed himself as F.A. Young. He worked on several other films, including Alfred Hitchcock's *Blackmail* (1929), which was the first British sound film. While working on *Victory,* Young met and married assistant director Marjorie Gaffney; the pair raised two adopted children. In the late 1920s Young became part of the creative team employed by producer Herbert Wilcox of the large British and Dominions studio. B&D spared no expense in its productions, and Young quickly mastered new technologies such as Technicolor, which he used on one reel of *Victoria the Great* (1937). He was the cinematographer on several key British films of the 1930s, including *Goodbye Mr. Chips* (1939).

Made Military Training Films

Young followed Wilcox to the United States in 1939 to make *Nurse Edith Cavell,* but then returned to Britain on an almost empty ship. During World War II he made military training and propaganda films for the British army, into which he was commissioned with the rank of captain. He also served as cinematographer on two major British films made from plays by George Bernard Shaw: *Major Barbara* (1941) and *Caesar and Cleopatra* (1945). According to Kevin Brownlow of the London *Independent,* while on the set of *Major Barbara,* assistant director David Lean barked an order to Young, prompting the reply ''Don't teach your grandmother to suck eggs.''

After the war Young found himself in demand on both sides of the Atlantic. In 1949 he became the first president of the British Society of Cinematographers. The 1950 version of *Treasure Island,* the first live-action film produced by Walt Disney Studios, was one of his many hits of the postwar period. Young earned his first Academy Award nomination for *Ivanhoe* (1952), and through the 1950s he worked with such top directors as John Ford, on *Mogambo* (1953), Vincente Minnelli, on *Lust for Life* (1956), and King Vidor, on the epic *Solomon and Sheba* (1959). The last of these was shot in the 70-millimeter wide screen format, one of many technical innovations to which Young quickly adapted during his career.

By the early 1960s, Young was recognized as perhaps Britain's top cinematographer. However, Lean, who was in the early stages of planning *Lawrence of Arabia,* remembered his unpleasant encounter with Young two decades earlier and refused to work with him. He later relented, with the result that Young's awe-inspiring desert photography became the film's trademark. Often Lean had an idea of the visuals he wanted for a particular scene, but had no idea how they might be technically realized, leaving it to Young to devise the actual procedures. One of the film's most famous scenes, in which actor Omar Sharif seems to emerge from a shimmering mirage, was essentially Young's work; he used a giant discarded telephoto lens he had salvaged from an American studio to capture close-up images of heat waves radiating from the desert floor.

A favorite film of both Young and Lean was Lean's next release, *Doctor Zhivago,* representing the Russian novel of Boris Pasternak but actually filmed in Spain. Again, Young composed memorable shots of the snow-covered countryside, created by grinding up hundreds of tons of marble. He was especially proud of a shot of actress Julie Christie's hand, as seen by the title character in a window in the darkness. ''I liked Doctor Zhivago because it was a bigger challenge for me,'' Young explained to Gary Crowdus of *Cineaste.* ''It was all done in Spain, but there was such a variety of things I had to do in that film. For example, since the story took place over many years, you had to photograph people aging—it's not just make-up, you know—to convey the impression of characters physically aging. The photography involved women, too, and in *Lawrence* there were no women.''

Invented Rain Deflector

For his next project with Lean, *Ryan's Daughter,* Young faced not desert conditions or artificial snow but the necessity of filming in major rainstorms in Lean's epic story of romance and struggle in Ireland. Again he rose to the technical challenge with a rain deflector— ''a round glass which revolves at tremendous speed so that any rain or water hitting it immediately becomes a plain sheet of water, so you don't see spots or anything,'' Young explained to Crowdus. ''I borrowed the idea from ships that had this sort of revolving glass over the windscreen. I had my camera mechanic make one for me with a plastic covering all over the camera. We could never have photographed that storm we did in *Ryan's Daughter* without it.'' As of the late 1990s, after Young's death, his original rain deflector could still be rented for use on location during storms.

His talent for on-the-spot technical solutions was not restricted to his work with Lean. When American director Sidney Lumet hoped to film *The Deadly Affair* (1966) in black-and-white but was forbidden from doing so by studio executives, Young fogged the film by pre-exposing it slightly and thus muted the colors. Young won Academy Awards for all three of his films with Lean, and in 1970 he was made a member of the Order of the British Empire. He worked on several other epic films, including the costume drama *Nicholas and Alexandra* (1971), and was active well into the 1980s. In 1984 he directed the British television film *Arthur's Hallowed Ground.*

After the death of his first wife in 1963, Young married Joan Morduch, and the couple had one son, David. After his retirement he devoted himself to painting, filling much of his country house in Roehampton with his own work. Young dictated his memoirs shortly before his death in London on December 1, 1998; they were published the following year as *Seventy Light Years: A Life in Movies.*

Books

Young, Freddie, *Seventy Light Years: A Life in the Movies,* Faber & Faber, 1999.

Periodicals

Cineaste, Summer 1995.
Independent (London, England), December 4, 1998.
New Statesman, March 12, 1999.
Scotsman (Edinburgh, Scotland), December 7, 1998.
Times (London, England), December 3, 1998.
Variety, December 7, 1998.

Online

"Young, Freddie," *Screenonline,* http://www.screenonline.org.uk/people/id/477394/(November 3, 2011). □

Atahualpa Yupanqui

The Argentine singer and songwriter Atahualpa Yupanqui (1908–1992) was an internationally known interpreter of the indigenous music of South America.

At a time when South America's native peoples had little representation in concert life in Argentina and around the rest of the continent, Yupanqui single-handedly built a career performing material inspired by their music. "All that the Indians feel but cannot or don't know how to say, I say it for them," he once said, according to the *New York Times.* Yupanqui wrote many famous songs himself. His identification with the downtrodden and with Argentina's nonwhite minority caused him problems during periods of right-wing rule, and he spent much of his life in exile, becoming a celebrated figure in western Europe in later life. The performers of the politically oriented *nueva canción* (new song) movement that flourished

all over Latin America beginning in the 1960s have repeatedly cited Yupanqui as a major influence.

Traveled Through Argentina as Child

Atahualpa Yupanqui was born Hector Roberto Chavero in the small Argentine city of Pergamino, in Buenos Aires province. His father, who was of Quechua Indian descent, was a small-time railroad official who traveled frequently, often bringing his family along to different parts of the country. He would bring a trunk full of novels and books of philosophy along on the trip. Yupanqui's mother's ancestors were members of the culturally distinct Basque ethnic group of Spain and southern France. In 1917 the family settled in Tucumán province in northwestern Argentina, where Yupanqui heard the music of Argentina's gauchos, or cowboys, and encountered the native people who were concentrated around Argentina's northern borders. He began contributing to a high school literary magazine, taking the pseudonym Atahualpa after the last king of the Incan empire. Later he added Yupanqui, the founder of that empire, as his surname.

Yupanqui was interested in music from the start, and played both violin and guitar as a youth. Soon he gravitated toward accompanying himself on the guitar, and he was adept at drawing an audience almost anywhere he went. As a teen he took a job delivering telegrams by mule so that he could see new places and find new kinds of music. During a period with his family in the city of Junín he found a guitar teacher, Bautista Almirón, whom he liked; the teacher's studio was 14 miles away from the Yupanqui family's dwelling, but he made the commute daily on horseback. He developed a fluent guitar style that blended classical and folk influences.

Yupanqui worked various job, including schoolteacher and print shop employee, as he worked on his music. One of his most famous songs, "Camino del Indio"

(Indian Trail) was written when he was 19. Yupanqui's travels among Argentina's downtrodden led him to join the Communist Party of Argentina, and in 1931 he participated in the unsuccessful attempt by brothers, Mario, Eduardo, and Roberto Kennedy to overthrow the coup-installed right-wing government of General José Félix Uriburu. Yupanqui was with the group as they hid in a forest from government bombing raids and encamped on an island to elude police pursuit. Finally Yupanqui began the first of several periods of exile from his native land, crossing the Plate River into neighboring Uruguay.

Performed on Radio

A 1934 government amnesty led to Yupanqui's return to Argentina, and he encountered a new round of influences from Indian music as he traveled with Swiss anthropologist Alfred Métraux on a research trip among the members of the Amaicha tribe. Back in Buenos Aires in 1935, Yupanqui found growing opportunities to perform, as the radio industry blossomed in Argentina and, as it did in the United States, put a new spotlight on the country's rural traditions. Performing as part of the sign-on of Radio El Mundo in 1935, he introduced listeners to such genres as the baguala, vidala, zamba, and gato (the cat), an old courtship dance. During this period Yupanqui met pianist Antonieta Paula "Nenette" Pepín Fitzpatrick, and the two were married. Using the pseudonym Pablo del Cerro, she contributed to many of his compositions.

Yupanqui made numerous recordings during the first part of his career, committing more than 12,000 songs to disc by one estimate. Many of his early recordings were made for small Argentine labels and are both out of print and rare; a careful reissue survey of his life's work would be valuable beyond the pleasure his recordings offer. Films of Yupanqui performing are available on Internet video services and show a sober figure who approached folk material with quiet respect, letting the words of the song carry the meaning. His guitar playing was exceptionally fluent and seemed capable of reproducing a wide variety of rhythms and instrumental sounds. Yupanqui had a mellifluous baritone voice that gained texture as he grew older, enabling him to maintain his career for many decades.

Yupanqui's vocal longevity became important, for developments in Argentine politics eventually made it necessary for him to leave Argentina and begin his career anew. After the ascent to power of nationalist leader Juan Perón in 1946, Yupanqui's affiliation with Communism made him increasingly suspect in the Argentine government's eyes. His music was censored, and he himself was jailed on several occasions. In 1949 Yupanqui left Argentina once again, making his first stop in Uruguay and moving on to tour the then-Communist countries of Hungary, Romania, Czechoslovakia, and Bulgaria. Though he later returned to Argentina to perform, he would never again make the country his primary residence.

Opened for Edith Piaf

In Paris, France, Yupanqui met the surrealist poet Paul Eluard, who invited both Yupanqui and French vocal star Edith Piaf to a party at his house. After hearing Yupanqui play the guitar, Piaf invited him to open for her on her next concert tour, even backing his nascent European career by having posters distributed that read "Edith Piaf sings for you and for Yupanqui." Yupanqui was also befriended by artist Pablo Picasso and by leading progressive figures of the French cultural scene. He was signed to the Le Chant du Monde record label and in 1950 released an LP that won a Charles Cross award from the French recording industry.

In 1952 Yupanqui renounced his affiliation with Communism and was allowed to return to Buenos Aires. He stated that he did not want to be involved with politics directly, but many of his songs of the 1950s and onward continued to explore themes of protest. Sometimes he wrote about the beauty of Argentina's landscape. Artists connected with the political nueva canción movement of the 1960s and 1970s looked directly to Yupanqui as an inspiration as they underwent their own struggles with government authority. The most popular nueva canción vocalist in Argentina, Mercedes Sosa, recorded an entire album of Yupanqui's songs, and her own music drew directly on folk roots in the same way Yupanqui's did. He appeared in two film documentaries about Argentine music, Argentísima and Argentísima II, but the rise to power of a new military dictatorship in 1976 forced him once again to limit his appearances in his home country.

In Europe, Yupanqui's popularity continued to expand. One of his albums won an award in Germany in 1985 as the best album recorded by a foreign artist, and in France, where he maintained his official residence, he continued to record and concertize extensively. He also published poetry and a translation of a novel, Cerro Bayo (Cream-Colored Hill), that he had written in the 1940s; that novel has also been translated into Dutch and Japanese. In 1989 Yupanqui wrote the text for a cantata celebrating the bicentennial of the French Revolution.

Yupanqui died in Nimes, France, on May 23, 1992, after performing a concert there and insisting on walking back to his hotel room. He was 84 years old. Yupanqui performed in countries around South America and Europe, made several tours of Japan, appeared in both Egypt and Israel, and remained very popular in France. He did appear at New York's Town Hall concert space in 1986, but his comparative obscurity in the United States makes him perhaps a ripe candidate for revival.

Periodicals

Globe & Mail (Toronto, Ontario, Canada), May 25, 1992.

Guardian (London, England), June 18, 1992.

New York Times, November 14, 1986; May 28, 1992.

Times (London, England), June 10, 1992.

Online

"Profile of Atahualpa Yupanqui—Pioneer of South American Indigenous Music," *Sounds and Colours,* http://www.soundsandcolours.com/articles/argentina/profile-of-atahualpa-yupanqui-pioneer-of-south-american-indigenous-music/ (October 7, 2011). □

Z

Marie Zakrzewska

The German-born physician Marie Zakrzewska (1829–1902) was a pioneer among women in the medical profession in the United States.

Z akrzewska's list of "firsts" is substantial. She was involved with the founding of the first two American hospitals staffed by women, and she founded the first American nursing school and the first hospital social service department. Zakrzewska's programs produced the first formally trained American nurse, the first trained African-American nurse, and the first women's medical society. Beyond these accomplishments, Zakrzewska was an effective advocate for a gender-blind commitment to science in the practice of medicine, and she was an energetic reformer whose political sense of commitment extended beyond the world of medicine.

Accompanied Midwife Mother on Rounds

Marie Elizabeth Zakrzewska (pronounced zock-SHEV-ska) was born in Berlin, then the capital of the Kingdom of Prussia, on September 6, 1829. She was descended from an old family that had been part of Poland's landowning class but fell on hard times after Poland was carved up by Prussia, Russia, and Austria at the end of the eighteenth century; her father, Ludwig Martin Zakrzewski, moved to Berlin and got a minor government job. Zakrzewska's maternal grandmother had been a veterinary surgeon, and her mother, to help support her seven children (Marie was the oldest), got training as a midwife at Berlin's Royal Charité Hospital. As a girl, Marie accompanied her mother on her rounds, and when she was 11 she was accidentally

locked in a morgue overnight. From her father she inherited a streak of political liberalism.

Zakrzewska showed obvious talent, not only as a midwife, but as a physician and surgeon; the training midwives received in the program did not differ greatly from that received by male doctors. She passed her exams with top scores that impressed the school's director and professor of obstetrics, Joseph Hermann Schmidt, who became a close friend. Schmidt paved the way for Zakrzewska to become head midwife and professor at the hospital's school of midwifery in 1852. This, however, caused dissension among male faculty members. Schmidt, who was in the last stages of a terminal illness, stuck to his decision, and it was respected. But Zakrzewska resigned after six months as director and left Germany for New York with her sister Anna.

Several factors may have played a role in her decision, including large-scale German emigration to the U.S. at the time, her difficulties at Royal Charité, and a perception that further medical education would be more easily available to her in America. Zakrzewska had heard about an all-female medical school in Philadelphia, but when she and her sister arrived in New York, making a living took first priority. Her organizational skills showed themselves immediately as she and her sister took in sewing piecework and were soon hiring other recent immigrants to help. But, living in New York's close-knit German community, she had trouble learning English and felt herself no closer to her dream.

Earned M.D. Degree

Zakrzewska's breakthrough came when she sought out and met Elizabeth Blackwell, who had graduated from upstate New York's Geneva Medical College in 1849 and become the world's first degreed female physician. Blackwell agreed to help, and with some help from Blackwell's

374

contacts, Zakrzewska was admitted to Cleveland Medical College (now part of Case Western Reserve University). Despite continuing problems with the English language, she completed her M.D. degree in 1856. Zakrzewska was lucky to have fit into a small window of opportunity: women had been admitted to the school only since 1847, and shortly after Zakrzewska's departure they were barred once again.

Zakrzewska repaid Blackwell's assistance by returning to New York and helping her to expand the New York Infirmary for Indigent Women and Children from a clinic into a full-fledged hospital, with Zakrzewska herself as resident physician. Depending on definitions, it was the first hospital in the United States operated exclusively by women. Zakrzewska also served as an instructor of nursing students, and as a fundraiser and housekeeper as well. She also opened her own private practice in New York. Her colleagues, flummoxed by her difficult Polish name, referred to her as Dr. Zak.

These activities led to Zakrzewska's appointment as Professor of Obstetrics at the New England Female Medical College in Boston, the world's first medical school for women. She seemed to have achieved her dreams, yet once again she clashed with largely male superiors. Zakrzewska intended to expand the school's curriculum beyond midwifery and other female-oriented areas of medicine, converting it into a state-of-the-art medical school, and she wanted to give students hands-on training in a new hospital associated with the school. When both these requests went nowhere with the school's trustees, Zakrzewska resigned in 1861 and embarked on a fresh round of fundraising.

Founded First American Nursing School

The result was the foundation of the New England Hospital for Women and Children, which opened in 1862 in Boston. The hospital still exists, as the Dimock Community Health Center. The staff was exclusively female. From its original ten beds, the hospital grew rapidly, and in 1872 Zakrzewska opened a nursing school at the hospital's new campus in the then-separate town of Roxbury; it was the first professional nursing school in the United States. The school attracted national attention among young women with medical ambitions, and trained the first African-American nurse (Mary Eliza Mahoney, class of 1879). By 1881 Zakrzewska could restrict her residency program to women who had already earned an M.D. degree.

Over the last four decades of the nineteenth century, the New England Hospital opened a variety of new buildings and clinics but never abandoned its initial commitment to serve the poor and needy. The hospital's social service department was the first in the United States. Never well endowed, the hospital held annual fundraising fairs to make ends meet. Zakrzewska, who served as the hospital's resident physician and head nurse, also maintained her private practice and eventually earned a reputation as New England's top female physician.

Zakrzewska's activities over the course of her career were not motivated simply by personal ambition but had roots in reform movements on both sides of the Atlantic. Even in her first years in New York, she had connections with German radicals who were refugees from the defeated revolutionary movements of the year 1848, and from them she absorbed a concept of science as a progressive force. In the words of her biographer Arleen Tuchman, Zakrzewska "thus grounded her moral values in a secular, materialist philosophy. This distinguished her from most other American women physicians, who...derived strength from 'the inviolable authority of religion.'" In later years, Zakrzewska became a steadfast supporter of such progressive causes as woman's suffrage and the abolition of slavery, and she numbered prominent Boston intellectuals such as abolitionist journalist William Lloyd Garrison among her friends.

Zakrzewska's domestic life was as unusual and pioneering as her career. For the last several decades of her life she maintained a household that included a longtime companion, Julia Sprague; Karl Heinzen, a fellow German emigré of radical political persuasion; and Heinzen's wife and child. It is an open question whether the relationship between Zakrzewska and Sprague was an intimate one; the fact that they shared a home and even a bedroom is not regarded as conclusive in a nineteenth-century cultural context. In her last years, Zakrzewska lived in a substantial house in Boston's Jamaica Plain neighborhood.

In 1899, at the age of 70, Zakrzewska retired. After several years of ill health, she died at her Boston home on May 12, 1902. A biography of Zakrzewska by Agnes Vietor, *A Woman's Quest: The Life of Marie E. Zakrzewska, M.D.,* was based on materials Zakrzewska herself had selected, and appeared in 1924. Zakrzewska was featured on an episode of the *Cavalcade of America* radio program during World War II, but after the war ended and most women returned to domestic roles, she was largely forgotten. A modern scholarly biography of Zakrzewska, Arleen Tuchman's *Science Has No Sex: The Life of Marie Zakrzewska,* appeared in 2006.

Books

Kelly, Howard Atwood, *A Cyclopedia of American Medical Biography,* Saunders, 1912.

Tuchman, Arleen, *Science Has No Sex: The Life of Marie Zakrzewska,* University of North Carolina, 2006.

Online

"Dr. Marie E. Zakrzewska," *Changing the Face of Medicine* (National Institutes of Health), http://www.nlm.nih.gov/changingthefaceofmedicine/physicians/biography_338.html (November 6, 2011).

"Marie Elizabeth Zakrzewska," *Distinguished Women of Past and Present,* http://www.distinguishedwomencom/biographies/zakrzews.html (November 6, 2011).

"Marie Zakrzewska: Medical Pioneer," *Jamaica Plain Historical Society,* http://www.jphs.org/people/2005/4/14/marie-zakrzewska-medical-pioneer.html (November 6, 2011). □

Cesare Zavattini

The Italian screenwriter Cesare Zavattini (1902–1989) contributed the screenplays to some of the greatest Italian films of all time. He was a key intellectual architect of the neorealist movement in Italian cinema.

Neorealism arose in Italy after World War II. In place of fanciful romantic plots and lavish sets inspired by the Hollywood value system, neorealist films offered scenes of everyday life, rendered in a hyper-realistic manner and often featuring nonprofessional actors. Such films accurately reflected the difficult economic conditions ordinary Italians faced during the post-war years. Highly influential in international cinema, neorealism is often associated with its directors, most often Vittorio de Sica. Yet Zavattini, in addition to contributing screenplays to key neorealist masterpieces, was the movement's central intellectual architect and theorist, and he began to explore neorealist ideas in advance of de Sica and the other famous directors of post-war Italy.

Worked as Journalist

Cesare Zavattini was born in the small town of Luzzara in central Italy's Emilia-Romagna district on April 20, 1902. After attending the University of Parma, he worked for several years, beginning in 1930, as a journalist in Milan. He had creative aspirations on the side from the beginning, and in the early 1930s he published several well-reviewed novels that displayed a surrealist streak. His first book, *Parliamo tanto di me,* appeared in 1931, and his novel-writing career continued into the period when he found success in the film world. As a journalist, Zavattini wrote some film criticism, and with the Italian film industry growing in the 1930s, he decided to try his hand at screenwriting himself.

Zavattini's first script was for the light comedy *Darò un milione,* which appeared in 1935 and was translated into English as *I'll Give a Million* in 1938. He continued to write various kinds of screenplays and to gain experience, becoming an in-demand creative contributor by the early 1940s. Between 1941 and 1943 he wrote 12 screenplays, with 1941's *Teresa Venerdi* marking his first collaboration with Vittorio de Sica. That film contained few signs of

neorealist ideas, but with his 1943 screenplay for Alessandro Blasetti's *Quattro passi fra le nuvole* (Four Steps in the Clouds) Zavattini began to explore social issues. In 1944 he reunited with de Sica for *I bambini ci guardano,* and that film marked a major step toward neorealist technique: the filmmakers left the studio in favor of filming on location, on Italy's streets.

Their motives at first might have been economic— by 1944 the war had slowed Italy's film industry considerably, and filmmakers were forced to rely on simple sets and low-cost lighting techniques. But neorealist ideas developed rapidly, as filmmakers struggled to come to grips with the scale of Italy's wartime disaster. The 1945 film *Open City,* directed by Roberto Rossellini, employed seemingly spontaneous camera work in its story of the Italian Resistance against fascism, and in 1946 Zavattini and de Sica decided to extend Rossellini's techniques in a story of the everyday streets of Italy. Zavattini wrote the script for *Shoe-Shine* (in Italian *Sciuscià),* which depicted a group of homeless street kids who become involved in black-market activities. The children were played by nonprofessional actors.

Nominated for Multiple Academy Awards

Like most of the early neorealist films, *Shoe-Shine* had little commercial success in Italy itself. But the film won international critical acclaim, and in the United States Zavattini shared in a Special Academy Award and won the first of three Oscar nominations for best screenplay. Six more films followed before Zavattini and de Sica collaborated once again, in 1948, on *The Bicycle Thief* (in Italian, *Ladri di biciclette,* which means "bicycle thieves"). This film, which was a commercial success in Italy as well as abroad, told the story of a man in desperate straits who makes a small amount of money by putting up advertising posters, traveling around the city on his bicycle; after it is stolen, the camera follows him almost in real time as, together with his young son, he searches for it.

Zavattini and de Sica collaborated again on the 1949 film *Miracle in Milan,* a sentimental film with supernatural elements. One of the most prolific screenwriters in Italian film history, Zavattini by no means restricted his output to neorealism.

The third of the classic of Zavattini–de Sica collaborations, *Umberto D,* appeared in 1952 and dealt with a poverty-stricken civil servant who is evicted from his apartment and ends up homeless, facing an uncertain fate. In its pure simplicity and its story of quiet desperation, *Umberto D* was a classic example of the neorealist style and one of the defining films of post-war cinema. Zavattini's scripts influenced filmmakers as far away as India, where writer-director Satyajit Ray emulated the structure of his screenplays in *Pather Panchali* and other films.

Zavattini outlined the ideas behind neorealism in a series of writings and interviews that, in the words of the *New York Times,* "placed him at the center of Italian intellectual life in the late 1940s and 1950s." "The old realism didn't express the real," he asserted in an interview quoted by the *Times.* "What I want to know is. . .the inner as well as the outer reality." In his essay *Some Ideas on the Cinema,* he argued that the camera itself was the primary creative force in film, and that plot was ultimately a distraction from deep observation of real life. Influential critics such as France's André Bazin began to write essays examining Zavattini's techniques.

Conceived Experimental Films

Zavattini even envisioned an experimental form of cinema that would eliminate plot altogether in favor of using the camera to record selected everyday scenes. He was unsuccessful in finding financing that would allow him to realize his ideas, however, and in the late 1950s he and de Sica had only intermittent success with realistic films that included strongly melodramatic elements. They were displaced to a degree by the rising star of Italian cinema, Federico Fellini, whose early stories of circus performers and the like were influenced by Zavattini's writing but went in new directions. Zavattini and de Sica enjoyed a comeback of sorts with the critically acclaimed *Two Women* (1960), which featured actress Sophia Loren in a story of a mother and daughter trying to survive in the countryside during World War II.

Zavattini wrote more films for de Sica and others in the 1960s, but these were poorly received critically. He was not involved with de Sica's later masterpiece, *The Garden of the Finzi-Continis*, but the two creative partners reunited one more time for *A Brief Vacation* (in Italian *Un breve vacanza*), made in 1973 and released in the United States in 1975). Many of his screenplays were published in book form in the 1970s, and he was a voluminous contributor to film magazines. In 1970 he published an autobiography, *Scenes from a Cinematic Life.* He continued to turn out new scripts for Italian films almost until the end of his life, but he never worked outside Italy or learned to speak English.

In later life, Zavattini pursued painting, printmaking, and poetry avidly, in addition to continuing to work in films. He maintained a large collection of postcard-sized paintings commissioned from various artists. In 1982, at the age of 80, Zavattini directed and starred in a surrealistic short film, *La veritàaa* (The Truth). Married to Olga Berni, who died in 1980, he had four children, Mario, Arturo, Marco, and Milly. Zavattini died in Rome on October 13, 1989, and was eulogized by *New Republic* critic Stanley Kauffman as a man who "had affected the film experience of millions around the world and yet was known to few of them."

Books

Bondanella, Peter, *Italian Cinema: From Neorealism to the Present,* Ungar, 1983.

International Dictionary of Films and Filmmakers, Gale, 2000.

Zavattini, Cesare, *Scenes from a Cinematic Life,* Prentice Hall, 1970.

Periodicals

CineAction, Spring 2007.

New Republic, November 27, 1989.

New York Times, October 16, 1989.

Times (London, England), October 16, 1989.

Online

"Biography of Cesare Zavattini," *RAI Italian Radio,* http://www.italica.rai.it/eng/principal/topics/bio/zavattini.htm (October 24, 2011).s

Contemporary Authors Online, Cengage Gale, http://www.gale.cengage.com (October 24, 2011).s□

Viktor Zhdanov

In 1958, Soviet virologist Viktor Zhdanov (1914-1987) persuaded the World Health Organization (WHO) to step up efforts to rid the world of smallpox, one of the most devastating diseases known to infect humans. Highly contagious, incredibly disfiguring, and frequently deadly, smallpox had plagued human populations for thousands of years. In addition to kick-starting the WHO's successful smallpox eradication program, Zhdanov initiated a trial of U.S. scientist Albert Sabin's live-virus polio vaccine during the late 1950s, which proved so successful that Sabin's vaccine enjoyed extensive use and ultimately helped snuff out the threat of polio worldwide.

Viktor Mikhailovich Zhdanov was born February 13, 1914, in Ukraine, an eastern European country that became part of the Soviet Union during Zhdanov's childhood. Zhdanov attended Ukraine's Kharkov Medical Institute and graduated in 1936. He spent the next decade working as a military doctor in Zabaikalye and Turkestan. During this time Zhdanov studied Hepatitis A and wrote his doctoral thesis on the infectious liver disease. In 1941, he joined the Communist Party of the Soviet Union.

Began Career in Public Health

In 1946, Zhdanov was appointed chief of the epidemiology department at the I.I. Mechnikov Institute of Epidemiology and Microbiology in Kharkov and moved up the ranks, becoming the institute's director within two years. Viruses fascinated Zhdanov and he began publishing papers on virus classification. This work led to Zhdanov's election to the International Committee on Taxonomy of Viruses (ICTV), a group comprising the world's leading virus experts. The ICTV was charged with maintaining a universal virus taxonomy database. Because of his depth of knowledge on the subject, Zhdanov was elected as a life member.

In 1950, Zhdanov joined the U.S.S.R.'s Ministry of Health, heading up the epidemiology department. In 1951 he was appointed the U.S.S.R.'s Deputy Minister of Health, which placed him in charge of overseeing programs to halt communicable diseases in the U.S.S.R. While serving in this position, Zhdanov naturally became interested in disease eradication and began studying its successes and failures.

By this time, the Soviet Union had successfully eliminated smallpox and dracunculiasis, a parasitic infection caused by a roundworm linked to stagnant drinking water. Zhdanov began studying other diseases, too, trying to figure out which ones might successfully be eradicated. Zhdanov reasoned that spending money upfront to eliminate a disease would save money in the long run.

OK'd Polio Vaccine Trial

During the 1950s, Zhdanov devoted a large portion of his time to the study of polio, realizing the public health threat the crippling disease posed to his nation. By the mid-1950s, U.S. scientists Jonas Salk and Albert Sabin had each developed a polio vaccine. Salk's "killed-virus" vaccine enjoyed extensive trials in the United States. Zhdanov agreed to try Sabin's vaccine in a Soviet trial.

Sabin's vaccine used a live, weakened form of the virus; Sabin believed the live virus was needed in order to ensure long-term immunity. Sabin's vaccine went through a trial in the Soviet Union under the direction of Soviet microbiologist Mikhail Chumakov. The Soviet team refined the vaccine, creating a version that could be taken orally. More than 70 million Soviet citizens received the Sabin vaccine and it became a worldwide standard.

Besides helping stem cases of polio in the Soviet Union, Zhdanov launched programs to help control the spread of other infectious diseases through extensive vaccination programs and improved hygiene. Under Zhdanov's watch, millions of Soviet children received vaccinations, leading to a decline in influenza and measles. To help spread information about his research, Zhdanov, in 1956, launched *Problems in Virology,* a journal aimed at educating researchers on recent findings in the field of virology. He edited the journal and contributed articles to it for the remainder of his life. In recognition of his work and knowledge in the area of virus research, Zhdanov became a member of the WHO's Expert Advisory Panel on Viral Diseases in 1957. He served on the panel for the remainder of his life.

Urged Smallpox Eradication

In 1958, Zhdanov traveled to the United States to attend the annual meeting of the World Health Assembly—the governing body of the World Health Organization (WHO). Zhdanov took the opportunity to give an inspiring speech, urging the WHO to work toward smallpox eradication. During his speech Zhdanov pointed out that citizens in smallpox-free nations, like the Soviet Union and the United States, still faced the possibility of contracting the disease from abroad and therefore continued costly national vaccination programs to protect against an outbreak. Zhdanov suggested that if smallpox was eradicated on a global level, routine vaccinations could come to an end.

Zhdanov pointed to successes in stopping the spread of the disease, citing the Soviet Union as an example. He pointed out that in 1936 the Soviet Union halted smallpox within its borders through the use of a primitive, non-heat stable liquid vaccine. Zhdanov noted that the vaccine had improved and with the new, highly-stable freeze-dried smallpox vaccine available, it was time to pursue global eradication so all nations could cease vaccinations.

During his speech Zhdanov quoted a letter former U.S. President Thomas Jefferson had written to British physician Edward Jenner in 1806. Jenner was the scientist who discovered the smallpox vaccine. According to a WHO publication on global smallpox eradication, Jefferson wrote that "in the future the peoples of the world will learn about this disgusting smallpox disease only from ancient traditions." Likewise, Zhdanov proposed that if the WHO launched a concerted effort to rid the world of smallpox, future generations would only know of the disease from reading history books. To get the effort started, Zhdanov said the Soviet Union would provide 25 million doses of the vaccine. While Zhdanov was sure the disease could be eliminated on a global scale, some virologists thought otherwise. No disease had ever been eliminated from the planet.

Smallpox, caused by the *variola virus,* was highly transmittable and could spread through the air during face-to-face contact. Symptoms started with a fever, followed by a rash. The rash spots started flat, then raised up becoming small, hard bubbles. As the disease progressed, the bubbles softened and filled with fluid and pus. Lesions in the throat and nose released the virus into the mouth, enabling it to spread quickly. Those who survived ended up with deeply pitted marks and, in a large number of survivors, blindness.

The disease's ghastly effects made it ripe for elimination. In 1959, the WHO created a Smallpox Eradication Program; however, efforts to eliminate the disease moved slowly. At the time, the WHO was involved in a malaria-eradication program and did not budget sufficient funds and equipment for the smallpox program. In 1965, U.S. President Lyndon Johnson threw his support behind the WHO's smallpox-elimination program, hoping to boost the United States' image in developing countries where the disease was prevalent. Johnson offered U.S. funding for the project and this influx of support prompted WHO officials to get serious about the problem. At the time, the disease had been eliminated in Europe, the United States, and most of the Americas but was still active in more than 30 countries, including India and South Asia.

The last known case of smallpox occurred in Somalia in 1977. According to Mark Caldwell of *Discover* magazine, on December 9, 1979, a WHO panel convened in Geneva, Switzerland, to sign a proclamation that read, in five languages, "We, the members of the global commission for the certification of smallpox eradication, certify that smallpox has been eradicated from the world." The eradication of smallpox saved countless lives, as the disease was estimated to have killed some 300 million people in the 20th century before the WHO's massive immunization program eliminated the disease at Zhdanov's prompting.

Continued Virus Research

In 1960 Zhdanov became a member of the Soviet Union's Academy of Sciences. Around that same time, Zhdanov left his position with the government's health ministry, having grown tired of Soviet Party politics. He devoted himself to research and became director of the D.I. Ivanovsky Institute of Virology, located in Moscow. Over the next several years, Zhdanov befriended western scientists, hoping to form collaborations. At the time, Zhdanov feared the Soviets were falling behind in the study of virology.

Zhdanov traveled to the United States in 1968 to visit virology labs. He became interested in molecular virology and began studying how viruses invade host cells. He spent several months working at St. Jude Children's Research Hospital in Memphis, working alongside David Kingsbury on replicating paramyxoviruses. Paramyxoviruses cause such diseases as mumps, measles, and RSV—or respiratory syncytial virus. In 1968, Zhdanov organized the First International Congress of Virology in Helsinki. Under Zhdanov's direction, the Ivanovsky Institute opened new laboratories and the staff increased, reaching more than 600.

Besides studying viruses and trying to figure out how host cells work, Zhdanov was also interested in influenza, using it to study viruses. He operated a WHO Collaborating Center for Influenza at the institute, whereby he isolated and stored all influenza strains that had invaded the U.S.S.R. In 1977, when an unusual influenza strain began spreading across the globe, Zhdanov made his virus collection available to other WHO Collaborating Centers so a vaccine could be created to stem the spread.

Concerned with AIDS Outbreak

During the 1980s, after doctors identified the AIDS virus, Zhdanov became interested in stopping the disease from spreading within the borders of the Soviet Union. He was frustrated, however, with Moscow's insistence that the disease had not spread to the Soviet Union. Zhdanov wanted to prepare for a large outbreak, whereas Soviet officials dismissed his warnings of a massive outbreak, calling it a faint possibility. Initially, Soviet intelligence insisted that HIV had been created by the U.S. government in a warfare laboratory. Despite pressure to tow the party line, Zhdanov studied HIV and published a paper on its origin, dismissing Soviet intelligence on the matter.

In 1986 Zhdanov traveled to Paris to attend the Second International Conference on AIDS. He hoped to pursue international cooperation in developing a vaccine against the disease. While there, he acknowledged that the Soviet government was lying when it claimed there were virtually no AIDS and HIV cases in the Soviet Union. Zhdanov noted that in fact there had been small outbreaks across his country.

When Zhdanov returned home, members of the Soviet security agency—the KGB—began harassing him. In addition, top Communist leaders in the scientific community launched a slander campaign against the noted virologist, questioning his scientific credibility and suggesting he was not to be trusted because he was not acting like a loyal Soviet citizen. "He was denounced as a CIA spy," fellow researcher Eduoard Karamov told Laurie Garrett in her book, *Betrayal of Trust: The Collapse of Global Public Health*. "He died less than a year after he returned from Paris, and I have no doubt that, despite his age, the witch hunt gave him that stroke." Zhdanov died of a cerebral hemorrhage in 1987. He was 73.

Books

Garrett, Laurie, *Betrayal of Trust: The Collapse of Global Public Health*, Oxford University Press, 2001.

Periodicals

Diplomatic History, April 2010.

Online

"Development of the Global Smallpox Eradication Programme, 1958-1966," World Health Organization, http://whqlibdoc.who.int/smallpox/9241561106_chp9.pdf (November 12, 2011).

"In Memory of Victor Zhdanov," *Virology Division News*, http://www.springerlink.com/content/m8205v513225303r/ (November 22, 2011).

"Polio: Two Vaccines," Smithsonian National Museum of American History, http://americanhistory.si.edu/polio/virusvaccine/vacraces2.htm (November 22, 2011).

"Vigil for a Doomed Virus," *Discover*, http://discovermagazine.com/1992/mar/vigilforadoomedv10 (November 22, 2011). □

Fritz Zwicky

Fritz Zwicky (1898-1974) was a Swiss astrophysicist best known for his theory of dark matter and for his work with supernovae. He is also known for his in-depth catalog of the stars. At the time of his death, Zwicky had discovered 122 supernovae and had 50 patents to his name, many of them in jet propulsion.

Fritz Zwicky was born in Varna, Bulgaria on February 14, 1898. The eldest of three children, Zwicky was born to Fridolin Zwicky, a Swiss accountant and merchant, and Franziska Wreck, a Czech woman. At the time of his birth, the Zwicky family was in Bulgaria while Fridolin Zwicky acted as the Norwegian consul to Bulgaria.

In 1904, Fridolin Zwicky moved his family back to Mollis, Switzerland. Even from a young age, Fritz Zwicky found himself to be very good at science, which led him to study engineering.

From 1914 to 1916 Zwicky attended the Oberrealischule secondary school in Zurich. Then he moved on to the Eidenössische Technische Hochschule (ETH), the Swiss Federal Institute of Technology, in Zurch. Zwicky switched from studying mechanical engineering to mathematics and earned his first degree in 1920, writing his diploma thesis under the notable German mathematician and physcist Hermann Weyl. In 1921, Zwicky published his first scholarly work, "The Second Virial Coefficient of the Rare Gases." He wrote a Ph.D. dissertation about the theory of ionic crystals under Peter Debye, a future Nobel Prize winner in chemistry, and Paul Scherrer, a Swiss physicist, finishing his doctorate in 1922. For the next three years, Zwicky worked as an assistant at Debye's Physical Institute at ETH.

Early Career

In 1925, Robert Millikan, president of Caltech (the California Institute of Technology), invited Zwicky to Pasadena, California, to study quantum theory related to solids and liquids. Zwicky received the Rockefeller Fellowship from the International Education Board to study there for two years specifically to work with Paul Epstein, a mathematician, and Millikan, himself a nobel laureate in physics, among others. Zwicky would work in the United States and at Caltech for the rest of his career, but would never renounce his Swiss citizenship. Zwicky would be an assistant at Caltech from 1927 to 1929, an associate professor of physics from 1929 to 1942, and the first professor of astrophysics at Caltech, a title that he held from 1942 to 1968.

Zwicky was still early in his career when his interests shifted from mathematics and chemistry to astrophysics. He began by pondering cosmic rays and how they were created. In 1929, Zwicky proposed an alternate theory to Hubble's law. Edwin Hubble, an American astronomer, believed that he could observe the expansion of the universe by looking at the correlation between the distance between interstellar objects and the redshift of their observable velocity to earth. Redshift is the tendency of waves to move towards the red end of the visible light spectrum as an object moves away from earth, much like the Doppler effect changes the pitch of sound as an object making a noise approaches and leaves. Hubble theorized that by looking at the correlation between the distance between interstellar objects and the redshift of those objects, he could prove that the universe was expanding.

Zwicky did not trust the measurement of redshift at the time. He believed that the redshift-related correlation that Hubble saw could be explained by "tired light," the fact that photons, small particles of light, become less energetic after they have traveled long distances. It is these less energetic photons that explain the redshift. Zwicky's idea was disproved 60 years later when supernovae showed that the expansion of the universe was real.

On March 25, 1932 Zwicky married Dorothy Vernon Gates, the daughter of a well-off California family. Gates's father, California State Senator Edgar J. Gates, would later help to finance one of Zwicky's telescopes, but Zwicky and Gates had no children and divorced in 1941.

Supernovae

In 1933, Zwicky began to move his interests further away from theoretical physics and closer to astrophysics. He was particularly interested in non-periodic novas; Zwicky renamed these supernovas. Zwicky believed that these supernovae were ordinary stars changing into neutron stars, what is left when a star collapses in on itself, which releases radiation and cosmic rays. In late 1933, Zwicky, working with Walter Baade, a German astronomer, began to study supernovae and how they could be used to determine the distances between galaxies. Eventually they would go on to study the cosmic rays that Zwicky believed radiated from supernovae.

In 1933, Zwicky convinced Caltech's Observatory Council to install an eighteen-inch Schmidt telescope at Palomar Mountain Observatory. Zwicky's ability to convince the university to build this telescope was particularly impressive considering that a 200-in Hale telescope was already being built for Palomar. This project was largely funded by Edgar Gates, Zwicky's then father-in-law, and was not finished until 1936.

In 1934, while waiting for the Schmidt telescope to be constructed, Zwicky mounted a small camera atop the Robinson Laboratory at Caltech. It was a small 3.5-in camera, which he used to photograph the Virgo cluster of galaxies. Zwicky never found a supernova with this camera, and many of his colleagues found this satisfying, as Zwicky's irascible manner made him very unpopular. It was not until the 18-in Schmidt telescope was finished that Zwicky found his first supernova. On February 1, 1937 Zwicky discovered his first supernova. Only a few short months later, on August 26, 1937, he found his second. Over the next five years, Zwicky with Baade and Rudolph Minkowski, a German-American astronomer, would record 18 supernovae.

Dark Matter

While he was working on supernovae, Zwicky was simultaneously working on another project. He had been measuring the redshifts for different galaxies in the Coma cluster, and concluded that none of the redshift velocities were the same. Zwicky published a paper in a German-Swiss journal suggesting that there had to be a very large mass in order to ensure that the gravitational pull was enough to hold the Cluster together. He coined a term to define this mass: "dunkle material." Now known as dark matter, Zwicky meant for this to be some combination of small, faint galaxies and diffuse gases, though modern astrophysics knows that these elements make up little of the mass of dark matter. It is this dark matter that holds the galaxies together. Not surprisingly, it took decades before the scientific community recognized this discovery for what it was. In part, this has to do with Zwicky's irritable attitude, which made his colleagues less than congenial towards him and his discoveries.

Military Research

During the Second World War, Zwicky spent much of his time working on rocketry and propulsion with the Aerojet Corporation, later Aerojet General Corporation. He founded the company with Theodore von Karman, a mathematician, physicist, and engineer, as well as other scientists and headquartered it in Azusa, California. From 1943 to 1949 Zwicky acted as the corporation's director of research and pioneered several kinds of jet and propulsion engines. By the end of his life, Zwicky would hold several patents in rocketry.

Starting in 1945, Zwicky worked with the United States military. From 1945 to 1946, he acted as a technical representative to the United States Army Air Forces factfinding team. They were sent to Germany and Japan to study the defeated countries' wartime research on jet propulsion after the war. From 1945 to 1949, Zwicky was a member of the United States Air Force Scientific Advisory Board. In 1946, he published a book for the air force entitled *Certain Phases of War Research in Germany.*

In 1949, Zwicky was awarded the Presidential Medal of Freedom for his work with Aerojet, but in that same year he stepped down from his position as head of research. Zwicky did continue on as a technical advisor and a research consultant with the company until 1961.

In 1955, Zwicky had his security clearance with the Department of Defense revoked. He was told that unless he became a United States citizen, he would not have his clearance reinstated. Zwicky refused, saying that naturalized citizens were treated as second-class citizens. He maintained his Swiss citizenship until his death, even though he lived the majority of his life in the United States.

More Controversy, Discoveries, and Lasting Impressions

In 1947, Zwicky published, "Morphology and Nomenclature of Jet Engines" in *Aviation.* On October 15 of that same year, Zwicky married Anna Margarita Zürcher, his second wife. She was the daughter of a hotel owner and the couple went on to have three daughters.

On May 12, 1948, Zwicky shocked the astrophysics world and ruffled more feathers when he delivered the Halley lecture, traditionally about celestial phenomena, on his own astronomy methodology. He would eventually go on to write a book entitled *Morphological Astronomy,* on the same topic, as an expansion of his Halley lecture. That same year the 48-in Schmidt telescope began operation at Palomar, a lens for which Zwicky had been a significant advocate.

Between 1961 and 1968 Zwicky began to compile his most lasting legacy to astronomy. The *Catalog of Galaxies, and of Clusters of Galaxies,* was a six volume set of clusters of galaxies which Zwicky and his team created with images taken by the 48-in Schmidt from the Palomar Observatory.

In 1968, Zwicky retired from Caltech, but he continued to work. In 1971 he released a *Catalog of Selected Compact Galaxies and of Post-Eruptive Galaxies,* which he compiled after the 1963 discovery of quasars. This book was co-authored with his oldest daughter, Margrit A. Zwicky. He would also create a catalog, with Milton Humason, of high-latitude B stars.

In addition to his other advances, Zwicky pioneered a lasting photographic handling technique used in astronomy. He determined how to subtract one negative from another positive to show parts of galaxies and nebulae that might have otherwise been missed by researchers.

Personal Life and Death

Zwicky's most notable trait was his irritable personality. Often derided and underestimated by his colleagues, many of Zwicky's discoveries went unnoticed and unheeded for many decades because Zwicky had few friends in the field and no followers to laud his efforts. It is often supposed that because of his attitude he received far fewer awards and accolades than he would have had he been more congenial. That being said, he was named the vice president of the International Academy of Astronautics and he did receive the Royal Astronomical Society's Gold Medal in 1972.

Zwicky enjoyed Alpine climbing and became well known for his charitable efforts including rebuilding European libraries after World War II. He was also named the chair of the Board of Trustees of the Pestalozzi Foundation in 1958, which housed war orphans. He had discovered 122 supernovae and had 50 patents to his name at the time of his death.

Fritz Zwicky died of a heart attack at the Huntington Memorial Hospital in Pasadena, California, on February 8, 1974. He is buried in Glarus, Switzerland.

Books

Clark, David H. and Matthew D.H. Clark, *Measuring the Cosmos: How Scientists Discovered the Dimensions of the Universe,* Rutgers University Press, 2004.

Complete Dictionary of Scientific Biography, Charles Scribner's Sons, 2008.

Dictionary of American Biography, Charles Scribner's Sons, 1994.

Hockey, Thomas, ed., *The Biographical Encyclopedia of Astronomers,* Springer, 2007.

Hoskin, Michael, ed., *Cambridge Illustrated History of Astronomy,* Cambridge University Press, 1997. □

HOW TO USE THE *SUPPLEMENT* INDEX

The *Encyclopedia of World Biography Supplement (EWB)* Index is designed to serve several purposes. First, it is a cumulative listing of biographies included in the entire second edition of *EWB* and its supplements (volumes 1-31). Second, it locates information on specific topics mentioned in volume 32 of the encyclopedia—persons, places, events, organizations, institutions, ideas, titles of works, inventions, as well as artistic schools, styles, and movements. Third, it classifies the subjects of *Supplement* articles according to shared characteristics. Vocational categories are the most numerous—for example, artists, authors, military leaders, philosophers, scientists, statesmen. Other groupings bring together disparate people who share a common characteristic.

The structure of the *Supplement* Index is quite simple. The biographical entries are cumulative and often provide enough information to meet immediate reference needs. Thus, people mentioned in the *Supplement* Index are identified and their life dates, when known, are given. Because this is an index to a *biographical* encyclopedia, every reference includes the *name* of the article to which the reader is directed as well as the volume and page numbers. Below are a few points that will make the *Supplement* Index easy to use.

Typography. All main entries are set in boldface type. Entries that are also the titles of articles in *EWB* are set entirely in capitals; other main entries are set in initial capitals and lowercase letters. Where a main entry is followed by a great many references, these are organized by subentries in alphabetical sequence. In certain cases—for example, the names of countries for which there are many references—a special class of subentries, set in small capitals and preceded by boldface dots, is used to mark significant divisions.

Alphabetization. The Index is alphabetized word by word. For example, all entries beginning with *New* as a separate word (*New Jersey, New York*) come before

Newark. Commas in inverted entries are treated as full stops (*Berlin; Berlin, Congress of; Berlin, University of; Berlin Academy of Sciences*). Other commas are ignored in filing. When words are identical, persons come first and subsequent entries are alphabetized by their parenthetical qualifiers (such as *book, city, painting*).

Titled persons may be alphabetized by family name or by title. The more familiar form is used—for example, *Disraeli, Benjamin* rather than *Beaconsfield, Earl of.* Cross-references are provided from alternative forms and spellings of names. Identical names of the same nationality are filed chronologically.

Titles of books, plays, poems, paintings, and other works of art beginning with an article are filed on the following word (*Bard, The*). Titles beginning with a preposition are filed on the preposition (*In Autumn*). In subentries, however, prepositions are ignored; thus *influenced by* would precede the subentry *in* literature.

Literary characters are filed on the last name. Acronyms, such as UNESCO, are treated as single words. Abbreviations, such as *Mr., Mrs.,* and *St.,* are alphabetized as though they were spelled out.

Occupational categories are alphabetical by national qualifier. Thus, *Authors, Scottish* comes before *Authors, Spanish,* and the reader interested in Spanish poets will find the subentry *poets* under *Authors, Spanish.*

Cross-references. The term *see* is used in references throughout the *Supplement* Index. The *see* references appear both as main entries and as subentries. They most often direct the reader from an alternative name spelling or form to the main entry listing.

This introduction to the *Supplement* Index is necessarily brief. The reader will soon find, however, that the *Supplement* Index provides ready reference to both highly specific subjects and broad areas of information contained in volume 32 and a cumulative listing of those included in the entire set.

INDEX

A

"A"
see Arnold, Matthew

"A.B."
see Pinto, Isaac

AALTO, HUGO ALVAR HENRIK
(1898-1976), Finnish architect, designer, and town planner **1** 1-2

AARON, HENRY LOUIS (Hank; born 1934), American baseball player **1** 2-3

ABAKANOWICZ, MAGDALENA (Marta Abakanowicz-Kosmowski; born 1930), Polish sculptor **25** 1-3

Abarbanel
see Abravanel

ABBA (music group)
Hallström, Lasse **32** 147-149

ABBA ARIKA (c. 175-c. 247), Babylonian rabbi **1** 3-4

ABBAS I (1571-1629), Safavid shah of Persia 1588-1629 **1** 4-6

ABBAS, FERHAT (1899-1985), Algerian statesman **1** 6-7

ABBAS, MAHMOUD (Abu Masen; born 1935), Palestinian statesman **27** 1-3

Abbas the Great
see Abbas I

Abbé Sieyès
see Sieyès, Comte Emmanuel Joseph

ABBEY, EDWARD (Edward Paul Abbey; 1927-1989), American author and environmental activist **27** 3-5

ABBOTT, BERENICE (1898-1991), American artist and photographer **1** 7-9

Abbott, Bud
see Abbott and Costello

ABBOTT, DIANE JULIE (born 1953), British politician and journalist **26** 1-3

ABBOTT, EDITH (1876-1957), American social reformer, educator, and author **26** 3-5

ABBOTT, GRACE (1878-1939), American social worker and agency administrator **1** 9-10

ABBOTT, LYMAN (1835-1922), American Congregationalist clergyman, author, and editor **1** 10-11

ABBOTT AND COSTELLO (Bud Abbott; 1895-1974, and Lou Costello; 1908-1959), American comedic acting team **32** 1-4

Abbott and Costello Show, The (television program)
Abbott and Costello **32** 1-4

ABBOUD, EL FERIK IBRAHIM (1900-1983), Sudanese general, prime minister, 1958-1964 **1** 11-12

ABC
see American Broadcasting Company (ABC)

ABC's Wide World of Sports (television program)
Arledge, Roone **32** 16-18
McKay, Jim **32** 247-249

ABD AL-MALIK (646-705), Umayyad caliph 685-705 **1** 12-13

ABD AL-MUMIN (c. 1094-1163), Almohad caliph 1133-63 **1** 13

ABD AL-RAHMAN I (731-788), Umayyad emir in Spain 756-88 **1** 13-14

ABD AL-RAHMAN III (891-961), Umayyad caliph of Spain **1** 14

Abd al-Rahman ibn Khaldun
see Ibn Khaldun, Abd al-Rahman ibn Muhammad

ABD AL-WAHHAB, MUHAMMAD IBN (Muhammad Ibn Abd al-Wahab; 1702-1703-1791-1792), Saudi religious leader **27** 5-7

ABD EL-KADIR (1807-1883), Algerian political and religious leader **1** 15

ABD EL-KRIM EL-KHATABI, MOHAMED BEN (c. 1882-1963), Moroccan Berber leader **1** 15-16

Abdallah ben Yassin
see Abdullah ibn Yasin

ABDELLAH, FAYE GLENN (born 1919), American nurse **24** 1-3

Abdu-l-Malik
see Abd al-Malik

ABDUH IBN HASAN KHAYR ALLAH, MUHAMMAD (1849-1905), Egyptian nationalist and theologian **1** 16-17

ABDUL-BAHA (Abbas Effendi; 1844-1921), Persian leader of the Baha'i Muslim sect **22** 3-5

ABDUL-HAMID II (1842-1918), Ottoman sultan 1876-1909 **1** 17-18

ABDUL RAHMAN, TUNKU (1903-1990), prime minister of Malaysia **18** 340-341

Abdul the Damned
see Abdul-Hamid II

ABDULLAH II (Abdullah bin al Hussein II; born 1962), king of Jordan **22** 5-7

ABDULLAH, MOHAMMAD (Lion of Kashmir; 1905-1982), Indian political leader who worked for an independent Kashmir **22** 7-9

'ABDULLAH AL-SALIM AL-SABAH, SHAYKH (1895-1965), Amir of Kuwait (1950-1965) **1** 18-19

ABDULLAH IBN HUSEIN (1882-1951), king of Jordan 1949-1951, of Transjordan 1946-49 **1** 19-20

ABDULLAH IBN YASIN (died 1059), North African founder of the Almoravid movement **1** 20

ABE, KOBO (born Kimifusa Abe; also transliterated as Abe Kobo; 1924-1993), Japanese writer, theater director, photographer **1** 20-22

385

ADAMS, JOHN (1735-1826), American statesman and diplomat, president 1797-1801 **1** 48-51
relatives
Adams, Louisa **32** 6-8

ADAMS, JOHN COUCH (1819-1892), English mathematical astronomer **1** 51-52

ADAMS, JOHN QUINCY (1767-1848), American statesman and diplomat, president 1825-29 **1** 52-54
relatives
Adams, Louisa **32** 6-8

ADAMS, LOUISA (born Louisa Catherine Johnson; 1775-1852), American first lady **32** 6-8

ADAMS, PETER CHARDON BROOKS (1848-1927), American historian **1** 54

ADAMS, SAMUEL (1722-1803), American colonial leader and propagandist **1** 55-56

ADAMSON, JOY (Friederike Victoria Gessner; 1910-1980), Austrian naturalist and painter **18** 7-9

ADDAMS, JANE (1860-1935), American social worker, reformer, and pacifist **1** 56-57

Addis Ababa, Duke of
see Badoglio, Pietro

ADDISON, JOSEPH (1672-1719), English essayist and politician **1** 57-58

ADDISON, THOMAS (1793-1860), English physician **1** 58-59

ADENAUER, KONRAD (1876-1967), German statesman, chancellor of the Federal Republic 1949-63 **1** 59-61

Adenosine triphosphate
Cohn, Mildred **32** 81-84

ADLER, ALFRED (1870-1937), Austrian psychiatrist **1** 61-63

ADLER, FELIX (1851-1933), American educator and Ethical Culture leader **1** 63-64

ADLER, LARRY (Lawrence Cecil Adler; 1914-2001), American harmonica player **26** 5-7

ADLER, MORTIMER JEROME (1902-2001), American philosopher and educator **22** 9-11

ADLER, RENATA (born 1938), American author **26** 8-9

Admiralty House (London)
Vassall, John **32** 350-352

Adolphe I
see Thiers, Adolphe

ADONIS ('Ali Ahmad Said; born 1930), Lebanese poet **1** 64-65

Adoption
Holt, Bertha **32** 168-171
Perkins, Rebecca Talbot **32** 297-298

ADORNO, THEODOR W. (1903-1969), German philosopher and leader of the Frankfurt School **1** 65-67

ADRIAN, EDGAR DOUGLAS (1st Baron Adrian of Cambridge; 1889-1977), English neurophysiologist **1** 67-69

Adventurers
French-Sheldon, May **32** 315-317

Adventures of Robin Hood, The (film)
Flynn, Errol **32** 117-119

ADZHUBEI, ALEKSEI IVANOVICH (1924-1993), Russian journalist and editor **18** 9-11

AELFRIC (955-c. 1012), Anglo-Saxon monk, scholar, and writer **1** 69-70

Aeronautics (science)
engineers
Blériot, Louis **32** 42-44

AEROSMITH (began 1969), American rock band **24** 4-7

AESCHYLUS (524-456 BCE), Greek playwright **1** 70-72

AESOP (c. 620 BCE-c. 560 BCE), Greek fabulist **24** 7-8

AFFONSO I (c. 1460-1545), king of Kongo **1** 72

AFINOGENOV, ALEKSANDR NIKOLAEVICH (1904-1941), Russian dramatist **1** 72-73

'AFLAQ, MICHEL (1910-1989), Syrian founder and spiritual leader of the Ba'th party **1** 73-74

African American art
see African American history

African American history
POLITICIANS
presidential candidates and presidents
Obama, Barack **32** 280-282
"SEPARATE BUT EQUAL" (1896-1954)
baseball
Gibson, Josh **32** 135-138
other rights cases
Desmond, Viola **32** 92-94
SOCIETY AND CULTURE
religion
Thurman, Howard **32** 334-335

African Americans
see African American history (United States)

African music
Bebey, Francis **32** 36-38

AGA KHAN (title), chief commander of Moslem Nizari Ismailis **1** 74-76

AGAOGLU, ADALET (Adalet Agoglu; born 1929), Turkish playwright, author, and human rights activist **22** 11-13

AGASSIZ, JEAN LOUIS RODOLPHE (1807-1873), Swiss-American naturalist and anatomist **1** 76-78

AGEE, JAMES (1909-1955), American poet, journalist, novelist, and screenwriter **1** 78-79

AGESILAUS II (c. 444-360 BCE), king of Sparta circa 399-360 B.C. **1** 79-80

Agglutinins
see Antibodies (biochemistry)

Agglutinogens
see Antigens (biochemistry)

AGHA MOHAMMAD KHAN (c. 1742-1797), shah of Persia **1** 80-81

AGIS IV (c. 262-241 BCE), king of Sparta **1** 81-82

AGNELLI, GIOVANNI (1920-2003), Italian industrialist **1** 82-83
Marchionne, Sergio **32** 232-234

AGNES (c. 292-c. 304), Italian Christian martyr **24** 8-10

AGNESI, MARIA (1718-1799), Italian mathematician, physicist, and philosopher **20** 4-5

AGNEW, DAVID HAYES (1818-1892), American physician **28** 3-5

AGNEW, HAROLD MELVIN (born 1921), American physicist **32** 8-10

AGNEW, SPIRO THEODORE (1918-1996), Republican United States vice president under Richard Nixon **1** 83-85

AGNODICE (born c. 300 BCE), Greek physician **20** 5-5

AGNON, SHMUEL YOSEPH (1888-1970), author **1** 85-86

AGOSTINO DI DUCCIO (1418-c. 1481), Italian sculptor **1** 86

Agricola
see Crèvecoeur, St. J.

AGRICOLA, GEORGIUS (1494-1555), German mineralogist and writer **1** 86-87

AGRIPPINA THE YOUNGER (Julia Agrippina; 15-59), wife of Claudius I, Emperor of Rome, and mother of Nero **20** 5-8

AGUINALDO, EMILIO (1869-1964), Philippine revolutionary leader **1** 88

Agustin I
see Iturbide, Augustin de

AHAD HAAM (pseudonym of Asher T. Ginsberg, 1856-1927), Russian-born author **1** 88-89

AHERN, BERTIE (Bartholomew Ahern; born 1951), Irish Prime Minister **18** 11-13

ALEIJADINHO, O (Antônio Francisco Lisbôa; 1738-1814), Brazilian architect and sculptor 1 125-126

ALEMÁN, MATEO (1547-c. 1615), Spanish novelist 1 126

ALEMÁN VALDÉS, MIGUEL (1902-1983), Mexican statesman, president 1946-1952 1 126-127

ALEMBERT, JEAN LE ROND D' (1717-1783), French mathematician and physicist 1 127-128
associates
Lespinasse, Julie de **32** 214-216

ALESSANDRI PALMA, ARTURO (1868-1950), Chilean statesman, president 1920-1925 and 1932-1938 1 128-129

ALESSANDRI RODRIGUEZ, JORGE (1896-1986), Chilean statesman, president 1958-1964 1 129-130

ALEXANDER I (1777-1825), czar of Russia 1801-1825 1 130-132

Alexander I, king of Yugoslavia
see Alexander of Yugoslavia

ALEXANDER II (1818-1881), czar of Russia 1855-1881 1 132-133
Nechaev, Sergei **32** 275-277

ALEXANDER III (Orlando Bandinelli; c. 1100-1181), Italian pope 1159-1181 **24** 12-14

ALEXANDER III (1845-1894), emperor of Russia 1881-1894 1 133-134

Alexander III, king of Macedon
see Alexander the Great

Alexander V, (Pietro di Candia; c. 1340-1410), antipope 1409-1410
Bracciolini, Poggio **32** 48-50

ALEXANDER VI (Rodrigo Borgia; 1431-1503), pope 1492-1503 1 134-135

ALEXANDER VII (Fabio Chigi; 1599-1667), Roman Catholic pope **25** 12-13

ALEXANDER, JANE (nee Jane Quigley; born 1939), American actress **26** 9-12

ALEXANDER, SADIE TANNER MOSSELL (1898-1989), African American lawyer **25** 13-15

ALEXANDER, SAMUEL (1859-1938), British philosopher 1 141

Alexander Karageorgevich (1888-1934)
see Alexander of Yugoslavia

Alexander Nevsky
see Nevsky, Alexander

ALEXANDER OF TUNIS, 1ST EARL (Harold Rupert Leofric George Alexander; born 1891), British field marshal 1 135-136

ALEXANDER OF YUGOSLAVIA (1888-1934), king of the Serbs, Croats, and Slovenes 1921-1929 and of Yugoslavia, 1929-1934 1 136-137

ALEXANDER THE GREAT (356-323 BCE), king of Macedon 1 137-141

Alexandria (city, Egypt)
museum library
Maria the Jewess **32** 234-236

Alexeyev, Constantin Sergeyevich
see Stanislavsky, Constantin

ALEXIE, SHERMAN (born 1966), Native American writer, poet, and translator 1 141-142

ALEXIS MIKHAILOVICH ROMANOV (1629-1676), czar of Russia 1645-1676 1 142-143

ALEXIUS I (c. 1048-1118), Byzantine emperor 1081-1118 1 143-144

ALFARO, JOSÉ ELOY (1842-1912), Ecuadorian revolutionary, president 1895-1901 and 1906-1911 1 144-145

ALFIERI, CONTE VITTORIA (1749-1803), Italian playwright 1 145-146

ALFONSÍN, RAÚL RICARDO (1927-2009), politician and president of Argentina (1983-89) 1 146-148

ALFONSO I (Henriques; c. 1109-1185), king of Portugal 1139-1185 1 148

Alfonso I, king of Castile
see Alfonso VI, king of León

ALFONSO III (1210-1279), king of Portugal 1248-1279 1 148-149

ALFONSO VI (1040-1109), king of León, 1065-1109, and of Castile, 1072-1109 1 149

ALFONSO X (1221-1284), king of Castile and León 1252-1284 1 150-151

ALFONSO XIII (1886-1941), king of Spain 1886-1931 1 151

Alfonso the Wise
see Alfonso X, king of Castile and León

ALFRED (849-899), Anglo-Saxon king of Wessex 871-899 1 151-153

Alfred the Great
see Alfred, king of Wessex

Algazel
see Ghazali, Abu Hamid Muhammad al-

ALGER, HORATIO (1832-1899), American author 1 153-154

Algonquian Indians (North America)
Manteo **32** 231-232

ALGREN, NELSON (Abraham; 1909-1981), American author 1 154-155

Alhazen
see Hassan ibn al-Haytham

ALI (c. 600-661), fourth caliph of the Islamic Empire 1 155-156

ALI, AHMED (1908-1998), Pakistani scholar, poet, author, and diplomat **22** 16-18

Ali, Haidar
see Haidar Ali

ALI, MUHAMMAD (Cassius Clay; born 1942), American boxer 1 156-158

ALI, MUSTAFA (1541-1600), Turkish historian and politician **31** 1-2

ALI, SUNNI (died 1492), king of Gao, founder of the Songhay empire 1 158-159

Ali Ber
see Ali, Sunni

Ali Shah (died 1885)
see Aga Khan II

Ali the Great
see Ali, Sunni

ALIA, RAMIZ (born 1925), president of Albania (1985-) 1 159

ALINSKY, SAUL DAVID (1909-1972), U.S. organizer of neighborhood citizen reform groups 1 161-162

All-American Girls Professional Baseball League
Wrigley, Philip K. **32** 365-367

ALLAL AL-FASSI, MOHAMED (1910-1974), Moroccan nationalist leader 1 162

ALLAWI, IYAD (born 1945), Iraqi prime minister **25** 15-17

Allegri, Antonio
see Correggio

ALLEN, ELSIE (Elsie Comanche Allen; 1899-1990), Native American weaver and educator **27** 10-11

ALLEN, ETHAN (1738-1789), American Revolutionary War soldier 1 163-164

ALLEN, FLORENCE ELLINWOOD (1884-1966), American lawyer, judge, and women's rights activist 1 164-165

ALLEN, GRACIE (1906-1964), American actress and comedian **22** 18-20

ALLEN, MEL (1913-1996), American broadcaster **32** 10-12

ALLEN, PAUL (Paul Gardner Allen; born 1953), American entrepreneur and philanthropist **25** 17-19

ALLEN, PAULA GUNN (born 1939), Native American writer, poet, literary critic; women's rights, environmental, and antiwar activist 1 165-167

ALLEN, RICHARD (1760-1831), African American bishop 1 168

ALLEN, SARAH (Sarah Bass Allen; 1764-1849), African American missionary **27** 12-13

ALLEN, STEVE (1921-2000), American comedian, author, and composer **22** 20-22

ALLEN, WOODY (born Allen Stewart Konigsberg; b. 1935), American actor, director, filmmaker, author, comedian **1** 169-171

ALLENBY, EDMUND HENRY HYNMAN (1861-1936), English field marshal **1** 171-172

ALLENDE, ISABEL (born 1942), Chilean novelist, journalist, dramatist **1** 172-174

ALLENDE GOSSENS, SALVADOR (1908-1973), socialist president of Chile (1970-1973) **1** 174-176

Alleyne, Ellen
see Rossetti, Christina Georgina

ALLSTON, WASHINGTON (1779-1843), American painter **1** 176-177

ALMAGRO, DIEGO DE (c. 1474-1538), Spanish conquistador and explorer **1** 177-178

ALMENDROS, NÉSTOR (Nestor Almendrod Cuyas; 1930-1992), Hispanic American cinematographer **27** 13-15

ALMODOVAR, PEDRO (Calmodovar, Caballero, Pedro; born 1949), Spanish film director and screenwriter **23** 6-9

Alompra
see Alaungpaya

Alonso (Araucanian chief)
see Lautaro

ALONSO, ALICIA (Alicia Ernestina de la Caridad dei Cobre Martinez Hoya; born 1921), Cuban ballerina **24** 14-17

ALP ARSLAN (1026/32-1072), Seljuk sultan of Persia and Iraq **1** 178-179

Alpetragius
see Bitruji, Nur al-Din Abu Ishaq al-

Alphabet, development of
Trubar, Primož **32** 336-338

ALPHONSA OF THE IMMACULATE CONCEPTION, ST. (1910-1946), Indian nun and Roman Catholic saint **30** 1-3

Alphonse the Wise
see Alfonso X, king of Castile

ALTAMIRA Y CREVEA, RAFAEL (1866-1951), Spanish critic, historian, and jurist **1** 179

ALTDORFER, ALBRECHT (c. 1480-1538), German painter, printmaker, and architect **1** 179-180

ALTERMAN, NATAN (1910-1970), Israeli poet and journalist **24** 17-18

ALTGELD, JOHN PETER (1847-1902), American jurist and politician **1** 180-182

ALTHUSSER, LOUIS (1918-1990), French Communist philosopher **1** 182-183

ALTIZER, THOMAS J. J. (born 1927), American theologian **1** 183-184

ALTMAN, ROBERT (1925-2006), American filmmaker **20** 12-14

ALTMAN, SIDNEY (born 1939), Canadian American molecular biologist **23** 9-11

ALUPI, CALIN (Calinic Alupi; 1906-1988), Romanian artist **24** 18-19

Alva, Duke of
see Alba, Duke of

ALVARADO, LINDA (Linda Martinez; born 1951), American businesswoman **25** 21-23

Alvarez, Jorge Guillén y
see Guillén y Alvarez, Jorge

ÁLVAREZ, JUAN (1780-1867), Mexican soldier and statesman, president 1855 **1** 184-185

ALVAREZ, JULIA (born 1950), Hispanic American novelist, poet **1** 185-187

ALVAREZ, LUIS W. (1911-1988), American physicist **1** 187-189
Agnew, Harold Melvin **32** 8-10

ÁLVAREZ BRAVO, MANUEL (1902-2002), Mexican photographer **31** 2-6

ALVARIÑO, ANGELES (Angeles Alvariño Leira; 1916-2005), Spanish American marine scientist **27** 15-17

AMADO, JORGE (1912-2001), Brazilian novelist **1** 189-190

Amazing Stories (periodical)
Ackerman, Forrest J **32** 4-6

AMBEDKAR, BHIMRAO RAMJI (1891-1956), Indian social reformer and politician **1** 190-191

AMBLER, ERIC (born 1909), English novelist **1** 191-192

Ambrogini, Angelo
see Poliziano, Angelo

AMBROSE, ST. (339-397), Italian bishop **1** 192-193

AMBROSE, STEPHEN E. (1936-2002), American historian **32** 12-14

AMENEMHET I (ruled 1991-1962 BCE), pharaoh of Egypt **1** 193-194

AMENHOTEP III (ruled 1417-1379 BCE), pharaoh of Egypt **1** 194-195

Amenhotep IV
see Ikhnaton

Amenophis IV
see Ikhnaton

American architecture
California style
Neff, Wallace **32** 277-279

American Broadcasting Company (ABC)
Arledge, Roone **32** 16-18

AMERICAN HORSE (aka Iron Shield; c. 1840-1876), Sioux leader **1** 195-198

American Medical Association
McManus, Louise **32** 251-253

American Michelangelo
see Rimmer, William

American Red Cross (established 1881)
Mosher, Clelia Duel **32** 263-265

American Rembrandt
see Johnson, Jonathan Eastman

American Telephone and Telegraph Co. (AT&T)
Bell Laboratories
Chu, Steven **32** 75-76

American Woodsman
see Audubon, John James

AMES, ADELBERT (1835-1933), American politician **1** 198

AMES, EZRA (1768-1836), American painter **29** 1-3

AMES, FISHER (1758-1808), American statesman **1** 199-200

AMHERST, JEFFERY (1717-1797), English general and statesman **1** 200-201

AMICHAI, YEHUDA (Yehuda Pfeuffer; Yehudah Amichai; 1924-2000), German-Israeli poet **24** 19-21

AMIET, CUNO (1868-1961), Swiss Postimpressionist painter **1** 201-202

AMIN DADA, IDI (born c. 1926), president of Uganda (1971-1979) **1** 202-204

AMINA OF ZARIA (Amina Sarauniya Zazzau; c. 1533-c. 1610), Nigerian monarch and warrior **21** 5-7

AMIS, KINGSLEY (Kingsley William Amis; 1922-1995), English author **28** 5-8

Amitabha Buddha
see Buddha (play)

AMMA (Amritanandamayi, Mata; Ammachi; Sudhamani; born 1953), Indian spiritual leader **28** 8-10

AMMANATI, BARTOLOMEO (1511-1592), Italian sculptor and architect **30** 3-5

AMONTONS, GUILLAUME (1663-1705), French physicist **29** 3-5

AMORSOLO, FERNANDO (1892-1972), Philippine painter **1** 204

ANNING, MARY (1799-1847), British fossil collector **20** 14-16

Annunzio, Gabriele d'
see D'Annunzio, Gabriel

ANOKYE, OKOMFO (Kwame Frimpon Anokye; flourished late 17th century), Ashanti priest and statesman **1** 242-243

ANOUILH, JEAN (1910-1987), French playwright **1** 243-244

ANSELM OF CANTERBURY, ST. (1033-1109), Italian archbishop and theologian **1** 244-245

ANSERMET, ERNEST (1883-1969), Swiss orchestral conductor **30** 9-11

Anson, Charles Edward
see Markham, Edwin

Anthoniszoon, Jeroen
see Bosch, Hieronymus

Anthony, Mark
see Antony, Mark

Anthony, Peter
see Shaffer, Peter Levin

ANTHONY, ST. (c. 250-356), Egyptian hermit and monastic founder **1** 246-248

ANTHONY, SUSAN BROWNELL (1820-1906), American leader of suffrage movement **1** 246-248

Anthony Abbott, St.
see Anthony, St.

Anthony of Egypt, St.
see Anthony, St.

ANTHONY OF PADUA, ST. (Fernando de Boullion; 1195-1231), Portuguese theologian and priest **21** 7-9

Anthropological Society of Paris
Broca, Pierre Paul **32** 53-55

Antibodies (biochemistry)
Harrison, James **32** 149-150

Antigens (biochemistry)
Blumberg, Baruch **32** 44-46

ANTIGONUS I (382-301 BCE), king of Macedon 306-301 B.C. **1** 248-249

ANTIOCHUS III (241-187 BCE), king of Syria 223-187 B.C. **1** 249-250

ANTIOCHUS IV (c. 215-163 BCE), king of Syria 175-163 B.C. **1** 250

Antiochus the Great
see Antiochus III

ANTISTHENES (c. 450-360 BCE), Greek philosopher **1** 250-251

ANTONELLO DA MESSINA (c. 1430-1479), Italian painter **1** 251-252

Antoninus, Marcus Aurelius
see Caracalla

Antonio, Donato di Pascuccio d'
see Bramante, Donato

ANTONIONI, MICHELANGELO (1912-2007), Italian film director **1** 252-253

Antonius, Marcus
see Antony, Mark

ANTONY, MARK (c. 82-30 BCE), Roman politician and general **1** 253-254

Anushervan the Just
see Khosrow I

ANZA, JUAN BAUTISTA DE (1735-1788), Spanish explorer **1** 254-255

AOUN, MICHEL (born 1935), Christian Lebanese military leader and prime minister **1** 255-257

Apache Napoleon
see Cochise

Apartheid (South Africa)
opponents
Papert, Seymour **32** 290-292

APELLES (flourished after 350 BCE), Greek painter **1** 257

APESS, WILLIAM (1798-1839), Native American religious leader, author, and activist **20** 16-18

APGAR, VIRGINIA (1909-1974), American medical educator, researcher **1** 257-259

Aphasia (psychology and medicine)
Broca, Pierre Paul **32** 53-55

APITHY, SOUROU MIGAN (1913-1989), Dahomean political leader **1** 259-260

Apocalypse
Argüelles, José **32** 14-16

APOLLINAIRE, GUILLAUME (1880-1918), French lyric poet **1** 260

APOLLODORUS (flourished c. 408 BCE), Greek painter **1** 261

APOLLONIUS OF PERGA (flourished 210 BCE), Greek mathematician **1** 261-262

Apostate, the
see Julian

Apostles
see Bible–New Testament

APPELFELD, AHARON (born 1932), Israeli who wrote about anti-Semitism and the Holocaust **1** 262-263

APPERT, NICOLAS (1749-1941), French chef and inventor of canning of foods **20** 18-19

APPIA, ADOLPHE (1862-1928), Swiss stage director **1** 263-264

APPLEBEE, CONSTANCE (1873-1981), American field hockey coach **24** 24-25

APPLEGATE, JESSE (1811-1888), American surveyor, pioneer, and rancher **1** 264-265

APPLETON, SIR EDWARD VICTOR (1892-1965), British pioneer in radio physics **1** 265-266

APPLETON, NATHAN (1779-1861), American merchant and manufacturer **1** 266-267

APULEIUS, LUCIUS (c. 124-170), Roman author, philosopher, and orator **20** 19-21

Apulia, Robert Guiscard, Count and Duke of
see Guiscard, Robert

Aquinas, St. Thomas
see Thomas Aquinas, St.

AQUINO, BENIGNO ("Nino"; 1933-1983), Filipino activist murdered upon his return from exile **1** 267-268

AQUINO, CORAZON COJOANGCO (born 1933), first woman president of the Republic of the Philippines **1** 268-270

Arabi Pasha, (Colonel Ahmed Arabi)
see ORABI, AHMED

ARAFAT, YASSER (also spelled Yasir; 1929-2004), chairman of the Palestinian Liberation Organization **1** 270-271

ARAGO, FRANÇOIS (1786-1853), French physicist **30** 11-14

ARAGON, LOUIS (1897-1982), French surrealist author **1** 271-272

ARAKCHEEV, ALEKSEI ANDREEVICH (1769-1834), Russian soldier and statesman **31** 9-10

ARAKIDA MORITAKE (1473-1549), Japanese poet **29** 287-288

ARÁMBURU, PEDRO EUGENIO (1903-1970), Argentine statesman, president 1955-1958 **30** 14-16

Arango, Doroteo
see Villa, Pancho

ARANHA, OSVALDO (1894-1960), Brazilian political leader **1** 272-273

ARATUS (271-213 BCE), Greek statesman and general **1** 273-274

Arbeiter Zeitung (newspaper)
Heartfield, John **32** 154-157

ARBENZ GUZMÁN, JACOBO (1913-1971), Guatemalan statesman, president 1951-1954 **1** 274-276

ARBER, AGNES ROBERTSON (nee Agnes Robertson; 1879-1960), English botanist **28** 14-16

Arblay, Madame d'
see Burney, Frances "Fanny"

ARBUS, DIANE NEMEROV (1923-1971), American photographer **1** 276-277

BADINGS, HENK (Hendrik Herman Badings; 1907-1987), Dutch composer **23** 26-28

BADOGLIO, PIETRO (1871-1956), Italian general and statesman **1** 428-429

BAECK, LEO (1873-1956), rabbi, teacher, hero of the concentration camps, and Jewish leader **1** 429-430

BAEKELAND, LEO HENDRIK (1863-1944), American chemist **1** 430-431

BAER, GEORGE FREDERICK (1842-1914), American businessman **22** 39-41

BAER, KARL ERNST VON (1792-1876), Estonian anatomist and embryologist **1** 431-432

BAEZ, BUENAVENTURA (1812-1884), Dominican statesman, five time president **1** 432-433

BAEZ, JOAN (born 1941), American folk singer and human rights activist **1** 433-435
    Parra, Violeta **32** 292-294

BAFFIN, WILLIAM (c. 1584-1622), English navigator and explorer **1** 435-436

BAGEHOT, WALTER (1826-1877), English economist **1** 436-437

BAGLEY, WILLIAM CHANDLER (1874-1946), educator and theorist of educational "essentialism" **1** 437-438

BAHÁ'U'LLÁH (Husayn-'Ali', Bahá'u'lláh Mírzá; 1817-1982), Iranian religious leader **28** 21-23

BAHR, EGON (born 1922), West German politician **1** 438-440

BAIKIE, WILLIAM BALFOUR (1825-1864), Scottish explorer and scientist **1** 440

BAILEY, F. LEE (born 1933), American defense attorney and author **1** 441-443

BAILEY, FLORENCE MERRIAM (1863-1948), American ornithologist and author **1** 443-444

BAILEY, GAMALIEL (1807-1859), American editor and politician **1** 444-445

BAILEY, JAMES A. (1847-1906), American circus owner **30** 26-28

BAILEY, MILDRED (Mildred Rinker, 1907-1951), American jazz singer **23** 28-30

BAILLIE, D(ONALD) M(ACPHERSON) (1887-1954), Scottish theologian **1** 445

BAILLIE, ISOBEL (Isabella Baillie; 1895-1983), British singer **26** 27-29

BAILLIE, JOANNA (1762-1851), Scottish playwright and poet **28** 23-25

BAILLIE, JOHN (1886-1960), Scottish theologian and ecumenical churchman **1** 445-447

BAIN, ALEXANDER (1818-1903), Scottish psychologist, philosopher, and educator **32** 28-30

BAIUS, MICHAEL (1513-1589), Belgian theologian **29** 31-33

BAKER, ELLA JOSEPHINE (1903-1986), African American human and civil rights activist **18** 26-28

BAKER, GEORGE PIERCE (1866-1935), American educator **29** 33-35

BAKER, HOWARD HENRY, JR. (born 1925), U.S. senator and White House chief of staff **18** 28-30

BAKER, JAMES ADDISON III (born 1930), Republican party campaign leader **1** 447-448

BAKER, JOSEPHINE (1906-1975), Parisian dancer and singer from America **1** 448-451

BAKER, NEWTON DIEHL (1871-1937), American statesman **1** 451

BAKER, RAY STANNARD (1870-1946), American author **1** 451-452

BAKER, RUSSELL (born 1925), American writer of personal-political essays **1** 452-454

BAKER, SIR SAMUEL WHITE (1821-1893), English explorer and administrator **1** 454-455

BAKER, SARA JOSEPHINE (1873-1945), American physician **1** 455-456

BAKHTIN, MIKHAIL MIKHAILOVICH (1895-1975), Russian philosopher and literary critic **1** 456-458

BAKSHI, RALPH (born 1938), American director **32** 30-32

BAKST, LEON (1866-1924), Russian painter **29** 35-37

BAKUNIN, MIKHAIL ALEKSANDROVICH (1814-1876), Russian anarchist **1** 458-460
    Nechaev, Sergei **32** 275-277

BALAGUER Y RICARDO, JOAQUÍN (1907-2002), Dominican statesman **1** 460-461

BALANCHINE, GEORGE (1904-1983), Russian-born American choreographer **1** 461-462

Balanchivadze, Georgi Melitonovitch
    see Balanchine, George

BALBO, ITALO (1896-1940), Italian air marshal **29** 37-39

BALBOA, VASCO NÚÑEZ DE (c. 1475-1519), Spanish explorer **1** 462-463

Balbulus, Notker
    see Notker Balbulus

BALCH, EMILY GREENE (1867-1961), American pacifist and social reformer **1** 463-464

BALDOMIR, ALFREDO (884-1948), Uruguayan president 1938-1943 **29** 39-41

BALDWIN I (1058-1118), Norman king of Jerusalem 1100-1118 **1** 464-465

BALDWIN, JAMES ARTHUR (1924-1987), African American author, poet, and dramatist **1** 465-466

BALDWIN, ROBERT (1804-1858), Canadian politician **1** 466-468

BALDWIN, ROGER NASH (1884-1981), American civil libertarian and social worker **25** 31-33

BALDWIN, STANLEY (1st Earl Baldwin of Bewdley; 1867-1947), English statesman, three times prime minister **1** 468-469

Baldwin of Bewdley, 1st Earl
    see Baldwin, Stanley

Baldwin of Boulogne
    see Baldwin I, king

BALENCIAGA, CRISTÓBAL (1895-1972), Spanish fashion designer **30** 28-30

BALFOUR, ARTHUR JAMES (1st Earl of Balfour; 1848-1930), British statesman and philosopher **1** 469-470

Baline, Israel
    see Berlin, Irving

BALL, GEORGE (1909-1994), American politician and supporter of an economically united Europe **1** 470-471

BALL, LUCILLE (Lucille Desiree Hunt; 1911-1989), American comedienne **1** 472-473

BALLA, GIACOMO (1871-1958), Italian painter **1** 473-474

BALLADUR, EDOUARD (born 1929), premier of the French Government **1** 474-475

BALLANCE, JOHN (1839-1893), New Zealand journalist and statesman **29** 42-44

BALLARD, J. G. (1930-2009), British author **30** 30-32

BALLARD, LOUIS WAYNE (1913-2007), Native American musician **26** 29-31

BALLARD, ROBERT (born 1942), American oceanographer **19** 10-12

Ballet (dance)
    Karsavina, Tamara **32** 177-180

Ballets Russes de Sergei Diaghilev (dance company)
    Karsavina, Tamara **32** 177-180

BAUER, EDDIE (1899-1986), American businessman **19** 13-14

Bauer, Georg
see Agricola, Georgius

BAULIEU, ÉTIENNE-ÉMILE (Étienne Blum; born 1926), French physician and biochemist who developed RU 486 **2** 63-66

BAUM, ELEANOR (born 1940), American engineer **30** 47-48

BAUM, HERBERT (1912-1942), German human/civil rights activist **2** 66-73

BAUM, L. FRANK (1856-1919), author of the Wizard of Oz books **2** 73-74

Baumfree, Isabella
see Truth, Sojourner

BAUR, FERDINAND CHRISTIAN (1792-1860), German theologian **2** 74-75

BAUSCH, PINA (born 1940), a controversial German dancer/choreographer **2** 75-76

BAXTER, RICHARD (1615-1691), English theologian **2** 76-77

BAYLE, PIERRE (1647-1706), French philosopher **2** 77-78

Bayley, Elizabeth
see Seton, Elizabeth Ann Bayley

BAYNTON, BARBARA (1857-1929), Australian author **22** 46-48

BAZIN, ANDRÉ (1918-1958), French film critic **28** 32-33

BEA, AUGUSTINUS (1881-1968), German cardinal **2** 79

BEACH, AMY (born Amy Marcy Cheney; 1867-1944), American musician **23** 30-32

BEACH, MOSES YALE (1800-1868), American inventor and newspaperman **2** 79-80

Beaconsfield, Earl of
see Disraeli, Benjamin

BEADLE, GEORGE WELLS (1903-1989), American scientist, educator, and administrator **2** 80-81

BEALE, DOROTHEA (1831-1906), British educator **2** 81-83

BEAN, ALAN (born 1932), American astronaut and artist **22** 48-50

BEAN, LEON LEONWOOD (L.L. Bean; 1872-1967), American businessman **19** 14-16

BEARD, CHARLES AUSTIN (1874-1948), American historian **2** 84

BEARD, MARY RITTER (1876-1958), American author and activist **2** 85-86

BEARDEN, ROMARE HOWARD (1914-1988), African American painter-collagist **2** 86-88

BEARDSLEY, AUBREY VINCENT (1872-1898), English illustrator **2** 88-89

BEATLES, THE (1957-1971), British rock and roll band **2** 89-92

BEATRIX, WILHELMINA VON AMSBERG, QUEEN (born 1938), queen of Netherlands (1980-) **2** 92-93

BEAUCHAMPS, PIERRE (1636-1705), French dancer and choreographer **21** 27-29

BEAUFORT, MARGARET (1443-1509), queen dowager of England **20** 29-31

BEAUJOYEULX, BALTHASAR DE (Balthasar de Beaujoyeux; Baldassare de Belgiojoso; 1535-1587), Italian choreographer and composer **21** 29-30

BEAUMARCHAIS, PIERRE AUGUST CARON DE (1732-1799), French playwright **2** 93-94

BEAUMONT, FRANCIS (1584/1585-1616), English playwright **2** 95

BEAUMONT, WILLIAM (1785-1853), American surgeon **2** 95-96

BEAUREGARD, PIERRE GUSTAVE TOUTANT (1818-1893), Confederate general **2** 96-97

Beaverbrook, Lord
see Aitken, William Maxwell

BEBEY, FRANCIS (1929-2001), Cameroonian musician **32** 36-38

BECARRIA, MARCHESE DI (1738-1794), Italian jurist and economist **2** 97-98

BECHET, SIDNEY (1897-1959), American jazz musician **22** 50-52

BECHTEL, STEPHEN DAVISON (1900-1989), American construction engineer and business executive **2** 98-99

BECK, JÓZEF (1894-1944), Polish statesman **29** 48-50

BECK, LUDWIG AUGUST THEODER (1880-1944), German general **2** 99-100

BECKER, CARL LOTUS (1873-1945), American historian **2** 100-101

BECKET, ST. THOMAS (c. 1128-1170), English prelate **2** 101-102

BECKETT, SAMUEL (1906-1989), Irish novelist, playwright, and poet **2** 102-104

BECKHAM, DAVID (David Robert Joseph Beckham; born 1975), British soccer player **26** 36-38

BECKMANN, MAX (1884-1950), German painter **2** 104-105

BECKNELL, WILLIAM (c. 1797-1865), American soldier and politician **2** 105-106

BECKWOURTH, JIM (James P. Beckwourth; c. 1800-1866), African American fur trapper and explorer **2** 106-107

BÉCQUER, GUSTAVO ADOLFO DOMINGUEZ (1836-1870), Spanish lyric poet **2** 107-108

BECQUEREL, ANTOINE HENRI (1852-1908), French physicist **2** 108-109

BEDE, ST. (672/673-735), English theologian **2** 109-110

BEDELL SMITH, WALTER (1895-1961), U.S. Army general, ambassador, and CIA director **18** 30-33

BEEBE, WILLIAM (1877-1962), American naturalist, oceanographer, and ornithologist **22** 52-54

BEECHAM, THOMAS (1879-1961), English conductor **24** 46-48

BEECHER, CATHARINE (1800-1878), American author and educator **2** 110-112

BEECHER, HENRY WARD (1813-1887), American Congregationalist clergyman **2** 112-113

BEECHER, LYMAN (1775-1863), Presbyterian clergyman **2** 113

Beer, Jakob Liebmann
see Meyerbeer, Giacomo

BEERBOHM, MAX (Henry Maximilian Beerbohm; 1872-1956), English author and critic **19** 16-18

BEETHOVEN, LUDWIG VAN (1770-1827), German composer **2** 114-117

Beethoven of America
see Heinrich, Anthony Philip

BEETON, ISABELLA MARY (Isabella Mary Mayson; Mrs. Beeton; 1836-1865), English author **28** 34-36

BEGAY, HARRISON (born 1917), Native American artist **2** 117-118

BEGIN, MENACHEM (1913-1992), Israel's first non-Socialist prime minister (1977-1983) **2** 118-120

BEHAIM, MARTIN (Martinus de Bohemia; c. 1459-1507), German cartographer **21** 30-32

Behmen, Jacob
see Boehme, Jacob

BEHN, APHRA (c. 1640-1689), English author **18** 33-34

BEHRENS, HILDEGARD (born 1937), German soprano **2** 120-121

BEHRENS, PETER (1868-1940), German architect, painter, and designer **2** 121-122

BEHRING, EMIL ADOLPH VON (1854-1917), German hygienist and physician **2** 122-123

BEHZAD (died c. 1530), Persian painter **2** 123

BEISSEL, JOHANN CONRAD (1690-1768), German-American pietist **2** 123-124

Bel canto (opera)
Horne, Marilyn **32** 171-172

BELAFONTE, HARRY (Harold George Belafonte, Jr.; born 1927), African American singer and actor **20** 31-32

BELASCO, DAVID (1853-1931), American playwright and director-producer **2** 124-125

BELAÚNDE TERRY, FERNANDO (1912-2002), president of Peru (1963-1968, 1980-1985) **2** 125-126

BELGRANO, MANUEL (1770-1820), Argentine general and politician **2** 126-127

BELINSKY, GRIGORIEVICH (1811-1848), Russian literary critic **2** 128

BELISARIUS (c. 506-565), Byzantine general **2** 128-129

Bell, Acton
see Brontë, Anne

BELL, ALEXANDER GRAHAM (1847-1922), Scottish-born American inventor **2** 129-131

BELL, ANDREW (1753-1832), Scottish educator **2** 131-132

Bell, Currer
see Brontë, Charlotte

BELL, DANIEL (born Daniel Bolotsky; 1919-2011), American sociologist **2** 132-133

Bell, Ellis
see Brontë, Emily

BELL, GERTRUDE (1868-1926), British archaeologist, traveler, and advisor on the Middle East **22** 54-55

BELL, GLEN (1923-2010), American restaurateur **31** 24-25

BELL, VANESSA (Vanessa Stephen; 1879-1961), British painter **25** 36-38

BELL BURNELL, SUSAN JOCELYN (born 1943), English radio astronomer **2** 133-134

BELLAMY, CAROL (born 1942), American activist and political servant **25** 38-40

BELLAMY, EDWARD (1850-1898), American novelist, propagandist, and reformer **2** 134-135

BELLÁN, ESTEBAN (1849-1932), Cuban baseball player **32** 38-40

BELLARMINE, ST. ROBERT (1542-1621), Italian theologian and cardinal **2** 135-136

Bellay, Joachim du
see Du Bellay, Joachim

BELLECOURT, CLYDE (born 1939), Native American activist **2** 136-137

Bellevue Hospital (New York City)
Blumberg, Baruch **32** 44-46

BELLI, GIACONDA (born 1948), Nicaraguan author and activist **24** 48-50

BELLINI, GIOVANNI (c. 1435-1516), Itlaian painter **2** 137-138

BELLINI, VINCENZO (1801-1835), Italian composer **2** 138-139

BELLMAN, CARL MICHAEL (1740-1794), Swedish poet and musician **25** 40-42

BELLO, ALHAJI SIR AHMADU (1909-1966), Nigerian politician **2** 139-140

BELLO Y LÓPEZ, ANDRÉS (1781-1865), Venezuelan humanist **2** 140-141

BELLOC, JOSEPH HILAIRE PIERRE (1870-1953), French-born English author and historian **2** 141

BELLOC LOWNDES, MARIE ADELAIDE (1868-1947), English novelist **30** 49-51

BELLOW, SAUL (1915-2005), American novelist and Nobel Prize winner **2** 141-143

BELLOWS, GEORGE WESLEY (1882-1925), American painter **2** 143

BELLOWS, HENRY WHITNEY (1814-1882), American Unitarian minister **2** 143-144

BELMONT, AUGUST (1816-1890), German-American banker, diplomat, and horse racer **22** 56-57

BELO, CARLOS FELIPE XIMENES (born 1948), East Timorese activist **25** 42-44

Beltov
see Plekhanov, Georgi Valentinovich

BEMBERG, MARIA LUISA (1922-1995), Argentine filmmaker **25** 44-46

BEMBO, PIETRO (1470-1547), Italian humanist, poet, and historian **2** 144-145

BEMIS, POLLY (Lalu Nathoy; 1853-1933), Chinese American pioneer and businesswoman **25** 46-47

BEN AND JERRY, ice cream company founders **18** 35-37

BEN BADIS, ABD AL-HAMID (1889-1940), leader of the Islamic Reform Movement in Algeria between the two world wars **2** 147-148

BEN BELLA, AHMED (1918-2012), first president of the Algerian Republic **2** 148-149

BEN-GURION, DAVID (1886-1973), Russian-born Israeli statesman **2** 160-161

BEN-HAIM, PAUL (Frankenburger; 1897-1984), Israeli composer **2** 161-162

BEN YEHUDA, ELIEZER (1858-1922), Hebrew lexicographer and editor **2** 181-182

BENACERRAF, BARUJ (1920-2011), American medical researcher **27** 42-44

BENALCÁZAR, SEBASTIÁN DE (died 1551), Spanish conquistador **2** 145-146

BENAVENTE Y MARTINEZ, JACINTO (1866-1954), Spanish dramatist **2** 146-147

BENCHLEY, ROBERT (1889-1945), American humorist **2** 150-151

BENDA, JULIEN (1867-1956), French cultural critic and novelist **2** 151-152

BENDIX, VINCENT (1881-1945), American inventor, engineer, and industrialist **19** 18-20

BENEDICT XIV (Prospero Lorenzo Lambertini; 1675-1758), pope, 1740-1758 **23** 32-35

BENEDICT XV (Giacomo della Chiesa; 1854-1922), pope, 1914-1922 **2** 153-154

BENEDICT XVI (Joseph Alois Ratzinger; born 1927), Roman Catholic pope (2005-) **26** 295-297

BENEDICT, RUTH FULTON (1887-1948), American cultural anthropologist **2** 154-155

BENEDICT, ST. (c. 480-547), Italian founder of the Benedictines **2** 154-155

Benedict of Nursia, St.
see Benedict, St.

BENEŠ, EDWARD (1884-1948), Czechoslovak president 1935-1938 and 1940-1948 **2** 155-157

BENÉT, STEPHEN VINCENT (1898-1943), American poet and novelist **2** 157-158

BENETTON, Italian family (Luciano, Giuliana, Gilberto, Carlo and Mauro) who organized a world-wide chain of colorful knitwear stores **2** 158-159

BENEZET, ANTHONY (1713-1784), American philanthropist and educator **2** 159-160

Bengan Korei
see Muhammad II, Askia

BENJAMIN, ASHER (1773-1845), American architect **2** 162-163

BENJAMIN, JUDAH PHILIP (1811-1884), American statesman **2** 163-164

BENJAMIN, WALTER (1892-1940), German philosopher and literary critic **20** 32-34

BENN, GOTTFRIED (1886-1956), German author **2** 164

BENN, TONY (Anthony Neil Wedgewood Benn; born 1925), British Labour party politician **2** 164-166

BENNETT, ALAN (born 1934), British playwright **2** 166-167

BENNETT, ARNOLD (1867-1931), English novelist and dramatist **2** 167-168

BENNETT, JAMES GORDON (1795-1872), Scottish-born American journalist and publisher **2** 168-169

BENNETT, JAMES GORDON, JR. (1841-1918), American newspaper owner and editor **2** 169-170

BENNETT, JOHN COLEMAN (1902-1995), American theologian **2** 170-171

BENNETT, RICHARD BEDFORD (1870-1947), Canadian statesman, prime minister 1930-1935 **2** 171-172

BENNETT, RICHARD RODNEY (born 1936), English composer **2** 172

BENNETT, ROBERT RUSSELL (1894-1981), American arranger, composer, and conductor **21** 32-34

BENNETT, WILLIAM JOHN (born 1943), American teacher and scholar and secretary of the Department of Education (1985-1988) **2** 172-174

Bennett of Mickleham, Calgary, and Hopewell, Viscount
see Bennett, Richard Bedford

BENNY, JACK (Benjamin Kubelsky; 1894-1974), American comedian and a star of radio, television, and stage **2** 174-176

Benso, Camillo
see Cavour, Conte di

BENTHAM, JEREMY (1748-1832), English philosopher, political theorist, and jurist **2** 176-178
influence of
Bain, Alexander **32** 28-30

BENTLEY, ARTHUR F. (1870-1957), American philosopher and political scientist **2** 178

BENTON, SEN. THOMAS HART (1782-1858), American statesman **2** 178-179

BENTON, THOMAS HART (1889-1975), American regionalist painter **2** 178-179

BENTSEN, LLOYD MILLARD (1921-2006), senior United States senator from Texas and Democratic vice-presidential candidate in 1988 **2** 180-181

BENZ, CARL (1844-1929), German inventor **2** 182-183

BERCHTOLD, COUNT LEOPOLD VON (1863-1942), Austro-Hungarian statesman **2** 183-184

BERDYAEV, NICHOLAS ALEXANDROVICH (1874-1948), Russian philosopher **2** 184-185

BERELSON, BERNARD (1912-1979), American behavioral scientist **2** 185-186

BERENSON, BERNARD (1865-1959), American art critic and historian **20** 34-35

BERENSON ABBOTT, SENDA (1868-1954), American athletic director **31** 26-27

BERG, ALBAN (1885-1935), Austrian composer **2** 186-187

BERG, MOE (1902-1972), American baseball player and spy **29** 50-52

BERG, PAUL (born 1926), American chemist **2** 187-189

BERGER, VICTOR LOUIS (1860-1929), American politician **2** 189-190

BERGIUS, FRIEDRICH KARL RUDOLPH (1884-1949), German chemist **30** 51-53

BERGMAN, (ERNST) INGMAR (1918-2007), Swedish film and stage director **2** 190-191
Harvey, Cyrus **32** 150-152

BERGMAN, INGRID (1917-1982), Swedish actress **20** 35-37

BERGSON, HENRI (1859-1941), French philosopher **2** 191-192

BERIA, LAVRENTY PAVLOVICH (1899-1953), Soviet secret-police chief and politician **2** 192-193

BERING, VITUS (1681-1741), Danish navigator in Russian employ **2** 193-194

BERIO, LUCIANO (1925-2003), Italian composer **2** 194-195

BERISHA, SALI (born 1944), president of the Republic of Albania (1992-) **2** 195-197

BERKELEY, BUSBY (William Berkeley Enos; 1895-1976), American filmmaker **20** 38-39

BERKELEY, GEORGE (1685-1753), Anglo-Irish philosopher and Anglican bishop **2** 197-198
Gaustad, Edwin **32** 130-131

BERKELEY, SIR WILLIAM (1606-1677), English royal governor of Virginia **2** 198-199

BERLAGE, HENDRICK PETRUS (1856-1934), Dutch architect **30** 53-55

BERLE, ADOLF AUGUSTUS, JR. (1895-1971), American educator **2** 199-200

BERLE, MILTON (1908-2002), American entertainer and actor **18** 37-39

BERLIN, IRVING (1888-1989), American composer **2** 200-201

BERLIN, ISAIAH (1909-1997), British philosopher **2** 201-203

Berlin, University of
chemistry
Bodenstein, Max Ernst **32** 46-48

BERLINER, ÉMILE (1851-1929), American inventor **20** 39-41

BERLIOZ, LOUIS HECTOR (1803-1869), French composer, conductor, and critic **2** 203-205

BERLUSCONI, SILVIO (born 1936), Italian businessman and politician **25** 48-50

BERMEJO, BARTOLOMÉ (Bartolomé de Cárdenas; flourished 1474-1498), Spanish painter **2** 205

Bermuda (archipelago; Atlantic Ocean)
Outerbridge, Mary Ewing **32** 288-289

BERNADETTE OF LOURDES, ST. (Marie Bernarde Soubirous; 1844-1879), French nun and Roman Catholic saint **21** 34-36

BERNADOTTE, JEAN BAPTISTE (1763-1844), king of Sweden 1818-1844 **2** 205-206

BERNANOS, GEORGES (1888-1948), French novelist and essayist **2** 206-207

BERNARD, CLAUDE (1813-1878), French physiologist **2** 208-210

BERNARD OF CLAIRVAUX, ST. (1090-1153), French theologian, Doctor of the Church **2** 207-208

Bernardi, Francesco
see Senesino

BERNARDIN, CARDINAL JOSEPH (1928-1996), Roman Catholic Cardinal and American activist **2** 210-211

Bernardone, Giovanni di
see Francis of Assisi, St.

BERNAYS, EDWARD L. (1891-1995), American public relations consultant **2** 211-212

BERNBACH, WILLIAM (1911-1982), American advertising executive **19** 20-22

BERNERS-LEE, TIM (born 1955), English computer scientist and creator of the World Wide Web **20** 41-43

BLUMBERG, BARUCH (1925-2011), American medical researcher **32** 44-46

BLUME, JUDY (born Judy Sussman, 1938), American fiction author **2** 344-345

BLUMENTHAL, WERNER MICHAEL (born 1926), American businessman and treasury secretary **2** 345-346

BLY, NELLIE (born Elizabeth Cochrane Seaman; 1864-1922), American journalist and reformer **2** 346-348

BLYDEN, EDWARD WILMOT (1832-1912), Liberian statesman **2** 348-349

Blythe, Vernon William
see Castle, I. and V.

Boadicia
see Boudicca

BOAL, AUGUSTO (1931-2009), Brazilian director and author **30** 63-65

Boal, Mark, (born 1973), American journalist
Bigelow, Kathryn **32** 40-42

Boanerges
see John, St.

BOAS, FRANZ (1858-1942), German-born American anthropologist **2** 349-351

BOCCACCIO, GIOVANNI (1313-1375), Italian author **2** 351-353

BOCCIONI, UMBERTO (1882-1916), Italian artist **2** 353-354

BÖCKLIN, ARNOLD (1827-1901), Swiss painter **2** 354-355

BODE, BOYD HENRY (1873-1953), American philosopher and educator **2** 355-356

Bodenstein, Andreas
see Karlstadt

BODENSTEIN, MAX ERNST (1871-1942), German chemist **32** 46-48

Bodhisattva Emperor
see Liang Wu-ti

BODIN, JEAN (1529/30-1596), French political philosopher **2** 356-357

BOECKH, AUGUST (1785-1867), German classical scholar **30** 63-67

BOEHME, JACOB (1575-1624), German mystic **2** 357

BOEING, WILLIAM EDWARD (1881-1956), American businessman **2** 357-358

BOERHAAVE, HERMANN (1668-1738), Dutch physician and chemist **2** 358-359

BOESAK, ALLAN AUBREY (born 1945), opponent of apartheid in South Africa and founder of the United Democratic Front **2** 359-360

BOETHIUS, ANICIUS MANLIUS SEVERINUS (c. 480-c. 524), Roman logician and theologian **2** 360-361

BOFF, LEONARDO (Leonardo Genezio Darci Boff; born 1938), Brazilian priest **22** 69-71

BOFFRAND, GABRIEL GERMAIN (1667-1754), French architect and decorator **2** 361

BOFILL, RICARDO (born 1939), post-modern Spanish architect **2** 362-363

BOGART, HUMPHREY (1899-1957), American stage and screen actor **2** 363-364
Harvey, Cyrus **32** 150-152

BOHEMUND I (of Taranto; c. 1055-1111), Norman Crusader **2** 364

BOHLEN, CHARLES (CHIP) EUSTIS (1904-1973), United States ambassador to the Soviet Union, interpreter, and presidential adviser **2** 364-366

BÖHM, GEORG (1661-1733), German organist **31** 28-29

BÖHM-BAWERK, EUGEN VON (1851-1914), Austrian economist **2** 366

Böhme, Jakob
see Boehme, Jacob

BOHR, AAGE NIELS (born 1922), Danish physicist **25** 53-55

BOHR, NIELS HENRIK DAVID (1885-1962), Danish physicist **2** 366-368

BOIARDO, MATTEO MARIA (Conte di Scandiano; 1440/41-1494), Italian poet **2** 369

BOILEAU-DESPRÉAUX, NICHOLAS (c. 1636-1711), French critic and writer **2** 369-371

Boisy, Francis
see Francis of Sales, St.

BOITO, ARRIGO (1842-1918), Italian composer, librettist, and poet **30** 67-69

BOIVIN, MARIE GILLAIN (née Marie Anne Victorine Gillain; 1773-1841), French midwife and author **25** 55-56

BOK, DEREK CURTIS (born 1930), dean of the Harvard Law School and president of Harvard University **2** 371-372

BOK, EDWARD WILLIAM (1863-1930), American editor and publisher **22** 71-73

BOK, SISSELA ANN (born 1934), American moral philosopher **2** 372-374

BOLAÑO, ROBERTO (1953-2003), Chilean author **28** 42-45

BOLEYN, ANNE (c. 1504-1536), second wife of Henry VIII **18** 47-49

Bolingbroke, Henry
see Henry IV (king of England)

BOLINGBROKE, VISCOUNT (Henry St. John; 1678-1751), English statesman **2** 374-375

BOLÍVAR, SIMÓN (1783-1830), South American general and statesman **2** 375-377

BOLKIAH, HASSANAL (Muda Hassanal Bolkiah Mu'izzaddin Waddaulah; born 1946), Sultan of Brunei **18** 49-51

BÖLL, HEINRICH (1917-1985), German writer and translator **2** 377-378

Bolsheviks (Russian politics)
supporters
Tukhachevsky, Mikhail **32** 340-342

BOLT, ROBERT (1924-1995), British screenwriter and playwright **30** 69-71

BOLTWOOD, BERTRAM BORDEN (1870-1927), American radiochemist **2** 378-379

BOLTZMANN, LUDWIG (1844-1906), Austrian physicist **2** 379-380

BOMANI, PAUL (1925-2005), Tanzanian politician **29** 63-65

BOMBAL, MARÍA LUISA (1910-1980), Chilean novelist and story writer **2** 380-381

Bonaparte, Charles Louis Napoleon
see Napoleon III

BONAPARTE, JOSEPH (1768-1844), French statesman, king of Naples 1806-1808 and of Spain 1808-1813 **2** 381-382

BONAPARTE, LOUIS (1778-1846), French statesman, king of Holland 1806-1810 **2** 382-383

Bonaparte, Napoleon
see Napoleon I

BONAVENTURE, ST. (1217-1274), Italian theologian and philosopher **2** 383-384

Boncompagni, Ugo
see Gregory XIII

BOND, HORACE MANN (1904-1972), African American educator **2** 384-386

BOND, JULIAN (born 1940), civil rights leader elected to the Georgia House of Representatives **2** 386-387

BONDEVIK, KJELL MAGNE (born 1947), Norwegian politician **27** 51-53

BONDFIELD, MARGARET GRACE (1873-1953), British union official and political leader **2** 388-389

BONDI, HERMANN (1919-2005), English mathematician and cosmologist **18** 51-52

BUBER, MARTIN (1878-1965), Austrian-born Jewish theologian and philosopher **3** 87-89

Buccleugh
see Monmouth and Buccleugh Duke of

BUCHALTER, LEPKE (Louis Bachalter; 1897-1944), American gangster **19** 42-44

BUCHANAN, JAMES (1791-1868), American statesman, president 1857-1861 **3** 89-90

BUCHANAN, PATRICK JOSEPH (born 1938), commentator, journalist, and presidential candidate **3** 90-91

BUCHWALD, ART (Arthur Buchwald; 1925-2007), American journalist **27** 55-57

BUCK, JACK (John Francis Buck; 1924-2002), American sportscaster **27** 57-59

BUCK, PEARL SYDENSTRICKER (1892-1973), American novelist **3** 91-93

BUCKINGHAM, 1ST DUKE OF (George Villiers; 1592-1628), English courtier and military leader **3** 93-94

BUCKINGHAM, 2D DUKE OF (George Villiers; 1628-1687), English statesman **3** 94-95

BUCKLE, HENRY THOMAS (1821-1862), English historian **3** 95-96

BUCKLEY, WILLIAM F., JR. (1925-2008), conservative American author, editor, and political activist **3** 96-97

BUDDHA (c. 560-480 BCE), Indian founder of Buddhism **3** 97-101

BUDDHADĀSA BHIKKHU (Nguam Phanich; 1906-1993), founder of Wat Suan Mokkhabalārama in southern Thailand and interpreter of Theravāda Buddhism **3** 101-102

BUDÉ, GUILLAUME (1467-1540), French humanist **3** 102-103

BUDGE, DON (J. Donald Budge; 1915-2000), American tennis player **21** 57-59

BUECHNER, FREDERICK (born 1926), American novelist and theologian **3** 103-105

BUEL, JESSE (1778-1839), American agriculturalist and journalist **3** 105

Buell, Sarah Josepha
see Hale, Sarah Josepha

BUFFALO BILL (William Frederick Cody; 1846-1917), American scout and publicist **3** 105-106

BUFFETT, WARREN (born 1930), American investment salesman **3** 106-109

BUFFON, COMTE DE (Georges Louis Leclerc; 1707-1788), French naturalist **3** 109-111

BUGEAUD DE LA PICONNERIE, THOMAS ROBERT (1784-1849), Duke of Isly and marshal of France **3** 111

Bugs Bunny (cartoon character)
Avery, Tex **32** 24-27

BUICK, DAVID (1854-1929), American inventor and businessman **19** 44-45

BUKHARI, MUHAMMAD IBN ISMAIL AL- (810-870), Arab scholar and Moslem saint **3** 111-112

BUKHARIN, NIKOLAI IVANOVICH (1858-1938), Russian politician **3** 112-113

Bukharin Jews
Malayev, Ilyas **32** 227-229

BUKOWSKI, CHARLES (1920-1994), American writer and poet **3** 113-115

BULATOVIC, MOMIR (born 1956), president of Montenegro (1990-1992) and of the new Federal Republic of Yugoslavia (1992-) **3** 115-116

BULFINCH, CHARLES (1763-1844), American colonial architect **3** 116-117

BULGAKOV, MIKHAIL AFANASIEVICH (1891-1940), Russian novelist and playwright **3** 117

BULGANIN, NIKOLAI (1885-1975), chairman of the Soviet Council of Ministers (1955-1958) **3** 118-119

Bulgaroctonus (Bulgar-Slayer)
see Basil II, (1415-1462)

BULL, OLE (Ole Bornemann Bull; 1810-1880), Norwegian violinist and composer **28** 54-56

Bullock, Anna Mae
see Turner, Tina

BULOSAN, CARLOS (1911-1956), American author and poet **21** 59-61

BULTMANN, RUDOLF KARL (1884-1976), German theologian **3** 119-120

BULWER-LYTTON, EDWARD (1st Baron Lytton of Knebworth; 1803-1873), English novelist **22** 87-88

BUNAU-VARILLA, PHILIPPE JEAN (1859-1940), French engineer and soldier **3** 120-121

BUNCH, CHARLOTTE (born 1944), American activist **31** 47-49

BUNCHE, RALPH JOHNSON (1904-1971), African American diplomat **3** 121-122

BUNDY, MCGEORGE (1919-1996), national security adviser to two presidents **3** 122-124

BUNIN, IVAN ALEKSEEVICH (1870-1953), Russian poet and novelist **3** 124

BUNSEN, ROBERT WILHELM (1811-1899), German chemist and physicist **3** 124-125

BUNSHAFT, GORDON (1909-1990), American architect **3** 125-127

BUNTING-SMITH, MARY INGRAHAM (Polly Bunting; 1910-1998), American educator **27** 59-61

BUNTLINE, NED (c. 1821-1886), American writer and publisher **30** 88-90

BUÑUEL, LUIS (1900-1983), Spanish film director **3** 127-128

BUNYAN, JOHN (1628-1688), English author and Baptist preacher **3** 128-129

BURBAGE, RICHARD (c. 1567-1619), British actor **24** 70-72

BURBANK, LUTHER (1849-1926), American plant breeder **3** 129-131

BURBIDGE, E. MARGARET (Eleanor Margaret Burbidge; born 1919), British-American astronomer and physicist **26** 48-50

BURCHFIELD, CHARLES (1893-1967), American painter **3** 131-132

BURCKHARDT, JACOB CHRISTOPH (1818-1897), Swiss historian **3** 132-133

BURCKHARDT, JOHANN LUDWIG (1784-1817), Swiss-born explorer **3** 133

BURGER, WARREN E. (1907-1986), Chief Justice of the United States Supreme Court (1969-1986) **3** 133-136

BURGESS, ANTHONY (John Anthony Burgess Wilson; 1917-1993), English author **3** 136-137

BURGOYNE, JOHN (1723-1792), British general and statesman **3** 137-138

BURKE, EDMUND (1729-1797), British statesman, political theorist, and philosopher **3** 138-141

BURKE, JOHN BERNARD (1814-1892), British genealogist and publisher **30** 90-91

BURKE, KENNETH (1897-1993), American literary theorist and critic **3** 141-142

BURKE, ROBERT O'HARA (1820-1861), Irish-born Australian policeman and explorer **3** 142-143

BURKE, SELMA (1900-1995), African American sculptor **3** 143-144

CATTELL, JAMES MCKEEN (1860-1944), American psychologist and editor 3 376-377

CATULUS, GAIUS VALERIUS (c. 84-c. 54 BCE), Roman poet 3 377-378

CAUCHY, AUGUSTIN LOUIS (1789-1857), French mathematician 3 378-380

Cauvin, John
see Calvin, John

CAVAFY, CONSTANTINE P. (Konstantinos P. Kabaphēs; 1863-1933), first modernist Greek poet 3 381-382

CAVALCANTI, GUIDO (c. 1255-1300), Italian poet 3 382

CAVALLI, PIETRO FRANCESCO (1602-1676), Italian composer 3 382-383

CAVAZOS, LAURO FRED (born 1927), American educator and public servant 25 79-81

Cavelier, René Robert
see La Salle, Sieur de

CAVENDISH, HENRY (1731-1810), English physicist and chemist 3 383-384

CAVENDISH, MARGARET LUCAS (1623-1673), English natural philosopher 23 66-67

CAVOUR, CONTE DI (Camillo Benso; 1810-1861), Italian statesman 3 385-386

CAXIAS, DUQUE DE (Luiz Alves de Lima e Silva; 1803-1880), Brazilian general and statesman 3 386

CAXTON, WILLIAM (1422-1491), English printer 3 386-387

CAYTON, SUSIE SUMNER REVELS (1870-1943), African American journalist and newspaper editor 27 79-81

CEAUSESCU, NICOLAE (1918-1989), Romanian statesman 3 387-388

CECCHETTI, ENRICO (1850-1928), Italian dancer, choreographer, and teacher 25 81-83

CECH, THOMAS ROBERT (born 1947), American biochemist 23 68-70

Cecil, Edward Algernon Robert
see Cecil of Chelwood, Viscount

CECIL OF CHELWOOD, VISCOUNT (Edgar Algernon Robert Cecil; 1864-1958), English statesman 3 388-389

CELA Y TRULOCK, CAMILO JOSÉ (1916-2002), Spanish author 3 389-390

CÉLINE, LOUIS FERDINAND (pen name of Ferdinand Destouches; 1894-1961), French novelist 3 390-391

Cell lines (biology)
Gey, George 32 134-135

CELLINI, BENVENUTO (1500-1571), Italian goldsmith and sculptor 3 391-392

CELSIUS, ANDERS (1701-1744), Swedish astronomer 3 392
Celsius, Olof 32 65-67

CELSIUS, OLOF (1670-1756), Swedish botanist 32 65-67

CELSUS, AULUS CORNELIUS (c. 25 BCE-c. A.D. 45), Roman medical author 3 393

Cenno de' Pepsi
see Cimabue

CENTLIVRE, SUSANNA (Susanna Carroll; Susanna Rawkins; c. 1666-1723), British author 28 65-67

Central Asia (Steppes-Turkestan)
Malayev, Ilyas 32 227-229

Central Powers (WWI)
see World War I (1914-1918)

Cepeda y Ahumada, Teresa de
see Theresa, St.

Cephas
see Peter, St.

Cerebral localization
Fritsch, Gustav Theodor 32 119-121
Hitzig, Eduard 32 164-166

Cerenkov, Pavel
see Cherenkov, Pavel

CERETA, LAURA (Laura Cereta Serina; 1469-1499), Italian author and feminist 24 75-77

CEREZO AREVALO, MARCO VINICIO (born 1942), president of Guatemala (1986-1991) 3 393-395

CERF, BENNETT (1898-1971), American editor, publisher, author, and television performer 22 98-100

CERNAN, GENE (Eugene Andrew Cernan; born 1934), American astronaut 22 100-102

CERVANTES, MIGUEL DE SAAVEDRA (1547-1616), Spanish novelist 3 395-398

CÉSAIRE, AIMÉ (1913-2008), Martinican writer and statesman 30 108-110

CÉSPEDES, CARLOS MANUEL DE (1819-1874), Cuban lawyer and revolutionary 3 398-399

CESTI, PIETRO (Marc'Antonio Cesti; 1623-1669), Italian composer 3 399-400

CETSHWAYO (Cetewayo; c. 1826-1884), king of Zululand 1873-1879 3 400

CÉZANNE, PAUL (1839-1906), French painter 3 400-402

CHABROL, CLAUDE (1930-2010), French filmmaker 28 67-69

CHADLI BENJEDID (born 1929), president of the Algerian Republic (1979-92) 3 402-404

CHADWICK, SIR EDWIN (1800-1890), English utilitarian reformer 3 404-405

CHADWICK, FLORENCE (1918-1995), American swimmer 19 64-66

CHADWICK, LYNN RUSSELL (1914-2003), English sculptor 18 88-90

CHADWICK, SIR JAMES (1891-1974), English physicist 3 405-406

CHAGALL, MARC (1887-1985), Russian painter 3 406-407

CHAHINE, YOUSSEF (1926-2008), Egyptian filmmaker 25 83-86

CHAI LING (born 1966), Chinese student protest leader 19 67-68

CHAIN, ERNST BORIS (1906-1979), German-born English biochemist 3 407-408

Chain reactions
Bodenstein, Max Ernst 32 46-48

CHALIAPIN, FEDOR IVANOVICH (1873-1938), Russian musician 24 77-79

CHALMERS, THOMAS (1780-1847), Scottish reformer and theologian 3 408-409

CHAMBERLAIN, ARTHUR NEVILLE (1869-1940), English statesman 3 409-411

CHAMBERLAIN, HOUSTON STEWART (1855-1927), English-born German writer 3 411

CHAMBERLAIN, JOSEPH (1836-1914), English politician 3 411-413

CHAMBERLAIN, OWEN (1920-2006), American physicist 25 86-88

CHAMBERLAIN, WILT (1936-1999), American basketball player 3 413-415

CHAMBERLIN, THOMAS CHROWDER (1843-1928), American geologist 3 415-416

CHAMBERS, WHITTAKER (Jay Vivian; 1901-1961), magazine editor who helped organize a Communist spy ring in the United States government 3 416-417

CHAMINADE, CÉCILE LOUISE STÉPHANIE (1857-1944), French composer and pianist 26 62-64

CHAMOISEAU, PATRICK (born 1953), Martiniquais writer 32 67-68

CHAMORRO, VIOLETA BARRIOS DE (born 1930), newspaper magnate, publicist, and first woman president of Nicaragua (1990) **3** 417-419

CHAMPLAIN, SAMUEL DE (c. 1570-1635), French geographer and explorer **3** 419-421

CHAMPOLLION, JEAN FRANÇOIS (1790-1832), French Egyptologist **3** 421

CHAN, JACKIE (Chan King-Sang; Sing Lung; born 1954), Chinese actor **27** 81-83

Chanakya
see Kautilya

CHANCELLOR, RICHARD (died 1556), English navigator **3** 422

CHANDLER, ALFRED DU PONT, JR. (1918-2007), American historian of American business **3** 422-423

CHANDLER, RAYMOND, JR. (1888-1959), American author **3** 423-425

CHANDLER, ZACHARIAH (1813-1879), American politician **3** 425-426

CHANDRAGUPTA MAURYA (died c. 298 BCE), emperor of India c. 322-298 **3** 426

CHANDRASEKHAR, SUBRAHMANYAN (1910-1995), Indian-born American physicist **3** 426-429

CHANEL, COCO (born Gabrielle Chanel; 1882-1971), French fashion designer **3** 429

CHANEY, LON (Alonzo Chaney; 1883-1930), American actor **19** 68-70

CHANG CHEH (c. 1923-2002), Chinese film director **31** 52-53

Chang Chiao
see Chang Chüeh

CHANG CHIEN (1853-1926), Chinese industrialist and social reformer **3** 429-430

CHANG CHIH-TUNG (1837-1909), Chinese official and reformer **3** 430-431

CHANG CHÜ-CHENG (1525-1582), Chinese statesman **3** 431-432

CHANG CHÜEH (died 184), Chinese religious and revolutionary leader **3** 432-433

CHANG HSÜEH-CH'ENG (1738-1801), Chinese scholar and historian **3** 433

Ch'ang-k'ang
see Ku K'ai-chih

CHANG PO-GO (died 846), Korean adventurer and merchant prince **3** 433-434

CHANG TSO-LIN (1873-1928), Chinese warlord **3** 434-435

CHANNING, EDWARD (1856-1931), American historian **3** 435

CHANNING, WILLIAM ELLERY (1780-1842), Unitarian minister and theologian **3** 435-436

CHAO, ELAINE (Elaine Lan Chao; born 1953), Asian American government adminstrator **27** 84-86

Chao K'uang-yin
see Zhao Kuang-yin

CHAO MENG-FU (1254-1322), Chinese painter **3** 436-437

CHAPIN, F(RANCIS) STUART (1888-1974), American sociologist **3** 437-438

CHAPLIN, CHARLES SPENCER (1889-1977), American film actor, director, and writer **3** 438-440

Chapman, Carrie Lane
see Catt, Carrie Chapman

CHAPMAN, EDDIE (Arnold Edward Chapman; 1914-1997), British criminal and spy **28** 69-72

CHAPMAN, GEORGE (c. 1559-1634), English poet, dramatist, and translator **3** 440-441

CHAPMAN, JOHN (Johnny Appleseed; c. 1775-1847), American horticulturist and missionary **21** 77-78

CHAPMAN, SYDNEY (1888-1970), English geophysicist **3** 441

CHAPONE, HESTER (Hester Mulso; 1727-1801), British author and critic **28** 72-74

CHARCOT, JEAN MARTIN (1825-1893), French psychiatrist **3** 442

CHARDIN, JEAN BAPTISTE SIMÉON (1699-1779), French painter **3** 442-443

CHARGAFF, ERWIN (1905-2002), American biochemist who worked with DNA **3** 444-445

CHARLEMAGNE (742-814), king of the Franks, 768-814, and emperor of the West, 800-814 **3** 445-447

CHARLES (born 1948), Prince of Wales and heir apparent to the British throne **3** 448-450

Charles I (king of Bohemia)
see Charles IV (Holy Roman emperor)

Charles I (king of Spain)
see Charles V (Holy Roman emperor)

CHARLES I (1600-1649), king of England 1625-1649 **3** 450-452

CHARLES II (1630-1685), king of England, Scotland, and Ireland 1660-1685 **3** 452-454
wife
      Catherine of Braganza **32** 62-55

CHARLES II (1661-1700), king of Spain 1665-1700 **3** 454

CHARLES III (1716-1788), king of Spain 1759-1788 **3** 454-455
    Lorenzana, Antonio **32** 220-222

Charles IV (king of Two Sicilies)
see Charles III (king of Spain)

CHARLES IV (1316-1378), Holy Roman emperor 1346-1378 **3** 455-456

CHARLES IV (1748-1819), king of Spain 1788-1808 **3** 456-457

CHARLES V (1337-1380), king of France 1364-1380 **3** 459-460

CHARLES V (1500-1558), Holy Roman emperor 1519-1556 **3** 457-459

CHARLES VI (1368-1422), king of France 1380-1422 **3** 460-461

CHARLES VII (1403-1461), king of France 1422-1461 **3** 461-462

CHARLES VIII (1470-1498), king of France 1483-1498 **3** 462-463

CHARLES X (1757-1836), king of France 1824-1830 **3** 463-464

CHARLES XII (1682-1718), king of Sweden 1697-1718 **3** 464-466

CHARLES, RAY (Robinson; 1930-2004), American jazz musician–singer, pianist, and composer **3** 469-470

CHARLES ALBERT (1798-1849), king of Sardinia 1831-1849 **3** 466

CHARLES EDWARD LOUIS PHILIP CASIMIR STUART (1720-1788), Scottish claimant to English and Scottish thrones **3** 466-467

Charles Louis Napoleon
see Napoleon III

Charles Martel
see Martel, Charles

Charles of Luxemburg
see Charles IV (Holy Roman emperor)

Charles Philippe (Count of Artois)
see Charles X (king of France)

CHARLES THE BOLD (1433-1477), duke of Burgundy 1467-1477 **3** 467-469

Charles the Great
see Charlemagne

Charles the Mad
see Charles VI (king of France)

Charlier, Jean
see Gerson, John

CHARNISAY, CHARLES DE MENOU (Seigneur d'Aulnay; c. 1604-1650), French governor of Acadia **3** 470-471

Charolais, Count of
see Charles the Bold

CLARKE, REBECCA THACHER (1886-1979), English composer and violist **24** 87-89

CLARKE, SAMUEL (1675-1729), English theologian and philosopher **4** 88

CLAUDE LORRAIN (1600-1682), French painter, draftsman, and etcher **4** 89-90

CLAUDEL, CAMILLE (1864-1943), French sculptor **22** 107-110

CLAUDEL, PAUL LOUIS CHARLES (1868-1955), French author and diplomat **4** 90-91

CLAUDIUS GERMANICUS, TIBERIUS (Claudius I; 10 BCE -A.D. 54), emperor of Rome 41-54 **4** 91-92

CLAUSEWITZ, KARL VON (Karl Philipp Gottlieb von Clausewitz; 1780-1831), Prussian military strategist **20** 89-91

CLAUSIUS, RUDOLF JULIUS EMANUEL (1822-1888), German physicist **4** 92-94

CLAVER, ST. PETER (1580-1654), Spanish Jesuit missionary **4** 94

CLAY, HENRY (1777-1852), American lawyer and statesman **4** 94-96

CLAYTON, JOHN MIDDLETON (1796-1856), American lawyer and statesman **4** 96-97

CLEARY, BEVERLY (nee Beverly Bunn; born 1916), American author of children's books **22** 110-112

CLEAVER, LEROY ELDRIDGE (1935-1998), American writer and Black Panther leader **4** 97-98

Cleft palate
von Graefe, Carl Ferdinand **32** 354-356

CLEISTHENES (flourished 6th century BCE), Athenian statesman **4** 98-99

CLEMENCEAU, GEORGES (1841-1929), French statesman **4** 99-101

Clemens, Samuel Langhorne
see Twain, Mark

Clemens, Titus Flavius
see Clement of Alexandria

CLEMENS NON PAPA, JACOBUS (c. 1510-c. 1556), Flemish composer **4** 101

CLEMENT I (died c. 100 A.D.), Bishop of Rome, pope **23** 78-81

CLEMENT V (1264-1314), pope 1304-1314 **4** 101-102

CLEMENT VII (Giulio de Medici; 1478-1534), pope (1523-1534) **21** 81-83

CLEMENT XI (Giovanni Francesco Albani; 1649-1721), Italian pope 1700-1721 **24** 90-92

CLEMENT OF ALEXANDRIA (c. 150-c. 215), Christian theologian **4** 102-103

Clement of Rome, St.
see Clement I, St.

CLEMENTE, ROBERTO (1934-1972), Hispanic American baseball player **19** 70-72

CLEOMENES I (flourished c. 520-490 BCE), Spartan king **4** 103

CLEOMENES III (c. 260-219 BCE), king of Sparta 235-219 **4** 103-104

CLEON (c. 475-422 BCE), Athenian political leader **4** 104-105

CLEOPATRA (69-30 BCE), queen of Egypt **4** 105-106

Cleophil
see Congreve, William

CLEVELAND, FRANCES FOLSOM (1864-1947), American first lady **32** 77-79

CLEVELAND, JAMES (1932-1991), African American singer, songwriter, and pianist **4** 106-108

CLEVELAND, STEPHEN GROVER (1837-1908), American statesman, twice president **4** 108-110
family
Cleveland, Frances Folsom **32** 77-79

Cleveland Indians (baseball team)
Maris, Roger **32** 236-240

CLIFFORD, ANNE (1590-1676), English author and philanthropist **27** 88-90

Climate change
Chu, Steven **32** 75-76

CLINE, PATSY (born Virginia Patterson Hensley; 1932-1963), American singer **4** 110-112

CLINTON, DEWITT (1769-1828), American lawyer and statesman **4** 112-113

CLINTON, GEORGE (1739-1812), American patriot and statesman **4** 113-114

CLINTON, SIR HENRY (c. 1738-1795), British commander in chief during the American Revolution **4** 114-115

CLINTON, HILLARY RODHAM (born 1947), American politician and first lady **4** 115-117
campaigns
Obama, Barack **32** 280-282

CLINTON, WILLIAM JEFFERSON (''Bill''; born 1946), 42nd president of the United States **4** 117-119
appointees
Sotomayor, Sonia **32** 320-321

CLIVE, ROBERT (Baron Clive of Plassey; 1725-1774), English soldier and statesman **4** 119-120

CLODION (1738-1814), French sculptor **4** 121

CLODIUS PULCHER, PUBLIUS (died 52 BCE), Roman politician **4** 121-122

CLOONEY, ROSEMARY (1928-2002), American singer and actress **27** 90-93

Clopinel, Jean
see Jean de Meun

Cloud computing
Gelernter, David **32** 131-133

CLOUET, FRANÇOIS (c. 1516-c. 1572), French portrait painter **4** 122-123

CLOUET, JEAN (c. 1485-c. 1541), French portrait painter **4** 122-123

CLOUGH, ARTHUR HUGH (1819-1861), English poet **4** 123-124

CLOVIS I (465-511), Frankish king **4** 124

Clyens, Mary Elizabeth
see Lease, Mary Elizabeth Clyens

Cnut
see Canute I

COACHMAN, ALICE (Alice Coachman Davis; born 1923), African American athlete **26** 71-73

COANDĂ, HENRI (1886-1972), Romanian engineer **31** 54-55

Coasters, The (music group)
Leiber and Stoller **32** 209-212
Ousley, Curtis **32** 182-184

COBB, JEWEL PLUMMER (born 1924), African American scientist and activist **22** 112-114

COBB, TYRUS RAYMOND (1886-1961), baseball player **4** 124-126

COBBETT, WILLIAM (1763-1835), English journalist and politician **4** 126-127

COBDEN, RICHARD (1804-1865), English politician **4** 127-128

COBOL (computer programming language)
Holberton, Betty **32** 166-168

Cobordism (mathematics)
Thom, René **32** 332-334

COCHISE (c. 1825-1874), American Chiricahua Apache Indian chief **4** 128

COCHRAN, JACQUELINE (Jackie Cochran; 1910-1980), American aviator and businesswoman **18** 94-96

COCHRAN, JOHNNIE (1937-2005), African American lawyer **4** 128-131

COCHRANE, THOMAS (Earl of Dundonald; 1775-1860), British naval officer **20** 91-93

COCKCROFT, JOHN DOUGLAS (1897-1967), English physicist **4** 131-132

COCTEAU, JEAN (1889-1963), French writer **4** 132-133
   Aumont, Jean-Pierre **32** 20-23

Cody, William Frederick
see Buffalo Bill

COE, SEBASTIAN (born 1956), English track athlete **20** 93-95

COEN, JAN PIETERSZOON (c. 1586-1629), Dutch governor general of Batavia **4** 133

COETZEE, J(OHN) M. (born 1940), South African novelist **4** 133-135

COFFIN, LEVI (1789-1877), American antislavery reformer **4** 135

Coffin, Lucretia
see Mott, Lucretia Coffin

COFFIN, WILLIAM SLOANE, JR. (1924-2006), Yale University chaplain and activist **4** 135-137

COHAN, GEORGE MICHAEL (1878-1942), American actor and playwright **4** 137-138

Cohen, Bennett, (Ben Cohen; born 1951)
see Ben & Jerry

Cohen, George Morris
see Brandes, Georg Morris

COHEN, HERMANN (1842-1918), Jewish-German philosopher **4** 138-139

COHEN, LEONARD (born 1934), Canadian musician and writer **32** 79-81

COHEN, MORRIS RAPHAEL (1880-1947), American philosopher and teacher **4** 139-140

COHEN, WILLIAM S. (born 1940), American secretary of defense **18** 96-98

Cohen-Tannoudji, Claude, French physicist
   Phillips, William D. **32** 301-302

COHN, FERDINAND (1829-1898), German botanist **20** 95-97

COHN, HARRY (1891-1958), American movie industry executive **31** 56-59

COHN, MILDRED (1913-2009), American biochemist **32** 81-84

COHN, ROY MARCUS (1927-1986), American lawyer and businessman **29** 116-118

COHN-BENDIT, DANIEL (born 1946), led "new left" student protests in France in 1968 **4** 140-141

COKE, SIR EDWARD (1552-1634), English jurist and parliamentarian **4** 141-142

Colbath, Jeremiah Jones
see Wilson, Henry

COLBERT, JEAN BAPTISTE (1619-1683), French statesman **4** 142-143

COLBY, WILLIAM E. (1920-1996), American director of the Central Intelligence Agency (CIA) **4** 143-145

Cold War (international politics)
   diplomacy during
     Dobrynin, Anatoly **32** 99-101

COLDEN, CADWALLADER (1688-1776), American botanist and politician **4** 145-146

COLDEN, JANE (1724-1766), American botanist **29** 118-119

COLE, GEORGE DOUGLAS HOWARD (1889-1959), English historian and economist **4** 146-147

COLE, JOHNNETTA (born 1936), African American scholar and educator **4** 147-149

COLE, NAT (a.k.a. Nat "King" Cole, born Nathaniel Adams Coles; 1919-1965), American jazz musician **4** 149-151

COLE, THOMAS (1801-1848), American painter **4** 151-152

COLEMAN, BESSIE (1892-1926), first African American to earn an international pilot's license **4** 152-154

COLERIDGE, SAMUEL TAYLOR (1772-1834), English poet and critic **4** 154-156

COLERIDGE-TAYLOR, SAMUEL (1875-1912), English composer and conductor **28** 80-83

COLES, ROBERT MARTIN (born 1929), American social psychiatrist, social critic, and humanist **4** 156-157

COLET, JOHN (c. 1446-1519), English theologian **4** 157-158

COLET, LOUISE (1810-1870), French poet **29** 119-121

COLETTE, SIDONIE GABRIELLE (1873-1954), French author **4** 158-159

COLIGNY, GASPARD DE (1519-1572), French admiral and statesman **4** 159-160

Collage (art form)
   Heartfield, John **32** 154-157

COLLETT, CAMILLA (nee Camilla Wergeland; 1813-1895), Norwegian author **26** 73-75

COLLETT VARE, GLENNA (1903-1989), American golfer **32** 84-86

COLLIER, JOHN (1884-1968), American proponent of Native American culture **4** 160-162

COLLINGWOOD, ROBIN GEORGE (1889-1943), English historian and philosopher **4** 162

COLLINS, BILLY (born 1941), American poet **28** 83-85

COLLINS, EDWARD KNIGHT (1802-1878), American businessman and shipowner **4** 162-163

COLLINS, EILEEN (born 1956), American astronaut **4** 163-165

COLLINS, MARVA (born Marva Deloise Nettles; b. 1936), African American educator **4** 165-167

COLLINS, MICHAEL (1890-1922), Irish revolutionary leader and soldier **4** 167-168

COLLINS, WILLIAM (1721-1759), English lyric poet **4** 168-169

COLLINS, WILLIAM WILKIE (1824-1889), English novelist **4** 169-170

COLLIP, JAMES BERTRAM (1892-1965), Canadian biochemist **29** 121-123

Collodi, Carlo
see Lorenzini, Carlo

COLLOR DE MELLO, FERNANDO (born 1949), businessman who became president of Brazil in 1990 **4** 170-172

COLOMBO, REALDO (c. 1516-1559), Italian anatomist **30** 120-122

Colonna, Oddone
see Martin V

COLT, SAMUEL (1814-1862), American inventor and manufacturer **4** 172-173

COLTRANE, JOHN (1926-1967), African American jazz saxophonist **4** 173-174

COLUM, MARY (1884-1957), Irish literary critic and writer **30** 123-124

COLUM, PADRAIC (1881-1972), Irish-American poet and playwright **4** 174-175

COLUMBA, ST. (c. 521-597), Irish monk and missionary **4** 175-176

COLUMBAN, ST. (c. 543-615), Irish missionary **4** 176

COLUMBUS, CHRISTOPHER (1451-1506), Italian navigator, discoverer of America **4** 176-179

COLVIN, RUTH JOHNSON (1916-1993), American literacy advocate **31** 60-61

COLWELL, RITA R. (born 1934), American marine microbiologist **4** 179-180

COMANECI, NADIA (Nadia Conner; born 1961), Romanian gymnast **18** 98-100

COMENIUS, JOHN AMOS (1592-1670), Moravian theologian and educational reformer **4** 180-181

Comics (cartoons)
   Avery, Tex **32** 24-27
   Dirks, Rudolph **32** 97-99
   Kurtzman, Harvey **32** 191-193

DAIMLER, GOTTLIEB (1834-1900), German mechanical engineer **4** 368

DALADIER, ÉDOUARD (1884-1970), French statesman **4** 369

DALAI LAMA (Lhamo Thondup; born 1935), 14th in a line of Buddhist spiritual and temporal leaders of Tibet **4** 369-371

DALE, SIR HENRY HALLETT (1875-1968), English pharmacologist and neuro-physiologist **4** 371-373

D'Alembert, Jean
see Alembert, Jean le Rond d'

DALEN, NILS GUSTAF (1869-1937), Swedish engineer and inventor **25** 99-101

DALEY, RICHARD J. (1902-1976), Democratic mayor of Chicago (1955-1976) **4** 373-375

DALEY, RICHARD M. (born 1942), mayor of Chicago **24** 102-104

DALHOUSIE, 1ST MARQUESS OF (James Andrew Broun Ramsay; 1812-1860), British statesman **4** 375-376

DALI, SALVADOR (1904-1989), Spanish painter **4** 376-377
Thom, René **32** 332-334

DALL, CAROLINE HEALEY (1822-1912), American reformer **31** 71-72

DALLAPICCOLA, LUIGI (1904-1975), Italian composer **4** 377-378

DALTON, JOHN (1766-1844), English chemist **4** 378-379

DALY, MARCUS (1841-1900), American miner and politician **4** 379-380

DALY, MARY (1928-2010), American feminist theoretician and philosopher **4** 380-381

DALZEL, ARCHIBALD (or Dalziel; 1740-1811), Scottish slave trader **4** 381-382

DAM, CARL PETER HENRIK (1895-1976), Danish biochemist **4** 382-383

DAMIEN, FATHER (1840-1889), Belgian missionary **4** 383

DAMPIER, WILLIAM (1652-1715), English privateer, author, and explorer **4** 384

DANA, CHARLES ANDERSON (1819-1897), American journalist **4** 384-385

DANA, RICHARD HENRY, JR. (1815-1882), American author and lawyer **4** 385-386

DANDOLO, ENRICO (c. 1107-1205), Venetian doge 1192-1205 **4** 386-387

DANDRIDGE, DOROTHY (1922-1965), African American actress and singer **18** 112-114

DANIELS, JOSEPHUS (1862-1948), American journalist and statesman **4** 387

Daniels, W.
see Wallace-Johnson, Isaac

D'ANNUNZIO, GABRIELE (1863-1938), Italian poet and patriot **4** 388
Brooks, Romaine **32** 55-57

DANQUAH, JOSEPH B. (1895-1965), Ghanaian nationalist and politician **4** 388-389

DANTE ALIGHIERI (1265-1321), Italian poet **4** 389-391

DANTON, GEORGES JACQUES (1759-1794), French revolutionary leader **4** 391-393

DANTZIG, GEORGE BERNARD (1914-2005), American mathematician **26** 81-83

Dar es Salaam (city, Tanzania)
Kambona, Oscar **32** 175-177

Dar es Salaam, University of (Tanzania)
Warioba, Joseph **32** 357-358

DARBY, ABRAHAM (1677-1717), English iron manufacturer **20** 106-107

DARÍO, RUBÉN (1867-1916), Nicaraguan poet **4** 393-394

DARIUS I (the Great; ruled 522-486 BCE), king of Persia **4** 394-395

Dark matter
Zwicky, Fritz **32** 379-381

DARROW, CLARENCE SEWARD (1857-1938), American lawyer **4** 396-397

DARWIN, CHARLES ROBERT (1809-1882), English naturalist **4** 397-399

DARWIN, ERASMUS (1731-1802), English physician, author, botanist and inventor **18** 114-116

DARWISH, MAHMUD (born 1942), Palestinian poet **4** 399-401

DAS, CHITTA RANJAN (1870-1925), Indian lawyer, poet, and nationalist **4** 401-402

Dashti
see Jami

DATSOLALEE (Dabuda; Wide Hips; 1835-1925), Native American weaver **22** 130-131

Datta, Narendranath
see Vivekananda

Dau
see Landau, Lev Davidovich

DAUBIGNY, CHARLES FRANÇOIS (1817-1878), French painter and etcher **4** 402

DAUDET, ALPHONSE (1840-1897), French novelist and dramatist **4** 402-403

DAUMIER, HONORÉ VICTORIN (1808-1879), French lithographer, painter, and sculptor **4** 403-405

DAVENANT, SIR WILLIAM (1606-1668), English poet laureate and dramatist **31** 73-75

DAVENPORT, JOHN (1597-1670), English Puritan clergyman **4** 405-406

DAVID (ruled c. 1010-c. 970 BCE), Israelite king **4** 406-407

DAVID I (1084-1153), king of Scotland **4** 407

DAVID, JACQUES LOUIS (1748-1825), French painter **4** 407-409

DAVID, ST. (Dewi; 520-601), Welsh monk and evangelist **23** 83-85

DAVID-NÉEL, ALEXANDRA (Eugénie Alexandrine Marie David; 1868-1969), French explorer and author **28** 90-92

DAVIES, ARTHUR BOWEN (1862-1928), American painter **4** 409-410

DAVIES, MARION (1897-1961), American film star **29** 135-138

DAVIES, RUPERT (1917-1976), British actor **18** 116-117

DAVIES, WILLIAM ROBERTSON (1913-1995), Canadian author **18** 117-119

DAVIGNON, VISCOUNT (ETIENNE) (born 1932), an architect of European integration and unity through the Commission of the European Communities **4** 410-411

DAVIS, ALEXANDER JACKSON (1803-1892), American architect **4** 411

DAVIS, ANGELA (Angela Yvonne Davis; born 1944), African American scholar and activist **4** 412-413

DAVIS, ARTHUR VINING (1867-1962), general manager of the Aluminum Company of America (ALCOA) **4** 413-414

DAVIS, BENJAMIN O., SR. (1877-1970), first African American general in the regular United States Armed Services **4** 414-415

DAVIS, BETTE (1908-1989), American actress **18** 119-121
Flynn, Errol **32** 117-119

DAVIS, COLIN REX (born 1927), British conductor **22** 131-133

DAVIS, ELMER HOLMES (1890-1958), American journalist and radio commentator **22** 133-136

DAVIS, GLENN (1925-2005), American football player **21** 101-103

DONLEAVY, JAMES PATRICK (born 1926), Irish author and playwright **19** 91-93

DONNE, JOHN (1572-1631), English metaphysical poet **5** 60-61

DONNELLY, IGNATIUS (1831-1901), American politician and author **5** 62

DONNER, GEORG RAPHAEL (1693-1741), Austrian sculptor **5** 63

DONOSO, JOSÉ (1924-1996), Chilean writer **5** 63-65

DONOVAN, WILLIAM JOSEPH (1883-1959), American lawyer and public servant **22** 147-149

DOOLITTLE, HILDA (1886-1961), American poet and novelist **5** 65-66

DOOLITTLE, JAMES HAROLD (1896-1993), American transcontinental pilot **5** 66-68

DOPPLER, CHRISTIAN (1803-1853), Austrian physicist **31** 87-88

DORATI, ANTAL (1906-1988), Hungarian-American conductor **32** 101-103

Dorchester, 1st Baron
see Carleton, Guy

DORIA, ANDREA (1466-1560), Italian admiral and politician **18** 123-125

DORR, RHETA CHILDE (1868-1948), American journalist **5** 68-69

DORSEY, JIMMY (James Dorsey; 1904-1957), American musician and bandleader **19** 93-95

DORSEY, THOMAS ANDREW (1900-1993), African American gospel singer and composer **22** 149-151

DOS PASSOS, RODERIGO (1896-1970), American novelist **5** 69-71

DOS SANTOS, JOSÉ EDUARDO (born 1942), leader of the Popular Movement for the Liberation of Angola and president of Angola **5** 71-72

DOS SANTOS, MARCELINO (born 1929), Mozambican nationalist insurgent, statesman, and intellectual **5** 72-74

DOSTOEVSKY, FYODOR (1821-1881), Russian novelist **5** 74-77
influenced by
Nechaev, Sergei **32** 275-277

DOUBLEDAY, FRANK NELSON (1862-1934), American publisher **29** 146-148

Douglas, Lord Alfred Bruce, (1870-1945), English author
Brooks, Romaine **32** 55-57

DOUGLAS, DONALD WILLS (1892-1981), American aeronautical engineer **5** 77

DOUGLAS, GAVIN (c. 1475-1522), Scottish poet, prelate, and courtier **5** 77-78

DOUGLAS, SIR JAMES (c. 1286-1330), Scottish patriot **5** 80-82

DOUGLAS, SIR JOHN SHOLTO (1844-1900), English boxing patron **29** 148-150

DOUGLAS, MARJORY STONEMAN (1890-1998), American conservationist **31** 89-91

DOUGLAS, MARY TEW (1921-2007), British anthropologist and social thinker **5** 79-80

DOUGLAS, STEPHEN ARNOLD (1813-1861), American politician **5** 80-82

Douglas, Thomas
see Selkirk, 5th Earl of

DOUGLAS, THOMAS CLEMENT (1904-1986), Canadian clergyman and politician, premier of Saskatchewan (1944-1961), and member of Parliament (1962-1979) **5** 82-83

DOUGLAS, WILLIAM ORVILLE (1898-1980), American jurist **5** 83-85

DOUGLAS-HOME, ALEC (Alexander Frederick Home; 1903-1995), Scottish politician **20** 117-119

DOUGLASS, FREDERICK (c. 1817-1895), African American leader and abolitionist **5** 85-86

DOUHET, GIULIO (1869-1930), Italian military leader **22** 151-152

DOVE, ARTHUR GARFIELD (1880-1946), American painter **5** 86-87

DOVE, RITA FRANCES (born 1952), United States poet laureate **5** 87-89

DOVZHENKO, ALEXANDER (Oleksandr Dovzhenko; 1894-1956), Ukrainian film director and screenwriter **25** 120-122

DOW, CHARLES (1851-1902), American journalist **19** 95-97

DOW, HERBERT H. (Herbert Henry Dow; 1866-1930), American chemist and businessman **28** 100-102

DOW, NEAL (1804-1897), American temperance reformer **5** 89-90

DOWLAND, JOHN (1562-1626), British composer and lutenist **5** 90

DOWNING, ANDREW JACKSON (1815-1852), American horticulturist and landscape architect **5** 90-91

DOYLE, SIR ARTHUR CONAN (1859-1930), British author **5** 91-92

D'Oyly Carte
see Carte, Richard D'Oyly

DRAGO, LUIS MARÍA (1859-1921), Argentine international jurist and diplomat **5** 92-93

DRAKE, DANIEL (1785-1852), American physician **5** 93-94

DRAKE, EDWIN (1819-1880), American oil well driller and speculator **21** 108-110

DRAKE, SIR FRANCIS (c. 1541-1596), English navigator **5** 94-96

DRAPER, JOHN WILLIAM (1811-1882), Anglo-American scientist and historian **5** 96-97

Drapier, M.B.
see Swift, Jonathan

DRAWBAUGH, DANIEL (1827-1911), American inventor **31** 92-93

DRAYTON, MICHAEL (1563-1631), English poet **5** 97-98

Dreams from My Father (autobiography)
Obama, Barack **32** 280-282

DREBBEL, CORNELIUS (Jacobszoon Drebbel; Cornelius Van Drebbel; 1572-1633), Dutch inventor and engineer **28** 102-104

DREISER, (HERMAN) THEODORE (1871-1945), American novelist **5** 98-100

DREW, CHARLES RICHARD (1904-1950), African American surgeon **5** 100-101

DREW, DANIEL (1797-1879), American stock manipulator **5** 101-102

Drew, Robert, (born 1924), American filmmaker
Leacock, Richard **32** 202-205

DREXEL, KATHERINE (1858-1955), founded a Catholic order, the Sisters of the Blessed Sacrament **5** 102-103

DREXLER, KIM ERIC (born 1955), American scientist and author **20** 119-121

DREYER, CARL THEODOR (1889-1968), Danish film director **22** 152-155

DREYFUS, ALFRED (1859-1935), French army officer **5** 103-105

DRIESCH, HANS ADOLF EDUARD (1867-1941), German biologist and philosopher **5** 105

Drifters, The (music group)
Leiber and Stoller **32** 209-212

Droopy Dog (cartoon character)
Avery, Tex **32** 24-27

DRUCKER, PETER (1909-2005), American author and business consultant **21** 110-112

Drummond, James Eric
see Perth, 16th Earl of

DURAND, ASHER BROWN (1796-1886), American painter and engraver **5** 156-157

DURANT, THOMAS CLARK (1820-1885), American railroad executive **5** 157-158

DURANT, WILLIAM CRAPO (1861-1947), American industrialist **5** 158

DURANTE, JIMMY (1893-1980), American actor **32** 103-106

DURAS, MARGUERITE (Marguerite Donnadieu; 1914-1996), French author and filmmaker **26** 92-95

DÜRER, ALBRECHT (1471-1528), German painter and graphic artist **5** 159-161

DURHAM, 1ST EARL OF (John George Lambton; 1792-1840), English statesman **5** 161-162

DURKHEIM, ÉMILE (1858-1917), French philosopher and sociologist **5** 162-163

DURRELL, GERALD MALCOLM (1925-1995), British naturalist and conservationist **24** 123-126

DURRELL, LAWRENCE (1912-1990), British author of novels, poetry, plays, short stories, and travel books **5** 163-164

DÜRRENMATT, FRIEDRICH (1921-1990), Swiss playwright **5** 164-165

DUSE, ELEONORA (1859-1924), Italian actress **30** 154-157

Dutch art and architecture
genre and portrait painting
Uijlenburgh, Saskia van **32** 346-347

DUVALIER, FRANÇOIS (Papa Doc; 1907-1971), Haitian president 1957-1971 **5** 165-166

DUVALIER, JEAN CLAUDE (Baby Doc; born 1949), president of Haiti (1971-1986) **5** 166-168

DVOŘÁK, ANTONIN (1841-1904), Czech composer **5** 168-169

DWIGHT, TIMOTHY (1752-1817), American educator and Congregational minister **5** 169

Dyck, Anthony van
see Van Dyck, Anthony

DYER, MARY BARRETT (c. 1611-1660), English martyr **31** 100-103

DYLAN, BOB (born Robert Allen Zimmerman, 1941), American singer, songwriter, and guitarist **5** 170-171

DYSON, FREEMAN JOHN (born 1923), British-American physicist **5** 171-173

DZERZHINSKY, FELIX EDMUNDOVICH (1877-1926), Soviet politician and revolutionary **5** 173-174

Dzhugashvili, Iosif Vissarionovich
see Stalin, Joseph

E

EADS, JAMES BUCHANAN (1820-1887), American engineer and inventor **5** 175-176

EAKINS, THOMAS (1844-1916), American painter **5** 176-177

EARHART, AMELIA MARY (1897-1937), American aviator **5** 177-179

EARL, RALPH (1751-1801), American painter **5** 179

EARLE, SYLVIA A. (Born Sylvia Alice Reade; born 1935), American marine biologist and oceanographer **5** 180-181

EARNHARDT, DALE (1951-2001), American race car driver **22** 156-158

EARP, WYATT BARRY STEPP (1848-1929), gun-fighting marshal of the American West **5** 181-182

EAST, CATHERINE (1916-1996), American government official and activist **31** 104-105

EAST, EDWARD MURRAY (1879-1938), American plant geneticist **5** 182-183

EASTMAN, CHARLES A. (1858-1939), Native American author **5** 183-185

EASTMAN, CRYSTAL (1881-1928), American lawyer **31** 106

EASTMAN, GEORGE (1854-1932), American inventor and industrialist **5** 186

EASTMAN, MAX (Max Forrester Eastman; 1883-1969), American poet, radical editor, translator, and author **5** 187-188

EASTWOOD, ALICE (1859-1953), American botanist **22** 158-160

EASTWOOD, CLINT (born 1930), American movie star and director **5** 188-190

EATON, DORMAN BRIDGMAN (1823-1899), American lawyer and author **5** 190-191

EBADI, SHIRIN (born 1947), Iranian author and human rights activist **25** 124-126

EBAN, ABBA (Abba Solomon Eban; 1915-2002), Israeli statesman, diplomat, and scholar **5** 191-192

EBB, FRED (1935-2004), American lyricist **21** 113-115

EBBERS, BERNIE (born 1941), American businessman **20** 122-124

EBBINGHAUS, HERMANN (1850-1909), German psychologist **5** 192-193

EBERT, FRIEDRICH (1871-1925), German president 1919-1925 **5** 193-194
Heartfield, John **32** 154-157

EBOUÉ, ADOLPHE FELIX SYLVESTRE (1885-1944), African statesman, governor of French Equatorial Africa **5** 194

E.C. Comics
Kurtzman, Harvey **32** 191-193

EÇA DE QUEIRÓS, JOSÉ MARIA (1845-1900), Portuguese writer **30** 158-160

ECCLES, SIR JOHN CAREW (1903-1997), Australian neurophysiologist **5** 195-196

ECCLES, MARRINER STODDARD (1890-1977), American banker **22** 160-162

ECEVIT, BÜLENT (1925-2006), Turkish statesman and prime minister **5** 196-197

Echaurren, Roberto Matta
see Matta Echaurren, Roberto Sebastian Antonio

ECHEVERRÍA, JOSÉ ESTÉBAN (1805-1851), Argentine author and political theorist **5** 197-198

ECHEVERRIA ALVAREZ, LUIS (born 1922), president of Mexico (1970-1976) **5** 198-200

ECK, JOHANN MAIER VON (1486-1543), German theologian **5** 200

ECKERT, JOHN PRESPER (1919-1995), American computer engineer **20** 124-126
Bartik, Jean **32** 34-36

ECKHART, (JOHANN) MEISTER (c. 1260-c. 1327), German Dominican theologian **5** 200-201

ECO, UMBERTO (born 1932), Italian scholar and novelist **18** 128-130

EDDINGTON, SIR ARTHUR STANLEY (1882-1944), English astronomer **5** 201-202

EDDY, MARY BAKER (1821-1910), American founder of the Christian Science Church **5** 202

EDELMAN, GERALD MAURICE (born 1929), American neuroscientist **27** 106-108

EDELMAN, MARIAN WRIGHT (born 1939), lobbyist, lawyer, civil rights activist, and founder of the Children's Defense Fund **5** 202-204

EDEN, ANTHONY (1897-1977), English statesman, prime minister 1955-1957 **5** 204-205

EDERLE, GERTRUDE (1906-2003), American swimmer **19** 98-100

EDGERTON, HAROLD EUGENE (1903-1990), American inventor **28** 109-111

EDGEWORTH, MARIA (1767-1849), British author **5** 205-206

EZRA (flourished 5th century BCE), Hebrew priest, scribe, and reformer **5** 356-357

F

FABERGÉ, CARL (Peter Carl Fabergé; Karl Gustavovich Fabergé; 1846-1920), Russian jeweler and goldsmith **21** 125-127

FABIUS, LAURENT (born 1946), prime minister of France in the 1980s **5** 358-359

FABRICI, GIROLAMO (1537-1619), Italian anatomist and surgeon **30** 167-169

Fabricius ab Aquapendente, Hieronymus see Fabrici, Girolamo

FACKENHEIM, EMIL LUDWIG (1916-2003), post-World War II Jewish theologian **5** 359-361

Facundo, Juan see Quiroga, Juan Facundo

FADIL AL-JAMALI, MUHAMMAD (1903-1997), Iraqi educator, writer, diplomat, and politician **5** 361-362

FADLALLAH, SAYYID MUHAMMAD HUSAYN (1935-2010), Shi'i Muslim cleric and Lebanese political leader **5** 362-364

FAHD IBN ABDUL AZIZ AL-SAUD (1920-2005), son of the founder of modern Saudi Arabia and king **5** 364-366

FAHRENHEIT, GABRIEL DANIEL (1686-1736), German physicist **5** 366

FAIDHERBE, LOUIS LÉON CÉSAR (1818-1889), French colonial governor **5** 366-367

Fair, A. A. see Gardner, Erle Stanley

FAIR, JAMES RUTHERFORD, JR. (1920-2010), American chemical engineer and educator **20** 131-131

FAIRBANKS, DOUGLAS (Douglas Elton Ulman; 1883-1939), American actor and producer **19** 107-108

FAIRCLOUGH, ELLEN LOUKS (1905-2004), Canadian Cabinet minister **5** 367-368

FAIRUZ (née Nuhad Haddad; born 1933), Arabic singer **5** 368-369

FAISAL I (1883-1933), king of Iraq 1921-33 **5** 370-371

FAISAL II (1935-1958), king of Iraq, 1953-1958 **20** 132-132

FAISAL IBN ABD AL AZIZ IBN SAUD (1904-1975), Saudi Arabian king and prominent Arab leader **5** 371-372

FALCONET, ÉTIENNE MAURICE (1716-1791), French sculptor **5** 372

FALLA, MANUEL DE (1876-1946), Spanish composer **5** 372-373

FALLACI, ORIANA (1929-2006), Italian journalist **27** 115-117

FALLETTA, JOANN (born 1954), American conductor **5** 373-375

FALLOPPIO, GABRIELE (1523-1562), Italian anatomist **29** 157-159

FALWELL, JERRY (1933-2007), fundamentalist religious leader who also promoted right-wing political causes **5** 375-376

Famous Monsters of Filmland (periodical) Ackerman, Forrest J **32** 4-6

FAN CHUNG-YEN (989-1052), Chinese statesman **5** 376-377

FANEUIL, PETER (1700-1743), American colonial merchant and philanthropist **5** 377

FANFANI, AMINTORE (1908-1999), Italian prime minister **5** 378-379

FANON, FRANTZ (1925-1961), Algerian political theorist and psychiatrist **5** 379-380

FARABI, AL- (Abou Nasr Mohammed ibn Tarkaw; 870-950), Turkish scholar and philosopher **22** 14-16

FARADAY, MICHAEL (1791-1867), English physicist and chemist **5** 380

FARAH, NURUDDIN (born 1945), Somali author **28** 114-116

FARGO, WILLIAM GEORGE (1818-1881), American businessman **5** 380-381

FARINA, MIMI (Margarita Mimi Baez Farina; 1945-2001), American singer and activist **27** 117-119

FARLEY, JAMES A. (1888-1976), Democratic Party organizer and political strategist **5** 381-383

FARMER, FANNIE MERRITT (1857-1915), American authority on cookery **5** 383

FARMER, JAMES (1920-1999), American civil rights activist who helped organize the 1960s ''freedom rides'' **5** 383-385

FARMER, MOSES GERRISH (1820-1893), American inventor and manufacturer **5** 385

Farnese, Alessandro (1468-1549) see Paul III

FARNESE, ALESSANDRO (Duke of Parma; 1545-1592), Italian general and diplomat **20** 132-135

FARNSWORTH, PHILO T. (1906-1971), American inventor of the television **5** 386-387

FAROUK I (1920-1965), king of Egypt 1937-1952 **5** 387-388

FARRAGUT, DAVID GLASGOW (1801-1870), American naval officer **5** 388-389

FARRAKHAN, LOUIS (Louis Eugene Walcott, born 1933), a leader of one branch of the Nation of Islam popularly known as Black Muslims and militant spokesman for Black Nationalism **5** 389-390

FARRAR, GERALDINE (1882-1967), American opera singer **23** 106-108

FARRELL, EILEEN (1920-2002), American singer **27** 119-121

FARRELL, JAMES THOMAS (1904-1979), American novelist and social and literary critic **5** 390-391

FARRELL, SUZANNE (née Roberta Sue Ficker; born 1945), American classical ballerina **5** 391-393

FARRENC, LOUISE (Jeanne Louise Dumont; 1804-1875), French pianist **27** 121-122

FASSBINDER, RAINER WERNER (1946-1982), German filmmaker **26** 101-103

Fatih see Mehmed the Conqueror

FAUCHARD, PIERRE (1678-1761), French dentist **26** 103-105

FAULKNER, BRIAN (1921-1977), prime minister of Northern Ireland (1971-1972) **5** 393-395

FAULKNER, WILLIAM (1897-1962), American novelist **5** 395-397

FAURÉ, GABRIEL URBAIN (1845-1924), French composer **5** 397-398

FAUSET, JESSIE REDMON (1882-1961), African American writer and editor **20** 135-138

FAUST, DREW GILPIN (Catherine Drew Gilpin; born 1947), American historian and university president **28** 116-118

FAVALORO, RENE GERONIMO (1923-2000), Argentine physician **24** 131-133

Female Man, The (novel) Russ, Joanna **32** 310-312

FAWCETT, MILLICENT GARRETT (1847-1929), British feminist **5** 398-400

FAWKES, GUY (Guido Fawkes; 1570-1606), English soldier and conspirator **27** 123-125

FAYE, SAFI (born 1943), Senegalese filmmaker and ethnologist **5** 400-401

G

(1950-1951) and leader of the Labour Party (1955-1963) **6** 173-174

Gaius Sallustius Crispus
see Sallust

GALAMB, JOSEPH (Jozsef Galamb; 1881-1955), Hungarian-American engineer **24** 154-155

Galaxy (astronomy)
Zwicky, Fritz **32** 379-381

GALBRAITH, JOHN KENNETH (1908-2006), economist and scholar of the American Institutionalist school **6** 174-177

GALDÓS, BENITO PÉREZ (1843-1920), Spanish novelist and dramatist **6** 177-178

GALEN (130-200), Roman physician **6** 178-180

GALERIUS, EMPEROR OF ROME (Gaius Galerius Valerius Maximianus; c. 250-311), Thracian emperor **28** 132-134

Galigai, Leonora, (1568-1617), Italian lady-in-waiting
Concini, Concino **32** 86-88

Galilei, Galileo
see Galileo Galilei

GALILEO GALILEI (1564-1642), Italian astronomer and physicist **6** 180-183

GALL, FRANZ JOSEPH (1758-1828), German founder of phrenology **29** 165-167
Broca, Pierre Paul **32** 53-55

GALLATIN, ALBERT (1761-1849), Swiss-born American statesman, banker, and diplomat **6** 183-184

GALLAUDET, THOMAS HOPKINS (1787-1851), American educator **6** 185

GALLEGOS FREIRE, RÓMULO (1884-1969), Venezuelan novelist, president 1948 **6** 185-186

GALLO, ROBERT CHARLES (born 1937), American virologist **22** 191-193

GALLOWAY, JOSEPH (c. 1731-1803), American politician **6** 186-187

GALLUP, GEORGE (1901-1984), pioneer in the field of public opinion polling and a proponent of educational reform **6** 187-189

GALSWORTHY, JOHN (1867-1933), English novelist and playwright **6** 189-190

GALT, SIR ALEXANDER TILLOCH (1817-1893), Canadian politician **6** 190-191

GALT, JOHN (1779-1839), Scottish novelist **18** 156-158

GALTIERI, LEOPOLDO FORTUNATO (1926-2003), president of Argentina (1981-1982) **6** 191-193

GALTON, SIR FRANCIS (1822-1911), English scientist, biometrician, and explorer **6** 193-194

GALVANI, LUIGI (1737-1798), Italian physiologist **6** 194-195

GÁLVEZ, BERNARDO DE (1746-1786), Spanish colonial administrator **6** 195-196

GÁLVEZ, JOSÉ DE (1720-1787), Spanish statesman in Mexico **6** 196

GALWAY, JAMES (born 1939), Irish flutist **18** 158-160

GAMA, VASCO DA (c. 1460-1524), Portuguese navigator **6** 196-198

GAMBARO, GRISELDA (born 1928), Argentine author **23** 115-117

GAMBETTA, LÉON (1838-1882), French premier 1881-1882 **6** 198-199

GAMOW, GEORGE (1904-1968), Russian-American nuclear physicist, astrophysicist, biologist, and author of books popularizing science **6** 199-200

GAMZATOV, RASUL (Rasul Gamzatovitch Gamzatov; 1923-2003), Russian poet **28** 134-136

GANCE, ABEL (1889-1981), French film director **25** 145-147

GANDHI, INDIRA PRIYADARSHINI (1917-1984), Indian political leader **6** 200-201

GANDHI, MOHANDAS KARAMCHAND (1869-1948), Indian political and religious leader **6** 201-204
influence of
Thurman, Howard **32** 334-335

GANDHI, RAJIV (1944-1991), Indian member of Parliament and prime minister **6** 204-205

GANDHI, SONIA (née Sonia Maino; born 1946), Indian politician **25** 147-149

GANNIBAL, ABRAM PETROVICH (c. 1696-1781), Russian military officer **32** 122-124

GAO XINGJIAN (born 1940), French Chinese author **25** 149-151

Gaon, Vilna
see Elijah ben Solomon

GARBER, MARY (1916-2008), American sportswriter **29** 167-169

GARBO, GRETA (1905-1990), Swedish-born American film star **6** 205-207

GARCIA, CARLOS P. (1896-1971), Philippine statesman, president 1957-61 **6** 207-208

GARCIA, JERRY (Jerome John Garcia; 1942-1995), American musician **21** 150-152

GARCÍA MÁRQUEZ, GABRIEL (born 1928), Colombian author **6** 208-209

GARCÍA MORENO, GABRIEL (1821-1875), Ecuadorian politician, president 1861-1865 and 1869-1875 **6** 209-210

GARCÍA ROBLES, ALFONSO (1911-1991), Mexican diplomat **23** 117-119

Garcia y Sarmientc, Félix Rubén
see Dario, Rubén

GARCILASO DE LA VEGA, INCA (1539-1616), Peruvian chronicler **6** 210-211

GARDEN, ALEXANDER (c. 1730-1791), Scottish-born American naturalist and physician **30** 176-178

GARDINER, SAMUEL RAWSON (1829-1902), English historian **6** 211

GARDNER, AVA (Ava Lavinia Gardner; 1922-1990), American actress **25** 151-154

GARDNER, ERLE STANLEY (1889-1970), American mystery writer **22** 193-195

GARDNER, GERALD (1884-1964), British witch and writer **30** 178-180

GARDNER, ISABELLA STEWART (1840-1924), American art patron and socialite **21** 152-155

GARDNER, JOHN W. (1912-2002), American educator, public official, and political reformer **6** 211-213

GARFIELD, JAMES ABRAM (1831-1881), American general, president 1881 **6** 213-214
family
Garfield, Lucretia Rudolph **32** 124-126

GARFIELD, LUCRETIA RUDOLPH (1832-1918), American first lady **32** 124-126

GARIBALDI, GIUSEPPE (1807-1882), Italian patriot **6** 215-217

GARLAND, HANNIBAL HAMLIN (1860-1940), American author **6** 217-218

GARLAND, JUDY (1922-1969), super star of films, musicals, and concert stage **6** 218-219

GARNEAU, FRANÇOIS-XAVIER (1809-1866), French-Canadian historian **6** 219-220

GARNER, JOHN NANCE (''Cactus Jack'' Garner; 1868-1967), American vice president (1933-1941) **21** 155-157

GARNET, HENRY HIGHLAND (1815-1882), African American clergyman, abolitionist, and diplomat **24** 155-158

GARNIER, FRANCIS (Marie Joseph François Garnier; 1839-1873), French naval officer **6** 220-221

GARNIER, JEAN LOUIS CHARLES (1825-1898), French architect **6** 221-222

GARRETT, JOHN WORK (1820-1884), American railroad magnate **6** 225

GARRETT, PATRICK FLOYD (1850-1908), American sheriff **30** 180-182

GARRETT, THOMAS (1789-1871), American abolitionist **6** 225-226

GARRETT (ANDERSON), ELIZABETH (1836-1917), English physician and women's rights advocate **6** 222-225

GARRISON, WILLIAM LLOYD (1805-1879), American editor and abolitionist **6** 226-228

GARROS, ROLAND (1888-1918), French aviator **32** 126-128

GARVEY, MARCUS MOSIAH (1887-1940), Jamaican leader and African nationalist **6** 228-229

GARY, ELBERT HENRY (1846-1927), American lawyer and industrialist **6** 229-230

GASCA, PEDRO DE LA (c. 1496-1567), Spanish priest and statesman **6** 230-231

Gascoyne-Cecil, Robert Arthur Talbot
see Salisbury, 3rd Marquess of

GASKELL, ELIZABETH (1810-1865), English novelist **6** 231-232

Gaspé, Philippe Aubert de
see Aubert de Gaspé, Philippe

GATES, HORATIO (c. 1728-1806), Revolutionary War general **29** 169-172

GATES, THOMAS SOVEREIGN (1873-1948), American educator and businessperson **32** 128-130

GATES, WILLIAM HENRY, III ("Bill"; born 1955), computer software company co-founder and executive **6** 232-234

GATLING, RICHARD JORDAN (1818-1903), American inventor of multiple-firing guns **6** 234-235

GAUDÍ I CORNET, ANTONI (1852-1926), Catalan architect and designer **6** 235-236

GAUGUIN, PAUL (1848-1903), French painter and sculptor **6** 236-238

GAULLI, GIOVANNI BATTISTA (1639-1709), Italian painter **6** 238-239

GAULTIER, JEAN PAUL (born 1952), French avant-garde designer **6** 239-240

GAUSS, KARL FRIEDRICH (1777-1855), German mathematician and astronomer **6** 240-242

GAUSTAD, EDWIN (1923-2011), American historian **32** 130-131

Gautama, Prince
see Buddha (play)

GAUTIER, THÉOPHILE (1811-1872), French writer **31** 133-134

GAVIRIA TRUJILLO, CESAR AUGUSTO (born 1947), president of Colombia **6** 242-243

GAY, JOHN (1685-1732), English playwright and poet **6** 243-244

GAY-LUSSAC, JOSEPH LOUIS (1778-1850), French chemist and physicist **6** 245-246

GAYE, MARVIN (Marvin Pentz Gay; 1939-1984), American musician **26** 119-123

GAYLE, HELENE DORIS (born 1955), African American epidemiologist and pediatrician **6** 244-245

Geber
see Jabir ibn Hayyan

GEDDES, SIR PATRICK (1854-1932), Scottish sociologist and biologist **6** 246-247

GEERTGEN TOT SINT JANS (Geertgen van Haarlem; c. 1460/65-1490/95), Netherlandish painter **6** 248

GEERTZ, CLIFFORD (1926-2006), American cultural anthropologist **6** 248-249

GEFFEN, DAVID LAWRENCE (born 1943), American record and film producer **23** 119-122

GEHRIG, LOU (Henry Louis Gehrig; 1903-1941), American baseball player **19** 119-121
    Allen, Mel **32** 10-12

GEHRY, FRANK O. (Goldberg; born 1929), American architect **6** 250-251

GEIGER, HANS (born Johannes Wilhelm Geiger; 1882-1945), German physicist **6** 251-253

GEISEL, ERNESTO (1908-1996), Brazilian army general, president of Brazil's national oil company (Petrobras), and president of the republic (1974-1979) **6** 253-255

GEISEL, THEODOR (a.k.a. Dr. Seuss; 1904-1991), American author of children's books **6** 255-256

Geiseric
see Gaiseric

GELERNTER, DAVID (born 1955), American computer scientist **32** 131-133

GELL-MANN, MURRAY (born 1929), American physicist **6** 257-258

Gellée, Claude
see Claude Lorrain

GELLER, MARGARET JOAN (born 1947), American astronomer **6** 256-257

GELLHORN, MARTHA ELLIS (1908-1998), American journalist and author **27** 141-143

GEMAYEL, AMIN (born 1942), Lebanese nationalist and Christian political leader; president of the Republic of Lebanon (1982-1988) **6** 258-259

GEMAYEL, BASHIR (1947-1982), Lebanese political and military leader **28** 136-138

GEMAYEL, PIERRE (1905-1984), leader of the Lebanese Phalangist Party **6** 259-261

GEMINIANI, FRANCESCO SAVERIO (Francesco Xaviero Geminiani; 1687-1762), Italian violinist and composer **26** 123-125

GENET, EDMOND CHARLES (1763-1834), French diplomat **6** 261-262

GENET, JEAN (1910-1986), French novelist and playwright **6** 262-263

GENEVIEVE, ST. (Genovefa; c. 422-512), French religious figure **26** 331-333

Genga, Annibale Francesco della
see Leo XII

GENGHIS KHAN (1167-1227), Mongol chief, creator of the Mongol empire **6** 263-265

GENSCHER, HANS-DIETRICH (born 1927), leader of West Germany's liberal party (the FDP) and foreign minister **6** 265-266

Genseric
see Gaiseric

GENTILE, GIOVANNI (1875-1944), Italian philosopher and politician **6** 267

GENTILE DA FABRIANO (Gentile di Niccolò di Giovanni di Massio; c. 1370-1427), Italian painter **6** 266-267

GENTILESCHI, ARTEMISIA (1593-1652), Italian painter **22** 195-196

GEOFFREY OF MONMOUTH (c. 1100-1155), English pseudohistorian **6** 268

Geometry (mathematics)
    catastrophe theory
        Thom, René **32** 332-334

GEORGE I (1660-1727), king of Great Britain and Ireland 1714-1727 **6** 268-269

GEORGE II (1683-1760), king of Great Britain and Ireland and elector of Hanover 1727-1760 **6** 269-270

GEORGE III (1738-1820), king of Great Britain and Ireland 1760-1820 **6** 270-272

GREER, GERMAINE (born 1939), author and authoritative commentator on women's liberation and sexuality **6** 528-530

GREGG, JOHN ROBERT (1867-1948), American inventor of system of shorthand writing **21** 178-180

GREGG, WILLIAM (1800-1867), American manufacturer **6** 530-531

GREGORY I, ST. (c. 540-604), pope 590-604 **6** 531-532

GREGORY VII (c. 1020-1085), pope 1073-85 **6** 532-534

GREGORY IX (Ugo [Ugolino] di Segni; 1145-1241), Roman Catholic pope (1227-1241) **21** 180-183

GREGORY XII (Angelo Corrario; c. 1327-1417), pope 1406-1415 **18** 169-171

GREGORY XIII (1502-1585), pope 1572-1585 **6** 534

GREGORY XVI (Bartolommeo Alberto Cappellari; Mauro; 1765-1846), Roman Catholic pope 1831-1846 **25** 165-166

GREGORY, LADY AUGUSTA (1852-1932), Irish dramatist **6** 535-536

GREGORY, DICK (Richard Claxton Gregory; born 1932), comedian and civil rights and world peace activist **6** 536-537

GREGORY OF TOURS, ST. (538-594), Frankish bishop and historian **6** 534-535

Gregory the Great, Saint
see Gregory I, Saint

GRENE, MARJORIE (1910-2009), American philosopher **30** 188-190

GRETZKY, WAYNE (born 1961), Canadian hockey star **6** 537-539

GREUZE, JEAN BAPTISTE (1725-1805), French painter **6** 539

GREVER, MARIA (nee Maria de la Portilla; 1894-1951), Mexican musician **24** 159-161

GREY, CHARLES (2nd Earl Grey; 1764-1845), English statesman, prime minister 1830-1834 **6** 539-540

GREY, SIR GEORGE (1812-1898), English explorer and colonial governor **6** 540-541

GREY, ZANE (Pearl Zane Gray; 1872-1939), American author **20** 160-162

GRIBEAUVAL, JEAN BAPTISTE VAQUETTE DE (1715-1789), French army officer **20** 162-163

GRIEG, EDVARD HAGERUP (1843-1907), Norwegian composer **6** 541-542

GRIERSON, JOHN (1898-1972), Canadian and British filmmaker **6** 542-543

GRIFFES, CHARLES TOMLINSON (1884-1920), American composer **6** 543-544

GRIFFIN, MERV (Mervyn Edward Griffin, Jr.; 1925-2007), American television personality and producer **28** 146-149

GRIFFITH, DAVID WARK (1875-1948), American filmmaker **6** 544-545

GRIFFITH, SIR SAMUEL WALKER (1845-1920), Australian statesman and jurist **6** 545-546

GRIFFITH JOYNER, FLORENCE (1959-1998), American athlete **19** 130-133

GRIFFITHS, MARTHA (1912-2003), American politician **31** 147-149

Grillet, Alain Robbe
see Robbe-Grillet, Alain

GRILLPARZER, FRANZ (1791-1872), Austrian playwright **6** 546-547

Grimaldi, Rainier de
see Rainier III, Prince of Monaco

GRIMKÉ, ANGELINA EMILY (1805-1879) AND SARAH MOORE (1792-1873), American abolitionists and women's rights agitators **7** 1-2

GRIMKÉ, ARCHIBALD HENRY (1849-1930), American editor, author, and diplomat **7** 1-2

GRIMM, JAKOB KARL (1785-1863) AND WILHELM KARL (1786-1859), German scholars, linguists, and authors **7** 3-4

GRIMMELSHAUSEN, HANS JAKOB CHRISTOFFEL VON (c. 1621-1676), German author **7** 4-5

GRIS, JUAN (1887-1927), Spanish painter **7** 5-6

GRISHAM, JOHN (born 1955), American author and attorney **7** 6-8

GRISI, CARLOTTA (1819-1899), Italian ballet dancer **30** 190-192

GRISSOM, VIRGIL IVAN (Gus Grissom; 1926-1967), American astronaut **25** 166-168

GROMYKO, ANDREI ANDREEVICH (1909-1988), minister of foreign affairs and president of the Union of Soviet Socialist Republic (1985-1988) **7** 9-11
Dobrynin, Anatoly **32** 99-101

GROOMS, RED (born 1937), American artist **7** 11-12

Groot, Huig de
see Grotius, Hugo

GROOTE, GERARD (1340-1384), Dutch evangelical preacher **7** 12-13

GROPIUS, WALTER (1883-1969), German-American architect, educator, and designer **7** 13-14

GROS, BARON (Antoine Jean Gros; 1771-1835), French romantic painter **7** 14-15

GROSS, AL (Alfred J. Gross; 1918-2000), Canadian inventor **28** 149-151

GROSS, SAMUEL DAVID (1805-1884), American surgeon, author, and educator **21** 183-185

GROSSETESTE, ROBERT (1175-1253), English bishop and statesman **7** 15

GROSSINGER, JENNIE (1892-1972), American hotel executive and philanthropist **7** 15-17

GROSZ, GEORGE (1893-1959), German-American painter and graphic artist **7** 17-18

GROTIUS, HUGO (1583-1645), Dutch jurist, statesman, and historian **7** 18-19

GROTOWSKI, JERZY (1933-1999), founder of the experimental Laboratory Theatre in Wroclaw, Poland **7** 19-20

GROVE, ANDREW (András Gróf; born 1936), American businessman **18** 171-174

GROVE, FREDERICK PHILIP (c. 1871-1948), Canadian novelist and essayist **7** 20-21

GROVES, LESLIE (1896-1970), military director of the Manhattan Project (atom bomb) during World War II **7** 21-22

GRUEN, VICTOR (1903-1980), Austrian-American architect **30** 192-194

GRÜNEWALD, MATTHIAS (c. 1475-1528), German painter **7** 23-24

GUARDI, FRANCESCO (1712-1793), Italian painter **7** 24-25

GUARINI, GUARINO (1624-1683), Italian architect, priest, and philosopher **7** 25-26

GUASTAVINO, RAFAEL (Rafael Guastavino Morano; 1842-1908), Spanish-American architect **23** 132-134

GUBAIDULINA, SOFIA (Sofia Asgatovna Gubaydulina; born 1931), Russian composer **26** 127-129

GUCCIONE, BOB, JR. (c. 1956), American publisher **7** 26

GUDERIAN, HEINZ (1888-1953), German military leader **20** 163-165

GUDJÓNSSON, HALLDÓR KILJAN (Halldór Laxness; 1902-1998), Icelandic author **25** 169-171

GÜEMES, MARTÍN (1785-1821), Argentine independence fighter **7** 26-27

H

HAGUE, FRANK (1876-1956), American politician **7** 63-64

HAHN, OTTO (1879-1968), German chemist **7** 64-65

HAHNEMANN, SAMUEL (Christian Friedrich Samuel Hahnemann; 1755-1843), German physician and chemist **21** 190-193

HAIDAR ALI (c. 1721-1782), Indian prince, ruler of Mysore 1759-1782 **7** 65-66

HAIG, ALEXANDER M., JR. (1924-2010), American military leader, diplomat, secretary of state, and presidential adviser **7** 66-67

HAIG, DOUGLAS (1st Earl Haig; 1861-1928), British field marshal **7** 67-68

HAIGNERE, CLAUDIE ANDRE-DESHAYS (born 1957), French astronaut and government official **25** 176-178

HAILE SELASSIE (1892-1975), emperor of Ethiopia **7** 68-70

HAKLUYT, RICHARD (1552/53-1616), English geographer and author **7** 70

HALBERSTAM, DAVID (1934-2007), American journalist, author and social historian **18** 180-183

HALDANE, JOHN BURDON SANDERSON (1892-1964), English biologist **7** 70-71

HALE, CLARA (nee Clara McBride; 1905-1992), American humanitarian and social reformer **20** 166-168

HALE, EDWARD EVERETT (1822-1909), American Unitarian minister and author **7** 71-72

HALE, GEORGE ELLERY (1868-1938), American astronomer **7** 72-74

HALE, SARAH JOSEPHA (née Buell; 1788-1879), American editor **7** 74-75

HALES, STEPHEN (1677-1761), English scientist and clergyman **7** 75

HALÉVY, ÉLIE (1870-1937), French philosopher and historian **7** 76

HALEY, ALEX (1921-1992), African American journalist and author **7** 76-78

HALEY, MARGARET A. (1861-1939), American educator and labor activist **7** 78-79

HALFFTER, CHRISTÓBAL (born 1930), Spanish composer **7** 79-80

HALIBURTON, THOMAS CHANDLER (1796-1865), Canadian judge and author **7** 80

Haliday, Bryant, (1928-1996), American actor, producer, and entrepreneur Harvey, Cyrus **32** 150-152

HALIDE EDIP ADIVAR (1884-1964), Turkish woman writer, scholar, and public figure **7** 80-82

HALIFAX, 1ST EARL OF (Edward Frederick Lindley Wood; 1881-1959), English statesman **7** 82-83

HALL, ASAPH (1829-1907), American astronomer **7** 83-84

HALL, DONALD (born 1928), New England memoirist, short story writer, essayist, dramatist, critic, and anthologist as well as poet **7** 84-85

HALL, EDWARD MARSHALL (1858-1927), British attorney **22** 204-205

HALL, GRANVILLE STANLEY (1844-1924), American psychologist and educator **7** 85-86

HALL, LLOYD AUGUSTUS (1894-1971), American scientist and inventor **28** 154-156

HALL, PETER REGINALD FREDERICK (born 1930), English theater director **24** 162-165

HALL, PRINCE (c. 1735-1807), African American abolitionist and founder of the first black masonic lodge **26** 136-138

HALL, RADCLYFFE (Marguerite Radclyffe Hall; 1880-1943), British author **20** 168-170

HALLAJ, AL-HUSAYN IBN MANSUR AL (857-922), Persian Moslem mystic and martyr **7** 86-87

HALLAM, LEWIS, SR. AND JR. (Lewis Sr. c. 1705-1755; Lewis Jr. 1740-1808), American actors and theatrical managers **7** 87

HALLAREN, MARY AGNES (1907-2005), American army colonel **31** 153-154

HALLECK, HENRY WAGER (1815-1872), American military strategist **22** 205-207 Ambrose, Stephen E. **32** 12-14

Hallelujah (song) Cohen, Leonard **32** 79-81

HALLER, ALBRECHT VON (1708-1777), Swiss physician **7** 87-88

HALLEY, EDMUND (1656-1742), English astronomer **7** 88-89

HALLSTRÖM, LASSE (born 1946), Swedish film director **32** 147-149

HALONEN, TARJA KAARINA (born 1943), Finnish president **25** 178-180

Halpin, Maria Cleveland, Frances Folsom **32** 77-79

HALS, FRANS (c.1581-1666), Dutch painter **7** 89-91

HALSEY, WILLIAM FREDERICK (1882-1959), American admiral **7** 91-92

HALSTED, WILLIAM STEWART (1852-1922), American surgeon **22** 207-209

HAMADA, SHOJI (1894-1978), Japanese potter **26** 138-140

HAMANN, JOHANN GEORG (1730-1788), German philosopher **7** 92

HAMER, FANNIE LOU (born Townsend; 1917-1977), American civil rights activist **7** 93-94

HAMILCAR BARCA (c. 285-229/228 BCE), Carthaginian general and statesman **7** 94-95

HAMILL, DOROTHY (born 1956), American figure skater **25** 180-183

HAMILTON, ALEXANDER (1755-1804), American statesman **7** 95-98

HAMILTON, ALICE (1869-1970), American physician **7** 98-99

HAMILTON, EDITH (1867-1963), American educator and author **22** 209-211

HAMILTON, SIR WILLIAM ROWAN (1805-1865), Irish mathematical physicist **7** 99-100

HAMM, MIA (born 1972), American soccer player **30** 197-199

HAMM-BRÜCHER, HILDEGARD (born 1921), Free Democratic Party's candidate for the German presidency in 1994 **7** 101-103

HAMMARSKJÖLD, DAG (1905-1961), Swedish diplomat **7** 100-101 Dobrynin, Anatoly **32** 99-101

HAMMER, ARMAND (1898-1990), American entrepreneur and art collector **7** 103-104

HAMMERSTEIN, OSCAR CLENDENNING II (1895-1960), lyricist and librettist of the American theater **7** 104-106

HAMMETT, (SAMUEL) DASHIELL (1894-1961), American author **7** 106-108

HAMMOND, JAMES HENRY (1807-1864), American statesman **7** 108-109

HAMMOND, JOHN (1910-1987), American music producer **31** 155-156 Christian, Charlie **32** 71-72

HAMMOND, JOHN LAWRENCE LE BRETON (1872-1952), English historian **7** 108-109

HAMMOND, LUCY BARBARA (1873-1961), English historian **7** 109

HAMMURABI (1792-1750 BCE), king of Babylonia **7** 109-110

I

Kalish, Sonya
see Tucker, Sophie

KALMAN, RUDOLF EMIL (born 1930), Hungarian scientist **24** 199-201

KALMUS, NATALIE (Natalie Mabelle Dunfee; c. 1883-1965), American inventor and cinematographer **21** 233-235

Kamako
see Fujiwara Kamatari

KAMARAJ, KUMARASWAMI (1903-1975), Indian political leader **8** 415

KAMBONA, OSCAR (1928-1997), Tanzanian statesman **32** 175-177

KAMEHAMEHA I (c. 1758-1819), king of the Hawaiian Islands 1795-1819 **8** 416

KAMEHAMEHA III (c. 1814-1854), king of the Hawaiian Islands 1825-1854 **8** 416-417

KAMENEV, LEV BORISOVICH (1883-1936), Russian politician **8** 417-418
Tukhachevsky, Mikhail **32** 340-342

KAMERLINGH ONNES, HEIKE (1853-1926), Dutch physicist **8** 418-420

Kamisori
see Tojo, Hideki

Kamitsumiya no Miko
see Shotoku Taishi

KAMMU (737-806), Japanese emperor 781-806 **8** 420

KAMROWSKI, GEROME (1914-2004), American artist **27** 197-199

KANDER, JOHN (born 1927), American composer and lyricist **21** 235-237

KANDINSKY, WASSILY (1866-1944), Russian painter **8** 420-422

KANE, JOHN (1860-1934), Scottish-born American primitive painter **8** 422

KANE, PAUL (1810-1871), Canadian painter and writer **8** 422-423

K'ANG-HSI (1654-1722), Chinese emperor 1661-1722 **8** 423-426

K'ANG YU-WEI (1858-1927), Chinese scholar and philosopher **8** 426-428

Kanis, Saint Peter
see Peter Canisius, Saint

KANISHKA (c. 78-c. 103), Kashan ruler **8** 428-429

Kankan Musa
see Musa Mansa

Kansas City Athletics (baseball team)
Maris, Roger **32** 236-240

KANT, IMMANUEL (1724-1804), German philosopher **8** 430-432

KAO-TSUNG (1107-1187), Chinese emperor **8** 433

KAPIOLANI, JULIA ESTHER (1834-1899), Hawaiian dignitary **31** 185-186

KAPITSA, PYOTR LEONIDOVICH (1894-1984), Soviet physicist **8** 433-435

KAPLAN, MORDECAI MENAHEM (1881-1983), American Jewish theologian and educator **8** 435-436

KAPP, WOLFGANG (1858-1922), German nationalist politician **8** 436

KAPTEYN, JACOBUS CORNELIS (1851-1922), Dutch astronomer **8** 436-437

KARADZIC, RADOVAN (born 1945), leader of the Serbian Republic **8** 437-440

KARAJAN, HERBERT VON (1908-1989), Austrian conductor **26** 190-192

Karakozov, Dmitry, (1840-1866), Russian revolutionary
Nechaev, Sergei **32** 275-277

KARAMANLIS, CONSTANTINE (1907-1998), Greek member of parliament, prime minister (1955-1963; 1974-1980), and president (1980-1985) **8** 440-441

KARAMZIN, NIKOLAI MIKHAILOVICH (1766-1826), Russian historian and author **8** 441-442

KARAN, DONNA (born 1948), American fashion designer and businesswoman **8** 442-444

KARENGA, MAULANA (born Ronald McKinley Everett; born 1941), African American author, educator, and proponent of black culturalism **8** 444-447

Karim, Prince
see Aga Khan IV

KARIM KHAN ZAND (died 1779), Iranian ruler, founder of Zand dynasty **8** 447

KARLE, ISABELLA (born 1921), American chemist and physicist **8** 447-449

KARLOFF, BORIS (William Henry Pratt; 1887-1969), English actor **26** 192-194

KARLSTADT, ANDREAS BODENHEIM VON (c. 1480-1541), German Protestant reformer **8** 449

KARMAL, BABRAK (1929-1996), Afghan Marxist and Soviet puppet ruler of the Democratic Republic of Afghanistan (1979-1986) **8** 449-451

KÁRMÁN, THEODORE VON (1881-1963), Hungarian-born American physicist **8** 451-452

KARP, NATALIA (1911-2007), Jewish Polish pianist **28** 192-194

KARSAVINA, TAMARA (1885-1978), Russian ballet dancer **32** 177-180

KARSH, YOUSUF (1908-2002), Canadian photographer **23** 184-187

KARTINI, RADEN AJENG (1879-1904), Indonesian activist **24** 201-203

KARUME, SHEIKH ABEID AMANI (1905-1972), Tanzanian political leader **8** 452-453

KASAVUBU, JOSEPH (c. 1913-1969), Congolese statesman **8** 453-455

Kasimir, Karl Theodore
see Meyerhold, Vsevolod Emilievich

KASPAROV, GARRY (Garri Kimovich Weinstein; born 1963), Russian chess player and politician **28** 194-196

KASSEBAUM, NANCY (born 1932), Republican senator from Kansas **8** 455-457

KASTRIOTI-SKANDERBEG, GJERGJ (1405-1468), Albanian military leader **23** 187-189

KATAYAMA, SEN (1860-1933), Japanese labor and Socialist leader **8** 457

Katzenjammer Kids (comic strip)
Dirks, Rudolph **32** 97-99

KAUFFMAN, ANGELICA (Maria Anna Angelica Catherina Kauffman; 1741-1807), Swedish artist **25** 229-231

KAUFMAN, GEORGE S. (1889-1961), American playwright **8** 457-458

KAUFMAN, GERALD BERNARD (born 1930), foreign policy spokesman of the British Labour Party **8** 458-460

KAUFMANN, EZEKIEL (1889-1963), Jewish philosopher and scholar **8** 460

KAUNDA, KENNETH DAVID (born 1924), Zambian statesman **8** 460-461

KAUTILYA (4th century BCE), Indian statesman and author **8** 462

KAUTSKY, KARL JOHANN (1854-1938), German Austrian Socialist **8** 462-463

KAWABATA, YASUNARI (1899-1972), Japanese novelist **8** 463-464

KAWAWA, RASHIDI MFAUME (1929-2009), Tanzanian political leader **8** 464-465

KAYE, DANNY (David Daniel Kaminsky; 1913-1987), American film and stage actor **25** 231-234

KAZAN, ELIA (1909-2003), American film and stage director **8** 465-466

KAZANTZAKIS, NIKOS (1883-1957), Greek author, journalist, and statesman **8** 466-468

KEAN, EDMUND (1789-1833), English actor 21 237-239

KEARNEY, DENIS (1847-1907), Irish-born American labor agitator **8** 468

KEARNY, STEPHEN WATTS (1794-1848), American general **8** 468-469

KEATING, PAUL JOHN (born 1944), federal treasurer of Australia (1983-1991) **8** 469-470

KEATON, BUSTER (Joseph Frank Keaton; 1895-1966), American comedian **20** 199-201
Durante, Jimmy **32** 103-106

KEATS, JOHN (1795-1821), English poet **8** 470-472

KECKLEY, ELIZABETH HOBBS (Elizabeth Hobbs Keckly; 1818-1907), African American seamstress and author **28** 196-199

KEENAN, BRIAN (1940-2008), Irish peace activist **29** 223-225

KEFAUVER, CAREY ESTES (1903-1963), U.S. senator and influential Tennessee Democrat **8** 472-474

KEILLOR, GARRISON (Gary Edward Keillor, born 1942), American humorist, radio host, and author **22** 271-273

KEITA, MODIBO (1915-1977), Malian statesman **8** 474-475

KEITEL, WILHELM (1882-1946), German general **18** 224-226

KEITH, SIR ARTHUR (1866-1955), British anatomist and physical anthropologist **8** 475-476

KEITH, MINOR COOPER (1848-1929), American entrepreneur **8** 476-477

KEKKONEN, URHO KALEVA (1900-1986), Finnish athlete and politician **23** 189-191

KEKULÉ, FRIEDRICH AUGUST (1829-1896), German chemist **8** 477-478

KELLER, ELIZABETH BEACH (Elizabeth Waterbury Beach; 1918-1997), American biochemist **25** 234-235

KELLER, GOTTFRIED (1819-1890), Swiss short-story writer, novelist, and poet **8** 478-479

KELLER, HELEN ADAMS (1880-1968), American lecturer and author **8** 479-480

KELLEY, FLORENCE (1859-1932), American social worker and reformer **8** 483-484

KELLEY, HALL JACKSON (1790-1874), American promoter **8** 480

KELLEY, OLIVER HUDSON (1826-1913), American agriculturalist **8** 480-481

KELLOGG, FRANK BILLINGS (1856-1937), American statesman **8** 481

KELLOGG, JOHN HARVEY (1852-1943), American health propagandist and cereal manufacturer **21** 239-242

KELLOGG, W. K. (Will Keith Kellogg; 1860-1951), American cereal manufacturer and philanthropist **28** 199-201

KELLOR, FRANCES (1873-1952), American activist and politician **8** 481-482

KELLY, ELLSWORTH (born 1923), American artist **8** 482-483

KELLY, GENE (born Eugene Curran Kelly; 1912-1996), American actor, dancer, and choreographer **8** 484-486

KELLY, GRACE (Grace, Princess; 1929-1982), princess of Monaco **19** 174-176

KELLY, LEONTINE (born 1920), American bishop **31** 187-188

KELLY, NED (1854-1880), Australian horse thief, bank robber, and murderer **29** 226-228

KELLY, PATRICK (1954-1990), African American fashion designer **22** 273-275

KELLY, PETRA (born 1947), West German pacifist and politician **8** 486-487

KELLY, WALT (Walter Crawford Kelly; 1913-1973), American cartoonist **22** 275-278

KELLY, WILLIAM (1811-1888), American iron manufacturer **8** 487-488

KELSEY, FRANCES OLDHAM (born 1914), Canadian American scientist **31** 189-190

KELSEY, HENRY (c. 1667-1724), English-born Canadian explorer **8** 488

KELVIN OF LARGS, BARON (William Thomson; 1824-1907), Scottish physicist **8** 488-489

Kemal, Mustapha (Kemal Atatürk)
see Atatürk, Ghazi Mustapha Kemal

KEMAL, YASHAR (born 1922), Turkish novelist **8** 489-491

KEMBLE, FRANCES ANNE (Fanny Kemble; 1809-1893), English actress **8** 491

KEMP, JACK FRENCH, JR. (1935-2009), Republican congressman from New York and secretary of housing and urban development **8** 491-493

KEMPE, MARGERY (1373-1440), English religious writer **29** 228-230

KEMPIS, THOMAS À (c. 1380-1471), German monk and spiritual writer **8** 493-494

KENDALL, AMOS (1789-1869), American journalist **8** 494

KENDALL, EDWARD CALVIN (1886-1972), American biochemist **8** 495

KENDALL, THOMAS HENRY (Henry Clarence Kendall; 1839-1882), Australian poet **23** 191-194

Kendrake, Carleton
see Gardner, Erle Stanley

KENDREW, JOHN C. (1917-1997), English chemist and Nobel Prize winner **8** 495-496

KENEALLY, THOMAS MICHAEL (born 1935), Australian author **18** 226-228

KENNAN, GEORGE F. (1904-2005), American diplomat, author, and scholar **8** 496-498

Kennedy, Aimee
see McPherson, Aimee Semple

KENNEDY, ANTHONY M. (born 1936), United States Supreme Court justice **8** 498-500

KENNEDY, EDWARD M. (Ted; 1932-2009), U.S. senator from Massachusetts **8** 500-502

KENNEDY, FLORYNCE RAE (1916-2000), African American activist and lawyer **27** 199-201

Kennedy, Jacqueline Lee Bouvier
see Onassis, Jacqueline Lee Bouvier Kennedy

KENNEDY, JOHN FITZGERALD (1917-1963), American statesman, president 1960-1963 **8** 502-506
foreign policy
Dobrynin, Anatoly **32** 99-101
media coverage
Leacock, Richard **32** 202-205

KENNEDY, JOHN FITZGERALD, JR. (1960-1999), American icon and publisher **25** 235-238

KENNEDY, JOHN PENDLETON (1795-1870), American author and politician **8** 506-507

KENNEDY, JOHN STEWART (1830-1909), American financier and philanthropist **8** 507-508

KENNEDY, JOSEPH (1888-1969), American financier, ambassador, and movie producer **19** 176-178

KENNEDY, ROBERT FRANCIS (1925-1968), American statesman **8** 508-509
Dobrynin, Anatoly **32** 99-101

KENNEDY, WILLIAM (born 1928), American author **19** 178-180

Kenny, Charles J.
see Gardner, Erle Stanley

KENNY, ELIZABETH (Sister Kenny; 1886-1952), Australian nursing sister **8** 509-510

KENT, JAMES (1763-1847), American jurist **8** 510-511

KENT, ROCKWELL (1882-1971), American painter and illustrator **8** 511

KENYATTA, JOMO (c. 1890-1978), Kenyan statesman **8** 512-514

KEOHANE, NANNERL OVERHOLSER (born 1940), American feminist activist and university chancellor **18** 229-230

KEOKUK (c. 1780-1848), American Sauk Indian chief **30** 238-240

KEPLER, JOHANNES (1571-1630), German astronomer **8** 514-516

KERENSKY, ALEKSANDR FEDOROVICH (1881-1970), Russian revolutionary and politician **8** 516-517

KERKORIAN, KIRK (Kerkor Kerkorian; born 1917), American financier **27** 201-203

KERN, JEROME DAVID (1885-1945), American composer **8** 517-518

KEROUAC, JEAN-LOUIS LEBRIS DE (Jack; 1922-1969), American writer of auto-biographical fiction **8** 518-519

KERR, CLARK (1911-2003), American economist, labor/management expert, and university president **8** 519-521

KERREY, J. ROBERT (born 1943), Democratic senator from Nebraska and 1992 presidential candidate **8** 521-522

KERRY, JOHN (born 1943), Democratic senator from Massachusetts and 2004 presidential candidate **25** 238-240

KESEY, KEN ELTON (1935-2001), American author **27** 203-205

KESSELRING, ALBERT (1885-1960), German field marshal **8** 522-523

KESSLER, DAVID A. (born 1951), commissioner of the Food and Drug Administration **8** 523-524

KETTERING, CHARLES F. (1876-1958), American engineer, industrial pioneer, and apostle of progress **8** 524-525

Ketterle, Wolfgang, (born 1957), German physicist
Cornell, Eric **32** 89-91
Wieman, Carl **32** 361-363

KEVORKIAN, JACK (1928-2011), American pathologist who practiced assisted suicide **19** 180-182

KEY, FRANCIS SCOTT (1779-1843), American poet and attorney **8** 525-527

KEY, VLADIMIR ORLANDO, JR. (1908-1963), American political scientist **8** 527-528

KEYNES, JOHN MAYNARD (1st Baron Keynes of Tilton; 1883-1946), English economist **8** 528-530

KGB (Komitet Gosudarstvennoy Bezopasnosti)
operatives
Vassall, John **32** 350-352

KHACHATURIAN, ARAM ILICH (or Khachaturov; 1903-1978), Russian composer **8** 530-531

KHALID BIN ABDUL AZIZ AL-SAUD (1912-1982), Saudi king and prime minister **23** 194-196

KHALIL, SAYYID ABDULLAH (1892-1970), Sudanese general, prime minister 1956-1958 **8** 531-532

KHAMA, SIR SERETSE M. (1921-1980), Botswana political leader **8** 532-533

KHAMENEI, AYATOLLAH SAYYID ALI (born 1939), supreme spiritual and political leader of the Islamic Republic of Iran **8** 533-535

Khammurapikh
see Hammurabi

KHAN, ALI AKBAR (1922-2009), Indian musician **24** 203-206

KHAN, A.Q. (Abdul Quadeer Khan; born 1936), Pakistani metallurgical engineer **27** 205-208

Khazars (Turkic people)
Pavić, Milorad **32** 295-297

Khmelnitskii, Bogdan
see Chmielnicki, Bogdan

KHOMEINI, AYATOLLAH RUHOLLAH MUSAVI (1902-1989), founder and supreme leader of the Islamic Republic of Iran **8** 535-537

KHORANA, HAR GOBIND (1922-2011), Indian organic chemist **8** 537-538

KHOSROW I (died 579), Sassanid king of Persia 531-576 **8** 538-539

Khosru
see Khosrow I

KHRUSHCHEV, NIKITA SERGEEVICH (1894-1971), Soviet political leader **8** 539-540
foreign policy
Dobrynin, Anatoly **32** 99-101

KHUFU (ruled 2590-2568 BCE), Egyptian king **8** 540-541

Khurram
see Shah Jahan

Khusrau
see Khosrow I

KHWARIZMI, MUHAMMAD IBN MUSA AL- (died c. 850), Arab mathematician, astronomer, and geographer **8** 541

KIBAKI, MWAI (born 1931), Kenyan presidnet **25** 240-242

Kibo-no Mabi
see Makibi, Kibi-no

KIDD, WILLIAM (c. 1645-1701), Scottish pirate **21** 242-244

KIDDER, ALFRED VINCENT (1885-1963), American archeologist **8** 541-542

KIDMAN, SIDNEY (1857-1935), ''The Cattle King'' of Australia **8** 542-544

KIEFER, ANSELM (born 1945), German artist **8** 544-546

KIENHOLZ, EDWARD (1927-1994), American Pop artist **8** 546-547

KIERKEGAARD, SØREN AABYE (1813-1855), Danish philosopher **8** 547-549

KIESLOWSKI, KRZYSZTOF (1941-1946), Polish film director **25** 242-244

KILBY, JACK ST. CLAIR (1923-2005), American electrical engineer and inventor **25** 244-246

Kilimanjaro, Mount
French-Sheldon, May **32** 315-317

KILPATRICK, WILLIAM H. (1871-1965), American educator, college president, and philosopher of education **9** 1-3

KIM DAE-JUNG (1925-2009), worked for the restoration of democracy and human rights in South Korea after 1971 **9** 3-4

KIM IL-SUNG (1912-1994), North Korean political leader **9** 4-6

KIM JONG IL (1941-2011), leader of the Democratic People's Republic of Korea **9** 6-7

KIM OK-KYUN (1851-1894), Korean politician **9** 7-8

KIM PUSIK (1075-1151), Korean statesman, historian, and general **9** 8-9

Kim Song-ju
see Kim Il-sung

KIM YOUNG SAM (born 1927), South Korean statesman **9** 9-10

KINCAID, JAMAICA (Elaine Potter Richardson; born 1949), African American author **23** 196-199

KINDI, ABU-YUSUF YAQUB IBN-ISHAQ AL- (died 873), Arab philosopher **9** 10-11

Kinetic theory of gases
reaction kinetics
Bodenstein, Max Ernst **32** 46-48

KNOPF, BLANCHE WOLF (1894-1966), American publisher **9** 61-62

KNOWLES, MALCOLM SHEPHERD (1913-1997), American adult education theorist and planner **9** 62-64

KNOX, HENRY (1750-1806), American Revolutionary War general **9** 64

KNOX, JOHN (c. 1505-1572), Scottish religious reformer **9** 65-66

KNOX, PHILANDER CHASE (1853-1921), American statesman **9** 66-67

KNUDSEN, WILLIAM S. (1879-1948), American auto industry leader **9** 67-68

KOBAYASHI, MASAKI (1916-1996), Japanese film director **23** 199-201

Kobo Daishi
see Kukai

KOCH, EDWARD I. (born 1924), New York City mayor **9** 68-69

KOCH, MARITA (Marita Meier-Koch; born 1957), German athlete **26** 197-199

KOCH, ROBERT HEINRICH HERMANN (1843-1910), German physician and bacteriologist **9** 69-70

KODÁLY, ZOLTÁN (1882-1967), Hungarian composer **9** 71

KOEPPE, LEONHARD (1884-1969), German ophthalmologist **30** 244-245

KOESTLER, ARTHUR (1905-1983), author of political novels **9** 71-73

KOGAWA, JOY NOZOMI (Na Kayama; born 1935), Japanese Canadian author and activist **25** 247-250

KOHL, HELMUT (born 1930), chancellor of West Germany (1982-1990) and first chancellor of a united Germany since World War II **9** 73-74

KOHN, WALTER (born 1923), German-American physicist **27** 214-216

KOIZUMI, JUNICHIRO (born 1942), Japanese prime minister **25** 250-252

Koizumi, Yakumo
see Hearn, Lafcadio

KOJONG (1852-1919), Korean king **9** 74-75

KOKOSCHKA, OSKAR (1886-1980), Austrian painter, graphic artist, and author **9** 75-76

KOLAKOWSKI, LESZEK (1927-2009), philosopher who wrote on broad themes of ethics, metaphysics, and religion **9** 76-77

KOLCHAK, ALEKSANDR VASILIEVICH (1873-1920), Russian admiral **9** 77-78
Tukhachevsky, Mikhail **32** 340-342

KOLLONTAI, ALEKSANDRA MIKHAILOVNA (1872-1952), Soviet diplomat **9** 79

KOLLWITZ, KÄTHE (1867-1945), German expressionist graphic artist and sculptor **9** 79-81

KOLMOGOROV, ANDREI (1903-1987), Russian mathematician and educator **32** 184-186

KOMITAS (1869-1935), Armenian composer **31** 194-195

KONEV, IVAN STEFANOVICH (1897-1973), Soviet marshal **9** 81-82

KONOE, PRINCE FUMIMARO (or Konoye; 1891-1945), Japanese premier 1937-1939 and 1940-1941 **9** 82-83

KOO, WELLINGTON (1888-1985), Chinese statesman and diplomat **29** 232-234

Kook, Abraham Isaac
see Kuk, Abraham Isaac

KOONS, JEFF (born 1955), American artist **9** 83-84

KOOP, C. EVERETT (born 1916), American surgeon general **18** 235-237

Koppel, Ted, (born 1940), American television journalist
Arledge, Roone **32** 16-18

KÖPRÜLÜ, AHMED (Köprülüzade Fazil Ahmed Pasha; 1635-1676), Turkish statesman and general **9** 84-85

KORBUT, OLGA (born 1955), Belarusian gymnast **24** 211-213

Korean War (1950-1953)
orphans
Holt, Bertha **32** 168-171

KOREMATSU, FRED (1919-2005), American political activist **29** 234-236

KORNBERG, ARTHUR (1918-2007), American biochemist **9** 85-87

Kornfeld, Gertrud, (1891-1955), German chemist
Bodenstein, Max Ernst **32** 46-48

KORNILOV, LAVR GEORGIEVICH (1870-1918), Russian general **9** 87-88

Kosan
see Yun Sondo

KOSCIUSZKO, TADEUSZ ANDRZEJ BONAWENTURA (1746-1817), Polish patriot, hero in the American Revolution **9** 88

KOSINSKI, JERZY (Jerzy Nikodem Lewinkopf; 1933-1991), Polish-American author **26** 199-201

KOSSUTH, LOUIS (1802-1894), Hungarian statesman **9** 88-90

Kostrowitsky, Wilhelm Apollinaris de
see Apollinaire, Guillaume

KOSYGIN, ALEKSEI NIKOLAEVICH (1904-1980), chairman of the U.S.S.R. Council of Ministers and head of the Soviet government (1964-1980) **9** 90-91

KOTZEBUE, OTTO VON (1787-1846), Russian explorer **9** 91-92

KOUFAX, SANDY (Sanford Braun; born 1945), American baseball player **20** 208-210

KOUSSEVITZKY, SERGE (Sergey Aleksandrovich Kusevitsky;1874-1951), Russian-born American conductor **24** 213-215

KOVACS, ERNIE (1919-1962), American comedian **19** 186-188

KOVALEVSKY, SOPHIA VASILEVNA (Sonya Kovalevsky; 1850-1891), Russian mathematician **22** 280-282

KOZYREV, ANDREI VLADIMIROVICH (born 1951), Russian minister of foreign affairs and a liberal, pro-Western figure in Boris Yeltsin's cabinet **9** 92-93

KRAMER, LARRY (born 1935), American AIDS activist and author **20** 210-212

KRAMER, STANLEY (1913-2001), American filmmaker **32** 186-189

KRASNER, LEE (Lenore; 1908-1984), American painter and collage artist **9** 93-94

KRAVCHUK, LEONID MAKAROVYCH (born 1934), president of Ukraine (1991-1994) **9** 94-95

KREBS, SIR HANS ADOLF (1900-1981), German British biochemist **9** 95-97

KREISKY, BRUNO (1911-1983), chancellor of Austria (1970-1983) **9** 97-98

KREISLER, FRITZ (Friedrich Kreisler; 1875-1962), Austrian violinist **26** 201-203

Kremer, Gerhard
see Mercator, Gerhardus

KRENEK, ERNST (1900-1991), Austrian composer **9** 98-99

KREPS, JUANITA MORRIS (1921-2010), economist, university professor, United States secretary of commerce (1977-1979), and author **9** 99-101

KRIEGHOFF, CORNELIUS (1815-1872), Dutch-born Canadian painter **9** 101

KRISHNAMURTI, JIDDU (1895-1986), Indian mystic and philosopher **9** 101-103

KRISHNAMURTI, UPPALURI GOPALA (1918-2007), Indian philosopher and author **28** 201-203

L

M

Masafuji
see Mabuchi, Kamo

Masahito
see Goshirakawa

Masanobu
see Mabuchi, Kamo

MASARYK, JAN (1886-1948), Czech foreign minister **20** 243-246

MASARYK, TOMÁŠ GARRIGUE (1850-1937), Czech philosopher and statesman, president 1919-1935 **10** 314-315

MASINA, GIULIETTA (1921-1994), Italian actress **29** 268-270

MASINISSA, KING OF NUMIDIA (240 BCE - 148 BCE), prince of the Massylians who consolidated the Numidian tribes to form a North African kingdom **10** 315-317

MASIRE, QUETT KETUMILE (born 1925), a leader of the fight for independence and president of Botswana **10** 318-319

MASON, BRIDGET (Biddy Mason; 1818-1891), African American nurse, midwife, and entrepreneur **22** 312-314

MASON, GEORGE (1725-1792), American statesman **10** 319-320

MASON, JAMES MURRAY (1796-1871), American politician and Confederate diplomat **10** 320-321

MASON, LOWELL (1792-1872), American composer and music educator **10** 321-322

Massachusetts Institute of Technology (Cambridge)
film
Leacock, Richard **32** 202-205
science
Cornell, Eric **32** 89-91
Papert, Seymour **32** 290-292
women
Cheney, Ednah Dow **32** 68-70

MASSAQUOI, HANS J. (born 1926), American journalist and author **29** 270-272

MASSASOIT (1580-1661), Native American tribal chief **10** 322-324

MASSEY, VINCENT (Charles Vincent Massey, 1887-1967), Canadian governor-general **24** 246-248

MASSEY, WILLIAM FERGUSON (1856-1925), New Zealand prime minister 1912-1925 **10** 324

MASSINGER, PHILIP (1583-1640), English playwright **10** 324-325

MASSYS, QUENTIN (1465/66-1530), Flemish painter **10** 325-326

Mastai-Ferretti, Giovanni Maria
see Pius IX

Master Meng
see Mencius

Master of Flémalle
see Campin, Robert

MASTERS, EDGAR LEE (1869-1950), American author and lawyer **10** 326-327

MASTERS, WILLIAM HOWELL (1915-2001), American psychologist and sex therapist **10** 327-328

MASTERSON, BAT (William Barclay Masterson; 1853-1921), American sheriff and sportswriter **29** 272-274

MASUDI, ALI IBN AL- HUSAYN AL- (died 956), Arab historian **10** 328-329

MASUR, KURT (born 1927), German conductor and humanist **20** 246-248

MATA HARI (Margaretha Geertruida Zelle; 1876-1917), Dutch spy **21** 279-282

MATAMOROS, MARINO (1770-1814), Mexican priest and independence hero **10** 329-330

Mathematics
geometry
Thom, René **32** 332-334

MATHER, COTTON (1663-1728), American Puritan clergyman and historian **10** 330-332

MATHER, INCREASE (1639-1723), American Puritan clergymen, educator, and author **10** 332-333

MATHEWSON, CHRISTY (Christopher Mathewson; 1880-1925), American baseball player **21** 282-284

MATHIAS, BOB (Robert Bruce Mathias; 1930-2006), American track and field star **21** 284-286

MATHIEZ, ALBERT (1874-1932), French historian **10** 333-334

MATILDA OF TUSCANY (c. 1046-1115), Italian countess **10** 334-336

MATISSE, HENRI (1869-1954), French painter and sculptor **10** 336-337

MATLIN, MARLEE (born 1965), American actress **19** 228-230

MATLOVICH, LEONARD (1943-1988), American gay rights activist **20** 248-250

Matoaka
see Pocahontas (ballet)

MATSUNAGA, SPARK MASAYUKI (1916-1990), Asian American U.S. senator **18** 279-281

MATSUSHITA, KONOSUKE (1918-1989), Japanese inventor and businessman **19** 230-232

Matsys, Quentin
see Massys, Quentin

MATTA ECHAURREN, ROBERTO SEBASTIAN ANTONIO (Matta, 1911-2002), Chilean artist **24** 248-250

MATTEI, ENRICO (1906-1962), Italian entrepreneur **10** 337-339

MATTEOTTI, GIACOMO (1885-1924), Italian political leader **10** 339-340

MATTHAU, WALTER (Walter Matthow; Walter Matuschanskayasky; 1920-2000), American Actor **22** 314-316

MATTHEW, ST. (flourished Ist century), Apostle and Evangelist **10** 340-341

MATTHEW PARIS (c. 1200-1259), English Benedictine chronicler **10** 341-342

MATTHEWS, MARJORIE SWANK (1916-1986), American bishop **32** 240-242

MATTHEWS, VICTORIA EARLE (1861-1907), American journalist and social reformer **32** 242-245

MATTINGLY, GARRETT (1900-1962), American historian, professor, and author of novel-like histories **10** 342-344

MATZELIGER, JAN (1852-1889), American inventor and shoemaker **19** 232-234

MAUCHLY, JOHN (1907-1980), American computer entrepreneur **20** 250-252
Bartik, Jean **32** 34-36

MAUDSLAY, HENRY (1771-1831), British engineer and inventor **21** 286-288

MAUGHAM, WILLIAM SOMERSET (1874-1965), English author **10** 344-345

MAULBERTSCH, FRANZ ANTON (1724-1796), Austrian painter **10** 345

MAULDIN, BILL (1921-2003), cartoon biographer of the ordinary GI in World War II **10** 345-346

MAUPASSANT, HENRI RENÉ ALBERT GUY DE (1850-1893), French author **10** 347

MAURIAC, FRANÇOIS (1885-1970), French author **10** 347-348

MAURICE, JOHN FREDERICK DENISON (1805-1872), English theologian and Anglican clergyman **10** 349-350

MAURICE OF NASSAU, PRINCE OF ORANGE (1567-1625), Dutch general and statesman **10** 348-349

MAURRAS, CHARLES MARIE PHOTIUS (1868-1952), French political writer and reactionary **10** 350-351

MAURY, ANTONIA (1866-1952), American astronomer and conservationist **20** 252-254

MOTLEY, JOHN LOTHROP (1814-1877), American historian and diplomat **11** 211-212

MOTLEY, WILLARD FRANCIS (1909-1965), African American author **22** 326-328

Motokiyo, Zeami
see Zeami, Kanze

MOTT, JOHN R. (1865-1955), American Protestant leader **11** 212

MOTT, LUCRETIA COFFIN (1793-1880), American feminist and abolitionist **11** 212-213

Moulton, Charles
see Marston, William Moulton

MOUNT, WILLIAM SIDNEY (1807-1868), American painter **11** 213-214

Mount Vernon Historical Site
Washington, Martha **32** 359-361

MOUNTAIN WOLF WOMAN (Kéhachiwinga; Wolf's Mountain Home Maker; Haksigaxunuminka; 1884-1960), Winnebago autobiographer **26** 269-272

MOUNTBATTEN, LOUIS FRANCIS ALBERT VICTOR NICHOLAS (1900-1979), English Navy officer and viceroy of India **18** 297-299

Mountjoy, 8th Baron, (Charles Blount, Earl of Devonshire; 1563-1606), English soldier
O'Donnell, Red Hugh **32** 282-284

MOYERS, BILLY DON ("Bill"; born 1934), television journalist, author, and press secretary to president Lyndon B. Johnson **11** 214-216

MOYNIHAN, DANIEL PATRICK ("Pat"; 1927-2003), United States senator from New York **11** 216-218
Sotomayor, Sonia **32** 320-321

MOZART, WOLFGANG AMADEUS (1756-1791), Austrian composer **11** 218-221

Mozee, Phoebe Anne Oakley
see Oakley, Annie

MPHAHLELE, EZEKIEL (a.k.a. Bruno Eseki; 1919-2008), South African author and scholar **11** 221-223

MQHAYI, SAMUEL EDWARD KRUNE (1875-1945), South African novelist and poet **11** 223

Mr. Tsungli Yaman
see Wen-hsiang

Mrs. Belloc Lowndes
see Belloc Lowndes, Marie Adelaide

MUAWIYA IBN ABU SUFYAN (died 680), Umayyad caliph **11** 223-224

MUBARAK, HOSNI (born 1928), president of Egypt **11** 225-226

MUDD, SAMUEL ALEXANDER (1833-1883), American physician **32** 265-268

MUELLER, OTTO (1874-1930), German expressionist painter **11** 226-227

Mufferaw, Joe
see Montferrand, Joseph

Mufti of Jerusalem
see Husagni, Al-Hajj Amin Al-

MUGABE, ROBERT GABRIEL (born 1924), Zimbabwe's first elected black prime minister **11** 227-229

MUHAMMAD, ELIJAH (Poole; 1897-1975), leader of the Nation of Islam ("Black Muslims") **11** 230-231

MUHAMMAD ALI PASHA (Mehmet Ali Pasha; Muhammad Ali; 1769-1849), Ottoman Turkish ruler of Egypt **27** 265-267

MUHAMMAD BIN TUGHLUQ (ruled 1325-1351), Moslem sultan of Delhi **11** 229

Muhammad ibn Daud
see Alp Arslan

Muhammad Shah (1877-1957)
see Aga Khan III

MUHAMMAD TURE, ASKIA (c. 1443-1538), ruler of the West African Songhay empire **11** 231-232

Muhibbi
see Suleiman I

MÜHLENBERG, HEINRICH MELCHIOR (1711-1787), German-born American Lutheran clergyman **11** 232-233

MUHLENBERG, WILLIAM AUGUSTUS (1796-1877), American Episcopalian clergyman **11** 233-234

MUIR, JOHN (1838-1914), American naturalist **11** 234

MUJIBUR RAHMAN, SHEIK (1920-1975), Bengal leader who helped found Bangladesh **11** 234-236

MUKERJI, DHAN GOPAL (1890-1936), Indian author and Hindu priest **22** 328-330

MULDOWNEY, SHIRLEY (born c. 1940), American race car driver **11** 236-238

MULLANY, KATE (1845-1906), Irish-American labor activist **31** 244-246

MULLER, HERMANN JOSEPH (1890-1967), American geneticist **11** 238-239

Müller, Johann
see Regiomontanus

MÜLLER, JOHANNES PETER (1801-1858), German physiologist and anatomist **11** 239-240

MÜLLER, KARL ALEXANDER (born 1927), Swiss-born solid-state physicist **11** 240-241

MÜLLER, PAUL HERMANN (1899-1965), Swiss chemist **11** 241-242

MULRONEY, MARTIN BRIAN (born 1939), prime minister of Canada **11** 242-246

Mumbai (city, India)
Catherine of Braganza **32** 62-55

MUMFORD, LEWIS (1895-1990), American social philosopher and architectural critic **11** 246-247

Mun Sun
see Yi Hwang

MUNCH, EDVARD (1863-1944), Norwegian painter and graphic artist **11** 247-248

MUNDELEIN, GEORGE WILLIAM (1872-1939), American Roman Catholic cardinal **11** 248-249

Mundinus
see Luzzi, Mondino de'

MUNI, PAUL (1895-1967), American actor **32** 268-271

MUÑOZ MARÍN, JOSÉ LUÍS ALBERTO (1898-1980), Puerto Rican political leader **11** 249-250

MUÑOZ RIVERA, LUÍS (1859-1916), Puerto Rican political leader **11** 250

MUNSEY, FRANK ANDREW (1854-1925), American publisher **11** 251

MÜNZER, THOMAS (c. 1489-1525), German Protestant reformer **11** 251-252

MURASAKI SHIKIBU (c. 976-c. 1031), Japanese writer **11** 252-253

MURAT, JOACHIM (1767-1815), French marshal, king of Naples 1808-1815 **11** 253-254

MURATORI, LODOVICO ANTONIO (1672-1750), Italian historian and antiquary **11** 254-255

MURCHISON, SIR RODERICK IMPEY (1792-1871), British geologist **11** 255-256

MURDOCH, JEAN IRIS (1919-1999), British novelist **11** 256-257

MURDOCH, RUPERT (born 1931), Australian newspaper publisher **11** 257-258

MURILLO, BARTOLOMÉ ESTEBAN (1617-1682), Spanish painter **11** 258-259

Murjebi, Hamed bin Mohammed el
see Tippu Tip

NOETHER, EMMY (born Amalie Emmy Noether; 1882-1935), German American mathematician **11** 414-416

NOGUCHI, ISAMU (1904-1988), American sculptor and designer **11** 416-418

Nol, Lon
see Lon Nol, (1913-1985)

NOLAN, SIDNEY ROBERT (1917-1992), Australian expressionist painter **11** 418

NOLAND, KENNETH (1924-2010), American color-field painter **11** 418-419

NOLDE, EMIL (1867-1956), German expressionist painter **11** 419-420

NONO, LUIGI (1924-1990), Italian composer **11** 420-421

NOONUCCAL, OODGEROO (Kath Wlaker; Kathleen Jean Mary Ruska; 1920-1993), Australian Aboriginal poet **27** 272-274

NOOYI, INDRA KRISHNAMURTHY (born 1955), Indian-American business woman **27** 274-276

NORDENSKJÖLD, BARON NILS ADOLF ERIK (1832-1901), Finnish-Swedish polar explorer and mineralogist **11** 421-422

NORDENSKOLD, NILS OTTO GUSTAF (1869-1928), Swedish polar explorer and geologist **11** 422-423

NORDSTROM, JOHN (Johan W. Nordstrom; 1871-1963), American shoe retailer **19** 270-272

NORFOLK, 3D DUKE OF (Thomas Howard; 1473-1554), English soldier and councilor **11** 423

NØRGÅRD, PER (born 1932), Danish composer **23** 265-267

NORIEGA, MANUEL A. (born 1934), strongman of Panama (1980s) forced out in 1989 by the United States **11** 423-425

NORMAN, JESSYE (born 1945), American singer **11** 425-427

NORMAND, MABEL (1895-1930), American actress **31** 251-253

Normandy, Duke of
see Charles V(king of France)

NORRIS, BENJAMIN FRANKLIN, JR. (1870-1902), American novelist and critic **11** 427-428

NORRIS, GEORGE WILLIAM (1861-1944), American statesman **11** 428-429

NORTH, FREDERICK (2nd Earl of Guilford; 1732-1792), English statesman **11** 429-430

NORTH, MARIANNE (1830-1890), English naturalist and painter **23** 268-270

NORTHROP, JOHN HOWARD (1891-1987), American biological chemist **11** 430-431

NORTHUMBERLAND, DUKE OF (John Dudley; c. 1502-1553), English soldier and statesman **11** 431-432

NORTON, ANDRE (Alice Mary Norton; 1912-2005), American science fiction and fantasy writer **28** 257-259

NOSTRADAMUS (born Michel de Notredame; 1503-1566), French physician, astrologist, and author **11** 432-434

NOTKER BALBULUS (c. 840-912), Swiss poet-musician and monk **11** 434-435

Nova Scotia (province; Canada)
Desmond, Viola **32** 92-94

Novak, Joseph
see Kosinsky, Jerzy

NOVALIS (1772-1801), German poet and author **11** 435

Novanglus
see Adams, John

Novel, development of (literature)
Pavić, Milorad **32** 295-297

NOVELLO, ANTONIA (Antonia Coello; born 1944), Puerto Rican American pediatrician **18** 308-310

NOVOTNÝ, ANTONÍN (1904-1975), Czechoslovak politician **29** 291-293

NOYCE, ROBERT (1927-1990), American physicist and inventor **11** 436-437

NOYES, JOHN HUMPHREY (1811-1886), American founder of the Oneida Community **11** 437-438

NOZICK, ROBERT (1938-2002), American philosopher and polemical advocate of radical libertarianism **11** 438-439

N'si Yisrael
see Bar Kochba, Simeon

NU, U (1907-1995), Burmese statesman **11** 439-441

Nueva canción (musical movement)
Parra, Violeta **32** 292-294
Yupanqui, Atahualpa **32** 372-373

NUJOMA, SHAFIIHUNA ("Sam"; born 1929), first president of independent Namibia **11** 441-443

Nukada-be, Princess
see Suiko

Núñez de Balboa, Vasco
see Balboa, Vasco Núñez de

NUNN, SAM (born 1938), United States senator from Georgia **11** 443-444

Nur-ad-Din
see Nureddin

Nur al-Din Abd al-Rahman, Maulana
see Jami

NUREDDIN (Malik al-Adil Nur-al-Din Mahmud; 1118-1174), sultan of Syria and Egypt **11** 444-445

NUREYEV, RUDOLPH (born 1938), Russian-born dancer and choreographer **11** 445-446

NURI AL-SA'ID (1888-1958), Iraqi army officer, statesman, and nationalist **11** 446-447

NURMI, PAAVO (1897-1973), Finnish runner **19** 272-274

Nurse, Malcolm Ivan Meredith
see Padmore, George

NURSÎ, SAID (Bediüzzaman Said Nursî; 1876-1960), Turkish theologian **28** 259-261

Nursing (medicine)
McManus, Louise **32** 251-253
Zakrzewska, Marie **32** 374-375

NUSSLEIN-VOLHARD, CHRISTIANE (born 1942), German biologist **25** 314-316

Nuvolara, Count of
see Castiglione, Baldassare

NYE, GERALD (1892-1971), American senator **21** 320-323

NYERERE, JULIUS KAMBERAGE (1922-1999), Tanzanian statesman **11** 447-449
Kambona, Oscar **32** 175-177
Warioba, Joseph **32** 357-358

NYGREN, ANDERS (1890-1978), Lutheran bishop of Lund and representative of the so-called Lundensian school of theology **11** 449-451

NYKVIST, SVEN (Sven Vilhelm Nykvist; 1922-2006), Swedish cinematographer **28** 261-263

NYRO, LAURA (1947-1997), American singer-songwriter **31** 254-256

NZINGA, ANNA (Pande Dona Ana Souza; 1582-1663), queen of Angola **23** 270-271

Nzinga Mvemba
see Affonso I

NZINGA NKUWU (died 1506), king of Kongo **11** 451-452

O

OAKLEY, ANNIE (1860-1926), American markswoman and Wild West star **11** 453-454

OATES, JOYCE CAROL (born 1938), American author **11** 454-456**

PÁEZ, JOSÉ ANTONIO (1790-1873), Venezuelan general and president 1831-46 **12** 58

PAGANINI, NICCOLO (1782-1840), Italian violinist and composer **12** 58-59

PAGE, THOMAS NELSON (1853-1922), American author and diplomat **12** 59-60

PAGE, WALTER HINES (1855-1918), American journalist and diplomat **12** 60-61

PAGELS, ELAINE HIESEY (born 1943), historian of religion **12** 61-62

PAGLIA, CAMILLE (born 1947), American author and social critic **23** 286-288

PAIGE, SATCHEL (Leroy Robert Paige; 1906-1982), African American baseball player **12** 62-65
   Gibson, Josh **32** 135-138

PAINE, JOHN KNOWLES (1839-1905), American composer **12** 65

PAINE, THOMAS (1737-1809), English-born American journalist and Revolutionary propagandist **12** 66-67

PAISLEY, IAN K. (born 1926), political leader and minister of religion in Northern Ireland **12** 67-69

Pak Chong-hŭi
   see Park, Chung Hee

PALACKÝ, FRANTIŠEK (1798-1876), Czech historian and statesman **12** 69-70

PALAMAS, KOSTES (1859-1943), Greek poet **12** 70

PALESTRINA, GIOVANNI PIERLUIGI DA (c. 1525-1594), Italian composer **12** 70-72

PALEY, GRACE (1922-2007), American author and activist **22** 348-350

PALEY, WILLIAM (1743-1805), English theologian and moral philosopher **12** 72

PALEY, WILLIAM S. (1901-1990), founder and chairman of the Columbia Broadcasting System **12** 72-75

PALLADIO, ANDREA (1508-1580), Italian architect **12** 75-77

PALMA, RICARDO (1833-1919), Peruvian poet, essayist, and short-story writer **12** 77

PALME, OLOF (Sven Olof Joachim Palme; 1927-1986), Swedish prime minister (1969-1973; 1982-1986) **28** 267-269

PALMER, ALEXANDER MITCHELL (1872-1936), American politician and jurist **12** 77-78

PALMER, ARNOLD DANIEL (born 1929), American golfer **12** 78-80

PALMER, NATHANIEL BROWN (1799-1877), American sea captain **12** 80-81

PALMER, PHOEBE WORRALL (1807-1847), American evangelist **23** 288-290

PALMERSTON, 3D VISCOUNT (Henry John Temple; 1784-1865), English prime minister 1855-65 **12** 81-83

Pamfili, Giovanni Batista
   see Innocent X

PAMUK, ORHAN (born 1952), Turkish novelist and Nobel Prize Winner **28** 269-272

PAN KU (32-92), Chinese historian and man of letters **12** 86-87

PANDIT, VIJAYA LAKSHMI (1900-1990), Indian diplomat and politician **12** 83-84

PANETTA, LEON E. (born 1938), Democratic congressman from California and chief of staff to President Clinton **12** 84-85

PANINI (flourished c. 5th century BCE), Indian grammarian **24** 293-295

PANKHURST, CHRISTABEL HARRIETTE (1880-1948), English reformer and suffragette **22** 350-352

PANKHURST, EMMELINE (1858-1928), English reformer **12** 85-86

PANKHURST, SYLVIA (1882-1960), English reformer **29** 309-311

PANNENBERG, WOLFHART (born 1928), German Protestant theologian **12** 87-88

PANUFNIK, ANDRZEJ (1914-1991), Polish/British composer and conductor **24** 295-298

Papal Schism (1378-1417)
   see Great Schism (1378-1417; Roman Catholic Church)

PAPANDREOU, ANDREAS (1919-1996), Greek scholar and statesman and prime minister **12** 88-91

PAPERT, SEYMOUR (born 1928), South African-born computer scientist and educator **32** 290-292

PAPINEAU, LOUIS-JOSEPH (1786-1871), French-Canadian radical political leader **12** 91

PARACELSUS, PHILIPPUS AUREOLUS (1493-1541), Swiss physician and alchemist **12** 91-93

Paramount Pictures (film studio)
   Arzner, Dorothy **32** 18-20

PARBO, ARVI (born 1926), Australian industrial giant **12** 93-94

PARÉ, AMBROISE (1510-1590), French military surgeon **12** 94-95

PARETO, VILFREDO (1848-1923), Italian sociologist, political theorist, and economist **12** 95-96

PARHAM, CHARLES FOX (1873-1929), American evangelist **23** 291-293

Paris, Matthew
   see Matthew Paris

PARIZEAU, JACQUES (born 1930), Canadian politician and premier of Quebec **12** 96-99

PARK, CHUNG HEE (1917-1979), Korean soldier and statesman **12** 99-102

PARK, MAUD WOOD (1871-1955), suffragist and first president of the League of Women Voters **12** 102

PARK, ROBERT E. (1864-1944), American sociologist **12** 102-104

PARK, WILLIAM HALLOCK (1863-1939), American physician **12** 104-105

PARKER, ARTHUR CASWELL (1881-1955), Native American anthropologist and museum administrator **26** 286-288

PARKER, CHARLES CHRISTOPHER, JR. (Charlie Parker; 1920-1955), American jazz musician **12** 105-106

PARKER, DOROTHY ROTHSCHILD (1893-1967), American writer **12** 106

PARKER, ELY SAMUEL (Ha-sa-no-an-da; 1828-1895), Native American tribal leader **12** 106-108

PARKER, HORATIO WILLIAM (1863-1919), American composer **12** 109

PARKER, QUANAH (c. 1845-1911), Native American religious leader **12** 109-112

PARKER, THEODORE (1810-1860), American Unitarian clergyman **12** 112-113

PARKER, TOM ("Colonel" Tom Parker; 1909-1997), Dutch-American talent manager **31** 273-274
   Leiber and Stoller **32** 209-212

PARKES, ALEXANDER (1813-1890), British metallurgist and inventor of plastic **21** 334-336

PARKES, SIR HENRY (1815-1896), Australian statesman **12** 113

PARKINSON, C. NORTHCOTE (Cyril Northcote Parkinson; 1909-1993), British historian and humorist **24** 298-300

PARKMAN, FRANCIS (1823-1893), American historian **12** 113-115

PARKS, GORDON (1912-2005), American photographer, composer, and filmmaker **19** 275-277

Paxton, Bill (born 1955), American actor
Bigelow, Kathryn **32** 40-42

PAYNE, JOHN HOWARD (1791-1852),
American actor, playwright, and
songwriter **12** 159

PAYNE-GAPOSCHKIN, CECILIA
(1900-1979), American astronomer **12**
159-161

PAYTON, WALTER (1954-1999),
American football player **20** 294-296

PAZ, OCTAVIO (1914-1998), Mexican
diplomat, critic, editor, translator, poet,
and essayist **12** 161-162

PAZ ESTENSSORO, VICTOR (1907-2001),
Bolivian statesman and reformer **12**
163-164

PAZ ZAMORA, JAIME (born 1939),
president of Bolivia (1989-) **12** 165-167

PÁZMÁNY, PÉTER (1570-1637),
Hungarian archbishop **12** 164-165

PEABODY, ELIZABETH PALMER
(1804-1894), American educator and
author **12** 167-168

PEABODY, GEORGE (1795-1869),
American merchant, financier, and
philanthropist **12** 168

PEACOCK, THOMAS LOVE (1785-1866),
English novelist and satirist **12** 169

PEALE, CHARLES WILLSON (1741-1827),
American painter and scientist **12**
169-171

PEALE, NORMAN VINCENT (1898-1993),
American religious leader who blended
psychotherapy and religion **12** 171-172

PEALE, REMBRANDT (1778-1860),
American painter **12** 172-173

PEARSE, PATRICK HENRY (1879-1916),
Irish poet, educator, and revolutionary
12 173-174

PEARSON, LESTER BOWLES (1897-1972),
Canadian statesman and diplomat,
prime minister **12** 174-175

PEARY, ROBERT EDWIN (1856-1920),
American explorer **12** 175-176

Pecci, Vincenzo Gioacchino
see Leo XIII

PECHSTEIN, HERMANN MAX
(1881-1955), German Expressionist
painter and graphic artist **12** 176-177

PECK, ANNIE SMITH (1850-1935),
American mountain climber **24** 304-306

PECK, MORGAN SCOTT (1936-2005),
American author and psychologist **26**
288-291

PECK, ROBERT NEWTON (born 1928),
American author of children's literature
12 177-178

PECKINPAH, SAM (1925-1984), American
film director **21** 338-340

PEDRARIAS (Pedro Arias de Ávila; c.
1440-1531), Spanish conqueror and
colonial governor **12** 179

PEDRO I (1798-1834), emperor of Brazil
and king of Portugal **12** 179-180

PEDRO II (1825-1891), emperor of Brazil
1831-89 **12** 180-181

Pedro III (king, Aragon)
see Peter III, (Peter Feodorovich;
1728-62)

Pedro IV (king, Portugal)
see Pedro I (emperor, Brazil)

PEEL, JOHN (John Robert Parker
Ravenscroft; 1939-2004), British disc
jockey **27** 286-288

PEEL, SIR ROBERT (1788-1850), English
statesman, prime minister 1834-35 and
1841-46 **12** 181-183

PÉGUY, CHARLES PIERRE (1873-1914),
French poet **12** 183-184

PEI, I. M. (Ieoh Ming Pei; born 1917),
Chinese-American architect **12** 184-187

PEIRCE, BENJAMIN (1809-1880),
American mathematician **21** 340-342

PEIRCE, CHARLES SANDERS (1839-1914),
American scientist and philosopher **12**
187-188

PEIXOTO, FLORIANO (1839-1895),
Brazilian marshal, president 1891-94 **12**
188-189

PELAGIUS (died c. 430), British theologian
12 189-190

PELE (Edson Arantes Do Nascimento Pele;
born 1940), Brazilian soccer player **12**
190-191

Peleliu, Battle of (1944)
Lea, Tom **32** 201-202

PELLI, CESAR (born 1926), Hispanic
American architect and educator **12**
191-192

PELOSI, NANCY (Nancy D'Alesandro; born
1940), American politician **25** 328-330

PELTIER, LEONARD (born 1944), Native
American activist **12** 193-195

PEMBERTON, JOHN STITH (1831-1888),
American inventor of Coca-Cola **28**
278-279

PEÑA, PACO (Francisco Peña Pérez; born
1942), Spanish guitarist and composer
23 299-301

PENDERECKI, KRZYSZTOF (born 1933),
Polish composer **12** 195-197

PENDERGAST, THOMAS J. (1872-1945),
American political boss **29** 313-315

PENDLETON, EDMUND (1721-1803),
American political leader **12** 197-198

PENDLETON, GEORGE HUNT
(1825-1889), American politician **12**
198

PENFIELD, WILDER GRAVES (1891-1976),
Canadian neurosurgeon **12** 198-200

PENN, WILLIAM (1644-1718), English
Quaker, founder of Pennsylvania **12**
200-202

PENNANT, THOMAS (1726-1798), British
naturalist, writer and antiquarian **31**
278-279

Pennebaker, Donn Alan, (born 1925),
American filmmaker
Leacock, Richard **32** 202-205

PENNEY, J. C. (James Cash Penney;
1875-1971), American chain store
executive and philanthropist **12** 202-203

PENNINGTON, MARY ENGLE
(1872-1952), American chemist **22**
352-355

Pennsylvania, University of (Philadelphia)
faculty
Cohn, Mildred **32** 81-84
Gates, Thomas Sovereign **32**
128-130

PENROSE, BOIES (1860-1921), American
senator and political boss **12** 203-204

PENROSE, ROGER (born 1931), British
mathematician and physicist **12**
204-205

Pensador Mexicano, El
see Fernández de Lizardi, Josè Joaquin

PENSKE, ROGER (born 1937), American
businessman and race car team owner
19 280-282

PENZIAS, ARNO ALLEN (born 1932),
German American physicist **23** 301-304

PEP, WILLIE (William Guiglermo Papaleo;
1922-2006), American boxer **21**
342-344

PEPPER, CLAUDE DENSON (1900-1989),
Florida attorney, state representative,
U.S. senator, and U.S. representative **12**
205-206

PEPPERELL, SIR WILLIAM (1696-1759),
American merchant and soldier **12**
206-207

PEPYS, SAMUEL (1633-1703), English
diarist **12** 207-208
Catherine of Braganza **32** 62-55

PERCY, WALKER (1916-1990), American
author **19** 282-284

PEREGRINUS, PETRUS (flourished
1261-69), French scholastic and scientist
12 208

PLATH, SYLVIA (1932-1963), American poet and novelist **12** 344-345

PLATO (428-347 BCE), Greek philosopher **12** 345-347

PLATT, THOMAS COLLIER (1833-1910), American politician **12** 347-348

PLAUTUS (c. 254-c. 184 BCE), Roman writer **12** 348-350

Playboy (magazine)
Vargas, Alberto **32** 348-350

PLAZA LASSO, GALO (1906-1987), Ecuadorian statesman **12** 350-351

PLEKHANOV, GEORGI VALENTINOVICH (1856-1918), Russian revolutionist and social philosopher **12** 351-352

PLENTY COUPS (c. 1848-1932), Native American tribal leader and Crow chief **12** 352-355

Plessis, Armand du
see Richelieu, Armand Jean Du Plessis De

PLIMPTON, GEORGE (1927-2003), American writer and editor **31** 282-283

PLINY THE ELDER (23/24-79), Roman encyclopedist **12** 355-356

PLINY THE YOUNGER (c. 61-c. 113), Roman author and administrator **12** 356

PLISETSKAYA, MAYA MIKHAILOVNA (born 1925), Russian ballet dancer **12** 356-358

PLOMER, WILLIAM (William Charles Franklyn Plomer; 1903-1973), South African/British author **24** 312-313

PLOTINUS (205-270), Greek philosopher, founder of Neoplatonism **12** 358-359

PLOTKIN, MARK (born 1955), American ethnobotanist and environmentalist **23** 308-310

PLUTARCH (c. 46-c. 120), Greek biographer **12** 359-360

PO CHÜ-I (772-846), Chinese poet **12** 362-363

POBEDONOSTSEV, KONSTANTIN PETROVICH (1827-1907), Russian statesman and jurist **12** 360-361

POCAHONTAS (c. 1595-1617), American Indian princess **12** 361-362

POE, EDGAR ALLAN (1809-1849), American writer **12** 363-365

Poets Laureate (England)
Meynell, Alice **32** 255-257

POINCARÉ, JULES HENRI (1854-1912), French mathematician **12** 365-366

POINCARÉ, RAYMOND (1860-1934), French statesman **12** 366-368

Point Break (film)
Bigelow, Kathryn **32** 40-42

POIRET, PAUL (1879-1944), French fashion designer **19** 291-293

POITIER, SIDNEY (born 1927), African American actor and director **12** 368-370
Kramer, Stanley **32** 186-189

POKORNY, JAN HIRD (1914-2008), Czech-American architect **29** 320-321

POL POT (1928-1998), Cambodian Communist and premier of Democratic Kampuchéa (1976-1979) **12** 382-384

POLANSKI, ROMAN (born 1933), Polish filmmaker and director **23** 310-312

POLANYI, JOHN CHARLES (born 1929), Canadian scientist and Nobel Prize winner **12** 370-372

POLANYI, KARL (1886-1964), Hungarian economic historian **12** 372

POLANYI, MICHAEL (1891-1976), Hungarian medical doctor, physical chemist, social thinker, and philosopher **12** 372-373

Poliomyelitis (disease)
vaccine
Zhdanov, Viktor Mikhailovich **32** 377-379

Politian
see Poliziano, Angelo

POLITKOVSKAYA, ANNA (Anna Stepanova Politkovskaya; 1958-2006), Russian journalist **27** 292-294

POLIZIANO, ANGELO (Politian; 1454-1494), Italian poet **12** 373-374

POLK, JAMES KNOX (1795-1849), American statesman, president 1845-49 **12** 374-376

POLK, LEONIDAS LAFAYETTE (1837-1892), American agrarian crusader and editor **12** 376-377

POLKE, SIGMAR (1941-2010), German painter **23** 312-315

POLLAIUOLO, ANTONIO (c. 1432-98), Italian painter, sculptor, goldsmith, and engraver **12** 377-378

POLLARD, ALBERT FREDERICK (1869-1948), English historian **12** 378

POLLOCK, JACKSON (1912-1956), American painter **12** 379-380

POLO, MARCO (c. 1254-c. 1324), Venetian traveler and writer **12** 380-382

POLYBIOS (c. 203-120 BCE), Greek historian **12** 384-385

POLYKLEITOS (flourished c. 450-420 BCE), Greek sculptor **12** 385-386

POMBAL, MARQUÊS DE (Sebastião José de Carvalho e Mello; 1699-1782), Portuguese statesman **12** 386-387

POMPEY (106-48 BCE), Roman general and statesman **12** 387-389

POMPIDOU, GEORGES (1911-1974), second president of the French Fifth Republic (1969-1974) **12** 389-390

POMPONAZZI, PIETRO (1462-1525), Italian Aristotelian philosopher **12** 390-391

PONCE, MANUEL (Manuel María Ponce; 1886-1948), Mexican composer and educator **28** 282-284

PONCE DE LEÓN, JUAN (c. 1460-1521), Spanish conqueror and explorer **12** 391-392

PONIATOWSKA, ELENA (born 1933), Mexican journalist, novelist, essayist, and short-story writer **12** 392-393

Pontedera, Andrea da
see Andrea Pisano

PONTIAC (c. 1720-69), Ottawa Indian chief **12** 393-394

PONTOPPIDAN, HENRIK (Rusticus; 1857-1943), Danish author **25** 336-338

PONTORMO (1494-1556), Italian painter **12** 394-395

POOL, JUDITH GRAHAM (1919-1975), American physiologist **23** 315-316

Pop, Iggy, (born 1947), American musician
Bangs, Lester **32** 32-34

POPE, ALEXANDER (1688-1744), English poet and satirist **12** 395-397

POPE, JOHN RUSSELL (1874-1937), American architect in the classical tradition **12** 397-399

POPHAM, WILLIAM JAMES (born 1930), American educator active in educational test development **12** 399-401

Popish Plot (England; 1678)
Catherine of Braganza **32** 62-55

POPOVA, LIUBOV SERGEEVNA (1889-1924), Russian and Soviet avant-garde artist **12** 401-402

POPPER, SIR KARL RAIMUND (1902-1994), Austrian philosopher **12** 402

Poquelin, Jean Baptiste
see Molière

Porky Pig (cartoon character)
Avery, Tex **32** 24-27

PORRES, MARTÍN DE, ST. (1579-1639), Peruvian patron saint of universal brotherhood **27** 295-297

ROBBINS, JEROME (Rabinowitz; 1918-1998), American director and choreographer **13** 190-192

ROBERT I (1274-1329), king of Scotland 1306-29 **13** 192-194

ROBERT II (1316-1390), king of Scotland 1371-90 **13** 194

ROBERT III (c. 1337-1406), king of Scotland 1390-1406 **13** 194-195

ROBERT, HENRY MARTYN (1837-1923), American engineer and parliamentarian **21** 367-370

ROBERT, SHAABAN (1909-1962), Tanzanian author who wrote in the Swahili language **14** 128-129

Robert Bruce
see Robert I (king, Scotland)

ROBERTS, ED (1941-2010), American computer designer **31** 299-300

ROBERTS, FREDERICK SLEIGH (1st Earl Roberts of Kandhar, Pretoria, and Waterford; 1832-1914), British field marshal **13** 195-196

ROBERTS, JOHN GLOVER, JR. (born 1955), American jurist, chief justice of the United States Supreme Court 2005-26 320-322
Sotomayor, Sonia **32** 320-321

ROBERTS, ORAL (Granville Oral Roberts; 1918-2009), American evangelist **28** 296-298

Roberts of Kandahar, Pretoria, and Waterford, 1st Earl
see Roberts, Frederick Sleigh

Robertson, Anna Mary
see Moses, Grandma

ROBERTSON, SIR DENNIS HOLME (1890-1963), English economist **13** 196

ROBERTSON, MARION G. (Pat Robertson; born 1930), television evangelist who founded the Christian Broadcasting Network and presidential candidate **13** 196-198

ROBERTSON, OSCAR (born 1938), African American basketball player **20** 311-313

ROBESON, ESLANDA GOODE (born Eslanda Cardozo Goode; 1896-1965), African American cultural anthropologist **23** 340-342

ROBESON, PAUL LEROY (1898-1976), American singer, actor, and political activist **13** 198-199

ROBESPIERRE, MAXIMILIEN FRANÇOIS MARIE ISIDORE DE (1758-1794), French Revolutionary leader **13** 199-201

ROBINSON, EDDIE (1919-2007), African American college football coach **18** 351-352

Robinson, Edward G., (1893-1973), American actor
Muni, Paul **32** 268-271

ROBINSON, EDWIN ARLINGTON (1869-1935), American poet and playwright **13** 201-202

ROBINSON, FRANK, JR. (born 1935), African American baseball player and manager **13** 202-203

ROBINSON, HARRIET HANSON (1825-1911), American author and suffragist **13** 203-207

ROBINSON, JACK ROOSEVELT (Jackie Robinson; 1919-1972), African American baseball player; first African American player in the major leagues **13** 207-208
Manley, Effa **32** 229-231

ROBINSON, JAMES HARVEY (1863-1936), American historian **13** 208

ROBINSON, JOAN VIOLET MAURICE (1903-1983), English economist **13** 209-210

ROBINSON, SIR JOHN BEVERLEY (1791-1863), Canadian political leader and jurist **13** 215-217

ROBINSON, JULIA (1919-1985), American mathematician **13** 210-211

ROBINSON, MARY BOURKE (born 1944), first woman president of Ireland **13** 211-213

ROBINSON, MAX (1939-1988), African American television news anchor **13** 213-215

ROBINSON, RANDALL (born 1941), American author and activist **23** 342-345

ROBINSON, SMOKEY (born 1940), African American performer and composer **13** 215-217

ROBINSON, SUGAR RAY (Walker Smith Jr.; 1921-1989), American boxer **19** 313-315

ROBINSON, THEODORE (1852-1896), American painter **13** 217

Robusti, Jacopo
see Tintoretto

ROCA, JULIO ARGENTINO (1843-1914), Argentine general and president **13** 218

ROCARD, MICHEL (born 1930), French left-wing politician **13** 218-220

ROCHAMBEAU, COMTE DE (Jean Baptiste Donatien de Vimeur, 1725-1807), French general **13** 220-221

ROCHBERG, GEORGE (1918-2005), American composer **13** 221-222

ROCHE, KEVIN (born 1922), Irish-American architect **13** 222-224

ROCK, ARTHUR (born 1926), American businessman **19** 316-317

ROCK, JOHN (1825-1866), American physician, lawyer, and abolitionist **21** 370-372

Rock and roll (music)
Bangs, Lester **32** 32-34
Leiber and Stoller **32** 209-212
Phillips, Sam **32** 298-301

Rock and Roll Hall of Fame
Cohen, Leonard **32** 79-81
King, Carole **32** 180-182
Leiber and Stoller **32** 209-212
Ousley, Curtis **32** 182-184
Phillips, Sam **32** 298-301

ROCKEFELLER, DAVID (born 1915), chairman of the Chase Manhattan Bank **13** 224-225

ROCKEFELLER, JOHN D., JR. (1874-1960), American philanthropist and industrial relations expert **13** 225-226

ROCKEFELLER, JOHN DAVISON (1839-1937), American industrialist and philanthropist **13** 226-228

ROCKEFELLER, NELSON ALDRICH (1908-1979), four-term governor of New York and vice-president of the United States **13** 228-230

Rocketry (science)
Opel, Fritz von **32** 284-286

ROCKINGHAM, 2D MARQUESS OF (Charles Watson-Wentworth; 1730-82), English statesman **13** 230-231

ROCKNE, KNUTE (1888-1931), American football coach **13** 231

ROCKWELL, NORMAN PERCEVEL (1894-1978), American illustrator **13** 231-233

RODAN, MENDI (Mendi Rosenblum; 1929-2009), Israeli musician **25** 356-358

RODCHENKO, ALEXANDER MIKHAILOVICH (1891-1956), Russian abstract painter, sculptor, photographer, and industrial designer **13** 233-234

RODDICK, ANITA (Anita Lucia Perilli; Dame Anita Roddick; 1942-2007), British businesswoman and activist **28** 298-301

RODGERS, JIMMIE (James Charles Rodgers; 1897-1933), American musician **19** 317-319

RODGERS, RICHARD CHARLES (1902-1972), American composer **13** 234-236

RODIN, AUGUSTE (1840-1917), French sculptor **13** 236-238

RODINO, PETER WALLACE, JR. (1909-2005), Democratic U.S. representative from New Jersey **13** 238-239

S

SABATIER, PAUL (1854-1941), French chemist **13** 398-399

SÁBATO, ERNESTO (1911-2011), Argentine novelist and essayist **13** 399-400

SABBATAI ZEVI (1626-1676), Jewish mystic and pseudo-Messiah **13** 400-401

Sabbatius, Flavius Petrus
see Justinian I

SABIN, ALBERT BRUCE (1906-1993), Polish-American physician and virologist who developed polio vaccine **13** 401-402
    Zhdanov, Viktor Mikhailovich **32** 377-379

SABIN, FLORENCE RENA (1871-1953), American anatomist **13** 402-405

Sabotino, Marchese of
see Badoglio, Pietro

SACAJAWEA (c. 1784-c. 1812), Native American translator/interpreter, and guide **13** 405-408

SACCO, NICOLA (1891-1927) AND VANZETTI, BARTOLOMEO (1887-1927), Italian-born American anarchists **13** 408-410

SACHS, HANS (1494-1576), German poet **13** 410-411

SACHS, NELLY (1891-1970), German-born Jewish poet and playwright **13** 411-412

SACKS, OLIVER WOLF (born 1933), British neurologist **26** 329-331

Sacred music
German
    Reincken, Johann Adam **32** 308-310

SADAT, ANWAR (1918-1981), Egyptian president **13** 412-414

SADAT, JIHAN (born 1933), Egyptian women's rights activist **13** 414-415

SADE, COMTE DE (Donatien Alphonse François, Marquis de Sade; 1740-1814), French writer **13** 416-418

SA'DI (c. 1200-1291), Persian poet **13** 418-419

SADI, SHAIKH MUSLIH-AL-DIN
see Sa'di

SADR, MUSA AL- (Imam Musa; 1928-c. 1978), Lebanese Shi'ite Moslem religious and political leader **13** 420-422

SAFIRE, WILLIAM (1929-2009), American journalist **13** 422-424

SAGAN, CARL E. (1934-1996), American astronomer and popularizer of science **13** 424-425

SAGER, RUTH (1918-1997), American biologist and geneticist **13** 425-426

Sagoyewatha
see Red Jacket

SAHA, MEGHNAD N. (1893-1956), Indian astrophysicist **30** 312-314

SAICHO (767-822), Japanese Buddhist monk **13** 426-428

SAID, EDWARD WADIE (1935-2003), American author and activist **27** 312-314

SAID, SEYYID (1790-1856), Omani sultan **13** 428-429

SAIGO, TAKAMORI (1827-1877), Japanese rebel and statesman **13** 429

St. Albans, Viscount
see Bacon, Sir Francis

ST. CLAIR, ARTHUR (1736-1818), Scottish-born American soldier and politician **13** 429-430

ST. DENIS, RUTH (c. 1878-1968), American dancer and choreographer **13** 430-431

SAINT-EXUPÉRY, ANTOINE DE (1900-1944), French novelist, essayist, and pilot **13** 431-432

St. Gallen, monastery (Germany)
    Bracciolini, Poggio **32** 48-50

SAINT-GAUDENS, AUGUSTUS (1848-1907), American sculptor **13** 432

SAINT-GEORGE, JOSEPH BOULOGNE, CHEVALIER DE (1745-1799), French musician, athlete and soldier **27** 314-316

St. John, Henry
see Bolingbroke, Viscount

St. John's College (Fordham, New York)
see Fordham University (New York City)

SAINT-JUST, LOUIS ANTOINE LÉON DE (1767-1794), French radical political leader **13** 433

ST. LAURENT, LOUIS STEPHEN (1882-1973), Canadian statesman **13** 434

ST. LAURENT, YVES (1936-2008), French fashion designer **20** 327-329

Saint-Léger Léger, Alexis
see Perse, Saint-John

St. Louis Cardinals (baseball team)
    Maris, Roger **32** 236-240

SAINT-PIERRE, ABBÉ DE (Charles Irénée Castel; 1658-1743), French political and economic theorist **13** 434-435

SAINT-SAËNS, CHARLES CAMILLE (1835-1921), French composer **13** 435-436

SAINT-SIMON, COMTE DE (Claude Henri de Rouvroy; 1760-1825), French social philosopher and reformer **13** 436-437

SAINT-SIMON, DUC DE (Louis de Rouvroy; 1675-1755), French writer **13** 436

SAINTE-BEUVE, CHARLES AUGUSTIN (1804-1869), French literary critic **13** 438

SAINTE-MARIE, BUFFY (Beverly Sainte-Marie; born 1941), Native American singer and songwriter **26** 334-336

SAIONJI, KIMMOCHI (1849-1940), Japanese elder statesman **13** 438-439

SAKHAROV, ANDREI (1921-1989), Russian theoretical physicist and "father of the Soviet atomic bomb" **13** 439-441

SALADIN (Salah-ad-Din Yusuf ibn Aiyub; 1138-93), Kurdish ruler of Egypt and Syria **13** 441-442

SALAM, ABDUS (1926-1996), Pakistani physicist **24** 344-346

SALAZAR, ANTÓNIO DE OLIVEIRA (1889-1970), Portuguese statesman **13** 442-443

Salcedo, Augusto Bernardino Leguía y
see Leguía y Salcedo, Augusto Bernardino

Salchow, Ulrich, (1877-1949), Swedish figure skater
    Syers, Madge **32** 329-331

SALIERI, ANTONIO (1750-1825), Italian composer **29** 333-335

SALIH, ALI'ABDALLAH (born 1942), president of the Yemeni Arab Republic (North Yemen) and first president of the United Republic of Yemen **13** 443-445

SALIH, TAYEB (1929-2009), Sudanese author **31** 317-318

SALINAS DE GORTARI, CARLOS (born 1948), president of Mexico (1988-) **13** 445-447

SALINGER, J. D. (1919-2010), American author **13** 447-448

SALISBURY, HARRISON EVANS (1908-1993), American journalist **13** 449-451

SALISBURY, 3D MARQUESS OF (Robert Arthur Talbot Gascoyne-Cecil; 1830-1903), English statesman and diplomat **13** 448-449

SALK, JONAS EDWARD (1914-1995), American physician, virologist, and immunologist **13** 451-452

SALLE, DAVID (born 1952), American artist **13** 452-453

SALLINEN, AULIS (born 1935), Finnish composer **25** 368-370

SALLUST (Gaius Sallustius Crispus; 86-c. 35 BCE), Roman statesman and historian **13** 454

Sato, Nobusuke
see Kishi, Nobusuke

SAUER, CARL ORTWIN (1889-1975), American geographer and anthropologist **13** 496-497

SAUGUET, HENRI (born 1901), French composer, writer, and thinker on art and music **13** 497-498

SAUL (c. 1020-1000 BCE), first King of Israel **13** 498

SAUND, DALIP SINGH (1899-1973), Indian-American U.S. congressman **28** 310-312

Saunders, Sir Alexander Morris Carr
see Carr-Saunders, Sir Alexander Morris

SAUNDERS, SIR CHARLES EDWARD (1867-1937), Canadian cerealist **13** 498-499

SAUNDERS, CICELY (Cicely Mary Strode Saunders; 1918-2005), English doctor and social worker **25** 376-378

SAVAGE, AUGUSTA CHRISTINE (born Augusta Christine Fells; 1892-1962), African American sculptor and teacher **13** 499-501

SAVAGE, MICHAEL JOSEPH (1872-1940), New Zealand labor leader, prime minister 1935-40 **13** 501-502

SAVARKAR, VINAYAK DAMODAR (Veer Savarkar; 1883-1966), Indian political leader **28** 312-314

SAVIGNY, FRIEDRICH KARL VON (1779-1861), German jurist **13** 502-503

SAVIMBI, JONAS MALHEIROS (1934-2002), founder and leader of UNITA (National Union for the Total Independence of Angola) **13** 503-505

SAVONAROLA, GIROLAMO (1452-1498), Italian religious reformer and dictator of Florence **13** 505-506

SAW MAUNG (1928-1997), leader of armed forces that took power in Burma (now Myanmar) in a 1988 military coup **13** 506-507

SAWALLISCH, WOLFGANG (born 1923), German orchestra conductor **28** 314-316

SAX, ADOLPHE (Antoine-Joseph Sax; 1814-1894), Belgian musician and inventor of musical instruments **28** 316-318

SAXE, COMTE DE (1696-1750), marshal of France **13** 507-508

Saxe-Coburg-Gotha dynasty (Great Britain)
see Great Britain-since 1901 (Windsor)

Saxophone (musical instrument)
Ousley, Curtis **32** 182-184

SAY, JEAN BAPTISTE (1767-1832), French economist **13** 508-509

SAYERS, DOROTHY L. (1893-1957), English author and translator **29** 335-337

SAYERS, GALE (born 1943), American football player **21** 377-379

SAYRE, FRANCIS BOWES (1885-1972), American lawyer and administrator **13** 509

SAYYID QUTB (1906-1966), Egyptian writer, educator, and religious leader **13** 509-511

SCALFARO, OSCAR LUIGI (born 1918), Christian Democratic leader and president of the Italian Republic **13** 511-512

SCALIA, ANTONIN (born 1936), U.S. Supreme Court justice **13** 513-514

Scandal, political
see Corruption, political (government)

Scandiano, Conte di
see Boiardo, Matteo Maria

Scarface (1932 film)
Muni, Paul **32** 268-271

SCARGILL, ARTHUR (born 1938), president of the British National Union of Mineworkers **13** 514-515

SCARLATTI, DOMENICO (1685-1757), Italian harpsichordist and composer **13** 515-517

SCARLATTI, PIETRO ALESSANDRO GASPARE (1660-1725), Italian composer **13** 517-518

SCHACHT, HJALMAR HORACE GREELEY (1877-1970), German economist and banker **13** 518-519

SCHAFF, PHILIP (1819-1893), Swiss-born American religious scholar **13** 519-520

SCHAPIRO, MIRIAM (born 1923), Artist **13** 520-521

SCHARNHORST, GERHARD JOHANN DAVID VON (1755-1813), Prussian general **13** 521-522

SCHARPING, RUDOLF (born 1947), minister-president of Rhineland-Palatinate and chairman of the German Social Democratic Party **13** 522-524

SCHECHTER, SOLOMON (1849-1915), Romanian-American Jewish scholar and religious leader **13** 524

SCHEELE, KARL WILHELM (1742-1786), Swedish pharmacist and chemist **13** 525-526

SCHELLING, FRIEDRICH WILHELM JOSEPH VON (1775-1854), German philosopher **13** 526-527

SCHEMBECHLER, BO (1929-2006), Glenn Edward Schembechler, Jr.; American football coach **31** 319-320

Scherer, Jean-Marie Maurice
see Rohmer, Éric

Scherrer, Paul, (1890-1969), Swiss physicist
Zwicky, Fritz **32** 379-381

SCHIELE, EGON (1890-1918), Austrian Expressionist painter and draftsman **14** 1-2

SCHIESS, BETTY BONE (born 1923), American Episcopalian priest **18** 360-362

SCHIFF, JACOB HENRY (1847-1920), German-American banker **14** 2-3

SCHILLEBEECKX, EDWARD (1914-2010), Belgian Roman Catholic theologian **14** 3-4

SCHILLER, JOHANN CHRISTOPH FRIEDRICH VON (1759-1805), German dramatist, poet, and historian **14** 4-7

SCHINDLER, ALEXANDER MOSHE (1925-2000), American Jewish leader **23** 360-362

SCHINDLER, OSKAR (1908-1974), German businessman and humanitarian **18** 362-365

SCHINDLER, SOLOMON (1842-1915), German-American rabbi and social theorist **14** 7-8

SCHINKEL, KARL FRIEDRICH (1781-1841), German architect, painter and designer **14** 8

Schism, Great (1378-1417)
see Great Schism

SCHLAFLY, PHYLLIS (born 1924), American political activist and author **14** 9-10

SCHLEGEL, FRIEDRICH VON (1772-1829), German critic and author **14** 10-11

SCHLEIERMACHER, FRIEDRICH ERNST DANIEL (1768-1834), German theologian and philosopher **14** 11-12

SCHLEMMER, OSKAR (1888-1943), German painter, sculptor, and stage designer **14** 12-13

SCHLESINGER, ARTHUR MEIER (1888-1965), American historian **14** 13

SCHLESINGER, ARTHUR MEIER, JR. (1917-2007), American historian and Democratic party activist **14** 13-15

SCHLESINGER, JAMES RODNEY (born 1929), American government official **14** 15-16

SCHLICK, FRIEDRICH ALBERT MORITZ (1882-1936), German physicist and philosopher **14** 16-17

URBAN VIII (Maffeo Barberini; 1568-1644), Italian Roman Catholic pope (1623-1644) **26** 301-302

URBAN, MATT (1919-1995), American solider **19** 391-392

UREY, HAROLD CLAYTON (1893-1981), American chemical physicist and geochemist **15** 394-396
Cohn, Mildred **32** 81-84

URQUIZA, JUSTO JOSÉ (1801-1870), Argentine dictator, general, and statesman **15** 396-397

URRACA (c. 1078-1126), Queen of Leon-Castilla) **23** 417-418

UTAMARO, KITAGAWA (1753-1806), Japanese printmaker **15** 397

MAN DON FODIO (1755-1816), Moslem teacher and theologian **15** 397-398

Uticensus, Marcus Porcius Cato
see Cato the Younger

Utilitarianism (philosophy)
expounders
Bain, Alexander **32** 28-30

Uzbekistan (nation, Central Asia)
Malayev, Ilyas **32** 227-229

V

Vaca, Álvar Núñez Cabeza de
see Cabeza de Vaca, Álvar Núñez

Vaccination
see Inoculation (immunology)

Vaccines
Blumberg, Baruch **32** 44-46
Zhdanov, Viktor Mikhailovich **32** 377-379

VADIM, ROGER (Roger Vadim Plemiannikov; 1928-2000), Russian/ French filmaker and author **22** 413-415

VAGANOVA, AGRIPPINA YAKOVLEVNA (1879-1951), Russian ballet dancer and teacher **24** 425-427

VAIL, THEODORE NEWTON (1845-1920), American businessman **23** 419-421

Vaillant, Sébastien, (1669-1722), French botanist
Celsius, Olof **32** 65-67

VAJPAYEE, ATAL BEHARI (born 1926), prime minister of India **19** 393-395

VALADON, SUZANNE (Marie Clémentine Valadon; 1865-1935), French artist and model **27** 354-356

VALDEZ, LUIS (born 1940), Hispanic American playwright and filmmaker **15** 399-400

VALDIVIA, PEDRO DE (c. 1502-53), Spanish conquistador and professional soldier **15** 400-401

VALENS, RITCHIE (Richard Steven Valenzuela; 1941-1959), Hispanic American musician **22** 415-417

VALENTI, JACK JOSEPH (1921-2007), presidential adviser and czar of the American film industry **15** 401-403

VALENTINO, RUDOLPH (Rodolfo Alfonso Raffaelo Pierre Filibert de Valentina d'Antonguolla Guglielmi; 1895-1926), Italian/American actor **20** 388-390
Arzner, Dorothy **32** 18-20

VALENZUELA, LUISA (born 1938), Argentine author **23** 421-423

VALERA Y ALCALÁ GALIANO, JUAN (1824-1905), Spanish novelist and diplomat **15** 403

VALERIAN (Publius Licinius Valerianus; c. 200-c. 260), Roman emperor 253-260 **15** 404-405

VALÉRY, PAUL AMBROISE (1871-1945), French poet, philosopher, and critic **15** 405-406

VALLA, LORENZO (c. 1407-57), Italian humanist **15** 406

VALLANDIGHAM, CLEMENT LAIRD (1820-1871), American politician **15** 406-407

VALLE INCLÁN, RAMÓN MARIA DEL (c. 1866-1936), Spanish novelist, playwright, and poet **15** 407-408

VALLEE, RUDY (Hubert Prior Vallee; 1901-1986), American vocalist **28** 359-361

VALLEJO, CÉSAR ABRAHAM (1892-1938), Peruvian poet **15** 408-409

VAN BUREN, MARTIN (1782-1862), American statesman, president 1837-41 **15** 410-411

VAN DER GOES, HUGO (flourished 1467-82), Flemish painter **15** 416-417

VAN DIEMEN, ANTHONY MEUZA (1593-1645), Dutch colonial official and merchant **15** 420

VAN DOESBURG, THEO (1883-1931), Dutch painter **15** 421

VAN DONGEN, KEES (Cornelis Theodorus Marie Van Dongen; 1877-1968), Fauvist painter, portraitist, and socialite **15** 421-422

VAN DUYN, MONA (1921-2004), first woman to be appointed poet laureate of the United States **15** 422-423

VAN DYCK, ANTHONY (1599-1641), Flemish painter **15** 423-425

VAN DYKE, DICK (Richard Wayne Van Dyke; born 1925), American actor, author, and producer **25** 416-418

VAN EEKELEN, WILLEM FREDERIK (born 1931), Dutch secretary-general of the Western European Union **15** 426-427

VAN GOGH, VINCENT (1853-1890), Dutch painter **15** 427-429

VAN HORNE, SIR WILLIAM CORNELIUS (1843-1915), American-born Canadian railroad entrepreneur **15** 429-430

Van Kuijk, Andreas Cornelius
see Parker, Tom

VAN PEEBLES, MELVIN (Melvin Peebles; born 1932), American film director and producer, actor, author, and musician **21** 414-416

VAN RENSSELAER, KILIAEN (c. 1580-1643), Dutch merchant and colonial official in America **15** 430-431

Van Schurman, Anna Maria
see Schurman, Anna Maria van

VAN VECHTEN, CARL (1880-1964), American writer and photographer **18** 400-402

VAN VLECK, JOHN HASBROUCK (1899-1980), American physicist **25** 418-420

VANBRUGH, SIR JOHN (1664-1726), English architect and dramatist **15** 409-410

VANCE, CYRUS R. (1917-2002), American secretary of the army and secretary of state **15** 411-413

VANCE, ZEBULON BAIRD (1830-1894), American politician **15** 413-414

VANCOUVER, GEORGE (1758-1798), English explorer and navigator **15** 414-415

VANDER ZEE, JAMES (1886-1983), photographer of the people of Harlem **15** 418-419

VANDERBILT, CORNELIUS (1794-1877), American financier, steamship and railroad builder **15** 415-416

VANDERBILT, GLORIA (born 1924), American designer, artist, and author **19** 395-397

VANDERLYN, JOHN (1775-1852), American painter **15** 417

VANDROSS, LUTHER (1951-2005), American singer **26** 364-366

VANE, SIR HENRY (1613-1662), English statesman **15** 425-426

Vannucci, Pietro
see Perugino

VAN'T HOFF, JACOBUS HENRICUS (1852-1911), Dutch physical chemist **15** 431-432
    Bodenstein, Max Ernst **32** 46-48

Vanzetti, Bartolomeo
see Sacco, Nicola and Vanzetti, Bartolomeo

VARDHAMANA MAHAVIRA (c. 540-470 BCE), Indian ascetic philosopher **10** 135-137

Varennes, Pierre Gaultier de
see La Verendrye, Sieur de

VARÈSE, EDGARD (1883-1965), French-American composer **15** 432-433

VARGAS, ALBERTO (1896-1982), Peruvian-American artist **32** 348-350

VARGAS, GETULIO DORNELLES (1883-1954), Brazilian political leader **15** 433-434

VARGAS LLOSA, MARIO (born 1936), Peruvian novelist, critic, journalist, screenwriter, and essayist **15** 434-436

VARMA, RAJA RAVI (1848-1906), Indian artist **31** 372-373

VARMUS, HAROLD ELIOT (born 1939), medical research expert and director of the National Institutes of Health (1993-) **15** 436-437

VARNHAGEN, FRANCISCO ADOLFO DE (1816-1878), Brazilian historian **15** 437-438

VARRO, MARCUS TERENTIUS (116-27 BCE), Roman scholar and writer **15** 438-439

VARTHEMA, LUDOVICO DI (c. 1470-c. 1517), Italian traveler and adventurer **15** 439-440

Vasa, Gustavus
see Gustavus I

VASARELY, VICTOR (1908-1997), Hungarian-French artist **15** 440-442

VASARI, GIORGIO (1511-1570), Italian painter, architect, and author **15** 442-443

VASCONCELOS, JOSÉ (1882-1959), Mexican educator and author **15** 443-444

Vassa, Gustavus
see Equiano, Olaudah

VASSALL, JOHN (1924-1996), British civil servant and spy **32** 350-352

VAUBAN, SEBASTIEN LE PRESTRE DE (1633-1707), French military engineer **18** 402-404

VAUDREUIL-CAVAGNAL, MARQUIS DE (Pierre François de Regaud; 1698-1778), Canadian-born governor of New France **15** 444

VAUGHAN, HENRY (1621/22-95), British poet **15** 444-445

VAUGHAN, SARAH LOIS (1924-1990), jazz singer **15** 445-446

VAUGHAN WILLIAMS, RALPH (1872-1958), English composer **15** 446-447

VAUGHT, WILMA L. (born 1930), U.S. Air Force officer **24** 427-429

VAVILOV, NIKOLAI IVANOVICH (1887-1943), Russian botanist and geneticist **15** 447-448

VÁZQUEZ, HORACIO (1860-1936), president of the Dominican Republic 1903-04 and 1924-30 **15** 448-449

VÁZQUEZ ARCE Y CEBALLOS, GREGORIO (1638-1711), Colombian artist **23** 423-425

VEBLEN, THORSTEIN BUNDE (1857-1929), American political economist and sociologist **15** 449-450

Vecellio, Tiziano
see Titian

VEECK, BILL (1914-1986), American sports team owner **30** 364-366

Vega, Inca Garcilaso de la
see Garcilaso de la Vega, Inca

Vega Carpio, Lope Félix
see Lope de Vega

VELASCO, JOSÉ MARÍA (1840-1912), Mexican painter **15** 450-451

VELASCO, LUIS DE (1511-1564), Spanish colonial administrator **15** 450-451

VELASCO ALVARADO, JUAN (1910-1977), Peruvian army officer who seized power in 1968 **15** 451-452

VELASCO IBARRA, JOSÉ MARÍA (1893-1979), Ecuadorian statesman, five time president **15** 452-454

VELASQUEZ, LORETA JANETA (1842-1897), Cuban American soldier and spy **28** 361-363

VELÁZQUEZ, DIEGO RODRÍGUEZ DE SILVA Y (1599-1660), Spanish painter **15** 454-456

VELÁZQUEZ, NYDIA MARGARITA (born 1953), Hispanic American politician **15** 456-459

VELÁZQUEZ DE CUÉLLAR, DIEGO (c. 1465-1523), Spanish conqueror, founder of Cuba **15** 459

VELDE, HENRY VAN DE (1863-1957), Belgian painter, designer, and architect **15** 419-420

Venerable Bede
see Bede, St.

Venezia, Domenico di Bartolomeo da
see Veneziano, Domenico

VENEZIANO, DOMENICO (Domenico di Bartolomeo da Venezia; c. 1410-1461), Italian painter **15** 459-460

Venice (city, Italy)
Republic of Venice (city-state)
Hayez, Francisco **32** 152-154

VENIZELOS, ELEUTHERIOS (1864-1936), Greek statesman **15** 460-461

VENTURI, ROBERT (born 1925), American architect **15** 461-463

VERA, YVONNE (1964-2005), Zimbabwean author **23** 425-427

VERCINGETORIX (c. 75-c. 46 BCE), Celtic chieftain and military leader **19** 397-399

VERDI, GIUSEPPE FORTUNINO FRANCESCO (1813-1901), Italian opera composer **15** 463-465

Vergerio, Pier Paolo, (1370-c. 1444), Italian lawyer, writer and translator
Chrysoloras, Manuel **32** 72-74

VERLAINE, PAUL MARIE (1844-1896), French poet **15** 465-466

VERMEER, JAN (1632-1675), Dutch painter **15** 466-467

VERNE, JULES (1828-1905), French novelist **15** 467-469

VERONESE, PAOLO (1528-1588), Italian painter **15** 469-470

VERRAZANO, GIOVANNI DA (c. 1485-c. 1528), Italian navigator and explorer **15** 470-471

VERROCCHIO, ANDREA DEL (1435-1488), Italian sculptor and painter **15** 471-472

VERSACE, GIANNI (1946-1997), Italian fashion designer **19** 399-401

VERTOV, DZIGA (Denis Abramovich Kaufman; 1896-1954), Russian film director **26** 366-368

Verulam, 1st Baron
see Bacon, Sir Francis

VERWOERD, HENDRIK FRENSCH (1901-1966), South African statesman, prime minister 1958-66 **15** 472-473

VESALIUS, ANDREAS (1514-1564), Belgian anatomist **15** 473-475

VESEY, DENMARK (1767-1822), American slave leader **15** 475

VESPASIAN (9-79), Roman emperor 69-79 **15** 475-476

Vespasianus, Titus Flavius
see Titus Flavius Vespasianus

VESPUCCI, AMERIGO (1454-1512), Italian navigator **15** 476-478

Vittorino da Feltre
see Feltre, Vittorino da

VIVALDI, ANTONIO (1678-1741), Italian violinist and composer **16** 3-4

VIVEKANANDA (1863-1902), Indian reformer, missionary, and spiritual leader **16** 4-5

VLADIMIR I (died 1015), grand prince of Kievan Russia 980-1015 **16** 5-6

Vladimir, St.
see Vladimir I

VLAMINCK, MAURICE (1876-1958), French painter **16** 6

VOEGELIN, ERIC (1901-1985), German-Austrian political theorist **16** 6-8

VOGEL, HANS-JOCHEN (born 1926), West German political leader **16** 8-9

VOGEL, SIR JULIUS (1835-1899), New Zealand statesman, twice prime minister **16** 9-10

VOGELWEIDE, WALTHER VON DER (c. 1170-1229), German poet, composer, and singer **16** 10-11

VOLCKER, PAUL (born 1927), chairman of the U.S. Federal Reserve Board (1979-1987) **16** 11-12

VOLTA, ALESSANDRO (1745-1827), Italian physicist **16** 12-14

VOLTAIRE (1694-1778), French poet, dramatist, historian, and philosopher **16** 14-16

VON AUE, HARTMANN (Aue von Hartman; c.1160 - c.1250), German poet and troubadour **22** 417-419

VON BINGEN, HILDEGARD (Hildegard of Bingen; 1098-1179), German composer, scientist, and theologian **22** 240-242

von Bora, Katharina
see Bora, Katharina Von

VON BRAUN, WERNHER (1912-1977), German-born American space scientist **16** 17-18

VON FURSTENBERG, DIANE (Diane Simone Michelle Halfin; born 1946), American fashion designer and businesswoman **16** 20-21

VON GLOEDEN, WILHELM (1956-1931), German photographer **32** 352-354

VON GRAEFE, CARL FERDINAND (1787-1840), German surgeon **32** 354-356

VON HÜGEL, BARON FRIEDRICH (1852-1925), philosopher of Christianity **16** 21-22

VON LAUE, MAX (1879-1960), German physicist **16** 23-24

VON MEHREN, ROBERT BRANDT (born 1922), American lawyer who helped create the International Atomic Energy Agency **16** 24-25

VON MISES, LUDWIG (1881-1973), Austrian economist and social philosopher **16** 25

VON NEUMANN, JOHN (1903-1957), Hungarian-born American mathematician **16** 27-28

VON PAPEN, FRANZ (1879-1969), conservative German politician who helped prepare the way for the Third Reich **16** 28-29

VON RAD, GERHARD (1901-1971), German theologian **16** 29-30

VON STROHEIM, ERICH (Erich Oswald Stroheim; 1885-1957), Austrian-American actor and director **29** 367-369

VON TRIER, LARS (born 1956), Danish filmmaker **30** 366-368

VON TROTTA, MARGARETHE (born 1942), German filmmaker and actor **25** 427-429

VONDEL, JOOST VAN DEN (1587-1679), Dutch poet and dramatist **16** 19-20

VONNEGUT, KURT, JR. (1922-2007), American author **16** 25-27

Voroshilov, K. E., (1881-1969), Soviet military and political leader
Tukhachevsky, Mikhail **32** 340-342

VORSTER, BALTHAZAR JOHANNES (1915-1983), South African political leader **16** 30-32

VOS SAVANT, MARILYN (born 1946), American columnist and consultant **16** 32-33

Voting rights
see Suffrage; Women's suffrage

VOZNESENSKY, ANDREI (1933-2010), Russian poet **31** 376-378

VREELAND, DIANA (1903-1989), American fashion journalist **30** 368-371

VUILLARD, JEAN ÉDOUARD (1868-1940), French painter **16** 36

VUITTON, LOUIS (1821-1892), French luggage maker and businessman **28** 365-367

VYSHINSKY, ANDREI (1883-1954), state prosecutor in Stalin's purge trials and head of the U.S.S.R.'s foreign ministry (1949-1953) **16** 36-37
Dobrynin, Anatoly **32** 99-101

VYSOTSKY, VLADIMIR (Vladimir Semyonovich Vysotsky; 1938-1980), Russian singer and poet **28** 367-369

W

W., BILL (1895-1971), American organization leader **30** 372-374
Wilson, Lois **32** 363-365

WAALS, JOHANNES DIDERIK VAN DER (1837-1923), Dutch physicist **15** 417-418

WADE, BENJAMIN FRANKLIN (1800-1878), American lawyer and politician **16** 38-39

WAGNER, HONUS (Johannes Peter Wagner; 1874-1955), American baseball player **20** 393-395

WAGNER, OTTO (1841-1918), Austrian architect and teacher **16** 39-40

WAGNER, RICHARD (1813-1883), German operatic composer **16** 40-43

WAGNER, ROBERT F. (1910-1991), New York City Tammany Hall mayor (1954-1965) **16** 44-45

WAGNER, ROBERT FERDINAND (1877-1953), American lawyer and legislator **16** 43

WAGONER, G. RICHARD (Richard Wagoner, Jr.; born 1953), American businessman **25** 430-432

WAHID, ABDURRAHMAN (1940-2009), Indonesian statesman, president 1999-2001 **31** 379-381

Wahlstatt, Prince of
see Blücher, G. L. von

WAINWRIGHT, JONATHAN MAYHEW (1883-1953), American general **16** 45-46

WAITE, MORRISON REMICK (1816-1888), American jurist, chief justice of U.S. Supreme Court 1874-88 **16** 46

WAITE, TERRY (born 1939), official of the Church of England and hostage in Lebanon **16** 47-48

WAITZ, GRETE (Grete Andersen; born 1953), Norwegian runner **24** 433-436

WAJDA, ANDRZEJ (Andrzei Wajda; born 1926), Polish film director and screenwriter **25** 432-434

WAKEFIELD, EDWARD GIBBON (1796-1862), British colonial reformer and promoter **16** 48-49

WAKSMAN, SELMAN ABRAHAM (1888-1973), American microbiologist **16** 49-50

WALCOTT, DEREK ALTON (born 1930), West Indian poet and dramatist **16** 50-51

WALCOTT, MARY VAUX (Mary Morris Vaux; 1860-1940), American artist and naturalist **25** 434-437